FREE GOVERNMENT IN THE MAKING
THIRD EDITION

FREE GOVERNMENT IN THE MAKING

READINGS IN AMERICAN POLITICAL THOUGHT

THIRD EDITION

Alpheus Thomas Mason

McCormick Professor of Jurisprudence
Department of Politics, Princeton University

NEW YORK
OXFORD UNIVERSITY PRESS
1965

Second Printing, 1966

Library of Congress Catalogue Card Number: 65-10151
Printed in the United States of America

To
my students in American Political Thought,
participants in a continuing symposium.

FOREWORD

The third edition of this book follows the pattern of the earlier versions; it continues to portray the American as a pragmatist. Pioneering men of action cleared the forest, conquered the foe, established the foundations of government. Among the scores of Americans represented in these readings, few have indulged in the isolated joy that separates the thinker from the doer. Jefferson is valued more for his statesmanship than his theorizing. The writings of John C. Calhoun, one of our most eminent theorists, were occasioned by specific issues and problems. John Marshall, Abraham Lincoln, David J. Brewer, Louis D. Brandeis—all had causes to serve, ends to achieve. The contemplative man—a Henry David Thoreau, a Thorstein Veblen, a Randolph Bourne—tends to be rated an eccentric loafer.

Theory has evolved slowly, usually appearing as the rationalization of *faits accomplis*. Ideological nuggets, such as the Gettysburg Address, have become effective tools in the governing process. Our nearest approach to a theoretical formulation, the Declaration of Independence, is among our more useful instruments for promoting the general welfare.

Featuring the ideas and deeds of men, and drawn from primary sources, these readings confront the student with living issues. On exhibit are our best minds—discussing, deliberating, opposing, compromising, deciding—building political institutions. For each problem divergent views are presented with sufficient fullness to bring out the weight and distinctive flavor of the argument. Introductory essays set the stage, introduce the actors, and acquaint the reader with relevant facts.

Space considerations limit the topics to what appears to be the main stream of political thought and action. Omissions may be less regrettable for those who believe, as I do, that knowledge of how things are done is quite as important as what was accomplished. Each chapter being a symposium, the reader may ponder the variety of points of view that can be sincerely and rationally entertained; he may realize that the desire to persuade and the willingness to be persuaded involve inescapable wastes, tedious methods, and cumbersome procedures—the essence as well as the strength of a free society.

As the panorama unfolds, the reader may observe the stark judgments of history stamped on actions taken. Whatever their merit or wisdom at crucial turning points—1776, 1789, 1861, 1933, 1954—things said and done fell short of final solutions. Chronological developments, highlighting the nation in crisis and transition, may quicken the reader's sense of history. By underscoring the relentless demands of Free Government, this book may enable him to see politics for what it is—an endless adventure.

Major modifications mark this new edition. Spurred by suggestions from colleagues (especially Sanford B. Gabin), from friends at other institutions (including David Cooperman, David Fellman, Richard P. Longaker, Arnold Rogow, and Robert G. McCloskey), and from former students (including William Janeway, Dan Martin, Edward Stettner, and Victor Wolfenstein), I sought to enrich the old product with fresh insights and new readings. A few earlier selections have been omitted; all have been edited anew with an eye to shortening and sharpening. The introductory essays have been recast and the selected references updated. The most significant changes have been made in the formative, the progressive, and the contemporary periods.

The long neglected, often ignored contribution of the Antifederalists to the Constitution, especially to the Bill of Rights, is reflected in Chapters IV, VI, and VII.

Chapter XVI adds prominent progressive thinkers, notably Herbert Croly, Walter Weyl, Theodore Roosevelt, and Walter Lippmann. Other new contributors include John Cotton, Orestes Brownson, Francis Lieber, Walter Rauschenbusch, James Bradley Thayer, Paul Elmer More, Sinclair Lewis, Thurman Arnold, Dwight D. Eisenhower, Robert Penn Warren, James Baldwin, Reinhold Niebuhr, J. William Fulbright, and John F. Kennedy.

Chapters XXI and XXII of the second edition have been condensed and combined, and the focus has been greatly broadened. Included are the explosive race problem, the perennial states' rights issue, the paradox of poverty and abundance, the implications of irresponsible power, the new 'radical right,' the strain of violence in our culture—all illustrating our continuing predicament.

The people at Oxford—Byron Hollinshead, Caroline Taylor, F. A. Guilford, to mention only those with whom I came in direct contact—assumed burdens beyond the call of duty, giving me the comfortable feeling that things were being done right.

A. T. M.

Princeton
18 September 1964

CONTENTS

I. NEW FOUNDATIONS FOR LIBERTY AND AUTHORITY IN THE OLD WORLD

II. AUTHORITARIAN THEOLOGY AND DEMOCRATIC DISSENT IN THE NEW WORLD

III. REVOLUTIONARY IDEAS IN FERMENT

IV. THE UNFINISHED REVOLUTION

V. TOWARD A MORE PERFECT UNION

VI. GETTING THE CONSTITUTION ADOPTED: THE RATIFICATION DEBATES

VII. GETTING THE BILL OF RIGHTS ADOPTED: JEFFERSON AND MADISON

XII. ROMANTIC INDIVIDUALISM

XIII. CHATTEL SLAVERY

XIV. THE NATURE OF THE UNION

XV. PLUTOCRACY OR SOCIAL DEMOCRACY?

XVI. THE PROGRESSIVE IMPULSE

XVII. JUDICIAL RESPONSE

XVIII. CYNICISM, NORMALCY, OPTIMISM, REALISM

XXI. CONTINUING PREDICAMENT

FREE GOVERNMENT IN THE MAKING

THIRD EDITION

I

NEW FOUNDATIONS FOR LIBERTY AND AUTHORITY IN THE OLD WORLD

The search for beginnings, no matter how far pressed, usually serves only to open more distant vistas of earlier developments. Origins recede as historical inquiry advances; ancient beginnings tend to become but the proximate ends of remoter outposts.

American political thought affords no exception to this general rule. Ideological landmarks, such as the Declaration of Independence and the Constitution of 1787, have antecedents reaching back through the long course of ancient and medieval European thought. It is useful, however, to distinguish between immediate and ultimate origins, and to confine our quest to the former. Chapters I and II portray certain intellectual ferments that influenced and informed American thought and action, posing issues still unresolved.

America's debt to the British was evident from the outset. John Locke (1632–1704), philosopher of the English Revolution of 1688, laid the theoretical foundations for the American Revolution of 1776. Key elements in Locke's system—natural rights, social contract, government by consent, right of revolution—had, however, been explored and agitated during the entire revolutionary period, beginning with Puritan resistance to Charles I. An illuminating discussion occurred in the General Council of the Parliamentary Army held at Putney, near London, from 28 October to 11 November 1647. Victorious over Charles I, the Army was in mutiny against Parliament, which had sought to disband it without making satisfactory provision either for the necessities of the mobilized troops or for the political rights of the English people. On 14 June 1647, under the leadership of Lieutenant General Ireton, the officers had issued a 'Declaration of the Army,' containing certain moderate demands for parliamentary reform as prerequsite to the restoration of the troops to obedience. This 'Declaration' failed to satisfy the Army's more radical elements. Mutiny worsened; the rank and file speedily associated themselves with Leveller elements in and out of the Army. The 'Agitators' formulated the 'Agreement of the People,' in substance a fundamental English constitutional compact designed to secure, among other things, manhood suffrage. Presentation of this 'Agreement of the People' to the officers of the Army touched off the grand debate in the General Council at Putney.

The case for the 'Agreement' was supported by Colonel Rainboro (also spelled Rainsborough, Rainborow, and variously) and Major Wildman, with considerable aid from Sexby, Pettus, Clarke, and one identified only as 'Bedfordshire Man.' Heading the opposition was Commissary (Lieutenant) General Ireton, who objected to the 'Agreement' at large and in detail. His opposition centered on the fact that the 'Agreement' conflicted with the earlier 'Declaration of the Army.' The 'Declaration,' he maintained, represented a firm engagement on the part of the Army, a compact with the Parliament and the people by which the Army remained inescapably bound. To adopt the 'Agreement,' however just, would involve repudiation of a binding compact, with disastrous results. Compact, Ireton insisted, constituted the basis of all civil institutions, including private property; to repudiate it threatened destruction of the foundation of civil society, especially property.

Against this argument, Rainboro and his associates arrayed the principles of natural law. The 'Agreement,' they contended, was designed to establish the people's rights in accordance with 'the law of nature and nations.' Insofar as the 'Declaration' conflicted with the 'Agreement,' the former remained in derogation of natural law and justice, and ought to be rejected. The Army—indeed all men—were under an engagement to obey civil authority, but they were under no obligation to sanction destruction of their just rights. The exchange between Ireton and Wildman posed enduring issues: on the one side, the notion of civil society founded on compact, which might legitimately deviate from the principles of natural law; on the other, the idea of the absolute paramountcy of natural law over all compacts.

The same conflict appeared in Ireton's more specific objection to the first Article of the 'Agreement,' proposing manhood suffrage in parliamentary elections. Rainboro's and Wildman's argument rested on the principle that government, to be legitimate, must be rooted in the consent of the governed. The right to vote for members of Parliament constituted the birthright of every Englishman; its denial to any man, rich or poor, rendered government, *pro tanto*, tyrannical. In Ireton's view, this argument simply amounted to the elevation of natural law over the kingdom's civil Constitution, threatening once again to subvert property and society itself. If the Constitution's suffrage provisions were to be set aside merely as violative of natural law, every man had a right to the franchise; private property could be similarly infringed; by the law of nature every man had a like right to every material thing required for his sustenance and support. Enfranchisement of the unpropertied, Ireton concluded, would inevitably enthrone the power to legislate private property out of existence.

These discussions of more than three centuries ago are couched in unfamiliar literary form and terminology, but the ideas explored and the dilemmas and predicaments posed are enduring. A. D. Lindsay, Master of Balliol, Oxford, commending them to 'all who wish to be able to give a reason for their democratic faith,' counsels any reader inclined to brush them aside as irrelevant to our modern discussions of democracy: 'Those who will take the trouble to get behind the theological language . . . will see how profound those democratic ideas are, how real and concrete and recurring is the situation which gives rise to them; and will see the tension there must always be between them as long as they are alive.'

The debates at Putney revealed sharp differences within an area of agreement. All parties recognized the existence of a higher law, *the law of nature.* All agreed that government rested upon compact. In varying degrees, all recognized the institution of property as basic in politics. Controversy centered on the relation of natural law to the constitutional compact and other civil institutions. Did natural law alone furnish the legitimate measure of men's rights in political society? Or were civil rights and political institutions shaped by constitutional compact, notwithstanding infraction of the law of nature? Controversy likewise turned upon the origin and status of property. Was property, as Ireton held, derived from the civil Constitution alone? Or was it, as Rainboro argued, founded on higher law? Was property, as Ireton suggested, the fundamental basis and end of government? Or were rights of personality also an object of governmental concern, as Rainboro contended in claiming the franchise for the unpropertied? Did the relationship of property and government, as Pettus stated it—property constituting the end of government—require a government founded on consent by all men?

Locke's *Two Treatises on Civil Government* (1690) embraced arguments from both sides of the debate at Putney. Like Rainboro, Locke derived property from higher law. Like Wildman, he insisted that natural law remained operative in civil society as the fundamental measure of individual rights. Locke endorsed the right of revolution, yet his philosophy, in effect, shows closer kinship with Ireton's. Locke accepts Wildman's view that natural law is carried over into civil society. Property, antedating civil society, is the true end of government. For its protection, revolution is a natural right. But for all practical purposes, revolution is a prerogative open only to a majority.

In the pamphlet war preceding revolution and independence, Locke furnished the American colonists with a full arsenal of arguments against arbitrary rule, whether of King or Parliament. Disgruntled American patriots quoted Locke with as much reverence as Communists today cite Karl Marx. The English philosopher was referred to deferentially as 'ingenious,' 'incomparable.' Locke's individualistic norms were especially meaningful. Frontier America suggested a state of nature, and the Mayflower Compact approximated his hypothetical social contract. The Constitutional Convention and the document resulting from it have been regarded as a remarkable fulfillment of Lockean theory. In the Declaration of Independence, Jefferson drew both ideas and phraseology from the *Second Treatise on Civil Government.*

Locke attempted to fuse liberty and restraint. Concern for the former is reflected in his stress on natural law and natural rights. But he provided no means, short of revolution, whereby aggrieved individuals or minorities could safeguard their rights against the arbitrary acts of a government enjoying majority support. Locke left unresolved the dilemma he posed toward the end of his *Second Treatise.* When the people's chosen representatives are alleged to have violated the trust imposed by the social compact and by 'promulgated established laws,' who is to judge the transgression? Locke's answer was that in the absence of a 'judicature on earth to decide . . . God in heaven is judge'—presumably a Lockean euphemism for force.

Locke's constitutionalism boiled down to political limitations on government—those imposed at elections, plus the hope that rulers and ruled alike would be guided by considerations of justice and common sense. Whether in a state of nature or in civil society, 'keeping of faith belongs to men as men.' It has been said that Locke was unreasonable 'only in his faith in reason.' The idea of a constitution limiting and superintending the operations of the supreme legislative authority forms no serious part of Locke's system. For Americans his politics was wanting on the institutional side. His contributions to the most unique aspect of American constitutionalism—judicial review—were inferential.

In the years since 1776, Locke's ideas have been a bulwark for conservatives seeking to maintain the *status quo*, or to reinforce constitutional safeguards for property. As recently as 1921, George Sutherland, subsequently Associate Justice of the United States Supreme Court, praised Locke's 'golden words that might have been written yesterday—so accurately do they describe the functions of our legislative, judicial, and executive departments and the great purpose of their aggregate powers.' Overlooked is Locke's authorship of the Fundamental Constitutions for the Carolinas, an abortive attempt to establish feudal relations in America.

About the time Ireton was arguing that those possessed of 'the permanent interest of the land' ought to rule, James Harrington (1611–77), seventeenth-century English aristocrat and opponent of the Stuarts, was beginning to discover that property does in fact govern. Harrington took specific issue with his Absolutist contemporary, Thomas Hobbes, who had tried to demonstrate that society and morals as well as the state rest on physical force. Harrington is almost ultramodern in defiant challenge of the author of *Leviathan* (1651), saying that an army is 'a beast that has a big belly and must be fed.'

Harrington had been to the Puritan Revolution and Oliver Cromwell what John Locke was to the Revolution of 1688 and (in Locke's own words) to 'our great Restorer, our present King William.' * Harrington's fictionalized political treatise, *Oceana* (1656), unlike the utopias of Plato and Sir Thomas More, was meant 'not for the skies nor for some spot on earth that did not exist, but for England.' The hero of the story is Cromwell, who had long pondered what one man, Lycurgus, could do for Sparta. Inspired by this noble example, the hero calls in experts who help frame a constitution. Cromwell is named Protector and the new order succeeds famously. At the height of its glory, the Protector, like Lycurgus, retires to private life, leaving England the happiest land in the world.

For Americans, Harrington has been a towering figure. James Otis described him in 1764 as 'the uncomparable Harrington.' John Adams devoted a long section in his *Defence of the Constitutions* . . . (1787–88) to the author of

* Peter Laslett demonstrates that the conventional view of Locke as the apologist of the Glorious Revolution is in error. He contends that 'the whole work was written before 1683.' See John Locke, *Two Treatises of Government*, Peter Laslett, ed., Cambridge, England, 1960, pp. 45–66.

Oceana, the first volume of Adams's work being available to members of the Philadelphia Convention that framed the Constitution of 1787. 'Harrington has shown,' Adams observed, 'that power always follows property. This I believe to be as infallible a maxim in politics as that action and reaction are equal, is in mechanics.' 'One of the most ingenious of political writers is Mr. Harrington,' Daniel Webster declared in the Massachusetts Constitutional Convention of 1820, seeking to prove that 'power naturally and necessarily follows property.'

Harrington supplied Americans with an enduring ideal, 'Empire of laws and not of men,' a paraphrase of which appears in the Massachusetts Constitution of 1780, largely the handiwork of John Adams. Still other familiar principles and axioms are found in *Oceana*: the written constitution, liberal suffrage coupled with short term of office, and separation of powers. All these maxims, ideas, and devices became prominent features of American constitutionalism in the years following publication of *Oceana* and especially after 1787.

English ideas also came indirectly to the attention of Americans through Charles Louis de Secondat, Baron de Montesquieu (1689–1755). The French aristocrat was inspired by his observations of the British Constitution to write *Spirit of the Laws*. The key principle Montesquieu saw (or thought he saw) at work in England was separation of powers and checks and balance—'the mirror of political liberty.' To Americans, 'no political truth is [or was] of greater intrinsic value than that embodied in Book XI—the 'most precious gift the present age has received,' Jefferson called it. Madison considered the Federal Constitution of 1787 a faithful embodiment of the Frenchman's recipe. Hamilton cited Montesquieu's Book IX as 'a luminous abridgement of the principal arguments in favor of the Union.'

Latter-day Americans continued to cite (some still do) these names to reinforce their own views on public policy and action. This does not imply that any of the now-familiar ideas and institutions can be traced directly to the materials contained in this chapter. But no one can deny that Locke, Harrington, and Montesquieu are conspicuous among the authorities confidently relied on in the discussion of American issues, especially during the revolutionary and formative periods of our history. It is, however, highly probable that Americans were influenced more by experience than by great names. 'Is it not the glory of the people of America,' Madison asks in *Federalist* 14, 'that, while they have paid a decent regard to the opinions of former times and other nations, they have not suffered a blind veneration for antiquity, for custom, or for names, to overrule the suggestions of their own good sense, the knowledge of their own situations, and the lessons of their own experience?' America 'reared the fabrics of government,' the father of the Constitution boasted, 'which have no models on the face of the globe.'

1. *The poorest in England has a life to live as the richest*

COL. THOMAS RAINBORO, *Debates on the Putney Project*, 1647 *

LIEUTENANT GENERAL CROMWELL: Truly this paper † does contain in it very great alterations of the very Government of the Kingdom, alterations from that Government that it has been under, I believe I may almost say since it was a Nation. . . Therefore, although the pretensions in it, and the expressions in it are very plausible, and if we could leap out of one condition into another, that had so specious things in it as this has, I suppose there would not be much dispute, though perhaps some of these things may be very well disputed. How do we know if while we are disputing these things another company of men shall gather together, and they shall put out a paper as plausible perhaps as this? . . . And not only another, and another, but many of this kind. And if so, what do you think of the consequence of that would be? Would it not be confusion? Would it not be utter confusion? Would it not make England like the Switzerland country, one canton of the Swiss against another, and one county against another? I ask you whether it be not fit for every honest man seriously to lay that upon his heart? And if so, what would that produce but an absolute desolation—an absolute desolation to the Nation—and we in the meantime tell the Nation, 'It is for your Liberty, 'Tis for your privilege,' ''Tis for your good.' Pray God it prove so whatsoever course we run. But truly, I think we are not only to consider what the consequences are (if there were nothing else but this paper), but we are to consider the probability of the ways and means to accomplish: that is to say [to consider] whether, according to reason and judgment, the spirits and temper of the people of this Nation are prepared to receive and to go on along with it. . . Give me leave to say this: There will be very great mountains in the way of this . . . and therefore we ought to consider the consequences, and God has given us our reason that we may do this. It is not enough to propose things that are good in the end, but suppose this model were an excellent model, and fit for England, and the Kingdom to receive, it is our duty as Christians and men to consider consequences. . .

This ought to be our consideration and yours, saving [that] in this you have the advantage of us—you that are the soldiers you have not—but you that are not [soldiers] you reckon yourselves at a loose and at a liberty, as men that have no obligation upon you. Perhaps we conceive we have; and therefore this is that I may say—both to those that come with you, and to my fellow officers and all others that hear me—that it concerns us as we would approve

* *The Clarke Papers*, C. H. Firth, ed., The Camden Society, new series XLIX, 1891, vol. I, pp. 236–69, 299–342, *passim*.

† The paper referred to is a document known as 'the Agreement of the People.' It demanded: (1) Equal electoral districts. (2) The dissolution of the Long Parliament on 30 September 1648. (3) Biennial Parliaments to be elected every March and sit for five months. (4) The limitation of the powers of future parliaments so as to guarantee complete toleration; a full indemnity for acts done during the late public differences, and good and equal laws.

ourselves [as honest men] before God, and before men that are able to judge of us, if we do not make good engagements, if we do not make good that that the world expects we should make good. I do not speak to determine what that is, but if I be not much mistaken we have in the time of our danger issued out Declarations; we have been required by the Parliament, because our Declarations were general, to declare particularly what we meant; and having done that how far that obliges or not obliges [us] that is by us to be considered, if we mean honestly and sincerely and to approve ourselves to God as honest men. . . He that departs from that that is a real engagement and a real tie upon him, I think he transgresses without faith, for faith will bear up men in every honest obligation, and God does expect from men the performance of every honest obligation. . .

MR. WILDMAN: . . . I conceive the chief weight of your Honor's speech lay in this, that you were first to consider what obligations lay upon you, and how far you were engaged, before you could consider what was just in this paper now propounded; adding, that God would protect men in keeping honest promises. To that I must only offer this, that according to the best knowledge [I have] of their apprehensions, they do apprehend that whatever obligation is past must be considered afterwards, when it is urged whether it were honest or just or no; and if [the obligation] were not just it does not oblige the persons, if it be an oath itself. But if, while there is not so clear a light, any person passes an Engagement, it is judged by them (and so I judge it), to be an act of honesty for that man to recede from his former judgment, and to abhor it. And therefore I conceive the first thing is to consider the honesty of what is offered, otherwise it cannot be considered of any obligation that does prepossess. . .

COMMISSARY GENERAL IRETON: . . . I can hardly think that man can be of that principle that no Engagement is binding further than that he thinks it just or no. For it hints that, if he that makes an Engagement (be it what it will be) have further light that this engagement was not good or honest, then he is free from it. . .

Truly Sir I have little to say at the present to that matter of the paper that is tendered to us. I confess there are plausible things in it, and there are things really good in it, and there are those things that I do with my heart desire, and there are those things for the most part of it [that] I shall be so free as to say if these Gentlemen, and other Gentlemen that will join with them can obtain, I would not oppose, I should rejoice to see obtained. . . But truly I do account we are under Engagements; and I suppose that whatsoever this Gentleman that spoke last does seem to deliver to us, holding himself absolved from all Engagements, if he thinks it, yet those men that came with him (that are in the case of the Army) * hold themselves more obliged; and therefore . . . I do wish that we may have a consideration of our former Engagements, of things which are the Engagements of the Army generally. Those we are to take notice of, and sure we are not to recede from them till we are convinced of them that they are unjust. And when we are

* That is, 'The soldier agitators contrasted with those who did not belong to the Army.'

convinced of them that they are unjust, truly yet I must not fully concur with the Gentleman's principle, that presently we are, as he says, absolved from them, that we are not bound to them, or we are not bound to make them good. . .

Bedfordshire Man: . . . I find that the Engagements of the Army are at present the things which is . . . to be considered. I confess my ignorance in those Engagements, but I apprehend, at least I hope, that those Engagements have given away nothing from the people that is the people's Right. . . If they have promised more than their Right to any person or persons, and have given away any thing from the people that is their Right, then I conceive they are unjust. And if they are unjust [they should be broken], though I confess for my own part I am very tender of breaking an Engagement when it concerns a particular person—I think that a particular person ought rather to set down and loose than to break an Engagement—but if any man have given way any thing from another whose Right it was to one or more whose Right it was not, I conceive these men may [break that engagement]—at least many of them think themselves bound not only to break this Engagement, but to place * to give everyone his due. I conceive that for the substance of the paper it is the people's due; and for the change of the Government which is so dangerous, I apprehend that there may be many dangers in it, and truly I apprehend there may be more dangers without it. . . And therefore . . . I must make this motion; that all those that upon a due consideration of the thing do find it to be just and honest, and do find that if they have engaged any thing to the contrary of this it is unjust and giving away the people's Rights, I desire that they and all others may have a free liberty of acting to any thing in this nature, or any other nature, that may be for the people's good, by petitioning or otherwise; whereby the fundamentals for a well-ordered Government for the people's Rights may be established. . .

Mr. Wildman: . . . A principle much spreading and much to any trouble . . . is this: that when persons once be engaged, though the Engagement appears to be unjust, yet the person must set down and suffer under it; and that therefore, in case a Parliament, as a true Parliament, does anything unjustly, if we be engaged to submit to the laws that they shall make, if they make an unjust law, though they make an unrighteous law, yet we must swear obedience.

I confess to me this principle is very dangerous, and I speak it the rather because I see it spreading abroad in the Army again. Whereas it is contrary to what the Army first declared: that they stood upon such principles of right and freedom, and the laws of nature and nations, whereby men were to preserve themselves though the persons to whom authority belonged should fail in it . . . and therefore if anything tends to the destruction of a people, because the thing is absolutely unjust and tends to their destruction [they may preserve themselves] † . . .

* The sense requires, 'to place it by a new engagement.'

† Wildman refers to the principles laid down in the *Declaration of the Army*, of 14 June 1647.

COMMISSARY GENERAL IRETON: . . . I am far from holding, that if a man have engaged himself to a thing that is not just—to a thing that is evil, that is sin if he do it—that that man is still bound to perform what he has promised; I am far from apprehending that. But when we talk of just, it is not so much of what is sinful before God, which depends upon many circumstances of indignation to that man and the like, but it intends of that which is just according to the foundation of justice between man and man. And for my part I account that the great foundation of justice between man and man, and that without which I know nothing of justice between man and man—in particular matters I mean, nothing in particular things that can come under human Engagement one way or other—there is no other foundation of right I know of, right to one thing from another man, no foundation of that justice or that righteousness, but this general justice, and this general ground of righteousness, that we should keep covenant one with another. Covenants freely made, freely entered into, must be kept one with another. Take away that I do not know what ground there is of any thing you can call any man's right. I would very fain know what you Gentlemen or any other do account the right you have to any thing in England, any thing of estate, land, or goods that you have, what ground, what right you have to it? What right has any man to any thing if you lay not that principle, that we are to keep covenant? If you will resort only to the law of Nature, by the law of Nature you have no more right to this land or anything else than I have. I have as much right to take hold of anything that is for my sustenance, [to] take hold of anything that I have a desire to for my satisfaction as you. But here comes the foundation of all right that I understand to be between men, as to the enjoying of one thing or not enjoying of it; we are under a contract, we are under an agreement, and that agreement is what a man has for matter of land that a man has received by a traduction from his ancestors, which according to the law does fall upon him to be his right. [The agreement is] that that he shall enjoy, he shall have the property of, the use of, the disposing of, with submission to that general authority which is agreed upon amongst us for the preserving of peace, and for the supporting of this law. This I take to be [the foundation of all right] for matter of land. For matter of goods, that which does fence me from that [right] which another man may claim by the law of nature of taking my goods, that which makes it mine really and civilly is the law. That which makes it unlawful originally and radically is only this: because that man is in covenant with me to live together in peace one with another, and not to meddle with that which another is possessed of, but that each of us should enjoy, and make use of, and dispose of, that which by the course of law is in his possession, and [another] shall not by violence take it away from him. This is the foundation of all the right any man has to anything but to his own person. This is the general thing: that we must keep covenant one with another when we have contracted one with another. . . And therefore when I hear men speak of laying aside all Engagements to [consider only] that wild or vast notion of what in every man's conception is just or unjust, I am afraid and do tremble at the boundless and endless consequences of it. . . You say, 'If these things in this paper, in this Engagement be just, then,' say you, 'never talk of any Engagement, for if anything in that Engagement be against this, your Engagement was unlawful; consider singly this paper, whether it be just.' In what sense do you think this is just? There is a great deal of equivocation [as to] what is just and unjust. . .

MR. WILDMAN: You repeat not the principle right—'To think that we are bound so absolutely to personal obedience to any Magistrates or personal authority that if they work to our destruction we may not oppose them.' . . .

COMMISSARY GENERAL IRETON: . . . But when men will first put in those terms of destruction, they will imagine any thing a destruction, if there could be any thing better [for them]; and so it is very easy and demonstrable that things are so counted abhorred and destructive, that at the utmost if a man should make it out by reason, that man would be in a better condition if it be not done, than if it be done. And though I cannot but subscribe to, that in such a visible way I may hold the hands of those that are in authority as I may the hands of a mad-man; but that no man shall think himself [bound] to acquiesce particularly, and to suffer for quietness' sake rather than to make a disturbance, or to raise a power if he can to make a disturbance in the State—I do apprehend and appeal to all men whether there be not more folly or destructiveness in the spring of that principle than there can be in that other principle of holding passive obedience? Now whatsoever we have declared in the Army [declarations] it is no more but this. The Parliament has commanded us [to do] this. We have said, no. First we have insisted upon [the] fundamental rights of the people. We have said we desire [first] to have the constitution of the supreme authority of this Kingdom reduced to that constitution which is due to the people of this Kingdom, and reducing the authority to this we will submit to it, we will acquiesce, we will cast our share into this common bottom; and if it go ill with us at one time, it will go well at another. The reducing of the supreme authority to that constitution, by success or election as near as may be, we have insisted upon as an essential right of the Kingdom; and no man can accuse the Army of disobedience, holding forth a principle of disobedience upon any other ground.

2. *If there be any foundation of liberty, it is that those who choose the law-makers shall be men freed from dependence on others*

LIEUT. GEN. HENRY IRETON, *Debates on the Putney Project*, 1647 *

COMMISSARY GENERAL IRETON: . . . It is said: 'The people of England' etc. . . . they are to be distributed 'according to the number of the in-

* C. H. Firth, ed., op. cit. Hereafter follows the debate on the first article of the Paper called the Agreement: 'That the people of England, Being at this day very unequally distributed by Counties, Cities, and Burroughs, for the election of their Deputies in Parliament ought to be more indifferently proportioned, according to the number of the Inhabitants. . .'

habitants'; and this does make me think that the meaning is, that every man that is an inhabitant is to be equally considered, and to have an equal voice in the election of the representors, those persons that are for the General Representative; and if that be the meaning then I have something to say against it. . .

MR. PETTUS: We judge that all inhabitants that have not lost their birthright should have an equal voice in Elections.

COLONEL RAINBORO: . . . Really I think that the poorest he that is in England has a life to live as the richest he; and therefore truly, Sir, I think it's clear, that every man that is to live under a Government ought first by his own consent to put himself under that Government; and I do think that the poorest man in England is not at all bound in a strict sense to that Government that he has not had a voice to put himself under; and I am confident that when I have heard the reasons against it, something will be said to answer those reasons, insomuch that I should doubt whether he was an Englishman or no that should doubt of these things.

COMMISSARY GENERAL IRETON: . . . Give me leave to tell you, that if you make this the rule I think you must fly for refuge to an absolute natural Right, and you must deny all Civil Right; and I am sure it will come to that in the consequence. . . For my part I think it is no right at all. I think that no person has a right to an interest or share in the disposing or determining of the affairs of the Kingdom, and in choosing those that shall determine what laws we shall be ruled by here, no person has a right to this, that has not a permanent fixed interest in this Kingdom; and those persons together are properly the Represented of this Kingdom, and consequently are to make up the Representors of this Kingdom, who taken together do comprehend whatsoever is of real or permanent interest in the Kingdom. . . We talk of birthright. Truly [by] birthright there is thus much claim. Men may justly have by birthright, by their very being born in England, that we should not seclude them out of England, that we should not refuse to give them air, and place, and ground, and the freedom of the highways and other things, to live amongst us; not [to] any man that is born here, though by his birth there come nothing at all to him that is part of the permanent interest of this Kingdom. That I think is due to a man by birth. But that by a man's being born here he shall have a share in that power that shall dispose of the lands here, and of all things here, I do not think it a sufficient ground. I am sure if we look upon that which is the utmost within man's view of what was originally the constitution of this Kingdom, [if we] look upon that which is the most radical and fundamental, and which if you take away . . . no man has any land, any goods [or] any civil interest, that is this: that those that choose the Representors for the making of Laws by which this State and Kingdom are to be governed, are the persons who taken together do comprehend the local interest of this Kingdom; that is, the persons in whom all land lies, and those in Corporations in whom all trading lies. This is the most fundamental Constitution of this Kingdom, which if you do not allow you allow none at all. This Constitution has limited and determined it that only those shall have voices in Elections. It is true as was said by a Gentleman [Rainboro] near me, the meanest man in England ought to have [a voice in the election of the government he lives under]. . . I say this, that those that have the meanest local interest, that man that has but forty shillings a year, he has as great voice in the Election of a Knight for the shire as he that has ten thousand a year or more, if he had never so much; and therefore there is that regard had to it. . . If we shall go to take away this fundamental part of the civil constitution we shall plainly go to take away all property and interest that any man has, either in land by inheritance, or in estate by possession, or anything else.

COLONEL RAINBORO: Truly, Sir . . . I do very much care whether [there be] a King or no King, Lords or no Lords, property or no property; and I think if we do not all take care, we shall all have none of these very shortly . . . I do hear nothing at all that can convince me, why any man that is born in England ought not to have his voice in Election of Burgesses. It is said, that if a man have not a permanent interest, he can have no claim, and we must be no freer than the laws will let us be. . . I do think that the main cause why Almighty God gave men reason, it was, that they should make use of that reason, and that they should improve it for that end and purpose that God gave it them.* And truly, I think that half a loaf is better than none if a man be hungry, yet I think there is nothing that God has given a man that any one else can take from him. Therefore I say, that either it must be the law of God or the law of man that must prohibit the meanest man in the Kingdom to have this benefit † as well as the greatest. I do not find anything in the law of God, that a Lord shall choose 20 Burgesses, and a Gentleman but two, or a poor man shall choose none. I find no such thing in the law of nature, nor in the law of nations. But I do find, that all Englishmen must be subject to English laws, and I do verily believe, that there is no man but will say, that the foundation of all law lies in the people, and if [it lie] in the people, I am to seek for this exemption. . . Therefore I do [think] and am still of the same opinion; that every man born in England cannot, ought not, neither by the law of God nor the law of nature, to be exempted from the choice of those who are to make laws, for him to live under, and for him, for aught I know, to lose his life under.

COMMISSARY GENERAL IRETON: . . . All the main thing that I speak for is because I would have an eye to property. . . Here is the case of the most fundamental part of the Constitution of the Kingdom, which if you take away, you take away all by that. Here are men of this and this quality are determined to be the Electors of men to the Parliament, and they are all those who have any permanent interest in the Kingdom, and who taken together do compre-

* A vote, the right of exercising his reason by electing a representative.

† Rainboro's argument seems to be: 'God gave man reason that he might use it, and though the poorest man may have no property yet he has his reason and he was meant to use it. It may be a small right but it is something, and you are not justified in taking from him any right God has given him.'

hend the whole interest of the Kingdom. I mean by permanent, local, that is not anywhere else. . .

Now I wish we may all consider of what right you will challenge, that all the people should have right to Elections. Is it by the right of nature? If you will hold forth that as your ground, then I think you must deny all property too, and this is my reason. . . By the same right of nature, whatever it be that you pretend . . . by the same right he has an equal right in any goods he sees: meat, drink, clothes, to take and use them for his sustenance. He has a freedom to the land, [to take] the ground, to exercise it, till it; he has the [same] freedom to anything that anyone does account himself to have any propriety in. Why now I say then, if you, against this most fundamental part of [the] civil Constitution (which I have now declared), will plead the law of nature, that a man should, paramount [to] this, and contrary, to this, have a power of choosing those men that shall determine what shall be law in this state, though he himself have no permanent interest in the State, [but] whatever interest he has he may carry about with him. If this be allowed, [because by the right of nature], we are free, we are equal, one man must have as much voice as another, then show me what step or difference [there is], why by the same right of necessity to sustain nature [I may not claim property as well]? . . .

COLONEL RAINBORO: . . . For my part, as I think, you forgot something that was in my speech, and you do not only yourselves believe that [we] are inclining to anarchy, but you would make all men believe that. And Sir, to say because a man pleads, that every man has a voice [by the right of nature], that therefore it destroys [by] the same [argument all property]—that there's a property the law of God says it; else why [has] God made that law, 'Thou shalt not steal?' . . . God has set down that thing as to propriety with this law of his, 'Thou shalt not steal.' For my part I am against any such thought, and as for yourselves I wish you would not make the world believe that we are for anarchy. . .

COMMISSARY GENERAL IRETON: I profess I must clear myself as to that point. . .

I have, with as much plainness and clearness of reason as I could, showed you how I did conceive the doing of this takes away that which is the most original, the most fundamental civil Constitution of this Kingdom, and which above all is that Constitution by which I have any property. . . I desire clearly to understand where then remains property?

Now then, as I say, I would misrepresent nothing; the answer which had anything of matter in it, the great and main answer upon which that which has been said against this rests, that seemed to be: that it will not make the breach of property: that there is a law, 'Thou shalt not steal.' The same law says, 'Honor thy Father and Mother'; and that law does likewise extend to all that are our governors in that place where we are in. So that, by that there is a forbidding of breaking a Civil Law when we may live quietly under it, and a Divine Law. . . Our property as well as our right of sending Burgesses descends from other things. That Divine Law does not determine particulars but generals, in relation to man and man, and to property, and all things else; and we should be as far to seek if we should go to prove a property in [a thing by] Divine Law as to prove that I have an interest in choosing Burgesses of the Parliament by Divine Law. . .

COLONEL RAINBORO: . . . I would fain know how it [i.e. the franchise] comes to be the property [of some men, and not of others]. As for estates, and those kind of things, and other things that belong to men, it will be granted that they are property; but I deny that that is a property, to a Lord, to a Gentleman, to any man more than another in the Kingdom of England. If it be a property, it is a property by a law; neither do I think, that there is very little property in this thing by the law of the land, because I think that the law of the land in that thing is the most tyrannical law under heaven, and I would fain know what we have fought for, and this is the old law of England and that which enslaves the people of England that they should be bound by laws in which they have no voice at all. . .

MR. PETTUS: I desire to add one word concerning the word Property.

It is for something that anarchy is so much talked of. For my own part, I cannot believe in the least that it can be clearly derived from that paper. 'Tis true, that somewhat may be derived in the paper against the power of the King, and somewhat against the power of the Lords; and the truth is when I shall see God going about to throw down King and Lords and property then I shall be contented. But I hope that they may live to see the power of the King and the Lords thrown down, that yet may live to see property preserved. And for this of changing the Representative of the Nation, of changing those that choose the Representative, making of them more full, taking more into the number than formerly, I had verily thought we had all agreed that more should have chosen, and that all had desired a more equal Representation than we now have. . . But [as] for this [argument] that it destroys all right [to property] that every Englishman that is an inhabitant of England should choose and have a choice in the Representatives, I suppose it is [on the contrary] the only means to preserve all property. For I judge every man is naturally free; and I judge the reason why men when they were in so great numbers [choose representatives was] that every man could not give his voice; and therefore men agreed to come into some form of Government that they who were chosen might preserve property. I would fain know, if we were to begin a Government, [whether you would say] 'you have not 40s. a year, therefore you shall not have a voice.' Whereas before there was a Government every man had such a choice, and afterwards for this very cause they did choose Representatives, and put themselves into forms of Government that they may preserve property, and therefore it is not to destroy it [to give every man a choice].

COMMISSARY GENERAL IRETON: . . . To that which this Gentleman spoke last. The main thing that he seemed to answer was this: that he would make it appear that the going about to establish this Government, [the constitution proposed in the 'Agreement of the People'] [or] such a Government, is not a destruction of property, nor does not tend to the destruction of property, because the people's falling into a Government is for the preservation of property. What weight there [is in it] lies in this: since there is a falling into a Government, and Government is to preserve property, therefore this cannot be against property. The objection does not lie in that, the making of it [i.e. The franchise more equal] but [in] the introducing of men into an equality of interest in this Government who have no property in this Kingdom, or who have no local permanent interest in it. . . I do not mean that I would have it [franchise] restrained to that proportion [it is now], but to restrain it still to men who have a local, a permanent interest in the Kingdom, who have such an interest that they may live upon it as freemen, and who have such an interest as is fixed upon a place, and is not the same everywhere equally . . . that is, that no person that has not a local and permanent interest in the Kingdom should have an equal dependance in Elections [with those that have]. But if you go beyond this law, if you admit any man that has a breath and being, I did show you how this will destroy property. It may come to destroy property thus: you may have such men chosen or at least the major part of them [as have no local and permanent interest.] Why may not those men vote against all property? . . . Show me what you will stop at, wherein you will fence any man in a property by this rule.

Colonel Rainboro: I desire to know how this [the franchise] comes to be a property in some men, and not in others.

Colonel Rich: I confess [there is weight in] that objection that the Commissary General Ireton last insisted upon; for you have five to one in this Kingdom that have no permanent interest. Some men [have] ten, some twenty servants, some more, some less. If the Master and servant shall be equal Electors, then clearly those that have no interest in the Kingdom will make it their interest to choose those that have no interest. It may happen, that the majority may by law, not in a confusion, destroy property; there may be a law enacted, that there shall be an equality of goods and estate. I think that either of the extremes may be urged to inconvenience. That is, men that have no interest as to Estate should have no interest as to Election . . . I remember there were as we have heard many workings and revolutions in the Roman Senate; and there was never a confusion that did appear, and that indeed was come to, till the State came to know this kind of distribution of Election. That the peoples voices were bought and sold, and that by the poor, and thence it came that he that was the richest man, and [a man] of some considerable power among the soldiers . . . made himself a perpetual dictator. And if we strain too far to avoid monarchy in Kings [let us take heed] that we do not call for Emperors to deliver us from more than one Tyrant.

Colonel Rainboro: . . . Truly, Sir, I should desire to go close to the business; and the thing that I am unsatisfied in is how it comes about that there is such a propriety in some free born Englishman, and not [in] others. . .

Mr. Wildman: Unless I be very much mistaken we are very much deviated from the first Question. . . I desire we may recall [ourselves to the question] whether it be right or no. I conceive all that has been said against it will be reduced to this . . . that it is against a fundamental law, [and] that every person ought to have a permanent interest, because it is not fit that those should choose Parliaments that have no lands to be disposed of by Parliament.

Commissary General Ireton: If you will take it by the way, it is not fit [fixed] that the Representees should choose the Representors, or the persons who shall make the law in the Kingdom, who have not a permanent fixed interest in the Kingdom.

Mr. Wildman: Sir I do so take it; and I conceive that that is brought in for the same reason, that foreigners might come to have a voice in our Elections as well as the native Inhabitants.

Commissary General Ireton: That is upon supposition that these [foreigners] should be all Inhabitants.

Mr. Wildman: I shall begin with the last first. The case is different from the native Inhabitant and foreigner. If a foreigner shall be admitted to be an Inhabitant in the Nation, so he will submit to that form of Government as the natives do, he has the same right as the natives, but in this particular. Our case is to be considered thus, that we have been under slavery. That's acknowledged by all. . . Every person in England has as clear a right to elect his Representative as the greatest person in England. I conceive that's the undeniable maxim of Government: that all government is in the free consent of the people. . . And therefore I should humbly move, that if the Question be stated—which would soon bring things to an issue—it might rather be this: whether any person can justly be bound by law, who does not give his consent that such persons shall make laws for him?

Commissary General Ireton: Let the Question be so; whether a man can be bound to any law that he does not consent to? And I shall tell you, that he may and ought to be [bound to a law] that he does not give a consent to. . . If a foreigner comes within this Kingdom, if that stranger will have liberty [to dwell here] who has no local interest here—he is a man it's true, has air that by nature * we must not expel [from] our Coasts . . . nor kill him because he comes upon our land, comes up our stream, arrives at our shore. It is a piece of hospitality, of humanity, to receive that man amongst us. But if that man be received to a being amongst us I think that man may very well be content to submit himself to the law of the land: that is, the law that is made by those people that have a property, a fixed property, in the land. I think if any man will receive protection from this people, this man ought to be subject to those laws, and be bound by those laws so long as he continues amongst them, though [neither] he nor his ancestors, not any between him and Adam, did ever give concurrence to this Constitution. . . And so the same reason does extend in my understanding

* Probably should be, 'hath a right by nature that.'

to that man that has no permanent interest in the Kingdom. If he has money, his money is as good in another place as here; he has nothing that does locally fix him to this Kingdom. If this man will live in this Kingdom or trade amongst us, that man ought to subject himself to the law made by the people who have the interest of this Kingdom in us . . . that man ought to give such a respect to the property of men that live in the land. . .

Colonel Rainboro: . . . The reason is, that the chief end of this Government is to preserve persons as well as estates, and if any law shall take hold of my person it is more dear than my estate. . .

Colonel Rich: . . . I did not at all urge that there should be a consideration [had of rich men only], and that [a] man that is [poor] shall be without consideration, or that he deserves to be made poor and not to live at all. All that I urged was this, that I think it worthy consideration, whether they should have an equality in their interest. . .

Colonel Rainboro: For my part I think we cannot engage one way or other in the Army if we do not think of the people's liberties. If we can agree where the liberty and freedom of the people lies, that will do all.

Commissary General Ireton: I cannot consent so far. As I said before: when I see the hand of God destroying King, and Lords, and Commons too, [or] any foundation of human Constitution, when I see God has done it, I shall I hope comfortably acquiesce in it. But first, I cannot give my consent to it because it is not good. . . If the principle upon which you move this alteration, or the ground upon which you press that we should make this alteration, do destroy all kind of property or whatsoever a man has by human Constitution [I cannot consent to it]. The law of God does not give me property, nor the law of nature, but property is of human Constitution. I have a property and this I shall enjoy. Constitution founds property. . .

Mr. Sexby: . . . We have engaged in this Kingdom and ventured our lives, and it was all for this: to recover our birthrights and privileges as Englishmen, and by the arguments urged there is none. There are many thousands of us soldiers that have ventured our lives; we have had little propriety in the Kingdom as to our estates, yet we have had a birthright. But it seems now except a man has a fixed estate in this Kingdom, he has no right in this Kingdom. I wonder we were so much deceived. If we had not a right to the Kingdom, we were mere mercenary soldiers. . . I do think the poor and meaner of this Kingdom (I speak as in that relation in which we are) have been the means of the preservation of this Kingdom. I say in their stations, and really I think to their utmost possibility; and their lives have not been dear for purchasing the good of the Kingdom. Those that act to this end are as free from anarchy or confusion as those that oppose it, and they have the law of God and the Law of their Conscience [with them]. . .

Commissary General Ireton: . . . If a man mean by birthright, whatsoever he can challenge by the law of nature, suppose there were no Constitution at all, supposing no Civil law and Civil Constitution—that that I am to contend for against Constitution, you leave no property, nor no foundation for any man to enjoy anything. . . If you merely upon a pretence of a birthright, of the right of nature, which is only true as for your better being; if you will upon that ground pretend, that this Constitution, the most fundamental Constitution, the thing that has reason and equity in it shall not stand in your way, [it] is the same principle to me say I, [as if] but for your better satisfaction you shall take hold of anything that a man calls his own.

Colonel Rainboro: Sir I see, that it is impossible to have liberty but all property must be taken away. . . But I would fain know what the soldier has fought for all this while? He has fought to enslave himself, to give power to men of riches, men of estates, to make him a perpetual slave. . .

Commissary General Ireton: . . . I tell you what the soldier of the Kingdom has fought for. First, the danger that we stood in was, that one man's will must be a law. The people of the Kingdom must have this right at least, that they should not be concluded [but] by the Representative of those that had the interest of the Kingdom. Some men fought in this, because they were immediately concerned and engaged in it. Other men who had no other interest in the Kingdom but this, that they should have the benefit of those laws made by the Representative, yet [fought] that they should have the benefit of this Representative. They thought it was better to be concluded by the common consent of those that were fixed men and settled men that had the interest of his Kingdom [in them], and from that way [said they] I shall know a law and have a certainty. . . And therefore this man I think had a great deal of reason to build up such a foundation of interest to himself: that is, that the will of one man should not be a law, but that the law of this Kingdom should be a choice of persons to represent, and that choice to be made by the generality of the Kingdom. Here was a right that induced men to fight, and those men that had this interest, though this be not the utmost interest that other men have, yet they had some interest. Now why we should go to plead whatsoever we can challenge by the right of nature against whatsoever any man can challenge by Constitution? I do not see where that man will stop as to point of property that he shall not use that right he has by the law of nature against that Constitution. I desire any man to show me where there is a difference. I have been answered 'now we see liberty cannot stand without [destroying] property.' Liberty may be had and property not be destroyed. First, the liberty of all those that have the permanent interest in the Kingdom, that is provided for; and in a general sense liberty cannot be provided for if property be preserved; for if property be preserved—that I am not to meddle with such a man's estate, his meat, his drink, his apparel, or other goods—then the right of nature destroys liberty. By the right of nature I am to have sustenance rather than perish, yet property destroys it for a man to have by the right of nature, suppose there be no human Constitution. . .

Mr. Pettus: The rich would very unwillingly be concluded by the poor; and there is as much reason, and indeed no reason that the rich should conclude the poor as the poor the rich. There should be an equal share in both. I understood your Engagement was, that you would use all your endeavours for the liberties of the people, that they should be secured. If there is a Constitution that the people are not free that should be annulled. But this Constitution does not make people free, that Constitution which is now set up is a Constitution of 40s. a year. . . The great reason that I have heard is [that this is] the Constitution of the Kingdom, the utmost Constitution of it; and if we destroy this Constitution there is no property. I suppose that it were very dangerous if Constitutions should tie up all men in this nature.

COMMISSARY GENERAL IRETON: First the thing itself were dangerous if it were settled to destroy property. But I say the principle that leads to this is destructive to property; for by the same reason that you will alter this Constitution merely that there's a greater Constitution by nature—by the same reason, by the law of nature, there is a greater liberty to the use of other men's goods which that property bars you of. . .

CAPTAIN CLARKE: I presume that the great stick here is this: that if everyone shall have his propiety [i.e. the franchise] it does bereave the Kingdom of its principal, fundamental Constitution that it has. I presume that all people and all nations whatsoever have a liberty and power to alter and change their Constitutions, if they find them to be weak and infirm. Now if the people of England shall find this weakness in their Constitution they may change it if they please. . .

COMMISSARY GENERAL IRETON: That you will alter that Constiution in my apprehension, from a better to a worse, from a just to a thing that is less just, and I will not repeat the reasons of that but refer to what I have declared before. . . Truly therefore I say for my part, to go on a sudden to make such a limitation as that [to inhabitants] in general—if you do extend the latitude [of it so far] that any man shall have a voice in Election who has not that interest in this Kingdom that is permanent and fixed, who has not that interest upon which he may have his freedom in this Kingdom without dependance, you will put it into the hands of men to choose, [instead] of men to preserve their liberty, [men] who will give it away. . .

If there be anything at all that is a foundation of liberty it is this, that those who shall choose the law makers shall be men freed from dependance upon others. . .

LIEUTENANT GENERAL CROMWELL: If we should go about to alter these things, I do not think that we are bound to fight for every particular proposition. Servants while servants are not included. Then you agree that he that receives alms is to be excluded. . .

MR. PETTUS: I conceive the reason why we would exclude apprentices, or servants, or those that take alms, is because they depend upon the will of other men and should be afraid to displease [them]. For servants and apprentices, they are included in their masters, and so for those that receive alms from door to door; but if there be any general way taken for those that are not [so] bound [to the will of other men] it would do well. . .

3. *The law of nature stands as an eternal rule to all men*

JOHN LOCKE, *Second Treatise on Civil Government*, 1690 *

CHAPTER II. OF THE STATE OF NATURE

To understand political power aright, and derive it from its original, we must consider what estate all men are naturally in, and that is, a state of perfect freedom to order their actions, and dispose of their possessions and persons as they think fit, within the bounds of the law of Nature, without asking leave or depending upon the will of any other man.

A state also of equality, where in all the power and jurisdiction is reciprocal, no one having more than another, there being nothing more evident than that creatures of the same species and rank, promiscuously born to all the same advantages of Nature, and the use of the same faculties, should also be equal one amongst another, without subordination or subjection, unless the lord and master of them all should, by any manifest declaration of his will, set one above another, and confer on him, by an evident and clear appointment, an undoubted right to dominion and sovereignty. . .

But though this be a state of liberty, yet it is not a state of license; though man in that state have an uncontrollable liberty to dispose of his person or possessions, yet he has not liberty to destroy himself, or so much as any creature in his possession, but where some nobler use than its bare preservation calls for it. The state of Nature has a law of Nature to govern it, which obliges every one, and reason, which is that law, teaches all mankind who will but consult it, that being all equal and independent, no one ought to harm another in his life, health, liberty or possessions. . . And, being furnished with like faculties, sharing all in one community of Nature, there cannot be supposed any such subordination among us that may authorise us to destroy one another, as if we were made for one another's uses, as the inferior ranks of creatures are for ours. Every one as he is bound to preserve himself, and not to quit his station wilfully, so by the like reason, when his own preservation comes not in competition, ought he as much as he can to preserve the rest of mankind, and not unless it be to do justice on an offender, take away or impair the life, or what tends to the preservation of the life, the liberty, health, limb, or goods of another.

And that all men may be restrained from invading others' rights, and from doing hurt to one another, and the law of Nature be observed, which willeth the peace and preservation of all mankind, the execution of the law of Nature is in that state put into every man's hands, whereby every one has a right to

* Everyman's Library, no. 751, 1924, pp. 118–242, *passim*.

punish the transgressors of that law to such a degree as may hinder its violation. For the law of Nature would, as all other laws that concern men in this world, be in vain if there were nobody that in the state of Nature had a power to execute that law, and thereby preserve the innocent and restrain offenders; and if any one in the state of Nature may punish another for any evil he has done, every one may do so. For in that state of perfect equality, where naturally there is no superiority or jurisdiction of one over another, what any may do in prosecution of that law, every one must needs have a right to do.

And thus, in the state of Nature, one man comes by a power over another, but yet no absolute or arbitrary power to use a criminal, when he has got him in his hands, according to the passionate heats or boundless extravagancy of his own will, but only to retribute to him so far as calm reason and conscience dictate, what is proportionate to his transgression, which is so much as may serve for reparation and restraint. . .

Every offence that can be committed in the state of Nature may, in the state of Nature, be also punished equally, and as far forth, as it may, in a commonwealth. For though it would be beside my present purpose to enter here into the particulars of the law of Nature, or its measures of punishment, yet it is certain there is such a law, and that too as intelligible and plain to a rational creature and a studier of that law as the positive laws of commonwealths, nay, possibly plainer; as much as reason is easier to be understood than the fancies and intricate contrivances of men, following contrary and hidden interests put into words. . .

To this strange doctrine—viz., That in the state of Nature every one has the executive power of the law of Nature—I doubt not but it will be objected that it is unreasonable for men to be judges in their own cases, that self-love will make men partial to themselves and their friends; and, on the other side, ill-nature, passion, and revenge will carry them too far in punishing others, and hence nothing but confusion and disorder will follow, and that therefore God hath certainly appointed government to restrain the partiality and violence of men. I easily grant that civil government is the proper remedy for the inconveniences of the state of Nature, which must certainly be great where men may be judges in their own case, since it is easy to be imagined that he who was so unjust as to do his brother an injury will scarce be so just as to condemn himself for it. But I shall desire those who make this objection to remember that absolute monarchs are but men; and if government is to be the remedy of those evils which necessarily follow from men being judges in their own cases, and the state of Nature is therefore not to be endured, I desire to know what kind of government that is, and how much better it is than the state of Nature, where one man commanding a multitude has the liberty to be judge in his own case, and may do to all his subjects whatever he pleases without the least question or control of those who execute his pleasure? and in whatsoever he doth, whether led by reason, mistake, or passion, must be submitted to? which men in the state of Nature are not bound to do one to another. And if he that judges, judges amiss in his own or any other case, he is answerable for it to the rest of mankind. . .

CHAPTER III. OF THE STATE OF WAR

. . . And hence it is that he who attempts to get another man into his absolute power does thereby put himself into a state of war with him; it being to be understood as a declaration of a design upon his life. For I have reason to conclude that he who would get me into his power without my consent would use me as he pleased when he had got me there, and destroy me too when he had a fancy to it; for nobody can desire to have me in his absolute power unless it be to compel me by force to that which is against the right of my freedom—i.e. make me a slave. To be free from such force is the only security of my preservation, and reason bids me look on him as an enemy to my preservation who would take away that freedom which is the fence to it; so that he who makes an attempt to enslave me thereby puts himself into a state of war with me. . .

And here we have the plain difference between the state of Nature and the state of war, which however some men have confounded, are as far distant as a state of peace, goodwill, mutual assistance, and preservation; and a state of enmity, malice, violence and mutual destruction are one from another. Men living together according to reason without a common superior on earth, with authority to judge between them, is properly the state of Nature. . . Want of a common judge with authority puts all men in a state of Nature; force without right upon a man's person makes a state of war both where there is, and is not, a common judge. . .

CHAPTER V. OF PROPERTY

. . . I shall endeavour to show how men might come to have a property in several parts of that which God gave to mankind in common, and that without any express compact of all the commoners.

God, who hath given the world to men in common, hath also given them reason to make use of it to the best advantage of life and convenience. The earth and all that is therein is given to men for the support and comfort of their being. And though all the fruits it naturally produces, and beasts it feeds, belong to mankind in common, as they are produced by the spontaneous hand of Nature, and nobody has originally a private dominion exclusive of the rest of mankind in any of them, as they are thus in their natural state, yet being given for the use of men, there must of necessity be a means to appropriate them some way or other before they can be of any use, or at all beneficial, to any particular men. The fruit or venison which nourishes the wild Indian, who knows no enclosure, and is still a tenant in common, must be his, and so his—i.e. a part of him, that another can no longer have any right to it before it can do him any good for the support of his life.

Though the earth and all inferior creatures be common to all men, yet every man has a 'property' in his own 'person.' This nobody has any right to but himself. The 'labour' of his body and the 'work' of his hands, we may say, are properly his. Whatsoever, then, he removes out of the state that Nature hath provided and left it in, he hath mixed his labour with it, and joined to it something that is his own, and thereby makes it his property. It being by him removed from the common state Nature placed it in, it hath by this labour something annexed to it that excludes the common right of other men. For this 'labour' being the unquestionable property of the laborer, no man but he can have a right to what that is once joined to, at least where there is enough, and as good left in common for others.

He that is nourished by the acorns he picked up under an oak, or the apples he gathered from the trees in the wood, has certainly appropriated them to himself. Nobody can deny but the nourishment is his. I ask, then, when did they begin to be his? when he digested? or when he ate? or when he boiled? or when he brought them home? or when he picked them up? And it is plain, if the first gathering made them not his, nothing else could. That labour put a distinction between them and common. That added something to them more than Nature, the common mother of all, had done, and so they became his private right. And will any one say he had no right to those acorns or apples he thus appropriated because he had not the consent of all mankind to make them his? Was it a robbery thus to assume to himself what belonged to all in common? If such a consent as that was necessary, man had starved, notwithstanding the plenty God had given him. We see in commons, which remain so by compact, that it is the taking any part of what is common, and removing it out of the state Nature leaves it in, which begins the property, without which the common is of no use. And the taking of this or that part does not depend on the express consent of all the commoners. Thus, the grass my horse has bit, the turfs my servant has cut, and the ore I have digged in any place, where I have a right to them in common with others, become my property without the assignation or consent of anybody. The labour that was mine, removing them out of that common state they were in, hath fixed my property in them. . .

It will, perhaps, be objected to this, that if gathering the acorns or other fruits of the earth, etc., makes a right to them, then any one may engross as much as he will. To which I answer, Not so. The same law of Nature that does by this means give us property, does also bound that property too. 'God has given us all things richly.' Is the voice of reason confirmed by inspiration? But how far has He given it us—'to enjoy'? As much as any one can make use of to any advantage of life before it spoils, so much he may by his labour fix a property in. Whatever is beyond this is more than his share, and belongs to others. Nothing was made by God for man to spoil or destroy. And thus considering the plenty of natural provisions there was a long time in the world, and the few spenders, and how small a part of that provision the industry of one man could extend itself and engross it to the prejudice of others, especially keeping within the bounds set by reason of what might serve for his use, there could be then little room for quarrels or contentions about property so established.

But the chief matter of property being now not the fruits of the earth and the beasts that subsist on it, but the earth itself, as that which takes in and carries with it all the rest, I think it is plain that property in that too is acquired as the former. As much land as a man tills, plants, improves, cultivates, and can use the product of, so much is his property. . .

. . . The same rule of propriety—viz., that every man should have as much as he could make use of, would hold still in the world . . . had not the invention of money, and the tacit agreement of men to put a value on it, introduced (by consent) larger possessions and a right to them. . .

The greatest part of things really useful to the life of man, and such as the necessity of subsisting made the first commoners of the world look after—as it doth the Americans now—are generally things of short duration, such as, if they are not consumed by use will decay and perish of themselves. Gold, silver, and diamonds are things that fancy or agreement hath put the value on, more than real use and the necessary support of life. Now of those good things which Nature hath provided in common, every one hath a right (as hath been said) to as much as he could use, and had a property in all he could effect with his labour; all that his industry could extend to, to alter from the state Nature had put it in, was his. He that gathered a hundred bushels of acorns or apples had thereby a property in them; they were his goods as soon as gathered. He was only to look that he used them before they spoiled, else he took more than his share, and robbed others. And, indeed, it was a foolish thing, as well as dishonest, to hoard up more than he could make use of. If he gave away a part to anybody else, so that it perished not uselessly in his possession, these he also made use of. And if he also bartered away plums that would have rotted in a week, for nuts that would last good for his eating a whole year, he did no injury; he wasted not the common stock; destroyed no part of the portion of goods that belonged to others, so long as nothing perished uselessly in his hands. Again, if he would give his nuts for a piece of metal, pleased with its colour, or exchange his sheep for shells, or wool for a sparkling pebble or a diamond, and keep those by him all his life, he invaded not the right of others; he might heap up as much of these durable things as he pleased; the exceeding of the bounds of his just property not lying in the largeness of his possession, but the perishing of anything uselessly in it.

And thus came in the use of money; some lasting thing that men might keep without spoiling, and that, by mutual consent, men would take in exchange for the truly useful but perishable supports of life.

And as different degrees of industry were apt to give men possessions in different proportions, so this invention of money gave them the opportunity to continue and enlarge them. . .

Thus, in the beginning, all the world was America, and more so than that is now; for no such thing as money was anywhere known. Find out something that hath the use and value of money amongst his neighbors, you shall see the same man will begin presently to enlarge his possessions.

But since gold and silver, being little useful to the life of man, in proportion to food, raiment, and carriage, has its value only from the consent of men—whereof labour yet makes in great part the measure—it is plain that the consent of men have agreed to a disproportionate and unequal possession of the earth—I mean out of the bounds of society and compact; for in governments the laws regulate it; they having, by consent, found out and agreed in a way how a man may, rightfully and without injury, possess more than he himself can make use of by receiving gold and silver, which may continue long in a man's possession without decaying for the overplus, and agreeing those metals should have a value.

And thus, I think, it is very easy to conceive, without any difficulty, how labour could at first begin a title of property in the common things of Nature, and how the spending it upon our uses bounded it; so that there could then be no reason of quarrelling about title, nor any doubt about the largeness of possession it gave. Right and conveniency went together. For as a man had a right to all he could employ his labour upon, so he had no temptation to labour for more than he could make use of. This left no room for controversy about the title, nor for encroachment on the right of others. What portion a man carved to himself was easily seen; and it was useless, as well as dishonest, to carve himself too much, or take more than he needed. . .

CHAPTER VIII. OF THE BEGINNING OF POLITICAL SOCIETIES

Men being, as has been said, by nature all free, equal, and independent, no one can be put out of this estate and subjected to the political power of another without his own consent, which is done by agreeing with other men, to join and unite into a community for their comfortable, safe, and peaceable living, one amongst another, in a secure enjoyment of their properties, and a greater security against any that are not of it. This any number of men may do, because it injures not the freedom of the rest; they are left, as they were, in the liberty of the state of Nature. When any number of men have so consented to make one community or government, they are thereby presently incorporated, and make one body politic, wherein the majority have a right to act and conclude the rest.

For, when any number of men have, by the consent of every individual, made a community, they have thereby made that community one body, with a power to act as one body, which is only by the will and determination of the majority. For that which acts any community, being only the consent of the individuals of it, and it being one body, must move one way, it is necessary the body should move that way whither the greater force carries it, which is the consent of the majority, or else it is impossible it should act or continue one body, one community, which the consent of every individual that united into it agreed that it should; and so every one is bound by that consent to be concluded by the majority. And therefore we see that in assemblies empowered to act by positive laws where no number is set by that positive law which empowers them, the act of the majority passes for the act of the whole, and of course determines as having, by the law of Nature and reason, the power of the whole.

And thus every man, by consenting with others to make one body politic under one government, puts himself under an obligation to every one of that society to submit to the determination of the majority, and to be concluded by it; or else this original compact, whereby he with others incorporates into one society, would signify nothing, and be no compact if he be left free under no other ties than he was in before in the state of Nature. For what appearance would there be of any compact? What new engagement if he were no farther tied by any decrees of the society than he himself thought fit and did actually consent to? This would be still as great a liberty as he himself had before his compact, or any one else in the state of Nature, who may submit himself and consent to any acts of it if he thinks fit.

For if the consent of the majority shall not in reason be received as the act of the whole, and conclude every individual, nothing but the consent of every individual can make anything to be the act of the whole, which, considering the infirmities of health and avocations of business, which in a number though much less than that of a commonwealth, will necessarily keep many away from the public assembly; and the variety of opinions and contrariety of interests which unavoidably happen in all collections of men, it is next impossible ever to be had. And, therefore, if coming into society be upon such terms, it will be only like Cato's coming into the theatre, *tantum ut exiret*. Such a constitution as this would make the mighty leviathan of a shorter duration than the feeblest creatures, and not let it outlast the day it was born in, which cannot be supposed till we can think that rational creatures should desire and constitute societies only to be dissolved. For where the majority cannot conclude the rest, there they cannot act as one body, and consequently will be immediately dissolved again.

Whosoever, therefore, out of a state of Nature unite into a community, must be understood to give up all the power necessary to the ends for which they unite into society to the majority of the community, unless they expressly agreed in any number greater than the majority. And this is done by barely agreeing to unite into one political society, which is all the compact that is, or needs be, between the individuals that enter into or make up a commonwealth. And thus, that which begins and actually constitutes any political society is nothing but the consent of any number of freemen capable of majority, to unite and incorporate into such a society. And this is that, and that only, which did or could give beginning to any lawful government in the world. . .

Every man being, as has been showed, naturally free, and nothing being able to put him into subjection to any earthly power, but only his own consent, it is to be considered what shall be understood to be a sufficient declaration of a man's consent to make him subject to the laws of any government. There is a common distinction of an express and tacit consent, which will concern our present case. Nobody doubts but an express consent of any man, entering into any society, makes him a perfect member of that society, a subject of that government. The difficulty is, what ought to be looked upon as a tacit consent, and how far it binds—i.e. how far any one shall be looked on to have consented, and thereby submitted to any government, where he has made no expression of it at all. And to this I say, that every man that hath any possession or enjoyment of any part of the dominions of any government doth hereby give his tacit consent, and is as far forth obliged to obedience to the laws of that government during such enjoyment, as any one under it, whether this his possession be of land to him and his heirs for ever, or a lodging only for a week; or whether it be barely travelling freely on the highway; and, in effect, it reaches as far as the very being of any one within the territories of that government. . .

CHAPTER IX. OF THE ENDS OF POLITICAL SOCIETY AND GOVERNMENT

If man in the state of Nature be so free as has been said, if he be absolute lord of his own persons and possessions, equal to the greatest and subject to nobody, why will he part with his freedom, this empire, and subject himself to the dominion and control of any other power? To which it is obvious to answer, that though in the state of Nature he hath such a right, yet the enjoyment of it is very uncertain and constantly exposed to the invasion of others; for all being kings as much as he, every man his equal, and the greater part no strict observers of equity and justice, the enjoyment of the property he has in this state is very unsafe, very insecure. This makes him willing to quit this condition which, however free, is full of fears and continual dangers; and it is not without reason that he seeks out and is willing to join in society with others who are already united, or have a mind to unite for the mutual preservation of their lives, liberties and estates, which I call by the general name—property.

The great and chief end, therefore, of men uniting into commonwealths, and putting themselves under government, is the preservation of their property; to which in the state of Nature there are many things wanting.

Firstly, there wants an established, settled, known law, received and allowed by common consent to be the standard of right and wrong, and the common measure to decide all controversies between them. For though the law of Nature be plain and intelligible to all rational creatures, yet men, being biased by their interest, as well as ignorant for want of study of it, are not apt to allow of it as a law binding to them in the application of it to their particular cases.

Secondly, in the state of Nature there wants a known and indifferent judge, with authority to determine all differences according to the established law. For every one in that state being both judge and executioner of the law of Nature, men being partial to themselves, passion and revenge is very apt to carry them too far, and with too much heat in their own cases, as well as negligence and unconcernedness, make them too remiss in other men's.

Thirdly, in the state of Nature there often wants power to back and support the sentence when right, and to give it due execution. They who by any injustice offended will seldom fail where they are able by force to make good their injustice. Such resistance many times makes the punishment dangerous, and frequently destructive to those who attempt it.

Thus mankind, notwithstanding all the privileges of the state of Nature, being but in an ill condition while they remain in it are quickly driven into society. Hence it comes to pass, that we seldom find any number of men live any time together in this state. The inconveniences that they are therein exposed to by the irregular and uncertain exercise of the power every man has of punishing the transgressions of others, make them take sanctuary under the established laws of government, and therein seek the preservation of their property. It is this makes them so willingly give up every one his single power of punishing to be exercised by such alone as shall be appointed to it amongst them, and by such rules as the community, or those authorised by them to that purpose, shall agree on. And in this we have the original right and rise of both the legislative and executive power as well as of the governments and societies themselves.

For in the state of Nature to omit the liberty he has of innocent delights, a man has two powers. The first is to do whatsoever he thinks fit for the preservation of himself and others within the permission of the law of Nature; by which law, common to them all, he and all the rest of mankind are one community, make up one society distinct from all other creatures, and were it not for the corruption and viciousness of degenerate men, there would be no need of any other, no necessity that men should separate from this great and natural community, and associate into lesser combinations. The other power a man has in the state of Nature is the power to punish the crimes committed against that law. Both these he gives up when he joins in a private, if I may so call it, or particular political society, and incorporates into any commonwealth separate from the rest of mankind.

The first power—viz., of doing whatsoever he thought fit for the preservation of himself and the rest of mankind, he gives up to be regulated by laws made by the society, so far forth as the preservation of himself and the rest of that society shall require; which laws of the society in many things confine the liberty he had by the law of Nature.

Secondly, the power of punishing he wholly gives up, and engages his natural force, which he might before employ in the execution of the law of Nature, by his own single authority, as he thought fit, to assist the executive power of the society as the law thereof shall require. For being now in a new state, wherein he is to enjoy many conveniences from the labour, assistance, and society of others in the same community, as well as protection from its whole strength, he is to part also with as much of his natural liberty, in providing for himself, as the good, prosperity, and safety of the society shall require, which is not only necessary but just, since the other members of the society do the like.

But though men when they enter into society give up the equality, liberty, and executive power they had in the state of Nature into the hands of the society, to be so far disposed of by the legislative as the good of the society shall require, yet it being only with an intention in every one the better to preserve himself, his liberty and property (for no rational creature can be supposed to change his condition with an intention to be worse), the power of the society or legislative constituted by them can never be supposed to extend farther than the common good, but is obliged to secure every one's property by providing against those three defects above mentioned that made the state of Nature so unsafe and uneasy. And so, whoever has the legislative or supreme power of any commonwealth, is bound to govern by established standing laws, promulgated and known to the people, and not by extemporary decrees, by indifferent and upright judges, who are to decide controversies by those laws; and to employ the force of the community at home only in the execution of such laws, or abroad to prevent or redress foreign injuries and secure the community from inroads and invasion. And all this to be directed to no other end but the peace, safety, and public good of the people. . .

CHAPTER XI. OF THE EXTENT OF THE LEGISLATIVE POWER

The great end of men's entering into society being the enjoyment of their properties in peace and safety, and the great instrument and means of that being the laws established in that society, the first and fundamental positive law of all commonwealths is the establishing of the legislative power, as the first and fundamental natural law, which is to govern even the legislative itself, is the preservation of the society and (as far as will consist with the public good) of every person in it. This legislative is not only the supreme power of the commonwealth, but sacred and unalterable in the hands where the community have once placed it. Nor can any edict of anybody else, in what form soever conceived, or by what power soever backed, have the force and obligation of a law which has not its sanction from that legislative which the public has chosen and appointed; for without this the law could not have that which is absolutely necessary to its being a law, the consent of the society, over whom nobody can have a power to make laws but by their own consent and by authority received from them. . .

Though the legislative, whether placed in one or more, whether it be always in being or only by intervals, though it be the supreme power in every commonwealth, yet, first, it is not, nor can possibly be, absolutely arbitrary over the lives and fortunes of the people. For it being but the joint power of every member of the society given up to that person or assembly which is legislator, it can be no more than those persons had in a state of Nature before they entered into society, and gave it up to the community. For nobody can transfer to another more power than he has in himself, and nobody has an absolute arbitrary power over himself, or over any other, to destroy his own life, or take away the life or property of another. A man, as has been proved, cannot subject himself to the arbitrary power of another; and having, in the state of Nature, no arbitrary power over the life, liberty, or possession of another, but only so much as the law of Nature gave him for the preservation of himself and the rest of mankind, this is all he doth, or can give up to the commonwealth, and by it to the legislative power, so that the legislative can have no more than this. Their power in the utmost bounds of it is limited to the public good of the society. It is a power that hath no other end but preservation, and therefore can never have a right to destroy, enslave, or designedly to impoverish the subjects; the obligations of the law of Nature cease not in society, but only in many cases are drawn closer, and have by human laws, known penalties annexed to them to enforce their observation. Thus the law of Nature stands as an external rule to all men, legislators as well as others. The rules that they make for other men's actions must, as well as their own and other men's actions, be conformable to the law of Nature—i.e., to the will of God, of which that is a declaration, and the fundamental law of Nature being the preservation of mankind, no human sanction can be good or valid against it. . .

These are the bounds which the trust that is put in them by the society and the law of God and Nature have set to the legislative power of every commonwealth, in all forms of government. First: They are to govern by promulgated established laws, not to be varied in particular cases, but to have one rule for rich and poor, for the favourite at Court, and the countryman at plough. Secondly: These laws also ought to be designed for no other end ultimately but the good of the people. Thirdly: They must not raise taxes on the property of the people without the consent of the people given by themselves or their deputies. And this properly concerns only such governments where the legislative is always in being, or at least where the people have not reserved any part of the legislative to deputies, to be from time to time chosen by themselves. Fourthly: Legislative neither must nor can transfer the power of making laws to anybody else, or place it anywhere but where the people have. . .

CHAPTER XIV. OF PREROGATIVE

Where the legislative and executive power are in distinct hands, as they are in all moderated monarchies and well-framed governments, there the good of the society requires that several things should be left to the discretion of him that has the executive power. For the legislators not being able to foresee and provide by laws for all that may be useful to the community, the executor of the laws, having the power in his hands, has by the common law of Nature a right to make use of it for the good of the society, in many cases where the municipal law has given no direction, till the legislative can conveniently be assembled to provide for it; nay, many things there are which the law can by no means provide for, and those must necessarily be left to the discretion of him that has the executive power in his hands, to be ordered by him as the public good and advantage shall require; nay, it is fit that the laws themselves should in some cases give way to the executive power, or rather to this fundamental law of Nature and government—viz., that as much as may be all the members of the society are to be preserved. For since many accidents may happen wherein a strict and rigid observation of the laws may do harm, as not to pull down an innocent man's house to stop the fire when the next to it is burning; and a man may come sometimes within the reach of the law, which makes no distinction of persons, by an action that may deserve reward and pardon; it is fit the ruler should have a power in many cases to mitigate the severity of the law, and pardon some offenders, since the end of government being the preservation of all as much as may be, even the guilty are to be spared where it can prove no prejudice to the innocent.

This power to act according to discretion for the public good, without the prescription of the law and sometimes even against it, is that which is called prerogative; for since in some governments the law-making power is not always in being and is usually too numerous, and so too slow for the dispatch requisite to execution, and because, also, it is impossible to foresee and so by laws to provide for all accidents and necessities that may concern the public, or make such laws as will do no harm, if they are executed with an inflexible rigour on all occasions and upon all persons that may come in their way, therefore there is a latitude left to the executive power to do many things of choice which the laws do not prescribe.

This power, whilst employed for the benefit of the community and suitably to the trust and ends of the government, is undoubted prerogative, and never is questioned. For the people are very seldom or never scrupulous or nice in the point or questioning of prerogative whilst it is in any tolerable degree employed for the use it was meant—that is, the good of the people, and not manifestly against it. But if there comes to be a question between the executive power and the people about a thing claimed as a prerogative, the tendency of the exercise of such prerogative, to the good or hurt of the people, will easily decide that question. . .

The old question will be asked in this matter of prerogative, 'But who shall be judge when this power is made a right use of?' I answer: Between an executive power in being, with such a prerogative, and a legislative that depends upon his will for their convening, there can be no judge on earth. As there can be none between the legislative and the people, should either the executive or the legislative, when they have got the power in their hands, design, or go about to enslave or destroy them, the people have no other remedy in this, as in all other cases where they have no judge on earth, but to appeal to Heaven; for the rulers in such attempts, exercising a power the people never put into their hands, who can never be supposed to consent that anybody should rule over them for their harm, do that which they have not a right to do. . . And therefore, though the people cannot be judge, so as to have, by the constitution of that society, any superior power to determine and give effective sentence in the case, yet they have reserved that ultimate determination to themselves which belongs to all mankind, where there lies no appeal on earth, by a law antecedent and paramount to all positive laws of men, whether they have just cause to make their appeal to Heaven. And this judgment they cannot part with, it being out of a man's power so to submit himself to another as to give him a liberty to destroy him; God and Nature never allowing a man so to abandon himself as to neglect his own preservation. And since he cannot take away his own life, neither can he give another power to take it. Nor let any one think this lays a perpetual foundation for disorder; for this operates not till the inconvenience is so great that the majority feel it, and are weary of it, and find a necessity to have it amended. And this the executive power, or wise princes, never need come in the danger of; and it is the thing of all others they have most need to avoid, as, of all others, the most perilous. . .

CHAPTER XIX. OF THE DISSOLUTION OF GOVERNMENT

He that will, with any clearness, speak of the dissolution of government, ought in the first place to distinguish between the dissolution of the society and the dissolution of the government. That which makes the community, and brings men out of the loose state of Nature into one politic society, is the agreement which every one has with the rest to incorporate and act as one body, and so be one distinct commonwealth. The usual, and almost only way whereby this union is dissolved, is the inroad of foreign force making a conquest upon them. For in that case (not being able to maintain and support themselves as one entire and independent body) the union belonging to that body, which consisted therein, must necessarily cease, and so every one return to the state he was in before, with a liberty to shift for himself and provide for his own safety, as he thinks fit, in some other society. Whenever the society is dissolved, it is certain the government of that society cannot remain. . .

Besides this overturning from without, governments are dissolved from within:

First. When the legislative is altered, civil society being a state of peace amongst those who are of it, from whom the state of war is excluded by the umpirage which they have provided in their legislative for the ending all differences that may arise amongst any of them; it is in their legislative that the members of a commonwealth are united and combined together into one coherent living body. This is the soul that gives form, life, and unity to the commonwealth; from hence the several members have their mutual influence, sympathy, and connections; and therefore when the legislative is broken, or dissolved, dissolution and death follow. For the essence and union of the society consisting in having one will, the legislative, when once established by the majority, has the declaring and, as it were, keeping of that will. The constitution of the legislative is the first and fundamental act of society, whereby provision is made for the continuation of their union under the direction of persons and bonds of laws, made by persons authorised thereunto, by the consent and appointment of the people, without which no one man, or number of men, amongst them can have authority of making laws that shall be binding to the rest. When any one, or more, shall take upon them to make laws whom the people have not appointed so to do, they make laws without authority, which the people are not therefore bound to obey; by which means they come again to be out of subjection, and may constitute to themselves a new legislative, as they think best, being in full liberty to resist the force of those who, without authority, would impose anything upon them. Every one is at the disposure of his own will, when those who had, by the delegation of the society, the declaring of the public will, are excluded from it, and others usurp the place who have no such authority or delegation.

This being usually brought about by such in the commonwealth, who misuse the power they have, it is hard to consider it aright, and know at whose door to lay it, without knowing the form of government in which it happens. Let us suppose, then, the legislative place in the concurrence of three distinct persons:—First, a single hereditary person having the constant, supreme, executive power, and with it the power of convoking and dissolving the other two within certain periods of time. Secondly, an assembly of hereditary nobility. Thirdly, an assembly of representatives chosen, *pro tempore*, by the people. Such a form of government supposed, it is evident:

First, that when such a single person or prince sets up his own arbitrary will in place of the laws which are the will of the society declared by the legislative, then the legislative is changed. . .

Secondly, when the prince hinders the legislative from assembling in its due time, or from acting freely, pursuant to those ends for which it was constituted the legislative is altered. . .

Thirdly, when, by the arbitrary power of the prince, the electors or ways of election are altered without the consent and contrary to the common interest of the people, there also the legislative is altered. . .

Fourthly, the delivery also of the people into the subjection of a foreign power, either by the prince or by the legislative, is certainly a change of the legislative, and so a dissolution of the government. . .

There is one way more whereby such a government may be dissolved, and that is: When he who has the supreme executive power neglects and abandons that charge, so that the laws already made can no longer be put in execution; this is demonstratively to reduce all to anarchy, and so effectively to dissolve the government. . .

In these, and the like cases, when the government is dissolved, the people are at liberty to provide for themselves by erecting a new legislative differing from the other by the change of persons, or form, or both, as they shall find it most for their safety and good. For the society can never, by the fault of another, lose the native and original right it has to preserve itself, which can only be done by a settled legislative and a fair and impartial execution of the laws made by it. But the state of mankind is not so miserable that they are not capable of using this remedy till it be too late to look for any. To tell people they may provide for themselves by erecting a new legislative, when, by oppression, artifice, or being delivered over to a foreign power, their old one is gone, is only to tell them they may expect relief when it is too late, and the evil is past cure. . .

There is, therefore, secondly, another way whereby governments are dissolved, and that is, when the legislative, or the prince either of them act contrary to their trust.

For the legislative acts against the trust reposed in them when they endeavour to invade the property of the subject, and to make themselves, or any part of the community, masters or arbitrary disposers of the lives, liberties, or fortunes of the people.

The reason why men enter into society is the preservation of their property; and the end while they choose and authorise a legislative is that there may be laws made, and rules set, as guards and fences to the properties of all the society, to limit the power and moderate the dominion of every part and member of the society. For since it can never be supposed to be the will of the society that the legislative should have a power to destroy that which every one designs to secure by entering into society, and for which the people submitted themselves to legislators of their own making: whenever the legislators endeavour to take away and destroy the property of the people, or to reduce them to slavery under arbitrary power, they put themselves into a state of war with the people, who are thereupon absolved from any farther obedience, and are left to the common refuge which God hath provided for all men against force and violence. Whensoever, therefore, the legislative shall transgress this fundamental rule of society, and either by ambition, fear, folly, or corruption, endeavour to grasp themselves, or put into the hands of any other, an absolute power over the lives, liberties, and estates of the people, by this breach of trust they forfeit the power the people had put into their hands for quite contrary ends, and it devolves to the people, who have a right to resume their original liberty, and by the establishment of a new legislative (such as they shall think fit), provide for their own safety and security, which is the end for which they are in society. . .

But it will be said this hypothesis lays a ferment for frequent rebellion. To which I answer:

First: no more than any other hypothesis. For when the people are made miserable, and find themselves exposed to the ill usage of arbitrary power, cry up their governors as much as you will for sons of Jupiter, let them be sacred and divine, descended or authorised from Heaven; give them out for whom or what you please, the same will happen. . .

Secondly: I answer, such revolutions happen not upon every little mismanagement in public affairs. Great mistakes in the ruling part, many wrong and inconvenient laws, and all the slips of human fraility will be borne by the people without mutiny or murmur. But if a long train of abuses, prevarications, and artifices, all tending the same way, make the design visible to the people, and they cannot but feel what they lie under, and see whither they are going, it is not to be wondered that they should then rouse themselves, and endeavour to put the rule into such hands which may secure to them the ends for which government was at first erected, and without which, ancient names and specious forms are so far from being better, that they are much worse than the state of Nature or pure anarchy; the inconveniencies being all as great and as near, but the remedy farther off and more difficult.

Thirdly: I answer, that this power in the people of providing for their safety anew by a new legislative when their legislators have acted contrary to their trust by invading their property, is the best fence against rebellion, and the probablest means to hinder it. For rebellion being an opposition, not to persons, but authority, which is founded only in the constitution and laws of the government: those, whoever they be, who, by force, break through, and, by force, justify their violation of them, are truly and properly rebels. For when men, by entering into society and civil government, have excluded force, and introduced laws for the preservation of property, peace, and unity amongst themselves, those who set up force again in opposition to the laws, do *rebell are*—that is, bring back again the state of war, and are properly rebels, which they who are in power, by the pretence they have to authority, the temptation of force they have in their hands, and the flattery of those about them being likeliest to do, the properest way to prevent the evil is to show them the danger and injustice of it who are under the greatest temptation to run into it.

In both the forementioned cases, when either the legislative is changed, or the legislators act contrary to the end for which they were constituted, those who are guilty are guilty of rebellion. And if those, who by force take away the legislative, are rebels, the legislators themselves, as has been shown, can be no less esteemed so, when they who were set up for the protection and preservation of the people, their liberties and properties shall by force invade and endeavour to take them away; and so they putting themselves into a state of war with those who made them the protectors and guardians of their peace, are properly, and with the greatest aggravation, *rebellantes*, rebels.

But if they who say it lays a foundation for rebellion mean that it may occasion civil wars or intestine broils to tell the people they are absolved from obedience when illegal attempts are made upon their liberties or properties, and may oppose the unlawful violence of those who were their magistrates when they invade their properties, contrary to the trust put in them, and that, therefore, this doctrine is not to be allowed, being so destructive to the peace of the world; they may as well say, upon the same ground, that honest men may not oppose robbers or pirates, because this may occasion disorder or bloodshed. . .

The end of government is the good of mankind; and which is best for mankind, that the people should be always exposed to the boundless will of tyranny, or that the rulers should be sometimes liable to be opposed when they grow exorbitant in the use of their power, and employ it for the destruction, and not the preservation, of the properties of their people?

Nor let any one say that mischief can arise from hence so often as it shall please a busy head or turbulent spirit to desire the alteration of the government. It is true such men may stir whenever they please, but it will be only to their own just ruin and perdition. For till the mischief be grown general, and the ill designs of the rulers become visible, or their attempts sensible to the greater part, the people, who are more disposed to suffer than right themselves by resistance, are not apt to stir. The examples of particular injustice or oppression of here and there an unfortunate man moves them not. But if they universally have a persuasion grounded upon manifest evidence that designs are carrying on against their liberties, and the general course and tendency of things cannot but give them strong suspicions of the evil intention of their governors, who is to be blamed for it? Who can help it if they, who might avoid it, bring themselves into this suspicion? Are the people to be blamed if they have the sense of rational creatures, and can think of things no otherwise than as they find and feel them? And is it not rather their fault who put things in such a posture that they would not have them thought as they are? . . .

Whosoever uses force without right—as every one does in society who does it without law—puts himself into a state of war with those against whom he so uses it, and in that state all former ties are cancelled, all other rights cease, and every one has a right to defend himself, and to resist the aggressor. . .

If a controversy arise betwixt a prince and some of the people in a matter where the law is silent or doubtful, and the thing be of great consequence, I should think the proper umpire in such a case should be the body of the people. . . But if the prince, or whoever they be in the administration, decline that way of determination, the appeal then lies nowhere but to Heaven. Force between either persons who have no known superior on earth, or which permits no appeal to a judge on earth, being properly a state of war, wherein the appeal lies only to Heaven; and in that state the injured party must judge for himself when he will think fit to make use of that appeal and put himself upon it.

To conclude. The power that every individual gave the society when he entered into it can never revert to the individuals again, as long as the society lasts, but will always remain in the community; because without this there can be no community—no commonwealth, which is contrary to the original agreement; so also when the society hath placed the legislative in any assembly of men, to continue in them and their successors, with direction and authority for providing such successors, the legislative can never revert to the people whilst that government lasts; because, having provided a legislative with power to continue for ever, they have given up their political power to the legislative, and cannot resume it. But if they have set limits to the duration of their legislative, and made this supreme power in any person or assembly only temporary; or else when, by the miscarriages of those in authority, it is forfeited; upon the forfeiture of their rulers, or at the determination of the time set, it reverts to the society, and the people have a right to act as supreme, and continue the legislative in themselves or place it in a new form, or new hands, as they think good.

4. *The liberty of a commonwealth consists in the empire of her laws*

JAMES HARRINGTON, *The Commonwealth of Oceana*, 1656 *

. . . Government (to define it *de jure*, or according to ancient prudence) is an art whereby a civil society of men is instituted and preserved upon the foundation of common right or interest; or (to follow Aristotle and Livy) it is the empire of laws, and not of men.

And government (to define it *de facto*, or according to modern prudence) is an art whereby some man, or some few men, subject a city or a nation, and rule it according to his or their private interest: which, because the laws in such cases are made according to the interest of a man, or of some few families, may be said to be the empire of men, and not of laws.

The former kind is that which Machiavel (whose books are neglected) is the only politician that has gone about to retrieve; and that *Leviathan* (who would have his book imposed upon the universities) goes about to destroy. For, *it is* (*says he*) *another error of Aristotle's politics, that in a well-ordered commonwealth not men should govern, but the laws. What man that has his natural senses, tho he can neither write nor read, does not find himself governed by them he fears, and believes can kill or hurt him when he obeys not? Or, who believes that the law can hurt him, which is but words and paper, without the hands and swords of men?* I confess, that the magistrate upon his bench is that to the law, which a gunner upon his platform is to his cannon. Nevertheless, I should not dare to argue with a man of any ingenuity after this manner. A whole army, tho they can neither write nor read, are not afraid of a platform, which they know is but earth or stone; nor of a cannon, which without a hand to give fire to it, is but cold iron; therefore a whole army is afraid of one man. . .

To go on therefore with his preliminary discourse, I shall divide it (according to the two definitions of government . . . in two parts. The first treating of the principles of government in general, and according to the ancients: the second treating of the late governments of *Oceana* in particular, and in that of modern prudence.

* Collected, methodized, and reviewed by John Toland, London, 1777, pp. 37–55 *passim*.

Government, according to the ancients, and their learned disciple Machiavel, the only politician of later ages, is of three kinds; the government of one man, or of the better sort, or of the whole people: which by their more learned names are called *monarchy, aristocracy,* and *democracy.* These they hold, thro their proneness to degenerate, to be all evil. For whereas they that govern should govern according to reason, if they govern according to passion, they do that which they should not do. Wherefore as reason and passion are two things, so government by reason is one thing, and the corruption of government by passion is another thing, but not always another government: as a body that is alive is one thing, and a body that is dead is another thing, but not always another creature, tho the corruption of one comes at length to be the generation of another. The corruption then of *monarchy* is called *tyranny;* that of *aristocracy, oligarchy;* and that of *democracy, anarchy.* But legislators having found these three governments at the best to be naught, have invented another consisting of a mixture of them all, which only is good. This is the doctrine of the ancients.

But *Leviathan* is positive, that they are all deceived, and that there is no other government in nature than one of the three; as also that the flesh of them cannot stink, the names of their corruptions being but the names of men's phansies. . .

To go my own way, and yet to follow the ancients, the principles of government are twofold; internal, or the goods of the mind; and external, or the goods of fortune. The goods of the mind are natural or acquired virtues, as wisdom, prudence, and courage, etc. The goods of fortune are riches. There are goods also of the body, as health, beauty, strength; but these are not to be brought into account upon this score, because if a man or an army acquires victory or empire, it is more from their discipline, arms, and courage, than from their natural health, beauty, or strength, in regard that a people conquered may have more natural strength, beauty and health, and yet find little remedy. The principles of government then are in the goods of the mind, or in the goods of fortune. To the goods of the mind answers authority; to the goods of fortune, power or empire. Wherefore *Leviathan,* tho he be right when he says that *riches are power,* is mistaken where he says that *prudence,* or *the reputation of prudence, is power:* for the learning or prudence of a man is no more power than the learning or prudence of a book or author, which is properly authority. A learned writer may have authority tho he has no power; and a foolish magistrate may have power, tho he has otherwise no esteem or authority. . .

Empire is of two kinds, domestic and national, or foreign and provincial.

Domestic empire is founded upon dominion.

Dominion is property real or personal, that is to say, in lands, or in money and goods.

Lands, or the parts and parcels of a territory, are held by the proprietor or proprietors, lords or lords of it, in some proportion; and such (except it be in a city that has little or no land, and whose revenue is in trade) as is the proportion or balance of dominion or property in land, such is the nature of the empire.

If one man be sole landlord of a territory, or overbalance the people, for example three parts in four, he is Grand Signior: for so the *Turk* is called from his property; and his empire is absolute monarchy. . .

And if the whole people be landlords, or hold the lands so divided among them, that no one man, or number of men, within the compass of the *few* or *aristocracy*, overbalance them, the empire (without the interposition of force) is a commonwealth.

If force be interposed in any of these three cases, it must either frame the government to the foundation, or the foundation to the government; or holding the government not according to the balance, it is not natural, but violent: and therefore if it be at the devotion of a prince, it is *tyranny;* if at the devotion of the few, *oligarchy;* or if in the power of the people, *anarchy*. Each of which confusions, the balance standing otherwise, is but of short continuance, because against the nature of the balance, which, not destroyed, destroys that which opposes it.

But there be certain other confusions, which, being rooted in the balance, are of longer continuance, and of worse consequence; as, first, where a nobility holds half the property, or about that proportion, and the people the other half; in which case, without altering the balance, there is no remedy but the one must eat out the other. . .

But *Leviathan* . . . has caught hold of the public sword, to which he reduces all manner and matter of government; as, where he affirms this opinion [*that any monarch receives his power by covenant, that is to say, upon conditions*] *to procede from the not understanding this easy truth, That covenants being but words and breath, have no power to oblige, contain, constrain, or protect any man, but what they have from the public sword.* But as he said of the law, that without this sword it is but paper; so he might have thought of this sword, that without a hand it is but cold iron. The hand which holds this sword is the militia of a nation; and the militia of a nation is either an army in the field, or ready for the field upon occasion. But an army is a beast that has a great belly, and must be fed; wherefore this will come to what pastures you have, and what pastures you have will come to the balance of property, without which the public sword is but a name or mere spitfrog. Wherefore to set that which *Leviathan* says of arms and of contracts a little straighter; he that can gaze this beast with the great belly . . . may well deride him that imagines he received his power by covenant, or is obliged to any such toy: it being in this case only that covenants are but words and breath. But if the property of the nobility, stocked with their tenants and retainers, be the pasture of that beast, the ox knows his master's crib; and it is impossible for a king in such a constitution to reign otherwise than by covenant; or if he breaks it, it is words that come to blows. . .

Machiavel has missed it very narrowly and more dangerously; for not fully perceiving that if a commonwealth be galled by the gentry, it is by their overbalance, he speaks of the gentry as hostile to popular governments, and of popular governments as hostile to the gentry; and makes us believe that the people in such are so enraged against them, that where they meet a gentleman they kill him; which can never be proved by any one example, unless in civil war; seeing that even in *Switzerland* the gentry are not only safe, but in honor.

But the balance, as I have laid it down, tho unseen by Machiavel, is that which interprets him, and that which he confirms by his judgment in many others as well as in this place, where he concludes, *That he who will go about to make a commonwealth where there be many gentlemen, unless he first destroys them, undertakes an impossibility. And that he who goes about to introduce monarchy where the condition of the people is equal, shall never bring it to pass, unless he cull out such of them as are the most turbulent and ambitious, and make them gentlemen or noblemen, not in name but in effect; that is, by enriching them with lands, castles, and treasures, that may gain them power among the rest, and bring in the rest to dependence upon themselves, to the end that they maintaining their ambition by the prince, the prince may maintain his power by them.*

Wherefore as in this place I agree with Machiavel, that a nobility or gentry, overbalancing a popular government, is the utter bane and destruction of it; so I shall show in another, that a nobility or gentry, in a popular government, not overbalancing it, is the very life and soul of it.

By what has been said, it should seem that we may lay aside further disputes of the public sword, or of the right of the militia; which, be the government what it will, or let it change how it can, is inseparable from the overbalance in dominion: nor, if otherwise stated by the law or custom (as in the commonwealth of *Rome*, where the people having the sword, the nobility came to have the overbalance) avails it to any other end than destruction. For as a building swaying from the foundation must fall, so it fares with the law swaying from reason, and militia from the balance of dominion. And thus much for the balance of national or domestic empire, which is in dominion. . .

I come to the principles of authority, which are internal, and founded upon the goods of the mind. These the legislator that can unite in his government with those of fortune, comes nearest to the work of God, whose government consists of heaven and earth: which was said by Plato, tho in different words, as, when princes should be philosophers, or philosophers princes, the world would be happy. . .

The *soul of man* (whose life or motion is perpetual contemplation or thought) is the mistress of two potent rivals, the one reason, the other passion, that are in continual suit; and, according as she gives up her will to these or either of them, is the felicity or misery which man partakes in this mortal life.

For as whatever was passion in the contemplation of a man, being brought forth by his will into action, is vice and the bondage of sin; so whatever was reason in the contemplation of a man, being brought forth by his will into action, is virtue and the freedom of soul. . .

Now government is no other than the soul of a nation or city: wherefore that which was reason in the debate of a commonwealth being brought forth by the result, must be virtue; and forasmuch as the soul of a city or nation is the sovereign power, her virtue must be law. But the government whose law is virtue, and whose virtue is law, is the same whose empire is authority, and whose authority is empire.

Again, if the liberty of a man consists in the empire of his reason, the absence whereof would betray him to the bondage of his passions; then the liberty of a commonwealth consists in the empire of her laws, the absence whereof would betray her to the lust of tyrants. . .

But seeing they that make the laws in commonwealth are but men, the main question seems to be, how a commonwealth comes to be an empire of laws, and not of men? or how the debate or result of a commonwealth is so sure to be according to reason; seeing they who debate, and they who resolve, be but men? *and as often as reason is against a man, so often will a man be against reason.*

This is thought to be a shrewd saying, but will do no harm; for be it so that reason is nothing but interest, there be diverse interests, and so diverse reasons. . .

Mankind then must either be less just than the creature, or acknowledge also his common interest to be common right. And if reason be nothing else but interest, and the interest of mankind be the right interest, then the reason of mankind must be right reason. Now compute well; for if the interest of popular government come the nearest to the interest of mankind, then the reason of popular government must come the nearest to right reason.

But it may be said, that the difficulty remains yet; for be the interest of popular government right reason, a man does not look upon reason as it is right or wrong in itself, but as it makes for him or against him. Wherefore unless you can show such orders of a government, as, like those of God in nature, shall be able to constrain this or that creature to shake off that inclination which is more peculiar to it, and take up that which regards the common good or interest; all this is to no more end, than to persuade every man in a popular government not to carve himself of that which he desires most, but to be mannerly at the public table, and give the best from himself to decency and the common interest. . .

A commonwealth is but a civil society of men: let us take any number of men (as twenty) and immediately make a commonwealth. Twenty men (if they be not all idiots, perhaps if they be) can never come so together, but there will be such a difference in them, that about a third will be wiser, or at least less foolish than all the rest; these upon acquaintance, tho it be but small, will be discovered, and (as stags that have the largest heads) lead the herd: for while the six discoursing and arguing one with another, show the eminence of their parts, the fourteen discover things that they never thought on; or are cleared in divers truths which had formerly perplexed them. Wherefore in matter of common concernment, difficulty, or danger, they hang upon their lips as children upon their fathers; and the influence thus acquired by the six, the eminence of whose parts are found to be a stay and comfort to the fourteen, is the *authority of the fathers*. . . The six then approved of, as in the present case, are the senate, not by hereditary right, or in regard of the greatness of their estates only (which would tend to such power as might force or draw the people) but by election for their excellent parts, which tends to the advancement of the influence of their virtue or authority that leads the people. Wherefore the office of the senate is not to be commanders, but counsellors of the people; and that which is proper to counsellors is first to debate, and afterward to give advice in the business whereupon they have debated. . . But to debate, is to discern or put a difference between things that, being alike, are not the same; or it is separating and weighing this reason against that, and that reason against this, which is dividing. . .

Dividing and choosing in the language of a commonwealth is debating and resolving; and whatsoever upon debate of the senate is proposed to the people, and resolved by them, is enacted by the authority of the fathers, and by the power of the people, which concurring, make a law.

But the law being made, says *Leviathan, is but words and paper without the hands and swords of men;* wherefore as these two orders of a commonwealth, namely the senate and the people, are legislative, so of necessity there must be a third to be executive of the laws made, and this is the magistracy; in which order, with the rest being wrought up by art, the commonwealth consists of *the senate proposing, the people resolving, and the magistracy executing:* whereby partaking of the *aristocracy* as in the senate, of the *democracy* as in the people, and of *monarchy* as in the magistracy, it is complete. . . But the magistracy both in number and function is different in different commonwealths. Nevertheless there is one condition of it that must be the same in every one. . . And this is no less than that as the hand of the magistrate is the executive power of the law, so the head of the magistrate is answerable to the people, that his execution be according to the law; by which *Leviathan* may see that the hand or sword that executes the law is in it, and not above it. . .

. . . Let me invite *Leviathan,* who of all other governments gives the advantage to monarchy for perfection, to a better disquisition of it by these three assertions.

The first, that the perfection of government lies upon such a libration in the frame of it, that no man or men in or under it can have the interest; or having the interest, can have the power to disturb it with sedition.

The second, that monarchy, reaching the perfection of the kind, reaches not to the perfection of government; but must have some dangerous flaw in it.

The third, that popular government, reaching the the perfection of the kind, reaches the perfection of government, and has no flaw in it. . .

For the proof of the third assertion; *Leviathan* yields it to me, that there is no other commonwealth, but monarchical or popular: wherefore if no monarchy be a perfect government, then either there is no perfect government, or it must be popular; for which kind of constitution I have something more to say, than *Leviathan* has said or ever will be able to say for monarchy. . .

An equal commonwealth is such a one as is equal both in the balance or foundation, and in the superstructure; that is to say, in her Agrarian law, and in her rotation.

An equal *Agrarian* is a perpetual law establishing and preserving the balance of dominion by such a distribution, that no one man or number of men, within the compass of the few or *aristocracy,* can come to overpower the whole people by their possessions in lands.

As the *Agrarian* answers to the foundation, so does *rotation* to the superstructures.

Equal *rotation* is equal vicissitude in government, or succession to magistracy conferred for such convenient terms, enjoying equal vacations, as take in the whole body by parts, succeeding others, thro the free election or suffrage of the people.

The contrary whereunto is prolongation of magistracy, which, trashing the wheel of rotation, destroys the life or natural motion of a commonwealth.

The election or suffrage of the people is most free, where it is made or given in such a manner, that it can neither oblige nor disoblige another; nor thro fear of an enemy, or bashfulness towards a friend, impair a man's liberty. . .

An *equal commonwealth* (by that which has been said) *is a government established upon equal Agrarian, arising into the superstructures or three orders, the senate debating and proposing, the people resolving, and the magistracy executing by an equal rotation thro the suffrage of the people given by the the ballot.* For tho rotation may be without the ballot, and the ballot without rotation, yet the ballot not only as to the insuing model includes both, but is by far the most equal way; for which cause under the name of the ballot I shall hereafter understand both that and rotation to. . .

5. *Every man invested with power is apt to abuse it*

BARON CHARLES-LOUIS DE SECONDAT DE MONTESQUIEU, *The Spirit of Laws*, 1721 *

DIFFERENT SIGNIFICATIONS OF THE WORD LIBERTY

There is no word that admits of more various significations, and has made more different impressions on the human mind, than that of *Liberty*. Some have taken it for a facility of deposing a person on whom they had conferred a tyrannical authority; others for the power of choosing a superior whom they are obliged to obey; others for the right of bearing arms, and of being thereby enabled to use violence; others, in fine, for the privilege of being governed by a native of their own country, or by their own laws. . . Some have annexed this name to one form of government exclusive of others: Those who had a republican taste, applied it to this species of polity; those who liked a monarchical state, gave it to monarchy. Thus they have all applied the name of *Liberty* to the government most suitable to their own customs and inclinations: and as in republics, the people have not so constant and so present a view of the causes of their misery, and as the magistrates seem to act only in conformity to the laws, hence liberty is generally said to reside in republics, and to be banished from monarchies. In fine, as in democracies the people seem to act almost as they please; this sort of government has been deemed the most free; and the power of the people has been confounded with their liberty.

IN WHAT LIBERTY CONSISTS

It is true, that in democracies the people seem to act as they please; but political

* Translated from the French by Thomas Nugent, 4th ed., London, Printed for J. Nourse and P. Vaillant, vol. 1, book 11, 1766.

liberty does not consist in an unlimited freedom. In governments, that is, in societies directed by laws, liberty can consist only in the power of doing what we ought to will, and in not being constrained to do, what we ought not to will.

We must have continually present to our minds the difference between independence and liberty. Liberty is a right of doing whatever the laws permit; and if a citizen could do what they forbid, he would be no longer possessed of liberty, because all his fellow citizens would have the same power.

Democratic and aristocratic states are not in their own nature free. Political liberty is to be found only in moderate governments: and even in these, it is not always found. It is there only when there is no abuse of power; but constant experience shows us, that every man invested with power is apt to abuse it; and to carry his authority as far as it will go. Is it not strange, though true, that virtue itself has need of limits?

To prevent this abuse, it is necessary from the very nature of things, power should be a check to power. A government may be so constituted, as no man shall be compelled to do things to which the law does not oblige him, nor forced to abstain from things which the law permits.

OF THE END OR VIEW OF DIFFERENT GOVERNMENTS

Though all governments have the same general end, which is that of preservation, yet each has another particular object. Increase of dominion was the object of Rome; war, that of Sparta; religion, that of the Jewish laws; commerce, that of Marseilles; public tranquillity, that of the laws of China; navigation, that of the laws of Rhodes; natural liberty, that of the policy of the Savages; in general, the pleasures of the prince, that of despotic states; that of monarchies, the prince's and the kingdom's glory: the independence of individuals is the end aimed at by the laws of Poland, from thence results the oppression of the whole.

One nation there is also in the world, that has for the direct end of its constitution political liberty. We shall presently examine the principles on which this liberty is founded; if they are found, liberty will appear in its highest perfection.

To discover political liberty in a constitution, no great labor is requisite. If we are capable of seeing it where it exists, it is soon found, and we need not go far in search of it.

OF THE CONSTITUTION OF ENGLAND

In every government there are three sorts of power: the legislative; the executive in respect to things dependent on the law of nations; and executive, in regard to matters that depend on the civil law.

By virtue of the first, the prince, or magistrate, enacts temporary or perpetual laws, and amends or abrogates those that have been already enacted. By the second, he makes peace or war, sends or receives embassies, establishes the public security, and provides against invasions. By the third, he punishes criminals, or determines the disputes that arise between individuals. The latter we shall call the judiciary power, and the other simply the executive power of the state.

The political liberty of the subject is a tranquillity of mind arising from the opinion each person has of his safety. In order to have this liberty, it is requisite the government be so constituted as one man need not be afraid of another.

When the legislative and executive powers are united in the same person, or in the same body of magistrates, there can be no liberty; because apprehensions may arise, lest the same monarch or senate should enact tyrannical laws, to execute them in a tyrannical manner.

Again, there is no liberty, if the judiciary power be not separated from the legislative and executive. Were it joined with the legislative, the life and liberty of the subject would be exposed to arbitrary control; for the judge would be then the legislator. Were it joined to the executive power, the judge might behave with violence and oppression.

There would be an end of everything, were the same man, or the same body, whether of the nobles or of the people, to exercise those three powers, that of enacting laws, that of executing the public resolutions, and of trying the causes of individuals. . .

The judiciary power ought not to be given to a standing senate, it should be exercised by persons taken from the body of the people, at certain times of the year, and consistently with a form and manner prescribed by law, in order to erect a tribunal that should last only so long as necessity requires.

By this method the judicial power so terrible to mankind, not being annexed to any particular state or profession, becomes, as it were, invisible. People have not then the judges continually present to their view; they fear the office, but not the magistrate.

In accusations of a deep or criminal nature, it is proper the person accused should have the privilege of choosing in some measure his judges in concurrence with the law; or at least he should have a right to except against so great a number, that the remaining part may be deemed his own choice.

The other two powers may be given rather to magistrates or permanent bodies, because they are not exercised on any private subject; one being no more than the general will of the state, and the other the execution of that general will.

But though the tribunals ought not to be fixed, the judgments ought; and to such a degree as to be ever conformable to the letter of the law. Were they to be the private opinion of the judge, people would then live in society, without exactly knowing the nature of their obligations.

The judges ought likewise to be of the same rank as the accused, or in other words, his peers; to the end that he may not imagine he is fallen into the hands of persons inclined to treat him with rigour.

If the legislature leaves the executive power in possession of a right to imprison those subjects, who can give security for their good behaviour, there is an end of liberty; unless they are taken up, in order to answer without delay to a capital crime; in which case they are really free, being subject only to the power of the law. . .

As in a country of liberty, every man who is supposed a free agent, ought to be his own governor; the legislative power should reside in the whole body of the people. But since this is impossible in large states, and in small ones is subject to many inconveniencies; it is fit the people should transact by their representatives, what they cannot transact by themselves.

The inhabitants of a particular town are much better acquainted with its wants and interests, than with those of other places; and are better judges of the capacity of their neighbours, than of that of the rest of their countrymen. The members therefore of the legislature should not be chosen from the general body of the nation; but it is proper that in every considerable place, a representative should be elected by the inhabitants.

The great advantage of representatives is their capacity of discussing public affairs. For this the people collectively are extremely unfit, which is one of the chief inconveniences of a democracy.

It is not at all necessary that the representatives who have received a general instruction from their constituents, should wait to be directed on each particular affair, as is practiced in the diets of Germany. True it is, that by this way of proceeding, the speeches of the deputies might with greater propriety be called the voice of the nation; but, on the other hand, this would occasion infinite delays; would give each deputy a power of controlling the assembly; and, on the most urgent and pressing occasions, the wheels of government might be stopped by the caprice of a single person. . .

Neither ought the representative body to be chosen for the executive part of the government, for which it is not so fit; but for the enacting of laws, or to see whether the laws in being are duly executed, a thing suited to their abilities, and which none indeed but themselves can properly perform.

In such a state there are always persons distinguished by their birth, riches, or honors: but were they to be confounded with the common people, and to have only the weight of a single vote like the rest, the common liberty would be their slavery, and they would have no interest in supporting it, as most of the popular resolutions would be against them. The share they have therefore in the legislature ought to be proportioned to their other advantages in the state; which happens only when they form a body that has a right to check the licentiousness of the people, as the people have a right to oppose any encroachment of theirs.

The legislative power is therefore committed to the body of the nobles, and to that which represents the people, each having their assemblies and deliberations apart, each their separate views and interests.

Of the three powers above mentioned, the judiciary is in some measure next to nothing: there remain therefore only two; and as these have need of a regulating power to moderate them, the part of the legislative body composed of the nobility, is extremely proper for this purpose.

The body of the nobility ought to be hereditary. In the first place it is so in its own nature; and in the next there must be a considerable interest to preserve its privileges; privileges that in themselves are obnoxious to popular envy, and of course in a free state are always in danger.

But as an hereditary power might be tempted to pursue its own particular interests, and forget those of the people; it is proper that where a singular advantage may be gained by corrupting the nobility, as in the laws relating to the supplies, they should have no other share in the legislation, than the power of rejecting, and not that of resolving.

By the *power of resolving*, I mean the right of ordaining by their own authority, or of amending what has been ordained by others. By the *power of rejecting*, I would be understood to mean the right of annulling a resolution taken by another. . .

The executive power ought to be in the hands of a monarch, because this branch of government, having need of dispatch, is better administered by one than by many: on the other hand, whatever depends on the legislative power, is oftentimes better regulated by many than by a single person.

But if there were no monarch, and the executive power should be committed to a certain number of persons selected from the legislative body, there would be an end then of liberty; by reason the two powers would be united, as the same persons would sometimes possess, and would be always able to possess, a share in both.

Were the legislative body to be a considerable time without meeting, this would likewise put an end to liberty. For of two things one would naturally follow; either that there would be no longer any legislative resolutions, and then the state would fall into anarchy; or that these resolutions would be taken by the executive power, which would render it absolute. . .

Were the executive power not to have a right of restraining the encroachments of the legislative body, the latter would become despotic; for as it might arrogate to itself what authority it pleased, it would soon destroy all the other powers.

But it is not proper, on the other hand, that the legislative power should have a right to stay the executive. For as the execution has its natural limits, it is useless to confine it; besides, the executive power is generally employed in momentary operations. . .

But if the legislative power in a free state, has no right to stay the executive, it has a right and ought to have the means of examining in what manner its laws have been executed. . .

But whatever may be the issue of that examination, the legislative body ought not to have a power of arraigning the person, nor of course the conduct of him who is intrusted with the executive power. His person should be sacred, because as it is necessary for the good of the state to prevent the legislative body from rendering themselves arbitrary, the moment he is accused or tried, there is an end of liberty.

In this case, the state would be no longer a monarchy, but a kind of republic, though not a free government. . .

Here then is the fundamental constitution of the government we are treating of. The legislative body being composed of two parts, they check one another by the mutual privilege of rejecting. They are both restrained by the executive power, as the executive is by the legislative.

These three powers should naturally form a state of repose or inaction. But as there is a necessity for movement in the course of human affairs, they are forced to move, but still in concert.

As the executive power has no other part in the legislative, than the privilege of rejecting, it can have no share in the public debates. It is not even necessary that it should propose, because as it may always disapprove of the resolutions that shall be taken, it may likewise reject the decisions on those proposals which were made against its will. . .

As all human things have an end, the state we are speaking of will lose its liberty, will perish. Have not Rome, Sparta, and Carthage perished? It will perish when the legislative power shall be more corrupt than the executive.

It is not my business to examine whether the English actually enjoy this liberty, or not. Sufficient it is for my purpose to observe, that it is established by their laws; and I inquire no farther.

Neither do I pretend by this to undervalue other governments, nor to say that this extreme political liberty ought to give uneasiness to those who have only a moderate share of it. How should I have any such design, I who think that even the highest refinement of reason is not always desirable, and that mankind generally find their account better in mediums than in extremes?

Harrington, in his *Oceana*, has also enquired into the utmost degree of liberty, to which the constitution of a state may be carried. But of him indeed it may be said, that for want of knowing the nature of real liberty, he busied himself in pursuit of an imaginary one; and that he built a Chalcedon, though he had a Byzantium before his eyes. . .

SELECTED REFERENCES

Jason Aronson, 'Shaftesbury on Locke,' *American Political Science Review*, December 1959, vol. 53, no. 4, pp. 1101–1

A. C. Coolidge, *Theoretical and Foreign Elements in the Formation of the American Constitution*, Freiburg, 1892.

Theodore D. Dwight, 'Harrington and His Influence upon American Political Institutions and Political Thought,' *Political Science Quarterly*, March 1887, vol. 2, pp 1–45.

J. W. Gough, 'Harrington and Contemporary Thought,' *Political Science Quarterly*, September 1930, vol. 45, pp. 395–404.

William G. Hastings, 'Montesquieu and Anglo-American Institutions,' *Illinois Law Review*, 1918–19, vol. 13, pp. 419–30.

John Locke, Two Treatises on Government, a critical edition, Peter Laslett, ed., Cambridge, England, 1960.

'The English Revolution and Locke's Two Treatises,' *Cambridge Historical Journal*, XII, 1956, pp. 40–45.

C. MacPherson, *The Political Theory of Possessive Individualism: Hobbes to Locke*, Oxford, The Clarendon Press, 1962.

James Monroe, *The People the Sovereign: Being a Comparison of the Government of the United States with Those of the Republics which have Existed Before, with the Causes of their Decadence and Fall*, Philadelphia, J. P. Lippincott, 1867. Pages 142–55 deal with the ideas of Locke and Montesquieu in their relation to America.

N. C. Phillips, 'Political Philosophy and Political Fact: The Evidence of John Locke,' in *Liberty and Learning: Essays in Honor of Sir James Hight*, Christchurch, Whitcombe & Tombs, 1950.

Florence A. Pooke, *Fountain-Sources of American Political Theory, A Study of the Origin and Meaning of the Democratic Political Theories in the American Declaration of Independence*, New York, Copeland, 1930.

George Sabine, *A History of Political Theory*, New York, Henry Holt, 1937. Pages 477–508, 517–42, 551–60 especially.

H. F. Russell Smith, *Harrington and His Oceana: A Study of a 17th Century Utopia and Its Influence in America*, Cambridge, Cambridge University Press, 1914.

Paul Merrill Spurlin, *Montesquieu in America, 1760–1801*, Baton Rouge, Louisiana State University Press, 1940.

Puritanism and Liberty, being the Army Debates (1647–9) from Clarke Manuscripts with Supplementary Documents, A. S. Woodhouse, ed., London, J. M. Dent, 1938. Foreword by A. D. Lindsay.

Francis D. Wormuth, *The Origins of Modern Constitutionalism*, New York, Harper, 1948. Parts II and III especially.

II

AUTHORITARIAN THEOLOGY AND DEMOCRATIC DISSENT IN THE NEW WORLD

'The popular movement of the American revolution,' John Quincy Adams noted in 1836, 'had been preceded by a foreseeing and directing mind.' Not by one mind, Adams said, 'but by a pervading mind, which in a preceding age had inspired the prophetic verses of Berkeley, and which may be traced back to the first Puritan Settlers of Plymouth and Massachusetts Bay.' The religious element in the American tradition, to which Adams referred, expressed itself most forcibly among the New England colonists of the seventeenth century in the rigid authoritarian theology of John Cotton, John Winthrop, and Nathaniel Ward, and in the bold insurgency of dissidents like Roger Williams and Jonathan Mayhew.

A great variety of considerations impelled these migrants to dare 'the desarts of America'—especially the desire to establish here a religious system. In the words of one: 'necessity may presse some, Novelties draw on others; hopes of gaine in time to come may prevaile with a third sort; but that the most and most sincere and godly part have the advancement of the *Gospel* for their maine scope I am confident.' The Puritans brought with them the common-law tradition and its institutions, also a profound sense of hierarchy and of social and economic class distinctions. The democratic idea of equality was non-existent. Massachusetts was settled for religious reasons; these included, John Winthrop observed, 'a due forme of Government both civill and ecclesiasticall.' But coloring and shaping their migration throughout was the all-pervasive ecclesiastical polity that glares at us still from the portraits of these pioneering Puritans.

More than practical politicians and astute churchmen, they were prolific literary exponents of church government. The ideas they espoused, the creed they defended, were ready-made from the outset. It was 'simply a part,' as Herbert L. Osgood has said, 'of a great movement, the wing of an army.' On this side of the Atlantic, however, old doctrines and old ways were destined to undergo rigorous testing. In time the same spirit that drove these sturdy souls to leave England and settle in America made them restive in their new habitat under the Puritan orthodoxy.

'From the first Institution of the Company of Massachusetts Bay,' wrote Dr. Donald Robertson, a public school teacher who helped prepare James Madison for Princeton, 'its members seem to have been animated with a spirit of innovation in civil policy as well as in religion; and by the habit of rejecting established usages in the one, they were prepared for deviating from them in the other. They had applied for a royal charter, in order to give legal effect to their operations in England, as acts of a body politic; but the persons whom they sent out to America as soon as they landed there, considered themselves as individuals, united together by voluntary association, possessing the natural right of men who form a society to adopt what mode of government and to enact what laws they deemed most conducive to general felicity.'

The Puritans came to America not to establish democracy but to found a more autonomous religious order, to win religious freedom not for others but for themselves. Puritanism meant unquestioning acceptance of God's sovereignty. The Bible containing His law had to be accepted as interpreted by the clergy, an official class, 'the elect,' who derived their authority from the church. To create that perfect Christian community, the state, a lesser sphere, was integrated with the church. Civil magistracy served to furnish the external conditions of public order and security. State and Church alike were of divine origin. Both were in the service of God, and to disobey or resist either was to subvert His sovereignty. 'Let no man here deceive himself, since he cannot resist God,' John Calvin declared in his *Institutes*. 'No polity can be successfully established unless piety be its first care.' But morality reinforced by religion was not enough. To secure property and public order, the state must punish idolarty, heresy, slander, blasphemy, and non-conformity. Presumably clear and explicit, truth was contained in the written word of God. In the society established on this continent, truth would forever reign supreme.

The Puritans thus set up theocracy in America just as John Calvin, reforming lawyer and theologian, had done in old Geneva, ruling by a small group, the 'elect.' As in Calvin's community of Geneva, so in John Winthrop's Massachusetts, non-church members could not hold civil office. Enjoyment of civil rights was likewise limited to 'saints,' foreordained for salvation. To Calvin, possessed of 'an autocrat's aversion to disorder and anarchy,' democracy was synonymous with chaos. It meant the elevation of the rabble above the devout and regenerate—a perversion of Christian values, a brazen insult to reason. Winthrop dubbed democracy 'the meanest and worst of all formes of Government . . . of least continuance and fullest of troubles . . . either for church or commonwealth.' 'God Almightie in his most holy and wise providence,' Winthrop averred, 'hath soe disposed of the condicion of mankinde, as in all times some must be rich, some poore, some high and eminent in power and dignity, others meane and in subieccion.' 'If the people be governors,' John Cotton blandly asked, 'who will be governed?' 'Democracy I do not conceive that ever God did ordain as fit government either in church or commonwealth. . . As for monarchy, and aristocracy, they are both of them clearly approved, and directed in scripture, yet so as referreth the Soveragntie to himselfe, and setteth up Theocracy in both, as the best forme of government in the Commonwealth, as well as in the Church.'

Among the most readable and ingenious defenses of Puritan theocracy is Nathaniel Ward's (1578–1652) *Simple Cobler of Aggawam*, leading the selections in this chapter. Ward had spent only twelve years in Massachusetts Bay, but he was an important and vital figure. Having earlier participated in the formation of the company, he contributed most of the material for the 'Body of Liberties,' the colony's legal code, adopted in 1641. Trained at Emanuel College, Cambridge, in both law and religion, he practiced law for fifteen years and then entered the ministry. Excommunicated from the Church of England for preaching Puritan doctrines, he came to America and accepted the pastorate at Aggawam (Ipswich), Massachusetts. In the New World he was as intolerant of unorthodox doctrines as Archbishop Laud had been in the Old World.

The *Simple Cobler* was 'Willing to help' mend his 'Native Country, lamentably tattered, both in the upper-Leather and sole, with all the honest stitches he can take.' The country was, as he saw it, rent and torn by 'diametrical contradictions' and a multimonstrous maufrey of heteroclytes and quicquidlibets'—that is, by tolerance of false opinions. As a remedy the punning shoemender suggested elimination of all false belief and imposition of that uniformity, that unity which God and truth required. The state to Ward was the agent of the Church, its primary duty to insure the latter against attack by false religionists. No argument of natural rights and liberties, of popular sovereignty, or of natural law could prevail against his devout authoritarianism. The God-given liberties must be protected and God's authority devoutly obeyed. The precise contours of such liberties Ward left quite vague, though his hatred of false opinions would seem to preclude any civil or religious views not in accord with his own.

The permissible range and scope of these all-important liberties were clarified somewhat by John Winthrop (1588–1649), the first governor of Massachusetts Bay. Non-cleric and lawyer, Winthrop, unlike Ward, did not come to America primarily for religious freedom. A member of a wealthy Suffolk family, he found that he could not maintain his social position there on his income. In England, he said 'no man's estate will suffice to keepe sail with his "equalls".' So he joined the Massachusetts Bay Company and came to America in 1630, where he remained for the rest of his life, serving as governor of the colony for nine years and as deputy governor for ten more. In 1645 he became involved in a serious controversy resulting in his trial before the general court. The 'people' of the town of Hingham had chosen a captain for the militia company, but the magistrates, including Winthrop, refused to confirm the election. A long conflict ensued, culminating in his impeachment on the ground that he had exceeded his power and 'that the people's liberty was thereby in danger.' Acquitted of all charges, he asked permission to give a 'little speech' in answer to those who had asserted natural rights against him and the other magistrates, and concluded that liberty was based on authority, on permission to do what is good, just and honest. Though his speech deals only with liberty, it clearly reflects a preference for mixed aristocracy and abhorrence of democracy in either Church or Commonwealth.

In the theocratic government of New England the dictators were not absolute and irresponsible. John Cotton (1584–1652), clerical spokesman for Massachusetts rulers, insisted 'that all power that is on earth be limited.' Preacher and theologian, Cotton was born in Derby, Derbyshire. Entering Trinity College, Cambridge, at the age of thirteen, he finished his education at Emmanuel College in 1606. He came to New England with Thomas Hooker, his nearest rival in reputation and learning, and immediately became teacher of the Boston church. A commanding figure in the councils of Congregationalism, his most famous utterance is the letter he wrote in 1636 to Lord Say and Seal defending, as the very foundation of the Bible Commonwealth, the Massachusetts requirement that made admission to citizenship, regardless of social position, dependent on church membership. 'Limitation of Government,' included in this chapter, furnishes the other side of Puritan political theory—limitations set by fundamental law and basic right.

Re-examination of the fundamentals of Church and State was first stimulated in Massachusetts Bay. Here the authoritarianism of the Puritan system was opposed by increasing numbers of stubborn democratic dissenters. Latent in its authoritarian form of organization were the seeds of democracy. In Congregationalism and Separatism may be found principles that contributed to the shaping of American democratic thought. The Separatists repulsed attempts to impose uniformity, by withdrawing from organized church systems and establishing their own, contributing thereby to that diversity so characteristic of latter-day American democracy. Likewise, the Congregationalists' form of church organization under which the congregation called and censored the minister was based upon the equality and sovereignty of the people—principles extending from church to civil government and thus contributing the doctrinal groundwork for revolution and democracy in later years.

Spearheading this reaction against authoritarianism in the Bay Colony, was Roger Williams (1603–82), 'a certain Windmill,' Cotton Mather called him, 'whirling round with extraordinary violence.' Williams began his pulpit career as an Anglican, turned to Separatism, and ended as a Seeker. Never certain that he had reached the absolute truth he sought, Williams was constantly striving for better understanding of both God and man. Such a liberal religious attitude fitted awkwardly into the Bay Colony authoritarianism, and it ultimately led to his removal from the Salem pastorate. Religious unorthodoxy was but a single facet of his betrayal. He opposed the required oath of fidelity, and denied the power of the magistrates to enforce purely religious commandments. He went even further, denouncing grants of land to the colonists as 'unjust usurpations upon others possessions'—that is, those of the Indians, from whom the land had been wrested without any semblance of legality. Tried in October 1635 for preaching 'newe and dangerous opinions, against the aucthoritie of magistrates,' he was ordered banished, but allowed to stay on through the winter on condition that he behave and desist from spreading his vicious ideas among the colonists. True to his nature, Williams did not behave but continued holding meetings at his house. For this offense he was ordered arrested. Escaping in mid-winter to the wild Narragansett country, he bought a tract of land from the Indians and established his 'Providence Plantations.' Here Williams began the first American experiment in democracy and tolerance, attempting to put into practice the ideas advanced in *The Bloudy Tenent of Persecution*, written during his controversy with John Cotton of Massachusetts Bay, and herein excerpted.

The Church and State need not be, Williams insisted, inextricably linked:

'A *Pagan* or *Antichristian Pilot* may be as skilful to carry the Ship to its desired Port, as any *Christian Mariner* or *Pilot* in the World, and may performe that worke with as much safety and speed.' 'God requireth not an *Uniformity* of Religion to be *inacted and inforced* in any Civill State,' he declared. Rather the tares in the field of Christian grain must be left alone; let man hold whatever religious opinions he choses provided he does not 'actually disturb civil peace,' ran a provision of the Rhode Island Charter of 1663; let civil government be based on the consent of the governed. 'The *Soveraigne*, originall, and *foundation* of *civil power* lies in the *People*,' Williams insisted. They 'may erect and establish what *forme* of *Government* seemes to them most meete for their *Civill* condition.'

Williams's plea for Separation of Church and State stemmed far less, Harold Laski writes, from tender concern for men's consciences than from 'a fear that their unity meant the government of the Church by civil men and thus a threat to its purity.' Popular control of the Church through elected magistrates Williams thought evil since it gave the Church 'to Satan himself, by whom all peoples natural are guided.' The precise intention of Scripture could not be ascertained, he believed, with the icy certainty claimed by the New England clergy. He wanted Church and State separated so the Church would not be corrupted by the State. Thomas Jefferson entertained the opposite conviction, fearing that the State would become contaminated by the Church.

It was not until 1715 that John Wise (1652–1729), son of an indentured servant, broadened and deepened the foundations of popular government, grounding it in 'natural reason,' in 'an original freedom of mankind.' In the treatise herein quoted Wise portrays democracy 'as agreeable with the light and laws of nature as any other whatever . . . and more accommodated to the concerns of religion than another.'

Wise attended Harvard and became a Congregational minister, serving as chaplain of the Quebec expedition in 1690. He was one of the few who protested against the witchcraft trials. Wise was fined, imprisoned, and removed from the ministry for his protest against arbitrary taxation. The *Vindication*, included in this chapter, was his answer to the Presbyterians who tried to bring the Congregational churches under their control to prevent the disruption of their theocracy. In attempting to establish the fundamentals of church government as it was known by the Congregationalists, he explored the basis of political government as well. The grounds on which he justified church authority were equally valid for political organizations, being based on natural rights and the doctrine that the people alone are the source of civil authority.

Another generation passed before Jonathan Mayhew (1720–66) reached the logical and more advanced democratic conclusion that utility and happiness are the sole ends of any government resting on consent. Any government that ignores these goals is evil and properly subject to the right of revolution.

Mayhew, the pastor of the West Church in Boston, was regarded as a radical agitator, so suspect that only two other ministers would attend his ordination ceremonies. He believed strongly in the principle of resistance to tyranny, and elevated it to the plane of religious duty, in direct opposition to the passive obedience preached by the Calvinists. When political rulers subvert the public good they were called to protect, they cease to be ministers of God and it becomes the duty of the people to remove them from office. Mayhew practiced his beliefs on the occasion of the Stamp Act and exhorted others to follow his example, giving it all systematic expression in the piece herein reprinted.

Thus, well before revolution flamed in America, insistent voices had proclaimed the limited character of government power, and the people's right to resist tyrannical kings and rulers. Mayhew's sermon fairly represents the libertarian political philosophy of many New England clergy whose opposition to authoritarian government was sharpened by the Dissenters' aversion to the Church of England with its historic relation to monarchy. Such sermons, emphasizing the limited, fiduciary character of government, had significant force in shaping the political mind of New England. The clergy wielded vast political influence; their sermons were important vehicles of popular education and enlightenment. Discourses like Mayhew's served at once to stimulate popular awareness of revolutionary theory and to canonize that theory.

Such sermons as these also effected a synthesis of revolutionary doctrine with Biblical texts—a matter of vast importance to a people whose religious traditions regarded Scripture as a divinely appointed code of conduct in political and all other human affairs.

'Our Democratic state,' Woodrow Wilson observed in 1893, 'was not a piece of developed theory, but a piece of developed habit. It was not created by mere aspirations or by new faith; it was built up by slow custom.' Wilson's observation is a half-truth at most; the materials contained in this chapter demonstrate the importance of theory, no less than of habit and experience. By the middle of the seventeenth century, the leaders of Yankee theocracy, though powerful and persistent, had begun to lose ground. For at least a generation before the obstinacy of George III and the shortsighted policies of his ministers made separation from Great Britain a political issue, the New England clergy had formulated and put into practice the doctrines on which Jefferson in 1776 could draw in asserting independence. The line of inheritance from John Wise and Jonathan Mayhew is direct. Just governments derive their powers from neither the Puritan God nor the English King; they rest on reason and the consent of the governed. More than that, the New England clergy suggested, as Alice Baldwin shows, judicial review as a device for enforcing what is probably the most fundamental principle of American constitutionalism—that 'no one is bound to obey an unconstitutional act.'

1. *He that is willing to tolerate any unsound opinion that his own may also be tolerated hangs God's Bible at the devil's girdle*

NATHANIEL WARD, *The Simple Cobler of Aggawam*, 1647 *

. . . I am the unablest adviser of a thousand, the unworthiest of ten thousand; yet I hope I may presume to assert what follows without just offence.

* From *Tracts and Other Papers, Collected by Peter Force*, Washington, D.C., 1844, vol. III, no. 8, pp. 6–11, 17–18, 28 *passim*.

First, such as have given or taken any unfriendly reports of us *New-English*, should do well to recollect themselves. We have been reputed a Colluvies of wild Opinionists, swarmed into a remote wilderness to find elbow-room for our Fhanatic Doctrines and practises; I trust our diligence past, and constant sedulity against such persons and courses, will plead better things for us. I dare take upon me, to be the Herald of *New-England* so far, as to proclaim to the World, in the name of our Colony, that all Familists, Antinomians, Anabaptists, and other Enthusiasts shall have free Liberty to keep away from us, and such as will come to be gone as fast as they can, the sooner the better.

Secondly, I dare aver, that God doth no where in his word tolerate Christian States, to give Tolerations to such adversaries of his Truth, if they have power in their hands to suppress them. . .

If the Devil might have his free option, I believe he would ask nothing else, but liberty to enfranchize all false Religions, and to embondage the true; nor should he need: It is much to be feared that lax Tolerations upon State-pretences and planting necessities, will be the next subtle Stratagem he will spread to distaste the Truth of God, and supplant the Peace of the Churches. Tolerations in things tolerable, exquisitely drawn out by the lines of the Scripture, and pencil of the Spirit, are the sacred favours of Truth, the due latitudes of Love, the fair Compartiments of Christian fraternity: but irregular dispensations, dealt forth by the facilities of men, are the frontiers of error, the redoubts of Schism, the perilous irritaments of carnal and spiritual enmity.

My heart hath naturally detested four things: The standing of the Apocrypha in the Bible; Foreigners dwelling in my Country, to crowd out Native Subjects into the corners of the Earth; Alchymized Coins; Tolerations of divers Religions, or of one Religion in segregant shapes: He that willingly assents to the last, if he examines his heart by daylight, his Conscience will tell him, he is either an Atheist, or an Heretic, or an Hypocrite, or at best a captive to some Lust: Poly-piety is the greatest impiety in the World. . .

Not to tolerate things merely indifferent to weak Consciences, argues a Conscience too strong: pressed uniformity in these, causes much disunity: To tolerate more than indifferenes, is not to deal indifferently with God: He that doth it, takes his Scepter out of his hand, and bids him stand by. Who hath to do to institute Religion but God. The power of all Religion and Ordinances, lies in their Purity, their Purity in their Simplicity: then are mixtures pernicious. I lived in a City, where a Papist Preached in one Church, a Lutheran in another, a Calvinist in a third; a Lutheran one part of the day, a Calvinist the other, in the same Pulpit: the Religion of that Place was but motly and meagre, their affections Leopard-like.

If the whole Creature should conspire to do the Creator a mischief, or offer him an insolency, it would be in nothing more, than in erecting untruths against his Truth, or by sophisticating his Truths with humane medleys: the removing of some one iota in Scripture, may draw out all the life, and traverse all the Truth of the whole Bible: but to authorize an untruth, by a Toleration of State, is to build a sconce against the walls of Heaven, to batter God out of his Chair: To tell a practical lie, is a great Sin, but yet transient; but to set up a Theorical untruth, is to warrant every lie that lies from its root to the top of every branch it hath, which are not a few. . .

That State is wise, that will improve all pains and patience rather to compose, than tolerate differences in Religion. There is no divine Truth, but hath much Celestial fire in it from the Spirit of Truth: nor no irreligious untruth, without its proportion of Antifire from the spirit of Error to contradict it: the zeal of the one, the virulency of the other, must necessarily kindle Combustions. Fiery diseases seated in the Spirit, imbroil the whole frame of the body: others more external and cool, are less dangerous. They which divide in Religion, divide in God; they who divide in him, divide beyond *Genus Generalissimum,* where there is no reconciliation, without atonement; that is, without uniting in him, who is One, and in his Truth, which is also one.

Wise are those men who will be persuaded rather to live within the pale of Truth, where they may be quiet, than in the purlieus, where they are sure to be hunted ever and anon, do Authority what it can. Every singular Opinion, hath a singular opinion of itself, and he that holds it a singular opinion of himself, and a simple opinion of all contra-sentients: he that confutes them, must confute all three at once, or else he does nothing; which will not be done without more stir than the Peace of the State or Church can indure.

And prudent are those Christians, that will rather give what may be given, than hazard all by yielding nothing. To sell all Peace of Country, to buy some Peace of Conscience unseasonably, is more avarice than thrift, imprudence than patience: they deal not equally, that set any Truth of God at such a rate; but they deal wisely that will stay till the Market is fallen. . .

He that is willing to tolerate any Religion, or discrepant way of Religion, besides his own, unless it be in matters merely indifferent, either doubts of his own, or is not sincere in it.

He that is willing to tolerate any unsound Opinion, that his own may also be tolerated, though never so sound, will for a need hang God's Bible at the Devil's girdle.

Every toleration of false Religions, or Opinions hath as many Errors and Sins in it, as all the false Religions and Opinions it tolerates, and one sound one more.

That State that will give Liberty of Conscience in matters of Religion, must give Liberty of Conscience and Conversation in their Moral Laws, or else the Fiddle will be out of Tune, and some of the strings crack.

He that will rather make an irreligious quarrel with other Religions than try the Truth of his own by valuable Arguments, and peaceable Sufferings; either his Religion, or himself is irreligious.

Experience will teach Churches and Christians, that it is far better to live in a State united, though a little Corrupt, than in a State, whereof some Part is incorrupt, and all the rest divided.

I am not altogether ignorant of the eight Rules given by Orthodox Divines about giving Tolerations, yet with their favour I dare affirm,

That there is no Rule given by God for any State to give an affirmative Toleration to any false Religion, or Opinion whatsoever; they must connive in some Cases, but may not concede in any. . .

It is said, That Men ought to have Liberty of their Conscience, and that it is Persecution to debar them of it: I can rather stand amazed than reply to this: it is an astonishment to think that the brains of men should be parboiled in such impious ignorance; Let all the wits under the Heavens lay their heads together and find an Assertion worse than this (one excepted) I will Petition to be chosen the universal Idiot of the World. . .

Hence it is, that God is so jealous of his Truths, that he hath taken order in his due justice: First, that no practical Sin is so Sinful as some error in judgment; no man so accursed with indelible infamy and dedolent impenitency, as Authors of Heresy. Secondly, that the least Error, if grown sturdy and pressed, shall set open the Spittle-door of all the squint-eyed, wry-necked, and brasen-faced Errors that are or ever were of that litter; if they be not enough to serve its turn, it will beget more, though it hath not one crust of reason to maintain them. Thirdly, that that State which will permit Errors in Religion, shall admit Errors in Policy unavoidably. Fourthly, that that Policy which will suffer irreligious Errors, shall suffer the loss of so much Liberty in one kind or other. . .

How all Religions should enjoy their liberty, Justice its due regularity, Civil cohabitation moral honesty, in one and the same Jurisdiction, is beyond the Artique of my comprehension. If the whole conclave of Hell can so compromise, exadverse, and diametrical contradictions, as to compolitize such a multimonstrous maufrey of heteroclytes and quicquidlibets quietly; I trust I may say with all humble reverence, they can do more than the Senate of Heaven. . .

It is greatly to be lamented, to observe the wanton fearlessness of this Age, especially of Younger Professors, to greet new Opinions and Opinionists: as if former truths were grown Superannuate, and Sapless, if not altogether antiquate. *Non senescet veritas.* No man ever saw a gray hair on the head or beard of any Truth, wrinkle, or morphew on its face: The bed of Truth is green all the year long. He that cannot solace himself with any saving truth, as affectionately as at the first acquaintance with it, hath not only a fastidious, but an adulterous Heart. . .

I fear, these differences and delays have occasioned men to make more new discoveries than otherwise they would. If Public Assemblies of Divines cannot agree upon a right way, private Conventicles of illiterate men, will soon find a wrong. Bivious demurs breed devious resolutions. Passengers to Heaven are in haste, and will walk one way or other. He that doubts of his way, thinks he loses his day: and when men are gone awhile, they will be loth to turn back. If God hide his path, Satan is at hand to turn Convoy: if any have a mind to ride post, he will help them with a fresh spavined Opinion at every Stage.

Where clocks will stand, and Dials have no light,
There men must go by guess, be't wrong or right. . .

2. *If you will be satisfied to enjoy such lawful liberties as God allows you, then you will cheerfully submit to that authority set over you*

JOHN WINTHROP, *'Little Speech' on Liberty*, 1645 *

I suppose something may be expected from me upon this charge that is befallen me, which moves me to speak now to you; yet I intend not to intermeddle in the proceedings of the court, or with any of the persons concerned therein. Only I bless God that I see an issue of this troublesome business. I also acknowledge the justice of the court, and, for mine own part, I am well satisfied, I was publicly charged, and I am publicly and legally acquitted, which is all I did expect or desire. And though this be sufficient for my justification before men, yet not so before the God who hath seen so much amiss in my dispensations (and even in this affair) as calls me to be humble. For to be publicly and criminally charged in this court is matter of humiliation (and I desire to make a right use of it), notwithstanding I be thus acquitted. If her father had spit in her face should she not have been ashamed seven days? Shame had lien upon her, whatever the occasion had been. I am unwilling to stay you from your urgent affairs, yet give me leave (upon this special occasion) to speak a little more to this assembly. It may be of some good use to inform and rectify the judgments of some of the people, and may prevent such distempers as have arisen amongst us. The great questions that have troubled the country are about the authority of the magistrates and the liberty of the people. It is yourselves who have called us to this office, and, being called by you, we have our authority from God, in way of an ordinance, such as hath the image of God eminently stamped upon it, the contempt and violation whereof hath been vindicated with examples of divine vengeance. I entreat you to consider that, when you choose magistrates, you take them from among yourselves, men subject to like passions as you are. Therefore, when you see infirmities in us, you should reflect upon your own, and that would make you bear the more with us, and not be severe censurers of the failings of your magistrates, when you have continual experience of the like infirmities in yourselves and others. We account him a good servant who breaks not his covenant. The covenant between you and us is the oath you have taken of us, which is to this purpose, that we shall govern you and judge your causes by the rules of God's laws and our own, according to our best skill. When you agree with a workman to build you a ship or house, etc., he undertakes as well for his skill as for his faithfulness; for it is his profession, and you pay him for both. But, when you call one to be a magistrate, he doth not profess nor undertake to have sufficient skill for that office, nor can you furnish him with gifts, etc., therefore you must run the hazard of his skill and ability. But if he fail in faithfulness, which by his oath he is bound unto, that he must answer for. If it fall out that the case be clear to common apprehension, and the rule clear also, if he transgress here, the error is not in the skill, but in the evil of the will: it must be required of him. But if the case be doubtful, or the rule doubtful, to

Old South Leaflets, vol. 3, no. 66, pp. 8–10.

men of such understanding and parts as your magistrates are, if your magistrates should err here, yourselves must bear it.

For the other point concerning liberty, I observe a great mistake in the country about that. There is a twofold liberty, natural (I mean as our nature is now corrupt) and civil or federal. The first is common to man with beasts and other creatures. By this, man as he stands in relation to man simply, hath liberty to do what he lists: it is a liberty to evil as well as to good. This liberty is incompatible and inconsistent with authority, and cannot endure the least restraint of the most just authority. The exercise and maintaining of this liberty makes men grow more evil, and in time to be worse than brute beasts: *omnes sumus licentia deteriores*. This is that great enemy of truth and peace, that wild beast, which all the ordinances of God are bent against, to restrain and subdue it. The other kind of liberty I call civil or federal; it may also be termed moral, in reference to the covenant between God and man, in the moral law, and the politic covenants and constitutions, amongst men themselves. This liberty is the proper end and object of authority, and cannot subsist without it; and it is a liberty to that only which is good, just, and honest. This liberty you are to stand for, with the hazard (not only of your goods, but) of your lives, if need be. Whatsoever crosseth this is not authority, but a distemper thereof. This liberty is maintained and exercised in a way of subjection to authority; it is of the same kind of liberty wherewith Christ hath made us free. The woman's own choice makes such a man her husband; yet, being so chosen, he is her lord, and she is to be subject to him, yet in a way of liberty, not of bondage; and a true wife accounts her subjection her honor and freedom, and would not think her condition safe and free but in her subjection to her husband's authority. Such is the liberty of the church under the authority of Christ, her king and husband; his yoke is so easy and sweet to her as a bride's ornaments; and if through forwardness or wantonness, etc., she shake it off, at any time, she is at no rest in her spirit until she take it up again; and whether her lord smiles upon her, and embraceth her in his arms, or whether he frowns, or rebukes, or smites her, she apprehends the sweetness of his love in all, and is refreshed, supported, and instructed by every such dispensation of his authority over her. On the other side, ye know who they are that complain of this yoke and say, let us break their bands, etc., we will not have this man to rule over us. Even so, brethren, it will be between you and your magistrates. If you stand for your natural corrupt liberties, and will do what is good in your own eyes, you will not endure the least weight of authority, but will murmur, and oppose, and be always striving to shake off that yoke; but if you will be satisfied to enjoy such civil and lawful liberties, such as Christ allows you, then will you quietly and cheerfully submit unto that authority which is set over you, in all the administrations of it, for your good. Wherein, if we fail at any time, we hope we shall be willing (by God's assistance) to hearken to good advice from any of you, or in any other way of God; so shall your liberties be preserved, in upholding the honor and power of authority amongst you.

3. *If there be power given to speak great things, then look for great blasphemies, look for a licentious abuse of it*

JOHN COTTON, *Limitation of Government,* 1646 *

This may serve to teach us the danger of allowing to any mortall man an inordinate measure of power to speak great things, to allow to any man uncontrollableness of speech, you see the desperate danger of it: Let all the world learn to give mortall men no greater power then they are content they shall use, for use it they will: and unlesse they be better taught of God, they will use it ever and anon, it may be make it the passage of their proceeding to speake what they will: And they that have liberty to speak great things, you will finde it to be true, they will speak great blasphemies. No man would think what desperate deceit and wickednesse there is in the hearts of men: And that was the reason why the Beast did speak such great things, hee might speak, and no body might controll him: What, saith the Lord in *Jer.* 3. 5. *Thou hast spoken and done evill things as thou couldst.* If a Church or head of a Church could have done worse, he would have done it: This is one of the straines of nature, it affects boundlesse liberty, and to runne to the utmost extent: What ever power he hath received, he hath a corrupt nature that will improve it in one thing or other; if he have liberty, he will think why may he not use it. Set up the Pope as Lord Paramount over Kings and Princes, and they shall know that he hath power over them, he will take liberty to depose one, and set up another. Give him power to make Laws, and he will approve, and disprove as he list; what he approves is Canonicall, what hee disproves is rejected: Give him that power, and he will so order it at length, he will make such a State of Religion, that he that so lives and dyes shall never be saved, and all this springs from the vast power that is given to him, and from the deep depravation of nature. Hee will open his mouth, *His tongue is his owne, who is Lord over him,* Psal, 12. 3, 4. It is therefore most wholsome for Magistrates and Officers in Church and Common-wealth, never to affect more liberty and authority then will do them good, and the People good; for what ever transcendant power is given, will certainly over-run those that give it, and those that receive it: There is a straine in a mans heart that will sometime or other runne out to excesse, unlesse the Lord restraine it, but it is not good to venture it: It is necessary therefore, that all power that is on earth be limited, Church-power or other: If there be power given to speak great things, then look for great blasphemies, look for a licentious abuse of it. It is counted a matter of danger to the State to limit Prerogatives; but it is a further danger, not to have them limited: They will be like a Tempest, if they be not limited: A Prince himselfe cannot tell where hee will confine himselfe, nor can the people tell: But if he have liberty to speak great things, then he will make and unmake, say and unsay, and undertake such things as are neither for his owne honour, nor for the safety of the State. It is therefore fit for every man to be studious of the bounds which the Lord hath set: and for the People, in whom fundamentally all power lyes,

* From Perry Miller and Thomas H. Johnson, *The Puritans,* New York, American Book Co., 1938, pp. 212–14.

to give as much power as God in his word gives to men: And it is meet that Magistrates in the Common-wealth, and so Officers in Churches should desire to know the utmost bounds of their own power, and it is safe for both: All intrenchment upon the bounds which God hath not given, they are not enlargements, but burdens and snares; They will certainly lead the spirit of a man out of his way sooner or later. It is wholsome and safe to be dealt withall as God deales with the vast Sea; *Hitherto shalt thou come, but there shalt thou stay thy proud waves:* and therefore if they be but banks of simple sand, they will be good enough to check the vast roaring Sea. And so for Imperiall Monarchies, it is safe to know how far their power extends; and then if it be but banks of sand, which is most slippery, it will serve, as well as any brazen wall. If you pinch the Sea of its liberty, though it be walls of stone or brasse, it will beate them downe: So it is with Magistrates, stint them where God hath not stinted them, and if they were walls of brasse, they would beate them downe, and it is meet they should: but give them the liberty God allows, and if it be but a wall of sand it will keep them: As this liquid Ayre in which we breath, God hath set it for the waters of the Clouds to the Earth; It is a Firmament, it is the Clouds, yet it stands firme enough, because it keeps the Climate where they are, it shall stand like walls of brasse: So let there be due bounds set, and I may apply it to Families; it is good for the Wife to acknowledg all power and authority to the Husband, and for the Husband to acknowledg honour to the Wife, but still give them that which God hath given them, and no more nor lesse: Give them the full latitude that God hath given, else you will finde you dig pits, and lay snares, and cumber their spirits, if you give them lesse: there is never peace where full liberty is not given, nor never stable peace where more then full liberty is granted: Let them be duely observed, and give men no more liberty then God doth, nor women, for they will abuse it: The Devill will draw them, and Gods providence leade them thereunto, therefore give them no more then God gives. And so for children; and servants, or any others you are to deale with, give them the liberty and authority you would have them use, and beyond that stretch not the tether, it will not tend to their good nor yours: And also from hence gather, and goe home with this meditation; That certainly here is this distemper in our natures, that we cannot tell how to use liberty, but wee shall very readily corrupt our selves: Oh the bottomlesse depth of sandy earth! of a corrupt spirit, that breaks over all bounds, and loves inordinate vastnesse; that is it we ought to be carefull of.

4. *God's people were and ought to be non-conformists*

ROGER WILLIAMS, *The Bloudy Tenent of Persecution for Cause of Conscience Discussed: and Mr. Cotton's Letter Examined and Answered*, 1644 *

First. That the blood of so many hundred thousand souls of protestants and papists, spilt in the wars of present and former ages, for their respective consciences, is not required nor accepted by Jesus Christ the Prince of Peace.

* The Hanserd Knollys Society, London, 1848, pp. B-2, 7–9, 19–21, 37–8, 46–7, 103–4, 119–29, 186–7 *passim*.

Secondly. Pregnant scriptures and arguments are throughout the work proposed against the doctrine of persecution for cause of conscience.

Thirdly. Satisfactory answers are given to scriptures and objections produced by Mr. Calvin, Beza, Mr. Cotton, and the ministers of the New English churches, and others former and later, tending to prove the doctrine of persecution for cause of conscience.

Fourthly. The doctrine of persecution for cause of conscience, is proved guilty of all the blood of the souls crying for vengeance under the altar.

Fifthly. All civil states, with their officers of justice, in their respective constitutions and administrations, are proved essentially civil, and therefore not judges, governors, or defenders of the spiritual, or Christian, state and worship.

Sixthly. It is the will and command of God that, since the coming of his Son the Lord Jesus, a permission of the most Paganish, Jewish, Turkish, or antichristian consciences and worships be granted to all men in all nations and countries: and they are only to be fought against with that sword which is only, in soul matters, able to conquer: to wit, the sword of God's Spirit, the word of God.

Seventhly. The state of the land of Israel, the kings and people thereof, in peace and war, is proved figurative and ceremonial, and no pattern nor precedent for any kingdom or civil state in the world to follow.

Eighthly. God requireth not an uniformity of religion to be enacted and enforced in any civil state; which enforced uniformity, sooner or later, is the greatest occasion of civil war, ravishing of conscience, persecution of Christ Jesus in his servants, and of the hypocrisy and destruction of millions of souls.

Ninthly. In holding an enforced uniformity of religion in a civil state, we must necessarily disclaim our desires and hopes of the Jews' conversion to Christ.

Tenthly. An enforced uniformity of religion throughout a nation or civil state, confounds the civil and religious, denies the principles of Christianity and civility, and that Jesus Christ is come in the flesh.

Eleventhly. The permission of other consciences and worships than a state professeth, only can, according to God, procure a firm and lasting peace; good assurance being taken, according to the wisdom of the civil state, for uniformity of civil obedience from all sorts.

Twelfthly. Lastly, true civility and Christianity may both flourish in a state or kingdom, notwithstanding the permission of divers and contrary consciences, either of Jew or Gentile. . .

While I plead the cause of truth and innocency against the bloody doctrine of persecution for cause of conscience, I judge it not unfit to give alarm to myself, and to [all] men, to prepare to be persecuted or hunted for cause of conscience. . .

THE ANSWER OF MR. JOHN COTTON, OF BOSTON, IN NEW ENGLAND

The question which you put is, whether persecution for cause of conscience be not against the doctrine of Jesus Christ, the King of kings?

Now, by persecution for cause of conscience, I conceive you mean, either for professing some point of doctrine which you believe in conscience to be the truth, or for practising some work which in conscience you believe to be a religious duty.

Now in points of doctrine some are fundamental, without right belief whereof a man cannot be saved; others are circumstantial, or less principal, wherein men may differ in judgment without prejudice of salvation on either part.

In like sort, in points of practice, some concern the weightier duties of the law, as, what God we worship, and with what kind of worship; whether such as, if it be right, fellowship with God is held; if corrupt, fellowship with him is lost.

Again, in points of doctrine and worship less principal, either they are held forth in a meek and peaceable way, Though the things be erroneous or unlawful: or they are held forth with such arrogance and impetuousness, as tendeth and reacheth (even of itself) to the disturbance of civil peace.

Finally, let me add this one distinction more: when we are persecuted for conscience' sake, it is either for conscience rightly informed, or for erroneous and blind conscience.

These things premised, I would lay down mine answer to the question in certain conclusions.

First, it is not lawful to persecute any for conscience' sake rightly informed; for in persecuting such, Christ himself is persecuted in them, Acts ix. 4.

Secondly, for an erroneous and blind conscience, (even in fundamental and weighty points) it is not lawful to persecute any, till after admonition once or twice; and so the apostle directeth, Tit. iii. 10, and giveth the reason, that in fundamental and principal points of doctrine or worship, the word of God in such things is so clear, that he cannot but be convinced in conscience of the dangerous error of his way after once or twice admonition, wisely and faithfully dispensed. And then if any one persist, it is not out of conscience, but against his conscience, as the apostle saith, ver. 11, He is subverted, and sinneth, being condemned of himself; that is, of his own conscience. So that if such a man, after such admonition, shall still persist in the error of his way, and be therefore punished, he is not persecuted for cause of conscience, but for sinning against his own conscience.

Thirdly. In things of lesser moment, whether points of doctrine or worship, if a man hold them forth in a spirit of Christian meekness and love, though with zeal and constancy, he is not to be persecuted, but tolerated, till God may be pleased to manifest his truth to him, Phil. iii. 17; Rom. xiv. 1–4.

But if a man hold forth, or profess, any error or falseway, with a boisterous and arrogant spirit, to the disturbance of civil peace, he may justly be punished according to the quality and measure of the disturbance caused by him. . .

A REPLY TO THE AFORESAID ANSWER OF MR. COTTON, IN A CONFERENCE BETWEEN TRUTH AND PEACE

Truth. In the answer, Mr. Cotton first lays down several distinctions and conclusions of his own, tending to prove persecution. . .

. . . I acknowledge that to molest any person, Jew or Gentile, for either professing doctrine, or practising worship merely religious or spiritual, it is to persecute him; and such a person, whatever his doctrine or practice be, true or false, suffereth persecution for conscience.

But withal I desire it may be well observed, that this distinction is not full and complete. For beside this, that a man may be persecuted because he holdeth or practiseth what he believes in conscience to be a truth, as Daniel did, for which he was cast into the lions' den, Dan. vi. 16, and many thousands of Christians, because they durst not cease to preach and practise what they believed was by God commanded, as the apostles answered, Acts iv. and v., I say, besides this, a man may also be persecuted because he dares not be constrained to yield obedience to such doctrines and worships as are by men invented and appointed. So the three famous Jews, who were cast into the fiery furnace for refusing to fall down, in a nonconformity to the whole conforming world, before the golden image, Dan. iii. 21. . .

Peace. The next distinction concerneth the manner of persons holding forth the aforesaid practices not only the weightier duties of the Law, but points of doctrine and worship less principal. . .

Truth. In the examination of this distinction we shall discuss,

First, what is civil peace, (wherein we shall vindicate thy name the better.)

Secondly, what it is to hold forth a doctrine or practice in this impetuousness or arrogancy.

First, for civil peace, what is it but *pax civitatis*, the peace of the city, whether an English city, Scotch, or Irish city, or further abroad, French, Spanish, Turkish city, etc. . . .

. . . God's people were and ought to be non-conformitants, not daring either to be restrained from the true, or constrained to false worship; and yet without breach of the civil or city peace, properly so called.

Peace. Hence it is that so many glorious and flourishing cities of the world maintain their civil peace; yea, the very Americans and wildest pagans keep the peace of their towns or cities, though neither in one nor the other can any man prove a true church of God in those places, and consequently no spiritual and heavenly peace. The peace spiritual, whether true or false, being of a higher and far different nature from the peace of the place or people, being merely and essentially civil and human.

Truth. Oh! how lost are the sons of men in this point! To illustrate this:—the church, or company of worshippers, whether true or false, is like unto a body or college of physicians in a city—like unto a corporation, society, or company of East India or Turkey merchants, or any other society or company in London; which companies may hold their courts, keep their records, hold disputations, and in matters concerning their society may dissent, divide, break into schisms and factions, sue and implead each other at the law, yea, wholly break up and dissolve into pieces and nothing, and yet the peace of the city not be in the least measure impaired or disturbed; because the essence or being of the city, and so the well being and peace thereof, is essentially distinct from those particular societies; the city courts, city laws, city punishments distinct from theirs. The city was before them, and stands absolute and entire when such a corporation or society is taken down.

. . . I observe, that he implies that beside the censure of the Lord Jesus, in the hands of his spiritual governors, for any spiritual evil in life or doctrine, the civil magistrate is also to inflict corporal punishment upon the contrary minded: whereas,

First, if the civil magistrate be a Christian, a disciple, or follower of the meek Lamb of God, he is bound to be far from destroying the bodies of men for refusing to receive the Lord Jesus Christ: for otherwise he should not know, according to this speech of the Lord Jesus, what spirit he was of, yea, and to be ignorant of the sweet end of the coming of the Son of man, which was not to destroy the bodies of men, but to save both bodies and souls, vers. 55, 56.

Secondly, if the civil magistrate being a Christian, gifted, prophesy in the church, 1 Cor. xiv. 1—although the Lord Jesus Christ, whom they in their own persons hold forth, shall be refused—yet they are here forbidden to call for fire from heaven, that is, to procure or inflict any corporal judgment, upon such offenders, remembering the end of the Lord Jesus' coming [was] not to destroy men's lives, but to save them.

Lastly, this also concerns the conscience of the civil magistrate. As he is bound to preserve the civil peace and quiet of the place and people under him, he is bound to suffer no man to break the civil peace, by laying hands of violence upon any, though as vile as the Samaritans, for not receiving of the Lord Jesus Christ.

It is indeed the ignorance and blind zeal of the second beast, the false prophet, Rev. xiii. 13, to persuade the civil powers of the earth to persecute the saints, that is, to bring fiery judgments upon men in a judicial way, and to pronounce that such judgments of imprisonment, banishment, death, proceed from God's righteous vengeance upon such heretics. So dealt divers bishops in France, and England too in Queen Mary's days, with the saints of God at their putting to death, declaiming against them in their sermons to the people, and proclaiming that these persecutions, even unto death, were God's just judgments from heaven upon these heretics. . .

Truth . . . to batter down idolatry, false worship, heresy, schism, blindness, hardness, out of the soul and spirit, it is vain, improper, and unsuitable to bring those weapons which are used by persecutors, stocks, whips, prisons, swords, gibbets, stakes, &c., (where these seem to prevail with some cities or kingdoms, a stronger force sets up again, what a weaker pulled down); but against these spiritual strongholds in the souls of men, spiritual artillery and weapons are proper, which are mighty through God to subdue and bring under the very thought to obedience, or else to bind fast the soul with chains of darkness, and lock it up in the prison of unbelieve and hardness to eternity.

2. I observe that as civil weapons are improper in this business, and never able to effect aught in the soul: so although they were proper, yet they are unnecessary; for if, as the Spirit here saith, and the answerer grants, spiritual weapons in the hand of church officers are able and ready to take vengeance on all disobedience, that is, able and mighty, sufficient and ready for the Lord's

work, either to save the soul, or to kill the soul of whomsoever be the party or parties opposite; in which respect I may again remember that speech of Job, 'How hast thou helped him that hath no power?' Job xxvi. 2. . .

Peace. Yea; but, say they, the godly will not persist in heresy, or turbulent schism, when they are convinced in conscience, &c.

Truth. Sweet Peace, if the civil court and magistracy must judge, as before I have written, and those civil courts are as lawful, consisting of natural men as of godly persons, then what consequences necessarily will follow I have before mentioned. And I add, according to this conclusion it must follow, that, if the most godly persons yield not to once or twice admonition, as is maintained by the answerer, they must necessarily be esteemed obstinate persons; for if they were godly, saith he, they would yield. Must it not then be said, as it was by one passing sentence of banishment upon some whose godliness was acknowledged, that he that commanded the judge not to respect the poor in the cause of judgment, commands him not to respect the holy or the godly person? . . .

Peace. Mr. Cotton concludes with a confident persuasion of having removed the grounds of that great error, viz., that persons are not to be persecuted for cause of conscience.

Truth. And I believe, dear Peace, it shall appear to them that, with fear and trembling at the word of the Lord, examine these passages, that the charge of error reboundeth back, even such an error as may well be called, The Bloody Tenent—so directly contradicting the spirit, and mind, and practice of the Prince of peace; so deeply guilty of the blood of souls, compelled and forced to hypocrisy in a spiritual and soul-rape; so deeply guilty of the blood of the souls under the altar, persecuted in all ages for the cause of conscience, and so destructive to the civil peace and welfare of all kingdoms, countries, and commonwealths.

5. *Man's original liberty ought to be cherished in all wise governments*

JOHN WISE, *A Vindication of the Government of New England Churches*, 1717 *

. . . Government . . . is necessary in that no society of men can subsist without it; and that particular form of government is necessary which best suits the temper and inclination of a people. Nothing can be God's ordinance, but what he has particularly declared to be such; there is no particular form of civil government described in God's word, neither does nature prompt it. . . Government is not formed by nature, as other births or productions; if it were, it would be the same in all countries; because nature keeps the same method, in the same thing, in all climates. . .

The prime immunity in man's state, is that he is most properly the subject of the law of nature. He is the favorite animal on earth; in that this part of God's image, *viz.* reason is congenate with his nature, wherein by a law immu-

* Boston, John Boyles, 1777, pp. 22–44 *passim.*

table, instampt upon his frame, God has provided a rule for men in all their actions, obliging each one to the performance of that which is right, not only as to justice, but likewise as to all other moral virtues. . . The way to discover the law of nature in our own state, is by a narrow watch, and accurate contemplation of our natural condition, and propensions. . . If a man any ways doubts, whether what he is going to do to another man be agreeable to the law of nature, then let him suppose himself to be in that other man's room; and by this rule effectually executed, a man must be a very dull scholar to nature not to make proficiency in the knowledge of her laws. But more particularly in pursuing our condition for the discovery of the law of nature, this is very obvious to view, *viz.*

1. A principle of self-love, and self-preservation, is very predominant in every man's being.

2. A sociable disposition.

3. An affection or love to mankind in general. And to give such sentiments the force of a law, we must suppose a God who takes care of all mankind, and has thus obliged each one, as a subject of higher principles of being, than mere instincts. . . Man is a creature extremely desirous of his own preservation; of himself he is plainly exposed to many wants, unable to secure his own safety and maintenance, without the assistance of his fellows; and he is also able of returning kindness by the furtherance of mutual good; but yet man is often found to be malicious, insolent, and easily provoked, and as powerful in effecting mischief, as he is ready in designing it. Now that such a creature may be preserved, it is necessary that he be sociable; that is, that he be capable and disposed to unite himself to those of his own species, and to regulate himself towards them, that they may have no fair reason to do him harm; but rather incline to promote his interests, and secure his rights and concerns. This then is a fundamental law of nature, that every man as far as in him lies, do maintain a sociableness with others, agreeable with the main end and disposition of human nature in general. For this is very apparent, that reason and society render man the most potent of all creatures. And finally, from the principles of sociableness it follows as a fundamental law of nature, that man is not so wedded to his own interest, but that he can make the common good the mark of his aim: and hence he becomes capacitated to enter into a civil state by the law of nature; for without this property in nature, *viz.* Sociableness which is for cementing of parts, every government would soon moulder and dissolve.

The second great immunity of man is an original liberty instampt upon his rational nature. He that intrudes upon this liberty, violates the law of nature. . .

The native internal liberty of man's nature implies, a faculty of doing or omitting things according to the direction of his judgment. But in a more special meaning, this liberty does not consist in a loose and ungovernable freedom, or in an unbounded licence of acting. Such licence of disagreeing with the condition and dignity of man, and would make man of a lower and meaner constitution than brute creatures; who in all their liberties are kept under a better and a more rational government, by their instincts. Therefore as Plutarch says, 'Those persons only who live in obedience to reason, are worthy to be accounted free: They alone live as they will, who have learnt what they ought to will.' So that the true natural liberty of man, such as really and truely agrees to him, must be understood, as he is guided and restrained by the ties of reason, and laws of nature; all the rest is brutal, if not worse. . .

The third capital immunity belonging to man's nature, is an equality amongst men; which is not to be denied by the law of nature, till man has resigned himself with all his rights for the sake of a civil state; and then his personal liberty and equality is to be cherished, and preserved to the highest degree, as will consist with all just distinctions amongst men of honor, and shall be agreeable with the public good. . . Since then human nature agrees equally with all persons; and since no one can live a sociable life with another that does not own or respect him as a man; it follows as a command of the law of nature, that every man esteem and treat another as one who is naturally his equal, or who is a man as well as he. There be many popular, or plausible reasons that greatly illustrate this equality, *viz.* that we all derive our being from one stock, the same common father of the human race. . .

. . . The noblest mortal in his entrance on the stage of life, is not distinguished by any pomp or of passage from the lowest of mankind; and our life hastens to the same general mark: Death observes no ceremony, but knocks as loud at the barriers of the court, as at the door of the cottage. This equality being admitted, bears a very great force in maintaining peace and friendship amongst men. For that he who would use the assistance of others, in promoting his own advantage, ought as freely to be at their service when they want his help on the like occasions. One good turn requires another, is the common proverb; for otherwise he must need esteem others unequal to himself, who constantly demands their aid, and as constantly denies his own. . . What! because you desire to be masters of all men, does it follow therefore that all men should desire to be your slaves, for that it is a command of nature's law, that no man that has not obtained a particular and special right, shall arrogate to himself a larger share than his fellows, but shall admit others to equal privileges with himself. So that the principle of equality in a natural state, is peculiarly transgressed by pride, which is when a man without sufficient reason, prefers himself to others. And though as Hensius, paraphrases upon Aristotle's politics to this purpose, *viz.* Nothing is more suitable to nature, than that those who excel in understanding and prudence should rule and controul those who are less happy in those advantages, etc. Yet we must note, that there is room for an answer. That it would be the greatest absurdity to believe, that nature actually invests the wise with a sovereignty over the weak; or with a right of forcing them against their wills; for that no sovereignty can be established, unless some human deed, or covenant precede: Nor does natural fitness for government make a man presently governor over another; for that as Ulpian says, 'by a natural right all men are born free'; and nature having set all men upon a level and made them equals, no servitude or subjection can be conceived without inequality; and this cannot be made without usurpation or force in others, or voluntary compliance in those who resign their freedom, and give away their degree of natural being. And thus we come,

To consider man in a civil state of being; wherein we shall observe the great difference between a natural, and political state; for in the latter state many great disproportions appear, or at least many obvious distinctions are soon made amongst men; which doctrine is to be laid open under a few heads.

Every man considered in a natural state, must be allowed to be free, and at his own dispose; yet to suit man's inclinations to society; and in a peculiar manner to gratify the necessity he is in of public rule and order, he is impelled to enter into a civil community; and divests himself of his natural freedom, and puts himself under government; which amongst other things comprehends the power of life and death over him, together with authority to enjoin him some things to which he has an utter aversion, and to prohibit him other things, for which he may have as strong an inclination; so that he may be often under this authority, obliged to sacrifice his private, for the public good. So that though man is inclined to society, yet he is driven to a combination by great necessity. For that the true and leading cause of forming governments, and yielding up natural liberty, and throwing man's equality into a common pile to be new cast by the rules of fellowship; was really and truly to guard themselves against the injuries men were liable to interchangeably; for none so good to man, as man, and yet none a greater enemy. So that,

The first human subject and original of civil power is the people. For as they have a power every man over himself in a natural state, so upon a combination they can and do bequeath this power unto others; and settle it according as their united discretion shall determine. For that this is very plain that when the subject of sovereign power is quite extinct, that power returns to the people again. And when they are free, they may set up what species of government they please; or if they rather incline to it, they may subside into a state of natural being, if it be plainly for the best. . .

The formal reason of government is the will of a community, yielded up and surrendered to some other subject, either of one particular person, or more, conveyed in the following manner.

Let us conceive in our mind a multitude of men, all naturally free and equal; going about voluntarily, to erect themselves into a new common-wealth. Now their condition being such, to bring themselves into a politic body, they must needs enter into divers covenants.

They must interchangeably each man covenant to join in one lasting society, that they may be capable to concert the measures of their safety, by a public vote.

A vote or decree must then nextly pass to set up some particular species of government over them. And if they are joined in their first compact upon absolute terms to stand to the decision of the first vote concerning the species of government: Then all are bound by the majority to acquiesce in that particular form thereby settled, though their own private opinion, incline them to some other model.

After a decree has specified the particular form of government, then there will be need of a new covenant, whereby those on whom sovereignty is conferred, engage to take care of the common peace, and welfare. And the subjects on the other hand, to yield them faithful obedience. In which covenant is included that submission and union of wills, by which a state may be conceived to be but one person. So that the most proper definition of a civil state, is this, *viz.* A civil state is a compound moral person whose will (united by those covenants before passed) is the will of all; to the end it may use, and apply the strength and riches of private persons towards maintaining the common peace, security, and well-being of all, which may be conceived as tho' the whole state was now become but one man; in which the aforesaid covenants may be supposed under God's providence, to be the divine *Fiat*, pronounced by God, let us make man. And by way of resemblance the aforesaid being may be thus anatomized.

1. The sovereign power is the soul infused, giving life and motion to the whole body.
2. Subordinate officers are the joints by which the body moves.
3. Wealth and riches are the strength.
4. Equity and laws are the reason.
5. Councellors the memory.
6. *Salus Populi*, or the happiness of the people, is the end of its being; or main business to be attended and done.
7. Concord amongst the members, and all estates, is the health.
8. Sedition is sickness, and civil war death.

The parts of sovereignty may be considered: So,

As it prescribes the rule of action: It is rightly termed legislative power.

As it determines the controversies of subjects by the standard of those rules. So it is justly termed judiciary power. . .

The chief end of civil communities, is, that men thus conjoined, may be secured against the injuries, they are liable to from their own kind. For if every man could secure himself singly; it would be great folly for him, to renounce his natural liberty, in which every man is his own king and protector. . .

The forms of a regular state are three only, which forms arise from the proper and particular subject, in which the supreme power resides. As,

A democracy, which is when the sovereign power is lodged in a council consisting of all the members, and where every member has the privilege of a vote. This form of government, appears in the greatest part of the world to have been the most ancient. For that reason seems to show it to be most probable, That when men (being originally in a condition of natural freedom and equality) had thoughts of joining in a civil body, would without question be inclined to administer their common affairs, by their common judgment, and so must necessarily to gratify that inclination establish a democracy . . .

A democracy is then erected, when a number of free persons, do assemble together, in order to enter into a covenant for uniting themselves in a body: And such a preparative assembly hath some appearance already of a democracy; it is a democracy in *embrio*, properly in this respect, that every man hath the privilege freely to deliver his opinion concerning the common affairs. Yet he who dissents from the vote of the majority, is not in the least obliged by what they determine, till by a second covenant, a popular form be actually established; for not before then can we call it a democratical government, *viz.* Till the right of determining all matters relating to the public safety, is actually placed in a general assembly of the whole people; or by their own compact and mutual agreement, determine themselves the proper subjects for the exercise of sovereign power. . .

The second species of regular government, is an aristocracy; and this is said then to be constituted when the people, or assembly united by a first covenant, and having thereby cast themselves into the first rudiments of a state; do then by common decree, devolve the sovereign power, on a council consisting of some select members; and these having accepted of the designation, are then properly invested with sovereign command; and then an aristocracy is formed.

The third species of a regular government, is a monarchy, which is settled when the sovereign power is conferred on some one worthy person. It differs from the former, because a monarch who is but one person in natural, as well as in moral account, and so is furnished with an immediate power of exercising sovereign command in all instances of government; but the forenamed must needs have particular time and place assigned; but the power and authority is equal in each. . .

A democracy. This is a form of government, which the light of nature does highly value, and often directs to, as most agreeable to the just and natural prerogatives of human beings. This was of great account, in the early times of the world. And not only so, but upon the experience of several thousand years, after the world had been tumbled, and tost from one species of government to another, at a great expense of blood and treasure, many of the wise nations of the world have sheltered themselves under it again; or at least have blendished, and balanced their governments with it.

It is certainly a great truth. That man's original liberty after it is resigned, (yet under due restrictions) ought to be cherished in all wise governments; or otherwise a man in making himself a subject, he alters himself from a freeman, into a slave, which to do is repugnant to the law of nature. Also the natural equality of men amongst men must be duly favored; in that government was never established by God or nature, to give one man a prerogative to insult over another; therefore in a civil, as well as in a natural state of being, a just equality is to be indulged so far, as that every man is bound to honor every man, which is agreeable both with nature and religion. . .

How can it consist with the honorable terms man holds upon here on earth; that the best sort of men that we can find in the world; such men as are adorned with a double set of ennobling immunities, the first from nature, the other from grace; that these men when they enter into charter-party to manage a trade for heaven, must *ipso facto* be clapt under a government, that is arbitrary and dispotic; yea that carries the plain symptoms of a tyranny in it, when the light of nature knows of a better species, and frequently has made use of it? It wants no farther demonstration, for it's most apparent, that nature is so much mistress of herself, that man in a natural state of being, is under God the first subject of all power, and therefore can make his own choice, and by deliberate compacts, settles his own conditions for the government of himself in a civil state of being; and when a government so settled shall throw itself from its foundations, or the subjects of sovereign power shall subvert or confound the constitution, they then degrade themselves; and so all power returns again to the people, who are the first owners. . . Nay, in a word, if the government of the churches be settled by God, either in the hands of a church monarch, or aristocracy, and the people are no ways the subject of church power: Nay, if they are not under Christ, the fountain of power; then the reformation so called, is but a mere cheat, a schism, and notorious rebellion; neither is there room left for the least palliation, or shadow of excuse, for the reformers in renouncing their obedience to their public governors. . .

But to wind up the whole discourse in a few words. . .

Three particulars; or so many golden maxims, securing the honor of congregational churches.

Particular 1. That the people or fraternity under the gospel, are the first subject of power; or else religion sinks the dignity of human nature into a baser capacity with relation to ecclesiastical, than it is in, in a natural state of being with relation to civil government.

Particular 2. That a democracy in church or state, is a very honorable and regular government according to the dictates of right reason. And therefore,

Particular 3. That these churches of New England, in their ancient constitution of church order; it being a democracy, are manifestly justified and defended by the law and light of nature. . .

6. *Rulers have no authority from God to do mischief*

JONATHAN MAYHEW, *A Discourse Concerning Unlimited Submission and Non-Resistance to the Higher Powers*, 30 January 1750 *

UNLIMITED SUBMISSION AND NON-RESISTANCE TO THE HIGHER POWERS

It is evident that the affairs of civil government may properly fall under a moral and religious consideration, at least so far forth as it relates to the general nature and end of magistracy, and to the grounds and extent of that submission which persons of a private character ought to yield to those who are vested with authority. This must be allowed by all who acknowledge the divine original of Christianity. For, although there be a sense, and a very plain and important sense, in which Christ's kingdom is not of this world, his inspired apostles have, nevertheless, laid down some general principles concerning the office of civil rulers, and the duty of subjects, together with the reason and obligation of that duty. . .

That the end of magistracy is the good of civil society, as *such*.

That civil rulers, as *such*, are the ordinance and ministers of God; it being by his permission and providence that any bear rule, and agreeable to his will that there should be *some persons* vested with authority in society, for the well-being of it.

* *The Pulpit of the American Revolution*, John Wingate Thornton, ed., Boston, D. Lothrop and Co., 2nd ed., 1876, pp. 53–104 *passim*.

That which is here said concerning civil rulers extends to all of them in common. It relates indifferently to monarchical, republican, and aristocratical government, and to all other forms which truly answer the sole end of government—the happiness of society; and to all the different degrees of authority in any particular state; to inferior officers no less than to the supreme.

That disobedience to civil rulers in the due exercise of their authority is not merely a political sin, but a heinous offence against God and religion. . .

There is one very important and interesting point which remains to be inquired into, namely, the *extent* of that subjection to the higher powers which is here enjoined as a duty upon all Christians. Some have thought it warrantable and glorious to disobey the civil powers in certain circumstances, and in cases of very great and general oppression, when humble remonstrances fail of having any effect; and, when the public welfare cannot be otherwise provided for and secured, to rise unanimously even against the sovereign himself, in order to redress their grievances; to vindicate their natural and legal rights; to break the yoke of tyranny, and free themselves and posterity from inglorious servitude and ruin. It is upon this principle that many royal oppressors have been driven from their thrones into banishment, and many slain by the hands of their subjects. . . It was upon this principle that King Charles I was beheaded before his own banqueting-house. It was upon this principle that King James II was made to fly that country which he aimed at enslaving; and upon this principle was that revolution brought about which has been so fruitful of happy consequences to Great Britain. But, in opposition to this principle it has often been asserted that the Scripture in general, and the passage under consideration in particular,* makes all resistance to princes a crime, in any case whatever. If they turn tyrants, and become the common oppressors of those whose welfare they ought to regard with a paternal affection, we must not pretend to right ourselves, unless it be by prayers, and tears, and humble entreaties. And if these methods fail of procuring redress, we must not have recourse to any other, but all suffer ourselves to be robbed and butchered at the pleasure of the 'Lord's anointed,' lest we should incur the sin of rebellion and the punishment of damnation!—for he has God's authority and commission to bear him out in the worst of crimes so far that he may not be withstood or controlled. . .

Now, there does not seem to be any necessity of supposing that an absolute, unlimited obedience, whether active or passive, is here enjoined, merely for this reason—that the precept is delivered in absolute terms, without any exception or limitation expressly mentioned. . .

There is, indeed, one passage in the New Testament where it may seem, at first view, that an unlimited submission to civil rulers is enjoined: 'Submit yourselves to every ordinance of man for the Lord's sake.' *To every ordinance of man.* . . But the true solution of this difficulty (if it be one) is this: By 'every ordinance of man' is not meant every command of the civil magistrate without exception, but every order of magistrates appointed by man, whether superior or inferior; for so the apostle explains himself in the very next words: 'Whether it be to the king as supreme, or to governors, as unto them that

* Rom. xiii. 1–8.

are sent,' etc. But although the apostle had not subjoined any such explanation, the reason of the thing itself would have obliged us to limit the expression 'every ordinance of man' to such human ordinances and commands as are not inconsistent with the ordinances and commands of God, the Supreme Lawgiver, or with any other higher and antecedent obligations. . .

And if we attend to the nature of the argument with which the apostle here enforces the duty of submission to the higher powers, we shall find it to be such a one as concludes not in favor of submission to all who bear the title of rulers in common, but only to those who actually perform the duty of rulers by exercising a reasonable and just authority for the good of human society. This is a point which it will be proper to enlarge upon, because the question before us turns very much upon the truth or falsehood of this position. It is obvious, then, in general, that the civil rulers whom the apostle here speaks of, and obedience to whom he presses upon Christians as a duty, are good rulers,* such as are, in the exercise of their office and power, benefactors to society. Such they are described to be throughout this passage. . . If those who bear the title of civil rulers do not perform the duty of civil rulers, but act directly counter to the sole end and design of their office; if they injure and oppress their subjects, instead of defending their rights and doing them good, they have not the least pretence to be honored, obeyed, and rewarded, according to the apostle's argument. For his reasoning, in order to show the duty of subjection to the higher powers, is, as was before observed, built wholly upon the supposition that they do, in fact, perform the duty of rulers. . .

Rulers have no authority from God to do mischief. . . It is blasphemy to call tyrants and oppressors God's ministers. They are more properly 'the messengers of Satan to buffet us.' † No rulers are properly God's ministers but such as are 'just, ruling in the fear of God' ‡. . .

I now add, further, that the apostle's argument is so far from proving it to be the duty of people to obey and submit to such rulers as act in contradiction to the public good, and so to the design of their office, that it proves the direct contrary. For, please to observe, that if the end of all civil government be the good of society; if this be the thing that is aimed at in constituting civil rulers; and if the motive and argument for submission to government be taken from the apparent usefulness of civil authority—it follows, that when no such good end can be answered by submission, there remains no argument or motive to enforce it; and if, instead of this good end's being brought about by submission, a contrary end is brought about, and the ruin and misery of society effected by it, here is a plain and positive reason against submission in all such cases, should they ever happen. And therefore, in such cases, a regard to the public welfare ought to make us withhold from our rulers that obedience and submission which it would otherwise be our duty to render to them.

* By 'good rulers,' are not intended such as are good in a moral or religious, but only in a political sense; those who perform their duty so far as their office extends, and so far as civil society, as such is concerned in their actions.

† 2 Cor. xii. 7.

‡ 2 Sam. xxiii. 3.

If it be our duty, for example, to obey our king merely for this reason, that he rules for the public welfare (which is the only argument the apostle makes use of), it follows, by a parity of reason, that when he turns tyrant, and makes his subjects his prey to devour and destroy, instead of his charge to defend and cherish, we are bound to throw off our allegiance to him, and to resist; and that according to the tenor of the apostle's argument in this passage. . .

Thus it appears that the common argument grounded upon this passage in favor of universal and passive obedience really overthrows itself, by proving too much, if it proves anything at all—namely, that no civil officer is, in any case whatever, to be resisted, though acting in express contradiction to the design of his office—which no man in his senses ever did or can assert.

If we calmly consider the nature of the thing itself, nothing can well be imagined more directly contrary to common sense than to suppose that millions of people should be subjected to the arbitrary, precarious pleasure of one single man—who has naturally no superiority over them in point of authority—so that their estates, and everything that is valuable in life, and even their lives also, shall be absolutely at his disposal, if he happens to be wanton and capricious enough to demand them. What unprejudiced man can think that God made *all* to be thus subservient to the lawless pleasure and frenzy of *one*, so that it shall always be a sin to resist him? Nothing but the most plain and express revelation from heaven could make a sober, impartial man believe such a monstrous, unaccountable doctrine; and, indeed, the thing itself appears so shocking, so out of all proportion, that it may be questioned whether all the miracles that ever were wrought could make it credible that this doctrine really came from God. . .

But, then, if unlimited submission and passive obedience to the higher powers, in all possible cases, be not a duty, it will be asked, 'How far are we obliged to submit? If we may innocently disobey and resist in some cases, why not in all? Where shall we stop? What is the measure of our duty? This doctrine tends to the total dissolution of civil government, and to introduce such scenes of wild anarchy and confusion as are more fatal to society than the worst of tyranny.'

After this manner some men object; and, indeed, this is the most plausible thing that can be said in favor of such an absolute submission as they plead for. But the worst, or, rather, the best of it is, that there is very little strength or solidity in it; for similar difficulties may be raised with respect to almost every duty of natural and revealed religion. . . It is indeed true, that turbulent, vicious-minded men may take occasion, from this principle that their rulers may in some cases be lawfully resisted, to raise factions and disturbances in the state, and to make resistance where resistance is needless, and therefore sinful. But it is not equally true that children and servants, of turbulent, vicious minds, may take occasion, from this principle that parents and masters may in some cases be lawfully resisted, to resist when resistance is unnecessary, and therefore criminal? Is the principle, in either case, false in itself merely because it may be abused, and applied to legitimate disobedience and resistance in those instances to which it ought not to be applied? According to this way of arguing, there will be no true principles in the world; for there are none but what may be wrested and perverted to serve bad purposes, either through the weakness or wickedness of men.

We may very safely assert these two things in general, without undermining government: One is, that no civil rulers are to be obeyed when they enjoin things that are inconsistent with the commands of God. All such disobedience is lawful and glorious. . . The only reason of the institution of civil government, and the only rational ground of submission to it, is the common safety and utility. If, therefore, in any case, the common safety and utility would not be promoted by submission to government, but the contrary, there is no ground or motive for obedience and submission, but for the contrary.

Whoever considers the nature of civil government, must indeed be sensible that a great degree of implicit confidence must unavoidably be placed in those that bear rule: this is implied in the very notion of authority's being originally a trust committed by the people to those who are vested with it—as all just and righteous authority is. All besides is mere lawless force, and usurpation; neither God nor nature having given any man a right of dominion over any society independently of that society's approbation and consent to be governed by him. Now, as all men are fallible, it cannot be supposed that the public affairs of any state should be always administered in the best manner possible, even by persons of the greatest wisdom and integrity. Nor is it sufficient to legitimate disobedience to the higher powers that they are not so administered, or that they are in some instances very ill-managed; for, upon this principle, it is scarcely supposable that any government at all could be supported, or subsist. Such a principle manifestly tends to the dissolution of government, and to throw all things into confusion and anarchy. But it is equally evident, upon the other hand, that those in authority may abuse their trust and power to such a degree, that neither the law of reason nor of religion requires that any obedience or submission should be paid to them; but, on the contrary, that they should be totally discarded, and the authority which they were before vested with transferred to others, who may exercise it more to those good purposes for which it is given. Nor is this principle, that resistance to the higher powers is in some extraordinary cases justifiable, so liable to abuse as many persons seem to apprehend it. For, although there will be always some petulant, querulous men in every state—men of factious, turbulent, and carping dispositions, glad to lay hold of any trifle to justify and legitimate their caballing against their rulers, and other seditious practices—yet there are, comparatively speaking, but few men of this contemptible character. It does not appear but that mankind in general have a disposition to be as submissive and passive and tame under government as they ought to be. Witness a great, if not the greatest, part of the known world, who are now groaning, but not murmuring, under the heavy yoke of tyranny! While those who govern do it with any tolerable degree of moderation and justice, and in any good measure act up to their office and character by being public benefactors, the people will generally be easy and peaceable, and be rather inclined to flatter and adore than to insult and resist them. . .

For what reason, then, was the resistance to King Charles made? The general answer to this inquiry is, that it was on account of the tyranny and oppression of his reign. . .

The next question which naturally arises is, whether this resistance which was made to the king by the Parliament was properly rebellion or not? The answer to which is plain—that it was not, but a most righteous and glorious stand, made in defence of the natural and legal rights of the people, against the unnatural and illegal encroachments of arbitrary power. Nor was this a rash and too sudden opposition. The nation had been patient under the oppressions of the crown, even to long-suffering, for a coarse of many years, and there was no rational hope of redress in any other way. Resistance was absolutely necessary, in order to preserve the nation from slavery, misery, and ruin. And who so proper to make this resistance as the Lords and Commons—the whole representative body of the people—guardians of the public welfare; and each of which was, in point of legislation, vested with an equal, coordinate power with that of the crown? . . .

To conclude: Let us all learn to be free and to be loyal; let us not profess ourselves vassals to the lawless pleasure of any man on earth; but let us remember, at the same time, government is sacred, and not to be trifled with. . . Let us prize our freedom but not 'use our liberty for a cloak of maliciousness.' There are men who strike at liberty under the term licentiousness; there are others who aim at popularity under the disguise of patriotism. Be aware of both. Extremes are dangerous. . .

SELECTED REFERENCES

Alice Baldwin, *The New England Clergy and the American Revolution*, Durham, North Carolina, Duke University Press, 1928.

John Calvin, *Institutes of the Christian Religion*, Philadelphia, Pennsylvania, 1816.

John Cotton, *The Way of the Churches in New England*, London, 1645.

James E. Ernst, *The Political Thought of Roger Williams*, Seattle, University of Washington Press, 1929.

H. D. Foster, 'The Political Theory of Calvinists before the Puritan Exodus to America,' *American Historical Review*, April 1916, vol. 21, pp. 481–503.

Thomas Cuming Hall, *The Religious Background of American Culture*, Boston, Little, Brown, 1930.

Thomas Hooker, *Survey of the Summe of Church Discipline*, London, 1648.

Roy N. Lokken, 'The Concept of Democracy in Colonial Political Thought,' *William and Mary Quarterly*, October 1959, 3rd Series, XVI, p. 568.

Perry Miller and Thomas H. Johnson, *The Puritans*, New York, American Book Company, 1938.

E. S. Morgan, *The Puritan Dilemma*, Boston, Little, Brown, 1958.

Lloyd R. Morris, *The Rebellious Puritan*, New York, Harcourt, Brace, 1927.

Herbert L. Osgood, 'The Political Ideas of the Puritans,' *Political Science Quarterly*, March 1891, vol. VI, pp. 1–28.

V. L. Parrington, *Main Currents in American Thought: The Colonial Mind, 1620–1800*, New York, Harcourt, Brace, 1927, vol. I.

Ralph Barton Perry, *Puritanism and Democracy*, New York, Vanguard, 1944.

Clinton L. Rossiter, *Seedtime of the Republic*, New York, Harcourt, Brace, 1953.

H. W. Schneider, *The Puritan Mind*, New York, Henry Holt, 1930.

T. J. Wertenbaker, *The Puritan Oligarchy: The Founding of American Civilization*, New York, Scribner's, 1947.

III

REVOLUTIONARY IDEAS IN FERMENT

'The true history of the American revolution,' John Adams observed in 1818, cannot be recovered, for 'the revolution was effected before the war commenced. The revolution was in the minds and hearts of the people.'

A passion for liberty and a hatred of oppression, along with much else of a protestant tendency, had indeed been present in the colonies since the earliest settlement. Carrying with them the traditions of Puritanism and the spirit of the Glorious Revolution, restive under sternly righteous theocratic rule, the colonists found much nourishment on American soil for the liberating doctrines of Colonel Rainboro and John Locke. A frontier people, ever striving to master their physical environment, early Americans were not naturally disposed to bear lightly the heavy restraint of distant authority. English policy, moreover, especially during the period of Prime Minister Walpole's 'salutary neglect' (1721–42), did much to stimulate self-reliance and sentiments of independence.

The Seven Years' War (1756–63) freed the colonies from the threat of France and Spain, and its aftermath imposed further strain on the ties of Empire. With the passage of the Stamp Act by Parliament in 1764, the currents of American political thought began to merge into a single channel flowing toward independence. In the heat of ensuing disputes between the King's centralizing representatives and the separatistic colonial assemblies, charges and counter-charges thundered across the council tables. 'Shall it depend upon the resolutions of a Philadelphia assembly,' cried one irate Englishman, 'whether our fellow subjects shall arm in defense of liberty and property? . . . Does the fate of a whole continent bear any proportion to an almost imperceptible encroachment upon the important privilege of an American, deliberating for a year or two, whether he will pay six-pence in the pound, to save himself and family from perdition?' His Majesty's Government could consider taxation the only effective means of raising colonial revenue, but to the colonists it seemed 'an intolerable outrage upon a free people.' Response to the Stamp Act was immediate, vociferous, and effective and, in an important sense, it marks a general awakening of American, as distinct from colonial, political thought.

Benjamin Franklin (1706–90), businessman, publisher, scientist, inventor, philosopher, and 'elder statesman,' gave this thought succinct utterance. The three letters to Governor William Shirley, the first of the readings in this chapter, grew out of Anglo-American discussion of the Albany Plan of 1754, which Franklin had drafted as a means of uniting the American colonies for military purposes. Franklin's Plan established a central executive, appointed by the Crown, and a central legislative council, with powers of taxation, which was to be elected by the representative assemblies of the several colonies. The British were well aware of the military advantages of an adequate revenue system throughout the American colonies; they were equally aware that danger of colonial insubordination lurked in any project whatever for a general council representative of the united colonies. It had been British policy since 1607 to keep the colonies separate and dependent on London. Instead of a system of taxation by an intercolonial representative council, the Crown proposed that taxes for military purposes (i.e. 'defense') be levied upon the several colonies *by act of Parliament*. Shirley, whom Franklin described in his *Autobiography* as 'sensible and sagacious in himself, and attentive to good advice from others, capable of forming judicious plans,' communicated to Franklin the Crown's proposal for colonial defense. Franklin's response, deprecating any scheme of government or taxation that left the colonists unrepresented, is a prescient foreshadowing of the taxation-representation principle which the colonists soon vigorously asserted. Yet Franklin couched his statement in persuasive terms of affection for England and belief in Empire. He seemed to hope that Americans would find membership in Parliament, thereby effecting a closer union between the colonies and Great Britain. But British political science was unable or unwilling to find any constitutional basis for doing this.

By 1767, Franklin's mood had changed. His years of service as agent in London for Pennsylvania and other colonies gave him deep insight into British imperial relations, and clear comprehension of the basic points in the Anglo-American dispute. He saw that British public law could not provide for an association of equals within a Commonwealth of Nations, and in his letter to Lord Kames, written before the Stamp Act controversy initiated the crisis phase of Anglo-American relations, he described in luminous fashion, as early as 1760, the future of the incipient nation. 'I have long been of opinion,' he wrote Kames, a friend of long standing, 'that the foundations of the future grandeur and stability of the British Empire lie in America; and though, like other foundations, they are low and little seen, they are, nevertheless, broad and strong enough to support the greatest political structure human wisdom ever yet erected.'

While Franklin addressed himself to specific issues, James Otis (1725–83) was inspired by events to seek a legal and plausible theory of government. His *Rights of the Colonists* provoked by the Stamp Act, and here excerpted, first appeared, 20 August, 1764, in the *Boston Gazette*. Exploring the foundations of political organization, Otis admitted that authority resided in Parliament, permitting appeal only to natural law or the 'will of God.' But he maintained—and this was his distinctive contribution—an act of Parliament might be against the 'fundamental constitution.' Three years before, arguing against the reprehensible Writs of Assistance, he had contended that 'no acts of Parliament can establish such a writ; though it should be made in the very words of the petition, it would be void. An act against the Constitution is void.' Elaborating the argument in 1764, he said: 'The supreme legislative and the supreme executive are a perpetual check and balance to each other. If the supreme executive errs, it is informed by the supreme legislative in parliament: if the supreme legislative errs, it is informed by the supreme executive in the King's courts of law. . . This is government! This, is a constitution!' Otis' concept of the courts as 'supreme executive,' exercising a constant check on legislative power, then relatively new on this side of the Atlantic, was destined to become the most conspicuous feature of American constitutionalism.

Unlike Otis, John Dickinson (1732–1808), Philadelphia lawyer and spokesman for prosperous colonial Whiggery, was concerned with the narrower legal case against taxation. His *Letters of a Farmer in Pennsylvania*, included in these readings, was published anonymously, beginning December 1767, as a statement of the temperate argument against British revenue acts. Reserved rather than radical, cautious rather than critical, moved by mercantile interests rather than by political considerations, he admonished both the colonists and Parliament: "If once we are separated from our mother country, what new form of government shall we adopt, or where shall we find another Britain, to supply our loss? . . . We cannot act with too much caution in our disputes. . .' The power to tax, he counseled Parliament, is a *new* power and must be given by consent, else 'oppressions and dissatisfactions being permitted to accumulate —if ever the governed throw off the load, they will do more. A people does not reform with moderation. . .'

James Wilson (1742–98), Scottish attorney of Philadelphia, had studied law with Dickinson. Like his mentor, Wilson was a moderate legalist whose mind moved slowly to acceptance of separation. Even in 1774, Wilson could not do more than question the absolute legislative authority of Parliament. Written in 1770, Wilson's *Considerations on the Authority of Parliament*, abridged in the readings, was not published until four years later. Parliament might err in the exercise of 'uncontrolled authority,' he said in his decidedly conciliatory argument, but the colonists were 'dependent' on the Crown. 'They are the subjects of the King of Great Britain. They owe him allegiance.'

Alexander Hamilton (1755–1804), youthful insurgent, did not share Wilson's inclination to indulge the British Sovereign. Born in the British West Indian St. Nevis, Hamilton was sent to New York in late 1772 to be educated and seek his fortune. Two years later, at the age of nineteen, he was already caught up in the heady business of revolution. 'To confess my weakness, Ned,' he wrote a boyhood friend, 'my ambition is prevalent, so that I condemn the groveling condition of a clerk or the like, to which my fortune, etc., condemns me, and would willingly risk my life, though not my character, to exalt my station. . . My folly makes me ashamed, and I beg you'll conceal it; yet, Neddy, we have seen such schemes successful when the projector is constant. I shall conclude saying, I wish there was a war.'

A Full Vindication, here reprinted, written in defense of the first Continental Congress, formed extra-legally in 1774, is Hamilton's first important contribution to the new doctrine of American empire. Trying to allay colonial fears of British boycott, he threw out a suggestion elaborated in his future *Report on Manufactures:* 'If, by the necessity of the thing, manufactures should once be established, and take root among us, they will pave the way still more to the future grandeur and glory of America.' The Continental Congress, Hamilton argued, spoke with 'the clear voice of natural justice. . . The idea of legislation, or taxation, when the subject is not represented, is inconsistent with that.' It contradicts 'the fundamental principles of the English constitution' as well as of the colonial charters. 'This being the case,' he concluded, 'we can have no recourse but in a restriction of our trade, or in a resistance *vi et armis*.'

The writings of Dr. Samuel Seabury (1729-96), who replied to Hamilton, and of Daniel Leonard (1740-1829) are here included as samplings of the Tory mind in the period before the Revolution. Seabury, eminent divine who later served as chaplain in the British forces, wrote in his *View of the Controversy* that government by consent had no foundation either in natural law or in the British constitution. The right to exercise a legislative power, he argued, does not derive 'from nature, but from the indulgence or grant of the parent state.' If, he added, with better logic than Wilson's, 'we obey the laws of the King, we obey the laws of the parliament. If we disown the authority of parliament, we disown the authority of the King.'

Daniel Leonard's *Letters* were published weekly from 12 December 1774, to 3 April 1775. A Boston lawyer of brilliant mind and aristocratic tastes, Leonard wrote under the pen name of 'Massachusettensis,' and his *Letters* marshalled the complete Tory doctrine. Following Hobbes and his *Leviathan* of 1651, Leonard found 'the security of the people from internal rapacity and violence, and from foreign invasion, [to be] the end and design of government.' The colonies, a part of the British Empire, 'must be subject to the supreme power of the state, which is vested in the estates of parliament. . .' Subversion of this principle, he warned, had planted the seed of sedition which 'has become a great tree . . . I now would induce you to go to work immediately with axes and hatchets, and cut it down. . .'

John Adams (1735-1826), political scientist and lawyer, on returning from the Continental Congress to Boston in 1775, 'found the Massachusetts Gazette teeming with political speculations, and *Massachusettensis* shining like a moon among the lesser stars.' Though it is claimed that Adams contemplated independence as early as 1755, his moves in that direction were juridically cautious and uncertain. He declared publicly against independence in 1774, and in that same year described it as 'a Hobgoblin of so frightful Mien, that it would throw a delicate person into fits to look it in the face.' His reply to Leonard a year later, included in these readings, was immediately prepared in the form of *Novanglus* or *Letters* to the people of Massachusetts Bay. Adams, a veteran politician immune to barbs, could like Zeus, hurl thunderbolts with devastating effect. 'Our rhetorical magician,' he wrote, referring to Leonard, can offer only one proposition in his 'long string of pretended absurdities.' To that proposition—'that it is absolutely necessary there should be a supreme power, coextensive with all the dominions'—Adams sharply disagreed.

Not content to build his case entirely on political theory or public law, Adams observed, if 'we enjoy, and are entitled to more liberty than the British constitution allows, where is the harm? . . . whose fault is this,' he asked, coyly, 'if we enjoy the British constitution in greater purity and perfection than they do in England?' Legislative authority, he added, was vested with the colonial assemblies in the same way that English law-making was lodged with Parliament. Any attempt to reduce English liberties in America, he warned, would be resisted.

Adams' attention was not confined to Loyalist 'rhetorical magicians.' 'That filthy Tom Paine,' he called the British citizen whom Franklin, in 1774, had enthusiastically sponsored and the man who, more than any other, made the Revolution popular with the mass of Americans. Thomas Paine (1737–1809), an agitator and pamphleteer of lowly origin, effectively translated the dialectics of the Revolutionary debate into a rousing bugle call for independence. In a time of doubt and hesitation, when many hoped for, or looked forward to, reconciliation with Britain, Paine fired up their courage, strengthened their will to revolt.

Paine's *Common Sense*, included in this chapter, was a call to arms, not a political treatise. First published in January, 1776, its total sales eventually running to half a million copies, this revolutionary classic proclaimed that economic self-interest, as well as common sense, dictated a bold assertion of 'Popular Sovereignty.' It is absurd, Paine clamored, for an island permanently to govern a continent. 'We have it in our power to make the world over again.'

The revolutionary mind had arrived at separation and independence with much reluctance and only after a careful sifting of alternatives. Franklin in 1754 had envisaged a confederation of equal states within the British Empire, but his plan came too late or too early for the colonists, and was even then too extreme for the Mother Country to accept, or even seriously to consider. Thereafter our discussion attacked the prerogatives of Parliament. Otis challenged the omnipotence of that body, Dickinson queried its precedents for taxation except for purposes of regulating trade, Wilson distinguished between allegiance to the Crown and allegiance to Parliament, while King's College undergraduate Hamilton found Parliament's acts contrary to principles of natural law and the British constitution. It remained for John Adams to declare that the colonial assemblies enjoyed authority equal to that of the Mother Country and, finally, for Paine to assert that 'the period of debate is over,' 'a government of our own is our natural right.'

The Tory argument had been tested at every step. Occasionally superior in logic and generally as profound in reasoning as that of the provincials, it had not been able to meet the peculiar needs of American life. Individualism, the gospel of our entrepreneurs, then and now, reacted sharply against the restrictive practices of British mercantilism; self-reliance, forced on men here by primitive conditions, did not permit dependence on a distant authority. The Tory case never actually engaged the American mind, was never adjusted to the realities of the emerging American empire.

'A decent respect for the opinions of mankind' impelled the colonial leaders to make formal announcement of the causes for separation, and state the basic doctrines to which the confederation was dedicated. Prepared by Thomas Jefferson for a committee of five consisting of John Adams, Benjamin Franklin, Roger Sherman, Robert R. Livingston, and Jefferson himself, the Declaration of Independence was designed to be, as Jefferson wrote Henry Lee many years later, 'an expression of the American mind,' fusing 'the harmonizing sentiments of the day, whether expressed in conversation, in letters, printed essays, or in elementary books of public right, as Aristotle, Cicero, Locke, Sidney, etc.' Not intending 'to find out new principles, or new arguments, never before thought of,' Jefferson sought, as he said, only 'to place before mankind the common sense of the subject,' and to do so 'in terms so plain and firm as to command their assent, and justify ourselves in the independent stand we [were] impelled to take.'

In the Virginia Bill of Rights, which preceded the Declaration by almost a month, property had been included among man's natural, unalienable rights: 'All Men are by Nature equally free and independent, and have certain inherent Rights, of which, when they enter into a State of Society, they cannot, by any Compact, deprive or divest their Posterity; namely, *the Enjoyment of Life and Liberty with the Means of acquiring and possessing Property, and pursuing and obtaining Happiness and Safety*.' Certain writers have made much of Jefferson's substitution of the phrase 'pursuit of Happiness' for the narrower term 'property,' as in the Virginia document of 12 June 1776. 'Samuel Adams and other followers of Locke had been content,' V. L. Parrington observes in his *Main Currents in American Thought*, 'with the classical enumeration of life, liberty, and property; but in Jefferson's hands the English doctrine was given a revolutionary shift.' Parrington interpreted Jefferson's change of phraseology as marking 'a complete break with the Whiggish doctrine of property rights that Locke had bequeathed to the English middle class, and the substitution of a broader sociological conception.' Dr. Julian P. Boyd sets the matter in truer perspective:

> What was new and revolutionary in the Declaration was the fact that here, for the first time, a political society formally declared the purpose of the state, enumerated some of man's natural rights, and affirmed the right of revolution. But this innovation was the act of a free people, not an invention of Jefferson. Even Jefferson's inclusion of the 'pursuit of happiness' as an indefeasible right does not warrant the assumption that this was a new philosophy of government, distinctively American . . . Jefferson only indicated in the Declaration certain unalienable rights and *among* these were life, liberty, and the pursuit of happiness. . . That he differed with Locke in the choice of this phrase is infinitely less important than that he and the people for whom he spoke grounded their Declaration upon Locke's great justification of revolution. For revolution, in both the Jeffersonian and the Lockian sense, is merely the ultimate means of pursuing happiness. . .

The long debate preceding revolution and independence was, in its broader aspects, a continuation of the Cromwellian discussions at Putney in 1647. What are the solid foundations of right and authority? Can government and laws be securely grounded in anything so vague as natural law? Can government action be tested by any such elusive standard? Or must individual rights and public authority be set in compact or constitution, and legal right and wrong be judged according to this more precise standard? Assuming that higher law, natural or constitutional, does provide the test of legitimate authority, who, ultimately, is to enforce the higher law?

The revolutionary controversy ignited other vexing issues: Did government, as Seabury claimed, exist to protect property rights, or was 'the happiness of individuals the ultimate end of political society'? Was Leonard correct in arguing that the end of government is 'the security of the people from internal rapacity and violence,' or, rather, did truth lie with Paine, that the final test of good government is its concern for the '*res publica*, the public affairs, or the public good'? Much of American political thought is the continuing search for answers to these questions.

1. *I look upon the colonies as so many countries gained to Great Britain*

BENJAMIN FRANKLIN to Governor William Shirley, 22 December 1754 *

LETTER I. 17 DECEMBER 1754.

SIR,

I return you the loose sheets of the plan, with thanks to your Excellency for communicating them.

I apprehend, that excluding the people of the colonies from all share in the choice of the grand council will give extreme dissatisfaction; as well as the taxing them by act of Parliament, where they have no representation. It is very possible, that this general government might be as well and faithfully administered without the people, as with them; but where heavy burthens are to be laid upon them, it has been found useful to make it as much as possible their own act; for they bear better, when they have, or think they have, some share in the direction; and when any public measures are generally grievous, or even distasteful, to the people, the wheels of government move more heavily.

LETTER II. 18 DECEMBER 1754.

Sir,

I mentioned it yesterday to your Excellency as my opinion, that excluding the people of the colonies from all share in the choice of the grand council would probably give extreme dissatisfaction, as well as the taxing them by act of Parliament, where they have no representation. In matters of general concern to the people, and especially where burthens are to be laid upon them, it is of use to consider, as well what they will be apt to think and say, as what they ought to think. I shall therefore, as your Excellency requires it of me briefly mention what of either kind occurs to me on this occasion.

* *The Works of Benjamin Franklin*, Jared Sparks, ed., Boston, 1840, vol. III, Letters I, II, and III, pp. 56–68.

First, they will say, and perhaps with justice, that the body of the people in the colonies are as loyal, and as firmly attached to the present constitution and reigning family, as any subjects in the king's dominions.

That there is no reason to doubt the readiness and willingness of the representatives they may choose to grant from time to time such supplies for the defence of the country, as shall be judged necessary, so far as their abilities will allow.

That the people in the colonies, who are to feel the immediate mischiefs of invasion and conquest by an enemy, in the loss of their estates, lives, and liberties, are likely to be better judges of the quantity of forces necessary to be raised and maintained, forts to be built and supported, and of their own abilities to bear the expense, than the Parliament of England, at so great a distance.

That governors often come to the colonies merely to make fortunes, with which they intend to return to Britain; are not always men of the best abilities or integrity; have many of them no estates here, nor any natural connexion with us, that should make them heartily concerned for our welfare; and might possibly be fond of raising and keeping up more forces than necessary, from the profits accruing to themselves, and to make provision for their friends and dependents.

That the counsellors in most of the colonies being appointed by the crown, on the recommendation of governors, are often persons of small estates, frequently dependent on the governors for offices, and therefore too much under influence.

That there is therefore great reason to be jealous of a power in such governors and councils to raise such sums, as they shall judge necessary, by drafts on the Lords of the Treasury, to be afterwards laid on the colonies by act of Parliament, and paid by the people here; since they might abuse it, by projecting useless expeditions, harassing the people, and taking them from their labor to execute such projects, merely to create offices and employments, and gratify their dependents, and divide profits.

That the Parliament of England is at a great distance, subject to be misinformed and misled by such governors and councils, whose united interests might probably secure them against the effect of any complaint from hence.

That it is supposed an undoubted right of Englishmen not to be taxed but by their own consent, given through their representatives.

That the colonies have no representatives in Parliament.

That to propose taxing them by Parliament, and refuse them the liberty of choosing a representative council to meet in the colonies, and consider and judge of the necessity of any general tax and the quantum, shows a suspicion of their loyalty to the crown, or of their regard for their country, or of their common sense and understanding, which they have not deserved.

That compelling the colonies to pay money without their consent, would be rather like raising contributions in an enemy's country, than taxing of Englishmen for their own public benefit. . .

That a tax laid by the representatives of the colonies might be easily lessened as the occasions should lessen; but, being once laid by Parliament under the influence of their representations made by governors, would probably be kept up and continued for the benefit of governors, to the grievous burthen and discontent of the colonies, and prevention of their growth and increase.

That a power in governors to march the inhabitants from one end of the British and French colonies to the other, being a country of at least one thousand five hundred miles long, without the approbation or the consent of their representatives first obtained to such expeditions, might be grievous and ruinous to the people. . .

That if the colonies in a body may be well governed by governors and councils appointed by the crown, without representatives, particular colonies may as well or better be so governed; a tax may be laid upon them all by act of Parliament for support of government, and their Assemblies may be dismissed as an useless part of the constitution. . .

That . . . the colonies pay yearly great sums to the mother country unnoticed; for

1. Taxes paid in Britain by the landholder or artificer must enter into and increase the price of the produce of land and manufactures made of it; and great part of this is paid by consumers in the colonies, who thereby pay a considerable part of the British taxes.

2. We are restrained in our trade with foreign nations; and where we could be supplied with any manufacture cheaper from them, but must buy the same dearer from Britain, the difference of price is a clear tax to Britain.

3. We are obliged to carry a great part of our produce directly to Britain; and where the duties laid upon it lessen its price to the planter, or it sells for less than it would in foreign markets, the difference is a tax paid to Britain.

4. Some manufactures we could make, but are forbidden, and must take them of British merchants; the whole price is a tax paid to Britain.

5. By our greatly increasing the demand and consumption of British manufactures, their price is considerably raised of late years; the advantage is clear profit to Britain, and enables its people better to pay great taxes; and much of it, being paid by us, is clear tax to Britain.

6. In short, as we are not suffered to regulate our trade, and restrain the importation and consumption of British superfluities, as Britain can the consumption of foreign superfluities, our whole wealth centres finally amongst the merchants and inhabitants of Britain; and if we make them richer, and enable them better to pay their taxes, it is nearly the same as being taxed ourselves, and equally beneficial to the crown.

These kinds of secondary taxes, however, we do not complain of, though we have no share in the laying or disposing of them; but to pay immediate heavy taxes, in the laying appropriation, and disposition of which we have no part, and which perhaps we may know to be as unnecessary as grievous, must seem hard measures to Englishmen, who cannot conceive, that, by hazarding their lives and fortunes in subduing and settling new countries, extending the dominion, and increasing the commerce of the mother nation, they have forfeited the native rights of Britons; which they think ought rather to be given to them, as due to such merit, if they had been before in a state of slavery.

These, and such kinds of things as these, I apprehend, will be thought and said by the people, if the proposed alteration of the Albany plan should take place. Then the administration of the board of governors and council so appointed, not having the representative body of the people to approve and unite in its measures, and conciliate the minds of the people to them, will probably become suspected and odious; dangerous animosities and feuds will arise between the governors and governed; and everything go into confusion. . .

LETTER III. 22 DECEMBER 1754.

Sir,

Since the conversation your Excellency was pleased to honor me with, on the subject of *uniting the colonies* more intimately with Great Britain, by allowing them *representatives in Parliament*, I have something further considered that matter, and am of opinion, that such a union would be very acceptable to the colonies, provided they had a reasonable number of representatives allowed them; and that all the old acts of Parliament restraining the trade or cramping the manufactures of the colonies be at the same time repealed, and the British subjects *on this side the water* put, in those respects, on the same footing with those in Great Britain, till the new Parliament, representing the whole, shall think it for the interest of the whole to reënact some or all of them. It is not that I imagine so many representatives will be allowed the colonies, as to have any great weight by their numbers; but I think there might be sufficient to occasion those laws to be better and more impartially considered, and perhaps to overcome the interest of a petty corporation, or of any particular set of artificers or traders in England, who heretofore seem, in some instances, to have been more regarded than all the colonies, or than was consistent with the general interest, or best national good. I think too, that the government of the colonies by a Parliament, in which they are fairly represented, would be vastly more agreeable to the people, than the method lately attempted to be introduced by royal instruction, as well as more agreeable to the nature of an English constitution, and to English liberty; and that such laws as now seem to bear hard on the colonies, would (when judged by such a Parliament for the best interest of the whole) be more cheerfully submitted to, and more easily executed.

I should hope too, that by such a union, the people of Great Britain, and the people of the colonies, would learn to consider themselves, as not belonging to different communities with different interests, but to one community with one interest; which I imagine would contribute to strengthen the whole, and greatly lessen the danger of future separations.

It is, I suppose, agreed to be the general interest of any state, that its people be numerous and rich; men enough to fight in its defence, and enough to pay sufficient taxes to defray the charge; for these circumstances tend to the security of the state, and its protection from foreign power. But it seems not of so much importance, whether the fighting be done by John or Thomas, or the tax paid by William or Charles. The iron manufacture employs and enriches British subjects, but is it of any importance to the state, whether the manufacturer lives at Birmingham, or Sheffield, or both; since they are still within its bounds, and their wealth and persons still at its command? Could the Goodwin Sands be laid dry by banks, and land equal to a large country thereby gained to England, and presently filled with English inhabitants, would it be right to deprive such inhabitants of the common privileges enjoyed by other Englishmen, the right of vending their produce in the same ports, or of making their own shoes, because a merchant or a shoemaker, living on the old land, might fancy it more for his advantage to trade or make shoes for them? Would this be right, even if the land were gained at the expense of the state? And would it not seem less right, if the charge and labor of gaining the additional territory to Britain had been borne by the settlers themselves? And would not the hardship appear yet greater, if the people of a new country should be allowed no representatives in the Parliament enacting such impositions?

Now I look on the colonies as so many countries gained to Great Britain, and more advantageous to it, than if they had been gained out of the seas around its coast, and joined to its lands; for being in different climates, they afford greater variety of produce, and materials for more manufactures; and, being separated by the ocean, they increase much more its shipping and seamen; and, since they are all included in the British empire, which has only extended itself by their means, and the strength and wealth of the parts are the strength and wealth of the whole, what imports it to the general state, whether a merchant, a smith, or a hatter, grows rich in Old or New England? And if, through increase of the people, two smiths are wanted for one employed before, why may not the *new* smith be allowed to live and thrive in the *new* country, as well as the *old* one in the *old?* In fine, why should the countenance of a state be *partially* afforded to its people, unless it be most in favor of those who have most merit? And if there be any difference, those who have most contributed to enlarge Britain's empire and commerce, increase her strength, her wealth, and the numbers of her people, at the risk of their own lives and private fortunes in new and strange countries, methinks ought rather to expect some preference. . .

2. *America must become a great country, populous and mighty*

BENJAMIN FRANKLIN to Lord Kames, 11 April 1767 *

I received your obliging favor of January the 19th. You have kindly relieved me from the pain I had long been under. You are goodness itself. I ought to have answered yours of December 25th, 1765. I never received a letter that contained sentiments more suitable to my own. It found me under much agitation of mind on the very important subject it treated. It fortified me greatly in the judgment I was inclined to form, though contrary to the general vogue, on the then delicate and critical situation of affairs between Great Britain and the colonies, and on that weighty point, their *union*. You guessed aright in suppos-

* Jared Sparks, ed., op. cit. vol. VII, pp. 327–34.

ing that I would not be a *mute in that play*. I was extremely busy, attending members of both Houses, informing, explaining, consulting, disputing, in a continual hurry from morning till night, till the affair was happily ended. During the course of its being called before the House of Commons, I spoke my mind pretty freely. . . You will there see how entirely we agree, except in a point of fact, of which you can not but be misinformed; the papers at that time being full of mistaken assertions, that the colonies had been the cause of the war, and had ungratefully refused to bear any part of the expense of it.

I send it you now, because I apprehend some late accidents are likely to revive the contest between the two countries. I fear it will be a mischievous one. It becomes a matter of great importance, that clear ideas should be formed on solid principles, both in Britain and America, of the true political relation between them, and the mutual duties belonging to that relation. Till this is done, they will be often jarring. . . I am fully persuaded with you, that a *consolidating union*, by a fair and equal representation of all the parts of this empire in Parliament, is the only firm basis on which its political grandeur and prosperity can be founded. Ireland once wished it, but now rejects it. The time has been, when the colonies might have been pleased with it; they are now *indifferent* about it; and, if it is much longer delayed, they too will *refuse* it. But the pride of this people cannot bear the thought of it, and therefore it will be delayed. Every man in England seems to consider himself as a piece of a sovereign over America; seems to jostle himself into the throne with the King, and talks of *our subjects in the colonies*. The Parliament cannot well and wisely make laws suited to the colonies, without being properly and truly informed of their circumstances, abilities, temper, &c. This it cannot be without representatives from thence; and yet it is fond of this power, and averse to the only means of acquiring the necessary knowledge for exercising it; which is desiring to be *omnipotent*, without being *omniscient*.

I have mentioned, that the contest is likely to be revived. It is on this occasion. In the same session with the Stamp Act, an act was passed to regulate the quartering of soldiers in America; when the bill was first brought in, it contained a clause, empowering the officers to quarter their soldiers in private houses; this we warmly opposed, and got it omitted. The bill passed, however, with a clause, that empty houses, barns, &c., should be hired for them; and that the respective provinces, where they were, should pay the expenses and furnish firing, bedding, drink, and some other articles to the soldiers, *gratis*. There is no way for any province to do this but by the Assembly's making a law to raise the money. The Pennsylvania Assembly has made such a law; the New York Assembly has refused to do it; and now all the talk here is, of sending a force to compel them.

The reasons given by the Assembly to the governor for the refusal are, that they understand the act to mean the furnishing such things to soldiers, only while on their march through the country, and not to great bodies of soldiers, to be fixed, as at present, in the province, the burden in the latter case being greater than the inhabitants can bear; that it would put it in the power of the captain-general to oppress the province at pleasure, &c. But there is supposed to be another reason at bottom, which they intimate, though they do not plainly express it; to wit, that it is of the nature of an *internal tax* laid on them by Parliament, which has no right so to do. Their refusal is here called *rebellion*, and punishment is thought of.

Now waiving that point of right, and supposing the legislatures in America subordinate to the legislature of Great Britain, one might conceive, I think, a power in the superior legislature to forbid the inferior legislatures making particular laws; but to enjoin it to make a particular law, contrary to its own judgment, seems improper; an Assembly or Parliament not being an *executive* officer of government, whose duty it is, in law making, to obey orders, but a *deliberative* body, who are to consider what comes before them, its propriety, practicability, or possibility, and to determine accordingly. The very nature of a Parliament seems to be destroyed by supposing it may be bound and compelled, by law of a superior Parliament, to make a law contrary to its own judgment.

Indeed, the act of Parliament in question has not as in other acts when a duty is enjoined, directed a penalty or neglect or refusal, and a mode of recovering that penalty. It seems, therefore, to the people in America, as a mere requisition, which they are at liberty to comply with or not, as it may suit or not suit the different circumstances of the different provinces. Pennsylvania has therefore voluntarily complied. New York, as I said before, has refused. The ministry that made the act, and all their adherents, call for vengeance. The present ministry are perplexed, and the measures they will finally take on the occasion are yet unknown. But sure I am, that, if *force* is used, great mischief will ensue; the affections of the people of America to this country will be alienated; your commerce will be diminished; and a total separation of interests will be the final consequence.

It is a common, but mistaken notion here, that the colonies were planted at the expense of Parliament, and that therefore the Parliament has a right to tax them, &c. The truth is, they were planted at the expense of private adventurers, who went over there to settle, with leave of the King, given by charter. On receiving this leave, and those charters, the adventurers voluntarily engaged to remain the King's subjects, though in a foreign country; a country which had not been conquered by either King or Parliament, but was possessed by a free people.

When our planters arrived, they purchased the lands of the natives, without putting King or Parliament to any expense. Parliament had no hand in their settlement, was never so much as consulted about their constitution, and took no kind of notice of them, till many years after they were established. I except only the two modern colonies, or rather attempts to make colonies (for they succeed but poorly, and as yet hardly deserve the name of colonies), I mean Georgia and Nova Scotia, which have hitherto been little better than Parliamentary jobs. Thus all the colonies acknowledge the King as their sovereign; his governors there represent his person; laws are made by their Assemblies or little parliaments, with the governor's assent, subject still to the King's pleasure to affirm or annul them. Suits arising in the colonies, and between colony and colony, are determined by the King in Council. In this view, they seem so many separate little states, subject to the same prince. The sovereignty of the King is therefore easily understood. But nothing is more common here than to talk of the *sovereignty* of PARLIAMENT, and the sovereignty of this nation over the colonies; a kind of sovereignty, the idea of which is not so clear, nor does it clearly appear on what foundation it is established. On the other hand, it seems necessary for the common good of the empire, that a power be lodged somewhere, to regulate its general commerce; this can be placed nowhere so properly as in the Parliament of Great Britain; and therefore, though that power has in some instances been executed with great partiality to Britain and prejudice to the colonies, they have nevertheless always submitted to it. Custom-houses are established in all of them, by virtue of laws made here, and the duties instantly paid, except by a few smugglers, such as are here and in all countries; but internal taxes laid on them by Parliament are still and ever will be objected to for the reason that you will see in the mentioned examination.

Upon the whole, I have lived so great a part of my life in Britain, and have formed so many friendships in it, that I love it, and sincerely wish it prosperity; and therefore wish to see that union, on which alone I think it can be secured and established. As to America, the advantages of such a union to her are not so apparent. She may suffer at present under the arbitrary power of this country; she may suffer for a while in a separation from it; but these are temporary evils which she will outgrow. Scotland and Ireland are differently circumstanced. Confined by the sea, they can scarcely increase in numbers, wealth, and strength, so as to overbalance England. But America, an immense territory, favored by nature with all advantages of climate, soils, great navigable rivers, lakes, &c., must become a great country, populous and mighty; and will, in a less time than is generally conceived, be able to shake off any shackles that may be imposed upon her, and perhaps place them on the imposers. In the mean time every act of oppression will sour their tempers, lessen greatly, if not annihilate, the profits of your commerce with them, and hasten their final revolt; for the seeds of liberty are universally found there, and nothing can eradicate them. And yet there remains among that people so much respect, veneration, and affection for Britain, that, if cultivated prudently, with a kind usage and tenderness for their privileges, they might be easily governed still for ages, without force or any considerable expense. But I do not see here a sufficient quantity of the wisdom, that is necessary to produce such a conduct, and I lament the want of it. . .

3. *Power in the nature of the thing is given in trust*

JAMES OTIS, *The Rights of the British Colonies*, 1764 *

The origin of *government* has in all ages no less perplexed the heads of lawyers and politicians, than the origin of *evil* has embarrassed divines and philosophers: And 'tis probable the world may receive a satisfactory solution on *both* those points of enquiry at the *same* time.

* From *The University of Missouri Studies*, Columbia, Mo., 1929, vol. IV, pp. 49–91 *passim*.

The various opinions on the origin of *government* have been reduced to four. (1) That dominion is founded in Grace. (2) On *force* or mere *power.* (3) On *compact.* (4) On *property.*

The first of these opinions is so absurd, and the world has paid so very dear for embracing it, especially under the administration of the *Roman pontiffs*, that mankind seem at this day to be in a great measure cured of their madness in this particular; and the notion is pretty generally exploded, and hissed off the stage.

To those who lay the foundation of government in *force* and mere *brutal power*, it is objected; that, their system destroys all distinction between right and wrong; that it overturns all morality, and leaves it to every man to do what is right in his own eyes; that it leads directly to *scepticism*, and ends in *atheism*. When a man's will and pleasure is his only rule and guide, what safety can there be either for him or against him but in the point of a sword?

On the other hand the gentlemen in favor of the *original compact* have been often told that their system is chimerical and unsupported by reason or experience. . .

With regard to the fourth opinion, that the *dominion is founded in property*, what is it but playing with words? Dominion in one sense of the term is synonymous with property, so one cannot be called the foundation of the other, but as one *name* may appear to be the foundation or cause of another.

Property cannot be the foundation of dominion as synonymous with government; for on the supposition that property has a precarious existence antecedent to government, and tho' it is also admitted that the security of property is one end of government, but that of little estimation even in the view of a *miser* when life and liberty of locomotion and further accumulation are placed in competition, it must be a very absurd way of speaking to assert that *one* end of government is the foundation of government. If the ends of government are to be considered as its foundation, it cannot with truth or propriety be said that government is founded on any *one* of those ends: . . . but at least on something else in conjunction. It is however true in fact and *experience*, as the great, the incomparable *Harrington* has most abundantly demonstrated in his *Oceana*, and other divine writings, that Empire follows the balance of *property*. 'Tis also certain that *property* in fact generally *confers* power, tho' the possessor of it may not have much more wit than a mole or a musquash: And this is too often the cause, that riches are fought after without the least concern about the right application of them. But is the fault in the riches, or the general law of nature, or the unworthy possessor? It will never follow from all this, that government is *rightfully* founded on *property*, alone. What shall we say then? Is not government founded on *grace?* No. Nor on *force?* No. Nor on *compact?* Nor *property?* Not altogether on either. Has it *any* solid foundation? any chief corner stone, but what accident, chance, or confusion may lay one moment and destroy the next? I think it has an everlasting foundation in the *unchangeable will of* God, the author of nature, whose laws never vary. *Government* is therefore most evidently founded *on the* necessities of our nature. It is by no means an *arbitrary* thing, depending merely on *compact* or *human* will for its existence. . .

Let no man think I am about to commence advocate for *despotism*, because I affirm that government is founded on the necessity of our natures; and that an original supreme Sovereign, absolute, and uncontrollable, *earthly* power *must* exist in and preside over every society; from whose final decisions there can be no appeal but directly to Heaven. . . I say supreme absolute power is *originally* and *ultimately* in the people; and they never did in fact *freely*, nor can they *rightfully* make an absolute, unlimited renunciation of this divine right.* It is ever in the nature of the thing given in *trust*, and on a condition, the performance of which no mortal can dispense with; namely, that the person or persons on whom the sovereignty is conferred by the people, shall incessantly consult *their* good. Tyranny of all kinds is to be abhorred, whether it be in the hands of one, or of the few, or of the many. . .

The *end* of government being the *good* of mankind, points out its great duties: It is above all things to provide for the security, the quiet, and happy enjoyment of life, liberty, and property. There is no one act which a government can have a right to make, that does not tend to the advancement of the security, tranquility, and prosperity of the people. . .

The form of government is by *nature* and by *right* so far left to the individuals of each society, that they may alter it from a simple democracy or government of all over all, to any other form they please. . .

The same law of nature and of reason is equally obligatory on a *democracy*, an *aristocracy*, and a *monarchy:* Whenever the administrators, in any of those forms, deviate from truth, justice and equity, they verge towards tyranny, and are to be opposed; and if they prove incorrigible, they will be *deposed* by the people, if the people are not rendered too abject. . .

OF THE NATURAL RIGHTS OF COLONISTS

In order to form an idea of the natural rights of the Colonists, I presume it will be granted that they are men, the common children of the same Creator with their brethren of Great Britain. Nature has placed all such in a state of equality and perfect freedom, to act within the bounds of the laws of nature and reason, without consulting the will or regarding the humor, the passions or whims of any other man, unless they are formed into a society or body politic. . .

By being or becoming members of society, they have not renounced their natural liberty in any greater degree than other good citizens, and if this be taken from them without their consent, they are so far enslaved. . .

OF THE POLITICAL AND CIVIL RIGHTS OF THE BRITISH COLONIES

I also lay it down as one of the first principles from whence I intend to deduce the civil rights of the British colonies, that all of them are subject to, and

* The power of God almighty is the only power that can properly and strictly be called supreme and absolute. In the order of nature immediately under him, comes the power of a simple *democracy*, or the power of the whole over the whole. Subordinate to both these, are all other political powers, from that of the French monarch to a petty constable.

dependent on Great Britain; and that therefore as over subordinate governments, the parliament of Great Britain has an undoubted power and lawful authority to make acts for the general good, that by naming them, shall and ought to be equally binding, as upon the subjects of Great Britain within the realm. This principle, I presume will be readily granted on the other side of the Atlantic. It has been practiced upon for twenty years to my knowledge, in the province of the *Massachusetts Bay;* and I have ever received it, that it has been so from the beginning, in this and the sister provinces, thro' the continent. . .

Every British subject born on the continent of America, or in any other of the British dominions, is by the law of God and nature, by the common law, and by act of parliament, (exclusive of all charters from the Crown) entitled to all the natural, essential, inherent, and inseparable rights of our fellow subjects in Great Britain. Among those rights are the following, which it is humbly conceived no man or body of men, not excepting the parliament, justly, equitably and consistently with their own rights and the constitution, can take away. . .

1st. *That the supreme and subordinate powers of the legislation should be free and sacred in the hands where the community have once rightfully placed them.*

2dly. *The supreme national legislative cannot be altered justly 'till the commonwealth is dissolved, nor a subordinate legislative taken away without forfeiture or other good cause.* Nor then can the subjects in the subordinate government be reduced to a state of slavery, and subject to the despotic rule of others. A state has no right to make slaves of the conquered. Even when the subordinate right of legislature is forfeited, and so declared, this cannot affect the natural persons either of those who were invested with it, or the inhabitants, so far as to deprive them of the rights of subjects and of men. The colonists will have an equitable right notwithstanding any such forfeiture of charter, to be represented in Parliament, or to have some new subordinate legislature among themselves. It would be best if they had both. Deprived however of their common rights as subjects, they cannot lawfully be while they remain such. A representation in Parliament from the several Colonies, since they are become so large and numerous, as to be called on not to maintain provincial government, civil and military, among themselves, for this they have cheerfully done, but to contribute towards the support of a national standing army, by reason of the heavy national debt, when they themselves owe a large one, contracted in the common cause, can't be thought an unreasonable thing, nor if asked, could it be called an immodest request. . .

No representation of the Colonies in parliament alone, would however be equivalent to a subordinate legislative among themselves; nor so well answer the ends of increasing their prosperity and the commerce of Great Britain. It would be impossible for the parliament to judge so well, of their abilities to bear taxes, impositions on trade, and other duties and burthens, or of the local laws that might be really needful, as a legislative here.

3rdly. *No legislative, supreme or subordinate, has a right to make itself arbitrary.*

It would be a most manifest contradiction, for a free legislative, like that of Great Britain, to make itself arbitrary.

4thly. *The supreme legislative cannot justly assume a power of ruling by extempore arbitrary decrees, but is bound to dispense justice by known settled rules*, and by duly *authorized independent judges.*

5thly. *The supreme power cannot take from any man any part of his property*, without his consent in *person, or by representation.*

6thly. *The legislature cannot transfer the power of making laws to any other hands.*

These are their bounds, which by God and nature are fixed, hitherto have they a right to come, and no further.

1. *To govern by stated laws.*

2. *Those laws should have no other end ultimately, but the good of the people.*

3. *Taxes are not to be laid on the people, but by their consent in person, or by deputation.*

4. *Their whole power is not transferable.*

These are the first principles of law and justice, and the great barriers of a free state, and of the British constitution in particular. I ask, I want no more—Now let it be shown how 'tis reconcilable with principles, or to many other fundamental maxims of the British constitution, as well as the natural and civil rights, which by the laws of their country, all British subjects are entitled to, as their best inheritance and birth-right, that all the northern colonies, who are without one representative in the house of Commons, should be taxed by the British parliament. . .

I can see no reason to doubt, but that the imposition of taxes, whether on trade, or on land, or houses, or ships, on real or personal, fixed or floating property, in the colonies, is absolutely irreconcilable with the rights of the Colonists, as British subjects, and as men. I say men, for in a state of nature, no man can take my property from me, without my consent: If he does, he deprives me of my liberty, and makes me a slave. If such a proceeding is a breach of the law of nature, no law of society can make it just—The very act of taxing, exercised over those who are not represented, appears to me to be depriving them of one of their most essential rights, as freemen; and if continued, seems to be in effect an entire disfranchisement of every civil right. For what one civil right is worth a rush, after a man's property is subject to be taken from him at pleasure, without his consent. If a man is not his own assessor in person, or by deputy, his liberty is gone, or lays entirely at the mercy of others. . .

The power of parliament is uncontrollable, but by themselves, and we must obey. They only can repeal their own acts. There would be an end of all government, if one or a number of subjects or subordinate provinces should take upon them so far to judge of the justice of an act of parliament, as to refuse obedience to it. If there was nothing else to restrain such a step, prudence ought to do it, for forcibly resisting the parliament and the King's laws, is high treason. Therefore let the parliament lay what burthens they please on us, we must, it is our duty to submit and patiently bear them, till they will be pleased to relieve us. And 'tis to be presumed, the wisdom and justice of that august assembly, always will afford us relief by repealing such acts, as through mistake, or other human infirmities, have been suffered to pass, if they can be convinced that their proceedings are not constitutional, or not for the common good. . .

To say the parliament is absolute and arbitrary, is a contradiction. The parliament cannot make 2 and 2, 5; Omnipotency cannot do it. The supreme power in a state, is *jus dicere* only;—*jus dare*, strictly speaking, belongs alone to God. Parliaments are in all cases to *declare* what is for the good of the whole; but it is not the declaration of Parliament that makes it so: There must be in every instance, a higher authority, viz. GOD. Should an act of parliament be against any of *his* natural laws, which are *immutably* true, their declaration would be contrary to eternal truth, equity and justice, and consequently void: and so it would be adjudged by the parliament itself, when convinced of their mistake. Upon this great principle, parliaments repeal such acts, as soon as they find they have been mistaken, in having declared them to be for the public good, when in fact they were not so. When such mistake is evident and palpable . . . the judges of the executive courts have declared the act 'of a whole parliament void.' See here the grandeur of the British constitution! See the wisdom of our ancestors! The supreme *legislative*, and the supreme *executive*, are a perpetual check and balance to each other. If the supreme executive errs, it is informed by the supreme legislative in parliament: If the supreme legislative errs, it is informed by the supreme executive in the King's courts of law —Here, the King appears, as represented by his judges, in the highest lustre and majesty, as supreme executor of the commonwealth; and he never shines brighter, but on his Throne, at the head of the supreme legislative. This is government! This, is a constitution! to preserve which, either from foreign or domestic foes, has cost oceans of blood and treasure in every age; and the blood and the treasure have upon the whole been well spent. . .

We all think ourselves happy under Great Britain. We love, esteem, and reverence our mother country, and adore our King. And could the choice of independency be offered the colonies, or subjection to Great Britain upon any terms above absolute slavery, I am convinced they would accept the latter. . .

These colonies are and always have been, 'entirely subject to the crown,' in the legal sense of the terms. But if any politician of 'tampering activity, of wrongheaded inexperience, wisted to be meddling,' means, by 'curbing the colonies in time,' and by 'being made entirely subject to the crown;' that this subjection should be absolute, and confined to the crown, he had better have suppressed his wishes. This never will nor can be done, without making the colonists vassals of the crown. . . A continuation of the same liberties that have been enjoyed by the colonists since the revolution, and the same moderation of government exercised towards them, will bind them in perpetual lawful and willing subjection, obedience and love to Great Britain: She and her colonies will both prosper and flourish: The monarchy will remain in sound health and full vigor at that blessed period, when the proud arbitrary tyrants of the continent shall either unite in the deliverance of the human race, or resign their crowns. Rescued, human nature must and will be, from the general slavery that has so long triumphed over the species. Great Britain has done much towards it: What a Glory will it be for her to complete the work throughout the world! . . .

The sum of my argument is, That civil government is of God: That the administrators of it were originally the whole people: That they might have devolved it on whom they pleased: That this devolution is fiduciary, for the good of the whole; That by the British constitution, this devolution is on the King, lords, and commons, the supreme, sacred, and uncontrollable legislative power, not only in the realm, but thro' the dominions: That by the abdication, the original compact was broken to pieces: That by the revolution, it was renewed, and more firmly established, and the rights and liberties of the subject in all parts of the dominions, more fully explained and confirmed: That in consequence of this establishment, and the acts of succession and union his Majesty GEORGE III is rightful king and sovereign, and with his parliament, the supreme legislative of Great Britain, France and Ireland, and the dominions thereto belonging: That this constitution is the most free one, and by far the best, now existing on earth: That by this constitution, every man in the dominion is a free man: That no parts of his Majesty's dominions can be taxed without their consent: That every part has a right to be represented in the supreme or some subordinate legislature: That the refusal of this, would seem to be a contradiction in practice to the theory of the constitution: That the colonies are subordinate dominions, and are now in such a state, as to make it best for the good of the whole, that they should not only be continued in the enjoyment of subordinate legislation, but be also represented in some proportion to their number and estates, in the grand legislature of the nation: That this would firmly unite all parts of the British empire, in the greatest peace and prosperity; and render it invulnerable and perpetual.

4. *The cause of liberty is a cause of too much dignity to be sullied by turbulence and tumult*

JOHN DICKINSON, *Letters from a Farmer*, 1767–68 *

LETTER I

. . . With a good deal of surprise I have observed, that little notice has been taken of an act of parliament, as injurious in its principle to the liberties of these colonies, as the stamp act: I mean the act for suspending the legislation of New York.

* *John Dickinson's Farmer's Letters*, reprinted from his political writings, Philadelphia, 1801, pp. 3–65 *passim*.

The assembly of that government complied with a former act of parliament, requiring certain provisions to be made for the troops in America, in every particular, I think, except the articles of salt, pepper and vinegar. In my opinion they acted imprudently, considering all circumstances, in not complying so far as would have given satisfaction, as several colonies did. But my dislike of their conduct in that instance has not blinded me so much, that I cannot plainly perceive, that they have been punished in a manner pernicious to American freedom, and justly alarming to all the colonies.

If the British parliament has a legal authority to order that we shall furnish a single article for the troops here, and to compel obedience to that order, they have the same right to issue an order for us to supply those troops with arms, clothes and every necessary; and to compel obedience to that order also; in short, to lay any burthens they please upon us. What is this but taxing us at a certain sum, and leaving to us only the manner of raising it? How is this mode more tolerable than the stamp act? Would that act have appeared more pleasing to Americans, if being ordered thereby to raise the sum total of the taxes, the mighty privilege had been left to them, of saying how much should be paid for an instrument of writing on paper, and how much for another on parchment?

An act of parliament, commanding us to do a certain thing, if it has any validity, is a tax upon us for the expense that accrues in complying with it; and for this reason, I believe every colony on the continent, that chose to give a mark of their respect for Great Britain, in complying with the act relating to the troops, cautiously avoided the mention of that act, lest their conduct should be attributed to its supposed obligation.

The matter being thus stated, the assembly of New York either had or had not, a right to refuse submission to that act. If they had, and I imagine no American will say they had not, then the parliament had no right to compel them to execute it. If they had not this right, they had no right to punish them for not executing it; and therefore no right to suspend their legislation, which is a punishment. In fact, if the people of New York cannot be legally taxed but by their own representatives, they cannot be legally deprived of the privilege of making laws only for insisting on that exclusive privilege of taxation. If they may be legally deprived in such a case, of the privilege of legislation, why may they not, with equal reason, be deprived of every other privilege? Or why may not every colony be treated in the same manner, when any of them shall dare to deny their assent to any impositions, that shall be directed? Or what signifies the repeal of the stamp act, if these colonies are to lose their other privileges, by not tamely surrendering that of taxation? . . .

LETTER II

. . . There is another late act of parliament, which appears to me to be unconstitutional, and as destructive to the liberty of these colonies, as that mentioned in my last letter; that is, the act for granting the duties on paper, glass, &c.

The parliament unquestionably possesses a legal authority to regulate the trade of Great Britain and all her colonies. Such an authority is essential to the relations between a mother country and its colonies, and necessary for the common good of all. He who considers these provinces as states distinct from the British empire, has very slender notions of justice, or of their interests. We are but parts of a whole; and therefore there must exist a power somewhere to preside, and preserve the connection in due order. This power is lodged in the parliament; and we are as much dependent on Great Britain as a perfectly free people can be on another.

I have looked over every statute relating to these colonies from their first settlement to this time, and I find every one of them founded on this principle, till the stamp act administration. All before are calculated to regulate trade, and preserve or promote a mutually beneficial intercourse between the several constituent parts of the empire; and though many of them imposed duties on trade, yet those duties were always imposed with design to restrain the commerce of one part, that were injurious to another, and thus to promote the general welfare. The raising a revenue thereby was never intended. . . Never did the British parliament, till the period above mentioned, think of imposing duties in America, for the purpose of raising a revenue. . .

Here we may observe an authority expressly claimed and exerted to impose duties on these colonies; not for the regulation of trade; not for the preservation or promotion of a mutually beneficial intercourse between the several constituent parts of the empire, heretofore the sole objects of parliamentary institutions; but for the single purpose of levying money upon us.

This I call an innovation; and a most dangerous innovation. It may perhaps be objected that Great Britain has a right to lay what duties she pleases upon her exports, and it makes no difference to us, whether they are paid here or there.

To this I answer. These colonies require many things for their use, which the laws of Great Britain prohibit them from getting anywhere but from her. Such are paper and glass.

That we may be legally bound to pay any general duties on these commodities, relative to the regulation of trade, is granted; but we being obliged by her laws to take them from Great Britain, any special duties imposed on their exportation to us only, with intention to raise a revenue from us only, are as much taxes upon us, as those imposed by the stamp act.

What is the difference in substance and right, whether the same sum is raised upon us by the rates mentioned in the stamp act, on the use of paper, or by these duties, on the importation of it. It is only the edition of a former book, shifting a sentence from the end to the beginning. . .

Some persons perhaps may say, that this act lays us under no necessity to pay the duties imposed, because we may ourselves manufacture the articles on which they are laid; whereas by the stamp act no instrument could be good, unless made on British paper, and that, too, stamped. . .

I am told there are but two or three glass-houses on this continent, and but very few paper-mills; and suppose more should be erected, a long course of years must elapse before they can be brought to perfection. This continent is a country of planters, farmers and fishermen; not of manufacturers. The difficulty of establishing particular manufactures in such a country is almost insuperable . . .

Great Britain has prohibited the manufacturing of iron and steel in these colonies, without any objection being made to her right of doing it. The like right she must have to prohibit any other manufacture among us. Thus she is possessed of an undisputed precedent on that point. This authority, she will say, is founded on the original intention of settling these colonies; that is, that she should manufacture for them, and that they should supply her with materials. . .

Here, then, my dear countrymen, rouse yourselves, and behold the ruin hanging over your heads. If you *once* admit that Great Britain may lay duties upon her exportations to us, for the purpose of levying money on us only, she then will have nothing to do, but to lay those duties on the articles which she prohibits us to manufacture—and the tragedy of American liberty is finished. . .

LETTER III

. . . Sorry I am to learn, that there are some few persons, who shake their heads with solemn motion, and pretend to wonder, what can be the meaning of these letters. 'Great Britain,' they say, 'is too powerful to contend with; she is determined to oppress us; it is in vain to speak of right on one side, when there is power on the other; when we are strong enough to resist, we shall attempt it; but now we are not strong enough, and therefore we had better be quiet; it signifies nothing to convince us that our rights are invaded, when we cannot defend them; and if we should get into riots and tumults about the late act, it will only draw down heavier displeasure upon us.'

What can such men design? What do their grave observations amount to, but this—that these colonies, totally regardless of their liberties, should commit them, with humble resignation, to chance, time and the tender mercies of ministers. . .

Do they condemn the conduct of these colonies, concerning the stamp act? Or have they forgotten its successful issue? Ought the colonies at that time, instead of acting as they did, to have trusted for relief, to the fortuitous events of futurity? If it is needless 'to speak of rights' now, it was as needless then . . . Therefore it becomes necessary to inquire whether 'our rights are invaded.' To talk of 'defending' them, as if they could be no otherwise 'defended' than by arms, is as much out of the way, as if a man, having a choice of several roads, to reach his journey's end, should prefer the worst, for no other reason but because it is the worst. . .

The cause of liberty is a cause of too much dignity to be sullied by turbulence and tumult. It ought to be maintained in a manner suitable to her nature. Those who engage in it should breathe a sedate, yet fervent spirit, animating them to actions of prudence, justice, modesty, bravery, humanity and magnanimity. . .

Every government at some time or other falls into wrong measures. These may proceed from mistake or passion. But every such measure does not dissolve the obligation between the government and the governed. The mistake may be corrected; the passion may subside. It is the duty of the governed to endeavour to rectify the mistake, and to appease the passion. They have not at first any other right, than to represent their grievances, and to pray for redress, unless an emergency is so pressing, as not to allow time for receiving an answer to their applications, which rarely happens. If their applications are disregarded, then that kind of opposition becomes justifiable, which can be made without breaking the laws, or disturbing the public peace. This consists in the prevention of the oppressors reaping advantage from their oppressions, and not in their punishment. For experience may teach them, what reason did not; and harsh methods cannot be proper till milder ones have failed.

If at length it becomes undoubted, that an inveterate resolution is formed to annihilate the liberties of the governed, the English history affords frequent examples of resistance by force. What particular circumstances will in any future case justify such resistance, can never be ascertained, till they happen. Perhaps it may be allowable to say generally, that it never can be justifiable, until the people are fully convinced, that any further submission will be destructive to their happiness.

When the appeal is made to the sword, highly probably is it, that the punishment will exceed the offence; and the calamities attending on war outweigh those preceding it. These considerations of justice and prudence, will always have great influence with good and wise men.

To these reflections on this subject, it remains to be added, and ought for ever to be remembered, that resistance, in the case of colonies against their mother country, is extremely different from the resistance of a people against their prince. A nation may change their king, or race of kings, and retaining their ancient form of government, be gainers by changing. . . But if once we are separated from our mother country, what new form of government shall we adopt, or where shall we find another Britain, to supply our loss? Torn from the body, to which we are united by religion, liberty, laws, affections, relations, language and commerce, we must bleed at every vein. . .

We cannot act with too much caution in our disputes. . .

The constitutional modes of obtaining relief are those which I wish to see pursued on the present occasion; that is, by petitions of our assemblies, or where they are not permitted to meet, of the people, to the powers that can afford us relief. . .

If, however, it shall happen by an unfortunate course of affairs, that our application to his majesty and the parliament for redress, prove ineffectual, let us then take another step, by withholding from Great Britain all the advantages she has been used to received from us. Then let us try, if our ingenuity, industry and frugality will not give weight to our remonstrances. . .

LETTER IV

. . . An objection, I hear, has been made against my second letter, which I would willingly clear up before I proceed. 'There is,' say these objectors, 'a material difference between the stamp act and the late act for laying a duty on paper, &c., that justifies the conduct of those who opposed the former, and yet are willing to submit to the latter. The duties imposed by the stamp act were internal taxes; but the present are external, and therefore the parliament may have a right to impose them.'

To this I answer, with a total denial of the power of parliament to lay upon these colonies any 'tax' whatever.

This point, being so important to this, and to succeeeding generations, I wish to be clearly understood.

To the word 'tax,' I annex that meaning which the constitution and history of England require to be annexed to it; that is—that it is an imposition on the subject, for the sole purpose of levying money. . .

Whenever we speak of 'taxes' among Englishmen let us therefore speak of them with reference to the principles on which, and the intentions with which they have been established. . .

In the national parliamentary sense insisted on, the word 'tax' was certainly understood by the congress at New York, whose resolves may be said to form the American 'bill of rights.'

The third, fourth, fifth and sixth resolves are thus expressed.

III. 'That it is inseparably essential to the freedom of a people and the undoubted right of Englishmen, that *no tax* be imposed on them but with their own consent, given personally, or by their representatives.'

IV. 'That the people of the colonies are not and from their local circumstances cannot be represented in the house of commons in Great Britain.'

V. 'That the only representative of the people of the colonies, are the persons chosen therein by themselves; and that *no taxes* ever have been, or can be constitutionally imposed on them, but by their respective legislatures.'

VI. 'That all supplies to the crown, being free gifts of the people, it is unreasonable, and inconsistent with the principles and spirit of the British constitution, for the people of Great Britain to grant his majesty the property of the colonies.'

Here is no distinction made between internal and external taxes. It is evident from the short reasoning thrown into these resolves, that every imposition 'to grant to his majesty the property of the colonies,' was thought 'a Tax'; and that every such imposition, if laid any other way, than with their consent, 'given personally, or by their representatives' was not only 'unreasonable, and inconsistent with the principles and spirit of the British constitution' but destructive 'to the freedom of a people'. . .

Such persons therefore as speak of internal and external 'taxes' I pray may pardon me, if I object to that expression, as applied to the privileges and interests of these colonies. There may be internal and external impositions, founded on different principles and having different tendencies; every 'tax' being an imposition, though every imposition is not a 'tax.' But all taxes are founded on the same principle; and have the same tendency.

External impositions, for the regulation of our trade, do not 'grant to his majesty the property of the colonies.' They only prevent the colonies acquiring property, in things not necessary, in a manner judged to be injurious to the welfare of the whole empire. But the last statute respecting us 'Grants to his majesty the property of the colonies,' by laying duties on the manufactures of Great Britain which they must take, and which she settled them, on purpose that they should take. . .

LETTER XI

. . . A perpetual jealousy, respecting liberty, is absolutely requisite in all free states. The very texture of their constitution, in mixt governments, demands it. For the cautions, with which power is distributed among the several orders, imply that each has that share which is proper for the general welfare, and therefore that any further acquisition must be pernicious. Machiavel employs a whole chapter in his discourses, to prove that a state, to be long lived, must be frequently corrected, and reduced to its first principles. But of all states that have existed, there never was any, in which this jealousy could be more proper than in these colonies. For the government here is not only mixt but dependent, which circumstance occasions a peculiarity in its forms, of a very delicate nature.

Two reasons induce me to desire, that this spirit of apprehension may be always kept up among us, in its utmost vigilance. The first is this—that as the happiness of these provinces indubitably consists in their connection with Great Britain, any separation between them is less likely to be occasioned by civil discords, if every disgusting measure is opposed singly, and while it is new, for in this manner of proceeding, every such measure is most likely to be rectified.—On the other hand, oppressions and dissatisfactions being permitted to accumulate—if ever the governed throw off the load, they will do more. A people does not reform with moderation. . .

This consideration leads me to the second reason, why I 'desire that the spirit of apprehension may be always kept up among us in its utmost vigilance.'

The first principles of government are to be looked for in human nature.—Some of the best writers have asserted, and it seems with good reasons, that 'government is founded on opinion'. . .

When an act injurious to freedom has been once done, and the people bear it, the repetition of it is most likely to meet with submission. For as the mischief of the one was found to be tolerable, they will hope that of the second will prove so too; and they will not regard the infamy of the last, because they are stained with that of the first.

Indeed nations, in general are not apt to think until they feel; and therefore nations in general have lost their liberty; for as violations of the rights of the governed are commonly not only specious, but small at the beginning, they spread over the multitude in such a manner, as to touch individuals but slightly. Thus they are disregarded. The power or profit that arises from these violations centering in a few persons, is to them considerable. For this reason the governors having in view their particular purposes, successively preserve an uniformity of conduct for attaining them. They regularly increase the first injuries till at length the inattentive people are compelled to perceive the heaviness of their burthens.—They begin to complain and inquire—but too late. They find their oppressors so strengthened by success and themselves so entangled in examples of express authority on the part of their rulers, and of tacit recognition on their own part, that they are quite confounded; for millions entertain no other idea of the legality of power, than that it is founded on the exercise of power. They voluntarily fasten their chains, by adopting a pusillanimous opinion, 'that there will be too much danger in attempting a remedy,'—or another opinion no less fatal—'that the government has a right to treat them as it does.' They then seek a wretched relief for their minds, by persuading themselves, that to yield their obedience is to discharge their duty. The deplorable poverty of spirit, that prostrates all the dignity bestowed by Divine Providence on our nature—of course succeeds.

From these reflections I conclude that every free state should incessantly watch, and instantly take alarm on any addition being made to the power exercised over them. . .

5. *Allegiance to the king and obedience to parliament are founded on different principles*

JAMES WILSON, *Considerations on the Nature and Extent of the Legislative Authority of the British Parliament,* 17 August 1774 *

No question can be more important to Great Britain, and to the colonies, than this—does the legislative authority of the British parliament extend over them? . . .

Those who allege that the parliament of Great Britain have power to make laws binding the American colonies, reason in the following manner. 'That there is and must be in every state a supreme, irresistible, absolute, uncontrolled authority, in which the *jura summi imperii*, or the rights of sovereignty, reside;' 'That this supreme power is, by the constitution of Great Britain, vested in the king, lords, and commons:' 'That, therefore, the acts of the king, lords, and commons, or, in other words, acts of parliament, have, by the British constitution, a binding force on the American colonies, they composing a part of the British empire.'

I admit that the principle, on which this argument is founded, is of great importance: its importance, however, is derived from its tendency to promote the ultimate end of all government. But if the application of it would, in any instance, destroy, instead of promoting, that end, it ought, in that instance, to be rejected: for to admit it, would be to sacrifice the end to the means, which are valuable only so far as they advance it.

All men are, by nature, equal and free: no one has a right to any authority over another without his consent: all lawful government is founded on the consent of those who are subject to it: such consent was given with a view to ensure and to increase the happiness of the governed, above what they

* *The Works of James Wilson,* James DeWitt Andrews, ed., Chicago, Callaghan and Company, 1896, vol. II, pp. 505–42 *passim.*

could enjoy in an independent and unconnected state of nature. The consequence is, that the happiness of the society is the *first* law of every government. . .

Such is the admirable temperament of the British constitution! such the glorious fabric of Britain's liberty—the pride of her citizens—the envy of her neighbors—planned by her legislators—erected by her patriots—maintained entire by numerous generations past! may it be maintained entire by numerous generations to come!

Can the Americans, who are descended from British ancestors, and inherit all their rights, be blamed—can they be blamed *by their brethren in Britain*—for claiming still to enjoy those rights? But can they enjoy them, if they are bound by the acts of a British parliament? Upon what principle does the British parliament found their power? Is it founded on the prerogative of the king? His prerogative does not extend to make laws to bind any of his subjects. Does it reside in the house of lords? The peers are a collective, and not a representative body. If it resides anywhere, then, it must reside in the house of commons. . .

But from what source does this mighty, this uncontrolled authority of the house of commons flow? From the collective body of the commons of Great Britain. This authority must, therefore, originally reside in them; for whatever they convey to their representatives, must ultimately be in themselves. And have those, whom we have hitherto been accustomed to consider as our fellow-subjects, an absolute and unlimited power over us? Have they a natural right to make laws, by which we may be deprived of our properties, of our liberties, of our lives? By what title do they claim to be our masters? What act of ours has rendered us subject to those, to whom we were formerly equal? Is British freedom denominated from the *soil*, or from the *people* of Britain? If from the latter, do they lose it by quitting the soil? Do those, who embark, freemen, in Great Britain, disembark, slaves, in America? . . . Is this the return made us for leaving our friends and our country—for braving the danger of the deep—for planting a wilderness, inhabited only by savage men and savage beasts—for extending the dominions of the British crown—for increasing the trade of the British merchants—for augmenting the rents of the British landlords—for heightening the wages of the British artificers? Britons should blush to make such a claim: Americans would blush to own it. . .

On what principles, then—on what motives of action, can we depend for the security of our liberties, of our properties, of everything dear to us in life, of life itself? Shall we depend on their veneration for the dictates of natural justice? A very little share of experience in the world—a very little degree of knowledge in the history of men, will sufficiently convince us, that a regard to justice is by no means the ruling principle in human nature. He would discover himself to be a very sorry statesman, who would erect a system of jurisprudence upon that slender foundation. 'He would make,' as my Lord Bacon says, 'imaginary laws for imaginary commonwealths; and his discourses, like the stars, would give little light, because they are so high'. . .

What has been already advanced will suffice to show, that it is repugnant to the essential maxims of jurisprudence, to the ultimate end of all governments, to the genius of the British constitution, and to the liberty and happiness of the colonies, that they should be bound by the legislative authority of the parliament of Great Britain. Such a doctrine is not less repugnant to the voice of her laws. In order to evince this, I shall appeal to some authorities from the books of the law, which show expressly, or by a necessary implication, that the colonies are not bound by the acts of the British parliament; because they have no share in the British legislature. . .

From this authority it follows, that it is by no means a rule, that the authority of parliament extends to all the subjects of the crown. The inhabitants of Ireland were the subjects of the king as of his crown of England; but it is expressly resolved, in the most solemn manner, that the inhabitants of Ireland are not bound by the statutes of England. Allegiance to the king and obedience to the parliament are founded on very different principles. The former is founded on protection; the latter on representation. An inattention to this difference has produced, I apprehend, much uncertainty and confusion in our ideas concerning the connection, which ought to subsist between Great Britain and the American colonies. . .

How came the colonists to be a conquered people? By whom was the conquest over them obtained? By the house of commons? By the constituents of that house? If the idea of conquest must be taken into consideration when we examine into the title by which America is held, that idea, so far as it can operate, will operate in favor of the colonists, and not against them. Permitted and commissioned by the crown, they undertook, at their own expense, expeditions to this distant country, took possession of it, planted it, and cultivated it. Secure under the protection of their king, they grew and multiplied, and diffused British freedom and British spirit, wherever they came. Happy in the enjoyment of liberty, and in reaping the fruits of their toils; but still more happy in the joyful prospect of transmitting their liberty and their fortunes to the latest posterity, they inculcated to their children the warmest sentiments of loyalty to their sovereign, under whose auspices they enjoyed so many blessings, and of affection and esteem for the inhabitants of the mother country, with whom they gloried in being intimately connected. Lessons of loyalty to parliament, indeed, they never gave: they never suspected that such unheard-of loyalty would be required. They never suspected that their descendants would be considered and treated as a conquered people; and therefore they never taught them the submission and abject behavior suited to that character. . .

It will be alleged, that I throw off all dependence on Great Britain. . .

Let us examine what is meant by a *dependence* on Great Britain: for it is always of importance clearly to define the terms that we use. . .

The original and true ground of the superiority of Great Britain over the American colonies is not shown in any book of the law, unless, as I have already observed, it be derived from the right of conquest. But I have proved, and I hope satisfactorily, that this right is altogether inapplicable to the colonists. The original of the superiority of Great Britain over the colonies is, then, unaccounted for; and when we consider the ingenuity and pains which have lately been employed at home on this subject, we may justly conclude, that the only reason why it is not accounted for, is, that it cannot be accounted for. The superiority of Great Britain over the colonies ought, therefore, to be rejected; and the dependence of the colonies upon her, if it is to be construed into 'an obligation to conform to the will or law of the superior state,' ought, in *this* sense, to be rejected also.

My sentiments concerning this matter are not singular. They coincide with the declarations and remonstrances of the colonies against the statutes imposing taxes on them. It was their unanimous opinion, that the parliament have no right to exact obedience to those statutes; and consequently, that the colonies are under no obligation to obey them. The dependence of the colonies on Great Britain was denied, in those instances; but a denial of it in those instances is, in effect, a denial of it in all other instances. For, if dependence is an obligation to conform to the will or law of the superior state, any exceptions to that obligation must destroy the dependence. If, therefore, by a dependence of the colonies on Great Britain, it is meant, that they are obliged to obey the laws of Great Britain, reason, as well as the unanimous voice of the Americans, teaches us to disown it. Such a dependence was never thought of by those who left Britain, in order to settle in America; nor by their sovereigns, who gave them commissions for that purpose. Such an obligation has no correspondent right: for the commons of Great Britain have no dominion over their equals and fellow-subjects in America; they can confer no right to their delegates to bind those equals and fellow-subjects by laws.

There is another, and a much more reasonable meaning, which may be intended by the dependence of the colonies on Great Britain. The phrase may be used to denote the obedience and loyalty, which the colonists owe to the *kings* of Great Britain. . .

Those who launched into the unknown deep, in quest of new countries and inhabitations, still considered themselves as subjects of the English monarchs, and behaved suitably to that character; but it nowhere appears, that they still considered themselves as represented in an English parliament, or that they thought the authority of the English parliament extended over them. They took possession of the country in the *king's* name: they treated, or made war with the Indians by *his* authority: they held the lands under *his* grants, and paid *him* the rents reserved upon them: they established governments under the sanction of *his* prerogative, or by virtue of *his* charters:—no application for those purposes was made to the parliament: no ratification of the charters or letters patent was solicited from that assembly, as is usual in England with regard to grants and franchises of much less importance. . .

The colonists ought to be dependent on the king, because they have hitherto enjoyed, and still continue to enjoy, his protection. . . Every subject, so soon as he is born, is under the royal protection, and is entitled to all the advantages arising from it. He therefore owes obedience to that royal power, from which the protection, which he enjoys, is derived. . .

Now we have explained the dependence of the Americans. They are the subjects of the king of Great Britain. They owe him allegiance. They have a right to the benefits which arise from preserving that allegiance inviolate. They are liable to the punishments which await those who break it. This is a dependence, which they have always boasted of. . .

From this dependence, abstracted from every other source, arises a strict connection between the inhabitants of Great Britain and those of America. They are fellow-subjects; they are under allegiance to the same prince; and this union of allegiance naturally produces a union of hearts. It is also productive of a union of measures through the whole British dominions. To the king is intrusted the direction and management of the great machine of government. He therefore is fittest to adjust the different wheels, and to regulate their motions in such a manner as to co-operate in the same general designs. He makes war: he concludes peace: he forms alliances: he regulates domestic trade by his prerogative, and directs foreign commerce by his treaties with those nations, with whom it is carried on. He names the officers of government; so that he can check every jarring movement in the administration. He has a negative on the different legislatures throughout his dominions, so that he can prevent any repugnancy in their different laws.

The connection and harmony between Great Britain and us, which it is her interest and ours mutually to cultivate, and on which her prosperity, as well as ours, so materially depends, will be better preserved by the operation of the legal prerogatives of the crown, than by the exertion of an unlimited authority by parliament.*

* After considering, with all the attention of which I am capable, the foregoing opinion —that all the different members of the British empire are distinct states, independent of each other, but connected together under the same sovereign in right of the same crown —I discover only one objection that can be offered against it. But this objection will, by many, be deemed a fatal one. 'How, it will be urged, can the trade of the British empire be carried on, without some power, extending over the whole to regulate it? . . .'

Permit me to answer these questions by proposing some others in my turn. How has the trade of Europe—how has the trade of the whole globe, been carried on? Have those widely extended plans been formed by one superintending power? Have they been carried into execution by one superintending power? Have they been formed—have they been carried into execution, with less conformity to the rules of justice and equality, than if they had been under the direction of one superintending power?

It has been the opinion of some politicians, of no inferior note, that all regulations of trade are useless; that the greatest part of them are hurtful; and that the stream of commerce never flows with so much beauty and advantage, as when it is not diverted from its natural channels. Whether this opinion is well founded or not, let others determine. Thus much may certainly be said, that commerce is not so properly the object of laws, as of treaties and compacts. In this manner, it has always been directed among the several nations of Europe.

But if the commerce of the British empire must be regulated by a general superintending power, capable of exerting its influence over every part of it, why may not this power be intrusted to the king, as a part of the royal prerogative? By making treaties, which it is his prerogative to make, he directs the trade of Great Britain with the other states of Europe: and his treaties with those states have, when considered with regard to his subjects, all the binding force of laws upon them. (1. Bl. Com. 252.) Where is the absurdity in supposing him vested with the same right to regulate the commerce of the distinct parts of his dominions with one another, which he has to regulate their commerce with foreign states? If the history of the British constitution, relating to this subject, be carefully traced, I apprehend we shall discover, that a prerogative in the crown, to regulate trade, is perfectly consistent with the principles of law. We find many

6. *Americans are entitled to freedom upon every rational principle*

ALEXANDER HAMILTON, *A Full Vindication*, 15 December 1774 *

. . . The only distinction between freedom and slavery consists in this: In the former state a man is governed by the laws to which he has given his consent, either in person, or by his representative: In the latter, he is governed by the will of another. In the one case, his life and property are his own: in the other, they depend upon the pleasure of a master. It is easy to discern which of these two states is preferable. No man in his senses can hesitate in choosing to be free, rather than a slave.

That Americans are entitled to freedom is incontestable upon every rational principle. All men have one common original: they participate in one common nature, and consequently have one common right. No reason can be assigned why one man should exercise any power or pre-eminence over his fellow-creatures more than another; unless they have voluntarily vested him with it. Since, then, Americans have not, by any act of theirs, empowered the British Parliament to make laws for them, it follows they can have no just authority to do it.

Besides the clear voice of natural justice in this respect, the fundamental principles of the English constitution are in our favor. It has been repeatedly demonstrated, that the idea of legislation, or taxation, when the subject is not represented, is inconsistent with *that*. Nor is this all; our charters, the express conditions on which our progenitors relinquished their native countries, and came to settle in this, preclude every claim of ruling and taxing us without our assent.

Every subterfuge that sophistry has been able to invent, to evade or obscure this truth, has been refuted by the most conclusive reasonings; so that we may pronounce it a matter of undeniable certainty, that the pretensions of Parliament are contradictory to the law of nature, subversive of the British constitution, and destructive of the faith of the most solemn compacts.

What, then, is the subject of our controversy with the mother country? It is this: Whether we shall preserve that security to our lives and properties, which the law of nature, the genius of the British constitution, and our charters, afford us; or whether we shall resign them into the hands of the British House of Commons, which is no more privileged to dispose of them than the Great Mogul? . . . The Parliament claims a right to tax us in all cases whatsoever: its late acts are in virtue of that claim. . .

The design of electing members to represent us in general Congress, was,

---

authorities that the king cannot lay impositions on traffic; and that he cannot restrain it *altogether*, nor confine it to monopolists; but none of the authorities, that I have had an opportunity of consulting, go any farther. Indeed many of them seem to imply a power in the crown to regulate trade, where that power is exerted for the great end of all prerogative—the public good. . .

* *The Works of Alexander Hamilton*, John C. Hamilton, ed., New York, Charles S. Francis and Company, 1851, vol. II, pp. 1–7 *passim*.

that the wisdom of America might be collected in devising the most proper and expedient means to repel this atrocious invasion of our rights. It has been accordingly done. Their decrees are binding upon all, and demand a religious observance. . .

If it should be objected, that they have not answered the end of their election, but have fallen upon an improper and ruinous mode of proceeding, I reply by asking, Who shall be the judge? Shall any individual oppose his private sentiment to the united counsels of men, in whom America has reposed so high a confidence? The attempt must argue no small degree of arrogance and self-sufficiency. . .

The only scheme of opposition, suggested by those who have been and are averse from a non-importation and non-exportation agreement, is, by REMONSTRANCE and PETITION. The authors and abettors of this scheme have never been able to invent a single argument to prove the likelihood of its succeeding. On the other hand, there are many standing facts and valid considerations against it.

In the infancy of the present dispute, we had recourse to this method only. We addressed the throne in the most loyal and respectful manner, in a legislative capacity; but what was the consequence? Our address was treated with contempt and neglect. . .

There is less reason now than ever to expect deliverance, in this way, from the hand of oppression. . .

What can we represent which has not already been represented? What petitions can we offer, that have not already been offered? The rights of America, and the injustice of parliamentary pretensions, have been clearly and repeatedly stated, both in and out of parliament. No new arguments can be framed to operate in our favor . . . Upon the whole, it is morally certain, this mode of opposition would be fruitless and defective. . .

This being the case, we can have no recourse but in a restriction of our trade, or in a resistance *vi et armis*. It is impossible to conceive any other alternative. Our Congress, therefore, have imposed what restraint they thought necessary. Those who condemn or clamor against it, do nothing more, nor less, than advise us to be slaves. . .

7. *The right of colonists to exercise a legislative power is no natural right*

SAMUEL SEABURY, *A View of the Controversy Between Great Britain and Her Colonies*, 24 December 1774. A Letter to the Author of *A Full Vindication.* *

. . . I wish you had explicitly declared to the public your ideas of the *natural rights of mankind*. Man in a *state of nature* may be considered as perfectly free from all restraints of law and government: And then the *weak* must submit

* *Letters of a Westchester Farmer* (1774–75), Charles H. Vance, ed., Publications of the Westchester County Historical Society, 1930, vol. VIII, pp. 103–27 *passim*.

to the *strong*. From such a state, I confess, I have a violent aversion. I think the form of government we lately enjoyed a much more eligible state to live in: And cannot help regretting our having *lost* it, by the *equity, wisdom,* and *authority* of the Congress, who have introduced in the room of it, confusion and violence; where all must submit to the power of a mob.

You have taken some pains to prove what would readily have been granted you—that *liberty* is a very *good* thing, and *slavery* a very *bad* thing. But then I must think that liberty under a *King, Lords* and *Commons* is as good as liberty under a republican Congress: And that slavery under a republican Congress is as bad, at least, as slavery under a *King, Lords* and *Commons:* And upon the whole, that *liberty* under the supreme authority and protection of Great Britain, is infinitely preferable to *slavery* under an American Congress. I will also agree with you, 'that Americans are intitled to freedom.' I will go further: I will own and acknowledge that not only Americans, but *Africans, Europeans, Asiatics,* all men, of all countries and degrees, of all sizes and complexions, have a right to as much freedom as is consistent with the security of civil society: And I hope you will not think me an 'enemy' to the *natural* 'rights of mankind' because I cannot wish them more. We must however remember, that more liberty may, without inconvenience, be allowed to individuals in a small government, than can be admitted of in a large empire.

But when you assert that 'since Americans have not by any act of theirs empowered the British parliament to make laws for them, it follows they can have no just authority to do it,' you advance a position subversive of the dependence which all colonies must, from their very nature, have on the mother-country. . .

Now the dependence of the colonies on the mother-country has ever been acknowledged. It is an impropriety of speech to talk of an independent colony. The words *independency* and *colony*, convey contradictory ideas . . . The British colonies make a part of the British Empire. As parts of the body they must be subject to the general laws of the body. To talk of a colony independent of the mother-country, is no better sense than to talk of a limb independent of the body to which it belongs.

In every government there must be a supreme, absolute authority lodged somewhere. In arbitrary governments this power is in the monarch; in aristocratical governments, in the nobles; in democratical, in the people; or the deputies of their electing. Our own government being a mixture of all these kinds, the supreme authority is vested in the King, Nobles and People, i.e. the King, House of Lords, and House of Commons elected by the people. This supreme authority extends as far as the British dominions extend. To suppose a part of the British dominions which is not subject to the power of the British legislature, is no better sense than to suppose a country, at one and the same time, to be and not to be a part of the British dominions. If therefore the colony of New York be a part of the British dominions, the colony of New York is subject, and dependent on the supreme legislative authority of Great Britain. . .

The position that we are bound by no laws to which we have not consented, either by ourselves, or our representatives, is a novel position, unsupported by any authoritative record of the British constitution, ancient or modern. It is republican in its very nature, and tends to the utter subversion of the English monarchy.

This position has arisen from an artful change of terms. To say that an Englishman is not bound by any laws, but those to which the representatives of the nation have given their consent, is to say what is true: But to say that an Englishman is bound by no laws but those to which *he* hath consented in person, or by *his* representative, is saying what never was true, and never can be true. A great part of the people in England have no vote in the choice of representatives and therefore are governed by laws to which they never consented either by *themselves* or by *their* representatives.

The right of colonists to exercise a legislative power, is no natural right. They derive it not from nature, but from the indulgence or grant of the parent state, whose subjects they were when the colony was settled, and by whose permission and assistance they made the settlement.

Upon supposition that every English colony enjoyed a legislative power independent of the parliament; and that the parliament has no just authority to make laws to bind them, this absurdity will follow—that there is no power in the British empire, which has authority to make laws for the whole empire; i.e. we have an empire, without government; or which amounts to the same thing, we have a government which has no supreme power. All our colonies are independent of each other: Suppose them independent of the British parliament,—what power do you leave to govern the whole? None at all. You split and divide the empire into a number of petty insignificant states. . .

To talk of being liege subjects to King George, while we disavow the authority of parliament is another piece of whiggish nonsense. I love my King as well as any whig in America or England either, and am as ready to yield him all lawful submission: But while I submit to the King, I submit to the authority of the laws of the state, whose guardian the King is. The difference between a good and a bad subject, is only this, that the one who obeys, the other transgresses the law. The difference between a loyal subject and a rebel, is, that the one yields obedience to, and faithfully supports the supreme authority of the state, and the other endeavours to overthrow it. If we obey the laws of the King, we obey the laws of the parliament. If we disown the authority of the parliament, we disown the authority of the King. There is no medium without ascribing powers to the King which the constitution knows nothing of:—without making him superior to the laws, and setting him above all restraint. These are some of the ridiculous absurdities of American whiggism.

I am utterly at a loss what ideas to annex to the phrases—*dependence on Great Britain;—subordination to the Parliament;—submission to the supreme legislative power;* unless they mean some degree of subjection to the British Parliament; some acknowledgment of its right to make laws to bind the colonies. . .

You have utterly failed in proving that 'the clear voice of natural justice,' and 'the fundamental principles of the English constitution,' set us free from the subordination here acknowledged. . .

. . . It has been proved, that the supreme authority of the British empire extends over all the dominions that compose the empire. The power, or right of the British Parliament to raise such a revenue as is necessary for the defense and support of the British government, in all parts of the British dominions, is therefore incontestable. For if no government can subsist without a power to raise the revenues necessary for its support, then, in fact, no government can extend any further than its power of raising such a revenue extends. If therefore the British Parliament has no power to raise a revenue in the colonies, it has no government over the colonies, i.e. no government can support itself. The burthen of supporting its government over the colonies must lie upon the other parts of the empire. But this is unreasonable. Government implies, not only a power of making and enforcing *laws*, but defence and protection. Now protection implies tribute. . . While therefore the colonies are under the British government, and share in its protection, the British government has a right to raise, and they are in reason and duty bound to pay, a reasonable and proportionable part of the expense of its administration.

The authority of the British Parliament, that is, of the supreme sovereign authority of the British empire, over the colonies, and its right to raise a proportional part of its revenue, for the support of its government, in the colonies, being established; it is to be considered what is the most reasonable and equitable method of doing it. . .

There are but two objections that can reasonably be made to what has been said upon this subject. The first is, that if the British Parliament has a right to make laws to bind the whole empire, our assemblies become useless. But a little consideration will remove this difficulty.

Our assemblies, from the very nature of things, can have but a delegated, subordinate, and local authority of legislation. Their power of making laws in conjunction with the other branches of the legislature, cannot extend beyond the limits of the province to which they belong. Their authority must be subordinate to the supreme sovereign authority of the nation, or there is *imperium in imperio:* two sovereign authorities in the same state; which is a contradiction. Every thing that relates to the internal policy and government of the province which they represent comes properly before them, whether they be matters of law or revenue. But all laws relative to the empire in general, or to all the colonies conjunctively, or which regulates the trade of any particular colony, in order to make it compatible with the general good of the whole empire, must be left to the parliament. There is no other authority which has a *right* to make such regulations, or *weight* sufficient to carry them into execution.

Our Assemblies are also the true, proper, legal guardians of our *rights, privileges* and *liberties*. If any laws of the British Parliament are thought oppressive; or if, in the administration of the British government, any unnecessary or unreasonable burthen be laid upon us, *they* are the proper persons to seek for redress: And they are the most likely to succeed. They have the legal and constitutional means in their hands. . .

Had our present contests with Great Britain been left to *their* management, I would not have said a word. But their authority is contravened and superseded by a power from without the province. . .

The other objection to what has been said upon the legislative authority of the British Parliament, is this: That if the Parliament have authority to make laws to bind the whole empire;—to regulate the trade of the whole empire;—and to raise a revenue upon the whole empire; then we have nothing that we can call our own:—By the same authority that they can take a penny, they can take a pound, or all we have got.

Let it be considered, that no scheme of human policy can be so contrived and guarded, but that something must be left to the integrity, prudence, and wisdom of those who govern. We are apt to think, and I believe justly, that the British constitution is the best scheme of government now subsisting: The rights and liberties of the people are better secured by it, than any other system now subsisting. And yet we find that the rights and liberties of Englishmen may be infringed by wicked and ambitious men. This will ever be the case, even after human sagacity has exerted its utmost ability. This is, however, not argument, that we should not secure ourselves as well as we can. It is rather an argument, that we should use our utmost endeavour to guard against the attempts of ambition or avarice.

A great part of the people in England, a considerable number of people in this province, are bound by laws, and taxed without their consent, or the consent of their representatives: for representatives they have none, unless the absurd position of a *virtual* representation be admitted. These people may object to the present mode of government. They may say, that they have nothing that they can call their own. That if they may be taxed a penny without their consent, they may be taxed a pound; and so on. You will think it a sufficient security to these people, that the representatives of the nation or province cannot hurt *them,* without hurting themselves; because, they cannot tax *them,* without taxing themselves. This security however may not be so effectual as at first may be imagined. The rich are never taxed so much in proportion to their estates as the poor: And even an equal proportion of that tax which a rich man can easily pay, may be a heavy burthen to a poor man. But the same security that these people have against being ruined by the representatives of the nation, or province where they live; the same security have we against being ruined by the British parliament. They cannot hurt us without hurting themselves. The principal profits of our trade center in England. If they lay unnecessary or oppressive burthens on it; or any ways restrain it, so as to injure us, they will soon feel the effect, and very readily remove the cause. . .

But the colonies have become so considerable by the increase of their inhabitants and commerce, and by the improvement of their lands, that they seem incapable of being governed in the same lax and precarious manner as formerly. They are arrived to that mature state of manhood which requires a different, and more exact policy of ruling, than was necessary in their infancy and childhood. They want, and are entitled to, a fixed determinate constitution of their own. A constitution which shall unite them firmly with Great Britain, and with one another;—which shall mark out the line of British supremacy, and colonial dependence, giving on the one hand full force to the supreme authority of the nation over all its dominions, and on the other, securing effectually the rights, liberty, and property of the colonists.—This is an event devoutly to be wished, by all good men; and which all ought to labour to obtain by all prudent, and probable means. Without obtaining this, it is idle to talk of obtaining a redress of the grievances complained of. They naturally, they necessarily result from the relation which we at present stand in to Great Britain.

You, Sir, argue through your whole pamphlet, upon an assumed point, viz: That the British government—the *King, Lords* and *Commons,* have laid a regular plan to enslave America; and that they are now deliberately putting it in execution. This point has never been proved, though it has been asserted over, and over, and over again. If you say, that they have declared their right of making laws, to *bind us in all cases whatsoever:* I answer; that the declarative act here referred to, means no more than to assert the supreme authority of Great Britain over all her dominions.—If you say, that they have exercised this power in a wanton, oppressive manner;—it is a point, that I am not enough acquainted with the *minutiae* of government to determine. It may be true. The colonies are undoubtedly alarmed on account of their liberties. Artful men have availed themselves of the opportunity, and have excited such scenes of contention between the parent state and the colonies, as afford none but dreadful prospects. Republicans smile at the confusion that they themselves have, in a great measure made, and are exerting all their influence, by sedition and rebellion, to shake the British empire to its very basis, that they may have an opportunity of erecting their beloved commonwealth on its ruins. If greater security to our rights and liberties be necessary than the present form and administration of the government can give us, let us endeavour to obtain it; but let our endeavours be regulated by prudence and probability of success. In this attempt all good men will join, both in England and America: All, who love their country, and wish the prosperity of the British empire, will be glad to see it accomplished.

Before we set out to obtain this security we should have had prudence enough to settle one point among ourselves. We should have considered what security it was we wanted;—what concessions, on the part of Great Britain would have been sufficient to have fixed our rights and liberties on a firm and permanent foundation. This was the proper business of our assemblies, and to them we ought to have applied. . .

I will here, Sir, venture to deliver my sentiments upon the line that ought to be drawn between the supremacy of Great Britain, and the dependency of the Colonies. And I shall do it with the more boldness, because, I know it to be agreeable to the opinions of many of the warmest advocates for America, both in England and in the colonies, in the time of the stamp-act.—I imagine that if all internal taxation be vested in our own legislatures, and the right of regulating trade by duties, bounties, &c. be left in the power of the Parliament; and also the right of enacting all general laws for the good of all the colonies, that we shall have all the security for our rights, liberties and property, which human policy can give us: The dependence of the colonies on the mother country will be fixed on a firm foundation; the sovereign authority of Parliament, over all the dominions of the empire will be established, and the mother-country and all her colonies will be knit together, in ONE GRAND, FIRM, AND COMPACT BODY. . .

If we should succeed in depriving Great Britain of the power, of regulating our trade, the colonies will probably be soon at variance with each other. Their commercial interests will interfere; there will be no supreme power to interpose, and discord and animosity must ensue.

And upon the whole—if the Parliament can regulate our trade, so as to make it conduce to the general good of the whole empire, as well as to our particular profit; if they can protect us in the secure enjoyment of an extensive and lucrative commerce, and at the same time can raise a part of the revenue necessary to support their naval power, without which our commerce cannot be safe, every reasonable man, I should imagine, would think it best to let them enjoy it in peace. . .

8. *Rebellion is the most atrocious offense that can be perpetrated by man*

DANIEL LEONARD, *Massachusettensis, Letters Addressed to the Inhabitants of the Province of Massachusetts Bay,* 1775 *

January, 9, 1775

. . . Perhaps the whole story of empire does not furnish another instance of a forcible opposition to government, with so much apparent and little real cause, with such apparent probability without any possibility of success. . . I intend to consider the acts of the British government, which are held up as the principal grievances, and inquire whether Great Britain is chargeable with injustice in any one of them. . .

The security of the people from internal rapacity and violence, and from foreign invasion, is the end and design of government. The simple forms of government are monarchy, aristocracy, and democracy; that is, where the authority of the state is vested in one, a few, or the many. Each of these species of government has advantages peculiar to itself, and would answer the ends of government, were the persons intrusted with the authority of the state, always guided, themselves, by unerring wisdom and public virtue; but rulers are not always exempt from the weakness and depravity which make government necessary to society. Thus monarchy is apt to rush headlong into tyranny, aristocracy to beget faction, and multiplied usurpation, and democracy, to degenerate into tumult, violence, and anarchy. A government formed upon these three principles, in due proportion, is the best calculated to answer the ends of government, and to endure. Such a government is the British constitution, consisting of king, lords and commons, which at once includes the principal excellencies, and excludes the principal defects of the other kinds of government. It is allowed, both by Englishmen and foreigners, to be the most perfect system that the wisdom of ages has produced. The distributions

* *Novanglus, and Massachusettensis,* Boston, Hews and Goss, 1819, pp. 169–226 *passim.*

of power are so just, and the proportions so exact, as at once to support and controul each other. An Englishman glories in being subject to, and protected by such a government. The colonies are a part of the British empire. The best writers upon the law of nations tell us, that when a nation takes possession of a distant country, and settles there, that country, though separated from the principal establishment, or mother country, naturally becomes a part of the state, equal with its ancient possessions. Two supreme or independent authorities cannot exist in the same state. It would be what is called *imperium in imperio*, the height of political absurdity. The analogy between the political and human body is great. Two independent authorities in a state would be like two distinct principles of volition and action in the human body, dissenting, opposing, and destroying each other. If, then, we are a part of the British empire, we must be subject to the supreme power of the state, which is vested in the estates of parliament, notwithstanding each of the colonies have legislative and executive powers of their own, delegated, or granted to them for the purposes of regulating their own internal police, which are subordinate to, and must necessarily be subject to the checks, controul, and regulation of the supreme authority.

This doctrine is not new, but the denial of it is. It is beyond a doubt, that it was the sense both of the parent country, and our ancestors, that they were to remain subject to parliament. It is evident from the charter itself; and this authority has been exercised by parliament, from time to time, almost ever since the first settlement of the country, and has been expressly acknowledged by our provincial legislatures. It is not less our interest, than our duty, to continue subject to the authority of parliament, which will be more fully considered hereafter. The principal argument against the authority of parliament, is this; the Americans are entitled to all the privileges of an Englishman; it is the privilege of an Englishman to be exempt from all laws, that he does not consent to in person, or by representative. The Americans are not represented in parliament, and therefore are exempt from acts of parliament, or in other words not subject to its authority. This appears specious; but leads to such absurdities as demonstrate its fallacy. If the colonies are not subject to the authority of parliament, Great Britain and the colonies must be distinct states, as completely so, as England and Scotland were before the union, or as Great Britain and Hanover are now. The colonies in that case will owe no allegiance to the imperial crown, and perhaps not to the person of the king, as the title to the crown is derived from an act of parliament, made since the settlement of this province, which act respects the imperial crown only. Let us waive this difficulty, and suppose allegiance due from the colonies to the person of the king of Great Britain. He then appears in a new capacity, of king of America, or rather in several new capacities, of king of Massachusetts, king of Rhode Island, king of Connecticut, &c., &c. For if our connexion with Great Britain by the parliament be dissolved, we shall have none among ourselves, but each colony become as distinct from the others, as England was from Scotland, before the union. Some have supposed that each state, having one and the same person for its king, is a sufficient connection. Were he an absolute monarch, it might be; but in a mixed government, it is no union at all. For as the king must govern each state, by its parliament, those several parliaments would pursue the particular interest of its own state; and however well disposed the king might be to pursue a line of interest, that was common to all, the checks and controul that he would meet with, would render it impossible. If the king of Great Britain has really these new capacities, they ought to be added to his titles; and another difficulty will arise, the prerogatives of these new crowns have never been defined or limited. Is the monarchical part of the several provincial constitutions to be nearer or more remote from absolute monarchy, in an inverted ratio to each one's approaching to, or receding from a republic? But let us suppose the same prerogatives inherent in the several American crowns, as are in the imperial crown of Great Britain, where shall we find the British constitution, that we all agree we are entitled to? We shall seek for it in vain in our provincial assemblies. They are but faint sketches of the estates of parliament. The houses of representatives, or Burgesses, have not all the powers of the house of commons; in the charter governments they have no more than what is expressly granted by their several charters. The first charters granted to this province did not empower the assembly to tax the people at all. Our council boards are as destitute of the constitutional authority of the house of lords, as their several members are of the noble independence, and splendid appendages of peerage. The house of peers is the bulwark of the British constitution, and through successive ages, has withstood the shocks of monarchy, and the sappings of democracy, and the constitution gained strength by the conflict. Thus the supposition of our being independent states, or exempt from the authority of parliament, destroys the very idea of our having a British constitution. The provincial constitutions, considered as subordinate, are generally well adapted to those purposes of government, for which they were intended; that is, to regulate the internal police of the several colonies; but have no principle of stability within themselves; they may support themselves in moderate times, but would be merged by the violence of turbulent ones, and the several colonies become wholly monarchical, or wholly republican, were it not for the checks, controuls, regulations, and support of the supreme authority of the empire. Thus the argument, that is drawn from their first principle of our being entitled to English liberties, destroys the principle itself, it deprives us of the bill of rights, and all the benefits resulting from the revolution of English laws, and of the British constitution.

Our patriots have been so intent upon building up American rights, that they have overlooked the rights of Great Britain, and our own interest. Instead of proving that we are entitled to privileges, that our fathers knew our situation would not admit us to enjoy, they have been arguing away our most essential rights. If there be any grievance, it does not consist in our being subject to the authority of parliament, but in our not having an actual representation in it. Were it possible for the colonies to have an equal representation in parliament, and were refused it upon proper application, I confess I should think it a grievance; but at present it seems to be allowed, by all parties, to be impracticable, considering the colonies are distant from Great Britain a thousand transmarine leagues. If that be the case, the right or privilege, that we complain of being deprived of, is not withheld by Britain, but the first principles of government, and the immutable laws of nature, render it impossible for us to enjoy it. . . Allegiance and protection are reciprocal. It is our highest interest to continue a part of the British empire; and equally our duty to remain subject to the authority of parliament. Our own internal police may generally be regulated by our provincial legislatures, but in national concerns, or where our own assemblies do not answer the ends of government with respect to ourselves, the ordinance or interposition of the great council of the nation is necessary. In this case, the major must rule the minor. After many more centuries shall have rolled away, long after we, who are now bustling upon the stage of life, shall have been received to the bosom of mother earth, and our names are forgotten, the colonies may be so far increased as to have the balance of wealth, numbers and power, in their favour, the good of the empire make it necessary to fix the seat of government here; and some future George, equally the friend of mankind, with him that now sways the British sceptre, may cross the Atlantic, and rule Great Britain, by an American parliament.

February 6, 1775

When we reflect upon the constitutional connection between Great Britain and the colonies, view the reciprocation of interest, consider that the welfare of Britain, in some measure, and the prosperity of America wholly depends upon that connection; it is astonishing, indeed, almost incredible, that one person should be found on either side of the Atlantic, so base, and destitute of every sentiment of justice, as to attempt to destroy or weaken it. If there are none such, in the name of Almighty God, let me ask, wherefore is rebellion, that implacable fiend to society, suffered to rear its ghastly front among us, blasting, with haggard look, each social joy, and embittering every hour?

Rebellion is the most atrocious offence, that can be perpetrated by man, save those which are committed more immediately against the supreme Governor of the Universe, who is the avenger of his own cause. It dissolves the social band, annihilates the security resulting from law and government; introduces fraud, violence, rapine, murder, sacrilege, and the long train of evils, that riot, uncontrouled, in a state of nature. Allegiance and protection are reciprocal. The subject is bound by the compact to yield obedience to government, and in return, is entitled to protection from it; thus the poor are protected against the rich; the weak against the strong; the individual against the many, and this protection is guaranteed to each member, by the whole community. But when government is laid prostrate, a state of war, of all against all commences; might overcomes right; innocence itself has no security, unless the individual sequesters himself from his fellowmen, inhabits his own cave, and seeks his own prey. This is what is called a state of nature. I once thought it chimerical. . .

April 3, 1775

. . . The advocates for the opposition to parliament often remind us of the rights of the people, repeat the latin adage *vox populi vox Dei*, and tell us that government in the dernier resort is in the people; they chime away melodiously, and to render their music more ravishing, tell us, that these are *revolution principles*. I hold the rights of the people as sacred, and revere the principles, that have established the succession to the imperial crown of Great Britain, in the line of the illustrious house of Brunswick; but that the difficulty lies in applying them to the cause of the whigs, *hic labor hoc opus est;* for admitting that the collective body of the people, that are subject to the British empire, have an inherent right to change their form of government, or race of kings, it does not follow, that the inhabitants of a single province, or of a number of provinces, or any given part under a majority of the whole empire, have such a right. By admitting that the less may rule or sequester themselves from the greater, we unhinge all government. . .

Novanglus abuses me, for saying, that the whigs aim at independence. The writer from Hampshire county is my advocate. He frankly asserts the independency of the colonies without any reserve; and is the only consistent writer I have met with on that side of the question. For by separating us from the king as well as the parliament, he is under no necessity of contradicting himself. Novanglus strives to hide the inconsistencies of his hypothesis, under a huge pile of learning. Surely he is not to learn, that arguments drawn from obsolete maxims, raked out of the ruins of the feudal system, or from principles of absolute monarchy, will not conclude to the present constitution of government. . . Public justice and generosity are no less characteristic of the English, than their private honesty and hospitality. The total repeal of the stamp act, and the partial repeal of the act imposing duties on paper, &c. may convince us that the nation has no disposition to injure us. We are blessed with a king that reflects honor upon a crown. He is so far from being avaricious, that he has relinquished a part of his revenue; and so far from being tyrannical, that he has generously surrendered part of his prerogative for the sake of freedom. . . We have only to cease contending with the supreme legislature, respecting its authority, with the king respecting his prerogatives, and with Great Britain respecting our subordination; to dismiss our illegal committees, disband our forces, despise the thraldom of *arrogant congresses,* and submit to constitutional government, to be happy. . .

9. *Our provincial legislatures are the only supreme authorities in the colonies*

JOHN ADAMS, *Novanglus, Letters Addressed to the Inhabitants of the Colony of Massachusetts Bay,* 1775 *

February 6, 1775

. . . Massachusettensis, conscious that the people of this continent have the utmost abhorrence of treason and rebellion, labours to avail himself of the magic in these words. But his artifice is vain. The people are not to be intimidated by hard words, from a necessary defence of their liberties: Their attachment to their constitution so dearly purchased by their own and their ancestors blood and treasure, their aversion to the late innovations, their horror of arbi-

* *Novanglus, and Massachusettensis,* Boston, Hews and Goss, 1819, pp. 26–102 *passim.*

trary power and the Romish religion, are much deeper rooted than their dread of rude sounds and unmannerly language. . . They know upon what hinge the whole dispute turns. That the *fundamentals* of the government over them, are disputed, that the minister pretends and had the influence to obtain the voice of the last parliament in his favour, that parliament is the only supreme, sovereign, absolute and uncontroulable legislative over all the Colonies, that therefore the minister and all his advocates will call resistance, to acts of parliament, by the names of treason and rebellion. But at the same time they know, that in their own opinions, and in the opinions of all the Colonies, parliament has no authority over them, excepting to regulate their trade, and this not by any principle of common law, but merely by the consent of the Colonies, founded on the obvious necessity of a case, which was never in contemplation of that law, nor provided for by it; that therefore they have as good a right to charge that minister, Massachusettensis and the whole army to which he has fled for protection, with treason and rebellion. For if the parliament has not a legal authority to overturn their constitution, and subject them to such acts as are lately passed, every man, who accepts of any commission and takes any steps to carry those acts into execution, is guilty of overt acts of treason and rebellion against his majesty, his royal crown and dignity, as much as if he should take arms against his troops, or attempt his sacred life. . .

March 6, 1775

. . . Our rhetorical magician, in his paper of January the 9th . . . comes to a great subject indeed, the British constitution; and undertakes to prove that 'the authority of parliament extends to the colonies.'

Why will not this writer state the question fairly? The whigs allow that from the necessity of a case not provided for by common law, and to supply a defect in the British dominions, which there undoubtedly is, if they are to be governed only by that law, America has all along consented, still consents, and ever will consent, that parliament being the most powerful legislature in the dominions, should regulate the trade of the dominions. This is founding the authority of parliament to regulate our trade, upon *compact* and *consent* of the colonies, not upon any principle of common or statute law, not upon any original principle of the English constitution, not upon the principle that parliament is the supreme and sovereign legislature, over them in all cases whatsoever.

The question is not therefore, whether the authority of parliament extends to the colonies in any case; for it is admitted by the whigs that it does in that of commerce: but whether it extends in all cases. . .

We are told, 'that the colonies are a part of the British empire.' But what are we to understand by this? Some of the colonies, most of them indeed, were settled before the kingdom of Great Britain was brought into existence. The union of England and Scotland, was made and established by act of parliament in the reign of queen Ann; and it was this union and statute which erected the kingdom of Great Britain. The colonies were settled long before, in the reigns of the Jameses and Charleses. What authority over them had Scotland? . . .

If the English parliament were to govern us, where did they get the right, without our consent to take the Scottish parliament into a participation of the government over us? When this was done, was the American share of the democracy of the constitution consulted? If not, were not the Americans deprived of the benefit of the democratical part of the constitution? And is not the democracy as essential to the English constitution, as the monarchy or aristocracy? . . .

If a new constitution was to be formed for the whole British dominions, and a supreme legislature coextensive with it, upon the general principles of the English constitution, an equal mixture of monarchy, aristocracy and democracy, let us see what would be necessary. England had six millions of people we will say: America had three. England has five hundred members in the house of commons we will say: America must have two hundred and fifty. Is it possible she should maintain them there, or could they at such a distance know the state, the sense or exigencies of their constituents? . . . Will the ministry thank Massachusettensis for becoming an advocate for such an union and incorporation of all the dominions of the king of Great Britain? Yet without such an union, a legislature which shall be sovereign and supreme in all cases whatsoever, and coextensive with the empire, can never be established upon the general principles of the English constitution, which Massachusettensis lays down, viz. an equal mixture of monarchy, aristocracy and democracy. . .

'The best writers upon the law of nations, tell us, that when a nation takes possession of a distant country and settles there, that country, though separated from the principal establishment, or mother country, naturally becomes a part of the state, equal with its ancient possessions.' We are not told who these 'best writers' are: I think we ought to be introduced to them. But their meaning may be no more, than that it is best they should be incorporated with the ancient establishment by contract, or by some new law and institution, by which the new country shall have equal right, powers and privileges, as well as equal protection; and be under equal obligations of obedience with the old. Has there been any such contract between Britain and the colonies? Is America incorporated into the realm? Is it a part of the realm? Is it a part of the kingdom? Has it any share in the legislative of the realm? The constitution requires that every foot of land should be represented in the third estate, the democratical branch of the constitution. How many millions of acres in America, how many thousands of wealthy landholders, have no representatives there.

But let these 'best writers' say what they will, there is nothing in the law of nations, which is only the law of right reason, applied to the conduct of nations, that requires that emigrants from a state that should continue, or be made a part of the state.

The practice of nations has been different. . .

But the sense and practice of nations is not enough. Their practice must be reasonable, just and right, or it will not govern Americans. . .

I deny, therefore, that the practice of free nations, or the opinions of the best writers upon the law of nations, will warrant the position of Massachusettensis, that when a nation takes possession of a distant territory, that becomes a part of the state equally with its ancient possessions. The practice of free nations, and the opinions of the best writers, are in general on the contrary.

I agree, that 'two supreme and independent authorities cannot exist in the same state,' any more than two supreme beings in one universe. And therefore I contend, that our provincial legislatures are the only supreme authorities in our colonies. Parliament, notwithstanding this, may be allowed an authority supreme and sovereign over the ocean, which may be limited by the banks of the ocean, or the bounds of our charters; our charters give us no authority over the high seas. Parliament has our consent to assume a jurisdiction over them. And here is a line fairly drawn between the rights of Britain and the rights of the colonies, viz. the banks of the ocean, or low water mark; the line of division between common law and civil, or maritime law. . .

'If then we are a part of the British empire, we must be subject to the supreme power of the state, which is vested in the estates in parliament.'

Here again we are to be conjured out of our senses by the magic in the words 'British empire,' and 'supreme power of the state.' But however it may sound, I say we are not a part of the British empire; because the British government is not an empire. . .

The question should be, whether we are a part of the kingdom of Great Britain: this is the only language, known in English laws. We are not then a part of the British kingdom, realm or state; and therefore the supreme power of the kingdom, realm, or state, is not upon these principles, the supreme power of us. That 'supreme power over America is vested in the estates in parliament,' is an affront to us; for there is not an acre of American land represented there—there are no American estates in parliament. . .

The only proposition in all this writer's long string of pretended absurdities, which he says follows from the position, that we are distinct states, is this: That, 'as the king must govern each state by its parliament, those several parliaments would pursue the particular interest of its own state; and however well disposed the king might be to pursue a line of interest that was common to all, the checks and controul that he would meet with, would render it impossible.' Every argument ought to be allowed its full weight: and therefore candour obliges me to acknowledge, that here lies all the difficulty that there is in this whole controversy. There has been, from first to last, on both sides of the Atlantic, an idea, an apprehension that it was necessary, there should be some superintending power, to draw together all the wills, and unite all the strength of the subjects in all the dominions, in case of war, and in the case of trade. The necessity of this, in case of trade, has been so apparent, that, as has often been said, we have consented that parliament should exercise such a power. In case of war, it has by some been thought necessary. But, in fact and experience, it has not been found so. . . The inconveniences of this were small, in comparison of the absolute ruin to the liberties of all which must follow the submission to parliament, in all cases, which would be giving up all the popular limitations upon the government. . .

But admitting the proposition in its full force, that it is absolutely necessary there should be a supreme power, co-extensive with all the dominions, will it follow that parliament, as now constituted, has a right to assume this supreme jurisdiction? By no means.

A union of the colonies might be projected, and an American legislature; for, if America has 3,000,000 people, and the whole dominions 12,000,000, she ought to send a quarter part of all the members to the house of commons, and instead of holding parliaments always at Westminster, the haughty members for Great Britain must humble themselves, one session in four, to cross the Atlantic, and hold the parliament in America.

There is no avoiding all inconveniences in human affairs. The greatest possible or conceivable would arise from ceding to parliament power over us, without a representation in it. The next greatest would accrue from any plan that can be devised for a representation there. The least of all would arise from going on as we began, and fared well for 150 years, by letting parliament regulate trade, and our own assemblies all other matters. . .

But perhaps it will be said that we are to enjoy the British constitution in our supreme legislature, the parliament, not in our provincial legislatures.

To this I answer, if parliament is to be our supreme legislature, we shall be under a complete oligarchy or aristocracy, not the British constitution, which this writer himself defines a mixture of monarchy, aristocracy, and democracy.—For king, lords and commons will constitute one great oligarchy, as will stand related to America, as much as the decemvirs did in Rome; with this difference for the worse, that our rulers are to be three thousand miles off. . . If our provincial constitutions are in any respect imperfect and want alteration, they have capacity enough to discern it, and power enough to effect it, without interposition of parliament. . . America will never allow that parliament has any authority to alter their constitution at all. She is wholly penetrated with a sense of the necessity of resisting it, at all hazards. . . The question we insist on most is not whether the alteration is for the better or not, but whether parliament has any right to make any alteration at all. And it is the universal sense of America, that it has none. . .

That a representation in parliament is impracticable we all agree: but the consequence is, that we must have a representation in our supreme legislatures here. This was the consequence that was drawn by kings, ministers, our ancestors, and the whole nation, more than a century ago, when the colonies were first settled, and continued to be the general sense until the last peace; and it must be the general sense again soon, or Great Britain will lose her colonies. . .

'It is our highest interest to continue a part of the British empire; and equally our duty to remain subject to the authority of parliament,' says Massachusettensis.

We are a part of the British dominions, that is of the king of Great Britain, and it is our interest and duty to continue so. It is equally our interest and duty to continue subject to the authority of parliament, in the regulation of our trade, as long as she shall leave us to govern our internal policy, and to give and grant our own money, and no longer. . .

March 13, 1775

'Our patriots most heroically resolved to become independent states, and flatly denied that parliament had a right to make any laws whatever that should be binding upon the colonies'. . .

Our patriots have never determined, or desired to be independent states, if a voluntary cession of a right to regulate their trade can make them dependent even on parliament, though they are clear in theory, that by the common law, and the English constitution, parliament has no authority over them. None of the patriots of this province, of the present age, have ever denied that parliament has a right, from our voluntary cession, to make laws which shall bind the colonies, as far as their commerce extends. . .

The patriots of this province desire nothing new; they wish only to keep their old privileges. They were for 150 years allowed to tax themselves, and govern their internal concerns, as they thought best. Parliament governed their trade as they thought fit. This plan, they wish may continue forever. But it is honestly confessed, rather than become subject to the absolute authority of parliament, in all cases of taxation and internal polity, they will be driven to throw off that of regulating trade. . .

10. *A government of our own is our natural right*

THOMAS PAINE, *Common Sense*, January 1776 *

ORIGIN AND DESIGN OF GOVERNMENT

Some writers have so confounded society with government, as to leave little or no distinction between them; whereas they are not only different, but have different origins. Society is produced by our wants, and government by our wickedness. . .

Society in every state is a blessing, but government even in its best state is but a necessary evil; in its worst state an intolerable one; for when we suffer, or are exposed to the same miseries by a *government*, which we might expect in a country *without government*, our calamity is heightened by reflecting that we furnish the means by which we suffer. . . [Man] . . . finds it necessary to surrender up a part of his property to furnish means for the protection of the rest; and this he is induced to do by the same prudence which in every other case advises him out of two evils to choose the least. *Wherefore*, security being the true design and end of government, it unanswerably follows, that whatever *form* thereof appears most likely to insure it to us, with the least expense and greatest benefit, is preferable to all others. . .

I know it is difficult to get over local or long standing prejudices, yet if

* *The Political Writings of Thomas Paine*, George Davidson, ed., 1824, Charleston [MS.], vol. I, pp. 19–47, 61–4 *passim.*

we will suffer ourselves to examine the component parts of the English constitution, we shall find them to be the base remains of two ancient tyrannies, compounded with some new republican materials.

1st, The remains of monarchical tyranny in the person of the king.

2d, The remains of aristocratical tyranny in the persons of the peers.

3d, The new republican materials, in the persons of the commons, on whose virtue depends the freedom of England.

The two first, by being hereditary, are independent of the people; wherefore in a *constitutional sense* they contribute nothing towards the freedom of the state. . .

To say that the commons is a check upon the king, pre-supposes two things:

1st, That the king is not to be trusted without being looked after; or in other words, that a thirst for absolute power is the natural disease of monarchy.

2d, That the commons, by being appointed for that purpose, are either wiser or more worthy of confidence than the crown.

But as the same constitution which gives the commons a power to check the king by withholding the supplies, gives afterwards the king a power to check the commons, by empowering him to reject their other bills; it again supposes that the king is wiser than those whom it has already supposed to be wiser than him. A mere absurdity!

There is something exceedingly ridiculous in the composition of monarchy; it first excludes a man from the means of information, yet empowers him to act in cases where the highest judgment is required. The state of a king shuts him from the world, yet the business of a king requires him to know it thoroughly; wherefore the different parts, by unnaturally opposing and destroying each other, prove the whole character to be absurd and useless. . .

How came the king by a power which the people are afraid to trust, and always obliged to check? Such a power could not be the gift of a wise people, neither can any power *which needs checking,* be from God; yet the provision, which the constitution makes, supposes such a power to exist. . .

OF MONARCHY AND HEREDITARY SUCCESSION

Mankind being originally equals in the order of creation, the equality could only be destroyed by some subsequent circumstance; the distinctions of rich and poor, may in a great measure be accounted for, and that without having recourse to the harsh, ill-sounding names of oppression and avarice. . .

But there is another and greater distinction, for which no truly natural or religious reason can be assigned, and that is, the distinction of men into *kings* and *subjects.* . .

In the early ages of the world, according to the scripture chronology, there were no kings; the consequence of which was there were no wars; it is the pride of kings which throws mankind into confusion. . .

To the evil of monarchy we have added that of hereditary succession; and as the first is a degradation and lessening of ourselves, so the second, claimed as a matter of right, is an insult and imposition on posterity. For all men being originally equals, no *one* by *birth,* could have a right to set up his own family, in perpetual preference to all others for ever, and though himself might deserve *some* degree of honors of his contemporaries, yet his descendants might be far too unworthy to inherit them. One of the strongest *natural* proofs of the folly of hereditary right in kings, is, that nature disapproves it, otherwise she would not so frequently turn it into ridicule, by giving mankind an *ass for a lion.*

Secondly, as no man at first could possess more public honors than were bestowed upon him, so the givers of those honors could have no power to give away the right of posterity, and though they might say, 'We choose you for *our head,*' they could not without manifest injustice to their children, say, that 'your children and your children's children shall reign over *ours* for ever.' Because such an unwise, unjust, unnatural compact might (perhaps) in the next succession put them under the government of a rogue or a fool. . .

This is supposing the present race of kings in the world to have had an honorable origin; whereas it is more than probable, that, could we take off the dark covering of antiquity, and trace them to their first rise, we should find the first of them nothing better than the principal ruffian of some restless gang, whose savage manners, or pre-eminence in subtlety obtained him title of chief among plunderers. . .

In England the king hath little more to do than to make war and give away places; which, in plain terms, is to impoverish the nation and set it together by the ears. A pretty business indeed for a man to be allowed eight hundred thousand sterling a year for, and worshipped into the bargain! Of more worth is one honest man to society, and in the sight of God, than all the crowned ruffians that ever lived.

THOUGHTS ON THE PRESENT STATE OF AMERICAN AFFAIRS

. . . Volumes have been written on the subject of the struggle between England and America. Men of all ranks have embarked in the controversy, from different motives, and with various designs: but all have been ineffectual, and the period of debate is closed. Arms, as the last resource, must decide the contest. . .

The sun never shined on a cause of greater worth. 'Tis not the affair of a city, a county, a province, or a kingdom, but of a continent—of at least one eighth part of the habitable globe. 'Tis not the concern of a day, a year, or an age; posterity are virtually involved in the contest, and will be more or less affected, even to the end of time, by the proceedings now. Now is the seed time of continental union, faith, and honor. The least fracture now will be like a name engraved with the point of a pin on the tender rind of a young oak; the wound will enlarge with the tree, and posterity read it in full grown characters. . .

As much hath been said of the advantages of reconciliation, which, like an agreeable dream, hath passed away and left us as we were, it is but right, that we should examine the contrary side of the argument, and inquire into some of the many material injuries which these colonies sustain, and always will sustain, by being connected with and dependant on Great Britain. . .

But Britain is the parent country, say some. Then the more shame upon her conduct. Even brutes do not devour their young, nor savages make war upon their families; wherefore, the assertion, if true, turns to her reproach; but it happens not to be true, or only partly so. . . Europe, and not England, is the parent country of America. This new world hath been the asylum for the persecuted lovers of civil and religious liberty from *every part* of Europe. . .

I challenge the warmest advocate for reconciliation, to show a single advantage that this continent can reap, by being connected with Great Britain. . .

Everything that is right or natural pleads for separation. The blood of the slain, the weeping voice of nature cries, *'tis time to part*. Even the distance at which the Almighty hath placed England and America, is a strong and natural proof, that the authority of one over the other, was never the design of heaven. . .

A government of our own is our natural right: and when a man seriously reflects on the precariousness of human affairs, he will become convinced, that it is infinitely wiser and safer, to form a constitution of our own in a cool deliberate manner, while we have it in our power, than to trust such an interesting event to time and chance. If we omit it now, some Massanello * may hereafter arise, who, laying hold of popular disquietudes, may collect together the desperate and the discontented, and by assuming to themselves the powers of government, finally sweep away the liberties of the continent like a deluge. . . Ye that oppose independence now, ye know not what ye do; ye are opening a door to eternal tyranny, by keeping vacant the seat of government. There are thousands and tens of thousands, who would think it glorious to expel from the continent that barbarous and hellish power, which hath stirred up the Indians and negroes to destroy us—the cruelty hath a double guilt, it is dealing brutally by us, and treacherously by them. . .

In short, independence is the only *bond* that can tie and keep us together. We shall then see our object, and our ears will be legally shut against the schemes of an intriguing, as well as cruel, enemy. We shall then, too, be on a proper footing to treat with Britain; for there is reason to conclude, that the pride of that court, will be less hurt by treating with the American states for terms of peace, than with those, whom she denominates 'rebellious subjects,' for terms of accommodation. It is our delaying it that encourages her to hope for conquest, and our backwardness tends only to prolong the war. As we have, without any good effect therefrom, withheld our trade to obtain a redress of our grievances, let us *now* try the alternative, by independently redressing them ourselves, and then offering to open the trade. The mercantile and reasonable part of England, will be still with us; because, peace, *with* trade, is preferable to war, *without* it. And if this offer be not accepted, other courts may be applied to.

On these grounds I rest the matter. . . Let the names of whig and tory be extinct; and let none other be heard among us, than those of *a good citizen; an*

* Thomas Anello, otherwise Massanello, a fisherman of Naples, who after spiriting up his countrymen in the public market place, against the oppression of the Spaniards, to whom the place was then subject, prompted them to revolt, and in the space of a day became king.

open and resolute friend; and a virtuous supporter of the RIGHTS *of* MANKIND, *and of the* FREE AND INDEPENDENT STATES OF AMERICA.

11. *We hold these truths*

The Unanimous Declaration of the Thirteen United States of America, 4 July 1776

When in the Course of human events, it becomes necessary for one people to dissolve the political bands which have connected them with another, and to assume among the Powers of the earth, the separate and equal station to which the Laws of Nature and of Nature's God entitle them, a decent respect to the opinions of mankind requires that they should declare the causes which impel them to the separation.

We hold these truths to be self-evident, that all men are created equal, that they are endowed by their Creator with certain unalienable Rights, that among these are Life, Liberty and the pursuit of Happiness. That to secure these rights, Governments are instituted among Men, deriving their just powers from the consent of the governed. That whenever any Form of Government becomes destructive of these ends, it is the Right of the People to alter or to abolish it, and to institute new Government, laying its foundation on such principles and organizing its powers in such form, as to them shall seem most likely to effect their Safety and Happiness. Prudence, indeed, will dictate that Governments long established should not be changed for light and transient causes; and accordingly all experience hath shown, that mankind are more disposed to suffer, while evils are sufferable, than to right themselves by abolishing the forms to which they are accustomed. But when a long train of abuses and usurpations, pursuing invariably the same Object evinces a design to reduce them under absolute Despotism, it is their right, it is their duty, to throw off such Government, and to provide new Guards for their future security. Such has been the patient sufferance of these Colonies; and such is now the necessity which constrains them to alter their former Systems of Government. . .

SELECTED REFERENCES

R. G. Adams, *Political Ideas of the American Revolution*, Durham, Duke University Press, 1922.

Carl Becker, *The Declaration of Independence: A Study in the History of Ideas*, New York, Knopf, 1942.

Julian P. Boyd, *The Declaration of Independence. The Evolution of the Text as Shown in Facsimiles of Various Drafts by Its Author, Thomas Jefferson*, Princeton, Princeton University Press, 1945.

W. F. Dana, 'The Declaration of Independence as Justification for Revolution.' *Harvard Law Review*, January 1900, vol. XIII, pp. 319–43.

O. M. Dickerson, 'Writs of Assistance as a Cause of Revolution,' *The Era of the American Revolution: Studies Subscribed to Evarts B. Greene*, Richard B. Morris, ed., New York, Columbia University Press, 1939.

Malcolm Rogers Eiselen, *Franklin's Political Theories*, Garden City, Doubleday, Doran, 1928.

Arnaud B. Leavelle, 'James Wilson and the Relation of the Scottish Metaphysics to American Political Thought,' *Political Science Quarterly*, September 1942, vol. 57, pp. 394–410.

C. H. McIlwain, *The American Revolution, A Constitutional Interpretation*, New York, Macmillan, 1923.

John C. Miller, *Origins of the American Revolution*, Boston, Little, Brown, 1943.

William H. Nelson, *The American Tory*, Oxford, The Clarendon Press, 1961.

V. L. Parrington, *Main Currents in American Thought: The Colonial Mind*, New York, Harcourt, Brace, 1927, vol. I, ch. III & IV.

Robert L. Schuyler, *Parliament and the British Empire*, New York, Columbia University Press, 1929.

Moses Cort Tyler, *The Literary History of the American Revolution*, New York, 1897.

C. H. Van Tyne, *History of the American Revolution, 1776–83*, New York, Harper, 1905.

IV

THE UNFINISHED REVOLUTION

Much of the special character of American political thought is in the Declaration of Independence and the Federal Constitution of 1787. The first takes into account human aspirations and ideals; the second builds on man's shortcomings, his inordinate greed, his drive for power. The Declaration, by its very nature, was comparatively easy to achieve. Richard Henry Lee introduced the resolution or act of independence in the Second Continental Congress on 7 June 1776. Within less than a month the declaration to assert and explain that act had been framed, revised, and approved. It was adopted 2 July 1776 and circulated throughout the thirteen states. In stating these 'self-evident truths' to which the emergent nation had dedicated itself, Jefferson could be abstract, dogmatic, bold—almost reckless. He took a stand—unsupported by our knowledge of either history or of human nature—that stable government could be established on reason and consent. Jefferson's immediate task was to attract effective support for a great effort. The task of the Constitutional Convention of 1787, on the other hand, was to lay solid and enduring foundations for national power, for effective government. This was far more difficult. The labors of fifty-five men over a period of five months, prolonged discussion, and arduous debate were required. The resulting document was finally ratified and put into operation two years later.

The Declaration of Independence and the Constitution are, as John Quincy Adams said in 1839, 'parts of one consistent whole'; each rests on the natural right of the people to dislodge or alter their government and to institute such forms as they see fit. Taken together, these two instruments embody the negative and positive aspects of the greatest of eighteen-century political achievements: the assertion of the right of revolution and the practical execution of the theory that governments 'derive their just powers from the consent of the governed.'

To assert this doctrine against a tyrannical mother country and ruler was one thing; to ground new institutions of government in such a high-toned principle was something else. 'There is nothing more common than to confound the terms of the *American Revolution* with those of the late American War,' Dr. Benjamin Rush observed in his address of 1787 to the people of the United States. 'The American War is over: but this is far from being the case with the American revolution. On the contrary, nothing but the first act of the great drama is closed. It remains yet to establish and perfect our new forms of government; and to prepare the principles, morals, and manners of our citizens, for these forms of government after they are established and brought to perfection.'

Even before the Declaration was signed, worried statesmen pondered the problem of establishing 'new forms of government' in an independent America. In 1811 John Adams recalled the situation:

> In the winter of 1776 there was much discussion in Congress concerning the necessity of independence, and advising the several states to institute governments for themselves under the immediate authority and original power of the people. Great difficulties occurred to many gentlemen in making a transition from the old governments to new, that is, from the royal to republican governments. . .

In January 1776, George Wythe of Virginia asked the New Englander to draw up a plan 'in order to get out of the old government and into a new one.' Adams's response, *Thoughts on Government*, the first selection in this chapter, remarkably approximates the scheme ultimately chosen by the Convention of 1787 as well as by several states. It required, however, the hard knocks of over a decade of experience under the Articles of Confederation and the early state constitutions for Adams's 'thoughts' to prevail.

Stemming from our colonial experience was a curious and persisting schizophrenia. Increased desire for union resulted in part from displeasure with British policy; resistance to union, grounded in our traditional distaste of all centralized authority, was reinforced by Great Britain's arbitrary rule. This tension manifested itself even before independence. In the First Continental Congress of 1774, James Duane, John Dickinson, and Robert Morris had urged the creation of a central government. In behalf of his Plan of Union, James Galloway had commented:

> Is it not necessary that the trade of the empire should be regulated by some power or other? Can the empire hold together without it? No. Who shall regulate it? Shall the Legislature of Nova Scotia or Georgia regulate it? Massachusetts or Virginia? Pennsylvania or New York? It can't be pretended. Our legislative powers extend no further than the limits of our governments. Where shall it then be placed? There is a necessity that an American Legislature should be set up, or else that we should give the power to Parliament or King.

In a similar vein, Samuel Seabury had observed: 'To talk of being liege subjects to King George, while we disavow the authority of parliament, is another piece of whiggish nonsense.' Yet Richard Henry Lee and Patrick Henry, in later years vehement Antifederalists, insisted not only on the independence of the colonies from Britain but also on their continued independence of each other.

The First Continental Congress rejected the Galloway Plan. The colonies had failed to come to grips with the difficulties inherent in any federal system—

the inevitable clash between central and local authority arising from the distribution of power between two authorities. America thus inherited the problem Britain and the colonies proved powerless to solve. Independence and war served only to shift the locus of responsibility for its solution. Independence had been achieved, but not union.

America's first attempt at constitution-making produced a document revealing, as Benjamin F. Wright has noted, both 'inexperience with federal government and distrust of any centralized power.' The Articles of Confederation, framed in 1777 but not put into effect until 1781, had no congeniality of principle with the Declaration of Independence. The Articles rested on the sovereignty of organized power, on the independence of separate, disunited states; the Declaration stressed the rights of man, proclaimed popular sovereignty and the right of revolution. John Dickinson's first draft of the Articles envisaged 'the United States of America.' Yet there was little likelihood that independent states would erect a centralized coercive authority of their own to replace the royal and imperial British tyranny so recently thrown off. The Articles represented a victory for state sovereignty, independence, and equality, for the belief that democracy was possible only in small political units.

Thomas Burke, who led the successful move to write into the Articles the provision that the states retain ultimate sovereignty, was 'much pleased to find the opinion of accumulating powers to Congress so little supported.' So effectively did Burke arouse states' rights sentiment that the Articles—even with his crippling amendments—evoked lurking suspicion that the power to be exercised by Congress might be dangerously excessive. The town of West Springfield, Massachusetts, objected that the Articles would grant Congress too much power; 'the sovereignty and independence' of the states would be 'nearly annihilated.' 'It is *freedom*, gentlemen,' the report affirmed, 'it is *freedom*, & not a choice of the *forms of servitude* for which we contend, and we rely on your fidelity, that you will not consent to the present *plan* of Union, till after the most calm & dispassionate examination you are fully convinced it is well calculated to secure so great & desirable an object.' West Springfield entertained 'no jealousy of the present [Continental] Congress,' but it could not be sure that 'in some future corrupt times there may be a Congress which will form a design upon the liberties of the people. . .'

Men like Duane, Morris, and Wilson, all supporters of Dickinson's original draft, faced an uphill struggle. Hardships under British rule could not be erased. '[T]he prejudices which the revolution had engendered against the arbitrary government of Great Britain,' William Plumer observed, 'made the people jealous of giving to their own officers so much power as was necessary to establish an efficient government.' Nevertheless, the Articles were a step—somewhat faltering—in America's long march toward union. They kept alive the *idea* of a 'great Federal Republic' at a time when the forces of disunion might easily have prevailed. By recognizing that the war power and foreign relations were national in character, they provided a base on which to build.

Perhaps the greatest service rendered by the Articles of Confederation was the impetus its shortcomings gave the nationalists, particularly James Wilson, John

Jay, Alexander Hamilton, James Madison, Thomas Jefferson, and John Adams. Despite defects in structure and power, the Articles, Julian Boyd has concluded, 'prepared the way not for anarchy and chaos but for a more perfect union.'

In practice, the Articles produced a constitutional dilemma. The supremacy of the states over Congress reinforced 'the most persistent problem of American constitutional law—the existence of a multiplicity of *local legislatures with indefinite powers*.' Inadequate power at the head meant that the central government was too weak to cope with problems national in scope; it was virtually powerless to check overbearing legislative majorities in the several states. State supremacy sanctioned the free play of thirteen state legislatures. The salutary effect was to spur the search for a truly Federalist solution.

Implementation of nationalist doctrine went hand in hand with overt demands for stronger central authority, tending to obscure evolution of the theory itself. Crucial in this development was the emergence of the doctrine of judicial review, a notion which pitted courts against the dominant legislative power of the thirteen states. Jefferson had early lamented legislative invasion of property and contract rights. In his own state of Virginia, he had seen that, 'One hundred and seventy-three despots would surely be as oppressive as one.'

While John Adams was arguing for an executive veto to check the excesses of legislative majorities, judicial power was being invoked as a remedy for abuses in the 'legislative vortex.' In certain states, courts set judicial knowledge 'against sheer legislative self-assertion,' destructive of the rights of property and contracts. Implied was the judicial duty to uphold higher law against legislative usurpations. Meanwhile, nationalists sought in vain to discover in the Articles of Confederation evidence of legal pre-eminence that might serve as a corrective of 'unconstitutional' state legislative enactments. Effective theoretical transformation of the Articles was contingent not only on repudiation of the states' claim to sovereignty but also on discovering a source of law which could claim higher status than that aspired to by the states. The drastic changes that had to be effected are measured by the lengths to which Hamilton, Wilson, and Jay went, prior to the Convention of 1787, in their gropings for the foundations of national sovereignty in the Articles of Confederation.

The spearhead in the 'conservative' campaign to restore at home a central power not unlike that which the 'radicals' had destroyed in the Revolution was Alexander Hamilton. Hamilton, at eighteen and still a student at Kings College (now Columbia University), had observed that 'when the minds [of the multitude] are loosened from their attachment to ancient establishments and courses, they . . . are apt more or less to run into anarchy.' Two years later he became aide-de-camp to General George Washington, with the rank of lieutenant colonel. From this vantage point he felt and studied the disintegrating forces impeding the war effort. Frustrated by failure in recruitment of men and with woefully inadequate supplies, the army of 1780 he described as 'a mob rather than an army; without clothing, without provision, without morals, without discipline.' Among the causes of this disaster, he pointed to the tendency to judge events by 'abstract calculations: which, though geometrically true are false as they relate to the concerns of beings governed more by passion and prejudice, than by an enlightened sense of their interests.' On this 'realtistic' theory of human nature Hamilton in November 1779 submitted detailed suggestions to General John Sullivan of New Hampshire for restoring financial stability and stabilizing the currency. Hamilton's objective was political as well as economic. 'A national bank,' he argued, 'will be a powerful cement to our union.' 'The only plan that can preserve the currency is one that will make it the *immediate* interest of the moneyed men to cooperate with the government in its support.' The political implications of his proposals are elaborated in the letter, here reprinted, to James Duane.

Duane, then a member of the Continental Congress from New York and a man of substance and influence, had come from Philadelphia to the camp in Morristown to confer with Washington and his generals, the main topic of discussion being the desperate financial situation. Duane found that Hamilton, more than anyone else, was specific not only in regard to what was wrong, but also concerning remedies. 'The fundamental defect is want of power in Congress,' he told Duane. 'It may be pleaded,' he went on, 'that Congress had never any definite powers granted them, and of course, could exercise none, could do nothing more than recommend.' Hamilton denied this:

> They have done many of the highest acts of sovereignty, which were always cheerfully submitted to: The Declaration of Independence; the declaration of war; the levying of an army; creating a navy; emitting money; making alliances with foreign powers; appointing a dictator, etc., etc. All these implications of a complete sovereignty were never disputed, and ought to have been a standard for the whole conduct of administration. Undefined powers are discretionary powers, limited only by the object for which they were given; in the present case, the independence and freedom of America. . .

Hamilton resigned from Washington's staff in 1781, after Yorktown, and began systematically to prepare for the reorganization of the powers of Congress along the lines suggested in his letter to Duane. On 12 July of that same year his ideas began to appear anonymously in a series of articles published under the title 'The Continentalist.' The last paper came out on 4 July 1782, just prior to his election to Congress. The selection here reprinted embodies Hamilton's objective—strong central government, 'a great Republic.' Included also are suggestions of policies and of the political techniques, some of rather Machiavellian flavor, whereby these might be achieved.

Hamilton was not alone in his efforts to infuse the Articles with the bases of national sovereignty. James Wilson, defending Congress' power to pass the act of 1781 incorporating the Bank of North America, argued in 1786:

> To many purposes the United States are to be considered as one undivided, independent nation; and as possessed of all the rights, and powers, and properties, by the law of nations incident to such. Whenever an object occurs, to the direction of which no state is competent, the management of it must, of necessity, belong to the United States in Congress assembled. There are many objects of this extended nature.

The same year John Jay, denying state authority to exercise the war power of confiscation, declared that the 'rights to make war, to make peace, and to make treaties, appertaining *exclusively* to the national sovereign, that is, to Congress . . . the thirteen state legislatures have no more authority to exercise the powers, or pass acts of sovereignty on those points, than any thirteen individual citizens.'

Challenged was not only the power of the states vis-à-vis the central government, but also the right of the states to withhold from Congress powers commensurate with national objectives. State legislative aggression had been opposed by judicial power; judicial review had been tied to the notion of higher law. It seemed logical to infer, as was *later* done, that the states were *never* sovereign. Independence and revolution had been, as Jefferson said, assertions of 'the right of the people.' The theoretical groundwork had yet to be laid for an effective national government. The arguments of Hamilton, Wilson, and Jay were ingenious rather than persuasive.

Someone has said that 'Hamilton began by writing to Washington's instructions and ended by divining, interpreting and anticipating his thoughts.' It would not be extreme to say that Hamilton did much more than 'anticipate'; he took the initiative in keeping before Washington the central issue. 'I congratulate Your Excellency on this happy conclusion of your labors,' he wrote Washington 24 March 1783. 'It now only remains to make solid establishments within, to perpetuate our union, to prevent our being a ball in the hands of European powers, bandied against each other at their pleasure; in fine, to make our independence truly a blessing. This,' he told Washington, 'will be an arduous work; for . . . the centrifugal is much stronger than the centripetal force in the states—the seeds of disunion much more numerous than those of union.'

With the war over Washington was confronted with the probability that the Army, soldiers and officers alike, long without pay, would be disbanded without any consideration of their claims. In June 1783, thinking he was about to retire to private life, Washington addressed a circular letter to various state governors expressing his deep concern not only for the welfare of his men but also (in the spirit of Hamilton) for the nation he had done so much to establish. Underscoring the need for drastic action, he wrote: 'It is indispensable to the happiness of the individual States that there should be lodged somewhere a Supreme Power, to regulate and govern the general concerns of the confederated Republic. . .'

Jefferson shared the prevailing sense of urgency. 'The want of power in the federal head was early perceived, and foreseen to be the flaw in our constitution which might endanger its destruction,' he wrote Richard Price from Paris in 1785. Two years earlier he had written Edmund Randolph, expressing his fear that, unless 'the band of our confederacy' were strengthened, 'the States will go to war with each other in defiance of Congress.'

While Hamilton was exploring the inadequacies of the Articles of Confederation, Jefferson had occasion to reflect on affairs in his own commonwealth. Later on he set his thoughts down in the only book he ever wrote, *Notes on*

Virginia. This volume, not intended originally for publication, yet embodying the most systematic statement we have of Jefferson's political doctrine, was the fortuitous result of twenty-three queries addressed to Jefferson and other leaders in the fall of 1780 by the Marquis de Barbé-Marbois, Secretary of the French legation at Philadelphia. The Frenchman's questionnaire was designed to elicit information about various American states. It happened that Jefferson, the man best qualified to supply answers on Virginia, was then about to quit the governorship, and would soon have the leisure necessary to reflect and write on matters ranging far and wide, including climate, soil, rivers, population, mountains, seaports, government, slavery, education, religion, weights, measures, and money. Jefferson was not content to supply, as he might have done, materials he had already collected or stored in his mind. In fields where his information was incomplete or uncertain—as in natural history—he addressed his own queries to experts or had them check his findings.

In the section of primary interest to us, and the one from which the material here included is drawn, Jefferson makes a critical analysis of his own state constitution. Three years as legislator and two as governor strengthened the conviction he had held since 1776, that the constitution was not genuinely representative. He objected not only to the existing suffrage qualifications as being too limited, but also to the county-unit system as being discriminatory against the more populous districts. He reserved his most vehement objections for the popularly elected legislatures, more particularly the despotic legislative majorities authorized under the Virginia Constitution to select the governor and other officers formerly appointed by the Crown. As a remedy he suggested the very principle which, a few years later, was so strongly favored by the Philadelphia Convention of 1787—that of separation of powers and checks and balances.

Jefferson, having reduced his own thought to permanent form, was soon off to France, where he served as our minister from 1784 to 1790. Sometime before taking up his duties abroad, James Madison had asked him for the name of 'a fit bookseller both in London and Paris.' Jefferson did more than supply this: he became Madison's 'literary explorer, buyer and agent,' finally supplying him with a literary cargo, as Madison called it, that enabled him, in the critical years prior to the meeting of the Philadelphia Convention, to engage exhaustively in an intensive study of confederacies, ancient and modern. Out of this effort came a booklet of 41 pages, and against this same rich background Madison, in the spring of 1787, wrote the brief essay, *Vices of the Political System of the United States*, included in this collection, finishing it only a few weeks before the Philadelphia Convention met on 25 May.

For Madison, the critical period posed a twofold problem: manifold evils in state governments and the alarming decline of national authority, especially 'the defect of legal and coercive sanctions,' experienced after a period of wartime unity and power. Two sides of the same coin were represented. Solutions for the 'multiplicity,' 'mutability,' and 'injustice' of state legislation were closely linked with the corrective for that other vice—'want of sanction to the laws and coercion in the Government of the Confederacy.' Later on, Madison suggested that the national government 'have a negative, in all cases whatsoever, on the Legislative acts of the States.' He conceived this check to be 'essential and the least possible abridgement of the State sovereignties.' That this method was ultimately rejected in favor of judicial review does not lessen its significance.

Madison's diagnosis is broader in scope than either Hamilton's or Jefferson's. Hamilton pointed to want of power in Congress as the major source of trouble, believing that 'the evil is not very great with respect to our state constitutions . . . and they seem to have in themselves . . . the seeds of improvement.' Jefferson, like Hamilton, did not consider outside help necessary to remedy Virginia's defective state constitution. Madison, on the other hand, not only looked to a new Federal Constitution as capable of affording correctives for want of power in the central government but also looked to the Philadelphia Convention as capable of providing a remedy for widespread complaints . . . 'that [state] measures are too often decided, not according to the rules of justice and rights of the minor party but by the superior force of an interested and overbearing majority.' Madison pointed up these ideas more sharply in a letter to James Monroe, 5 October 1786:

'There is no maxim, in my opinion, which is more liable to be misapplied, and which therefore needs more elucidation, than the current one, that the interest of the majority is the political standard of right and wrong. Taking the word interest as synonymous with ultimate happiness, in which sense it is qualified with every moral ingredient, it is, no doubt true. But taking it in the popular sense, as referring to the immediate augmentation of property and wealth, nothing can be more false. In the latter sense it would be the interest of the majority, in every community, to despoil and enslave the minority of individuals, and in a Federal community to make a similar sacrifice of the minority of the component parts. In fact, it is only re-establishing, under another name, and a more specious form, force as a measure of right. . .'

Meanwhile, foreign observers turned a critical eye on America's first effort at constitution-building. Among these was the learned Frenchman, M. Turgot, who criticized American state constitutions on the score that they did not 'collect all authority into one centre, the nation.'

The sagacious Turgot had elaborated his views in a letter of 22 March 1778 to Dr. Richard Price: 'I see in the greatest number [of the American State Constitutions] an unreasonable imitation of the usages of England. Instead of bringing all the authorities into one, that of the nation, they have established different bodies—a House of Representatives, a council, a governor—because England has a House of Commons, lords, and a King. They undertake to balance these different authorities, as if the same equilibrium of powers which has been thought necessary to balance the enormous preponderance of royalty could be of any use in republics, formed upon the equality of all citizens; and as if every article which constitutes different bodies was not a source of divisions. By striking to escape imaginary dangers, they have created real ones.'

John Adams, certainly among the best-informed men in the country on political science, queried Turgot in the work here quoted, *Defence of the Constitutions of Government of the United States of America*. He took this occasion to answer also the radicalism of the Englishman, Marchamont Nedham, expressed in his book, *The Excellency of a Free State*, published in 1656.

Ransacking history from the dawn of civilization down to his own times, Adams concluded that 'if there is one certain truth to be collected from the history of all ages, it is this: that the people's rights and liberties, and the democratic mixture in a constitution, can never be preserved without a strong executive, or, in other words without separating the executive power from the legislature.'

Adams did not share Hamilton's belief in the moral superiority of the rich, the able, and wellborn, or Jefferson's supreme confidence in 'the people,' preferably rural and agrarian. Adams followed James Harrington in holding that 'dominion follows property'; political power will therefore reside with an aristocracy of ownership. Since, however, in any society the rich tend to exploit the poor, and the poor to usurp the rights of property, freedom and security can best be preserved by a system of 'balanced powers.'

The first volume of Adams's *Defence* was available to the Philadelphia Convention of 1787, and certain delegates cited it with approval. Dr. Benjamin Rush, who, though not a member of the Convention, was in close touch with the delegates, testified to its influence: 'Mr. Adams' book has diffused such excellent principles among us that there is little doubt of our adopting a vigorous and compounded Federal legislature. Our illustrious minister [at the Court of St. James, 1785] in this gift to his country has done us more service than if he had obtained alliances for us with all the nations of Europe.'

Toward the end of his life Adams could take satisfaction in noting that the federal system followed his basic principle to an extraordinary degree, including, as he saw it, no less than eight balances: (1) states and territories against the central government; (2) the House of Representatives against the Senate; (3) the President against Congress; (4) the Judiciary against Congress; (5) the Senate against the President in matters of appointments and treaties; (6) the people against their Representatives; (7) the state legislatures against the Senate; (8) the Electoral College against the people.

Nationalist reactions to the defects of the Articles, combined with the aggressive campaign to augment its central authority, only served to intensify opposition. Defenders of the Articles of Confederation, most of whom would later become Antifederalists, reiterated the same arguments which had earlier proved so successful in defeating the Galloway Plan of Union and in emasculating John Dickinson's original draft of the Articles. Since amendment of the Articles required unanimity among the thirteen states, even the effort to confer upon Congress a limited power to raise an independent income failed. Dogged resistance to Congress inspired the instructions of Fairfax County, Virginia, of 30 May 1783, to the state legislature: 'The proposed duties may be proper, but the separate States only can safely have *the power of levying taxes*. Congress should not have even the appearance of such a power.' Congress' plea for power to levy an impost was 'found to exhibit strong proofs of lust of power. . .' These instructions were authored by George Mason, in later years an Antifederalist, one of three who refused to sign the Constitution. Rhode Island delegates had submitted a similar message to the Governor of Rhode Island on 15 October 1782. An impost grant would effect fundamental alterations of the present system; it might 'disturb the general harmony, derange the elegant proportions and endanger the welfare of the whole building.'

During the pre-Convention decade, this basic distrust, a nagging fear that a new aristocracy was in the making, pervaded the states' rights literature. Power begat power, the theme went; once granted, it was never surrendered but rather expanded. When the power in question happened to be taxation, the implications were all the more serious. 'Taxation is the necessary instrument of tyranny,' wrote *The Plain Dealer*, 10 May 1783. 'There is no tyranny without it.' Taxation was the most dangerous of all powers; 'power, among civilized people as we are, is necessarily connected with the direction of the public money.' Abraham Yates, Jr., reminded his readers, 21 April 1785, that it was not accidental that the Articles of Confederation denied Congress the power to raise money by direct taxation. Yates recalled that taxes had been crucial in the dispute with Great Britain; indeed, all history proved that 'no important revolutions have taken place in any government, till the power of raising money from the people has been put into different hands. . .' 'This power is the center of gravity,' he concluded, 'for it will eventually draw into its vortex all other powers.'

Just as the forces of union and disunion had produced a dualism in early American political thought, so they also effected a division within the body of early Antifederalist thinking. Most of them recognized the need to bolster central authority, but they were reluctant to operate outside the confining framework of the Articles of Confederation. Skeptical of any radical move, they suspected the motives of those who advocated it. This attitude is reflected in the reaction of Massachusetts delegates in Congress to instructions sent to them in September 1785 by the Massachusetts legislature, recommending that the delegates introduce a resolution calling for a constitutional convention. Any commercial power granted Congress, the delegates replied, should be temporary and restricted. A convention might be tempted to alter the basic structure of government. While measures ought to be taken 'to guard against the evils arising from the want in one or two particulars of power in Congress, we are in great danger of incurring the other extreme. . . We are for increasing the power of Congress as far as it will promote the happiness of the people, but at the same time are clearly of opinion that every measure should be avoided which would strengthen the hands of the enemies to a free government. . .'

It would be a mistake to conclude that all these precursors of Antifederalism were impervious to the defects inherent in the Articles. Some were as narrow in their political outlook as the advocates of reform charged, but the great majority did not oppose all effort to revise the Articles. All agreed that some revision was necessary. Shays' Rebellion did not impress Federalists alone. Included among those who favored stronger government before 1787 were George Mason, Patrick Henry, Elbridge Gerry, George Clinton, James Monroe, William Grayson, John Francis Mercer, and James Warren. All were destined to become staunch Antifederalists.

When the call for a convention was issued at Annapolis in 1786, opponents of major change found themselves in a dilemma. Conceding that the Articles were imperfect and recognizing that amendments were nearly impossible to obtain by the mode prescribed, they could not consistently block the drive for a convention so long as it was authorized only to *recommend* reforms *within* the existing constitutional framework. George Bryan later recalled the circumstances that narrowed the range of Antifederalist action prior to the Philadelphia Convention:

> Previous to the appointment of the Convention there seemed to be in Pennsylvania a general wish for a more efficient Confederation. The public debt was unpaid & unfunded. We were deluged with foreign goods, which it was evident might have paid large sums to the Continental Treasury, if duties could have been generally laid & collected, & at the same time the levying such duties would have checked the extravagant consumption. Whilst Congress could refuse to execute them it was obvious that we were in danger of falling to pieces.

Antifederalist thought may have been ambivalent, but it was not ambiguous. Most Antifederalists of this period agreed that the central government under the Articles needed invigoration. The basic character of the Articles must, however, remain unaltered. Above all, they did not want the central government removed from control of the state legislatures. Union, not unity, was their goal. Fundamental disagreement with the nationalists lay in the conflict between their desire for some change and their distrust of nationalist objectives.

Experience under the Articles of Confederation eventually culminated in the establishment of a more perfect union, created in spite of, rather than because of, the Articles. Though the Articles cannot be blamed directly for the conditions that made the critical years critical, the central government's lack of coercive power contributed to the crisis. The Articles marked, as John Quincy Adams suggests, a break with the political theory of the Declaration and of the Revolution. Whereas the earlier experience was founded on the notion of *one people*, if not yet one nation, acting in a united, sovereign capacity, the Articles were explicitly grounded in the idea of state sovereignty. In this sense, the Articles represented a usurpation by the states of the original sovereignty vested in the people, the authority asserted in both independence and revolution.

The definition of a constitution that Judge William Paterson fashioned in his famous charge to the jury in Vanhorne's Lessee *v.* Dorrance (2 Dallas 304, 1795) had yet to be met:

> What is a constitution? It is the form of government, delineated by the mighty hand of the people, in which certain first principles or fundamental laws are established. The constitution is certain and fixed; it contains the permanent will of the people, and is the supreme law of the land; it is paramount to the power of the legislature, and can be revoked or altered only by the authority that made it. What are legislatures? Creatures of the constitution, they owe their existence to the constitution—they derive their powers from the constitution. It is their commission, and therefore all their acts must be conformable to it, or else void. The *constitution* is the work or will of the *people* themselves, in their original, sovereign, and unlimited

capacity. Law is the work or will of the legislature in their derivative capacity.

The Articles fell far short of the goal. The architects of this system had 'wasted their time, their talent,' as John Quincy Adams said, 'in erecting and roofing and buttressing a frail and temporary shed to shelter the nation from the storm.' The experience was not, however, without its advantages. These early fruits of Antifederalism should perhaps be tested not so much by the bitter taste they left as by the ultimate result they inspired. Afforded was 'an experiment of inestimable value, even in its failure.' 'It taught our fathers the lesson,' Adams observed, 'that they had more, infinitely more to do than merely to achieve their Independence by War. That they must form their Social compact upon principles never before attempted on earth.'

In his Circular Letter of 1783, Washington had urged that 'our Federal government be given such tone . . . as will enable it to answer the ends of its institution.' 'Binding ligaments' were needed and these could properly be imposed by 'no earthly power other than the People themselves.' Americans had still to demonstrate whether they could meet the challenge Jefferson underscored many years later: 'A generation that commences a revolution rarely completes it.'

1. *The blessings of society depend entirely on the constitutions of government*

JOHN ADAMS, *Thoughts on Government*, 1776 *

If I was equal to the task of forming a plan for the government of a colony, I should be flattered with your request, and very happy to comply with it; because, as the divine science of politics is the science of social happiness, and the blessings of society depend entirely on the constitutions of government, which are generally institutions that last for many generations, there can be no employment more agreeable to a benevolent mind than a research after the best.

Pope flattered tyrants too much when he said,

> 'For forms of government let fools contest,
> That which is best administered is best.'

Nothing can be more fallacious than this. But poets read history to collect flowers, not fruits; they attend to fanciful images, not the effects of social institutions. Nothing is more certain, from the history of nations and nature of man, than that some forms of government are better fitted for being well administered than others.

We ought to consider what is the end of government, before we determine which is the best form. Upon this point all speculative politicians will agree, that the happiness of society is the end of government, as all divines and

* *The Works of John Adams*, Charles Francis Adams, ed., Boston, Little, Brown, 1851, vol. IV, pp. 193–200 *passim*.

moral philosophers will agree that the happiness of the individual is the end of man. From this principle it will follow, that the form of government which communicates ease, comfort, security, or, in one word, happiness, to the greatest number of persons, and in the greatest degree, is the best. . .

Fear is the foundation of most governments; but it is so sordid and brutal a passion, and renders men in whose breasts it predominates so stupid and miserable, that Americans will not be likely to approve of any political institution which is founded on it.

Honor is truly sacred, but holds a lower rank in the scale of moral excellence than virtue. Indeed, the former is but a part of the latter, and consequently has not equal pretensions to support a frame of government productive of human happiness.

The foundation of every government is some principle or passion in the minds of the people. The noblest principles and most generous affections in our nature, then, have the fairest chance to support the noblest and most generous models of government. . .

As good government is an empire of laws, how shall your laws be made? In a large society, inhabiting an extensive country, it is impossible that the whole should assemble to make laws. The first necessary step, then, is to depute power from the many to a few of the most wise and good. But by what rules shall you choose your representatives? Agree upon the number and qualifications of persons who shall have the benefit of choosing, or annex this privilege to the inhabitants of a certain extent of ground.

The principal difficulty lies, and the greatest care should be employed, in constituting this representative assembly. It should be in miniature an exact portrait of the people at large. It should think, feel, reason, and act like them. That it may be the interest of this assembly to do strict justice at all times, it should be an equal representation, or, in other words, equal interests among the people should have equal interests in it. Great care should be taken to effect this, and to prevent unfair, partial, and corrupt elections. Such regulations, however, may be better made in times of greater tranquillity than the present; and they will spring up themselves naturally, when all the powers of government come to be in the hands of the people's friends. At present, it will be safest to proceed in all established modes, to which the people have been familiarized by habit.

A representation of the people in one assembly being obtained, a question arises, whether all the powers of government, legislative, executive, and judicial, shall be left in this body? I think a people cannot be long free, nor ever happy, whose government is in one assembly. . .

The dignity and stability of government in all its branches, the morals of the people, and every blessing of society depend so much upon an upright and skilful administration of justice, that the judicial power ought to be distinct from both the legislative and executive, and independent upon both, that so it may be a check upon both, as both should be checks upon that. The judges, therefore, should be always men of learning and experience in the laws, of exemplary morals, great patience, calmness, coolness, and attention. Their minds should not be distracted with jarring interests; they should not be dependent upon any man, or body of men. To these ends, they should hold estates for life in their offices; or, in other words, their commissions should be during good behavior, and their salaries ascertained and established by law. For misbehavior, the grand inquest of the colony, the house of representatives, should impeach them before the governor and council, where they should have time and opportunity to make their defence; but, if convicted, should be removed from their offices, and subjected to such other punishment as shall be thought proper. . .

A constitution founded on these principles introduces knowledge among the people, and inspires them with a conscious dignity becoming freemen; a general emulation takes place, which causes good humor, sociability, good manners, and good morals to be general. That elevation of sentiment inspired by such a government, makes the common people brave and enterprising. That ambition which is inspired by it makes them sober, industrious, and frugal. You will find among them some elegance, perhaps, but more solidity; a little pleasure, but a great deal of business; some politeness, but more civility. . .

If the colonies should assume governments separately, they should be left entirely to their own choice of the forms; and if a continental constitution should be formed, it should be a congress, containing a fair and adequate representation of the colonies, and its authority should sacredly be confined to these cases, namely, war, trade, disputes between colony and colony, the post-office, and the unappropriated lands of the crown, as they used to be called.

These colonies, under such forms of government, and in such a union, would be unconquerable by all the monarchies of Europe.

You and I, my dear friend, have been sent into life at a time when the greatest lawgivers of antiquity would have wished to live. How few of the human race have ever enjoyed an opportunity of making an election of government, more than of air, soil, or climate, for themselves or their children! When, before the present epocha, had three millions of people full power and a fair opportunity to form and establish the wisest and happiest government that human wisdom can contrive? I hope you will avail yourself and your country of that extensive learning and indefatigable industry which you possess, to assist her in the formation of the happiest governments and the best character of a great people.

2. *Unlimited power can not be safely trusted to any man or set of men on earth*

THOMAS BURKE to the Governor of North Carolina, 11 March and 29 April 1777 *

11 MARCH 1777

The more experience I acquire, the stronger is my conviction that *unlimited power can not be safely trusted* to any man or set of men on earth. No men

* *Letters of Members of the Continental Congress*, E. C. Burnett, ed., Washington, D.C., 1921–38, vol. II, pp. 294–6, 345–6.

have undertaken to exercise authority with intentions more generous and disinterested than the Congress and none seem to have fewer or more feeble motives for increasing the power of their body politic. What could induce individuals blest with peaceable domestic affluence to forego all the enjoyment of a pleasing home, to neglect their private affairs, and at the expense of all their time and some part of their private fortunes, to attend public business under many insurmountable difficulties and inconveniences? What but a generous zeal for the public? And what can induce such men to endeavor at increasing the power with which they are invested, when their tenure of it must be exceedingly dangerous and precarious and can bring them individually neither pleasure or profit? This is a question I believe cannot be answered but by a plain declaration that power of all kinds has an irresistible propensity to increase a desire for itself. It gives the passion of ambition a velocity which increases in its progress, and this is a passion which grows in proportion as it is gratified. . . Great part of our time is consumed in debates, whose object on one side is to increase the power of Congress, and on the other to restrain it. The advocates do not always keep the same side of the contest. The same persons who on one day endeavor to carry through some resolutions, whose tendency is to increase the power of Congress, are often on another day very strenuous advocates to restrain it. From this I infer that no one has entertained a concerted design to increase the power; and the attempts to do it proceed from ignorance of what such a being ought to be, and from the delusive intoxication which power naturally imposes on the human mind. . .

These and many other considerations make me earnestly wish that the power of Congress was accurately defined and that there were adequate check provided to prevent any excess. . .

I enclose you an abstract of the debates in Congress on every question of any consequence that has been determined in Congress since my last. . .

. . . The last matter in the abstract will show you that even thus early, men so eminent as members of Congress are willing to explain away any power that stands in the way of their particular purposes. What may we not expect some time hence when the seat of power shall become firm by habit and men will be accustomed to obedience, and perhaps forgetful of the original principles which gave rise thereto. I believe Sir the root of the evil is deep in human nature. Its growth may be kept down but it cannot be entirely extirpated. Power will sometime or other be abused unless men are well watched, and checked by something they cannot remove when they please.

29 APRIL 1777

At present, nothing but executive business is done, except the Confederation, and on mere executive business there are seldom any debates; (and still more seldom any worth remembering). We have agreed to three articles: one containing the name; the second a declaration of the sovereignty of the States, and an express provision that they be considered as retaining every power not expressly delegated; and the third an agreement mutually to assist each other against every enemy. The first and latter passed without opposition or dissent, the second occasioned two days debate. It stood originally the third article; and expressed only a reservation of the power of regulating the internal police, and consequently resigned every other power. It appeared to me that this was not what the States expected, and, I thought, it left it in the power of the future Congress or General Council to explain away every right belonging to the States and to make their own power as unlimited as they please. I proposed, therefore an amendment which held up the principle that all sovereign power was in the States separately, and that particular acts of it, which should be expressly enumerated, would be exercised in conjunction, and not otherwise; but that in all things else each state would exercise all the rights and power of sovereignty, uncontrolled. This was at first so little understood that it was some time before it was seconded, and South Carolina first took it up. The opposition was made by Mr. Wilson of Pennsylvania, and Mr. R. H. Lee of Virginia. In the end, however, the question was carried for my proposition, eleven ayes, one no, and one divided. The no was Virginia; the divided, New Hampshire. I was much pleased to find the opinion of accumulating powers to Congress so little supported, and I promise myself, in the whole business I shall find my ideas relative thereto nearly similar to those of most of the States. In a word, Sir, I am of opinion the Congress should have power enough to call out and apply the common strength for the common defence, but not for the partial purposes of ambition. . .

3. *The fundamental defect is want of power in Congress*

ALEXANDER HAMILTON to James Duane, 3 September 1780 *

Dear Sir,—Agreeably to your request, and my promise, I sit down to give you my ideas of the defects of our present system, and the changes necessary to save us from ruin. . .

The fundamental defect is a want of power in Congress. It is hardly worth while to show in what this consists, as it seems to be universally acknowledged; or to point out how it has happened, as the only question is how to remedy it. It may, however, be said that it has originated from three causes: an excess of the spirit of liberty, which has made the particular states show a jealousy of all power not in their own hands, and this jealousy has led them to exercise a right of judging, in the last resort, of the measures recommended by Congress, and of acting according to their own opinions of their propriety or necessity; a diffidence in Congress of their own powers, by which they have been timid and indecisive in their resolutions; constantly making concessions to the States, till they have scarcely left themselves the shadow of power; a want of sufficient means at their disposal to answer the public exigencies, and of vigour to draw forth those means, which have occasioned them to depend on the States, individually, to fulfil their engagements with the army, the conse-

* *The Works of Alexander Hamilton*, Henry Cabot Lodge, ed., New York, G. P. Putnam's Sons, 1904, vol. 1, pp. 213–39 *passim*.

quence of which has been to ruin their influence and credit with the army, to establish its dependence on each state, separately, rather than *on them*, that is, than on the whole collectively.

It may be pleaded that Congress had never any definitive powers granted them, and of course could exercise none, could do nothing more than recommend. The manner in which Congress was appointed would warrant, and the public good required, that they should have considered themselves as vested with full power *to preserve the republic from harm*. They have done many of the highest acts of sovereignty, which were always cheerfully submitted to: The declaration of independence, the declaration of war, the levying of an army, creating a navy, emitting money, making alliances with foreign powers, appointing a dictator, etc. All these implications of a complete sovereignty were never disputed, and ought to have been a standard for the whole conduct of administration. Undefined powers are discretionary powers, limited only by the object for which they were given; in the present case, the independence and freedom of America. . .

But the Confederation itself is defective, and requires to be altered. It is neither fit for war, nor peace. The idea of an uncontrollable sovereignty in each State, over its internal police, will defeat the other powers given to Congress, and make our union feeble and precarious. There are instances, without number, where acts necessary for the general good, and which rise out of the powers given to Congress, must interfere with the internal police of the States; and there are as many instances in which the particular States, by arrangements of internal police, can effectually, though indirectly, counteract the arrangements of Congress. . .

The Confederation gives the States, individually, too much influence in the affairs of the army. They should have nothing to do with it. The entire formation and disposal of our military forces ought to belong to Congress. It is an essential cement of the union; and it ought to be the policy of Congress to destroy all ideas of State attachments to the army, and make it look up wholly to them. For this purpose all appointments, promotions, and provisions whatsoever, ought to be made by them. It may be apprehended that this may be dangerous to liberty. But nothing appears more evident to me, than that we run much greater risk of having a weak and disunited federal government, than one which will be able to usurp upon the rights of the people. . .

The forms of our State constitutions must always give them great weight in our affairs, and will make it too difficult to bend them to the pursuit of a common interest, too easy to oppose whatever they do not like, and to form partial combinations, subversive to the general one. There is a wide difference between our situation and that of an empire under one simple form of government, distributed into counties, provinces, or districts, which have no Legislatures, but merely magistratical bodies to execute the laws of a common sovereign. Here the danger is that the sovereign will have too much power, and oppress the parts of which it is composed. In our case, that of an empire composed of confederated States, each with a government completely organized within itself, having all the means to draw its subjects to a close dependence on itself, the danger is directly the reverse. It is that the common sovereign will not have power sufficient to unite the different members together, and direct the common forces to the interest and happiness of the whole. . . A little time hence, some of the States will be powerful empires; and we are so remote from other nations, that we shall have all the leisure and opportunity we can wish to cut each other's throats. . .

The Confederation, too, gives the power of the purse too entirely to the State Legislatures. It should provide perpetual funds, in the disposal of Congress, by a land tax, poll tax, or the like. All imposts upon commerce ought to be laid by Congress, and appropriated to their use; for without certain revenues, a government can have no power. That power which holds the purse-strings absolutely, must rule. This seems to be a medium, which, without making Congress altogether independent, will tend to give reality to its authority.

Another defect in our system is want of method and energy in the administration. This has partly resulted from the other defect; but in a great degree from prejudice and the want of a proper executive. Congress have kept the power too much in their own hands, and have meddled too much with details of every sort. Congress is properly a deliberative corps, and it forgets itself when it attempts to play the executive. It is impossible that a body, numerous as it is, constantly fluctuating, can ever act with sufficient decision, or with system. . .

A single man in each department of the administration . . . would give us a chance of more knowledge, more activity, more responsibility, and, of course, more zeal and attention. Boards partake of a part of the inconveniences of larger asemblies. Their decisions are slower, their energy less, their responsibility more diffused. They will not have the same abilities and knowledge as an administration by single men. Men of the first pretensions will not so readily engage in them, because they will be less conspicuous, of less importance, have less opportunity of distinguishing themselves. . . All these reasons conspire to give a preference to the plan of vesting the great executive departments of the State in the hands of individuals. As these men will be, of course, at all times under the direction of Congress, we shall blend the advantages of a monarchy and republic in our constitution. . .

A third defect is, the fluctuating constitution of our army. This has been a pregnant source of evil; all our military misfortunes, three-fourths of our civil embarrassments, are to be ascribed to it. . .

The imperfect and unequal provision made for the army, is a fourth defect. Without a speedy change, the army must dissolve. It is now a mob rather than an army, without clothing, without pay, without provision, without morals, without discipline. . .

The present mode of supplying the army, by State purchases, is not one of the least considerable defects of our system. It is too precarious a dependence, because the States will never be sufficiently impressed with our necessities. . .

These are the principal defects in the present system that now occur to me. . .

I shall now propose the remedies which appear to me applicable to our circumstances, and necessary to extricate our affairs from their present deplorable situation.

The first step must be to give Congress powers competent to the public exigencies. This may happen in two ways: one by resuming and exercising the discretionary powers I suppose to have been originally vested in them for the safety of the States, and resting their conduct on the candour of their countrymen and the necessity of the conjuncture; the other, by calling immediately a Convention of all the States, with full authority to conclude finally upon a General Confederation, stating to them beforehand, explicitly, the evils arising from a want of power in Congress, and the impossibility of supporting the contest on its present footing, that the delegates may come possessed of proper sentiments, as well as proper authority, to give efficacy to the meeting. Their commission should include a right of vesting Congress with the whole or a proportion of the unoccupied lands, to be employed for the purpose of raising a revenue, reserving the jurisdiction to the States by whom they are granted.

The first plan, I expect, will be thought too bold an expedient by the generality of Congress; and, indeed, their practice hitherto has so riveted the opinion of their want of power, that the success of this experiment may very well be doubted.

I see no objection to the other mode that has any weight in competition with the reasons for it. The Convention should assemble the first of November next. The sooner the better. Our disorders are too violent to admit of a common or lingering remedy. The reasons for which I require them to be vested with plenipotentiary authority are that the business may suffer no delay in the execution, and may, in reality, come to effect. A Convention may agree upon a Confederation; the States, individually, hardly ever will. We must have one, at all events, and a vigorous one, if we mean to succeed in the contest and be happy hereafter. As I said before, to engage the States to comply with this mode, Congress ought to confess to them, plainly and unanimously, the impracticability of supporting our affairs on the present footing, and without a solid coercive union. I ask that the Convention should have a power of vesting the whole or a part of the unoccupied lands in Congress; because it is necessary that body should have some property as a fund for the arrangements of finance; and I know of no other kind that can be given them.

The Confederation, in my opinion, should give Congress a complete sovereignty; except as to that part of internal police which relates to the rights of property and life among individuals, and to raising money by internal taxes. It is necessary that everything belonging to this should be regulated by the State Legislatures. Congress should have complete sovereignty in all that relates to war, peace, trade, finance, and to the management of foreign affairs; the right of declaring war; of raising armies, officering, paying them, directing their motions in every respect; of equipping fleets, and doing the same with them; of building fortifications, arsenals, magazines, &c., &c.; of making peace on such conditions as they think proper; of regulating trade, determining with what countries it shall be carried on; granting indulgences; laying prohibitions on all the articles of export or import; imposing duties, granting bounties and premiums for raising, exporting or importing; and applying to their own use the product of these duties, only giving credit to the States on whom they are raised in the general account of revenues and expense; instituting admiralty courts, &c.; of coining money, establishing banks on such terms, and with such privileges, as they think proper; appropriating funds, and doing whatever else relates to the operations of finance; transacting everything with foreign nations, making alliances, offensive and defensive, treaties of commerce, &c., &c.

The Confederation should provide certain perpetual revenues, productive and easy of collection; a land tax, poll tax, or the like, which, together with the duties on trade, and the unlocated lands, would give Congress a substantial existence, and a stable foundation for their schemes of finance. What more supplies were necessary, should be occasionally demanded of the States, in the present mode of quotas.

The second step I would recommend is, that Congress should instantly appoint the following great officers of State: A Secretary for Foreign Affairs; a President of War; a President of Marine; A Financier; a President of Trade. Instead of this last, a Board of Trade may be preferable, as the regulations of trade are slow and gradual, and require prudence and experience more than other qualities for which boards are very well adapted.

Congress should choose for these offices, men of the first abilities, property, and character, in the Continent; and such as have had the best opportunities of being acquainted with the several branches. . .

In my opinion, a plan of this kind would be of inconceivable utility to our affairs; its benefits would be very speedily felt. It would give new life and energy to the operations of government. . .

I have only skimmed the surface of the different subjects I have introduced. . . I am persuaded a solid confederation, a permanent army, a reasonable prospect of subsisting it, would give us treble consideration in Europe, and produce a peace this winter.

If a Convention is called, the minds of all the States and the people ought to be prepared to receive its determinations by sensible and popular writings, which should conform to the views of Congress. There are epochs in human affairs, when *novelty* even is useful. If a general opinion prevails that the old way is bad, whether true or false, and this obstructs or relaxes the operations of the public service, a change is necessary, if it be but for the sake of change. This is exactly the case now. It is an universal sentiment that our present system is a bad one, and that things do not go right on this account. The measure of a Convention would revive the hopes of the people and give a new direction to their passions, which may be improved in carrying points of substantial utility. . .

And in future, my dear sir, two things let me recommend as fundamental rules of conduct to Congress: to attach the army to them by every motive; to maintain an air of authority (not domineering) in all their measures with the States. The manner in which a thing is done has more influence than is commonly imagined. Men are governed by opinion; this opinion is as much influenced by appearances as by realities. If a government appears to be confident of its own powers, it is the surest way to inspire the same confidence in others. If it is diffident, it may be certain there will be a still greater diffidence in others, and that its authority will not only be distrusted, controverted, but contemned.

I wish, too, Congress would always consider, that a kindness consists as much in the manner as in the thing. The best things, done hesitatingly, and with an ill grace, lose their effect, and produce disgust rather than satisfaction or gratitude. In what Congress have at any time done for the army, they have commonly been too late. They have seemed to yield to importunity, rather than to sentiments of justice, or to a regard to the accommodation of their troops. An attention to this idea is of more importance than it may be thought. I, who have seen all the workings and progress of the present discontents, am convinced that a want of this has not been among the most inconsiderable causes. . .

4. *As too much power leads to despotism, too little leads to anarchy*

ALEXANDER HAMILTON, *The Continentalist*, 12 July 1781 and 4 July 1782 *

It would be the extreme of vanity in us not to be sensible that we began this revolution with very vague and confined notions of the practical business of government. To the greater part of us it was a novelty; of those who under the former constitution had had opportunities of acquiring experience, a large proportion adhered to the opposite side, and the remainder can only be supposed to have possessed ideas adapted to the narrow colonial sphere in which they had been accustomed to move, not of that enlarged kind suited to the government of an independent nation. . .

On a retrospect, however, of our transactions, under the disadvantages with which we commenced, it is perhaps more to be wondered at that we have done so well than that we have not done better. There are, indeed, some traits in our conduct as conspicuous for sound policy as others for magnanimity. But, on the other hand, it must also be confessed, there have been many false steps, many chimerical projects and utopian speculations, in the management of our civil as well as of our military affairs. A part of these were the natural effects of the spirit of the times, dictated by our situation. An extreme jealousy of power is the attendant on all popular revolutions, and has seldom been without its evils. It is to this source we are to trace many of the fatal mistakes which have so deeply endangered the common cause; particularly that defect which will be the object of these remarks—a want of power in Congress. . .

In the first stages of the controversy, it was excusable to err. Good intentions, rather than great skill, were to have been expected from us. But we have now had sufficient time for reflection, and experience as ample as unfortunate, to rectify our errors. To persist in them becomes disgraceful, and even criminal, and belies that character of good sense, and a quick discernment of our interests, which, in spite of our mistakes, we have been hitherto allowed. It will prove that our sagacity is limited to interests of inferior moment, and

* Henry Cabot Lodge, ed., op. cit. vol. 1, pp. 243–87 *passim*.

that we are incapable of those enlightened and liberal views necessary to make us a great and a flourishing people.

History is full of examples where, in contests for liberty, a jealousy of power has either defeated the attempts to recover or preserve it, in the first instance, or has afterward subverted it by clogging government with too great precautions for its felicity, or by leaving too wide a door for sedition and popular licentiousness. In a government framed for durable liberty, not less regard must be paid to giving the magistrate a proper degree of authority to make and execute the laws with rigor, than to guard against encroachments upon the rights of the community. As too much power leads to despotism, too little leads to anarchy, and both, eventually, to the ruin of the people. These are maxims well known, but never sufficiently attended to, in adjusting the frames of governments. Some momentary interest or passion is sure to give a wrong bias, and pervert the most favorable opportunities. . .

In comparison of our governments with those of the ancient republics, we must, without hesitation, give the preference to our own; because every power with us is exercised by representation, not in tumultuary assemblies of the collective body of the people, where the art or impudence of the *Orator* or *Tribune*, rather than the utility or justice of the measure, could seldom fail to govern. Yet, whatever may be the advantage on our side in such a comparison, men who estimate the value of institutions, not from prejudices of the moment, but from experience and reason, must be persuaded that the same *jealousy of power* has prevented our reaping all the advantages from the examples of other nations which we ought to have done, and has rendered our constitutions in many respects feeble and imperfect.

Perhaps the evil is not very great in respect to our State constitutions; for notwithstanding their imperfections, they may for some time be made to operate in such a manner as to answer the purposes of the common defence and the maintenance of order; and they seem to have, in themselves, and in the progress of society among us, the seeds of improvement.

But this is not the case with respect to the Federal Government; if it is too weak at first, it will continually grow weaker. The ambition and local interests of the respective members will be constantly undermining and usurping upon its prerogatives till it comes to a dissolution, if a partial combination of some of the more powerful ones does not bring it to a more *speedy* and *violent end*. . .

Political societies in close neighborhood must either be strongly united under one government, or there will infallibly exist emulations and quarrels; this is in human nature, and we have no reason to think ourselves wiser or better than other men. Some of the larger States, a small number of years hence, will be in themselves populous, rich, and powerful in all those circumstances calculated to inspire ambition and nourish ideas of separation and independence. Though it will ever be their true interest to preserve the Union, their vanity and self-importance will be very likely to overpower that motive, and make them seek to place themselves at the head of particular confederacies independent of the general one. A schism once introduced, competitions of boundary and rivalships of commerce will easily afford pretexts for war.

European powers may have many inducements for fomenting these divisions and playing us off against each other; but without such a disposition in them, if separations once take place we shall, of course, embrace different interests and connections. . .

We already see symptoms of the evils to be apprehended. . .

Where the blame of this may lie is not so much the question as what are the proper remedies, yet it may not be amiss to remark that too large a share has fallen upon Congress. That body is no doubt chargeable with mistakes, but perhaps its greatest has been too much readiness to make concessions of the powers implied in its original trust. This is partly to be attributed to an excessive complaisance to the spirit which has evidently actuated a majority of the States, a desire of monopolizing all power in themselves. Congress has been responsible for the administration of affairs, without the means of fulfilling that responsibility. . .

The vesting Congress with the power of regulating trade ought to have been a principal object of the Confederation for a variety of reasons. It is as necessary for the purposes of commerce as of revenue. There are some who maintain that trade will regulate itself, and is not to be benefited by the encouragements or restraints of government. Such persons will imagine that there is no need of a common directing power. This is one of those wild speculative paradoxes, which have grown into credit among us, contrary to the uniform practice and sense of the most enlightened nations. . .

Commerce, like other things, has its fixed principles, according to which it must be regulated. If these are understood and observed, it will be promoted by the attention of government; if unknown, or violated, it will be injured—but it is the same with every other part of administration.

To preserve the balance of trade in favor of a nation ought to be a leading aim of its policy. The avarice of individuals may frequently find its account in pursuing channels of traffic prejudicial to that balance, to which the government may be able to oppose effectual impediments. There may, on the other hand, be a possibility of opening new sources, which, though accompanied with great difficulties in the commencement, would in the event amply reward the trouble and expense of bringing them to perfection. The undertaking may often exceed the influence and capitals of individuals, and may require no small assistance, as well from the revenue as from the authority of the state.

The contrary opinion which has grown into a degree of vogue among us, has originated in the injudicious attempts made at different times to effect a regulation of prices. It became a cant phrase among the opposers of these attempts, that trade must regulate itself; by which at first was only meant that it had its fundamental laws, agreeable to which its general operations must be directed, and that any violent attempts in opposition to these would commonly miscarry. In this sense the maxim was reasonable, but it has since been extended to militate against all interference by the sovereign; an extreme as little reconcilable with experience or common sense as the practice it was first framed to discredit. . .

Perhaps it may be thought that the power of regulation will be best placed in the governments of the several States, and that a general superintendence is unnecessary. If the States had distinct interests, were unconnected with each other, their own governments would then be the proper, and could be the only, depositories of such a power; but as they are parts of a whole, with a common interest in trade, as in other things, there ought to be a common direction in that as in all other matters. It is easy to conceive that many cases may occur in which it would be beneficial to all the States to encourage or suppress a particular branch of trade, while it would be detrimental to either to attempt it without the concurrence of the rest, and where the experiment would probably be left untried for fear of a want of that concurrence.

No mode can be so convenient as a source of revenue to the United States. It is agreed that imposts on trade, when not immoderate, or improperly laid, are one of the most eligible species of taxation. They fall in a great measure upon articles not of absolute necessity, and being partly transferred to the price of the commodity, are so far imperceptibly paid by the consumer. It is therefore that mode which may be exercised by the Federal Government with least exception or disgust. Congress can easily possess all the information necessary to impose the duties with judgment, and the collection can without difficulty be made by their own officers.

They can have no temptation to abuse this power, because the motive of revenue will check its own extremes. Experience has shown that moderate duties are more productive than high ones. When they are low, a nation can trade abroad on better terms, its imports and exports will be larger, the duties will be regularly paid, and arising on a greater quantity of commodities, will yield more in the aggregate than when they are so high as to operate either as a prohibition, or as an inducement to evade them by illicit practices.

It is difficult to assign any good reason why Congress should be more liable to abuse the powers with which they are entrusted than the State Assemblies. . . It is to be presumed that Congress will be in general better composed for abilities, as well as for integrity, than any assembly on the continent. . .

It is too much characteristic of our national temper to be ingenious in finding out and magnifying the minutest disadvantages, and to reject measures of evident utility, even of necessity, to avoid trivial and sometimes imaginary evils. We seem not to reflect that in human society there is scarcely any plan, however salutary to the whole and to every part, by the share each has in the common prosperity, but in one way, or another, and under particular circumstances, will operate more to the benefit of some parts than of others. Unless we can overcome this narrow disposition and learn to estimate measures by their general tendencies, we shall never be a great or a happy people, if we remain a people at all.

Let us see what will be the consequences of not authorizing the Federal Government to regulate the trade of these States. Besides the want of revenue and of power, besides the immediate risk to our independence and the dangers of all the future evils of a precarious Union, besides the deficiency of a wholesome concert and provident superintendence to advance the general prosperity of trade, the direct consequence will be that the landed interest and the laboring poor will in the first place fall a sacrifice to the trading interest, and the whole eventually to a bad system of policy made necessary by the want of such regulating power.

Each State will be afraid to impose duties on its commerce, lest the other States, not doing the same, should enjoy greater advantages than itself, by being able to afford native commodities cheaper abroad and foreign commodities cheaper at home.

A part of the evils resulting from this would be a loss to the revenue of those moderate duties which, without being injurious to commerce, are allowed to be the most agreeable species of taxes to the people. . .

Many branches of trade, hurtful to the common interest, would be continued for want of proper checks and discouragements. As revenues must be found to satisfy the public exigencies in peace and in war, too great a proportion of taxes will fall directly upon land, and upon the necessaries of life—the produce of that land. The influence of these evils will be to render landed property fluctuating and less valuable; to oppress the poor by raising the prices of necessaries; to injure commerce by encouraging the consumption of foreign luxuries, by increasing the value of labor, by lessening the quantity of home productions, enhancing their prices at foreign markets, of course obstructing their sale, and enabling other nations to supplant us. . .

Nothing can be more mistaken than the collision and rivalship which almost always subsist between the landed and trading interests, for the truth is they are so inseparably interwoven that one cannot be injured without injury nor benefited without benefit to the other. Oppress trade, lands sink in value; make it flourish, their value rises. Incumber husbandry, trade declines; encourage agriculture, commerce revives. The progress of this mutual reaction might be easily delineated, but it is too obvious to every man who turns his thoughts, however superficially, upon the subject to require it. It is only to be regretted that it is too often lost sight of when the seductions of some immediate advantage or exemption tempt us to sacrifice the future to the present. . .

There is something noble and magnificent in the perspective of a great Federal Republic, closely linked in the pursuit of a common interest, tranquil and prosperous at home, respectable abroad; but there is something proportionably diminutive and contemptible in the prospect of a number of petty States, with the appearance only of union, jarring, jealous, and perverse, without any determined direction, fluctuating and unhappy at home, weak and insignificant by their dissensions in the eyes of other nations.

Happy America, if those to whom thou hast intrusted the guardianship of thy infancy know how to provide for thy future repose, but miserable and undone, if their negligence or ignorance permits the spirit of discord to erect her banner on the ruins of thy tranquillity!

5. *We desire and instruct you strenuously to oppose all encroachments upon the sovereignty and jurisdiction of the separate states*

Instructions from Fairfax County, Virginia, to its representatives in the Virginia legislature, 30 May 1783 *

We desire and instruct you strenuously to oppose all encroachments of the American Congress upon the sovereignty and jurisdiction of the separate States; and every assumption of power, not expressly vested in them, by the Articles of Confederation. If experience shall prove that further powers are necessary and safe, they can be granted only by additional articles to the Confederation, duly acceded to by all the States; for if Congress, upon the plea of necessity, or upon any pretence whatever, can arrogate powers not warranted by the Articles of Confederation, in one instance, they may in another, or in an hundred; every repetition will be strengthened and confirmed by precedents.

And in particular we desire and instruct you to oppose any attempts which may be made by Congress to obtain a perpetual revenue, or the appointment of revenue officers. Were these powers superadded to those they already possess, the Articles of Confederation, and the Constitutions of Government in the different States would prove mere parchment bulwarks to American liberty.

We like not the language of the late address from Congress to the different States, and of the report of their committee upon the subject of revenue, published in the same pamphlet. If they are carefully and impartially examined, they will be found to exhibit strong proofs of lust of power. . . After having reluctantly given up part of what they found they could not maintain, they still insist that the several States shall invest *the United States in Congress assembled with a power to levy*, for the use of the United States, the following duties, &c., and that the revenue officers shall be amenable to Congress. The very style is alarming. The proposed duties may be proper, but the separate States only can safely have *the power of levying taxes*. Congress should not have even the appearance of such a power. Forms generally imply substance, and such a precedent may be applied to dangerous purposes hereafter. When the same man, or set of men, holds both the sword and the purse, there is an end of liberty. . .

6. *Our independence is acknowledged only in our united character as an empire*

GEORGE WASHINGTON to Governor William Livingston, 12 June 1783 †

. . . The Citizens of America, placed in the most enviable condition as the sole Lords and Proprietors of a vast tract of Continent, comprehending all the

* Kate Mason Rowland, *The Life of George Mason*, New York, 1892, vol. II, pp. 50–51.

† *The Collector*, Mary A. Benjamin, ed., New York, February 1947, vol. LX, no. 2, whole no. 657, pp. 25–30.

various Soils and climates of the World, and abounding with all the necessaries and conveniences of life, are now, by the late satisfactory pacification, acknowledged to be possessed of absolute freedom and Independency. They are from this period to be considered as the Actors on a most conspicuous theatre, which seems to be peculiarly designated by Providence for the display of human greatness and felicity. Here they are not only surrounded with every thing which can contribute to the completion of private and domestic enjoyment, but Heaven has crowned all its other blessings, by giving a fairer Opportunity for political happiness, than any other Nation has ever been favored with.—Nothing can illustrate these observations more forcibly, than a recollection of the happy conjuncture of times and circumstances, under which our Republic assumed its Rank among the Nations. The foundation of our Empire was not laid in the gloomy Age of ignorance and superstition, but at an Epocha when the rights of mankind were better understood, and more clearly defined than at any former period, the researches of the human mind, after social happiness, have been carried to a great extent, the Treasures of knowledge acquired by the labours of Philosophers, Sages and Legislators through a long succession of years, are laid open for our use, and their collected wisdom may be happily applied in the establishment of our forms of Government, the free cultivation of Letters, the unbounded extension of Commerce, the progressive refinement of manners, the growing liberality of sentiment, and above all the pure and benign light of Revelation have had a meliorating influence on mankind, and encreased the blessings of Society—At this auspicious period, the United States came into existence as a Nation, and if the Citizens should not be completely free and happy, the fault will be entirely their own.

Such is our situation, and such are our prospects; but notwithstanding the cup of blessing is thus reached out to us, notwithstanding happiness is ours if we have a disposition to seize the occasion & make it our own; yet, it appears to me there is an option still left to the United States of America, that it is in their choice, and depends upon their conduct, whether they will be respectable and prosperous, or contemptible and miserable as a Nation—This is the time of their political probation—this is the moment when the Eyes of the whole World are turned upon them—this is the moment to establish or ruin their national Character for ever—this is the favorable moment to give such a tone to our Federal Government as will enable it to answer the ends of its institution—or this may be the ill-fated moment for relaxing the powers of the Union, annihilating the cement of the Confederation, and exposing us to become the sport of European Politics, which may play one State against another to prevent their growing importance, and to serve their own interested purposes. . .

With this conviction of the importance of the present crisis, silence in me would be a crime; I will therefore speak to your Excellency the language of freedom and of sincerity without disguise. . .

There are four things which I humbly conceive are essential to the well being, I may even venture to say, to the existence of the United States as an independent Power.

1st An indissoluble Union of the States under one Federal Head

2d A sacred Regard to Public Justice

3d The adoption of a proper Peace establishment and

4thly The prevalence of that pacific and friendly disposition among the people of the United States, which will induce them to forget their local prejudices and policies, to make those mutual concessions which are Requisite to the general prosperity, and in some instances, to sacrifice their individual advantages to the interests of the community.

These are the Pillars on which the glorious fabric of our Independency and National Character must be supported;—Liberty is the basis—and whoever would dare to sap the foundation, or overturn the Structure, under whatever specious pretext, he may attempt it, will merit the bitterest execration and the severest punishment which can be inflicted by his injured Country.

On the three first Articles I will make a few observations, leaving the last to the good sense and serious consideration of those immediately concerned.

Under the first head, altho' it may not be necessary or proper for me in this place to enter into a particular disquisition of the principles of the Union, and to take up the great question which has been frequently agitated, whether it be expedient and requisite for the States to delegate a larger proportion of Power to Congress, or not—Yet it will be a part of my duty and that of every true Patriot to assert without reserve & to insist upon, the following positions—That unless the States will suffer Congress to exercise those prerogatives they are undoubtedly invested with by the Constitution, every thing must very rapidly tend to Anarchy and confusion—That it is indispensable to the happiness of the individual States, that there should be lodged some where a Supreme Power, to regulate and govern the general concerns of the confederated Republic, without which the Union cannot be of long duration—That there must be a faithful & pointed compliance on the part of every State with the late proposals and demands of Congress, or the most fatal consequences will ensue—That whatever measures have a tendency to dissolve the Union, or contribute to violate or lessen the Sovereign Authority ought to be considered as hostile to the Liberty and Independency of America, and the Authors of them treated accordingly—and lastly that unless we can be enabled by the concurrence of the States to participate of the Fruits of the Revolution, and enjoy the essential benefits of civil Society, under a form of Government so free & uncorrupted, so happily guarded against the danger of oppression, as has been devised and adopted by the Articles of Confederation, that it will be a subject of regret that so much blood and treasure have been lavished for no purpose, that so many sufferings have been encountered without a compensation, and that so many sacrifices have been in vain.

Many other considerations might here be adduced to prove, that without an entire conformity to the spirit of the Union, we cannot exist as an Independent Power; it will be sufficient for my purposes to mention but one or two which seem to me of the greatest importance—It is only in our united Character as an Empire that our Independence is acknowledged, that our power can be regarded, or our Credit supported, among foreign Nations—The Treaties of the European Powers with the United States of America, will have no validity on a dissolution of the Union—We shall be left nearly in a State of Nature, or we may find by our own unhappy experience, that there is a natural and necessary progression from the extreme of Anarchy, to the extreme of Tyranny; and that arbitrary power is most easily established, on the ruins of Liberty abused to licentiousness.

As to the second Article—which respects the performance of Public Justice. . .

The ability of the Country to discharge the debts which have been incurred in its defence is not to be doubted, an inclination, I flatter myself, will not be wanting—the path of our duty is plain before us—honesty will be found, on every experiment, to be the best and only true policy—let us then as a nation be just—let us fulfill the public Contracts, which Congress had undoubtedly a right to make for the purpose of carrying on the War, with the same good faith we suppose ourselves bound to perform our private engagements; in the mean time, let an attention to the cheerful performance of their proper business as Individuals and as members of society, be earnestly inculcated in the Citizens of America,—then will they strengthen the hands of Government and be happy under its protection: every one will reap the fruit of his Labours—every one will enjoy his own acquisitions without molestation and without danger.

In this State of absolute freedom and perfect security, who will grudge to yield a very little of his property to support the common interests of society, and ensure the protection of Government? Who does not remember the frequent declarations at the commencement of the War, that we should be completely satisfied, if at the expence of one half, we could defend the Remainder of our possessions? Where is the man to be found who wishes to remain indebted for the defence of his own person and property, to the exertions, the bravery, and the blood of others, without making one generous effort to repay the debt of honor and of gratitude:—In what part of the Continent shall we find any Man, or body of Men, who would not blush to stand up & propose measures, purposely calculated to rob the soldier of his Stipend, and the public Creditor of his due? and were it possible that such a flagrant instance of Injustice could ever happen, would it not excite the general indignation, and tend to bring down upon the Authors of such measures the aggravated vengeance of Heaven?—

If after all, a spirit of disunion or a temper of obstinacy & perverseness should manifest itself in any of the States, if such an ungracious disposition should attempt to frustrate all the happy effects that might be expected to flow from the Union, if there should be a refusal to comply with the requisitions for funds to discharge the Annual Interest of the public debts, and if that refusal should revive again all those jealousies, and produce all those evils which are now happily removed,—Congress, who have in all their Transactions shown a great degree of Magnanimity and justice, will stand justified in the sight of God and Man—and the State alone which puts itself in opposition to the aggregate Wisdom of the Continent, & follows such mistaken & pernicious Councils, will be responsible for all the consequences. . .

It is necessary to say but a few words on the third topic which was proposed, and which regards particularly the defence of the Republic—As there can be little doubt that Congress will recommend a proper Peace Establishment for the United States, in which a due attention will be paid to the importance of placing the Militia of the Union, upon a regular & respectable footing; If this should be the case, I would beg leave to urge the great advantage of it in the strongest terms.—The Militia of this Country must be considered as the Palladium of our security, and the first effectual resort in case of hostility. It is essential therefore, that the same system should pervade the whole—that the formation and discipline of the Militia of the Continent should be absolutely Uniform, and that the same species of Arms—Accoutrements, & Military Apparatus, should be introduced in every part of the United States; No one who has not learned it from experience can conceive the difficulty, expence, & confusion which result from a contrary system, or the vague Arrangements which have hitherto prevailed.

If in treating of political points, a greater latitude than usual has been taken in the course of this address—the importance of the Crisis, and the magnitude of the objects in discussion, must be my apology—It is, however, neither my wish nor expectation that the preceding observations should claim any regard, except so far as they shall appear to be dictated by a good intention—consonant to the immutable rules of Justice—calculated to produce a liberal system of policy, and founded on whatever experience may have been acquired, by a long and close attention to public business—Here I might speak with the more confidence from my actual observations and, if it would not swell this Letter (already too prolix) beyond the bounds I had prescribed my self, I could demonstrate to every mind open to conviction, that in less time, and with much less expence than has been incurred, the War might have been brought to the same happy conclusion, if the resources of the Continent could have been properly brought forth—that the distresses & disappointments which have very often ocurred, have in too many instances resulted more from a want of energy in the Continental Government, than a deficiency of means in the particular States—That the inefficacy of measures arising from the want of an adequate authority in the supreme Power, from a partial compliance with the Requisitions of Congress in some of the States, and from a failure of punctuality in others, while it tended to damp the zeal of those which were more willing to exert themselves; served also to accumulate the expences of the War, and to frustrate the best concerted Plans—and that the discouragement occasioned by the complicated difficulties & embarrassments, in which our affairs were by this means involved, would have long ago produced the dissolution of any Army less patient, less virtuous, and less persevering, than that which I have had the honor to command. But while I mention these things, which are notorious facts, as the defects of our Federal Constitution, particularly in the prosecution of a War—I beg it may be understood, that as I have ever taken a pleasure in gratefully acknowledging the assistance and support I have derived from every class of Citizens, so shall I always be happy to do justice to the unparalleled exertions of the individual States, on many interesting occasions. . .

7. *We are apprehensive . . .*

Reply of Massachusetts delegates in Congress to instructions from the Massachusetts legislature directing them to introduce a resolution in Congress calling for a constitutional convention, 3 September 1785 *

The great object of the Revolution was the establishment of good government, and each of the states, in forming their own, as well as the federal constitution, have adopted republican principles. Notwithstanding this, plans have been artfully laid, and vigorously pursued, which had they been successful, we think would inevitably have changed our republican governments into baleful aristocracies. Those plans are frustrated, but the same spirit remains in their abettors. And the institution of the Cincinnati, honorable and beneficent as the views may have been of the officers who compose it, we fear, if not totally abolished, will have the same fatal tendency. What the effect then may be of calling a Convention to revise the Confederation generally, we leave with your Excellency and the honorable Legislature to determine. We are apprehensive and it is our duty to declare it, that such a measure would produce thro'out the Union, an exertion of the friends of an aristocracy to send members who would promote a change of government, and we can form some judgment of the plan which such members would report to Congress. But should the members be altogether republican, such have been the declamation of designing men against the Confederation generally; against the rotation of members, which perhaps is the best check to corruption, and against the mode of altering the Confederation by the unanimous consent of the Legislatures, which effectually prevents innovations in the Articles by intrigue or surprise, that we think there is great danger of a report which would invest Congress with powers that the honorable legislature have not the most distant intention to delegate. Perhaps it may be said this can produce no ill effect because Congress may correct the report however exceptionable, or if passed by them, any of the states may refuse to ratify it. True it is that Congress and the states have such powers, but would not such a report affect the tranquility and weaken the government of the Union? We have already considered the operation of the report as it would respect Congress; and if animosities and parties would naturally arise from their rejecting it, how much would these be increased it the report approved by Congress and some of the states, should be rejected by other states? Would there not be danger of a party spirit's being thus more generally diffused and warmly supported? Far distant we know it to be from the honorable legislature of Massachusetts to give up a single principle of republicanism, but when a general revision shall have proceeded from their motion, and a report which to them may be highly offensive, shall have been confirmed by seven states in Congress, and ratified by several Legislatures, will not these be ready to charge Massachusetts with inconsistency in being the first to oppose a measure which the state will be said to have originated? Massachusetts

* *Letters of Members of the Continental Congress*, E. C. Burnett, ed., vol. VIII, pp. 208–9.

has great weight and is considered as one of the most republican states in the Union; and when it is known that the legislature have proposed a general revision, there can be no doubt that they will be represented as being convinced of the necessity of increasing generally the powers of Congress, and the opinion of the state will be urged with such art as to convince numbers that the Articles of the Confederation are altogether exceptionable. Thus, whilst measures are taken to guard against the evils arising from the want in one or two particulars of power in Congress, we are in great danger of incurring the other extreme. 'More power in Congress' has been the cry from all quarters, but especially of those whose views, not being confined to a government that will best promote the happiness of the people, are extended to one that will afford lucrative employments, civil and military. Such a government is an aristocracy, which would require a standing army and a numerous train of pensioners and placemen to prop and support its exalted administration. To recommend one's self to such an administration would be to secure an establishment for life and at the same time to provide for his posterity. These are pleasing prospects, which republican governments do not afford, and it is not to be wondered at that many persons of elevated views and idle habits in these states are desirous of the change. We are for increasing the power of Congress as far as it will promote the happiness of the people, but at the same time are clearly of opinion that every measure should be avoided which would strengthen the hands of the enemies to a free government. And that an administration of the present Confederation with all its inconveniences, is preferable to the risk of general dissensions and animosities which may approach to anarchy and prepare the way to a ruinous system of government.

8. *An elective despotism was not the government we fought for*

THOMAS JEFFERSON, *Notes on Virginia*, 1781–82 *

QUERY XIII

The Constitution of the State [Virginia, 1776] and Its Several Charters.

. . . This constitution was formed when we were new and unexperienced in the science of government. It was the first, too, which was formed in the whole United States. No wonder then that time and trial have discovered very capital defects in it.

1. The majority of the men in the State, who pay and fight for its support, are unrepresented in the legislature, the roll of freeholders entitled to vote not including generally the half of those on the roll of the militia, or of the tax-gatherers.

2. Among those who share the representation, the shares are very unequal. Thus the county of Warwick, with only one hundred fighting men, has an

* *The Writings of Thomas Jefferson*, H. A. Washington, ed., 1854, New York, Riker, Thorne & Co., Washington, D.C., Taylor and Maury, vol. VIII, pp. 352–91 *passim*.

equal representation with the county of London, which has one thousand seven hundred and forty-six. . .

. . . It will appear at once that nineteen thousand men, living below the falls of the rivers, possess half the senate, and want four members only of possessing a majority of the house of delegates; a want more than supplied by the vicinity of their situation to the seat of government, and of course the greater degree of convenience and punctuality with which their members may and will attend in the legislature. These nineteen thousand, therefore, living in one part of the country, give law to upwards of thirty thousand living in another, and appoint all their chief officers, executive and judiciary. From the difference of their situation and circumstances, their interests will often be very different.

3. The senate is, by its constitution, too homogenous with the house of delegates. Being chosen by the same electors, at the same time, and out of the same subjects, the choice falls of course on men of the same description. The purpose of establishing different houses of legislation is to introduce the influence of different interests or different principles. Thus in Great Britain it is said their constitution relies on the house of commons for honesty, and the lords for wisdom; which would be a rational reliance, if honesty were to be bought with money, and if wisdom were hereditary. In some of the American States, the delegates and senators are so chosen, as that the first represent the persons, and the second the property of the State. But with us, wealth and wisdom have equal chance for admission into both houses. We do not, therefore, derive from the separation of our legislature into two houses, those benefits which a proper complication of principles are capable of producing, and those which alone can compensate the evils which may be produced by their dissensions.

4. All the powers of government, legislative, executive, and judiciary, result to the legislative body. The concentrating these in the same hands is precisely the definition of despotic government. It will be no alleviation that these powers will be exercised by a plurality of hands, and not by a single one. One hundred and seventy-three despots would surely be as oppressive as one. Let those who doubt it turn their eyes on the republic of Venice. As little will it avail us that they are chosen by ourselves. An *elective despotism* was not the government we fought for, but one which should not only be founded on free principles, but in which the powers of government should be so divided and balanced among several bodies of magistracy, as that no one could transcend their legal limits, without being effectually checked and restrained by the others. For this reason that convention which passed the ordinance of government, laid its foundation on this basis, that the legislative, executive, and judiciary departments should be separate and distinct, so that no person should exercise the powers of more than one of them at the same time. But no barrier was provided between these several powers. The judiciary and executive members were left dependent on the legislative, for their subsistence in office, and some of them for their continuance in it. If, therefore, the legislature assumes executive and judiciary powers, no opposition is likely to be made; nor, if made, can it be effectual; because in that case they may put their

proceedings into the form of an act of assembly, which will render them obligatory on the other branches. They have, accordingly, in many instances, decided rights which should have been left to judiciary controversy; and the direction of the executive, during the whole time of their session, is becoming habitual and familiar. . . And this will probably be the case for some time to come. But it will not be a very long time. Mankind soon learn to make interested uses of every right and power which they possess, or may assume. The public money and public liberty, intended to have been deposited with three branches of magistracy, but found inadvertently to be in the hands of one only, will soon be discovered to be sources of wealth and dominion to those who hold them. . . Nor should our assembly be deluded by the integrity of their own purposes, and conclude that these unlimited powers will never be abused, because themselves are not disposed to abuse them. They should look forward to a time, and that not a distant one, when a corruption in this, as in the country from which we derive our origin, will have seized the heads of government, and be spread by them through the body of the people; when they will purchase the voices of the people, and make them pay the price. Human nature is the same on every side of the Atlantic, and will be alike influenced by the same causes. The time to guard against corruption and tyranny, is before they shall have gotten hold of us. It is better to keep the wolf out of the fold, than to trust to drawing his teeth and talons after he shall have entered. To render these considerations the more cogent, we must observe in addition:

5. That the ordinary legislature may alter the constitution itself. On the discontinuance of assemblies, it became necessary to substitute in their place some other body, competent to the ordinary business of government, and to the calling forth the powers of the State for the maintenance of our opposition to Great Britain. Conventions were therefore introduced, consisting of two delegates from each county, meeting together and forming one house, on the plan of the former house of burgesses, to whose places they succeeded. These were at first chosen anew for every particular session. But in March 1775, they recommended to the people to choose a convention, which should continue in office a year. This was done, accordingly, in April 1775, and in the July following that convention passed an ordinance for the election of delegates in the month of April annually. . . Under this ordinance, at the annual election in April 1776, a convention for the year was chosen. Independence, and the establishment of a new form of government, were not even yet the objects of the people at large. . .

So far as a temporary organization of government was necessary to render our opposition energetic, so far their organization was valid. But they received in their creation no power but what were given to every legislature before and since. They could not, therefore, pass an act transcendent to the powers of other legislatures. . . So far, and no farther authorized, they organized the government by the ordinance entitled a constitution or form of government. It pretends to no higher authority than the other ordinances of the same session; it does not say that it shall be perpetual; that it shall be unalterable by other legislatures; that it shall be transcendent above the powers of those who they knew would have equal power with themselves. . . The other States in the union have been of opinion that to render a form of government unalterable by ordinary acts of assembly, the people must delegate persons with special powers. They have accordingly chosen special conventions to form and fix their governments. The individuals then who maintain the contrary opinion in this country, should have the modesty to suppose it possible that they may be wrong, and the rest of America right. But if there be only a possibility of their being wrong, if only a plausible doubt remains of the validity of the ordinance of government, is it not better to remove that doubt by placing it on a bottom which none will dispute? If they be right we shall only have the unnecessary trouble of meeting once in convention. If they be wrong, they expose us to the hazard of having no fundamental rights at all. . .

6. That the assembly exercises a power of determining the quorum of their own body which may legislate for us. After the establishment of the new form they adhered to the *Lex majoris partis*, founded in common law as well as common right. It is the natural law of every assembly of men, whose numbers are not fixed by any other law. They continued for some time to require the presence of a majority of their whole number, to pass an act. But the British parliament fixes its own quorum; our former assemblies fixed their own quorum; and one precedent in favor of power is stronger than an hundred against it. The house of delegates, therefore, have [June 4, 1781] lately voted that, during the present dangerous invasion, forty members shall be a house to proceed to business. . . When, therefore, it is considered, that there is no legal obstacle to the assumption by the assembly of all the powers legislative, executive, and judiciary, and that these may come to the hands of the smallest rag of delegation, surely the people will say, and their representatives, while yet they have honest representatives, will advise them to say, that they will not acknowledge as laws any acts not considered and assented to by the major part of their delegates.

In enumerating the defects of the constitution, it would be wrong to count among them what is only the error of particular persons. In December 1776, our circumstances being much distressed, it was proposed in the house of delegates to create a *dictator*, invested with every power legislative, executive, and judiciary, civil and military, of life and of death, over our persons and over our properties; and in June 1781, again under calamity, the same proposition was repeated, and wanted a few votes only of being passed. One who entered into this contest from a pure love of liberty, and a sense of injured rights, who determined to make every sacrifice, and to meet every danger, for the re-establishment of those rights on a firm basis, who did not mean to expend his blood and substance for the wretched purpose of changing this matter for that, but to place the powers of governing him in a plurality of hands of his own choice, so that the corrupt will of no one man might in future oppress him, must stand confounded and dismayed when he is told, that a considerable portion of that plurality had meditated the surrender of them into a single hand, and, in lieu of a limited monarchy, to deliver him over to a despotic one! . . . In God's name, from whence have they derived this power? . . . Is it from any principle in our new constitution expressed or implied? Every lineament expressed or implied, is in full opposition to it. Its fundamental principle is, that the State shall be governed as a commonwealth. It provides a republican organization, proscribes under the name of *prerogative* the exercise of all powers undefined by the laws; places on this basis the whole system of our laws; and by consolidating them together, chooses that they should be left to stand or fall together, never providing for any circumstances, nor admitting that such could arise, wherein either should be suspended; no, not for a moment. Our ancient laws expressly declare, that those who are but delegates themselves shall not delegate to others powers which require judgment and integrity in their exercise. . . The same laws forbid the abandonment of that post, even on ordinary occasions; and much more a transfer of their powers into other hands and other forms, without consulting the people. They never admit the idea that these, like sheep or cattle, may be given from hand to hand without an appeal to their own will. Was it from the necessity of the case? Necessities which dissolve a government, do not convey its authority to an oligarchy or a monarchy. They throw back, into the hands of the people, the powers they had delegated, and leave them as individuals to shift for themselves. A leader may offer, but not impose himself, nor be imposed on them. Much less can their necks be submitted to his sword, their breath to be held at his will or caprice. The necessity which should operate these tremendous effects should at least be palpable and irresistible. Yet in both instances, where it was feared, or pretended with us, it was belied by the event. It was belied, too, by the preceding experience of our sister States, several of whom had grappled through greater difficulties without abandoning their forms of government. . . The very thought alone was treason against the people; was treason against mankind in general; as rivetting forever the chains which bow down their necks, by giving to their oppressors a proof, which they would have trumpeted through the universe, of the imbecility of republican government, in times of pressing danger, to shield them from harm. Those who assume the right of giving away the reins of government in any case, must be sure that the herd, whom they hand on to the rods and hatchet of the dictator, will lay their necks on the block when he shall nod to them. But if our assemblies supposed such a recognition in the people, I hope they mistook their character. . . Searching for the foundations of this proposition, I can find none which may pretend a color of right or reason, but the defect before developed, that there being no barrier between the legislative, executive, and judiciary departments, the legislature may seize the whole; that having seized it, and possessing a right to fix their own quorum, they may reduce that quorum to one, whom they may call a chairman, speaker, dictator, or by any other name they please. Our situation is indeed perilous, and I hope my countrymen will be sensible of it, and will apply, at a proper season, the proper remedy, which is a convention to fix the constitution, to amend its defects, to bind up the several branches of government by certain laws, which, when they transgress, their acts shall become nullities; to render unnecessary an appeal to the people, or in other words a rebellion, on every infraction of their rights, on the peril that their acquiescence shall be construed into an intention to surrender those rights. . .

The rights of conscience we never submitted, we could not submit. We are answerable for them to our God. The legitimate powers of government extend to such acts only as are injurious to others. But it does me no injury for my neighbor to say there are twenty gods, or no God. It neither picks my pocket nor breaks my leg. If it be said, his testimony in a court of justice cannot be relied on, reject it then, and be the stigma on him. Constraint may make him worse by making him a hypocrite, but it will never make him a truer man. It may fix him obstinately in his errors, but will not cure them. Reason and free inquiry are the only effectual agents against error. Give a loose to them, they will support the true religion by bringing every false one to their tribunal, to the test of their investigation. They are the natural enemies of error, and of error only. Had not the Roman government permitted free inquiry, Christianity could never have been introduced. Had not free inquiry been indulged at the era of the reformation, the corruptions of Christianity could not have been purged away. If it be restrained now, the present corruptions will be protected, and new ones encouraged. Was the government to prescribe to us our medicine and diet, our bodies would be in such keeping as our souls are now. Thus in France the emetic was once forbidden as a medicine, and the potato as an article of food. Government is just as infallible, too, when it fixes systems in physics. Galileo was sent to the Inquisition for affirming that the earth was a sphere; the government had declared it to be as flat as a trencher, and Galileo was obliged to abjure his error. This error, however, at length prevailed, the earth became a globe, and Descartes declared it was whirled round its axis by a vortex. The government in which he lived was wise enough to see that this was no question of civil jurisdiction, or we should all have been involved by authority in vortices. In fact, the vortices have been exploded, and the Newtonian principle of gravitation is now more firmly established, on the basis of reason, than it would be were the government to step in, and to make it an article of necessary faith. Reason and experiment have been indulged, and error has fled before them. It is error alone which needs the support of government. Truth can stand by itself. Subject opinion to coercion: whom will you make your inquisitors? Fallible men; men governed by bad passions, by private as well as public reasons. And why subject it to coercion? To produce uniformity. But is uniformity of opinion desirable? No more than of face and stature. Introduce the bed of Procrustes then, and as there is danger that the large men may beat the small, make us all of a size, by lopping the former and stretching the latter. Difference of opinion is advantageous in religion. The several sects perform the office of a *censor morum* over such other. Is uniformity attainable? Millions of innocent men, women, and children, since the introduction of Christianity, have been burnt, tortured, fined, imprisoned; yet we have not advanced one inch towards uniformity. What has been the effect of coercion? To make one half the world fools, and the other half hypocrites. To support roguery and error all over the earth. Let us reflect that it is inhabited by a thousand millions of people. That these profess probably a thousand different systems of religion. That ours is but one of that thousand. That if there be but one right, and ours that one, we should wish to see the nine hundred and ninety-nine wandering sects gathered into the fold of truth. But against such a majority we cannot effect this by force. Reason and persuasion are the only practicable instruments. To make way for these, free inquiry must be indulged; and how can we wish others to indulge it while we refuse it ourselves. . .

9. *The injustice of state laws has brought into question the fundamental principle that the majority is the safest guardian of public good and private rights*

JAMES MADISON, *Vices of the Political System of the United States,* April 1787 *

1. Failure of the States to comply with the Constitutional requisitions.

This evil has been so fully experienced both during the war and since the peace, results so naturally from the number and independent authority of the States and has been so uniformly exemplified in every similar Confederacy, that it may be considered as not less radically and permanently inherent in than it is fatal to the object of the present system.

2. Encroachments by the States on the federal authority. . .

3. Violations of the law of nations and of treaties. . .

4. Trespasses of the States on the rights of each other. . .

5. Want of concert in matters where common interest requires it. . .

6. Want of Guaranty to the States of their Constitutions and laws against internal violence. . .

7. Want of sanction to the laws, and of coercion in the Government of the Confederacy.

A sanction is essential to the idea of law, as coercion is to that of Government. The federal system being destitute of both, wants the great vital principles of a Political Constitution. Under the form of such a constitution, it is in fact nothing more than a treaty of amity of commerce and of alliance, between independent and Sovereign States. From what cause could so fatal an omission have happened in the articles of Confederation? from a mistaken confidence that the justice, the good faith, the honor, the sound policy, of the several legislative assemblies would render superfluous any appeal to the ordinary motives by which the laws secure the obedience of individuals: a confidence which does honor to the enthusiastic virtue of the compilers, as much as the inexperience of the crisis apologizes for their errors. The time which has since elapsed has had the double effect, of increasing the light and tempering the warmth, with which the arduous work may be revised. It is no longer doubted that a unanimous and punctual obedience of 13 independent bodies, to the acts of the federal Government ought not to be calculated on. . . How indeed could it be otherwise? In the first place, Every general act of the Union must necessarily bear unequally hard on some particular member or members of it,

* *The Writings of James Madison,* Gaillard Hunt, ed., New York, G. P. Putnam's Sons, 1901, vol. II, pp. 361–9. These views, formulated in April 1787, served as a basis for Madison's long speech in the Federal Convention, 19 June 1787. See Farrand, *Records of the Federal Convention,* vol. I, p. 314.

secondly the partiality of the members to their own interests and rights, a partiality which will be fostered by the courtiers of popularity, will naturally exaggerate the inequality where it exists, and even suspect it where it has no existence, thirdly a distrust of the voluntary compliance of each other may prevent the compliance of any, although it should be the latent disposition of all. . .

8. Want of ratification by the people of the articles of Confederation. . .

9. Multiplicity of laws in the several States. . .

10. Mutability of the laws of the States. . .

11. Injustice of the laws of the States.

If the multiplicity and mutability of laws prove a want of wisdom, their injustice betrays a defect still more alarming: more alarming not merely because it is a greater evil in itself; but because it brings more into question the fundamental principle of republican Government, that the majority who rule in such governments are the safest Guardians both of public Good and private rights. To what causes is this evil to be ascribed?

These causes lie (1) in the Representative bodies, (2) in the people themselves.

1. Representative appointments are sought from 3 motives. (1) ambition; (2) personal interest; (3) public good. Unhappily the two first are proved by experience to be most prevalent. Hence the candidates who feel them, particularly, the second, are most industrious, and most successful in pursuing their object; and forming often a majority in the legislative Councils, with interested views, contrary to the interest and views of their constituents, join in a perfidious sacrifice of the latter to the former. . .

How frequently too will the honest but unenlightened representative be the dupe of a favorite leader, veiling his selfish views under the professions of public good, and varnishing his sophistical arguments with the glowing colours of popular eloquence?

2. A still more fatal if not more frequent cause, lies among the people themselves. All civilized societies are divided into different interests and factions, as they happen to be creditors or debtors—rich or poor—husbandmen, merchants or manufacturers—members of different religious sects—followers of different political leaders—inhabitants of different districts—owners of different kinds of property etc. etc. In republican Government the majority however composed, ultimately give the law. Whenever therefore an apparent interest or common passion unites a majority what is to restrain them from unjust violations of the rights and interests of the minority, or of individuals? Three motives only: (1) a prudent regard to their own good as involved in the general and permanent good of the community. This consideration although of decisive weight in itself, is found by experience to be too often unheeded. It is too often forgotten, by nations, as well as by individuals, that honesty is the best policy, (2) respect for character. However strong this motive may be in individuals, it is considered as very insufficient to restrain them from injustice. In a multitude its efficacy is diminished in proportion to the number which is to share the praise or the blame . . . (3) will Religion, the only remaining motive, be a sufficient restraint? It is not pretended to be such on men individually

considered. Will its effect be greater on them considered in an aggregate view? quite the reverse. . . Place three individuals in a situation wherein the interest of each depends on the voice of the others; and give to two of them an interest opposed to the rights of the third? Will the latter be secure? The prudence of every man would shun the danger. The rules and forms of justice suppose and guard against it. Will two thousand in a like situation be less likely to encroach on the rights of one thousand? The contrary is witnessed by the notorious factions and oppressions which take place in corporate towns limited as the opportunities are, and in little republics when uncontrouled by apprehensions of external danger. If an enlargement of the sphere is found to lessen the insecurity of private rights, it is not because the impulse of a common interest or passion is less predominant in this case with the majority; but because a common interest or passion is less apt to be felt and the requisite combinations less easy to be formed by a great than by a small number. The Society becomes broken into a greater variety of interests, of pursuits of passions, which check each other, whilst those who may feel a common sentiment have less opportunity of communication and concert. It may be inferred that the inconveniences of popular States contrary to the prevailing Theory, are in proportion not to the extent, but to the narrowness of their limits.

The great desideratum in Government is such a modification of the sovereignty as will render it sufficiently neutral between the different interests and factions, to controul one part of the society from invading the rights of another, and at the same time sufficiently controuled itself, from setting up an interest adverse to that of the whole Society. In absolute Monarchies the prince is sufficiently neutral towards his subjects, but frequently sacrifices their happiness to his ambition or his avarice. In small Republics, the sovereign will is sufficiently controuled from such a sacrifice of the entire Society, but is not sufficiently neutral towards the parts composing it. As a limited monarchy tempers the evils of an absolute one; so an extensive Republic meliorates the administration of a small Republic.

An auxiliary desideratum for the melioration of the Republican form is such a process of elections as will most certainly extract from the mass of the society the purest and noblest characters which it contains; such as will at once feel most strongly the proper motives to pursue the end of their appointment, and be most capable to devise the proper means of attaining it.

10. *To give the people uncontrolled power is not the way to preserve liberty*

JOHN ADAMS, *A Defence of the Constitutions of Government of the United States of America*, 1787–88 *

. . . The people in America have now the best opportunity and the greatest trust in their hands, that Providence ever committed to so small a number, since

* *The Works of John Adams*, Charles Francis Adams, ed., Boston, Charles C. Little and James Brown, 1851, vol. IV, pp. 271–588 *passim*, vol. VI, pp. 6–89, 506–21 *passim*.

the transgression of the first pair; if they betray their trust, their guilt will merit even greater punishment than other nations have suffered, and the indignation of Heaven. If there is one certain truth to be collected from the history of all ages, it is this; that the people's rights and liberties, and the democratical mixture in a constitution, can never be preserved without a strong executive, or, in other words, without separating the executive from the legislative power. If the executive power, or any considerable part of it, is left in the hands either of an aristocratical or a democratical assembly, it will corrupt the legislature as necessarily as rust corrupts iron, or as arsenic poisons the human body; and when the legislature is corrupted, the people are undone. . .

The United States of America have exhibited, perhaps, the first example of governments erected on the simple principles of nature; and if men are now sufficiently enlightened to disabuse themselves of artifice, imposture, hypocrisy, and superstition, they will consider this event as an era in their history. Although the detail of the formation of the American governments is at present little known or regarded either in Europe or in America, it may hereafter become an object of curiosity. It will never be pretended that any persons employed in that service had interviews with the gods, or were in any degree under the inspiration of Heaven, more than those at work upon ships or houses, or laboring in merchandise or agriculture; it will forever be acknowledged that these governments were contrived merely by the use of reason and the senses. . . Thirteen governments thus founded on the natural authority of the people alone, without a pretence of miracle or mystery, and which are destined to spread over the northern part of that whole quarter of the globe, are a great point gained in favor of the rights of mankind. The experiment is made, and has completely succeeded; it can no longer be called in question, whether authority in magistrates and obedience of citizens can be grounded on reason, morality, and the Christian religion, without the monkery of priests, or the knavery of politicians. As the writer was personally acquainted with most of the gentlemen in each of the states, who had the principal share in the first draughts, the following work was really written to lay before the public a specimen of that kind of reading and reasoning which produced the American constitutions. . .

PRELIMINARY OBSERVATIONS

M. Turgot, in his letter to Dr. Price, confesses, 'that he is not satisfied with the constitutions which have hitherto been formed for the different states of America.' He observes, 'that by most of them the customs of England are imitated, without any particular motive. Instead of collecting all authority into one centre, that of the nation, they have established different bodies, a body of representatives, a council, and a governor, because there is in England a house of commons, a house of lords, and a king. They endeavor to balance these different powers, as if this equilibrium, which in England may be a necessary check to the enormous influence of royalty, could be of any use in republics founded upon the equality of all the citizens, and as if establishing different orders of men was not a source of divisions and disputes. . .'

It was not so much because the legislature in England consisted of three branches, that such a division of power was adopted by the states, as because their own assemblies had ever been so constituted. It was not so much from attachment by habit to such a plan of power that it was continued, as from conviction that it was founded in nature and reason.

M. Turgot seems to be of a different opinion, and is for 'collecting all authority into one centre, the nation.' It is easily understood how all authority may be collected into 'one centre' in a despot or monarch; but how it can be done when the centre is to be the nation, is more difficult to comprehend. Before we attempt to discuss the notions of an author, we should be careful to ascertain his meaning. It will not be easy, after the most anxious research, to discover the true sense of this extraordinary passage. If, after the pains of 'collecting all authority into one centre,' that centre is to be the nation, we shall remain exactly where we began, and no collection of authority at all will be made. . . Not one will have any authority over any other. The first 'collection' of authority must be an unanimous agreement to form themselves into a *nation, people, community,* or *body politic,* and to be governed by the majority of suffrages or voices. But even in this case, although the authority is collected into one centre, that centre is no longer the nation, but the majority of the nation. Did M. Turgot mean that the people of Virginia, for example, half a million of souls scattered over a territory of two hundred leagues square, should stop here, and have no other authority by which to make or execute a law, or judge a cause, but by a vote of the whole people, and the decision of a majority! Where is the plain large enough to hold them; and what are the means, and how long would be the time, necessary to assemble them together?

A simple and perfect democracy never yet existed among men. If a village of half a mile square, and one hundred families, is capable of exercising all the legislative, executive, and judicial powers, in public assemblies of the whole, by unanimous votes, or by majorities, it is more than has ever yet been proved in theory or experience. In such a democracy, for the most part, the moderator would be king, the town-clerk legislator and judge, and the constable sheriff; and, upon more important occasions, committees would be only the counsellors of both the former, and commanders of the latter.

Shall we suppose, then, that M. Turgot intended that an assembly of representatives should be chosen by the nation, and vested with all the powers of government; and that this assembly should be the centre in which all the authority was to be collected, and should be virtually deemed the nation? After long reflection, I have not been able to discover any other sense in his words, and this was probably his real meaning. . . I shall not then esteem my time misspent, in placing this idea of M. Turgot in all its lights; in considering the consequences of it; and in collecting a variety of authorities against it. [Adams's elaborate examination of certain contemporary European governments has been omitted.]. . .

RECAPITULATION

. . Among every people, and in every species of republics, we have constantly found a *first magistrate, a head, a chief,* under various denominations, indeed, and with different degrees of authority. . . If there is no example, then, in any free government, any more than in those which are not free, of a society without a principal personage, we may fairly conclude that the body politic cannot subsist, any more than the animal body, without a head . . . and, therefore, that the Americans are not justly liable to censure for instituting *governors.*

In every form of government we have seen a *senate,* or *little council,* a composition, generally, of those officers of state who have the most experience and power, and a few other members selected from the highest ranks and most illustrious reputations. On these lesser councils, with the first magistrate at their head, generally rests the principal burden of administration, a share in the legislative, as well as executive and judicial authority of government. The admission of such senates to a participation of these three kinds of power, has been generally observed to produce in the minds of their members an ardent aristocratical ambition, grasping equally at the prerogatives of the first magistrate, and the privileges of the people, and ending in the nobility of a few families, and a tyrannical oligarchy. But in those states, where the senates have been debarred from all executive power, and confined to the legislative, they have been observed to be firm barriers against the encroachments of the crown, and often great supporters of the liberties of the people. The Americans, then, who have carefully confined their senates to the legislative power, have done wisely in adopting them.

We have seen, in every instance, another and a larger assembly, composed of the body of the people, in some little states; of representatives chosen by the people, in others; of members appointed by the senate, and supposed to represent the people, in a third sort; and of persons appointed by themselves or the senate, in certain aristocracies; to prevent them from becoming oligarchies. The Americans, then, whose assemblies are the most adequate, proportional, and equitable representations of the people, that are known in the world, will not be thought mistaken in appointing houses of representatives.

In every republic,—in the smallest and most popular, in the larger and more aristocratical, as well as in the largest and most monarchical,—we have observed a multitude of curious and ingenious inventions to balance, in their turn, all those powers; to check the passions peculiar to them, and to control them from rushing into those exorbitancies to which they are most addicted. The Americans will then be no longer censured for endeavoring to introduce an equilibrium, which is much more profoundly meditated, and much more effectual for the protection of the laws, than any we have seen, except in England. We may even question whether that is an exception.

In every country we have found a variety of *orders,* with very great distinctions. In America, there are different orders of *offices,* but none of *men.* Out of office, all men are of the same species, and of one blood; there is neither a greater nor a lesser nobility. Why, then, are the Americans accused of establishing different orders of men? To our inexpressible mortification, we must have observed, that the people have preserved a share of power, or an existence in the government, in no country out of England, except upon the tops of a few inaccessible mountains, among rocks and precipices, in territories so narrow that you may span them with a hand's breadth, where, living unenvied, in extreme poverty, chiefly upon pasturage, destitute of manufactures and commerce, they still exhibit the most charming picture of life, and the most dignified character of human nature.

Wherever we have seen a territory somewhat larger, arts and sciences more cultivated, commerce flourishing, or even agriculture improved to any great degree, an aristocracy has risen up in a course of time, consisting of a few rich and honorable families, who have united with each other against both the people and the first magistrate. . .

We have seen these noble families . . . anxious to preserve to themselves as large a share as possible of power in the executive and judicial, as well as the legislative departments of the state. . .

We have seen no one government in which is a distinct separation of the legislative from the executive power, and of the judicial from both, or in which any attempt has been made to balance these powers with one another, or to form an equilibrium between the one, the few, and the many, for the purpose of enacting and executing equal laws, by common consent, for the general interest, excepting in England.

Shall we conclude, from these melancholy observations, that human nature is incapable of liberty, that no honest equality can be preserved in society, and that such forcible causes are always at work as must reduce all men to a submission to despotism, monarchy, oligarchy, or aristocracy?

By no means. We have seen one of the first nations in Europe, possessed of ample and fertile territories at home and extensive dominions abroad, of a commerce with the whole world, immense wealth, and the greatest naval power which ever belonged to any nation, which has still preserved the power of the people by the equilibrium we are contending for, by the trial by jury, and by constantly refusing a standing army. The people of England alone, by preserving their share in the legislature, at the expense of the blood of heroes and patriots, have enabled their king to curb the nobility, without giving him a standing army.

After all, let us compare every constitution we have seen with those of the United States of America, and we shall have no reason to blush for our country. On the contrary, we shall feel the strongest motives to fall upon our knees, in gratitude to heaven for having been graciously pleased to give us birth and education in that country, and for having destined us to live under her laws! We shall have reason to exult, if we make our comparison with England and the English constitution. Our people are undoubtedly sovereign; all the landed and other property is in the hands of the citizens; not only their representatives, but their senators and governors, are annually chosen; there are no hereditary titles, honors, offices, or distinctions; the legislative, executive, and judicial powers are carefully separated from each other; the powers of the one, the few, and the many are nicely balanced in the legislatures; trials by jury are preserved in all their glory, and there is no standing army; the *habeas corpus* is in full force; the press is the most free in the world. Where all these circumstances take place, it is unnecessary to add that the laws alone can govern. [Adams's review of the opinions of philosophers and historians, and his examination of ancient republics, have been omitted]. . .

CONCLUSION

By the authorities and examples already recited, you will be convinced that three branches of power have an unalterable foundation in nature; that they exist in every society natural and artificial; and that if all of them are not acknowledged in any constitution of government, it will be found to be imperfect, unstable, and soon enslaved; that the legislative and executive authorities are naturally distinct; and that liberty and the laws depend entirely on a separation of them in the frame of government; that the legislative power is naturally and necessarily sovereign and supreme over the executive; and, therefore, that the latter must be made an essential branch of the former, even with a negative, or it will not be able to defend itself, but will be soon invaded, undermined, attacked, or in some way or other totally ruined and annihilated by the former. This is applicable to every state in America, in its individual capacity; but is it equally applicable to the United States in their federal capacity?

The people of America and their delegates in congress were of opinion, that a single assembly was every way adequate to the management of all their federal concerns; and with very good reason, because congress is not a legislative assembly, nor a representative assembly, but only a diplomatic assembly.* A single council has been found to answer the purposes of confederacies very well. But in all such cases the deputies are responsible to the states; their authority is clearly ascertained; and the states, in their separate capacities, are the checks. These are able to form an effectual balance, and at all times to control their delegates. The security against the dangers of this kind of government will depend upon the accuracy and decision with which the governments of the separate states have their own orders arranged and balanced.

The necessity we are under of submitting to a federal government, is an additional and a very powerful argument for three branches, and a balance by an equal negative, in all the separate governments. Congress will always be composed of members from the natural and artificial aristocratical body in every

* This sentence drew from Mr. Jefferson a remonstrating comment. In a letter, 23 February 1787, he wrote:

'I have read your book with infinite satisfaction and improvement. It will do great good in America. Its learning and its good sense will, I hope, make it an institute for our politicians, old as well as young. There is one opinion in it, however, which I will ask you to reconsider, because it appears to me not entirely accurate, and not likely to do good. "Congress is not a legislative, but a diplomatic assembly." Separating into parts the whole sovereignty of our states, some of these parts are yielded to congress. Upon these I should think them both legislative and executive, and that they could have been judiciary also, had not the confederation required them for certain purposes to appoint a judiciary. It has accordingly been the decision of our courts, that the confederation is a part of the law of the land, and superior in authority to the ordinary laws, because it cannot be altered by the legislature of any one state. I doubt whether they are at all a diplomatic assembly.'

state, even in the northern, as well as in the middle and southern states. Their natural dispositions, then, in general will be, (whether they shall be sensible of it or not, and whatever integrity or abilities they may be possessed of,) to diminish the prerogatives of the governors and the privileges of the people, and to augment the influence of the aristocratical parties. There have been causes enough to prevent the appearance of this inclination hitherto; but a calm course of prosperity would very soon bring it forth, if effectual provision against it be not made in season. It will be found absolutely necessary, therefore, to give negatives to the governors, to defend the executive against the influence of this body, as well as the senate and representatives in their several states. The necessity of a negative in the house of representatives will be called in question by nobody. . .

In the present state of society and manners in America, with a people living chiefly by agriculture, in small numbers, sprinkled over large tracts of land, they are not subject to those panics and transports, those contagions of madness and folly, which are seen in countries where large numbers live in small places, in daily fear of perishing for want. We know, therefore, that the people can live and increase under almost any kind of government, or without any government at all. But it is of great importance to begin well; misarrangements now made, will have great, extensive, and distant consequences; and we are now employed, how little soever we may think of it, in making establishments which will affect the happiness of a hundred millions of inhabitants at a time, in a period not very distant. All nations, under all governments, must have parties; the great secret is to control them. There are but two ways, either by a monarchy and standing army, or by a balance in the constitution. Where the people have a voice, and there is no balance, there will be everlasting fluctuations, revolutions, and horrors, until a standing army, with a general at its head, commands the peace, or the necessity of an equilibrium is made appear to all, and is adopted by all. . .

MARCHAMONT NEDHAM; THE RIGHT CONSTITUTION OF A COMMONWEALTH EXAMINED

Marchamont Nedham lays it down as a fundamental principle and an undeniable rule, 'that the people, (that is, such as shall be successively chosen to represent the people,) are the best keepers of their own liberties, and that for many reasons. First, because they never think of usurping over other men's rights, but mind which way to preserve their own.' . .

But who are the people? . .

If by *the people* is meant the whole body of a great nation, it should never be forgotten, that they can never act, consult, or reason together, because they cannot march five hundred miles, nor spare the time, nor find a space to meet; and, therefore, the proposition, that they are the best keepers of their own liberties, is not true. They are the worst conceivable; they are no keepers at all. They can neither act, judge, think, or will, as a body politic or corporation. If by *the people* is meant all the inhabitants of a single city, they are not in a general assembly, at all times, the best keepers of their own liberties, nor perhaps at any time, unless you separate from them the executive and judicial power, and temper their authority in legislation with the maturer counsels of the one and the few. If it is meant by *the people*, as our author explains himself, a representative assembly, 'such as shall be successively chosen to represent the people,' still they are not the best keepers of the people's liberties or their own, if you give them all the power, legislative, executive, and judicial. They would invade the liberties of the people, at least the majority of them would invade the liberties of the minority, sooner and oftener than an absolute monarchy. . .

All kinds of experience show, that great numbers of individuals do oppress great numbers of other individuals; that parties often, if not always, oppress other parties; and majorities almost universally minorities. All that this observation can mean then, consistently with any color of fact, is, that the people will never unanimously agree to oppress themselves. But if one party agrees to oppress another, or the majority the minority, the people still oppress themselves, for one part of them oppress another.

'The people never think of usurping over other men's rights.'

What can this mean? Does it mean that the people never *unanimously* think of usurping over other men's rights? This would be trifling; for there would, by the supposition, be no other men's rights to usurp. . . Now, grant, but this truth, and the question is decided. If a majority are capable of preferring their own private interest, or that of their families, counties, and party, to that of the nation collectively, some provision must be made in the constitution, in favor of justice, to compel all to respect the common right, the public good, the universal law, in preference to all private and partial considerations.

The proposition of our author, then, should be reversed, and it should have been said, that they mind so much their own, that they never think enough of others. Suppose a nation, rich and poor, high and low, ten millions in number, all assembled together; not more than one or two millions will have lands, houses, or any personal property; if we take into the account the women and children, or even if we leave them out of the question, a great majority of every nation is wholly destitute of property, except a small quantity of clothes, and a few trifles of other movables. . . Property is surely a right of mankind as really as liberty. Perhaps, at first, prejudice, habit, shame, or fear, principle or religion, would restrain the poor from attacking the rich, and the idle from usurping on the industrious; but the time would not be long before courage and enterprise would come, and pretexts be invented by degrees, to countenance the majority in dividing all the property among them, or at least, in sharing it equally with its present possessors. . . What would be the consequence of this? The idle, the vicious, the intemperate, would rush into the utmost extravagance of debauchery, sell and spend all their share, and then demand a new division of those who purchased from them. The moment the idea is admitted into society, that property is not as sacred as the laws of God, and that there is not a force of law and public justice to protect it, anarchy and tyranny commence. . .

If the first part of the proposition, namely, that 'the people never think of usurping over other men's rights,' cannot be admitted, is the second, namely, 'they mind which way to preserve their own,' better founded?

There is in every nation and people under heaven a large proportion of persons who take no rational and prudent precautions to preserve what they have, much less to acquire more. Indolence is the natural character of man, to such a degree that nothing but the necessities of hunger, thirst, and other wants equally pressing, can stimulate him to action, until education is introduced in civilized societies, and the strongest motives of ambition to excel in arts, trades, and professions, are established in the minds of all men. Until this emulation is introduced, the lazy savage holds property in too little estimation to give himself trouble for the preservation or acquisition of it. . .

'The case is far otherwise among kings and grandees,' says our author, 'as all nations in the world have felt to some purpose.' . .

There is no reason to believe the one much honester or wiser than the other; they are all of the same clay; their minds and bodies are alike. The two latter have more knowledge and sagacity, derived from education, and more advantages for acquiring wisdom and virtue. As to usurping others' rights, they are all three equally guilty when unlimited in power. No wise man will trust either with an opportunity; and every judicious legislator will set all three to watch and control each other. . . The majority has eternally, and without one exception, usurped over the rights of the minority. . .

Though we allow benevolence and generous affections to exist in the human breast, yet every moral theorist will admit the selfish passions in the generality of man to be the strongest. . . Self-interest, private avidity, ambition, and avarice, will exist in every state of society, and under every form of government. A succession of powers and persons, by frequent elections, will not lessen these passions in any case, in a governor, senator, or representative; nor will the apprehension of an approaching election restrain them from indulgence if they have the power. The only remedy is to take away the power, by controlling the selfish avidity of the governor, by the senate and house; of the senate, by the governor and house; and of the house, by the governor and senate. . .

To expect self-denial from men, when they have a majority in their favor, and consequently power to gratify themselves, is to disbelieve all history and universal experience; it is to disbelieve Revelation and the Word of God, which informs us, the heart is deceitful above all things and desperately wicked. There have been examples of self-denial, and will be again; but such exalted virtue never yet existed in any large body of men, and lasted long; and our author's argument requires it to be proved, not only that individuals, but that nations and majorities of nations, are capable, not only of a single act, or a few acts, of disinterested justice and exalted self-denial, but of a course of such heroic virtue for ages and generations; and not only that they are capable of this, but that it is probable they will practice it. There is no man so blind as not to see, that to talk of founding a government upon a supposition that nations and great bodies of men, left to themselves, will practice a course of self-denial, is either to babble like a new-born infant, or to deceive like an unprincipled impostor. . .

There is, in short, no possible way of defending the minority . . . from the tyranny of the majority, but by giving the former a negative on the latter. . . As the major may bear all possible relations of proportion to the minor part, it may be fifty-one against forty-nine in an assembly of a hundred, or it may be ninety-nine against one only. It becomes therefore necessary to give the negative to the minority, in all cases, though it be ever so small. Every member must possess it, or he can never be secure that himself and his constituents shall not be sacrificed by all the rest. . .

The passions and desires of the majority of the representatives in an assembly being in their nature insatiable and unlimited by any thing within their own breasts, and having nothing to control them without, will crave more and more indulgence, and, as they have the power, they will have the gratification. . .

It is agreed that the people are the best keepers of their own liberties, and the only keepers who can be always trusted; and, therefore, the people's fair, full, and honest consent, to every law, by their representatives, must be made an essential part of the constitution; but it is denied that they are the best keepers, or any keepers at all, of their own liberties, when they hold collectively, or by representation, the executive and judicial power, or the whole and uncontrolled legislative; on the contrary, the experience of all ages has proved, that they instantly give away their liberties into the hand of grandees, or kings, idols of their own creation. The management of the executive and judicial powers together always corrupts them, and throws the whole power into the hands of the most profligate and abandoned among themselves. The honest men are generally nearly equally divided in sentiment, and, therefore, the vicious and unprincipled, by joining one party, carry the majority; and the vicious and unprincipled always follow the most profligate leader, him who bribes the highest, and sets all decency and shame at defiance. It becomes more profitable, and reputable too, except with a very few, to be a party man than a public-spirited one.

It is agreed that 'the end of all government is the good and ease of the people, in a secure enjoyment of their rights, without oppression'; but it must be remembered, that the rich are *people* as well as the poor; that they have rights as well as others; that they have as clear and as *sacred* a right to their large property as others have to theirs which is smaller; that oppression to them is as possible and as wicked as to others; that stealing, robbing, cheating, are the same crimes and sins, whether committed against them or others. The rich, therefore, ought to have an effectual barrier in the constitution against being robbed, plundered, and murdered, as well as the poor; and this can never be without an independent senate. The poor should have a bulwark against the same dangers and oppressions; and this can never be without a house of representatives of the people. But neither the rich nor the poor can be defended by their respective guardians in the constitution, without an executive power, vested with a negative, equal to either, to hold the balance even between them, and decide when they cannot agree. If it is asked, When will this negative be used: it may be answered, Perhaps never. The known existence of it will prevent all occasion to exercise it; but if it has not a being, the want of it will be felt every day. . .

In every society where property exists, there will ever be a struggle between rich and poor. Mixed in one assembly, equal laws can never be expected. They will either be made by numbers, to plunder the few who are rich, or by influence, to fleece the many who are poor. Both rich and poor, then, must be made independent, that equal justice may be done, and equal liberty enjoyed by all. To expect that in a single sovereign assembly no load shall be laid upon any but what is common to all, nor to gratify the passions of any, but only to supply the necessities of their country, is altogether chimerical. Such an assembly, under an awkward, unwieldy form, becomes at once a simple monarchy in effect. Some one overgrown genius, fortune, or reputation, becomes a despot, who rules the state at his pleasure, while the deluded nation, or rather a deluded majority, thinks itself free; and in every resolve, law, and act of government, you see the interest, fame, and power of that single individual attended to more than the general good. . .

The way to secure liberty is to place it in the people's hands, that is, to give them a power at all times to defend it in the legislature and in the courts of justice. But to give the people, uncontrolled, all the prerogatives and rights of supremacy, meaning the whole executive and judicial power, or even the whole undivided legislative, is not the way to preserve liberty. . .

We certainly know, from the known constitution of the human mind and heart and from uniform experience, that the law of nature, the decalogue, and all the civil laws, will be violated, if men's passions are not restrained; and, therefore, to presume that an unmixed democratical government will preserve the laws, is as mad as to presume that a king or senate will do it. . . Swerving from rules is no more the fault of standing kings and senates, than it is of standing or successive popular assemblies. Of the three, the last have the strongest disposition to swerve, and always do swerve the soonest when unbalanced. But the fault of permitting the continuance of power in particular hands, is incurable in the people, when they have the power. The people think you a fool, when you advise them to reject the man you acknowledge to be the ablest, wisest, and best, and whom you and they know they love best, and appoint another, who is but second in their confidence. They ever did, and ever will continue him, nay, and augment his power; for their love of him, like all their other passions, never stands still; it constantly grows, until it exceeds all bounds. These continual reelections, this continuance of power in particular men, gives them 'an opportunity to create parties of their own among the people, and for their own ends to inveigle, engage, and entangle them in popular tumults and divisions.' . .

The people are tumultuous when sensible of oppression, although naturally of a peaceable temper, minding nothing but a free enjoyment; but if circumvented, misled, or squeezed by such as they have trusted, they swell like the sea, overrun the bounds of justice and honesty, ruining all before them; but unhappily they very often mistake and swell against the most honest and faithful men, and insist upon being misled by the most artful and knavish. A great majority of the people, and those as honest as any, are too fond of ease and peace to trouble themselves with public affairs, which leaves an opportunity to the profligate and dissolute to have more influence than they ought, to set up such idols as will flatter and seduce them, by gifts, by offices, and by partiality in judgments; which shows, that although they are very competent to the choice of one branch of the legislative, they are altogether incapable of well managing the executive power. It is really unaccountable, but by that party spirit which destroys the understanding as well as the heart, that our author should conclude, 'there is not one precedent of tumults or sedition, which can be cited out of all stories, where the pople were in fault.' It was even their fault to be drawn in or provoked; it was their fault to set up idols, whose craft or injustice, and whose fair pretences had designs upon the public liberty. They ought to know that such pretenders will always arise, and that they never are to be trusted uncontrolled. . .

Tumults arise in all governments; but they are certainly most remediless and certainly fatal in a simple democracy. Cheats and tricks of great men will as certainly take place in simple democracy as in simple aristocracy or monarchy, and will be less easily resisted or remedied; and, therefore, our author has not vindicated his project from the objection of its danger from tumults. A mixed government, of all others, is best calculated to prevent, to manage, and to remedy tumults, by doing justice to all men on all occasions, to the minority as well as majority; and by forcing all men, majority as well as minority, to be contented with it. . .

A prospect into futurity in America, is like contemplating the heavens through the telescopes of Herschell. Objects stupendous in their magnitudes and motions strike us from all quarters, and fill us with amazement! When we recollect that the wisdom or the folly, the virtue or the vice, the liberty or servitude, of those millions now beheld by us, only as Columbus saw these times in vision, are certainly to be influenced, perhaps decided, by the manners, examples, principles, and political institutions of the present generation, that mind must be hardened into stone that is not melted into reverence and awe. . .

The former confederation of the United States was formed upon the model and example of all the confederacies, ancient and modern, in which the federal council was only a diplomatic body. . . The magnitude of territory, the population, the wealth and commerce, and especially the rapid growth of the United States, have shown such a government to be inadequate to their wants; and the new system, which seems admirably calculated to unite their interests and affections, and bring them to an uniformity of principles and sentiments, is equally well combined to unite their wills and forces as a single nation. A result of accommodation cannot be supposed to reach the ideas of perfection of any one; but the conception of such an idea, and the deliberate union of so great and various a people in such a plan, is, without all partiality or prejudice, if not the greatest exertion of human understanding, the greatest single effort of national deliberation that the world has ever seen. That it may be improved is not to be doubted, and provision is made for that purpose in the report itself. A people who could conceive, and can adopt it, we need not fear will be able to amend it, when, by experience, its inconveniences and imperfections shall be seen and felt. . .

SELECTED REFERENCES

John Quincy Adams, *The Jubilee of the Constitution. A Discourse Delivered April 30, 1839, Being the Fiftieth Anniversary of the Inauguration of General Washington*, New York, Samuel Colman, 1839.

———, *An Eulogy on the Life and Character of James Madison. Delivered in Boston September 27, 1836*, Boston, John H. Eastburn, 1836.

The Articles of Confederation and Perpetual Union, Julian P. Boyd, ed., Boston, The Old South Association, 1960.

Irving Brant, *James Madison: The Nationalist, 1780–1787*, Indianapolis, Bobbs-Merrill, 1948.

Edward S. Corwin, 'Progress of Constitutional Theory between the Declaration of Independence and the Meeting of the Philadelphia Convention,' *American Historical Review*, April 1925, vol. 30, pp. 511–36.

John Fiske, *The Critical Period of American History*, Boston, Houghton Mifflin, 1888.

Ruth Henline, 'A Study of *Notes on the State of Virginia* as an Evidence of Jefferson's Reaction Against the Theories of the French Naturalists,' *Virginia Magazine*, vol. 55, pp. 233–46.

Merrill Jensen, *The Articles of Confederation: An Interpretation of the Social-Constitutional History of the American Revolution, 1774, 1781*, Madison, University of Wisconsin Press, 1940.

———, *The New Nation: A History of the United States During the Confederation, 1781–1789*, New York, Knopf, 1950.

Marie Kimball, *Jefferson, War and Peace, 1776 to 1784*, New York, Coward-McCann, 1947.

Dumas Malone, *Jefferson the Virginian*, Boston, Little, Brown, 1948.

Andrew C. McLaughlin, *The Confederation and Constitution, 1783–1789*, New York, Harper, 1905.

Forrest McDonald, *We the People: The Economic Origins of the Constitution*, Chicago, University of Chicago Press, 1958.

Allan Nevins, *The American States During and After the Revolution*, New York, Macmillan, 1924.

Frederick Scott Oliver, *Alexander Hamilton, An Essay on American Union*, New York, G. P. Putnam, 1906.

V. L. Parrington, *Main Currents in American Thought: The Colonial Mind, 1620–1800*, New York, Harcourt, Brace, 1927, vol. 1.

Nathan Schachner, *Alexander Hamilton*, New York, D. Appleton-Century Co., 1946.

J. Allen Smith, *The Spirit of American Government: A Study of the Constitution, Its Origin, Influence, and Relation to Democracy*, New York, Macmillan, 1912, chap. 2, 'The Revolutionary Period.'

C. M. Walsh, *The Political Science of John Adams: A Study in the Theory of Mixed Government and Bicameral System*, New York, G. P. Putnam, 1915.

B. F. Wright, *Consensus and Continuity, 1776–1787*, Boston, Boston University Press, 1958.

V

TOWARD A MORE PERFECT UNION

'What astonishing changes a few years are capable of producing,' Washington wrote John Jay from Mount Vernon 1 August 1786. 'What a triumph for the advocates of despotism to find that we are incapable of governing ourselves and that systems founded on the basis of equal liberty are merely ideal and fallacious! Would to God that wise measures may be taken in time to avert the consequence we have but too much reason to apprehend.'

Later that same year General Henry Knox, adding to Washington's disquiet, wrote of 'people who are insurgents'—the Shaysites in Massachusetts and those of like sentiment in Rhode Island, Connecticut, and New Hampshire. 'Their creed,' Knox told Washington, is 'that the property of the United States has been protected from the confiscations of Britain by the joint exertions of all, and therefore ought to be the common property of all. And he that attempts opposition to this creed is an enemy to equity and justice, and ought to be swept from the face of the earth.'

Knox enlarged on the awful spectacle: how after British rule was thrown off, the lower orders took base advantage both of the Articles of Confederation, and of the state constitutions. Small farmers, debtors, and squatters were arrayed against merchants, investors, creditors, and large landowners, frightening the possessing classes, intensifying their distrust of democracy, fixing in them the determination not only to set up government with power to regulate commerce and deal with foreign nations but also to fortify constitutional restrictions against such popular outbursts as Shays' Rebellion in Massachusetts. Radicalism had won victories in currency inflation, stay-laws, and legislative intervention in private controversies pending in, or already decided by, the ordinary courts. 'This dreadful situation has alarmed every man of principle and property in New England,' Knox wrote Washington. 'Our government must be braced, changed, or altered to secure our lives and property.'

All this tends to support the theory that the Constitution of 1787 was 'the outcome of a conflict between radical and agrarian forces on the one side and the forces of reaction on the other.' Recent investigations indicate still other influences at work. 'I am of the opinion,' the late Charles A. Beard has noted, that 'besides the radicals and the conservatives there was an influential group on the extreme right of the conservatives—a group that was ripe and ready for a resort to the sword, especially after Daniel Shays and his followers in Massachusetts had taken up arms against the grinding creditors and the bigots who would yield nothing. Had the movement for forming a new Constitution by peaceful processes failed, there is no doubt in my mind that the men of the sword would have made a desperate effort to set up a dictatorship by arms.'

Beard marshals support for this hypothesis. Governor George Clinton of New York, arch enemy of constitutional ratification, recalled in 1788 that a 'dangerous attempt was made [in 1780–81] to subvert our liberties by creating a supreme dictator.' A few days before the Philadelphia Convention assembled, in May 1787, Madison, in a letter to John Armstrong, commented on 'the alarming flame' in Massachusetts: 'Shall I tell you in confidence, I have now twice heard, nor from low authority [some principal men of that state] begin to talk of wishing one general *Head* to the union, in the room of Congress!'

Virginia took the first direct step to avoid any such calamity when she invited the other commonwealths to join in a conference, set for early September 1786 at Annapolis, to discuss trade and commerce among the several states. The meeting was poorly attended and, measured solely in terms of its stated objectives, was a dismal failure. The Commissioners, twelve in number representing five states, convened on 11 September and broke up 14 September, but the session was long enough for them to discover that a remedy even for the evils affecting commerce and trade must be found in some broader constitutional framework. To achieve one, all states would have to join and the Commissioners' authority would have to be considerably extended. At Annapolis only New Jersey had empowered her delegates to discuss 'other important matters.'

The upshot was that the Convention adopted the forward-looking resolutions framed by Alexander Hamilton, declaring that the small attendance alone precluded the Commissioners from proceeding 'to the business of their mission.' They must therefore confine themselves to stating 'their earnest and unanimous wish that speedy measures may be taken to effect a general meeting of the states in a future convention for the same and such other purposes as the situation of public affairs may be found to require.' The resolution went on to record that further reflection had led the Commissioners to the conclusion that 'the power of regulating trade is of such comprehensive extent, and will enter so far into the general system of the Federal Government, that to give it efficacy, and to obviate questions and doubts concerning its precise nature and limits, may require a correspondent adjustment of the federal system.' The resolutions ended with the proposal that all the states appoint Commissioners 'to meet at Philadelphia on the second Monday in May next, to take into consideration the situation of the United States, to devise such further provisions as shall appear to them necessary to render the Constitution of the Federal Government *adequate to the exigencies of the Union*.' (Editor's italics.)

Hamilton had originally prepared a much stronger statement, but toned it down to meet the opposition of Governor Edmund Randolph of Virginia. But even as qualified it contained 'the weapons,' as Nathan Schachner observes, 'by which Hamilton intended to forge a new government and a new nation.'

Here the New Yorker was but following his own maxim of statesmanship: 'Wise men ought to walk at the head of affairs and produce the event.'

In a memorandum found among Madison's papers after his death, one discovers a suggestion of the politics motivating the proceedings at Annapolis. Madison, himself a Commissioner, recorded that several of his colleagues deliberately stayed away, or delayed their coming from 'a belief that the time has not yet arrived for such a political reform as might be expected from a further experience of its necessity.' A more complete disclosure of what went on in the minds of our nationalist leaders is contained in a letter of 10 October 1786 from the French minister Otto to his chief, Count Vergennes:

> Although there are no nobles in America, there is a class of men denominated 'gentlemen,' who, by reason of their wealth, their talents, their education, their families, or the offices they hold, aspire to a preëminence which the people refuse to grant them; and although many of these men have betrayed the interests of their order to gain popularity, there reigns among them a connection so much the more intimate as they almost all of them dread the efforts of the people to despoil them of their possessions, and, moreover, they are creditors, and therefore interested in strengthening the government and watching over the execution of the laws. . . The attempt, my lord, has been vain, by pamphlets and other publications, to spread notions of justice and integrity, and to deprive the people of a freedom which they have so misused. By proposing a new organization of the general government, all minds would have been revolted; circumstances ruinous to the commerce of America have happily arisen to furnish the reformers with a pretext for introducing innovations.

About the motives prompting the projectors of the Annapolis Convention, Otto continues:

> The authors of this proposition had no hope, nor even desire, to see the success of this assembly of commissioners, which was only intended to prepare a question much more important than that of commerce. The measures were so well taken that at the end of September no more than five states were represented at Annapolis, and the commissioners from the Northern states tarried several days at New York in order to retard their arrival. The states which assembled, after having waited nearly three weeks, separated under the pretext that they were not in sufficient numbers to enter on the business, and, to justify this dissolution, they addressed to the different legislatures and to Congress a report, the translation of which I have the honor to enclose you.

The report of the Annapolis Commissioners came before the Congress in October with the expectation that it would recommend the action suggested. This was opposed, however, on technical grounds by Nathan Dane and Rufus King of Massachusetts. Worsening of the situation not only among but within states left Congress with little or no choice but to adopt, on 21 February 1787, the Annapolis resolutions. The states, with the exception of Rhode Island, began immediately to choose delegates to represent them in the forthcoming convention. Even before the Congress had adopted the resolutions, Virginia provided the project with an aspect of buoyant expectancy by choosing George Washington as one of her delegates.

The members were slow in arriving and the Convention did not get under way until 25 May. Meeting in Philadelphia in the same brick building from which, eleven years before, the Declaration of Independence had been promulgated to an astonished world, the delegates constituted a varied and distinguished gathering—'the wisest council in the world,' one of its members, William Pierce of Georgia, called it. The youngest delegate was Jonathan Dayton of New Jersey, aged twenty-six; the oldest, Benjamin Franklin, President of Pennsylvania, eighty-one. Twenty-nine were university graduates, and the twenty-six nongraduates included two of the most eminent citizens in the land—Washington and Franklin. Certain noted agitators and revolutionaries were conspicuous by their absence. Jefferson was still at his diplomatic post in France. Patrick Henry 'smelt a rat' and declined to serve as a delegate. Samuel Adams of Massachusetts and Richard Henry Lee of Virginia shied off from any move that might lead to their pet aversion—'consolidated' government.

Predominantly lawyers, merchants, planters, and investors, these men were moved by political experience and practical considerations rather than by philosophic abstractions. Bitter defeat through six years of frustration since Yorktown's victory had built up in them a profound distrust of human nature and democracy. A twofold objective prompted their efforts: to provide more adequate power and energy in the central government; to secure private rights against the evil of factions, which they identified as 'the superior force of an interested and overbearing majority.'

Delegates exerting greatest influence in the proceedings included:

George Washington—the Convention's unanimous choice as presiding officer.

Benjamin Franklin—'the greatest philosopher of the present age'; 'all the operations of nature he seems to understand,' William Pierce of Georgia records in his *Notes*. 'The very heavens obey him, and the clouds yield up their lightning to be imprisoned in his rod.'

Alexander Hamilton—'practitioner of the law,' 'finished scholar,' 'able, convincing, and engaging in his eloquence—the Head and Heart sympathize in approving him.'

William Paterson (New Jersey)—'a classic, a lawyer, and an orator,' 'one of those kind of men whose powers break in upon you, and create wonder and astonishment.'

James Wilson (Pennsylvania)—'ranks among the foremost in legal and political knowledge.'

Gouverneur Morris (Pennsylvania)—'one of those geniuses in whom every species of talents combine to render him conspicuous and flourishing in public debate.'

Rufus King (Massachusetts)—'distinguished for his eloquence and great parliamentary talents. . . Take him *tout ensemble*,' Pierce records, 'he may with propriety be ranked among the luminaries of the present age.'

Edmund Randolph—'a young gentleman in whom unite all the accomplishments of the scholar, and the statesman.'

James Madison—'the best-informed man on any point in debate.'

Madison not only made major contributions to the discussion on all crucial issues but also recorded the notes reprinted in this chapter. In an introduction to his *Notes*, published in 1840, four years after his death, he wrote:

> I chose a seat in front of the presiding member, with the members, on my right and left hand. In this favorable position for hearing all that passed I noted in terms legible and in abbreviations and marks intelligible to myself what was read from the chair or spoken by the members; and losing not a moment unnecessarily between the adjournment and reassembling of the Convention I was able to write out my daily notes during the session or within a few finishing days after its close.

The Randolph-Virginia plan, introduced four days after the Convention assembled, is generally credited to Madison's influence. Six weeks before the Convention, Madison formulated 'some leading propositions' and submitted them on 8 April 1787 to Edmund Randolph. Contained in this letter, herein reprinted, are the essential ingredients of the Randolph plan. It struck at the heart of the evils suffered under the Articles of Confederation by authorizing the new government to act directly on individuals rather than on states. Introduction of this bold proposal precipitated sharp and prolonged debate, ultimately revealing the Convention as a revolutionary body. 'He [Randolph] came forward with the postulation, or first principles, on which the Convention acted,' Pierce recorded, 'and he supported them with a force of eloquence and reasoning that did him great honor.' Luther Martin of Maryland denounced the Randolph plan as swallowing up the sovereign states, and William Paterson of New Jersey countered with a plan of his own. Aiming to amend rather than supplant the Articles of Confederation, supporters of the New Jersey plan argued that the general government was 'meant,' as Martin said, 'to preserve the state governments, not to govern individuals.' At one point Madison stated the extreme alternatives as 'a perfect separation' or 'a perfect incorporation, of the thirteen states.' Doctor William Samuel Johnson of Connecticut suggested a middle course: 'In some respects, the states are to be considered in their political capacity, and in others as districts of individual citizens; the two ideas embraced on different sides, instead of being opposed to each other ought to be combined; that in one branch the people ought to be represented; in the other the states.' In this lay the essence of the famous Connecticut compromise, without which it is hardly likely the Convention would have succeeded in erecting the foundations of a stable government.

The Constitution was revolutionary, not only in the sense that it went into effect on ratification by nine states instead of by all, as required for amendment of the Articles of Confederation, but in the more fundamental sense that the proposed Constitution derived its authority from *the people*, and rested on their consent. Madison himself admitted in *Federalist* 40 that the Convention deviated from the tenor of their Commission 'in not reporting a plan requiring the confirmation of the legislatures of all the states' and in reporting 'a plan which is to be confirmed by the *people*.' He justified these departures in *Federalist* 43, 'by recurring to the absolute necessity of the case; to the great principle of self-preservation; to the transcendent law of nature and of nature's God, which declares that the safety and happiness of society are the objects at which all political institutions aim, and to which all such institutions must be sacrificed.'

Basically the issue between Martin and Madison concerned the proper scope of the Right of Revolution. Martin saw revolution negatively in terms of *right* rather than positively in the sense of power; he conceived of it as properly asserted only against acts of oppression. Madison, on the other hand, like Dr. Benjamin Rush, gave it positive connotation, holding that revolution was available as an original *power* in the people to secure their safety and happiness.

Even the revolutionary Randolph plan failed to satisfy Hamilton. Frankly expressing his admiration for the British system and even for monarchy, he naturally found the Paterson plan hopelessly inadequate. As to its alternative, Yates reports him as casting it aside disdainfully: 'What ever is the Virginia plan, but *pork still, with a little change of sauce*.'

Hamilton, speaking behind closed doors and among members pledged to secrecy, could afford to be frank. Little wonder, however, that Washington insisted that the rule of secrecy be strictly observed. Once when a copy of the proceedings happened to be picked up by a delegate outside the Convention Hall, Washington warned: 'I must entreat gentlemen to be more careful, lest our transactions get into the newspapers, and disturb public repose by premature speculations. I know not whose paper it is, but there it is [throwing it down on the table], let him who owns it take it.' Delegate William Pierce of Georgia relates how Washington then 'bowed, picked up his hat, and quitted the room with a dignity so severe that every person seemed alarmed.' No person, Pierce tells us, ever had enough courage to claim the paper.

In the secrecy of the Convention, prejudices and preferences had free rein; economic motives and class interests were openly acknowledged. The theory that society tends to divide into classes along economic lines was accepted without argument. Property was freely equated with liberty or happiness, and Hamilton spoke of it as 'the great and fundamental distinction of society.' Madison conceded that suffrage is one of the fundamental articles of Republican government, but held that 'freeholders' are the 'safest depositories of Republican liberty.' All agreed with Elbridge Gerry that 'the evils we experience flow from the excesses of democracy,' but certain members, notably Franklin and George Mason, cautioned the Convention against the possibility, as Mason put it, that 'we should incautiously run to the opposite extreme.' 'The genius of the people is in favor of it [democracy],' Mason said, 'and the genius of the people must be consulted.' And the venerable Franklin was prompted to express his distaste of 'everything that tended to debase the common people.'

'The virtue and public spirit of our common people' during the Revolution, he recalled, contributed 'principally to the favorable issue of it.'

Especially disturbing to the Convention delegates, notably Madison, was the almost certain prospect that the masses would in time become politically dominant. Madison queried Charles Pinckney's easy assumption that the prevailing condition of economic equality would continue to be characteristic of American society, pointing out that 'we cannot . . . be regarded, even at this time, as one homogeneous mass.'

'In future time,' the Father of the Constitution warned, 'a great majority of the people will not only be without land, but any other sort of property.' When this happens, Madison predicted, 'these [the masses] will either combine under the influence of their common situation,—in which case the rights of property and public liberty will not be secure,—or what is more probable, they will become tools of opulence and ambitions; in which case, there will be equal danger on the other side.'

Madison's forebodings make it clear that he had not yet developed any theory of public power rooted in the people. Nor did he have confidence in the ability of average people to govern themselves. One notices also the unmistakable inference that leadership resting on broad popular support was for him necessarily demagogic. That is why the factions he defined and feared were those of majorities, and also why he was determined to embody in the structure of the Constitution provisions and devices whereby the baneful effects of such factions could be controlled.

The Constitution of 1787 has been described caustically as 'the triumph of a skillfully directed reactionary movement.' That this should have been so is not at all unnatural. The revolutionaries, a decade earlier, dedicated themselves to the proposition that government originates in the people and to the theory that man is created with certain natural rights; the framers of the Constitution, taking into account human frailties, especially man's inordinate greed and lust for power, proclaimed the necessity of constitutional safeguards to control his violent passions. In the political institutions born of the Revolution, the legislature tended to absorb all power into its vortex; the federalists emphasized the necessity of balance among the various organs of government. The revolutionaries stressed weak government and its responsiveness to the popular will; the framers of the Constitution underscored efficiency, order, and stability, and fashioned various devices for placing government beyond the direct influence of mass passions.

On 17 September, the last day of the Convention, a question was raised as to what disposition should be made of the records. After perfunctory debate it was agreed that Washington, as president of the Convention, be authorized to 'retain the journal and other papers subject to the order of Congress, if ever formed under the Constitution.' The conditional nature of the resolution indicates that the framers of the Constitution were more certain that what they proposed was sound than that the states would ratify their work. Contrary to the views of certain of the framers' critics, these men sincerely believed—indeed some of them, Hamilton, Madison, Franklin and Washington, among others, stated in precise terms—that they were then deciding the fate of Republican government. In the stands taken and things done they were fully conscious of having a rendezvous with history. There must be no compromise with basic principles merely to win popular support. 'It is too probable,' Washington, according to the report of Gouverneur Morris, solemnly told the delegates, 'that no plan we propose will be adopted. Perhaps another dreadful conflict is to be sustained. If, *to please the people,* we offer what we ourselves disapprove, how can we afterward defend our work? Let us raise a standard to which the wise and the honest can repair; the event is in the hand of God . . .' (Editor's italics.)

Another chapter in the march of great events was concluded on 20 September, when Washington transmitted a draft of the proposed Constitution to the Congress.

1. *Let it be tried, then, whether any middle ground can be taken*

JAMES MADISON to Edmund Randolph, 8 April 1787 *

. . . I am glad to find that you are turning your thoughts towards the business of May next. My despair of your finding the necessary leisure, as signified in one of your letters, with the probability that some leading propositions at least would be expected from Virginia, had engaged me in a closer attention to the subject than I should otherwise have given. I will just hint the ideas that have occurred, leaving explanations for our interview.

I think with you, that it will be well to retain as much as possible of the old Confederation, though I doubt whether it may not be best to work the valuable articles into the new system, instead of engrafting the latter on the former. I am also perfectly of your opinion, that, in framing a system, no material sacrifices ought to be made to local or temporary prejudices. An explanatory address must of necessity accompany the result of the Convention on the main object. I am not sure that it will be practicable to present the several parts of the reform in so detached a manner to the States, as that a partial adoption will be binding. Particular States may view different articles as conditions of each other, and would only ratify them as such. Others might ratify them as independent propositions. The consequence would be that the ratifications of both would go for nothing. I have not, however, examined this point thoroughly. In truth, my ideas of a reform strike so deeply at the old Confederation, and lead to such a systematic change, that they scarcely admit of the expedient.

I hold it for a fundamental point, that an individual independence of the States is utterly irreconcilable with the idea of an aggregate sovereignty. I think,

* *The Writings of James Madison,* Gaillard Hunt, ed., New York, 1904, vol. II, pp. 336-40. The same material is contained in Madison's letter to Washington, April 16, 1787, ibid., vol. II, pp. 344-52.

at the same time, that a consolidation of the States into one simple republic is not less unattainable than it would be inexpedient. Let it be tried, then, whether any middle ground can be taken, which will at once support a due supremacy of the national authority, and leave in force the local authorities so far as they can be subordinately useful.

The first step to be taken is, I think, a change in the principle of representation. According to the present form of the Union, an equality of suffrage, if not just towards the larger members of it, is at least safe to them, as the liberty they exercise of rejecting or executing the acts of Congress, is uncontrollable by the nominal sovereignty of Congress. Under a system which would operate without the intervention of the States, the case would be materially altered. A vote from Delaware would have the same effect as one from Massachusetts or Virginia.

Let the national Government be armed with a positive and complete authority in all cases where uniform measures are necessary, as in trade, &c., &c. Let it also retain the powers which it now possesses.

Let it have a negative, in all cases whatsoever, on the Legislative acts of the States, as the King of Great Britain heretofore had. This I conceive to be essential and the least possible abridgement of the State sovereignties. Without such a defensive power, every positive power that can be given on paper will be unavailing. It will also give internal stability to the States. There has been no moment since the peace at which the Federal assent would have been given to paper-money, &c., &c.

Let this national supremacy be extended also the Judiciary department. If the Judges in the last resort depend on the States, and are bound by their oaths to them and not to the Union, the intention of the law and the interests of the nation may be defeated by the obsequiousness of the tribunals to the policy or prejudices of the States. It seems at least essential that an appeal should lie to some national tribunals in all cases which concern foreigners, or inhabitants of other States. The admiralty jurisdiction may be fully submitted to the National Government.

A Government formed of such extensive powers ought to be well organized. The Legislative department may be divided into two branches. One of them to be chosen every ——— years by the Legislatures or the people at large; the other to consist of a more select number, holding their appointments for a longer term, and going out in rotation. Perhaps the negative on the State laws may be most conveniently lodged in this branch. A Council of Revision may be superadded, including the great ministerial officers.

A national Executive will also be necessary. I have scarcely ventured to form my own opinion yet, either of the manner in which it ought to be constituted, or of the authorities with which it ought to be clothed.

An article ought to be inserted expressly guaranteeing the tranquility of the States against internal as well as external dangers.

To give the new system its proper energy, it will be desirable to have it ratified by the authority of the people, and not merely by that of the Legislatures.

I am afraid you will think this project, if not extravagant, absolutely unattainable and unworthy of being attempted. Conceiving it myself to go no further than is essential, the objections drawn from this source are to be laid aside. I flatter myself, however, that they may be less formidable on trial than in contemplation. The change in the principle of representation will be relished by a majority of the States, and those too of most influence. The northern States will be reconciled to it by the actual superiority of their populousness; the Southern by their expected superiority on this point. This principle established, the repugnance of the large States to part with power will in a great degree subside, and the smaller States must ultimately yield to the predominant will. It is also already seen by many, and must by degrees be seen by all, that, unless the Union be organized efficiently on republican principles, innovations of a much more objectionable form may be obtruded, or, in the most favorable event, the partition of the Empire, into rival and hostile confederacies will ensue. . .

2. *I doubt whether any other Convention will be able to make a better Constitution*

BENJAMIN FRANKLIN, in *The Federal Convention,* 1787 *

PLANS OF GOVERNMENT: RANDOLPH PLAN

Tuesday May 29

. . . Mr. Randolph opened the main business. He expressed his regret, that it should fall to him, rather than those, who were of longer standing in life and political experience, to open the great subject of their mission. But, as the convention had originated from Virginia, and his colleagues supposed, that some proposition was expected from them, they had imposed this task on him.

He then commented on the difficulty of the crisis, and the necessity of preventing the fulfilment of the prophecies of the American downfall.

He observed that in revising the federal system we ought to inquire (1) into the properties, which such a government ought to possess, (2) the defects of the confederation, (3) the danger of our situation and (4) the remedy.

1. The character of such a government ought to secure (1) against foreign invasion; (2) against dissentions between members of the Union, or seditions in particular states; (3) to procure to the several States various blessings, of which an isolated situation was incapable; (4) to be able to defend itself against incroachment; and (5) to be paramount to the state constitutions.

2. In speaking of the defects of the confederation he professed a high respect for its authors, and considered, them as having done all that patriots could do, in the then infancy of the science of constitutions, and of confed-

* *The Records of the Federal Convention of 1787*, Max Farrand, ed., New Haven, Yale University Press, 1911, vol. I, pp. 18–606 *passim;* vol. II, pp. 29–430, 641–50 *passim.*

eracies,—when the inefficiency of requisitions was unknown—no commercial discord had arisen among any states—no rebellion had appeared as in Massachusetts—foreign debts had not become urgent—the havoc of paper money had not been foreseen—treaties had not been violated—and perhaps nothing better could be obtained from the jealousy of the states with regard to their sovereignty. . .

He proposed as conformable to his ideas the following resolutions, which he explained one by one.

1. Resolved that the articles of Confederation ought to be so corrected and enlarged as to accomplish the objects proposed by their institution; namely, 'common defence, security of liberty and general welfare.'

2. Resolved therefore that the rights of suffrage in the National Legislature ought to be proportioned to the quotas of contribution, or to the number of free inhabitants, as the one or the other rule may seem best in different cases.

3. Resolved that the National Legislature ought to consist of two branches.

4. Resolved that the members of the first branch of the National Legislature ought to be elected by the people of the several States. . .

5. Resolved that the members of the second branch of the National Legislature ought to be elected by those of the first, out of a proper number of persons nominated by the individual Legislatures. . .

6. Resolved that each branch ought to possess the right of originating Acts; that the National Legislature ought to be empowered to enjoy the legislative rights vested in Congress by the Confederation and moreover to legislate in all cases to which the separate States are incompetent, or in which the harmony of the United States may be interrupted by the exercise of individual Legislation; to negative all laws passed by the several States, contravening in the opinion of the National Legislature the articles of Union; and to call forth the force of the Union against any member of the Union failing to fulfill its duty under the articles thereof.

7. Resolved that a National Executive be instituted; to be chosen by the National Legislature . . . and to be ineligible a second time; and that besides a general authority to execute the National laws, it ought to enjoy the Executive rights vested in Congress by the Confederation.

8. Resolved that the Executive and a convenient number of the National Judiciary, ought to compose a council of revision with authority to examine every act of the National Legislature before it shall operate, and every act of a particular Legislature before a negative thereon shall be final; and that the dissent of the said Council shall amount to a rejection, unless the Act of the National Legislature be again passed, or that of a particular Legislature be again negatived by . . . each branch.

9. Resolved that a National Judiciary be established to consist of one or more supreme tribunals, and of inferior tribunals to be chosen by the National Legislature, to hold their offices during good behavior. . .

He concluded with an exhortation, not to suffer the present opportunity of establishing general peace, harmony, happiness and liberty in the United States to pass away unimproved. . .

PATERSON PLAN

Friday *June 15*

. . . The propositions from New Jersey moved by Mr. Paterson were in the words following.

1. Resolved that the articles of Confederation ought to be so revised, corrected and enlarged, as to render the federal Constitution adequate to the exigences of Government, and the preservation of the Union.

2. Resolved that in addition to the powers vested in the United States in Congress, by the present existing articles of Confederation, they be authorized to pass acts for raising a revenue, by levying a duty or duties on all goods or merchandizes of foreign growth or manufacture, imported into any part of the United States . . . to pass Acts for the regulation of trade and commerce as well with foreign nations as with each other: provided that all punishments, fines, forfeitures and penalties to be incurred for contravening such acts rules and regulations shall be adjudged by the Common law Judiciarys of the State in which any offence contrary to the true intent and meaning of such Acts rules and regulations shall have been committed or perpetrated, with liberty of commencing in the first instance all suits and prosecutions for that purpose in the superior Common law Judiciary in such State, subject nevertheless, for the correction of all errors, both in law and fact in rendering judgment, to an appeal to the Judiciary of the United States.

3. Resolved that whenever requisitions shall be necessary, instead of the rule for making requisitions mentioned in the articles of Confederation, the United States in Congress be authorized to make such requisitions in proportion to the whole number of white and other free citizens and inhabitants of every age, sex and condition including those bound to servitude for a term of years and three fifths of all other persons not comprehended in the foregoing description, except Indians not paying taxes; that if such requisitions be not complied with, in the time specified therein, to direct the collection thereof in the non complying States and for that purpose to devise and pass acts directing and authorizing the same; provided that none of the powers hereby vested in the United States in Congress shall be exercised without the consent of at least — States, and in that proportion if the number of Confederated States should hereafter be increased or diminished.

4. Resolved that the United States in Congress be authorized to elect a federal Executive to consist of — persons . . . to be paid out of the federal treasury . . . to be ineligible a second time, and removeable by Congress on application by a majority of the Executives of the several States; that the Executives besides their general authority to execute the federal acts ought to appoint all federal officers not otherwise provided for, and to direct all military operations, provided that none of the persons composing the federal Executive shall on any occasion take command of any troops, so as personally to conduct any enterprise as General, or in other capacity.

5. Resolved that a federal Judiciary be established to consist of a supreme Tribunal and Judges of which to be appointed by the Executive, and to hold their offices during good behaviour. . .

6. Resolved that all Acts of the United States in Congress, made by virtue and in pursuance of the powers hereby and by the articles of Confederation vested in them, and all Treaties made and ratified under the authority of the United States shall be the supreme law of the respective States so far forth as those Acts or Treaties shall relate to the said States or their Citizens, and that the Judiciary of the several States shall be bound thereby in their decisions, any thing in the respective laws of the Individual States to the contrary notwithstanding; and that if any State, or any body of men in any State shall oppose or prevent the carrying into execution such acts or treaties, the federal Executive shall be authorized to call forth the power of the Confederated States, or so much thereof as may be necessary to enforce and compel an obedience to such Acts, or an Observance of such Treaties. . .

PATERSON'S EXPLANATION

Saturday *June 16*

Mr. Paterson said . . . he would now avoiding repetition as much as possible give his reasons in favor of that proposed by himself. He preferred it because it accorded (1) with the powers of the Convention; (2) with the sentiments of the people. If the confederacy was radically wrong, let us return to our States, and obtain larger powers, not assume them of ourselves. . . Our object is not such a Government as may be best in itself, but such a one as our Constituents have authorized us to prepare, and as they will approve. If we argue the matter on the supposition that no Confederacy at present exists, it can not be denied that all the States stand on the footing of equal sovereigny. All therefore must concur before any can be bound. If a proportional representation be right, why do we not vote so here? If we argue on the fact that a federal compact actually exists, and consult the articles of it we still find an equal Sovereignty to be the basis of it. He reads the 5th article of the Confederation giving each State a vote—and the 13th declaring that no alteration shall be made without unanimous consent. This is the nature of all treaties. What is unanimously done, must be unanimously undone. It was observed [by Mr. Wilson] that the larger State gave up the point, not because it was right, but because the circumstances of the moment urged the concession. Be it so. Are they for that reason at liberty to take it back. Can the donor resume his gift Without the consent of the donee. This doctrine may be convenient, but it is a doctrine that will sacrifice the lesser States. The large States acceded readily to the confederacy It was the small ones that came in reluctantly and slowly. New Jersey and Maryland were the two last, the former objecting to the want of power in Congress over trade: both of them to the want of power to appropriate the vacant territory to the benefit of the whole. If the sovereignty of the States is to be maintained, the Representatives must be drawn immediately from the States, not from the people: and we have no power to vary the idea of equal sovereignty. The only expedient that will cure the difficulty, is that of throwing the States into Hotchpot. To say that this is impracticable, will not make it so. Let it be tried, and we shall see wheher the Citizens of Massachusetts, Pennsylvania, and Virginia accede to it. It will be objected that Coercion will be impracticable. But will it be more so in one plan than the other? Its efficacy will depend on the quantum of power collected, not on its being drawn from the States, or from the individuals; and according to his plan it may be exerted on individuals as well as according that of Mr. R. a distinct executive and Judiciary also were equally provided by this plan. It is urged that two branches in the Legislature are necessary. Why? for the purpose of a check. But the reason of the precaution is not applicable to this case. Within a particular State, when party heats prevail, such a check may be necessary. In such a body as Congress it is less necessary, and besides, the delegations of the different States are checks on each other. Do the people at large complain of Congress? No: what they wish is that Congress may have more power. If the power now proposed be not enough the people hereafter will make additions to it. With proper powers Congress will act with more energy and wisdom than the proposed National Legislature; being fewer in number, and more secreted and refined by the mode of election. The plan of Mr. R. will also be enormously expensive. Allowing Georgia and Delaware two representatives each in the popular branch the aggregate number of that branch will be 180. Add to it half as many for the other branch and you have 270 members coming once at least a year from the most distant parts as well as the most central parts of the republic. In the present deranged State of our finances can so expensive a system be seriously thought of? By enlarging the powers of Congress the greatest part of this expense will be saved, and all purposes will be answered. At least a trial ought to be made. . .

HAMILTON'S PLAN AND HIS CRITIQUE OF THE RANDOLPH AND PATERSON PLANS

Monday *June* 18

. . . Mr. Hamilton, had been hitherto silent on the business before the Convention, partly from respect to others whose superior abilities age and experience rendered him unwilling to bring forward ideas dissimilar to theirs, and partly from his delicate situation with respect to his own State, to whose sentiments as expressed by his Colleagues, he could by no means accede. The crisis however which now marked our affairs, was too serious to permit any scruples whatever to prevail over the duty imposed on every man to contribute his efforts for the public safety and happiness. He was obliged therefore to declare himself unfriendly to both plans. He was particularly opposed to that from New Jersey, being fully convinced, that no amendment of the confederation, leaving the States in possession of their sovereignty could possibly answer the purpose. On the other hand he confessed he was much discouraged by the amazing extent of Country in expecting the desired blessings from any general sovereignty that could be substituted.—As to the powers of the Convention, he thought that doubts started on the subject had arisen from distinctions and reasonings to subtle. A *federal* Government he conceived to mean an association of independent Communities into one. Different Confederacies have different powers, and exercise them in different ways. In some instances the powers are exercised over collective bodies; in others over individuals, as in the German Diet—and among ourselves in cases of piracy. Great latitude therefore must be given to the signification of the term. The plan last proposed departs itself from the *federal* idea, as understood by some, since it is to operate eventually on individuals. He agreed moreover with the Honorable gentleman from Virginia [Mr. R.] that we owed it to our Country, to do on this emergency whatever we should deem essential to its happiness. The States sent us here to provide for the exigences of the Union. To rely on and propose any plan not adequate to these exigences, merely because it was not clearly within our powers, would be to sacrifice the means to the end. It may be said that the *States* can not *ratify* a plan not within the purview of the article of Confederation providing for alterations and amendments. But may not the States themselves in which no constitutional authority equal to this purpose exists in the Legislatures, have had in view a reference to the people at large. In the Senate of New York, a proviso was moved, that no act of the Convention should be binding until it should be referred to the people and ratified; and the motion was lost by a single voice only, the reason assigned against it, being that it [might possibly] be found an inconvenient shackle.

The great question is what provision shall we make for the happiness of our Country? He would first make a comparative examination of the two plans—prove that there were essential defects in both—and point out such changes as might render a *national one*, efficacious.—The great and essential principles necessary for the support of Government are (1) an active and constant interest in supporting it. This principle does not exist in the States in favor of the federal Government. They have evidently in a high degree, the esprit de corps. They constantly pursue internal interests adverse to those of the whole. They have their particular debts—their particular plans of finance etc. all these when opposed to, invariably prevail over the requisitions and plans of Congress. (2) the love of power, Men love power. The same remarks are applicable to this principle. The States have constantly shown a disposition rather to regain the powers delegated by them than to part with more, or to give effect to what they had parted with. The ambition of their demagogues is known to hate the control of the General Government. It may be remarked too that the Citizens have not that anxiety to prevent a dissolution of the General Government as of the particular Governments. A dissolution of the latter would be fatal: of the former would still leave the purposes of Government attainable to a considerable degree. Consider what such a State as Virginia will be in a few years, a few compared with the life of nations. How strongly will it feel its importance and self-sufficiency? (3) an habitual attachment of the people. The whole force of this tie is on the side of the State Government. Its sovereignty is immediately before the eyes of the people: its protection is immediately enjoyed by them. From its hand distributive justice, and all those acts which familiarize and endear Government to a people, are dispensed to them. (4) *Force* by which may be understood a *coercion of laws* or *coercion of arms*. Congress, have not the former except in few cases. In particular States, this coercion is nearly sufficient; though he held it in most cases, not entirely so. A certain portion of military force is absolutely necessary in large communities. Massachusetts is now feeling this necessity and making provision for it. But how can this force be exerted on the States collectively. It is impossible. It amounts to a war between the parties. Foreign powers also will not be idle spectators. They will interpose, the confusion will increase, and a dissolution of the Union ensue. (5) *influence*, he did not mean corruption, but a dispensation of those regular honors and emoluments, which produce an attachment to the Government almost all the weight of these is on the side of the States; and must continue so as long as the States continue to exist. All the passions then we see, of avarice, ambition, interest, which govern most individuals, and all public bodies, fall into the current of the States, and do not flow in the stream of the General Government; the former therefore will generally be an overmatch for the General Government and render any confederacy, in its very nature precarious. . . How then are all these evils to be avoided? only by such a complete sovereignty in the general Government as will turn all the strong principles and passions above mentioned on its side. Does the scheme of New Jersey produce this effect? does it afford any substantial remedy whatever? On the contrary it labors under great defects, and the defect of some of its provisions will destroy the efficacy of others. It gives a direct revenue to Congress, but this will not be sufficient. The balance can only be supplied by requisitions; which experience proves can not be relied on. If States are to deliberate on the mode, they will also deliberate on the object of the supplies, and will grant or not grant as they approve or disapprove of it. The delinquency of one will invite and countenance it in others. Quotas too must in the nature of things be so unequal as to produce the same evil. To what standard will you resort? Land is a fallacious one. . . Take numbers of inhabitants for the rule and make like comparison of different countries, and you will find it to be equally unjust. The different degrees of industry and improvement in different Countries render the first object a precarious measure of wealth. Much depends too on *situation*. Connecticut, New Jersey, and North Carolina, not being commercial States and contributing to the wealth of the commercial ones, can never bear quotas assessed by the ordinary rules of proportion. They will and must fail [in their duty]—their example will be followed, and the Union itself be dissolved. Whence then is the national revenue to be drawn? from Commerce, even from exports which notwithstanding the common opinion are fit objects of moderate taxation, from excise, etc. etc. These though not equal, are less unequal than quotas. Another destructive ingredient in the plan, is that equality of suffrage which is so much desired by the small States. It is not in human nature that Virginia and the large States should consent to it, or if they did that they should long abide by it. It shocks too much the ideas of Justice, and every human feeling. Bad principles in a Government though slow are sure in their operation, and will gradually destroy it. A doubt has been raised whether Congress at present have a right to keep ships or troops in time of peace. He leans to the negative. Mr. Paterson's plan provides no remedy.—If the powers proposed were adequate, the organization of Congress is such that they could never be properly and effectually exercised. The members of Congress being chosen by the

States and subject to recall, represent all the local prejudices. Should the powers be found effectual, they will from time to time be heaped on them, till a tyrannic sway shall be established. The general power whatever be its form if it preserves itself, must swallow up the State powers, otherwise it will be swallowed up by them. It is against all the principles of a good Government to vest the requisite powers in such a body as Congress. Two Sovereignties can not co-exist within the same limits. Giving powers to Congress must eventuate in a bad Government or in no Government. The plan of New Jersey therefore will not do. What then is to be done? Here he was embarrassed. The extent of the Country to be governed, discouraged him. The expense of a general Government was also formidable; unless there were such a diminution of expense on the side of the State Governments as the case would admit. If they were extinguished, he was persuaded that great economy might be obtained by substituting a general Government. He did not mean however to shock the public opinion by proposing such a measure. On the other hand he saw no other necessity for declining it. They are not necessary for any of the great purposes of commerce, revenue, or agriculture. Subordinate authorities he was aware would be necessary. There must be district tribunals: corporations for local purposes. But cui bono, the vast and expensive apparatus now appertaining to the States. The only difficulty of a serious nature which occurred to him, was that of drawing representatives from the extremes to the center of the Community. What inducements can be offered that will suffice? The moderate wages for the 1st branch, would only be a bait to little demagogues. Three dollars or thereabouts he supposed would be the Utmost. The Senate he feared from a similar cause, would be filled by certain undertakers who wish for particular offices under the Government. This view of the subject almost led him to despair that a Republican Government could be established over so great an extent. He was sensible at the same time that it would be unwise to propose one of any other form. In his private opinion he had no scruple in declaring, supported as he was by the opinions of so many of the wise and good, that the British Government was the best in the world: and that he doubted much whether any thing short of it would do in America. He hoped Gentlemen of different opinions would bear with him in this, and begged them to recollect the change of opinion on this subject which had taken place and was still going on. It was once thought that the power of Congress was amply sufficient to secure the end of their institution. The error was now seen by every one. The members most tenacious of republicanism, he observed, were as loud as any in declaiming against the vices of democracy. This progress of the public mind led him to anticipate the time, when others as well as himself would join in the praise bestowed . . . on the British Constitution, namely, that it is the only Government in the world 'which unites public strength with individual security.'—In every community where industry is encouraged, there will be a division of it into a few and the many. Hence separate interests will arise. There will be debtors and creditors etc. Give all power to the many, they will oppress the few. Give all power to the few they will oppress the many. Both therefore ought to have power, that each may defend itself against the other. To the want of this check we owe our paper money—instalment laws etc. To the proper adjustment of it the British owe the excellence of their Constitution. Their house of Lords is a most noble institution. Having nothing to hope for by a change, and a sufficient interest by means of their property, in being faithful to the National interest, they form a permanent barrier against every pernicious innovation, whether attempted on the part of the Crown or of the Commons. No temporary Senate will have firmness enough to answer the purpose. . . Gentlemen differ in their opinions concerning the necessary checks, from the different estimates they form of the human passions. They suppose seven years a sufficient period to give the Senate an adequate firmness, from not duly considering the amazing violence and turbulence of the democratic spirit. When a great object of Government is pursued, which seizes the popular passions, they spread like wild fire, and become irresistable. He appealed to the gentlemen from the New England States whether experience had not there verified the remark. As to the Executive, it seemed to be admitted that no good one could be established on Republican principles. Was not this giving up the merits of the question; for can there be a good Government without a good Executive. The English model was the only good one on this subject. The Hereditary interest of the King was so interwoven with that of the Nation, and his personal emoluments so great, that he was placed above the danger of being corrupted from abroad—and at the same time was both sufficiently independent and sufficiently controlled, to answer the purpose of the institution at home. One of the weak sides of Republics was there being liable to foreign influence and corruption. Men of little character, acquiring great power become easily the tools of intermedling neighbours. . . What is the inference from all these observations? That we ought to go as far in order to attain stability and permanency, as republican principles will admit. Let one branch of the Legislature hold their places for life or at least during good-behaviour. Let the Executive also be for life. He appealed to the feelings of the members present whether a term of seven years, would induce the sacrifices of private affairs which an acceptance of public trust would require, so as to ensure the services of the best Citizens. On this plan we should have in the Senate a permanent will, a weighty interest, which would answer essential purposes. But is this a Republican Government it will be asked? Yes, if all the Magistrates are appointed, and vacancies are filled, by the people, or a process of election originating with the people. He was sensible that an Executive constituted as he proposed would have in fact but little of the power and independence that might be necessary. On the other plan of appointing him for 7 years, he thought the Executive ought to have but little power. He would be ambitious, with the means of making creatures; and as the object of his ambition would be to *prolong* his power, it is probable that in case of a war, he would avail himself of the emergency, to evade or refuse a degradation from his place. An Executive for life has not this motive for forgetting his fidelity, and will therefore be a safer depositary of power. It will be objected probably, that such an Executive will be an *elective* Monarch, and will give birth to the tumults which characterise that form of Government. He would reply that Monarch is an indefinite term. It marks not either the degree or duration of power. If this Executive Magistrate would be a monarch for life—the other proposed by the Report from the Committee of the whole, would be a monarch for seven years. The circumstance of being elective was also applicable to both. It had been observed by judicious writers that elective monarchies would be the best if they could be guarded against the *tumults* excited by the ambition and intrigues of competitors. He was not sure that tumults were an inseparable evil. He rather thought this character of Elective Monarchies had been taken rather from particular cases than from general principles. . . Might not such a mode of election be devised among ourselves as will defend the community against these effects in any dangerous degree? Having made these observations he would read to the Committee a sketch of a plan which he should prefer to either of those under consideration. He was aware that it went beyond the ideas of most members. But will such a plan be adopted out of doors? In return [he would ask] will the people adopt the other plan? At present they will adopt neither. But he sees the Union dissolving or already dissolved—he sees evils operating in the States which must soon cure the people of their fondness for democracies—he sees that a great progress has been already made and is still going on in the public mind. He thinks therefore that the people will in time be unshackled from their prejudices; and whenever that happens, they will themselves not be satisfied at stopping where the plan of Mr. R. would place them, but be ready to go as far at least as he proposes. He did not mean to offer the paper he had sketched as a proposition to the Committee. It was meant only to give a more correct view of his ideas, and to suggest the amendments which he should probably propose to the plan of Mr. R. in the proper stages of its future discussion. He reads his sketch in the words following:

I. The Supreme Legislative power of the United States of America to be vested in two different bodies of men; the one to be called the Assembly, the other the Senate who together shall form the Legislature of the United States with power to pass all laws whatsoever subject to the Negative hereafter mentioned.

II. The Assembly to consist of persons elected by the people to serve for three years.

III. The Senate to consist of persons elected to serve during good behaviour; their election to be made by electors chosen for that purpose by the people; in order to this the States to be divided into election districts. On the death, removal or resignation of any Senator his place to be filled out of the district from which he came.

IV. The supreme Executive authority of the United States to be vested in a Governour to be elected to serve during good behaviour—the election to be made by Electors chosen by the people in the Election Districts aforesaid—The authorities and functions of the Executive to be as follows: to have a negative on all laws about to be passed, and the execution of all laws passed, to have the direction of war when authorized or begun; to have with the advice and approbation of the Senate the power of making all treaties; to have the sole appointment of the heads or chief officers of the departments of Finance, War and Foreign Affairs; to have the nomination of all other officers (Ambassadors to foreign Nations included) subject to the approbation or rejection of the Senate; to have the power of pardoning all offences except Treason; which he shall not pardon without the approbation of the Senate.

V. On the death resignation or removal of the Governour his authorities to be exercised by the President of the Senate till a Successor be appointed.

VI. The Senate to have the sole power of declaring war, the power of advising and approving all Treaties, the power of approving or rejecting all appointments of officers except the heads or chiefs of the departments of Finance War and foreign affairs.

VII. The Supreme Judicial authority to be vested in — Judges to hold their offices during good behaviour with adequate and permanent salaries. This Court to have original jurisdiction in all causes of capture, and an appellative jurisdiction in all causes in which the revenues of the general Government or the citizens of foreign nations are concerned.

VIII. The Legislature of the United States to have power to institute Courts in each State for the determination of all matters of general concern.

IX. The Governour, Senators and all officers of the United States to be liable to impeachment for mal—and corrupt conduct; and upon conviction to be removed from office, and disqualified for holding any place of trust or profit—all impeachments to be tried by a court to consist of the Chief ——— or Judge of the Superior Court of Law of each State, provided such Judge shall hold his place during good behavior, and have a permanent salary.

X. All laws of the particular States contrary to the Constitution or laws of the United States to be utterly void; and the better to prevent such laws being passed, the Governour or president of each state shall be appointed by the General Government and shall have a negative upon the laws about to be passed in the State of which he is Governour or President.

XI. No State to have any forces land or Naval; and the Militia of all the States to be under the sole and exclusive direction of the United States, the officers of which to be appointed and commisioned by them. . .

POSITION OF THE STATES IN THE UNION

Saturday *June 9*

. . . Mr. Paterson considered the proposition for a proportional representation as striking at the existence of the lesser States. He would premise however to an investigation of this question some remarks on the nature structure and powers of the Convention. The Convention he said was formed in pursuance of an Act of Congress that this act was recited in several of the Commissions, particularly that of Massachusetts which he required to be read: That the amendment of the confederacy was the object of all the laws and commissions on the subject; that the articles of the confederation were therefore the proper basis of all the proceedings of the Convention. We ought to keep within its limits, or we should be charged by our constituents with usurpation. . . The idea of a national Government as contradistinguished from a federal one, never entered into the mind of any of them, and to the public mind we must accommodate ourselves. . . *The proposition* could not be maintained whether considered in reference to us as a nation, or as a confederacy. A confederacy supposes sovereignty in the members composing it and sovereignty supposes equality. . . He said there was no more reason that a great individual State contributing much, should have more votes than a small one contributing little, than that a rich individual citizen should have more votes than an indigent one. . . Give the large States an influence in proportion to their magnitude, and what will be the consequence? Their ambition will be proportionally increased, and the small States will have every thing to fear. . . It has been said that if a National Government is to be formed so as to operate on the people and not on the States, the representatives ought to be drawn from the people. But why so? May not a Legislature filled by the State Legislatures operate on the people who choose the State Legislatures? or may not a practicable coercion be found? He admitted that there was none such in the existing System. He was attached strongly to the plan of the existing confederacy, in which the people choose their Legislative representatives; and the Legislatures their federal representatives. No other amendments were wanting than to mark the orbits of the State with due precision, and provide for the use of coercion, which was the great point. . . New Jersey will never confederate on the plan before the Committee. She would be swallowed up. He had rather submit to a monarch, to a despot, than to such a fate. He would not only oppose the plan here but on his return home do everything in his power to defeat it there.

Mr. Wilson . . . entered elaborately into the defence of a proportional representation, stating for his first position that as all authority was derived from the people, equal numbers of people ought to have an equal number of representatives, and different numbers of people different numbers of representatives. This principle had been improperly violated in the Confederation, owing to the urgent circumstances of the time. . . Mr. P. admitted persons, not property to be the measure of suffrage. Are not the citizens of Pennsylvania equal to those of New Jersey? does it require 150 of the former to balance 50 of the latter? Representatives of different districts ought clearly to hold the same proportion to each other, as their respective constituents hold to each other. . . We have been told that each State being sovereign, all are equal. So each man is naturally a sovereign over himself, and all men are therefore naturally equal. Can he retain this equality when he becomes a member of civil Government? He can not. As little can a Sovereign State, when it becomes a member of a federal Government. If New Jersey will not part with her Sovereignty it is in vain to talk of Government. . .

Tuesday *June 19*

. . . Mr. Wilson observed that by a National Government he did not mean one that would swallow up the State Governments as seemed to be wished by some gentlemen. He was tenacious of the idea of preserving the latter. He thought, contrary to the opinion of Col. Hamilton that they might not only subsist but subsist on friendly terms with the former. They were absolutely necessary for certain purposes which the former could not reach. All large Governments must be subdivided into lesser jurisdictions. . .

Col. Hamilton . . . He had not been understood yesterday. By an abolition of the States, he meant that no boundary could be drawn between the National and State Legislatures; that the former must therefore have indefinite authority. If it were limited at all, the rivalship of the States would gradually subvert it. Even as Corporations the extent of some of them as Virginia, Massachusetts, etc. would be formidable. As *States*, he thought they ought to be abolished. But he admitted the necessity of leaving in them, subordinate jurisdictions. . .

Mr. King . . . conceived that the import of the terms 'States' 'Sovereignty' '*national*' 'federal,' had been often used and applied in the discussion inaccurately and delusively. The States were not 'sovereigns' in the sense contended for by some. They did not possess the peculiar features of sovereignty. They could not make war, nor peace, nor alliances, nor treaties. Considering them as political Beings, they were dumb, for they could not speak to any foreign Sovereign whatever. They were deaf, for they could not hear any propositions from such Sovereign. They had not even the organs or faculties of defence or offence, for they could not of themselves raise troops, or equip vessels, for war. On the other side, if the Union of the States comprises the idea of a confederation, it comprises that also of consolidation. A Union of the States is a union of the men composing them, from whence a *national* character results to the whole. Congress can act alone without the States—they can act and their acts will be binding against the Instructions of the States. If they declare war, war is de jure declared, captures made in pursuance of it are lawful. No acts of the States can vary the situation, or prevent the judicial consequences. If the States therefore retained some portion of their sovereignty, they had certainly divested themselves of essential portions of it. If they formed a confederacy in some respects—they formed a Nation in others. . . He doubted much the practicability of annihilating the States; but thought that much of their power ought to be taken from them.

Mr. Martin said he considered that the separation from Great Britain placed the 13 States in a state of nature towards each other; that they would have remained in that state till this time, but for the confederation; that they entered into the confederation on the footing of equality; that they met now to amend it on the same footing, and that he could never accede to a plan that would introduce an inequality and lay 10 States at the mercy of Virginia, Massachusetts, and Pennsylvania.

Mr. Wilson could not admit the doctrine that when the Colonies became independent of Great Britain, they became independent also of each other. He read the Declaration of Independence, observing thereon that the *United Colonies were* declared to be free and independent States; and inferring that they were independent, not *Individually* but *Unitedly* and that they were confederated as they were independent, States.

Col. Hamilton assented to the doctrine of Mr. Wilson. . .

Wednesday *June 27*

. . . Mr. L. Martin contended at great length and with great eagerness that the General Government was meant merely to preserve the State Governments: not to govern individuals: that its powers ought to be kept within narrow limits; that if too little power was given to it, more might be added; but that if too much, it could never be resumed: that individuals as such have little to do but with their own States; that the General Government has no more to apprehend from the States composing [the Union] while it pursues proper measures, than a Government over individuals has to apprehend from its subjects: that to resort to the Citizens at large for their sanction to a new Government will be throwing them back into a State of Nature: that the dissolution of the State Governments is involved in the nature of the process: that the people have no right to do this without the consent of those to whom they have delegated their power for State purposes; through their tongue only they can speak, through their ears, only, can hear: that the States have shown a good disposition to comply with the Acts of Congress weak, contemptibly weak as that body has been; and have failed through inability alone to comply: that the heaviness of the private debts, and the waste of property during the war, were the chief causes of this inability . . . that an equal vote in each State was essential to the federal idea, and was founded in justice and freedom, not merely in policy: that though the States may give up this right of sovereignty, yet they had not, and ought not: that the States like individuals were in a State of nature equally sovereign and free. In order to prove that individuals in a State of nature are equally free and independent he read passages from Locke, Vattel, Lord Summers—Priestly. To prove that the case is the same with States till they surrender their equal sovereignty, he read other passages in Locke and Vattel, and also Rutherford: that the States being equal cannot treat or confederate so as to give up an equality of votes without giving up their liberty. . .

Thursday *June 28*

. . . Mr. Madison said he was much disposed to concur in any expedient not inconsistent with fundamental principles, that could remove the difficulty concerning the rule of representation. But he could neither be convinced that the rule contended for was just, nor necessary for the safety of the small States against the large States. . . The fallacy of the reasoning drawn from the equality of Sovereign States in the formation of compacts, lay in confounding mere Treaties, in which were specified certain duties to which the parties were to be bound, and certain rules by which their subjects were to be reciprocally governed in their intercourse, with a compact by which an authority was created paramount to the parties, and making laws for the government of them. . . By the plan [proposed] a complete power of taxation, the highest prerogative of supremacy is proposed to be vested in the National Government. Many other powers are added which assimilate it to the Government of individual States. The negative [on the State laws] proposed, will make it an essential branch of the State Legislatures and of course will require that it should be exercised by a body established on like principles with the other branches of those Legislatures.—That it is not necessary to secure the small States against the large ones he conceived to be equally obvious: Was a combination of the large ones dreaded? this must arise either from some interest common to Virginia, Massachusetts, and Pennsylvania and distinguishing them from the other States [or from the mere circumstance of similarity of size]. Did any such common interest exist? In point of situation they could not have been more effectually separated from each other by the most jealous citizen of the most jealous State. In point of manners, Religion and the other circumstances, which sometimes beget affection between different communities, they were not more assimilated than the other States.—In point of the staple productions they were as dissimilar as any three other States in the union. . . . Was a Combination to be apprehended from the mere circumstance of equality of size? Experience suggested no such danger. The journals of Congress did not present any peculiar association of these States in the votes recorded. . . Were the large States formidable *singly* to their smaller neighbours? On this supposition the latter ought to wish for such a general Government as will operate with equal energy on the former as on themselves. The more lax the band, the more liberty the larger will have to avail themselves of their superior force. . . In a word; the two extremes before us are a perfect separation and a perfect incorporation, of the 13 States. In the first case they would be independent nations subject to no law, but the law of nations. In the last, they would be mere counties of one entire republic, subject to one common law. In the first case the smaller states would have every thing to fear from the larger. In the last they would have nothing to fear. The true policy of the small States therefore lies in promoting those principles and that form of Government which will most approximate the States to the condition of Counties. Another consideration may be added. If the General Government be feeble, the large States distrusting its continuance, and foreseeing that their importance and security may depend on their own size and strength, will never submit to a partition. Give to the General Government sufficient energy and permanency, and you remove the objection. . .

Mr. Sherman. The question is not what rights naturally belong to men; but how they may be most equally and effectually guarded in Society. And if some give up more than others in order to obtain this end, there can be no room for complaint. To do otherwise, to require an equal concession from all, if it would create danger to the rights of some, would be sacrificing the end to the means. The rich man who enters into Society along with the poor man, gives up more than the poor man, yet with an equal vote he is equally safe. Were he to have more votes than the poor man in proportion to his superior stake, the rights of the poor man would immediately cease to be secure. This consideration prevailed when the articles of confederation were formed. . .

Friday *June 29*

Dr. Johnson. The controversy must be endless whilst Gentlemen differ in the grounds of their arguments; Those on one side considering the States as districts of people composing one political Society; those on the other considering them as so many political societies. The fact is that the States do exist as political Societies, and a Government is to be formed for them in their political capacity, as well as for the individuals composing them. Does it not seem to follow, that if the States as such are to exist they must be armed with some power of self-defence. This is the idea of Col. Mason who appears to have looked to the bottom of this matter. Besides the Aristocratic and other interests, which ought to have the means of defending themselves, the States have their interests as such, and are equally entitled to like means. On the whole he thought that as in some respects the States are to be considered in their political capacity, and in others as districts of individual citizens, the two ideas embraced on different sides, instead of being opposed to each other, ought to be combined; that in *one* branch the *people*, ought to be represented; in the *other*, the *States*. . .

Mr. Madison agreed with Dr. Johnson, that the mixed nature of the Government ought to be kept in view; but thought too much stress was laid on the rank of the States as political societies. There was a gradation, he observed from the smallest corporation, with the most limited powers, to the largest empire with the most perfect sovereignty. He pointed out the limitations on the sovereignty of the States as now confederated; [their laws in relation to the paramount law of the Confederacy were analogous to that of bye laws to the supreme law, within a State.] Under the proposed Govt. the powers of the States will be much farther reduced. According to the views of every member, the General Government will have powers far beyond those exercised by the British Parliament when the States were part of the British Empire. It will in particular have the power, without the consent of the State Legislatures, to levy money directly on the people themselves; and therefore not to divest such *unequal* portions of the people as composed the several States, of an *equal* voice, would subject the system to the reproaches and evils which have resulted from the vicious representation in Great Britain. . .

Mr. Hamilton observed that individuals forming political Societies modify their rights differently, with regard to suffrage. Examples of it are found in all the States. In all of them some individuals are deprived of the right altogether, not having the requisite qualification of property. In some of the States the right of suffrage is allowed in some cases and refused in others. To vote for a member in one branch, a certain quantum of property, to vote for a member in another branch of the Legislature, a higher quantum of property is required. In like manner States may modify their right of suffrage differently, the larger exercising a larger, the smaller a smaller share of it. But as States are a collection of individual men which ought we to respect most, the rights of the people composing them, or of the artificial beings resulting from the composition. Nothing could be more preposterous or absurd than to sacrifice the former to the latter. It has been said that if the smaller States renounce their *equality* they renounce at the same time their *liberty*. The truth is it is a contest for power, not for liberty. Will the men composing the small States be less free than those composing the larger. The State of Delaware having 40,000 souls will *lose power*, if she has 1/10 only of the votes allowed to Pennsylvania having 400,000: but will the people of Delaware *be less free,* if each citizen has an equal vote with each citizen of Pennsylvania. . .

Mr. Elseworth moved that the rule of suffrage in the 2d branch be the same with that established by the articles of confederation. . . He hoped it would become a ground of compromise with regard to the 2d branch. We are partly national; partly federal. The proportional representation in the first branch was conformable to the national principle and would secure the large States against the small. An equality of voices was conformable to the federal principle and was necessary to secure the Small States against the large. He trusted that on this middle ground a compromise would take place. . .

Saturday *June 30*

Mr. Wilson did not expect such a motion after the establishment of the contrary principle in the 1st branch . . . Can we forget for whom we are forming a Government? Is it for *men,* or for the imaginary beings called States? Will our honest Constituents be satisfied with metaphysical distinctions? . . . Much has been said of an imaginary combination of three States. Sometimes a danger of monarchy, sometimes of aristocracy has been charged on it. . . Are the people of the three large States more aristocratic than those of the small ones? Whence then the danger of aristocracy from their influence? It is all a mere illusion of names. We talk of States, till we forget what they are composed of. Is a real and fair majority, the natural hot-bed of aristocracy? It is a part of the definition of this species of Government or rather of tyranny, that the smaller number governs the greater. It is true that a majority of States in the 2d branch can not carry a law against a majority of the people in the 1st. But this removes half only of the objection. Bad Governments are of two sorts. (1.) that which does too little. (2.) that which does too much: that which fails through weakness; and that which destroys through oppression. Under which of these evils do the United States at present groan? under the weakness and inefficiency of its Government. To remedy this weakness we have been sent to this Convention. If the motion should be agreed to, we shall leave the United States fettered precisely as heretofore; with the additional mortification of seeing the good purposes of the fair representation of the people in the 1st branch, defeated in the 2d. . .

Mr. Elseworth. The capital objection of Mr. Wilson 'that the minority will rule the majority' is not true. The power is given to the few to save them from being destroyed by the many. If an equality of votes had been given to them in both branches, the objection might have had weight. Is it a novel thing that the few should have a check on the many? Is it not the case in the British Constitution the wisdom of which so many gentlemen have united in applauding? Have not the House of Lords, who form so small a proportion of the nation a negative on the laws, as a necessary defence of their peculiar rights against the encroachments of the Commons. No instance [of a Confederacy] has existed in which an equality of voices has not been exercised by the members of it. We are running from one extreme to another. We are razing the foundations of the building. When we need only repair the roof. . .

Mr. King observed . . . that he was . . . filled with astonishment that if we were convinced that every *man* in America was secured in all his rights, we should be ready to sacrifice this substantial good to the phantom of *State* sovereignty . . . that he could not therefore but repeat his amazement that when a just Government founded on a fair representation of the *people* of America was within our reach, we should renounce the blessing, from an attachment to the ideal freedom and importance of *States*. . .

THE LEGISLATIVE

Thursday *May 31*

. . . [The 3d Resolution] 'that the national Legislature ought to consist of two branches' was agreed to without debate or dissent, [except that of Pennsylvania, given probably from complaisance to Dr. Franklin who was understood to be partial to a single House of Legislation.]

[Resolution 4 first clause] 'that the members of the first branch of the National Legislature ought to be elected by the people of [the several] States' [being taken up].

Mr. Sherman opposed the election by the people, insisting that it ought to be by the [State] Legislatures. The people he said, [immediately] should have as little to do as may be about the Government. They want information and are constantly liable to be misled.

Mr. Gerry. The evils we experience flow from the excess of democracy. The people do not want virtue; but are the dupes of pretended patriots. In Massachusetts it has been fully confirmed by experience that they are daily misled into the most baneful measures and opinions by the false reports circulated by designing men, and which no one on the spot can refute. One principal evil arises from the want of due provision for those employed in the administration of Government. It would seem to be a maxim of democracy to starve the public servants. He mentioned the popular clamour in Massachusetts for the reduction of salaries and the attack made on that of the Governor though secured by the spirit of the Constitution itself. He had he said been too republican heretofore: he was still however republican, but had been taught by experience the danger of the levelling spirit.

Mr. Mason argued strongly for an election of the larger branch by the people. It was to be the grand depository of the democratic principle of the Government. It was, so to speak, to be our House of Commons—It ought to know and sympathise with every part of the community; and ought therefore to be taken not only from different parts of the whole republic. . . He admitted that we had been too democratic but was afraid we should incautiously run into the opposite extreme. We ought to attend to the rights of every class of the people. He had often wondered at the indifference of the superior classes of society to this dictate of humanity and policy, considering that however affluent their circumstances, or elevated their situations, might be, the course of a few years, not only might but certainly would, distribute their posterity throughout the lowest classes of Society. Every selfish motive therefore, every family attachment, ought to recommend such a system of policy as would provide no less carefully for the rights—and happiness of the lowest than of the highest orders of Citizens.

Mr. Wilson contended strenuously for drawing the most numerous branch of the Legislature immediately from the people. He was for raising the federal pyramid to a considerable altitude, and for that reason wished to give it as broad a basis as possible. No government could long subsist without the confidence of the people. In a republican Government this confidence was peculiarly essential. He also thought it wrong to increase the weight of the State Legislatures by making them the electors of the national Legislature. All interference between the general and local Governments should be obviated as much as possible. On examination it would be found that the opposition of States to federal measures had proceeded much more from the Officers of the States, than from the people at large.

Mr. Madison considered the popular election of one branch of the national Legislature as essential to every plan of free Government. He observed that in some of the States one branch of the Legislature was composed of men already removed from the people by an intervening body of electors. That if the first branch of the general legislature should be elected by the State Legislatures, the second branch elected by the first—the Executive by the second together with the first; and other appointments again made for subordinate purposes by the Executive, the people would be lost sight of altogether; and the necessary sympathy between them and their rulers and officers, too little felt. He was an advocate for the policy of refining the popular appointments by successive filtrations, but thought it might be pushed too far. He wished the expedient to be resorted to only in the appointment of the second branch of the Legislature, and in the Executive and judiciary branches of the Government. He thought too that the great fabric to be raised would be more stable and durable if it should rest on the solid foundation of the people themselves, than if it should stand merely on the pillars of the Legislatures.

Mr. Gerry did not like the election by the people. The maxims taken from the British constitution were often fallacious when applied to our situation which was extremely different. Experience he said had shown that the State Legislatures drawn immediately from the people did not always possess their confidence. He had no objection however to an election by the people if it were so qualified that men of honor and character might not be unwilling to be joined in the appointments. He seemed to think the people might nominate a certain number out of which the State legislatures should be bound to choose. . .

Wednesday *June 6*

. . . Mr. Sherman. If it were in view to abolish the State Governments the elections ought to be by the people. If the State Governments are to be continued, it is necessary in order to preserve harmony between the national and State Governments that the elections to the former should be made by the latter. The right of participating in the National Government would be sufficiently secured to the people by their election of the State Legislatures. The objects of the Union, he thought were few. (1.) defence against foreign danger. (2.) against internal disputes and a resort to force. (3.) treaties with foreign nations. (4.) regulating foreign commerce, and drawing revenue from it. These and perhaps a few lesser objects alone rendered a Confederation to the States necessary. All other matters civil and criminal would be much better in the hands of the States. The people are more happy in small than large States. States may indeed be too small as Rhode Island, and thereby be too subject to faction. Some others are perhaps too large, the powers of Government not being able to pervade them. He was for giving the General Government power to legislate and execute within a defined province. . .

Mr. Madison . . . differed from the member from Connecticut [Mr. Sherman] in thinking the objects mentioned to be all the principal ones that required a National Government. Those were certainly important and necessary objects; but he combined with them the necessity, of providing more effectually for the security of private rights, and the steady dispensation of Justice. Interference with these were evils which had more perhaps than any thing else, produced this convention. Was it to be supposed that republican liberty could long exist under the abuses of it practiced in [some of] the States. The gentleman [Mr. Sherman] had admitted that in a very small State, faction and oppression would prevail. It was to be inferred then that wherever these prevailed the State was too small. Had they not prevailed in the largest as well as the smallest though less than in the smallest; and were we not thence admonished to enlarge the sphere as far as the nature of the Government would admit. This was the only defence against the inconveniences of democracy consistent with the democratic form of Government. All civilized Societies would be divided into different Sects, Factions, and interests, as they happened to consist of rich and poor, debtors and creditors, the landed, the manufacturing, the commercial interests, the inhabitants of this district, or that district, the followers of this political leader or that political leader, the disciples of this religious sect or that religious sect. In all cases where a majority are united by a common interest or passion, the rights of the minority are in danger. What motives are to restrain them? A prudent regard to the maxim that honesty is the best policy is found by experience to be as little regarded by bodies of men as by individuals. Respect for character is always diminished in proportion to the number among whom the blame or praise is to be divided. Conscience, the only remaining tie is known to be inadequate in individuals: In large numbers, little is to be expected from it. Besides, Religion itself may become a motive to persecution and oppression— These observations are verified by the Histories of every Country ancient and modern. In Greece and Rome the rich and poor, the creditors and debtors, as well as the patricians and plebeians alternately oppressed each other with equal unmercifulness. . . Why was America so justly apprehensive. . . The holders of one species of property have thrown a disproportion of taxes on the holders of another species. The lesson we are to draw from the whole is that where a majority are united by a common sentiment and have an opportunity, the rights of the minor party become insecure. In a Republican Government the Majority if united have always an opportunity. The only remedy is to enlarge the sphere, and thereby divide the community into so great a number of interests and parties, that in the 1st place a majority will not be likely at the same moment to have a common interest separate from that of the whole or of the minority; and in the 2d place, that in case they should have such an interest, they may not be apt to unite in the pursuit of it. It was incumbent on us then to try this remedy, and with that view to frame a republican system on such a scale and in such a form as will control all the evils which have been experienced.

Mr. Dickinson considered it as essential that one branch of the Legislature should be drawn immediately from the people; and as expedient that the other should be chosen by the Legislatures of the States. This combination of the State Governments with the National Government was as politic as it was unavoidable. In the formation of the Senate we ought to carry it through such a refining process as will assimilate it as near as may be to the House of Lords in England. He repeated his warm eulogisms on the British Constitution. He was for a strong National Government but for leaving the states a considerable agency in the System. . .

Mr. Pierce was for an election by the people as to the 1st branch and by the States as to the 2d branch; by which means the citizens of the States would be represented both *individually* and *collectively*. . .

Thursday *June 7*

. . . Mr. Dickinson now moved 'that the members of the 2d branch ought to be chosen by the individual Legislatures.' . .

Mr. Wilson. If we are to establish a national Government, that Government ought to flow from the people at large. If one branch of it should be chosen by the Legislatures, and the other by the people, the two branches will rest on different foundations, and dissentions will naturally arise between them. He wished the Senate to be elected by the people as well as the other branch, and the people might be divided into proper districts for the purpose and moved to postpone the motion of Mr. Dickinson, in order to take up one of that import. . .

Mr. Madison. If the motion of Mr. Dickinson should be agreed to, we must either depart from the doctrine of proportional representation; or admit into the Senate a very large number of members. The first is inadmissible, being evidently unjust. The second is inexpedient. The use of the Senate is to consist in its proceeding with more coolness, with more system, and with more wisdom, than the popular branch. Enlarge their number and you communicate to them the vices which they are meant to correct. He differed from Mr. D. who thought that the additional number would give additional weight to the body. On the contrary it appeared to him that their weight would be an inverse ratio to their number. The example of the Roman Tribunes was applicable. They lost their influence and power, in proportion as their number was augmented. The reason seemed to be obvious: They were appointed to take care of the popular interests and pretensions at Rome, because the people by reason of their numbers could not act in concert, were liable to fall into factions among themselves, and to become a prey to their aristocratic adversaries.

The more the representatives of the people therefore were multiplied, the more they partook of the infirmities of their constituents, the more liable they became to be divided among themselves either from their own indiscretions or the artifices of the opposite factions, and of course the less capable of fulfilling their trust. When the weight of a set of men depends merely on their personal characters; the greater the number the greater the weight. When it depends on the degree of political authority lodged in them the smaller the number the greater the weight. . .

Mr. Wilson . . . The British Government cannot be our model. We have no materials for a similar one. Our manners, our laws, the abolition of entails and of primogeniture, the whole genius of the people, are opposed to it. He did not see the danger of the States being devoured by the National Government. On the contrary, he wished to keep them from devouring the national Government. He was not however for extinguishing these planets as was supposed by Mr. D.—neither did he on the other hand, believe that they would warm or enlighten the Sun. Within their proper orbits they must still be suffered to act for subordinate purposes [for which their existence is made essential by the great extent of our Country]. . .

Mr. Madison . . . The great evils complained of were that the State Legislatures run into schemes of paper money etc, whenever solicited by the people, and sometimes without even the sanction of the people. Their influence then, instead of checking a like propensity in the National Legislature, may be expected to promote it. Nothing can be more contradictory than to say that the National Legislature without a proper check will follow the example of the State legislatures, and in the same breath, that the State Legislatures are the only proper check. . .

Tuesday *June 12*

. . . Mr. Spaight moved to fill the blank for the duration of the appointments to the 2d branch of the National [Legislature] with the words '7 years.' . .

Mr. Randolph was for the term of 7 years. The Democratic licentiousness of the State Legislatures proved the necessity of a firm Senate. The object of this 2d branch is to control the democratic branch of the National Legislature. . .

Mr. Madison considered 7 years as a term by no means too long. What we wished was to give to the Government that stability which was every where called for, and which the enemies of the Republican form alleged to be inconsistent with its nature. He was not afraid of giving too much stability by the term of seven years. His fear was that the popular branch would still be too great an overmatch for it. It was to be much lamented that we had so little direct experience to guide us. . . He conceived it to be of great importance that a stable and *firm* Government organized in the republican form should be held out to the people. If this be not done, and the people be left to judge of this species of Government by the operations of the defective systems under which they now live, it is much to be feared the time is not distant when, in universal disgust, they will renounce the blessing which they have purchased at so dear a rate, and be ready for any change that may be proposed to them. . .

Tuesday *June 26*

. . . Mr. Madison. In order to judge of the form to be given to this institution, it will be proper to take a view of the ends to be served by it. These were first to protect the people against their rulers: secondly to protect the people against the transient impressions into which they themselves might be led. A people deliberating in a temperate moment, and with the experience of other nations before them, on the plan of Government most likely to secure their happiness, would first be aware, that those charged with the public happiness, might betray their trust. An obvious precaution against this danger would be to divide the trust between different bodies of men, who might watch and check each other. In this way they would be governed by the same prudence which has prevailed in organizing the subordinate departments of Government where all business liable to abuses is made to pass through separate hands, the one being a check on the other. It would next occur to such a people, that they themselves were liable to temporary errors, through want of information as to their true interest, and that men chosen for a short term, and employed but a small portion of that in public affairs, might err from the same cause. This reflection would naturally suggest that the Government be so constituted, as that one of its branches might have an opportunity of acquiring a competent knowledge of the public interests. Another reflection equally becoming a people on such an occasion, would be that they themselves, as well as a numerous body of Representatives, were liable to err also, from fickleness and passion. A necessary fence against this danger would be to select a portion of enlightened citizens, whose limited number, and firmness might seasonably interpose against impetuous counsels. It ought finally to occur to a people deliberating on a Government for themselves, that as different interests necessarily result from the liberty meant to be secured, the major interest might under sudden impulses be tempted to commit injustice on the minority. In all civilized Countries the people fall into different classes having a real or supposed difference of interests. There will be creditors and debtors, farmers, merchants, and manufacturers. There will be particularly the distinction of rich and poor. It was true as had been observed (by Mr. Pinckney), we had not among us those hereditary distinctions, of rank which were a great source of the contests in the ancient Governments as well as the modern States of Europe, nor those extremes of wealth or poverty which characterize the latter. We cannot however be regarded even at this time, as one homogeneous mass, in which every thing that affects a part will affect in the same manner the whole. In framing a system which we wish to last for ages, we should not lose sight of the changes which ages will produce. An increase of population will of necessity increase the proportion of those who will labour under all the hardships of life, and secretly sigh for a more equal distribution of its blessings. These may in time outnumber those who are placed above the feelings of indigence. According to the equal laws of suffrage, the power will slide into the hands of the former.

No agrarian attempts have yet been made in this Country, but symptoms of a leveling spirit, as we have understood, have sufficiently appeared in certain quarters to give notice of the future danger. How is this danger to be guarded against on republican principles? How is the danger in all cases of interested co-alitions to oppress the minority to be guarded against? Among other means by the establishment of a body in the Government sufficiently respectable for its wisdom and virtue, to aid on such emergencies, the preponderance of justice by throwing its weight into that scale. Such being the objects of the second branch in the proposed Government he thought a considerable duration ought to be given to it. He did not conceive that the term of nine years could threaten any real danger; but in pursuing his particular ideas on the subject, he should require that the long term allowed to the 2d branch should not commence till such a period of life as would render a perpetual disqualification to be re-elected little inconvenient either in a public or private view. He observed that as it was more than probable we were now digesting a plan which in its operation would decide forever the fate of Republican Government we ought not only to provide every guard to liberty that its preservation could require, but be equally careful to supply the defects which our own experience had particularly pointed out.

Mr. Sherman. Government is instituted for those who live under it. It ought therefore to be so constituted as not to be dangerous to their liberties. The more permanency it has the worse if it be a bad Government. Frequent elections are necessary to preserve the good behavior of rulers. They also tend to give permanency to the Government, by preserving that good behavior, because it ensures their re-election. . .

Mr. Hamilton . . . He concurred with Mr. Madison in thinking we were now to decide for ever the fate of Republican Government; and that if we did not give that form due stability and wisdom, it would be disgraced and lost among ourselves, disgraced and lost to mankind for ever. He acknowledged himself not to think favorably of Republican Government; but addressed his remarks to those who did think favorably of it, in order to prevail on them to tone their Government as high as possible. He professed himself to be as zealous an advocate for liberty as any man whatever, and trusted he should be as willing a martyr to it though he differed as to the form in which it was most eligible.—He concurred also in the general observations of (Mr. Madison) on the subject, which might be supported by others if it were necessary. It was certainly true that nothing like an equality of property existed: that an inequality would exist as long as liberty existed, and that it would unavoidably result from that very liberty itself. This inequality of property constituted the great and fundamental distinction in Society. When the Tribunitial power had levelled the boundary between the *patricians* and *plebeians* what followed? The distinction between rich and poor was substituted. . .

Mr. Gerry wished we could be united in our ideas concerning a permanent Government. All aim at the same end, but there are great differences as to the means. One circumstance he thought should be carefully attended to. There were not 1/1000th part of our fellow citizens who were not against every approach towards Monarchy. Will they ever agree to a plan which seems to make such an approach. The Convention ought to be extremely cautious in what they hold out to the people. . . He did not deny the position of Mr.— [Madison.] that the majority will generally violate justice when they have an interest in so doing; But did not think there was any such temptation in this Country. Our situation was different from that of Great Britain: and the great body of lands yet to be parcelled out and settled would very much prolong the difference. Notwithstanding the symptoms of injustice which had marked many of our public Councils, they had not proceeded so far as not to leave hopes, that there would be a sufficient sense of justice and virtue for the purpose of Government. He admitted the evils arising from a frequency of elections: and would agree to give the Senate a duration of four or five years. A longer term would defeat itself. It never would be adopted by the people. . .

Monday *July 2*

. . . Mr. Governeur Morris . . . The mode of appointing the 2d branch tended he was sure to defeat the object of it. What is this object? to check the precipitation, changeableness, and excesses of the first branch. Every man of observation had seen in the democratic branches of the State Legislatures, precipitation—in Congress changeableness, in every department excesses against personal liberty, private property and personal safety. What qualities are necessary to constitute a check in this case? *Abilities* and *virtue*, are equally necessary in both branches. Something more then is wanted. (1.) The Checking branch must have a personal interest in checking the other branch. One interest must be opposed to another interest. Vices as they exist, must be turned against each other. (2.) It must have great personal property, it must have the aristocratic spirit; it must love to lord it through pride, pride is indeed the great principle that actuates both the poor and the rich. It is this principle which in the former resists, in the latter abuses authority. (3.) It should be independent. In Religion the Creature is apt to forget its Creator. That it is otherwise in political affairs. The late debates here are an unhappy proof. The aristocratic body, should be as independent and as firm as the democratic. If the members of it are to revert to a dependence on the democratic choice, the democratic scale will preponderate. All the guards contrived by America have not restrained the Senatorial branches of the Legislatures from a servile complaisance to the democratic. If the 2d branch is to be dependent we are better without it. To make it independent, it should be for life. It will then do wrong, it will be said. He believed so: He hoped so. The Rich will strive to establish their dominion and enslave the rest. They always did. They always will. The proper security against them is to form them into a separate interest. The two forces will then control each other. Let the rich mix with the poor and in a Commercial Country, they will establish an Oligarchy. Take away commerce, and the democracy will triumph. Thus it has been all the world over. So it will be among us. Reason tells us we are but men: and we are not to expect any particular interference of Heaven in our favor. By thus combining and setting apart, the aristocratic interest, the popular interest will be combined against it. There will be a mutual check and mutual security. (4.) An independence for life, involves the necessary permanency. . . He was also against paying the Senators. They will pay themselves if they can. If they can not they will be rich and can do without it. . . A firm Government alone can protect our liberties. He fears the influence of the rich. They will have the same effect here as elsewhere if we do not by such a Government keep them within their proper sphere. We should remember that the people never act from reason alone. The rich will take advantage of their passions and make these the instruments for oppressing them. The Result of the Contest will be a violent aristocracy, or a more violent despotism. The schemes of the Rich will be favored by the extent of the Country. The people in such distant parts can not communicate and act in concert. They will be the dupes of those who have more Knowledge and intercourse. The only security against encroachments will be a select and sagacious body of men, instituted to watch against them on all sides. . .

THE EXECUTIVE

Friday *June 1*

. . . [The] Committee of the whole proceeded to Resolution 7 'that a national Executive be instituted, to be chosen by the national Legislature . . . to be ineligible thereafter, to possess the executive powers of Congress etc.' . .

Mr. Pinckney was for a vigorous Executive but was afraid the Executive powers of [the existing] Congress might extend to peace and war, etc. which would render the Executive a Monarchy, of the worst kind, to wit an elective one.

Mr. Wilson moved that the Executive consist of a single person. . .

A considerable pause ensuing and the Chairman asking if he should put the question, Dr. Franklin observed that it was a point of great importance and wished that the gentlemen would deliver their sentiments on it before the question was put.

Mr. Rutlidge . . . said he was for vesting the Executive power in a single person, though he was not for giving him the power of war and peace. A single man would feel the greatest responsibility and administer the public affairs best.

Mr. Sherman said he considered the Executive magistracy as nothing more than an institution for carrying the will of the Legislature into effect, that the person or persons ought to be appointed by and accountable to the Legislature only, which was the depositary of the supreme will of the Society. As they were the best judges of the business which ought to be done by the Executive department, and consequently of the number necessary from time to time for doing it, he wished the number might [not] be fixed, but that the legislatures should be at liberty to appoint one or more as experience might dictate.

Mr. Wilson preferred a single magistrate, as giving most energy, dispatch and responsibility to the office. He did not consider the Prerogatives of the British Monarch as a proper guide in defining the Executive powers. Some of these prerogatives were of a Legislative nature. Among others that of war and peace, etc. The only powers he conceived strictly Executive were those of executing the laws, and appointing officers, not [appertaining to and] appointed by the Legislature.

Mr. Gerry favored the policy of annexing a Council [to the Executive] in order to give weight and inspire confidence.

Mr. Randolph strenuously opposed a unity in the Executive magistracy. He regarded it as the foetus of monarchy. We had he said no motive to be governed by the British Government as our prototype. He did not mean however to throw censure on that Excellent fabric. If we were in a situation to copy it he did not know that he should be opposed to it; but the fixt genius of the people of America required a different form of Government. He could not see why the great requisites for the Executive department, vigor, despatch and responsibility could not be found in three men, as well as in one man. The Executive ought to be independent. It ought therefore [in order to support its independence] to consist of more than one.

Mr. Wilson said that Unity in the Executive instead of being the foetus of Monarchy would be the best safeguard against tyranny. He repeated that he was not governed by the British Model which was inapplicable to the situation of this Country; the extent of which was so great, and the manners so republican, that nothing but a great confederated Republic would do for it. . .

Saturday *June 2*

. . . Dr. Franklin moved that what related to the compensation for the services of the Executive be postponed, in order to substitute—'whose necessary expenses shall be defrayed, but who shall receive no salary, stipend, fee, or reward whatsoever for their services.' . .

Sir, there are two passions which have a powerful influence on the affairs of men. These are ambition and avarice; the love of power, and the love of money. Separately each of these has great force in prompting men to action; but when united in view of the same object, they have in many minds the most violent effects. Place before the eyes of such men a post of *honour* that shall at the same time be a place of *profit*, and they will move heaven and earth to obtain it. The vast number of such places it is that renders the British Government so tempestuous. The struggles for them are the true sources of all those factions which are perpetually dividing the Nation, distracting its councils, hurrying sometimes into fruitless and mischievous wars, and often compelling a submission to dishonorable terms of peace.

And of what kind are the men that will strive for this profitable preeminence, through all the bustle of cabal, the heat of contention, the infinite mutual abuse of parties, tearing to pieces the best of characters? It will not be the wise and moderate, the lovers of peace and good order, the men fittest for the trust. It will be the bold and the violent, the men of strong passions and indefatigable activity in their selfish pursuits. These will thrust themselves into your Government and be your rulers. . .

Besides these evils, Sir, though we may set out in the beginning with moderate salaries, we shall find that such will not be of long continuance. Reasons will never be wanting for proposed augmentations. And there will always be a party for giving more to the rulers, that the rulers may be able in return to give more to them. . . It will be said, that we don't propose to establish Kings. I know it. But there is a natural inclination in mankind to Kingly Government. It sometimes relieves them from Aristocratic domination. They had rather have one tyrant than five hundred. It gives more of the appearance of equality among Citizens, and that they like. I am apprehensive therefore, perhaps too apprehensive, that the Government of these States, may in future times, end in a Monarchy. But this Catastrophe I think may be long delayed, if in our proposed system we do not sow the seeds of contention, faction and tumult, by making our posts of honor, places of profit. . .

Monday *June 4*

. . . [First] Clause [of Proposition 8] relating to a *Council of Revision* taken into consideration.

Mr. Gerry . . . moves to postpone the clause [in order] to propose 'that the National Executive shall have a right to negative any Legislative act which shall not be afterwards passed by . . . parts of each branch of the national Legislature.' . .

Dr. Franklin said he was sorry to differ from his colleague for whom he had a very great respect, on any occasion, but he could not help it on this. He had had some experience of this check in the Executive on the Legislature, under the proprictary Government of Pennsylvania. The negative of the Governor was constantly made use of to extort money. No good law whatever could be passed without a private bargain with him. An increase of his salary, or some donation, was always made a condition; till at last it became the regular practice, to have orders in his favor on the Treasury, presented along with the bills to be signed, so that he might actually receive the former before he should sign the latter. . . It was true the King of Great Britain had not, as was said, exerted his negative since the Revolution: but that matter was easily explained. The bribes and emoluments now given to the members of parliament rendered it unnecessary, everything being done according to the will of the Ministers. He was afraid, if a negative should be given as proposed, that more power and money would be demanded, till at last enough would be gotten to influence and bribe the Legislature into a complete subjection to the will of the Executive.

Mr. Sherman was against enabling any one man to stop the will of the whole. No one man could be found so far above all the rest in wisdom. He thought we ought to avail ourselves of his wisdom in revising the laws, but not permit him to overrule the decided and cool opinions of the Legislature.

Mr. Madison supposed that if a proper proportion of each branch should be required to overrule the objections of the Executive, it would answer the same purpose as an absolute negative. It would rarely if ever happen that the Executive constituted as ours is proposed to be would, have firmness enough to resist the Legislature, unless backed by a certain part of the body itself. The King of Great Britain with all his splendid attributes would not be able to withstand the unanimous and eager wishes of both houses of Parliament. To give such a prerogative would certainly be obnoxious to the [temper of this country; its present temper at least.]

Mr. Wilson believed as others did that this power would seldom be used. The Legislature would know that such a power existed, and would refrain from such laws, as it would be sure to defeat. Its silent operation would therefore preserve harmony and prevent mischief. . .

Col. Mason observed that . . . probable abuses of a negative had been well explained by Dr. F. as proved by experience, the best of all tests. Will not the same door be opened here? The Executive may refuse its assent to necessary measures till new appointments shall be referred to him; and having by degrees engrossed all these into his own hands, the American Executive, like the British, will by bribery and influence, save himself the trouble and odium of exerting his negative afterwards. We are Mr. Chairman going very far in this business. We are not indeed constituting a British Government, but a more dangerous monarchy, an elective one. We are introducing a new principle into our system, and not necessary as in the British Government where the Executive has greater rights to defend. Do gentlemen mean to pave the way to hereditary Monarchy? Do they flatter themselves that the people will ever consent to such an innovation? If they do I venture to tell them, they are mistaken. The people never will consent. And do gentlemen consider the danger of delay, and the still greater danger of a rejection not for a moment but forever, of the plan which shall be proposed to them. Notwithstanding the oppressions and injustice experienced among us from democracy; the genius of the people is in favor of it, and the genius of the people must be consulted. . . He hoped that nothing like a monarchy would ever be attempted in this Country. A hatred to its oppressions had carried the people through the late Revolution. Will it not be enough to enable the Executive to suspend offensive laws, till they shall be coolly revised, and the objections to them overruled by a greater majority than was required in the first instance? He never could agree to give up all the rights of the people to a single Magistrate. If more than one had been fixed on, greater powers might have been entrusted to the Executive. He hoped this attempt to give such powers would have its weight hereafter [as an argument] for increasing the number of the Executive. . .

Tuesday *July 17*

. . . 9th Resolution. 'that National Executive consist of a single person . . . to be chosen by the National Legislature.'

Mr. Governeur Morris was pointedly against his being so chosen. He will be the mere creature of the Legislature if appointed and impeachable by that body. He ought to be elected by the people at large, by the freeholders of the Country. . . If the people should elect, they will never fail to prefer some man of distinguished character, or services; some man, if he might so speak, of continental reputation. If the Legislature elect, it will be the work of intrigue, of cabal, and of faction: it will be like the election of a pope by a conclave of cardinals; real merit will rarely be the title to the appointment. [He moved to strike out 'National Legislature' and insert 'citizens of U. S.'] . . .

Mr. Wilson. . . A particular objection with him against an absolute election by the Legislature was that the Executive in that case would be too dependent to stand the mediator between the intrigues and sinister views of the Representatives and the general liberties and interests of the people.

Mr. Pinkney did not expect this question would again have been brought forward; An Election by the people being liable to the most obvious and striking objections. They will be led by a few active and designing men. The most populous States by combining in favor of the same individual will be able to carry their points. The National Legislature being most immediately interested in the laws made by themselves, will be most attentive to the choice of a fit man to carry them properly into execution.

Mr. Governeur Morris. It is said that in case of an election by the people the populous States will combine and elect whom they please. Just the reverse. The people of such States cannot combine. If there be any combination it must be among their representatives in the Legislature. It is said the people will be led by a few designing men. This might happen in a small district. It can never happen throughout the continent. In the election of a Governor of New York, it sometimes is the case in particular spots, that the activity and intrigues of little partizans are successful, but the general voice of the State is never influenced by such artifices. It is said the multitude will be uninformed. It is true they would be uninformed of what passed in the Legislative Conclave, if the election were to be made there; but they will not be uninformed of those great and illustrious characters which have merited their esteem and confidence. If the Executive be chosen by the National Legislature, he will not be independent of it; and if not independent, usurpation and tyranny on the part of the Legislature will be the consequence. . .

Col. Mason. . . At one moment we are told that the Legislature is entitled to thorough confidence, and to indefinite power. At another, that it will be governed by intrigue and corruption, and cannot be trusted at all. But not to dwell on this inconsistency he would observe that a Government which is to last ought at least to be practicable. Would this be the case if the proposed election should be left to the people at large. He conceived it would be as unnatural to refer the choice of a proper character for chief Magistrate to the people, as it would, to refer a trial of colours to a blind man. The extent of the Country renders it impossible that the people can have the requisite capacity to judge of the respective pretensions of the Candidates. . .

Mr. Broom was for a shorter term since the Executive Magistrate was now to be re-eligible. Had he remained ineligible a 2d time, he should have preferred a longer term.

Dr. McClurg moved to strike out 7 years, and insert 'during good behavior' . . . he conceived the independence of the Executive to be equally essential with that of the Judiciary department.

Mr. Governeur Morris seconded the motion. He expressed great pleasure in hearing it. This was the way to get a good Government. His fear that so valuable an ingredient would not be attained had led him to take the part he had done. He was indifferent how the Executive should be chosen, provided he held his place by this tenure. . .

Mr. Madison. If it be essential to the preservation of liberty that the Legislative, Executive, and Judiciary powers be separate, it is essential to a maintenance of the separation that they should be independent of each other. The Executive could not be independent of the Legislature, if dependent on the pleasure of that branch for a re-appointment. Why was it determined that the Judges should not hold their places by such a tenure? Because they might be tempted to cultivate the Legislature, by an undue complaisance, and thus render the Legislature the virtual expositor, as well the maker of the laws. In like manner a dependence of the Executive on the Legislature, would render it the Executor as well as the maker of laws; and then according to the observations of Montesquieu, tyrannical laws may be made that they may be executed in a tyrannical manner. . . He conceived it to be absolutely necessary to a well constituted Republic that the two . . . should be kept distinct and independent of each other. . .

Col. Mason . . . considered an Executive during good behavior as a softer name only for an Executive for life. And that the next would be an easy step to hereditary Monarchy. If the motion should finally succeed, he might himself live to see such a Revolution. If he did not it was probable his children or grandchildren would. He trusted there were few men in that House who wished for it. No state he was sure had so far revolted from Republican principles as to have the least bias in its favor.

Mr. Madison was not apprehensive of being thought to favor any step towards monarchy. The real object with him was to prevent its introduction. Experience had proved a tendency in our governments to throw all power into the Legislative vortex. The Executives of the States are in general little more than Cyphers; the legislatures omnipotent. If no effectual check be devised for restraining the instability and encroachments of the latter, a revolution of some kind or other would be inevitable. The preservation of Republican Govt. therefore required some expedient for the purpose, but required evidently at the same time that in devising it, the genuine principles of that form should be kept in view.

Mr. Governeur Morris was as little a friend to monarchy as any gentleman. He concurred in the opinion that the way to keep out monarchial Government was to establish such a Republican Government as would make the people happy and prevent a desire of change.

Dr. McClurg was not so much afraid of the shadow of monarchy as to be unwilling to approach it; nor so wedded to Republican Government as not to be sensible of the tyrannies that had been and may be exercised under that form. It was an essential object with him to make the Executive independent of the Legislature. . .

Thursday *July* 19

On reconsideration of the vote rendering the Executive re-eligible a 2d time. . .

Mr. Governeur Morris. . . It has been a maxim in political Science that Republican Government is not adapted to a large extent of Country, because the energy of the Executive Magistracy can not reach the extreme parts of it. Our Country is an extensive one. We must either then renounce the blessings of the Union, or provide an Executive with sufficient vigor to pervade every part of it. . . One great object of the Executive is to control the Legislature. The Legislature will continually seek to aggrandize and perpetuate themselves; and will seize those critical moments produced by war, invasion or convulsion for that purpose. It is necessary then that the Executive Magistrate should be the guardian of the people, even of the lower classes, against Legislative tyranny, against the Great and the wealthy who in the course of things will necessarily compose—the Legislative body. Wealth tends to corrupt the mind and to nourish its love of power, and to stimulate it to oppression. History proves this to be the spirit of the opulent. . . The Executive therefore ought to be so constituted as to be the great protector of the Mass of the people. . . He finds too that the Executive is not to be re-eligible. What effect will this have? (1.) it will destroy the great incitement to merit public esteem by taking away the hope of being rewarded with a reappointment. It may give a dangerous turn to one of the strongest passions in the human breast. The love of fame is the great spring to noble and illustrious actions. Shut the Civil road to Glory and he may be compelled to seek it by the sword. (2.) It will tempt him to make the most of the Short space of time allotted him, to accumulate wealth and provide for his friends. (3.) It will produce violations of the very constitution it is meant to secure. In moments of pressing danger the tried abilities and established character of a favorite Magistrate will prevail over respect for the forms of the Constitution. . . These then are the faults of the Executive establishments as now proposed. Can no better establishment be devised? If he is to be the Guardian of the people let him be appointed by the people. If he is to be a check on the Legislature let him not be impeachable. Let him be of short duration, that he may with propriety be re eligible.—It has been said that the candidates for this office will not be known to the people. If they be known to the Legislature, they must have such a notoriety and eminence of Character, that they cannot possibly be unknown to the people at large. It cannot be possible that a man shall have sufficiently distinguished himself to merit this high trust without having his character proclaimed by fame throughout the Empire. . . He saw no alternative for making the Executive independent of the Legislature but either to give him his office for life, or make him eligible by the people. . . The extent of the Country would secure his re-election against the factions and discontents of particular States. It deserved consideration also that such an ingredient in the plan would render it extremely palatable to the people. . .

Mr. King did not like the ineligibility. He thought there was great force in the remark of Mr. Sherman, that he who has proved himself to be most fit for an Office, ought not to be excluded by the constitution from holding it. He would therefore prefer any other reasonable plan that could be substituted. He was much disposed to think that in such cases the people at large would choose wisely. There was indeed some difficulty arising from the improbability of a general concurrence of the people in favor of any one man. On the whole he was of opinion that an appointment by electors chosen by the people for the purpose, would be liable to fewest objections. . .

Mr. Madison . . . There is the same and perhaps greater reason why the

Executive should be independent of the Legislature, than why the Judiciary should: A coalition of the two former powers would be more immediately and certainly dangerous to public liberty. . . He was disposed for these reasons to refer the appointment to some other Source. The people at large was in his opinion the fittest in itself. . . There was one difficulty however of a serious nature attending an immediate choice by the people. The right of suffrage was much more diffusive in the Northern than the Southern States; and the latter could have no influence in the election on the score of the Negroes. The substitution of electors obviated this difficulty and seemed on the whole to be liable to the fewest objections.

Mr. Gerry. If the Executive is to be elected by the Legislature he certainly ought not to be re-eligible. This would make him absolutely dependent. He was against a popular election. The people are uninformed, and would be misled by a few designing men. . .

THE JUDICIARY

Saturday *July* 21

. . . Mr. Wilson moved as an amendment to Resolution 10 'that the [supreme] National Judiciary should be associated with the Executive in the Revisionary power.' This proposition had been before made, and failed but he was so confirmed by reflection in the opinion of its utility, that he thought it incumbent on him to make another effort: The Judiciary ought to have an opportunity of remonstrating against projected encroachments on the people as well as on themselves. It had been said that the Judges, as expositors of the Laws would have an opportunity of defending their constitutional rights. There was weight in this observation; but this power of the Judges did not go far enough. Laws may be unjust, may be unwise, may be dangerous, may be destructive; and yet not be so unconstitutional as to justify the Judges in refusing to give them effect. Let them have a share in the Revisionary power, and they will have an opportunity of taking notice of these characters of a law, and of counteracting, by the weight of their opinions the improper views of the Legislature.—Mr. Madison seconded the motion.

Mr. Ghorum did not see the advantage of employing the Judges in this way. As Judges they are not to be presumed to possess any peculiar knowledge of the mere policy of public measures. Nor can it be necessary as a security for their constitutional rights. The Judges in England have no such additional provision for their defence, yet their jurisdiction is not invaded. He thought it would be best to let the Executive alone be responsible, and at most to authorize him to call on Judges for their opinions.

Mr. Elseworth approved heartily of the motion. The aid of the Judges will give more wisdom and firmness to the Executive. They will possess a systematic and accurate knowledge of the Laws, which the Executive can not be expected always to possess. The law of Nations also will frequently come into question. Of this the Judges alone will have competent information.

Mr. Madison—considered the object of the motion as of great importance to the meditated Constitution. It would be useful to the Judiciary department by giving it an additional opportunity of defending itself against Legislative encroachments: It would be useful to the Executive, by inspiring additional confidence and firmness in exerting the revisionary power: It would be useful to the Legislature by the valuable assistance it would give in preserving a consistency, conciseness, perspicuity and technical propriety in the laws, qualities peculiarly necessary; and yet shamefully wanting in our republican codes. It would moreover be useful to the Community at large as an additional check against a pursuit of those unwise and unjust measures which constituted so great a portion of our calamities. If any solid objection could be urged against the motion, it must be on the supposition that it tended to give too much strength either to the Executive or Judiciary. He did not think there was the least ground for this apprehension. It was much more to be apprehended that notwithstanding this co-operation of the two departments, the Legislature would still be an overmatch for them. Experience in all the States had evinced a powerful tendency in the Legislature to absorb all power into its vortex. This was the real source of danger to the American Constitutions; and suggested the necessity of giving every defensive authority to the other departments that was consistent with republican principles.

Mr. Mason said he had always been a friend to this provision. It would give a confidence to the Executive, which he would not otherwise have, and without which the Revisionary power would be of little avail.

Mr. Gerry did not expect to see this point which had undergone full discussion, again revived. The object he conceived of the Revisionary power was merely to secure the Executive department against legislative encroachment. The Executive therefore who will best know and be ready to defend his rights ought alone to have the defence of them. The motion was liable to strong objections. It was combining and mixing together the Legislative and the other departments. It was establishing an improper coalition between the Executive and Judiciary departments. It was making Statesmen of the Judges; and setting them up as the guardians of the Rights of the people. He relied for his part on the Representatives of the people as the guardians of their Rights and interests. It was making the Expositors of the Laws, the Legislators which ought never to be done. A better expedient for correcting the laws, would be to appoint as had been done in Pennsylvania a person or persons of proper skill, to draw bills for the Legislature.

Mr. Strong thought with Mr. Gerry that the power of making ought to be kept distinct from that of expounding, the laws. No maxim was better established. The Judges in exercising the function of expositors might be influenced by the part they had taken, in framing the laws. . .

Mr. L. Martin considered the association of the Judges with the Executive as a dangerous innovation; as well as one which, could not produce the particular advantage expected from it. A knowledge of mankind, and of Legislative affairs cannot be presumed to belong in a higher degree to the Judges than to the Legislature. And as to the Constitutionality of laws, that point will come before the Judges in their proper official character. In this character they have a negative on the laws. Join them with the Executive in the Revision and they will have a double negative. It is necessary that the Supreme Judiciary should have the confidence of the people. This will soon be lost, if they are employed in the task of remonstrating against popular measures of the Legislature. . .

Mr. Madison could not discover in the proposed association of the Judges with the Executive in the Revisionary check on the Legislature any violation of the maxim which requires the great departments of power to be kept separate and distinct. On the contrary he thought it an auxiliary precaution in favor of the maxim. If a Constitutional discrimination of the departments on paper were a sufficient security to each against encroachments of the others, all further provisions would indeed be superfluous. But experience had taught us a distrust of that security; and that it is necessary to introduce such a balance of powers and interests, as will guarantee the provisions on paper. Instead therefore of contenting ourselves with laying down the theory in the Constitution that each department ought to be separate and distinct, it was proposed to add a defensive power to each which should maintain the theory in practice. In so doing we did not blend the departments together. We erected effectual barriers for keeping them separate. . .

Col. Mason observed that the defence of the Executive was not the sole object of the Revisionary power. He expected even greater advantages from it. Notwithstanding the precautions taken in the Constitution of the Legislature, it would so much resemble that of the individual States, that it must be expected frequently to pass unjust and pernicious laws. This restraining power was therefore essentially necessary. It would have the effect not only of hindering the final passage of such laws; but would discourage demagogues from attempting to get them passed. It had been said (by Mr. L. Martin) that if the Judges were joined in this check on the laws, they would have a double negative, since in their expository capacity of Judges they would have one negative. He would reply that in this capacity they could impede in one case only, the operation of laws. They could declare an unconstitutional law void. But with regard to every law however unjust, oppressive or pernicious, which did not come plainly under this description, they would be under the necessity as Judges to give it a free course. He wished the further use to be made of the Judges, of giving aid in preventing every improper law. . .

Mr. Wilson. The separation of the departments does not require that they should have separate objects but that they should act separately though on the same objects. It is necessary that the two branches of the Legislature should be separate and distinct, yet they are both to act precisely on the same object.

Mr. Gerry had rather give the Executive an absolute negative for its own defence than thus to blend together the Judiciary and Executive departments. It will bind them together in an offensive and defensive alliance against the Legislature, and render the latter unwilling to enter into a contest with them. . .

Mr. Rutlidge thought the Judges of all men the most unfit to be concerned in the revisionary Council. The Judges ought never to give their opinion on a law until it comes before them. . .

Wednesday *August 15*

. . . Mr. Madison moved that all acts before they became laws should be submitted both to the Executive and Supreme Judiciary Departments, that if either of these should object ⅔rds of each House, if both should object, ¾ths of each House, should be necessary to overrule the objections. . .

Mr. Mercer heartily approved the motion. It is an axiom that the Judiciary ought to be separate from the Legislative: but equally so that it ought to be independent of that department. The true policy of the axiom is that legislative usurpation and oppression may be obviated. He disapproved of the doctrine that the Judges as expositors of the Constitution should have authority to declare a law void. He thought laws ought to be well and cautiously made, and then to be uncontrolable. . .

Mr. Dickenson was strongly impressed with the remark of Mr. Mercer as to the power of the Judges to set aside the law. He thought no such power ought to exist. He was at the same time at a loss what expedient to substitute. . .

Mr. Governeur Morris . . . could not agree that the Judiciary which was part of the Executive, should be bound to say that a direct violation of the Constitution was law. A control over the legislature might have its inconveniences. But view the danger on the other side. The most virtuous citizens will often as members of a legislative body concur in measures which afterwards in their private capacity they will be ashamed of. . .

APPORTIONMENT OF REPRESENTATION IN HOUSE OF REPRESENTATIVES

Thursday *July 5*

. . . The 1st proposition in the Report for fixing the representation in the 1st branch, one member for every 40,000 inhabitants, being taken up.

Mr. Governeur Morris objected to that scale of apportionment. He thought property ought to be taken into the estimate as well as the number of inhabitants. Life and liberty were generally said to be of more value, than property. An accurate view of the matter would nevertheless prove that property was the main object of Society. The savage State was more favorable to liberty than the Civilized; and sufficiently so to life. It was preferred by all men who had not acquired a taste for property. . . If property then was the main object of Government certainly it ought to be one measure of the influence due to those who were to be affected by the Government. . .

Mr. Rutlidge . . . Property was certainly the principal object of Society. If numbers should be made the rule of representation, the Atlantic States will be subjected to the Western. He moved that the first proposition in the report be postponed in order to take up the following viz. 'that the suffrages of the several States be regulated and proportioned according to the sums to be paid towards the general revenue by the inhabitants of each State respectively . . .'

Friday *July 6*

. . . Mr. Ghorum . . . thought the number of Inhabitants the true guide . . .

Mr. Gerry . . . thought that Representation ought to be in the Combined ratio of numbers of Inhabitants and of wealth, and not of either singly.

Mr. King . . . thought . . . that the number of inhabitants was not the proper index of ability and wealth; that property was the primary object of Society; and that in fixing a ratio this ought not to be excluded from the estimate. . .

Mr. Butler . . . was persuaded that the more the subject was examined, the less it would appear that the number of inhabitants would be a proper rule of proportion. If there were no other objection the changeableness of the standard would be sufficient. He concurred with those who thought some balance was necessary between the old and New States. He contended strenuously that property was the only just measure of representation. This was the great object of Government: the great cause of war, the great means of carrying it on.

Mr. Pinckney . . . The value of land had been found on full investigation to be an impracticable rule. The contributions of revenue including imports and exports, must be too changeable in their amount; too difficult to be adjusted; and too injurious to the non-commercial States. The number of inhabitants appeared to him the only just and practicable rule. He thought the blacks ought to stand on an equality with whites . . .

Monday *July 9*

. . . Mr. Governeur Morris delivered a report from the Committee of 5 members to whom was committed the clause . . . stating the proper ratio of Representatives in the 1st branch, to be as 1 to every 40,000 inhabitants . . .

Mr. Sherman wished to know on what principles or calculations the Report was founded. . .

Mr. Gorham. Some provision of this sort was necessary in the outset. The number of blacks and whites with some regard to supposed wealth was the general guide. . .

Mr. Paterson considered the proposed estimate for the future according to the combined rule of numbers and wealth, as too vague. For this reason New Jersey was against it. He could regard negroes slaves in no light but as property. They are no free agents, have no personal liberty, no faculty of acquiring property, but on the contrary are themselves property, and like other property entirely at the will of the Master. Has a man in Virginia a number of votes in proportion to the number of his slaves? and if Negroes are not represented in the States to which they belong, why should they be represented in the General Government? What is the true principle of Representation? It is an expedient by which an assembly of certain individuals chosen by the people is substituted in place of the inconvenient meeting of the people themselves. If such a meeting of the people was actually to take place, would the slaves vote? they would not. Why then should they be represented. . .

Mr. Butler urged warmly the justice and necessity of regarding wealth in the apportionment of Representation.

Mr. King had always expected that as the Southern States are the richest, they would not league themselves with the Northern unless some respect were paid to their superior wealth. . . Eleven out of 13 of the States had agreed to consider Slaves in the apportionment of taxation; and taxation and Representation ought to go together. . .

Tuesday *July* 10

. . . Mr. Governeur Morris . . . thought the Southern States have by the report more than their share of representation. Property ought to have its weight; but not all the weight. . .

Wednesday *July* 11

Mr. Butler and General Pinkney insisted that blacks be included in the rule of Representation, *equally* with the Whites: [and for that purpose moved that the words 'three fifths' be struck out.]

Mr. Gerry thought that ⅗ths of them was to say the least the full proportion that could be admitted. . .

Mr. Butler insisted that the labour of a slave in South Carolina was as productive and valuable as that of a freeman in Massachusetts, that as wealth was the great means of defence and utility to the Nation they are equally valuable to it with freemen; and that consequently an equal representation ought to be allowed for them in a Government which was instituted principally for the protection of property, and was itself to be supported by property.

Mr. Mason could not agree to the motion, notwithstanding it was favorable to Virginia because he thought it unjust. It was certain that the slaves were valuable, as they raised the value of land, increased the exports and imports and of course the revenue, would supply the means of feeding and supporting an army, and might in cases of emergency become themselves soldiers As in these important respects they were useful to the community at large, they ought not to be excluded from the estimate of Representation. He could not however regard them as equal to freemen and could not vote for them as such. He added as worthy of remark, that the Southern States have this peculiar species of property, over and above the other species of property common to all the States. . .

On Mr. Butler's motion for considering blacks as equal to Whites in the apportionment of Representation

Massachusetts: no. Connecticut: no. (New York not on floor.) New Jersey: no. Pennsylvania: no. Delaware: ay. Maryland: no. Virginia: no. North Carolina: no. South Carolina: ay. Georgia: ay. [Ayes—3; noes—7.]

Mr. Governeur Morris . . . If slaves were to be considered as inhabitants, not as wealth, then the said Resolution would not be pursued: If as wealth, then why is no other wealth but slaves included? . . . His great objection was that the number of inhabitants was not a proper standard of wealth. . . Numbers might with greater propriety be deemed a measure of strength, than of wealth, yet the late defence made by Great Britain against her numerous enemies proved in the clearest manner, that it is entirely fallacious even in this respect. . .

Mr. Wilson . . . considered wealth as an impracticable rule. . .

Mr. Governeur Morris . . . could not persuade himself that numbers would be a just rule at any time. . . Among other objections it must be apparent they would not be able to furnish men equally enlightened, to share in the administration of our common interests. The busy haunts of men not the remote wilderness, was the proper School of political talents. If the Western people get the power into their hands they will ruin the Atlantic interests. The Back members are always most averse to the best measures. . .

Mr. Madison . . . The truth was that all men having power ought to be distrusted to a certain degree. . . He could not agree that any substantial objection lay against fixing numbers for the perpetual standard of Representation. It was said that Representation and taxation were to go together; that taxation and wealth ought to go together, that population and wealth were not measures of each other. . .

Mr. King being much opposed to fixing numbers as the rule of representation, was particularly so on account of the blacks. He thought the admission of them along with Whites at all, would excite great discontents among the States having no slaves. . .

Mr. Wilson did not well see on what principle the admission of blacks in the proportion of three fifths could be explained. Are they admitted as Citizens? Then why are they not admitted on an equality with White Citizens? Are they admitted as property? then why is not other property admitted into the computation? These were difficulties however which he thought must be overruled by the necessity of compromise. He had some apprehensions also from the tendency of the blending of the blacks with the whites, to give disgust to the people of Pennsylvania as had been intimated by his colleague (Mr. Governeur Morris). But he differed from him in thinking numbers of inhabitants so incorrect a measure of wealth. . .

Thursday *July 12*

. . . Dr. Johnson thought that wealth and population were the true, equitable rule of representation; but he conceived that these two principles resolved themselves into one; population being the best measure of wealth. He concluded therefore that the number of people ought to be established as the rule, and that all descriptions including blacks *equally* with the whites, ought to fall within the computation. . .

General Pinkney desired that the rule of wealth should be ascertained and not left to the pleasure of the Legislature; and that property in slaves should not be exposed to danger under a Government instituted for the protection of property. . .

Mr. Randolph . . . urged strenuously that express security ought to be provided for including slaves in the ratio of Representation. He lamented that such a species of property existed. But as it did exist the holders of it would require this security. It was perceived that the design was entertained by some of excluding slaves altogether; the Legislature therefore ought not to be left at liberty. . .

. . . On the question on the whole proposition; [as proportioning representation to direct taxation and both to the white and 3/5ths of black inhabitants, and requiring a census within six years—and within every ten years afterwards.]

Massachusetts: divided. Connecticut: ay. New Jersey: no. Pennsylvania: ay. Delaware: no. Maryland: ay. Virginia: ay. North Carolina: ay. South Carolina: divided. Georgia: ay. [Ayes—6; noes—2; divided—2.]

Friday *July* 13

. . . On the motion of Mr. Randolph, the vote of Saturday last authorizing the Legislature to adjust from time to time, the representation upon the principles of *wealth* and numbers of inhabitants was reconsidered by common consent in order to strike out 'Wealth' and adjust the resolution to that requiring periodical revisions according to the number of whites and three fifths of the blacks. . .

Mr. Governeur Morris opposed the alteration as leaving still an incoherence. If Negroes were to be viewed as inhabitants, and the revision was to proceed on the principle of numbers of inhabitants they ought to be added in their entire number, and not in the proportion of 3/5ths. If as property, the word wealth was right, and striking it out would produce the very inconsistency which it was meant to get rid of.— The train of business and the late turn which it had taken, had led him he said, into deep meditation on it, and he would candidly state the result. A distinction had been set up and urged, between the Northern and Southern States. He had hitherto considered this doctrine as heretical. He still thought the distinction groundless. . .

Mr. Wilson . . . Conceiving that all men wherever placed have equal rights and are equally entitled to confidence, he viewed without apprehension the period when a few States should contain the superior number of people. The majority of people wherever found ought in all questions to govern the minority. If the interior Country should acquire this majority they will not only have the right, but will avail themselves of it whether we will or no. This jealousy misled the policy of Great Britain with regard to America. The fatal maxims espoused by her were that the Colonies were growing too fast, and that their growth must be stinted in time. What were the consequences? first, enmity on our part, then actual separation. Like consequences will result on the part of the interior settlements, if like jealousy and policy be pursued on ours. Further, if numbers be not a proper rule, why is not some better rule pointed out. No one has yet ventured to attempt it. . . Again he could not agree that property was the sole or the primary object of Government and Society. The cultivation and improvement of the human mind was the most noble object. With respect to this object, as well as to other *personal* rights, numbers were surely the natural and precise measure of Representation. . .

OFFICIAL QUALIFICATIONS

Thursday *July 26*

. . . Mr. Mason moved 'that the Committee of detail be instructed to receive a clause requiring certain qualifications of landed property and citizenship [of the United States] in members of the Legislature . . .

Mr. Governeur Morris. If qualifications are proper, he would prefer them in the electors rather than the elected. . .

Mr. King observed that there might be great danger in requiring landed property as a qualification since it would exclude the monied interest, whose aids may be essential in particular emergencies to the public safety.

Mr. Dickinson was against any recital of qualifications in the Constitution. . . The best defence lay in the freeholders who were to elect the Legislature. Whilst this Source should remain pure, the public interest would be safe. . . He doubted the policy of interweaving into a Republican constitution a veneration for wealth. He had always understood that a veneration for property and virtue, were the objects of republican encouragement. It seemed improper that any man of merit should be subjected to disabilities in a Republic where merit was understood to form the great title to public trust, honors and rewards.

Mr. Gerry. If property be one object of Government, provisions for securing it can not be improper.

Mr. Madison moved to strike out the word *landed*, before the word, 'qualifications.' If the proposition should be agreed to he wished the Committee to be at liberty to report the best criterion they could devise. Landed possessions were no certain evidence of real wealth. Many enjoyed them to a great extent who were more in debt than they were worth. The unjust laws of the States had proceeded more from this class of men, than any others. It had often happened that men who had acquired landed property on credit, got into the Legislatures with a view of promoting an unjust protection against their Creditors. In the next place, if a small quantity of land should be made the standard, it would be no security—if a large one, it would exclude the proper representatives of those classes of Citizens who were not landholders. It was politic as well as just that the interests and rights of every class should be duly represented and understood in the public Councils. . . The three principal classes into which our citizens were divisible, were the landed, the commercial, and the manufacturing. The 2d and 3rd class, bear as yet a small proportion to the first. The proportion however will daily increase. We see in the populous Countries in Europe now, what we shall be hereafter. These classes understand much less of each others interests and affairs, than men of the same class inhabiting different districts. It is particularly requisite therefore that the interests of one or two of them should not be left entirely to the care, or the impartiality of the third. . . He concurred with Mr. Governeur Morris in thinking that qualifications in the Electors would be much more effectual than in the elected. The former would discriminate between real and ostensible property in the latter; But he was aware of [the difficulty of] forming any uniform standard that would suit the different circumstances and opinions prevailing in the different States. . .

Friday *August 10*

Art. VI. Sect. 2. ['The Legislature of the United States shall have authority to establish such uniform qualifications of the members of each House, with regard to property, as to the said Legislature shall seem expedient.']

Mr. Pinkney—The Committee as he had conceived were instructed to report the proper qualifications of property for the members of the National Legislature . . . He was opposed to the establishment of an undue aristocratic influence in the Constitution but he thought it essential that the members of the Legislature, the Executive, and the Judges—should be possessed of competent property to make them independent and respectable. . .

Dr. Franklin expressed his dislike of every thing that tended to debase the spirit of the common people. If honesty was often the companion of wealth, and if poverty was exposed to peculiar temptation, it was not less true that the possession of property increased the desire of more property—Some of the greatest rogues he was ever acquainted with, were the richest rogues. . . This Constitution will be much read and attended to in Europe, and if it should betray a great partiality to the rich—will not only hurt us in the esteem of the most liberal and enlightened men there, but discourage the common people from removing to this Country. . .

Mr. Rutlidge was opposed to leaving the power to the Legislature—He proposed that the qualifications should be the same as for members of the State Legislatures. . .

SUFFRAGE QUALIFICATIONS

Tuesday *August 7*

Art. IV. Sect. 1. ['The members of the House of Representatives shall be chosen every second year, by the people of the several States comprehended within this Union. The qualifications of the electors shall be the same, from time to time, as those of the electors in the several States, of the most numerous branch of their own legislatures']. . .

Mr. Wilson . . . It was difficult to form any uniform rule of qualifications for all the States. . .

Mr. Elseworth . . . The right of suffrage was a tender point, and strongly guarded by most of the [State] Constitutions. The people will not readily subscribe to the National Constitution, if it should subject them to be disfranchised. The States are the best Judges of the circumstances and temper of their own people.

Col. Mason. The force of habit is certainly not attended to by those gentlemen who wish for innovations on this point. Eight or nine States have extended the right of suffrage beyond the freeholders. What will the people there say, if they should be disfranchised. . .

Mr. Butler. There is no right of which the people are more jealous than that of suffrage. Abridgments of it tend to the same revolution as in Holland, where they have at length thrown all power into the hands of the Senates, who fill up vacancies themselves, and form a rank aristocracy.

Mr. Dickinson had a very different idea of the tendency of vesting the right of suffrage in the freeholders of the Country. He considered them as the best guardians of liberty; and the restriction of the right to them as a necessary defence against the dangerous influence of those multitudes without property and without principle, with which our Country like all others, will in time abound. As to the unpopularity of the innovation it was in his opinion chimerical. The great mass of our Citizens is composed at this time of freeholders, and will be pleased with it.

Mr. Elseworth. How shall the freehold be defined? Ought not every man who pays a tax to vote for the representative who is to levy and dispose of his money? Shall the wealthy merchants and manufacturers, who will bear a full share of the public burdens be not allowed a voice in the imposition of them—[taxation and representation ought to go together.]

Mr. Governeur Morris. He had long learned not to be the dupe of words. The sound of Aristocracy therefore, had no effect on him. It was the thing, not the name, to which he was opposed, and one of his principal objections to the Constitution as it is now before us, is that it threatens this Country with an Aristocracy. The aristocracy will grow out of the House of Representatives. Give the votes to people who have no property, and they will sell them to the rich who will be able to buy them. We should not confine our attention to the present moment. The time is not distant when this Country will abound with mechanics and manufacturers who will receive their bread from their employers. Will such men be the secure and faithful Guardians of liberty? Will they be the impregnable barrier against aristocracy?—He was as little duped by the association of the words, 'taxation and Representation'—The man who does not give his vote freely is not represented. It is the man who dictates the vote. . . As to merchants etc. if they have wealth and value the right they can acquire it. If not they don't deserve it.

Col. Mason. We all feel too strongly the remains of ancient prejudices, and view things too much through a British Medium. A Freehold is the qualification in England, and hence it is imagined to be the only proper one. The true idea in his opinion was that every man having evidence of attachment to and permanent common interest with the Society ought to share in all its rights and privileges. Was this qualification restrained to freeholders? Does no other kind of property but land evidence a common interest in the proprietor? does nothing besides property mark a permanent attachment? Ought the merchant, the monied man, the parent of a number of children whose fortunes are to be pursued in their own [Country], to be viewed as suspicious characters, and unworthy to be trusted with the common rights of their fellow Citizens.

Mr. Madison. The right of suffrage is certainly one of the fundamental articles of republican Government, and ought not to be left to be regulated by the Legislature. A gradual abridgment of this right has been the mode in which Aristocracies have been built on the ruins of popular forms. Whether the Constitutional qualification ought to be a freehold, would with him depend much on the probable reception such a change would meet with in States where the right was now exercised by every description of people. In several of the States a freehold was now the qualification. Viewing the subject in its merits alone, the freeholders of the Country would be the safest depositories of Republican liberty. In future times a great majority of the people will not only be without landed, but any other sort of property. These will either combine under the influence of their common situation; in which case, the rights of property and the public liberty, [will not be secure in their hands:] or which is more probable, they will become the tools of opulence and ambition, in which case there will be equal danger on another side. . .

Dr. Franklin. It is of great consequence that we should not depress the virtue and public spirit of our common people; of which they displayed a great deal during the war, and which contributed principally to the favorable issue of it. He related the honorable refusal of the American seamen who were carried in great numbers into the British Prisons during the war, to redeem themselves from misery or to seek their fortunes, by entering on board the Ships of the Enemies to their Country; contrasting their patriotism with a contemporary instance in which the British seamen made prisoners by the Americans, readily entered on the ships of the latter on being promised a share of the prizes that might be made out of their own Country. This proceeded he said, from the different manner in which the common people were treated in America and Great Britain. He did not think that the elected had any right in any case to narrow the privileges of the electors. . . He was persuaded also that such a restriction as was proposed would give great uneasiness in the populous States. The sons of a substantial farmer, not being themselves freeholders, would not be pleased at being disfranchised, and there are a great many persons of that description.

Mr. Mercer. The Constitution is objectionable in many points, but in none more than the present. He objected to the footing on which the qualification was put, but particularly to the *mode of election* by the people. The people can not know and judge of the characters of Candidates. The worse possible choice will be made. . .

Mr. Rutlidge thought the idea of restraining the right of suffrage to the freeholders a very unadvised one. It would create division among the people and make enemies of all those who should be excluded. . .

SIGNING THE CONSTITUTION

Monday *September 17*

In Convention, the 109th day, the engrossed Constitution being read, Dr. Franklin rose with a speech in his hand, which he had reduced to writing for his own conveniency, and which Mr. Wilson read in the words following.

Mr. President:

I confess that there are several parts of this constitution which I do not at present approve, but I am not sure I shall never approve them; for having lived long, I have experienced many instances of being obliged by better information or fuller consideration, to change opinions even on important subjects, which I once thought right, but found to be otherwise. It is therefore that the older I grow, the more apt I am to doubt my own judgment, and to pay more respect to the judgment of others. Most men indeed as well as most sects in Religion, think themselves in possession of all truth, and that wherever others differ from them it is so far error. Steele, a Protestant in a Dedication tells the Pope, that the only difference between our Churches in their opinions of the certainty of their doctrine is, the Church of Rome is infallible and the Church of England is never in the wrong. But though many private persons think almost as highly of their own infallibility as that of their sect, few express it so naturally as a certain French lady, who in a dispute with her sister, said, 'I don't know how it happens, Sister but I meet with no body but myself, that's always in the right,'—*Il n'y a que moi qui a tojours raison.*

In these sentiments, Sir, I agree to this Constitution with all faults, if they are such; because I think a general Government necessary for us, and there is no form of Government but what may be a blessing to the people if well administered, and believe farther that this is likely to be well administered for a course of years, and can only end in Despotism, as other forms have done before it, when the people shall become so corrupted as to need despotic Government, being incapable of any other. I doubt too whether any other Convention we can obtain may be able to make a better Constitution. For when you assemble a number of men to have the advantage of their joint wisdom, you inevitably assemble with those men, all their prejudices, their passions, their errors of opinion, their local interests, and their selfish views. From such an Assembly can a perfect production be expected? It therefore astonishes me, Sir, to find this system approaching so near to perfection as it does; and I think it will astonish our enemies, who are waiting with confidence to hear that our councils are confounded like those of the Builders of Babel; and that our States are on the point of separation, only to meet hereafter for the purpose of cutting one another's throats. Thus I consent, Sir, to this Constitution because I expect no better, and because I am not sure, that it is not the best. The opinions I have had of its errors, I sacrifice to the public good—I have never whispered a syllable of them abroad—Within these walls they are born, and here they shall die—If every one of us in returning to our Constituents were to report the objections he has had to it, and endeavor to gain partizans in support of them, we might prevent its being generally received, and thereby lose all the salutary effects and great advantages resulting naturally in our favor among foreign Nations as well as among ourselves, from our real or apparent unanimity. Much of the strength and efficiency of any Government in procuring and securing happiness to the people, depends on opinion, on the general opinion of the goodness of the Government, as well as of the wisdom and integrity of its Governors. I hope therefore that for the sake of posterity, we shall act heartily and unanimously in recommending this Constitution (if approved by Congress and confirmed by the Conventions) wherever our influence may extend, and turn our future thoughts and endeavors to the means of having it well administered.

On the whole, Sir, I cannot help expressing a wish that every member of the Convention who may still have objections to it, would with me, on this occasion doubt a little of his own infallibility—and to make manifest our unanimity, put his name to this instrument.—He then moved that the Constitution be signed by the members and offered the following as a convenient form *viz.* 'Done in Convention, by the unanimous consent of *the States* present the 17th of September—In Witness whereof we have hereunto subscribed our names' . . .

Mr. Randolph then rose and with an allusion to the observations of Dr. Franklin, apologized for his refusing to sign the Constitution, notwithstanding the vast majority and venerable names that would give sanction to its wisdom and its worth. He said however that he did not mean by this refusal to decide that he should oppose the Constitution without doors. He meant only to keep himself free to be governed by his duty as it should be prescribed by his future judgment—He refused to sign, because he thought the object of the convention would be frustrated by the alternative which it presented to the people. Nine States will fail to ratify the plan and confusion must ensue. With such a view of the subject he ought not, he could not, by pledging himself to support the plan, restrain himself from taking such steps as might appear to him most consistent with the public good.

Mr. Gouverneur Morris said that he too had objections, but considering the present plan as the best that was to be attained, he should take it with all its faults. The majority had determined in its favor and by that determination he should abide. The moment this plan goes forth all other considerations will be laid aside—and the great question will be, shall there be a national Government or not? and this must take place or a general anarchy will be the alternative. . .

Mr. Hamilton expressed his anxiety that every member should sign. . . No man's ideas were more remote from the plan than his own were known to be; but it is impossible to deliberate between anarchy and Convulsion on one side, and the chance of good to be expected from the plan on the other. . .

Mr. Gerry described the painful feelings of his situation, and the embarrassment under which he rose to offer any further observations on the subject which had been finally decided. Whilst the plan was depending, he had treated it with all the freedom he thought it deserved. He now felt himself bound as he was to treat it with the respect due to the Act of the Convention—He hoped he should not violate that respect in declaring on this occasion his fears that a Civil war may result from the present crisis of the United States—In Massachusetts, particularly he saw the danger of this calamitous event—In that State there are two parties, one devoted to Democracy, the worst he thought of all political evils, the other as violent in the opposite extreme. From the collision of these in opposing and resisting the Constitution, confusion was greatly to be feared. He had thought it necessary for this and other reasons that the plan should have been proposed in a more mediating shape, in order to abate the heat and opposition of parties—As it had been passed by the Convention, he was persuaded it would have a contrary effect—

He could not therefore by signing the Constitution pledge himself to abide by it at all events. . . Alluding to the remarks of Dr. Franklin, he could not he said but view them as levelled at himself and the other gentlemen who meant not to sign; . . .

On motion of Dr. Franklin.

New Hampshire: ay. Massachusetts: ay. Connecticut: ay. New Jersey: ay. Pennsylvania: ay. Delaware: ay. Maryland: ay. Virginia, ay. North Carolina: ay. South Carolina: divided. Georgia: ay. (Ayes—10; noes—0; divided—1.) . . .

The members then proceeded to sign the instrument.

Whilst the last members were signing it Dr. Franklin looking towards the President's Chair, at the back of which a rising sun happened to be painted, observed to a few members near him, that Painters had found it difficult to distinguish in their art a rising from a setting sun. I have, said he, often and often in the course of the Session, and the vicissitudes of my hopes and fears as to its issue, looked at that behind the President without being able to tell whether it was rising or setting; But now at length I have the happiness to know that it is a rising and not a setting Sun.

The Constitution being signed by all the Members except Mr. Randolph, Mr. Mason, and Mr. Gerry who declined giving it the sanction of their names, the Convention dissolved itself by the Adjournment sine die—

SELECTED REFERENCES

Charles A. Beard, *An Economic Interpretation of the Constitution*, New York, Macmillan, 1913.

A. C. Coolidge, *Theoretical and Foreign Elements in the Formation of the American Constitution*, Freiburg, 1892.

E. S. Corwin, *The Doctrine of Judicial Review*, Princeton, Princeton University Press, 1914, chap. 2, 'We the People.'

———, 'Review of Beard's Economic Interpretation,' *History Teachers' Magazine*, February 1914, vol v, pp. 65–6.

Louise B. Dunbar, *A Study of 'Monarchical' Tendencies in the United States from 1776 to 1801*, Urbana, 1922.

Max Farrand, *The Framing of the Constitution of the United States*, New Haven, Yale University Press, 1913.

———, 'George Washington in the Federal Convention,' *The Yale Review*, November 1907, vol. 16, pp. 280–87.

Henry Jones Ford, *Rise and Growth of American Politics*, New York, Macmillan, 1898.

Essays on the Constitution of the United States, 1787–1788, Paul Leicester Ford, ed., Brooklyn, N. Y., Historical Printing Club, 1892.

Pamphlets on the Constitution, Paul Leicester Ford, ed., Brooklyn, N. Y., Historical Printing Club, 1888.

Richard Hofstadter, *The American Political Tradition*, New York, Knopf, 1948, chap. 1, 'The Founding Fathers: An Age of Reason.'

R. McKeon, 'The Development of the Concept of Property in Political Philosophy: A Study of the Background of the Constitution,' *Ethics*, April 1938, vol. 48, pp. 297–366.

Luther Martin, *The Genuine Information Delivered to the State of Maryland Relative to the Proceedings of the General Convention, held at Philadelphia in 1787.*

Alpheus T. Mason, *The States Rights Debate: Antifederalism and the Constitution*, Englewood Cliffs, N. J., Prentice-Hall, 1964, chap. 2.

'Notes of Major William Pierce on the Federal Convention of 1787,' *American Historical Review*, vol. III, pp. 310–34.

John C. Ranney, 'The Bases of American Federalism,' *The William and Mary Quarterly*, January 1946, 3rd series, vol. III, no. 1.

The Delegate from New York, or, Proceedings of the Federal Convention of 1787, from the notes of John Lansing, Jr., Joseph R. Strayer, ed., Princeton, Princeton University Press, 1939.

Carl Van Doren, *The Great Rehearsal: The Story of the Making and Ratifying of the Constitution of the United States*, New York, Viking, 1948.

VI

GETTING THE CONSTITUTION ADOPTED: THE RATIFICATION DEBATES

Only three of the forty-two present on the closing day of the Convention refused to sign the proposed Constitution—Edmund Randolph and George Mason of Virginia and Elbridge Gerry of Massachusetts. (Randolph finally supported ratification; the others resisted to the bitter end.) Yet the Congress to which the instrument was reported gave it cool reception. Richard Henry Lee, joined by Nathan Dane of Massachusetts and Melancton Smith of New York, pounced fiercely upon it, raising technical objections and demanding amendments. Finally, without a favorable word, the Congress voted unanimously that the Constitution 'be transmitted to the several legislatures in order to be submitted to a Convention of delegates chosen in each state by the people thereof, in conformity to the resolves of the Convention.'

Although early response in the states was encouraging, Antifederalists waged a stubborn fight throughout. Even Jefferson's first reaction was one of disappointment. 'I am sorry they [the Convention] began their deliberations by so abominable a precedent as that of tying up the tongues of their members,' he had written John Adams on 30 August. 'Nothing can justify this example, but the innocence of their intentions, and ignorance of the value of public discussions. I have no doubt that all their other measures will be good and wise. It really is an assembly of demigods.'

On examination of the document itself, Jefferson tempered his approval with specific criticisms. These, together with his warm endorsement of the Confederate Government, 'with all its imperfections,' as 'the best existing, or that ever did exist,' were potent ammunition in Antifederalist hands. 'I think all the good of this new Constitution,' he wrote John Adams, 13 November 1787, 'might have been couched in three or four new articles, to be added to the good old venerable fabric, which should have been preserved even as a religious relique.' Unfortunately, Jefferson failed to specify which articles ought to have been added.

Certain of the Constitution's bitterest foes, among them Robert Yates and John Lansing of New York, had been Convention delegates. Yates was a State Supreme Court judge, known for his 'great legal talents.' 'Some of his enemies,' Pierce noted cryptically, 'say he is an anti-federal man.' Lansing was Mayor of Albany, a lawyer whose 'legal knowledge,' Pierce records, 'is not very extensive, nor his education a good one.' In early July, Yates and Lansing had become alarmed by the Convention's bold disregard of the limited authority the states had conferred upon it. 'The scheme itself is totally novel,' Lansing had said of the Virginia plan on 16 June. 'There is no parallel to it to be found.' Strongly favoring the New Jersey plan and convinced that their very presence in a convention determined to ignore the Articles of Confederation was in violation of their instructions, the New Yorkers quit Philadelphia on 10 July.

But no such squeamishness inhibited them on their return to Albany. Violating the Convention's rule of secrecy, they conveyed to Governor George Clinton their conviction that 'a general government, however guarded by declarations of rights, or cautionary provisions, must unavoidably, in a short time, be productive of the destruction of the civil liberty of such citizens as could be effectually coerced by it.' The letter Yates and Lansing addressed to Clinton, here reprinted, was but part of a concerted campaign to inflame Clinton and his huge popular following, and 'educate' the Constitution's wavering opponents.

Opposition of a higher order came from George Mason, delegate to the Convention from Virginia. Veteran statesman and famous author of the Virginia Declaration of Rights, Mason has been described by Jefferson as 'a man of the first order of wisdom among those who acted on the theatre of the Revolution, of expansive mind, profound judgment, cogent in argument, learned in the lore of our former Constitution (Virginia, 1776) and earnest for the republican change on democratic principles.' Mason had been mildly optimistic when the Convention opened. He approved strengthening the central government but, from conversation with delegates, he early sensed the 'most prevalent idea in the principal states' for 'total alteration of the present system.' He was much disturbed that men, 'tired and disgusted with the unexpected evils they have experienced [with democracy] and anxious to remove them as far as possible, are very apt to run into the opposite extreme.'

As the proceedings advanced, Mason not only objected to specific provisions but also to 'the precipitate and intemperate, not to say indecent manner, in which the business was conducted during the last weeks of the Convention after the patrons of this new plan had a decided majority in their favor.' Writing Jefferson shortly before the opening of the ratifying Convention in Virginia, Mason informed him that 'upon the most mature consideration I was capable of, and from motives of sincere patriotism, I was under the necessity of refusing my signature . . . and drew up some general objections.' Portions of his 'Objections,' published in the *Pennsylvania Packet*, 4 October 1787, are here reprinted.

Luther Martin, later known as 'the bulldog of Federalism,' was the leading Antifederalist in Maryland. A staunch defender of states' rights at the Convention, he detailed his case against the Constitution in 'Genuine Information,' delivered to the Maryland state legislature, 29 November 1787, and excerpted here. The Constitution, 'in its very *introduction*,' Martin complained, was declared to be 'a compact between the people of the United States, as individuals; and it is to be ratified by the *people* at large, in their capacity *as individuals.*' This 'would be quite right and proper,' he explained, 'if there were *no State Governments, if all the people* of this continent were in a *state of nature,* and we were forming one *national government* for *them as individuals.*'

Elbridge Gerry enjoyed the distinction of being the only northern member of the Convention who refused to sign the Constitution. A signer of the Declaration, minister to France, governor of Massachusetts, patron of gerrymandering, and later Vice President of the United States, Gerry had refused to attend the Annapolis Convention of 1786, contending that its competence was inadequate. Elected a delegate to the Federal Convention, he had joined the advocates of strong central government, but before the proceedings were concluded he reversed his position, being convinced that the proposed Constitution 'will lay the foundation of Government of *force* and *fraud,* that the people will bleed with taxes at every pore, and that the existence of their liberties will soon be terminated.' When the Constitution was ratified, he insisted that it must be supported. In due course, he was able to overcome his earlier Antifederalist leanings and support Hamilton's program for establishing energetic government, including the United States Bank in which he was a stockholder. Pierce, a fellow delegate at the Philadelphia Convention, stressed Gerry's 'integrity and perseverance,' and marked 'as his first virtue, a love for his country.' Carl Van Doren's more recent appraisal seems nearer the truth: 'Captious and inconsistent, theoretically a republican but practically full of contempt for the people, in the habit of opposing any proposal in the Constitution which he had not made himself.' Certainly Gerry's opposition was lacking in the restraint that pervades the objections cogently stated by George Mason and Richard Henry Lee.

V. L. Parrington gives high praise to Lee's *Letters from the Federal Farmer to the Republican,* extracted in these readings. Parrington speaks of it as 'a frank and disinterested examination of the proposed instrument of government,' and sharply contrasts it with the *Federalist* for 'calmness and fair-mindedness.' Lee, like Mason, approached the Convention and the Constitution with mixed emotions. For reasons not altogether clear he declined Governor Randolph's appointment to be a Virginia delegate to the Philadelphia Convention. On his way to New York in the summer of 1787, he passed through Philadelphia and, despite the enforced secrecy, he learned enough to venture the opinion that 'we shall hear of a government not unlike the British Constitution.' But when the Constitution became known, his reaction was remarkably temperate. He proposed amendment, not rejection.

'The constitution has a great many excellent regulations in it,' he wrote George Mason, 1 October, 1787, 'and if it could be reasonably amended, would be a fine system.' The Bill of Rights he proposed was based on a thousand years of struggle for Anglo-Saxon liberties, and rooted in the firm conviction that the Constitution, if adopted unamended, would 'put Civil Liberty and happiness of the people at the mercy of Rulers who may possess the great unguarded powers given.' He wanted such amendments 'as will give security to the just rights of human nature, and better secure from injury the discordant interests of the different parts of this union.' Lee was certain 'that the good people of the United States' in contending for 'free government' had 'no idea of being brought under despotic rule' under the notion of 'strong government, or in the form of *elective despotism:* Chains being still Chains, whether made of gold or iron.' Feeling this way, Lee, like Mason, naturally deplored the 'unseemly haste of its advocates.'

Perhaps the most knowledgeable advocate of the Constitution was James Wilson of Pennsylvania. A leading nationalist at the Convention and later a distinguished Associate Justice of the Supreme Court, he formulated and expounded the standard arguments used by all supporters of ratification. Excerpted herein is his famous State House speech, delivered in Philadelphia, 10 October 1787, just prior to the Pennsylvania ratifying convention.

The issues dividing Federalists and Antifederalists were brilliantly illuminated in Pennsylvania. Challenging the redoubtable Wilson were Findley, Smilie, and Whitehill, delegates from the western counties. At the outset, Wilson posed the burning question of the day: 'Of what description is the constitution before us?' To the inquiry which continues to vex scholars, he replied:

> In its principles, Sir, it is purely democratical; varying indeed, in its form, in order to admit all the advantages, and to exclude all the disadvantages which are incidental to the known and established constitutions of government. But when we take an extensive and accurate view of the streams of power that appear through this great and comprehensive plan, when we contemplate the variety of their directions, the force and dignity of their currents . . . we shall be able to trace them all to one great and noble source, THE PEOPLE.

The grandiloquent words 'We, the people' are 'the fee simple of freedom and government . . . declared to be in the people . . . an inheritance with which they will not part.'

Wilson's unremitting insistence that the people—to the complete exclusion of the states—were the only proper source of sovereignty led to admissions which fed more and more fuel to the fire raging in Antifederalist minds. He confessed that 'the Federal convention had exceeded the powers given to them by the several legislatures. . . The Federal convention did not act at all upon the powers given to them by the States . . . they proceeded upon original principles, and having framed a constitution which they thought would promote the happiness of their country, they have submitted it to their consideration, who may either adopt or reject it, as they please.'

The Pennsylvania debate reached an emotional and intellectual peak when Findley, on 6 December 1787, 'delivered an eloquent and powerful speech, to prove that the proposed plan of government amounted to a consolidation, and not a confederation of the states.' The *Pennsylvania Packet* reported:

> Mr. Wilson had before admitted that if this was a just objection, it would be strongly against the system; and it seems from the subsequent silence of all its advocates upon the subject (except Dr. Rush, who . . . insinuated that he saw and rejoiced at the eventual annihilation of the state sovereignties) Mr. Findley had established his

> position. Previous to an investigation of the plan, that gentleman . . . showed that we were in an eligible position to attempt the improvement of the Federal Government, but not so desperately circumstanced as to be obliged to adopt any system, however destructive to the liberties of the people, and the sovereign rights of the states.

Findley went on to argue 'that the proposed constitution established a general government and destroyed the individual governments,' basing his case on 'evidence taken from the system itself.'

Findley's speech evoked serious response from Wilson. 'The secret is now disclosed,' he replied solemnly, 'and it is discovered to be a dread that the boasted state sovereignties will, under this system, be disrobed of part of their power.' Mounting a frontal attack, Wilson queried the very foundation of state sovereignty. 'Upon what principle,' he asked, 'is it contended that the sovereign power resides in the state governments?' Findley had contended that 'there can be no subordinate sovereignty.' Wilson joined issue:

> Now if there can not, my position is, that sovereignty resides in the people. They have not parted with it; they have only dispensed such portions of power as were conceived necessary for the public welfare. This constitution stands upon this broad principle. I know very well, Sir, that the people have hitherto been shut out of the federal government, but it is not meant that they should any longer be dispossessed of their rights. In order to recognize this leading principle, the proposed system sets out with a declaration that its existence depends upon the supreme authority of the people alone. . .

Here, then, was the crucial point—the people were always sovereign; the states were mere pretenders, perhaps usurpers. How dared the states question the sovereignty of their masters? '[H]ow comes it, Sir,' Wilson asked, 'that these State governments dictate to their superiors?—to the majesty of the people?'

Findley, Whitehill, and Smilie had met a formidable adversary, one who pulled no punches in his defense of the 'leading principle'—popular sovereignty. Making crystal clear the unbridgeable gap separating the two positions, Wilson proceeded:

> His position [Findley's] is, that the supreme power resides in the States, as governments; and mine is, that it *resides* in the PEOPLE, as the fountain of government; that the people have not—that the people mean not—and that the people ought not, to part with it to any government whatsoever. In their hands it remains secure. They can delegate it in such proportions, to such bodies, on such terms, and under such limitations, as they think proper. I agree with the members in opposition, that there cannot be two sovereign powers on the same subject.

To underscore the impasse, Wilson drew on the immortal Declaration, confirming 'the inherent and unalienable right of the people . . . to form either a general government, or state governments, in what manner they please. . .' 'The broad basis on which our independence was placed' was that '*governments* are instituted among men, *deriving their just powers from the consent of the governed*.' 'On the same certain and solid foundation this system is erected.' Antifederalists argued that thirteen sovereign states won their independence from Great Britain; Wilson contended that the sovereign people rebelled. Antifederalists contended that the Articles of Confederation constituted a legitimate expression of state sovereignty; Wilson insisted that the Articles were an aberration. Because popular sovereignty underlay the proposed Constitution, Wilson explained, 'we are told it is a violation of the present confederation—a CONFEDERATION of SOVEREIGN STATES.' But for Wilson this meant only that the Articles were not founded on 'the principle of free governments.' 'The true and only safe principle for a free people, is a practical recognition of their original and supreme authority.' There was no middle ground. 'I am astonished to hear the ill-founded doctrine,' Wilson declared, 'that States alone ought to be represented in the federal government. . .'

> No: let us *reascend* to first principles. That expression is not strong enough to do my ideas justice. Let us RETAIN first principles. The people of the United States are now in the possession and exercise of their original rights, and while this doctrine is known and operates, we shall have a cure for every disease.

Though the expression 'free government' was frequently on the lips of Americans prior to 1787, no definition had been attempted. James Wilson fashioned this description:

> A free government has often been compared to a pyramid. This allusion is made with peculiar propriety in the system before you; it is laid on the broad basis of the people; its powers gradually rise while they are confined, in proportion as they ascend, until they end in that most permanent of all forms. When you examine all its parts, they will invariably be found to preserve that essential mark of free government—a chain of connection with the people.

Wilson's outspoken defiance of state sovereignty confirmed the Antifederalists' worst fears. Charges that the Convention had produced a 'consolidated' system, designed ultimately, if not immediately, to 'swallow up' the states, echoed and re-echoed throughout the country. 'I confess,' lamented Samuel Adams in Massachusetts, 'as I enter the Building I stumble at the Threshold. I meet with a National Government, instead of a Federal Union.'

> I am not able to conceive why the Wisdom of the Convention led them to give Preference to the former [the national government] before the latter [the sovereign states]. If the several states in the Union are to become one entire Nation, under one Legislature, the

> powers of which shall extend to every Subject of Legislation, and its laws be Supreme and control the whole, the Idea of Sovereignty in those States must be lost. . .

In North Carolina, James Iredell, like Wilson destined for the Supreme Court, joined the refrain in defense of the Constitution. Portions of his reply to George Mason's 'Objections' are included herein.

Iredell's rebuttal did not go unchallenged. Lenoir's speech in the North Carolina convention, contained in these readings, is fairly representative of the American mind of the period. It reflects the deep-seated distrust of power so fundamental to an understanding of America's unrelenting search for union without unity.

Prior to the Constitution's adoption, no one, Federalist or Antifederalist, so accurately forecast the judicial construction of the Constitution as did Robert Yates in the 'Letters of Brutus,' herein excerpted. Yates took judicial review for granted. The Supreme Court, he predicted, could be expected to extend national power, including its own, to unconscionable limits, and 'abolish entirely the State governments.' 'You have given us a good Constitution,' a friend told Gouverneur Morris soon after the Convention adjourned. 'That depends,' Morris answered soberly, 'on how it is construed.' Later, Antifederalists John Taylor and Hugh Legaré interpreted the constitutional jurisprudence of Chief Justice John Marshall as a complete vindication of Yates's words.

To allay the fears aroused by Yates's ominous forecast, Hamilton wrote essays 78 and 81 of *The Federalist*. Said he, 'Some perplexity respecting the rights of courts to pronounce legislative acts void, because, contrary to the Constitution, has arisen from an imagination that the doctrine [judicial review] would imply a superiority of the judiciary to the legislative power.' In combating this proposition, Hamilton fused reason and magic, concluding: 'Nor does this conclusion [that the Constitution ought to be preferred to a statute] by any means suppose a superiority of the judicial to the legislative power. It only supposes that the power of the people is superior to both [court and legislature]; and that if the will of the legislature, declared in statutes, stands in opposition to that of the people declared in the Constitution, the judges ought to be governed by the latter rather than by the former.'

The Federalist, a propaganda book, as we would call it today, of approximately 175,000 words, was published under the pseudonym *Publius* in various New York papers at regular intervals between 27 October 1787, and 15 August 1788—the period in which the Constitution was being hotly debated. Written primarily to win ratification in New York state, but broadcast in other states, the preparation had to be done in great haste. 'It frequently happened,' Madison recalled many years later, 'that, whilst the printer was putting into type parts of a number, the following parts were under the pen and to be furnished in time for the press.' Yet *The Federalist* ranks today among the world's classics. Its high excellence was immediately recognized and its fame has grown through the years. Jefferson read the papers 'with care, pleasure and improvement,' and then wrote Madison from Paris praising them as 'the best commentary on the principles of government ever written.' Washington was equally enthusiastic: 'As the perusal of the political papers under the signature of Publius has afforded me great satisfaction,' he wrote Hamilton from Mount Vernon, 'I shall consider them as claiming a most distinguished place in my library.'

Despite such reception, neither Hamilton nor Madison, for political reasons, was inclined for some years thereafter to identify the particular numbers they wrote. The result is that the authorship of *The Federalist*, long shrouded in mystery, has been a subject of lively contention among scholars and scholar-politicians, such as Henry Cabot Lodge, down to our own time. An article published in 1944 by Professor Douglass Adair goes far toward resolving the controversy. Briefly the story is this:

Two days before his fatal duel with Burr, Hamilton went to the law office of his friend, Egbert Benson, and 'ostentatiously' concealed in the lawyer's bookcase a slip of paper identifying the authors of the various numbers. Of the 85 essays, Hamilton claimed 63 as his own. In 1818 Jacob Gideon published a corrected list, claiming 29 essays for Madison instead of the 14 conceded to him by Hamilton. The Gideon edition, moreover, was checked and approved by Madison himself. Because of this conflict, editors of various editions have been accustomed to 'resolve' this historic controversy easily by placing the words 'Hamilton or Madison' over the disputed numbers. This is no longer necessary. The research of recent years makes it reasonably clear that of the 85 essays John Jay wrote 5 (2–5 and 64); Hamilton did numbers 1, 6–9, 11–13, 15–17, 21–36, 59–61, and 65–85, inclusive; numbers 18, 19, and 20 appear to have been the result of Madison's and Hamilton's joint effort. The remaining essays were written by Madison, making the authenticated tally Hamilton, 51, Madison, 26. These findings have been given statistical support by feeding 'marker' and 'color' words, drawn from the disputed numbers, into a computer.

The Federalist embodies four main arguments: (1). The necessity of prompt and effective action because of acknowledged defects in the Articles of Confederation; (2). The urgency of a unitary system, acting directly on individuals and possessed of coercive power to avoid that worst of all political monsters—an *imperium in imperio;* (3). The peculiar adaptability of the republican form of government to a great extent of territory and widely divergent interests, as in the United States; (4). The necessity of providing more effectually for the securing of private rights, especially of property and contract, harassed and violated in the several states by 'interested and over-bearing majorities.'

The scope of the task and the necessity of expediting preparation and publication called for a division of labor along the lines of Hamilton's and Madison's special aptitudes and interests, a division such as would enable them to utilize material already in hand. Since 1780 Hamilton had been citing want of power in Congress as the crucial defect in the existing system. It was natural therefore that he should devote his major effort to demonstrating how the Constitution provided the requisite remedy. Madison, though not ignoring the need for greater energy and power in the central government, had denounced legislative encroachments on vested rights as among the most grievous wrongs to be righted. His most significant numbers, 10 and 51, are accordingly devoted to showing how the Constitution corrects the evil which more than any other had, as he said, produced the Convention.

Differing emphases in advocacy served to strengthen rather than weaken the case made for the Constitution. Also, certain essential areas of agreement enabled the major authors to co-operate effectively. Practical experience during the years since 1776 had tended to undermine faith in human nature, no less than in the revolutionary abstractions such as natural law and natural rights. The supreme confidence in reason, of earlier years, had also been shaken. 'What is government itself,' Madison inquired in number 51, 'but the greatest of all reflections on human nature? If men were angels no government would be necessary. If angels were to govern men, neither external nor internal controls on government would be necessary.' 'Why has government been instituted at all?,' Hamilton asks, in essay 15. 'Because the passions of men will not conform to the dictates of reason and justice, without constraint.'

In number 28 Hamilton denounced that popular but, as he thought, misguided principle 'of governing at all times by the simple force of law (which we have been told is the only admissible principle of republican government).' Such a principle, he said, 'has no place but in the reveries of those political doctors whose sagacity disdains the admonition of experimental instruction.' Madison did not labor the point in such stately fashion but he freely disparaged the effectiveness of religion, patriotism, and principles of justice as factors in politics, and called for a government with at least as much coercive energy as that provided in the Constitution.

Both Hamilton and Madison saw society as plagued by 'factions.' They agreed, too, that inequality results inevitably from liberty. Both addressed themselves to finding a remedy for the chaos inherent in a society certain to be increasingly torn by conflicts between rich and poor. Both presumed to find a republican remedy for the affliction to which popular governments are particularly addicted—the evil of faction. But these areas of essential agreement should not blind us to important points of difference. Careful allocation of the subjects discussed tended to prevent any highlighting of divergencies between the two authors, but an independent reading of the essays attributed to them reveals *The Federalist* as a 'split personality.' 'It is not difficult to perceive,' John Quincy Adams observed in 1836, 'that diversity of genius and of character which afterwards separated them so widely from each other on questions of political interest, affecting the construction of the Constitution which they so ably defended, and so strenuously urged their countrymen to adopt.'

Running through Hamilton's numbers is an undertone of Hobbesian monism. In Philadelphia Hamilton was certain that nothing short of monarchy, a permanent will in government independent of society, would suffice to remedy the evils suffered from existing inadequacies. He was naturally less outspoken in *The Federalist*, but he makes clear his belief in numbers 9, 70, 71, and 78 that an independent will in government, immune from fluctuating gusts of popular passion, is altogether compatible with republican principles.

Madison, on the other hand, though rejecting democracy, stressed dependence on the people as the essential attribute of republicanism, and proposed a pluralistic remedy for a republican disease—factions. The Constitution, as he interpreted it, makes functional use not only of the states, but also of the vast expanse of territory and the great multiplicity of social and economic interests. Faction must be balanced against faction. Ambition must be pitted against ambition. All interests are to act as checks on all other interests within the societal framework. Justice will result, Madison suggested, from the mutual opposition of natural forces. With good reason John Quincy Adams described Hamilton's number 9 and Madison's number 10 as 'rival dissertations upon Faction and its remedy.'

Other differences may be noted. For Hamilton the capital infirmity of the existing system was congenital—'it never had ratification by the People.' To avoid the 'gross heresy' that a 'party to a compact has a right to revoke that compact, the fabric of American empire *ought* to rest on the solid basis of *the consent of the People*.' In essay 15 he had likewise portrayed the Constitution as the proper corrective of 'the great and radical vice'—'legislation for states . . . as contradistinguished from the individuals of which they consist.' There follows his classic expression of the doctrine of Federalism:

> If we are unwilling to be placed in this perilous situation; if we still adhere to the design of a national government, or, which is the same thing, of a superintending power, under the direction of a Common council, we must resolve to incorporate into our plan those ingredients which may be considered as forming the characteristic difference between a league and a government; we must extend the authority of the Union to the persons of the citizens,—the only proper objects of government.

Madison's position is not so unequivocal:

> The assent and ratification is to be given by the people, not as individuals composing one entire nation, but as composing the distinct and independent states to which they respectively belong. It is to be the assent and ratification of the several states, derived from the supreme authority in each state,—the authority of the people themselves. The act, therefore, establishing the Constitution, will not be a *national*, but a *federal* act.

For Madison the distinction was fundamental. This clearly does not accord with Hamilton's position that the Constitution establishes a 'government,' not a 'league,' and one which is 'national,' not 'federal.' A distinction that Madison labored in essay 39, Hamilton passed over lightly in number 9 as 'a distinction more subtle than accurate.'

Nor were Hamilton and Madison fully agreed about the nature and scope of the power granted to the national government. In essay 40 Madison argued that the 'great principles' of the Constitution were not 'absolutely new' but an 'expansion of principles which are found in the Articles of Confederation.' 'The powers delegated by the proposed Constitution are few and defined,' Madison observed in number 45. 'The change which it [the Constitution] proposes consists much less in the addition of new powers to the union, than in the invigoration of its original powers.' Hamilton, on the other hand, took the position that the objects of the national government were general and undefined—indeed undefinable. Therefore the powers granted to secure them differed in kind, not in degree, as Madison suggested, from those provided for under the Articles of Confederation. What was necessary in his mind was far more than 'invigoration.' The exigencies required nothing short of a complete change of system, as he makes clear in essays 9, 15, and 22. Nor was the force of the new government to be applied so exclusively, as Madison suggested, in the field of foreign relations. Hamilton conceived of the central government as an essential force in domestic affairs as well—especially as a safeguard against faction and insurrection.

Neither of the major contributors to *The Federalist* tried to hide his misgivings. 'I shall not dissemble,' Hamilton said in his concluding essay, 'that I feel an entire confidence in the arguments which recommend the proposed system to your adoption; and that I am unable to discern any real force in those by which it has been assailed. I am persuaded that it is the best which our political situation, habits, and opinions will admit, and superior to any the revolution has produced.' Perhaps at best the Constitution was a workable makeshift to avoid, as Hamilton suggested, 'civil war . . . a dismemberment of the Union and monarchies in different portions of it.' There may have been other motivating considerations, for he frankly avowed in the opening essay that while his 'arguments' would 'be open to all and may be judged by all' his 'motives must remain in the depository of my own breast.' Madison divulged that 'certain of the deputations at the Convention may have been induced to accede to the Constitution by a deep conviction of the necessity of sacrificing private opinions and partial interests to the public good.' The authors' own lack of entire confidence in the instrument they supported may account for the exalted spirit of tolerance that animates their argument from start to finish.

'We are not always sure,' Hamilton observed in the first essay, 'that those who advocate the truth are influenced by purer principles than their antagonists.' 'We upon many occasions,' he added, 'see wise and good men on the wrong as well as on the right side of questions of the first magnitude to society.' Hamilton ends the closing essay on the same magnanimous note:

> I never expect to see a perfect work from imperfect man. The result of the deliberations of all collective bodies must necessarily be a compound, as well of the errors and prejudices, as of the good sense and wisdom, of the individuals of whom they are composed. The compacts which are to embrace thirteen distinct States in a common bond of amity and union, must as necessarily be a compromise of as many dissimilar interests and inclinations. How can perfection spring from such materials?

The Federalist may have been, as someone has said, 'a propaganda barrage,' but no one can deny that it spread the faith effectively. In 1825 Jefferson called it 'an authority to which appeal is habitually made by all, and rarely declined or denied by any, as evidence of the general opinion of those who framed and of those who accepted the Constitution of the United States as to its genuine meaning.' These are strong words—ironically, words with which

Federalists and Antifederalists alike could and did agree. When John Taylor set out to prove that Chief Justice Marshall had, through spurious interpretation, converted a compact of sovereign states into a consolidated empire, he drew indiscriminately from Hamilton's and Madison's numbers of *The Federalist*. Marshall had enlisted the support of America's political classic—that 'great authority,' he called it—to demonstrate that federal judicial power must extend to Supreme Court review of state court decisions arising under the federal Constitution or laws of the United States. Yet Spencer Roane resorted to this same resourceful arsenal for the ammunition he used to blast Marshall's alleged usurpations.

Marshall was accustomed to reiterate the telling reminder: 'we must never forget, that it is a *Constitution* we are expounding.' Like an oracle, it speaks ambiguously. *The Federalist* is even more ambiguous than the document it sought to illuminate.

1. *We object to consolidation of the United States into one government*

ROBERT YATES AND JOHN LANSING, to the Governor of New York, Containing Their Reasons for not Subscribing to the Federal Convention, 1787 *

. . . It is with the sincerest concern we observe, that, in the prosecution of the important objects of our mission, we have been reduced to the disagreeable alternative, of either exceeding the powers delegated to us, and giving assent to measures which we conceive destructive to the political happiness of the citizens of the United States, or opposing our opinions to that of a body of respectable men, to whom those citizens had given the most unequivocal proofs of confidence.—Thus circumstanced, under these impressions, to have hesitated, would have been to be culpable; we, therefore, gave the principles of the constitution, which has received the sanction of a majority of the convention, our decided and unreserved dissent; but we must candidly confess, that we should have been equally opposed to any system however modified, which had in object the consolidation of the United States into one government.

We beg leave, briefly, to state some cogent reasons which, among others, influenced us to decide against a consolidation of the state. These are reducible into two heads:

1st. The limited and well defined powers under which we acted, and which could not, on any possible construction, embrace an idea of such magnitude, as to assent to a general constitution, in subversion of that of the state.

2d. A conviction of the impracticability of establishing a general government, pervading every part of the United States, and extending essential benefits to all.

Our powers were explicit, and confined to the sole and express purpose of revising the articles of confederation, and reporting such alterations and provi-

* Senate Documents, vol. 15, 60th Congress, 2nd session, 7 December 1908–4 March 1909, Washington, D.C., Government Printing Office, 1909, pp. 190–92 *passim*.

sions therein, as should render the federal constitution adequate to the exigencies of government, and the preservation of the union.

From these expressions, we were led to believe, that a system of consolidated government could not in the remotest degree, have been in contemplation of the legislature of this state, for that so important a trust, as the adopting measures which tended to deprive the state government of its most essential rights of sovereignty, and to place it in a dependant situation, could not have been confided by implication; and the circumstances, that the acts of the convention were to receive a state approbation in the last resort, forcibly corroborated the opinion, that our powers could not involve the subversion of a constitution, which being immediately derived from the people, could only be abolished by their express consent and not by a legislature, possessing authority vested in them for its preservation. Nor could we suppose, that if it had been the intention of the legislature, to abrogate the existing confederation, they would, in such pointed terms, have directed the attention of their delegates to the revision and amendment of it, in total exclusion of every other idea.

Reasoning in this manner, we were of opinion, that the leading feature of every amendment, ought to be the preservation of the individual states, in their uncontrolled constitutional rights, and that in reserving these, a mode might have been devised of granting to the confederacy, the moneys arising from a general system of revenue; the power of regulating commerce, and enforcing the observance of foreign treaties and other necessary matters of less moment.

Exclusive of our objections originating from the want of power, we entertained an opinion, that a general government, however guarded by declarations of rights, or cautionary provisions, must unavoidably, in a short time, be productive of the destruction of the civil liberty of such citizens who could be effectually coerced by it; by reason of the extensive territory of the United States, the dispersed situation of its inhabitants and the insuperable difficulty of controlling or counteracting the views of a set of men (however unconstitutional and oppressive their acts might be) possessed of all the powers of government; and who from their remoteness from their constituents and necessary permanency of office, could not be supposed to be uniformly actuated by an attention to their welfare and happiness; that however wise and energetic the principles of the general government might be, the extremities of the United States could not be kept in due submission and obedience to its laws, at the distance of many hundred miles from the seat of government; that if the general legislature was composed of so numerous a body of men, as to represent the interests of all the inhabitants of the United States, in the usual and true ideas of representation, the expense of supporting it would become intolerably burthensome and that if a few only were vested with a power of legislation, the interests of a great majority of the inhabitants of the United States, must necessarily be unknown; or if known, even in the first stages of the operations of the new government, unattended to.

These reasons were, in our opinion, conclusive against any system of consolidated government. . .

We were not present at the completion of the new constitution; but before we left the convention, its principles were so well established, as to convince us, that no alteration was to be expected to conform it to our ideas of expediency and safety. . .

2. *The time may come when it shall be the duty of a state to have recourse to the sword*

LUTHER MARTIN, *Genuine Information . . . Relative to the Proceedings of the General Convention*, delivered to the Legislature of the State of Maryland, 1787 *

By the principles of the American revolution arbitrary power may, and ought to be resisted even by arms if necessary. The time may come when it shall be the duty of a state, in order to preserve itself from the oppression of the general government, to have recourse to the sword. In which case the proposed form of government declares, that the state and every one of its citizens who act under its authority, are guilty of a direct act of treason; reducing by this provision the different states to this alternative, that they must tamely and passively yield to despotism, or their citizens must oppose it at the hazard of the halter if unsuccessful, and reducing the citizens of the state which shall take arms, to a situation in which they must be exposed to punishment, let them act as they will, since if they obey the authority of their state government, they will be *guilty of treason against the United States*, if they join the general government they will be guilty of treason against their own state. . .

I was of opinion, that the states considered as states, in their political capacity, are the members of a federal government; that the states in their political capacity, or as sovereignties, are entitled, and *only entitled* originally to agree upon the form of, and submit themselves to, a federal government, and afterwards by mutual consent to dissolve or alter it. That every thing which relates to the formation, the dissolution or the alteration of a federal government over states equally free, sovereign and independent, is the peculiar province of the state in their *sovereign* or *political* capacity, in the same manner as what relates to forming alliances or treaties of peace, amity or commerce, and that the people at large in their individual capacity, have no more right to interfere in the one case than in the other: That according to these principles we originally acted in forming our confederation; it was the states as states, by their representatives in Congress, that formed the articles of confederation; it was the states as states, by their legislatures, who ratified those articles, and it was there established and provided, that the states as states, that is, by their legislatures, should agree to any alterations that should hereafter be proposed in the federal government, before they should be binding, and any alterations agreed to any manner cannot release the states from the obligation they are under to each other by virtue of the original articles of confederation. The people of the different states never made any objection to the manner the articles of confederation were formed or ratified, or to the mode by which alterations were to be made in that government, with the rights of their respective

* *The Debates in the Several State Conventions on the Adoption of the Federal Constitution*, Jonathan Elliot, ed., Washington, D.C., 1836, vol. 1, pp. 430, 436–7.

states they wished not to interfere. Nor do I believe the people in their individual capacity, would ever have expected or desired to have appealed to on the present occasion, in violation of the rights of their respective states, if the favorers of the proposed constitution, imagining they had a better chance of forcing it to be adopted by a hasty appeal to the people at large, who could not be so good judges of the dangerous consequence, had not insisted upon this mode. Nor do these positions in the least interfere with the principle, that all power originates from the people, because when once the people have *exercised their power*, in establishing and forming themselves into a *state government*, it never devolves back to them, nor have they a right to resume or again to exercise that power until such events take place as will amount to a dissolution of their state government. And it is an established principle that a dissolution or alteration of a federal government doth not dissolve the state governments which compose it. It was also my opinion, that upon principles of sound policy, the agreement or disagreement to the proposed system, ought to have been by the state legislatures, in which case, let the event have been what it would, there would have been but little prospect of the public peace being disturbed thereby—Whereas, the attempt to force down this system, although Congress and the respective state legislatures should disapprove, by appealing to the people, and to procure its establishment in a manner totally unconstitutional, has a tendency to set the state governments and their subjects at variance with each other—to lessen the obligations of government—to *weaken the bands of society*—to introduce *anarchy* and *confusion*—and to light the torch of discord and civil war throughout this continent. All these considerations weighed with me most forcibly against giving my assent to the mode by which it is resolved by this system is to be ratified, and were urged by me in opposition to the measure.

3. *The change now proposed transfers power from the many to the few*

RICHARD HENRY LEE, *Letters from the Federal Farmer to the Republican*, 1787 *

LETTER I — *8 October* 1787

. . . My uniform federal attachments, and the interest I have in the protection of property, and a steady execution of the laws, will convince you, that, if I am under any bias at all, it is in favor of any general system which shall promise those advantages. The instability of our laws increases my wishes for firm and steady government; but then, I can consent to no government, which, in my opinion, is not calculated equally to preserve the rights of all orders of men in the community. . . I am not disposed to unreasonably contend about forms. I know our situation is critical, and it behooves us to make the best of it. A federal government of some sort is necessary. We have suffered the present to

* *Pamphlets on the Constitution of the United States*, Paul Leicester Ford, ed., 1888, pp. 277–324 *passim*.

languish; and whether the confederation was capable or not originally of answering any valuable purposes, it is now but of little importance. . . A constitution is now presented which we may reject, or which we may accept with or without amendments, and to which point we ought to direct our exertions is the question. To determine this question with propriety, we must attentively examine the system itself, and the probable consequences of either step. . .

The first principal question that occurs is, Whether, considering our situation, we ought to precipitate the adoption of the proposed constitution? If we remain cool and temperate, we are in no immediate danger of any commotions; we are in a state of perfect peace, and in no danger of invasions; the state governments are in the full exercise of their powers; and our governments answer all present exigencies, except the regulation of trade, securing credit, in some cases, and providing for the interest, in some instances, of the public debts; and whether we adopt a change three or nine months hence, can make but little odds with the private circumstances of individuals; their happiness and prosperity, after all, depend principally upon their own exertions. We are hardly recovered from a long and distressing war: The farmers, fishmen, etc. have not fully repaired the waste made by it. Industry and frugality are again assuming their proper station. Private debts are lessened, and public debts incurred by the war have been, by various ways, diminished; and the public lands have now become a productive source for diminishing them much more. I know uneasy men, who with very much to precipitate, do not admit all these facts; but they are facts well known to all men who are thoroughly informed in the affairs of this country. It must, however, be admitted, that our federal system is defective, and that some of the state governments are not well administered; but, then, we impute to the defects in our governments many evils and embarrassments which are most clearly the result of the late war. . .

It is natural for men, who wish to hasten the adoption of a measure, to tell us, now is the crisis—now is the critical moment which must be seized or all will be lost; and to shut the door against free enquiry, whenever conscious the thing presented has defects in it, which time and investigation will probably discover. This has been the custom of tyrants, and their dependents in all ages. If it is true, what has been so often said, that the people of this country cannot change their condition for the worse, I presume it still behooves them to endeavour deliberately to change it for the better. . .

Our object has been all along, to reform our federal system, and to strengthen our governments—to establish peace, order and justice in the community—but a new object now presents. The plan of government now proposed is evidently calculated totally to change, in time, our condition as a people. Instead of being thirteen republics, under a federal head, it is clearly designed to make us one consolidated government. . . This consolidation of the states has been the object of several men in this country for some time past. Whether such a change can ever be effected, in any manner; whether it can be effected without convulsions and civil wars; whether such a change will not totally destroy the liberties of this country—time only can determine.

To have a just idea of the government before us, and to show that a consolidated one is the object in view, it is necessary not only to examine the plan, but also its history, and the politics of its particular friends.

The confederation was formed when great confidence was placed in the voluntary exertions of individuals, and of the respective states; and the framers of it, to guard against usurpation, so limited, and checked the powers, that, in many respects, they are inadequate to the exigencies of the union. We find, therefore, members of congress urging alterations in the federal system almost as soon as it was adopted. It was early proposed to vest congress with powers to levy an impost, to regulate trade, etc. but such was known to be the caution of the states in parting with power, that the vestment even of these, was proposed to be under several checks and limitations. During the war, the general confusion, and the introduction of paper money, infused in the minds of people vague ideas respecting government and credit. We expected too much from the return of peace, and of course we have been disappointed. Our governments have been new and unsettled; and several legislatures, by making tender, suspension, and paper money laws, have given just cause of uneasiness to creditors. By these and other causes, several orders of men in the community have been prepared, by degrees, for a change of government; and this very abuse of power in the legislatures, which in some cases has been charged upon the democratic part of the community, has furnished aristocratical men with those very weapons, and those very means, with which, in great measure, they are rapidly effecting their favourite object. And should an oppressive government be the consequence of the proposed change, posterity may reproach not only a few overbearing, unprincipled men, but those parties in the states which have misused their powers.

The conduct of several legislatures, touching paper money, and tender laws, has prepared many honest men for changes in government, which otherwise they would not have thought of—when by the evils, on the one hand, and by the secret instigations of artful men, in the other, the minds of men were become sufficiently uneasy, a bold step was taken, which is usually followed by a revolution, or a civil war. . .

The first interesting question, therefore suggested, is, how far the states can be consolidated into one entire government on free principles. In considering this question extensive objects are to be taken into view, and important changes in the forms of government to be carefully attended to in all their consequences. The happiness of the people at large must be the great object with every honest statesman, and he will direct every movement to this point. If we are so situated as a people, as not to be able to enjoy equal happiness and advantages under one government, the consolidation of the states cannot be admitted. . .

LETTER II — *9 October 1787*

. . . There are certain unalienable and fundamental rights, which in forming the social compact, ought to be explicitly ascertained and fixed—a free and enlightened people, in forming this compact, will not resign all their rights to those who govern, and they will fix limits to their legislators and rulers, which will soon be plainly seen by those who are governed, as well as by those who govern: and the latter will know they cannot be passed unperceived by the former, and without giving a general alarm—These rights should be made the basis of every constitution; and if a people be so situated, or have such different opinion that they cannot agree in ascertaining and fixing them, it is a very strong argument against their attempting to form one entire society, to live under one system of laws only. . .

LETTER III 10 *October* 1787

. . . I am fully convinced that we must organize the national government on different principles, and make the parts of it more efficient, and secure in it more effectually the different interests in the community. . . It is not my object to multiply objections, or to contend about inconsiderable powers or amendments. I wish the system adopted with a few alterations; but those, in my mind, are essential ones. . .
. . . It is necessary . . . to examine the extent, and the probable operations of some of those extensive powers proposed to be vested in this government. These powers, legislative, executive, and judicial, respect internal as well as external objects. Those respecting external objects, as all foreign concerns, commerce, imposts, all causes arising on the seas, peace and war, and Indian affairs can be lodged no where else, with any propriety, but in this government. Many powers that respect internal objects ought clearly to be lodged in it; as those to regulate trade between the states, weights and measures, the coin or current monies, post-offices, naturalization, etc. These powers may be exercised without essentially effecting the internal police of the respective states: But powers to lay and collect internal taxes, to form the militia, to make bankrupt laws, and to decide on appeals, questions arising on the internal laws of the respective states, are of a very serious nature, and carry with them almost all other powers. These taken in connection with the others, and powers to raise armies and build navies, proposed to be lodged in this government, appear to me to comprehend all the essential powers in this community, and those which will be left to the states will be of no great importance. . .

LETTER IV 12 *October* 1787

. . . There appears to me to be not only a premature deposit of some important powers in the general government—but many of those deposited there are undefined, and may be used to good or bad purposes as honest or designing men shall prevail. . .

It is to be observed that when the people shall adopt the proposed constitution it will be their last and supreme act; it will be adopted not by the people of New Hampshire, Massachusetts, &c., but by the people of the United States; and wherever this constitution, or any part of it, shall be incompatible with the ancient customs, rights, the laws or the constitutions heretofore established in the United States, it will entirely abolish them and do them away: And not only this, but the laws of the United States which shall be made in pursuance of the federal constitution will be also supreme laws, and wherever they shall be incompatible with those customs, rights, laws or constitutions heretofore established, they will also entirely abolish them and do them away.

By the [supremacy clause] treaties also made under the authority of the United States, shall be the supreme law: It is not said that these treaties shall be made in pursuance of the constitution—nor are there any constitutional bounds set to those who shall make them: The president and two-thirds of the senate will be empowered to make treaties indefinitely, and when these treaties shall be made, they will also abolish all laws and state constitutions incompatible with them. This power in the president and senate is absolute, and the judges will be bound to allow full force to whatever rule, article or thing the president and senate shall establish by treaty, whether it be practicable to set any bounds to those who make treaties, I am not able to say; if not, it proves that this power ought to be more safely lodged.

The federal constitution, the laws of congress made in pursuance of the constitution, and all treaties must have full force and effect in all parts of the United States; and all other laws, rights and constitutions which stand in their way must yield: It is proper the national laws should be supreme, and superior to state or district laws; but then the national laws ought to yield to unalienable or fundamental rights—and national laws, made by a few men, should extend only to a few national objects. This will not be the case with the laws of congress: To have any proper idea of their extent, we must carefully examine the legislative, executive and judicial powers proposed to be lodged in the general government, and consider them in connection with a general clause in art. 1, sect. 8 in these words (after enumerating a number of powers) "To make all laws which shall be necessary and proper for carrying into execution the foregoing powers, and all other powers vested by this constitution in the government of the United States, or in any department or officer thereof." —The powers of this government as has been observed, extend to internal as well as external objects, and to those objects to which all others are subordinate; it is almost impossible to have a just conception of their powers, or of the extent and number of the laws which may be deemed necessary and proper to carry them into effect, till we shall come to exercise those powers and make the laws. In making laws to carry those powers into effect, it is to be expected, that a wise and prudent congress will pay respect to the opinions of a free people, and bottom their laws on those principles which have been considered as essential and fundamental in the British, and in our government: But a congress of a different character will not be bound by the constitution to pay respect to those principles.

It is said that when people make a constitution, and delegate powers, that all power not delegated by them to those who govern, is reserved in the people; and that the people, in the present case, have reserved in themselves, and in their state governments, every right and power not expressly given by the federal constitution to those who shall administer the national government. It is said, on the other hand, that the people, when they make a constitution, yield all power not expressly reserved to themselves. The truth is, in either case, it is mere matter of opinion, and men usually take either side of the argument, as will best answer their purposes: But the general presumption being, that men who govern, will in doubtful cases, construe laws and constitutions most favourably for increasing their own powers; all wise and prudent people, in forming constitutions, have drawn the line, and carefully described the powers parted with and the powers reserved. By the state constitutions, certain rights have been reserved in the people; or rather, they have been recognized and established in such a manner, that state legislatures are bound to respect them, and to make no laws infringing upon them. The state legislatures are obliged to take notice of the bills of rights of their respective states. The bills of rights, and the state constitutions, are fundamental compacts only between those who govern, and the people of the same state.

In the year 1787 the people of the United States made a federal constitution, which is a fundamental compact between them and their federal rulers; these rulers, in the nature of things, cannot be bound to take notice of any other compact. It would be absurd for them, in making laws, to look over thirteen, fifteen, or twenty state constitutions, to see what rights are established as fundamental, and must not be infringed upon, in making laws in the society. It is true, they would be bound to do it if the people, in their federal compact, should refer to the state constitutions, recognize all parts not inconsistent with the federal constitution, and direct their federal rulers to take notice of them accordingly; but this is not the case, as the plan stands proposed at present; and it is absurd, to suppose so unnatural an idea is intended or implied. I think my opinion is not only founded in reason, but I think it is supported by the report of the convention itself. If there are a number of rights established by the state constitutions, and which will remain sacred, and the general government is bound to take notice of them—it must take notice of one as well as another; and if unnecessary to recognize or establish one by the federal constitution, it would be unnecessary to recognize or establish another by it. If the federal constitution is to be construed so far in connection with the state constitution, as to leave the trial by jury in civil causes, for instance, secured; on the same principles it would have left the trial by jury in criminal causes, the benefits of the writ of habeas corpus, &c. secured; they all stand on the same footing; they are the common rights of Americans, and have been recognized by the state constitutions: But the convention found it necessary to recognize or reestablish the benefits of that writ, and the jury trial in criminal cases. As to *expost facto* laws, the convention has done the same in one case, and gone further in another. It is a part of the compact between the people of each state and their rulers, that no *expost facto laws* shall be made. But the convention, by Art. 1, Sect. 10, have put a sanction upon this part even of the state compacts. In fact, the 9th and 10th Sections in Art. 1, in the proposed constitution, are no more nor less, than a partial bill of rights; they establish certain principles as part of the compact upon which the federal legislators and officers can never infringe. It is here wisely stipulated, that the federal legislature shall never pass a bill of attainder, or *expost facto* law; that no tax shall be laid on articles exported, &c. The establishing of one right implies the necessity of establishing another and similiar one.

On the whole, the position appears to me to be undeniable, that this bill of rights ought to be carried farther, and some other principles established, as a part of this fundamental compact between the people of the United States and their federal rulers.

It is true, we are not disposed to differ much, at present, about religion; but when we are making a constitution, it is to be hoped, for ages and millions yet unborn, why not establish the free exercise of religion, as a part of the national compact. There are other essential rights, which we have justly understood to be the rights of freemen; as freedom from hasty and unreasonable search warrants, warrants not founded on oath, and not issued with due caution, for searching and seizing men's papers, property, and persons. The trials by jury in civil causes, it is said, varies so much in the several states, that no words could be found for the uniform establishment of it. If so, the federal legislation will not be able to establish it by any general laws. I confess I am of opinion it may be established, but not in that beneficial manner in which we may enjoy it, for the reasons beforementioned. When I speak of the jury trial of the vicinage, or the trial of the fact in the neighborhood, I do not lay so much stress upon the circumstance of our being tried by our neighbors: in this enlightened country men may be probably impartially tried by those who do not live very near them: but the trial of facts in the neighbourhood is of great importance in other respects. Nothing can be more essential than the cross examining witnesses, and generally before the triers of the facts in question. The common people can establish facts with much more ease with oral than written evidence; when trials of facts are removed to a distance from the homes of the parties and witnesses, oral evidence becomes intolerably expensive, and the parties must depend on written evidence, which to the common people is expensive and almost useless; it must be frequently taken ex parte, and but very seldom leads to the proper discovery of truth. . .

I confess I do not see in what cases the congress can, with any pretence of right, make a law to suppress the freedom of the press; though I am not clear, that congress is restrained from laying any duties whatever on printing, and from laying duties particularly heavy on certain pieces printed, and perhaps congress may require large bonds for the payment of these duties. Should the printer say, the freedom of the press was secured by the constitution of the state in which he lived, congress might, and perhaps, with great propriety, answer, that the federal constitution is the only compact existing between them and the people; in this compact the people have named no others, and therefore congress, in exercising the powers assigned them, and in making laws to carry them into execution, are restrained by nothing beside the federal constitution, any more than a state legislature is restrained by a compact between the magistrates and people of a county, city, or town of which the people, in forming the state constitution, have taken no notice.

It is not my object to enumerate rights of inconsiderable importance; but there are others, no doubt, which ought to be established as a fundamental part of the national system. . .

LETTER V *15 October 1787*

. . . There are, however, in my opinion, many good things in the proposed system. It is founded on elective principles, and the deposits of powers in different hands, is essentially right. The guards against those evils we have experienced in some states in legislation are valuable indeed; but the value of every feature in this system is vastly lessened for the want of that one important feature in a free government, a representation of the people. Because we have sometimes abused democracy, I am not among those men who think a democratic branch a nuisance; which branch shall be sufficiently numerous to admit some of the best informed men of each order in the community into the administration of government. . .

I have admitted that we want a federal system—that we have a system presented, which, with several alterations may be made a tolerable good one. . . In this situation of things, you ask me what I think ought to be done? . . . It is true there may be danger in delay; but there is danger in adopting the system in its present form; and I see the danger in either case will arise principally from the conduct and views of two very unprincipled parties in the United States—two fires, between which the honest and substantial people have long found themselves situated. One party is composed of little insurgents, men in debt, who want no law, and who want a share of the property of others; these are called levellers, Shayites, etc. The other party is composed of a few, but more dangerous men, with their servile dependents; these avariciously grasp at all power and property; you may discover in all the actions of these men, an evident dislike to free and equal government, and they will go systematically to work to change, essentially, the forms of government in this country. . . Between these two parties is the weight of the community; the men of middling property, men not in debt on the one hand, and men, on the other, content with republican governments, and not aiming at immense fortunes, offices and power. In 1786, the little insurgents, the levellers, came forth, invaded the rights of others, and attempted to establish governments according to their wills. Their movements evidently gave encouragement to the other party, which, in 1787, has taken the political field, and with its fashionable dependants, and the tongue and the pen, is endeavoring to establish in a great haste, a politer kind of government. These two parties, which will probably be opposed or united as it may suit their interests and views, are really insignificant, compared with the solid, free, and independent part of the community. . . The sensible and judicious part of the community will carefully weigh all these circumstances; they will view the late convention as a respectable body of men—America probably never will see an assembly of men, of a like number, more respectable. But the members of the convention met without knowing the sentiments of one man in ten thousand in these states respecting the new ground taken. Their doings are but the first attempts in the most important scene ever opened. Though each individual in the state conventions will not, probably, be so respectable as each individual in the federal convention, yet as the state conventions will probably consist of fifteen hundred or two thousand men of abilities, and versed in the science of government, collected from all parts of the community and from all orders of men, it must be acknowledged that the weight of respectability will be in them—In them will be collected the solid sense and the real political character of the country. Being revisers of the subject, they will possess peculiar advantages. To say that these conventions ought not to attempt, coolly and deliberately, the revision of the system, or that they cannot amend it is very foolish and very assuming. . .

4. *I am bold to assert that it is the best form of government ever offered to the world*

JAMES WILSON, State House Speech in Philadelphia, 10 October 1787 *

It will be proper . . . before I enter into the refutation of the charges that are alleged, to mark the leading discrimination between the State constitutions and the constitution of the United States. When the people established the powers of legislation under their separate governments, they invested their representatives with every right and authority which they did not in explicit terms reserve; and therefore upon every question respecting the jurisdiction of the House of Assembly, if the frame of government is silent, the jurisdiction is efficient and complete. But in delegating federal powers, another criterion was necessarily introduced, and the congressional power is to be collected, not from tacit implication, but from the positive grant expressed in the instrument of the union. Hence, it is evident, that in the former case everything which is not reserved is given; but in the latter the reverse of the proposition prevails, and everything which is not given is reserved.

This distinction being recognized, will furnish an answer to those who think the omission of a bill of rights a defect in the proposed constitution; for it would have been superfluous and absurd to have stipulated with a federal body of our own creation, that we should enjoy those privileges of which we are not divested, either by the intention or the act that has brought the body into existence. For instance, the liberty of the press, which has been a copious source of declamation and opposition—what control can proceed from the Federal government to shackle or destroy that sacred palladium of national freedom? If, indeed, a power similar to that which has been granted for the regulation of commerce had been granted to regulate literary publications, it would have been as necessary to stipulate that the liberty of the press should be preserved inviolate, as that the impost should be general in its operation. . . In truth,

* *Pennsylvania and the Federal Constitution, 1787–1788*, John Bach McMaster and Frederick D. Stone, eds., The Historical Society of Pennsylvania, 1888, pp. 143–78 *passim*.

then, the proposed system possesses no influence whatever upon the press, and it would have been merely nugatory to have introduced a formal declaration upon the subject—nay, that very declaration might have been construed to imply that some degree of power was given, since we undertook to define its extent.

Another objection that has been fabricated against the new constitution, is expressed in this disingenious form—'The trial by jury is abolished in civil cases.' . . Let it be remembered . . . that the business of the Federal Convention was not local, but general—not limited to the views and establishments of a single State, but co-extensive with the continent, and comprehending the views and establishments of thirteen independent sovereignities. When, therefore, this subject was in discussion, we were involved in difficulties which pressed on all sides, and no precedent could be discovered to direct our course. The cases open to a trial by jury differed in the different States. It was therefore impracticable, on that ground, to have made a general rule. The want of uniformity would have rendered any reference to the practice of the States idle and useless; and it could not with any propriety be said that, 'The trial by jury shall be as heretofore,' since there has never existed any federal system of jurisprudence, to which the declaration could relate. Besides, it is not in all cases that the trial by jury is adopted in civil questions; for depending in courts of admiralty, such as relate to maritime captures, and such as are agitated in courts of equity, do not require the intervention of that tribunal. How, then was the line of discrimination to be drawn? The Convention found the task too difficult for them, and they left the business as it stands, in the fullest confidence that no danger could possibly ensure, since the proceedings of the Supreme Court are to be regulated by the Congress, which is a faithful representation of the people; and the oppression of government is effectually barred, by declaring that in all criminal cases the trial by jury shall be preserved.

This constitution, it has been further urged, is of a pernicious tendency, because it tolerates a standing army in the time of peace. This has always been a topic of popular declamation; and yet I do not know a nation in the world which has not found it necessary and useful to maintain the appearance of strength in a season of the most profound tranquility. Nor is it a novelty with us; for under the present articles of confederation, Congress certainly possesses this reprobated power, and the exercise of that power is proved at this moment by her cantonments along the banks of the Ohio. But what would be our national situation were it otherwise? Every principle of policy must be subverted, and the government must declare war, before they are prepared to carry on. Whatever may be the provocation, however important the object in view, and however necessary dispatch and secrecy may be, still the declaration must precede the preparation, and the enemy will be informed of your intention, not only before you are equipped for an attack, but even before you are fortified for a defence. The consequence is too obvious to require any further delineation, and no man who regards the dignity and safety of his country can deny the necessity of a military force, under the control and with the restrictions which the new constitution provides. . .

The next accusation I shall consider is that which represents the federal constitution, as not only calculated, but designedly framed, to reduce the State governments to mere corporations, and eventually to annihilate them. Those who have employed the term corporation upon this occasion are not perhaps aware of its extent. In common parlance, indeed, it is generally applied to petty associations for the ease and convenience of a few individuals; but in its enlarged sense, it will comprehend the government of Pennsylvania, the existing union of the States, and even this projected system is nothing more than a formal act of incorporation. But upon what pretence can it be alleged that it was designed to annihilate the State governments? For I will undertake to prove that upon their existence depends the existence of the Federal plan. For this purpose, permit me to call your attention to the manner in which the President, Senate and House of Representatives are proposed to be appointed. The President is to be chosen by electors, nominated in such manner as the legislature of each State may direct; so that if there is no legislature there can be no electors, and consequently the office of President cannot be supplied.

The Senate is to be composed of two Senators from each State, chosen by the Legislature; and, therefore, if there is no Legislature, there can be no Senate. The House of Representatives is to be composed of members chosen every second year by the people of the several States, and the electors in each State shall have the qualifications requisite for electors of the most numerous branch of the State Legislature; unless, therefore, there is a State Legislature, that qualification cannot be ascertained, and the popular branch of the federal constitution must be extinct. From this view, then, it is evidently absurd to suppose that the annihilation of the separate governments will result from their union; or, that having that intention, the authors of the new system would have bound their connection with such indissoluble ties. Let me here advert to an arrangement highly advantageous, for you will perceive, without prejudice to the powers of the Legislature in the election of Senators, the people at large will acquire an additional privilege in returning members to the House of Representatives; whereas, by the present confederation, it is the Legislature alone that appoints the delegates to Congress.

The power of direct taxation has likewise been treated as an improper delegation to the federal government; but when we consider it as the duty of that body to provide for the national safety, to support the dignity of the union, and to discharge the debts contracted upon the collected faith of the States for their common benefit, it must be acknowledged that those upon whom such important obligations are imposed, ought in justice and in policy to possess every means requisite for a faithful performance of their trust. But why should we be alarmed with visionary evils? I will venture to predict that the great revenue of the United States must, and always will, be raised by impost, for, being at once less obnoxious and more productive, the interest of the government will be best promoted by the accommodation of the people. Still, however, the objects of direct taxation should be within reach in all cases of emergency; and there is no more reason to apprehend oppresssion in the mode of collecting a revenue from this resource, than in the form of an impost, which, by universal assent, is left to the authority of the federal government. In either case, the force of civil institutions will be adequate to the purpose; and the dread of military violence, which has been assiduously disseminated, must eventually prove the mere effusion of a wild imagination or a factious spirit. But the salutary consequences that must flow from thus enabling the government to receive and support the credit of the union, will afford another answer to the objections upon this ground. . .

. . . I will confess . . . that I am not a blind admirer of this plan of government, and that there are some parts of it which, if my wish had prevailed, would certainly have been altered. . . If there are errors, it should be remembered that the seeds of reformation are sown in the work itself, and the concurrence of two-thirds of the Congress may at any time introduce alterations and amendments. Regarding it, then, in every point of view, with a candid and disinterested mind, I am bold to assert that it is the best form of government which has ever been offered to the world.

5. *I anticipate annihilation of the state governments, which would destroy civil liberties*

ANTIFEDERALIST WHITEHILL, in the Pennsylvania Ratifying Convention, 1787 *

MR. WHITEHILL. I differ, Sir, from the honorable member from the city [Wilson] as to the impropriety or necessity of a bill of rights. If, indeed, the constitution itself so well defined the powers of the government that no mistake could arise, and we were well assured that our governors would always act right, then we might be satisfied without an explicit reservation of those rights with which the people ought not, and mean not to part. But, Sir, we know that it is the nature of power to seek its own augmentation, and thus the loss of liberty is the necessary consequence of a loose or extravagant delegation of authority. National freedom has been, and will be the sacrifice of ambition and power, and it is our duty to employ the present opportunity in stipulating such restrictions as are best calculated to protect us from oppression and slavery. Let us then, Mr. President, if other countries cannot supply an adequate example, let us proceed upon our own principles, and with the great end of government in view, the happiness of the people, it will be strange if we err. Government, we have been told, Sir, is yet in its infancy: we ought not therefore to submit to the shackles of foreign schools and opinions. In entering into the social compact, men ought not to leave their rulers at large, but erect a permanent land-mark by which they may learn the extent of their authority, and the people be able to discover the first encroachments on their liberties. But let us attend to the language of the system before us. 'We the people of the United States,' is a sentence that evidently shows the old foundation of the union is destroyed, the principle of confederation excluded, and a new and unwieldy system of consolidated empire is set up, upon the ruins of the present compact between the states. Can this be denied? No, Sir:

* *Pennsylvania and the Federal Constitution,* 1787–1788, McMaster and Stone, eds., pp. 254–63, 267–71, 283–7.

It is artfully indeed, but it is incontrovertibly designed to abolish the independence and sovereignty of the states individually, an event which cannot be the wish of any good citizen of America, and therefore it ought to be prevented, by rejecting the plan which is calculated to produce it. What right indeed have we in the manner here proposed to violate the existing confederation? It is declared, that the agreement of nine states shall be sufficient to carry the new system into operation, and consequently to abrogate the old one. Then, Mr. President, four of the present confederated states may not be comprehended in the compact: shall we, Sir, force these dissenting states into the measure? The consequences of that attempt are evidently such as no man can either justify or approve. But reverse the idea—would not these states have a fair pretext to charge the rest with an unconstitutional and unwarrantable abandonment of the nature and obligation of the union of 1776? And having shown sufficient reason why they could not accede to the proposed government, would they not still be entitled to demand a performance of the original compact between the states? Sir, these questions must introduce a painful anticipation of the confusion, contest, and a civil war, which, under such circumstances, the adoption of the offered system must produce. It will be proper, perhaps, to review the origin of this business. It was certainly, Mr. President, acknowledged on all hands, that an additional share of power for federal purposes ought to be delegated to Congress; and with a view to enquire how far it was necessary to strengthen and enlarge the jurisdiction of that body, the late convention was appointed under the authority, and by legislative acts of the several states. But how, Sir, did the convention act upon this occasion? Did they pursue the authority which was given to them? . . .

. . . [I]t appears that no other power was given to the delegates from this state (and I believe the power given by the other states was of the same nature and extent) than to increase in a certain degree the strength and energy of Congress; but it never was in the contemplation of any man that they were authorized to dissolve the present union, to abrogate the state sovereignties, and to establish one comprehensive government, novel in its structure, and in its probable operation oppressive and despotic. Can it then be said that the late convention did not assume powers to which they had no legal title? On the contrary, Sir, it is clear that they set aside the laws under which they were appointed, and under which alone they could derive any legitimate authority, they arrogantly exercised any powers that they found convenient to their object, and in the end they have overthrown that government which they were called upon to amend, in order to introduce one of their own fabrication.

True it is, Mr. President, that if the people intended to engage in one comprehensive system of continental government, the power to frame that system must have been conferred by them; for the legislatures of the states are sworn to preserve the independence of their respective constitutions, and therefore they could not, consistently with their most sacred obligations, authorize an act which sacrificed the individual to the aggregate sovereignty of the states. But it appears from the origin and nature of the commission under which the late convention assembled, that a more perfect confederation was the only object submitted to their wisdom, and not, as it is attempted by this plan, the total destruction of the government of Pennsylvania, and of every other state. So far, Sir, the interference of the legislatures was proper and efficient; but the moment the convention went beyond that object, they ceased to act under any legitimate authority, for the assemblies could give them none, and it cannot be pretended that they were called together by the people; for, till the preamble was produced, it never was understood that the people at large had been consulted upon the occasion, or that otherwise than through their representatives in the several states, they had given a sanction to the proceedings of that body. If, indeed, the federal convention, finding that the old system was incapable of repair, had represented the incurable defects to the Congress, and advised that the original and inherent power of the people might be called into exercise for the institution of a new government, then, Sir, the subject would have come fairly into view, and we should have known upon what principles we proceeded. At present we find a convention appointed by one authority, but acting under the arbitrary assumption of another; and instead of transacting the business which was assigned to them, behold! they have produced a work of supererogation, after a mysterious labor of three months. Let us, however, Sir, attend for a moment to the constitution. And here we shall find, in a single line, sufficient matter for weeks of debate, and which it will puzzle any one member to investigate and define. But, besides the powers enumerated, we find in this constitution an authority is given to make all laws that are necessary to carry it effectually into operation, and what laws are necessary is a consideration left for Congress to decide. In constituting the representative body, the interposition of the Congress is likewise made conclusive; for, with the power of regulating the place and manner of elections, it is easy to perceive that the returns will always be so managed as to answer their purpose. It is strange to mark, however, what a sudden and striking revolution has taken place in the political sentiments of America; for, Sir, in the opening of our struggle with Great Britain, it was often insisted that annual parliaments were necessary to secure the liberties of the people, and yet it is here proposed to establish a house of representatives which shall continue for two, a senate for six, and a president for four years! What is there in this plan indeed, which can even assure us that the several departments shall continue no longer in office? Do we not know that an English parliament elected for three years, by a vote of their own body, extended their existence to seven, and with this example, Congress possessing a competent share of power may easily be tempted to exercise it. The advantages of annual elections are not at this day to be taught, and when every other security was withheld, I should still have thought there was some safety in the government, had this been left. The seats of Congress being held for so short a period, and by a tenure so precarious as popular elections, there could be no inducement to invade the liberties of the people, nor time enough to accomplish the schemes of ambition and tyranny. But when the period is protracted, an object is presented worthy of contention, and the duration of the office affords an opportunity for perpetuating the influence by which it was originally obtained. Another power designed to be vested in the new government, is the superlative power of taxation, which may be carried to an inconceivable excess, swallowing up every object of taxation, and consequently plundering the several states of every means to support their governments, and to administer their laws. Then, Sir, can it longer be doubted that this is a system of consolidation? That government which possesses all the powers of raising and maintaining armies, of regulating and commanding the militia, and of laying imposts and taxes of every kind, must be supreme, and will (whether in twenty or in one year, it signifies little to the event) naturally absorb every subordinate jurisdiction. It is in vain, Sir, to flatter ourselves that the forms of popular elections will be the means of self-preservation, and that the officers of the proposed government will uniformly act for the happiness of the people—for why should we run a risk which we may easily avoid? The giving such extensive and undefined power is a radical wrong that cannot be justified by any subsequent merit in the exercise; for in framing a new system, it is our duty rather to indulge a jealousy of the human character, than an expectation of unprecedented perfection. . . A bill of rights, Mr. President, it has been said, would not only be unnecessary, but it would be dangerous, and for this special reason, that because it is not practicable to enumerate all the rights of the people, therefore it would be hazardous to secure such of the rights as we can enumerate! Truly, Sir, I will agree that a bill of rights may be a dangerous instrument, but it is to the views and projects of the aspiring ruler, and not the liberties of the citizen. Grant but this explicit criterion, and our governors will not venture to enroach; refuse it, and the people cannot venture to complain. From the formal language of magna charta we are next taught to consider a declaration of rights as superfluous; but, Sir, will the situation and conduct of Great Britain furnish a case parallel to that of America? It surely will not be contended that we are about to receive our liberties as a grant or concession from any power upon earth; so that if we learn anything from the English charter, it is this: that the people having negligently lost or submissively resigned their rights into the hands of the crown, they were glad to recover them upon any terms; their anxiety to secure the grant by the strongest evidence will be an argument to prove, at least, the expediency of the measure, and the result of the whole is a lesson instructing us to do by an easy precaution, what will hereafter be an arduous and perhaps insurmountable task. . . Will it still be said, that the state governments would be adequate to the task of correcting the usurpations of Congress? Let us not, however, give the weight of proof to the boldness of assertion; for, if the opposition is to succeed by force, we find both the purse and the sword are almost exclusively transferred to the general government; and if it is to succeed by legislative remonstrance, we shall find that expedient rendered nugatory by the law of Congress, which is to be the supreme law of the land. Thus, Mr. President, must the powers and sovereignty of the several states be eventually destroyed. . . Upon the whole, therefore, I wish it to be seriously considered, whether we have a right to leave the liberties of the people to such future constructions and expositions as may possibly be made upon this system. . . I am not anxious, Mr. President, about forms—it is the substance which I wish to obtain; and therefore I acknowledge, if our liberties are secured by the frame of government itself, the supplementary instrument of a declaration of rights may well be dispensed with. . . The question at present, Sir, is, however, of a preliminary kind—does the plan now in discussion propose a consolidation of the states? and will a consolidated government be most likely to promote the interests and happiness of America? If it is satisfactorily demonstrated, that in its principles or in its operation, the dissolution of the state sovereignties is not a necessary consequence, I shall then be willing to accompany the gentlemen on the other side in weighing more particularly its merits and demerits. But my judgment, according to the information I now possess, leads me to anticipate the annihilation of the several state governments—an event never expected by the people, and which would, I fervently believe, destroy the civil liberties of America.

MR. SMILIE. I am happy, Mr. President, to find the argument placed upon the proper ground, and that the honorable member from the city has so fully spoken on the question, whether this system proposes a consolidation or a confederation of the states, as that is, in my humble opinion, the source of the greatest objection, which can be made to its adoption. I agree likewise with him, Sir, that it is, or ought to be, the object of all governments, to fix upon the intermediate point between tyranny and licentiousness; and therefore, it will be one of the great objects of our enquiry, to ascertain how far the proposed system deviates from that point of political happiness. . . I think however, Mr. President, it has been clearly argued, that the proposed system does not directly abolish, the governments of the several States, because its organization, and, for some time, perhaps, its operations, naturally pre-suppose their existence. But, Sir, it is not said, nor is thought, that the words of this instrument expressly announce that the sovereignty of the several States, their independency, jurisdiction, and power, are at once absorbed and annihilated by the general government. To this position and to this alone, the arguments of the honorable gentlemen can effectually apply, and there they must undoubtedly hold as long as the forms of State Government remain, at least, till a change takes place in the federal constitution. It is, however, upon other principles that the final destruction of the individual governments is asserted to be a necessary consequence of their association under this general form,—for, Sir, it is the silent but certain operation of the powers, and not the cautious, but artful tenor of the expressions contained in this system, that can excite terror, or generate oppression. . . Hence, Sir, we may trace that passage which has been pronounced by the honorable delegate to the late convention with exultation and applause; but when it is declared that 'We the people of the United States do ordain and establish this constitution,' is not the very foundation a proof of a consolidated government, by the manifest subversion of the principle that constitutes a union of States, which are sovereign and independent, except in the specific objects of confederation? These words have a plain and positive meaning, which could not be misunderstood by those who employed them; and therefore, Sir, it is fair and reasonable to infer, that it was in contemplation of the framers of this system, to absorb and abolish the efficient sovereignty and independent powers of the several States, in order to invigorate and aggrandize the general government. The plan before us, then, explicitly proposes the formation of a new constitution upon the original authority of the people, and not an association of States upon the authority of their respective governments. On that ground, we perceive that it contains all the necessary parts of a complete system of government, the executive, legislative and judicial establishments; and when two separate governments are at the same time in operation, over the same people, it will be difficult indeed to provide for each the means of safety and defence against the other; but if those means are not provided, it will be easily foreseen, that the stronger must eventually subdue and annihilate the weaker institution. Let us then examine the force and influence of the new system, and enquire whether the small remnant of power left to the States can be adequate even to the trifling charge of its own preservation. Here, Sir, we find the right of making laws for every purpose is invested in the future governors of America, and in this is included the uncontrolled jurisdiction over the purses of the people. The power of raising money is indeed the soul, the vital prop of legislation, without which legislation itself cannot for a moment exist. It will, however, be remarked that the power of taxation, though extended to the general government, is not taken from the States individually. Yes, Sir!—but it will be remembered that the national government may take from the people just what they please, and if anything should afterwards remain, then indeed the exigencies of the State governments may be supplied from the scanty gleanings of the harvest. Permit me now, Sir, to call your attention to the powers enumerated in the 8th section of the first article, and particularly to that clause which authorizes the proposed Congress, 'to lay and collect taxes, duties, imposts and excises, to pay the debts and provide for the common defence and general welfare of the United States.' With such powers, Mr. President, what cannot the future governors accomplish? It will be said, perhaps, that the treasure, thus accumulated, is raised and appropriated for the general welfare and the common defence of the States; but may not this pretext be easily perverted to other purposes, since those very men who raise and appropriate the taxes, are the only judges of what shall be deemed the general welfare and common defence of the national government? If then, Mr. President, they have unlimited power to drain the wealth of the people in every channel of taxation, whether by imposts on our commercial intercourse with foreign nations, or by direct levies on the people, I repeat it, that this system must be too formidable for any single State, or even for a combination of the States, should an attempt be made to break and destroy the yoke of domination and tyranny which it will hereafter set up. . . To assemble a military force would be impracticable; for the general government, foreseeing the attempt would anticipate the means, by the exercise of its indefinite control over the purses of the people; and, in order to act upon the consciences as well as the persons of men, we find it is expressly stipulated, that every officer of the State government shall be sworn to support the constitution of the United States. Hence likewise, Sir, I conclude that in every point of rivalship, in every contention for power on the one hand, and for freedom on the other, the event must be favorable to the views and pretensions of a government gifted with so decisive a pre-eminence. . . For, Sir, the attachment of citizens to their government and its laws is founded upon the benefits which they derive from them, and it will last no longer than the duration of the power to confer those benefits. When, therefore, the people of the respective States shall find their governments grown torpid, and divested of the means to promote their welfare and interests, they will not, Sir, vainly idolize a shadow, nor disburse their hard earned wealth without the prospect of a compensation. The constitution of the States having become weak and useless to every beneficial purpose, will be suffered to dwindle and decay, and thus if the governors of the Union are not too impatient for the accomplishment of unrivalled and absolute dominion, the destruction of State jurisdiction will be produced by its own insignificance. . .

6. *In parting with the coercive authority over the states as states, there must be a coercion allowed as to individuals*

JAMES IREDELL, Reply to George Mason's Objections, 1788 *

I. OBJECTION.

'There is no declaration of rights, and the laws of the general government being paramount to the laws and constitutions of the several States, the declarations of rights in the separate States are no security. Nor are the people secured even in the enjoyment of the benefit of the common law, which stands here upon no other foundation than its having been adopted by the respective acts forming the Constitutions of the several States.'

ANSWER.

1. As to the want of a declaration of rights. The introduction of these in England, from which the idea was originally taken, was in consequence of usurpations of the Crown, contrary, as was conceived, to the principles of their government. But there no original constitution is to be found, and the only meaning of a declaration of rights in that country is, that in certain particulars specified, the Crown had no authority to act. Could this have been necessary had there been a constitution in being by which it could have been clearly discerned whether the Crown had such authority or not? Had the people, by a solemn instrument, delegated particular powers to the Crown at the formation of their government, surely the Crown, which in that case could claim under that instrument only, could not have contended for more power than was conveyed by it. So it is in regard to the new Constitution here: the future government which may be formed under that authority certainly cannot act beyond the warrant of that authority. . .

2. As to the common law, it is difficult to know what is meant by that part of the objection. So far as the people are now entitled to the benefit of the common law, they certainly will have a right to enjoy it under the new Con-

* *Pamphlets on the Constitution of the United States,* P. L. Ford, ed., pp. 335–70 *passim.*

stitution until altered by the general legislature, which even in this point has some cardinal limits assigned to it. . . The principles of the common law, as they now apply, must surely always hereafter apply, except in those particulars in which express authority is given by this constitution; in no other particulars can the Congress have authority to change it. . .

IV. OBJECTION.

'The judiciary of the United States is so constructed and extended, as to absorb and destroy the judiciaries of the several States; thereby rendering law as tedious, intricate and expensive and justice as unattainable by a great part of the community, as in England; and enabling the rich to oppress and ruin the poor.'

ANSWER.

. . . How is this the case? Are not the State judiciaries left uncontrolled as to the affairs of that *State* only? In this, as in all other cases, where there is a wise distribution, power is commensurate to its object. With the mere internal concerns of a State, Congress are to have nothing to do: In no case but where the Union is in some measure concerned, are the federal courts to have any jurisdiction. The State Judiciary will be a satellite waiting upon its proper planet: That of the Union, like the sun, cherishing and preserving a whole planetary system.

In regard to a possible ill construction of this authority, we must depend upon our future legislature in this case as well as others, in respect to which it is impracticable to define every thing, that it will be provided for so as to occasion as little expense and distress to individuals as can be. *In parting with the coercive authority over the States as States, there must be a coercion allowed as to individuals. The former power no man of common sense can any longer seriously contend for; the latter is the only alternative.* . .

VIII. OBJECTION.

'Under their own construction of the general clause at the end of the enumerated powers, the Congress may grant monopolies in trade and commerce, constitute new crimes, inflict unusual and severe punishment, and extend their power as far as they shall think proper; so that the State Legislatures have no security for the powers now presumed to remain to them; or the people for their rights. There is no declaration of any kind for preserving the liberty of the press, the trial by jury in civil causes, nor against the danger of standing armies in time of peace.'

ANSWER.

The general clause at the end of the enumerated power is as follows:

'To make all laws which shall be necessary and proper for carrying into execution the *foregoing powers, and all other powers vested by this Constitution in the United States, or in any department or office thereof.'*

Those powers would be useless, except acts of legislation could be exercised upon them. It was not possible for the Convention, nor is it for any human body, to foresee and provide for all contingent cases that may arise. Such cases must therefore be left to be provided for by the general Legislature as they shall happen to come into existence. If Congress, under pretence of exercising the power delegated to them, should in fact, by the exercise of any other power, usurp upon the rights of the different Legislatures, or of any private citizens, the people will be exactly in the same situation as if there had been an express provision against such power in particular, and yet they had presumed to exercise it. It would be an act of tyranny, against which no parchment stipulations can guard; and the Convention surely can be only answerable for the propriety of the powers given, not for the future virtues of all with whom those powers may be intrusted. It does not therefore appear to me that there is any weight in this objection more than in others.

7. *This system does not secure the unalienable rights of free men*

ANTIFEDERALIST LENOIR in the North Carolina Ratifying Convention, 1788 *

. . . I think it [the constitution] not proper for our adoption, as I consider that it endangers our liberties. When we consider this system collectively, we must be surprised to think, that any set of men who were delegated to amend the confederation, should propose to annihilate it. For that and this system are utterly different, and cannot exist together. It has been said that the fullest confidence should be put in those characters who formed this constitution. We will admit them in private and public transactions to be good characters. But, sir, it appears to me . . . that they exceeded their powers. Those gentlemen had no sort of power to form a new constitution altogether, neither had the citizens of this country such an idea in their view. I cannot undertake to say what principles actuated them. I must conceive they were mistaken in their politics, and that this system does not secure the unalienable rights of freemen. It has some aristocratical and some monarchical features, and perhaps some of them intended the establishment of one of these governments. Whatever might be their intent . . . it will lead to the most dangerous aristocracy that ever was thought of—an aristocracy established on a constitutional bottom! I conceive that this is so dangerous, that I should like as well to have no constitution at all. Their powers are almost unlimited. . .

My constituents instructed me to oppose the adoption of this constitution. The principal reasons are as follow: The right of representation is not fairly and explicitly preserved to the people, it being easy to evade that privilege as provided in this system, and the terms of election being too long. . . The senators are chosen for six years, and two-thirds of them with the president have

* *The Debates in the Several State Conventions* . . ., J. Elliot, ed., vol. IV, pp. 203–7.

most extensive powers. They may enter into a dangerous combination. And they may be continually re-elected. The president may be as good a man as any in existence, but he is but a man. He may be corrupt. He has an opportunity of forming plans dangerous to the community at large. I shall not enter into the minutiæ of this system, but I conceive that whatever may have been the intention of its framers, that it leads to a most dangerous aristocracy. It appears to me that instead of securing the sovereignty of the states, it is calculated to melt them down into one solid empire. If the citizens of this state like a consolidated government, I hope they will have virtue enough to secure their rights. I am sorry to make use of the expression, but it appears to me to be a scheme to reduce this government to an aristocracy. It guarantees a republican form of government to the states; when all these powers are in congress it will only be a form. It will be past recovery, when congress has the power of the purse and the sword. The power of the sword is in explicit terms given to it. The power of direct taxation gives the purse. They may prohibit the trial by jury, which is a most sacred and valuable right. There is nothing contained in this constitution to bar them from it. The federal courts have also appellate cognizance of law and fact: the sole cause of which is to deprive the people of that trial, which it is optional in them to grant or not. We find no provision against infringement on the rights of conscience. Ecclesiastical courts may be established, which will be destructive to our citizens. They may make any establishment they think proper. They have also an exclusive legislation in their ten miles square, to which may be added their power over the militia, who may be carried thither and kept there for life. Should any one grumble at their acts, he would be deemed a traitor, and perhaps taken up and carried to the exclusive legislation, and there tried without a jury. We are told there is no cause to fear. When we consider the great powers of congress, there is great cause of alarm. They can disarm the militia. If they were armed, they would be a resource against great oppressions. The laws of a great empire are difficult to be executed. If the laws of the union were oppressive they could not carry them into effect, if the people were possessed of proper means of defence.

It was cried out that we were in a most desperate situation, and that congress could not discharge any of their most sacred contracts. I believe it to be the case. But why give more power than is necessary? The men who went to the federal convention, went for the express purpose of amending the government, by giving it such additional powers as were necessary. If we should accede to this system, it may be thought proper by a few designing persons to destroy it in a future age, in the same manner that the old system is laid aside. The confederation was binding on all the states. It could not be destroyed but with the consent of all the states. There was an express article to that purpose. The men who were deputed to the convention, instead of amending the old, as they were solely empowered and directed to do, proposed a new system. If the best characters departed so far from their authority, what may not be apprehended from others who may be agents in the new government?

It is natural for men to aspire to power—it is the nature of mankind to be tyrannical, therefore it is necessary for us to secure our rights and liberties as far as we can; but it is asked why we should suspect men who are to be chosen by ourselves, while it is their interest to act justly, and while men have self-interest at heart? I think the reasons which I have given are sufficient to answer that question. We ought to consider the depravity of human nature, the predominant thirst of power which is in the breast of every one, the temptations our rulers may have, and the unlimited confidence placed in them by this system. These are the foundation of my fears. They would be so long in the general government that they would forget the grievances of the people of the states.

But it is said we shall be ruined if separated from the other states, which will be the case if we do not adopt. If so, I would put less confidence in those states. The states are all bound together by the confederation, and the rest cannot break from us without violating the most solemn compact. If they break that, they will this.

But it is urged that we ought to adopt, because so many other states have In those states which have patronized and ratified it, many great men have opposed it. The motives of those states I know not. It is the goodness of the constitution we are to examine. We are to exercise our own judgments, and act independently. And as I conceive we are not out of the union, I hope this constitution will not be adopted till amendments are made. . .

8. *This power in the judicial will enable them to mould the Government into almost any shape they please*

ROBERT YATES, *Letters of Brutus*, 1788 *

BRUTUS, NO. XI 31 *January* 1788

. . . Much has been said and written upon the subject of this new system on both sides, but I have not met with any writer, who has discussed the judicial powers with any degree of accuracy. And yet it is obvious, that we can form but very imperfect ideas of the manner in which this government will work, or the effect it will have in changing the internal police and mode of distributing justice at present subsisting in the respective states, without a thorough investigation of the powers of the judiciary and of the manner in which they will operate. This government is a complete system, not only for making, but for executing laws. And the courts of law, which will be constituted by it, are not only to decide upon the constitution and the laws made in pursuance of it, but by officers subordinate to them to execute all their decisions. The real effect of this system of government, will therefore be brought home to the feelings of the people, through the medium of the judicial power. It is, moreover, of great importance, to examine with care the nature and extent of the judicial power, because those who are to be vested with it, are to be placed in a

* Published in the *New York Journal and Weekly Register*. Numbers 11, 12, and 15 are reprinted in full in E. S. Corwin, *Court over Constitution*, Princeton, N.J., Princeton University Press, 1938, Appendix, pp. 231–62.

situation altogether unprecedented in a free country. They are to be rendered totally independent, both of the people and the legislature, both with respect to their offices and salaries. No errors they may commit can be corrected by any power above them, if any such power there be, nor can they be removed from office for making ever so many erroneous adjudications.

The only causes for which they can be displaced, is, conviction of treason, bribery, and high crimes and misdemeanors.

This part of the plan is so modelled, as to authorize the courts, not only to carry into execution the powers expressly given, but where these are wanting or ambiguously expressed, to supply what is wanting by their own decisions. . .

They [the courts] will give the sense of every article of the constitution, that may from time to time come before them. And in their decisions they will not confine themselves to any fixed or established rules, but will determine, according to what appears to them, the reason and spirit of the constitution. The opinions of the supreme court, whatever they may be, will have the force of law; because there is no power provided in the constitution, that can correct their errors, or controul their adjudications. From this court there is no appeal. And I conceive the legislature themselves, cannot set aside a judgment of this court, because they are authorized by the constitution to decide in the last resort. The legislature must be controuled by the constitution, and not the constitution by them. They have therefore no more right to set aside any judgment pronounced upon the construction of the constitution, than they have to take from the president, the chief command of the army and navy, and commit it to some other person. The reason is plain; the judicial and executive derive their authority from the same source, that the legislature do theirs; and therefore in all cases, where the constitution does not make the one responsible to, or controulable by the other, they are altogether independent of each other.

The judicial power will operate to effect, in the most certain, but yet silent and imperceptible manner, what is evidently the tendency of the constitution: —I mean, an entire subversion of the legislative, executive and judicial powers of the individual states. Every adjudication of the supreme court, on any question that may arise upon the nature and extent of the general government, will affect the limits of the state jurisdiction. In proportion as the former enlarge the exercise of their powers, will that of the latter be restricted.

That the judicial power of the United States, will lean strongly in favour of the general government, and will give such an explanation to the constitution, as will favour an extension of its jurisdiction, is very evident from a variety of considerations.

1st. The constitution itself strongly countenances such a mode of construction. Most of the articles in this system, which convey powers of any considerable importance, are conceived in general and indefinite terms, which are either equivocal, ambiguous, or which require long definitions to unfold the extent of their meaning. The two most important powers committed to any government, those of raising money, and of raising and keeping up troops, have already been considered, and shewn to be unlimited by anything but the discretion of the legislature. The clause which vests the power to pass all laws which are proper and necessary, to carry the powers given into execution, it has been shewn, leaves the legislature at liberty, to do every thing, which in their judgment is best. It is said, I know, that this clause confers no power on the legislature, which they would not have had without it—though I believe this is not the fact, yet, admitting it to be, it implies that the constitution is not to receive an explanation strictly, according to its letter; but more power is implied than is expressed. And this clause, if it is to be considered, as explanatory of the extent of the powers given, rather than giving a new power, is to be understood as declaring, that in construing any of the articles conveying power, the spirit, intent and design of the clause, should be attended to, as well as the words in their common acceptation.

This constitution gives sufficient colour for adopting an equitable construction, if we consider the great end and design it professedly has in view—this appears from its preamble to be, 'to form a more perfect union, establish justice, insure domestic tranquility, provide for the common defense, promote the general welfare, and secure the blessings of liberty to ourselves and posterity.' The design of this system is here expressed, and it is proper to give such a meaning to the various parts, as will best promote the accomplishment of the end; this idea suggests itself naturally upon reading the preamble, and will countenance the court in giving the several articles such a sense, as will the most effectually promote the ends the constitution had in view—how this manner of explaining the constitution will operate in practice, shall be the subject of future enquiry.

2d. Not only will the constitution justify the courts in inclining to this mode of explaining it, but they will be interested in using this latitude of interpretation. Every body of men invested with office are tenacious of power; they feel interested, and hence it has become a kind of maxim, to hand down their offices, with all its rights and privileges, unimpaired to their successors; the same principle will influence them to extend their power, and increase their rights; this of itself will operate strongly upon the courts to give such a meaning to the constitution in all cases where it can possibly be done, as will enlarge the sphere of their own authority. Every extension of the power of the general legislature, as well as of the judicial powers, will increase the powers of the courts; and the dignity and importance of the judges, will be in proportion to the extent and magnitude of the powers they exercise. I add, it is highly probable that emolument of the judges will be increased, with the increase of the business they will have to transact and its importance. From these considerations the judges will be interested to extend the powers of the courts, and to construe the constitution as much as possible, in such a way as to favour it; and that they will do it, appears probable.

3d. Because they will have precedent to plead, to justify them in it. It is well known, that the courts in England, have by their own authority, extended their jurisdiction far beyond the limits set them in their original institution, and by the laws of the land. . .

When the courts will have a president [precedent] before them of a court which extended its jurisdiction in opposition to an act of the legislature, is it not to be expected that they will extend theirs, especially when there is nothing in the constitution expressly against it? and they are authorized to construe its meaning, and are not under any controul?

This power in the judicial, will enable them to mould the government, into almost any shape they please. . .

BRUTUS, NO. XII 14 *February* 1788

. . . To discover the spirit of the constitution, it is of the first importance to attend to the principal ends and designs it has in view. These are expressed in the preamble. . . If the end of the government is to be learned from these words, which are clearly designed to declare it, it is obvious it has in view every object which is embraced by any government. The preservation of internal peace—the due administration of justice—and to provide for the defence of the community, seems to include all the objects of government; but if they do not, they are certainly comprehended in the words, 'to provide for the general welfare.' If it be further considered, that this constitution, if it is ratified, will not be a compact entered into by states, in their corporate capacities, but an agreement of the people of the United States, as one great body politic, no doubt can remain, but that the great end of the constitution, if it is to be collected from the preamble, in which its end is declared, is to constitute a government which is to extend to every case for which any government is instituted, whether external or internal. The courts, therefore, will establish this as a principle in expounding the constitution, and will give every part of it such an explanation, as will give latitude to every department under it, to take cognizance of every matter, not only that affects the general and national concerns of the union, but also of such as relate to the administration of private justice, and to regulating the internal and local affairs of the different parts.

Such a rule of exposition is not only consistent with the general spirit of the preamble, but it will stand confirmed by considering more minutely the different clauses of it.

The first object declared to be in view is, 'To form a perfect union.' It is to be observed, it is not an union of states or bodies corporate; had this been the case the existence of the state governments, might have been secured. But it is a union of the people of the United States considered as one body, who are to ratify this constitution, if it is adopted. Now to make a union of this kind perfect, it is necessary to abolish all inferior governments, and to give the general one compleat legislative, executive and judicial powers to every purpose. The courts there will establish it as a rule in explaining the constitution. To give it such a construction as will best tend to perfect the union or take from the state governments every power of either making or executing laws. The second object is 'to establish justice.' This must include not only the idea of instituting the rule of justice, or of making laws which shall be the measure or rule of right, but also of providing for the application of this rule or of administering justice under it. And under this the courts will in their decisions extend the power of the government to all cases they possibly can, or otherwise they will be restricted in doing what appears to be the intent of the constitution they should do, to wit, pass laws and provide for the execution of them, for the general distribution of justice between man and man. Another end declared is 'to insure domestic tranquility.' This comprehends a provision against all private breaches of the peace, as well as against all public commotions or general insurrections; and to attain the object of this clause fully, the government must exercise the power of passing laws on these subjects, as well as of appointing magistrates with authority to execute them. And the courts will adopt these ideas in their expositions. I might proceed to the other clause, in the preamble, and it would appear by a consideration of all of them separately, as it does by taking them together, that if the spirit of this system is to be known from its declared end and design in the preamble, its spirit is to subvert and abolish all the powers of the state government, and to embrace every object to which any government extends.

As it sets out in the preamble with this declared intention, so it proceeds in the different parts with the same idea. Any person, who will peruse the 8th section with attention, in which most of the powers are enumerated, will perceive that they either expressly or by implication extend to almost every thing about which any legislative power can be employed. But if this equitable mode of construction is applied to this part of the constitution; nothing can stand before it.

This will certainly give the first clause in that article a construction which I confess I think the most natural and grammatical one, to authorize the Congress to do any thing which in their judgment will tend to provide for the general welfare, and this amounts to the same thing as general and unlimited powers of legislation in all cases.

BRUTUS, NO. XV — 20 *March* 1788

I said in my last number, that the supreme court under this constitution would be exalted above all other powers in the government, and subject to no control. The business of this paper will be to illustrate this, and to shew the danger that will result from it. I question whether the world ever saw, in any period of it, a court of justice invested with such immense powers, and yet placed in a situation so little responsible. . .

The framers of this constitution appear to have followed that of the British, in rendering the judges independent, by granting them their offices during good behavior, without following the constitution of England, in instituting a tribunal in which their errors may be corrected; and without adverting to this, that the judicial under this system have a power which is above the legislative, and which indeed transcends any power before given to a judicial by any free government under heaven.

I do not object to the judges holding their commissions during good behaviour. I suppose it a proper provision provided they were made properly responsible. But I say, this system has followed the English government in this, while it has departed from almost every other principle of their jurisprudence, under the idea, of rendering the judges independent; which, in the British constitution, means no more than that they hold their places during good behaviour, and have fixed salaries, they have made the judges *independent*, in the fullest sense of the word. There is no power above them, to controul any of their decisions. There is no authority than can remove them, and they cannot be controuled by the laws of the legislature. In short, they are independent of the people, of the legislature, and of every power under heaven. Men placed in this situation will generally soon feel themselves independent of heaven itself. . .

The supreme court then have a right, independent of the legislature, to give a construction of the constitution and every part of it, and there is no power provided in this system to correct their construction or do it away. If, therefore, the legislature pass any laws, inconsistent with the sense the judges put upon the constitution, they will declare it void; and therefore in this respect their power is superior to that of the legislature. . .

I have, in the course of my observation on this constitution, affirmed and endeavored to shew, that it was calculated to abolish entirely the state governments, and to melt down the states into one entire government, for every purpose as well internal and local, as external and national. In this opinion the opposers of the system have generally agreed—and this has been uniformly denied by its advocates in public. Some individuals indeed, among them, will confess, that it has this tendency, and scruple not to say, it is what they wish; and I will venture to predict, without the spirit of prophecy, that if it is adoption without amendments, or some such precautions as will ensure amendments immediately after its adoption, that the same gentlemen who have employed their talents and abilities with such success to influence the public mind to adopt this plan, will employ the same to persuade the people, that it will be for their good to abolish the state governments as useless and burdensome.

Perhaps nothing could have been better conceived to facilitate the abolition of the state government than the constitution of the judicial. They will be able to extend the limits of the general government gradually, and by insensible degrees, and to accommodate themselves to the temper of the people. . .

Had the construction of the constitution been left with the legislature, they would have explained it at their peril; if they exceed their powers, or sought to find, in the spirit of the constitution, more than was expressed in the letter, the people from whom they derived their power could remove them, and do themselves right; and indeed I can see no other remedy that the people can have against their rulers for encroachments of this nature. A constitution is a compact of a people with their rulers; if the rulers break the compact, the people have a right and ought to remove them and do themselves justice; but in order to enable them to do this with the greater facility, those whom the people chuse at stated periods, should have the power in the last resort to determine the sense of the compact; if they determine contrary to the understanding of the people, an appeal will lie to the people at the period when the rulers are to be elected, and they will have it in their power to remedy the evil; but when this power is lodged in the hands of men independent of the people, and of their representatives, and who are not, constitutionally, accountable for their opinions, no way is left to controul them but *with a high hand and an outstretched arm.*

9. *The fabric of American empire ought to rest on the solid consent of the people*

ALEXANDER HAMILTON, *The Federalist*, 1787–88 *

NO. LXXVIII (HAMILTON'S REPLY TO 'BRUTUS')

We proceed now to an examination of the judiciary department of the proposed government. . .

Whoever attentively considers the different departments of power must perceive, that, in a government in which they are separated from each other, the judiciary, from the nature of its functions, will always be the least dangerous to the political rights of the Constitution; because it will be least in a capacity to annoy or injure them. . . The judiciary . . . has no influence over either the sword or the purse; no direction either of the strength or of the wealth of the society; and can take no active resolution whatever. It may truly be said to have neither FORCE nor WILL, but merely judgment; and must ultimately depend upon the aid of the executive arm even for the efficacy of its judgments.

This simple view of the matter suggests several important consequences. It proves incontestably, that the judiciary is beyond comparison the weakest of the three departments of power; that it can never attack with success either of the other two; and that all possible care is requisite to enable it to defend itself against their attacks. It equally proves, that though individual oppression may now and then proceed from the courts of justice, the general liberty of the people can never be endangered from that quarter; I mean so long as the judiciary remains truly distinct from both the legislature and the Executive. . .

Some perplexity respecting the rights of the courts to pronounce legislative acts void, because contrary to the Constitution, has arisen from an imagination that the doctrine would imply a superiority of the judiciary to the legislative power. It is urged that the authority which can declare the acts of another void, must necessarily be superior to the one whose acts may be declared void. As this doctrine is of great importance in all the American constitutions, a brief discussion of the ground on which it rests cannot be unacceptable.

There is no position which depends on clearer principles, than that every act of a delegated authority, contrary to the tenor of the commission under which it is exercised, is void. No legislative act, therefore, contrary to the Constitution, can be valid. To deny this, would be to affirm, that the deputy is greater than his principal; that the servant is above his master; that the representatives of the people are superior to the people themselves; that men acting by virtue of

* *The Federalist*, Henry Cabot Lodge, ed., New York, G. P. Putnam's Sons, 1904.

powers, may do not only what their powers do not authorize, but what they forbid.

If it be said that the legislative body are themselves the constitutional judges of their own powers, and that the construction they put upon them is conclusive upon the other departments, it may be answered, that this cannot be the natural presumption, where it is not to be collected from any particular provisions in the Constitution. It is not otherwise to be supposed, that the Constitution could intend to enable the representatives of the people to substitute their *will* to that of their constituents. It is far more rational to suppose, that the courts were designed to be an intermediate body between the people and the legislature, in order, among other things, to keep the latter within the limits assigned to their authority. The interpretation of the laws is the proper and peculiar province of the courts. A constitution is, in fact, and must be regarded by the judges, as a fundamental law. It therefore belongs to them to ascertain its meaning, as well as the meaning of any particular act proceeding from the legislative body. If there should happen to be an irreconcilable variance between the two, that which has the superior obligation and validity ought, of course, to be preferred; or, in other words, the Constitution ought to be preferred to the statute, the intention of the people to the intention of their agents.

Nor does this conclusion by any means suppose a superiority of the judicial to the legislative power. It only supposes that the power of the people is superior to both; and that where the will of the legislature, declared in its statutes, stands in oppisition to that of the people, declared in the Constitution, the judges ought to be governed by the latter rather than the former. They ought to regulate their decisions by the fundamental laws, rather than by those which are not fundamental. . .

If, then, the courts of justice are to be considered as the bulwarks of a limited Constitution against legislative encroachments, this consideration will afford a strong argument for the permanent tenure of judicial offices, since nothing will contribute so much as this to that independent spirit in the judges which must be essential to the faithful performance of so arduous a duty.

This independence of the judges is equally requisite to guard the Constitution and the rights of individuals from the effects of those ill humors, which the arts of designing men, or the influence of particular conjunctures, sometimes disseminate among the people themselves, and which, though they speedily give place to better information, and more deliberate reflection, have a tendency, in the meantime, to occasion dangerous innovations in the government, and serious oppressions of the minor party in the community. Though I trust the friends of the proposed Constitution will never concur with its enemies, in questioning that fundamental principle of republican government, which admits the right of the people to alter or abolish the established Constitution, whenever they find it inconsistent with their happiness, yet it is not to be inferred from this principle, that the representatives of the people, whenever a momentary inclination happens to lay hold of a majority of their constituents, incompatible with the provisions in the existing Constitution, would, on that account, be justifiable in a violation of those provisions; or that the courts would be under a greater obligation to connive at infractions in this shape, than when they had proceeded wholly from the cabals of the representative body. Until the people have, by some solemn and authoritative act, annulled or changed the established form, it is binding upon themselves collectively, as well as individually and no presumption, or even knowledge, of their sentiments, can warrant their representatives in a departure from it, prior to such an act. But it is easy to see, that it would require an uncommon portion of fortitude in the judges to do their duty as faithful guardians of the Constitution, where legislative invasions of it had been instigated by the major voice of the community.

But it is not with a view to infractions of the Constitution only, that the independence of the judges may be an essential safeguard against the effects of occasional ill humors in the society. These sometimes extend no farther than to the injury of the private rights of particular classes of citizens, by unjust and partial laws. Here also the firmness of the judicial magistracy is of vast importance in mitigating the severity and confining the operation of such laws. . . This is a circumstance calculated to have more influence upon the character of our governments, than but few may be aware of. The benefits of the integrity and moderation of the judiciary have already been felt in more States than one; and though they may have displeased those whose sinister expectations they may have disappointed, they must have commanded the esteem and applause of all the virtuous and disinterested. . .

There is yet a further and a weightier reason for the permanency of the judicial offices, which is deducible from the nature of the qualifications they require. It has been frequently remarked, with great propriety, that a voluminous code of laws is one of the inconveniences necessarily connected with the advantages of a free government. To avoid an arbitrary discretion in the courts, it is indispensable that they should be bound down by strict rules and precedents, which serve to define and point out their duty in every particular case that comes before them; and it will readily be conceived from the variety of controversies which grow out of the folly and wickedness of mankind, that the records of those precedents must unavoidably swell to a very considerable bulk, and must demand long and laborious study to acquire a competent knowledge of them. Hence it is, that there can be but few men in the society who will have sufficient skill in the laws to qualify them for the stations of judges. And making the proper deductions for the ordinary depravity of human nature, the number must be still smaller of those who unite the requisite integrity with the requisite knowledge. These considerations apprise us, that the government can have no great option between fit character; and that a temporary duration in office, which would naturally discourage such characters from quitting a lucrative line of practice to accept a seat on the bench, would have a tendency to throw the administration of justice into hands less able, and less well qualified, to conduct it with utility and dignity. . .

NO. IX (HAMILTON.)

A firm Union will be of the utmost moment to the peace and liberty of the

States, as a barrier against domestic faction and insurrection. It is impossible to read the history of the petty republics of Greece and Italy without feeling sensations of horror and disgust at the distractions with which they were continually agitated, and at the rapid succession of revolutions by which they were kept in a state of perpetual vibration between the extremes of tyranny and anarchy. . .

From the disorders that disfigure the annals of those republics the advocates of despotism have drawn arguments, not only against the forms of republican government, but against the very principles of civil liberty. They have decried all free government as inconsistent with the order of society. . .

The science of politics, however, like most other sciences, has received great improvement. The efficacy of various principles is now well understood, which were either not known at all, or imperfectly known to the ancients. The regular distribution of power into distinct departments; the introduction of legislative balances and checks; the institution of courts composed of judges holding their offices during good behavior; the representation of the people in the legislature by deputies of their own election: these are wholly new discoveries, or have made their principal progress towards perfection in modern times. They are means, and powerful means, by which the excellences of republican government may be retained and its imperfections lessened or avoided. To this catalogue of circumstances that tend to the amelioration of popular systems of add one more . . . I mean the *enlargement* of the *orbit* within which such systems are to revolve, either in respect to the dimensions of a single State, or to the consolidation of several smaller States into one great Confederacy. . .
civil Government, I shall venture, however novel it may appear to some, to

The utility of a Confederacy, as well to suppress faction and to guard the internal tranquillity of States, as to increase their external force and security, is in reality not a new idea. It has been practised upon in different countries and ages, and has received the sanction of the most approved writers on the subjects of politics. The opponents of the plan proposed have, with great assiduity, cited and circulated the observations of Montesquieu on the necessity of a contracted territory of a republican government. . .

When Montesquieu recommends a small extent for republics, the standards he had in view were of dimensions far short of the limits of almost every one of these States. Neither Virginia, Massachusetts, Pennsylvania, New York, North Carolina, nor Georgia can by any means be compared with the models from which he reasoned and to which the terms of his description apply. If we therefore take his ideas on this point as the criterion of truth, we shall be driven to the alternative either of taking refuge at once in the arms of monarchy, or of splitting ourselves into an infinity of little, jealous, clashing, tumultuous commonwealths, the wretched nurseries of unceasing discord, and the miserable objects of universal pity or contempt. . .

So far are the suggestions of Montesquieu from standing in opposition to a general Union of the States, that he explicitly treats of a *confederate republic* as the expedient for extending the sphere of popular government, and reconciling the advantages of monarchy with those of republicanism. . .

A distinction, more subtle than accurate, has been raised between a con-

federacy and a *consolidation* of the States. The essential characteristic of the first is said to be, the restriction of its authority to the members in their collective capacities, without reaching to the individuals of whom they are composed. It is contended that the national council ought to have no concern with any object of internal administration. An exact equality of suffrage between the members has also been insisted upon as a leading feature of a confederate government. These positions are, in the main, arbitrary; they are supported neither by principle nor precedent. . .

The definition of a *confederate republic* seems simply to be 'an assemblage of societies,' or an association of two or more states into one state. The extent, modifications, and objects of the federal authority, are mere matters of discretion. So long as the separate organization of the members be not abolished; so long as it exists, by a constitutional necessity, for local purposes; though it should be in perfect subordination to the general authority of the union, it would still be, in fact and in theory, an association of states, or a confederacy. The proposed Constitution, so far from implying an abolition of the State governments, makes them constituent parts of the national sovereignty, by allowing them a direct representation in the Senate, and leaves in their possession certain exclusive and very important portions of sovereignty power. This fully corresponds, in every rational import of the terms, with the idea of a federal government. . .

NO. XV (HAMILTON.)

. . . The point next in order to be examined is the 'insufficiency of the present Confederation to the preservation of the Union.' . .

We may indeed with propriety be said to have reached almost the last stage of national humiliation. There is scarcely any thing that can wound the pride or degrade the character of an independent nation which we do not experience. . .

Facts, too stubborn to be resisted, have produced a species of general assent to the abstract proposition that there exist material defects in our national system; but the usefulness of the concession, on the part of the old adversaries of federal measures, is destroyed by a strenuous opposition to a remedy, upon the only principles that can give it a chance of success. While they admit that the government of the United States is destitute of energy, they contend against conferring upon it those powers which are requisite to supply that energy. They seem still to aim at things repugnant and irreconcilable; at an augmentation of federal authoritly, without a diminution of State authority; at sovereignty in the Union, and complete independence in the members. They still, in fine, seem to cherish with blind devotion the political monster of an *imperium in imperio*. This renders a full display of the principal defects of the Confederation necessary, in order to show that the evils we experience do not proceed from minute or partial imperfections, but from fundamental errors in the structure of the building, which cannot be amended otherwise than by an alteration in the first principles and main pillars of the fabric.

The great and radical vice in the construction of the existing Confederation is the principle of LEGISLATION for STATES OR GOVERNMENTS, in their CORPORATE OR COLLECTIVE CAPACITIES, and as contradistinguished from the INDIVIDUALS of which they consist. Though this principle does not run through all the powers delegated to the Union, yet it pervades and governs those on which the efficacy of the rest depends. . .

Government implies the power of making laws. It is essential to the idea of a law, that it be attended with a sanction; or, in other words, a penalty or punishment for disobedience. If there be no penalty annexed to disobedience, the resolutions or commands which pretend to be laws will, in fact, amount to nothing more than advice or recommendation. This penalty, whatever it may be, can only be inflicted in two ways: by the agency of the courts and ministers of justice, or by military force; by the COERCION of the magistracy, or by the COERCION of arms. The first kind can evidently apply only to men; the last kind must of necessity, be employed against bodies politic or communities, or States. It is evident that there is no process of a court by which the observance of the laws can, in the last resort, be enforced. Sentences may be denounced against them for violations of their duty; but these sentences can only be carried into execution by the sword. In an association where the general authority is confined to the collective bodies of the communities that compose it, every breach of the laws must involve a state of war; and military execution must become the only instrument of civil obedience. Such a state of things can certainly not deserve the name of government, nor would any prudent man choose to commit his happiness to it.

There was a time when we were told that breaches, by the States, of the regulations of the federal authority were not to be expected; that a sense of common interest would preside over the conduct of the respective members, and would beget a full compliance with all the constitutional requisitions of the Union. This language, at the present day, would appear as wild as a great part of what we now hear from the same quarter will be thought, when we shall have received further lessons from that best oracle of wisdom, experience. It at all times betrayed an ignorance of the true springs by which human conduct is actuated, and belied the original inducements to the establishment of civil power. Why has government been instituted at all? Because the passions of men will not conform to the dictates of reason and justice, without constraint. Has it been found that bodies of men act with more rectitude or greater disinterestedness than individuals? The contrary of this has been inferred by all accurate observers of the conduct of mankind; and the inference is founded upon obvious reasons. Regard to reputation has a less active influence, when the infamy of a bad action is to be divided among a number, than when it is to fall singly upon one. A spirit of faction, which is apt to mingle its poison in the deliberations of all bodies of men, will often hurry the persons of whom they are composed into improprieties and excesses, for which they would blush in a private capacity.

In addition to all this, there is, in the nature of sovereign power, an impatience of control, that disposes those who are invested with the exercise of it, to look with an evil eye upon all external attempts to restrain or direct its operations. From this spirit it happens, that in every political association which is formed upon the principle of uniting in a common interest a number of lesser sovereignties, there will be found a kind of eccentric tendency in the subordinate or inferior orbs, by the operation of which there will be a perpetual effort in each to fly off from the common centre. This tendency is not difficult to be accounted for. It has its origin in the love of power. Power controlled or abridged is almost always the rival and enemy of that power by which it is controlled or abridged. This simple proposition will teach us, how little reason there is to expect, that the persons intrusted with the administration of the affairs of the particular members of a confederacy will at all times be ready, with perfect good-humor, and an unbiased regard to the public weal, to execute the resolutions or decrees of the general authority. The reverse of this results from the constitution of human nature. . .

NO. XVII (HAMILTON.)

An objection . . . may perhaps be . . . urged against the principle of legislation for the individual citizens of America. It may be said that it would tend to render the government of the Union too powerful, and to enable it to absorb those residuary authorities, which it might be judged proper to leave with the States for local purposes. Allowing the utmost latitude to the love of power which any reasonable man can require, I confess I am at a loss to discover what temptation the persons intrusted with the administration of the general government could ever feel to divest the States of the authorities of that description. The regulation of the mere domestic police of a State appears to me to hold out slender allurements to ambition. Commerce, finance, negotiation, and war seem to comprehend all the objects which have charms for minds governed by that passion; and all the powers necessary to those objects ought, in the first instance, to be lodged in the national depository. The administration of private justice between the citizens of the same State, the supervision of agriculture and of other concerns of a similar nature, all those things, in short, which are proper to be provided for by local legislation, can never be desirable cares of a general jurisdiction. It is therefore improbable that there should exist a disposition in the federal councils to usurp the powers with which they are connected; because the attempt to exercise those powers would be as troublesome as it would be nugatory; and the possession of them, for that reason, would contribute nothing to the dignity, to the importance, or to the splendor of the national government.

But let it be admitted, for argument's sake, that mere wantonness and lust of domination would be sufficient to beget that disposition; still it may be safely affirmed, that the sense of the constituent body of the national representatives, or, in other words, the people of the several States, would control the indulgence of so extravagant an appetite. It will always be far more easy for the State governments to encroach upon the national authorities, than for the national government to encroach upon the State authorities. The proof of this proposition turns upon the greater degree of influence which the State governments, if they administer their affairs with uprightness and prudence, will generally possess over the people; a circumstance which at the same time teaches us that there is an inherent and intrinsic weakness in all federal constitutions, and that too much pains cannot be taken in their organization, to give them all the force which is compatible with the principles of liberty. . .

There is one transcendent advantage belonging to the province of the State governments, which alone suffices to place the matter in a clear and satisfactory light,—I mean the ordinary administration of criminal and civil justice. This, of all others, is the most powerful, most universal, and most attractive source of popular obedience and attachment. . .

The operations of the national government, on the other hand, falling less immediately under the observation of the mass of the citizens, the benefits derived from it will chiefly be perceived and attended to by speculative men. Relating to more general interests, they will be less apt to come home to the feelings of the people; and, in proportion, less likely to inspire an habitual sense of obligation, and an active sentiment of attachment. . .

NO. XXII (HAMILTON.)

. . . A circumstance which crowns the defects of the Confederation remains yet to be mentioned,—the want of a judiciary power. Laws are a dead letter without courts to expound and define their true meaning and operation. The treaties of the United States, to have any force at all, must be considered as part of the law of the land. Their true import, as far as respects individuals, must, like all other laws, be ascertained by judicial determinations. To produce uniformity in these determinations, they ought to be submitted, in the last resort, to one SUPREME TRIBUNAL. And this tribunal ought to be instituted under the same authority which forms the treaties themselves. These ingredients are both idispensable. If there is in each State a court of final jurisdiction, there may be as many different final determinations on the same point as there are courts. . . To avoid the confusion which would unavoidably result from contradictory decisions of a number of independent judicatories, all nations have found it necessary to establish one court paramount to the rest, possessing a general superintendence, and authorized to settle and declare in the last resort a uniform rule of civil justice. . .

In this review of the Confederation, I have confined myself to the exhibition of its most material defects. . . It must be by this time evident to all men of reflection, who can divest themselves of the prepossessions of preconceived opinions, that it is a system so radically vicious and unsound, as to admit not of amendment but by an entire change in its leading features and characters. . .

It has not a little contributed to the infirmities of the existing federal system, that it never had a ratification by the PEOPLE. Resting on no better foundation than the consent of the several legislatures, it has been exposed to frequent and intricate questions concerning the validity of its powers, and has, in some instances, given birth to the enormous doctrine of a right of legislative repeal. Owing its ratification to the law of a State, it has been contended that the same authority might repeal the law by which it was ratified. However gross a heresy it may be to maintain that a *party* to a *compact* has a right to revoke that *compact*, the doctrine itself has had respectable advocates.* The possibility of a question of this nature proves the necessity of laying the foundations of our national government deeper than in the mere sanction of delegated authority. The fabric of American Empire ought to rest on the solid basis of THE CONSENT OF THE PEOPLE. The streams of national power ought to flow immediately from that pure, original fountain of all legitimate authority.

NO. XXXIII (HAMILTON.)

. . . These two clauses ('Supremacy,' Art. 6, par. 2 and 'Necessary and Proper,' Art. 1, Sec. VIII, par. 18) have been the source of much virulent invective and petulant declamation against the proposed Constitution. . . And yet, strange as it may appear, after all this clamor, to those who may not have happened to contemplate them in the same light, it may be affirmed with perfect confidence that the constitutional operation of the intended government would be precisely the same, if these clauses were entirely obliterated. . . They are only declaratory of a truth which would have resulted by necessary and unavoidable implication from the very act of constituting a federal government, and vesting it with certain specified powers. . .

What is a power, but the ability or faculty of doing a thing? What is the ability to do a thing, but the power of employing the *means* necessary to its execution? What is a *legislative* power, but a power of making LAWS? What are the *means* to execute a *legislative* power, but LAWS? What is the power of laying and collecting taxes, but a *legislative power*, or a power of *making laws*, to lay and collect taxes? What are the proper means of executing such a power, but *necessary* and *proper* laws?

This simple train of inquiry furnishes us at once with a test by which to judge of the true nature of the clause complained of. It conducts us to this palpable truth, that a power to lay and collect taxes must be a power to pass all laws *necessary* and *proper* for the execution of that power; and what does the unfortunate and calumniated provision in question do more than declare the same truth, to wit, that the national legislature, to whom the power of laying and collecting taxes had been previously given, might, in the execution of that power, pass all laws *necessary* and *proper* to carry it into effect? I have applied these observations thus particularly to the power of taxation, because it is the immediate subject under consideration, and because it is the most important of the authorities proposed to be conferred upon the Union. But the same process will lead to the same result, in relation to all other powers declared in the Constitution. And it is *expressly* to execute these powers that the sweeping clause, as it has been affectedly called, authorizes the national legislature to pass all *necessary* and *proper* laws. If there is anything exceptionable, it must be sought for in the specific powers upon which this general declaration is predicated. The declaration itself, though it may be chargeable with tautology or redundancy, is at least perfectly harmless.

But SUSPICION may ask, Why then was it introduced? The answer is, that it

* Compare Madison's words in *The Federalist* 46, *infra*.

could only have been done for greater caution, and to guard against all cavilling refinements in those who might hereafter feel a disposition to curtail and evade the legitimate authorities of the Union.* The Convention probably foresaw, what it has been a principal aim of these papers to inculcate, that the danger which most threatens our political welfare is that the State governments will finally sap the foundations of the Union; and might therefore think it necessary, in so cardinal a point, to leave nothing to construction. Whatever may have been the inducement to it, the wisdom of the precaution is evident from the cry which has been raised against it; as that very cry betrays a disposition to question the great and essential truth which it is manifestly the object of that provision to declare.

But it may be again asked, Who is to judge of the *necessity* and *propriety* of the laws to be passed for executing the powers of the Union? I answer, first, that this question arises as well and as fully upon the simple grant of those powers as upon the declaratory clause; and I answer, in the second place, that the national government, like every other, must judge, in the first instance, of the proper exercise of its powers, and its constituents in the last. If the federal government should overpass the just bounds of its authority and make a tyrannical use of its powers, the people, whose creature it is, must appeal to the standard they have formed, and take such measures to redress the injury done to the Constitution as the exigency may suggest and prudence justify. The propriety of a law, in a constitutional light, must always be determined by the nature of the powers upon which it is founded. . .

But it is said that the laws of the Union are to be the *supreme law* of the land. But what inference can be drawn from this, or what would they amount to, if they were not to be supreme? It is evident they would amount to nothing. A LAW, by the very meaning of the term, includes supremacy. It is a rule which those to whom it is prescribed are bound to observe. This results from every political association. If individuals enter into a state of society, the laws of that society must be the supreme regulator of their conduct. If a number of political societies enter into a larger political society, the laws which the latter may enact, pursuant to the powers intrusted to it by its constitution, must necessarily be supreme over those societies, and the individuals of whom they are composed. It would otherwise be a mere treaty, dependent on the good faith of the parties, and not a government, which is only another word for POLITICAL POWER AND SUPREMACY. But it will not follow from this doctrine that acts of the larger society which are *not pursuant* to its constitutional powers, but which are invasions of the residuary authorities of the smaller societies, will become the supreme law of the land. These will be merely acts of usurpation, and will deserve to be treated as such. . .

* Compare Madison's analysis, nos. 44 and 45, *infra*.

10. *The proposed constitution is, in strictness, neither a national nor a federal constitution, but a composition of both*

JAMES MADISON, *The Federalist*, 1787–88 *

NO. X (MADISON.)

Among the numerous advantages promised by a well-constructed Union, none deserves to be more accurately developed than its tendency to break and control the violence of faction. The friend of popular governments never finds himself so much alarmed for their character and fate, as when he contemplates their propensity to this dangerous vice. . . The instability, injustice, and confusion introduced into the public councils, have, in truth, been the mortal diseases under which popular governments have everywhere perished. . . Complaints are everywhere heard from our most considerate and virtuous citizens, equally the friends of public and private faith, and of public and personal liberty, that our governments are too unstable, that the public good is disregarded in the conflicts of rival parties, and that measures are too often decided, not according to the rules of justice and the rights of the minor party, but by the superior force of an interested and overbearing majority. However anxiously we may wish that these complaints had no foundation, the evidence of known facts will not permit us to deny that they are in some degree true. It will be found, indeed, on a candid review of our situation, that some of the distresses under which we labor have been erroneously charged on the operation of our governments; but it will be found, at the same time, that other causes will not alone account for many of our heaviest misfortunes; and, particularly, for that prevailing and increasing distrust of public engagements, and alarm for private rights, which are echoed from one end of the continent to the other. These must be chiefly, if not wholly, effects of the unsteadiness and injustice with which a factious spirit has tainted our public administrations.

By a faction, I understand a number of citizens, whether amounting to a majority or minority of the whole, who are united and actuated by some common impulse of passion, or of interest, adverse to the rights of other citizens, or to the permanent and aggregate interests of the community.

There are two methods of curing the mischiefs of faction: the one, by removing its causes; the other, by controlling its effects.

There are again two methods of removing the causes of faction: the one, by destroying the liberty which is essential to its existence; the other, by giving to every citizen the same opinions, the same passions, and the same interests.

It could never be more truly said than of the first remedy, that it was worse than the disease. Liberty is to faction what air is to fire, an aliment without which it instantly expires. But it could not be less folly to abolish liberty, which is essential to political life, because it nourishes faction, than it would be

* *The Federalist*, Henry Cabot Lodge, ed.

to wish the annihilation of air, which is essential to animal life, because it imparts to fire its destructive agency.

The second expedient is as impracticable as the first would be unwise. As long as the reason of man continues fallible, and he is at liberty to exercise it, different opinions will be formed. As long as the connection subsists between his reason and his self-love, his opinions and his passions will have a reciprocal influence on each other; and the former will be objects to which the latter will attach themselves. The diversity in the faculties of men, from which the rights of property originate, is not less an insuperable obstacle to a uniformity of interests. The protection of these faculties is the first object of government. From the protection of different and unequal faculties of acquiring property, the possession of different degrees and kinds of property immediately results; and from the influence of these on the sentiments and views of the respective proprietors, ensues a division of the society into different interests and parties.

The latent causes of faction are thus sown in the nature of man; and we see them everywhere brought into different degrees of activity, according to the different circumstances of civil society. A zeal for different opinions concerning religion, concerning government, and many other points, as well of speculation as of practice; an attachment to different leaders ambitiously contending for pre-eminence and power; or to persons of other descriptions whose fortunes have been interesting to the human passions, have, in turn, divided mankind into parties, inflamed them with mutual animositly, and rendered them much more disposed to vex and oppress each other than to co-operate for their common good. So strong is this propensity of mankind to fall into mutual animosities, that where no substantial occasion presents itself, the most frivolous and fanciful distinctions have been sufficient to kindle their unfriendly passions and excite their most violent conflicts. But the most common and durable source of factions has been the various and unequal distribution of property. Those who hold and those who are without property have ever formed distinct interests in society. Those who are creditors, and those who are debtors, fall under a like discrimination. A landed interest, a manufacturing interest, a mercantile interest, a moneyed interest, with many lesser interests, grow up of necessity in civilized nations, and divide them into different classes, actuated by different sentiments and views. The regulation of these various and interfering interests forms the principal task of modern legislation, and involves the spirit of party and faction in the necessary and ordinary operations of the government.

No man is allowed to be a judge in his own cause, because his interest would certainly bias his judgment, and, not improbably, corrupt his integrity. With equal, nay with greater reason, a body of men are unfit to be both judges and parties at the same time; yet what are many of the most important acts of legislation, but so many judicial determinations, not indeed concerning the rights of single persons, but concerning the rights of large bodies of citizens? And what are the different classes of legislators but advocates and parties to the causes which they determine? Is a law proposed concerning private debts? It is a question to which the creditors are parties on one side and the debtors on the other. Justice ought to hold the balance between them. Yet the parties are, and must be, themselves the judges; and the most numerous party, or, in other words, the most powerful faction must be expected to prevail. Shall domestic manufacturers be encouraged, and in what degree, by restrictions on foreign manufactures? are questions which would be differently decided by the landed and the manufacturing classes, and probably by neither with a sole regard to justice and the public good. The apportionment of taxes on the various descriptions of property is an act which seems to require the most exact impartiality; yet there is, perhaps, no legislative act in which greater opportunity and temptation are given to a predominant party to trample on the rules of justice. . .

It is in vain to say that enlightened statesmen will be able to adjust these clashing interests, and render them all subservient to the public good. Enlightened statesmen will not always be at the helm. Nor, in many cases, can such an adjustment be made at all without taking into view indirect and remote considerations, which will rarely prevail over the immediate interest which one party may find in disregarding the rights of another or the good of the whole.

The inference to which we are brought is, that the *causes* of faction cannot be removed, and that relief is only to be sought in the means of controlling its *effects*.

If a faction consists of less than a majority, relief is supplied by the republican principle, which enables the majority to defeat its sinister views by regular vote. It may clog the administration, it may convulse the society; but it will be unable to execute and mask its violence under the forms of the Constitution. When a majority is included in a faction, the form of popular government, on the other hand, enables it to sacrifice to its ruling passion or interest both the public good and the rights of other citizens. To secure the public good and private rights against the danger of such a faction, and at the same time to preserve the spirit and the form of popular government, is then the great object to which our inquiries are directed. . .

By what means is this object attainable? Evidently by one of two only. Either the existence of the same passion or interest in a majority at the same time must be prevented, or the majority, having such coexistent passion or interest, must be rendered, by their number and local situation, unable to concert and carry into effect schemes of oppression. If the impulse and the opportunity be suffered to coincide, we well know that neither moral nor religious motives can be relied on as an adequate control. . .

From this view of the subject it may be concluded that a pure democracy, by which I mean a society consisting of a small number of citizens, who assemble and administer the government in person, can admit of no cure for the mischiefs of faction. A common passion or interest will, in almost every case, be felt by a majority of the whole; a communication and concert result from the form of government itself; and there is nothing to check the inducements to sacrifice the weaker party or an obnoxious individual. Hence it is that such democracies have ever been spectacles of turbulence and contention; have ever been found incompatible with personal security or the rights of property; and have in general been as short in their lives as they have been violent in their deaths. Theoretic politicians, who have patronized this species of government, have erroneously supposed that by reducing mankind to a perfect equality in their political rights, they would, at the same time, be perfectly equalized and assimilated in their possessions, their opinions, and their passions.

A republic, by which I mean a government in which the scheme of representation takes place, opens a different prospect, and promises the cure for which we are seeking. Let us examine the points in which it varies from pure democracy, and we shall comprehend both the nature of the cure and the efficacy which it must derive from the Union.

The two great points of difference between a democracy and a republic are: first, the delegation of the government, in the latter, to a small number of citizens elected by the rest; secondly, the greater number of citizens, and greater sphere of country, over which the latter may be extended.

The effect of the first difference is, on the one hand, to refine and enlarge the public views, by passing them through the medium of a chosen body of citizens, whose wisdom may best discern the true interest of their country, and whose patriotism and love of justice will be least likely to sacrifice it to temporary or partial considerations. Under such a regulation, it may well happen that the public voice, pronounced by the representatives of the people, will be more consonant to the public good than if pronounced by the people themselves, convened for the purpose. On the other hand, the effect may be inverted. Men of factious tempers, of local prejudices, or of sinister designs, may, by intrigue, by corruption, or by other means, first obtain the suffrages, and then betray the interests, of the people. The question resulting is, whether small or extensive republics are more favorable to the election of proper guardians of the public weal; and it is clearly decided in favor of the latter by two obvious considerations:

In the first place, it is to be remarked that, however small the republic may be, the representatives must be raised to a certain number, in order to guard against the cabals of a few; and that, however large it may be, they must be limited to a certain number, in order to guard against the confusion of a multitude. Hence, the number of representatives in the two cases not being in proportion to that of the two constituents, and being proportionally greater in the small republic, it follows that, if the proportion of fit characters be not less in the large than in the small republic, the former will present a greater option, and consequently a greater probability of a fit choice.

In the next place, as each representative will be chosen by a greater number of citizens in the large than in the small republic, it will be more difficult for unworthy candidates to practise with success the vicious arts by which elections are too often carried; and the suffrages of the people being more free, will be more likely to center in men who possess the most attractive merit and the most diffusive and established characters.

It must be confessed that in this, as in most other cases, there is a mean, on both sides of which inconveniences will be found to lie. By enlarging too much the number of electors, you render the representative too little acquainted with all their local circumstances and lesser interests; as by reducing it too much, you render him unduly attached to these, and too little fit to comprehend and pursue great and national objects. The federal Constitution forms a happy combination in this respect; the great and aggregate interests being referred to the national, the local and particular to the State legislatures.

The other point of difference is, the greater number of citizens and extent of territory which may be brought within the compass of republican than of democratic government; and it is this circumstance principally which renders factious combinations less to be dreaded in the former than in the latter. The smaller the society, the fewer probably will be the distinct parties and interests composing it; the fewer the distinct parties and interests, the more frequently will a majority be found of the same party; and the smaller the number of individuals composing a majority, and the smaller the compass within which they are placed, the more easily will they concert and execute their plans of oppression. Extend the sphere, and you take in a greater variety of parties and interests; you make it less probable that a majority of the whole will have a common motive to invade the rights of other citizens; or if such a common motive exists, it will be more difficult for all who feel it to discover their own strength, and to act in unison with each other. Besides other impediments, it may be remarked that, where there is a consciousness of unjust or dishonorable purposes, communication is always checked by distrust in proportion to the number whose concurrence is necessary.

Hence, it clearly appears, that the same advantage which a republic has over a democracy, in controlling the effects of faction, is enjoyed by a large over a small republic,—is enjoyed by the Union over the States composing it. Does the advantage consist in the substitution of representatives whose enlightened views and virtuous sentiments render them superior to local prejudices and to schemes of injustice? It will not be denied that the representation of the Union will be most likely to possess these requisite endowments. Does it consist in the greater security afforded by a greater variety of parties, against the event of any one party being able to outnumber and oppress the rest? In an equal degree does the increased variety of parties comprised within the Union, increase this security. Does it, in fine, consist in the greater obstacles opposed to the concert and accomplishment of the secret wishes of an unjust and interested majority? Here, again, the extent of the Union gives it the most palpable advantage.

The influence of factious leaders may kindle a flame within their particular States, but will be unable to spread a general conflagration through the other States. A religious sect may degenerate into a political faction in a part of the Confederacy; but the variety of sects dispersed over the entire face of it must secure the national councils against any danger from that source. A rage for paper money, for an abolition of debts, for an equal division of property, or for any other improper or wicked project, will be less apt to pervade the whole body of the Union than a particular member of it; in the same proportion as such a malady is more likely to taint a particular county or district, than an entire State.

In the extent and proper structure of the Union, therefore, we behold a republican remedy for the diseases most incident to republican government. . .

NO. XXXVII (MADISON.)

. . . Among the difficulties encountered by the convention, a very important one must have lain in combining the requisite stability and energy in government, with the inviolable attention due to liberty and to the republican form. . . The genius of republican liberty seems to demand on one side, not only that all power should be derived from the people, but that those intrusted with it should be kept in dependence on the people, by a short duration of their appointments; and that even during this short period the trust should be placed not in a few, but a number of hands. Stability, on the contrary, requires that the hands in which power is lodged should continue for a length of time the same. A frequent change of men will result from a frequent return of elections; and a frequent change of measures from a frequent change of men: whilst energy in government requires not only a certain duration of power, but the execution of it by a single hand. . .

Not less arduous must have been the task of marking the proper line of partition between the authority of the general and that of the State governments. Every man will be sensible of this difficulty, in proportion as he has been accustomed to contemplate and discriminate objects extensive and complicated in their nature. The faculties of the mind itself have never yet been distinguished and defined, with satisfactory precision, by all the efforts of the most acute and metaphysical philosophers. Sense, perception, judgment, desire, volition, memory, imagination, are found to be separated by such delicate shades and minute gradations that their boundaries have eluded the most subtle investigations, and remain a pregnant source of ingenious disquisition and controversy. . .

When we pass from the works of nature, in which all the delineations are perfectly accurate, and appear to be otherwise only from the imperfections of the eye which surveys them, to the institutions of man, in which the obscurity arises as well from the object itself as from the organ by which it is contemplated, we must perceive the necessity of moderating still further our expectations and hopes from the efforts of human sagacity. Experience has instructed us that no skill in the science of government has yet been able to discriminate and define, with sufficient certainty, its three great provinces—the legislative, executive, and judiciary; or even the privileges and powers of the different legislative branches. Questions daily occur in the course of practice, which prove the obscurity which reigns in these subjects, and which puzzle the greatest adepts in political science. . .

Here, then, are three sources of vague and incorrect definitions: indistinctness of the object, imperfection of the organ of conception, inadequateness of the vehicle of ideas. Any one of these must produce a certain degree of obscurity. The convention, in delineating the boundary between the federal and State jurisdictions, must have experienced the full effect of them all. . .

Would it be wonderful if, under the pressure of all these difficulties, the convention should have been forced into some deviations from that artificial structure and regular symmetry which an abstract view of the subject might lead an ingenious theorist to bestow on a Constitution planned in his closet or in his imagination? The real wonder is that so many difficulties should have been surmounted, and surmounted with a unanimity almost as unprecedented as it must have been unexpected. . .

NO. XXXIX (MADISON.)

. . . It is evident that no other form [than one strictly republican] would be reconcilable with the genius of the people of America; with the fundamental principles of the Revolution; or with that honorable determination which animates every votary of freedom, to rest all our political experiments on the capacity of mankind for self-government. . .

What, then, are the distinctive characters of the republican form? . .

If we resort for a criterion to the different principles on which different forms of government are established, we may define a republic to be, or at least may bestow that name on, a government which derives all its powers directly or indirectly from the great body of the people, and is administered by persons holding their offices during pleasure, for a limited period, or during good behavior. It is *essential* to such a government that it be derived from the great body of the society, not from an inconsiderable proportion, or a favored class of it; otherwise a handful of tyrannical nobles, exercising their oppressions by a delegation of their powers, might aspire to the rank of republicans, and claim for their government the honorable title of republic. It is *sufficient* for such a government that the persons administering it be appointed, either directly or indirectly, by the people; and that they hold their appointments by either of the tenures just specified; otherwise every government in the United States, as well as every other popular government that has been or can be well organized or well executed, would be degraded from the republican character. . .

'But it was not sufficient,' say the adversaries of the proposed Constitution, 'for the convention to adhere to the republican form. They ought, with equal care, to have preserved the *federal* form, which regards the Union as a *Confederacy* of sovereign states; instead of which, they have framed a *national* government, which regards the Union as a *consolidation* of the States.' And it is asked by what authority this bold and radical innovation was undertaken? . .

Without inquiring into the accuracy of the distinction on which the objection is founded, it will be necessary to a just estimate of its force, first, to ascertain the real character of the government in question; secondly, to inquire how far the Convention were authorized to propose such a government; and thirdly, how far the duty they owed to their country could supply any defect of regular authority. . .

On examining the first relation, it appears, on one hand, that the Constitution is to be founded on the assent and ratification of the people of America, given by deputies elected for the special purpose; but, on the other, that this assent and ratification is to be given by the people, not as individuals composing one entire nation, but as composing the distinct and independent States to which they respectively belong. It is to be the assent and ratification of the several States, derived from the supreme authority in each State,—the authority of the people themselves. The act, therefore, establishing the Constitution, will not be a *national*, but a *federal* act.

That it will be a federal and not a national act, as these terms are understood by the objectors; the act of the people, as forming so many independent States, not as forming one aggregate nation, is obvious from this single consideration, that it is to result neither from the decision of a *majority* of the people of the Union, nor from that of a *majority* of the States. It must result from the *unanimous* assent of the several States that are parties to it, differing no otherwise from their ordinary assent than in its being expressed, not by the legislative authority, but by that of the people themselves. Were the people regarded in this transaction as forming one nation, the will of the majority of the whole people of the United States would bind the minority, in the same manner as the majority in each State must bind the minority; and the will of the majority must be determined either by a comparison of the individual votes, or by considering the will of the majority of the States as evidence of the will of a majority of the people of the United States. Neither of these rules has been adopted. Each State, in ratifying the Constitution, is considered as a sovereign body, independent of all others, and only to be bound by its own voluntary act. In this relation, then, the new Constitution will, if established, be a *federal*, and not a *national* constitution.

The next relation is, to the sources from which the ordinary powers of government are to be derived. The House of Representatives will derive its powers from the people of America; and the people will be represented in the same proportion, and on the same principle, as they are in the legislature of a particular State. So far the government is *national*, not *federal*. The Senate, on the other hand, will derive its powers from the States, as political and coequal societies; and these will be represented on the principle of equality in the Senate, as they now are in the existing Congress. So far the government is *Federal*, not national. The executive power will be derived from a very compound source. The immediate election of the President is to be made by the States in their political characters. The votes allotted to them are in a compound ratio, which considers them partly as distinct and coequal societies, partly as unequal members of the same society. The eventual election, again, is to be made by that branch of the legislature which consists of the national representatives; but in this particular act they are to be thrown into the form of individual delegations, from so many distinct and coequal bodies politic. From this aspect of the government, it appears to be of a mixed character, presenting at least as many *federal* as *national* features.

The difference between a federal and national government, as it relates to the *operation of the government*, is supposed to consist in this, that in the former the powers operate on the political bodies composing the Confederacy, in their political capacities; in the latter, on the individual citizens composing the nation, in their individual capacites. On trying the Constitution by this criterion, it falls under the *national*, not the *federal* character; though perhaps not so completely as has been understood. In several cases, and particularly in the trial of controversies to which States may be parties, they must be viewed and proceeded against in their collective and political capacities only. So far the national countenance of the government on this side seems to be disfigured by a few federal features. But this blemish is perhaps unavoidable in any plan; and the operation of the government on the people, in their individual capacities in its ordinary and most essential proceedings, may, on the whole, designate it, in this relation, a *national* government.

But if the government be national with regard to the *operation* of its powers, it changes its aspect again when we contemplate it in relation to the *extent* of its powers. The idea of a national government involves in it, not only an authority over the individual citizens, but an indefinite supremacy over all persons and things, so far as they are objects of lawful government. Among a people consolidated into one nation, this supremacy is completely vested in the national legislature. Among communities united for particular purposes, it is vested partly in the general and partly in the municipal legislatures. In the former case, all local authorities are subordinate to the supreme; and may be controlled, directed, or abolished by it at pleasure. In the latter, the local or municipal authorities form distinct and independent portions of the supremacy, no more subject, within their respective spheres, to the general authority, than the general authority is subject to them, within its own sphere. In this relation, then, the proposed government cannot be deemed a *national* one; since its jurisdiction extends to certain enumerated objects only, and leaves to the several States a residuary and inviolable sovereignty over all other objects. It is true that in controversies relating to the boundary between the two jurisdictions the tribunal which is ultimately to decide, is to be established under the general government. But this does not change the principle of the case. The decision is to be impartially made, according to the rules of the Constitution; and all the usual and most effectual precautions are taken to secure this impartiality. Some such tribunal is clearly essential to prevent an appeal to the sword and a dissolution of the compact; and that it ought to be established under the general rather than under the local governments, or, to speak more properly, that it could be safely established under the first alone, is a position not likely to be combated.

If we try the Constitution by its last relation to the authority by which amendments are to be made, we find it neither wholly *national* nor wholly *federal*. Were it wholly national, the supreme and ultimate authority would reside in the *majority* of the people of the Union; and this authority would be competent at all times, like that of a majority of every national society, to alter or abolish its established government. Were it wholly federal, on the other hand, the concurrence of each State in the Union would be essential to every alteration that would be binding on all. The mode provided by the plan of the convention is not founded on either of these principles. In requiring more than a majority, and particularly in computing the proportion by *States*, not by *citizens*, it departs from the *national* and advances toward the *federal* character; in rendering the concurrence of less than the whole number of States sufficient, it loses again the *federal* and partakes of the *national* character.

The proposed Constitution, therefore, is, in strictness, neither a national nor a federal Constitution, but a composition of both. In its foundation it is federal, not national; in the sources from which the ordinary powers of the government are drawn, it is partly federal and partly national; in the operation of these powers, it is national, not federal; in the extent of them, again, it is federal, not national; and, finally, in the authoritative mode of introducing amendments, it is nether wholly federal nor wholly national. . .

NO. XLIV (MADISON.)

. . . Few parts of the Constitution have been assailed with more intemperance than this: [Article 1, Section 8, Paragraph 18: Congress shall have 'power to make all laws which shall be necessary and proper for carrying into execution the foregoing powers, and all other powers vested by this Constitution in the government of the United States, or in any department or officer thereof.'] Yet on a fair investigation of it, no part can appear more completely invulnerable. Without the *substance* of this power, the whole Constitution would be a dead letter. Those who object to the article, therefore, as a part of the Constitution, can only mean that the *form* of the provision is improper. But have they considered whether a better form could have been substituted?

There are four other possible methods which the Convention might have taken on this subject. They might have copied the second article of the existing Confederation, which would have prohibited the exercise of any power not *expressly* delegated; they might have attempted to positive enumeration of the powers comprehended under the general terms 'necessary and proper'; they might have attempted a negative enumeration of them, by specifying the powers excepted from the general definition; they might have been altogether silent on the subject, leaving these necessary and proper powers to construction and inference. . .

Had the Constitution been silent on this head, there can be no doubt that all the particular powers requisite as means of executing the general powers would have resulted to the government, by unavoidable implication. No axiom is more clearly established in law, or in reason, than that wherever the end is required, the means are authorized; wherever a general power to do a thing is given, every particular power necessary for doing it is included. Had this last method, therefore, been pursued by the convention, every objection now urged against their plan would remain in all its plausibility; and the real inconveniency would be incurred of not removing a pretext which may be seized on critical occasions for drawing into question the essential powers of the Union.

If it be asked what is to be the consequence, in case the Congress shall misconstrue this part of the Constitution, and exercise powers not warranted by its true meaning, I answer, the same as if they should misconstrue or enlarge any other power vested in them; as if the general power had been reduced to particulars, and any one of these were to be violated; the same, in short, as if the State legislatures should violate their respective constitutional authorities. In the first instance, the success of the usurpation will depend on the executive and judiciary departments, which are to expound and give effect to the legislative acts; and in the last resort a remedy must be obtained from the people, who can, by the election of more faithful representatives, annul the acts of the usurpers. The truth is, that this ultimate redress may be more confided in against unconstitutional acts of the federal than of the State legislatures, for this plain reason, that as every such act of the former will be an invasion of the rights of the latter, these will be ever ready to mark the innovation, to sound the alarm of the people, and to exert their local influence in effecting a change of federal representatives. . .

NO. XLV (MADISON.)

. . . The adversaries to the plan of the convention, instead of considering in the first place what degree of power was absolutely necessary for the purposes of the federal government, have exhausted themselves in a secondary inquiry into the possible consequences of the proposed degree of power to the governments of the particular States. But if the Union, as has been shown, be essential to the security of the people of America against foreign danger; if it be essential to their security against contentions and wars among the different States; if it be essential to guard them against those violent and oppressive factions which embitter the blessings of liberty, and against those military establishments which must gradually poison its very fountain; if, in a word, the Union be essential to the happiness of the people of America, is it not preposterous, to urge as an objection to a government, without which the objects of the Union cannot be attained, that such a government may derogate from the importance of the governments of the individual States? Was, then, the American Revolution effected, was the American Confederacy formed, was the precious blood of thousands spilt, and the hard-earned substance of millions lavished, not that the people of America should enjoy peace, liberty, and safety, but that the government of the individual States, that particular municipal establishments, might enjoy a certain extent of power, and be arrayed with certain dignities and attributes of sovereignty? We have heard of the impious doctrine in the Old World, that the people were made for kings, not kings for the people. Is the same doctrine to be revived in the New, in another shape—that the solid happiness of the people is to be sacrificed to the views of political institutions of a different form? It is too early for politicians to presume on our forgetting that the public good, the real welfare of the great body of the people, is the supreme object to be pursued; and that no form of government whatever has any other value than as it may be fitted for the attainment of this object. Were the plan of the convention adverse to the public happiness, my voice would be, reject the plan. Were the Union itself inconsistent with the public happiness, it would be, abolish the Union. In like manner, as far as the sovereignty of the States cannot be reconciled to the happiness of the people, the voice of every good citizen must be, Let the former be sacrificed to the latter. How far the sacrifice is necessary, has been shown. . .

Several important considerations have been touched in the course of these papers, which discountenance the supposition that the operation of the federal government will by degrees prove fatal to the State governments. The more I revolve the subject, the more fully I am persuaded that the balance is much more likely to be disturbed by the preponderancy of the last than of the first scale. . .

The powers delegated by the proposed Constitution to the federal government are few and defined. Those which are to remain in the State governments are numerous and indefinite. The former will be exercised principally on external objects, as war, peace, negotiation, and foreign commerce; with which last the power of taxation will, for the most part, be connected. The powers reserved to the several States will extend to all the objects which, in the ordinary course of affairs, concern the lives, liberties, and properties of the people, and the internal order, improvement, and prosperity of the States.

The operations of the federal government will be most extensive and important in times of war and danger; those of the State governments, in times of peace and security. As the former periods will probably bear a small proportion to the latter, the State governments will here enjoy another advantage over the federal government. The more adequate, indeed, the federal powers may be rendered to the national defence, the less frequent will be those scenes of danger which might favor their ascendancy over the governments of the particular States.

If the new Constitution be examined with accuracy and candor, it will be found that the change which it proposes consists much less in the addition of NEW POWERS to the Union, than in the invigoration of its ORIGINAL POWERS. The regulation of commerce, it is true, is a new power; but that seems to be an addition which few oppose, and from which no apprehensions are entertained. The powers relating to war and peace, armies and fleets, treaties and finance, with the other more considerable powers, are all vested in the existing Congress by the Articles of Confederation. The proposed change does not enlarge these powers; it only substitutes a more effectual mode of administering them. The change relating to taxation may be regarded as the most important; and yet the present Congress have as complete authority to REQUIRE of the States indefinite supplies of money for the common defence and general welfare, as the future Congress will have to require them of individual citizens; and the latter will be no more bound than the States themselves have been, to pay the quotas respectively taxed on them. Had the States complied punctually with the Articles of Confederation, or could their compliance have been enforced by as peaceable means as may be used with success towards single persons, our past experience is very far from countenancing an opinion, that the State governments would have lost their constitutional powers, and have gradually undergone an entire consolidation. To maintain that such an event would have ensued, would be to say at once, that the existence of the State governments is incompatible with any system whatever that accomplishes the essential purposes of the Union.

NO. XLVI (MADISON.)

. . . The federal and State governments are in fact but different agents and trustees of the people, constituted with different powers, and designed for different purposes. The adversaries of the Constitution seem to have lost sight of the people altogether in their reasonings on this subject; and to have viewed these different establishments, not only as mutual rivals and enemies, but as uncontrolled by any common superior in their efforts to usurp the authorities of each other. These gentlemen must here be reminded of their error. They must be told that the ultimate authority, wherever the derivative may be found, resides in the people alone, and that it will not depend merely on the comparative ambition or address of the different governments, whether either, or which of them will be able to enlarge its sphere of jurisdiction at the expense of the other. . .

Were it admitted, however, that the federal government may feel an equal disposition with the State governments to extend its power beyond the due limits, the latter would still have the advantage in the means of defeating such encroachments. . . Should an unwarrantable measure of the federal government be unpopular in particular States, which would seldom fail to be the case, or even a warrantable measure be so, which may sometimes be the case, the means of opposition to it are powerful and at hand. The disquietude of the people; their repugnance and, perhaps, refusal to cooperate with the officers of the Union; the frowns of the executive magistracy of the State; the embarrassments created by legislative devices, which would often be added on such occasions, would oppose, in any State, difficulties not to be despised; would form, in a large State, very serious impediments; and where the sentiments of several adjoining States happened to be in unison, would present obstructions which the federal government would hardly be willing to encounter.

But ambitious encroachments of the federal government, on the authority of the State governments, would not excite the opposition of a single State, or of a few States only. They would be signals of general alarm. Every government would espouse the common cause. A correspondence would be opened. Plans of resistance would be concerted. One spirit would animate and conduct the whole. The same combinations, in short, would result from an apprehension of the federal, as was produced by the dread of a foreign yoke; and unless the projected innovations should be voluntarily renounced, the same appeal to a trial of force would be made in the one case as was made in the other. But what degree of madness could ever drive the federal government to such an extremity. . .

NO. LI (MADISON.)

To what expedient . . . shall we . . . resort, for maintaining in practice the necessary partition of power among the several departments, as laid down in the Constitution? The only answer that can be given is, that as all these exterior provisions are found to be inadequate, the defect must be supplied, by so contriving the interior structure of the government as that its several constituent parts may, by their mutual relations, be the means of keeping each other in their proper places. . .

The great security against a gradual concentration of the several powers in the same department, consists in giving to those who administer each department the necessary constitutional means and personal motives to resist encroachments of the others. The provision for defence must in this, as in all other cases, be made commensurate to the danger of attack. Ambition must be made to counteract ambition. The interest of the man must be connected with the constitutional rights of the place. It may be a reflection on human nature, that such devices should be necessary to control the abuses of government. But what is government itself, but the greatest of all reflections on human nature? If men were angels, no government would be necessary. If angels were to govern men, neither external nor internal controls on government would be necessary. In framing a government which is to be administered by men over men, the great difficulty lies in this: you must first enable the government to control the governed; and in the next place oblige it to control itself. A dependence on the people is, no doubt, the primary control on the government; but experience has taught mankind the necessity of auxiliary precautions.

This policy of supplying, by opposite and rival interests, the defect of better motives, might be traced through the whole system of human affairs, private as well as public. We see it particularly displayed in all the subordinate distributions of power, where the constant aim is to divide and arrange the several offices in such a manner as that each may be a check on the other—that the private interest of every individual may be a sentinel over the public rights. These inventions of prudence cannot be less requisite in the distribution of the supreme powers of the State.

But it is not possible to give to each department an equal power of self-defence. In republican government, the legislative authority necessarily predominates. The remedy for this inconveniency is to divide the legislature into different branches; and to render them, by different modes of election and different principles of action, as little connected with each other as the nature of their common functions and their common dependence on the society will admit. It may even be necessary to guard against dangerous encroachments by still further precautions. As the weight of the legislative authority requires that it should be thus divided, the weakness of the executive may require, on the other hand, that it should be fortified. An absolute negative on the legislature appears, at first view, to be the natural defence with which the executive magistrate should be armed. But perhaps it would be neither altogether safe nor alone sufficient. On ordinary occasions it might not be exerted with the requisite firmness, and on extraordinary occasions it might be perfidiously abused. May not this defect of an absolute negative be supplied by some qualified connection between this weaker department and the weaker branch of the stronger department, by which the latter may be led to support the constitutional rights of the former, without being too much detached from the rights of its own department? . .

There are, moreover, two considerations particularly applicable to the federal system of America, which place that system in a very interesting point of view.

First. In a single republic, all the power surrendered by the people is submitted to the administration of a single government; and the usurpations are guarded against by a division of the government into distinct and separate departments. In the compound republic of America, the power surrendered by the people is first divided between two distinct governments, and then the portion allotted to each subdivided among distinct and separate departments. Hence a double security arises to the rights of the people. The different governments will control each other, at the same time each will be controlled by itself.

Second. It is of great importance in a republic not only to guard the society against the oppression of its rulers, but to guard one part of the society against the injustice of the other part. Different interests necessarily exist in different classes of citizens. If a majority be united by a common interest, the rights of the minority will be insecure. There are but two methods of providing against this evil: the one by creating a will in the community independent of the majority—that is, of the society itself; the other, by comprehending in the society so many separate descriptions of citizens as will render an unjust combination of a majority of the whole very improbable, if not impracticable. The first method prevails in all governments possessing an hereditary or self-appointed authority. This, at best, is but a precarious security; because a power independent of the society may as well espouse the unjust views of the major, as the rightful interests of the minor party, and may possibly be turned against both parties. The second method will be exemplified in the federal republic of the United States. Whilst all authority in it will be derived from and dependent on the society, the society itself will be broken into so many parts, interests, and classes of citizens, that the rights of individuals, or of the minority, will be in little danger from interested combinations of the majority. In a free government the security for civil rights must be the same as that for religious rights. It consists in the one case in the multiplicity of interests, and in the other in the multiplicity of sects. The degree of security in both cases will depend on the number of interests and sects; and this may be presumed to depend on the extent of country and number of people comprehended under the same government. This view of the subject must particularly recommend a proper federal system to all the sincere and considerate friends of republican government, since it shows that in exact proportion as the territory of the Union may be formed into more circumscribed Confederacies, or States, oppressive combinations of a majority will be facilitated; the best security, under the republican forms, for the rights of every class of citizens, will be diminished; and consequently the stability and independence of some member of the government, the only other security, must be proportionally increased. Justice is the end of government. It is the end of civil society. It ever has been and ever will be pursued until it be obtained, or until liberty be lost in the pursuit. In a society under the forms of which the stronger faction can readily unite and oppress the weaker, anarchy may as truly be said to reign as in a state of nature, where the weaker individual is not secured against the violence of the stronger; and as, in the latter state, even the stronger individuals are prompted, by the uncertainty of their condition, to submit to a government which may protect the weak as well as themselves; so, in the former state, will the more powerful factions or parties be gradually induced, by a like motive, to wish for a government which will protect all parties, the weaker as well as the more powerful. It can be little doubted that if the State of Rhode Island was separated from the Confederacy and left to itself, the insecurity of rights under the popular form of government within such narrow limits would be displayed by such reiterated oppressions of factious majorities that some power altogether independent of the people would soon be called for by the voice of the very factions whose misrule had proved the necessity of it. In the extended republic of the United States, and among the great variety of interests, parties, and sects which it embraces, a coalition of a majority of the whole society could seldom take place on any other principles than those of justice and the general good; whilst there being thus less danger to a minor from the will of a major party, there must be less pretext, also, to provide for the security of the former, by introducing into the government a will not dependent on the latter, or, in other words, a will independent of the society itself. It is no less certain than it is important, notwithstanding the contrary opinions which have been entertained, that the larger the society, provided it lie within a practical sphere, the more duly capable it will be of self-government. And happily for the *republican cause*, the practicable sphere may be carried to a very great extent, by a judicious modification and mixture of the *federal principle*.

SELECTED REFERENCES

Douglass Adair, 'The Authorship of the Disputed Federalist Papers,' *William and Mary Quarterly*, 3rd series vol. I, 1944, pp. 97, 235.

James T. Austin, *The Life of Elbridge Gerry*, Boston, Wells & Lilly, 1829.

James Curtis Ballagh, *The Letters of Richard Henry Lee, 1779–1794*, New York, Macmillan, 1914, vol. II.

Irving Brant, 'Settling the Authorship of the Federalist,' 67 *American Historical Review*, 1961, p. 71.

Gottfried Dietze, *The Federalist: A Classic on Federalism and Free Government*, Baltimore, Johns Hopkins Press, 1960.

The Debates in the Several State Conventions on the Adoption of the Federal Constitution, Jonathan Elliot, ed., 5 vols., Washington, D.C., 1836–45.

The Records of the Federal Convention of 1787, Max Farrand, ed., New Haven, Yale University Press, 1911, vol. III.

Essays on the Federal Constitution of the United States, P. L. Ford, ed., Brooklyn, N.Y., Historical Printing Club, 1892.

Cecelia M. Kenyon, 'Men of Little Faith: The Anti-Federalists on the Nature of Representative Government; 12 *William and Mary Quarterly*, 1955, 3rd. Ser., pp. 3–43.

Pennsylvania and the Federal Constitution, 1787–1788, J. B. McMaster and F. D. Stone, eds., Philadelphia, 1888.

Jackson Turner Main, *The Anti-Federalists: Critics of the Constitution*, Chapel Hill, University of North Carolina Press, 1961.

Luther Martin, *The Genuine Information . . .* , Philadelphia, 1788.

A. T. Mason, *The States' Rights Debate: Antifederalism and the Constitution*, Englewood Cliffs, N.J., Prentice-Hall, 1964.

———, 'Our Federal Union Reconsidered,' 55 *Political Science Quarterly*, 1950.

———, '*The Federalist*: A Split Personality,' 57 *American Historical Review*, 1952, p. 625.

S. E. Morison, 'Elbridge Gerry, Gentleman-Democrat,' *The New England Quarterly*, January 1929, vol. II, no. 1, pp. 6–33.

Kate Mason Rowland, *The Life of George Mason, 1725–1792*, 2 vols., New York, G. P. Putnam, 1892.

E. W. Spaulding, *His Excellency, George Clinton*, New York, Macmillan, 1938.

Benjamin F. Wright, 'The Federalist on the Nature of Man,' *Ethics*, January 1949, vol. LIX, no. 2, pt. 2.

VII

GETTING THE BILL OF RIGHTS ADOPTED: JEFFERSON AND MADISON

The Federalists had only partially succeeded in resolving John Locke's dilemma posed by his query, who shall judge in case of conflict between the government and the people? They had recognized the need for *judges* to ascertain when the people's representatives had broken the social compact, but had refused to provide *standards*. Smilie of Pennsylvania stated the problem:

> . . . So loosely, so inaccurately are the powers which are enumerated in this constitution defined, that it will be impossible, without a test of that kind [a bill of rights], to ascertain the limits of authority, and to declare when government has degenerated into oppression. In that event the contest will arise between the people and the rulers: 'You have exceeded the powers of your office, you have oppressed us,' will be the language of the suffering citizen. The answer of the government will be short—'We have not exceeded our power; you have no test by which you can prove it.' Hence, Sir, it will be impracticable to stop the progress of tyranny, for there will be no check but the people, and their exertions must be futile and uncertain; since it will be difficult, indeed, to communicate to them the violation that has been committed, and their proceedings will be neither systematical nor unanimous. . .

Without a bill of rights fixing the limits of national power in relation to the rights of individuals—and states—the Constitution inadequately filled the yawning hiatus in Locke's system. Antifederalists would have carried the Federalist solution to the Lockean dilemma one crucial step further. To the mechanism of judicial review, they would have tied a bill of rights.

'Without promise of a limiting Bill of Rights,' the late Justice Jackson commented in 1943, 'it is doubtful if our Constitution could have mustered enough strength to enable its ratification.' If the Justice meant that nine states would not have ratified unless a bill of rights were guaranteed, he was perhaps mistaken. Delaware, the first state to consider the Constitution, discussed it four days and ratified unanimously. In Pennsylvania, Robert Whitehill proposed that there be no ratification without a Bill of Rights, but the convention voted two to one to join the union. The New Jersey convention was in session only seven days and gave unanimous endorsement of an unamended Constitution. The Georgia delegates met on Christmas Day 1787 and approved unanimously on the second day of the new year. In Connecticut, debate lasted less than seven days. On being assured by Lieutenant Governor Oliver Wolcott that the Constitution was so well guarded that 'it seems impossible that the rights either of the States or of the people should be destroyed,' the delegates voted 128 to 40 in favor of ratification.

The Constitution first encountered powerful opposition in Massachusetts. For a while it seemed doubtful that enough votes in favor could be mustered. Samuel Adams, whose democratic convictions had highlighted the prerevolutionary years, noted signs of reaction against 'the Natural Rights of Man' developing even before the conclusion of that struggle. John Hancock, initially inclined to be negative, finally supplied the formula that won Adams's acquiescence. 'I give my assent to the Constitution,' Adams said, 'in full confidence that the amendments proposed will soon become a part of the system. 'Recommendatory'—not 'conditional'—amendments was the price exacted. This outcome created 'a blemish,' Madison admitted, but one 'least offensive' in form. The size of the minority, 187 to 168, was 'disagreeably large'; but its temper supplied 'some atonement.'

Meanwhile, Maryland and South Carolina ratified with comfortable margins. New Hampshire became the ninth to ratify by vote of 57 to 47.

The Bay State's procedure had worked so well that Madison advocated its use wherever the vote promised to be close. 'My idea is,' Virginia delegate Francis Corbin observed, 'that we should go hand in hand with Massachusetts; adopt it first, and then propose amendments. . .' Jefferson, who had earlier urged that ratification be delayed until a bill of rights could be added, surrendered. '[T]he plan of Massachusetts is far preferable,' he agreed, 'and will I hope be followed by those who are yet to decide.' 'It will be more difficult, if we lose this instrument, to recover what is good in it, than to correct what is bad after we shall have adopted it.'

Virginia posed the most crucial hurdle. Even if enough states ratified to put the Constitution into effect, no one entertained the slightest hope for its success without New York and Virginia, where the Bill of Rights issue was most hotly and narrowly contested. In Virginia, the Constitution, at first, had evoked great enthusiasm. Then the tide took 'a sudden and strong turn in the opposite direction.' Nowhere was the opposition so well organized or so well led. Patrick Henry, George Mason, and Richard Henry Lee constituted a formidable trio. It was said that Henry's purpose was to amend the Constitution and 'leave the fate of the measures to depend on all the other States conforming to the will of Virginia,' the theory being that 'other States cannot do without us. . .'

George Wythe of Virginia took a decisive step on 24 June 1788, when he admitted the Constitution's imperfections, and 'the propriety of some amendments.' Wythe then proposed 'that whatsoever amendments might be deemed necessary, should be recommended to consideration of the congress which should first assemble under the constitution. . .' Notwithstanding misgivings as to their efficacy, Madison finally acquiesced. Two days earlier—on 22 June—he had written Rufus King that rather than incur the dangers implicit in a temporary adjournment, which he thought the Henry-led Antifederalist forces were seeking, he would support a Bill of Rights. 'It has been judged prudent,' he wrote, '. . . to maintain so exemplary a fairness on our part, (and even in some points to give way to unreasonable pretensions) as will withhold every pretext for so rash a step.' Madison was adamant in his opposition to *prior* amendments or to *any* amendments which would materially alter the structure of the new government.

In the end the issue which clinched victory in Virginia did not concern 'recommendatory' versus 'conditional' amendments. It was the one Governor Randolph stated in his final dramatic appeal:

> . . . *I went to the federal Convention*, with the strongest affection for the union . . . I acted there, in full conformity with this affection: . . . *I refused to subscribe, because I had as I still have objections to the Constitution*, and wished a free inquiry into its merits; and . . . the accession of eight states reduced our *deliberations* to the single question of *union or no union*.

The decision for union stood 89 to 79.

In New York, the Antifederalists, led by Governor Clinton, were strong. Success was by no means assured. During the last days of the convention word came that New Hampshire and Virginia had ratified. It was now certain that the Constitution would be given a trial.

While news of Virginia gladdened the hearts of the Federalists, it served only to harden Antifederalist opposition. Enemies of the new Constitution now proposed conditional ratification—ratification with the right of withdrawal if amendments were not adopted. Alarmed by this move, Hamilton insisted on *recommendatory* amendments only. The Federalists would only 'concur in rational recommendations.' To stall the Antifederalist drive for prior amendments, Federalists moved for temporary adjournment. Outvoted, 40 to 22, they had no recourse but to debate the issue. The situation looked grim. Hamilton, having just received a propitious reply from Madison, repulsed the opposition by apt quotation:

> My opinion is, that a reservation of a right to withdraw, if amendments be not decided on under the form of the constitution within a certain time, is a *conditional* ratification; that it does not make New York a member of the new union, and, consequently, that she could not be received on that plan. The constitution requires an adoption *in toto* and *forever*. It has been so adopted by the other states. An adoption for a limited time would be as defective as an adoption of some of the articles only. In short, any *condition* whatever must vitiate the ratification.

In New York, as in Virginia, the vote, though close (30 to 27), was for union. Eleven states had now ratified; the new system of government would be put in operation.* None had joined with anything more than recommendations attached. Justice Jackson's inference that want of a bill of rights weighed heavily in the discussions on ratification is entirely justified.

Jefferson was elated. Previously a staunch, uncompromising advocate, he now took a more balanced view. Bills of rights were, he agreed, 'like all other human blessings alloyed with some inconveniences.' Their presence might, under some circumstances, 'cramp government.' Not all rights could ever be made secure, but it was better to protect some than none. Transcending all other considerations was his conviction that the inconveniences attending omission of a bill of rights would be 'permament, afflicting and irreparable . . . in constant progression from bad to worse.' Almost as an afterthought, it seems, he alerted Madison to a crucial oversight: 'In the arguments in favor of a declaration of rights, you omit one which has great weight with me, the legal check which it puts into the hands of the judiciary. This is a body which if rendered independent, and kept strictly to their own department merits great confidence for their learning and integrity. . . [W]hat degree of confidence would be too much for a body composed of such men as Wythe, Blair and Pendleton? On characters like these, the "civium ardor prava jubentium" would make no impression.' Jefferson shared the distrust that has always obsessed Americans, and for which the judiciary is expected to provide safeguards—'passion of the citizen ordaining perverse things.'

Under pressure from Jefferson, Madison had capitulated; he now recognized that 'political truths declared in that solemn manner' might 'acquire by degrees the character of fundamental maxims of free Government.' As these became incorporated into national sentiment, the effect might be to 'counteract the impulses of interest and passion.' He now believed that amendments, 'if pursued with a proper moderation and in a proper mode,' might serve the 'double purpose of satisfying the minds of well meaning opponents, and of providing additional guards in favour of liberty.' A bill of rights being 'anxiously desired by others,' it seemed prudent to acquiesce, especially when 'the precaution can do no injury.' A bill of rights had thus become recognized as a sensible expedient 'were it only to conciliate the opposition.'

Ratification in the key state of New York had been achieved, but only at

* Order, dates, and votes on ratification:

Delaware	7 December 1787; yeas, 30 (unanimous).
Pennsylvania . .	12 December 1787; yeas, 46; nays, 23.
New Jersey . . .	18 December 1787; yeas, 38 (unanimous).
Georgia	2 January 1788; yeas, 26 (unanimous).
Connecticut . . .	9 January 1788; yeas, 128; nays, 40.
Massachusetts . .	6 February 1788; yeas, 187; nays, 168.
Maryland . . .	28 April 1788; yeas, 63; nays, 11.
South Carolina . .	23 May 1788; yeas, 149; nays, 73.
New Hampshire .	21 June 1788; yeas, 57; nays, 47.
Virginia	26 June 1788; yeas, 89; nays, 79.
New York . . .	26 July 1788; yeas, 30; nays, 27.
North Carolina . .	21 November 1789; yeas, 194; nays, 77.
Rhode Island . .	29 May 1790; yeas, 34; nays, 32.

the price of a Circular letter to other states calling for another convention to provide the amendments demanded. George Mason considered this maneuver the last hope. Some suspected ulterior motives. The Circular letter, Washington warned, was designed 'to set everything afloat again.'

Madison had earlier speculated that 'if a second Convention should be formed, it is as little to be expected that the same spirit of compromise will prevail in it as produced an amicable result to the first.' 'It will be easy also,' he had written Jefferson, 'for those who have latent views of disunion, to carry them on under the mask of contending for alterations popular in some but inadmissible in other parts of the U. States.'

Everywhere the opposition seized the Circular letter 'as the signal for united exertions in pursuit of early amendments.' Sending a copy to Jefferson, Madison warned that 'mischiefs are apprehended.'

> The great danger in the present crisis is that if another Convention should be soon assembled, it would terminate in discord, or in alterations of the federal system which would throw back *essential* powers into the State Legislatures. The delay of a few years will assuage the jealousies which have been artificially created by designing men and will at the same time point out the faults which really call for amendment. At present the public mind is neither sufficiently cool nor sufficiently informed for so delicate an operation.

Less than two weeks later Madison wrote Jefferson again, lamenting North Carolina's failure to ratify the Constitution and 'the tendency of the circular letter from the Convention of N. York. . .' Events there had 'somewhat changed the aspect of things' and had 'given fresh hopes and exertions to those who opposed the Constitution.'

A month later Madison was still pondering the impact of New York's Circular letter. It had 'rekindled an ardor among the opponents of the federal Constitution for an *immediate* revision of it by another General Convention.' Madison noted ominous signs in Pennsylvania and Virginia of a push for a second convention. While the effect of the Circular letter 'on other States is less well known,' Madison concluded 'it will be the same every where among those who opposed the Constitution, or contended for a conditional ratification of it.'

It turned out that the Circular letter produced much more smoke than fire. While serious efforts for a second convention were made in Pennsylvania, New York, Rhode Island, Virginia, and North Carolina, they were all effectively rebutted. As Madison had predicted, the drive for a second convention would 'certainly be industriously opposed in some parts of the Union, not only by those who wish for no alterations, but by others who would prefer the other mode provided in the Constitution.'

By December 8, 1788, Madison seemed set on utilizing that 'other mode' to procure unobjectionable 'supplemental safeguards to liberty'—if only to placate the Antifederalists. Another letter, describing his strategy and the situation compelling it, went out to Jefferson. Success seemed assured. Writing

Jefferson on 12 December 1788, he reported that the results of Pennsylvania's congressional election clinched Federalist domination in the first Congress but did not alter the desirability of securing unobjectionable amendments.

> . . . There will be seven representatives of the federal party, and one a moderate antifederalist [representing Pennsylvania]. I consider this choice as ensuring a majority of friends to the federal Constitution, in both branches of the Congress; as securing the Constitution against the hazardous experiment of a Second Convention; and if prudence should be the character of the first Congress, as leading to measures which will conciliate the well-meaning of all parties, and put our affairs into an auspicious train.

Three months later, Madison reported to Jefferson that

> the disaffected party in the Senate amounts to two or three members only; and that in the other House it does not exceed a very small minority, some of which will also be restrained by the federalism of the States from which they come. Notwithstanding this character of the Body, I hope and expect that some conciliatory sacrifices will be made, in order to extinguish opposition to the system, or at least break the force of it, by detaching the deluded opponents from their designing leaders. . .

Federalist acquiescence rendered the task relatively easy—less so, however, than was perhaps anticipated. In the months preceding election of the new Congress, it was rumored that the Federalists had no intention of pressing for amendments. Not only did revision, prior to putting the new system into operation, seem untimely, but friends of the Constitution, including Madison, were concerned lest precipitous change jeopardize the main goal—energetic government. Madison himself was the object of suspicion. In his campaign for a seat in the new Congress, he was charged with abandoning the cause of religious freedom. Now modifying his previous stand as to the wisdom of including a bill of rights, he took the position that ratification, without prior attempts at alteration, made amendments safe and proper.

> Under this change of circumstances, it is my sincere opinion that the Constitution ought to be revised, and that the first Congress meeting under it ought to prepare and recommend to the States for ratification, the most satisfactory provision for all essential rights, particularly the rights of Conscience in the fullest latitude, the freedom of press, trials by jury, security against general warrants etc. . . [so as] to put the judiciary department into such a form as will render vexatious appeals impossible.

As a member of the first Congress, Madison felt 'bound in honor and duty' to fulfill this election pledge. Federalist members were inclined to delay 'till the more pressing business is dispatched.' Having learned that Antifederalists were eager to take the initiative and promote amendments damaging to national power, Madison announced that on June 8, 1789, he would place the promised amendments before the House. From the list then submitted came the first ten amendments of the Constitution, including guarantees of freedom of speech, press, religion, petition, and assembly; safeguards against unreasonable search, seizure, and warrants of arrest. Besides the blanket provision that no person be deprived of life, liberty, or property without due process of law, Madison proposed specific protections for accused persons—the right to a speedy and public trial, the right to counsel, the right to be confronted with one's accusers, and to be protected against self-incrimination and against being placed twice in jeopardy for the same offense.

In piloting the proposed amendments through Congress, Madison stressed the very point Jefferson had earlier called to his attention as a glaring omission: 'If they [the Bill of Rights] are incorporated into the constitution, independent tribunals of justice will consider themselves in a peculiar manner the guardians of those rights; they will be an impenetrable bulwark against every assumption of power in the legislative or executive; they will be naturally led to resist every encroachment upon rights expressly stipulated for in the constitution by the declaration of rights.' 'The great object in view,' according to the now converted Madison, 'is to limit the power of government, by excepting out of the grant of power those cases in which the Government ought not to act, or to act only in a particular mode.'

Specific safeguards against government enroachment on individual rights, though of first importance, was not enough. Antifederalists had conjured up the image of the central government as a colossus, destined to swallow up or destroy the defenseless states. To quiet these fears, Madison included among the amendments submitted on 8 June the following: 'The powers not delegated by this constitution, nor prohibited by it to the States, are reserved to the States respectively. . .' In explanation he said:

> I find from looking into the amendments proposed by the State conventions, that several are particularly anxious that it should be declared in the Constitution, that the powers not therein delegated should be reserved to the several States. Perhaps words which may define this more precisely than the whole of the instrument now does, may be considered as superfluous. I admit they may be deemed unnecessary; but there can be no harm in making such a declaration, if gentlemen will allow that the fact is as stated. I am sure I understand it so, and do therefore propose it. . .

On three occasions it was proposed that the word 'expressly' be inserted before 'delegated.' Madison objected 'because it was impossible to confine a Government to the exercise of express powers; there must necessarily be admitted powers by implication, unless the constitution descended to recount every minutia.' He remembered the word 'expressly' had been moved in the convention of Virginia, by the opponents to ratification, and, after full and fair discussion, was given up by them, and the system allowed to retain its present form. Roger Sherman, concurring, observed that 'corporate bodies are supposed to possess all powers incident to a corporate capacity, without being absolutely expressed.' Congressman Tucker, joined by Gerry, pressed for insertion of the word 'expressly,' but the proposal was defeated 17 to 32.

Once again men of states' rights persuasion were defeated in their attempt to draw a precise line limiting the national government with respect to an area considered free from federal control.

The unavailing struggle to put teeth into the Tenth Amendment underscores the conclusion that for many Antifederalists *states'* rights weighed more heavily than their concern for *personal* rights.

Spurring the Antifederalist campaign was the unshakeable conviction that the proposed Constitution would enthrone a consolidated government, thereby rendering *state* protection of individual rights insecure. It seemed not unreasonable, as Spencer and Adams contended, that if state sovereignty in the new system could be adequately safeguarded, this would obviate, in effect, the need for a bill of rights. Thus, Adams had maintained that an amendment reserving to the states all power not expressly delegated to the new national government would be 'a summary of a bill of rights. . .' It would remove 'a doubt which many have entertained respecting the matter,' and would give 'assurance that if any law made by the federal government shall be extended beyond the power granted by the proposed constitution, and inconsistent with the constitution of this state, it will be an error, and adjudged by the courts of law to be void. . .' Spencer, in North Carolina, had admitted, 'It might not be so necessary to have a bill of rights in the government of the United States, if such means had not been made use of, as endanger a consolidation of all the states. . .'

Antifederalist motives are hard to disentangle. Persistent attempts to secure *states'* rights seem consistent with their expressed concern for *individual* rights—given the logical connection between state power in the federal system and continued state protection of the rights of their citizens. Subsequent behavior, however, renders any desire to give them the benefit of the doubt at best gratuitous. The conclusion that states' rights—regardless of individual rights—was the primary concern becomes inescapable. Yates and Lansing, in their letter to Governor Clinton, strongly opposed the new 'consolidated system'—however guarded it might be 'by declarations of rights, or cautionary provisions. . .' As the struggle for a bill of rights reached its consummation in the first Congress, the word 'amendments' came to mean different things to Federalists and Antifederalists. '"Amendments" to Madison meant a bill of rights,' Robert Rutland observes. 'To Clinton and Henry the word "amendments" also connoted a weakening of the federal system in favor of the states on such all-important questions as direct taxation and the treaty-making power.' Madison had agreed to a Bill of Rights to protect *individual* liberties. He firmly opposed any amendments which might sap the energy of the new government.

Antifederalist response to the *kind* of amendments Madison sought—and finally procured—reveals the values they wished most to protect. William Grayson, writing Patrick Henry in June 1789, objected to Madison's proposed amendments as greatly overemphasizing the protection of personal rights at the expense of states' rights. 'Some gentlemen here [in the first Congress] from motives of policy, have it in contemplation to effect amendments which shall effect personal liberty alone, leaving the great points of the judiciary, direct taxation, &c., to stand as they are . . . after this I presume many of the most sanguine expect to go on coolly in sapping the independence of the state legislatures. . .' Pierce Butler had the same low regard for the Bill of Rights. Instead of 'substantial amendments,' Madison had proposed a 'few *milk-and-water* amendments . . . such as liberty of conscience, a free press, and one or two general things already well secured.' 'I suppose it was done to keep his promise with his constituents, to move for alterations,' Butler speculated, 'but if I am not greatly mistaken, he is not hearty in the cause of amendments.'

As Madison's amendments emerged from the first Congress, the reaction among Antifederalists was one of disappointment. To Grayson the new amendments were 'so multilated and gutted that in fact they are good for nothing. . .' Patrick Henry, according to David Stuart, thought 'the single amendment proposed in our Convention [Virginia ratifying convention], respecting direct taxes, worth all the rest.' Not even Jefferson was entirely satisfied, but his concern had to do with minutia, not fundamentals.

The most bitter criticism came from Richard Henry Lee. Writing his brother, Lee lamented the 'much mutilated and enfeebled' amendments. 'It is too much the fashion now to look at the rights of the People, as a miser inspects a Security, to find a flaw.' Expanding on this theme, Lee told Patrick Henry the next day how much he deplored 'the idea of subsequent amendments,' a procedure 'little better than putting oneself to death first, in expectation that the doctor, who wished our destruction, would afterwards restore us to life.' Personal rights had been secured, but the 'great points'—such as 'the unlimited rights of taxation, and standing armies, remain as they were.'

> The most essential danger from the present system arises, in my opinion, from its tendency to a consolidated government, instead of a union of Confederated States. . . [T]herefore it becomes the friends of liberty to guard with perfect vigilance every right that belongs to the states, and to protest against every invasion of them, taking care always to procure as many protesting states as possible; this kind of vigilance will create caution, and establish such a mode of conduct as will create a system of precedent that will prevent a consolidative effect from taking place by slow but sure degrees. A sufficient number of legislatures cannot be got at present to agree in demanding a convention, but I shall be very much mistaken indeed, if ere long a great sufficiency will not concur in this measure. . . A careless reader would be apt to suppose that the amendments desired by the states had been graciously granted, but when the thing done is compared with that desired, nothing can be more unlike. Some valuable rights are indeed declared, but the power to violate them to all intents and purposes remains unchanged.

Lee and Grayson, the two senators from Virginia to the first Congress, summed up their opposition to the new amendments in reports to the Governor of Virginia and to the Speaker of the Virginia House of Representatives. They had hoped to be able to transmit 'effectual Amendments' for ratification, 'and it is with grief that we now send forward propositions inadequate to the purpose of real and substantial Amendments, and so far short of the wishes of our Country. . .' 'It is impossible for us not to see the necessary tendency to consolidated empire in the natural operation of the Constitution, if not further amended than as now proposed,' they wrote the Speaker of the House. 'Such Amendments therefore as may secure against the annihilation of the state governments we devoutly wish to see adopted.' The letter closed with the hope that an aroused demand by the states for a second convention might achieve that purpose.

Jefferson thought he had divined what lay behind much of the Antifederalist drive. Clinton and Henry, among others, were 'moving heaven and earth to have a new Convention to make capital changes,' he wrote John Paul Jones in the spring of 1789. 'But they will not succeed. There has been just opposition enough to produce probably further safeguards to liberty without touching the energy of the government. . .' And that is precisely the way it turned out.

The campaign for a bill of rights had begun as a seemingly partisan move, a strategic maneuver, some believed, to defeat ratification. In the end, the goals sought were generally accepted by all. '[S]ecurity for liberty,' through a bill of rights, was demanded 'by the general voice of America.' Fundamental maxims of a free society gained no greater moral sanctity by incorporation in our basic law. Yet a signficant gain had been made. Rights formerly natural became civil. Individuals could thereafter look to courts for their protection; courts—thanks to the Antifederalists—could look to the Constitution for standards. The Constitution had been infused with '*the means of its own preservation*'; the likelihood of violent revolution had been minimized.

1. *A bill of rights is what the people are entitled to against every government on earth*

THOMAS JEFFERSON to James Madison, 20 December 1787 *

. . . I like much the general idea of framing a government which should go on of itself peaceably, without needing continual recurrence to the state legislatures. I like the organization of the government into Legislative, Judiciary and Executive. I like the power given the Legislature to levy taxes; and for that reason solely approve of the greater house being chosen by the people directly. For tho' I think a house chosen by them will be, very illy qualified to legislate for the Union, for foreign nations &c. yet this evil does not weigh against the good of preserving inviolate the fundamental principle that the people are not to be taxed but by representatives chosen immediately by themselves. I am captivated by the compromise of the opposite claims of the great and little states, of the latter to equal, and the former to proportional influence. I am

* *The Papers of Thomas Jefferson*, Julian P. Boyd, ed., Princeton, Princeton University Press, 1955, vol. XII, pp. 439–42.

much pleased too with the substitution of the method of voting by persons, instead of that of voting by states: and I like the negative given to the Executive with a third of either house, though I should have liked it better had the Judiciary been associated for that purpose, or invested with a similar and separate power. There are other good things of less moment. I will now add what I do not like. First the omission of a bill of rights providing clearly and without the aid of sophisms for freedom of religion, freedom of the press, protection against standing armies, restriction against monopolies, the eternal and unremitting force of the habeas corpus laws, and trials by jury in all matters of fact triable by the laws of the land and not by the law of Nations. To say, as Mr. Wilson does that a bill of rights was not necessary because all is reserved in the case of the general government which is not given, while in the particular ones all is given which is not reserved might do for the Audience to whom it was addressed, but is surely gratis dictum, opposed by strong inferences from the body of the instrument, as well as from the omission of the clause of our present confederation which had declared that in express terms. It was a hard conclusion to say because there has been no uniformity among the states as to the cases triable by jury, because some have been so incautious as to abandon this mode of trial, therefore the more prudent states shall be reduced to the same level of calamity. It would have been much more just and wise to have concluded the other way that as most of the states had judiciously preserved this palladium, those who had wandered should be brought back to it, and to have established general right instead of general wrong. Let me add that a bill of rights is what the people are entitled to against every government on earth, general or particular, and what no just government should refuse, or rest on inference. The second feature I dislike, and greatly dislike, is the abandonment in every instance of the necessity of rotation in office, and most particularly in the case of the President. Experience concurs with reason in concluding that the first magistrate will always be reelected if the constitution permits it. He is then an officer for life. . . If once elected, and at a second or third election outvoted by one or two votes, he will pretend false votes, foul play, hold possession of the reins of government, be supported by the states voting for him, especially if they are the central ones lying in a compact body themselves and separating their opponents. . . It may be said that if elections are to be attended with these disorders, the seldomer they are renewed the better. But experience shews that the only way to prevent disorder is to render them uninteresting by frequent changes. An incapacity to be elected a second time would have been the only effectual preventative. The power of removing him every fourth year by the vote of the people is a power which will not be exercised. The king of Poland is removeable every day by the Diet, yet he is never removed. . . I do not pretend to decide what would be the best method of procuring the establishment of the manifold good things in this constitution, and of getting rid of the bad. Whether by adopting it in hopes of future amendment, or, after it has been duly weighed and canvassed by the people, after seeing the parts they generally dislike, and those they generally approve, to say to them 'We see now what you wish. Send together your deputies again, let them frame a constitution for you omitting what you have condemned, and establishing the powers you approve. Even these will be a great addition to the energy of your government.'—At all events I hope you will not be discouraged from other trials, if the present one should fail of it's full effect.—I have thus told you freely what I like and dislike: merely as a matter of curiosity for I know your own judgment has been formed on all these points after having heard every thing which could be urged on them. I own I am not a friend to a very energetic government. It is always oppressive. The late rebellion in Massachusetts has given more alarm than I think it should have done. Calculate that one rebellion in 13 states in the course of 11 years, is but one for each state in a century and a half. No country should be so long without one. Nor will any degree of power in the hands of government prevent insurrections. France with all it's despotism, and two or three hundred thousand men always in arms has had three insurrections in the three years I have been here in every one of which greater numbers were engaged than in Massachusetts and a great deal more blood was spilt. . . After all, it is my principle that the will of the Majority should always prevail. If they approve the proposed Convention in all it's parts, I shall concur in it cheerfully, in hopes that they will amend it whenever they shall find it works wrong. . .

2. *I have never found the omission of a bill of rights a material defect*

James Madison to Thomas Jefferson, 17 October 1788 *

. . . My own opinion has always been in favor of a bill of rights, provided it be so framed as not to imply powers not meant to be included in the enumeration. At the same time I have never thought the omission a material defect, nor been anxious to supply it even by *subsequent* amendment, for any other reason than that it is anxiously desired by others. I have favored it because I supposed it might be of use, and if properly executed could not be of disservice. I have not viewed it in an important light—1. because I conceive that in a certain degree, though not in the extent argued by Mr. Wilson, the rights in question are reserved by the manner in which the federal powers are granted. 2. because there is great reason to fear that a positive declaration of some of the most essential rights could not be obtained in the requisite latitude. I am sure that the rights of conscience in particular, if submitted to public definition would be narrowed much more than they are likely ever to be by an assumed power. One of the objections in New England was that the Constitution by prohibiting religious tests, opened a door for Jews Turks & infidels. 3. because the limited powers of the federal Government and the jealousy of the subordinate Governments, afford a security which has not existed in the case of the State Governments, and exists in no other. 4. because experience proves the inefficacy of a bill of rights on those occasions when its controul is most needed. Repeated violations of these parchment barriers have been committed by over-

* *The Papers of Thomas Jefferson*, Julian P. Boyd, ed., vol. xiv, pp. 18–21.

bearing majorities in every State. In Virginia I have seen the bill of rights violated in every instance where it has been opposed to a popular current. Notwithstanding the explicit provision contained in that instrument for the rights of Conscience, it is well known that a religious establishment wd have taken place in that State, if the Legislative majority had found as they expected, a majority of the people in favor of the measure; and I am persuaded that if a majority of the people were now of one sect, the measure would still take place and on narrower ground than was then proposed, notwithstanding the additional obstacle which the law has since created. Wherever the real power in a Government lies, there is the danger of oppression. In our Government, the real power lies in the majority of the Community, and the invasion of private rights is *chiefly* to be apprehended, not from acts of Government contrary to the sense of its constituents, but from acts in which the Government is the mere instrument of the major number of the Constituents. This is a truth of great importance, but not yet sufficiently attended to; and is probably more strongly impressed on my mind by facts, and reflections suggested by them, than on yours which has contemplated abuses of power issuing from a very different quarter. Wherever there is an interest and power to do wrong, wrong will generally be done, and not less readily by a powerful & interested party than by a powerful and interested prince. The difference so far as it relates to the superiority of republics over monarchies, lies in the less degree of probability that interest may prompt more abuses of power in the former than in the latter; and in the security in the former agst an oppression of more than the smaller part of the Society, whereas in the former [latter] it may be extended in a manner to the whole. The difference so far as it relates to the point in question —the efficacy of a bill of rights in controuling abuses of power—lies in this: that in a monarchy the latent force of the nation is superior to that of the Sovereign, and a solemn charter of popular rights must have a great effect, as a standard for trying the validity of public acts, and a signal for rousing & uniting the superior force of the community; whereas in a popular Government, the political and physical power may be considered as vested in the same hands, that it is a majority of the people, and, consequently the tyrannical will of the Sovereign is not [to] be controuled by the dread of an appeal to any other force within the community. What use then it may be asked can a bill of rights serve in popular Governments? I answer the two following which, though less essential than in other Governments, sufficiently recommend the precaution: 1. The political truths declared in that solemn manner acquire by degrees the character of fundamental maxims of free Governments, and as they become incorporated with the national sentiment, counteract the impulses of interest and passion. 2. Altho, it be generally true as above stated that the danger of oppression lies in the interested majorities of the people rather than in usurped acts of the Government, yet there may be occasions on which the evil may spring from the latter source; and on such, a bill of rights will be a good ground for an appeal to the sense of the community. Perhaps too there may be a certain degree of danger, that a succession of artful and ambitious rulers may be gradual & well timed advances, finally erect an independent Government on the subversion of liberty. Should this danger exist at all, it is prudent to guard ag[st] it, especially when the precaution can do no injury. At the same time I must own that I see no tendency in our Governments to danger on that side. It has been remarked that there is a tendency in all Governments to an augmentation of power at the expence of liberty. But the remark as usually understood does not appear to me well founded. Power when it has attained a certain degree of energy and independence goes on generally to further degrees. But when below that degree, the direct tendency is to further degrees of relaxation, until the abuses of liberty beget a sudden transition to an undue degree of power. With this explanation the remark may be true; and in the latter sense only is it, in my opinion applicable to the Governments in America. It is a melancholy reflection that liberty should be equally exposed to danger whether the Government have too much or too little power, and that the line which divides these extremes should be so inaccurately defined by experience.

Supposing a bill of rights to be proper the articles which ought to compose it, admit of much discussion. I am inclined to think that *absolute* restrictions in cases that are doubtful, or where emergencies may overrule them, ought to be avoided. The restrictions however strongly marked on paper will never be regarded when opposed to the decided sense of the public, and after repeated violations in extraordinary cases they will lose even their ordinary efficacy. Should a Rebellion or insurrection alarm the people as well as the Government, and a suspension of the Hab. Corp. be dictated by the alarm, no written prohibitions on earth would prevent the measure. Should an army in time of peace be gradually established in our neighborhood by Brit. or Spain, declarations on paper would have as little effect in preventing a standing force for the public safety. The best security ag[st] these evils is to remove the pretext for them. With regard to Monopolies, they are justly classed among the greatest nuisances in Government. But is it clear that as encouragements to literary works and ingenious discoveries, they are not too valuable to be wholly renounced? Would it not suffice to reserve in all cases a right to the public to abolish the privilege at a price to be specified in the grant of it? Is there not also infinitely less danger of this abuse in our Governments than in most others? Monopolies are sacrifices of the many to the few. Where the power is in the few it is natural for them to sacrifice the many to their own partialities and corruptions. Where the power as with us is in the many not in the few the danger cannot be very great that the few will be thus favored. It is much more to be dreaded that the few will be unnecessarily sacrificed to the many. . .

3. *You omit an argument which has great weight with me*

THOMAS JEFFERSON to James Madison, 15 March 1789 *

. . . Your thoughts on the subject of the Declaration of rights in the letter of Oct. 17, I have weighed with great satisfaction. Some of them had not occurred to me before, but were acknoleged [sic] just in the moment they were presented

* *The Papers of Thomas Jefferson*, Julian P. Boyd, ed., vol. XIV, pp. 659–61.

to my mind. In the arguments in favor of a declaration of rights, you omit one which has great weight with me, the legal check which it puts into the hands of the judiciary. This is a body, which if rendered independent, and kept strictly to their own department merits great confidence for their learning and integrity. In fact, what degree of confidence would be too much for a body composed of such men as Wythe, Blair, and Pendleton? On characters like these the 'civium ardor prava jubentium' would make no impression. I am happy to find that on the whole you are a friend to this amendment. The Declaration of rights is like all other human blessings alloyed with some inconveniences, and not accomplishing fully it's object. But the good in this instance vastly overweighs the evil. I cannot refrain from making short answers to the objections which your letter states to have been raised. 1. That the rights in question are reserved by the manner in which the federal powers are granted. Answer. A constitutive act may certainly be so formed as to need no declaration of rights. The act itself has the force of a declaration as far as it goes: and if it goes to all material points nothing more is wanting. In the draught of a constitution which I had once a thought of proposing in Virginia, and printed afterwards, I endeavored to reach all the great objects of public liberty, and did not mean to add a declaration of rights. Probably the object was imperfectly executed: but the deficiencies would have been supplied by others in the course of discussion. But, in a constitutive act which leaves some precious articles unnoticed, and raises implications against others, a declaration of rights becomes necessary by way of supplement. This is the case of our new federal constitution. This instrument forms us into one state as to certain objects, and gives us a legislative and executive body for these objects. It should therefore guard us against their abuses of power within the field [sic] submitted to them. 2. A positive declaration of some essential rights could not be obtained in the requisite latitude. Answer. Half a loaf is better than no bread. If we cannot secure all our rights, let us secure what we can. 3. The limited powers of the federal government and jealousy of the subordinate governments afford a security which exists in no other instance. Answer. The first member of this seems resolvable into the 1st. objection before stated. The jealousy of the subordinate governments is a precious reliance. But observe that those governments are only agents. They must have principles furnished them whereon to found their opposition. The declaration of rights will be the text whereby they will try all the acts of the federal government. In this view it is necessary to the federal government also: as by the same text they may try the opposition of the subordinate governments. 4. Experience proves the inefficacy of a bill of rights. True. But tho it is not absolutely efficacious under all circumstances, it is of great potency always, and rarely inefficacious. A brace the more will often keep up the building which would have fallen with that brace the less. There is a remarkable difference between the characters of the inconveniences which attend a Declaration of rights, and those which attend the want of it. The inconveniences of the Declaration are that it may cramp government in it's useful exertions. But the evil of this is shortlived, moderate, and reparable. The inconveniences of the want of a Declaration are permanent, afflicting and irreparable: they are in constant progression from bad to worse.

The executive in our governments is not the sole, it is scarcely the principal object of my jealousy. The tyranny of the legislatures is the most formidable dread at present, and will be for long years. That of the executive will come in it's turn, but it will be at a remote period. I know there are some among us who would now establish a monarchy. But they are inconsiderable in number and weight of character. The rising race are all republicans. We were educated in royalism: no wonder if some of us retain that idolatry still. Our young people are educated in republicanism. An apostacy from that to royalism is unprecedented and impossible. I am much pleased with the prospect that a declaration of rights will be added: and hope it will be done in that way which will not endanger the whole frame of the government, or any essential part of it. . .

4. *We act the part of wise and liberal men to make these alterations*

JAMES MADISON, Speech Placing the Proposed Bill of Rights Amendments before the House of Representatives, 8 June 1789 *

Mr. Madison rose, and reminded the House that this was the day that he had heretofore named for bringing forward amendments to the constitution, as contemplated in the fifth article of the constitution. . . As I considered myself bound in honor and in duty to do what I have done on this subject, I shall proceed to bring the amendments before you as soon as possible, and advocate them until they shall be finally adopted or rejected by a constitutional majority of this House. With a view of drawing your attention to this important object, I shall move that this House do now resolve itself into a Commitee of the whole on the state of the Union; by which an opportunity will be given, to bring forward some propositions, which I have strong hopes will meet with the unanimous approbation of this House, after the fullest discussion and most serious regard. I therefore move you, that the House now go into a committee on this business.

Mr. Smith was not inclined to interrupt the measures which the public were so anxiously expecting, by going into a Committee of the whole at this time. . . For, said he, it must appear extremely impolitic to go into the consideration of amending the Government, before it is organized, before it has begun to operate. . .

Mr. Jackson.—I am of opinion we ought not to be in a hurry with respect to altering the constitution. . . What experience have we had of the good or bad qualities of this constitution? Can any gentleman affirm to me one proposition that is a certain and absolute amendment? I deny that he can. Our constitution, sir, is like a vessel just launched, and lying at the wharf; she is untried, you can hardly discover any one of her properties. It is not known how she will answer her helm, or lay her course; whether she will bear with safety the precious freight to be deposited in her hold. . .

* *Annals U.S. Congress*, 1st Congress (1789–91), vol. 1, pp. 440–60.

When the propriety of making amendments shall be obvious from experience, I trust there will be virtue enough in my country to make them. . . .

Mr. Madison.—. . . But if we continue to postpone from time to time, and refuse to let the subject come into view, it may occasion suspicions, which, though not well founded, may tend to inflame or prejudice the public mind against our decisions. They may think we are not sincere in our desire to incorporate such amendments in the constitution as will secure those rights, which they consider as not sufficiently guarded. The applications for amendments come from a very respectable number of our constituents, and it is certainly proper for Congress to consider the subject, in order to quiet that anxiety which prevails in the public mind. Indeed, I think it would have been of advantage to the Government, if it had been practicable to have made some propositions for amendments the first business we entered upon; it would have stifled the voice of complaint, and made friends of many who doubted the merits of the constitution. Our future measures would then have been more generally agreeably supported; but the justifiable anxiety to put the Government into operation prevented that; it therefore remains for us to take it up as soon as possible. . . I only wish to introduce the great work, and, as I said before, I do not expect it will be decided immediately; but if some step is taken in the business, it will give reason to believe that we may come to a final result. This will inspire a reasonable hope in the advocates for amendments, that full justice will be done to the important subject; and I have reason to believe their expectation will not be defeated. . .

I will state my reasons why I think it proper to propose amendments, and state the amendments themselves, so far as I think they ought to be proposed. . . It appears to me that this House is bound by every motive of prudence, not to let the first session pass over without proposing to the State Legislatures some things to be incorporated into the constitution, that will render it as acceptable to the whole people of the United States, as it has been found acceptable to a majority of them. I wish, among other reasons why something should be done, that those who have been friendly to the adoption of this constitution may have the opportunity of proving to those who were opposed to it that they were as sincerely devoted to liberty and a Republican Government, as those who charged them with wishing the adoption of this constitution in order to lay the foundation of an aristocracy or despotism. It will be a desirable thing to extinguish from the bosom of every member of the community, any apprehensions that there are those among his countrymen who wish to deprive them of the liberty for which they valiantly fought and honorably bled. And if there are amendments desired of such a nature as will not injure the constitution, and they can be ingrafted so as to give satisfaction to the doubting part of our fellow-citizens, the friends of the Federal Government will evince that spirit of deference and concession for which they have hitherto been distinguished.

It cannot be a secret to the gentlemen in this House, that, notwithstanding the ratification of this system of Government by eleven of the thirteen United States, in some cases unanimously, in others by large majorities; yet still there is a great number of our constituents who are dissatisfied with it; among whom are many respectable for their talents and patriotism, and respectable for the jealousy they have for their liberty, which, though mistaken in its object, is laudable in its motive. There is a great body of the people falling under this description, who at present feel much inclined to join their support to the cause of Federalism, if they were satisfied on this one point. We ought not to disregard their inclination, but, on principles of amity and moderation, conform to their wishes, and expressly declare the great rights of mankind secured under this constitution. The acquiescence which our fellow-citizens show under the Government, calls upon us for a like return of moderation. But perhaps there is a stronger motive than this for our going into a consideration of the subject. It is to provide those securities for liberty which are required by a part of the community; I allude in a particular manner to those two States [Rhode Island and North Carolina] that have not thought fit to throw themselves into the bosom of the Confederacy. It is a desirable thing, on our part as well as theirs, that a re-union should take place as soon as possible. . .

But I will candidly acknowledge, that, over and above all these considerations, I do conceive that the constitution may be amended; that is to say, if all power is subject to abuse, that then it is possible the abuse of the powers of the General Government may be guarded against in a more secure manner than is now done, while no one advantage arising from the exercise of that power shall be damaged or endangered by it. We have in this way something to gain, and, if we proceed with caution, nothing to lose. And in this case it is necessary to proceed with caution; for while we feel all these inducements to go into a revisal of the constitution, we must feel for the constitution itself, and make that revisal a moderate one. I should be unwilling to see a door opened for a reconsideration of the whole structure of the Government—for a re-consideration of the principles and the substance of the powers given; because I doubt, if such a door were opened, we should be very likely to stop at that point which would be safe to the Government itself. But I do wish to see a door opened to consider, so far as to incorporate those provisions for the security of rights, against which I believe no serious objection has been made by any class of our constituents: such as would be likely to meet with the concurrence of two-thirds of both Houses, and the approbation of three-fourths of the State Legislatures. I will not propose a single alteration which I do not wish to see take place, as intrinsically proper in itself, or proper because it is wished for by a respectable number of my fellow-citizens; and therefore I shall not propose a single alteration but is likely to meet the concurrence required by the constitution. There have been objections of various kinds made against the constitution. Some were levelled against its structure because the President was without a council; because the Senate, which is a legislative body, had judicial powers in trials on impeachments; and because the powers of that body were compounded in other respects, in a manner that did not correspond with a particular theory; because it grants more power than is supposed to be necessary for every good purpose, and controls the ordinary powers of the State Governments. I know some respectable characters who opposed this Government on these grounds; but I believe that the great mass of the people who opposed it, disliked it because it did not contain effectual provisions against encroachments on particular rights, and those safeguards which they have been long accustomed to have interposed between them and the magistrate who exercises the sovereign power; nor ought we to consider them safe, while a great number of our fellow-citizens think these securities necessary.

It is a fortunate thing that the objection to the Government has been made on the ground I stated; because it will be practicable, on that ground, to obviate the objection, so far as to satisfy the public mind that their liberties will be perpetual, and this without endangering any part of the constitution, which is considered as essential to the existence of the Government by those who promoted its adoption.

[Madison then proceeded to list the amendments.]

The first of these amendments relates to what may be called a bill of rights. I will own that I never considered this provision so essential to the federal constitution, as to make it improper to ratify it, until such an amendment was added; at the same time, I always conceived, that in a certain form, and to a certain extent, such a provision was neither improper nor altogether useless. . .

It has been said, that it is unnecessary to load the constitution with this provision, because it was not found effectual in the constitution of the particular States. It is true, there are a few particular States in which some of the most valuable articles have not, at one time or other, been violated; but it does not follow but they may have, to a certain degree, a salutary effect against the abuse of power. If they are incorporated into the constitution, independent tribunals of justice will consider themselves in a peculiar manner the guardians of those rights; they will be an impenetrable bulwark against every assumption of power in the legislative or executive; they will be naturally led to resist every encroachment upon rights expressly stipulated for in the constitution by the declaration of rights. Besides this security, there is a great probability that such a declaration in the federal system would be enforced; because the State Legislatures will jealously and closely watch the operations of this Government, and be able to resist with more effect every assumption of power, than any other power on earth can do; and the greatest opponents to a Federal Government admit the State Legislatures to be sure guardians of the people's liberty. I conclude, from this view of the subject, that it will be proper in itself, and highly politic, for the tranquility of the public mind, and the stability of the Government, that we should offer something, in the form I have proposed, to be incorporated in the system of Government, as a declaration of the rights of the people. . .

I wish also, in revising the constitution, we may throw into that section, which interdicts the abuse of certain powers in the State Legislatures, some other provisions of equal, if not greater importance than those already made. The words, 'No State shall pass any bill of attainder, *ex post facto* law,' &c. were wise and proper restrictions in the constitution. I think there is more danger of those powers being abused by the State Governments than by the Government of the United States. The same may be said of other powers which they possess, if not controlled by the general principle, that laws are unconstituional which infringe the rights of the community. I should therefore wish to extend this interdiction, and add that no State shall violate the equal right of conscience, freedom of the press, or trial by jury in criminal cases; because it is proper that every Government should be disarmed of powers which trench upon those particular rights. I know, in some of the State constitutions, the power of the Government is controlled by such a declaration; but others are not. I cannot see any reason against obtaining even a double security on those points; and nothing can give a more sincere proof of the attachment of those who opposed this constitution to these great and important rights, than to see them join in obtaining the security I have now proposed; because it must be admitted, on all hands, that the State Governments are as liable to attack these invaluable privileges as the General Government is, and therefore ought to be as cautiously guarded against. . .

I find, from looking into the amendments proposed by the State conventions, that several are particularly anxious that it should be declared in the constitution, that the powers not therein delegated should be reserved to the several States. Perhaps words which may define this more precisely than the whole of the instrument now does, may be considered as superfluous. I admit they may be deemed unnecessary; but there can be no harm in making such a declaration, if gentlemen will allow that the fact is as stated. I am sure I understand it so, and do therefore propose it.

There are the points on which I wish to see a revision of the constitution take place. How far they will accord with the sense of this body, I cannot take upon me absolutely to determine; but I believe every gentleman will readily admit that nothing is in contemplation, so far as I have mentioned, that can endanger the beauty of the Government in any one important feature, even in the eyes of its most sanguine admirers. I have proposed nothing that does not appear to me as proper in itself, or eligible as patronized by a respectable number of our fellow-citizens; and if we can make the constitution better in the opinion of those who are opposed to it, without weakening its frame, or abridging its usefulness, in the judgment of those who are attached to it, we act the part of wise and liberal men to make such alterations as shall produce that effect.

SELECTED REFERENCES

The Great Rights, Edmond Cahn, ed., New York, Macmillan, 1963.

Zechariah Chafee, *How Human Rights Got into the Constitution*, Boston, Boston University Press, 1952.

Adrienne Koch, *Jefferson and Madison: the Great Collaboration*, New York, Knopf, 1950.

Milton R. Konvitz, *A Century of Civil Rights*, New York, Columbia University Press, 1961.

Leonard W. Levy, *Legacy of Suppression: Freedom of Speech and Press in Early American History*, Cambridge, Harvard University Press, 1960.

Jackson Turner Main, *The Anti-Federalists: Critics of the Constitution*, Chapel Hill, University of North Carolina Press, 1961.

A. T. Mason, *The States' Rights Debate*, Englewood Cliffs, N.J., Prentice-Hall, 1964.

Robert Rutland, *The Birth of the Bill of Rights*, Chapel Hill, University of North Carolina Press, 1955.

Edward P. Smith, 'The Movement Towards a Second Constitutional Convention in 1788,' J. Franklin Jameson, ed., *Essays in the Constitutional History of the United States in the Formative Period, 1775–1789*, Boston, Houghton, Mifflin, 1889, pp. 46–115.

VIII

ESTABLISHING NATIONAL POWER: HAMILTON AND MARSHALL

Even before successful termination of the Revolution the states were faced with a dilemma. Should the confederacy of states, individually strong, collectively weak, be patched up and confirmed? Or should an attempt be made to set in motion a counter tendency, making for centralized, coercive power, leading, as Hamilton said, to a Great Republic, 'tranquil and prosperous at home and respectable abroad'? In the Convention, Hamilton had dramatized the issue, telling the delegates that they were called upon to decide the fate of republican government. If they did not give to that form 'due stability and wisdom it would be disgraced and lost to mankind forever.' When he threw down this caveat, months of debating and altercation, maneuvers and strategems, were still ahead. 'The Constitution,' as John Quincy Adams truly said, had to be 'extorted from the grinding necessity of a reluctant nation.'

It was one thing to lay the foundations of government in a constitutional text, to blueprint the machinery of rulership; it was something else to supply the motive power of governing, to strike out a bold new course, break away from the bias and prejudice of old ways and old institutions. A constitution is a lifeless thing, a paper contrivance, at most a license to begin governing. However meritorious the document of 1787 as it came from the framers, the new political system might be good or bad depending on the character of the men empowered to launch it. With energetic leaders of insight, daring, and imagination, the experiment might succeed. In the hands of weak men, blind to what the nation might become, the Constitution, prepared with so much care and accepted with reservation, might well have failed. 'Governments, like clocks,' William Penn once observed, 'go from the motion men give them.'

The Constitution, as framed, fell far short of Hamilton's ideal of complete national sovereignty, states reduced to the status of corporations. Nevertheless, he gave it wholehearted support on the common-sense ground that it was not possible to deliberate between anarchy and the *possibility* of good government. Washington had his doubts, too. As he forsook his beloved Mt. Vernon and took up the reins of government under the new constitution, he confessed feelings 'not unlike those of a culprit who is going to the place of his execution.'

Hamilton, at thirty-four, appointed by President Washington in 1789 as

Secretary of the Treasury, knew that to succeed as Finance Minister and as directing head of the new administration, he would have to battle at every step the predominant interests and prejudices of the times—agrarianism in economics and jealous localism in politics. He would have to inaugurate his own policy at once and entrench it in a fortress of precedent that only revolution could dislodge. This was a large undertaking, but Hamilton's adventurous qualities heightened the chance of success. A foreigner by birth, uninhibited by state or local loyalties, he was able to consider the burning issues of the day in a spirit of cool detachment unequaled among his contemporaries.

The Antifederalists, stunned by defeat in the state ratifying conventions, sought to rally and get their bearings. Hamilton seized the opportunity to translate paper grants of power into a workable program of government. The day after the first Congress assembled, the Secretary of the Treasury announced that he was ready to submit a full report on public credit. The national government must assume all debts, state and federal, take full responsibility toward various creditors, and pay all interest in arrears.

The political objective underlying his proposal had been in Hamilton's mind since 1780. Now, as then, the ultimate purpose was to bind the moneyed interests firmly to the union cause, to induce them to look to the central government rather than to the states for security of their capital.

To put his policies into effect, Hamilton recommended a sinking fund and the establishment of a national bank. Congressional authorization of the bank, 8 February 1791, violated Jefferson's dogma of *laisser-faire* and ran head on into constitutional objections. In its support Hamilton espoused the famous doctrine of implied powers, elaborated in the paper here reprinted. Jefferson contended that Hamilton's proposal did not come within Congress's powers, express or implied. 'To take a single step beyond the boundaries thus especially drawn around the powers of Congress,' Jefferson argued 'is to take possession of a boundless field of power, no longer susceptible of any definition.' Greatly perturbed by such divergence of opinion within his official family, Washington affixed his signature to the bill embodying Hamilton's proposal only after careful consideration.

Even before the fate of his bank proposal was settled, Hamilton came forward, on 28 January, with his Report on the Establishment of a Mint, laying down principles for the minting of coins and establishing monetary standards. The Secretary of the Treasury pushed this measure through with such dispatch that he was hailed as 'all-powerful . . . fails in nothing he attempts.'

A harder fight loomed ahead—to win Congressional authorization of government encouragement to industry. Manufactures as one of the keys to empire had long been in Hamilton's contemplation. When threat of a British boycott loomed ominously on the horizon in 1774, the youthful pamphleteer calmly suggested: 'If, by the necessity of the thing, manufactures should once be established, and take root among us, they will pave the way still more to the future grandeur and glory of America.' That same prospect was in full view by February 1791, when he urged government aid to manufactures on two closely related grounds, familiar and convincing today: military security and national economic development. 'For over a year while head over heels immersed in a tremendous sea of other business,' Nathan Schachner observes, 'he had been carefully, painstakingly and incessantly gathering materials on which to base such a report.' Letters of inquiry went out to all parts of the world. As the answers came in, they were read, digested, and filed. Such were the painstaking procedures leading to a state paper that ranks with the world's best.

Within two years after the national government was inaugurated, Hamilton had laid the bases on which America stands today as the greatest political-industrial power in modern world. He not only contributed immeasurably, at all stages, to the achievement of a more perfect union and the establishment of national power, but he also took important initial steps in the development of American capitalism. By his grasp of credit, finance, and the factory system, he inaugurated policies that helped release those forces which were in time to transform America from Jefferson's agrarian localism to a country dominated by finance and industry—the fulfillment of Jefferson's worst fears.

'There are some,' Hamilton had observed, 18 April 1782, with reference to the current doctrines of *laisser-faire*, 'who maintain that trade will regulate itself, and is not to be benefited by the encouragements or restraints of government. Such persons will imagine that there is no need of a common directing power. This is one of those wild speculative paradoxes, which have grown into credit among us, contrary to the uniform practice and sense of the most enlightened nations.' In 1791 Hamilton still believed 'that the interference and aid of . . . governments are indispensable' to the effective functioning of the American economy.

He did not subscribe, of course, to social planning, as we know it today. In fact, he expressed views on the employment of women and children that indicate lack of sympathy with any such notion. But he did expressly reject the idea, still current among our industrialists, that production, prices, and profits are governed automatically by the operation of natural economic laws. Hamilton not only advocated government regulation of economic forces, but also claimed for the national government power sufficient in scope to do this. On the basis of the theories he then formulated our government today seeks to meet the needs of a vastly changed society, more remote from Hamilton than he was from Julius Caesar.

Hamilton's bold disregard of Jefferson's minimized state stirred profound suspicion. In May 1792 Jefferson wrote Washington complaining that a 'corrupt squadron' in Congress aimed to destroy the states and replace them with a consolidated system, thus paving the way for monarchy. 'There might be desires,' Washington conceded in reply, but he did not believe 'there were designs.'

Jefferson was not convinced. Mutual suspicion deepened. Certain that Hamilton was a scheming monarchist * and Washington acquiescent, Jefferson soon began to keep a secret notebook in which he jotted down conversations and observations that confirmed, or seemed to confirm, his suspicions. Years later he published it under the title *Anas*—after, as he explained, 'the passions of the time are passed away.' But he still believed 'that the contests of that day

* See Julian P. Boyd, *Number 7: Alexander Hamilton's Secret Attempts to Control American Foreign Policy*, Princeton, Princeton University Press, 1964.

were contests of principle, between the advocates of republican, and those of kingly government.'

Hamilton countered, denouncing 'pretended republicans' as inspired by French revolutionaries, characterized as 'mere speculatists,' 'philosophic politicians.' One can get the flavor of the feud, in which Madison, member of the House of representatives, was now joined with Jefferson, from Hamilton's letter to Colonel Edward Carrington. Against this background, too, one can better understand the fierce determination with which Hamilton put down the Whisky Rebellion.

To help amass the resources necessary to carry out national assumption of state debts, Hamilton recommended an excise tax on the domestic manufacture of whisky. This immediately roused the farmers in western Pennsylvania, Virginia, and North Carolina. A tax on the one commodity most easily converted into cash seemed to backwoods distillers an intolerable burden. They stubbornly refused to pay, threatened the lives of the revenue collectors, and taunted the government with explosive revolutionary slogans. All this for Hamilton was symptomatic of the Jacobin radicalism he accused Jefferson and others of fostering in America. It was a bold challenge, as he saw it, to the power, integrity, and dignity of the new national government.

Hamilton may have welcomed this so-called rebellion as an opportunity to test national power. He knew, as Washington said in connection with the Shays' Rebellion, that 'influence is not government.' Supporting evidence of his eagerness to put the force of government to the test may be found in the papers he wrote under the pseudonym, Tully, excerpted in this volume. The trivial dimensions of the uprising make Hamilton's solemn appeal 'To the People of the United States' slightly ludicrous: 'Shall the majority govern or be governed?' he challenged. 'Shall the nation rule or be ruled? Shall the general will prevail, or the will of a faction? Shall there be government or no government?' The issue was not then quite so sharp.

Having rounded out his national program, Hamilton resigned, 31 January 1795, from Washington's cabinet. It remained for John Marshall, appointed Chief Justice of the United States Supreme Court by President John Adams in 1801 at the end of his term, to anchor it in judicial precedents. Jefferson regarded Marshall's appointment as a Federalist conspiracy to maintain their diabolical rule. 'The Federalists,' he wrote, 'have retired into the judiciary as a stronghold and from that battery all the works of Republicanism are to be beaten down and erased.'

Marshall moved systematically, logically, with the precision of a military strategist. As the first plank in the reinforcement of national power, the Supreme Court had to achieve for itself supreme authority to interpret the Constitution, not only in relation to the power of Congress but also as to state acts and state court decisions. The first step was taken, 1803, in the great case of Marbury v. Madison.

Among the appointees Adams installed in the judicial fortress of Federalism was William Marbury, appointed Justice of the Peace in the District of Columbia. Marbury's commission had been signed but not delivered, and President Jefferson instructed his Secretary of State, James Madison, not to surrender it.

Marbury brought an original suit in the Supreme Court under the Judiciary Act of 1789, authorizing the Court to hear such suits in the exercise of its original jurisdiction.

Three questions were involved: Did Marbury have a right to his commission? The Court answered 'yes.' Conceding that he had such a right, did the laws of the country afford him a remedy? Again the answer was 'yes.' Was he entitled to the remedy he sought? Marshall agreed that a writ of mandamus was the proper remedy, but held that the Supreme Court was not the proper tribunal. The Chief Justice was not required to deliver the first part of his opinion touching the merits of the case, and this has frequently been termed *obiter*—Jefferson being one of the critics. The Court had only to explain why it did not have jurisdiction and this afforded Marshall opportunity to deliver the part of the opinion given herein, in answer to the question whether the Supreme Court must enforce an act of Congress that exceeds the bounds set by the Constitution—in this instance an act enlarging the Court's original jurisdiction.

Marshall's decision and opinion constituted a political coup of the first magnitude. It clinched a power Hamilton had insisted upon in *Federalist* 78, and thus laid the foundation for our entire system of constitutional law.

The charter of 1791 establishing the national bank expired in 1811, and in 1816 Congress granted a second charter. It was exceedingly unpopular in the states and Maryland, among others, passed discriminatory legislation against it. It was this act that came before Chief Justice Marshall in McCulloch v. Maryland. In the course of his opinion Marshall leaned heavily on Hamilton's argument of 1791, but reinforced, refined, and illuminated it all with masterful constitutional theory.

Varying appraisals have been made of Hamilton's and Marshall's contribution to the development of national power. In 1882, Henry Cabot Lodge described Marshall as 'a nation-maker, a state-builder,' and accorded equal, if not larger, credit to Hamilton. Years later Woodrow Wilson spoke of Hamilton as 'a great man, but not a great American,' while Justice Holmes, mindful of Hamilton's achievements before 1801, gave the great Chief Justice relatively scant praise. 'I should feel a . . . doubt,' Holmes wrote in 1901, 'whether, after Hamilton and the Constitution itself, Marshall's work proved more than a strong intellect, a good style, personal ascendancy in his Court, courage, justice and the convictions of his party.'

Surely an important element in appraising the stature of both Hamilton and Marshall is what they accomplished. As for Marshall, one must realize that when he took office, Jeffersonian Republicans held sway in the political branches of the government, also that Hamilton was in an extremely pessimistic mood, berating the Constitution, 27 February 1802, as 'a weak and worthless fabric.' Not the least of the reasons for its great strength lay in the achievements of his own statesmanship. The First Bank was not even challenged judicially; the Second Bank was bolstered by compelling constitutional theory. In judging Marshall first importance must be given to the fact that he interpreted and enforced national power broadly at a time when the forces of disunion had already espoused the right of secession.

1. *A national debt is a national blessing, but . . .*

ALEXANDER HAMILTON, *First Report on the Public Credit*, 14 January, 1790 *

The Secretary of the Treasury . . . has felt, in no small degree, the anxieties which naturally flow . . . from a deep and solemn conviction of the momentous nature of the truth contained in the resolution under which his investigations have been conducted,—'That an adequate provision for the support of the public credit is a matter of high importance to the honor and prosperity of the United States.' . .

In the opinion of the Secretary, the wisdom of the House, in giving their explicit sanction to the proposition which has been stated, cannot but be applauded by all who will seriously consider and trace, through their obvious consequences, these plain and undeniable truths:

That exigencies are to be expected to occur, in the affairs of nations, in which there will be a necessity for borrowing.

That loans in time of public danger, especially from foreign war, are found an indispensable resource, even to the wealthiest of them.

And that, in a country which, like this, is possessed of little active wealth, or, in other words, little moneyed capital, the necessity for that resource must, in such emergencies, be proportionably urgent.

And as, on the one hand, the necessity for borrowing in particular emergencies cannot be doubted, so, on the other, it is equally evident that, to be able to borrow upon good terms, it is essential that the credit of a nation should be well established. . .

To attempt to enumerate the complicated variety of mischiefs, in the whole system of the social economy, which proceed from a neglect of the maxims that uphold public credit, and justify the solicitude manifested by the House on this point, would be an improper intrusion on their time and patience.

In so strong a light, nevertheless, do they appear to the Secretary, that, on their due observance, at the present critical juncture, materially depends, in his judgment, the individual and aggregate prosperity of the citizens of the United States; their relief from the embarrassments they now experience; their character as a people; the cause of good government.

If the maintenance of public credit, then, be truly so important, the next inquiry which suggests itself is: By what means is it to be effected? The ready answer to which question is, by good faith; by a punctual performance of contracts. States, like individuals, who observe their engagements are respected and trusted, while the reverse is the fate of those who pursue an opposite conduct.

Every breach of the public engagements, whether from choice or necessity, is, in different degrees, hurtful to public credit. When such a necessity does truly exist, the evils of it are only to be palliated by a scrupulous attention, on the part of the Government, to carry the violation no further than the neces-

* *The Works of Alexander Hamilton*, Henry Cabot Lodge, ed., New York. G. P. Putnam's Sons, 1904, vol. II, pp. 227–34, 283 *passim.*

sity absolutely requires, and to manifest, if the nature of the case admit of it, a sincere disposition to make reparation whenever circumstances shall permit. But, with every possible mitigation, credit must suffer, and numerous mischiefs ensue. It is, therefore, highly important, when an appearance of necessity seems to press upon the public councils, that they should examine well its reality, and be perfectly assured that there is no method of escaping from it, before they yield to its suggestions. For, though it cannot safely be affirmed that occasions have never existed, or may not exist, in which violations of the public faith, in this respect, are inevitable; yet there is great reason to believe that they exist far less frequently than precedents indicate, and are oftenest either pretended, through levity or want of firmness; or supposed, through want of knowledge. Expedients often have been devised to effect, consistently with good faith, what has been done in contravention of it. Those who are most commonly creditors of a nation, are generally speaking, enlightened men; and there are signal examples to warrant a conclusion that, when a candid and fair appeal is made to them they will understand their true interest too well to refuse their concurrence in such modifications of their claims as any real necessity may demand.

While the observance of that good faith, which is the basis of public credit, is recommended by the strongest inducements of political expediency, it is enforced by considerations of still greater authority. These are arguments for it which rest on the immutable principles of moral obligation. And in proportion as the mind is disposed to contemplate, in the order of Providence, an intimate connection between public virtue and public happiness, will be its repugancy to a violation of those principles.

This reflection derives additional strength from the nature of the debt of the United States. It was the price of liberty. The faith of America has been repeatedly pledged for it, and with solemnities that give peculiar force to the obligation. There is, indeed, reason to regret that it has not hitherto been kept; that the necessities of the war, conspiring with inexperience in the subjects of finance, produced direct infractions; and that the subsequent period has been a continued scene of negative violation or non-compliance. But a diminution of this regret arises from the reflection, that the last seven years have exhibited an earnest and uniform effort, on the part of the Government of the Union, to retrieve the national credit, by doing justice to the creditors of the nation; and that the embarrassments of a defective Constitution, which defeated this laudable effort, have ceased.

From this evidence of a favorable disposition given by the former Government, the institution of a new one, clothed with powers competent to calling forth the resources of the community, has excited correspondent expectations. A general belief accordingly prevails, that the credit of the United States will quickly be established on the firm foundation of an effectual provision for the existing debt. The influence which this has had at home is witnessed by the rapid increase that has taken place in the market value of the public securities. From January to November, they rose thirty-three and a third per cent.; and, from that period to this time, they have risen fifty per cent. more; and the intelligence from abroad announces effects proportionably favorable to our national credit and consequence.

It cannot but merit particular attention, that, among ourselves, the most enlightened friends of good government are those whose expectations are the highest.

To justify and preserve their confidence; to promote the increasing respectability of the American name; to answer the calls of justice; to restore landed property to its due value; to furnish new resources, both to agriculture and commerce; to cement more closely the union of the States; to add to their security against foreign attack; to establish public order on the basis of an upright and liberal policy;—these are the great and invaluable ends to be secured by a proper and adequate provision, at the present period, for the support of public credit.

To this provision we are invited, not only by the general considerations which have been noticed, but by others of a more particular nature. It will procure, to every class of the community, some important advantages, and remove some no less important disadvantages.

The advantage to the public creditors, from the increased value of that part of their property which constitutes the public debt, needs no explanation.

But there is a consequence of this, less obvious, though not less true, in which every other citizens is interested. It is a well-known fact, that, in countries in which the national debt is properly funded, and an object of establish confidence, it answers most of the purposes of money. Transfers of stock or public debt are there equivalent to payments in species; or, in other words, stock in the principal transactions of business, passes current as specie. The same thing would, in all probability, happen here under the like circumstances.

The benefits of this are various and obvious:

First.—Trade is extended by it, because there is a larger capital to carry it on, and the merchant can, at the same time, afford to trade for smaller profits; as his stock, which, when unemployed, brings him an interest from the Government, serves him also as money when he has a call for it in his commercial operations.

Secondly.—Agriculture and manufactures are also promoted by it, for the like reason, that more capital can be commanded to be employed in both; and because the merchant, whose enterprise in foreign trade gives to them activity and extension, has greater means for enterprise.

Thirdly.—The interest of money will be lowered by it; for this is always in a ratio to the quantity of money, and to the quickness of circulation. This circumstance will enable both the public and individuals to borrow on easier and cheaper terms.

And from the combination of these effects, additional aids will be furnished to labor, to industry, and to arts of every kind. . .

Persuaded, as the Secretary is, that the proper funding of the present debt will render it a national blessing, yet he is so far from acceding to the position, in the latitude in which it is sometimes laid down, that 'public debts are public benefits'—a position inviting to prodigality and liable to dangerous abuse—that he ardently wishes to see it incorporated as a fundamental maxim in the system of public credit of the United States, that the creation of debt should always be accompanied with the means of extinguishment. This he regards as the true secret for rendering public credit immortal. . .

2. *Every power vested in government is in its nature sovereign*

ALEXANDER HAMILTON, *Opinion on the Constitutionality of the Bank of the United States*, 23 February 1791 *

The Secretary of the Treasury having perused with attention the papers containing the opinions of the Secretary of State † and the Attorney-General,‡ concerning the constitutionality of the bill for establishing a national bank, proceeds, according to the order of the President, to submit the reasons which have induced him to entertain a different opinion. . .

In entering upon the argument, it ought to be premised that the objections of the Secretary of State and the Attorney-General are founded on a general denial of the authority of the United States to erect corporations. The latter, indeed, expressly admits, that if there be anything in the bill which is not warranted by the Constitution, it is the clause of incorporation.

Now it appears to the Secretary of the Treasury that this *general principle* is *inherent* in the very *definition* of government, and *essential* to every step of the progress to be made by that of the United States, namely: That every power vested in a government is in its nature *sovereign*, and includes, by *force* of the *term*, a right to employ all the *means* requisite and fairly applicable to the attainment of the *ends* of such *power*, and which are not precluded by restrictions and exceptions specified in the Constitution, or not immoral, or not contrary to the *essential ends* of political society. . .

The circumstance that the powers of sovereignty are in this country divided between the National and State governments, does not afford the distinction required. It does not follow from this, that each of the portion of powers delegated to the one or to the other, is not sovereign with *regard to its proper objects*. It will only *follow* from it, that each has sovereign power as to *certain things*, and not as to *other things*. To deny that the Government of the United States has sovereign power, as to its declared purposes and trusts, because its power does not extend to all cases, would be equally to deny that the State governments have sovereign power in any case, because their power does not extend to every case. The tenth section of the first article of the Constitution exhibits a long list of very important things which they may not do. And thus the United States would furnish the singular spectacle of a *political society* without *sovereignty*, or of a people governed, without *government*.

If it would be necessary to bring proof to a proposition so clear, as that which affirms that the powers of the Federal Government, as to *its objects*,

* *The Works of Alexander Hamilton*, Henry Cabot Lodge, ed., vol. III, pp. 445–58 *passim*.
† Thomas Jefferson.
‡ Edmund Randolph.

were sovereign, there is a clause of its Constitution which would be decisive. It is that which declares that the Constitution, and the laws of the United States made in pursuance of it, and all treaties made, or which shall be made, under their authority, shall be the *supreme law of the land.* The power which can create the *supreme law of the land* in *any case,* is doubtless *sovereign* as to such case.

This general and indisputable principle puts at once an end to the *abstract* question, whether the United States have power to erect a *corporation;* that is to say, to give a *legal* or *artificial capacity* to one or more persons, distinct from the *natural.* For it is unquestionably incident to *sovereign power* to erect corporations, and consequently to *that* of the United States, in *relation* to the *objects* intrusted to the management of the government. The difference is this: where the authority of the government is general, it can create corporations in *all cases;* where it is confined to certain branches of legislation, it can create corporations *only* in those cases.

Here, then, as far as concerns the reasonings of the Secretary of State and the Attorney-General, the affirmative of the constitutionality of the bill might be permitted to rest. It will occur to the President, that the principle here advanced has been untouched by either of them.

For a more complete elucidation of the point, nevertheless, the arguments which they had used against the power of the government to erect corporations, however foreign they are to the great and fundamental rule which has been stated, shall be particularly examined. And after showing that they do not tend to impair its force, it shall also be shown that the power of incorporation, incident to the government in certain cases, does fairly extend to the particular case which is the object of the bill.

The first of these arguments is, that the foundation of the Constitution is laid on this ground: 'That all powers not delegated to the United States by the Constitution, nor prohibited by it to the States, are reserved to the States, or to the people.' Whence it is meant to be inferred, that Congress can in no case exercise any power not included in those enumerated in the Constitution. And it is affirmed, that the power of erecting a corporation is not included in any of the enumerated powers.

The main proposition here laid down, in its true signification, is not to be questioned. It is nothing more than a consequence of this republican maxim, that all government is a delegation of power. But how much is delegated in each case is a question of fact, to be made out by fair reasoning and construction, upon the particular provisions of the Constitution, taking as guides the general principles and general ends of governments.

It is not denied that there are *implied,* as well as *express powers,* and that the *former* are as effectually delegated as the *latter.* And for the sake of accuracy it shall be mentioned that there is another class of powers, which may be properly denominated *resulting powers.* It will not be doubted that if the United States should make a conquest of any of the territories of its neighbors, they would possess sovereign jurisdiction over the conquered territory. This would be rather a result from the whole mass of the powers of the government, and from the nature of political society, than a consequence of either of the powers specially enumerated.

But be this as it may, it furnishes a striking illustration of the general doctrine contended for; it shows an extensive case, in which a power of erecting corporations is either implied in, or would result from, some or all of the powers vested in the National Government. The jurisdiction acquired over such conquered country would certainly be competent to any species of legislation.

To return:—It is conceded that *implied powers* are to be considered as delegated equally with *express ones*. Then it follows, that as a power of erecting a corporation may as well be *implied* as any other thing, it may as well be employed as an *instrument* or *means* of carrying into execution any of the specified powers, as any other *instrument* or *means* whatever. The only question must be in this, as in every other case, whether the means to be employed, or, in this instance, the corporation to be erected, has a natural relation to any of the acknowledged objects or lawful ends of the government. Thus a corporation may not be erected by Congress for superintending the police of the city of Philadelphia, because they are not authorized to *regulate* the *police* of that city. But one may be erected in relation to the collection of taxes, or to the trade with foreign countries, or to the trade between the States, or with the Indian tribes; because it is the province of the Federal Government to *regulate* those objects, and because it is incident to a general *sovereign* or *legislative* power to *regulate* a thing, to employ all the means which relate to its regulation to the best and greatest advantage. . .

Through this mode of reasoning respecting the right of employing all the means requisite to the execution of the specified powers of the government, it is to be objected, that none but necessary and proper means are to be employed; and the Secretary of State maintains, that no means are to be considered *necessary* but those without which the grant of the power would be *nugatory*. Nay, so far does he go in his restrictive interpretation of the word, as even to make the case of necessity which shall warrant the constitutional exercise of the power to depend on *casual* and *temporary* circumstances; an idea which alone refutes the construction. . .

It is essential to the being of the national government, that so erroneous a conception of the meaning of the word *necessary* should be exploded.

It is certain, that neither the grammatical nor popular sense of the term requires that construction. According to both, *necessary* often means no more than *needful, requisite, incidental, useful,* or *conducive to.* It is a common mode of expression to say, that it is *necessary* for a government or a person to do this or that thing, when nothing more is intended or understood, than that the interests of the government or person require, or will be promoted by, the doing of this or that thing. The imagination can be at no loss for exemplifications of the use of the word in this sense. And it is the true one in which it is to be understood as used in the Constitution. The whole turn of the clause containing it indicates, that it was the intent of the Convention, by that clause, to give a liberal latitude to the exercise of the specified powers.

The expressions have peculiar comprehensiveness. They are, 'to make all *laws* necessary and proper for *carrying into execution* the *foregoing powers*, and all other powers vested by the Constitution in the *Government* of the United States, or in any *department* or *officer* thereof.'

To understand the word as the Secretary of States does, would be to depart from its obvious and popular sense, and to give it a restrictive operation, an idea never before entertained. It would be to give it the same force as if the word *absolutely* or *indispensably* had been prefixed to it. . .

It may be truly said of every government, as well as of that of the United States, that it has only a right to pass such laws as are necessary and proper to accomplish the objects intrusted to it. For no government has a right to do *merely what it pleases*. Hence, by a process of reasoning similar to that of the Secretary of State, it might be proved that neither of the State governments has the right to incorporate a bank. It might be shown that all the public business of the State could be performed without a bank, and inferring thence that it was unnecessary, it might be argued that it could not be done, because it is against the rule which has been just mentioned. A like mode of reasoning would prove that there was no power to incorporate the inhabitants of a town, with a view to a more perfect police. For it is certain that an incorporation may be dispensed with, though it is better to have one. It is to be remembered that there is no *express* power in any State constitutions to erect corporations.

The *degree* in which a measure is necessary can never be a *test* of the legal right to adopt it; that must be a matter of opinion, and can only be a *test* of expediency. The *relation* between the measure and the *end*; between the *nature* of the *means* employed towards the execution of a power, and the object of that power, must be the criterion of constitutionality, not the more or less of *necessity* or *utility*.

The practice of the government is against the rule of construction advocated by the Secretary of State. Of this, the act concerning lighthouses, beacons, buoys, and public piers is a decisive example. This, doubtless, must be referred to the powers of regulating trade, and is fairly relative to it. But it cannot be affirmed that the exercise of that power in this instance was strictly *necessary*, or that the power itself would be *nugatory*, without that of regulating establishments of this nature.

This restrictive interpretation of the word *necessary* is also contrary to this sound maxim of construction; namely, that the powers contained in a constitution of government, especially those which concern the general administration of the affairs of a country, its finances, trade, defence, etc., ought to be construed liberally in advancement of the public good. This rule does not depend on the particular form of a government, or on the particular demarcation of the boundaries of its powers, but on the nature and objects of government itself. The means by which national exigencies are to be provided for, national inconveniences obviated, national prosperity promoted, are of such infinite variety, extent, and complexity, that there must of necessity be great latitude of discretion in the selection and application of those means. Hence, consequently, the necessity and propriety of exercising the authorities intrusted to a government on principles of liberal construction. . .

But while on the one hand the construction of the Secretary of State is deemed inadmissible, it will not be contended, on the other, that the clause in question gives any *new* or *independent* power. But it gives an explicit sanction to the doctrine of *implied powers,* and is equivalent to an admission of the proposition that the government, as to its *specified powers* and *objects,* has plenary and sovereign authority, in some cases paramount to the States; in others, co-ordinate with it. For such is the plain import of the declaration, that it may pass all *laws* necessary and proper to carry into execution those powers.

It is no valid objection to the doctrine to say, that it is calculated to extend the power of the General Government throughout the entire sphere of State legislation. The same thing has been said . . . with regard to every exercise of power by *implication* or *construction.* . .

The truth is, that difficulties on this point are inherent in the nature of the Federal Constitution; they result inevitably from a division of the legislative power. The consequence of this division is, that there will be cases clearly within the power of the National Government; others, clearly without its powers; and a third class, which will leave room for controversy and difference of opinion, and concerning which a reasonable latitude of judgment must be allowed.

But the doctrine which is contended for is not chargeable with the consequences imputed to it. It does not affirm that the National Government is sovereign in all respects, but that it is sovereign to a certain extent—that is, to the extent of the objects of its specified powers.

It leaves, therefore, a criterion of what is constitutional, and of what is not so. This criterion is the *end,* to which the measure relates as a *means.* If the *end* be clearly comprehended within any of the specified powers, and if the measure have an obvious relation to that *end,* and is not forbidden by any particular provision of the Constitution, it may safely be deemed to come within the compass of the national authority. . .

3. *What can be so useful as promoting and improving industry?*

Alexander Hamilton, *Report on Manufactures,* 1791 *

. . . The expediency of encouraging manufactures in the United States, which was not long since deemed very questionable, appears at this time to be pretty generally admitted. The embarrassments which have obstructed the progress of our external trade, have led to serious reflections on the necessity of enlarging the sphere of our domestic commerce. The restrictive regulations, which, in foreign markets, abridge the vent of the increasing surplus of our agricultural produce, serve to beget an earnest desire that a more extensive demand for that surplus may be created at home; and the complete success which has rewarded manufacturing enterprise in some valuable branches, con-

* *The Works of Alexander Hamilton,* Henry Cabot Lodge, ed., vol. IV, pp. 70–198 *passim.* 'Report on Manufactures' was communicated to the House of Representatives, 5 December 1791.

spiring with the promising symptoms which attend some less mature essays in others, justify a hope that the obstacles to the growth of this species of industry are less formidable than they were apprehended to be, and that it is not difficult to find, in its further extension, a full indemnification for any external disadvantages, which are or may be experienced, as well as an accession of resources, favorable to national independence and safety.

There still are, nevertheless, respectable patrons of opinions unfriendly to the encouragement of manufactures. . .

'In every country (say those who entertain them) agriculture is the most beneficial and productive object of human industry. . . Nothing, equally with this, can contribute to the population, strength, and real riches of the country.

'To endeavor, by the extraordinary patronage of government, to accelerate the growth of manufactures, is, in fact, to endeavor, by force and art, to transfer the natural current of industry from a more to a less beneficial channel. . . To leave industry to itself, therefore, is, in almost every case, the soundest as well as the simplest policy.

'This policy is not only recommended to the United States, by considerations which affect all nations; it is, in a manner, dictated to them by the imperious force of a very peculiar situation. The smallness of their population compared with their territory; the constant allurements to emigration from the settled to the unsettled parts of the country, the facility with which the less independent condition of an artisan can be exchanged for the more independent condition of a farmer; these, and similar causes, conspire to produce, and, for a length of time, must continue to occasion, a scarcity of hands for manufacturing occupation, and dearness of labor generally. . .

'If, contrary to the natural course of things, an unseasonable and premature spring can be given to certain fabrics, by heavy duties, prohibitions, bounties, or by other forced expedients, this will only be to sacrifice the interests of the community to those of particular classes. Besides the misdirection of labor, a virtual monopoly will be given to the persons employed on such fabrics; and an enhancement of price, the inevitable consequence of every monopoly, must be defrayed at the expense of the other parts of society. It is far preferable, that those persons should be engaged in the cultivation of the earth, and that we should procure, in exchange for its productions, the commodities with which foreigners are able to supply us in greater perfection, and upon better terms.' . .

It ought readily to be conceded that the cultivation of the earth, as the primary and most certain source of national supply; as the immediate and chief source of subsistence to man; as the principal source of those materials which constitute the nutriment of other kinds of labor; as including a state most favorable to the freedom and independence of the human mind—one, perhaps, most conducive to the multiplication of the human species, has intrinsically a strong claim to pre-eminence over every other kind of industry.

But, that it has a title to any thing like an exclusive predilection, in any country, ought to be admitted with great caution; that it is even more productive than every other branch of industry, requires more evidence than has yet been given in support of the position. That its real interests, precious and important as, without the help of exaggeration, they truly are, will be advanced, rather than injured, by the due encouragement of manufactures, may, it is believed, be satisfactorily demonstrated. . .

It has been maintained, that agriculture is not only the most productive, but the only productive species of industry. The reality of this suggestion, in either respect, has, however, not been verified by any accurate detail of facts and calculations; and the general arguments which are adduced to prove it, are rather subtle and paradoxical, than solid or convincing. . .

But without contending for the superior productiveness of manufacturing industry, it may conduce to a better judgment of the policy which ought to be pursued respecting its encouragement, to contemplate the subject under some additional aspects, tending not only to confirm the idea that this kind of industry has been improperly represented as unproductive in itself, but to evince, in addition, that the establishment and diffusion of manufactures have the effect of rendering the total mass of useful and productive labor, in a community, greater than it would otherwise be. . .

To affirm that the labor of the manufacturer is unproductive, because he consumes as much of the produce of land as he adds value to the raw material which he manufactures, is not better founded, than it would be to affirm that the labor of the farmer, which furnishes materials to the manufacturer, is unproductive, because he consumes an equal value of manufactured articles. Each furnishes a certain portion of the produce of his labor to the other, and each destroys a correspondent portion of the produce of the labor of the other. In the meantime, the maintenance of two citizens, instead of one, is going on; the State has two members instead of one; and they, together, consume twice the value of what is produced from the land.

If, instead of a farmer and artificer, there were a farmer only, he would be under the necessity of devoting a part of his labor to the fabrication of clothing, and other articles, which he would procure of the artificer, in the case of there being such a person; and of course he would be able to devote less labor to the cultivation of his farm, and would draw from it a proportionably less product. . .

Again, if there were both an artificer and a farmer, the latter would be left at liberty to pursue exclusively the cultivation of his farm. A greater quantity of provisions and raw materials would, of course, be produced, equal, at least, as has been already observed, to the whole amount of the provisions, raw materials, and manufactures, which would exist on a contrary supposition. The artificer, at the same time, would be going on in the production of manufactured commodities, to an amount sufficient, not only to repay the farmer, in those commodities, for the provisions and materials which were procured from him, but to furnish the artificer himself, with a supply of similar commodities for his own use. Thus, then, there would be two quantities or values in existence, instead of one; and the revenue and consumption would be double, in one case, what it would be in the other. . .

The labor of the artificer replaces to the farmer that portion of his labor with which he provides the materials of exchange with the artificer, and which he would otherwise have been compelled to apply to manufactures; and while the artificer thus enables the farmer to enlarge his stock of agricultural industry, a portion of which he purchases for his own use, he also supplies himself with the manufactured articles, of which he stands in need. He does still more. Besides this equivalent, which he gives for the portion of agricultural labor consumed by him, and this supply of manufactured commodities for his own consumption, he furnishes still a surplus, which compensates for the use of the capital advanced, either by himself or some other person, for carrying on the business. This is the ordinary profit of the stock employed in the manufactory, and is, in every sense, as effective an addition to the income of the society as the rent of land.

The produce of the labor of the artificer, consequently, may be regarded as composed of three parts. One, by which the provisions for his subsistence and the materials for his work are purchased of the farmer; one, by which he supplies himself with manufactured necessaries; and a third, which constitutes the profit on the stock employed. The two last portions seem to have been overlooked in the system which represents manufacturing industry as barren and unproductive. . .

It is now proper . . . to enumerate the principal circumstances from which it may be inferred that manufacturing establishments not only occasion a positive augmentation of the produce and revenue of the society, but that they contribute essentially to rendering them greater than they could possibly be without such establishments. These circumstances are:

1. The division of labor.

2. An extension of the use of machinery.

3. Additional employment to classes of the community not ordinarily engaged in the business.

4. The promoting of emigration from foreign countries.

5. The furnishing greater scope for the diversity of talents, and dispositions, which discriminate men from each other.

6. The affording a more ample and various field for enterprise.

7. The creating, in some instances, a new, and securing, in all, a more certain and steady demand for the surplus produce of the soil. . .

1. *As to the division of labor.*

It has justly been observed that there is scarcely anything of greater moment in the economy of a nation than the proper division of labor. The separation of occupations causes each to be carried to a much greater perfection than it could possibly acquire if they were blended. . .

2. *As to an extension of the use of machinery.* . .

The employment of machinery forms an item of great importance in the general mass of national industry. It is an artificial force brought in aid of the natural force of man; and, to all the purposes of labor, is an increase of hands, an accession of strength, unencumbered too by the expense of maintaining the laborer. May it not, therefore, be fairly inferred, that those occupations which give greatest scope to the use of this auxiliary, contribute most to the general stock of industrious effort, and, in consequence, to the general product of industry? . . .

3. *As to the additional employment of classes of the community not originally engaged in the particular business.*

. . . In places where those institutions prevail, besides the persons regularly engaged in them, they afford occasional and extra employment to industrious individuals and families, who are willing to devote the leisure resulting from the intermissions of their ordinary pursuits to collateral labors, as a resource for multiplying their acquisitions or their enjoyments. The husbandman himself experiences a new source of profit and support from the increased industry of his wife and daughters, invited and stimulated by the demands of the neighboring manufactories.

Besides this advantage of occasional employment to classes having different occupations, there is another, of a nature allied to it, and of a similar tendency. This is the employment of persons who would otherwise be idle, and in many cases a burthen on the community, either from the bias of temper, habit, infirmity of body, or some other cause, indisposing or disqualifying them for the toils of the country. It is worthy of particular remark, that, in general, women and children are rendered more useful, and the latter more early useful, by manufacturing establishments, than they would otherwise be. Of the number of persons employed in the cotton manufactories of Great Britain, it is computed that four-sevenths, nearly, are women and children; of whom the greatest proportion are children, and many of them of a tender age. . .

6. *As to the affording a more ample and various field for enterprise.*

This also is of greater consequence in the general scale of national exertion than might, perhaps, on a superficial view be supposed. . . To cherish and stimulate the activity of the human mind, by multiplying the objects of enterprise, is not among the least considerable of the expedients by which the wealth of a nation may be promoted. Even things in themselves not positively advantageous sometimes becomes so, by their tendency to provoke exertion. Every new scene which is opened to the busy nature of man to rouse and exert itself, is the addition of a new energy to the general stock of effort.

The spirit of enterprise, useful and prolific as it is, must necessarily be contracted or expanded, in proportion to the simplicity or variety of the occupations and productions which are to be found in a society. It must be less in a nation of mere cultivators, than in a nation of cultivators and merchants; less in a nation of cultivators and merchants, than in a nation of cultivators, artificers, and merchants.

7. *As to the creating, in some instances, a new, and securing, in all, a more certain and steady demand for the surplus produce of the soil.*

This is among the most important of the circumstances which have been indicated. It is a principal means by which the establishment of manufactures contributes to an augmentation of the produce of revenue of a country, and has an immediate and direct relation to the prosperity of agriculture.

It is evident that the exertions of the husbandman will be steady or fluctuating, vigorous or feeble, in proportion to the steadiness or fluctuation, adequateness or inadequateness, of the markets on which he must depend for the vent of the surplus which may be produced by his labor; and that such surplus, in the ordinary course of things, will be greater or less in the same proportion.

For the purpose of this vent, a domestic market is greatly to be preferred to a foreign one; because it is, in the nature of things, far more to be relied upon. . .

This idea of an extensive domestic market for the surplus produce of the soil, is of the first consequence. It is, of all things, that which most effectually conduces to a flourishing state of agriculture. If the effect of manufactories should be to detach a portion of the hands which would otherwise be engaged in tillage, it might possibly cause a smaller quantity of lands to be under cultivation; but, by their tendency to procure a more certain demand for the surplus produce of the soil, they would, at the same time, cause the lands which were in cultivation to be better improved and more productive. And while, by their influence, the condition of each individual farmer would be meliorated, the total mass of agricultural production would probably be increased. For this must evidently depend as much upon the degree of improvement, if not more, than upon the number of acres under culture. . .

The . . . objections to a particular encouragement of manufactures in the United States now require to be examined.

One of these turns on the proposition, that industry, if left to itself, will naturally find its way to the most useful and profitable employment. Whence it is inferred that manufactures, without the aid of government, will grow up as soon and as fast as the natural state of things and the interest of the community may require. . .

Experience teaches, that men are often so much governed by what they are accustomed to see and practise, that the simplest and most obvious improvements, in the most ordinary occupations, are adopted with hesitation, reluctance, and by slow gradations. The spontaneous transition to new pursuits, in a community long habituated to different ones, may be expected to be attended with proportionably greater difficulty. . .

The apprehension of failing in new attempts, is, perhaps, a more serious impediment. There are dispositions apt to be attracted by the mere novelty of an undertaking; but these are not always the best calculated to give it success. To this it is of importance that the confidence of cautious, sagacious capitalists, both citizens and foreigners, should be excited. And to inspire this description of persons with confidence, it is essential that they should be made to see in any project which is new—and for that reason alone, if for no other, precarious—the prospect of such a degree of countenance and support from government, as may be capable of overcoming the obstacles inseparable from first experiments. . .

But the greatest obstacle of all to the successful prosecution of a new branch of industry in a country in which it was before unknown, consists, as far as the instances apply, in the bounties, premiums, and other aids which are granted, in a variety of cases, by the nations in which the establishments to be imitated are previously introduced. It is well known (and particular examples, in the course of this report, will be cited) that certain nations grant bounties on the exportation of particular commodities, to enable their own workmen to undersell and supplant all competitors in the countries to which these commodities are sent. Hence the undertakers of a new manufacture have to contend, not only with the natural disadvantages of a new undertaking, but with the gratuities and remunerations which other governments bestow. To be enabled to contend with success, it is evident that the interference and the aid of their own governments are indispensable. . .

There remains to be noticed an objection to the encouragement of manufactures, of a nature different from those which question the probability of success. This is derived from its supposed tendency to give a monopoly of advantages to particular classes, at the expense of the rest of the community, who, it is affirmed, would be able to procure the requisite supplies of manufactured articles on better terms from foreigners than from our own citizens; and who, it is alleged, are reduced to the necessity of paying an enhanced price for whatever they want, by every measure which obstructs the free competition of foreign commodities.

It is not an unreasonable supposition that measures which serve to abridge the free competition of foreign articles, have a tendency to occasion an enhancement of prices. . . But, though it were true that the immediate and certain effect of regulations controlling the competition of foreign with domestic fabrics was an increase of price, it is universally true that the contrary is the ultimate effect with every successful manufacture. . . The internal competition which takes place soon does away with everything like monoply, and by degrees reduces the price of the article to a minimum of a reasonable profit on the capital employed. This accords with the reason of the thing, and with experience. . .

Not only the wealth but the independence and security of a country appear to be materially connected with the prosperity of manufactures. Every nation, with a view to those great objects, ought to endeavor to possess within itself, all the essentials of national supply. These comprise the means of subsistence, habitation, clothing, and defence.

The possession of these is necessary to the perfection of the body politic; to the safety as well as to the welfare of the society. The want of either is the want of an important organ of political life and motion; and in the various crises which await a state, it must severely feel the effects of any such deficiency. The extreme embarrassments of the United States during the late war, from an incapacity of supplying themselves, are still matter of keen recollection. . .

One more point of view only remains, in which to consider the expediency of encouraging manufactures in the United States.

It is not uncommon to meet with an opinion, that, though the promoting of manufactures may be the interest of a part of the Union, it is contrary to that of another part. The Northern and Southern regions are sometimes represented as having adverse interests in this respect. Those are called manufacturing, these agricultural States; and a species of opposition is imagined to subsist between the manufacturing and agricultural interests. . .

Ideas of a contrariety of interests between the Northern and Southern regions of the Union are, in the main, as unfounded as they are mischievous.

The diversity of circumstances, on which such contrariety is usually predicated, authorized a directly contrary conclusion. Mutual wants constitute one of the strongest links of political connection; and the extent of these bear a natural proposition to the diversity in the means of mutual supply. . .

But there are more particular considerations which serve to fortify the idea that the encouragement of manufactures is the interest of all parts of the Union. If the Northern and Middle States should be the principal scenes of such establishments, they would immediately benefit the more Southern, by creating a demand for productions, some of which they have in common with the other States, and others which are either peculiar to them, or more abundant, or of better quality, than elsewhere. These productions, principally, are timber, flax, hemp, cotton, wool, raw silk, indigo, iron, lead, furs, hides, skins, and coal. . .

A question has been made concerning the constitutional right of the Government of the United States to apply this species of encouragement, but there is certainly no good foundation for such a question. The National Legislature has express authority to lay and collect taxes, duties, imports and excises, to pay the debts, and provide for the common defence and general welfare. . . The power to raise money is plenary and indefinite, and the objects to which it may be appropriated are no less comprehensive than the payment of the public debts, and the providing for the common defence and general welfare. The terms 'general welfare' were doubtless intended to signify more than was expressed or imported in those which preceded; otherwise, numerous exigencies incident to the affairs of a nation would have been left without a provision. The phrase is as comprehensive as any that would have been used, because it was not fit that the constitutional authority of the Union to appropriate its revenues should have been restricted within narrower limits than the 'general welfare,' and because this necessarily embraces a vast variety of particulars, which are susceptible neither of specification nor of definition.

It is therefore, of necessity, left to the discretion of the National Legislature to pronounce upon the objects which concern the general welfare, and for which, under that description, an appropriation of money is requisite and proper. And there seems to be no room for a doubt that whatever concerns the general interests of learning, of agriculture, of manufactures, and of commerce, are within the sphere of the national councils, as far as regards an application of money. . .

4. *Among those disposed to narrow federal authority—Jefferson and Madison*

ALEXANDER HAMILTON to Colonel Edward Carrington, 26 May 1792 *

Believing that I possess a share of your personal friendship and confidence, and yielding to that which I feel towards you; persuaded also, that our political

* *The Works of Alexander Hamilton*, Henry Cabot Lodge, ed., vol. IX, pp. 513–35 *passim*.

creed is the same on two essential points—first, the necessity of Union to the respectability and happiness of this country, and second, the necessity of an efficient general government to maintain the Union, I have concluded to unbosom myself to you, on the present state of political parties and views. . . When I accepted the office I now hold, it was under full persuasion, that from similarity of thinking, conspiring with personal good-will, I should have the firm support of Mr. Madison, in the general course of my administration. Aware of the intrinsic difficulties of the situation, and of the powers of Mr. Madison, I do not believe I should have accepted under a different supposition. I have mentioned the similarity of thinking between that gentleman and myself. This was relative, not merely to the general principles of national policy and government, but to the leading points, which were likely to constitute questions in the administration of the finances. I mean, first, the expediency of funding the debt; second, the inexpediency of discrimination between original and present holders; third, the expediency of assuming the State debts. . .

Under these circumstances you will naturally imagine that it must have been matter of surprise to me when I was apprised that it was Mr. Madison's intention to oppose my plan on both the last-mentioned points. . .

At this time and afterwards repeated intimations were given to me that Mr. Madison, from a spirit of rivalship, or some other cause, had become personally unfriendly to me; and one gentleman in particular, whose honor I have no reason to doubt, assured me that Mr. Madison, in a conversation with him, had made a pretty direct attempt to insinuate unfavorable impressions of me. Still I suspended my opinion on the subject. . . It was not till the last session that I became unequivocally convinced of the following truth: 'that Mr. Madison, cooperating with Mr. Jefferson, is at the head of a faction decidedly hostile to me and my administration; and actuated by views, in my judgment, subversive of the principles of good government and dangerous to the Union, peace, and happiness of the country.' . .

Mr. Jefferson is an avowed enemy to a funded debt. Mr. Madison disavows in public, any intention to undo what has been done, but, in private conversation . . . he favored the sentiment . . . that a Legislature had no right to fund the debt by mortgaging permanently the public revenues, because they had no right to bind posterity. The inference is that what has been unlawfully done may be undone. . .

What are we to think of those maxims of government by which the power of a Legislature is denied to bind the nation, by a contract in the affair of property for twenty-four years? For this is precisely the case of the debt. What are to become of all the legal rights of property, of all charters to corporations, nay, of all grants to a man, his heirs and assigns, for ever, if this doctrine be true? What is the term for which a government is in capacity to contract? Questions might be multiplied without end, to demonstrate the perniciousness and absurdity of such a doctrine.

In almost all the questions, great and small, which have arisen since the first session of Congress, Mr. Jefferson and Mr. Madison have been found among those who are disposed to narrow the federal authority. The question of a national bank is one example. The question of bounties to the fisheries is another. Mr. Madison resisted it on the ground of constitutionality, till it was evident, by the intermediate questions taken, that the bill would pass; and he then, under the wretched subterfuge of a change of a single word, 'bounty' for 'allowance,' went over to the majority, and voted for the bill. On the militia bill, and in a variety of minor cases, he has leaned to abridging the exercise of federal authority, and leaving as much as possible to the States; and he lost no opportunity of sounding the alarm, with great affected solemnity, at encroachments, meditated on the rights of the States, and of holding up the bugbear of a faction in the government having designs unfriendly to liberty.

This kind of conduct has appeared to me the more extraordinary on the part of Mr. Madison, as I know for a certainty, it was a primary article in his creed, that the real danger in our system was the subversion of the national authority by the preponderancy of the State governments. All his measures have proceeded on an opposite supposition. . . In respect to foreign politics, the views of these gentlemen are, in my judgment, equally unsound and dangerous. They have a womanish attachment to France and a womanish resentment against Great Britain. They would draw us into the closest embrace of the former, and involve us in all the consequences of her politics; and they would risk the peace of the country in their endeavors to keep us at the greatest possible distance from the latter. This disposition goes to a length, particularly in Mr. Jefferson, of which, till lately, I had no adequate idea. Various circumstances prove to me that if these gentlemen were left to pursue their own course, there would be, in less than six months, an open war between the United States and Great Britain. I trust I have a due sense of the conduct of France towards this country in the late revolution; and that I shall always be among the foremost in making her very suitable return; but there is a wide difference between this and implicating ourselves in all her politics; between bearing good-will to her and hating and wrangling with all those whom she hates. The neutral and the pacific policy appears to me to mark the true path to the United States.

Having delineated to you what I conceive to be a true complexion of the politics of these gentlemen, I will not attempt a solution of these strange appearances. Mr. Jefferson, it is known, did not in the first instance cordially acquiesce in the new Constitution for the United States; he had many doubts and reserves. He left this country before we had experienced the imbecilities of the former.

In France, he saw government only on the side of its abuses. He drank freely of the French philosophy, in religion, in science, in politics. He came from France in the moment of a fermentation, which he had a share in exciting, and in the passions and feelings of which he shared both from temperament and situation. He came here probably with a too partial idea of his own powers; and with the expectation of a greater share in the direction of our councils than he has in reality enjoyed. I am not sure that he had not peculiarly marked out for himself the department of the finances.

He came, electrified with attachment to France, and with the project of knitting together the two countries in the closest political bands.

Mr. Madison had always entertained an exalted opinion of the talents, knowledge, and virtues of Mr. Jefferson. The sentiment was probably reciprocal. A close correspondence subsisted between them during the time of Mr. Jefferson's absence from the country. A close intimacy arose upon his return.

Whether any peculiar opinions of Mr. Jefferson's concerning the public debt wrought a change in the sentiments of Mr. Madison (for it is certain that the former is more radically wrong than the latter), or whether Mr. Madison, seduced by the expectation of popularity, and possibly by the calculation of advantage to the State of Virginia, was led to change his own opinion, certain it is that a very material change took place, and that the two gentlemen were united in the new ideas. . . The course of this business and a variety of circumstances which took place left Mr. Madison a very discontented and chagrined man, and begot some degree of ill-humor in Mr. Jefferson. Attempts were made by these gentlemen, in different ways, to produce a commercial warfare with Great Britain. In this, too, they were disappointed. And, as they had the liveliest wishes on the subject, their dissatisfaction has been proportionately great; and, as I had not favored the project, I was comprehended in their displeasure. . .

Another circumstance has contributed to widening the breach. It is evident, beyond a question, from every movement, that Mr. Jefferson aims with ardent desire at the Presidential chair. . . You know how much it was a point to establish the Secretary of State, as the officer who was to administer the government in defect of the President and Vice-President. Here, I acknowledge, though I took far less part than was supposed, I ran counter to Mr. Jefferson's wishes; but if I had had no other reason for it, I had already experienced opposition from him, which rendered it a measure of self-defence. . . Under the influence of all these circumstances the attachment to the government of the United States, originally weak in Mr. Jefferson's mind, has given way to something very like dislike in Mr. Madison's. It is so counteracted by personal feelings as to be more an affair of the head than of the heart; more the result of a conviction of the necessity of Union than of cordiality to the thing itself. I hope it does not stand worse than this with him. In such a state of mind both these gentlemen are prepared to hazard a great deal to effect a change. Most of the important measures of every government are connected with the treasury. To subvert the present head of it, they deem it expedient to risk rendering the government itself odious; perhaps foolishly thinking that they can easily recover the lost affections and confidence of the people, and not appreciating, as they ought to do, the natural resistance to government, which in every community results from the human passions, the degree to which this is strengthened by the organized rivality of State governments, and the infinite danger that the national government, once rendered odious, will be kept so by these powerful and indefatigable enemies. They forget an old, but a very just, though a coarse saying, that it is much easier to raise the devil than to lay him. . .

A word on another point. I am told that serious apprehensions are disseminated in your State as to the existence of a monarchical party meditating the destruction of State and republican government. If it is possible that so absurd an idea can gain ground, it is necesary that it should be combated. I assure you, on my private faith and honor as a man, that there is not, in my judgment, a shadow of foundation for it. A very small number of men indeed may entertain theories less republican than Mr. Jefferson and Mr. Madison, but I am persuaded there is not a man among them who would not regard as both criminal and visionary any attempt to subvert the republican system of the country. Most of these men rather fear that it may not justify itself by its fruit, than feel a predilection of a different form; and their fears are not diminished by the factious and fanatical politics which they find prevailing among a certain set of gentlemen and threatening to disturb the tranquility and order of the government.

As to the destruction of State governments, the great and real anxiety is to be able to preserve the national from the too potent and counteracting influence of those governments. As to my own political creed, I give it to you with the utmost sincerity. I am affectionately attached to the republican theory. I desire above all things to see the equality of political rights, exclusive of all hereditary distinction, firmly established by a practical demonstration of its being consistent with the order and happiness of socetiy. As to State governments, the prevailing bias of my judgment is that if they can be circumscribed within bounds, consistent with the preservation of the national government, they will prove useful and salutary. If the States were all of the size of Connecticut, Maryland, or New Jersey, I should decidedly regard the local governments as both safe and useful. As the thing now is, however, I acknowledge the most serious apprehensions, that the government of the United States will not be able to maintain itself against their influence. I see that influence already penetrating into the national councils and preventing their direction. Hence, a disposition on my part towards a liberal construction of the powers of the national government, and to erect every fence, to guard it from depredations which is, in my opinion, consistent with constitutional propriety. As to any combination to prostrate the State governments, I disavow and deny it. From an apprehension lest the judiciary should not work efficiently or harmoniously, I have been desirous of seeing some national scheme of connection adopted as an amendment to the Constitution, otherwise I am for maintaining things as they are; though I doubt much the possibility of it, from a tendency in the nature of things towards the preponderancy of the State governments.

I said that I was affectionately attached to the republican theory. This is the real language of my heart, which I open to you in the sincerity of friendship; and I add that I have strong hopes of the success of that theory; but, in candor, I ought also to add that I am far from being without doubts. I consider its success as yet a problem. It is yet to be determined by experience whether it be consistent with that stability and order in government which are essential to public strength and private security and happiness.

On the whole, the only enemy which Republicanism has to fear in this country is in the spirit of faction and anarchy. If this will not permit the ends of government to be attained under it, if it engenders disorders in the community, all regular and orderly minds will wish for a change, and the demagogues who have produced the disorder will make it for their own aggrandizement. This is the old story. If I were disposed to promote monarchy and overthrow State governments, I would mount the hobby-horse of popularity; I would cry out 'usurpation,' 'danger to liberty,' etc., etc.; I would endeavor to prostrate the national government, raise a ferment, and then 'ride in the whirlwind, and direct the storm.' That there are men acting with Jefferson and Madison who have this in view, I verily believe; I could lay my finger on some of them. That Madison does not mean it, I also verily believe; and I rather believe the same of Jefferson, but I read him upon the whole thus: 'A man of profound ambition and violent passions.' . .

5. *A well-organized republic can scarcely lose its liberty from any other source than that of anarchy*

ALEXANDER HAMILTON, on the Whisky Rebellion, 28 August 1794 *

If it were to be asked, What is the most sacred duty, and the greatest source of security in a republic? the answer would be, An inviolable respect for the Constitution and laws—the first growing out of the last. It is by this, in a great degree, that the rich and the powerful are to be restrained from enterprises against the common liberty—operated upon by the influence of a general sentiment, by their interest in the principle, and by the obstacles which the habit it produces erects against innovation and encroachment. It is by this, in a still greater degree, that caballers, intriguers, and demagogues are prevented from climbing on the shoulders of faction to the tempting seats of usurpation and tyranny.

Were it not that it might require too long a discussion, it would not be difficult to demonstrate that a large and well-organized republic can scarcely lose its liberty from any other cause than that of anarchy, to which a contempt of the laws is the high-road.

But without entering into so wide a field, it is sufficient to present to your view a more simple and a more obvious truth, which is this: that a sacred respect for the constitutional law is the vital principle, the sustaining energy of a free government.

Government is frequently and aptly classed under two descriptions—a government of FORCE, and a government of LAWS; the first is the definition of despotism—the last, of liberty. But how can a government of laws exist when the laws are disrespected and disobeyed? Government supposes control. It is that POWER by which individuals in society are kept from doing injury to each other, and are brought to co-operate to a common end. The instruments by which it must act are either the AUTHORITY of the laws or FORCE. If the first be destroyed, the last must be substituted; and where this becomes the ordinary instrument of government, there is an end to liberty.

* *The Works of Alexander Hamilton*, Henry Cabot Lodge, ed., vol. VI, pp. 418–24 *passim*.

Those therefore, who preach doctrines, or set examples which undermine or subvert the authority of the laws, lead us from freedom to slavery; they incapacitate us for a GOVERNMENT OF LAWS, and consequently prepare the way for one of FORCE, for mankind must have GOVERNMENT OF ONE SORT OR ANOTHER. There are, indeed, great and urgent cases where the bounds of the Constitution are manifestly transgressed, or its constitutional authorities so exercised as to produce unequivocal oppression on the community, and to render resistance justifiable. But such cases can give no color to the resistance by a comparatively inconsiderable part of a community, of constitutional laws distinguished by no extraordinary features of rigor or oppression, and acquiesced in by the body of the community.

Such a resistance is treason against society, against liberty, against every thing that ought to be dear to a free, enlightened, and prudent people. To tolerate it, were to abandon your most precious interests. Not to subdue it, were to tolerate it. Those who openly or covertly dissuade you from exertions adequate to the occasion, are your worst enemies. They treat you either as fools or cowards, too weak to perceive your interest or your duty, or too dastardly to pursue them. They therefore merit and will, no doubt, meet your contempt. To the plausible but hollow harangue of such conspirators you cannot fail to reply, How long, ye Catalines, will ye abuse our patience? . . .

Fellow-citizens: A name, a sound, has too often had influence on the affairs of nations; an EXCISE has too long been the successful watchword of party. It has even sometimes led astray well-meaning men. The experiment is now to be tried whether there be any spell in it of sufficient force to unnerve the arm which may be found necessary to be raised in defence of law and order.

The jugglers who endeavor to cheat us with the sound, have never dared to venture into the fair fields of argument. They are conscious that it is easier to declaim than to reason on the subject. They know it to be better to play a game with the passions and prejudices, than to engage seriously with the understanding of the auditory. You have already seen that the merits of excise laws are immaterial to the question to be decided, that you have prejudged the point by a solemn constitutional act, and that until you shall have revoked or modified that act, resistance to its operation is a criminal infraction of the social compact, an inversion of the fundamental principles of republican government, and a daring attack upon YOUR sovereignty, which you are bound, by every motive of duty and self-preservation, to withstand and defeat. The matter might safely be suffered to rest here; but I shall take a future opportunity to examine the reasonableness of the prejudice which is inculcated against excise laws, and which has become the pretext for excesses tending to dissolve the bands of society.

Fellow-citizens: You are told that it will be intemperate to urge the execution of the laws which are resisted. What? Will it be indeed intemperate in your Chief Magistrate, sworn to maintain the Constitution, charged faithfully to execute the laws, and authorized to employ for that purpose force, when the ordinary means fail—will it be intemperate in him to exert that force, when the Constitution and the laws are opposed by force? Can he answer it to his conscience, to you, not to exert it?

Yes, it is said; because the execution of it will produce civil war—the consummation of human evil.

Fellow-citizens: Civil war is, undoubtedly, a great evil. It is one that every good man would wish to avoid, and will deplore if inevitable. But it is incomparably a less evil than the destruction of government. The first brings with it serious but temporary and partial ills; the last undermines the foundations of our security and happiness. And where should we be if it were once to grow into a maxim, that force is not to be used against the seditious combinations of parts of the community to resist the laws? This would be to give a CARTE BLANCHE to ambition, to licentiousness, to foreign intrigue, to make you the prey of the gold of other nations—the sport of the passions and vices of individuals among yourselves. The hydra Anarchy would rear its head in every quarter. The goodly fabric you have established would be rent asunder, and precipitated into the dust. You knew how to encounter civil war rather than surrender your liberty to foreign domination; you will not hesitate now to brave it rather than to surrender your sovereignty to the tyranny of a faction; you will be as deaf to the apostles of anarchy now as you were to the emissaries of despotism then. Your love of liberty will guide you now as it did then; you know that the POWER of the majority and LIBERTY are inseparable. Destroy that, and this perishes. But, in truth, that which properly can be called civil war is not to be apprehended—unless from the act of those who endeavor to fan the flame, by rendering the government odious. A civil war is a contest between two GREAT parts of the same empire. The exertion of the strength of the nation to suppress resistance to its laws, by a sixtieth part of itself, is not of that description.

After endeavoring to alarm you with the horrors of civil war, an attempt is made to excite your sympathy in favor of the armed faction, by telling you that those who compose it are men who understand the principles of freedom, and know the horrors and distresses of anarchy, and must therefore have been prompted to hostility against the laws by radical defect EITHER in the government OR in its administration. Fellow-citizens, for an answer to this you have only to consult your senses. The natural consequences of radical defect in a government, or in its administration, are national distress and suffering. Look around you—where is it? Do you feel it? Do you see it?

Go in quest of it beyond the Allegheny, and instead of it you will find that there also a scene of unparalleled prosperity upbraids the ingratitude and madness of those who are endeavoring to cloud the bright face of our political horizon, and to mar the happiest lot that beneficent Heaven ever indulged to undeserving mortals.

When you have turned your eyes towards that scene, examine well the men whose knowledge of the principles of freedom is so emphatically vaunted—where did they get their better knowledge of those principles than that which you possess? How is it that you have been so blind or tame as to remain quiet, while they have been goaded into hostility against the laws by a RADICAL DEFECT in the government or its administration? Are you willing to yield them the palm of discernment, of patriotism, or of courage? . . .

6. *The very essence of judicial duty*

CHIEF JUSTICE JOHN MARSHALL, Marbury *v.* Madison, 1803 *

. . . The question whether an act repugnant to the Constitution can become the law of the land, is a question deeply interesting to the United States; but, happily, not of an intricacy proportioned to its interests. It seems only necessary to recognize certain principles, supposed to have been long and well established to decide it.

That the people have an original right to establish, for their future government, such principles as, in their opinion, shall most conduce to their own happiness, is the basis on which the whole American fabric has been erected. The exercise of this original right is a very great exertion; nor can it nor ought it to be frequently repeated. The principles, therefore, so established, are deemed fundamental. And as the authority from which they proceed is supreme, and can seldom act, they are designed to be permanent.

This original and supreme will organizes the government, and assigns to different departments their respective powers. It may either stop here, or establish certain limits not to be transcended by those departments.

The government of the United States is of the latter description. The powers of the legislature are defined and limited; and that those limits may not be mistaken, or forgotten, the Constitution is written. To what purpose are powers limited, and to what purpose is that limitation committed to writing, if these limits may, at any time, be passed by those intended to be restrained? The distinction between a government with limited and unlimited powers is abolished, if those limits do not confine the persons on whom they are imposed, and if acts prohibited and acts allowed are of equal obligation. It is a proposition too plain to be contested, that the Constitution controls any legislative act repugnant to it; or, that the legislature may alter the Constitution by an ordinary act.

Between these alternatives there is no middle ground. The Constitution is either a superior paramount law, unchangeable by ordinary means, or it is on a level with ordinary legislative acts, and, like other acts, is alterable when the legislature shall please to alter it.

If the former part of the alternative be true, then a legislative act contrary to the Constitution is not law; if the latter part be true, then written constitutions are absurd attempts, on the part of the people, to limit a power in its own nature illimitable.

Certainly all those who have framed written constitutions contemplate them as forming the fundamental and paramount law of the nation, and, consequently, the theory of every such government must be, that an act of the legislature, repugnant to the Constitution, is void.

This theory is essentially attached to a written constitution, and is consequently to be considered, by this Court, as one of the fundamental principles

* 1 Cranch, 137.

of our society. It is not, therefore, to be lost sight of in the further consideration of this subject.

If an act of the legislature, repugnant to the Constitution, is void, does it, notwithstanding its invalidity, bind the courts, and oblige them to give it effect? Or, in other words, though it be not law, does it constitute a rule as operative as if it were a law? This would be to overthrow in fact what was established in theory; and would seem, at first view, an absurdity too gross to be insisted on. It shall, however, receive more attentive consideration.

It is emphatically the province and duty of the judicial department to say what the law is. Those who apply the rule to particular cases, must of necessity expound and interpret that rule. If two laws conflict with each other, the courts must decide on the operation of each.

So if a law be in opposition to the Constitution; if both the law and the Constitution apply to a particular case, so that the court must either decide that case conformably to the law, disregarding the Constitution, or conformably to the Constitution, disregarding the law, the court must determine which of these conflicting rules governs the case. This is of the very essence of judicial duty.

If, then, the courts are to regard the Constitution, and the Constitution is superior to any ordinary act of the Legislature, the Constitution, and not such ordinary act, must govern the case to which they both apply.

Those, then, who controvert the principle that the Constitution is to be considered, in court, as a paramount law, are reduced to the necessity of maintaining that courts must close their eyes on the Constitution, and see only the law.

This doctrine would subvert the very foundation of all written constitutions. It would declare that an act which, according to the principles and theory of our government, is entirely void, is yet, in practice, completely obligatory. It would declare that if the legislature shall do what is expressly forbidden, such act, notwithstanding the express prohibition, is in reality effectual. It would be giving to the legislature a practical and real omnipotence, with the same breath which profess to restrict their powers within narrow limits. It is prescribing limits, and declaring that those limits may be passed at pleasure.

That it thus reduces to nothing what we have deemed the greatest improvement on political institutions, a written constitution, would of itself be sufficient, in America, where written constitutions have been viewed with so much reverence, for rejecting the construction. But the peculiar expressions of the Constitution of the United States furnish additional arguments in favor of its rejection.

The judicial power of the United States is extended to all cases arising under the Constitution.

Could it be the intention of those who gave this power, to say that in using it, the Constitution should not be looked into? That a case arising under the Constitution should be decided without examining the instrument under which it arises?

This is too extravagant to be maintained.

In some cases, then, the Constitution must be looked into by the judges. And if they can open it at all, what part of it are they forbidden to read or to obey? . . .

Why does a judge swear to discharge his duties agreeably to the Constitution of the United States, if that Constitution forms no rule for his government? if it is closed upon him, and cannot be inspected by him?

If such be the real state of things, this is worse than solemn mockery. To prescribe, or to take this oath, becomes equally a crime.

It is also not entirely unworthy of observation, that in declaring what shall be the supreme law of the land, the Constitution itself is first mentioned; and not the laws of the United States generally, but those only which shall be made in pursuance of the Constitution, have that rank.

Thus, the particular phraseology of the Constitution of the United States confirms and strengthens the principle, supposed to be essential to all written constitutions, that a law repugnant to the Constitution is void; and that courts, as well as other departments, are bound by that instrument. . .

7. *The power to create implies the power to preserve*

CHIEF JUSTICE JOHN MARSHALL, M'Culloch *v.* Maryland, 1819 *

In the case now to be determined, the defendant, a sovereign state, denies the obligation of a law enacted by the legislature of the Union, and the plaintiff, on his part, contests the validity of an act which has been passed by the legislature of that state. The constitution of our country, in its most interesting and vital parts, is to be considered; the conflicting powers of the government of the Union and of its members, as marked in that constitution, are to be discussed; and an opinion given, which may essentially influence the great operations of the government. No tribunal can approach such a question without a deep sense of its importance, and of the awful responsibility involved in its decision. But it must be decided peacefully, or remain a source of hostile legislation, perhaps of hostility of a still more serious nature; and if it is to be so decided, by this tribunal alone can the decision be made. On the Supreme Court of the United States has the constitution of our country devolved this important duty.

The first question made in the cause is, has Congress power to incorporate a bank? . . .

In discussing this question, the counsel for the state of Maryland have deemed it of some importance, in the construction of the constitution, to consider that instrument not as emanating from the people, but as the act of sovereign and independent states. The powers of the general government, it has been said, are delegated by the states, who alone are truly sovereign;

* 4 Wheaton, 316.

and must be exercised in subordination to the states, who alone possess supreme dominion.

It would be difficult to sustain this proposition. The convention which framed the constitution was indeed elected by the state legislatures. But the instrument, when it came from their hands, was a mere proposal, without obligation, or pretensions to it. It was reported to the then existing Congress of the United States, with a request that it might 'be submitted to a convention of delegates, chosen in each state by the people thereof, under the recommendation of its legislature, for their assent and ratification.' This mode of proceeding was adopted; and by the convention, by Congress, and by the state legislatures, the instrument was submitted to the people. They acted upon it in the only manner in which they can act safely, effectively, and wisely, on such a subject, by assembling in convention. It is true, they assembled in their several states—and where else should they have assembled? No political dreamer was ever wild enough to think of breaking down the lines which separate the states, and of compounding the American people into one common mass. Of consequence, when they act, they act in their states. But the measures they adopt do not, on that account, cease to be the measures of the people themselves, or become the measures of the state governments.

From these conventions the constitution derives its whole authority. The government proceeds directly from the people; is 'ordained and established' in the name of the people; and is declared to be ordained, 'in order to form a more perfect union, establish justice, insure domestic tranquility, and secure the blessings of liberty to themselves and to their posterity.' The assent of the states, in their sovereign capacity, is implied in calling a convention, and thus submitting that instrument to the people. But the people were at perfect liberty to accept or reject it; and their act was final. It required not the affirmance, and could not be negatived, by the state governments. The constitution, when thus adopted, was of complete obligation, and bound the state sovereignties. . .

The government of the Union, then (whatever may be the influence of this fact on the case), is, emphatically, and truly, a government of the people. In form and in substance it emanates from them. Its powers are granted by them, and are to be exercised directly on them, and for their benefit.

This government is acknowledged by all to be one of enumerated powers. The principle, that it can exercise only the powers granted to it, would seem too apparent to have required to be enforced by all those arguments which its enlightened friends, while it was pending before the people, found it necessary to urge. That principle is now universally admitted. . .

If any one proposition could command the universal assent of mankind, we might expect it would be this—that the government of the Union, though limited in its powers, is supreme within its sphere of action. This would seem to result necessarily from its nature. It is the government of all; its powers are delegated by all; it represents all, and acts for all. Though any one state may be willing to control its operations, no state is willing to allow others to control them. The nation, on those subjects on which it can act, must necessarily bind its component parts. But this question is not left to mere reason; the people have, in express terms, decided it by saying, 'this constitution, and the laws of the United States, which shall be made in pursuance thereof,' 'shall be the supreme law of the land,' and by requiring that the members of the state legislatures, and the officers of the executive and judicial departments of the states shall take the oath of fidelity to it. . .

Among the enumerated powers, we do not find that of establishing a bank or creating a corporation. But there is no phrase in the instrument which, like the articles of confederation, excludes incidental or implied powers; and which requires that everything granted shall be expressly and minutely described. Even the 10th amendment, which was framed for the purpose of quieting the excessive jealousies which had been excited, omits the word 'expressly,' and declares only that the powers 'not delegated to the United States, nor prohibited to the states, are reserved to the states or to the people'; thus leaving the question, whether the particular power which may become the subject of contest has been delegated to the one government, or prohibited to the other, to depend on a fair construction of the whole instrument. The men who drew and adopted this amendment had experienced the embarrassments resulting from the insertion of this word in the articles of confederation, and probably omitted it to avoid those embarrassments. A constitution, to contain an accurate detail of all the subdivisions of which its great powers will admit, and of all the means by which they may be carried into execution, would partake of a prolixity of a legal code, and could scarcely be embraced by the human mind. It would probably never be understood by the public. Its nature, therefore, requires that only its great outlines should be marked, its important objects designated, and the minor ingredients which compose those objects be deduced from the nature of the objects themselves. . . In considering this question, then, we must never forget that it is a constitution we are expounding.

Although, among the enumerated powers of government, we do not find the word 'bank' or 'incorporation,' we find the great powers to lay and collect taxes; to borrow money; to regulate commerce; to declare and conduct a war; and to raise and support armies and navies. The sword and the purse, all the external relations, and no inconsiderable portion of the industry of the nation, are entrusted to its government. It can never be pretended that these vast powers draw after them others of inferior importance, merely because they are inferior. Such an idea can never be advanced. But it may with great reason be contended, that a government, entrusted with such ample powers, on the due execution of which the happiness and prosperity of the nation so vitally depends, must also be entrusted with ample means for their execution. The power being given, it is the interest of the nation to facilitate its execution. It can never be their interest, and cannot be presumed to have been their intention, to clog and embarrass its execution by withholding the most appropriate means. . . Can we adopt that construction (unless the words imperiously require it) which would impute to the framers of that instrument, when granting these powers for the public good, the intention of impeding their exercise by withholding a choice of means? If, indeed, such be the mandate of the constitution, we have only to obey; but that instrument does not profess to enumerate the means by which the powers it confers may be executed; nor does it prohibit the creation of a corporation, if the existence of such a being be essential to the beneficial exercise of those powers. It is, then, the subject of fair inquiry, how far such means may be employed. It is not denied that the powers given to the government imply the ordinary means of execution. . . But it is denied that the government has its choice of means; or, that it may employ the most convenient means, if, to employ them, it be necessary to erect a corporation. . .

The creation of a corporation, it is said, appertains to sovereignty. This is admitted. But to what portion of sovereignty does it appertain? Does it belong to one more than to another? In America, the powers of sovereignty are divided between the government of the Union, and those of the States. They are each sovereign, with respect to the objects committed to it, and neither sovereign with respect to the objects committed to the other. . . The power of creating a corporation, though appertaining to sovereignty, is not, like the power of making war, or levying taxes, or of regulating commerce, a great substantive and independent power, which cannot be implied as incidental to other powers, or used as a means of executing them. It is never the end for which other powers are exercised, but a means by which other objects are accomplished. No contributions are made to charity for the sake of an incorporation, but a corporation is created to administer the charity; no seminary of learning is instituted in order to be incorporated, but the corporate character is conferred to subserve the purposes of education. No city was ever built with the sole object of being incorporated, but is incorporated as affording the best means of being well governed. The power of creating a corporation is never used for its own sake, but for the purpose of effecting something else. No sufficient reason is, therefore, perceived, why it may not pass as incidental to those powers which are expressly given, if it be a direct mode of executing them.

But the constitution of the United States has not left the right of Congress to employ the necessary means for the execution of the powers conferred on the government to general reasoning. To its enumeration of powers is added that making 'all laws which shall be necessary and proper, for carrying into execution the foregoing powers, and all other powers vested by this constitution, in the government of the United States, or in any department thereof.'

The counsel for the State of Maryland have urged various arguments, to prove that this clause, though in terms a grant of power, is not so in effect; but is really restrictive of the general right, which might otherwise be implied, of selecting means for executing the enumerated powers.

In support of this proposition, they have found it necessary to contend, that this clause was inserted for the purpose of conferring on Congress the power of making laws. . .

But could this be the object for which it was inserted? . . Could it be necessary to say that a legislature should exercise legislative powers in the shape of legislation? . . That a legislature, endowed with legislative powers, can legislate, is a proposition too self-evident to have been questioned.

But the argument on which most reliance is placed, is drawn from the peculiar language of this clause. Congress is not empowered by it to make all laws, which may have relation to the powers conferred on the government, but such only as may be 'necessary and proper' for carrying them into execution. The word 'necessary' is considered as controlling the whole sentence, and as limiting the right to pass laws for the execution of the granted powers, to such as are indispensable, and without which the power would be nugatory. That it excludes the choice of means, and leaves to Congress, in each case, that only which is most direct and simple.

Is it true that this is the sense in which the word 'necessary' is always used? Does it always import an absolute physical necessity, so strong that one thing, to which another may be termed necessary, cannot exist without that other? We think it does not. . . Such is the character of human language, that no word conveys to the mind, in all situations, one single definite idea; and nothing is more common than to use words in a figurative sense. Almost all compositions contain words, which, taken in their rigorous sense, would convey a meaning different from that which is obviously intended. . . The word 'necessary' is of this description. It has not a fixed character peculiar to itself. It admits of all degrees of comparison; and is often connected with other words, which increase or diminish the impression the mind receives of the urgency it imports. A thing may be necessary, very necessary, absolutely or indispensably necessary. To no mind would the same idea be conveyed to these several phrases. . . This word, then, like others, is used in various senses; and, in its construction, the subject, the context, the intention of the person using them, are all to be taken into view.

Let this be done in the case under consideration. The subject is the execution of those great powers on which the welfare of a nation essentially depends. It must have been the intention of those who gave these powers, to insure, as far as human prudence could insure, their beneficial execution. This could not be done by confining the choice of means of such narrow limits as not to leave it in the power of Congress to adopt any which might be appropriate, and which were conducive to the end. This provision is made in a constitution intended to endure for ages to come, and, consequently, to be adapted to the various crises of human affairs. To have prescribed the means by which government should, in all future time, execute its powers, would have been to change, entirely, the character of the instrument, and give it the properties of a legal code. It would have been an unwise attempt to provide, by immutable rules, for exigencies which, if foreseen at all, must have been seen dimly, and which can be best provided for as they occur. To have declared that the best means shall not be used, but those alone without which the power given would be nugatory, would have been to deprive the legislature of the capacity to avail itself of experience, to exercise its reason, and to accommodate its legislation to circumstances. If we apply this principle of construction to any of the powers of the government, we shall find it so pernicious in its operation that we shall be compelled to discard it. . .

But the argument which most conclusively demonstrates the error of the construction contended for by the counsel for the state of Maryland, is founded on the intention of the convention, as manifested in the whole clause. To waste time and argument in proving that without it Congress might carry its powers into execution, would be not much less idle than to hold a lighted taper to the sun. As little can it be required to prove, that in the absence of this clause, Congress would have some choice of means. . . This clause, as construed by the state of Maryland, would abridge, and almost annihilate this useful and necessary right of the legislature to select its means. That this could not be intended, is, we should think, had it not been already controverted, too apparent for controversy. We think so for the following reasons:

1st. The clause is placed among the powers of Congress, not among the limitations on those powers.

2d. Its terms purport to enlarge, not to diminish the powers vested in the government. It purports to be an additional power, not a restriction on those already granted. . .

The result of the most careful and attentive consideration bestowed upon this clause is, that if it does not enlarge, it cannot be construed to restrain the powers of Congress, or to impair the right of the legislature to exercise its best judgment in the selection of measures to carry into execution the constitutional powers of the government. If no other motive for its insertion can be suggested, a sufficient one is found in the desire to remove all doubts respecting the right to legislate on that vast mass of incidental powers which must be involved in the constitution, if that instrument be not a splendid bauble.

We admit, as all must admit, that the powers of the government are limited, and that its limits are not to be transcended. But we think the sound construction of the constitution must allow to the national legislature that discretion, with respect to the means by which the powers it confers are to be carried into execution, which will enable that body to perform the high duties assigned to it, in the manner most beneficial to the people. Let the end be legitimate, let it be within the scope of the constitution, and all means which are appropriate, which are plainly adapted to that end, which are not prohibited, but consist with the letter and spirit of the constitution, are constitutional. . .

If a corporation may be employed indiscriminately with other means to carry into execution the powers of the government, no particular reason can be assigned for excluding the use of a bank, if required for its fiscal operations. To use one, must be within the discretion of Congress, if it be an appropriate mode of executing the powers of government. That it is a convenient, a useful, and essential instrument in the prosecution of its fiscal operations, is not now a subject of controversy. . .

It being the opinion of the court that the act incorporating the bank is constitutional, and that the power of establishing a branch in the state of Maryland might be properly exercised by the bank itself, we proceed to inquire:

2. Whether the state of Maryland may, without violating the constitution, tax that branch?

That the power of taxation is one of vital importance; that it is retained by the states; that it is not abridged by the grant of a similar power to the government of the Union; that it is to be concurrently exercised by the two governments: are truths which have never been denied. But, such is the paramount character of the constitution that its capacity to withdraw any subject from the action of even this power, is admitted. . .

On this ground the counsel for the bank place its claim to be exempted from the power of a state to tax its operations. There is no express provision for the case, but the claim has been sustained on a principle which so entirely pervades the constitution, is so intermixed with the materials which compose it, so interwoven with its web, so blended with its texture, as to be incapable of being separated from it without rending it into shreds.

This great principle is, that the constitution and the laws made in pursuance thereof are supreme; that they control the constitution and laws of the respective states, and cannot be controlled by them. From this, which may be almost termed an axiom, other propositions are deduced as corollaries, on the truth or error of which, and on their application to this case, the cause has been supposed to depend. These are 1st. That a power to create implies a power to preserve. 2d. That a power to destroy, if wielded by a different hand, is hostile to, and incompatible with these powers to create and to preserve. 3d. That where this repugancy exists, that authority which is supreme must control, not yield to that over which it is supreme. . .

That the power of taxing it by the states may be exercised so as to destroy it, is too obvious to be denied. But taxation is said to be an absolute power, which acknowledges no other limits than those expressly prescribed in the constitution, and like sovereign power of every other description, is trusted to the discretion of those who use it. But the very terms of this argument admit that the sovereignty of the state, in the article of taxation itself, is subordinate to, and may be controlled by the constitution of the United States. How far it has been controlled by that instrument must be a question of construction. . .

The sovereignty of a state extends to everything which exists by its own authority, or is introduced by its permission; but does it extend to those means which are employed by Congress to carry into execution powers conferred on that body by the people of the United States? We think it demonstrable that it does not. Those powers are not given by the people of a single state. They are given by the people of the United States, to a government whose laws, made in pursuance of the constitution, are declared to be supreme. Consequently, the people of a single state cannot confer a sovereignty which will extend over them. . .

We find, then, on just theory, a total failure of this original right to tax the means employed by the government of the Union, for the execution of its powers. The right never existed, and the question whether it has been surrendered, cannot arise.

But, waiving this theory for the present, let us resume the inquiry, whether this power can be exercised by the respective states, consistently with a fair construction of the constitution.

That the power to tax involves the power to destroy; that the power to destroy may defeat and render useless the power to create; that there is a plain repugnance, in conferring on one government a power to control the constitutional measures of another, which other, with respect to those very measures, is declared to be supreme over that which exerts the control, are propositions not to be denied. But all inconsistencies are to be reconciled by the magic of the word CONFIDENCE. Taxation, it is said, does not necessarily and unavoidably destroy. To carry it to the excess of destruction would be an abuse, to presume which, would banish that confidence which is essential to all government.

But is this a case of confidence? Would the people of any one state trust those of another with a power to control the most insignificant operations of their state government? We know they would not. Why, then, should we suppose that the people of any one state should be willling to trust those of another with a power to control the operations of a government to which they have confided the most important and most valuable interests? In the legislature of the Union alone, are all represented. The legislature of the Union alone, therefore, can be trusted by the people with the power of controlling measures which concern all, in the confidence that it will not be abused. This, then, is not a case of confidence, and we must consider it as it really is.

If we apply the principle for which the state of Maryland contends, to the constitution generally, we shall find it capable of changing totally the character of that instrument. We shall find it capable of arresting all the measures of the government, and of prostrating it at the foot of the states. The American people have declared their constitution, and the laws made in pursuance thereof, to be supreme; but this principle would transfer the supremacy, in fact, to the states.

If the states may tax one instrument, employed by the government in the execution of its powers, they may tax any and every other instrument. They may tax the mail; they may tax the mint; they may tax patent-rights; they may tax the papers of the custom-house; they may tax judicial process; they may tax all the means employed by the government, to an excess which would defeat all the ends of government. . .

This is not all. If the controlling power of the states be established; if their supremacy as to taxation be acknowledged; what is to restrain their exercising this control in any shape they may please to give it? Their sovereignty is not confined to taxation. That is not the only mode in which it might be displayed. The question is, in truth, a question of supremacy; and if the right of the states to tax the means employed by the general governments be conceded, the declaration that the constitution, and the laws made in pursuance thereof, shall be the supreme law of the land, is empty and unmeaning declamation. . .

It has also been insisted, that, as the power of taxation in the general and state governments is acknowledged to be concurrent, every argument which would sustain the right of the general government to tax banks chartered by the states, will equally sustain the right of the states to tax banks chartered by the general government. But the two cases are not on the same reason. The people of all the states have created the general government, and have conferred upon it the general power of taxation. The people of all the states, and the states themselves, are represented in congress, and, by their representatives, exercise this power. When they tax the chartered institutions of the states, they tax their constituents; and these taxes must be uniform. But when a state taxes the operations of the government of the United States, it acts upon institutions created, not by their own constituents, but by people over whom they claim no control. It acts upon the measures of a government created by others as well as themselves, for the benefit of others in common with themselves. The difference is that which always exists, and always must exist, between the action of the whole on a part, and the action of a part on the whole—between the laws of a government declared to be supreme, and those of a government which, when in opposition to those laws, is not supreme. . .

SELECTED REFERENCES

Albert J. Beveridge, *The Life of John Marshall*, 4 vols., Boston, Houghton Mifflin, 1916–19.

Claude G. Bowers, *Jefferson and Hamilton: The Struggle for Democracy*, Boston, Houghton Mifflin, 1925.

——————, *Jefferson in Power: The Death Struggle of the Federalists*, Boston, Houghton Mifflin, 1936.

Harold W. Bradley, 'The Political Thinking of George Washington,' *Journal of Southern History*, November 1945, vol. XI, pp. 469–86.

Edward S. Corwin, *John Marshall and the Constitution*, New Haven, Yale University Press, 1921.

Louis M. Hacker, *Alexander Hamilton in the American Tradition*, New York, McGraw-Hill, 1957.

O. W. Holmes, *Collected Legal Papers*, New York, Harcourt, Brace & Howe, 1920, 'Essay on Chief Justice Marshall,' pp. 266–71.

Hugh Swinton Legaré, *Writings*, Charleston, S. C., Burger & James, 1845. Vol. II, pp. 101–41, contains a penetrating critique of Marshall's opinion in McCulloch *v.* Maryland.

John C. Miller, *Alexander Hamilton: Portrait in Paradox*, New York, Harper, 1959.

——————, *The Federalist Era*, New York, Harper, 1960.

Broadus Mitchell, *Heritage from Hamilton*, New York, Columbia University Press, 1957.

——————, *Alexander Hamilton: Youth to Maturity, 1755–1788*, New York, Macmillan, 1957.

F. S. Oliver, *Alexander Hamilton: An Essay on American Union*, New York, G. P. Putnam, 1907.

Nathan Schachner, *Alexander Hamilton*, New York, D. Appleton-Century, 1946.

Rexford Guy Tugwell and Joseph Dorfman, 'Alexander Hamilton, Nation Maker,' *Columbia University Quarterly*, December 1937–March 1938.

Leonard White, *The Federalists*, New York, Macmillan, 1948.

IX

ESTABLISHING NATIONAL POWER: JEFFERSON AND TAYLOR

After brief flirtation, as a youthful revolutionary, with 'wild and enthusiastic democracy,' Hamilton had, as we have seen, queried or rejected a considerable part of the creed he endorsed in 1776. Building on more mature assumptions, he began in 1780 the long and arduous task of laying the foundations of 'the American Empire.' Great success rewarded his effort. By 1802, with Jefferson as head of the national administration and John Marshall as Chief Justice, the outlook was less bright, but was it altogether hopeless? Hamilton seemed to think so. Writing Gouverneur Morris in February of that year, he bemoaned: 'Mine is an odd destiny. Perhaps no man in the United States has sacrificed or done more for the present Constitution than myself; and contrary to all my anticipations of its fate, as you know from the very beginning, I am still laboring to prop the frail and worthless fabric.'

No such dramatic lamentations marred Jefferson's prospect as he took the oath of office, 4 March 1801, as third President of the United States. 'The revolution of 1800 was,' he said two days later, 'as real a revolution in the principles of our government as that of 1776 was in its form.' Therefore as head of the triumphant Democratic-Republican party, he portrayed the nation as in 'the full tide of successful experiment,' and rated the national government as 'the best world's hope.' 'I know,' the inaugural message continued, 'that some honest men have feared that a republican government cannot be strong; that this government is not strong enough . . . I believe this, on the contrary, the strongest government on earth.'

In a letter to John Dickinson, 6 March, Jefferson made a more specific indictment of the course the Federalists had steered, and expressed his determination to effect a 'perfect consolidation':

> The storm through which we have passed has been tremendous indeed. The tough sides of our Argosie have been thoroughly tried. Her strength has stood the waves into which she was steered with a view to sink her. We shall put her on her republican tack, and she will now show by the beauty of her motion the skill of her builders . . . I hope to see shortly a perfect consolidation, to effect which

> nothing shall be spared on my part, short of the abandonment of the principles of our revolution. A just and solid republican government maintained here, will be a standing monument and example for the aim and imitation of the people of other countries; and I join with you in the hope and belief that they will see from our example that a free government is of all others the most energetic, that the enquiry which has been excited among the mass of mankind by our revolution and its consequences will ameliorate the condition of man over a great portion of the globe. What a satisfaction have we in the contemplation of the benevolent effects of our efforts, compared with those of the leaders of the other side, who have discountenanced all advances in science as dangerous innovations, have endeavored to render philosophy and republicanism terms of reproach, to persuade us that man cannot be governed but by the rod, etc. I shall have the happiness of living and dying in the contrary hope.

Obviously the ingredients of national strength here suggested bear little or no resemblance to those Hamilton and Marshall deemed essential, and no one was more acutely conscious of these divergencies than the protagonists themselves. After 1780 Hamilton had emphasized coercive force, energy, and stability in the central government as the primary ballast of his Empire. 'The safest reliance of every government is on men's interests,' Hamilton believed. 'By this interest we must govern him, and, by means of it, make him cooperate to the public good, notwithstanding this insatiable avarice and ambition.' In early October 1787 he confessed that he was not 'much attached to the majesty of the multitude,' and expressed distrust of those citizens 'who to gain their own private ends inflame the minds of the well-meaning though less intelligent parts of the community, by sating their vanity with that cordial and unfailing specific, that all power is seated in the people.'

In 1776, as in 1787, in 1801, and to the end, Jefferson, on the other hand, upheld responsiveness to an informed populace as the hallmark of free government. The people were 'the most honest and safe, although not the most wise depository of the public interest . . .' 'To render even them safe, their minds must be improved to a certain degree.' Responsibility, he said, 'is a tremendous engine in a free government.' 'I would rather be exposed,' he observed, 'to the inconveniences attending too much liberty than those attending too small a degree.' 'It is not by consolidation or concentration of powers, but by their distribution that good government is effected.' 'The true barriers of liberty in this country are our state governments.' These are among the elements on which Jefferson relied for effecting 'a perfect consolidation.'

In the letters and in other materials collected in this chapter, he 'unbosomed' himself fully. The starting point of his Democratic-Republicanism was the individual, the 'free' man, born with God-given unalienable rights and with a mind 'perfectible to a degree of which we cannot as yet form any conception.' To violate individual rights or ignore man's infinite capacity for development is, he believed, to sever the very roots of national strength. Jefferson anticipated John Stuart Mill in holding that 'the worth of the state is the worth of the individuals composing it.' He voiced a conviction which tragic world experience has since confirmed, that any nation that makes its citizens docile instruments, even for beneficent purposes, will discover that with small men no great things are possible.

Jefferson made freedom—especially of speech, press, and religion—central to everything. On this solid foundation he built his 'Empire of Liberty.' Having, as he said, sworn hostility 'to every form of tyranny over the mind of man,' he would invigorate man and society, quicken and inform public policy and action by exposure to all the divergent and shifting winds of doctrine. 'Reason and free inquiry are the only effectual agents against error,' he proclaimed in his *Notes on Virginia*. 'It is error alone which needs the support of government. Truth can stand by itself.' In a letter to Elbridge Gerry he reiterated unwavering conviction: 'I am for freedom of religion, and against all manoeuvres to bring about legal ascendancy of one sect over another; for freedom of the press, and against all violations of the Constitution to silence by force and not by reason the complaints or criticisms, just or unjust, of our citizens against the conduct of their agents.' Fresh experience under the abominably unconstitutional Alien and Sedition laws of 1798 validated his doctrine, and in his first inaugural address, he re-echoed it with the challenge: 'If there be any among us who would wish to dissolve this Union or change its republican form, let them stand undisturbed as monuments of the safety with which error of opinion may be tolerated when reason is left free to combat it.'

In his day Jefferson believed that men could find their fullest growth in an agrarian economy, under localized, frugal government with limited powers. 'I own I am not a friend of very energetic government,' he wrote Madison 20 December 1787. Jefferson was especially distrustful of centralized government. 'Were we directed from Washington when to sow and when to reap,' runs a G.O.P. favorite since 1932, 'we should soon want bread.' Government must, however, have authority enough to prevent men from injuring one another, enough to eliminate artificial barriers to equality of opportunity, enough to spread the advantages of education among rich and poor, and thus create that natural aristocracy of 'virtue and talents'—'the most precious gift of nature for the instruction, the trusts, and government of society.' He abhorred Hamilton's artificial aristocracy of family and fortune and denounced it for always contriving 'to nestle themselves into the places of power and profit.' Jefferson realized 'equal division of property is impractical,' but in view of 'the consequences of this enormous inequality producing so much misery to the bulk of mankind, legislators cannot invent too many devices for subdividing property.' G.O.P. adherents to Jeffersonian principles have not featured these sentiments.

As conditions changed, Jefferson modified his policy and action. For him no man-made thing, whether law or Constitution, was immune to the inexorable forces of change. As means serving human ends, contracts, compacts, and constitutions carried no peculiar sanctity. '*The earth*,' he insisted in 1789, '*belongs in usufruct to the living*.' 'The idea that institutions established for the use of the nation cannot be touched or modified, even to make them answer their end,' he wrote in 1816, 'is most absurd . . . yet our lawyers and priests generally inculcate this doctrine, and suppose that preceding generations held the earth more freely than we do . . . in fine, that the earth belongs to the dead and not to the living.'

Jefferson therefore freely shifted his position when the ground he was standing on went soft. In 1787, he regretted that the judiciary was not associated with the President, under the proposed Constitution, in the exercise of the veto power, suggesting that the Supreme Court might have been 'invested with a similar or separate function.' Years later he not only denied that the Constitution had conferred an 'exclusive' power of judicial review but said it 'is a misnomer to call a government republican, in which a branch of the supreme power is independent of the nation.' In 1782 he saw the greatness of America tied to agrarianism: 'While we have land to labor, let us never wish to see our citizens occupied at a workbench, or twirling a distaff. . . For the general operations of manufacture, let our work-shops remain in Europe.' But in 1801 he included manufacture, along with agriculture, navigation and commerce, among the 'four pillars of our prosperity.' From 1790 onward, he upbraided the Federalists, Hamilton and Marshall in particular, for broad construction of national power. Yet as President he himself stretched national power to the breaking point in the Louisiana Purchase and in the Embargo of 1807 against British and French preying on American trade. In explanation of his alleged inconsistencies and 'unconstitutional' acts, he said, writing J. B. Colvin, 20 September 1810:

> To lose our country by a scrupulous adherence to written law, would be to lose the law itself, with life, liberty and property and all those who are enjoying them with us; thus absurdly sacrificing the end to the means. . . The line of discrimination between cases may be difficult, but the good officer is bound to draw it at his own peril, and throw himself on the justice of his country and the rectitude of his motives.

While Jefferson freely changed his stand on public issues, he never swerved from his adherence to 'the rights which God, and the law (natural) have given equally to all.' 'Nothing,' he said, 'is unchangeable but the inherent and inalienable rights of man.' On the altar of this doctrine, he asserted the right of revolution, the right of a whole people to dislodge their government and rest it on new foundations deemed more conducive to their safety and happiness. In 1782 he invoked these same eternal verities against elective despotism, under the Virginia State Constitution. In 1801 he raised the same barriers against 'the vital principle of republics'—'absolute acquiescence in the decisions of the majority.' The will of the majority, he said in his first inaugural address, 'to be rightful must be reasonable: that the minority possess their equal rights, which equal laws must protect, and to violate would be oppression.'

Jefferson did not so much oppose the Hamiltonian goal of a Great Republic as query Federalist policies for achieving it. National power, he held, had to be written indelibly in the hearts, minds, and aspirations of men. As keenly aware of human frailties as Hamilton, he would safeguard society from the resulting pitfalls less by coercion and force, more by education, believing that 'no other sure foundation can be devised for the preservation of freedom and happiness.' Indeed certain Jeffersonians are inclined even to elevate his contributions to national power at the expense of Hamilton and Marshall, and to divert the charge of inconsistency from Jefferson to them. Having embraced with Jefferson the revolutionary ideals in youth, Hamilton and Marshall, as Dr. Julian P. Boyd, an acute student of our tradition, observes, 'faltered in mid-course, and came at last to oppose its implications if not its terms. Theirs was the ultimate opportunism, his the settled and unchanging course.' 'The salient fact that we have too long overlooked,' Boyd concludes, 'is that the cardinal principle of Jefferson's life was his uncompromising devotion to the union because of its identity with human rights.'

In imputing so much to Jefferson one should bear in mind his stand-offish, or at least stand-by, role during those arduous months of 1786–89 (he was in Paris at the time) when the bonds of union were being forged. Nor should one forget that it was Jefferson who, in 1799, formulated the first clear and unequivocal statement of the doctrine of nullification, laying the foundations for the doctrine of secession. In the same pessimistic spirit which motivated the Kentucky resolutions, he seemed to lose all faith in man's capacity for self-government:

> . . . [I]t would be a dangerous delusion were a confidence in the men of our choice to silence our fears for the safety of our rights: . . . confidence is everywhere the parent of despotism—free government is founded in jealousy, and not in confidence; it is jealousy and not confidence which prescribes limited constitutions, to bind down those whom we are obliged to trust with power . . . In questions of power, then, let no more be heard of confidence in man, but bind him down from mischief by the chains of the Constitution. . .

On 16 June 1826, Jefferson, who was in his eighty-third year and nearing the end—he died the following fourth of July—received a letter from R. C. Weightman, mayor of Washington, D.C., inviting him, 'as one of the signers of the ever-memorable' Declaration of Independence to join in celebrating its fiftieth anniversary 'in a manner worthy of the Metropolis of the nation.' Jefferson, declining because of ill health, wrote in part:

> I should, indeed, with peculiar delight, have met and exchanged . . . congratulations personally, with the small band, the remnant of that host of worthies, who joined with us, on that day, in the bold and doubtful election we were to make for our country, between submission, or the sword; and to have enjoyed with them the consolatory fact that our fellow citizens, after half a century of experience and prosperity, continue to approve the choice we made. May it be to the world what I believe it will be, (to some parts sooner, to others later, but finally to all,) the Signal of arousing men to burst the chains, under which Monkish ignorance and superstition had persuaded them to bind themselves and to assume the

> blessings and security of self government. The form which we have substituted restores the free right to the unbounded exercise of reason and freedom of opinion. All eyes are opened, or opening to the rights of man. The general spread of the light of science has already laid open to every view the palpable truth that the mass of mankind has not been born, with saddles on their backs, nor a favored few booted and spurred, ready to ride them legitimately, by the grace of God. These are grounds of hope for others. For [our] selves let the annual return of this day, for ever refresh our recollections of these rights and an undiminished devotion to them.

Toward the end of his life Jefferson had set himself the question: 'Is my Country the Better for my Having Lived at All?' In reply, he listed the achievements with which his name is usually associated—The Declaration of Independence, the Virginia Statute on Religious Freedom, the act abolishing primogeniture and entail, the act against the importation of slaves. Along with these notable accomplishments, he solemnly included an achievement of 1790: 'I got a cart of heavy upland rice, from the river Denhigh, in Africa . . . which I sent to Charleston, in hopes it might supersede the culture of wet rice, which renders South Carolina and Georgia so pestilential through the summer.' This list, particularly the last item, provides a clue to Jefferson's peculiar significance. All these contributions, like the three services he specified for his own epitaph, were not so much measures for governing men as for freeing and emancipating them. The man who had been twice elected to the presidency and who refused to run for a third term could not only omit any mention of this distinction, but could also say that 'the greatest service which can be rendered any country is, to add an useful plant to its culture.' Perhaps Woodrow Wilson grasped the true measure of Jefferson's greatness when he said that it did not consist 'in any one of his achievements, but in his attitude toward mankind.'

Jefferson never crystallized his political philosophy in a systematic statement. Nor did he make any full-dress appraisal or criticism of the Federalists' doctrines he so roundly opposed. For an elaboration of the Jeffersonian principles in their relation to Federalist policies, we must turn to John Taylor (1753–1824) of Caroline County, Virginia, with whom Jefferson, as he himself said, 'rarely, if ever differed in any political principle of importance.' Member of the Virginia house of Delegates, a United States Senator (1792–94, 1803, 1822), a prolific writer, one of the most influential Antifederalists in Virginia, Taylor dealt specifically and at length with the Federalist leaders—Hamilton, Adams, and Marshall. In his volume, *An Inquiry into the Principles and Policy of the Government of the United States*, 1814, which Charles A. Beard praises as the 'single immortal work in political science since . . . *The Federalist*,' Taylor makes a frontal attack on Hamilton's financial policies as creating a new aristocracy of wealth and, perhaps, goes beyond Jefferson himself in his defense of agrarianism. Included also is a vehement assault on John Adams's theory of natural aristocracy. Taylor agreed that 'wherever a few possess the mass of the renown, virtue, talents and wealth of a nation, that they will become an aristocracy, and probably ought to'; but, he added, 'wherever no such body is to be found, an aristocracy ought not to be created by legal assignments of wealth and poverty,' as in Hamilton's financial and tariff policies.

Taylor's full blast against the protective tariff is in *Tyranny Unmasked*, 1822. The tariff, as he saw it, was an artificial restriction on competition, an embargo in disguise, in violation of the 'natural right of free trade,' serving to enhance the profits of manufacturers at the expense of agriculture and the community at large. It is 'a tax upon the rich and poor of the whole community, all consumers, for the exclusive benefit of the rich of one occupation. This is aristocracy in its worst character.' As to the proposition that bounties to manufacturing would make America independent of Europe and thus provide a greater market for agriculture, Taylor answered: 'It would be sounder reasoning to contrast the high price of manufactures here, with the low price there, to prove that they ought to give bounties to provide a market for manufactures.'

In *Construction Construed and Constitutions Vindicated*, 1820, Taylor joined issue with the third member of the Federalist triumvirate, Chief Justice John Marshall, whose great opinion in McCulloch *v.* Maryland claims no less than five chapters. The selection here reprinted comes from Taylor's last book, *New Views of the Constitution of the United States*, and constitutes a prelude to the doctrine of secession:

> There remains a right, anterior to every political power whatsoever, and alone sufficient to put the subject of slavery at rest; the natural right of self-defense. . . It is allowed on all hands, that danger to the slave-holding states lurks in their existing situation, however it has been produced, and it must be admitted, that the right of self-defense applies to that situation, of the necessity for which the parties exposed to the danger are the natural judge: otherwise this right, the most sacred of all possessed by men, would be no right at all. I leave to the reader the application of these observations.

Turning to the historical record, Taylor sought to show that the Convention refused to authorize 'centralized supremacy,' and that John Marshall had secured by judicial interpretation what national leaders had failed to win in 1787. It should be noted, however, that certain of the Antifederalists themselves might be cited against Taylor, including Samuel Adams, Richard Henry Lee, Robert Yates, and Luther Martin, all of whom opposed the Constitution because they believed the document itself made for a consolidated system without any assistance from John Marshall.

1. *The earth belongs in usufruct to the living*

THOMAS JEFFERSON to James Madison, 6 September 1789 *

. . . The question whether one generation of men has a right to bind another, seems never to have been stated either on this or our side of the water. Yet it is a question of such consequences as not only to merit decision, but place also, among the fundamental principles of every government. The course of reflection in which we are immersed here on the elementary principles of society has presented this question to my mind; and that no such obligation can be so transmitted I think very capable of proof.—I set out on this ground, which I suppose to be self evident, *'that the earth belongs in usufruct to the living'*: that the dead have neither powers nor rights over it. The portion occupied by any individual ceases to be his when himself ceases to be, and reverts to the society. If the society has formed no rules for the appropriation of its lands in severality, it will be taken by the first occupants. These will generally be the wife and children of the decedent. If they have formed rules of appropriation, those rules may give it to the wife and children, or to some one of them, or to the legatee of the deceased. So they may give it to his creditor. But the child, the legatee, or creditor takes it, not by any natural right, but by a law of the society of which they are members, and to which they are subject. Then no man can, by *natural right*, oblige the lands he occupied, or the persons who succeed him in that occupation, to the payment of debts contracted by him. For if he could, he might, during his own life, eat up the usufruct of the lands for several generations to come, and then the lands would belong to the dead, and not to the living, which would be the reverse of our principle.

What is true of every member of the society individually, is true of them all collectively, since the rights of the whole can be no more than the sum of the rights of the individuals.—To keep our ideas clear when applying them to a multitude, let us suppose a whole generation of men to be born on the same day, to attain mature age on the same day, and to die on the same day, leaving a succeeding generation in the moment of attaining their mature age all together. Let the ripe age be supposed of 21 years, and their period of life 34 years more, that being the average term given by the bills of mortality to persons who have already attained 21 years of age. Each successive generation would, in this way, come on, and go off the stage at a fixed moment, as individuals do now. Then I say the earth belongs to each of these generations, during it's course, fully, and in their own right. The 2d. generation receives it clear of the debts and incumberances of the 1st. the 3d of the 2d. and so on. For if the 1st could charge it with a debt, then the earth would belong to the dead and not the living generation. Then no generation can contract debts greater than may be paid during the course of its own existence.

. . . On similar ground it may be proved that no society can make a perpetual constitution, or even a perpetual law. The earth belongs always to the living

* *The Papers of Thomas Jefferson*, Julian P. Boyd, ed., Princeton, Princeton University Press, 1958, vol. xv, pp. 392–6 *passim.*

generation. They may manage it then, and what proceeds from it, as they please, during their usufruct. They are masters too of their own persons, and consequently may govern them as they please. But persons and property make the sum of the objects of government. The constitution and the laws of their predecessors extinguished then in their natural course with those who gave them being. This could preserve that being till it ceased to be itself, and no longer. Every constitution then, and every law, naturally expires at the end of 19 years. If it be enforced longer, it is an act of force, and not of right.—It may be said that the succeeding generation exercising in fact the power of repeal, this leaves them as free as if the constitution or law had been expressly limited to 19 years only. In the first place, this objection admits the right, in proposing an equivalent. But the power of repeal is not an equivalent. It might be indeed if every form of government were so perfectly contrived that the will of the majority could always be obtained fairly and without impediment. But this is true of no form. The people cannot assemble themselves. Their representation is unequal and vicious. Various checks are opposed to every legislative proposition. Factions get possession of the public councils. Bribery corrupts them. Personal interests lead them astray from the general interests of their constituents: and other impediments arise so as to prove to every practical man that a law of limited duration is much more manageable than one which needs a repeal. . .

2. *I unbosom myself fully*

THOMAS JEFFERSON to Elbridge Gerry, 26 January 1799 *

. . . I shall make to you a profession of my political faith; in confidence that you will consider every future imputation on me of a contrary complexion, as bearing on its front the mark of falsehood and calumny.

I do then, with sincere zeal, wish an inviolable preservation of our present federal constitution, according to the true sense in which it was adopted by the States, that in which it was advocated by its friends, and not that which its enemies apprehended, who therefore became its enemies; and I am opposed to the monarchising its features by the forms of its administration, with a view to conciliate a first transition to a President and Senate for life, and from that to a hereditary tenure of these offices, and thus to worm out the elective principle. I am for preserving to the States the powers not yielded by them to the Union, and to the legislature of the Union its constitutional share in the division of powers; and I am not for transferring all the powers of the States to the general government, and all those of that government to the Executive branch. I am for a government rigorously frugal and simple, applying all the possible savings of the public revenue to the discharge of the national debt; and not for a multiplication of officers and salaries merely to make partisans, and for increasing, by every device, the public debt, on the principle

* *The Writings of Thomas Jefferson*, P. L. Ford, ed., New York, G. P. Putnam's Sons, 1896, vol. VII, pp. 325–36 *passim*.

of its being a public blessing.* I am for relying, for internal defence, on our militia solely, till actual invasion, and for such a naval force only as may protect our coasts and harbors from such depredations as we have experienced; and not for a standing army in time of peace, which may overawe the public sentiment; nor for a navy, which, by its own expenses and the eternal wars in which it will implicate us, will grind us with public burdens, and sink us under them. I am for free commerce with all nations; political connection with none; and little or no diplomatic establishment. And I am not for linking ourselves by new treaties with the quarrels of Europe; entering that field of slaughter to preserve their balance, or joining in the confederacy of kings to war against the principles of liberty. I am for freedom of religion, and against all maneuvres to bring about a legal ascendancy of one sect over another; for freedom of the press, and against all violations of the constitution to silence by force and not by reason the complaints or criticisms, just or unjust, of our citizens against the conduct of their agents. And I am for encouraging the progress of science in all its branches; and not for raising a hue and cry against the sacred name of philosophy; for awing the human mind by stories of raw head and bloody bones to a distrust of its own vision, and to repose implicitly on that of others; to go backwards instead of forwards to look for improvements; to believe that government, religion, morality, and every other science were in the highest perfection in ages of the darkest ignorance, and that nothing can ever be devised more perfect than what was established by our forefathers. To these I will add, that I was a sincere well-wisher to the success of the French revolution, and still wish it may end in the establishment of a free and well-ordered republic; but I have not been insensible under the atrocious depredations they have committed on our commerce. The first object of my heart is my own country. In that is embarked my family, my fortune, and my own existence. I have not one farthing of interest, nor one fibre of attachment out of it, nor a single motive of preference of any one nation to another, but in proportion as they are more or less friendly to us. But though deeply feeling the injuries of France, I did not think war the surest means of redressing them. I did believe, that a mission sincerely disposed to preserve peace, would obtain for us a peaceable and honorable settlement and retribution; and I appeal to you to say, whether this might not have been obtained, if either of your colleagues had been of the same sentiment with yourself.

These, my friend, are my principles; they are unquestionably the principles of the great body of our fellow citizens, and I know there is not one of them which is not yours also. In truth, we never differed but on one ground, the funding system; and as, from the moment of its being adopted by the constituted authorities, I became religiously principled in the sacred discharge of it to the uttermost farthing, we are united now even on that single ground of difference. . .

* Hamilton had said in his letter to Robert Morris, 30 April 1781: 'A national debt, if not excessive, will be to us a national blessing. It will be a powerful cement of our union. It will also create a necessity for keeping up taxation to a degree which, without being oppressive, will be a spur to industry, remote as we are from Europe, and shall be from danger.' (*Works*, ed. by J. C. Hamilton, vol. 1, p. 257.)

When I sat down to answer your letter, but two courses presented themselves, either to say nothing or everything; for half-confidences are not in my character. I could not hesitate which was due to you. I have unbosomed myself fully; and it will certainly be highly gratifying if I receive like confidence from you. For even if we differ in principle more than I believe we do, you and I know too well the texture of the human mind, and the slipperiness of human reason, to consider differences of opinion otherwise than differences of form or feature. Integrity of views more than their soundness, is the basis of esteem.

3. *Our country is too large to have all its affairs directed by a single government*

THOMAS JEFFERSON to Gideon Granger, 13 August 1800 *

I received with great pleasure your favor of June 4th, and am much comforted by the appearance of a change of opinion in your State [Connecticut]; for tho' we may obtain, and I believe shall obtain, a majority in the Legislature of the United States, attached to the preservation of the Federal constitution according to its obvious principles, and those on which it was known to be received; attached equally to the preservation to the States of those rights unquestionably remaining with them; friends to the freedom of religion, freedom of the press, trial by jury and to economical government; opposed to standing armies, paper systems, war, and all connection, other than commerce, with any foreign nation; in short, a majority firm in all those principles which we have espoused and the federalists have opposed uniformly; still, should the whole body of New England continue in opposition to these principles of government, either knowingly or through delusion, our government will be a very uneasy one. It can never be harmonious and solid, while so respectable a portion of its citizens support principles which go directly to a change of the federal constitution, to sink the State governments, consolidate them into one, and to monarchize that. Our country is too large to have all its affairs directed by a single government. Public servants at such a distance, and from under the eye of their constituents, must, from the circumstance of distance, be unable to administer and overlook all the details necessary for the good government of the citizens, and the same circumstance, by rendering detection impossible to their constituents, will invite the public agents to corruption, plunder, and waste. And I do verily believe that if the principle were to prevail of a common law being in force in the United States (which principle possesses the general government at once of all the powers of the state governments, and reduces us to a single consolidated government), it would become the most corrupt government on the earth. You have seen the practises by which the public servants have been able to cover their conduct, or, where that could not be done, delusions by which they have varnished it for the eye of their constituents. What an augmentation of the field for jobbing, speculating,

* *The Writings of Thomas Jefferson*, P. L. Ford, ed., vol. VII, pp. 450–52.

plundering, office-building and office-hunting would be produced by an assumption of all the State powers into the hands of the General Government. The true theory of our constitution is surely the wisest and best, that the States are independent as to everything within themselves, and united as to everything respecting foreign nations. Let the General Government be reduced to foreign concerns only, and let our affairs be disentangled from those of all other nations, except as to commerce, which the merchants will manage the better, the more they are left free to manage for themselves, and our general government may be reduced to a very simple organization, and a very unexpensive one; a few plain duties to be performed by a few servants. But I repeat, that this simple and economical mode of government can never be secured, if the New England States continue to support the contrary system. I rejoice, therefore, in every appearance of their returning to those principles which I had always imagined to be almost innate in them. . .

4. *In a republic there must be absolute acquiescence in the will of the majority, but that will to be rightful must be reasonable*

THOMAS JEFFERSON, First Inaugural Address, 4 March 1801 *

. . . During the contest of opinion through which we have passed the animation of discussions and of exertions has sometimes worn an aspect which might impose on strangers unused to think freely and to speak and to write what they think; but this being now decided by the voice of the nation, announced according to the rules of the Constitution, all will, of course, arrange themselves under the will of the law, and unite in common efforts for the common good. All, too, will bear in mind this sacred principle, that though the will of the majority is in all cases to prevail, that will to be rightful must be reasonable; that the minority possess their equal rights, which equal law must protect, and to violate would be oppression. Let us, then, fellow-citizens, unite with one heart and one mind. Let us restore to social intercourse that harmony and affection without which liberty and even life itself are but dreary things. And let us reflect that, having banished from our land that religious intolerance under which mankind so long bled and suffered, we have yet gained little if we countenance a political intolerance as despotic, as wicked, and capable of as bitter and bloody persecutions. During the throes and convulsions of the ancient world, during the agonizing spasms of infuriated man, seeking through blood and slaughter his long-lost liberty, it was not wonderful that the agitation of the billows should reach even this distant and peaceful shore; that this should be more felt and feared by some and less by others, and should divide opinions as to measure of safety. But every difference of opinion is not a difference of principle. We have called by different names brethren of the same principle. We are all Republicans, we are all Federalists.

* *Messages and Papers of the Presidents, 1789–1902*, 20 vols., J. D. Richardson, ed., Washington, D.C., 1917, vol. 1, pp. 309–12 *passim*.

If there be any among us who would wish to dissolve this Union or to change its republican form, let them stand undisturbed as monuments of the safety with which error of opinion may be tolerated where reason is left free to combat it. I know, indeed, that some honest men fear that a republican government can not be strong, that this Government is not strong enough; but would the honest patriot, in the full tide of successful experiment, abandon a government which has so far kept us free and firm on the theoretic and visionary fear that this Government, the world's best hope, may by possibility want energy to preserve itself? I trust not. I believe this, on the contrary, the strongest Government on earth. I believe it the only one where every man, at the call of the law, would fly to the standard of the law, and would meet invasions of the public order as his own personal concern. Sometimes it is said that man cannot be trusted with the government of himself. Can he, then, be trusted with the government of others? Or have we found angels in the forms of kings to govern him? Let history answer this question.

Let us, then, with courage and confidence pursue our own Federal and Republican principles, our attachment to union and representative government. Kindly separated by nature and a wide ocean from the exterminating havoc of one quarter of the globe; too high-minded to endure the degradations of the others; possessing a chosen country, with room enough for our descendants to the thousandth and thousandth generation; entertaining a due sense of our equal right to the use of our own faculties, to the acquisitions of our own industry, to honor and confidence from our fellow-citizens, resulting not from birth, but from our actions and their sense of them; enlightened by a benign religion, professed, indeed, and practiced in various forms, yet all of them inculcating honesty, truth, temperance, gratitude, and the love of man; acknowledging and adoring an overruling Providence, which by all its dispensations proves that it delights in the happiness of man here and his greater happiness hereafter—with all these blessings, what more is necessary to make us a happy and a prosperous people? Still one thing more, fellow-citizens—a wise and frugal Government, which shall restrain men from injuring one another, shall leave them otherwise free to regulate their own pursuits of industry and improvement, and shall not take from the mouth of labor the bread it has earned. This is the sum of good government, and this is necessary to close the circle of our felicities.

About to enter, fellow-citizens, on the exercise of duties which comprehend everything dear and valuable to you, it is proper you should understand what I deem the essential principles of our Government, and consequently those which ought to shape its Administration. I will compress them within the narrowest compass they will bear, stating the general principle, but not all limitations. Equal and exact justice to all men, of whatever state or persuasion, religious or political; peace, commerce, and honest friendship with all nations, entangling alliances with none; the support of the State governments in all their rights, as the most competent administrations for our domestic concerns and the surest bulwarks against anti-republican tendencies; the preservation of the General Government in its whole constitutional vigor, as the sheet anchor of our peace at home and safety abroad; a jealous care of the right of election by the people—a mild and safe corrective of abuses which are lopped by the sword of revolution where peaceable remedies are unprovided; absolute acquiescence in the decisions of the majority, the vital principle of republics, from which is no appeal but to force, the vital principle and immediate parent of despotism; a well-disciplined militia, our best reliance in peace and for the first moments of war, till regulars may relieve them; the supremacy of the civil over the military authority; economy in the public expense, that labor may be lightly burthened; the honest payment of our debts and sacred preservation of the public faith; encouragement of agriculture, and of commerce as its handmaid; the diffusion of information and arraignment of all abuses at the bar of the public reason; freedom of religion; freedom of the press, and freedom of person under the protection of the habeas corpus, and trial by juries impartially selected. These principles form the bright constellation which has gone before us and guided our steps through an age of revolution and reformation. The wisdom of our sages and blood of our heroes have been devoted to their attainment. They should be the creed of our political faith, the text of civic instruction, the touchstone by which to try the services of those we trust; and should we wander from them in moments of error or of alarm, let us hasten to retrace our steps and to regain the road which alone leads to peace, liberty, and safety. . .

5. *Two principles divide our fellow citizens into two parties*

THOMAS JEFFERSON to Dr. Benjamin Rush, 16 January 1811 *

. . . You know the perfect coincidence of principle and of action, in the early part of the Revolution, which produced a high degree of mutual respect and esteem between Mr. [John] Adams and myself. Certainly no man was ever truer than he was, in that day, to those principles of rational republicanism which, after the necessity of throwing off our monarchy, dictated all our efforts in the establishment of a new government. And although he swerved, afterwards, towards the principles of the English constitution, our friendship did not abate on that account. While he was Vice-President, and I Secretary of State, I received a letter from President Washington, then at Mount Vernon, desiring me to call together the heads of departments, and to invite Mr. Adams to join us (which, by-the-bye, was the only instance of that being done), in order to determine on some measure which required despatch; and he desired me to act on it, as decided, without again recurring to him. I invited them to dine with me, and after dinner, sitting at our wine, having settled our question, other conversation came on, in which a collision of opinion arose between Mr. Adams and Colonel Hamilton, on the merits of the British constitution, Mr. Adams giving it as his opinion, that, if some of its defects and abuses were corrected, it would be the most perfect constitution of government ever devised by man. Hamilton, on the contrary, asserted, that with its existing

* *The Writings of Thomas Jefferson*, P. L. Ford, ed., vol. XI, pp. 165–71 *passim*.

vices, it was the most perfect model of government that could be formed; and that the correction of its vices would render it an impracticable government. And this you may be assured was the real line of difference between the political principles of these two gentlemen. Another incident took place on the same occasion, which will further delineate Mr. Hamilton's political principles. The room being hung around with a collection of the portraits of remarkable men, among them were those of Bacon, Newton, and Locke, Hamilton asked me who they were. I told him they were my trinity of the three greatest men the world had ever produced, naming them. He paused for some time: 'The greatest man,' said he, 'that ever lived, was Julius Caesar.' Mr. Adams was honest as a politician, as well as a man; Hamilton honest as a man, but, as a politician, believing in the necessity of either force or corruption to govern men.

You remember the machinery which the federalists played off, about that time, to beat down the friends to the real principles of our Constitution, to silence by terror every expression in their favor, to bring us into war with France and alliance with England, and finally to homologize our constitution with that of England. Mr. Adams, you know, was overwhelmed with feverish addresses, dictated by the fear, and often by the pen, of the *bloody buoy*, and was seduced by them into some open indications of his new principles of government, and in fact, was so elated as to mix with his kindness a little superciliousness towards me. . . The nation at length passed condemnation on the political principles of the federalists, by refusing to continue Mr. Adams in the Presidency. On the day on which we learned in Philadelphia the vote of the city of New York, which it was well known would decide the vote of the State, and that, again, the vote of the Union, I called on Mr. Adams on some official business. He was very sensibly affected, and accosted me with these words: 'Well, I understand that you are to beat me in this contest, and I will only say that I will be as faithful a subject as any you will have.' 'Mr. Adams,' said I, 'this is no personal contest between you and me. Two system of principles on the subject of government divide our fellow citizens into two parties. With one of these you concur, and I with the other. As we have been longer on the public stage than most of those now living, our names happened to be more generally known. One of these parties, therefore, has put your name at its head, the other mine. Were we both to die to-day, to-morrow two other names would be in the place of ours, without any change in the motion of the machinery. Its motion is from its principle, not from you or myself.' 'I believe you are right,' said he, 'that we are but passive instruments, and should not suffer this matter to affect our personal dispositions.' But he did not long retain this just view of the subject. I have always believed that the thousand calumnies which the federalists, in bitterness of heart, and mortification at their ejection, daily invented against me, were carried to him by their busy intriguers, and made some impression. When the election between Burr and myself was kept in suspense by the federalists, and they were mediating to place the President of the Senate at the head of the government, I called on Mr. Adams with a view to have this desperate measure prevented by his negative. He grew warm in an instant, and said with a vehemence he had not used towards me before, 'Sir, the event of the election is within your own power. You have only to say you will do justice to the public creditors, maintain the navy, and not disturb those holding offices, and the government will instantly be put into your hands. We know it is the wish of the people it should be so.' 'Mr. Adams,' said I, 'I know not what part of my conduct, in either public or private life, can have authorized a doubt of my fidelity to the public engagements. I say, however, I will not come into the government by capitulation. I will not enter on it, but in perfect freedom to follow the dictates of my own judgment.' I had before given the same answer to the same intimation from Governeur [Robert] Morris. 'Then,' said he, 'things must take their course.' I turned the conversation to something else, and soon took my leave. It was the first time in our lives we had ever parted with anything like dissatisfaction. And then followed those scenes of midnight appointment, which have been condemned by all men. The last day of his political power, the last hours, and even beyond the midnight, were employed in filling all offices, and especially permanent ones, with the bitterest federalists, and providing for me the alternative, either to execute the government by my enemies, whose study it would be to thwart and defeat all my measures, or to incur the odium of such numerous removals from office, as might bear me down. A little time and reflection effaced in my mind this temporary dissatisfaction with Mr. Adams, and restored me to that just estimate of his virtues and passions, which a long acquaintance had enabled me to fix. And my first wish became that of making his retirement easy by any means in my power; for it was understood he was not rich. I suggested to some republican members of the delegation from his State, the giving him, either directly or indirectly, an office, the most lucrative in that State, and then offered to be resigned, if they thought he would not deem it affrontive. They were of opinion he would take great offence at the offer, and moreover, that the body of Republicans would consider such a step in the outset as arguing very ill of the course I meant to pursue. I dropped the idea, therefore, but did not cease to wish for some opportunity of renewing our friendly understanding. . .

6. *The party called Republican is steadily for the support of the present Constitution*

THOMAS JEFFERSON to John Melish, 13 January 1813 *

I received duly your favor of December the 15th, and with it the copies of your map and travels, for which be pleased to accept my thanks. The book I have read with extreme satisfaction and information. . . I had no conception that manufactures had made such progress there, and particularly of the number of carding and spinning machines dispersed through the whole coun-

* *The Writings of Thomas Jefferson*, P. L. Ford, ed., vol. XI, pp. 272–80.

try . . . I have not formerly been an advocate for great manufactories.* I doubted whether our labor, employed in agriculture, and aided by the spontaneous energies of the earth, would not procure us more than we could make ourselves of other necessaries. But other considerations entering into the question have settled my doubts.

The candor with which you have viewed the manners and condition of our citizens is so unlike the narrow prejudices of the French and English travellers preceding you, who, considering each the manners and habits of their own people as the only orthodox, have viewed everything differing from that test as boorish and barbarous, that your work will be read here extensively, and operate great good.

Amidst this mass of approbation which is given to every other part of the work, there is a single sentiment which I cannot help wishing to bring to what I think the correct one; and, on a point so interesting, I value your opinion too highly not to ambition its concurrence with my own. Stating in volume

* Jefferson had stated his earlier views in *Notes on Virginia*, 1782:
'The political economists of Europe have established it as a principle, that every State should endeavour to manufacture for itself; and this principle, like many others, we transfer to America, without calculating the difference of circumstance which should often produce a difference of result. In Europe the lands are either cultivated, or locked up against the cultivator. Manufacture must therefore be resorted to, of necessity, not of choice, to support the surplus of their people. But we have an immensity of land courting the industry of the husbandman. Is it best then that all our citizens should be employed in its improvement, or that one half should be called off from that to exercise manufactures and handicraft arts for the other? Those who labour in the earth are the chosen people of God, if ever he had a chosen people, whose breasts he has made his peculiar deposit for substantial and genuine virtue. It is the focus in which he keeps alive that sacred fire, which otherwise might escape from the face of the earth. Corruption of morals in the mass of cultivators is a phenomenon of which no age nor nation has furnished an example. It is the mark set on those, who not looking up to heaven, to their own soil and industry, as does the husbandman, for their subsistence, depend for it on casualties and caprice of customers. Dependence begets subservience and venality, suffocates the germ of virtue, and prepares fit tools for the designs of ambition. This, the natural progress and consequence of the arts, has sometimes perhaps been retarded by accidental circumstances: but, generally speaking the proportion which the aggregate of the other classes of citizens bears in any state to that of its husbandmen, is the proportion of its unsound to its healthy parts, and is a good enough barometer whereby to measure its degree of corruption. While we have land to labour then, let us never wish to see our citizens occupied at a workbench, or twirling a distaff. Carpenters, masons, smiths, are wanting in husbandry: but, for the general operations of manufacture, let our work-shops remain in Europe. It is better to carry provisions and materials to workmen there, than bring them to the provisions and materials, and with them their manners and principles. The loss by the transportation of commodities across the Atlantic will be made up in happiness and permanence of government. The mobs of great cities add just so much to the support of pure government, as sores do to the strength of the human body. It is the manners and spirit of a people which preserve a republic in vigour. A degeneracy in these is a canker which soon eats to the heart of its laws and constitution.' (*The Writings of Thomas Jefferson*, P. L. Ford, ed., vol. III, pp. 268–9.)

Greatly changed circumstances since 1782 brought considerable qualifications in Jefferson's views. Writing Benjamin Austin, 9 Jan. 1816, he said, "We must now place the manufacturer by the side of agriculturists.' Ford, ed., op. cit. vol. x, pp. 7–11.

one, page sixty-three, the principle of difference between the two great political parties here, you conclude it to be, 'whether the controlling power shall be vested in this or that set of men.' That each party endeavors to get into the administration of the government, and exclude the other from power, is true, and may be stated as a motive of action; but this is only secondary; the primary motive being a real and radical difference of political principle. . .

The party called republican is steadily for the support of the present constitution. They obtained at its commencement all the amendments to it they desired. These reconciled them to it perfectly, and if they have any ulterior view, it is only, perhaps, to popularize it further, by shortening the Senatorial term, and devising a process for the responsibility of judges, more practical than that of impeachment. They esteem the people of England and France equally, and equally detest the governing powers of both.

This I verily believe, after an intimacy of forty years with the public councils and characters, is a true statement of the grounds on which they are at present divided, and that it is not merely an ambition for power. An honest man can feel no pleasure in the exercise of power over his fellow citizens. And considering as the only offices of power those conferred by the people directly, that is to say, the executive and legislative functions of the General and State governments, the common refusal of these, and multiplied resignations, are proofs sufficient that power is not alluring to pure minds, and is not, with them, the primary principle of contest. This is my belief of it; it is that on which I have acted; and had it been a mere contest who should be permitted to administer the government according to its genuine republican principles, there has never been a moment of my life in which I should have relinquished for it the enjoyments of my family, my farm, my friends and books.

You expected to discover the difference of our party principles in General Washington's valedictory, and my inaugural address. Not at all. General Washington did not harbor one principle of federalism. He was neither an Angloman, a monarchist, nor a separatist. He sincerely wished the people to have as much self-government as they were competent to exercise themselves. The only point on which he and I ever differed in opinion, was, that I had more confidence than he had in the natural integrity and discretion of the people, and in the safety and extent to which they might trust themselves with a control over their government. He has asseverated to me a thousand times his determination that the existing government should have a fair trial, and that in support of it he would spend the last drop of his blood. He did this the more repeatedly, because he knew General Hamilton's political bias, and my apprehensions from it. It is a mere calumny, therefore, in the monarchists, to associate General Washington with their principles. But that may have happened in this case which has been often seen in ordinary cases, that, by oft repeating an untruth, men come to believe it themselves. It is a mere artifice in this party to bolster themselves up on the revered name of that first of our worthies. . .

7. *The natural aristocracy I consider the most precious gift of nature*

THOMAS JEFFERSON to John Adams, 28 October 1813 *

. . . I agree with you that there is a natural aristocracy among men. The grounds of this are virtue and talents. Formerly, bodily powers gave place among the *aristoi*. But since the invention of gunpowder has armed the weak as well as the strong with missile death, bodily strength, like beauty, good humor, politeness, and other accomplishments, has become but an auxiliary ground of distinction. There is also an artificial aristocracy, founded on wealth and birth, without either virtue or talents; for with these it would belong to the first class. The natural aristocracy I consider as the most precious gift of nature, for the instruction, the trusts, and government of society. And indeed, it would have been inconsistent in creation to have formed man for the social state, and not to have provided virtue and wisdom enough to manage the concerns of the society. May we not even say, that that form of government is the best, which provides the most effectually for a pure selection of these natural *aristoi* into the offices of government? The artificial aristocracy is a mischievous ingredient in government, and provision should be made to prevent its ascendency. On the question, what is the best provision, you and I differ; but we differ as rational friends, using the free exercise of our own reason, and mutually indulging its errors. You think it best to put the *pseudo-aristoi* into a separate chamber of legislation, where they may be hindered from doing mischief by their co-ordinate branches, and where, also, they may be a protection to wealth against the Agrarian and plundering enterprises of the majority of the people. I think that to give them power in order to prevent them from doing mischief, is arming them for it, and increasing instead of remedying the evil. For if the co-ordinate branches can arrest their action, so may they that of the co-ordinates. Mischief may be done negatively as well as positively. Of this, a cabal in the Senate of the United States has furnished many proofs. Nor do I believe them necessary to protect the wealthy; because enough of these will find their way into every branch of the legislation, to protect themselves. From fifteen to twenty legislatures of our own, in action for thirty years past, have proved that no fears of an equalization of property are to be apprehended from them. I think the best remedy is exactly that provided by all our constitutions, to leave to the citizens the free election and separation of the *aristoi* from the *pseudo-aristoi*, of the wheat from the chaff. In general they will elect the really good and wise. In some instances, wealth may corrupt, and birth blind them; but not in sufficient degree to endanger the society.

It is probable that our difference of opinion may, in some measure, be produced by a difference of character in those among whom we live. From what I have seen of Massachusetts and Connecticut myself, and still more from what I have heard, and the character given of the former by yourself, who know them so much better, there seems to be in those two States a traditionary

* *The Writings of Thomas Jefferson*, P. L. Ford, ed., vol. XI, pp. 341–9.

reverence for certain families; which has rendered the offices of the government nearly hereditary in those families. I presume that from an early period of your history, members of those families happening to possess virtue and talents, have honestly exercised them for the good of the people, and by their services have endeared their names to them. In coupling Connecticut with you, I mean it politically only, not morally. For having made the Bible the common law of their land, they seem to have modeled their morality on the story of Jacob and Laban. But although this hereditary succession to office with you, may, in some degree, be founded in real family merit, yet in a much higher degree, it has proceeded from your strict alliance of Church and State. These families are canonized in the eyes of the people on common principles, 'you tickle me, and I will tickle you.' In Virginia we have nothing of this. Our clergy, before the Revolution, having been secured against rivalship by fixed salaries, did not give themselves the trouble of acquiring influence over the people. Of wealth, there were great accumulations in particular families, handed down from generation to generation, under the English law of entails. But the only object of ambition for the wealthy was a seat in the King's Council. All their court then was paid to the crown and its creatures; and they Philipized in all collisions between the King and the people. Hence they were unpopular; and that unpopularity continues attached to their names. A Randolph, a Carter, or a Burwell must have great personal superiority over a common competitor to be elected by the people even at this day. At the first session of our legislature after the Declaration of Independence, we passed a law abolishing entails. And this was followed by one abolishing the privilege of primogeniture, and dividing the lands of intestates equally among all their children, or other representatives. These laws, drawn by myself, laid the axe to the foot of pseudo-aristocracy. And had another which I prepared been adopted by the legislature, our work would have been complete. It was a bill for the more general diffusion of learning. This proposed to divide every county into wards of five or six miles square, like your townships; to establish in each ward a free school for reading, writing, and common arithmetic; to provide for the annual selection of the best subjects from these schools, who might receive, at the public expense, a higher degree of education at a district school; and from these district schools to select a certain number of the most promising subjects, to be completed at an university, where all the useful sciences should be taught. Worth and genius would thus have been sought out from every condition of life, and completely prepared by education for defeating the competition of wealth and birth for public trusts. My proposition had, for a further object, to impart to these wards those portions of self-government for which they are best qualified, by confiding to them the care of their poor, their roads, police, elections, the nomination of jurors, administration of justice in small cases, elementary exercises of militia; in short, to have made them little republics, with a warden at the head of each, for all those concerns which, being under their eye, they would better manage than the larger republics of the county or State. A general call of ward meetings by their wardens on the same day through the State would at any time produce the genuine sense of the people on any required point, and would enable the State to act in mass, as your people have so often done, and with so much effect by their town meetings. The law for religious freedom,* which made a part of this system, having put down the aristocracy of the clergy, and restored to the citizen the freedom of the mind, and those of entails and descents nurturing an equality of condition among them, this on education would have

* JEFFERSON'S DRAFT OF AN ACT OF 1786 FOR ESTABLISHING RELIGIOUS FREEDOM IN VIRGINIA READS AS FOLLOWS:

SECTION I. Whereas Almighty God hath created the mind free; that all attempts to influence it by temporal punishments or burthens, or by civil incapacitations, tend only to beget habits of hypocrisy and meanness, and are a departure from the plan of the Holy Author of our religion, who being Lord both of body and mind, yet chose not to propagate it by coercions on either, as was in his Almighty power to do; that the impious presumption of Legislators and rulers, civil as well as ecclesiastical, who being themselves but fallible and uninspired men, have assumed dominion over the faith of others, setting up their own opinions and modes of thinking as the only true and infallible, and as such endeavouring to impose them on others, hath established and maintained false religions over the the greatest part of the world, and through all time; that to compel a man to furnish contributions of money for the propagation of opinions which he disbelieves, is sinful and tyrannical; that even the forcing him to support this or that teacher of his own religious persuasion, is depriving him of the comfortable liberty of giving his contributions to the particular pastor, whose morals he would make his pattern, and whose powers he feels most persuasive to righteousness, and is withdrawing from the ministry those temporary rewards, which proceeding from an approbation of their personal conduct, are an additional incitement to earnest and unremitting labours for the instruction of mankind; that our civil rights have no dependence on our religious opinions, any more than our opinions in physics or geometry; that therefore the proscribing any citizen as unworthy the public confidence, by laying upon him an incapacity of being called to the offices of trust and emolument, unless he profess or renounce this or that religious opinion, is depriving him injuriously of those privileges and advantages to which in common with his fellow-citizens he has a natural right; that it tends only to corrupt the principles of that religion it is meant to encourage, by bribing with a monopoly of worldly honours and emoluments, those who will externally profess and conform to it; that though indeed these are criminal who do not withstand such temptation, yet neither are those innocent who lay the bait in their way; that to suffer the civil Magistrate to intrude his powers into the field of opinion, and to restrain the profession or propagation of principles on supposition of their ill tendency, is a dangerous fallacy, which at once destroys all religious liberty, because he being of course judge of that tendency will make his opinions the rule of judgement, and approve or condemn the sentiments of others only as they shall square with or differ from his own; that it is time enough for the rightful purposes of civil government, for its officers to interfere when principles break out into overt acts against peace and good order; and finally, that truth is great and will prevail if left to herself, that she is the proper and sufficient antagonist to error, and has nothing to fear from the conflict, unless by human interposition disarmed of her natural weapons, free argument and debate, errors ceasing to be dangerous when it is permitted freely to contradict them:

SECT. II. BE *it enacted by the General Assembly,* That no man shall be compelled to frequent or support any religious worship, place, or Ministry whatsoever, nor shall be enforced, restrained, molested, or burthened in his body or goods, nor shall otherwise suffer on account of his religious opinions or belief; but that all men shall be free to profess, and by argument to maintain, their opinions in matters of religion, and that the same shall in no wise diminish, enlarge, or affect their civil capacities.

SECT. III. AND though we well know this Assembly elected by the people for the ordinary purposes of legislation only, have no power to restrain the Acts of succeeding Assemblies, constituted with powers equal to our own, and that therefore to declare this Act to be irrevocable, would be of no effect in law; yet we are free to declare, and do declare, that the rights hereby asserted, are of the natural rights of mankind, raised the mass of the people to the high ground of moral respectability necessary to their own safety, and to orderly government; and would have completed the great object of qualifying them to select the veritable *aristoi*, for the trusts of government, . . . I have great hope that some patriotic spirit will . . . make it the keystone of the arch of our government.

With respect to aristocracy, we should further consider, that before the establishment of the American States, nothing was known to history but the man of the old world, crowded within limits either small or overcharged, and steeped in the vices which that situation generates. A government adapted to such men would be one thing; but a very different one, than for the man of these States. Here every one may have land to labor for himself, if he chooses; or, preferring the exercise of any other industry, may exact for it such compensation as not only to afford a comfortable subsistence, but wherewith to provide for a cessation from labor in old age. Every one, by his property, or by his satisfactory situation, is interested in the support of law and order. And such men may safely and advantageously reserve to themselves a wholesome control over their public affairs, and a degree of freedom, which, in the hands of the *canaille* of the cities of Europe, would be instantly perverted to the demolition and destruction of everything public and private. . .

But even in Europe a change has sensibly taken place in the mind of man. Science had liberated the ideas of those who read and reflect, and the American example had kindled feelings of right in the people. An insurrection has consequently begun, of science, talents, and courage, against rank and birth, which have fallen into contempt. It has failed in its first effort, because the mobs of the cities, the instrument used for its accomplishment, debased by ignorance, poverty, and vice, could not be restrained to rational action. But the world will recover from the panic of this first catastrophe. Science is progressive, and talents and enterprise on the alert. Resort may be had to the people of the country, a more governable power from their principles and subordination; and rank, and birth, and tinsel-aristocracy will finally shrink into significance, even there. This, however, we have no right to meddle with. It suffices for us, if the moral and physical condition of our own citizens qualifies them to select the able and good for the direction of their government, with a recurrence of elections at such short periods as will enable them to displace an unfaithful servant, before the mischief he meditates may be irremediable. . .

---

and that if any Act shall be hereafter passed to repeal the present, or to narrow its operation, such Act will be an infringement of natural right.

Ch. xxxiv of *Acts Passed at a General Assembly of the Commonwealth of Virginia*, October session, 1785, Richmond, 1786.

8. *There is not a word in the Constitution giving judges exclusive authority to declare laws invalid*

THOMAS JEFFERSON to W. H. Torrance, 11 June 1815 *

. . . The . . . question, whether the judges are invested with exclusive authority to decide on the constitutionality of a law, has been heretofore a subject of consideration with me in the exercise of official duties. Certainly there is not a word in the constitution which has given that power to them more than to the executive or legislative branches. Questions of property, of character and of crime being ascribed to the judges, through a definite course of legal proceeding, laws involving such questions belong, of course, to them; and as they decide on them ultimately and without appeal, they of course decide *for themselves*. The constitutional validity of the law or laws again prescribing executive action, and to be administered by that branch ultimately and without appeal, the executive must decide for *themselves* also, whether, under the constitution, they are valid or not. So also as to laws governing the proceedings of the legislature, that body must judge for *itself* the constitutionality of the law, and equally without appeal or control from its co-ordinate branches. And, in general, that branch which is to act ultimately, and without appeal, on any law, is the rightful expositor of the validity of the law, uncontrolled by the opinions of the other co-ordinate authorities. It may be said that contradictory decisions may arise in such case, and produce inconvenience. This is possible, and is a necessary failing in all human proceedings. Yet the prudence of the public functionaries, and authority of public opinion, will generally produce accommodation. . . This is what I believe myself to be sound. But there is another opinion entertained by some men of such judgment and information as to lessen my confidence in my own. That is, that the legislature alone is the exclusive expounder of the sense of the constitution, in every part of it whatever. And they allege in its support, that this branch has authority to impeach and punish a member of either of the others acting contrary to its declaration of the sense of the constitution. It may indeed be answered, that an act may still be valid although the party is punished for it, right or wrong. However, this opinion which ascribes exclusive exposition to the legislature, merits respect for its safety, there being in the body of the nation a control over them, which, if expressed by rejection on the subsequent exercise of their elective franchise, enlists public opinion against their exposition, and encourages a judge or executive on a future occasion to adhere to their former opinion. Between these two doctrines, every one has a right to choose, and I know of no third meriting any respect. . .

* *The Writings of Thomas Jefferson*, P. L. Ford, ed., vol. XI, pp. 471–5.

9. *Our governments have much less of republicanism than ought to have been expected*

THOMAS JEFFERSON to John Taylor, 28 May 1816 *

On my return from a long journey and considerable absence from home, I found here the copy of your 'Enquiry into the Principles of our Government,' which you had been so kind as to send me. . .

Besides much other good matter, it settles unanswerably the right of instructing representatives, and their duty to obey. The system of banking we have both equally and ever reprobated. I contemplate it as a blot left in our constitutions, which, if not covered, will end in their destruction, which is already hit by the gamblers in corruption, and is sweeping away in its progress the fortunes and morals of our citizens. Funding I consider as limited, rightfully, to a redemption of the debt within the lives of a majority of the generation contracting it; every generation coming equally, by the laws of the Creator of the world, to the free possession of the earth he made for their subsistence, unincumbered by their predecessors, who, like them, were but tenants for life. You have successfully and completely pulverized Mr. Adams' system of orders, and his opening the mantle of republicanism to every government of laws, whether consistent or not with natural right. Indeed, it must be acknowledged, that the term *republic* is of very vague application in every language. Witness the self-styled republics of Holland, Switzerland, Genoa, Venice, Poland. Were I to assign to this term a precise and definite idea, I would say, that, purely and simply, it means a government by its citizens in mass, acting directly and personally, according to rules established by the majority: and that every other government is more or less republican, in proportion as it has in its composition more or less of this ingredient of the direct action of the citizens. Such a government is evidently restrained to very narrow limits of space and population. I doubt if it would be practicable beyond the extent of a New England township. The first shade from this pure element, which, like that of pure vital air, cannot sustain life of itself, would be where the powers of the government, being divided, should be exercised each by representatives chosen by the citizens either *pro hac vice*, or for such short terms as should render secure the duty of expressing the will of their constituents. This I should consider as the nearest approach to a pure republic, which is practicable on a large scale of country or population. And we have examples of it in some of our State constitutions, which, if not poisoned by priestcraft, would prove its excellence over all mixtures with other elements; and, with only equal doses of poison, would still be the best. Other shades of republicanism may be found in other forms of government, where the executive, judiciary, and legislative functions, and the different branches of the latter, are chosen by the people more or less directly, for longer terms of years, or for life, or made hereditary; or where there are mixtures of authorities, some dependent on, and others independent of the people. The further the departure from direct and constant control by the citi-

* *The Writings of Thomas Jefferson*, P. L. Ford, ed., vol. x, pp. 27–31 *passim*.

zens, the less has the government of the ingredient of republicanism; evidently none where the authorities are hereditary, as in France, Venice, etc., or self-chosen, as in Holland; and little, where for life, in proportion as the life continues in being after the act of election.

The purest republican feature in the government of our own State, is the House of Representatives. The Senate is equally so the first year, less the second, and so on. The Executive still less, because not chosen by the people directly. The Judiciary seriously anti-republican, because for life; and the national arm wielded, as you observe, by military leaders, irresponsible but to themselves. Add to this the vicious constitution of our county courts (to whom the justice, the executive administration, the taxation, police, the military appointments of the county, and nearly all our daily concerns are confided), self-appointed, self-continued, holding their authorities for life, and with an impossibility of breaking in on the perpetual succession of any faction once possessed of the bench. They are, in truth, the executive, the judiciary, and the military of their respective counties, and the sum of the counties make the State. And add, also, that one half of our brethren who fight and pay taxes, are excluded, like Helots, from the rights of representation, as if society were instituted for the soil, and not for the men inhabiting it; or one half of these could dispose of the rights and the will of the other half, without their consent.

> 'What constitutes a State?
> Not high-raised battlements, or labor'd mound,
> Thick wall, or moated gate;
> Not cities proud, with spires and turrets crown'd;
> No: men, high-minded men;
> Men, who their duties know;
> But know their rights; and, knowing, dare maintain.
> These constitute a State.'

In the General Government, the House of Representatives is mainly republican; the Senate scarcely so at all, as not elected by the people directly, and so long secured even against those who do elect them; the Executive more republican than the Senate, for its shorter term, its election by the people, *in practice* (for they vote for A only on an assurance that he will vote for B) and because, *in practice, also*, a principle of rotation seems to be in a course of establishment; the judiciary independent of the nation, their coercion by impeachment being found nugatory.

If, then, the control of the people over the organs of their government be the measure of its republicanism (and I confess I know no other measure), it must be agreed that our governments have much less of republicanism than ought to have been expected; in other words, that the people have less regular control over their agents, than their rights and their interest require. And this I ascribe, not to any want of republican dispositions in those who formed these constitutions, but to a submission of true principle to European authorities, to speculators on government, whose fears of the people have been inspired by the populace of their own great cities, and were unjustly entertained against the independent, the happy, and therefore orderly citizens of the United States. Much I apprehend that the golden moment is past for reforming these heresies. The functionaries of public power rarely strengthen in their dispositions to abridge it, and an unorganized call for timely amendment is not likely to prevail against an organized opposition to it. We are always told that things are going on well; why change them? '*Chi sta bene, non si muova*,' said the Italian, 'let him who stands well, stand still.' This is true; and I verily believe they would go on well with us under an absolute monarch, while our present character remains, of order, industry, and love of peace, and restrained, as he would be, by the proper spirit of the people. But it is while it remains such, we should provide against the consequences of its deterioration. And let us rest in the hope that it will yet be done, and spare ourselves the pain of evils which may never happen.

On this view of the import of the term *republic*, instead of saying, as has been said, 'that it may mean any thing or nothing,' we may say with truth and meaning, that governments are more or less republican, as they have more or less of the element of popular election and control in their composition: and believing, as I do, that the mass of the citizens is the safest depository of their own rights, and especially, that the evils flowing from the duperies of the people, are less injurious than those from the egoism of their agents, I am a friend to that composition of government which has in it the most of this ingredient. And I sincerely believe, with you, that banking establishments are more dangerous than standing armies; and that the principle of spending money to be paid by posterity, under the name of funding, is but swindling futurity on a large scale. . .

10. *An idea quite unfounded—on entering into society, we give up any natural right*

THOMAS JEFFERSON to Francis W. Gilmer, 7 June 1816 *

. . . Our legislators are not sufficiently apprised of the rightful limits of their power; that their true office is to declare and enforce only our natural rights and duties, and to take none of them from us. No man has a natural right to commit aggression on the equal rights of another; and this is all from which the laws ought to restrain him; every man is under the natural duty of contributing to the necessities of the society; and this is all the laws should enforce on him; and, no man having a natural right to be the judge between himself and another, it is his natural duty to submit to the umpirage of an impartial third. When the laws have declared and enforced all this, they have fulfilled their functions; and the idea is quite unfounded, that on entering into society we give up any natural right. . . There is a work of the first order of merit now in the press at Washington, by Destutt Tracy, on the subject of political economy. . . In a preliminary discourse on the origin of

* *The Writings of Thomas Jefferson*, P. L. Ford, ed., vol. x, pp. 31-3.

the right of property, he coincides much with the principles of the present manuscript; but is more developed, more demonstrative. He promises a future work on morals, in which I lament to see that he will adopt the principles of Hobbes, or humiliation to human nature; that the sense of justice and injustice is not derived from our natural organization, but founded on convention only. . . Man was created for social intercourse; but social intercourse cannot be maintained without a sense of justice; than man must have been created with a sense of justice. There is an error into which most of the speculators on government have fallen, and which the well-known state of society of our Indians ought, before now, to have corrected. In their hypothesis of the origin of government, they suppose it to have commenced in the patriarchal or monarchical form. Our Indians are evidently in that state of nature which has passed the association of a single family; and not yet submitted to the authority of positive laws, or of any acknowledged magistrate. Every man, with them, is perfectly free to follow his own inclinations. But if, in doing this, he violates the rights of another, if the case be slight, he is punished by the disesteem of his society, or, as we say, by public opinion; if serious, he is tomahawked as a dangerous enemy. Their leaders conduct them by the influence of their character only; and they follow, or not, as they please, him of whose character for wisdom or war they have the highest opinion. Hence the origin of the parties among them adhering to different leaders, and governed by their advice, not by their command. The Cherokees, the only tribe I know to be contemplating the establishment of regular laws, magistrates, and government, propose a government of representatives, elected from every town. But of all things, they least think of subjecting themselves to the will of one man. This, the only instance of actual fact within our knowledge, will be then a beginning by republican, and not by patriarchal or monarchical government, as speculative writers have generally conjectured. . .

11 *I am not among those who fear the people*

THOMAS JEFFERSON to Samuel Kercheval, 12 July 1816 *

. . . The question you propose, on equal representation, has become a party one, in which I wish to take no public share. Yet, if it be asked for your own satisfaction only, and not to be quoted before the public, I have no motive to withhold it, and the less from you, as it coincides with your own. At the birth of our republic, I committed that opinion to the world, in the draught of a constitution annexed to the 'Notes on Virginia,' in which a provision was inserted for a representation permanently equal. The infancy of the subject at that moment, and our inexperience of self-government, occasioned gross departures in that draught from genuine republican canons. In truth, the abuses of monarchy had so much filled all the space of political contemplation, that we imagined everything republican which was not monarchy. We had

* *The Writings of Thomas Jefferson*, P. L. Ford, ed., vol. x, pp. 37–45.

not yet penetrated to the mother principle, that 'governments are republican only in proportion as they embody the will of their people, and execute it.' Hence, our first constitutions had really no leading principles in them. But experience and reflection have but more and more confirmed me in the particular importance of the equal representation then proposed. . .

Inequality of representation in both Houses of our legislature, is not the only republican heresy in this first essay of our revolutionary patriots at forming a constitution. For let it be agreed that a government is republican in proportion as every member composing it has his equal voice in the direction of its concerns (not indeed in person, which would be impracticable beyond the limits of a city, or small township, but) by representatives chosen by himself, and responsible to him at short periods, and let us bring to the test of this canon every branch of our constitution.

In the legislature, the House of Representatives is chosen by less than half the people, and not at all in proportion to those who do choose. The Senate are still more disproportionate, and for long terms of irresponsibility. In the Executive, the Governor is entirely independent of the choice of the people, and of their control; his Council equally so, and at best but a fifth wheel to a wagon. In the Judiciary, the judges of the highest courts are dependent on none but themselves. In England, where judges were named and removable at the will of an hereditary executive, from which branch most misrule was feared, and has flowed, it was a great point gained, by fixing them for life, to make them independent of that executive. But in a government founded on the public will, this principle operates in an opposite direction, and against that will. There, too, they were still removable on a concurrence of the executive and legislative branches. But we have made them independent of the nation itself. They are irremovable, but by their own body, for any depravities of conduct, and even by their own body for the imbecilities of dotage. The justices of the inferior courts are self-chosen, are for life, and perpetuate their own body in succession forever, so that a faction once possessing themselves of the bench of a county, can never be broken up, but hold their county in chains, forever indissoluble. Yet these justices are the real executive as well as judiciary, in all our minor and most ordinary concerns. They tax us at will; fill the office of sheriff, the most important of all the executive officers of the county; name nearly all our military leaders, which leaders, once named, are removable but by themselves. The juries, our judges of all fact, and of law when they choose it, are not selected by the people, nor amenable to them. They are chosen by an officer named by the court and executive. Chosen, did I say? Picked up by the sheriff from the loungings of the court yard, after everything respectable has retired from it. Where then is our republicanism to be found? Not in our constitution certainly, but merely in the spirit of our people. That would oblige even a despot to govern us republicanly. Owing to this spirit, and to nothing in the form of our constitution, all things have gone well. But this fact, so triumphantly misquoted by the enemies of reformation, is not the fruit of our constitution, but has prevailed in spite of it. Our functionaries have done well, because generally honest men. If any were not so, they feared to show it.

But it will be said, it is easier to find faults than to amend them. I do not think their amendment so difficult as is pretended. Only lay down true principles, and adhere to them inflexibly. Do not be frightened into their surrender by the alarms of the timid, or the croakings of wealth against the ascendency of the people. If experience be called for, appeal to that of our fifteen or twenty governments for forty years, and show me where the people have done half the mischief in these forty years, that a single despot would have done in a single year; or show half the riots and rebellions, the crimes and the punishments, which have taken place in any single nation, under kingly government, during the same period. The true foundation of republican government is the equal right of every citizen, in his person and property, and in their management. Try by this, as a tally, every provision of our constitution and see if it hangs directly on the will of the people. Reduce your legislature to a convenient number for full, but orderly discussion. Let every man who fights or pays exercise his just and equal right in their election. Submit them to approbation or rejection at short intervals. Let the executive be chosen in the same way, and for the same term, by those whose agent he is to be; and leave no screen of a council behind to skulk from responsibility. It has been thought that the people are not competent electors of judges *learned in the law.* But I do not know that this is true, and, if doubtful, we should follow principle. In this, as in many other elections, they would be guided by reputation, which would not err oftener, perhaps, than the present mode of appointment. In one State of the Union, at least, it has long been tried, and with the most satisfactory success. The judges of Connecticut have been chosen by the people every six months, for nearly two centuries, and I believe there had hardly ever been an instance of change; so powerful is the curb of incessant responsiblity. If prejudice, however, derived from a monarchical institution, is still to prevail against the vital elective principle of our own, and if the existing example among ourselves of periodical election of judges by the people be still mistrusted, let us at least not adopt the evil, and reject the good, of the English precedent; let us retain a movability on the concurrence of the executive and legislative branches, and nomination by the executive alone. Nomination to office is an executive function. To give it to the legislature, as we do, is a violation of the principle of the separation of powers. It swerves the members from correctness, by temptations to intrigue for office themselves, and to corrupt barter of votes; and destroys responsibility by dividing it among a multitude. By leaving nominations in its proper place, among executive functions, the principle of the distribution of power is preserved, and responsibility weighs with its heaviest force on a single head.

The organization of our county administrations may be thought more difficult. But follow principle, and the knot unties itself. Divide the counties into wards of such size as that every citizen can attend, when called on, and act in person. Ascribe to them the government of their wards in all things relating to themselves exclusively. A justice, chosen by themselves, in each, a constable, a military company, a patrol, a school, the care of their own poor, their own portion of the public roads, the choice of one or more jurors to serve in some court, and the delivery, within their own wards, of their own votes for all elective officers of higher sphere, will relieve the county administration of nearly all its business, will have it better done, and by making every citizen an acting member of the government, and in the offices nearest and most interesting to him, will attach him by his strongest feelings to the independence of his country, and its republican constitution. The justices thus chosen by every ward, would constitute the county court, would do its judiciary business, direct roads and bridges, levy county and poor rates, and administer all the matters of common interest to the whole country. These wards, called townships in New England, are the vital principle of their governments, and have proved themselves the wisest invention ever devised by the wit of man for the perfect exercise of self-government, and for its preservation. We should thus marshal our government into, 1, the general federal republic, for all concerns foreign and federal; 2, that of the State, for what relates to our own citizens exclusively; 3, the county republics, for the duties and concerns of the county; and 4, the ward republics, for the small, and yet numerous and interesting concerns of the neighborhood; and in government, as well as in every other business of life, it is by division and subdivision of duties alone, that all matters, great and small, can be managed to perfection. And the whole is cemented by giving to every citizen, personally, a part in the administration of the public affairs.

The sum of these amendments is, 1. General Suffrage. 2. Equal representation in the legislature. 3. An executive chosen by the people. 4. Judges elective or amovable. 5. Justices, jurors, and sheriffs elective. 6. Ward divisions. And 7. Periodical amendments of the constitution.

I have thrown out these as loose heads of amendment, for consideration and correction; and their object is to secure self-government by the republicanism of our constitution, as well as by the spirit of the people; and to nourish and perpetuate that spirit. I am not among those who fear the people. They, and not the rich, are our dependence for continued freedom. And to preserve their independence, we must not let our rulers load us with perpetual debt. We must make our election between *economy and liberty*, or *profusion and servitude*. If we run into such debts, as that we must be taxed in our meat and in our drink, in our necessaries and our comforts, in our labors and our amusements, for our callings and creeds, as the people of England are, our people, like them, must come to labor sixteen hours in the twenty-four, give the earnings of fifteen of these to the government for their debts and daily expenses; and the sixteenth being insufficient to afford us bread, we must live, as they now do, on oatmeal and potatoes; have no time to think, no means of calling the mismanagers to account; but be glad to obtain subsistence by hiring ourselves to rivet their chains on the necks of our fellow-suffers. Our landholders, too, like theirs, retaining indeed the title and stewardship of estates called theirs, but held really in trust for the treasury, must wander, like theirs, in foreign countries, and be contented with penury, obscurity, exile, and the glory of the nation. This example reads to us the salutary lesson, that private fortunes are destroyed by public as well as by private extravagence. And this is the tendency of all human governments. A departure from principle in one instance becomes a precedent for a second, that second for a third; and so on, till the bulk of the society is reduced to be mere automatons of misery, and to have no sensibilities left but for sinning and suffering. Then begins, indeed, the *bellum omnium in omnia*, which some philosophers observing to be so general in this world, have mistaken it for the natural, instead of the abusive state of man. And the fore horse of this frightful team is public debt. Taxation follows that, and in its train wretchedness and oppression.

Some men look at constitutions with sanctimonious reverence, and deem them like the arc of the covenant, too sacred to be touched. They ascribe to the men of the preceding age a wisdom more than human, and suppose what they did to be beyond amendment. I knew that age well; I belonged to it, and labored with it. It deserved well of its country. It was very like the present, but without the experience of the present; and forty years of experience in government is worth a century of bookreading; and this they would say themselves, were they to rise from the dead. I am certainly not an advocate for frequent and untried changes in laws and constitutions. I think moderate imperfections had better be borne with; because, when once known, we accommodate ourselves to them, and find practical means of correcting their ill effects. But I know also, that laws and institutions must go hand in hand with the progress of the human mind. As that becomes more developed, more enlightened, as new discoveries are made, new truths disclosed, and manners and opinions change with the change of circumstances, institutions must advance also, and keep pace with the times. We might as well require a man to wear still the coat which fitted him when a boy, as civilized society to remain ever under the regimen of their barbarous ancestors. It is this preposterous idea which has lately deluged Europe in blood. Their monarchs, instead of wisely yielding to the gradual change of circumstances, of favoring progressive accommodation to progressive improvement, have clung to old abuses, entrenched themselves behind steady habits, and obliged their subjects to seek through blood and violence rash and ruinous innovations, which, had they been referred to the peaceful deliberations and collected wisdom of the nation, would have been put into acceptable and salutary forms. Let us follow no such examples, nor weakly believe that one generation is not as capable as another of taking care of itself, and of ordering its own affairs. Let us, as our sister States have done, avail ourselves of our reason and experience, to correct the crude essays of our first and unexperienced, although wise, virtuous, and well-meaning councils. And lastly, let us provide in our constitution for its revision at stated periods. What these periods should be, nature herself indicates. By the European tables of mortality, of the adults living at any one moment of time, a majority will be dead in about nineteen years. At the end of that period, then, a new majority is come into place; or, in other words, a new generation. Each generation is as independent as the one preceding, as that was of all which had gone before. It has then, like them, a right to choose for itself the form of government it believes most promotive of its own happiness; consequently, to accommodate to the circumstances in which it finds itself, that received from its predecessors; and it is for the peace and good of mankind, that a solemn opportunity of doing this every nineteen or twenty years, should be provided by the constitution; so that it may be handed on, with periodical repairs, from generation to generation, to the end of time, if anything human can so long endure. It is now forty years since the constitution of Virginia was formed. The same tables inform us, that, within that period, two-thirds of the adults then living are now dead. Have then the remaining third, even if they had the wish, the right to hold in obedience to their will, and to laws heretofore made by them, the other two-thirds, who, with themselves, compose the present mass of adults? If they have not, who has? The dead? But the dead have no rights. They are nothing; and nothing cannot own something. Where there is no substance, there can be no accident. This corporeal globe, and everything upon it, belong to its present corporeal inhabitants, during their generation. They alone have a right to direct what is the concern of themselves alone, and to declare the law of that direction; and this declaration can only be made by their majority. That majority, then, has a right to depute representatives to a convention, and to make the constitution what they think will be the best for themselves. But how collect their voice? This is the real difficulty. If invited by private authority, or county or district meetings, these divisions are so large that few will attend; and their voice will be imperfectly, or falsely pronounced. Here, then, would be one of the advantages of the ward divisions I have proposed. The mayor of every ward, on a question like the present, would call his ward together, take the simple yea or nay of its members, convey these to the county court, who would hand on those of all its wards to the proper general authority; and the voice of the whole people would be thus fairly, fully, and peaceably expressed, discussed, and decided by the common reason of the society. If this avenue be shut to the call of sufferance, it will make itself heard through that of force, and we shall go on, as other nations are doing, in the endless circle of oppression, rebellion, reformation; and oppression, rebellion, reformation, again; and so on forever.

These, Sir, are my opinions of the governments we see among men, and of the principles by which alone we may prevent our own from falling into the same dreadful track. I have given them at greater length than your letter called for. But I cannot say things by halves; and I confide them to your honor, so to use them to preserve me from the gridiron of the public papers. If you shall approve and enforce them, as you have done that of equal representation, they may do some good. If not, keep them to yourself as the effusions of withered age and useless time. I shall, with not the less truth, assure you of my great respect and consideration.

12. *The Constitution did not create a concentrated supremacy in the national government*

JOHN TAYLOR, *New Views of the Constitution of the United States*, 1823 *

Had the journal of the convention which framed the constitution of the United States, though obscure and incomplete, been published immediately after its ratification, it would have furnished lights towards a true construction, sufficiently clear to have prevented several trespasses upon its principles, and tendencies towards its subversion. Perhaps it may not be yet too late to lay before the public the important evidence it furnishes. . .

On the 29th of May, 1787, the convention was organized, and Mr. Randolph, of Virginia, offered sundry resolutions resuming the word national though it had been rejected by all the states, and proposing 'that a *national* legislature shall have the right to legislate in all cases in which the harmony of the United States may be interrupted by the exercise of *individual legislation, and to negative all laws passed by the several states, contravening, in the opinion of the national legislature, the articles of the union*, or any treaty under the union.' The resolutions also proposed 'a *national* executive and a *national* judiciary; that the executive and a convenient number of the *national* judiciary ought to compose a *council of revision*, with authority to examine every act of the national legislature, before it shall operate, and every act of a *particular legislature*, before a negative thereon shall be final; and that the *dissent* of the said council shall amount to a *rejection* unless the act of the national legislature be again passed, or that of a particular legislature be again negatived by ——— of the members of each branch.'

It is worthy of particular observation, that in this project, the constructive supremacy now claimed for the federal government *'over the articles of the union,'* was proposed to be given to a national government; because the actual consideration of this identical power, and its absence from the constitution as it was finally adopted, seems to be irresistible evidence that it does not exist. Throughout Mr. Randolph's resolutions, fifteen in number, the word national is adopted, and the word Congress rejected, except in reference to the Congress under the confederation of 1777, proving that the word was applicable to a federal union, but not to a national government.

The proposed national form of government was ultimately renounced or rejected, but the negative power over state laws with which it was invested, was much less objectionable than that now constructively contended for on behalf of the federal government. The president was to be one of a council of revision, and the influence of the states in his election might have afforded to them some feeble security, a little better than could be expected from a council of revision composed of a few federal judges. Both the legislative branches which were to pronounce the first veto upon state laws, were also to be exposed to popular influence, and might feel all the responsibility of

* John Taylor, *New Views of the Constitution of the United States*, Washington, D.C., Way and Gideon, 1823, pp. 11–246 *passim*.

which a body of men are susceptible in extending its own power by its own vote. A judicial veto, as now contended for, is exposed to no responsibility whatever. The council of revision, with the president at its head, were only to be controlled by more than a majority of the national legislature. This was evidently a better security for the small states, than a power in the majority of Congress to abrogate state laws. But all these alleviations of the power in a national form of government to negative state laws, were unsuccessful, because the principle itself, however modified, was inconsistent with the federal form adopted. It can never be conceived that the principle of a negative over state laws, audibly proposed and rejected, had silently crept into the constitution. This was quite consistent with the national form of government proposed, but quite inconsistent with the federal form adopted. The project for a national form of government was deduced from the doctrine, as we shall hereafter see, that the declaration of independence had committed the gross blunder of making the states dependent corporations; that it was in fact a declaration of dependence. When this doctrine failed in the convention, the national negative over state laws died with it. Revived by construction, it assumes a far more formidable and consolidating aspect than as it was originally offered, because the usurped negative over states laws, by a majority of a court or of Congress, would not have its malignity to the states alleviated by the checks to which the project itself resorted. Without these checks, even the advocates for a national form of government thought such a negative intolerable. The project contemplated a mixed legislative, executive, and judicial supremacy over state laws, so that one department of this sovereignty, like that of the English, might check the other, in construing 'the articles of the union,' and did not venture even to propose, that a government should be established, in which a single court was to be invested with a supreme power over these articles, or the constitution. The idea seems to be a political monster never seen in fable or in fact. . .

The project for a national government, gave a supremacy over the articles of the constitution it advocated, to the legislative, judiciary, and executive, and did not propose that the constitution should be supreme over these departments, because it would have involved a contradiction. As they were to have had a supreme power of construing its articles, these articles could not possess a supreme power over their constructions. But a federal system required that the articles of union should be invested with supremacy, over the instruments created to obey and execute them. Hence they are declared to be so in reference to all these instruments, without excepting the federal court. . . In all treaties, the right of construction must be attached to the right of alteration, or the latter right would be destroyed. . . But the right of alteration being placed in the states, because they made it, and not in a consolidated people, because such a people did not make it; the right of construction is attached to the altering power, and not given to its own agents under the fictions assumed to sustain a national government, namely, that a consolidated people existed. . .

The supremacy of the constitution is an admonition to all departments, both state and federal, that they were bound to obey the restrictions it imposes.

In relation to the federal government, it literally declares that its laws must conform to its exclusive and concurrent powers; and in relation to the state governments, it implies, that theirs must also conform to their exclusive and concurrent powers. It neither enlarges nor abridges the powers delegated or reserved. And it is enforced, not by an oath to be faithful to the supreme constructions of the federal departments, but by an oath to be faithful to the supremacy of the constitution. . .

Sovereignty is the highest degree of political power, and the establishment of a form of government, the highest proof which can be given of its existence. The states could not have reserved any rights by the articles of their union, if they had not been sovereign, because they could have no rights unless they flowed from that source. In the creation of the federal government, the states exercised the highest act of sovereignty, and they may, if they please, repeat the proof of their sovereignty, by its annihilation. But the union possesses no innate sovereignty, like the states; it was not self-constituted, it is conventional, and of course subordinate to the sovereignties by which it was formed. . . I have no idea of a sovereignty constituted upon better ground than that of each state, nor of one which can be pretended to on worse, than that claimed for the federal government, or some portion of it. . . The sovereignties which imposed the limitations upon the federal government, far from supposing that they perished by the exercise of a part of their faculties, were vindicated, by reserving powers in which their deputy, the federal government, could not participate; and the usual right of sovereigns to alter or revoke its commissions. . .

The federal legislative and judicial powers are both plainly intended to be limited by the constitution, and any mode by which this limitation can be evaded, must destroy our federal system, or be destroyed by it. If Congress can give a judicial supremacy to a federal court, the federal legislative power must be itself supreme, and may extend its boundary to the executive also. . .

There are some principles necessary for the existence of the political system of the United States. One of these is, the supremacy, both of the state and federal constitutions, over the repositories of power created by their articles. Another, that this is a limited supremacy in both cases, subject in one, to the supremacy of the people in each state, and in the other, to the supremacy of three-fourths of the states. And a third, that no power created by these constitutions, can violate their articles, or evade the supremacies to which the constitutions are themselves subject. From these principles it results, that neither laws nor judgments are valid, which do not conform to constitutions; and that a mutual control of political departments, is the only mode of enforcing this doctrine, necessary to sustain both the supremacy of constitutions, and of those who make them. The federal judges do not take an oath to obey the state constitutions, because, as they derive no jurisdiction from them, there is no privity between the rights and powers which they establish, and these judges. If the federal courts could abridge these rights and powers, it would defeat the principle of the supremacy of the people of each state, over their constitutions. This would vitally destroy the federal compact, supposed to exist between republics, because the states would not be republics, if their constitutions were made subordinate to the will or the power of the court, instead of being only subordinate to the will or power of the people. . . As state constitutions are subject to the supremacy of the people of each state, and the federal constitution to three-fourths of the states, neither are subject to laws or judgments state or federal, or to a consolidated American nation. A supremacy in a federal court to construe the articles of the declaration of independence, and of the federal and state constitutions, united with a power to enforce its constructions, would as effectually destroy the supremacy of the people, and of three-fourths of the states, as the same species of supreme power in state legislatures would destroy the supremacy of state constitutions, and of the people of each state.

If the constitution of a state should be so altered, as to bestow on the legislature a supreme power of construing its articles, and excluding the judiciary from the right or the duty of disobeying unconstitutional laws; or if the constitution of the United States should invest the federal judiciary with the same supreme power as to the construction of the federal constitution; the principles, necessary for the existence of our political system, would be abolished, and both the federal and state governments would substantially be reinstated, according to the English policy, by which the government itself can modify its own powers. . .

Liberty and power are adverse pleaders, and the arguments or temptations offered by both, have never failed to make proselytes. Between the tyranny of concentrated power, and of unbridled licentiousness, is a space filled with materials for computing the effects produced by controlling both extremes, and estimating the chances for promoting human liberty and happiness. It seems to be nature's law, that every species of concentrated sovereignty over extensive territories, whether monarchical, aristocratical, democratical, or mixed, must be despotic. In no case has a concentrated power over great territories been sustained, except by mercenary armies; and wherever power is thus sustained, despotism is the consequence. . . Between this conclusion, dictated by the laws of nature, and a territorial division of powers, lies our alternative. The geography of our country and the character of our people, unite to demonstrate that the ignorance and partiality of a concentrated form of government, can only be enforced by armies; and the peculiar ability of the states to resist, promises that resistance would be violent; so that a national government must either be precarious or despotic. By dividing power between the federal and state governments, local partialities and oppressions, the common causes of revolution, are obliterated from our system. . .

Communities possessed of sufficient knowledge to discriminate between liberty and slavery, have uniformly laboured to invest governments with a portion of power sufficient to secure social happiness, but insufficient for its destruction. The United States understood the discrimination, and in the formation of the federal government endeavoured, by limitations and prohibitions, to reserve and secure as many of their individual rights as might be retained without defeating the end of providing for their common interest. The two principles of a division or a concentration of power, are the adversaries contending for preference. . . The United States saw that any geographical interest, if invested with supremacy by the establishment of a consolidated national government, would oppress some other geographical interest; and made a new effort to avoid this natural malignity of a concentrated supreme power. . .

Against this beautiful theory, an appetite for power in all ages, urges the same objection. It uniformly asserts that divisions of power obstruct, paralyze, or defeat, the splendid actions to be expected from a concentrated supremacy. Before this argument can have any force, it ought to be settled, whether the achievements of concentrated power are good or bad things; since, according to the determination of this fact, the argument becomes an objection to the principle of dividing power, or its recommendation. Will this principle defeat most good or bad measures? Its value should be ascertained, not by a partial exhibition of the good measures it may have obstructed, but by its general tendency to prevent oppression. The fact that mankind have suffered the sorest evils from a supreme concentrated power, is undoubtedly well established; and it is equally a fact, that no remedy against these universal calamities, has ever been suggested, except divisions of power. . .

The principles of division and control are applied extensively to the state governments, whereas they are not applied at all, or ineffectually applied, to the concentrated baronial, monarchical, or mixed governments of Europe. This difference accounts for the exclusive blessings we have reaped from our modes of dividing and controlling power. If we should exchange them for a concentrated supremacy in the federal government, the internal divisions of the state governments would be rendered useless, the state elections for controlling state departments, would dwindle into an idle ceremony. The European supremacies possess no principles sufficient to secure the liberty and happiness of the people, and are naturally guided by the worst passions; the states have united, not to awaken these bad passions by creating a concentrated supremacy, but to secure the liberty and happiness of the people, or the most holy interests of mankind. . .

The objection, that the state governments may obstruct federal measures, unless they are subordinate to some federal supremacy, is only equivalent to the objection, that the federal government may obstruct state measures, unless it is subordinate to a state supremacy. . . Reason, compact, and a common interest, and not a supreme power, are the only resources for settling such collisions, compatible with a division of power. These umpires have inspired the king, lords, and commons, of Britain, with a mutual moderation towards each other. If the preservation of the rights of free states and free men, cannot inspire the state and federal governments with mutual moderation, it will unfortunately prove that the children of mammon are wiser than the children of liberty. If the common interest of the states to preserve the federal government, will not be regarded, a government by force must succeed, and all our social improvements founded upon a common interest, will be lost. But have not the states as strong and better motives for nourishing their federal, as well as local prosperity, than the king, lords, and commons of England have for nourishing their concentrated supremacy? What checks against tyranny can be devised, if those founded in a common interest are unsuccessful? and can they be unsuccessful, except by exchanging them for a concentrated supremacy?

Society, well constructed, must be compounded of restraint and freedom, and this was carefully attended to in framing our union. . . Freedom without restraint, or restraint without freedom, is either anarchy or despotism. . . A concentrated power destroys the counterpoise between freedom and restraint, and never fails to become the executioner of human happiness. The constitution, with consummate wisdom, has effected this counterpoise, and also provided against foreign and state collisions, without sacrificing state prosperity. It did not design to embitter the best fruits of government, by tacitly creating a concentrated supremacy. . .

SELECTED REFERENCES

Gordon E. Baker, 'Thomas Jefferson and Academic Freedom,' American Association of University Professors, *Bulletin* XXXIX, Autumn 1953, p. 377.

Julian P. Boyd, 'Thomas Jefferson's "Empire of Liberty,"' *The Virginia Quarterly Review*, Autumn 1948, vol. 24, no. 4.

Manning J. Dauer and Hans Hammond, 'John Taylor: Democrat or Aristocrat?' *Journal of Politics*, November 1944, vol. VI, pp. 381–403.

W. E. Dodd, 'John Taylor of Caroline, Prophet of Secession,' *John P. Branch Historical Papers of Randolph-Macon College*, Ashland, Virginia, 1908, vol. 2, pp. 214–52.

Clement Eaton, 'The Jeffersonian Tradition of Liberalism in America,' *South Atlantic Quarterly*, 1944, vol. 43, pp. 1–10.

Joseph Dorfman, 'The Economic Philosophy of Thomas Jefferson,' *Political Science Quarterly*, March 1940, vol. 55, pp. 98–121.

G. P. Fisher, 'Jefferson and the Social Compact Theory,' *Annual Report, American Historical Association*, 1893, Washington, D.C., 1894, pp. 165–77.

A. Whitney Griswold, *Farming and Democracy*, New York, Harcourt, Brace, 1948.

Adrienne Koch, *The Philosophy of Thomas Jefferson*, New York, Columbia University Press, 1943.

——— and Harry Ammon, 'The Virginia and Kentucky Resolutions: An Episode in Jefferson's and Madison's Defence of Civil Liberties,' *William and Mary Quarterly*, April 1948, vol. 5, p. 166.

Karl Lehmann, *Thomas Jefferson, American Humanist*, New York, Macmillan, 1947.

Leonard Levy, *Jefferson and Civil Liberties: The Darker Side*, Cambridge, Harvard University Press, 1963.

E. T. Mudge, *The Social Philosophy of John Taylor of Caroline*, New York, Columbia University Press, 1939.

V. L. Parrington, *Main Currents in American Thought: The Colonial Mind*, New York, Harcourt, Brace, 1927, vol. I, pp. 342–56.

Merrill Peterson, *The Jefferson Image in the American Mind*, New York, Oxford University Press, 1960.

C. S. Thomas, 'Jefferson and the Judiciary,' *Constitutional Review*, 1926, vol. 10, pp. 67–76.

Francis G. Wilson, 'On Jeffersonian Tradition,' *Review of Politics*, July 1943, vol. V, pp. 302–21.

Charles Maurice Wiltse, 'Jeffersonian Democracy: A Dual Tradition,' *American Political Science Review*, 1934, vol. 28, pp. 838–51.

———, *The Jeffersonian Tradition in American Democracy*, Chapel Hill, N. C., 1935.

Benjamin F. Wright, 'The Philosopher of Jeffersonian Democracy,' *American Political Science Review*, 1928, vol. XXII, pp. 870–92.

———, *American Interpretations of Natural Law*, Cambridge, Harvard University Press, 1931.

X

EXPANDING THE BASE OF POPULAR POWER

The original state constitutions, framed in revolution, were not calculated to endure. 'We all knew,' P. R. Livingston observed, 5 September 1821, in the Convention called to revise New York's Constitution of 1777, that 'it was adopted in an hour of extreme peril, amidst the noise of musketry and the thunder of cannon.' 'Is it to be wondered at,' he queried, 'that their deliberations, under such circumstances, were in some measure erroneous?' In the years immediately following 1776, the preferred position accorded men of property was an expedient easily justified. 'Nearly all the freehold property in the State was then possessed by a few families,' Chief Justice Ambrose Spencer of New York explained, 24 September 1821, 'and unless they were indulged in this favorite discrimination, it would lead to disaffection, which the most imperious considerations of safety urged them to prevent.'

Conditions after 1820, however, were greatly changed, and public opinion, reflecting these changes, expressed itself in widespread movements for extending, in various ways, the range of popular power. So while Democratic-Republicans supported such Federalist measures as the United States Bank and the protective tariff, popular discontent stirred in the states and rose to the breaking point. In a single decade, 1820–30, Massachusetts, New York, and Virginia called conventions to liberalize their fundamental laws. Other states followed in rapid succession.

Assembled in these conventions were some of the most eminent statesmen in the land, men whose services to the nation dated from the revolutionary period. Massachusetts delegates included the venerable John Adams (1735–1826), revolutionary leader and second President of the United States; Joseph Story (1779–1845), Associate Justice of the Supreme Court; and Daniel Webster (1782–1852)—all ardent defenders of the *status quo*. Chancellor James Kent (1763–1847) headed New York's delegation, while the Virginia convention included two ex-Presidents, James Madison (1751–1836) and James Monroe (1758–1831), as well as Chief Justice John Marshall (1755–1835) and John Randolph (1773–1833) of Roanoke. Associated with these notables were men less distinguished who were strongly determined to achieve drastic constitutional change. So while Chancellor Kent and men of equal rank in other states staunchly defended 'our Constitution formed by those illustrious sages and patriots who adorned the revolution,' obscure delegates argued that failure to liberalize the state constitutions would mean a continuing breach of those fundamental principles for which American patriots had spent their blood and treasure.

Among other things, the debates centered on the proposal to remove the freehold restrictions on suffrage contained in the Virginia Constitution of 1777, and on proposals to amend those provisions in the original constitutions of Massachusetts and New York that made the Senate 'the guardian of property,' as Jonathan Blake of the Bay State put it, 'the rich man's citadel.'

In his letter to Samuel Kercheval, 12 July 1816, Jefferson referred to the 'gross departures . . . from genuine republican canons'—lack of adequate and equal representation, restrictions on suffrage, and judicial supremacy—that characterized the Virginia Constitution of 1776. To win amendments, the non-freeholders of Richmond recalled the familiar natural rights doctrine, only to meet open and categorical resistance at the hands of conservative leaders such as Upshur and Randolph; extension of the suffrage would forge for the masses a political weapon, enabling them, as Webster said, to break in upon the rights of property. This argument, the non-freeholders insisted, was blind to the motives prompting their efforts. They were not thinking in terms of class struggle. Property was sacrosanct in the minds of rich and poor alike. Most men, they explained, 'desire to become owners of property. . . It can never be in their interest to overburthen, or render precarious, what they themselves desire to enjoy in peace.'

John Randolph was inclined to hear these protestations of good will 'in words the most courteous and soft,' but he was 'not so soft as to swallow them.' 'King Numbers' still remained the threat. Nor could any realist accept the revolutionary doctrine of natural law as civil society's measure of right and wrong. For Upshur, too, numbers and property were the 'majorities' to be considered. Each was entitled to formal statutory protection. He who enters society with rights of person and rights of property has the greatest stake and must 'possess an authority proportioned to that interest, and adequate to its protection.' Once again James Madison, now aged and infirm, rose to invoke the calm and conciliatory council that had marked his career throughout. The immediate issue concerned the Negro population of the commonwealth and their relations as persons and property in the matter of representation. He began:

> It is sufficiently obvious that persons and property are the two great objects on which Governments are to act; that the rights of persons and the rights of property are the objects for the protection of which Government was instituted. These rights cannot well be separated. The personal right to acquire property which is a natural right, gives to property when acquired, a right to protection, as a social right.
>
> It is due to justice; due to humanity; to the sympathies of our nature in fine, to our character as a people, both abroad and at home; that the colored part of our population should be considered,

> as much as possible, in the light of human beings, and not as mere property. As such they are acted upon by our laws, and have an interest in our laws.
>
> In framing a constitution, great difficulties are necessarily to be overcome; and nothing can ever overcome them but the spirit of compromise. Other nations are surprised at nothing so much as our having been able to form constitutions in the manner which has been exemplified in this country. Even the union of so many states, is, in the eyes of the world, a wonder; the harmonious establishment of a common Government over all, a miracle. I cannot but flatter myself that without a miracle, we shall be able to arrange all difficulties. I never have despaired, notwithstanding all the threatening appearances we have passed through. I have now more than a hope—a consoling confidence—that we shall at last find that our labors have not been in vain.

Another major issue in the Virginia Convention concerned the Judiciary, which John Marshall's biographer, Albert J. Beveridge, characterized as 'the very negation of democracy,' a 'rigid self-perpetuating oligarchy,' which had even assumed the right of nominating the new appointments the governor was to make to the bench. One member of the Convention charged that the inability of the legislature to get rid of a judge established 'a privileged corps in a free community.' But Marshall blandly stated in reply that 'a Judge ought to be responsible only to God and to his conscience.' A judge removable at the will of the legislature would lose all value as the protector of property and individual rights. The Judiciary must, he said, remain the bulwark of property against the tyranny of the majority.

One cannot read these discussions without a sense of the great and continuing paradox that permeates free government: the moral ideals of political freedom and equality coupled with impassioned insistence that inevitable economic inequality must be maintained by constitutional safeguards. As Kent in New York, Upshur and Randolph in Virginia, Story and Webster in Massachusetts tried to grapple realistically with the facts of an American society already clearly destined for industrialism, they were taunted by opposing delegates who spoke in terms of our exalted eighteenth-century ideals. Randolph, flabbergasted, said: 'It is the first time in my life that I have ever heard of a government which was to divorce property from power.' 'Universal suffrage,' Chancellor Kent had said, is 'inconsistent with liberty.' Once granted, it is granted forever. 'There is no retrograde step,' he observed sadly, 'in the rear of democracy.'

Such fears and wild forebodings were blind to the motivations of the so-called common man. 'Every member of the convention was,' P. R. Livingston said, 'a friend of property, and to the landed interest.' Furthermore, in America, unlike Europe, 'real property will be,' Buel of New York predicted, 'in the hands of the many' because with us 'the desire of acquiring property is a universal passion.' In a country like ours, rich in natural resources and educational opportunities, the European analogy was patently false.

In the 1820's conservative leaders charted a course for America not unlike that developed two decades later in Marx's *Communist Manifesto*. The Kents, Randolphs, and Upshurs conceived of society deeply stratified along economic lines, torn by fierce conflict between rich and poor. They wanted to maintain high constitutional barriers for the few against the many. On the other hand the liberals—the Livingstons, Cramers, and Buels—saw America destined to follow a course altogether different from that of Europe. There would be no class struggle here, for all would respect and attain property.

After the liberal triumph in the state constitutional conventions and the election of Jackson in 1828, the conservatives found themselves in an awkward situation. If the liberals accepted at face value the argument that inevitable antagonism divides society, it was logical for them to use the newly won power to attack property. Faced with this dangerous possibility, the conservatives did a quick about-face. They accepted the liberals' central argument that America is different from Europe, that class war does not apply here, that all elements in the population do have a common interest in maintaining the institution of private property. Webster went so far as to say that 'a great equality of condition . . . is the true basis most certainly of popular government.'

Herein the great orator profoundly forecast the dynamic dichotomy in American politics after 1870; as political power became diffused, economic power became increasingly concentrated. Casting himself in the role of a prophet, he suggested that if the tendency of the laws were to create a rapid accumulation of property in a few hands and to render the great masses dependent and penniless, 'the popular power must break in upon the rights of property or else the influence of property must limit and control the exercise of popular power.' Webster clearly foreshadowed both conservative and liberal strategy in the years ahead.

1. *It must always be a question of highest moment how the property-holding part of the community may be sustained against the inroads of poverty and vice*

JOSEPH STORY, Massachusetts Constitutional Convention, 1820 *

MR. JOSEPH STORY. . . The proposition of my friend from Roxbury [Henry A. S. Dearborn] is to make population the basis for apportioning the senate. . . Those who contend on the other hand, for the basis of valuation, propose nothing new, but stand upon the letter and spirit of the present constitution. . .

The qualifications are to remain as before, and the rich and the poor, and

* *Journal of Debates and Proceedings in the Convention of Delegates Chosen to Revise the Constitution of Massachusetts, new edition,* revised and corrected, Boston, 1853, pp. 283–8 *passim.*

the high and the low are to meet at the polls upon the same level of equality. . . I agree that the poor man is not to be deprived of his rights any more than the rich man, nor have I as yet heard of any proposition to that effect; and if it should come, I should feel myself bound to resist it. The poor man ought to be protected in his rights, not merely of life and liberty, but of his scanty and hard earnings. I do not deny that the poor man may possess as much patriotism as the rich; but it is unjust to suppose that he necessarily possesses more. Patriotism and poverty do not necessarily march hand in hand; nor is wealth that monster which some imaginations have depicted, with a heart of adamant and a sceptre of iron, surrounded with scorpions stinging every one within its reach, and planting its feet of oppression upon the needy and the dependent. Such a representation is not just with reference to our country. There is no class of very rich men in this happy land, whose wealth is fenced in by hereditary titles, by entails, and by permanent elevation to the highest offices. Here there is a gradation of property from the highest to the lowest, and all feel an equal interest in its preservation. . .

When I look around and consider the blessings which property bestows, I cannot persuade myself that gentlemen are serious in their views, that it does not deserve our utmost protection. I do not here speak of your opulent and munificent citizens, whose wealth has spread itself into a thousand channels of charity and public benevolence . . . I speak not of these, not because they are not worthy of all praise; but because I would dwell rather on those general blessings, which prosperity diffuses through the whole mass of the community. Who is there that has not a friend or relative in distress, looking up to him for assistance? Who is there that is not called upon to administer to the sick and the suffering, to those who are in the depth of poverty and distress, to those of his own household, or to the stranger beside the gate? The circle of kindness commences with the humblest, and extends wider and wider as we rise to the highest in society, each person administering in his own way to the wants of those around him. It is thus that property becomes the source of comforts of every kind, and dispenses its blessings in every form. In this way it conduces to the public good by promoting private happiness; and every man from the humblest, possessing property, to the highest in the State, contributes his proportion to the general mass of comfort. The man without any property may desire to do the same; but he is necessarily shut out from this most interesting charity. It is in this view that I consider property as the source of all the comforts and advantages we enjoy, and every man, from him who possesses but a single dollar up to him who possesses the greatest fortune, is equally interested in its security and its preservation. Government indeed stands on a combination of interests and circumstances. It must always be a question of the highest moment, how the property-holding part of the community may be sustained against the inroads of poverty and vice. Poverty leads to temptation, and temptation often leads to vice, and vice to military despotism. The rights of man are never heard in a despot's palace. The very rich man, whose estate consists in personal property, may escape from such evils by flying for refuge to some foreign land. But the hardy yeoman, the owner of a few acres of the soil, and supported by it, cannot leave his home without becoming a wanderer on the face of the earth. In the preservation of property and virtue, he has, therefore, the deepest and most permanent interest.

Gentlemen have argued as if personal rights only were the proper objects of government. But what, I would ask, is life worth, if a man cannot eat in security the bread earned by his own industry? . . I will say no more about the rich and the poor. There is no parallel to be run between them, founded on permanent constitutional distinctions. The rich help the poor, and the poor in turn administer to the rich. In our country, the highest man is not *above* the people; the humblest is not *below* the people. If the rich may be said to have additional protection, they have not additional power. Nor does wealth here form a permanent distinction of families. Those who are wealthy today pass to the tomb, and their children divide their estates. Property thus is divided quite as fast as it accumulates. No family can, without its own exertions, stand erect for a long time under our statute of descents and distributions, the only true and legitimate agrarian law. . . It is a mistaken theory, that government is founded for one object only. It is organized for the protection of life, liberty and property, and all the comforts of society—to enable us to indulge in our domestic affections, and quietly to enjoy our homes and our firesides. . .

It has been also suggested, that great property, of itself, gives great influence, and that it is unnecessary that the constitution should secure to it more.* I have already stated what I conceive to be the true answer; that a representation in the senate founded on valuation, is not a representation of property in the abstract. . . The basis of valuation was undoubtedly adopted by the framers of our constitution, with reference to a just system of checks, and balances, and the principles of rational liberty. Representation and taxation was the doctrine of those days—a doctrine for which our fathers fought and bled, in the battles of the revolution. Upon the basis of valuation, property is not directly represented; but property in the aggregate, combined with personal rights—where the greatest burthen of taxation falls, there the largest representation is apportioned; but still the choice depends upon the will of the majority of voters, and not upon that of the wealthier class within the district. There is a peculiar beauty in our system of taxation and equalizing the public burthens. . . But even if it were true that the representation in the senate were founded on property, I would respectfully ask gentlemen, if its natural influence would be weakened or destroyed by assuming the basis of population. I presume not. It would still be left to exert that influence over friends and dependents in the same manner that it now does; so that the change would not in the slightest degree aid the asserted object, I mean the suppression of the supposed predominating authority of wealth.

Gentlemen have argued, as though it was universally conceded as a political axiom, that population is in all cases and under all circumstances the safest and best basis of representation. I beg leave to doubt the proposition.

*Jefferson had taken precisely this position. See his letter to John Adams, 28 October 1813, *supra* p. 385 [A.T.M.]

2. *Political power naturally goes into the hands of those which hold property*

DANIEL WEBSTER, Speech in the Massachusetts Convention, 1820–21 *

The immediate question, now under discussion is, *in what manner* shall the Senators be elected? . . . shall they be chosen, in proportion to the *number of inhabitants* in each district, or in proportion to the *taxable property* of each district, or in other words, *in proportion to the part which each district bears in the public burdens of the state.* The latter is the existing provision of the constitution; and to this I give my support. . .

. . . If the two houses are to be chosen in the manner proposed by the resolutions of the member from Roxbury [Dearborn], there is obviously no other check or control than a division into separate chambers. The members of both houses are to be chosen at the same time, by the same electors, in the same districts, and for the same term of office. They will of course, all be actuated by the same feelings and interests. Whatever motives may, at the moment exist, to elect particular members of one house, will operate, equally on the choice of members of the other. There is so little of real utility in this mode, that, if nothing more be done, it would be more expedient to choose all the members of the Legislature, without distinction, simply as members of the Legislature, and to make the division into two houses, either by lot, or otherwise, after these members thus chosen, should have come up to the Capital.

I understand the reason of *checks* and *balances*, in the Legislative power, to arise from the truth, that, in Representative governments, that Department is the leading and predominating power; and if its will may be, at any time, suddenly and hastily expressed, there is great danger that it may overflow all other powers.—Legislative bodies naturally feel strong, because they are numerous, and because they consider themselves as the immediate Representatives of the people. As if Montesquieu had never demonstrated the necessity of separating the departments of governments; as if Mr. Adams had not done the same thing, with equal ability, and more clearness, in his defence of the American Constitution; as if the sentiments of Mr. Hamilton and Mr. Madison, were already forgotten; we see, all around us, a tendency to extend the Legislative power over the proper sphere of the other Departments. And as the Legislature, from the very nature of things, is the most powerful department, it becomes necessary to provide, in the mode of forming it, some check, which shall ensure deliberation, and caution, in its measures. If all Legislative power rested in one house, it is very problematical, whether any proper independence could be given, either to the Executive or the Judiciary. Experience does not speak encouragingly, on that point. If we look through the several constitutions of the states, we shall perceive that generally the Departments are most distinct and independent, where the Legislature is composed of two houses, with equal authority, and mutual checks. If all Legislative power be in one popular body, all other power, sooner or later, will be there also.

* Op. cit. pp. 304–17 *passim.*

I wish, now, Sir, to correct a most important mistake, in the manner in which this question has been stated. It has been said, that we propose to give to property, merely as such, a control over the people, numerically considered. But this I take not to be at all the true nature of the proposition. The Senate is not to be a check on the *People*, but on the *House of Representatives*. It is the case of an authority, given to *one* agent, to check or control the acts of *another*. The people, having conferred on the House of Representatives, powers which are great, and from their nature, liable to abuse, require, for their own security, another house, which shall possess an effectual negative on the first. This does not limit the power of the people; but only the authority of their agents. It is not a restraint on their rights, but a restraint on that power which they have delegated. It limits the authority of agents, in making laws to bind their principals. And if it be wise to give one agent the power of checking or controlling another, it is equally wise, most manifestly, that there should be some difference of character, sentiment, feeling, or origin, in that agent, who is to possess this control. Otherwise, it is not at all probable that the control will ever be exercised. To require the consent of two agents to the validity of act, and yet to appoint agents so similar, in all respects, as to create a moral certainty that what one does the other will do also, would be inconsistent, and nugatory. There can be no effectual control without some difference of origin, or character, or interest, or feeling, or sentiment. And the great question, in this country, has been, where to find, or how to create, this difference, in governments entirely elective and popular? Various modes have been attempted, in various states. In some, a difference of qualification has been required, in the persons to be elected.—This obviously produces little or no effect. . . In this state the qualification of the voters is the same, and there is no essential difference in that of the persons chosen.—But, in apportioning the Senate to the different districts of the state, the present Constitution assigns to each district, a number proportioned to its public taxes. Whether this be the best mode, of producing a difference in the construction of the two houses, is not now the question; but the question is whether this be better than no mode. . .

The best authority, for the support of a particular principle or provision, in Government, is experience; and, of all experience, our own, if it have been long enough to give the principle a fair trial, should be most decisive. This provision has existed, for forty years, and while so many gentlemen contend that it is wrong in theory, no one has shewn that it has been either injurious or inconvenient in practice. No one pretends, that it has caused a bad law to be enacted, or a good one to be rejected. To call on us, then, to strike out this provision, because we should be able to find no authority for it, in any Book on Government, would seem to be like requiring a mechanic to abandon the use of an implement, which had always answered all the purposes designed by it, because he could find no model of it, in the patent office.

But, sir, I take the *principle* to be well established by writers of the greatest authority. In the first place, those who have treated of natural law, have maintained, as a principle of that law, that as far as the object of society is the protection of something in which the members possess unequal shares, it is just that the weight of each person, in the common councils, should bear a relation and proportion to his interest. Such is the sentiment of Grotius, and he refers, in support of it, to several institutions, among the ancient states.

Those authors who have written more particularly on the subject of political institutions, have, many of them, maintained similar sentiments.—Not, indeed, that every man's power should be in exact proportion to his property, but that, in a general sense, and in a general form, property, as such, should have its weight and influence, in political arrangement. Montesquieu speaks, with approbation, of the early Roman regulation, made by Servius Tullius, by which the people were distributed into classes, according to their property, and the public burdens apportioned to each individual, according to the degree of power which he possessed in the government. By which regulation, he observes, some bore with the greatness of their tax, because of their proportionable participation in power and credit; others consoled themselves, for the smallness of their power and credit, by the smallness of their tax. One of the most ingenious of political writers, is Mr. Harrington; an author not now read so much as he deserves. It is his leading object, in his Oceana, to prove, that power *naturally* and *necessarily* follows property.—He maintains that a government, founded on property, is legitimately founded; and that a government founded on the disregard of property, is founded in injustice, and can only be maintained by military force. 'If one man, says he, be sole landlord like the grand seignior, his empire is absolute. If a few possess the land, this makes the Gothic or Feudal Constitution. If the *whole people* be landlords, then is it a Commonwealth.' 'It is strange,' says Mr. Pope, in one of his recorded conversations, 'that Harrington should be the first man to find out so evident and demonstrable a truth, as that of property being the true basis and measure of power.' In truth, he was not the first. The idea is as old as political science itself. It may be found in Aristotle, Lord Bacon, Sir Walter Raleigh, and other writers. Harrington seems however to be the first writer who has illustrated, and expanded the principle, and given to it the effect and prominence which justly belong to it.

To this sentiment, sir, I entirely agree. It seems to me to be plain, that in the absence of military force, political power naturally and necessarily goes into the hands which hold the property. In my judgment, therefore, a republican form of government rests, not more on political Constitutions, than on those laws which regulate the descent and transmission of property.—Governments like ours could not have been maintained, where property was holden according to the principles of the feudal system; nor, on the other hand, could the feudal Constitution possibly exist with us. . . The character of their [our New England ancestry] political institutions was determined by the fundamental laws, respecting property. The laws rendered estates divisible, among sons, and daughters. The right of primogeniture, at first limited, and curtailed was afterwards abolished. The property was all freehold. The entailment of estates, long trusts and the other processes for fettering and tying up inheritances, were not applicable to the condition of society, and seldom made use of. On the contrary, alienation of the land was, every way, facilitated, even to the subjecting of it to every species of debt. . . The consequence of all these causes has been, a great subdivision of the soil, and a great equality, of condition; the true basis most certainly of a popular government.—'If the People,' says Harrington, 'held three parts in four of the territory, it is plain there can neither be any single person nor nobility able to dispute the government with them; in this case, therefore, *except force be interposed,* they govern themselves.' . .

The true principle of a free and popular government would seem to be so to construct it as to give to all, or at least to a very great majority, an interest in its preservation. To found it, as other things are founded, on men's interest. The stability of government requires that those who desire its continuance should be more powerful than those who desire its dissolution. This power, of course, is not always to be measured by mere numbers.—Education, wealth, talents, are all parts and elements of the general aggregate of power; but numbers, nevertheless, constitute ordinarily the most important consideration, unless indeed there be a *military force* in the hands of the few, by which they can control the many. In this country we have actual existing systems of government, in the protection of which it would seem a great majority, both in numbers and in other means of power and influence, must see their interest. But this state of things is not brought about merely by written political constitutions, or the mere manner of organizing the government; but also by the laws which regulate the descent and transmission of property. The freest government, if it could exist, would not be long acceptable, if the tendency of the laws were to create a rapid accumulation of property in few hands, and to render the great mass of the population dependent and pennyless. In such a case, the popular power must break in upon the rights of property, or else the influence of property must limit and control the exercise of popular power.—Universal suffrage, for example, could not long exist in a community, where there was great inequality of property. The holders of estates would be obliged in such case, either, in some way, to restrain the right of suffrage; or else such right of suffrage would, ere long divide the property. In the nature of things, those who have not property, and see their neighbours possess much more than they think them to need, cannot be favorable to laws made for the protection of property. When this class becomes numerous, it grows clamorous. It looks on property as its prey and plunder, and is naturally ready, at all times, for violence and revolution.

It would seem, then, to be the part of political wisdom to found government on property; and to establish such distribution of property, by the laws which regulate its transmission and alienation, as to interest the great majority of society in the protection of the government. This is, I imagine, the true theory and the actual practice of our republican institutions. With property divided, as we have it, no other government than that of a republic could be maintained, even were we foolish enough to desire it. There is reason, therefore, to expect a long continuance of our systems. Party and passion, doubtless, may prevail at times, and much temporary mischief be done. Even modes and forms may be changed, and perhaps for the worse. But a great revolution, in regard to property, must take place, before our governments can be moved from their republican basis, unless they be violently struck off by military power. The people possess the property, more emphatically than it could ever be said of the people of any other country, and they can have no interest to overturn a government which protects that property by equal laws.

If the nature of our institutions be to found government on property, and that it should look to those who hold property for its protection, it is entirely just that property should have its due weight and consideration, in political arrangements. Life, and personal liberty, are, no doubt, to be protected by law; but property is also to be protected by law, and is the fund out of which the means for protecting life and liberty are usually furnished. We have no experience that teaches us, that any other rights are safe, where property is not safe. Confiscation and plunder are generally in revolutionary commotions not far before banishment, imprisonment and death. It would be monstrous to give even the name of government, to any association, in which the rights of property should not be competently secured. The disastrous revolutions which the world has witnessed, those political thunderstorms, and earthquakes which have overthrown the pillars of society from their very deepest foundations, have been revolutions *against property*. . .

The English revolution of 1688 was a revolution *in favor of property*, as well as of other rights. It was brought about by the men of property, for their security; and our own immortal revolution was undertaken, not to shake or plunder property, but to protect it. The acts of which the country complained, were such as violated rights of property. An immense majority of all those who had an interest in the soil were in favor of the revolution; and they carried it through, looking to its results for the security of their possessions. It was the property of the frugal yeomanry of New-England, hard earned, but freely given, that enabled her to act her proper part, and perform her full duty, in achieving the independence of the country. . .

I will beg leave to ask, sir, whether property may not be said to *deserve* this portion of respect and power in the government? It pays, at this moment, I think, *five sixths* of all the public taxes;—*one sixth* only being raised on persons. Not only, sir, do these taxes support those burdens, which all governments require, but we have, in New-England, from early times holden property to be subject to *another* great public use;—I mean the support of *schools*. . .

Does any history show property more beneficently applied? Did any government ever subject the property of those who have estates, to a burden, for a purpose more favorable to the poor, or more useful to the whole community? Sir, *property* and the power which the law exercises over it, for the purpose of instruction, is the basis of the system. It is entitled to the respect and protection of government, because, in a very vital respect, it aids and sustains government. . . If we take away from the towns the power of assessing taxes on property, will the school houses remain open? If we deny to the poor, the benefit which they now derive from the property of the rich, will their children remain on their farms, or will they not, rather, be in the streets, in idleness and in vice? . . .

I will now proceed to ask, sir, whether we have not seen, and whether we do not at this moment see, the advantage and benefit, of giving security to property, by this, and all other reasonable and just provisions? The Constitution has stood, on its present basis, forty years. Let me ask, what State has been more distinguished for wise and wholesome legislation? . . I do not know how much of this stability of government and of the general respect for it, may be fairly imputed to this particular mode of organizing the Senate. It has, no doubt, had some effect—It has shewn a respect for the rights of property, and may have operated on opinion, as well as upon measures. Now to strike out and obliterate it, as it seems to me, would be, in a high degree, unwise and improper.

As to the *right* of apportioning Senators upon this principle, I do not understand how there can be a question about it. All government is a modification of general principles and general truths, with a view to practical utility. Personal liberty, for instance, is a clear right, and is to be provided for; but it is not a clearer right than the right of property, though it may be more important. It is therefore entitled to protection. But property is also to be protected; and when it is remembered, how great a portion of the people of this state possess property, I cannot understand how its protection or its influence is hostile to their rights and privileges.

For these reasons, sir, I am in favor of maintaining that *check* in the constitution of the Legislature, which has so long existed there. . .

3. *The tendency of universal suffrage is to jeopardize the rights of property and principles of liberty*

CHANCELLOR JAMES KENT, New York Constitutional Convention, 1821 *

. . . I must beg leave to trespass for a few moments upon the patience of the committee, while I state the reasons which have induced me to wish, that the senate should continue, as heretofore, the representative of the landed interest, and exempted from the control of universal suffrage. . .

This state has existed for forty-four years under our present constitution, which was formed by those illustrious sages and patriots who adorned the revolution. It has wonderfully fulfilled all the great ends of civil government. During that long period, we have enjoyed in an eminent degree, the blessings of civil and religious liberty. We have had our lives, our privileges, and our property, protected. We have had a succession of wise and temperate legislatures. The code of our statute law has been again and again revised and corrected, and it may proudly bear a comparison with that of any other people. We have had, during that period, (though I am, perhaps, not the fittest person to say it) a regular, stable, honest, and enlightened administration of justice. All the peaceable pursuits of industry, and all the important interests of education and science, have been fostered and encouraged. We have trebled our numbers within the last twenty-five years, have displayed mighty resources, and have made unexampled progress in the career of prosperity and greatness.

* *Reports of the Proceedings and Debates of the Convention of 1821, Assembled for the Purpose of Amending the Constitution of the State of New York*, Albany, 1821, pp. 219–22 *passim*.

Our financial credit stands at an enviable height; and we are now successfully engaged in connecting the great lakes with the ocean by stupendous canals, which excite the admiration of our neighbours, and will make a conspicuous figure even upon the map of the United States.

These are some of the fruits of our present government; and yet we seem to be dissatisfied with our condition, and we are engaged in the bold and hazardous experiment of remodelling the constitution. Is it not fit and discreet: I speak as to wise men; is it not fit and proper that we should pause in our career, and reflect well on the immensity of the innovation in contemplation? Discontent in the midst of so much prosperity, and with such abundant means of happiness, looks like ingratitude, and as if we were disposed to arraign the goodness of Providence. Do we not expose ourselves to the danger of being deprived of the blessings we have enjoyed?—When the husbandman has gathered in his harvest, and has filled his barns and his granaries with the fruits of his industry, if he should then become discontented and unthankful, would he not have reason to apprehend, that the Lord of the harvest might come in his wrath, and with his lightning destroy them?

The senate has hitherto been elected by the farmers of the state—by the free and independent lords of the soil, worth at least $250 in freehold estate, over and above all debts charged thereon. The governor has been chosen by the same electors, and we have hitherto elected citizens of elevated rank and character. Our assembly has been chosen by freeholders, possessing a freehold of the value of $50, or by persons renting a tenement of the yearly value of $5, and who have been rated and actually paid taxes to the state. By the report before us, we propose to annihilate, at one stroke, all those property distinctions and to bow before the idol of universal suffrage. That extreme democratic principle, when applied to the legislative and executive departments of government, has been regarded with terror, by the wise men of every age, because in every European republic, ancient and modern, in which it has been tried, it has terminated disastrously, and been productive of corruption, injustice, violence, and tyranny. And dare we flatter ourselves that we are a peculiar people, who can run the career of history, exempted from the passions which have disturbed and corrupted the rest of mankind? If we are like other races of men, with similar follies and vices, then I greatly fear that our posterity will have reason to deplore in sackcloth and ashes, the delusion of the day.

It is not my purpose at present to interfere with the report of the committee, so far as respects the qualifications of electors for governor and members of assembly. I shall feel grateful if we may be permitted to retain the stability and security of a senate, bottomed upon the freehold property of the state. Such a body, so constituted, may prove a sheet anchor amidst the future factions and storms of the republic. The great leading and governing interest of this state, is, at present, the agricultural; and what madness would it be to commit that interest to the winds. The great body of the people, are now the owners and actual cultivators of the soil. With that wholesome population we always expect to find moderation, frugality, order, honesty, and a due sense of independence, liberty, and justice. It is impossible that any people can lose their liberties by internal fraud or violence, so long as the country is parcelled out among freeholders of moderate possessions, and those freeholders have a sure and efficient control in the affairs of the government. Their habits, sympathies, and employments, necessarily inspire them with a correct spirit of freedom and justice; they are the safest guardians of property and the laws: We certainly cannot too highly appreciate the value of the agricultural interest: It is the foundation of national wealth and power. . .

I wish those who have an interest in the soil, to retain the exclusive possession of a branch in the legislature, as a strong hold in which they may find safety through all the vicissitudes which the state may be destined, in the course of Providence, to experience. I wish them to be always enabled to say that their freeholds cannot be taxed without their consent. The men of no property, together with the crowds of dependents connected with great manufacturing and commercial establishments, and the motley and undefinable population of crowded ports, may, perhaps, at some future day, under skilful management, predominate in the assembly, and yet we should be perfectly safe if no laws could pass without the free consent of the owners of the soil. That security we at present enjoy; and it is that security which I wish to retain.

The apprehended danger from the experiment of universal suffrage applied to the whole legislative department, is no dream of the imagination. It is too mighty an excitement for the moral constitution of men to endure. The tendency of universal suffrage, is to jeopardize the rights of property, and the principles of liberty. There is a constant tendency in human society, and the history of every age proves it; there is a tendency in the poor to covet and to share the plunder of the rich; in the debtor to relax or avoid the obligation of contracts; in the majority to tyrannize over the minority, and trample down their rights; in the indolent and the profligate, to cast the whole burthens of society upon the industrious and the virtuous; and *there is a tendency in ambitious and wicked men, to inflame these combustible materials.* It requires a vigilant government, and a firm administration of justice, to counteract that tendency. Thou shalt not covet; thou shalt not steal; are divine injunctions induced by this miserable depravity of our nature. Who can undertake to calculate with any precision, how many millions of people, this great state will contain in the course of this and the next century, and who can estimate the future extent and magnitude of our commercial ports? The disproportion between the men of property, and the men of no property, will be in every society in a ratio to its commerce, wealth, and population. We are no longer to remain plain and simple republics of farmers, like the New-England colonists, or the Dutch settlements on the Hudson. We are fast becoming a great nation, with great commerce, manufactures, population, wealth, luxuries, and with the vices and miseries that they engender. One seventh of the population of the city of Paris at this day subsists on charity, and one third of the inhabitants of that city die in the hospitals; what would become of such a city with universal suffrage? France has upwards of four, and England upwards of five millions of manufacturing and commercial labourers without property. Could these kingdoms sustain the weight of universal suffrage? The radicals in England, with the force of that mighty engine, would at once sweep away the property, the laws, and the liberties of that island like a deluge.

The growth of the city of New-York is enough to startle and awaken those who are pursuing the *ignis fatuus* of universal suffrage. . .

It is rapidly swelling into the unwieldy population, and with the burdensome pauperism, of an European metropolis. New-York is destined to become the future London of America; and in less than a century, that city, with the operation of universal suffrage, and under skilful direction, will govern this state.

The notion that every man that works a day on the road, or serves an idle hour in the militia, is entitled as of right to an equal participation in the whole power of the government, is most unreasonable, and has no foundation in justice. We had better at once discard from the report such a nominal test of merit. If such persons have an equal share in one branch of the legislature, it is surely as much as they can in justice or policy demand. Society is an association for the protection of property as well as of life, and the individual who contributes only one cent to the common stock, ought not to have the same power and influence in directing the property concerns of the partnership, as he who contributes his thousands. He will not have the same inducements to care, and diligence, and fidelity. His inducements and his temptation would be to divide the whole capital upon the principles of an agrarian law.

Liberty, rightly understood, is an inestimable blessing, but liberty without wisdom, and without justice, is no better than wild and savage licentiousness. The danger which we have hereafter to apprehend, is not the want, but the abuse, of liberty. We have to apprehend the oppression of minorities, and a disposition to encroach on private right—to disturb chartered privileges—and to weaken, degrade, and overawe the administration of justice; we have to apprehend the establishment of unequal, and consequently, unjust systems of taxation, and all the mischiefs of a crude and mutable legislation. A stable senate, exempted from the influence of universal suffrage, will powerfully check these dangerous propensities, and such a check becomes the more necessary, since this Convention has already determined to withdraw the watchful eye of the judicial department from the passage of laws. . .

Universal suffrage once granted, is granted forever, and never can be recalled. There is no retrograde step in the rear of democracy. However mischievous the precedent may be in its consequences, or however fatal in its effects, universal suffrage never can be recalled or checked, but by the strength of the bayonet. We stand, therefore, this moment, on the brink of fate, on the very edge of the precipice. If we let go our present hold on the senate, we commit our proudest hopes and our most precious interests to the waves. . .

4. *Character does not spring from the ground*

P. R. LIVINGSTON, New York Constitutional Convention, 1821 *

He was well persuaded, that every member of the convention was a friend to property, and to the landed interest. But he thought that the views of some

* Op. cit. pp. 224–5 *passim*.

gentlemen, if adopted, were not calculated to advance the cause of civil liberty.

Allusions had been made to the formation of the Constitution under which we live; and what was the first feature in our remonstrance against the usurpations of Britain? Was it not that taxation and representation were reciprocal; and that no imposition could be laid upon us without our consent? Was it the paltry tax on tea that led to the revolution? No, sir; it was the *principle*, for which we contended: and the same principle, in my judgment, requires a rejection of the proposition now on your table. . .

It is concluded, however, that the measure proposed by the original amendment jeopardizes the landed interest. Sir, it is the landed interest, in common with others, that have demanded this measure at our hands: and will they resort to projects which are calculated to injure ourselves? France has been alluded to. The French revolution, sir, has produced incalculable blessings to that country. Before that revolution one third of the property of the kingdom was in the hands of the clergy; the rest in the hands of the nobility. Where the interest of one individual has been sacrificed, the interests of thousands have been promoted. After dining with that friend of universal liberty, the patriotic La Fayette, he once invited me to a walk upon the top of his house, that commanded a view of all the surrounding country. Before the revolution, said he, all the farms and hamlets you can see were mine. I am now reduced to a thousand acres, and I exult in the diminution; since the happiness of others is promoted by participation.

This, sir, is the language of true patriotism; the language of one whose heart, larger than his possessions, embraced the whole family of man in the circuit of its beneficence. And shall we, with less ample domains, refuse to our poorer neighbours the common privileges of freemen?

But, sir, we are told and warned of the rotten boroughs of England. By whom are they owned? By men of wealth. They confer the right of representation on the few, to the exclusion of the many. They are always found in the views of the monarch; and while aristocracy is supported by the house of lords, the house of commons is borne down by the boroughs.

It is said that wealth builds our churches, establishes our schools, endows our colleges, and erects our hospitals. But have these institutions been raised without the hand of labour? No, sir; and it is the same hand that has levelled the sturdy oak, the lofty pine, and the towering hemlock, and subdued your forests to a garden. It is not the fact, in this country, that money controls labour; but labour controls money. When the farmer cradles his wheat and harvests his hay, he does not find the labourer on his knees before him at the close of the day, solicitous for further employment; but it is the farmer who takes off his hat, pays him his wages, and requests his return on the morrow.

Apprehensions are professed to be entertained, that the merchant and manufacturer will combine to the prejudice of the landed interest. But is not agriculture the legitimate support of both? And do gentlemen really suppose that they will madly combine to destroy themselves? If the title to land contributed to the elevation of the mind, or if it gave stability to independence, or added wisdom to virtue, there might be good reason for proportioning the right of suffrage to the acres of soil. But experience has shewn that property forms not the scale of worth, and that character does not spring from the ground. It seems, indeed, to be thought, that poverty and vice are identified. But look to the higher classes of society. Do you not often discover the grossest abuse of wealth? Look to the republics of Greece. They were all destroyed by the wealth of the aristocracy bearing down the people.

And how were the victories of Greece achieved in her better days? By the militia. How were the liberties of Rome sustained? By her militia. How were they lost? By her standing armies. How have we been carried triumphantly through two wars? By the militia—by the very men whom it is now sought to deprive of the inestimable privilege of freemen. And whom do you find in your armies in time of war? The miser? The monied Shylock? The speculator? No, sir; it is the poor and hardy soldier who spills his blood in defence of his country; the veteran to whom you allow the privilege to fight, but not to vote. If there is value in the right of suffrage, or reliance to be placed upon our fellow citizens in time of war, where, I ask, is the justice of withholding that right in times of peace and safety? . . .

5. *Let us not brand the Constitution with any odious distinction as to property*

JOHN CRAMER, New York Constitutional Convention, 1821 *

I had supposed that the great fundamental principle, that all men were equal in their rights, was settled, and forever settled, in this country. I had supposed, sir, that there was some meaning in those words, and some importance in the benefits resulting from them. I had supposed from the blood and treasure which its attainment had cost, that there was something invaluable in it: and that in pursuance of this principle it ought to be the invariable object of the framers of our civil compact, to render all men equal in their political enjoyments as far as could be, consistent with order and justice. But, sir, this, the honourable gentleman from Albany,† for whose opinion on such subjects, I have entertained a profound respect, and who has presented the amendment now under consideration, has informed us with great assurance and emphasis, is a most egregious mistake, and that in it consists the very essence of aristocracy. However, he has the charity to suppose that the mistake arose in the committee of which I had the honour of being a member, and who presented the report on your table, not from design, but from ignorance, and that a careful examination of proper authorities, on this subject, would convince any person of the correctness of his position; and as a lawyer and a distinguished jurist, he has referred us to certain authorities which I shall endeavour to examine as to their bearing on the subject under discussion, in the same order in which they were presented. And first, the 62d number of 'The Federalist,' said to be written

*Op. cit. pp. 235–9 *passim.*
† Kent.

by the venerated Hamilton; I have read it, and it contains no such principles. . . But, the gentleman has said, that whatever had fallen from the pen of that distinguished statesman, is entitled to great consideration, and is to be considered as a political text book to the framers of free government, and has also said that he entertains the most profound veneration for all his political writings. I have read, sir, other productions of what venerable gentleman, in the secret debates of the Convention which formed the constitution of the United States; I have read there, sir, the plan which he submitted to that Convention in which he recommends a president for life, a senate for life, and that the president should have the power of appointing the state executives. Is this, the political text book which the gentleman from Albany, so much admires? Is this, the form of government which this gentleman, wishes to see adopted? I presume not. I too, sir, have a high estimation of the character of the departed Hamilton; he had talents, he had integrity of a superior, I had almost said, of a celestial order; but he was mortal and subject to the frailties of our nature; he had entertained too degrading an opinion of his fellow man, his political opinions, therefore, I never did respect. . . Next, we were invited to behold the glorious inequality in property and in the civil privileges of the people of England, and among other causes it was ascribed, and justly so, to their system of borough elections, the very system which the gentleman would by his amendment adopt here; for as in that, so in his system, territory and not population is the basis of representation; there, sir, many little deserted villages and boroughs, which do not contain fifty families, have the right to elect two representatives to the house of commons; and are equal rights and equal enjoyments, recognized there? No, sir, privileged orders and a landed aristocracy, the natural effects of a monarchical government, are, and ever have been, the order of the day; thus much, for the authorities of the gentleman; and in turn I would refer him, and this committee, to a few plain, practical, modern commentators on the rights of man and on civil government, in our own country: namely, the constitutions of the several states. . . In fact, but two states * in the union, with the exception of this state, have any freehold distinction as to electors; . . And when in opposition to these we find that all the different constitutions which have been formed or amended within the last thirty years, have discarded this odious, this aristocratical, this worse than useless, feature, from their political charts, will any gentleman of this committee say that all this affords no evidence to his mind, of the impropriety of retaining this freehold distinction? To me, it is satisfactory and conclusive. . .

I have heard much on this subject for several years past, and so far as I have been able to judge, there is but one sentiment among the intelligent and virtuous, which is 'grant universal suffrage to all, except those excluded by crime, and abolish the distinction, in regard to electors which now prevails, because of one man's possessing more of the soil than another.' . .

But it has been said, that the landed interest of this state, bears more than its equal proportion of the burthens of taxation. This, sir, I deny. All property, real and personal, is equally taxed, and bears its just proportion of the public

* Virginia and North Carolina.

burthens; but, sir, is not life and liberty dearer than property, and common to all, and entitled to equal protection? No, sir. That gentleman appeared to be impressed with the ideas, that the *turf* is of all things the most sacred, and that for its security, you must have thirty-two grave turf senators from the soil, in that *Sanctum Sanctorum*, the senate chamber, and then all your rights will be safe. No matter whether they possess intelligence, if they are selected by your rich landholders, all is well.—But it is alleged by gentlemen, who have spoken on that side of the house, that the poor are a degraded class of beings, have no will of their own, and would not exercise this high prerogative with independence and sound discretion if entrusted with it: and, therefore, it would be unwise to trust them with ballots.—This, sir, is unfounded: for more integrity and more patriotism are generally found in the labouring class of the community than in the higher orders. These are the men, who add to the susbtantial wealth of the nation, in peace. These are the men, who constitute your defence in war. Of such men, consisted your militia, when they met and drove the enemy at Plattsburgh, Sacket's Harbour, Queenston, and Erie; for you found not the rich landholder or speculator in your ranks; and are we told, that these men, because they have no property, are not to be trusted at the ballot boxes! Men, who in defence of their liberties, and to protect the property of this country, have hazarded their lives; and who, to shield your wives and children from savage brutality, have faced the destructive cannon, and breasted the pointed steel? All this they could be trusted to do. They could, without apprehension, be permitted to handle their muskets, bayonets, powder and balls; but, say the gentlemen, it will not answer to trust them with tickets at the ballot boxes. I would admonish gentlemen of this committee, to reflect, who they are about to exclude from the right of suffrage, if the amendment under consideration should prevail.- They will exclude your honest industrious mechanics, and many farmers, for many there are, who do not own the soil which they till. And what for? Because your farmers wish it? No, sir, they wish no such thing; they wish to see the men who have defended their soil, participate equally with them in the election of their rulers. Nay, now you exclude most of the hoary headed patriots, who achieved your independence, to whom we are indebted for the very ground we stand upon, and for the liberties we enjoy. But for the toil and sufferings of these men, we should not now be here debating as to forms of government. No, sir, the legitimates would soon have disposed of all this business. And why are these men to be excluded? Not because they are not virtuous, not because they are not meritorious; but, sir, because they are poor and dependant, and can have no will of their own, and will vote as the man who feeds them and clothes them may direct, as one of the honourable gentlemen has remarked. I know of no men in this country, who are not dependant. The rich man is as much dependant upon the poor man for his labour, as the poor man is upon the rich for his wages. I know of no men, who are more dependant upon others for their bread and raiment, than the judges of your supreme court are upon the legislature, and who will pretend that this destroys their independence, or makes them subservient to the views of the legislature. Let us not, sir, disgrace ourselves in the eyes of the world, by expressing such degrading opinions of our fellow citizens. Let us grant universal suffrage, for after all, it is upon the virtue and intelligence of the people that the stability of your government must rest. Let us not brand this constitution with any odious distinctions as to property, and let it not be said of us as has been truly said of most republics, that we have been ungrateful to our best benefactors.

6. *Arguments drawn from the state of European society are not applicable here*

DAVID BUEL, JR., New York Constitutional Convention, 1821 *

The subject now before the committee, is thought by many gentlemen to be the most important that will fall under our deliberations. . . The question whether it is safe and proper to extend the right of suffrage to other classes of our citizens, besides the landholders, is decided as I think, by the sober sense and deliberate acts of the great American people. . .

It is supposed, however, by the honourable member before me (Chancellor Kent) that landed property will become insecure under the proposed extension of the right of suffrage, by the influx of a more dangerous population. That gentleman has drawn a picture from the existing state of society in European kingdoms, which would be indeed appalling, if we could suppose such a state of society could exist here. But are arguments, drawn from the state of society in Europe, applicable to our situation? . . .

It is conceded by my honourable friend, that the great landed estates must be cut up by the operation of our laws of descent; that we have already seen those laws effect a great change; and that it is the inevitable tendency of our rules of descent, to divide up our territory into farms of moderate size. The real property, therefore, will be in the hands of the *many*. But in England, and other European kingdoms, it is the policy of the aristocracy to keep the lands in few hands. . . Hence we find in Europe, the landed estates possessed by a few rich men; and the great bulk of the population poor, and without that attachment to the government which is found among the owners of the soil. Hence, also, the poor envy and hate the rich, and mobs and insurrections sometimes render property insecure. Did I believe that our population would degenerate into such a state, I should, with the advocates for the amendment, hesitate in extending the right of suffrage; but I confess I have no such fears. . .

There are in my judgment, many circumstances which will forever preserve the people of this state from the vices and the degradation of European population, beside those which I have already taken notice of. The provision already made for the establishment of common schools, will, in a very few years, extend the benefit of education to all our citizens. The universal diffusion of informa-

* Op. cit. pp. 239–44 *passim*.

tion will forever distinguish our population from that of Europe. Virtue and intelligence are the true basis on which every republican government must rest. When these are lost, freedom will no longer exist. The diffusion of education is the only sure means of establishing these pillars of freedom. I rejoice in this view of the subject, that our common school fund will (if the report on the legislative department be adopted,) be consecrated by a constitutional provision; and I feel no apprehension, for myself, or my posterity, in confiding the right of suffrage to the great mass of such a population as I believe ours will always be. . .

The supposition that, at some future day, when the poor shall become numerous, they may imitate the radicals of England, or the Jacobins of France; that they may rise, in the majesty of their strength, and usurp the property of the landholders, is so unlikely to be realized, that we may dismiss all fear arising from that source. Before that can happen, wealth must lose all its influence; public morals must be destroyed; and the nature of our government changed, and it would be in vain to look to a senate, chosen by landholders, for security in a case of such extremity. I cannot but think, that all the dangers which it is predicted will flow from doing away the exclusive right of the landholders to elect the senators, are groundless.

I contend, that by the true principle of our government, property, as such, is not the basis of representation. Our community is an association of persons —of human beings—not a partnership founded on property. The declared object of the people of this state in associating, was, to 'establish such a government as they deemed best calculated to secure the rights and liberties of the good people of the state, and most conducive to their happiness and safety.' Property, it is admitted, is one of the rights to be protected and secured; and although the protection of life and liberty is the highest object of attention, it is certainly true, that the security of property is a most interesting and important object in every free government. Property is essential to our temporal happiness; and is necessarily one of the most interesting subjects of legislation. The desire of acquiring property is a universal passion. . . Property is only one of the incidental rights of the person who possesses it; and, as such, it must be made secure; but it does not follow, that it must therefore be represented specifically in any branch of the government. It ought, indeed, to have an influence—and it ever will have, when properly enjoyed. So ought talents to have an influence. It is certainly as important to have men of good talents in your legislature, as to have men of property; but you surely would not set up men of talents as a separate order, and give them exclusive privileges.

The truth is, that both wealth and talents will ever have a great influence; and without the aid of exclusive privileges, you will always find the influence of both wealth and talents predominant in our halls of legislation.

7. *The very desire for property implies the desire to possess it securely*

JOHN R. COOKE, Virginia Constitutional Convention, 1829–30 *

On motion of Mr. [Philip] Doddridge, the Convention proceeded to consider the report of the Committee on the Legislative Department of Government. The report was read at the Clerk's table, and the first section having then been read by the Chairman for amendment, as follows:

'*Resolved*, That in the apportionment of representation in the House of Delegates, regard should be had to the white population exclusively.'

Mr. [John W.] Green moved to amend it by striking out the word '*exclusively*,' and adding in lieu thereof the words '*and taxation combined*.'

Mr. [Benjamin W.] Leigh of Chesterfield said that he did hope that the friends . . . of these new proportions, new at least in our State, if not new throughout the world, would give to those who differed from themselves, some reasons in support of their scheme; some better reasons than that such principles were unknown to our English ancestors, from whom we have derived our institutions; better than the rights of man as held in the French school; better than that they were calculated in their nature to lead to rapine, anarchy and bloodshed, and in the end, to military despotism: a scheme, which has respect to numbers alone; and considers property as unworthy of regard. . .
Mr. Cooke said, that he could not but express his unfeigned astonishment, that the able gentleman from Chesterfield (Mr. Leigh) should have ventured to say to that assembly, that the principle of representation recommended by the Legislative Committee, was 'new to him, and new in the history of the world.' Can the gentleman have forgotten, (said Mr. Cooke,) that the principle which he treats as a novelty, and an innovation, is asserted in the 'Declaration of the Rights of the people of Virginia?' And does he not know, that when the Convention of 1776 promulgated, in that instrument, the principles of Government on which their infant Republic was founded, they did but announce, in solemn form, to the people of Virginia, principles which had received, a *century before*, the deliberate sanction of the most enlightened friends of liberty, throughout the world?

Sir, the fathers of the Revolution did but *reiterate* those great and sacred truths which had been illustrated by the genius of Locke, and Sydney, and Milton: truths for which Hampden, and a host of his compatriots, had poured out their blood in vain.

Driven from Europe, by Kings, and Priests, and Nobles, those simple truths were received, with favour, by the sturdy yeomanry who dwelt on the western shores of the Atlantic. The love of liberty, aye, Sir, and of *equality* too, grew with the growth, and strengthened with the strength, of the Colonies. It declared war, at last, not only against the *power* of the *King*, but against the

* *Proceedings and Debates of the Virginia State Convention of 1829–30*, Richmond, Ritchie and Cook, 1830, pp. 53–61 *passim*.

privilege of the *Noble*, and laid the deep foundations of our Republic on the *sovereignty of the people* and *the equality of men*.

The sacred instrument, for sacred I will dare to call it, notwithstanding the sneers which its very name excites in this assembly of *Republicans*, the sacred instrument in which those great principles were declared, was ushered into existence under circumstances the most impressive and solemn. The 'Declaration of the Rights of the people of Virginia,' was made by an assembly of sages and patriots, who had just involved their country in all the horrors of war, in all the dangers of an unequal contest with the most powerful nation on earth, for the sake of the noble and elevated principles which that instrument announces and declares. For the sake of those principles, they had imperilled their lives, their fortunes, their wives, their children, their country; and, in one word, all that is dear to man. For the sake of those principles, they had spread havoc and desolation over their native land, and consigned to ruin and poverty a whole generation of the people of Virginia.

And for what did they make these mighty sacrifices! For wild 'abstractions, and metaphysical subleties!' No, Sir. For principles of eternal truth; as practical, in character, as they are vital, in importance; for principles deep-seated in the nature of man, by whose development, alone, he can attain the happiness which is the great object of his being. Those principles are,

'That all power is vested in, and consequently derived from, *the people*.'

'That all men are, by nature, *equally* free.' And

'That *a majority of the community* possesses, by the law of nature and necessity, a right to control its concerns. . .

I say, then, Sir, with a confidence inspired by a deep conviction of the truth of what I advance, that the principles of the *sovereignty of the people, the equality of men*, and the *right of the majority*, set forth in the 'Declaration of the Rights of the people of Virginia,' so far from being 'wild and visionary,' so far from being 'abstractions and metaphysical subleties,' are the very principles which alone give a *distinctive* character to our institutions, are the principles which have had the *practical* effect in Virginia, of abolishing *kingly power*, and *aristocratic privilege*, substituting for them an elective magistracy, deriving their power *from* the people, and responsible *to* the people.

But it has been said that the authors of the Declaration of Rights themselves, admitted, in effect, the abstract and *unpractical* character of the principles which it contains, by establishing a Government whose practical regulations are wholly inconsistent with those theoretical principles. That while, in the Declaration of Rights, they asserted that all power is vested in the *people*, and should be exercised by a *majority* of the people, they established a Goverment in which *unequal counties*, expressing their sense by the representatives of a *selected few* in those counties, to wit, the *freeholders*, were the real political *units*, or essential *elements* of political power. . .

Sir, the argument would be a good one if the premises which support it were correct. But it is *not true* that the authors of the Declaration of Rights *established* the anomalous Government under which we have lived these fifty years and more. There can be no grosser error than to suppose that the

Constitution of Virginia was *formed* in 1776. Its two great distinctive features, the *sectional* and the *aristocratic* had been given to it a century before. . .

What then, was the situation in which the framers of the Constitution were placed?—While they framed that instrument they were almost within hearing of the thunder of the hostile cannon. . . It would have been the very height of folly, at such a crisis, to create disaffection in the minds of the *freeholders,* by stripping them of their exclusive powers, and to exasperate the smaller *counties* by degrading them from the rank which they had held under the royal Government. In leaving the *freeholders* and the *counties* as they found them, the framers of the Constitution bowed to the supreme law of necessity, and acted like wise and *practical* statesmen.

No, Sir, it was not reserved for *us* to discover the inconsistency between their theoretical principles, and their practical regulations. They saw it themselves, and deplored it. In the very heat of the war which was waged for these 'abstractions'—in the hurly-burly of the conflict, *one* statesman, at least, was found, to point out those inconsistencies, and to urge home on the people of Virginia the 'new and unheard of' principle, that in the apportionment of representation, regard should be had to the white population only. As early as 1781, Mr. Jefferson exhorted the people of Virginia, in the most earnest and impressive language, to reduce the principle to practice, 'so soon as leisure should be afforded them, for intrenching, within good forms, the rights for which they had bled.'

From that time to this, the spirit of reform has never slept. From that time to this, the friends of liberty have continually lifted up their voices against the inequality and injustice of our system of Government. Incessantly baffled and defeated, they have not abandoned their purpose; and after a struggle for fifty years, the purpose seems at length on the eve of accomplishment. The Representatives of the people of Virginia have at length assembled in Convention to revise the Constitution of the State. A special committee of this Convention has recommended, among other measures of reform, the adoption of a resolution,

'That in the apportionment of representation, in the House of Delegates, regard should be had to white population exclusively.' . . .

It is alleged, then, Sir, that . . . there is a great *practical* principle, wholly overlooked in the resolution of the Select Committee, of vital and *paramount* importance. The principle in question, and the argument by which it is sustained, when broadly and fairly developed, amount to this:

1. That the security of property is one of the most essential elements of the prosperity and happiness of a community, and should be sedulously provided for by its institutions.

2. That men naturally love property, and the comforts and advantages it will purchase.

3. That this love of wealth is so strong, that the *poor* are the natural enemies of the *rich,* and feel a strong and habitual inclination to strip them of their wealth, or, at least, to throw on them alone all the burthens of society.

4. That the *poor,* being more numerous in every community than all the classes above them, would have the *power,* as well as the *inclination,* thus to

oppress the rich, if admitted to an equal participation with them in political power; and

5. That it is therefore necessary to restrain, limit and diminish the power of this natural majority; of this many-headed and hungry monster, *the many*, by some artificial regulation in *the Constitution*, or *fundamental law*, of every community. And if this be not done, either directly, by limitations on the right of suffrage, or indirectly, by some artificial distribution of political power, in the apportionment of representation, like that contained in the amendment, property will be invaded, all the multiplied evils of anarchy will ensue, till the society, groaning under the yoke of unbridled democracy, will be driven to prefer to its stormy sway, the despotic Government of a single master. And this is said to be the natural death of the Government of *numbers*.

Sir, if this statement of the argument be a little over-coloured by imputing to those who advance it epithets which they are too prudent to use, it is nevertheless, like all good caricatures, a striking likeness.

To this argument I answer that, like most unsound arguments, it is founded on a bold assumption of false premises. It is founded on the assumption that men are, by nature, *robbers*, and are restrained from incessant invasions of the rights of each other, only by fear or coercion. But, is this a just picture of that compound creature *man?* Sir, I conceive it to be a libel on the race, disproved by every page of its history. If you will look there you will find that man, thought sometimes driven by stormy passions to the commission of atrocious crimes, is by nature and habit neither a wolf nor a tiger. That he is an *affectionate*, a *social*, a *patriotic*, a *conscientious* and a *religious* creature. In him, alone, of all animals, has nature implanted the feeling of *affection for his kindred*, after the attainment of maturity. This alone is a restraint on the excess of his natural desire for property as extensive as the ties of blood that bind him to his fellow man. Designing, moreover, that man shall live in *communities*, where alone he can exist, nature has given to him the *social feeling*; the feeling of attachment to those around him. Intending that for the most perfect development of his high faculties, and for the attainment of the greatest degree of comfort and happiness of which he is susceptible, man should associate in *nations*, she implanted in him a feeling, the glorious displays of which had shed lustre around so many pages of his history. I mean *the love of country* or *patriotism*. Designing that he should attain to happiness through the practice of virtue, and in that way only, she erected in each man's bosom the tribunal of *conscience*, which passes in review all the actions of the individual, and pronounces sentence of condemnation on every manifest deviation from moral rectitude. To add sanctions to the decisions of conscience, she also implanted in his bosom an intuitive belief in the existence of an intelligence governing the world, who would reward virtue and punish vice in a future state of being. Man is therefore, by nature a *religious* creature, whose conduct is more or less regulated by the love or fear of the unknown governor of the Universe. Above all, the light of revealed religion has shone for ages on the world, and that Divine system of morals which commands us 'to do unto others as we would have them do unto us,' has shed its benign influence on the hearts of countless thousands, of the high and the low, the wise and the foolish, the *rich* and the *poor*. But we are asked to believe that all these natural feelings, all these social affections, all these monitions of conscience, all these religious impressions, all these Christian charities, all these hopes of future rewards and fears of future punishments, are dead, and silent, and inoperative in the bosom of man. The love of property is the great engrossing passion which swallows up all other passions, and feelings, and principles; and this not in particular cases only, but in all men. The poor man is fatally and inevitably the enemy of the rich, and will wage a war of rapine against him, if once let loose from the restraints of the fundamental law. A doctrine monstrous, hateful and incredible!

But, Sir, if I were even to admit, for a moment, the truth of the revolting proposition that the desire for property swallows up all the other feelings of man, does it follow that the aspirants after the enjoyments that property confers, will seek to attain their object in the manner which the argument in question supposes? If it be contended that man is greedy and avaricious, it will, still, not be denied, that he is a reasoning and calculating, animal. When he desires to *attain* property, it is in order that he may *possess and enjoy it*. But if he join in establishing the rule that the right of the strongest is the best right, what security has he that he, in his turn, will not soon be deprived of his property by some one stronger than himself? Sir, the *very* desire for property implies the desire to possess it *securely*. And he who has a strong desire to possess it, and a high relish, in anticipation, of the pleasure of enjoying it securely, will be a firm supporter of the laws which secure that possession, and a decided enemy to every systematic invasion of the rule of *meum* and *tuum*. In other words, man is sagacious enough to know that as a general and public rule of action, the maxim that honesty is the best policy, is the safest and best maxim. And when he deviates from that rule he always hopes that the violation will go undiscovered, or otherwise escape punishment. So true is this, that I am persuaded that if a nation could be found consisting exclusively of rogues and swindlers, there would not be found in the legislative code of that nation a systematic invasion of the right of property, such as the argument for the proposed amendment apprehends and seeks to provide against.

Communities of men are sagacious enough to know and follow their *real* interest. And, Sir, I do not, and cannot believe that it is, or ever was the real interest of any class in the community, or of any community to commit gross and flagrant abuses of power, to disregard the monitions of conscience, to break down the barriers and obliterate the distinctions between right and wrong, and thus to involve society in all the horrors of anarchy. The principles of justice are the foundation of the social fabric, and rash and foolish is he and blind to his true interest, who undermines the foundation and tumbles the fabric in ruins.

Thus far I have reasoned *a priori*. But what are the lessons which history and experience teach us, in pursuing this enquiry?—We need not go far for examples. Let us look at the experience of our good old Commonwealth of Virginia. From the foundation of the Commonwealth the slave-holding population of Virginia has held the supreme power in the State. From the foundation of the Commonwealth there has existed and there still exists, a numerous population of our western frontier, who are comparatively destitute of slave-property, and whose wealth has ever consisted in cattle more than in any other description of property. Now if the argument of those who support the proposed amendment be a sound one, it would follow that as it is and always has been the interest (according to *their* views of interest) of the slave-holding population to shift for themselves, and to lay on others, the burthens of Government, they would impose heavy taxes on the cattle, the property of the helpless minority, and oppress them by this and every other species of fiscal exaction. And yet the very reverse is the fact. For the slave-holders, invested with supreme power, and urged to its exercise by their '*interest*,' have not only not overtaxed the cattle of their western brethren, but have, in fact, imposed on them, except at one period of danger and distress from foreign war, no tax at all, and when the pressure ceased the law imposing the tax was instantly repealed. And why?—Because they were governed by the principles of justice, and the feelings of honour. Because they thought, and justly, that the people of the frontier, burthened as they were with 'the first expenses of society,' and engaged in laying the very foundations of the social fabric, could ill endure the additional burthen of a tax on their flocks and herds. Because the non-slave holders of the west were at their mercy, and every feeling of honor and magnanimity forbade them to oppress the weak. I say, then, Sir, that the slave-holders of Virginia have shewn by their conduct in this particular case, the incorrectness of the theory which supposes man to be habitually governed by a blind and reckless cupidity; by the sordid feelings alone of his nature, to the exclusion of the nobler. . .

8. *There is a majority in interest as well as a majority in numbers*

JUDGE ABEL P. UPSHUR, Virginia Constitutional Convention, 1829–30 *

It is contended by our opponents, that the proper basis of representation in the General Assembly, is white population alone, because this principle results necessarily from the right which the majority possess, to rule the minority. I have been forcibly struck with the fact, that in all the arguments upon this subject here and elsewhere, this right in a majority is assumed as a postulate. It has not yet been proved, nor have I even heard an attempt to prove it. . .

There are two kinds of majority. There is a majority in interest, as well as a majority in number. If the first be within the contemplation of gentlemen, there is an end of all discussion. It is precisely the principle for which we contend, and we shall be happy to unite with them in so regulating this matter, that those who have the greatest stake in the Government, shall have the greatest share of power in the administration of it. But this is not what gentlemen mean. They mean, for they distinctly say so, that a majority in number only, without regard to property, shall give the rule. It is the propriety of this rule, which I now propose to examine.

* Op. cit. pp. 65–73 *passim.*

If there be, as our opponents assume, an original, *a priori*, inherent and indestructible right in a majority to control a minority, from what source permit me to inquire, is that right derived? If it exist at all, it must I apprehend, be found either in some positive compact or agreement conferring it, or else in some order of our nature, independent of all compact, and consequently prior to all Government. If gentlemen claim the right here as springing from positive compact, from *what compact* does it spring? Not certainly from that Constitution of Government which we are now revising; for the chief purpose for which we have been brought together, is to correct a supposed defect in the Constitution, in this very particular. Not certainly from any other Constitution or form of Government, for to none other are we at liberty to look, for any grant of power, or any principle which can bind us. The right then, is not conventional. Its source must be found beyond all civil society, prior to all social compact, and independent of its sanctions. We must look for it in the law of nature; we have indeed been distinctly told, that it exists in 'necessity and nature;' and upon that ground only, has it hitherto been claimed. I propose now to inquire whether the law of nature does indeed, confer this right or not.

Let me not be misunderstood, Sir. I am not inquiring whether, according to the form and nature of our institutions, a majority ought or ought not to rule. That inquiry will be made hereafter. At present, I propose only to prove that there is *no original a priori* principle in the law of nature, which gives to a majority a right to control a minority; and of course, that we are not bound by any obligation *prior to society*, to adopt that principle in our civil institutions.

If there be any thing in the law of nature which confers the right now contended for, in what part of her code, I would ask, is it to be found? For my own part, I incline strongly to think, that, closely examined, the law of nature will be found to confer no other right than this: the right in every creature to use the powers derived from nature, in such mode as will best promote its own happiness. If this be not the law of nature, she is certainly but little obeyed in any of the living departments of her *empire*. Throughout her boundless domain, the law of force gives the only rule of right. The lion devours the ox; the ox drives the lamb from the green pasture; the lamb exerts the same law of power over the animal that is weaker and more timid than itself; and thus the rule runs, throughout all the gradations of life, until at last, the worm devours us all. But, if there be another law independent of force, which gives to a greater number a right to control a smaller number, to what consequence does it lead? Gentlemen must themselves admit, that all men are by nature *equal*, for this is the very foundation of their claim of right in a majority. If this be so, each individual has his rights, which are precisely equal to the rights of his fellow. But the right of a majority to rule, necessarily implies a right to impose restraints, in some form or other; either upon the freedom of opinion or the freedom of action. And what follows? Each one of the three, enjoys the same rights with each one of the four, and yet it is gravely said, that because four is a majority of the seven, *that* majority has a right to restrain, to abridge, and consequently, to destroy all the rights of the lesser number. That is to say, while all are by nature equal, and all derive from nature the same rights in every respect, there shall yet be a number, only one less than a majority of the whole, who may not by the law of nature possess any rights at all! . . .

To such absurdities are we inevitably driven when we attempt to apply principles deduced from a state of nature, to a state of society; a state which pre-supposes that nature with all her rights and all her laws, has been shaken off! Indeed, Sir, the whole reasoning is fallacious, because it is founded on a state of things which in all probability, never had existence at all. It goes back to a state prior to all history, and about which we know nothing beyond mere conjecture. The first accounts which we have of man, are of man, in a social state. Wherever he has been found, and however rude his condition, he has been bound to his fellows by some form of association, in advance of a state of nature. If we may indulge any conjecture upon such a subject, the probability is that he was first urged into society, by a strong *feeling of property* implanted in his nature; by a feeling that he had, or at least, that he ought to have, a better title than another, to whatever his own labour had appropriated. The necessity of securing this right and protecting him in the enjoyment of it, in all probability, first suggested the idea of the social compact. Although property therefore, is strictly speaking the creature of society, yet a *feeling of property* was probably its creator. The result would be, that at the very moment that two human beings first came together, the social compact was formed. . .

The subject, Mr. Chairman, is scarcely worth the examination it has received. I will pursue it no farther, since I have no intention to give you a treatise on natural law, instead of an argument upon the practical subject of Government. I have thought it necessary to go thus far into an examination of the subject, because gentlemen have founded themselves upon what they are pleased to consider an axiom, that there is in a majority, an *a priori, inherent* and *indestructible* right to rule a minority, under all circumstances, and in every conceivable condition of things. And one of them at least has been understood by me, as referring this right to the law of nature; a law which he supposes, society cannot repeal, and which therefore, is of original and universal authority. Surely this is a very great mistake. Nay, Sir, there is proof enough before us that gentlemen themselves, who claim this right, and who seek to give it solemnity by referring it to the very law of our being, do not venture to carry it into the details of their own system. If there be a right in a majority of persons or of *white* persons, to rule a minority, upon what principle is it that the right of suffrage is restricted? *All* are counted, in making up the majority; and each one of the majority ought of consequence, to possess a share in its rights. Why then do you not admit women to the polls? Nature has stamped no such inferiority upon that sex, as to disqualify it under all circumstances, for a safe and judicious exercise of the right of suffrage. And why exclude minors? Infants who have not acquired language, or whose intellects are not sufficiently unfolded to enable them to understand their own actions, may be excluded from the necessity of the case. But at what time, in the ordinary course of nature, do these disabilities cease? Gentlemen say, at the age of twenty-one years. And why so? Not certainly because nature declares it; for the faculties attain maturity at different periods, in different latitudes of the earth. In one latitude we are ripe at sixteen; in another, not until 30; and even among ourselves, we see many, under the age of twenty-one who possess more wisdom and more power of general usefulness, than can be found in others of fifty; far more than in those who have approached their second childhood. What is there then, which indicates the precise period of twenty-one years, as the earliest at which these members of the ruling majority, may exercise the rights which belong to them? This, and this only: that the rule which is furnished by nature, is unfit for a state of society, and we are compelled, in our own defence, to adopt an arbitary rule of our own, which is better suited to our actual condition. There is no one among us so wild and visionary, as to desire universal suffrage, and yet it is perfectly certain that, at the moment when you limit that right, in however small a degree, you depart from the *principle* that a majority shall rule. If you establish any disqualification whatever, there is no *natural necessity*, nor even a *moral certainty*, that a majority in any given community, will not come within the exception. . .

In truth, Mr. Chairman, *there are no original principles of Government at all*. Novel and strange as the idea may appear, it is nevertheless, strictly true, in the sense in which I announce it. There are no original principles, existing in the nature of things and independent of agreement, to which Government must of necessity conform, in order to be either legitimate or philosophical. The principles of Government, are those principles only, which the people who form the Government, choose to *adopt and apply to themselves*. Principles do not precede, but spring out of Government. If this should be considered a dangerous novelty in this age of improvement, when all old fashioned things are rejected as worthless; let us test the doctrine by reference to examples. In Turkey, the Government is centered in one man; in England, it resides in King, Lords, and Commons, and in the Republics of the United States, we profess to repose it in the people alone. The principles of all these Governments are essentially different; and yet will it be said that the Governments of Turkey and England are no Governments at all, or not legitimate Governments, because in them, the will of a majority does not give the rule? Or, will it be said, that our own Governments are not legitimate, because they do not conform to the despotic principles of Turkey, nor recognise the aristocracy of England? If there be these original principles at all, we must presume that they are uniform in themselves, and universal in their application. It will not do to say that there is one principle for one place, and another principle for another place. The conclusion resulting from the reasoning of gentlemen will be, that there is one Government in the world which is *really* a Government, rightful and legitimate; and all other forms of social compact, however long, or however firmly established, are no Governments at all. Every Government is legitimate which springs directly from the will of the people, or to which the people have consented to give allegiance. And I am not going too far, in asserting that Governments are free or otherwise, only in proportion as the people have been consulted in forming them, and as their rulers are directly responsible to them for the execution of their will. It matters not what form they assume, nor who are the immediate depositories of political power. It may suit the purposes of the people, as it once suited those of Rome, to invest all authority in a Dictator; and if the people choose this form of Government; if their interest and safety require that they shall submit to it, what original principle is there which renders it illegitimate? If the majority possesses all power, they possess the power to *surrender* their power. And if it be just and wise that they should do so, it is still their own Government, and no one can impugn its legitimacy.

I have thus, Mr. Chairman, endeavored to prove, that there is not in nature, nor even in sound political science, any fundamental principle applicable to this subject, which is mandatory upon us. We are at perfect liberty to choose our own principle; . . .

I admit, as a general proposition, that in free Governments, power ought to be given to the majority; and why? The rule is founded in the idea that there is an identity, though not an *equality* of interests, in the several members of the body politic: in which case the presumption naturally arises, that the greater number possess the greater interest. But the rule no longer applies, when the reason of it fails. . . If the interests of the several parts of the Commonwealth were identical, it would be, we admit, safe and proper that a majority of *persons only* should give the rule of political power. But our interests are not identical, and the difference between us arises from property alone. We therefore contend that property ought to be considered, in fixing the basis of representation.

What, Sir, are the constituent elements of society? Persons *and property*. What are the subjects of Legislation? Persons *and property*. Was there ever a society seen on earth, which consisted only of men, women and children? The very idea of society, carries with it the idea of property, as its necessary and inseparable attendant. History cannot show any form of the social compact, at any time, or in any place, into which property did not enter as a constituent element, nor one in which that element did not enjoy protection in a greater or less degree. Nor was there ever a society in which the protection once extended to property, was afterwards withdrawn, which did not fall an easy prey to violence and disorder. Society cannot exist without property; it constitutes the full half of its being. Take away all protection from property, and our next business is to cut each other's throats. All experience proves this. The safety of men depends on the safety of property; the rights of persons must mingle in the ruin of the rights of property. And shall it not then be protected? Sir, your Government cannot move an inch without property. . . And what are the subjects upon which the law-making power is called to act? Persons *and property*. To these two subjects, and not to one of them alone, is the business of legislation confined. . . If then, Sir, property is thus necessary to the very being of society; thus indispensable to every movement of Government; if it be that subject upon which Government chiefly acts; is it not, I would ask, entitled to such protection as shall be above all suspicion, and free from every hazard? It appears to me that I need only announce the proposition, to secure the assent of every gentleman present.

Sir, the obligations of man in his social state are two-fold; to bear arms, and to pay taxes for the support of Government. The obligation to bear arms, results from the duty which society owes him, to protect his rights of person. The society which protects me, I am bound to protect in return. The obligation to pay taxes, results from the protection extended to property. Not a protection against foreign enemies; not a protection by swords and bayonets merely; but a protection derived from a prompt and correct administration of justice; a protection against the violence, the fraud, or the injustice of my neighbor. In this protection, the owner of property is alone interested. Here, then, is the plain agreement between Government on the one hand, and the tax-paying citizen on the other. It is an agreement which results, of necessity, from the social compact; and when the consideration is fairly paid, how can you honestly withhold the equivalent? . . .

If men enter into the social compact upon unequal terms; if one man brings into the partnership, his rights of person alone, and another brings into it, equal rights of person and all the rights of property beside, can they be said to have an equal interest in the common stock? Shall not he who has most at stake; who has, not only a *greater* interest, but a *peculiar* interest in society, possess an authority proportioned to that interest, and adequate to its protection? . . .

I must remind the gentlemen, that they have admitted the principle, that property must be protected, and protected in the very form now proposed; they are obliged to admit it. It would be a wild and impracticable scheme of Government, which did not admit it. Among all the various and numerous propositions, lying upon your table, is there one which goes the length of proposing *universal suffrage?* There is none. Yet this subject is in direct connexion with that. Why do you not admit a pauper to vote? He is a person: he counts one in your numerical majority. In rights strictly personal, he has as much interest in the Government as any other citizen. He is liable to commit the same offences, and to become exposed to the same punishments as the rich man. Why, then, shall he not vote? Because, thereby, he would receive an influence over property; and all who own it, feel it to be unsafe, to put the power of controlling it, into the hands of those who are not the owners. If you go on population as the basis of representation, you will be obliged to go the length of giving the elective franchise to every human being over twenty-one years; yes, and under twenty-one years, on whom your penal laws take effect; an experiment, which has met with nothing but utter and disastrous failure, wherever it has been tried. No, Mr. Chairman: Let us be consistent. Let us openly acknowledge the truth; let us boldly take the bull by the horns, and incorporate this influence of property as a leading principle in our Constitution. . .

9. *The two sexes do no more certainly gravitate to each other than power and property*

JOHN RANDOLPH, Virginia Constitutional Convention, 1829–30 *

As long as I have had any fixed opinions, I have been in the habit of considering the Constitution of Virginia, under which I have lived for more than half a century, with all its faults and failings, and with all the objections which practical men—not theorists and visionary speculators, have urged or can urge against it, as the very best Constitution; not for Japan; not for China; not for New England; or for Old England; but for this, our ancient Commonwealth of Virginia.

But, I am not such a bigot as to be unwilling, under any circumstances, however imperious, to change the Constitution under which I was born; I may say, certainly under which I was brought up, and under which, I had hoped to be carried to my grave. My principles on that subject are these: the grievance must first be clearly specified, and fully proved; it must be vital, or rather, deadly in its effect; its magnitude must be such as will justify prudent and reasonable men in taking the always delicate, often dangerous step, of making innovations in their fundamental law; and the remedy proposed must be reasonable and adequate to the end in view. When the grievance shall have been thus made out, I hold him to be not a loyal subject, but a political bigot, who would refuse to apply the suitable remedy.

But, I will not submit my case to a political physician; come his diploma from whence it may; who would at once prescribe all the medicines in the Pharmacopoeia, not only for the disease I now have, but for all the diseases of every possible kind I ever might have in future. These are my principles, and I am willing to carry them out; for, I will not hold any principles which I may not fairly carry out in practice.

Judge, then, with what surprise and pain, I found that not one department of this Government—no, not one—Legislative, Executive or Judicial—nor one branch of either, was left untouched by the spirit of *innovation*. . .

I have by experience learned that changes, even in the ordinary law of the land, do not always operate as the drawer of the bill, or the Legislative body, may have anticipated; and of all things in the world, a Government, whether ready made, to suit casual customers, or made per order, is the very last that operates as its framers intended. Governments are like revolutions: you may put them in motion, but I defy you to control them after they are *in* motion. . .

Mr. Chairman, since I have been here, the scene has recalled many old recollections. At one time, I thought myself in the House of Representatives, listening to the debate on the Tariff; at another time, I imagined myself listening to the debate on the Missouri Question; and sometimes I fancied myself listening to both questions debated at once. Are we men? met to consult about the affairs of men? Or are we, in truth, a Robinhood Society? discussing rights

* Op. cit. pp. 313–21 *passim.*

in the abstract? Have we no house over our heads? Do we forget, that we are living under a Constitution, which has shielded us for more than half a century —that we are not a parcel of naked and forlorn savages, on the shores of New Holland; and that the worst that can come is, that we shall live under the same Constitution that we lived under, freely and happily, for half a century? To their monstrous claims of power, we plead this prescription; but then we are told, that *nullum tempus occurrit Regi*—King whom? King Numbers. And they will not listen to a prescription of fifty-four years—a period greater, by four years, than would secure a title to the best estate in the Commonwealth, unsupported by any other shadow of right. Nay, Sir, in this case, prescription operates *against* possession. They tell us, it is only a case of long-continued, and, therefore, of aggravated injustice. They say to us, in words the most courteous and soft, (but I am not so soft as to swallow them,) 'we shall be—we will be—we must be your masters, and you shall submit.' To whom do they hold this language? To dependents? weak, unprotected, and incapable of defence? Or is it to the great tobacco-growing and slave-holding interest, and to every other interest on this side the Ridge? 'We are numbers, you have property.' I am not so obtuse, as to require any further explanation on this head. 'We are numbers, you have property.' Sir, I understand it perfectly. Mr. Chairman, since the days of the French Revolution, when the Duke of Orleans, who was the richest subject, not only in France, but in all Europe, lent himself to the *mountain* party in the Convention, in the vain and weak hope of grasping political power, perhaps of mounting the throne, still slippery with the blood of the last incumbent—from that day to this, so great a degree of infatuation, has not been shown by any individual, as by the tobacco-grower, and slave-holder of Virginia, who shall lend his aid to rivet this yoke on the necks of his brethren, and on his own. . .

I hold with one of the greatest masters of political philosophy, that 'no rational man ever did govern himself by abstractions and universals.' . .

'A Statesman differs from a Professor in an University. The latter has only the general view of society; the former, the Statesman, has a number of circumstances to combine with those general ideas, and to take into his consideration. Circumstances are infinite, are infinitely combined, are variable and transient: he who does not take them into consideration, is not erroneous, but stark mad—*dat operam ut cum ratione insanat*—he is metaphysically mad. A Statesman, never losing sight of principles, is to be guided by circumstances, and judging contrary to the exigencies of the moment, he may ruin his country forever.' . .

Mr. Chairman, I am a practical man. I go for solid security, and I never will, knowingly, take any other. But, if the security on which I have relied, is insufficient, and my property is in danger, it is better that I should know it in time, and I may prepare to meet the consequences, while it is yet called to-day, than to rest on a security that is fallacious and deceptive. Sir, I would not give a button for your mixed basis in the Senate. Give up this question, and I have nothing more to lose. This is the entering wedge, and every thing else must follow. We are told, indeed, that we must rely on a restriction of the Right of

Suffrage; but, gentlemen, know, that after you shall have adopted the report of the Select Committee, you can place no restriction upon it. When this principle is in operation, the waters are out. It is as if you would ask an industrious and sagacious Hollander, that you may cut his dykes, provided you make your cut only of a certain width. A rat hole will let in the ocean. Sir, there is an end to the security of all property in the Commonwealth, and he will be unwise, who shall not abandon the ship to the underwriters. It is the first time in my life, that I ever heard of a Government, which was to divorce property from power. Yet, this is seriously and soberly proposed to us. Sir, I know it is practicable, but it can be done only by a violent divulsion, as in France—but the moment you have separated the two, that very moment property will go in search of power, and power in search of property. 'Male and female created he them;' and the two sexes do not more certainly, nor by a more unerring law, gravitate to each other, than power and property. You can only cause them to change hands. . . It is of the nature of man. Man always has been in society—we always find him in possession of property, and with a certain appetite for it, which leads him to seek it, if not *per fas,* sometimes *per nefas;* and hence the need of laws to protect it, and to punish its invaders.

But, I am subjecting myself, I know, to a most serious reproach. It will be said that I am not a friend of the poor. . . I wish to say a word as to the 'friends of the poor.' Whenever I see a man, especially a rich man, endeavoring to rise and to acquire consequence in society, by standing out as the especial champion of the poor, I am always reminded of an old acquaintance of mine, one Signor Manuel Ordonez, who made a comfortable living, and amassed an opulent fortune by administering the funds of the poor. Among the strange notions which have been broached since I have been on the political theatre, there is one which has lately seized the minds of men, that all things must be done for them by the Government, and that they are to do nothing for themselves: The Government is not only to attend to the great concerns which are its province, but it must step in and ease indviduals of their natural and moral obligations. A more pernicious notion cannot prevail. Look at that ragged fellow staggering from the whiskey shop, and see that slattern who has gone there to reclaim him; where are their children? Running about, ragged, idle, ignorant, fit candidates for the penitentiary. Why is all this so? Ask the man and he will tell you, 'Oh, the Government has undertaken to educate our children for us. It has given us a premium for idleness, and I now spend in liquor, what I should otherwise be obliged to save to pay for their schooling. My neighbor there, that is so hard at work in his field yonder with his son, can't spare that boy to attend, except in the winter months, the school which he is taxed to support for mine. He has to scuffle hard to make both ends meet at the end of the year, and keep the wolf from the door. His children can't go to this school, yet he has to pay a part of the tax to maintain it.' Sir, is it like friends of the poor to absolve them from what Nature, what God himself has made their first and most sacred duty? For the education of their children is the first and most obvious duty of every parent, and one which the worthless alone are ever known wholly to neglect.

Mr. Chairman, these will be deemed, I fear, unconnected thoughts; but they have been the ailment of my mind for years. Rumination and digestion can do no more; they are thoroughly concocted.

In the course of not a short or uneventful life, I have had correspondence with various persons in all parts of the Union, and I have seen gentlemen on their return from the North and East, as well as from the new States of the West; and I never heard from any of them, but one expression of opinion as it related to us in Virginia. It was in the sentiment, if not in the language of Virgil; Oh, fortunate, if we knew our own blessedness. They advise us with one voice, 'Stick to what you have got; stick to your Constitution; stick to your Right of Suffrage. Don't give up your freehold representation. We have seen enough of the opposite system and too much.' . .

SELECTED REFERENCES

W. C. Bruce, *John Randolph of Roanoke, 1773–1833*, New York, G. P. Putnam, 1922.

F. W. Coker, 'American Traditions Concerning Property and Liberty,' *American Political Science Review*, February 1936, vol. 30, pp. 1–23.

A Voice from America, by an American Gentleman (Calvin Colton), London, 1839.

Louis Hartz, *The Liberal Tradition in America: An Interpretation of American Political Thought since the Revolution*, New York, Harcourt, Brace, 1955.

Richard Hofstadter, *The American Political Tradition*, New York, Alfred A. Knopf, Inc., 1948, ch. III.

J. T. Horton, *James Kent, A Study in Conservatism*, New York, 1939.

John Krout and Dixon Ryan Fox, *The Completion of Independence, 1740–1830*, New York, Macmillan, 1944.

Arthur M. Schlesinger, Jr., *The Age of Jackson*, Boston, Little, Brown, 1946, chaps. 2, 22, and 26.

Alexis de Tocqueville, *Democracy in America*, translated by Henry Reeve, Boston, John Allyn, 1882.

Benjamin F. Wright, *American Interpretations of Natural Law*, Cambridge, Harvard University Press, 1931.

XI

JACKSON AND REVOLUTION

The age of Jackson has become a favorite topic for scholarly and semi-popular research. Yet Jackson himself is still an almost impenetrable enigma. Charles M. Wiltse, writing in 1948, observed: 'Those who have succeeded in giving Jackson either a consistent policy or an intelligible political philosophy have been able to do so . . . only on the basis of incomplete analysis or misinterpretation of essential facts.' The selection of materials contained in this chapter is made with full knowledge that they may give undue coherence to a most complex and widely variegated movement.

By 1825 the Federalist versus Republican two-party system had disappeared. The 'era of good feeling' had dawned. National power, serving great commercial and financial interests through the agency of the United States Bank, the protective tariff, bounties, and internal improvements, was settled policy. Even Madison and Monroe, the Virginians who occupied the White House from 1809 to 1825, had, as practical politicians, abandoned the strict Jeffersonian principles they once endorsed. In 1816 President Madison approved the second National Bank, the very institution he, along with other Democratic-Republicans, had vigorously opposed twenty-five years earlier. That same year he endorsed the protective tariff. President James Monroe yielded still further, signing a bill for internal improvements. Jefferson himself to some extent had joined the rout, saying in 1816, when the first all-out attempt was made to enact Hamilton's Report on Manufactures: 'Experience has taught me that manufactures are as necessary to our independence as to our comfort.' Only John Taylor of Caroline adhered doggedly and unqualifiedly to the 'old Republican School.'

Elected President of the United States in 1828 and re-elected in 1832, Andrew Jackson (1767–1845) built his strength on the frontier conditions and ideas of the New West and the South. Helping swell the Jacksonian tide were farmers of the eastern seaboard, joined by the rising mechanics and factory workers, who recognized a community of interest with western agrarians in the war on the United States Bank and other institutions of commercial power. Jackson succeeded in welding these incongruous elements into an aggressive middle-class movement, dedicated to the 'common man.' Extension of the suffrage and the leveling of restrictive constitutional barriers were but part of a fairly well integrated program designed to bring government closer to the people. This was done by means of the longer ballot and rotation in office—'a leading principle in the Republican creed,' Jackson called it—and by the national nominating convention, eliminating 'King Caucus.' All this enabled Jackson to present himself over Congress as the one representative of all the people. Executive power grew enormously, as shown by his extended use of patronage and the presidential veto, by his bold challenge to Chief Justice Marshall and the whole Federal judiciary. Jackson may not have used the exact words often attributed to him apropos the Supreme Court's judgment in Worcester *v.* Georgia (1832), but they clearly expressed his attitude: 'John Marshall has made his decision, now let him enforce it.'

Jackson's confidence in the average man's capacity for politics comes out strongly in his first annual message to Congress, which opens this chapter. 'The duties of all public officers are . . . so plain and simple,' runs a much quoted line, 'that men of intelligence may readily qualify themselves for their performance. . . In a country where offices are created solely for the benefit of the people, no one man has any more intrinsic right to official station than another.'

Marshall, Justice Story, and Chancellor Kent saw the problem of government primarily in terms of 'how the property-holding part of the community may be sustained against inroads of poverty and vice.' Yet even they recognized that a certain correlation must exist between political and economic power. 'With property divided as we have it,' Webster had said, 'no other government than that of a republic could be maintained, even were we foolish enough to desire it.' But what was the prospect for popular government where economic power was becoming increasingly concentrated?

The Federalists had seen property as the basis of civilized society. To promote the general welfare, government must give it absolute protection and help along any trade or industry that needed support. In the leading case of the Trustees of Dartmouth College against Woodward, Chief Justice Marshall found adequate safeguards for rights of property and contract in Article 1, Section 10, of the Constitution, holding that any direct interference by the state with such rights must have been authorized in the charter. The result was that individual rights of property and contract fixed the contours within which the states could exercise their power. Nor was this doctrine confined, as in the Dartmouth College case, to the charters of charitable or educational institutions. It applied with equal force to profit-seeking corporate monopolies. That is why the Jacksonian democrats were so profoundly concerned lest the foundation of popular government be undermined by corporations enjoying exclusive privileges under charters granted by government and construed by John Marshall as inviolable.

The dynamism of the Jacksonian revolution stemmed, above all, from a situation in which, as it was said, 'the bargaining and trading away of chartered privileges is the whole business of our legislature.' Or again, 'We cannot pass the bounds of the city without paying tribute to monopoly; our bread, our meat, our vegetables, our fuel, all, all pay tribute to monopolists.' 'Not a road can be opened, not a bridge can be built, not a canal can be dug,' William

Leggett of the *New York Post* observed, 'but a charter of exclusive privilege must be granted for the purpose.' Old Hickory expressed sentiments not unlike these in his refusal to approve renewal of a charter for Nicholas Biddle's bank, and the presidential veto message, largely prepared by his Attorney General, Roger B. Taney, embodies a forthright statement of the belief that privilege is as wrong, as undemocratic, in economics as in politics.

> It is to be regretted that the rich and powerful too often bend the acts of government to their selfish purposes. Distinctions in society will always exist under every just government. Equality and talents, of education, or of wealth cannot be produced by human institutions. In the full enjoyment of the gifts of Heaven and the fruits of superior industry, economy, and virtue, every man is equally entitled to protection by law; but when the laws undertake to add to these natural and just advantages artificial distinctions, to grant titles, gratuities, and exclusive privileges, to make the rich richer and the potent more powerful, the humble members of society—the farmers, mechanics, and laborers—who have neither the time nor means of securing like favors to themselves, have a right to complain of the injustice of their Government. . . If we cannot at once, in justice to interests vested under improvident legislation, make our Government what it ought to be, we can at least take a stand against all new grants of monopolies and exclusive privileges, against any prostitution of our Government to the advancement of the few at the expense of the many, and in favor of compromise and gradual reform in our code of laws and system of political economy.

Chief Justice Taney's opinion in the Charles River Bridge case, herein excerpted, is written in the same spirit, representing at the state level the same devotion to free enterprise and genuine *laisser-faire*. In 1785 Harvard College received from the State legislature a charter authorizing construction of the Charles River Bridge. The corporation flourished as population and business expanded, and the Massachusetts legislature authorized in 1828 a second bridge, the Warren, which was in time to be operated free of toll. Daniel Webster, one of the counsel for the Charles River Bridge, argued on the basis of Marshall's reasoning in the Dartmouth College case that there was an implied contract that no second bridge would be authorized or built. The case thus involved a clear conflict between vested rights on one side and public power on the other. Did the legislature of Massachusetts, in interfering with the profits of this private corporation, impair its charter? In 1831 Marshall had resolved the issue, without decision, in favor of the vested interests of the Charles River Bridge, but on re-argument two years after his death Marshall's successor narrowed the immunities of the corporation so as to promote free enterprise. Chief Justice Taney held that no rights were to be construed as granted except those conferred specifically by the charter itself. 'The object and end of all government is,' he said, 'to promote the happiness and prosperity of the community by which it is established, and it never can be assumed that the government intended to diminish its power of accomplishing the end for which it was created.'

As to the rights of private property, they must be 'sacredly guarded,' Taney agreed, but 'we must not forget that the community also have rights, and that the happiness and well being of every citizen depends on their faithful preservation.' The important thing was to keep the channels of enterprise free and opportunities untrammeled. 'In a country like ours,' Taney pointed out, 'free, active, and enterprising, continually advancing in numbers and wealth,' new channels of communication and travel are continually found necessary, all being essential to the comfort, convenience, and prosperity of the people.

In Taney's opinion, one finds no trace of the spirit of leveling, no suggestion that it is the business of government itself to undertake, by positive action, promotion of the public good. Lacking in Taney is the utopianism of Orestes A. Brownson (1803–1876), New England liberal and harsh critic of the capitalist system. Taney does, however, bluntly repudiate the Federalist notion that the absolute protection of private property is the surest way to secure the welfare of all. What Jackson and Taney asked of government was even-handed justice. What they desired was elimination of economic privilege. Far from assailing property or business enterprise, their primary concern was to protect it against privilege-seeking corporations. In thus insisting that industry, commerce, and finance be liberated from government-created monopoly privilege, the Jacksonians were apostles of *laisser-faire* equalled only by Jefferson himself. Jackson's successor, Martin Van Buren, and the founder of the *United States Magazine* and *Democratic Review*, John L. O'Sullivan (1813–95), whose introductory statement of principles is included in this chapter, are clearly in the same tradition.

In October 1836 Jackson, looking forward to retirement, wrote Taney that he contemplated making a farewell address. What should go into it? 'Your farewell address,' Taney replied, 'should be exclusively devoted to those great and enduring principles upon which our institutions are founded, and without which the blessings of freedom cannot be preserved.' The address of 1837, written according to these specifications, largely by Taney in close collaboration with Jackson, is included in this chapter.

Recently certain students have been wont to interpret Jacksonian democracy as a sort of forerunner of Franklin D. Roosevelt and his New Deal. There are, of course, suggestive points of comparison. Both were manifestations of electoral and popular revolt against economic power and greed. In their day Nicholas Biddle and the United States Bank were the spearhead of economic power, just as Charles E. Mitchell, the National City Bank, and the American Liberty League symbolized latter-day economic privilege. Leading the popular revolt in both instances was a towering political leader. These similarities must not, however, blur the important difference of circumstances and environment. Professor Richard Hofstadter observes: *

> The New Deal was frankly based upon the premise that economic expansion had come to an end and economic opportunities were disappearing. It attempted to cope with the situation by establish-

* *The American Political Tradition*, copyright 1948 by Alfred A. Knopf, Inc.

> ing governmental ascendancy over the affairs of business. The Jacksonian movement grew out of expanding opportunities and a common desire to enlarge these opportunities still further by removing restrictions and privileges that had their origin in acts of government; thus, with some qualifications, it was essentially a movement of laissez-faire, an attempt to divorce government from business. . . The Jacksonian movement was a phase in the expansion of democracy . . . it was also a phase in the expansion of liberated capitalism.

Jacksonian democracy was above all else alive with unbounded faith in the expanding opportunities of America wherein all could rise and none need be pulled down. This process was to be accelerated not by any positive act of government, but by erasing those privileges, both economic and political, that government itself had been powerfully instrumental in creating. Jackson's veto of the bank bill and the clamorous war he waged against financial privilege is but a conspicuous example of a far-flung policy.

Barring slavery, America in the second quarter of the nineteenth century may well have come closer to realizing the ideals of our Declaration of Independence than at any time before or since. Democracy had not been fully achieved, it is true, even in the elementary sense of universal manhood suffrage, but the country was moving progressively in that direction. The constitutions of the six western states admitted to the Union between 1812 and 1821 either provided for or approximated universal white manhood suffrage. The original states, too, were in the process of breaking down the constitutional barriers guarding economic privilege. Nor is this all. Liberty meant more then than later, because it was coupled more closely with economic equality. Tools of production were still relatively simple and inexpensive, their ownership rather easily obtainable and widely diffused. The corporate form of business organization was not the dominant thing it is today, and even if one man was hired to work for another, he could and did look forward, usually not in vain, to independence in his own shop and on his own land. Moreover the Great West beckoned and government land policy now enhanced individual opportunity and stimulated the American drive for equality. In 1820 the minimum price of public land was $2 per acre; by 1830 it had been reduced to $1.25, and sales were authorized in smaller units. During Jackson's time alone over 63 million acres of the public domain were distributed. This, in short, was a period in which the philosophy of rugged individualism had real basis in fact. Any individual by his own effort might rise to the top. Despite Brownson's plea that hereditary property be destroyed, there was no thought of transferring wealth by government action from the few to the many. With property resources almost limitless, free men could be trusted to want what was right and get it.

Few then realized that another revolution, industrial in character, was already in progress, destined to forge new chains on man's freedom as paralyzing as the institutional and constitutional restrictions which were soon to be thrown off. Society was to be confronted with yet another baffling dilemma, to prove once more Walt Whitman's discerning truism: 'It is provided in the very essence of things that from any fruition of success, no matter what, shall come forth something to make a greater struggle necessary.'

1. *The duties of public officers are so plain and simple that men of intelligence may readily qualify themselves for their performance*

ANDREW JACKSON, First Annual Message to Congress, 8 December 1829 *

I consider it one of the most urgent of my duties to bring to your attention the propriety of amending that part of our Constitution which relates to the election of President and Vice-President. Our system of government was by its framers deemed an experiment, and they therefore consistently provided a mode of remedying its defects.

To the people belongs the right of electing their Chief Magistrate; it was never designed that their choice should in any case be defeated, either by the intervention of electoral colleges or by the agency confided, under certain contingencies, to the House of Representatives. Experience proves that in proportion as agents to execute the will of the people are multiplied there is danger of their wishes being frustrated. Some may be unfaithful; all are liable to err. So far, therefore, as the people can with convenience speak, it is safer for them to express their own will. . .

One may err from ignorance of the wishes of his constituents; another from a conviction that it is his duty to be governed by his own judgment of the fitness of the candidates; finally, although all were inflexibly honest, all accurately informed of the wishes of their constituents, yet under the present mode of election a minority may often elect a President, and when this happens it may reasonably be expected that efforts will be made on the part of the majority to rectify this injurious operation of their institutions. But although no evil of this character should result from such a perversion of the first principle of our system—*that the majority is to govern*—it must be very certain that a President elected by a minority cannot enjoy the confidence necessary to the successful discharge of his duties.

In this as in all other matters of public concern policy requires that as few impediments as possible should exist to the free operation of the public will. Let us, then, endeavor so to amend our system that the office of Chief Magistrate may not be conferred upon any citizen but in pursuance of a fair expression of the will of the majority. . .

There are, perhaps, a few men who can for any great length of time enjoy office and power without being more or less under the influence of feelings unfavorable to the faithful discharge of their public duties. Their integrity may be proof against improper considerations immediately addressed to themselves, but they are apt to acquire a habit of looking with indifference upon the public

* *Messages and Papers of the Presidents,* James D. Richardson, ed., vol. II, pp. 442, 447–52 *passim.*

interests and of tolerating conduct from which an unpracticed man would revolt. Office is considered as a species of property, and government rather as a means of promoting individual interests than as an instrument created solely for the service of the people. Corruption in some and in others a perversion of correct feelings and principles divert government from its legitimate ends and make it an engine for the support of the few at the expense of the many. The duties of all public officers are, or at least admit of being made, so plain and simple that men of intelligence may readily qualify themselves for their performance; and I cannot but believe that more is lost by the long continuance of men in office than is generally to be gained by their experience. I submit, therefore, to your consideration whether the efficiency of the Government would not be promoted and official industry and integrity better secured by a general extension of the law which limits appointments to four years.

In a country where offices are created solely for the benefit of the people no one man has any more intrinsic right to official station than another. Offices were not established to give support to particular men at the public expense. No individual wrong is, therefore, done by removal, since neither appointment to nor continuance in office is matter of right. The incumbent became an officer with a view to public benefits, and when these require his removal they are not to be sacrificed to private interests. It is the people, and they alone, who have a right to complain when a bad officer is substituted for a good one. He who is removed has the same means of obtaining a living that are enjoyed by the millions who never held office. The proposed limitation would destroy the idea of property now so generally connected with official station, and although individual distress may be sometimes produced, it would, by promoting that rotation which constitutes a leading principle in the republican creed, give healthful action to the system.

No very considerable change has occurred during the recess of Congress in the condition of either our agriculture, commerce, or manufactures. . .

To regulate its conduct so as to promote equally the prosperity of these three cardinal interests is one of the most difficult tasks of Government; and it may be regretted that the complicated restrictions which now embarrass the intercourse of nations could not by common consent be abolished, and commerce allowed to flow in those channels to which individual enterprise, always its surest guide, might direct it. But we must ever expect selfish legislation in other nations, and are therefore compelled to adapt our own to their regulations in the manner best calculated to avoid serious injury and to harmonize the conflicting interests of our agriculture, our commerce, and our manufactures. Under these impressions I invite your attention to the existing tariff, believing that some of its provisions require modification.

The general rule to be applied in graduating the duties upon articles of foreign growth or manufacture is that which will place our own in fair competition with those of other countries; and the inducements to advance even a step beyond this point are controlling in regard to those articles which are of primary necessity in time of war. When we reflect upon the difficulty and delicacy of this operation, it is important that it should never be attempted but with the utmost caution. Frequent legislation in regard to any branch of industry, affecting its value, and by which its capital may be transferred to new channels, must always be productive of hazardous speculation and loss.

In deliberating, therefore, on these interesting subjects local feelings and prejudices should be merged in the patriotic determination to promote the great interests of the whole. All attempts to connect them with the party conflicts of the day are necessarily injurious, and should be discountenanced. Our action upon them should be under the control of higher and purer motives. Legislation subjected to such influences can never be just, and will not long retain the sanction of a people whose active patriotism is not bounded by sectional limits nor insensible to that spirit of concession and forbearance which gave life to our political compact and still sustains it. Discarding all calculations of political ascendency, the North, the South, the East, and the West should unite in diminishing any burthen of which either may justly complain.

The agricultural interest of our country is so essentially connected with every other and so superior in importance to them all that it is scarcely necessary to invite to it your particular attention. It is principally as manufactures and commerce tend to increase the value of agricultural productions and to extend their application to the wants and comforts of society that they deserve the fostering care of Government. . .

After the extinction of the public debt it is not probable that any adjustment of the tariff upon principles satisfactory to the people of the Union will until a remote period, if ever, leave the Government without a considerable surplus in the Treasury beyond what may be required for its current service. As, then, the period approaches when the application of the revenue to the payment of debt will cease, the disposition of the surplus will present a subject for the serious deliberation of Congress; and it may be fortunate for the country that it is yet to be decided. Considered in connection with the difficulties which have heretofore attended appropriations for purposes of internal improvement, and with those which this experience tells us will certainly arise whenever power over such subjects may be exercised by the General Government, it is hoped that it may lead to the adoption of some plan which will reconcile the diversified interests of the States and strengthen the bonds which unite them. Every member of the Union, in peace and in war, will be benefited by the improvement of inland navigation and the construction of highways in the several States. Let us, then, endeavor to attain this benefit in a mode which will be satisfactory to all. That hitherto adopted has by many of our fellow-citizens been deprecated as an infraction of the Constitution, while by others it has been viewed as inexpedient. All feel that it has been employed at the expense of harmony in the legislative councils.

To avoid these evils it appears to me that the most safe, just, and federal disposition which could be made of the surplus revenue would be its apportionment among the several States according to their ratio of representation, and should this measure not be found warranted by the Constitution that it would be expedient to propose to the States an amendment authorizing it. I regard an appeal to the source of power in cases of real doubt, and where its exercise is deemed indispensable to the general welfare, as among the most sacred of all our obligations. Upon this country more than any other has, in the providence of God, been cast the special guardianship of the great principle of adherence to written constitutions. If it fail here, all hope in regard to it will be extinguished. That this was intended to be a government of limited and specific, and not general, powers must be admitted by all, and it is our duty to preserve for it the character intended by its framers. If experience points out the necessity for an enlargement of these powers, let us apply for it to those for whose benefit it is to be exercised, and not undermine the whole system by a resort to overstrained constructions. The scheme has worked well. It has exceeded the hopes of those who devised it, and become an object of admiration to the world. We are responsible to our country and to the glorious cause of self-government for the preservation of so great a good. The great mass of legislation relating to our internal affairs was intended to be left where the Federal Convention found it—in the State governments. Nothing is clearer, in my view, than that we are chiefly indebted for the success of the Constitution under which we are now acting to the watchful and auxiliary operation of the State authorities. This is not the reflection of a day, but belongs to the most deeply rooted convictions of my mind. I cannot, therefore, too strongly or too earnestly, for my own sense of its importance, warn you against all encroachments upon the legitimate sphere of State sovereignty. Sustained by its healthful and invigorating influence the federal system can never fall. . .

2. *Rich men have besought us to make them richer by act of Congress*

ANDREW JACKSON, Veto of the Bank Bill, 10 July 1832 *

The bill 'to modify and continue' the act entitled 'An act to incorporate the subscribers to the Bank of the United States' was presented to me on the 4th July instant. Having . . . come to the conclusion that it ought not to become law, I herewith return it to the Senate, in which it originated, with my objections. . .

The present corporate body . . . enjoys an exclusive privilege of banking under the authority of the General Government, a monopoly of its favor and support, and, as a necessary consequence, almost a monopoly of the foreign and domestic exchange. The powers, privileges, and favors bestowed upon it in the original charter, by increasing the value of the stock far above its par value, operated as a gratuity of many millions to the stockholders. . .

The act before me proposes another gratuity to the holders of the same stock. . . On all hands it is conceded that its passage will increase at least 20 or 30 per cent more the market price of the stock, subject to the payment of the annuity of $200,000 per year secured by the act, thus adding in a

* *Messages and Papers of the Presidents*, James D. Richardson, ed., vol. II, pp. 576–91 *passim.*

moment one-fourth to its par value. It is not our own citizens only who are to receive the bounty of our Government. More than eight millions of the stock of this bank are held by foreigners. By this act the American Republic proposes virtually to make them a present of some millions of dollars. For these gratuities to foreigners and to some of our own opulent citizens the act secures no equivalent whatever. . . Every monopoly and all exclusive privileges are granted at the expense of the public which ought to receive a fair equivalent. . . But the act does not permit competition in the purchase of this monopoly. It seems to be predicated on the erroneous idea that the present stockholders have a prescriptive right not only to the favor but to the bounty of government. . .

It is maintained by the advocates of the bank that its constitutionality in all its features ought to be considered as settled by precedent and by the decision of the Supreme Court. To this conclusion I cannot assent. Mere precedent is a dangerous source of authority, and should not be regarded as deciding questions of constitutional power except where the acquiescence of the people and the States can be considered as well settled. So far from this being the case on this subject, an argument against the bank might be based on precedent. One Congress, in 1791, decided in favor of a bank; another, in 1811, decided against it. One Congress, in 1815, decided against a bank; another, in 1816, decided in its favor. Prior to the present Congress, therefore, the precedents drawn from that source were equal. If we resort to the States, the expressions of legislative, judicial, and executive opinions against the bank have been probably to those in its favor as 4 to 1. . .

If the opinion of the Supreme Court covered the whole ground of this act, it ought not to control the co-ordinate authorities of this Government. The Congress, the Executive, and the Court must each for itself be guided by its own opinion of the Constitution. Each public officer who takes an oath to support the Constitution swears that he will support it as he understands it, and not as it is understood by others. It is as much the duty of the House of Representatives, of the Senate, and of the President to decide upon the constitutionality of any bill or resolution which may be presented to them for passage or approval as it is of the supreme judges when it may be brought before them for judicial decision. The opinion of the judges has no more authority over Congress than the opinion of Congress has over the judges, and on that point the President is independent of both. The authority of the Supreme Court must not, therefore, be permitted to control the Congress or the Executive when acting in their legislative capacities, but to have only such influence as the force of their reasoning may deserve.

But in the case relied upon the Supreme Court have not decided that all the features of this corporation are compatible with the Constitution. It is true that the court have said that the law incorporating the bank is a constitutional exercise of power by Congress; but taking into view the whole opinion of the court and the reasoning by which they have come to that conclusion, I understand them to have decided that inasmuch as a bank is an appropriate means for carrying into effect the enumerated powers of the General Government, therefore the law incorporating it is in accordance with that provision of the Constitution which declares that Congress shall have power 'to make all laws which shall be necessary and proper for carrying those powers into execution.' Having satisfied themselves that the word 'necessary' in the Constitution means 'needful,' 'requisite,' 'essential,' 'conducive to,' and that 'a bank' is a convenient, a useful, and essential instrument in the prosecution of the Government's 'fiscal operations,' they conclude that to 'use one must be within the discretion of Congress' and that 'the act to incorporate the Bank of the United States is a law made in pursuance of the Constitution'; 'but,' say they, '*where the law is not prohibited and is really calculated to effect any of the objects intrusted to the Government, to undertake here to inquire into the degree of its necessity would be to pass the line which circumscribes the judicial department and to tread on legislative ground.*'

The principle here affirmed is that the 'degree of its necessity,' involving all the details of the banking institution, is a question exclusively for legislative consideration. A bank is constitutional, but it is the province of the Legislature to determine whether this or that particular power, privilege, or exemption is 'necessary and proper' to enable the bank to discharge its duties to the Government, and from their decision there is no appeal to the courts of justice. Under the decision of the Supreme Court, therefore, it is the exclusive province of Congress and the President to decide whether the particular features of this act are *necessary* and *proper* in order to enable the bank to perform conveniently and efficiently the public duties assigned to it as a fiscal agent, and therefore constitutional, or *unnecessary* and *improper*, and therefore unconstitutional. . .

If our power over means is so absolute that the Supreme Court will not call in question the constitutionality of an act of Congress the subject of which 'is not prohibited, and is really calculated to effect any of the objects intrusted to the Government,' although, as in the case before me, it takes away powers expressly granted to Congress and rights scrupulously reserved to the States, it becomes us to proceed in our legislation with the utmost caution. Though not directly, our own powers and the rights of the States may be indirectly legislated away in the use of means to execute substantive powers. We may not enact that Congress shall not have the power of exclusive legislation over the District of Columbia, but we may pledge the faith of the United States that as a means of executing other powers it shall not be exercised for twenty years or forever. We may not pass an act prohibiting the States to tax the banking business carried on within their limits, but we may, as a means of executing our powers over other objects, place that business in the hands of our agents and then declare it exempt from State taxation in their hands. Thus may our own powers and the rights of the States, which we cannot directly curtail or invade, be frittered away and extinguished in the use of means employed by us to execute other powers. That a bank of the United States, competent to all the duties which may be required by the Government, might be so organized as not to infringe on our own delegated powers or the reserved rights of the States I do not entertain a doubt. . .

The bank is professedly established as an agent of the executive branch of the Government, and its constitutionality is maintained on that ground. Neither upon the propriety of present action nor upon the provisions of this act was the Executive consulted. It has had no opportunity to say that it neither needs nor wants an agent clothed with such powers and favored by such exemptions. There is nothing in its legitimate functions which makes it necessary or proper. Whatever interest or influence, whether public or private, has given birth to this act, it cannot be found either in the wishes or necessities of the executive department, by which present action is deemed premature, and the powers conferred upon its agent not only unnecessary, but dangerous to the Government and country.

It is to be regretted that the rich and powerful too often bend the acts of government to their selfish purposes. Distinctions in society will always exist under every just government. Equality of talents, of education, or of wealth cannot be produced by human institutions. In the full enjoyment of the gifts of Heaven and the fruits of superior industry, economy, and virtue, every man is equally entitled to protection by law; but when the laws undertake to add to these natural and just advantages artificial distinctions, to grant titles, gratuities, and exclusive privileges to make the rich richer, and the potent more powerful, the humble members of society—the farmers, mechanics, and laborers—who have neither the time nor the means of securing like favor to themselves, have a right to complain of the injustice of their government. There are no necessary evils in government. Its evils exist only in its abuses. If it would confine itself to equal protection, and, as Heaven does its rains, shower its favors alike on the high and the low, the rich and the poor, it would be an unqualified blessing. In the act before me there seems to be a wide and unnecessary departure from these just principles. . .

Experience should teach us wisdom. Most of the difficulties our Government now encounters and most of the dangers which impend over our Union have sprung from an abandonment of the legitimate objects of Government by our national legislation, and the adoption of such principles as are embodied in this act. Many of our rich men have not been content with equal protection and equal benefits, but have besought us to make them richer by act of Congress. By attempting to gratify their desires we have in the results of our legislation arrayed section against section, interest against interest, and man against man, in a fearful commotion which threatens to shake the foundations of our Union. It is time to pause in our career to review our principles, and if possible revive that devoted patriotism and spirit of compromise which distinguished the sages of the Revolution and the fathers of our Union. If we cannot at once, in justice to interests vested under improvident legislation, make our government what it ought to be, we can at least take a stand against all new grants of monopolies and exclusive privileges, against any prostitution of our government to the advancement of the few at the expense of the many, and in favor of compromise and gradual reform in our code of laws and system of political economy.

3. *Our Constitution is no longer a doubtful experiment, but . . .*

ANDREW JACKSON, Farewell Address, 4 March 1837 *

We have now lived almost fifty years under the Constitution framed by the sages and patriots of the Revolution. . . Our Constitution is no longer a doubtful experiment, and at the end of nearly half a century we find that it has preserved unimpaired the liberties of the people, secured the rights of property, and that our country has improved and is flourishing beyond any former example in the history of nations.

In our domestic concerns there is everything to encourage us, and if you are true to yourselves nothing can impede your march to the highest point of national prosperity. . .

These cheering and grateful prospects and these multiplied favors we owe, under Providence, to the adoption of the Federal Constitution. It is no longer a question whether this great country can remain happily united and flourish under our present form of government. Experience, the unerring test of all human undertakings, has shown the wisdom and foresight of those who formed it, and has proved that in the union of these States there is a sure foundation for the brightest hopes of freedom and for the happiness of the people. At every hazard and by every sacrifice this Union must be preserved.

The necessity of watching with jealous anxiety for the preservation of the Union was earnestly pressed upon his fellow-citizens by the Father of his Country in his Farewell Address. He has there told us that 'while experience shall not have demonstrated its impracticability, there will always be reason to distrust the patriotism of those who in any quarter may endeavor to weaken its bands'; and he has cautioned us in the strongest terms against the formation of parties on geographical discriminations, as one of the means which might disturb our Union and to which designing men would be likely to resort.

The lessons contained in this invaluable legacy of Washington to his countrymen should be cherished in the heart of every citizen to the latest generation; and perhaps at no period of time could they be more usefully remembered than at the present moment. . . The trial has been made. It has succeeded beyond the proudest hopes of those who framed it. Every quarter of this widely extended nation has felt its blessings and shared in the general prosperity produced by its adoption. But amid this general prosperity and splendid success the dangers of which he warned us are becoming every day more evident, and the signs of evil are sufficiently apparent to awaken the deepest anxiety in the bosom of the patriot. We behold systematic efforts publicly made to sow the seeds of discord between different parts of the United States and to place party divisions directly upon geographical distinctions; to excite the *South* against the *North* and the *North* against the *South*, and to force into the controversy the most delicate and exciting topics—topics upon which it is impossible that a large portion of the Union can ever speak without strong emotion. . . Let it

* *Messages and Papers of the Presidents*, James D. Richardson, ed., vol. III, pp. 292–308 *passim*.

not be supposed that I impute to all of those who have taken an active part in these unwise and unprofitable discussions a want of patriotism or of public virtue. The honorable feeling of State pride and local attachments finds a place in the bosoms of the most enlightened and pure. But while such men are conscious of their own integrity and honesty of purpose, they ought never to forget that the citizens of other States are their political brethren, and that however mistaken they may be in their views, the great body of them are equally honest and upright with themselves. Mutual suspicions and reproaches may in time create mutual hostility, and artful and designing men will always be found who are ready to foment these fatal divisions and to inflame the natural jealousies of different sections of the country. The history of the world is full of such examples, and especially the history of republics.

What have you to gain by division and dissension? Delude not yourselves with the belief that a breach once made may be afterwards repaired. If the Union is once severed, the line of separation will grow wider and wider, and the controversies which are now debated and settled in the halls of legislation will then be tried in fields of battle and determined by the sword. . .

There is too much at stake to allow pride or passion to influence your decision. Never for a moment believe that the great body of the citizens of any State or States can deliberately intend to do wrong. They may, under the influence of temporary excitement or misguided opinions, commit mistakes; they may be misled for a time by the suggestions of self-interest; but in a community so enlightened and patriotic as the people of the United States argument will soon make them sensible of their errors, and when convinced they will be ready to repair them. If they have no higher or better motives to govern them, they will at least perceive that their own interest requires them to be just to others, as they hope to receive justice at their hands.

But in order to maintain the Union unimpaired it is absolutely necessary that the laws passed by the constituted authorities should be faithfully executed in every part of the country, and that every good citizen should at all times stand ready to put down, with the combined force of the nation, every attempt at unlawful resistance, under whatever pretext it may be made or whatever shape it may assume. Unconstitutional or oppressive laws may no doubt be passed by Congress, either from erroneous views or the want of due consideration; if they are within the reach of judicial authority, the remedy is easy and peaceful; and if, from the character of the law, it is an abuse of power not within the control of the judiciary, then free discussion and calm appeals to reason and to the justice of the people will not fail to redress the wrong. But until the law shall be declared void by the courts or repealed by Congress no individual or combination of individuals can be justified in forcibly resisting its execution. It is impossible that any government can continue to exist upon any other principles. It would cease to be a government and be unworthy of the name if it had not the power to enforce the execution of its own laws within its own sphere of action. . .

The Constitution cannot be maintained nor the Union preserved, in opposition to public feeling, by the mere exertion of the coercive powers confided to the General Government. The foundations must be laid in the affections of the people, in the security it gives to life, liberty, character, and property in every quarter of the country, and in the fraternal attachment which the citizens of the several States bear to one another as members of one political family, mutually contributing to promote the happiness of each other. Hence the citizens of every States should studiously avoid everything calculated to wound the sensibility or offend the just pride of the people of other States, and they should frown upon any proceedings within their own borders likely to disturb the tranquillity of their political brethren in other portions of the Union. In a country so extensive as the United States, and with pursuits so varied, the internal regulations of the several States must frequently differ from one another in important particulars, and this difference is unavoidably increased by the varying principles upon which the American colonies were originally planted—principles which had taken deep root in their social relations before the Revolution, and therefore of necessity influencing their policy since they became free and independent States. But each State has the unquestionable right to regulate its own internal concerns according to its own pleasure, and while it does not interfere with the rights of the people of other States or the rights of the Union, every State must be the sole judge of the measures proper to secure the safety of its citizens and promote their happiness; and all efforts on the part of the people of the other States to cast odium upon their institutions, and all measures calculated to disturb their rights of property or to put in jeopardy their peace and internal tranquillity, are in direct opposition to the spirit in which the Union was formed, and must endanger its safety. . .

It is well known that there have always been those amongst us who wish to enlarge the powers of the General Government, and experience would seem to indicate that there is a tendency on the part of this Government to overstep the boundaries marked out for it by the Constitution. Its legitimate authority is abundantly sufficient for all the purposes for which it was created, and its powers being expressly enumerated, there can be no justification for claiming anything beyond them. Every attempt to exercise power beyond these limits should be promptly and firmly opposed, for one evil example will lead to other measures still more mischievous; and if the principle of constructive powers or supposed advantages or temporary circumstances shall ever be permitted to justify the assumption of a power not given by the Constitution, the General Government will before long absorb all the powers of legislation, and you will have in effect but one consolidated government. From the extent of our country, its diversified interests, different pursuits, and different habits, it is too obvious for argument that a single consolidated government would be wholly inadequate to watch over and protect its interests; and every friend of our free institutions should be always prepared to maintain unimpaired and in full vigor the rights and sovereignty of the States and to confine the action of the General Government strictly to the sphere of its appropriate duties.

There is, perhaps, no one of the powers conferred on the Federal Government so liable to abuse as the taxing power. . . Congress has no right under the Constitution to take money from the people unless it is required to execute some one of the specific powers intrusted to the Government; and if they raise more than is necessary for such purposes, it is an abuse of the power of taxation, and unjust and oppressive. It may indeed happen that the revenue will sometimes exceed the amount anticipated when the taxes were laid. When, however, this is ascertained, it is easy to reduce them, and in such a case it is unquestionably the duty of the Government to reduce them, for no circumstances can justify it in assuming a power not given to it by the Constitution nor in taking away the money of the people when it is not needed for the legitimate wants of the Government.

Plain as these principles appear to be, you will yet find there is a constant effort to induce the General Government to go beyond the limits of its taxing power and to impose unnecessary burdens upon the people. Many powerful interests are continually at work to procure heavy duties on commerce and to swell the revenue beyond the real necessities of the public service, and the country has already felt the injurious effects of their combined influence. They succeeded in obtaining a tariff of duties bearing most oppressively on the agricultural and laboring classes of society and producing a revenue that could not be usefully employed within the range of the powers conferred upon Congress, and in order to fasten upon the people this unjust and unequal system of taxation extravagant schemes of internal improvement were got up in various quarters to squander the money and to purchase support. Thus one unconstitutional measure was intended to be upheld by another, and the abuse of the power of taxation was to be maintained by usurping the power of expending the money in internal improvements. You cannot have forgotten the severe and doubtful struggle through which we passed when the executive department of the Government by its veto endeavored to arrest this prodigal scheme of injustice and to bring back the legislation of Congress to the boundaries prescribed by the Constitution.* The good sense and practical judgment of the people when the subject was brought before them sustained the course of the Executive, and this plan of unconstitutional expenditures for the purposes of corrupt influence is, I trust, finally overthrown.

. . . The various interests which have combined together to impose a heavy tariff and to produce an overflowing Treasury are too strong and have too much at stake to surrender the contest. The corporations and wealthy individuals who are engaged in large manufacturing establishments desire a high tariff to increase their gains. Designing politicians will support it to conciliate their favor and to obtain the means of profuse expenditure for the purpose of purchasing influence in other quarters; and since the people have decided that the Federal Government cannot be permitted to employ its income in internal improvements, efforts will be made to seduce and mislead the citizens of the several States by holding out to them the deceitful prospect of benefits to be derived from a surplus revenue collected by the General Government and annually divided among the States. . . There is but one safe rule, and that is to confine the General Government rigidly within the sphere of its appropriate duties. It has no power to raise a revenue or impose taxes except for the purposes enumerated in the Constitution, and if its income is found to exceed these wants it should be forthwith reduced and the burden of the people so far lightened.

* The Maysville Road Veto of 1830. [A.T.M.]

In reviewing the conflicts which have taken place between different interests in the United States and the policy pursued since the adoption of our present form of Government, we find nothing that has produced such deep-seated evil as the course of legislation in relation to the currency. . .

Recent events have proved that the paper-money system of this country may be used as an engine to undermine your free institutions, and that those who desire to engross all power in the hands of the few and to govern by corruption or force are aware of its power and prepared to employ it. . .

When the charter for the Bank of the United States was obtained from Congress it perfected the schemes of the paper system and gave to its advocates the position they have struggled to obtain from the commencement of the Federal Government to the present hour. The immense capital and peculiar privileges bestowed upon it enabled it to exercise despotic sway over the other banks in every part of the country. From its superior strength it could seriously injure, if not destroy, the business of any one of them which might incur its resentment; and it openly claimed for itself the power of regulating the currency throughout the United States. . .

We are not left to conjecture how the moneyed power, thus organized and with such a weapon in its hands, would be likely to use it. The distress and alarm which pervaded and agitated the whole country when the Bank of the United States waged war upon the people in order to compel them to submit to its demands cannot yet be forgotten. The ruthless and unsparing temper with which whole cities and communities were oppressed, individuals impoverished and ruined, and a scene of cheerful prosperity suddenly changed into one of gloom and despondency ought to be indelibly impressed on the memory of the people of the United States. If such was its power in a time of peace, what would it not have been in a season of war, with an enemy at your doors? No nation but the freemen of the United States could have come out victorious from such a contest; yet, if you had not conquered, the Government would have passed from the hands of the many to the hands of the few, and this organized money power from its secret conclave would have dictated the choice of your highest officers and compelled you to make peace or war, as best suited their own wishes. The forms of your Government might for a time have remained, but its living spirit would have departed from it.

4. *All communities are apt to look to government for too much*

Martin Van Buren, Special Session Message, 4 September 1837 *

. . . Those who look to the action of this Government for specific aid to the citizen to relieve embarrassments arising from losses by revulsions in commerce and credit lose sight of the ends for which it was created and the powers with

* *Messages and Papers of the Presidents*, James D. Richardson, ed., vol. III, pp. 344–5 *passim*.

which it is clothed. It was established to give security to us all in our lawful and honorable pursuits under the lasting safeguard of republican institutions. It was not intended to confer special favors on individuals or on any classes of them, to create systems of agriculture, manufactures, or trade, or to engage in them either separately or in connection with individual citizens or organized associations. If its operations were to be directed for the benefit of any one class, equivalent favors must in justice be extended to the rest, and the attempt to bestow such favors with an equal hand, or even to select those who should most deserve them, would never be successful.

All communities are apt to look to government for too much. Even in our own country, where its powers and duties are so strictly limited, we are prone to do so, especially at periods of sudden embarrassment and distress. But this ought not to be. The framers of our excellent Constitution and the people who approved it with calm and sagacious deliberation acted at the time on a sounder principle. They wisely judged that the less government interferes with private pursuits the better for the general prosperity. It is not its legitimate object to make men rich or to repair by direct grants of money or legislation in favor of particular pursuits, losses not incurred in the public service. This would be substantially to use the property of some for the benefit of others. But its real duty—that duty the performance of which makes a good government the most precious of human blessings—is to enact and enforce a system of general laws commensurate with, but not exceeding, the objects of its establishment, and to leave every citizen and every interest to reap under its benign protection the rewards of virtue, industry, and prudence.

I cannot doubt that on this as on all similar occasions the Federal Government will find its agency most conducive to the security and happiness of the people when limited to the exercise of its conceded powers. In never assuming, even for a well-meant object, such powers as were not designed to be conferred upon it, we shall in reality do most for the general welfare. To avoid every unnecessary interference with the pursuits of the citizen will result in more benefit than to adopt measures which could only assist limited interests, and are eagerly, but perhaps naturally, sought for under the pressure of temporary circumstances. If, therefore, I refrain from suggesting to Congress any specific plan for regulating the exchanges of the country, relieving mercantile embarrassments, or interfering with the ordinary operations of foreign or domestic commerce, it is from a conviction that such measures are not within the constitutional province of the General Government, and that their adoption would not promote the real and permanent welfare of those they might be designed to aid.

5. *The best government governs least*

JOHN L. O'SULLIVAN, *Democratic Review,* 1837 *

DEMOCRACY IMPLIES AND REQUIRES SELF-GOVERNMENT

So many false ideas have insensibly attached themselves to the term 'democracy,' as connected with our party politics, that we deem it necessary here, at the outset, to make a full and free profession of the cardinal principles of political faith on which we take our stand. . .

We believe . . . in the principle of democratic republicanism, in its strongest and purest sense. We have an abiding confidence in the virtue, intelligence, and full capacity for self-government, of the great mass of our people, our industrious, honest, manly, intelligent millions of freemen.

We are opposed to all self-styled 'wholesome restraints' on the free action of the popular opinion and will, other than those which have for their sole object the prevention of precipitate legislation. This latter object is to be attained by the expedient of the division of power, and by causing all legislation to pass through the ordeal of successive forms; to be sifted through the discussions of co-ordinate legislative branches with mutual suspensive veto powers. Yet all should be dependent with equal directness and promptness on the influence of public opinion; the popular will should be equally the animating and moving spirit of them all, and ought never to find in any of its own creatures a self-imposed power, capable, when misused either by corrupt ambition or honest error, of resisting itself and defeating its own determined object. We cannot, therefore, look with an eye of favor on any such forms of representation as, by length of tenure of delegated power, tend to weaken that universal and unrelaxing responsibility to the vigilance of public opinion which is the true conservative principle of our institutions.

The great queston here occurs, which is of vast importance to this country (Was it not once near dissolving the Union, and plunging it into the abyss of civil war?), of the relative rights of majorities and minorities. Though we go for the republican principle of the supremacy of the will of the majority, we acknowledge, in general, a strong sympathy with minorities and consider that their rights have a high moral claim on the respect and justice of majorities; a claim not always fairly recognized in practice by the latter, in the full sway of power, when flushed with triumph and impelled by strong interests. This has ever been the point of the democratic cause most open to assault and most difficult to defend. This difficulty does not arise from any intrinsic weakness. The democratic theory is perfect and harmonious in all its parts; and if this point is not so self-evidently clear as the rest is generally, in all candid discussion, conceded to be, it is because of certain false principles of government which have, in all practical experiments of the theory, been interwoven

* From the Introduction to *The United States Magazine and Democratic Review,* October 1837.

with the democratic portions of the system, being borrowed from the example of anti-democratic systems of government. . . The great argument against pure democracy, drawn from this source, is this:

Though the main object with reference to which all social institutions ought to be modelled is undeniably, as stated by the democrat, 'the greatest good of the greatest number,' yet it by no means follows that the greatest number always rightly understands its own greatest good. Highly pernicious error has often possessed the minds of nearly a whole nation; while the philosopher in his closet, and an enlightened few about him, powerless against the overwhelming current of popular prejudice and excitement, have alone possessed the truth, which the next generation may perhaps recognize and practice, though its author, now sainted, has probably, in his own time, been its martyr. The original adoption of the truth would have saved perhaps oceans of blood and mountains of misery and crime. How much stronger, then, the case against the absolute supremacy of the opinion and will of the majority, when its numerical preponderance is, as often happens, comparatively small. And if the larger proportion of the more wealthy and cultivated classes of the society are found on the side of the minority, the disinterested observer may well be excused if he hesitate long before he awards the judgment, in a difficult and complicated question, in favor of the mere numerical argument. Majorities are often as liable to error of opinion, and not always free from a similar proneness to selfish abuse of power, as minorities; and a vast amount of injustice may often be perpetrated, and consequent general social injury be done, before the evil reaches that extreme at which it rights itself by revolution, moral or physical.

We have here, we believe, correctly stated the anti-democratic side of the argument on this point. It is not to be denied that it possesses something more than plausibility. It has certainly been the instrument of more injury to the cause of the democratic principle than all the bayonets and cannon that have ever been arrayed in support of it against that principle. The inference from it is that the popular opinion and will must not be trusted with the supreme and absolute direction of the general interests; that it must be subjected to the 'conservative checks' of minority interests, and to the regulation of the 'more enlightened wisdom' of the 'better classes,' and those to whom the possession of a property 'test of merit' gives what they term 'a stake in the community.' And here we find ourselves in the face of the great stronghold of the anti-democratic, or aristocratic, principle.

It is not our purpose, in this place, to carry out the discussion of this question. The general scope and tendency of the present work are designed to be directed towards the refutation of this sophistical reasoning and inference. It will be sufficient here to allude to the leading ideas by which they are met by the advocate of the pure democratic cause.

In the first place, the greatest number are more likely, at least, as a general rule, to understand and follow their own greatest good, than is the minority.

In the second, a minority is much more likely to abuse power for the promotion of its own selfish interests, at the expense of the majority of numbers, the substantial and producing mass of the nation, than the latter is to oppress unjustly the former. The social evil is also, in that case, proportionately greater. This is abundantly proved by the history of all aristocratic interests that have existed, in various degrees and modifications, in the world. A majority cannot subsist upon a minority; while the natural, and in fact uniform, tendency of a minority entrusted with governmental authority is to surround itself with wealth, splendor, and power, at the expense of the producing mass, creating and perpetuating those artificial social distinctions which violate the natural equality of rights of the human race and at the same time offend and degrade the true dignity of human nature.

In the third place, there does not naturally exist any such original superiority of a minority class above the great mass of a community in intelligence and competence for the duties of government, even putting out of view its constant tendency to abuse from selfish motives, and the safer honesty of the mass. The general diffusion of education, the facility of access to every species of knowledge important to the great interests of the community; the freedom of the press, whose very licentiousness cannot materially impair its permanent value, in this country at least, make the pretensions of those self-styled 'better classes' to the sole possession of the requisite intelligence for the management of public affairs too absurd to be entitled to any other treatment than an honest, manly contempt. As far as superior knowledge and talent confer on their possessor a natural charter of privilege to control his associates and exert an influence on the direction of the general affairs of the community, the free and natural action of that privilege is best secured by a perfectly free democratic system which will abolish all artificial distinctions, and, preventing the accumulation of any social obstacles to advancement, will permit the free development of every germ of talent, wherever it may chance to exist, whether on the proud mountain summit, in the humble valley, or by the wayside of common life.

But the question is not yet satisfactorily answered, how the relation between majorities and minorities, in the frequent case of a collision of sentiments and particular interests, is to be so adjusted as to secure a mutual respect of rights, to preserve harmony and good will, and save society from the *malum extremum discordia*, from being as a house divided against itself, and thus to afford free scope to that competition, discussion, and mutual moral influence which cannot but result, in the end, in the ascendancy of the truth and in 'the greatest good of the greatest number.' On the one side, it has only been shown that the absolute government of the majority does not always afford a perfect guarantee against the misuse of its numerical power over the weakness of the minority. On the other, it has been shown that this chance of misuse is, as a general rule, far less than in the opposite relation of the ascendancy of a minority; and that the evils attendant upon it are infinitely less, in every point of view, in the one case than the other. But this is not yet a complete or satisfactory solution of the problem. Have we but a choice of evils? Is there, then, such a radical deficiency in the moral elements implanted by its Creator in human society that no other alternative can be devised by which both evils shall be avoided, and a result attained more analogous to the beautiful and glorious harmony of the rest of his creation?

It were scarcely consistent with a true and living faith in the existence and attributes of that Creator, so to believe; and such is not the democratic belief. The reason of the plausibility with which appeal may be made to the experience of so many republics to sustain this argument against democratic institutions is that the true theory of national self-government has been hitherto but imperfectly understood; bad principles have been mixed up with the good; and the republican government has been administered on ideas and in a spirit borrowed from the strong governments of the other forms; and to the corruptions and manifold evils which have never failed, in the course of time, to evolve themselves out of these seeds of destruction is ascribable the eventual failure of those experiments, and the consequent doubt and discredit which have attached themselves to the democratic principles on which they were, in the outset, mainly based.

It is under the word 'government' that the subtle danger lurks. Understood as a central consolidated power, managing and directing the various general interests of the society, all government is evil, and the parent of evil. A strong and active democratic government, in the common sense of the term, is an evil, differing only in degree and mode of operation, and not in nature, from a strong despotism. This difference is certainly vast, yet, inasmuch as these strong governmental powers must be wielded by human agents, even as the powers of the despotism it is, after all, only a difference in degree; and the tendency to demoralization and tyranny is the same, though the development of the evil results is much more gradual and slow in the one case than in the other. Hence the demagogue; hence the faction; hence the mob; hence the violence, licentiousness, and instability; hence the ambitious struggles of parties and their leaders for power; hence the abuses of that power by majorities and their leaders; hence the indirect oppressions of the general by partial interests; hence (fearful symptom) the demoralization of the great men of the nation, and of the nation itself, proceeding, unless checked in time by the more healthy and patriotic portion of the mind of the nation rallying itself to reform the principles and sources of the evil, gradually to that point of maturity at which relief from the tumult of moral and physical confusion is to be found only under the shelter of an energetic armed despotism.

The best government is that which governs least. No human depositories can, with safety, be trusted with the power of legislation upon the general interests of society so as to operate directly or indirectly on the industry and property of the community. Such power must be perpetually liable to the most pernicious abuse, from the natural imperfection, both in wisdom of judgment and purity of purpose, of all human legislation, exposed constantly to the pressure of partial interests; interests which, at the same time that they are essentially selfish and tyrannical, are ever vigilant, persevering, and subtle in all the arts of deception and corruption. In fact, the whole history of human society and government may be safely appealed to, in evidence that the abuse of such power a thousandfold more than overbalances its beneficial use. Legislation has been the fruitful parent of nine-tenths of all the evil, moral and physical, by which mankind has been afflicted since the creation of the world, and by which human nature has been self-degraded, fettered, and oppressed. Government should have as little as possible to do with the general business and interests of the people. If it once undertake these functions as its rightful province of action, it is impossible to say to it, 'Thus far shalt thou go, and no farther.' It will be impossible to confine it to the public interests of the commonwealth. It will be perpetually tampering with private interests, and sending forth seeds of corruption which will result in the demoralization of the society. Its domestic action should be confined to the administration of justice, for the protection of the natural equal rights of the citizen and the preservation of social order.

In all other respects, the voluntary principle, the principle of freedom, suggested to us by the analogy of the divine government of the Creator, and already recognized by us with perfect success in the great social interests of religion, affords the true 'golden rule' which is alone abundantly competent to work out the best possible general result of order and happiness from that chaos of characters, ideas, motives, and interests: human society. Afford but the single nucleus of a system of administration of justice between man and man, and, under the sure operation of this principle, the floating atoms will distribute and combine themselves, as we see in the beautiful natural process of crystallization, into a far more perfect and harmonious result than if government, with its 'fostering hand,' undertake to disturb, under the plea of directing, the process. The natural laws which will establish themselves and find their own level are the best laws. The same hand was the Author of the moral, as of the physical world; and we feel clear and strong in the assurance that we cannot err in trusting, in the former, to the same fundamental principles of spontaneous action and self-regulation which produce the beautiful order of the latter.

This is then, we consider, the true theory of government, the one simple result towards which the political science of the world is gradually tending, after all the long and varied experience by which it will have dearly earned the great secret, the elixir of political life. This is the fundamental principle of the philosophy of democracy, to furnish a system of administration of justice, and then leave all the business and interests of society to themselves, to free competition and association; in a word, to the voluntary principle. . .

It is borrowed from the example of the perfect self government of the physical universe, being written in letters of light on every page of the great bible of Nature. It contains the idea of full and fearless faith in the providence of the Creator. It is essentially involved in Christianity, of which it has been well said that its pervading spirit of democratic equality among men is its highest fact and one of its most radiant internal evidences of the divinity of its origin. It is the essence and the one general result of the science of political economy. And this principle alone, we will add, affords a satisfactory and perfect solution of the great problem, otherwise unsolved, of the relative rights of majorities and minorities.

We deem it scarcely necessary to say that we are opposed to all precipitate radical changes in social institutions. Adopting 'Nature as the best guide,' we cannot disregard the lesson which she teaches when she accomplishes her most mighty results of the good and beautiful by the silent and slow operation of great principles, without the convulsions of too rapid action. *Festina lente* is an invaluable precept, if it be not abused. On the other hand, that specious sophistry ought to be no less watchfully guarded against, by which old evils always struggle to perpetuate themselves by appealing to our veneration for 'the wisdom of our fathers,' to our inert love of present tranquillity, and our natural apprehension of possible danger from the untried and unknown. . .

We are not afraid of that much dreaded phrase, 'untried experiment,' which looms so fearfully before the eyes of some of our most worthy and valued friends. The whole history of the progress hitherto made by humanity, in every respect of social amelioration, records but a series of 'experiments.' The American Revolution was the greatest of experiments, and one of which it is not easy at this day to appreciate the gigantic boldness. Every step in the onward march of improvement by the human race is an experiment; and the present is most emphatically an age of experiments. The eye of man looks naturally forward; and as he is carried onward by the progress of time and truth, he is far more likely to stumble and stray if he turn his face backward, and keep his looks fixed on the thoughts and things of the past. We feel safe under the banner of the democratic principle, which is borne onward by an unseen hand of Providence, to lead our race toward the high destinies of which every human soul contains the God-implanted germ; and of the advent of which—certain, however distant—a dim prophetic presentiment has existed, in one form or another, among all nations in all ages. We are willing to make every reform in our institutions that may be commanded by the test of the democratic principle, to democratize them, but only so rapidly as shall appear, to the most cautious wisdom, consistent with a due regard to the existing development of public opinion and to the permanence of the progress made. Every instance in which the action of government can be simplified, and one of the hundred giant arms curtailed, with which it now stretches around its fatal protecting grasp over almost all the various interests of society, to substitute the truly healthful action of the free voluntary principle, every instance in which the operation of the public opinion and will, fairly signified, can be brought to bear more directly upon the action of delegated powers, we would regard as so much gained for the true interest of the society and of mankind at large. In this path we cannot go wrong; it is only necessary to be cautious not to go too fast.

Such is, then, our democracy. It of course places us in the school of the strictest construction of the Constitution; and in that appears to be involved a full committal of opinion on all the great political questions which now agitate the public mind, and to which we deem it unnecessary here to advert in detail. One necessary inference from the views expressed above is that we consider the preservation of the present ascendancy of the Democratic party as of great, if not vital, importance to the future destinies of this holy cause. . .

6. *The object and end of all government is to promote the happiness and prosperity of the community*

CHIEF JUSTICE R. B. TANEY in Charles River Bridge *v.* Warren Bridge, 1837 *

. . . Borrowing, as we have done, our system of jurisprudence from the English law . . . it would present a singular spectacle, if, while the courts in England are restraining, within the strictest limits, the spirit of monopoly, and exclusive privileges in nature of monopolies, and confining corporations to the privileges plainly given to them in their charter, the courts of this country should be found enlarging these privileges by implication; and construing a statute more unfavorably to the public, and to the right of the community than would be done in a like case in an English court of justice.

But we are not now left to determine for the first time the rules by which public grants are to be construed in this country. The subject has already been considered in this court, and the rules of construction above stated fully established in the case of the *United States* v. *Arredondo*, 8 Pet. 738, the leading cases upon this subject are collected together by the learned judge who delivered the opinion of the court, and the principle recognized that, in grants by the public nothing passes by implication. . .

But the case most analogous to this, and in which the question came more directly before the court, is the case of *Providence Bank* v. *Billings*, 4 Pet. 514, which was decided in 1830. In that case it appeared that the legislature of Rhode Island had chartered the bank, in the usual form of such acts of incorporation. The charter contained no stipulation on the part of the state that it would not impose a tax on the bank, nor any reservation of the right to do so. It was silent on this point. Afterwards a law was passed imposing a tax on all banks in the State, and the right to impose this tax was resisted by the Providence Bank upon the ground that if the State could impose a tax, it might tax so heavily as to render the franchise of no value, and destroy the institution; that the charter was a contract, and that a power which may in effect destroy the charter is inconsistent with it, and is impliedly renounced in granting it. But the court said that the taxing power is of vital importance and essential to the existence of government, and that the relinquishment of such a power is never to be assumed. . . The case now before the court, in principle, is precisely the same. It is a charter from a state; the act of incorporation is silent in relation to the contested power. The argument in favor of the proprietors of the Charles River bridge is the same, almost in words, with that used by the Providence Bank; that is, that the power claimed by the state, if it exists, may be so used as to destroy the value of the franchise they have granted to the corporation. The argument must receive the same answer; and the fact that the power has been already exercised, so as to destroy the value of the franchise, cannot in any degree affect the principle. The existence of the power does not, and cannot, depend upon the circumstance of its having been exercised or not.

* 11 Peters, 420.

It may, perhaps, be said, that in the case of the Providence Bank, this court were speaking of the taxing power; which is of vital importance to the very existence of every government. But the object and end of all government is to promote the happiness and prosperity of the community by which it is established; and it can never be assumed that the government intended to diminish its power of accomplishing the end for which it was created. And in a country like ours, free, active, and enterprising, continually advancing in numbers and wealth, new channels of communication are daily found necessary, both for travel and trade, and are essential to the comfort, convenience, and prosperity of the people. A state ought never to be presumed to surrender this power, because, like the taxing power, the whole community have an interest in preserving it undiminished. And when a corporation alleges that a state has surrendered, for seventy years, its power of improvement and public accommodation in a great and important line of travel, along which a vast number of its citizens must daily pass, the community have a right to insist, in the language of this court, above quoted, 'that its abandonment ought not to be presumed, in a case in which the deliberate purpose of the state to abandon it does not appear.' The continued existence of a government would be of no great value, if, by implications and presumptions, it was disarmed of the powers necessary to accomplish the ends of its creation, and the functions it was designed to perform transferred to the hands of privileged corporations. The rule of construction announced by the court was not confined to the taxing power, nor is it so limited in the opinion delivered. On the contrary, it was distinctly placed on the ground that the interests of the community were concerned in preserving, undiminished, the power then in question; and whenever any power of the state is said to be surrendered or diminished, whether it be the taxing power, or any other affecting the public interest, the same principle applies, and the rule of construction must be the same. No one will question that the interests of the great body of the people of the state would in this instance be affected by the surrender of this great line of travel to a single corporation, with the right to exact toll, and exclude competition, for seventy years. While the rights of private property are sacredly guarded, we must not forget that the community also have rights, and that the happiness and well-being of every citizen depends on their faithful preservation.

Adopting the rule of construction above stated as the settled one, we proceed to apply it to the charter of 1785 to the proprietors of the Charles River bridge. This act of incorporation is in the usual form, and the privileges such as are commonly given to corporations of that kind. It confers on them the ordinary faculties of a corporation, for the purpose of building the bridge; and establishes certain rates of toll, which the company are authorized to take. This is the whole grant. There is no exclusive privilege given to them over the waters of Charles River, above or below their bridge; no right to erect another bridge themselves, nor to prevent other persons from erecting one; no engagement from the State, that another shall not be erected; and no undertaking not to sanction competition, nor to make improvements that may diminish the amount of its income. Upon all these subjects the charter is silent; and nothing is said in it about a line of travel, so much insisted on in the argument, in which they are to have exclusive privileges. No words are used from which an intention to grant any of these rights can be inferred. If the plaintiff is entitled to them, it must be implied, simply from the nature of the grant, and cannot be inferred from the words by which the grant is made. . .

The inquiry then is, does the character contain such a contract on the part of the State? Is there any such stipulation to be found in that instrument? It must be admitted on all hands, that there is none—no words that even relate to another bridge, or to the diminution of their tolls, or to the line of travel. If a contract on that subject can be gathered from the charter, it must be by implication, and cannot be found in the words used. Can such an agreement be implied? The rule of construction before stated is an answer to the question. In charters of this description, no rights are taken from the public, or given to the corporation, beyond those which the words of the charter, by their natural and proper construction, purport to convey. There are no words which import such a contract as the plaintiffs in error contend for, and none can be implied; and the same answer must be given to them that was given by this court to the Providence Bank. The whole community are interested in this inquiry, and they have a right to require that the power of promoting their comfort and convenience, and of advancing the public prosperity, by providing safe, convenient, and cheap ways for the transportation of produce and purposes of travel, shall not be construed to have been surrendered or diminished by the State, unless it shall appear by plain words that it was intended to be done. . .

Indeed, the practice and usage of almost every State in the Union old enough to have commenced the work of internal improvement is opposed to the doctrine contended for on the part of the plaintiffs in error. Turnpike roads have been made in succession, on the same line of travel; the later ones interfering materially with the profits of the first. These corporations have, in some instances, been utterly ruined by the introduction of newer and better modes of transportation and traveling. In some cases, railroads have rendered the turnpike roads on the same line of travel so entirely useless that the franchise of the turnpike corporation is not worth preserving. Yet in none of these cases have the corporations supposed that their privileges were invaded, or any contract violated on the part of the State. . .

And what would be the fruits of this doctrine of implied contracts on the part of the States, and of property in a line of travel by a corporation, if it should now be sanctioned by this court? To what results would it lead us? If it is to be found in the charter to this bridge, the same process of reasoning must discover it, in the various acts which have been passed within the last forty years for turnpike companies. . . If this court should establish the principles now contended for, what is to become of the numerous railroads established on the same line of travel with turnpike companies, and which have rendered the franchises of the turnpike corporations of no value? Let it once be understood that such charters carry with them these implied contracts, and give this unknown and undefined property in a line of traveling, and you will soon find the old turnpike corporations awakening from their sleep and calling upon this court to put down the improvements which have taken their place. The millions of property which have been invested in railroads and canals upon lines of travel which had been before occupied by turnpike corporations will be put in jeopardy. We shall be thrown back to the improvements of the last century, and obliged to stand still until the claims of the old turnpike corporations shall be satisfied, and they shall consent to permit these States to avail themselves of the lights of modern science, and to partake of the benefit of those imporvements which are now adding to the wealth and prosperity, and the convenience and comfort, of every other part of the civilized world. . .

7. *The great work for this age and the coming is to raise up the laborer*

ORESTES A. BROWNSON, *The Laboring Classes*, 1840 *

No one can observe the signs of the times with much care without perceiving that a crisis as to the relation of wealth and labor is approaching. It is useless to shut our eyes to the fact, and like the ostrich fancy ourselves secure because we have so concealed our heads that we see not the danger. We or our children will have to meet this crisis. The old war between the King and the Barons is well nigh ended, and so is that between the Barons and the Merchants and Manufacturers, landed capital and commercial capital. The businessman has become the peer of my Lord. And now commences the new struggle between the operative and his employer, between wealth and labor. Every day does this struggle extend further and wax stronger and fiercer; what or when the end will be God only knows.

In this coming contest there is a deeper question at issue than is commonly imagined, a question which is but remotely touched in your controversies about United States banks and sub-treasuries, chartered banking and free banking, free trade and corporations, although these controversies may be paving the way for it to come up. . .

What we would ask is, throughout the Christian world, the actual condition of the laboring classes, viewed simply and exclusively in their capacity of laborers? They constitute at least a moiety of the human race. We exclude the nobility, we exclude also the middle class, and include only actual laborers, who are laborers and not proprietors, owners of none of the funds of production, neither houses, shops, nor lands, nor implements of labor, being therefore solely dependent on their hands. We have no means of ascertaining their precise proportion to the whole number of the race, but we think we may estimate them at one half. . . Now here is the system which prevails, and here is its

* *Boston Quarterly Review*, July 1840, vol. III, pp. 358–95; October 1840, vol. III, pp. 420–512.

result. The whole class of simple laborers are poor and in general unable to procure any thing beyond the bare necessaries of life.

In regard to labor two systems obtain: one that of slave labor, the other that of free labor. Of the two, the first is, in our judgment, except so far as the feelings are concerned, decidedly the least oppressive. If the slave has never been a free man, we think, as a general rule, his sufferings are less than those of the free laborer at wages. As the actual freedom one has just about as much as the other. The laborer at wages has all the disadvantages of freedom and none of its blessings, while the slave, if denied the blessings, is freed from the disadvantages. We are no advocates of slavery; we are as heartily opposed to it as any modern abolitionist can be; but we say frankly that, if there must always be a laboring population distinct from proprietors and employers, we regard the slave system as decidedly preferable to the system at wages. It is no pleasant thing to go days without food, to lie idle for weeks, seeking work and finding none, to rise in the morning with a wife and children you love, and know not where to procure them a breakfast, and to see constantly before you no brighter prospect than the almshouse. Yet these are no unfrequent incidents in the lives of our laboring population. . .

They are industrious; they do all that they can find to do, but yet the little there is for them to do, and the miserable pittance they receive for it is hardly sufficient to keep soul and body together. And yet there is a man who employs them to make shirts, trousers, etc., and grows rich on their labors. He is one of our respectable citizens, perhaps is praised in the newspapers for his liberal donations to some charitable institution. He passes among us as a pattern of morality and is honored as a worthy Christian. And why should he not be, since our *Christian* community is made up of such as he, and since our clergy would not dare question his piety lest they should incur the reproach of infidelity and lose their standing and their salaries? . . .

The slave system . . . in name and form, is gradually disappearing from Christendom. It will not subsist much longer. But its place is taken by the system of labor at wages, and this system, we hold, is no improvement upon the one it supplants. Nevertheless the system of wages will triumph. It is the system which in name sounds honester than slavery and in substance is more profitable to the master. It yields the wages of inquity, without its opprobrium. It will therefore supplant slavery and be sustained, for a time. . .

In our own country this condition has existed under its most favorable aspects and has been made as good as it can be. It has reached all the excellence of which it is susceptible. It is now not improving but growing worse. The actual condition of the workingman today, viewed in all its bearings, is not so good as it was fifty years ago. If we have not been altogether misinformed, fifty years ago, health and industrious habits constituted no mean stock in trade, and with them almost any man might aspire to competence and independence. But it is so no longer. The wilderness has receded, and already the new lands are beyond the reach of the mere laborer, and the employer has him at his mercy. If the present relation subsist, we see nothing better for him in reserve than what he now possesses, but something altogether worse. . .

Now the great work for this age and the coming is to raise up the laborer, and to realize in our own social arrangements and in the actual condition of all men that equality between man and man which God has established between the rights of one and those of another. In other words, our business is to emancipate the proletaries as the past has emancipated the slaves. This is our work. There must be no class of our fellow men doomed to toil through life as mere workmen at wages. If wages are tolerated it must be, in the case of the individual operative, only under such conditions that, by the time he is of a proper age to settle in life, he shall have accumulated enough to be an independent laborer on his own capital, on his own farm or in his own shop. Here is our work. How is it to be done?

Reformers in general answer this question, or what they deem its equivalent, in a manner which we cannot but regard as very unsatisfactory. They would have all men wise, good, and happy; but in order to make them so, they tell us that we want not external changes; but internal. And therefore, instead of declaiming against society and seeking to disturb existing social arrangements, we should confine ourselves to the individual reason and conscience, seek merely to lead the individual to repentance and to reformation of life, make the individual a practical, a truly religious man; and all evils will either disappear, or be sanctified to the spiritual growth of the soul.

For our part, we yield to none in our reverence for science and religion; but we confess that we look not for the regeneration of the race from priests and pedagogues. They have had a fair trial. They cannot construct the temple of God. They cannot conceive its plan, and they know not how to build. They daub with untempered mortar, and the walls they erect tumble down if so much as a fox attempt to go up thereon. In a word they always league with the people's masters, and seek to reform without disturbing the social arrangements which render reform necessary. They would change the consequents without changing the antecedents, secure to men the rewards of holiness, while they continue their allegiance to the devil. We have no faith in priests and pedagogues. They merely cry peace, peace, and that too when there is no peace, and can be none.

We admit the importance of what Dr. Channing in his lectures on the subject we are treating recommends as "self-culture." Self-culture is a good thing, but it cannot abolish inequality nor restore men to their rights. As a means of quickening moral and intellectual energy, exalting the sentiments, and preparing the laborer to contend manfully for his rights, we admit its importance and insist as strenuously as anyone on making it as universal as possible; but as constituting in itself a remedy for the vices of the social state, we have no faith in it. As a means it is well, as the end it is nothing.

The truth is the evil we have pointed out is not merely individual in its character. It is not, in the case of any single individual, of any one man's procuring, nor can the efforts of any one man, directed solely to his own moral and religious perfection, do aught to remove it. What is purely individual in its nature, efforts of individuals to perfect themselves may remove. But the evil we speak of is inherent in all our social arrangements, and cannot be cured without a radical change of those arrangements. . .

The only way to get rid of its evils is to change the system, not its managers. The evils of slavery do not result from the personal characters of slave masters. They are inseparable from the system, let who will be masters. Make all your rich men good Christians, and you have lessened not the evils of existing inequality in wealth. The mischievous effects of this inequality do not result from the personal characters of either rich or poor, but from itself, and they will continue just so long as there are rich men and poor men in the same community. You must abolish the system or accept its consequences. No man can serve both God and Mammon. If you will serve the devil, you must look to the devil for your wages; we know no other way. . .

Having, by breaking down the power of the priesthood and the Christianity of the priests, obtained an open field and freedom for our operations, and by preaching the true Gospel of Jesus, directed all minds to the great social reform needed, and quickened in all souls the moral power to live for it or to die for it, our next resort must be to government, to legislative enactments. Government is instituted to be the agent of society, or more properly the organ through which society may perform its legitimate functions. It is not the master of society; its business is not to control society, but to be the organ through which society effects its will. Society has never to petition government; government is its servant and subject to its commands. . .

Now the evils of which we have complained are of a social nature. That is, they have their root in the constitution of society as it is; and they have attained to their present growth by means of social influences, the action of government, of laws, and of systems and institutions upheld by society, and of which individuals are the slaves. This being the case, it is evident that they are to be removed only by the action of society, that is, by government, for the action of society is government.

But what shall government do? Its first doing must be an undoing. There has been thus far quite too much government, as well as government of the wrong kind. The first act of government we want is a still further limitation of itself. It must begin by circumscribing within narrower limits its powers. And then it must proceed to repeal all laws which bear against the laboring classes, and then to enact such laws as are necessary to enable them to maintain their equality. We have no faith in those systems of elevating the working classes which propose to elevate them without calling in the aid of government. We must have government and legislation expressly directed to this end. . . It is obvious then that, if our object be the elevation of the laboring classes, we must destroy the power of the banks over the Government and place the Government in the hands of the laboring classes themselves or in the hands of those, if such there be, who have an identity of interest with them. But this cannot be done so long as the banks exist. Such is the subtle influence of credit and such the power of capital that a banking system like ours, if sustained, necessarily and inevitably becomes the real and efficient government of the country. . .

The present character, standing, and resources of the bank party prove to a demonstration that the banks must be destroyed or the laborer not elevated. Uncompromising hostility to the whole banking system should therefore be the motto of every workingman and of every friend of humanity. The system must be destroyed. On this point there must be no misgiving, no subterfuge, no palliation. The system is at war with the rights and interest of labor, and it must go.

Following the destruction of the banks, must come that of all monopolies, of all privilege. There are many of these. We cannot specify them all. . .

We only say now that we have abolished hereditary monarchy and hereditary nobility we must complete the work by abolishing hereditary property. A man shall have all he honestly acquires, so long as he himself belongs to the world in which he acquires it. But his power over his property must cease with his life, and his property must then become the property of the State, to be disposed of by some equitable law for the use of the generation which takes his place. Here is the principle without any of its details, and this is the grand legislative measure to which we look forward. We see no means of elevating the laboring classes which can be effectual without this. And is this a measure to be easily carried? Not at all. It will cost infinitely more than it cost to abolish either hereditary monarchy or hereditary nobility. It is a great measure, and a startling. The rich, the business community, will never voluntarily consent to it, and we think we know too much of human nature to believe that it will ever be effected peaceably. It will be effected only by the strong arm of physical force. It will come, if it ever come at all, only at the conclusion of war, the like of which the world as yet has never witnessed, and from which, however inevitable it may seem to the eye of philosophy, the heart of Humanity recoils with horror.

SELECTED REFERENCES

Social Theories of Jacksonian Democracy: Representative Writings of the Period 1825-1850, Joseph L. Blau, ed., New York, Hafner, 1947.

R. C. H. Catteral, *The Second Bank of the United States*, Chicago, University of Chicago Press, 1903.

Francis W. Coker, 'American Traditions Concerning Property and Liberty,' February 1936, *The American Political Science Review*, vol. xxx, pp. 1–23.

Calvin Colton, *A Voice from America*, Colburn, 1839.

Joseph Dorfman, *The Economic Mind in American Civilization, 1606–1865*, New York, Viking, 1946, vol. 2, chaps. XXIII and XXIV.

———, The 'Jackson Wage-Earner Thesis,' *American Historical Review*, January 1949, vol. LIV, no. 2.

Bray Hammond, *Banks and Politics in America*, Princeton, Princeton University Press, 1957.

Louis Hartz, *Economic Policy and Democratic Thought: Pennsylvania, 1776–1860*, Cambridge, Harvard University Press, 1948.

David Henshaw, *Remarks Upon the Rights and Powers of Corporations*, Boston, Beals & Greene, 1837.

Richard Hofstadter, *The American Political Tradition*, New York, Knopf, 1948, chap. 3.

W. M. Holland, *Life and Political Opinions of Martin Van Buren*, Startford, Belnaps & Hamersley, 1836.

Marvin Meyers, *The Jacksonian Persuasion*, Stanford, Stanford University Press, 1957.

Francis Lieber, *Essays on Property and Labor*, New York, Harper, 1847.

Arthur M. Schlesinger, Jr., *The Age of Jackson*, Boston, Little, Brown, 1946.

H. W. Schneider, *A History of American Philosophy*, New York, Columbia University Press, 1946, chap. III.

Thomas Skidmore, *The Rights of Man to Property*, New York, The Author, 1829.

Carl B. Swisher, *Roger B. Taney*, New York, Macmillan, 1935.

Jonathan Mayhew Wainwright, *Inequality of Individual Wealth the Ordinance of Providence, and Essential to Civilization*, Boston, Dutton & Wentworth, 1835.

J. W. Ward, *Andrew Jackson: Symbol for an Age*, New York, Oxford University Press, 1955.

Charles M. Wiltse, *John C. Calhoun, Nullifier, 1829–1839*, Indianapolis, Bobbs-Merrill, 1949.

Benjamin F. Wright, Jr., 'American Democracy and the Frontier,' *Yale Review*, vol. XX, pp. 349–65.

———, *The Contract Clause and the Constitution*, Cambridge, Harvard University Press, 1936.

XII

ROMANTIC INDIVIDUALISM

D. W. Brogan, discerning British observer of contemporary America, remarked, 14 November 1948, that 'the wellsprings of American strength are not just iron mines and oil fields, natural gas and fertile soil. . . The best and most effective Americans have always remembered that even more than riches, righteousness exalteth a nation.'

'What, then, is the source of our strength,' David E. Lilienthal asked, 6 March 1949. His answer reinforces Brogan: 'That source is our ethical and moral standards of precepts, and our democratic faith in man. This faith is the chief armament of our democracy.'

Long before the development of our natural resources had made this country fabulously wealthy in material things, long before the inventions of applied science had given us at least temporary military supremacy, Ralph Waldo Emerson, Henry David Thoreau, and Walt Whitman, pointed each in his own way to other and more substantial resources. Much that passed for Jacksonian democracy—the incessant drive for gain, the vugarity and 'spoils' of politics, the glorification of the untutored common man—all this was anathema to the romantic individualists whose writings are featured in this chapter.

Emerson (1803–82), American poet, essayist, critic, transcendentalist, was born of a Brahmin line of ministers in Boston. Graduated from Harvard, he taught for a while in his brother's private school for young ladies. He then entered divinity school and prepared himself for the Unitarian pulpit. But after a few years of preaching, he resigned his pastorate to become, as Parrington says, 'the most searching critic of contemporary America.'

Emerson hated the gross materialism of his day—its ostentation, its overbearing rich and its greedy poor, its lack of thought, beauty, friendship, and love. Men spent their money on trifles and neglected their own personalities, lost their souls in vain seeking after 'fine garments, handsome apartments, access to public houses and places of amusement.' It was not so much that the commercial spirit was bad in itself, but rather that it received undue emphasis. 'This invasion of Nature by Tıadc with its Money, its Credit, its Steam, its Railroad, threatens to upset the balance of man and establish a new universal Monarchy more tyrannical than Babylon or Rome.'

The Jacksonian emphasis on political equality led to much the same result, according equal significance to saint and sinner, philosopher and fool. 'Away with this hurrah of the masses,' Emerson implored, 'and let us have the considerate vote of single men spoken on their honor and their conscience. In old Egypt it was established law that the vote of a prophet be reckoned equal to a hundred hands. I think it was much underestimated.' Instead of the religion of material progress, and the bare level of mediocrity, Emerson preached the doctrine of individual spirituality and superiority; for the doctrine of the masses, 'rude, lame, unmade, pernicious in their demands,' he substituted the full-grown, well-rounded individual. He deplored a society in which 'members . . . suffered amputation from the trunk, and strut about so many walking monsters—a good finger, a neck, a stomach, an elbow, but never a man.' Genuine equality he measured in terms of equal possession of ability to live according to divine Reason, no longer a part, but a whole individual, a vibrant expression of the Over-soul. Thus Emerson's wise man was one in harmony with the cosmos, one who realized the divinity of his own nature, one who through the experience of reason achieved a morality, placing him in a new relation to his fellows and to the world. Such a man needs no instrument of force, no government, no social institutions. The power of love alone will suffice.

Though man's first duty was to develop the fullness of his spiritual personality and power, he remains an animal and must, by his own effort, fulfil his animal needs. Not even the wise man is justified in living on the labor of others, for work is more than a means of sustaining life; it is a process whereby one comes closer to nature, finds himself. 'As a tree exists for its fruit, so a man for his work. What is a weed? A plant whose virtues have not yet been discovered.'

Emerson dealt no less harshly with the 'property-mindedness' of the whigs than with the 'mob-mindedness' of the democrats. Government had no special duty toward property. Left to shift for itself, and to regulation by its own natural laws, it would flow 'from the idle and imbecile to the industrious, brave and persevering.' 'The only safe rule is found in the self-adjusting meter of demand and supply. Do not legislate. . .'

Such sentiments enabled latter-day *laisser-faire* theorists to claim this transcendentalist as their own. But it seems quite clear that he would not have approved any economic order that narrowed individual opportunity. The individual must be free to pursue self-realization unencumbered by either political or economic restrictions.

Politics for Emerson was immaterial, irrelevant, not only because there was little or nothing government could do to change the fundamental laws of social development, but also because politics would disappear with the emergence of a higher level of civilization. That is why all political and social laws were to him trivial compared to the emancipation of the individual and the development of his divine soul. For much the same reason Emerson was skeptical of reform and reformers. 'Nature . . . does not like our benevolence or our learning much better than she likes our frauds and wars. When we come out of the caucus, or the bank, or the Abolition-convention, or the

Temperance-meeting, or the Transcendental-club into the fields and woods, she says to us, "So hot? my little Sir." '

'We are all a little worried here with numberless projects of social reform,' Emerson wrote his English friend, Thomas Carlyle, in the fall of 1840. 'Not a reading man but has a draft of a new community in his waistcoat pocket.' Emerson was mildly interested in the Brook Farm experiments and other good causes then occupying the 'come-outers,' as he called reformers, but he remained coolly aloof. He distrusted their unbounded enthusiasm, and even more the potential danger to the individual implicit in any form of collectivism. Current reform objectives seemed to him temporary rather than enduring, superficial not basic. What in his day passed for root-and-branch imperatives—abolition of war, gambling, intemperance, and even of slavery—were for him only 'medicating the symptoms' of a basic malady—the stunted, dwarfed individual.

Yet Emerson himself was a reformer eagerly entreated and besought by 'come-outers' on all sides. He resisted their solicitations, however, to follow the one course he deemed fundamental: 'I think *that* the soul of reform; the conviction that not sensuality, not slavery, not war, not imprisonment, not even government are needed,—but in lieu of them all, reliance on the sentiment of man which will work best the more it is trusted.' Aside from love and persuasion by example, the only sure means of reform he recognized, the only effective way of revitalizing society he endorsed and advocated, was education. 'We must begin higher up,' he insisted, 'namely in education.' For him the highest end of government 'is the culture of man.'

Emerson became an abolitionist by gradual stages. First inclined to accept slavery as a decree of nature, as an insurmountable barrier marking off 'different degrees of intellect to these different races,' he later endorsed the abolitionist purpose but denounced their methods as philanthropic, as more concerned in bringing reform abroad than at home. 'I have not yet conquered my own house. It irks and repents me. Shall I raise the siege of this hencoop,' he asked disdainfully, and 'march baffled away to a pretended siege of Babylon?' In time, however, he berated the 'old indecent nonsense about the nature of the negro,' saying: 'It now appears that the negro race is, more than any other, susceptible of rapid civilization.' As sectional struggles grew ever more bitter, slavery became increasingly an economic and political issue. Then when the pro-slavery element fought for the annexation of Texas, Emerson urged New England to resist 'tooth and nail.' He attended several anti-annexation meetings, and at one of them delivered the address on 'Politics,' here reprinted. Even at the very end when friends like Henry David Thoreau, William Lloyd Garrison, and Wendell Phillips threw themselves wholeheartedly into the struggle, Emerson remained more or less detached. There were more impelling duties to discharge: 'I have quite other slaves to free than those negroes, to wit, imprisoned spirits, imprisoned thoughts, far back in the brain of man,—far retired in the heaven of invention, and which, important to the republic of Man, have no watchman, no lover, or defender but I.'

The utopia Emerson envisaged, the America he admired was the ideal—what this country might be. The constitution in which he put his trust was not that one so dear to the heart of James Madison and John Adams, with its mechanical contrivances for holding men to their moral and legal obligations. Even less did he subscribe to Hamilton's 'coercive,' over-all sovereignty. The crux of his system, if such it be, finds expression in his essay, 'New England Reformers':

> Men will live and communicate, and plough, and reap and govern, as by added ethereal power, when once they are united. . . This union must be inward, and not one of covenants, and is to be reached by a reverse of the methods they use. The union is only perfect when all the uniters are isloated. . . Each man, if he attempts to join himself to others, is on all sides cramped and diminished of his proportion; and the stricter the union the smaller and more pitiful he is. But leave him alone, to recognize in every hour and place the secret soul; he will go up and down doing the works of a true member, and, to the astonishment of all, the work will be done with concert, though no man spoke. Government will be adamantine without any governor. The union must be ideal in actual individualism.

Emerson's influence was deep and abiding. Men differing as widely in temperament and method as Justices Holmes and Brandeis bear the imprint of his persuasive power. As a friend of the famous father, Emerson was often a visitor in the Holmes' household in Boston. Emerson's ideas and sometimes his words appear in the Justice's writing, the most conspicuous instance being in Holmes' attitude toward reform and reformers. During his years on the Supreme Court Holmes liked to recall 'Uncle Waldo' spurring him as a youth with the admonition: 'When you strike at a King, you must kill him.' 'I used to say that Emerson's great gift,' Holmes wrote John C. H. Wu, 27 January 1925, 'was that of imparting a ferment.' Certainly this was the case with Louis D. Brandeis. While a student at the Harvard Law School, he copied in his notebooks long passages from Emerson's essays, the favorite being 'Self-Reliance.' 'I have read a few sentences of his,' Brandeis recorded in 1876, 'which are alone enough to make the man immortal.'

Among others Emerson influenced was his fellow-townsman and friend, Henry David Thoreau (1817–62), essayist, poet, naturalist, surveyor, mystic, and social critic. Son of a lead pencil manufacturer, and educated at Harvard, Thoreau taught for a while at a private school, but finally eschewed any craft or profession, believing that the less labor a man does the better—for himself and the country. Life, he insisted, should be reduced to bare essentials, in order that one might devote himself to the study of nature and of one's self. 'I came into this world,' he wrote, 'not chiefly to make this a good place to live in, but to *live* in it, be it good or bad.' 'If we stay at home and mind our business, who will want railroads?' he asked. 'Superfluous wealth can buy superfluities only. Money is not required to buy one necessary for the soul.'

When Thoreau wanted money, he resorted to agreeable manual labor, supplying his meager needs by short turns rather than prolonged employment. He was, as Emerson said, 'a protestant *à outrance* . . . bred to no profession, lived alone, never went to church, refused to pay taxes, ate no flesh, drank no wine, used no tobacco.' An idealist, he stood for the abolition of slavery, tariffs and government or at least bad government and for him there was hardly any other.

Emerson was content to live in the community, at least physically, and abide its abuse. Thoreau, on the other hand, withdrew in 1847 to his Walden Pond hut, where he lived for two years, finding and demonstrating there, in close communion with the birds, beasts, and flowers, the individualism he lived. He did not abandon society because he disliked people, or repelled communion with his fellows. Quite the contrary; he sought closer union with them, deeper understanding of the natural world in which all men existed and few lived. 'What sort of space is that which separates a man from his fellows and makes him solitary? I have found that no exertion of the legs can bring two minds much nearer to one another.'

Back of his desire for physical retreat lay the conviction that to be a philosopher one must do more than have subtle thoughts, write erudite essays, or give learned lectures, enunciating one's doctrines and beliefs, or urging government aid for this or that, or backing organized reform. Nor was he running away from society's puzzles. He was proving them: living his philosophy, trying to discover important truths of a mystical nature. When he refused to pay tax to a state that tolerated slavery; when he was seized and put in jail, where he remained for one night (or until someone paid the tax for him), he explained his action in the discourse, here reproduced, 'Civil Disobedience'—an essay rivaling his most famous work, *Walden; or Life in the Woods*, published in 1854. When Thoreau said 'that government is best which governs not at all,' note that he was not pleading 'at once for better government,' 'not at once, [for] no government.' Only when men are 'prepared for it' will men be governed 'not at all.' He urged disobedience to tyrannical government, not to all authority—which would seem to make him a rebel rather than a philosophical anarchist, as usually supposed.

Though Thoreau lived in Emerson's household for two years, the latter seems not to have grasped fully the subtlety of Thoreau's effort and the significance of his life. At any rate, the host deplored in a memorial essay his friend's lack of ambition, believing that with his energy and practical ability, his achievements in the world of affairs might have been great indeed. 'Wanting this,' Emerson complained, 'instead of engineering for all America, he was the captain of a huckleberry-party. Pounding beans is good to the end of pounding empires one of these days; but if, at the end of years, it is still only beans!' It seems too bad that we have no memorial appraisal of Emerson by Thoreau!

In 1854 a small quarto of less than a hundred pages appeared bearing the obscure title, *Leaves of Grass*, written by the equally obscure Walt Whitman (1819–92). The book attracted no attention until the New York *Tribune* published a letter from Emerson to the author, characterizing this slim volume as 'the most extraordinary piece of wisdom that America has yet contributed.' Poet, newspaper editor, one-time government clerk, Walt Whitman was the son of a carpenter and farmer, and born on Long Island, New York. Largely self-educated and a writer who learned to write by writing, Whitman promoted pound weight:—and the attributes of a person, his wit and his moral energy, will exercise, under any law or extinguishing tyranny, their proper force,—if not overtly, then covertly; if not for the law, then against it; if not wholesomely, then poisonously; with right, or by might.

The boundaries of personal influence it is impossible to fix, as persons are organs of moral or supernatural force. Under the dominion of an idea which possesses the minds of multitudes, as civil freedom, or the religious sentiment, the powers of persons are no longer subjects of calculation. A nation of men unanimously bent on freedom or conquest can easily confound the arithmetic of statists, and achieve extravagant actions, out of all proportion to their means; as the Greeks, the Saracens, the Swiss, the Americans, and the French have done.

In like manner to every particle of property belongs its own attraction. A cent is the representative of a certain quantity of corn or other commodity. Its value is in the necessities of the animal man. It is so much warmth, so much bread, so much water, so much land. The law may do what it will with the owner of property; its just power will still attach to the cent. The law may in a mad freak say that all shall have power except the owners of property; they shall have no vote. Nevertheless, by a higher law, the property will, year after year, write every statute that respects property. The non-proprietor will be the scribe of the proprietor. What the owners wish to do, the whole power of property will do, either through the law or else in defiance of it. Of course I speak of all the property, not merely of the great estates. When the rich are outvoted, as frequently happens, it is the joint treasury of the poor which exceeds their accumulations. Every man owns something, if it is only a cow, or a wheel-barrow, or his arms, and so has that property to dispose of.

The same necessity which secures the rights of persons and property against the malignity or folly of the magistrate, determines the form and methods of governing, which are proper to each nation and to its habit of thought, and nowise transferable to other states of society. In this country we are very vain of our political institutions, which are singular in this, that they sprung, within the memory of living men, from the character and condition of the people, which they still express with sufficient fidelity,—and we ostentatiously prefer them to any other in history. They are not better, but only fitter for us. We may be wise in asserting the advantage in modern times of the democratic form, but to other states of society, in which religion consecrated the monarchical, that and not this was expedient. Democracy is better for us, because the religious sentiment of the present time accords better with it. Born democrats, we are nowise qualified to judge of monarchy, which, to our fathers living in the monarchical idea, was also relatively right. But our institutions, though in coincidence with the spirit of the age, have not any exemption from the practical defects which have discredited other forms. Every actual State is corrupt. Good men must not obey the laws too well. What satire on government can equal the severity of censure conveyed in the word *politic*, which now for ages has signified *cunning*, intimating that the State is a trick?

The same benign necessity and the same practical abuse appear in the parties, into which each State divides itself, of opponents and defenders of the

no cause, joined no movement. An incurable optimist, he lived and moved with work-a-day people, befriended and tolerated them, an experience that permeates all his writing. Like Rousseau's, his conclusions derived 'from observing and wandering among men.' The central idea of his poems and of his essay 'Democratic Vistas,' excerpted herein, is the conviction that the genius of the United States is 'most in the common people,' 'in the bulk quality of the whole.' The America he envisaged was the ideal—what it might be when 'carried far beyond politics into the region of taste, the standards of manners and beauty, and even into philosophy and religion.'

Science had 'already burst well upon the world,' he observed in 'Democratic Vistas,' and its far-reaching transformation would win for America a conspicuous place in the sun. But science alone could not enable America, or any people, to realize its highest moral and spiritual destiny. 'Bear in mind,' he warned, 'that nothing less than the mightiest original non-subordinated soul has ever really gloriously led, or ever can lead.' In the individual, not in science or material wealth, lies the well-spring of free, vibrant, democratic America. 'One's self I sing, a simple separate person, yet utter the word, democratic, the word, en-masse.' That is why he would lead a great chorus where the voice of every man, woman, and child would be heard, and the sovereignty of the people realized.

> It is not the earth, it is not
> America who is so great,
> It is I who am great or to be great,
> it is You up there, or any one,
> It is to walk rapidly through
> civilization, governments, theories,
> Through poems, pageants, shows,
> to form individuals.
> Underneath all, individuals, I swear
> nothing is good to me now that
> ignores individuals * * *

1. *The antidote to the abuse of formal government is the growth of the individual*

Ralph Waldo Emerson, *Politics*, 1841 *

The theory of politics which has possessed the mind of men, and which they have expressed the best they could in their laws and in their revolutions, considers persons and property as the two objects for whose protection government exists. Of persons, all have equal rights, in virtue of being identical in nature. This interest of course with its whole power demands a democracy. Whilst the rights of all as persons are equal, in virtue of their access to reason, their

* *Essays*, second series, vol. III, Riverside edition, 1895, pp. 191–211 *passim*.

rights in property are very unequal. One man owns his clothes, and anoth
owns a county. This accident, depending primarily on the skill and virtue
the parties, of which there is every degree, and secondarily on patrimony, fa
unequally, and its rights of course are unequal. Personal rights, universally t
same, demand a government framed on the ratio of the census; property d
mands a government framed on the ratio of owners and of owning. . .

In the earliest society the proprietors made their own wealth, and so lo
as it comes to the owners in the direct way, no other opinion would arise
any equitable community than that property should make the law for propert
and persons the law for persons.

But property passes through donation or inheritance to those who do n
create it. Gift, in one case, makes it as really the new owner's, as labor ma
it the first owner's: in the other case, of patrimony, the law makes an owne
ship which will be valid in each man's view according to the estimate whic
he sets on the public tranquillity.

It was not however found easy to embody the readily admitted princip
that property should make law for property, and persons for persons; sin
persons and property mixed themselves in every transaction. At last it seeme
settled that the rightful distinction was that the proprietors should have mo
elective franchise than non-proprietors. . .

That principle no longer looks so self-evident as it appeared in form
times, partly because doubts have arisen whether too much weight had not bee
allowed in the laws to property, and such a structure given to our usages
allowed the rich to encroach on the poor, and to keep them poor; but mainl
because there is an instinctive sense, however obscure and yet inarticulate, th
the whole constitution of property, on its present tenures, is injurious, and i
influence on persons deteriorating and degrading; that truly the only intere
for the consideration of the State is persons; that property will always follo
persons; that the highest end of gvernment is the culture of men; and that i
men can be educated, the institutions will share their improvement and th
moral sentiment will write the law of the land.

If it be not easy to settle the equity of this question, the peril is less whe
we take note of our natural defences. We are kept by better guards than th
vigilance of such magistrates as we commonly elect. Society always consists i
greater part of young and foolish persons. The old, who have seen throug
the hypocrisy of courts and statesmen, die and leave no wisdom to their sons
They believe their own newspaper, as their fathers did at their age. With suc
an ignorant and deceivable majority, States would soon run to ruin, but tha
there are limitations beyond which the folly and ambition of governors canno
go. Things have their laws, as well as men; and things refuse to be trifle
with. Property will be protected. Corn will not grow unless it is planted an
manured; but the farmer will not plant or hoe it unless the chances are a hun
dred to one that he will cut and harvest it. Under any forms, persons an
property must and will have their just sway. They exert their power as steadil
as matter its attraction. Cover up a pound of earth never so cunningly, divid
and subdivide it; melt it to liquid, convert it to gas; it will always weigh
pound; it will always attract and resist other matter by the full virtue of on

administration of the government. Parties are also founded on instincts, and have better guides to their own humble aims than the sagacity of their leaders. They have nothing perverse in their origin, but rudely mark some real and lasting relation. We might as wisely reprove the east wind or the frost, as a political party, whose members, for the most part, could give no account of their position, but stand for the defense of those interests in which they find themselves. Our quarrel with them begins when they quit this deep natural ground at the bidding of some leader, and obeying personal considerations, throw themselves into the maintenance and defence of points nowise belonging to their svstem. A party is perpetually corrupted by personality. Whilst we absolve the association from dishonesty, we cannot extend the same charity to their leaders. They reap the rewards of the docility and zeal of the masses which they direct. Ordinarily our parties are parties of circumstance, and not of principle; as the planting interest in conflict with the commercial; the party of capitalists and that of operatives: parties which are identical in their moral character, and which can easily change ground with each other in the support of many of their measures. Parties of principle, as, religious sects, or the party of free-trade, of universal suffrage, of abolition of slavery, of abolition of capital punishment,—degenerate into personalities, or would inspire enthusiasm. The vice of our leading parties in this country (which may be cited as a fair specimen of these societies of opinion) is that they do not plant themselves on the deep and necessary grounds to which they are respectively entitled, but lash themselves to fury in the carrying of some local and momentary measure, nowise useful to the commonwealth. Of the two great parties which at this hour almost share the nation between them, I should say that one has the best cause, and the other contains the best men. The philosopher, the poet, or the religious man, will of course wish to cast his vote with the democrat, for free-trade, for wide suffrage, for the abolition of legal cruelties in the penal code, and for facilitating in every manner the access of the young and the poor to the sources of wealth and power. But he can rarely accept the persons whom the so-called popular party propose to him as representatives of these liberalities. They have not at heart the ends which give to the name of democracy what hope and virtue are in it. The spirit of our American radicalism is destructive and aimless: it is not loving; it has no ulterior and divine ends, but is destructive only out of hatred and selfishness. On the other side, the conservative party, composed of the most moderate, able, and cultivated part of the population, is timid, and merely defensive of property. It vindicates no right, it aspires to no real good, it brands no crime, it proposes no generous policy; it does not build, nor write, nor cherish the arts, nor foster religion, nor establish schools, nor encourage science, nor emancipate the slave, nor befriend the poor, or the Indian, or the immigrant. From neither party, when in power, has the world any benefit to expect in science, art, or humanity, at all commensurate with the resources of the nation.

I do not for these defects despair of our republic. We are not at the mercy of any waves of chance. In the strife of ferocious parties, human nature always finds itself cherished; as the children of the convicts at Botany Bay are found to have as healthy a moral sentiment as other children. Citizens of feudal states are alarmed at our democratic institutions lapsing into anarchy, and the older and more cautious among ourselves are learning from Europeans to look with some terror at our turbulent freedom. It is said that in our license of construing the Constitution, and in the despotism of public opinion, we have no anchor; and one foreign observer thinks he has found the safeguard in the sanctity of Marriage among us; and another thinks he has found it in our Calvinism. Fisher Ames expressed the popular security more wisely, when he compared a monarchy and a republic, saying that a monarchy is a merchantman, which sails well, but will sometimes strike on a rock and go to the bottom; whilst a republic is a raft, which would never sink, but then your feet are always in water. No forms can have any dangerous importance whilst we are befriended by the laws of things. It makes no difference how many tons weight of atmosphere presses on our heads, so long as the same pressure resists it within the lungs. Augment the mass a thousand fold, it cannot begin to crush us, as long as reaction is equal to action. The fact of two poles, of two forces, centripetal and centrifugal, is universal, and each force by its own activity develops the other. Wild liberty develops iron conscience. Want of liberty, by strengthening law and decorum, stupefies conscience. 'Lynch-law' prevails only where there is greater hardihood and self-subsistency in the leaders. A mob cannot be a permanency; everybody's interest requires that it should not exist, and only justice satisfies all.

We must trust infinitely to the beneficent necessity which shines through all laws. Human nature expresses itself in them as characteristically as in statues, or songs, or railroads; and an abstract of the codes of nations would be a transcript of the common conscience. Governments have their origin in the moral identity of men. Reason for one is seen to be reason for another, and for every other. There is a middle measure which satisfies all parties, be they never so many or so resolute for their own. Every man finds a sanction for his simplest claims and deeds, in decisions of his own mind, which he calls Truth and Holiness. In these decisions all the citizens find a perfect agreement, and only in these; not in what is good to eat, good to wear, good use of time, or what amount of land or of public aid each is entitled to claim. This truth and justice men presently endeavor to make application of to the measuring of land, the apportionment of service, the protection of life and property. Their first endeavors, no doubt, are very awkward. Yet absolute right is the first governor; or, every government is an impure theocracy. The idea after which each community is aiming to make and mend its law, is the will of the wise man. The wise man it cannot find in nature, and it makes awkward but earnest efforts to secure his government by contrivance; as by causing the entire people to give their voices on every measure; or by a double choice to get the representation of the whole; or by a selection of the best citizens; or to secure the advantages of efficiency and internal peace by confiding the government to one, who may himself select his agents. All forms of government symbolize an immortal government, common to all dynasties and independent of numbers, perfect where two men exist, perfect where there is only one man.

Every man's nature is a sufficient advertisement to him of the character of his fellows. My right and my wrong is their right and their wrong. Whilst I do what is fit for me, and abstain from what is unfit, my neighbor and I shall often agree in our means, and work together for a time to one end. But whenever I find my dominion over myself not sufficient for me, and undertake the direction of him also, I overstep the truth, and come into false relations to him. I may have so much more strength or skill than he that he cannot express adequately his sense of wrong, but it is a lie, and hurts like a lie both him and me. Love and nature cannot maintain the assumption; it must be executed by a practical lie, namely by force. This undertaking for another is the blunder which stands in colossal ugliness in the governments of the world. It is the same thing in numbers, as in a pair, only not quite so intelligible. I can see well enough a great difference between my setting myself down to a self-control, and my going to make somebody else act after my views; but when a quarter of the human race assume to tell me what I must do, I may be too much disturbed by the circumstances to see so clearly the absurdity of their command. Therefore all public ends look vague and quixotic beside private ones. For any laws but those which men make for themselves, are laughable. If I put myself in the place of my child, and we stand in one thought and see that things are thus or thus, that perception is law for him and me. We are both there, both act. But if, without carrying him into the thought, I look over into his plot, and, guessing how it is with him, ordain this or that, he will never obey me. This is the history of governments,—one man does something which is to bind another. A man who cannot be acquainted with me, taxes me; looking from afar at me ordains that a part of my labor shall go to this or that whimsical end,—not as I, but as he happens to fancy. Behold the consequence. Of all debts men are least willing to pay the taxes. What a satire is this on government! Everywhere they think they get their money's worth, except for these.

Hence the less government we have the better,—the fewer laws, and the less confided power. The antidote to this abuse of formal Government is the influence of private character, the growth of the Individual; the appearance of the principal to supersede the proxy; the appearance of the wise man; of whom the existing government is, it must be owned, but a shabby imitation. That which all things tend to educe; which freedom, cultivation, intercourse, revolutions, go to form and deliver, is character; that is the end of Nature, to reach unto this coronation of her king. To educate the wise man the State exists, and with the appearance of the wise man the State expires. The appearance of character makes the State unnecessary. The wise man is the State. He needs no army, fort, or navy,—he loves men too well; no bribe, or feast, or palace, to draw friends to him; no vantage ground, no favorable circumstance. He needs no library, for he has not done thinking; no church, for he is a prophet; no statute book, for he has the lawgiver; no money, for he is value; no road, for he is at home where he is; no experience, for the life of the creator shoots through him, and looks from his eyes. . .

We think our civilization near its meridian, but we are yet only at the cock-crowing and the morning star. In our barbarous society the influence of character is in its infancy. As a political power, as the rightful lord who is to tumble all rulers from their chairs, its presence is hardly yet suspected. Malthus and Ricardo quite omit it; the Annual Register is silent; in the Conversations'

Lexicon it is not set down; the President's Message, the Queen's Speech, have not mentioned it; and yet it is never nothing. Every thought which genius and piety throw into the world, alters the world. The gladiators in the lists of power feel, through all their frocks of force and stimulation, the presence of worth. I think the very strife of trade and ambition is confession of this divinity; and successes in those fields are the poor amends, the fig-leaf with which the shamed soul attempts to hide its nakedness. I find the like unwilling homage in all quarters. It is because we know how much is due from us that we are impatient to show some petty talent as a substitute for worth. We are haunted by a conscience of this right to grandeur of character, and are false to it. But each of us has some talent, can do somewhat useful, or graceful, or formidable, or amusing, or lucrative. That we do, as an apology to others and to ourselves for not reaching the mark of a good and equal life. But it does not satisfy us, whilst we thrust it on the notice of our companions. It may throw dust in their eyes, but does not smooth our own brow, or give us the tranquillity of the strong when we walk abroad. We do penance as we go. Our talent is a sort of expiation, and we are constrained to reflect on our splendid moment with a certain humiliation, as somewhat too fine, and not as one act of many acts, a fair expression of our permanent energy. Most persons of ability meet in society with a kind of tacit appeal. Each seems to say, 'I am not all here.' Senators and presidents have climbed so high with pain enough, not because they think the place specially agreeable, but as an apology for real worth, and to vindicate their manhood in our eyes. This conspicuous chair is their compensation to themselves for being of a poor, cold, hard nature. They must do what they can. Like one class of forest animals, they have nothing but a prehensile tail; climb they must, or crawl. If a man found himself so rich-natured that he could enter into strict relations with the best persons and make life serene around him by the dignity and sweetness of his behavior, could he afford to circumvent the favor of the caucus and the press, and covet relations so hollow and pompous as those of a politician? Surely nobody would be a charlatan who could afford to be sincere.

The tendencies of the times favor the idea of self-government, and leave the individual, for all code, to the rewards and penalties of his own constitution; which work with more energy than we believe whilst we depend on artificial restraints. The movement in this direction has been very marked in modern history. Much has been blind and discreditable, but the nature of the revolution is not affected by the vices of the revolters; for this is a purely moral force. It was never adopted by any party in history, neither can be. It separates the individual from all party, and unites him at the same time to the race. It promises a recognition of higher rights than those of personal freedom, or the security of property. A man has a right to be employed, to be trusted, to be loved, to be revered. The power of love, as the basis of a State, has never been tried. We must not imagine that all things are lapsing into confusion if every tender protestant be not compelled to bear his part in certain social conventions; nor doubt that roads can be built, letters carried, and the fruit of labor secured, when the government of force is at an end. Are our methods now so excellent that all competition is hopeless? could not a nation of friends even devise better ways? On the other hand, let not the most conservative and timid fear anything from a premature surrender of the bayonet and the system of force. For, according to the order of nature, which is quite superior to our will, it stands thus; there will always be a government of force where men are selfish; and when they are pure enough to abjure the code of force they will be wise enough to see how these public ends of the post-office, of the highway, of commerce and the exchange of property, of museums and libraries, of institutions of art and science can be answered. . .

2. *There will never be a really free state until the individual is recognized as a higher and independent power*

HENRY DAVID THOREAU, *Civil Disobedience*, 1849 *

I heartily accept the motto, 'That government is best which governs least'; and I should like to see it acted up to more rapidly and systematically. Carried out, it finally amounts to this, which also I believe,—'That government is best which governs not at all'; and when men are prepared for it, that will be the kind of government which they will have. Government is at best but an expedient; but most governments are usually, and all governments are sometimes, inexpedient. . .

This American government,—what is it but a tradition, though a recent one, endeavoring to transmit itself unimpaired to posterity, but each instant losing some of its integrity? It has not the vitality and force of a single living man; for a single man can bend it to his will. It is a sort of wooden gun to the people themselves. But it is not the less necessary for this; for the people must have some complicated machinery or other, and hear its din, to satisfy that idea of government which they have. Governments show thus how successfully men can be imposed on, even impose on themselves, for their own advantage. It is excellent, we must all allow. Yet this government never of itself furthered any enterprise, but by the alacrity with which it got out of its way. *It* does not keep the country free. *It* does not settle the West. *It* does not educate. The character inherent in the American people has done all that has been accomplished; and it would have done somewhat more, if the government had not sometimes got in its way. For government is an expedient by which men would fain succeed in letting one another alone; and, as has been said, when it is most expedient, the governed are most let alone by it. Trade and commerce, if they were not made of india-rubber, would never manage to bounce over the obstacles which legislators are continually putting in their way; and, if one were to judge these men wholly by the effects of their actions and not partly by their intentions, they would deserve to be classed and punished with those mischievous persons who put obstructions on the railroads.

But, to speak practically and as a citizen, unlike those who call themselves

* *The Writings of Henry David Thoreau*, 1906, vol. IV, 'Cape Cod and Miscellanies,' pp. 356-87 *passim*.

no-government men, I ask for, not at once no government, but *at once* a better government. Let every man make known what kind of government would command his respect, and that will be one step toward obtaining it.

After all, the practical reason why, when the power is once in the hands of the people, a majority are permitted, and for a long period continue, to rule is not because they are most likely to be in the right, nor because this seems fairest to the minority, but because they are physically the strongest. But a government in which the majority rule in all cases cannot be based on justice, even as far as men understand it. Can there not be a government in which majorities do not virtually decide right and wrong, but conscience?—in which majorities decide only those questions to which the rule of expediency is applicable? Must the citizen ever for a moment, or in the least degree, resign his conscience to the legislator? Why has every man a conscience, then? I think that we should be men first, and subjects afterward. It is not desirable to cultivate a respect for the law, so much as for the right. The only obligation which I have a right to assume is to do at any time what I think right. It is truly enough said that a corporation has no conscience; but a corporation of conscientious men is a corporation *with* a conscience. Law never made men a whit more just; and, by means of their respect for it, even the well-disposed are daily made the agents of injustice. A common and natural result of an undue respect for law is, that you may see a file of soldiers, colonel, captain, corporal, privates, powder-monkeys, and all, marching in admirable order over hill and dale to the wars, against their wills, ay, against their common sense and consciences, which makes it very steep marching indeed, and produces a palpitation of the heart. . .

The mass of men serve the state thus, not as men mainly, but as machines, with their bodies. They are the standing army, and the militia, jailers, constables, *posse comitatus*, etc. In most cases there is no free exercise whatever of the judgment or of the moral sense; but they put themselves on a level with wood and earth and stones; and wooden men can perhaps be manufactured that will serve the purpose as well. Such command no more respect than men of straw or a lump of dirt. They have the same sort of worth only as horses and dogs. Yet such as these even are commonly esteemed good citizens. Others—as most legislators, politicians, lawyers, ministers, and office-holders—serve the state chiefly with their heads; and, as they rarely make any moral distinctions, they are as likely to serve the devil, without *intending* it, as God. A very few—as heroes, patriots, martyrs, reformers in the great sense, and *men*—serve the state with their consciences also, and so necessarily resist it for the most part; and they are commonly treated as enemies by it. . .

How does it become a man to behave toward this American government to-day? I answer, that he cannot without disgrace be associated with it. I cannot for an instant recognize that political organization as *my* government which is the *slave's* government also.

All men recognize the right of revolution; that is, the right to refuse allegiance to, and to resist, the government, when its tyranny or its inefficiency are great and unendurable. But almost all say that such is not the case now. But such was the case, they think, in the Revolution of '75. If one were to tell me that this was a bad government because it taxed certain foreign commodities brought to its ports, it is most probable that I should not make an ado about it, for I can do without them. All machines have their friction; and possibly this does enough good to counterbalance the evil. At any rate, it is a great evil to make a stir about it. But when the friction comes to have its machine, and oppression and robbery are organized, I say, let us not have such a machine any longer. In other words, when a sixth of the population of a nation which has undertaken to be the refuge of liberty are slaves, and a whole country is unjustly overrun and conquered by a foreign army, and subjected to military law, I think that it is not too soon for honest men to rebel and revolutionize. What makes this duty the more urgent is the fact that the country so overrun is not our own, but ours is the invading army. . .

How can a man be satisfied to entertain an opinion merely, and enjoy *it?* Is there any enjoyment in it, if his opinion is that he is aggrieved? If you are cheated out of a single dollar by your neighbor, you do not rest satisfied with knowing that you are cheated, or with saying that you are cheated, or even with petitioning him to pay you your due; but you take effectual steps at once to obtain the full amount, and see that you are never cheated again. Action from principle, the perception and the performance of right, changes things and relations; it is essentially revolutionary, and does not consist wholly with anything which was. It not only divides States and churches, it divides families; ay, it divides the *individual,* separating the diabolical in him from the divine.

Unjust laws exist; shall we be content to obey them, or shall we endeavor to amend them and obey them until we have succeeded, or shall we transgress them at once? Men generally, under such a government as this, think that they ought to wait until they have persuaded the majority to alter them. They think that, if they should resist, the remedy would be worse than the evil. But it is the fault of the government itself that the remedy *is* worse than the evil. *It* makes it worse. Why is it not more apt to anticipate and provide for reform? Why does it not cherish its wise minority? Why does it cry and resist before it is hurt? Why does it not encourage its citizens to be on the alert to point out its faults, and *do* better than it would have them? Why does it always crucify Christ, and excommunicate Copernicus and Luther, and pronounce Washington and Franklin rebels? . .

I do not hesitate to say, that those who call themselves Abolitionists should at once effectually withdraw their support, both in person and property, from the government of Massachusetts, and not wait till they constitute a majority of one, before they suffer the right to prevail through them. I think that it is enough if they have God on their side, without waiting for that other one. Moreover, any man more right than his neighbors constitutes a majority of one already. . .

Under a government which imprisons any unjustly, the true place for a just man is also a prison. The proper place to-day, the only place which Massachusetts has provided for her freer and less desponding spirits, is in her prisons, to be put out and locked out of the State by her own act, as they have already put themselves out by their principles. It is there that the fugitive slave, and the Mexican prisoner on parole, and the Indian come to plead the wrongs of his race should find them; on that separate, but more free and honorable, ground, where the State places those who are not *with* her, but *against* her,—the only house in a slave State in which a free man can abide with honor. If any think that their influence would be lost there, and their voices no longer afflict the ear of the State, that they would not be as an enemy within its walls, they do not know by how much truth is stronger than error, nor how much more eloquently and effectively he can combat injustice who has experienced a little in his own person. Cast your whole vote, not a strip of paper merely, but your whole influence. A minority is powerless while it conforms to the majority; it is not even a minority then; but it is irresistible when it clogs by its whole weight. If the alternative is to keep all just men in prison, or give up war and slavery, the State will not hesitate which to choose. If a thousand men were not to pay their tax-bills this years, that would not be a violent and bloody measure, as it would be to pay them, and enable the State to commit violence and shed innocent blood. This is, in fact, the definition of a peaceable revolution, if any such is possible. If the tax-gatherer, or any other public officer, asks me, as one has done, 'But what shall I do?' my answer is, 'If you really wish to do anything, resign your office.' When the subject has refused allegiance, and the officer has resigned his office, then the revolution is accomplished. But even suppose blood should flow. Is there not a sort of blood shed when the conscience is wounded? Through this wound a man's real manhood and immortality flow out, and he bleeds to an everlasting death. I see this blood flowing now. . .

Some years ago, the State met me in behalf of the Church, and commanded me to pay a certain sum toward the support of a clergyman whose preaching my father attended, but never I myself. 'Pay,' it said, 'or be locked up in the jail.' I declined to pay. But, unfortunately, another man saw fit to pay it. I did not see why the schoolmaster should be taxed to support the priest, and not the priest the schoolmaster; for I was not the State's schoolmaster, but I supported myself by voluntary subscription. I did not see why the lyceum should not present its tax-bill, and have the State to back its demand, as well as the Church. However, at the request of the selectmen, I condescended to make some such statement as this in writing:—'Know all men by these presents, that I, Henry Thoreau, do not wish to be regarded as a member of any incorporated society which I have not joined.' This I gave to the town clerk; and he has it. The State, having thus learned that I did not wish to be regarded as a member of that church, has never made a like demand on me since; though it said that it must adhere to its original presumption that time. If I had known how to name them, I should then have signed off in detail from all the societies which I never signed on to; but I did not know where to find a complete list.

I have paid no poll-tax for six years. I was put into a jail once on this account, for one night; and, as I stood considering the walls of stone, two or three feet thick, the door of wood and iron, a foot thick, and the iron grating which strained the light, I could not help being struck with the foolishness of that institution which treated me as if I were mere flesh and blood and bones, to be locked up. I wondered that it should have concluded at length that this was the best use it could put me to, and had never thought to avail itself of my services in some way. I saw that, if there was a wall of stone between me and my townsmen, there was a still more difficult one to climb or break through before they could get to be as free as I was. I did not for a moment feel confined, and the walls seemed a great waste of stone and mortar. I felt as if I alone of all my townsmen had paid my tax. They plainly did not know how to treat me, but behaved like persons who are underbred. In every threat and in every compliment there was a blunder; for they thought that my chief desire was to stand the other side of that stone wall. I could not but smile to see how industriously they locked the door on my meditations, which followed them out again without let or hindrance, and *they* were really all that was dangerous. As they could not reach me, they had resolved to punish my body; just as boys, if they cannot come at some person against whom they have a spite, will abuse his dog. I saw that the State was half-witted, that it was timid as a lone woman with her silver spoons, and that it did not know its friends from its foes, and I lost all my remaining respect for it, and pitied it.

Thus the State never intentionally confronts a man's sense, intellectual or moral, but only his body, his senses. It is not armed with superior wit or honesty, but with superior physical strength. I was not born to be forced. I will breathe after my own fashion. Let us see who is the strongest. What force has a multitude? They only can force me who obey a higher law than I. They force me to become like themselves. I do not hear of *men* being *forced* to live this way or that by masses of men. What sort of life were that to live? When I meet a government which says to me, 'Your money or your life,' why should I be in haste to give it my money? It may be in a great strait, and not know what to do: I cannot help that. It must help itself; do as I do. It is not worth the while to snivel about it. I am not responsible for the successful working of the machinery of society. I am not the son of the engineer. I perceive that, when an acorn and a chestnut fall side by side, the one does not remain inert to make way for the other, but both obey their own laws, and spring and grow and flourish as best they can, till one, perchance, overshadows and destroys the other. If a plant cannot live according to its nature, it dies; and so a man. . .

The night in prison was novel and interesting enough. The prisoners in their shirt-sleeves were enjoying a chat and the evening air in the doorway, when I entered. But the jailer said, 'Come, boys, it is time to lock up'; and so they dispersed, and I heard the sound of their steps returning into the hollow apartments. My room-mate was introduced to me by the jailer as 'a first-rate fellow and a clever man.' When the door was locked, he showed me where to hang my hat, and how he managed matters there. The rooms were whitewashed once a month; and this one, at least, was the whitest, most simply furnished, and probably the neatest apartment in the town. He naturally wanted to know where I came from, and what brought me there; and, when I had told him, I asked him in my turn how he came there, presuming him to be an honest man, of course; and, as the world goes, I believe he was. 'Why,' said he, 'they accuse me of burning a barn; but I never did it.' As near as I could discover, he had probably gone to bed in a barn when drunk, and smoked his pipe there; and so a barn was burnt. He had the reputation of being a clever man, had been there some three months waiting for his trial to come on, and would have to wait as much longer; but he was quite domesticated and contented, since he got his board for nothing, and thought that he was well treated.

He occupied one window, and I the other; and I saw that if one stayed there long, his principal business would be to look out the window. I had soon read all the tracts that were left there, and examined where former prisoners had broken out, and where a grate had been sawed off, and heard the history of the various occupants of that room; for I found that even here there was a history and a gossip which never circulated beyond the walls of the jail. Probably this is the only house in the town where verses are composed, which are afterward printed in a circular form, but not published. I was shown quite a long list of verses which were composed by some young men who had been detected in an attempt to escape, who avenged themselves by singing them.

I pumped my fellow-prisoner as dry as I could, for fear I should never see him again; but at length he showed me which was my bed, and left me to blow out the lamp. . .

In the morning, our breakfasts were put through the hole in the door, in small oblong-square tin pans, made to fit, and holding a pint of chocolate, with brown bread, and an iron spoon. When they called for the vessels again, I was green enough to return what bread I had left; but my comrade seized it, and said that I should lay that up for lunch or dinner. Soon after he was let out to work at haying in a neighboring field, whither he went every day, and would not be back till noon; so he bade me good-day, saying that he doubted if he should see me again.

When I came out of prison—for some one interfered, and paid that tax—I did not perceive that great changes had taken place on the common, such as he observed who went in a youth and emerged a tottering and gray-headed man; and yet a change had to my eyes come over the scene—the town, and State, and country—greater than any that mere time could effect. I saw yet more distinctly the State in which I lived. I saw to what extent the people among whom I lived could be trusted as good neighbors and friends; that their friendship was for summer weather only; that they did not greatly propose to do right; that they were a distinct race from me by their prejudices and superstitions, as the Chinamen and Malays are; that in their sacrifices to humanity they ran no risks, not even to their property; that after all they were not so noble but they treated the thief as he had treated them, and hoped, by a certain outward observance and a few prayers, and by walking in a particular straight though useless path from time to time, to save their souls. This may be to judge my neighbors harshly; for I believe that many of them are not aware that they have such an institution as the jail in their village. . .

I have never declined paying the highway tax, because I am as desirous of being a good neighbor as I am being a bad subject; and as for supporting schools, I am doing my part to educate my fellow-countrymen now. It is for no particular item in the tax-bill that I refuse to pay it. I simply wish to refuse allegiance to the State, to withdraw and stand aloof from it effectually. I do not care to trace the course of my dollar, if I could, till it buys a man or a musket to shoot one with—the dollar is innocent—but I am concerned to trace the effects of my allegiance. In fact, I quietly declare war with the State, after my fashion, though I will still make what use and get what advantage of her I can, as is usual in such cases.

If others pay the tax which is demanded of me, from a sympathy with the State, they do but what they have already done in their own case, or rather they abet injustice to a greater extent than the State requires. If they pay the tax from a mistaken interest in the individual taxed, to save his property, or prevent his going to jail, it is because they have not considered wisely how far they let their private feelings interfere with the public good.

This, then, is my position at present. But one cannot be too much on his guard in such a case, lest his action be biased by obstinacy or an undue regard for the opinions of men. Let him see that he does only what belongs to himself and to the hour. . .

I do not wish to quarrel with any man or nation. I do not wish to split hairs, to make fine distinctions, or set myself up as better than my neighbors. I seek rather, I may say, even an excuse for conforming to the laws of the land. I am but too ready to conform to them. Indeed, I have reason to suspect myself on this head; and each year, as the tax-gatherer comes round, I find myself disposed to review the acts and position of the general and State governments, and the spirit of the people, to discover a pretext for conformity.

> We must affect our country as our parents,
> And if at any time we alienate
> Our love or industry from doing it honor,
> We must respect effects and teach the soul
> Matter of conscience and religion,
> And not desire of rule or benefit.

I believe that the State will soon be able to take all my work of this sort out of my hands, and then I shall be no better a patriot than my fellow-countrymen. Seen from a lower point of view, the Constitution, with all its faults, is very good; the law and the courts are very respectable; even this State and this American government are, in many respects, very admirable, and rare things, to be thankful for, such as a great many have described them; but seen from a point of view a little higher, they are what I have described them; seen from a higher still, and the highest, who shall say what they are, or that they are worth looking at or thinking of at all? . . .

I know that most men think differently from myself; but those whose lives are by profession devoted to the study of these or kindred subjects content me as little as any. Statesmen and legislators, standing so completely within the institution, never distinctly and nakedly behold it. They speak of moving society, but have no resting-place without it. They may be men of a certain experience and discrimination, and have no doubt invented ingenious and even useful systems, for which we sincerely thank them; but all their wit and usefulness lie within certain not very wide limits. They are wont to forget that the world is not governed by policy and expediency. Webster never goes behind government, and so cannot speak with authority about it. His words are wisdom to those legislators who contemplate no essential reform in the existing government; but for thinkers, and those who legislate for all time, he never once glances at the subject. I know of those whose serene and wise speculations on this theme would soon reveal the limits of his mind's range and hospitality. Yet, compared with the cheap professions of most reformers, and the still cheaper wisdom and eloquence of politicians in general, his are almost the only sensible and valuable words, and we thank Heaven for him. Comparatively, he is always strong, original, and, above all, practical. Still, his quality is not wisdom, but prudence. The lawyer's truth is not Truth, but consistency or a consistent expediency. Truth is always in harmony with herself, and is not concerned chiefly to reveal the justice that may consist with wrong-doing. He well deserves to be called, as he has been called, the Defender of the Constitution. There are really no blows to be given by him but defensive ones. He is not a leader, but a follower. His leaders are the men of '87. 'I have never made an effort,' he says, 'and never propose to make an effort; I have never countenanced an effort, and never mean to countenance an effort, to disturb the arrangement as originally made, by which the various States came into the Union.' Still thinking of the sanction which the Constitution gives to slavery, he says, 'Because it was a part of the original compact,—let it stand.' Nothwithstanding his special acuteness and ability, he is unable to take a fact out of its merely political relations, and behold it as it lies absolutely to be disposed of by the intellect. . .

They who know of no purer sources of truth, who have traced up its stream no higher, stand, and wisely stand, by the Bible and the Constitution, and drink at it there with reverence and humility; but they who behold where it comes trickling into this lake or that pool, gird up their loins once more, and continue their pilgrimage toward its fountain-head.

The authority of government, even such as I am willing to submit to,—for I will cheerfully obey those who know and can do better than I, and in many things even those who neither know nor can do so well,—is still an impure one: to be strictly just, it must have the sanction and consent of the governed. It can have no pure right over my person and property but what I concede to it. The progress from an absolute to a limited monarchy, from a limited monarchy to a democracy, is a progress toward a true respect for the individual. Even the Chinese philosopher was wise enough to regard the individual as the basis of the empire. Is a democracy, such as we know it, the last improvement possible in government? Is it not possible to take a step further towards recognizing and organizing the rights of man? There will never be a really free and enlightened State until the State comes to recognize the individual as a higher and independent power, from which all its own power and authority are derived, and treats him accordingly. I please myself with imagining a State at last which can afford to be just to all men, and to treat the individual with respect as a neighbor; which even would not think it inconsistent with its own repose if a few were to live aloof from it, not meddling with it, nor embraced by it, who fulfilled all the duties of neighbors and fellow-men. A State which bore this kind of fruit, and suffered it to drop off as fast as it ripened, would prepare the way for a still more perfect and glorious State, which also I have imagined, but not yet anywhere seen.

3. *The purpose of democracy is to illustrate that man properly trained in sanest, highest freedom may and must become a law unto himself*

WALT WHITMAN, *Democratic Vistas*, 1871 *

America, filling the present with greatest deeds and problems, cheerfully accepting the past, including Feudalism . . . counts, as I reckon, for her justification and success, . . . almost entirely on the future. Nor is that hope unwarranted. To-day, ahead, though dimly yet, we see, in vistas, a copious, sane, gigantic offspring. . .

I will not gloss over the appalling dangers of universal suffrage in the United States. In fact, it is to admit and face these dangers I am writing. To him or her within whose thought rages the battle, advancing, retreating, between Democracy's convictions, aspirations, and the People's crudeness, vice, caprices, I mainly write this book.

I shall use the words America and Democracy as convertible terms. . . The United States are destined either to surmount the gorgeous history of Feudalism, or else prove the most tremendous failure of time. Not the least doubtful am I on any prospects of their material success. The triumphant future of their business, geographic, and productive departments, on larger scales and in more varieties than ever, is certain. In those respects the Republic must soon (if she does not already) outstrip all examples hitherto afforded, and dominate the world.

Admitting all this, with the priceless value of our political institutions, general suffrage (and cheerfully acknowledging the latest, widest opening of the doors,) I say that, far deeper than these, what finally and only is to make of our Western World a Nationality superior to any hitherto known, and outtopping the past, must be vigorous, yet unsuspected Literatures, perfect personalities and sociologies, original, transcendental, and expressing (what, in highest sense, are not yet expressed at all,) Democracy and the Modern. With these, and out of these, I promulge new races of Teachers, and of perfect Women, indispensable to endow the birth-stock of a New World. . .

I say that Democracy can never prove itself beyond cavil, until it founds and luxuriantly grows its own forms of arts, poems, schools, theology, displacing all that exists, or that has been produced anywhere in the past, under opposite influences.

It is curious to me that while so many voices, pens, minds, in the press, lecture-rooms, in our Congress, etc., are discussing intellectual topics, pecuniary dangers, legislative problems, the suffrage, tariff and labor questions, and the various business and benevolent needs of America, with propositions, remedies, often worth deep attention, there is one need, a hiatus, and the profoundest, that no eye seems to perceive, no voice to state. Our fundamental want to-day in the United States, with closest, amplest reference to present conditions, and

* Published as a pamphlet, Washington, D.C., 1871.

to the future, is of a class, and the clear idea of a class, of native Authors, Literatures far different, far higher in grade than any yet known, sacerdotal, modern, fit to cope with our occasions, lands, permeating the whole mass of American mentality, taste, belief, breathing into it a new breath of life, giving it decision, affecting politics far more than the popular superficial suffrage, with results inside and underneath the elections of Presidents or Congresses, radiating, begetting appropriate teachers and schools, manners, costumes, and, as its grandest result, accomplishing, (what neither the schools nor the churches and their clergy have hitherto accomplished, and without which this nation will no more stand, permanently, soundly, than a house will stand without a substratum,) a religious and moral character beneath the political and productive and intellectual bases of The States. . .

First, let us see what we can make out of a brief, general, sentimental consideration of political Democracy, and whence it has arisen, with regard to some of its current features, as an aggregate, and as the basic structure of our future literature and authorship. We shall, it is true, quickly and continually find the origin-idea of the singleness of man, individualism, asserting itself, and cropping forth, even from the opposite ideas. But the mass, or lump character, for imperative reasons, is to be ever carefully weighed, borne in mind, and provided for. Only from it, and from its proper regulation and potency, comes the other, comes the chance of Individualism. The two are contradictory, but our task is to reconcile them.

The political history of the past may be summed up as having grown out of what underlies the words Order, Safety, Caste, and especially out of the need of some prompt deciding Authority, and of Cohesion, at all cost. . .

For after the rest is said—after the many time-honored and really true things for subordination, experience, rights of property, etc., have been listened to and acquiesced in—after the valuable and well-settled statement of our duties and relations in society is thoroughly conned over and exhausted—it remains to bring forward and modify everything else with the idea of that Something a man is, (last precious consolation of the drudging poor,) standing apart from all else, divine in his own right, and a woman in hers, sole and untouchable by any canons of authority, or any rule derived from precedent, state-safety, the acts of legislatures, or even from what is called religion, modesty, or art.

The radiation of this truth is the key of the most significant doings of our immediately preceding three centuries, and has been the political genesis and life of America. Advancing visibly, it still more advances invisibly. Underneath the fluctuations of the expressions of society, as well as the movements of the politics of the leading nations of the world, we see steadily pressing ahead, and strengthening itself, even in the midst of immense tendencies toward aggregation, this image of completeness in separatism, of individual personal dignity, of a single person, either male or female, characterized in the main, not from extrinsic acquirements or position, but in the pride of himself or herself alone; and, as an eventful conclusion and summing up, (or else the entire scheme of things is aimless, a cheat, a crash,) the simple idea that the last, best dependence is to be upon Humanity itself, and its own inherent, normal, full-grown qualities, without any superstitious support whatever. This idea of perfect individualism it is indeed that deepest tinges and gives character to the idea of the Aggregate. For it is mainly or altogether to serve independent separatism that we favor a strong generalization, consolidation. As it is to give the best vitality and freedom to the rights of the States, (every bit as important as the right of Nationality, the union,) that we insist on the identity of the Union at all hazards.

The purpose of Democracy—supplanting old belief in the necessary absoluteness of established dynastic rulership, temporal, ecclesiastical, and scholastic, as furnishing the only security against chaos, crime, and ignorance—is, through many transmigrations, and amid endless ridicules, arguments, and ostensible failures, to illustrate, at all hazards, this doctrine or theory that man, properly trained in sanest, highest freedom, may and must become a law, and series of laws, unto himself, surrounding and providing for, not only his own personal control, but all his relations to other individuals, and to the State; and that, while other theories, as in the past histories of nations, have proved wise enough, and indispensable perhaps for their conditions, *this*, as matters now stand in our civilized world, is the only Scheme worth working for, as warranting results like those of Nature's laws, reliable, when once established, to carry on themselves. . .

As to the political section of Democracy, which introduces and breaks ground for further and vaster sections, few probably are the minds, even in These Republican States, that fully comprehend the aptness of that phrase, 'THE GOVERNMENT OF THE PEOPLE, BY THE PEOPLE, FOR THE PEOPLE,' which we inherit from the lips of Abraham Lincoln; a formula whose verbal shape is homely wit, but whose scope includes both the totality and all minutiae of the lesson.

The People! Like our huge earth itself, which, to ordinary scansion, is full of vulgar contradictions and offence, Man, viewed in the lump, displeases, and is a constant puzzle and affront to the merely educated classes. The rare, cosmical, artist-mind, lit with the Infinite, alone confronts his manifold and oceanic qualities, but taste, intelligence and culture, (so-called,) have been against the masses, and remain so. There is plenty of glamour about the most damnable crimes and hoggish meannesses, special and general, of the Feudal and dynastic world over there, with its *personnel* of lords and queens and courts, so well-dressed and so handsome. But the People are ungrammatical, untidy, and their sins gaunt and ill-bred. . .

I know nothing more rare, even in this country, than a fit scientific estimate and reverent appreciation of the People—of their measureless wealth of latent power and capacity, their vast, artistic contrasts of lights and shades—with, in America, their entire reliability in emergencies, and a certain breadth of historic grandeur, of peace or war, far surpassing all the vaunted samples of book-heroes, or any *haut ton* coteries, in all the records of the world.

The movements of the late Secession war, and their results, to any sense that studies well and comprehends them, show that Popular Democracy, whatever its faults and dangers, practically justifies itself beyond the proudest claims and wildest hopes of its enthusiasts. Probably no future age can know, but I well know, how the gist of this fiercest and most resolute of the world's warlike contentions resided exclusively in the unnamed, unknown rank and file; and how the brunt of its labor of death was, to all essential purposes, Volunteered. The People, of their own choice, fighting, dying for their own idea, insolently attacked by the Secession-Slave-Power, and its very existence imperiled. Descending to detail, entering any of the armies, and mixing with the private soldiers, we see and have seen august spectacles. We have seen the alacrity with which the American-born populace, the peaceablest and most good-natured race in the world, and the most personally independent and intelligent, and the least fitted to submit to the irksomeness and exasperation of regimental discipline, sprang, at the first tap of the drum, to arms—not for gain, nor even glory, nor to repel invasion—but for an emblem, a mere abstraction—for the life, *the safety of the Flag*. We have seen the unequaled docility and obedience of these soldiers. We have seen them tried long and long by hopelessness, mismanagement, and the defeat; have seen the incredible slaughter toward or through which armies (as at first Fredericksburg, and afterward at the Wilderness,) still unhesitatingly obeyed orders to advance. We have seen them in trench, or crouching behind breastwork, or tramping in deep mud, or amid pouring rain or thick-falling snow, or under forced marches in hottest summer (as on the road to get to Gettysburg)—vast suffocating swarms, divisions, corps, with every single man so grimed and black with sweat and dust, his own mother would not have known him—his clothes all dirty, stained and torn, with sour, accumulated sweat for perfume—many a comrade, perhaps a brother, sun-struck, staggering out, dying, by the roadside, of exhaustion—yet the great bulk bearing steadily on, cheery enough, hollow-bellied from hunger, but sinewy with unconquerable resolution. . .

What have we here, if not, towering above all talk and argument, the plentifully-supplied, last-needed proof of Democracy, in its personalities? Curiously enough, too, the proof on this point comes, I should say, every bit as much from the South, as from the North. Although I have spoken only of the latter, yet I deliberately include all. Grand, common stock! to me the accomplished and convincing growth, prophetic of the future; proof undeniable to sharpest sense, of perfect beauty, tenderness and pluck, that never Feudal Lord, nor Greek, nor Roman breed, yet rivaled. . .

I, as Democrat, see clearly enough, (as already illustrated,) the crude, defective streaks in all the strata of the common people; the specimens and vast collections of the ignorant, the credulous, the unfit and uncouth, the incapable, and the very low and poor. The eminent person just mentioned, sneeringly asks whether we expect to elevate and improve a Nation's politics by absorbing such morbid collections and qualities therein. The point is a formidable one, and there will doubtless always be numbers of solid and reflective citizens who will never get over it. Our answer is general, and is involved in the scope and letter of this essay. We believe the ulterior object of political and all other government, (having, of course, provided for the police, the safety of life, property, and for the basic statute and common law, and their administration, always first in order,) to be, among the rest, not merely to rule, to repress disorder, etc., but to develop, to open up to cultivation, to encourage the possibilities of all beneficent and manly outcroppage, and of that aspiration for independence, and the pride and self-respect latent in all characters. (Or, if there be exceptions, we cannot, fixing our eyes on them alone, make theirs the rule for all.)

I say the mission of government, henceforth, in civilized lands, is not repression alone, and not authority alone, not even of law, nor by that favorite standard of the eminent writer, the rule of the best men, the born heroes and captains of the race, (as if such ever, or one time out of a hundred, got into the big places, elective or dynastic!)—but, higher than the highest arbitrary rule, to train communities through all their grades, beginning with individuals and ending there again, to rule themselves. . .

To be a voter with the rest is not so much; and this, like every institute, will have its imperfections. But to become an enfranchised man, and now, impediments removed, to stand and start without humiliation, and equal with the rest; to commence, or have the road cleared to commence, the grand experiment of development, whose end, (perhaps requiring several generations,) may be the forming of a full-grown man or woman—that *is* something. To ballast the State is also secured, and in our times is to be secured, in no other way.

We do not, (at any rate I do not,) put it either on the ground that the People, the masses, even the best of them, are, in their latent or exhibited qualities, essentially sensible and good—nor on the ground of their rights; but that, good or bad, rights or no rights, the Democratic formula is the only safe and preservative one for coming times. We endow the masses with the suffrage for their own sake, no doubt; then, perhaps still more, from another point of view, for community's sake. . .

I say of all dangers to a Nation, as things exist in our day, there can be no greater one than having certain portions of the people set off from the rest by a line drawn—they not privileged as others, but degraded, humiliated, made of no account. Much quackery teems, of course, even on Democracy's side, yet does not really affect the orbic quality of the matter. To work in, if we may so term it, and justify God, his divine aggregate, the People, (or, the veritable horned and sharp-tailed Devil, *his* aggregate, if there be who convulsively insist upon it,)—this, I say, is what Democracy is for; and this is what our America means, and is doing—may I not say, has done? . . .

And, truly, whatever may be said in the way of abstract argument, for or against the theory of a wider democratizing of institutions in any civilized country, much trouble might well be saved to all European lands by recognizing this palpable fact, (for a palpable fact it is,) that some form of such democratizing is about the only resource now left. . .

The eager and often inconsiderate appeals of reformers and revolutionists are indispensable to counter-balance the inertness and fossilism making so large a part of human institutions. The latter will always take care of themselves—the danger being that they rapidly tend to ossify us. The former is to be treated with indulgence, and even respect. As circulation to air, so is agitation and a plentiful degree of speculative license to political and moral sanity. Indirectly, but surely, goodness, virtue, law, (of the very best,) follow Freedom. These, to Democracy, are what the keel is to the ship, or saltness to the ocean.

The true gravitation-hold of Liberalism in the United States will be a more universal ownership of property, general homesteads, general comfort—a vast, intertwining reticulation of wealth. As the human frame, or, indeed, any object in this manifold Universe, is best kept together by the simple miracle of its own cohesion, and the necessity, exercise and profit thereof, so a great and varied Nationality, occupying millions of square miles, were firmest held and knit by the principle of the safety and endurance of the aggregate of its middling property owners.

So that, from another point of view, ungracious as it may sound, and a paradox after what we have been saying, Democracy looks with suspicious, ill-satisfied eye upon the very poor, the ignorant, and on those out of business. She asks for men and women with occupations, well-off, owners of houses and acres, and with cash in the bank—and with some cravings for literature, too; and must have them, and hastens to make them. Luckily, the seed is already well-sown, and has taken ineradicable root. . .

Political Democracy, as it exists and practically works in America, with all its threatening evils, supplies a training-school for making grand young men. It is life's gymnasium, not of good only, but of all. We try often, though we fall back often. A grave delight, fit for freedom's athletes, fills these arenas, and fully satisfies, out of the action in them, irrespective of success. Whatever we do not attain, we at any rate attain the experiences of the fight, the hardening of the strong campaign, and throb with currents of attempt at least. Time is ample. Let the victors come after us. Not for nothing does evil play its part among men. Judging from the main portions of the history of the world, so far, justice is always in jeopardy, peace walks amid hourly pitfalls, and of slavery, misery, meanness, the craft of tyrants and the credulity of the populace, in some of their protean forms, no voice can at any time say, They are not. The clouds break a little, and the sun shines out—but soon and certain the lowering darkness falls again, as if to last forever. Yet is there an immortal courage and prophecy in every sane soul that cannot, must not, under any circumstances, capitulate. *Vive*, the attack—the perennial assault! *Vive*, the unpopular cause—the spirit that audaciously aims—the never-abandoned efforts, pursued the same amid opposing proofs and precedents. . .

The average man of a land at last only is important. He, in These States, remains immortal owner and boss, deriving good uses, somehow, out of any sort of servant in office, even the basest; because, (certain universal requisites, and their settled regularity and protection, being first secured,) a Nation like ours, in a sort of geological formation state, trying continually new experiments, choosing new delegations, is not served by the best men only, but sometimes more by those that provoke it—by the combats they arouse. Thus national rage, fury, discussion, etc., better than content. Thus, also, the warning signals, invaluable for after times.

What is more dramatic than the spectacle we have seen repeated, and doubtless long shall see—the popular judgment taking the successful candidates on trial in the offices—standing off, as it were, and observing them and their doings for a while, and always giving, finally, the fit, exactly due reward?

I think, after all, the sublimest part of political history, and its culmination, is currently issuing from the American people. I know nothing grander, better exercise, better digestion, more positive proof of the past, the triumphant result of faith in humankind, than a well-contested American national election. . .

As I perceive, the tendencies of our day, in The States, (and I entirely respect them,) are toward those vast and sweeping movements, influences, moral and physical, of humanity, now and always current over the planet, on the scale of the impulses of the elements. Then it is also good to reduce the whole matter to the consideration of a single self, a man, a woman, on permanent grounds. Even for the treatment of the universal, in politics, metaphysics, or anything, sooner or later we come down to one single, solitary Soul.

There is, in sanest hours, a consciousness, a thought that rises, independent, lifted out from all else, calm, like the stars, shining eternal. This is the thought of Identity—yours for you, whoever you are, as mine for me. Miracle of miracles, beyond statement, most spiritual and vaguest of earth's dreams, yet hardest basic fact, and only entrance to all facts. In such devout hours, in the midst of the significant wonders of heaven and earth, (significant only because of the Me in the centre,) creeds, conventions, fall away and become of no account before this simple idea. Under the luminousness of real vision, it alone takes possession, takes value. Like the shadowy dwarf in the fable, once liberated and looked upon, it expands over the whole earth, and spreads to the roof of heaven.

The quality of BEING in the object's self, according to its own central idea and purpose, and of growing therefrom and thereto—not criticism by other standards, and adjustments thereto—is the lesson of Nature. True, the full man wisely gathers, culls, absorbs; but if, engaged disproportionately in that, he slights or overlays the precious idiocrasy and special nativity and intention that he is, the man's self, the main thing, is a failure, however wide his general cultivation. Thus, in our times, refinement and delicatesse are not only attended to sufficiently, but threaten to eat us up, like a cancer. Already, the Democratic genius watches, ill-pleased, these tendencies. Provision for a little healthy rudeness, savage virtue, justification of what one has in one's self, whatever it is, is demanded. Negative qualities, even deficiencies, would be a relief. Singleness and normal simplicity, and separation, amid this more and more complex, more and more artificialized, state of society—how pensively we yearn for them! how we would welcome their return! . . .

SELECTED REFERENCES

Daniel Aaron, *Men of Good Hope*, New York, Oxford University Press, 1951.

Newton Arvin, *Whitman*, New York, Macmillan, 1938.

Richmond C. Beatty, 'Whitman's Political Thought,' *The South Atlantic Quarterly*, January 1947, vol. 46, no. 1, pp. 72–83.

Joseph L. Blau, *Social Theories of Jacksonian Democracy, Representative Writings of the Period 1825–1850*, New York, Hafner, 1947, pp. 128–36.

D. W. Brogan, 'A Plea to America Not To Undersell Itself,' *New York Times Magazine*, 14 November 1948.

Van Wyck Brooks, *The Life of Emerson*, New York, E. P. Dutton, 1932.

———, *The Times of Melville and Whitman*, New York, E. P. Dutton, 1947.

John Jay Chapman, 'Emerson, Sixty Years After,' *The Atlantic Monthly*, February 1897, vol. LXXIX, pp. 222–40.

Avery Craven, 'The 1840's and the Democratic Process,' *Journal of Southern History*, vol. XVI, May 1950, pp. 161–76.

R. W. Emerson, *Lectures and Biographical Sketches*, Cambridge, Riverside Press, 1883. Essay on Thoreau, delivered as a memorial, May 1862, pp. 421–52.

Henry David Gray, *Emerson: A Statement of New England Transcendentalism as Expressed in the Philosophy of Its Chief Exponent*, Stanford, Stanford University Press, 1917.

Joseph Wood Krutch, *Henry David Thoreau*, New York, William Sloane Associates, 1948.

David E. Lilienthal, 'Our Faith Is Mightier Than Our Atom Bomb,' *New York Times Magazine*, 6 March 1949.

F. O. Matthiessen, *American Renaissance: Art and Expression in the Age of Emerson and Whitman*, New York, Oxford University Press, 1941.

Raymer McQuiston, 'The Relation of Ralph Waldo Emerson to Public Affairs,' *Bulletin of the University of Kansas Humanistic Studies*, 15 April 1923, vol. III, no. 1.

Marjory M. Moody, 'The Evolution of Emerson as an Abolitionist,' *American Literature*, March 1945–January 1946, vol. 17, pp. 1–21.

Jerome Nathanson, *Forerunners of Freedom*, American Council on Public Affairs, 1947.

Constance Mayfield Rourke, *Trumpets of Jubilee*, New York, Harcourt, Brace, 1927.

Charles Child Walcutt, 'Thoreau in the Twentieth Century,' *South Atlantic Quarterly*, April 1940, vol. 39, no. 2, pp. 168–84.

XIII

CHATTEL SLAVERY

The chattel slave trade, which first reached American shores at Jamestown, Virginia, in 1619, unloaded with its human cargo a problem as old as mankind. From earliest times, perhaps from that ancient day when man took his first step erect and stumbled upon a fellow-creature less advanced in evolution and yet useful to him, slavery has been a grim fact in the history of nations. The Greeks inherited it from even earlier cultures, and tended to regard the institution as stemming from natural differences. 'Those men therefore who are as much inferior to others as the body is to the soul,' Aristotle wrote in his *Politics*, 'are to be thus disposed of, as the proper use of them is their bodies, in which their excellence consists; and if what I have said be true, they are slaves by nature, and it is advantageous to them to be always under government.'

In America the economic advantage of slave labor was immediately apparent to Southern planters of rice, cotton, and tobacco. These staple crops were in great demand, especially for export abroad. Cotton, particularly after the first stages of the Industrial Revolution, and Eli Whitney's invention of the cotton gin, was needed in increasing amounts to feed the textile mills of England and northern America. Production of these crops (at the expense of soil destruction) required few tools, little equipment, and only primitive techniques easily understood by and enforced upon the slaves. This essential variety of property could be imported, or bred in the slave states, in great numbers at relatively low cost. They were worked long hours at hard labor, and required a minimum of subsistence, amounting to very little besides what they produced for themselves. The Negroes were a form of capital, the value of which rose constantly as the plantation system became more profitable. As the Negroes learned mechanical trades, they could easily be exchanged for all kinds of goods or sold for cash. Finally, slaves made possible the creation of a planter aristocracy, which, freed from the necessity of labor and faithfully tended from the cradle to the grave, could devote itself to varied civic and social pursuits.

The slavery system, however, did not benefit the South as a whole. Slave owners were apt to be poor managers, rash gamblers, and easily cheated by the merchants who dealt with them. Early economists agreed that it did not yield returns proportionate to effort and capital expended, in comparison with the more diversified economy of the North. Too much was left to managers and overseers. Accounting was crude and little understood. The plantation system, by favoring investment of surplus capital only into more land and more slaves, indefinitely delayed the rise of any sufficient Southern industrialism that would bring in a generally higher standard of living. Some argued that under slavery, the South itself must remain in economic peonage, increasingly dependent on Northern and imported manufactures, increasingly specialized in agriculture and practically bound to a ruinous single-crop economy. These analyses were rife at the turn of the eighteenth century, and as late as 1857, H. R. Helper, in his *Impending Crisis in the South*, amassed ladders of figures and statistics to prove that the plantation system must disappear and slavery be abolished if the South were to prosper as fully as its potential resources allowed:

> The causes which have impeded the progress and prosperity of the South, which have dwindled our commerce, and other similar pursuits, into the most contemptible insignificance; sunk a large majority of the people in galling poverty and ignorance; rendered a small minority conceited and tyrannical, and driven the rest away from their homes; entailed upon us a humiliating dependence on the Free States; disgraced us in the recesses of our own souls, and brought us under reproach in the eyes of all civilized and enlightened nations—may be traced to one common source . . . slavery.

The political thought of the time, though less interested in the economics of slavery, reached the same conclusion—that slavery could not and would not adjust itself to the new conditions of American life. Revolutionary figures like Madison, George Mason, Patrick Henry, and Jefferson, their minds rooted in concepts of natural law, saw chattel slavery in sharp conflict with the principles of the Declaration of Independence. Among the charges Jefferson leveled against the King in the original draft of the Declaration was that he had evinced determination 'to keep a market where men should be bought and sold' and 'has at length prostituted his negative for suppressing any legislative attempt to prohibit and restrain this execrable commerce.' 'What a stupendous, what an incomprehensive machine is man!' Jefferson exclaimed later on, 'who can endure toil, famine, stripes, imprisonment, and death itself, in vindication of his own liberty, and, the next moment be deaf to all those motives whose power supported him through his trial, and inflict on his fellow man a bondage, one hour of which is fraught with more misery than ages of that which he rose in rebellion to oppose. . . I tremble for my country when I reflect God is just.' Washington, a more temperate critic, could still avow, 9 September 1786: 'I never mean . . . to possess another slave by purchase, it being my *first wishes* to see some plan adopted by which slavery in this country, may be abolished by law." Washington, Jefferson, and Jackson freed their slaves in the wills that disposed of their estates. The Massachusetts Constitution of 1780 declared that 'all men are born free and equal.' Under this provision Quock Walker, in 1781, won a suit for freedom brought against his master. This ended slavery in the Bay State. New Jersey provided for eventual extinction of slavery by the Bloomfield Act of 1804.

These examples, along with the economic analyses of slavery, had an important influence on the early emancipation societies, which, until the 1830's, were located mainly in the South. By control of several newspapers and constant debate in public forums, these antagonists of American slavery were able to generate a persistent sentiment in favor of abolition. Slave owners were urged to free their slaves for resettlement in Africa. Congress in 1807 banned further importation of Negroes. In 1820, the Missouri Compromise, prohibiting slavery 'forever' in the region north of the parallel 36′30″ (the southern boundary of Missouri), seemed to make more certain the eventual peaceful solution of the problem.

Yet after 1830 the textile trades boomed, especially in England, cotton went to fantastic prices, and the whole slavery question again swelled into high and hot debate. Northern manufacturers, demanding higher tariffs, subsidized railroad building, and internal improvements at public expense for their 'infant industries,' found themselves hindered in successive Congresses dominated by Southern planter interests, especially in the Senate. These same interests succeeded in pushing chattel slavery into the Southwest as the nation expanded, and were largely instrumental in precipitating annexation of Texas and the Mexican War. The 1850's saw the Fugitive Slave Law, which enlisted the forces of the federal government to search out, seize, and return escaped slaves; the Kansas-Nebraska Act, repealing the Missouri Compromise, opening Northern territory in the Western area to slavery; and the Dred Scott case, which shocked the North by insisting that the Negro had no rights under law, and that the Northern states could do nothing about it.

The abolitionist argument, meanwhile, had lost Southern support by taking on the broad refinement of an inclusive social crusade. Its doctrine, based on religion, philosophy, and political theory in fairly equal measure, led gradually to a total indictment of the slavery system. Some abolitionists saw in it a contemptible ethic or immorality handed down from vilest practices of barbarism. Others found it repugnant to the true principles of Christianity. Still others held slavery to be inconsistent with republican government, which, it was pointed out, referring to Jefferson and many other authorities, rested upon the consent of *all*, not merely on that of a male, white majority. As militancy sharpened and hardened among enlightened social thinkers, Abolition became concerned with a host of related humanitarian issues: women's rights, universal suffrage, and the interests of working-men.

Pro-slavery advocates, on the other hand, were united in the faith and obstinacy of traditional conservatism. Property, they argued, was the principal end of government, and the slave as property, as Robert Carter Nicholas was told in the Virginia Revolutionary Convention of 1776, was therefore beyond the scope of abolishing legislation. Compulsory emancipation, it was said, by tyrannically depriving slave-holders of their property, would dissolve the bond that held the states together. As apt at Scripture as the Abolitionists, the slaveholders were able to contend that the Almighty had not made men equal in their natural powers; the Negro slave, they maintained, was not fit to govern himself. 'Curst be Cain; a servant of servants shall he be, a hewer of wood and a drawer of water all the days of his life in the house of the Lord forever.' The

Negro was Cain. Finally, and on this point there was general agreement throughout the slave states, if the Constitution were not to be broken, the problem of slavery could be dealt with only by the states in which it existed. 'I detest it as the political and domestic curse of our Southern country,' one clergyman of emancipationist temper wrote in 1831, 'and yet I would *contend to the death* against Northern interference with Southern rights.' Above the Mason and Dixon line these arguments were widely echoed, especially in the Senate, by 'doughfaces,' as Theodore Parker called Northern men with Southern principles.

The Southern clergyman's sentiments were in part reaction against the fiery exhortations of William Lloyd Garrison (1805–79), self-chosen leader of militant Abolitionists. In Garrison, New England journalist and editor, both ardent supporters and mild critics of slavery had an uncompromising opponent who imparted to Abolition the burning zeal of a religious crusade. A bitter opponent of the Southern slave-holders, who in several states put a price upon his head, he was utterly intolerant of those who advocated temporary expedients or partial solutions. 'Has not the experience of two centuries,' he wrote, 'shown that gradualism in theory is perpetuity in practice? Is there an instance, in the history of the world, where slaves have been educated for freedom by their task-masters?'

The American Anti-Slavery Society, organized by Garrison in 1833, was designed to unite all Abolitionists into a single front. Entrusted with drafting the Society's famous Declaration of Sentiments, Garrison composed this drastic catalogue of slavery's moral indignities in one night at the home of a Negro woman in Philadelphia. For practical measures it urged Congress to prohibit slavery in the territories it controlled, meanwhile calling on 'the people of the free States to remove slavery by moral and political action.'

Garrison's friend, William Ellery Channing (1780–1842), a Unitarian minister, brought to the movement a philosophy distilled from the liberal humanitarian thought of the New England 'Revival.' An admirer of Rousseau and confidant of Emerson, Channing found slavery in bitter contrast to the new idealism. Property in men, he wrote, denies the doctrine of natural rights which all possess, and negates the theory of equality of individuals: 'Justice is a greater good than property, not greater in degree, but in kind.'

Channing's words fitted John C. Calhoun (1782–1851) with uncanny precision. In this Yale graduate of 1804, the 'Marx of the Master Class,' as he has been aptly described, pro-slavery thought found an incomparably lucid political thinker. Twice Vice President of the United States, cabinet member, and long-time Senator from South Carolina, Calhoun became an early exponent of sectional issues. His bitter opposition to economic measures benefiting Northern capitalism, which he saw would inevitably overthrow the plantation system, led him to make an impressive critique of democratic principles. 'No government based on the naked principle that the majority ought to govern,' he wrote in 1828, 'however true the maxim in its proper sense and under proper restrictions, can preserve its liberties even for a single generation.' Andrew Jackson was elected President in 1828 and Calhoun was his Vice President.

Calhoun's doctrine of state nullification was designed to block tariffs and other federal legislation inimical to Southern interests, a later version of the secession idea sponsored by the Hartford Convention of 1815. The *Disquisition on Government*, published after his death, is the mature statement of his political philosophy. In it he, somewhat like Hamilton, maintained that inequality of condition is a necessary consequence of liberty. As society developed, he explained, the tendency would be for property and wealth to be concentrated in the hands of the few, and political power to be vested in the great propertyless majority. Without political collaboration between property-owners—both North and South—government must degenerate into a tyranny of numbers. The main energies of his political life were given to preventing any such eventuality.

George Fitzhugh (1806–81), Southern planter and pamphleteer, a sort of Hitlerite born too soon, put the underlying issues of slavery in terms much more familiar today. Abolition he regarded as a specter, 'a surrender to Socialism and Communism . . . to no private property, no church, no law, to free love, free lands, free women and free children.' His *Cannibals All!* published four years before the Civil War, featured pious respect for all forms of property and simulated concern for the slave's welfare. Negroes, Fitzhugh argued, are better cared for on the plantations than 'free' labor in Northern cities. Talk of liberty and equality is mere cant. No one is free, no one is equal; government rests upon force rather than consent.

Fitzhugh's book brought from Garrison a scathing review in the pages of the *Liberator*. 'Mr. Fitzhugh,' he wrote in a style suggestive of John Adams, 'is the Don Quixote of Slavedom . . . only still more demented than his predecessor. As the latter saw in a harmless windmill a giant of frightful aspect, and lustily assailed it with all the success possible under the circumstances, so the former sees in freedom a terriffic monster which is devouring its millions, and valiantly essays to drive it from the earth. . . He is certainly crack-brained, and deserves pity rather than ridicule or censure.'

Fitzhugh's coadjutor in the pro-slavery argument, William Harper (1790–1847), drafted his 'Memoir on Slavery,' included herein, in 1837, as a refinement of the conservative position. A judge of the South Carolina Court of Chancery, Harper seemed to Southerners especially well qualified to place slavery in the proper perspective of their social life. In his *Memoir*, which Charles A. Beard accepted as 'one of the most important pro-slavery arguments in the history of the controversy,' Harper makes States' Rights central to the structure of his thought and Southern interests paramount. For him slavery marked the progress, not the retrogression, of our civilization. It is the order of nature. The slave is 'born to subjection as he is born in sin and ignorance.' It is as natural that some men should exploit other men 'as that other animals should prey upon each other.' Slaves were wealth, both as property and as creators of capital, and to this extent slavery benefits civilization: 'Property—the accumulation of capital, as it is commonly called—is the first element of civilization.' Thus the whole theory of unalienable rights of the Declaration of Independence became for him a 'sentimental phrase . . . either palpably false' or without precise meaning.

Abraham Lincoln (1809–65), according to his law partner and biographer, William Herndon, read Fitzhugh's book on slavery with distaste and rising indignation. Although he was never an abolitionist (indeed, he did not publicly condemn slavery until 1854), Lincoln revolted at Fitzhugh's caveat that 'Slavery will everywhere be abolished, or everywhere be reinstituted.' Slavery, Lincoln thought, could safely be confined to the states where it existed, restricted from the western territory, neither totally abolished nor totally permitted. Even on the eve of the Civil War, he was not willing to take a more radical stand.

Lincoln's early attitude was determined by the economics of western agrarianism. With each extension of slavery into the west, the free soilers for whom Lincoln spoke saw their homesteads menaced. Cotton became a monster that consumed the land, degraded the labor market, and drove free white farmers out of existence. Although the agrarians had contempt for the Negro as an individual, they came to agree with the abolitionists that slavery spelled pauperism for white and black alike.

Lincoln's speech at Peoria, Illinois, 16 October 1854, was made in reply to Senator Stephen A. Douglas' efforts on behalf of the Kansas-Nebraska Act, which had been passed the preceding May. The Act had sorely split the Democratic party, and Lincoln tried to attract offended Whigs and Democrats to the newly begun Republican party. His strategy was to voice an outspoken opposition to any slavery extension while, at the same time, showing careful understanding of the South's problems. In his speech at Springfield, Illinois, 17 June 1858, and after the Dred Scott decision, he injected a stronger note, took a more advanced position: 'A house divided against itself cannot stand. I believe this government cannot endure permanently half-slave and half-free.' The principles of the Declaration of Independence, he declared, were intended to apply to all men, though not to declare equality 'in all respects.' Equality did not operate in social spheres, Lincoln conceded. Nevertheless, it was basic to a consideration of political and economic rights. It is 'counterfeit logic,' he suggested, in a paragraph still significant, 'to insist that, because I do not want a black woman for a slave I must necessarily want her for a wife. I need not have her for either. I can just leave her alone. In some respects she certainly is not my equal; but in her natural right to eat bread she earns with her own hands without asking leave of any one else, she is my equal, and the equal of all others.'

A Jeffersonian in politics, Lincoln repulsed any theory of racial persecution. Men given equal chances would have equal success whatever their origins. 'I had thought,' he said, addressing conservatives everywhere, 'the Declaration [of Independence] contemplated the progressive improvement in the condition of all men. . .' In essence Lincoln's thought, his conception of democracy was the simple one: 'As I would not be a *slave*, so I would not be a *master*—This expresses my idea of democracy. Whatever differs from this, to the extent of the difference, is no democracy.'

1. *Man cannot hold property in man*

WILLIAM LLOYD GARRISON, *Declaration of Sentiments of the American Anti-Slavery Convention*, 1833 *

More than fifty-seven years have elapsed, since a band of patriots convened in this place, to devise measures for the deliverance of this country from a foreign yoke. The corner-stone upon which they founded the Temple of Freedom was broadly this—'that all men are created equal; that they are endowed by their Creator with certain inalienable rights; that among these are life, LIBERTY, and the pursuit of happiness.' At the sound of their trumpet-call, three millions of people rose up as from the sleep of death, and rushed to the strife of blood; deeming it more glorious to die instantly as freemen, than desirable to live one hour as slaves. They were few in number—poor in resources; but the honest conviction that Truth, Justice and Right were on their side, made them invincible. . .

Their grievances, great as they were, were trifling in comparison with the wrongs and sufferings of those for whom we plead. Our fathers were never slaves—never bought and sold like cattle—never shut out from the light of knowledge and religion—never subjected to the lash of brutal taskmasters.

But those, for whose emancipation we are striving—constituting at the present time at least one-sixth part of our countrymen—are recognized by law, and treated by their fellow-beings, as marketable commodities, as goods and chattels, as brute beasts; are plundered daily of the fruits of their toil without redress; really enjoy no constitutional nor legal protection from licentious and murderous outrages upon their persons; and are ruthlessly torn asunder—the tender babe from the arms of its frantic mother—the heart-broken wife from her weeping husband—at the caprice or pleasure of irresponsible tyrants. For the crime of having a dark complexion, they suffer the pangs of hunger, the infliction of stripes, the ignominy of brutal servitude. They are kept in heathenish darkness by laws expressly enacted to make their instruction a criminal offence.

These are the prominent circumstances in the condition of more than two millions of our people, the proof of which may be found in thousands of indisputable facts, and in the laws of the slaveholding States.

Hence we maintain—that, in view of the civil and religious privileges of this nation, the guilt of its oppression is unequalled by any other on the face of the earth; and, therefore, that it is bound to repent instantly, to undo the heavy burdens, and to let the oppressed go free.

We further maintain—that no man has a right to enslave or imbrute his brother—to hold or acknowledge him, for one moment, as a piece of merchandize—to keep back his hire by fraud—or to brutalize his mind, by denying him the means of intellectual, social and moral improvement.

The right to enjoy liberty is inalienable. To invade it is to usurp the preroga-

* *Selections from the Writings and Speeches of William Lloyd Garrison*, Boston, R. F. Wallcut, 21 Cornhill, 1852, pp. 66–70 *passim.*

tive of Jehovah. Every man has a right to his own body—to the products of his own labor—to the protection of law—and to the common advantages of society. It is piracy to buy or steal a native African, and subject him to servitude. Surely, the sin is as great to enslave an American as an African.

Therefore, we believe and affirm—that there is no difference, in principle, between the African slave trade and American slavery:

That every American citizen, who detains a human being in involuntary bondage as his property, is, according to Scripture (Ex. xxi. 16), a man-stealer:

That the slaves ought instantly to be set free, and brought under the protection of law:

That if they had lived from the time of Pharaoh down to the present period, and had been entailed through successive generations, their right to be free could never have been alienated, but their claims would have constantly risen in solemnity:

That all those laws which are now in force, admitting the right of slavery, are therefore, before God, utterly null and void; being an audacious usurpation of the Divine prerogative, a daring infringement on the law of nature, a base overthrow of the very foundations of the social compact, a complete extinction of all the relations, endearments and obligations of mankind, and a presumptious transgression of all the holy commandments; and that therefore they ought instantly to be abrogated.

We further believe and affirm—that all persons of color, who possess the qualifications which are demanded of others, ought to be admitted forthwith to the enjoyment of the same privileges, and the exercise of the same prerogatives, as others; and that the paths of preferment, of wealth, and of intelligence, should be opened as widely to them as to persons of a white complexion.

We maintain that no compensation should be given to the planters emancipating their slaves:

Because it would be a surrender of the great fundamental principle, that man cannot hold property in man:

Because slavery is a crime, and therefore is not an article to be sold:

Because the holders of slaves are not the just proprietors of what they claim; freeing the slave is not depriving them of property, but restoring it to its rightful owner; it is not wronging the master, but righting the slave—restoring him to himself:

Because immediate and general emancipation would only destroy nominal, not real property; it would not amputate a limb or break a bone of the slaves, but by infusing motives into their breasts, would make them doubly valuable to the masters as free laborers; and

Because, if compensation is to be given at all, it should be given to the outraged and guiltless slaves, and not to those who have plundered and abused them.

We regard as delusive, cruel and dangerous, any scheme of expatriation which pretends to aid, either directly or indirectly, in the emancipation of the slaves, or to be a substitute for the immediate and total abolition of slavery.

We fully and unanimously recognise the sovereignty of each State, to legislate exclusively on the subject of the slavery which is tolerated within its limits; we concede that Congress, under the present national compact, has no right to interfere with any of the slave States, in relation to this momentous subject:

But we maintain that Congress has a right, and is solemnly bound, to suppress the domestic slave trade between the several States, and to abolish slavery in those portions of our territory which the Constitution has placed under its exclusive jurisdiction.

We also maintain that there are, at the present time, the highest obligations resting upon the people of the free States to remove slavery by moral and political action, as prescribed in the Constitution of the United States. They are now living under a pledge of their tremendous physical force, to fasten the galling fetters of tyranny upon the limbs of millions in the Southern States; they are liable to be called at any moment to suppress a general insurrection of the slaves; they authorize the slave owner to vote for three-fifths of his slaves as property, and thus enable him to perpetuate his oppression; they support a standing army at the South for its protection; and they seize the slave, who has escaped into their territories, and send him back to be tortured by an enraged master or a brutal driver. This relation to slavery is criminal, and full of danger: IT MUST BE BROKEN UP.

These are our views and principles—these our designs and measures. With entire confidence in the overruling justice of God, we plant ourselves upon the Declaration of our Independence and the truths of Divine Revelation, as upon the Everlasting Rock.

2. *The liberties of a people ought to tremble until every man is free*

WILLIAM ELLERY CHANNING, *Slavery*, 1841 *

The slave-holder claims the slave as his Property. The very idea of a slave is, that he belongs to another, that he is bound to live and labor for another, to be another's instrument, and to make another's will his habitual law, however adverse to his own. Another owns him, and, of course, has a right to his time and strength, a right to the fruits of his labor, a right to task him without his consent, and to determine the kind and duration of his toil, a right to confine him to any bounds, a right to extort the required work by stripes, a right, in a word, to use him as a tool, without contract, against his will, and in denial of his right to dispose of himself, or to use his power for his own good. 'A slave,' says the Louisiana code, 'is in the power of the master to whom he belongs. The master may sell him, dispose of his person, his industry, his labor; he can do nothing, possess nothing, nor acquire any thing, but which must belong to his master.' 'Slaves shall be deemed, taken, reputed, and adjudged,' says the South Carolina laws, 'to be chattels personal in the hands of their

* *Works of William E. Channing*, Boston, American Unitarian Association, 1871, vol. II, *passim*.

masters, and possessions to all intents and purposes whatsoever.' Such is slavery, a claim to man as property.

Now this claim of property in a human being is altogether false, groundless. No such right of man in man can exist. A human being cannot be justly owned. To hold and treat him as property is to inflict a great wrong, to incur the guilt of oppression. . .

I will endeavor, however, to illustrate the truth which I have stated.

1. It is plain, that, if one man may be held as property, then every other man may be so held. If there be nothing in human nature, in our common nature, which excludes and forbids the conversion of him who possesses it into an article of property; if the right of the free to liberty is founded, not on their essential attributes as rational and moral beings, but on certain adventitious, accidental circumstances, into which they have been thrown; then every human being, by a change of circumstances, may justly be held and treated by another as property. If one man may be rightfully reduced to slavery, then there is not a human being on whom the same chain may not be imposed. . . This deep assurance, that we cannot be rightfully made another's property, does not rest on the hue of our skins, or the place of our birth, or our strength, or wealth. These things do not enter our thoughts. The consciousness of indestructible rights is a part of our moral being. The consciousness of our humanity involves the persuasion, that we cannot be owned as a tree or a brute. As men, we cannot justly be made slaves. Then no man can be rightfully enslaved. . .

2. A man cannot be seized and held as property, because he has *Rights*. What these rights are, whether few or many, or whether all men have the same, are questions for future discussion. All that is assumed now is, that every human being has *some* rights. This truth cannot be denied, but by denying to a portion of the race that moral nature which is the sure and only foundation of rights. This truth has never, I believe, been disputed. It is even recognized in the very codes of slave legislation, which, while they strip a man of liberty, affirm his right to life, and threaten his murderer with punishment. Now, I say, a being having rights cannot justly be made property; for this claim over him virtually annuls all his rights. It strips him of all power to assert them. It makes it a crime to assert them. The very essence of slavery is, to put a man defenceless into the hands of another. The right claimed by the master, to task, to force, to imprison, to whip, and to punish the slave, at discretion, and especially to prevent the least resistance to his will, is a virtual denial and subversion of all the rights of the victim of his power. The two cannot stand together. Can we doubt which of them ought to fall?

3. Another argument against property is to be found in the Essential Equality of men. I know that this doctrine, so venerable in the eyes of our fathers, has lately been denied. Verbal logicians, have told us that men are 'born equal' only in the sense of being equally born. They have asked whether all are equally tall, strong, or beautiful; or whether nature, Procrustes-like, reduces all her children to one standard of intellect and virtue. By such arguments it is attempted to set aside the principle of equality, on which the soundest moralists have reared the structure of social duty; and in these ways

the old foundations of despotic power, which our fathers in their simplicity thought they had subverted, are laid again by their sons.

It is freely granted, that there are innumerable diversities among men; but be it remembered, they are ordained to bind men together, and not to subdue one to the other; ordained to give means and occasions of mutual aid, and to carry forward each and all, so that the good of all is equally intended in this distribution of various gifts. Be it also remembered, that these diversities among men are as nothing in comparison with the attributes in which they agree; and it is this which constitutes their essential equality. All men have the same rational nature and the same power of conscience, and all are equally made for indefinite improvement of these divine faculties, and for the happiness to be found in their virtuous use. . . Let it be added, that the natural advantages, which distinguish one man from another, are so bestowed as to counterbalance one another, and bestowed without regard to rank or condition in life. Whoever surpasses in one endowment is inferior in others. Even genius, the greatest gift, is found in union with strange infirmities, and often places its possessors below ordinary men in the conduct of life. Great learning is often put to shame by the mother-wit and keen good sense of uneducated men. Nature, indeed, pays no heed to birth or condition in bestowing her favors. The noblest spirits sometimes grow up in the obscurest spheres. Thus equal are men; and among these equals, who can substantiate his claim to make others his property, his tools, the mere instruments of his private interest and gratification? . . .

4. That a human being cannot be justly held and used as property, is apparent from the very nature of property. Property is an exclusive right. It shuts out all claim but that of the possessor. What one man owns, cannot belong to another. What then, is the consequence of holding a human being as property? Plainly this. He can have no right to himself. His limbs are, in truth, not morally his own. He has not a right to his own strength. It belongs to another. His will, intellect, and muscles, all the powers of body and mind which are exercised in labor, he is bound to regard as another's. Now, if there be property in any thing, it is that of a man in his own person, mind, and strength. All other rights are weak, unmeaning, compared with this, and, in denying this, all right is denied. It is true, that an individual may forfeit by crime his right to the use of his limbs, perhaps to his limbs, and even to life. But the very idea of forfeiture implies, that the right was originally possessed. It is true, that a man may by contract give to another a limited right to his strength. But he gives only because he possesses it, and gives it for considerations which he deems beneficial to himself; and the right conferred ceases at once on violation of the conditions on which it was bestowed. To deny the right of a human being to himself, to his own limbs and faculties, to his energy of body and mind, is an absurdity too gross to be confuted by any thing but a simple statement. Yet this absurdity is involved in the idea of his belonging to another. . .

6. Another argument against the right of property in man, may be drawn from a very obvious principle of moral science. It is a plain truth, universally received, that every right supposes or involves a corresponding obligation. If,

then, a man has a right to another's person or powers, the latter is under obligation to give himself up as a chattel to the former. This is his duty. He is bound to be a slave, and bound not merely by the Christian law, which enjoins submission to injury, not merely by prudential considerations, or by the claims of public order and peace; but bound because another has a right of ownership, has a moral claim to him, so that he would be guilty of dishonesty, of robbery, in withdrawing himself from this other's service. It is his duty to work for his master, though all compulsion were withdrawn; and in deserting him he would commit the crime of taking away another man's property, as truly as if he were to carry off his owner's purse. Now do we not instantly feel, can we help feeling, that this is false? Is the slave thus morally bound? When the African was first brought to these shores, would he have violated a solemn obligation by slipping his chain, and flying back to his native home? Would he not have been bound to seize the precious opportunity of escape? Is the slave under a moral obligation to confine himself, his wife, and children, to a spot where their union in a moment may be forcibly dissolved? Ought he not, if he can, to place himself and his family under the guardianship of equal laws? Should we blame him for leaving his yoke? Do we not feel, that, in the same condition, a sense of duty would quicken our flying steps? Where, then, is the obligation which would necessarily be imposed, if the right existed which the master claims? The absence of obligation proves the want of the right. The claim is groundless. It is a cruel wrong.

7. I come now to what is to my own mind the great argument against seizing and using a man as property. He cannot be property in the sight of God and justice, because he is a Rational, Moral, Immortal Being; because created in God's image, and therefore in the highest sense his child; because created to unfold godlike faculties, and to govern himself by a Divine Law written on his heart, and republished in God's Word. His whole nature forbids that he should be seized as property. From his very nature it follows, that so to seize him is to offer an insult to his Maker, and to inflict aggravated social wrong. Into every human being God has breathed an immortal spirit, more precious than the whole outward creation. No earthly or celestial language can exaggerate the worth of a human being. No matter how obscure his condition. Thought, Reason, Conscience, the capacity of Virtue, the capacity of Christian Love, an immortal Destiny, an intimate moral connection with God —here are attributes of our common humanity which reduce to insignificance all outward distinctions, and make every human being unspeakably dear to his Maker. No matter how ignorant he may be. The capacity of Improvement allies him to the more instructed of his race, and places within his reach the knowledge and happiness of higher worlds. Every human being has in him the germ of the greatest idea in the universe, the idea of God; and to unfold this is the end of his existence. Every human being has in his breast the elements of that Divine, Everlasting Law, which the highest orders of the creation obey. . . Every human being has affections, which may be purified and expanded into a Sublime Love. He has, too, the idea of Happiness, and a thirst for it which cannot be appeased. Such is our nature. Wherever we see a man, we see the possessor of these great capacities. Did God make such a

being to be owned as a tree or a brute? How plainly was he made to exercise, unfold, improve his highest powers, made for a moral, spiritual good! and how is he wronged, and his Creator opposed, when he is forced and broken into a tool to another's physical enjoyment!

Such a being was plainly made for an End in Himself. He is a Person, not a Thing. He is an End, not a mere Instrument or Means. . .

Having considered the great fundamental right of human nature, particular rights may easily be deduced. Every man has a right to exercise and invigorate his intellect or the power of knowledge, for knowledge is the essential condition of successful effort for every good; and whoever obstructs or quenches the intellectual life in another, inflicts a grievous and irreparable wrong. Every man has a right to inquire into his duty, and to conform himself to what he learns of it. Every man has a right to use the means, given by God and sanctioned by virtue, for bettering his condition. He has a right to be respected according to his moral worth; a right to be regarded as a member of the community to which he belongs, and to be protected by impartial laws; and a right to be exempted from coercion, stripes, and punishment, as long as he respects the rights of others. He has a right to an equivalent for his labor. He has a right to sustain domestic relations, to discharge their duties, and to enjoy the happiness which flows from fidelity in these and other domestic relations. Such are a few of human rights; and if so, what a grievous wrong is slavery! . . .

I cannot leave the subject of the evils of slavery without saying a word of its Political influence. Under this head, I shall not engage in discussions which belong to the economists. I shall not repeat, what has been often proved, that slave-labor is less productive than free. . . I wish only to speak of the influence of slavery on Free Institutions. This influence, we are gravely told, is favorable, and therefore I am bound to give it a brief notice. Political liberty is said to find strength and security in domestic servitude. Strange mode, indeed, of ensuring freedom to ourselves, to violate it in the persons of others! Among the new lights of the age, the most wonderful discovery is, that to spoil others of their rights is the way to assert the sacredness of our own. . .

But the great argument in favor of the political benefits of slavery, remains to be stated. In plain language it amounts to this, that slavery excludes the laboring or poorer classes from the elective franchise, from political powers; and it is the turbulence of these classes which is supposed to constitute the chief peril of liberty. . . Whoever knows the state of society in the Free States, can testify, that the love of liberty, pride in our free institutions, and jealousy of rights, are nowhere more active than in those very classes which in a slave-holding country are reduced to servitude. Undoubtedly the jealousies, passions, and prejudices of the laboring portion of the community may work evil, and even ruin to the state; and so may the luxury, the political venality, the gambling spirit of trade, and the cupidity, to be found in other ranks or conditions. If freedom must be denied wherever it will be endangered, then every class in society must be reduced to slavery.

Free institutions rest on two great political virtues, the love of liberty and the love of order. The slave-holder (I mean the slave-holder by choice) is of necessity more or less wanting in both. How plain is it, that no man can love liberty with a true love, who has the heart to wrest it from others! Attachment to freedom does not consist in spurning indignantly a yoke prepared for our own necks; for this is done even by the savage and the beast of prey. It is a moral sentiment, an impartial desire and choice, that others as well as ourselves may be protected from every wrong, may be exempted from every unjust restraint. . .

Slave-holding in a republic tends directly to lawlessness. It gives the habit of command, not of obedience. The absolute master is not likely to distinguish himself by subjection to the civil power. The substitution of passion and self-will for law, is nowhere so common as in the Slave-holding States. In these it is thought honorable to rely on one's own arm, rather than on the magistrate, for the defence of many rights. . .

Slavery is a strange element to mix with free institutions. It cannot but endanger them. It is a pattern for every kind of wrong. The slave brings insecurity on the free. Whoever holds one human being in bondage, invites others to plant the foot on his own neck. Thanks to God, not one human being can be wronged with impunity. The liberties of a people ought to tremble until every man is free. Tremble they will. Their true foundation is sapped by the legalized degradation of a single innocent man to slavery. That foundation is impartial justice, is respect for human nature, is respect for the rights of every human being. . .

A republican government, bought by the sacrifice of half or more than half of a people, by stripping them of their most sacred rights, by degrading them to a brutal condition, would cost too much. A freedom so tainted with wrong ought to be our abhorrence. They, who tell us that slavery is a necessary condition of a republic, do not justify the former, but pronounce a sentence of reprobation on the latter. If they speak truth, we are bound as a people to seek more just and generous institutions, under which the rights of all will be secure. . .

3. *The greatest truths are often the most unpopular and exasperating*

WILLIAM ELLERY CHANNING, *Tribute to the American Abolitionists*, 1836 *

It is not my purpose to speak of the Abolitionists as Abolitionists. They now stand before the world in another character, and to this I shall give my present attention. . . Had the Abolitionists been left to pursue their object with the freedom which is guaranteed to them by our civil institutions; had they been resisted only by those weapons of reason, rebuke, reprobation, which the laws allow, I should have no inducement to speak of them again, either in praise or censure. But the violence of their adversaries has driven them to a new

* *Tribute of William Ellery Channing to the American Abolitionists for Their Vindication of Freedom of Speech*, New York, The American Anti-Slavery Society, 1861, pp. 3–24 *passim*.

position. Abolitionism forms an era in our history, if we consider the means by which it has been opposed. Deliberate, systematic efforts have been made, not here, or there, but far and wide, to wrest from its adherents that liberty of speech and the press, which our fathers asserted unto blood, and which our National and State Governments are pledged to protect as our most sacred right. . . The Abolitionists, then, not only appear in the character of the champions of the colored race. In their persons, the most sacred rights of the white man and the free man have been assailed. They are sufferers for the liberty of thought, speech and the press; and, in maintaining this liberty amid insult and violence, they deserve a place among its most honorable defenders. In this character I shall now speak of them.

In regard to the methods adopted by the Abolitionists of promoting emancipation, I might find much to censure; but when I regard their firm, fearless assertion of the rights of free discussion, of speech and the press, I look on them with unmixed respect. I see nothing to blame, and much to admire. To them has been committed the most important bulwark of liberty, and they have acquitted themselves of the trust like men and Christians. No violence has driven them from their post. Whilst, in obedience to conscience, they have refrained from opposing force to force, they have still persevered amidst menace and insult, in bearing their testimony against wrong, in giving utterance to their deep convictions. Of such men, I do not hesitate to say, that they have rendered to freedom a more essential service than any body of men among us. The defenders of freedom are not those who claim and exercise rights which no one assails, or who win shouts of applause by well-turned compliments to liberty in the days of her triumph. They are those who stand up for rights which mobs, conspiracies, or single tyrants put in jeopardy; who contend for liberty in that particular form which is threatened at the moment by the many or the few. To the Abolitionists this honor belongs. The first systematic effort to strip the citizen of freedom of speech, they have met with invincible resolution. From my heart I thank them. I am myself their debtor. I am not sure that I should this moment write in safety, had they shrunk from the conflict, had they shut their lips, imposed silence on their presses, and hid themselves before their ferocious assailants. I know not where these outrages would have stopped, had they not met resistance from their first destined victims. The newspaper press, with a few exceptions, uttered no genuine indignant rebuke of the wrong-doers, but rather countenanced, by its gentle censures, the reign of Force. The mass of the people looked supinely on this new tryanny, under which a portion of their fellow-citizens seemed to be sinking. . . I thank the Abolitionists that, in this evil day, they were true to the rights which the multitude were ready to betray. Their purpose to suffer, to die, rather than surrender their dearest liberties, taught the lawless that they had a foe to contend with, whom it was not safe to press, whilst, like all manly appeals, it called forth reflection and sympathy in the better portion of the community. In the name of freedom and humanity, I thank them. Through their courage, the violence, which might have furnished a precedent fatal to freedom, is to become, I trust, a warning to the lawless of the folly as well as crime of attempting to crush opinion by force.

Of all powers, the last to be intrusted to the multitude of men is that of determining what questions shall be discussed. The greatest truths are often the most unpopular and exasperating; and were they to be denied discussion, till the many should be ready to accept them, they would never establish themselves in the general mind. The progress of society depends on nothing more than on the exposure of time-sanctioned abuses, which cannot be touched without offending multitudes, than on the promulgation of principles, which are in advance of public sentiment and practice, and which are consequently at war with the habits, prejudices, and immediate interests of large classes of the community. Of consequence, the multitude, if once allowed to dictate or proscribe subjects of discussion, would strike society with spiritual blindness and death. The world is to be carried forward by truth, which at first offends, which wins its way by degrees, which the many hate, and would rejoice to crush. The right of free discussions is, therefore, to be guarded by the friends of mankind with peculiar jealousy. It is at once the most sacred and most endangered of all our rights. He who would rob his neighbor of it should have a mark set on him as the worst enemy of freedom. . .

How strange, in a free country, that the men from whom the liberty of speech is to be torn, are those who use it in pleading for freedom, who devote themselves to the vindication of human rights! What a spectacle is presented to the world by a republic, in which sentence of proscription is passed on citizens who labor, by addressing men's consciences, to enforce the truth, that slavery is the greatest of wrongs! Through the civilized world, the best and greatest men are bearing joint witness against slavery. Christians of all denominations and conditions, rich and poor, learned and ignorant, are bound in a holy league against this most degrading form of oppression. But in free America, the language which despots tolerate must not be heard. One would think that freemen might be pardoned, if the view of fellow-creatures stripped of all human rights should move them to vehemence of speech. But whilst, on all other subjects, the deeply-stirred feelings may overflow in earnest remonstrance, on slavery, the freeman must speak in whispers, or pay the penalty of persecution for the natural utterance of strong emotion. . .

Allow me to say a few words on a topic which has given me many painful thoughts, the more painful, because so few have seemed to share my feelings. I refer to that gross outrage on rights and liberty, the burning of the Hall of Freedom in Philadelphia. I have felt this the more, because this Hall was erected for free discussion, was dedicated to Liberty of Speech. Undoubtedly, it was especially designed to give the Abolitionists a chance of being heard; but it was also intended to give the same privilege to others, who, in consequence of having adopted unpopular opinions, might be excluded from the places commonly devoted to public meetings. This building was associated with the dearest right of an intelligent, spiritual being, that of communicating thought, and receiving such communication in return—more intimately associated with it than any other edifice in the country. And this was stormed by a mob; a peaceful assemblage was driven from its walls; and afterwards it was levelled to the earth by fire. . .

This outrage against the Abolitionists made little impression on the country at large. It was pronounced wrong, of course; but, then, we were told that the Abolitionists were so imprudent, so fierce, so given to denunciation, so intolerant towards all who differ from them, that they had no great claim to sympathy! Everywhere the excesses of the Abolitionists are used to palliate the persecution which they suffer. But are they the only intolerant people in the country? Is there a single political party, which does not deal as freely in denunciation? Is there a religious sect, which has not its measure of bitterness? I ask, as before, if fierce denunciation is to be visited with flames, where will the conflagration stop? . . .

There are many whose testimony against slavery is very much diluted by the fact of its having been so long sanctioned, not only by usage, but by law, by public force, by the forms of civil authority. They bow before numbers and prescription. But in an age of inquiry and innovation, (when other institutions must make good their title to continuance,) it is a suspicious tenderness which fears to touch a heavy yoke, because it has grown by time into the necks of our fellow-creatures. . .

What is more common among ourselves than a courteous, apologetic disapprobation of slavery, which differs little from taking its part? This is one of its worst influences. It taints the whole country. The existence, the perpetual presence of a great, prosperous, unrestrained system of wrong in a community, is one of the sorest trials to the moral sense of the people, and needs to be earnestly withstood. . . The dead know not their want of life; and so a people, whose moral sentiments are palsied by the interweaving of all their interests with a system of oppression, become degraded without suspecting it. In consequence of this connection with slave countries, the idea of Human Rights, that great idea of our age, and on which we profess to build our institutions, is darkened, weakened, among us, so as to be to many little more than a sound.

4. *Inequality of condition is a necessary consequence of liberty*

JOHN C. CALHOUN, *Disquisition on Government*, 1850 *

. . . To perfect society, it is necessary to develop the faculties, intellectual and moral, with which man is endowed. But the main spring to their development, and, through this, to progress, improvement and civilization, with all their blessings, is the desire of individuals to better their condition. For, this purpose, liberty and security are indispensable. Liberty leaves each free to pursue the course he may deem best to promote his interest and happiness as far as it may be compatible with the primary end for which goverment is ordained;—while security gives assurance to each, that he shall not be deprived of the fruits of his exertions to better his condition. These combined, give to this desire the strongest impulse of which it is susceptible. For, to extend

* *The Works of John C. Calhoun*, Richard K. Crallé, ed., New York, D. Appleton and Co., 1853–55, vol. 1, pp. 52–9 *passim*.

liberty beyond the limits assigned, would be to weaken the government and to render it incompetent to fulfil its primary end,—the protection of society against dangers, internal and external. The effect of this would be, insecurity; and, of insecurity—to weaken the impulse of individuals to better their condition, and thereby retard progress and improvement. On the other hand, to extend the powers of the government, so as to contract the sphere assigned to liberty, would have the same effect, by disabling individuals in their efforts to better their condition.

Herein is to be found the principle which assigns to power and liberty their proper spheres, and reconciles each to the other under all circumstances. For, if power be necessary to secure to liberty the fruits of its exertions, liberty, in turn, repays power with interest, by increased population, wealth, and other advantages, which progress and improvement bestow on the community. By thus assigning to each its appropriate sphere, all conflicts between them cease; and each is made to co-operate with and assist the other, in fulfilling the great ends for which government is ordained.

But the principle, applied to different communities, will assign to them different limits. It will assign a larger sphere to power and a more contracted one to liberty, or the reverse, according to circumstances. To the former, there must ever be allotted, under all circumstances, a sphere sufficiently large to protect the community against danger from without and violence and anarchy within. The residuum belongs to liberty. More cannot be safely or rightly allotted to it. . .

The principle, in all communities, according to these numerous and various causes, assigns to power and liberty their proper spheres. To allow to liberty, in any case, a sphere of action more extended than this assigns, would lead to anarchy; and this, probably, in the end, to a contraction instead of an enlargement of its sphere. Liberty, then, when forced on a people unfit for it, would, instead of a blessing, be a curse; as it would, in its reaction, lead directly to anarchy,—the greatest of all curses. No people, indeed, can long enjoy more liberty than that to which their situation and advanced intelligence and morals fairly entitle them. If more than this be allowed, they must soon fall into confusion and disorder,—to be followed, if not by anarchy and despotism, by a change to a form of government more simple and absolute; and, therefore, better suited to their condition. . .

It follows, from what has been stated, that it is a great and dangerous error to suppose that all people are equally entitled to liberty. It is a reward to be earned, not a blessing to be gratuitously lavished on all alike;—a reward reserved for the intelligent, the patriotic, the virtuous and deserving;—and not a boon to be bestowed on a people too ignorant, degraded and vicious, to be capable either of appreciating or of enjoying it. Nor is it any disparagement to liberty, that such is, and ought to be the case. On the contrary, its greatest praise,—its proudest distinction is, that an all-wise Providence has reserved it, as the noblest and highest reward for the development of our faculties, moral and intellectual. A reward more appropriate than liberty could not be conferred on the deserving;—nor a punishment inflicted on the undeserving more just, than to be subject to lawless and despotic rule. . .

There is another error, not less great and dangerous, usually associated with the one which has just been considered. I refer to the opinion, that liberty and equality are so intimately united, that liberty cannot be perfect without perfect equality.

That they are united to a certain extent,—and that equality of citizens, in the eyes of the law, is essential to liberty in a popular government, is conceded. But to go further, and make equality of *condition* essential to liberty, would be to destroy both liberty and progress. The reason is, that inequality of condition, while it is a necessary consequence of liberty, is, at the same time, indispensable to progress. In order to understand why this is so, it is necessary to bear in mind, that the main spring to progress is, the desire of individuals to better their condition; and that the strongest impulse which can be given to it is, to leave individuals free to exert themselves in the manner they may deem best for that purpose, as far at least as it can be done consistently with the ends for which government is ordained,—and to secure to all the fruits of their exertions. Now, as individuals differ greatly from each other, in intelligence, sagacity, energy, perseverance, skill, habits of industry and economy, physical power, position and opportunity,—the necessary effect of leaving all free to exert themselves to better their condition, must be a corresponding inequality between those who may possess these qualities and advantages in a high degree, and those who may be deficient in them. The only means by which this result can be prevented are, either to impose such restrictions on the exertions of those who may possess them in a high degree, as will place them on a level with those who do not; or to deprive them of the fruits of their exertions. But to impose such restrictions on them would be destructive of liberty,—while, to deprive them of the fruits of their exertions, would be to destroy the desire of bettering their condition. It is, indeed, this inequality of condition between the front and rear ranks, in the march of progress which gives so strong an impulse to the former to maintain their position, and to the latter to press forward into their files. This gives to progress its greatest impulse. To force the front rank back to the rear, or attempt to push forward the rear into line with the front, by the interposition of the government, would put an end to the impulse, and effectually arrest the march of progress.

These great and dangerous errors have their origin in the prevalent opinion that all men are born free and equal;—than which nothing can be more unfounded and false. It rests upon the assumption of a fact, which is contrary to universal observation, in whatever light it may be regarded. It is, indeed, difficult to explain how an opinion so destitute of all sound reason, ever could have been so extensively entertained, unless we regard it as being confounded with another, which has some semblance of truth;—but which, when properly understood, is not less false and dangerous. I refer to the assertion, that all men are equal in the state of nature; meaning, by a state of nature, a state of individuality, supposed to have existed prior to the social and political state; and in which men lived apart and independent of each other. If such a state ever did exist, all men would have been, indeed, free and equal in it; that is, free to do as they pleased, and exempt from the authority or control of others —as, by supposition, it existed anterior to society and government. But such a state is purely hypothetical. It never did, nor can exist; as it is inconsistent with the preservation and perpetuation of the race. It is, therefore, a great misnomer to call it *the state of nature*. Instead of being the natural state of man, it is, of all conceivable states, the most opposed to his nature—most repugnant to his feelings, and most incompatible with his wants. His natural state is, the social and political—the one for which his Creator made him, and the only one in which he can preserve and perfect his race. As, then, there never was such a state as the, so called, state of nature, and never can be, it follows, that men, instead of being born in it, are born in the social and political state; and of course, instead of being born free and equal, are born subject, not only to parental authority, but to the laws and institutions of the country where born, and under whose protection they draw their first breath. . .

5. *The Negro slaves of the South are the freest people in the world*

GEORGE FITZHUGH, *Cannibals All!* 1856 *

We are, all, North and South, engaged in the White Slave Trade, and he who succeeds best, is esteemed most respectable. It is far more cruel than the Black Slave Trade, because it exacts more of its slaves, and neither protects nor governs them. . . But we not only boast that the White Slave Trade is more exacting and fraudulent (in fact, though not in intention,) than Black Slavery; but we also boast, that it is more cruel, in leaving the laborer to take care of himself and family out of the pittance which skill or capital have allowed him to retain. When the day's labor is ended, he is free, but is overburdened with the cares of family and household, which make his freedom an empty and delusive mockery. But his employer is really free, and may enjoy the profits made by others' labor, without a care, or a trouble, as to their well-being. The Negro slave is free, too, when the labors of the day are over, and free in mind as well as body; for the master provides food, raiment, house, fuel, and everything else necessary to the physical well-being of himself and family. The master's labors commence just when the slave's end. No wonder men should prefer white slavery to capital, to Negro slavery, since it is more profitable, and is free from all the cares and labors of black slave-holding.

Now, reader, if you wish to know yourself—to 'descant on your own deformity'—read on. But if you would cherish self-conceit, self-esteem, or self-appreciation, throw down our book; for we will dispel illusions which have promoted your happiness, and shew you that what you have considered and practiced as virtue, is little better than moral Cannibalism. But you will find yourself in numerous and respectable company; for all good and respectable people are 'Cannibals all," who do not labor, or who are successfully trying to live without labor, on the unrequited labor of other people. . .

But, reader, we do not wish to fire into the flock. 'Thou art the man!' You

* Richmond, Virginia, A. Morris, Publisher, 1857, pp. 25–361 *passim*.

are a Cannibal! and if a successful one, pride yourself on the number of your victims, quite as much as any Feejee chieftain, who breakfasts, dines and sups on human flesh.—And your conscience smites you, if you have failed to succeed, quite as much as his, when he returns from an unsuccessful foray.

Probably, you are a lawyer, or a merchant, or a doctor, who have made by your business fifty thousand dollars, and retired to live on your capital. But, mark! not to spend your capital. That would be vulgar, disreputable, criminal. That would be, to live by your own labor; for your capital is your amassed labor. That would be, to do as common working men do; for they take the pittance which their employers leave them, to live on. They live by labor; for they exchange the results of their own labor for the products of other people's labor. It is, no doubt, an honest, vulgar way of living; but not at all a respectable way. The respectable way of living is, to make other people work for you, and to pay them nothing for so doing—and to have no concern about them after their work is done. Hence, white slave-holding is much more respectable than Negro slavery—for the master works nearly as hard for the Negro, as he for the master. But you, my virtuous, respectable reader, exact three thousand dollars per annum from white labor, (for your income is the product of white labor,) and make not one cent of return in any form. You retain your capital, and never labor, and yet live in luxury on the labor of others. Capital commands labor, as the master does the slave. Neither pays for labor; but the master permits the slave to retain a larger allowance from the proceeds of his own labor, and hence 'free labor is cheaper than slave labor.' You, with the command over labor which your capital gives you, are a slave owner—a master, without the obligations of a master. They who work for you, who create your income, are slaves, without the rights of slaves. Slaves without a master! Whilst you were engaged in amassing your capital, in seeking to become independent, you were in the White Slave Trade. To become independent, is to be able to make other people support you, without being obliged to labor for *them*. Now, what man in society is not seeking to attain this situation? He who attains it, is a slave owner, in the worst sense. He who is in pursuit of it, is engaged in the slave trade. You, reader, belong to the one or other class. The men without property, in free society, are theoretically in a worse condition than slaves. Practically, their condition corresponds with this theory, as history and statistics every where demonstrate. The capitalists, in free society, live in ten times the luxury and show that Southern masters do, because the slaves to capital work harder and cost less, than negro slaves.

The Negro slaves of the South are the happiest, and, in some sense, the freest people in the world. The children and the aged and infirm work not at all, and yet have all the comforts and necessaries of life provided for them. They enjoy liberty, because they are oppressed neither by care nor labor. The women do little hard work, and are protected from the despotism of their husbands by their masters. The Negro men and stout boys work, on the average, in good weather, not more than nine hours a day. The balance of their time is spent in perfect abandon. Besides, they have their Sabbaths and holidays. White men, with so much of license and liberty, would die of ennui; but Negroes luxuriate in corporeal and mental repose. With their faces upturned to the sun, they can sleep at any hour; and quiet sleep is the greatest of human enjoyments. . .

Free laborers have not a thousandth part of the rights and liberties of negro slaves. Indeed, they have not a single right or a single liberty, unless it be the right or liberty to die. But the reader may think that he and other capitalists and employers are freer than negro slaves. Your capital would soon vanish, if you dared indulge in the liberty and abandon of Negroes. You hold your wealth and position by the tenure of constant watchfulness, care and circumspection. You never labor; but you are never free.

Where a few own the soil, they have unlimited power over the balance of society, until domestic slavery comes in, to compel them to permit this balance of society to draw a sufficient and comfortable living from 'terra mater.' Free society, asserts the right of a few to the earth—slavery, maintains that it belongs, in different degrees, to all. . .

'Property in man' is what all are struggling to obtain. Why should they not be obliged to take care of man, their property, as they do of their horses and their hounds, their cattle and their sheep. Now, under the delusive name of liberty, you work him, 'from morn to dewy eve'—from infancy to old age—then turn him out to starve. You treat your horses and hounds better. Capital is a cruel master. The free slave trade, the commonest, yet the cruelest of trades. . .

PRIVATE PROPERTY DESTROYS LIBERTY AND EQUALITY

The Abolitionists and Socialists, who, alone, have explored the recesses of social science, well understand that they can never establish their Utopia until private property is abolished or equalized. The man without property is theoretically and, too often, practically, without a single right. Air and water, 'tis generally believed, are the common property of mankind; but nothing is falser in fact as well as theory. The ownership of land gives to the proprietor the exclusive right to everything above and beneath the soil. The lands are all appropriated, and with them the air above them, the waters on them, and the mines beneath them. The pauper, to breathe the air or drink the waters, must first find a place where he may rightfully enjoy them. He can find, at all times, no such place, and is compelled, by his necessities, to inhale the close and putrid air of small rooms, damp cellars and crowded factories, and to drink insufficient quantities of impure water, furnished to him at a price he can ill afford. He pays for the water which he drinks, because it has ceased to be common property. He is not free, because he has no where that he may rightfully lay his head. Private property has monopolized the earth, and destroyed both his liberty and equality. He has no security for his life, for he cannot live without employment and adequate wages, and none are [sic] bound to employ him. If the earth were in common, he could always enjoy not only air and water, but by his industry might earn the means of subsistence. His situation is theoretically and practically desperate and intolerable. Were he a slave, he would enjoy in fact as well as in legal fiction, all necessary and essential rights. Pure air and water, a house, sufficient food, fire, and clothing, would be his at all times. Slavery is a form of communism, and as the Abolitionists and Socialists have resolved to adopt a new social system, we recommend it to their consideration. The manner in which the change shall be made from the present form of society to that system of communism which we propose is very simple. Negro slaves are now worth seven hundred dollars a head. As whites work harder, they are worth about a thousand. Make the man who owns a thousand dollars of capital the guardian (the term master is objectionable) of one white pauper of average value; give the man who is worth ten thousand dollars ten paupers, and the millionaire a thousand. This would be an act of simple mercy and justice; for the capitalists now live entirely by the proceeds of poor men's labor, which capital enables them to command; and they command and enjoy it in almost the exact proportions which we have designated. Thus, a family of poor laborers, men, women, and children, ten in number, can support themselves, and make about six hundred dollars, for their employer, which is the interest on ten thousand. They would work no harder than they do now, would be under no greater necessity to work, would be relieved of most of the cares of life, and let into the enjoyment of all valuable and necessary rights. What would they lose in liberty and equality? Just nothing. Having more rights, they would have more liberty than now, and approach nearer to equality. It might be, that their security and exemption from care would render their situation preferable to that of their employers. We suspect it would be easier to find wards or slaves than guardians or masters—for the gain would be all on the laborer's side, and the loss all on that of the capitalist.

Set your miscalled free laborers actually free, by giving them enough property or capital to live on, and then call on us at the South to free our Negroes. At present, you Abolitionists know our Negro slaves are much the freer of the two; and it would be a great advance towards freeing your laborers, to give them guardians, bound, like our masters, to take care of them, and entitled, in consideration thereof, to the proceeds of their labor. . .

GOVERNMENT A THING OF FORCE, NOT OF CONSENT

We do not agree with the authors of the Declaration of Independence, that governments 'derive their just powers from the consent of the governed.' The women, the children, the Negroes, and but few of the non-property holders were consulted, or consented to the Revolution, or the governments that ensued from its success. As to these, the new governments were self-elected despotisms, and the governing class self-elected despots. Those governments originated in force, and have been continued by force. All governments must originate in force, and be continued by force. The very term, government, implies that it is carried on against the consent of the governed. . . The ancient republics were governed by a small class of adult male citizens, who assumed and exercised the government, without the consent of the governed. The South is governed just as those ancient republics were. In the county in which we live, there are eighteen thousand souls, and only twelve hundred voters. But we twelve hundred, the governors, never asked and never intend to ask the consent of the sixteen thousand eight hundred whom we govern. Were we to do so, we should soon have an 'organized anarchy.' The governments of Europe could not exist a week without the positive force of standing armies.

They are all governments of force, not of consent. Even in our North, the women, children, and free Negroes, constitute four-fifths of the population; and they are governed without their consent. But they mean to correct this gross and glaring iniquity at the North. They hold that all men, women, and Negroes, and smart children, are equals, and entitled to equal rights. The widows and free Negroes begin to vote in some of those States, and they will have to let all colors and sexes and ages vote soon, or give up the glorious principles of human equality and universal emancipation. . .

Whilst we hold that all government is a matter of force, we yet think the governing class should be numerous enough to understand, and so situated as to represent fairly, all interests. . .

A word, at parting, to Northern Conservatives. A like danger threatens North and South, proceeding from the same source. Abolitionism is maturing what Political Economy began. With inexorable sequence 'Let Alone' is made to usher in No-Government. North and South our danger is the same, and our remedies, though differing in degree, must in character be the same. 'Let Alone' must be repudiated, if we would have any Government. We must, in all sections, act upon the principle that the world is 'too little governed.' You of the North need not institute Negro slavery; far less reduce white men to the state of Negro slavery. But the masses require more of protection, and the masses and philosophers equally require more of control. Leave it to time and circumstances to suggest the necessary legislation; but, rely upon it, 'Anarchy, plus the street constable,' won't answer any longer. . .

. . . More of despotic discretion, and less of Law, is what the world wants. We take our leave by saying, 'THERE IS TOO MUCH OF LAW AND TOO LITTLE OF GOVERNMENT IN THIS WORLD.'

6. *Man is born to subjection*

WILLIAM HARPER, *Slavery in the Light of Social Ethics*, 1837 *

. . . The coercion of slavery alone is adequate to form man to habits of labor. Without it, there can be no accumulation of property, no providence for the future, no tastes for comfort or elegancies, which are the characteristics and essentials of civilization. He who has obtained the command of another's labor, first begins to accumulate and provide for the future, and the foundations of civilization are laid. We find confirmed by experience that which is so evident in theory. Since the existence of man upon the earth, with no exception whatever, either of ancient or modern times every society which has attained civilization, has advanced to it through this process. . .

There seems to be something in this subject which blunts the perceptions,

* *Cotton Is King, and Pro-Slavery Arguments*, E. N. Elliott, ed., Augusta, Pritchard, Abbott and Loomis, 1860, pp. 552–71 *passim*.

and darkens and confuses the understandings and moral feelings of man. Tell them that, of necessity, in every civilized society, there must be an infinite variety of conditions and employments, from the most eminent and intellectual, to the most servile and laborious; that the Negro race, from their temperament and capacity, are peculiarly suited to the situation which they occupy, and not less happy in it than any corresponding class to be found in the world; prove incontestably that no scheme of emancipation could be carried into effect without the most intolerable mischiefs and calamities to both master and slave, or without probably throwing a large and fertile portion of the earth's surface out of the pale of civilization—and you have done nothing. They reply, that whatever may be the consequence, you are bound to do *right*; that man has a right to himself, and man cannot have property in man; that if the Negro race be naturally inferior in mind and character, they are not less entitled to the rights of humanity; that if they are happy in their condition, it affords but the stronger evidence of their degradation, and renders them still more objects of commiseration. They repeat, as the fundamental maxim of our civil policy, that all men are born free and equal, and quote from our Declaration of Independence, 'that men are endowed by their Creator with certain inalienable *rights*, among which are life, liberty, and the pursuit of happiness.' . .

All men are born free and equal. Is it not palpably nearer the truth to say that no man was ever born free, and that no two men were ever born equal? Man is born in a state of the most helpless dependence on others. He continues subject to the absolute control of others and remains without many of the civil and all of the political privileges of his society, until the period which the laws have fixed as that at which he is supposed to have attained the maturity of his faculties. Then inequality is further developed, and becomes infinite in every society, and under whatever form of government. Wealth and poverty, fame or obscurity, strength or weakness, knowledge or ignorance, ease or labor, power or subjection, mark the endless diversity in the condition of men.

But we have not arrived at the profundity of the maxim. This inequality is, in a great measure, the result of abuses in the institutions of society. They do not speak of what exists, but of what ought to exist. Everyone should be left at liberty to obtain all the advantages of society which he can compass, by the free exertion of his faculties, unimpeded by civil restraints. It may be said that this would not remedy the evils of society which are complained of. The inequalities to which I have referred, with the misery resulting from them, would exist in fact under the freest and most popular form of government that man could devise. But what is the foundation of the bold dogma so confidently announced? Females are human and rational beings. They may be found of better faculties, and better qualified to exercise political privileges, and to attain the distinctions of society, than many men; yet who complains of the order of society by which they are excluded from them? For I do not speak of the few who would desecrate them; do violence to the nature which their Creator has impressed upon them; drag them from the position which they necessarily occupy for the existence of civilized society, and in which they constitute its blessings and ornament—the only position which they have ever occupied in any human society—to place them in a situation in which they would be alike miserable and degraded. Low as we descend in combating the theories of presumptuous dogmatists, it cannot be necessary to stoop to this. A youth of eighteen may have powers which cast into the shade those of any of his more advanced contemporaries. He may be capable of serving or saving his country, and if not permitted to do so now, the occasion may have been lost forever. But he can exercise no political privilege, or aspire to any political distinction. It is said that, of necessity, society must exclude from some civil and political privileges those who are unfitted to exercise them, by infirmity, unsuitableness of character, or defect of discretion; that of necessity there must be some general rule on the subject, and that any rule which can be devised will operate with hardship and injustice on individuals. This is all that can be said, and all that need be said. It is saying, in other words, that the privileges in question are no matter of natural rights, but to be settled by convention, as the good and safety of society may require. If society should disfranchise individuals convicted of infamous crimes, would this be an invasion of natural rights? Yet this would not be justified on the score of their moral guilt, but that the good of society required or would be promoted by it. We admit the existence of a moral law, binding on societies as on individuals. Society must act in good faith. No man, or body of men, has a right to inflict pain or privation on others, unless with a view, after full and impartial deliberation, to prevent a greater evil. If this deliberation be had, and the decision made in good faith, there can be no imputation of moral guilt. Has any politician contended that the very existence of governments in which there are orders privileged by law, constitutes a violation of morality; that their continuance is a crime, which men are bound to put an end to, without any consideration of the good or evil to result from the change? Yet this is the natural inference from the dogma of the natural equality of men as applied to our institution of slavery—an equality not to be invaded without injustice and wrong, and requiring to be restored instantly, unqualified, and without reference to consequences. . .

Man is born to subjection. Not only during infancy is he dependent, and under the control of others; at all ages, it is the very bias of his nature, that the strong and the wise should control the weak and ignorant. . . The existence of some form of slavery in all ages and countries, is proof enough of this. He is born to subjection as he is born in sin and ignorance. To make any considerable progress in knowledge, the continued efforts of successive generations, and the diligent training and unwearied exertions of the individual, are requisite. To make progress in moral virtue, not less time and effort, aided by superior help, are necessary; and it is only by the matured exercise of his knowledge and his virtue, that he can attain to civil freedom. Of all things, the existence of civil liberty is most the result of artificial institution. The proclivity of the natural man is to domineer or to be subservient. A noble result, indeed, but in the attaining of which, as in the instances of knowledge and virtue, the Creator, for his own purposes, has set a limit beyond which we cannot go. . .

So when the greatest progress in civil liberty has been made, the enlightened lover of liberty will know that there must remain much inequality, much injustice, much *slavery*, which no human wisdom or virtue will ever be able wholly to prevent or redress. . .

Man has been endowed by his Creator with certain inalienable rights, among which are life, liberty, and the pursuit of happiness. What is meant by the *inalienable* right of liberty? Has any one who has used the words ever asked himself this question? Does it mean that a man has no right to alienate his own liberty—to sell himself and his posterity for slaves? This would seem to be the more obvious meaning. When the word *right* is used, it has reference to some law which sanctions it, and would be violated by its invasion. It must refer either to the general law of morality, or the law of the country—the law of God or the law of man. If the law of any country permitted it, it would of course be absurd to say that the law of that country was violated by such alienation. If it have any meaning in this respect, it must mean that though the law of the country permitted it, the man would be guilty of an immoral act who should thus alienate his liberty. . . Yet who will say that the man pressed by famine, and in prospect of death, would be criminal for such an act? Self-preservation, as is truly said, is the first law of nature. High and peculiar characters, by elaborate cultivation, may be taught to prefer death to slavery, but it would be folly to prescribe this as a duty to the mass of mankind. . .

7. *Most governments have been based on the denial of equal rights of men; ours began by affirming those rights*

ABRAHAM LINCOLN, *Fragments on Slavery*, 1 July 1854(?) *

The ant, who has toiled and dragged a crumb to his nest, will furiously defend the fruit of his labor, against whatever robber assails him. So plain, that the most dumb and stupid slave that ever toiled for a master, does constantly *know* that he is wronged. So plain that no one, high or low, ever does mistake it, except in a plainly *selfish* way; for although volume upon volume is written to prove slavery a very good thing, we never hear of the man who wishes to take the good of it, *by being a slave himself.*

Most governments have been based, practically, on the denial of equal rights of men, as I have, in part, stated them; *ours* began, by *affirming* those rights. They said, some men are too *ignorant*, and *vicious*, to share in government. Possibly so, said we; and, by your system, you would always keep them ignorant, and vicious. We proposed to give *all* a chance; and we expected the weak to grow stronger, the ignorant, wiser; and all better, and happier together. . .

If A. can prove, however conclusively, that he may, of right, enslave B.—why may not B. snatch the same argument, and prove equally, that he may enslave A.?—

You say A. is white, and B. is black. It is *color*, then; the lighter, having the

* *Selected Speeches, Messages and Letters*, T. Harry Williams, ed., New York, Rinehart, 1957, pp. 39–40.

right to enslave the darker? Take care, By this rule, you are to be slave to the first man you meet, with fairer skin than your own.

You do not mean *color* exactly?—You mean the whites are intellectually the superiors of the blacks, and, therefore have the right to enslave them? Take care again. By this rule, you are to be slave to the first man you meet, with an intellect superior to your own.

But, say you, it is a question of *interest;* and, if you can make it your *interest,* you have the right to enslave another. Very well. And if he can make it his interest, he has the right to enslave you.

8. *Slavery is founded in the selfishness of man's nature*

ABRAHAM LINCOLN, Speech at Peoria, Illinois, In Reply to Senator Stephen A. Douglas, 16 October 1854 *

. . . The repeal of the Missouri Compromise, and the propriety of its restoration, constitute the subject of what I am about to say. . .

And as this subject is no other than part and parcel of the larger general question of domestic slavery, I wish to make and to keep the distinction between the existing institution and the extension of it, so broad and so clear that no honest man can misunderstand me, and no dishonest one successfully misrepresent me. . .

This declared indifference, but, as I must think, covert real zeal, for the spread of slavery, I cannot but hate. I hate it because of the monstrous injustice of slavery itself. I hate it because it deprives our republican example of its just influence in the world; enables the enemies of free institutions with plausibility to taunt us as hypocrites; causes the real friends of freedom to doubt our sincerity; and especially because it forces so many good men among ourselves into an open war with the very fundamental principles of civil liberty, criticizing the Declaration of Independence, and insisting that there is no right principle of action but self interest.

Before proceeding let me say that I think I have no prejudice against the Southern people. They are just what we would be in their situation. If slavery did not now exist among them, they would not introduce it. If it did now exist among us, we should not instantly give it up. This I believe of the masses North and South. Doubtless there are individuals on both sides who would not hold slaves under any circumstances, and others who would gladly introduce slavery anew if it were out of existence. We know that some Southern men do free their slaves, go North and become tip-top Abolitionists, while some Northern ones go South and become most cruel slave-masters.

When Southern people tell us they are no more responsible for the origin of slavery than we are, I acknowledge the fact. When it is said that the institu-

* *Abraham Lincoln, Complete Works,* Comprising His Speeches, Letters, State Papers, and Miscellaneous Writings, John G. Nicolay and John Hay, eds., New York, The Century Co., 1894, vol. II, pp. 190–241 *passim.*

tion exists, and that it is very difficult to get rid of it in any satisfactory way, I can understand and appreciate the saying. I surely will not blame them for not doing what I should not know how to do myself. If all earthly power were given me, I should not know what to do as to the existing institution. My first impulse would be to free all the slaves, and send them to Liberia, to their own native land. But a moment's reflection would convince me that whatever of high hope (as I think there is) there may be in this in the long run, its sudden execution is impossible. If they were all landed there in a day, they would all perish in the next ten days; and there are not surplus shipping and surplus money enough to carry them there in many times ten days. What then? Free them all, and keep them among us as underlings? Is it quite certain that this betters their condition? I think I would not hold one in slavery at any rate, yet the point is not clear enough for me to denounce people upon. What next? Free them, and make them politically and socially our equals. My own feelings will not admit of this, and if mine would, we well know that those of the great mass of whites will not. Whether this feeling accords with justice and sound judgment is not the sole question, if indeed it is any part of it. A universal feeling, whether well or ill founded, cannot be safely disregarded. We cannot then make them equals. It does seem to me that systems of gradual emancipation might be adopted, but for their tardiness in this I will not undertake to judge our brethren of the South.

When they remind us of their constitutional rights, I acknowledge them—not grudgingly, but fully and fairly; and I would give them any legislation for the reclaiming of their fugitives which should not in its stringency be more likely to carry a free man into slavery than our ordinary criminal laws are to hang an innocent one.

But all this, to my judgment, furnishes no more excuse for permitting slavery to go into our own free territory than it would for reviving the African slave-trade by law. The law which forbids the bringing of slaves from Africa, and that which has so long forbidden the taking of them into Nebraska, can hardly be distinguished on any moral principle, and the repeal of the former could find quite as plausible excuses as that of the latter. . .

Equal justice to the South, it is said, requires us to consent to the extension of slavery to new countries. That is to say, inasmuch as you do not object to my taking my hog to Nebraska, therefore I must not object to you taking your slave. Now I admit that this is perfectly logical, if there is no difference between hogs and negroes. But while you thus require me to deny the humanity of the negro, I wish to ask whether you of the South, yourselves, have ever been willing to do as much? It is kindly provided that of all those who come into the world only a small percentage are natural tyrants. That percentage is no larger in the slave States than in the free. The great majority South, as well as North, have human sympathies, of which they can no more divest themselves than they can of their sensibility to physical pain. These sympathies in the bosoms of the Southern people manifest, in many ways, their sense of the wrong of slavery, and their consciousness that, after all, there is humanity in the Negro. If they deny this, let me address them a few plain questions. In 1820 you joined the North, almost unanimously, in declaring the African slave-trade piracy, and in annexing to it the punishment of death. Why did you do this? If you did not feel that it was wrong, why did you join in providing that men should be hung for it? The practice was no more than bringing wild negroes from Africa to such as would buy them. But you never thought of hanging men for catching and selling wild horses, wild buffaloes, or wild bears.

Again, you have among you a sneaking individual of the class of native tyrants known as the 'Slave-Dealer.' He watches your necessities, and crawls up to buy your slave, at a speculating price. If you cannot help it, you sell to him; but if you can help it, you drive him from your door. You despise him utterly. . . Now why is this? You do not so treat the man who deals in corn, cotton, or tobacco.

And yet again. There are in the United States and Territories, including the District of Columbia, 433,643 free blacks. At five hundred dollars per head they are worth over two hundred millions of dollars. How comes this vast amount of property to be running about without owners? We do not see free horses or free cattle running at large. How is this? All these free blacks are the descendants of slaves, or have been slaves themselves; and they would be slaves now but for something which has operated on their white owners, inducing them at vast pecuniary sacrifice to liberate them. What is that something? Is there any mistaking it? In all these cases it is your sense of justice and human sympathy continually telling you that the poor Negro has some natural right to himself—that those who deny it and make mere merchandise of him deserve kickings, contempt, and death.

And now why will you ask us to deny the humanity of the slave, and estimate him as only the equal of the hog? Why ask us to do what you will not do yourselves? Why ask us to do for nothing what two hundred millions of dollars could not induce you to do?

But one great argument in support of the repeal of the Missouri Compromise is still to come. That argument is the 'sacred right of self-government.' It seems our distinguished senator has found great difficulty in getting his antagonists, even in the Senate, to meet him fairly on this argument. Some poet has said:

Fools rush in where angels fear to tread.

At the hazard of being thought one of the fools of this quotation, I meet that argument—I rush in—I take that bull by the horns. I trust I understand and truly estimate the right of self-government. My faith in the proposition that each man should do precisely as he pleases with all which is exclusively his own lies at the foundation of the sense of justice there is in me. I extend the principle to communities of men as well as to individuals. I so extend it because it is politically wise in saving us from broils about matters which do not concern us. Here, or at Washington, I would not trouble myself with the oyster laws of Virginia, or the cranberry laws of Indiana. The doctrine of self-government is right,—absolutely and eternally right,—but it has no just application as here attempted. Or perhaps I should rather say that whether it has such application depends upon whether a Negro is not or is a man. If he is not a man, in that case he who is a man may as a matter of self-government do just what he pleases with him. But if the Negro is a man, is it not to that extent a total destruction of self-government to say that he too shall not govern himself? When the white man governs himself, that is self-government; but when he governs himself and also governs another man, that is more than self-government—that is despotism. If the Negro is a man, why then my ancient faith teaches me that 'all men are created equal,' and that there can be no moral right in connection with one man's making a slave of another.

Judge Douglas frequently, with bitter irony and sarcasm, paraphrases our argument by saying, 'The white people of Nebraska are good enough to govern themselves, but they are not good enough to govern a few miserable Negroes!'

Well! I doubt not that the people of Nebraska are and will continue to be as good as the average of people elsewhere. I do not say the contrary. What I do say is that no man is good enough to govern another man without that other's consent. I say this is the leading principle, the sheet-anchor of American republicanism. . .

But Nebraska is urged as a great Union-saving measure. Well, I too go for saving the Union. Much as I hate slavery, I would consent to the extension of it rather than see the Union dissolved, just as I would consent to any great evil to avoid a greater one. But when I go to Union-saving, I must believe, at least, that the means I employ have some adaptation to the end. To my mind, Nebraska has no such adaptation. It hath no relish of salvation in it. It is an aggravation, rather, of the only one thing which ever endangers the Union. When it came upon us, all was peace and quiet. . . Every inch of territory we owned already had a definite settlement of the slavery question, by which all parties were pledged to abide. . .

In this state of affairs the Genius of Discord himself could scarcely have invented a way of again setting us by the ears but by turning back and destroying the peace measures of the past. The counsels of that Genius seem to have prevailed. The Missouri Compromise was repealed; and here we are in the midst of a new slavery agitation, such, I think, as we have never seen before. . .

Argue as you will and long as you will, this is the naked front and aspect of the measure. And in this aspect it could not but produce agitation. Slavery is founded in the selfishness of man's nature—opposition to it in his love of justice. These principles are an eternal antagonism, and when brought into collision so fiercely as slavery extension brings them, shocks and throes and convulsions must ceaselessly follow. Repeal the Missouri Compromise, repeal all compromises, repeal the Declaration of Independence, repeal all past history, you still cannot repeal human nature. It still will be the abundance of man's heart that slavery extension is wrong, and out of the abundance of his heart his mouth will continue to speak. . .

The Missouri Compromise ought to be restored. For the sake of the Union, it ought to be restored. . .

We thereby restore the national faith, the national confidence, the national feeling of brotherhood. We thereby reinstate the spirit of concession and compromise, that spirit which has never failed us in past perils, and which may be safely trusted for all the future. The South ought to join in doing this. The peace of the nation is as dear to them as to us. In memories of the past and hopes of the future, they share as largely as we. It would be on their part a great act—great in its spirit, and great in its effect. It would be worth to the nation a hundred years' purchase of peace and prosperity. . .

9. *The Declaration of Independence looks toward a progressive improvement in the condition of all men*

ABRAHAM LINCOLN, Speech in Springfield, Illinois, 26 June 1857 *

. . . And now as to the Dred Scott decision. That decision declares two propositions—first, that a Negro cannot sue in the United States courts; and secondly, that Congress cannot prohibit slavery in the Territories. It was made by a divided court—dividing differently on the different points. Judge Douglas does not discuss the merits of the decision, and in that respect I shall follow his example. . .

He denounces all who question the correctness of that decision, as offering violent resistance to it. But who resists it? Who has, in spite of the decision, declared Dred Scott free, and resisted the authority of his master over him?

Judicial decisions have two uses—first, to absolutely determine the case decided; and secondly, to indicate to the public how other similar cases will be decided when they arise. For the latter use, they are called 'precedents' and 'authorities.'

We believe as much as Judge Douglas (perhaps more) in obedience to, and respect for, the judicial department of government. We think its decisions on constitutional questions, when fully settled, should control not only the particular cases decided, but the general policy of the country, subject to be disturbed only by amendments of the Constitution as provided in that instrument itself. More than this would be revolution. But we think the Dred Scott decision is erroneous. We know the court that made it has often overruled its own decisions, and we shall do what we can to have it to overrule this. We offer no resistance to it. . .

But Judge Douglas considers this view awful. Hear him:

> The courts are the tribunals prescribed by the Constitution and created by the authority of the people to determine, expound, and enforce the law. Hence, whoever resists the final decision of the highest judicial tribunal aims a deadly blow at our whole republican system of government—a blow which, if successful, would place all our rights and liberties at the mercy of passion, anarchy, and violence. I repeat, therefore, that if resistance to the decisions of the Supreme Court of the United States, in a matter like the points

* *Abraham Lincoln, Complete* Works, John G. Nicolay and John Hay, eds., vol. II, pp. 315–39 *passim.*

> decided in the Dred Scott case, clearly within their jurisdiction as defined by the Constitution, shall be forced upon the country as a political issue, it will become a distinct and naked issue between the friends and enemies of the Constitution—the friends and the enemies of the supremacy of the laws.

Why, this same Supreme Court once decided a national bank to be constitutional; but General Jackson, as President of the United States, disregarded the decision, and vetoed a bill for a recharter, partly on constitutional ground declaring that each public functionary must support the Constitution, 'as he understands it.' . .

Again and again have I heard Judge Douglas denounce that bank decision and applaud General Jackson for disregarding it. It would be interesting for him to look over his recent speech, and see how exactly his fierce philippics against us for resisting Supreme Court decisions fall upon his own head. It will call to mind a long and fierce political war in this country, upon an issue which, in his own language, and, of course, in his own changeless estimation, was 'a distinct issue between the friends and the enemies of the Constitution,' and in which war he fought in the ranks of the enemies of the Constitution.

I have said, in substance, that the Dred Scott decision was in part based on assumed historical facts which were not really true, and I ought not to leave the subject without giving some reasons for saying this; I therefore give an instance or two, which I think fully sustain me. Chief Justice Taney, in delivering the opinion of the majority of the court, insists at great length that Negroes were no part of the people who made, or for whom was made, the Declaration of Independence, or the Constitution of the United States. . .

Chief Justice Taney says:

> It is difficult at this day to realize the state of public opinion, in relation to that unfortunate race, which prevailed in the civilized and enlightened portions of the world at the time of the Declaration of Independence, and when the Constitution of the United States was framed and adopted.

And again, after quoting from the Declaration, he says:

> The general words above quoted would seem to include the whole human family, and if they were used in a similar instrument at this day, would be so understood.

In these the Chief Justice does not directly assert, but plainly assumes, as a fact, that the public estimate of the black man is more favorable now than it was in the days of the Revolution. This assumption is a mistake. In some trifling particulars the condition of that race has been ameliorated; but as a whole, in this country, the change between then and now is decidedly the other way; and their ultimate destiny has never appeared so hopeless as in the last three or four years. In two of the five States—New Jersey and North Carolina—that then gave the free Negro the right of voting, the right has since been taken away, and in a third—New York—it has been greatly abridged; while it has not been extended, so far as I know, to a single additional State, though the number of the States has doubled. In those days, as I understand, masters could, at their own pleasure, emancipate their slaves; but since then such legal restraints have been made upon emancipation as to amount almost to prohibition. In those days legislatures held the unquestioned power to abolish slavery in their respective States, but now it is becoming quite fashionable for State constitutions to withhold that power from the legislatures. In those days, by common consent, the spread of the black man's bondage to the new countries was prohibited, but now Congress decides that it will not continue the prohibition, and the Supreme Court decides that it could not if it would. In those days our Declaration of Independence was held sacred by all, and thought to include all; but now, to aid in making the bondage of the Negro universal and eternal, it is assailed and sneered at and construed, and hawked at and torn, till, if its framers could rise from their graves, they could not at all recognize it. All the powers of earth seem rapidly combining against him. Mammon is after him, ambition follows, philosophy follows, and the theology of the day is fast joining the cry. . .

It is grossly incorrect to say or assume that the public estimate of the Negro is more favorable now than it was at the origin of the government. . .

There is a natural disgust in the minds of nearly all white people at the idea of an indiscriminate amalgamation of the white and black races; and Judge Douglas evidently is basing his chief hope upon the chances of his being able to appropriate the benefit of this disgust to himself. If he can, by much drumming and repeating, fasten the odium of that idea upon his adversaries, he thinks he can struggle through the storm. He therefore clings to this hope, as a drowning man to the last plank. He makes an occasion for lugging it in from the opposition to the Dred Scott decision. He finds the Republicans insisting that the Declaration of Independence includes *all* men, black as well as white, and forthwith he boldly denies that it includes Negroes at all, and proceeds to argue gravely that all who contend it does, do so only because they want to vote, and eat, and sleep, and marry with Negroes! He will have it that they cannot be consistent else. Now I protest against the counterfeit logic which concludes that, because I do not want a black woman for a slave I must necessarily want her for a wife. I need not have her for either. I can just leave her alone. In some respects she certainly is not my equal; but in her natural right to eat bread she earns with her own hands without asking leave of any one else, she is my equal, and the equal of all others.

Chief Justice Taney, in his opinion in the Dred Scott case, admits that the language of the Declaration is broad enough to include the whole human family, but he and Judge Douglas argue that the authors of that instrument did not intend to include Negroes, by the fact that they did not at once actually place them on an equality with the whites. Now this grave argument comes to just nothing at all, by the other fact that they did not at once, or ever afterward, actually place all white people on an equality with one another. And this is the staple argument of both the chief justice and the senator for doing this obvious violence to the plain, unmistakable language of the Declaration.

I think the authors of that notable instrument intended to include *all* men, but they did not intend to declare all men equal *in all respects*. They did not mean to say all were equal in color, size, intellect, moral developments, or social capacity. They defined with tolerable distinctness in what respects they did consider all men created equal—equal with 'certain inalienable rights, among which are life, liberty, and the pursuit of happiness.' This they said, and this they meant. They did not mean to assert the obvious untruth that all were then actually enjoying that equality nor yet that they were about to confer it immediately upon them. In fact, they had no power to confer such a boon. They meant simply to declare the right, so that enforcement of it might follow as fast as circumstances should permit.

They meant to set up a standard maxim for free society, which should be familiar to all, and revered by all; constantly looked to, constantly labored for, and even though never perfectly attained, constantly approximated, and thereby constantly spreading and deepening its influence and augmenting the happiness and value of life to all people of all colors everywhere. The assertion that 'all men are created equal' was of no practical use in effecting our separation from Great Britain; and it was placed in the Declaration not for that, but for future use. Its authors meant it to be—as, thank God, it is now proving itself—a stumbling-block to all those who in after times might seek to turn a free people back into the hateful paths of despotism. They knew the proneness of prosperity to breed tyrants, and they meant when such should reappear in this fair land and commence their vocation, they should find left for them at least one hard nut to crack.

I have now briefly expressed my view of the meaning and object of that part of the Declaration of Independence which declares that 'all men are created equal.'

Now let us hear Judge Douglas's view of the same subject, as I find it in the printed report of his late speech. Here it is:

> No man can vindicate the character, motives, and conduct of the signers of the Declaration of Independence, except upon the hypothesis that they referred to the white race alone, and not to the African, when they declared all men to have been created equal; that they were speaking of British subjects on this continent being equal to British subjects born and residing in Great Britain; that they were entitled to the same inalienable rights, and among them were enumerated life, liberty, and the pursuit of happiness. The Declaration was adopted for the purpose of justifying the colonists in the eyes of the civilized world in withdrawing their allegiance from the British crown, and dissolving their connection with the mother country.

My good friends, read that carefully over some leisure hour, and ponder well upon it; see what a mere wreck—mangled ruin—it makes of our once glorious Declaration. . .

I had thought the Declaration contemplated the progressive improvement in the condition of all men everywhere; but no, it merely 'was adopted for the purpose of justifying the colonists in the eyes of the civilized world in withdrawing their allegiance from the British crown, and dissolving their connection with the mother country.' Why, that object having been effected some eighty years ago, the Declaration is of no practical use now—mere rubbish—old wadding left to rot on the battlefield after the victory is won.

I understand you are preparing to celebrate the 'Fourth,' tomorrow week. . . Suppose, after you read it once in the old-fashioned way, you read it once more with Judge Douglas's version. It will then run thus: 'We hold these truths to be self-evident, that all British subjects who were on this continent eighty-one years ago, were created equal to all British subjects born and then residing in Great Britain.'

And now I appeal to all—to Democrats as well as others—are you really willing that the Declaration shall thus be frittered away?—thus left no more, at most, than an interesting memorial of the dead past?—thus shorn of its vitality and practical value, and left without the germ or even the suggestion of the individual rights of man in it? . .

10. *Republicans are for both the* man *and the* dollar; *but in cases of conflict the man* before *the dollar*

ABRAHAM LINCOLN to Henry L. Pierce and other Boston Republicans, 6 April 1859 *

Gentlemen Springfield, Ill.

Your kind note inviting me to attend a Festival in Boston, on the 13th. Inst. in honor of the birth-day of Thomas Jefferson, was duly received. My engagements are such that I can not attend.

Bearing in mind that about seventy years ago, two great political parties were first formed in this country, that Thomas Jefferson was the head of one of them, and Boston the headquarters of the other, it is both curious and interesting that those supposed to descend politically from the party opposed to Jefferson, should now be celebrating his birth-day in their own original seat of empire, while those claiming political descent from him have nearly ceased to breathe his name everywhere.

Remembering too, that the Jefferson party were formed upon their supposed superior devotion to the *personal* rights of men holding the rights of *property* to be secondary only, and greatly inferior, and then assuming that the so-called democracy of to-day, are the Jefferson, and their opponents, the anti-Jefferson parties, it will be equally interesting to note how completely the two have changed hands as to the principle upon which they were originally supposed to be divided.

The democracy of to-day hold the *liberty* of one man to be absolutely nothing, when in conflict with another man's right of *property*. Republicans, on

* *Selected Speeches, Messages and Letters*, T. Harry Williams, ed., pp. 112–18.

the contrary, are for both the *man* and the *dollar;* but in cases of conflict, the man *before* the *dollar.*

I remember once being much amused at seeing two partially intoxicated men engage in a fight with their great-coats on, which fight, after a long, and rather harmless contest, ended in each having fought himself *out* of his own coat, and *into* that of the other. If the two leading parties of this day are really identical with the two in the days of Jefferson and Adams, they have performed about the same feat as the two drunken men.

But soberly, it is now no child's play to save the principles of Jefferson from total overthrow in this nation.

One would start with great confidence that he could convince any sane child that the simpler propositions of Euclid are true; but, nevertheless, he would fail, utterly, with one who should deny the definitions and axioms. The principles of Jefferson are the definitions and axioms of free society. And yet they are denied, and evaded, with no small show of success. One dashingly calls them 'glittering generalities'; another bluntly calls them 'self evident lies'; and still others insidiously argue that they apply only to 'superior races.'

These expressions, differing in form, are identical in object and effect—the supplanting the principles of free government, and restoring those of classification, caste, and legitimacy. They would delight a convocation of crowned heads, plotting against the people. They are the van-guard—the miners, and sappers—of returning despotism. We must repulse them, or they will subjugate us.

This is a world of compensations; and he who would *be* no slave, must consent to *have* no slave. Those who deny freedom to others, deserve it not for themselves; and, under a just God, can not long retain it.

All honor to Jefferson—to the man who, in the concrete pressure of a struggle for national independence by a single people, had the coolness, forecast, and capacity to introduce into a merely revolutionary document, an abstract truth, applicable to all men and all times, and so to embalm it there, that to-day, and in all coming days, it shall be a rebuke and a stumblingblock to the very harbingers of re-appearing tyranny and oppression. . .

SELECTED REFERENCES

Alice Dana Adams, *The Neglected Period of Anti-Slavery in America, 1808–1831*, Boston, Ginn, 1908.

Albert T. Bledsoe, *An Essay on Liberty and Slavery*, Philadelphia, J. B. Lippincott, 1856.

H. S. Commager, *Theodore Parker*, Boston, Little, Brown, 1936.

Thomas R. Dew, *An Assay on Slavery*, 2nd ed., Richmond, Va., J. W. Randolph, 1849.

Charles Dickens, *American Notes, 1841*, New York, E. P. Dutton, 1908, chap. XVII, 'Slavery,' pp. 225–41.

David Donald, *An Excess of Democracy: The American Civil War and the Social Process*, Oxford, Clarendon Press, 1960.

———, *Lincoln Reconsidered: Essays on the Civil War Era*, New York, Knopf, 1956.

E. N. Elliott, ed., *Cotton Is King and Pro-Slavery Arguments*, Augusta, Ga., Pritchard, Abbott, & Loomis, 1860.

A. B. Hart, *Slavery and Abolition, 1831–41*, New York, Harper, 1906.

Hinton R. Helper, *The Impending Crisis of the South: How To Meet It*, New York, A. B. Burdick, 1860.

W. S. Jenkins, *Pro-Slavery Thought in the Old South*, Chapel Hill, University of North Carolina Press, 1935.

Arnaud Leavelle and Thomas I. Cook, 'George Fitzhugh and the Theory of American Conservatism,' *Journal of Politics*, May 1945, vol. VII, pp. 145–68.

Eric L. McKitrick, ed., *Slavery Defended: The Views of the Old South*, Englewood Cliffs, N. J., Prentice-Hall, 1963.

Josiah Priest, *Bible Defense of Slavery; and Origin, Fortunes, and History of the Negro Race*, 5th ed., Glasgow, Ky., W. S. Brown, 1852.

Francis Wayland, *The Elements of Moral Science*, New York, Printed for Cooke and Co., 1835.

Harvey Wish, *George Fitzhugh: Propagandist of the Old South*, Baton Rouge, Louisiana State University Press, 1943.

C. Vann Woodward, *The Strange Career of Jim Crow*, New York, Oxford University Press, 1957.

XIV

THE NATURE OF THE UNION

The slavery controversy and the civil conflict growing out of it precipitated discussion of a continuing issue. What was the nature of the union established in 1787–89? Though much of what was said and done after 1789 served to blur and confuse rather than sharpen and clarify, the end result has been to quicken the realization of American nationality and union.

The Constitution had not drawn the boundary line between the General Government and the States in colors so distinct and clear as to escape diversity of opinion. Indeed, grave and protracted dispute had raged since the Convention of 1787. And yet if there be any single proposition to which Americans were and are dedicated, it is this: that the people have a right to change their government, 'laying its foundations on such principles, and organizing its powers in such form, as to them shall seem most likely to effect their safety and happiness.' The Declaration of Independence had declared that the people alone are the rightful source of legitimate government. James Wilson called this (and many others agreed with him) 'the leading principle in politics and that which pervades the American Constitution.' The thirteen colonies had long acted on this Lockian precept and most notably in the separation of 1776. They declared themselves, as *united* colonies, free and independent states, by the authority of the whole people. Nor was this proclamation capable of serving only negative purposes. When government under the Articles of Confederation exhibited fatal weakness because sovereign states linked in that 'League of Friendship' could ignore or resist with impunity the resolutions and requisitions of Congress, that same 'leading principle' was constructively invoked. The Confederation was therefore, as John Quincy Adams said in 1836, 'an experiment of inestimable value even by its failure. It taught our fathers the lesson that they had more, infinitely more to do than merely to achieve their independence by war. That they must form their social compact upon principles never before attempted upon earth.'

Adams went on to observe that the idea of continuing as 'one people' under one organized government was 'in itself so simple, and addressed itself at once so forcibly to the reason, to the imagination, and to the benevolent feelings of all, that it can scarcely be supposed to have escaped the mind of any reflecting man from Maine to Georgia.' And yet, when this 'simple' idea was projected and acted upon in the Philadelphia Convention, it stirred 'state sovereignties, corporate feudal baronies, tenacious of their own liberty, impatient of a superior and jealous, and disdainful of a paramount sovereign, even in the whole democracy of the nation.' The people, that is to say, could exert themselves negatively and unitedly against the tyrannous oppression of Great Britain, but when that same ultimate American authority moved constructively in the face of well-nigh insurmountable internal complexities, vested interests and prejudices were profoundly aroused.

To deal effectively with the exigencies of the situation it had been as necessary in 1787 as in 1776 to return, as Rufus King said, 'to first principles'; or, as Wilson put it, 'to go to the original powers of society'—the people. The Convention, in short, was a revolutionary body, acting in accordance with the proposition that 'all authority is derived from the people.' Evidence that the changes effected by the Constitution were in fact revolutionary comes not only from those who supported it, but also from those who opposed it.

How, in the face of the historical record could the doctrine that the Constitution was a mere compact between sovereign states, so boldly asserted and acted upon by the slave states, receive any credibility whatsoever? How could our 'leading principle in politics . . . that the supreme power resides in the people,' be converted into the self-stultifying notion that the Constitution was a compact of independent and sovereign corporate entities? How could states' rights advocates, John C. Calhoun in particular, claim for entities called States a prerogative that belongs, under our theory of government, only to the people or populations? How, in short, could the highest political capacity of *the people* of the states be 'transmuted into the highest capacity of the States themselves?'

Calhoun executed the suggested legerdemain with assistance, paradoxically enough, from certain of the Constitution's most ardent defenders, notably Madison and Jefferson. In seeking to allay, in 1787, widespread fear that the central government would encroach on the states, even Hamilton took a position seemingly at odds with his assertion, in number 22 of the *Federalist*, that 'the fabric of the American empire ought to rest on the solid basis of the consent of the people.' 'The state legislatures,' Hamilton observed in number 26, 'who will always be not only vigilant but also suspicious and jealous guardians of the rights of the citizens against encroachments from the federal government, will constantly have their attention awake to the conduct of the national rulers, and will be ready enough, if anything improper appears, to sound the alarm to the people, and not only to be the voice, but, if necessary, the *Arm* of their discontent.' Is this an assertion of the right of revolution or the doctrine of nullification?

Dealing with the same subject, Madison says in essay 46: 'But ambitious encroachments of the federal government, on the authority of the state governments, would not excite the opposition of a single state or of a few states only. They would be the signal for general alarm. Every government would espouse the common cause. A correspondence would be opened. Plans of resistance would be concerted.'

Was Hamilton himself guilty of that 'gross heresy' he so roundly denounced, or were both he and Madison only voicing that 'leading principle' we had adhered to since 1776? 'It is a plain statement of the doctrine of the right of revolution, which is a right not of governments but of the governed,' Professor Corwin insists. Maybe so, but there remains a doubt whether Madison's stand, at least, does not approximate Calhoun's doctrine of nullification.

No such doubt clouds the Virginia Resolutions of 1798, drawn by Madison against the 'Usurpations' of President John Adams, declaring that 'the powers of the federal government' are 'limited by the plain sense and intention of [the Constitution] . . . and that, in case of a deliberate, palpable and dangerous exercise of other powers, not granted . . . the states . . . have the right, and are in duty bound, to interpose, for arresting the progress of the evil, and for maintaining within the respective limits, the authority, rights, and liberties pertaining to them.'

The Jefferson-inspired Kentucky resolutions of 1799 were even more explicit in declaring 'that the several states who formed that instrument [the Constitution] being sovereign and independent, have the unquestionable right to judge of the infraction; and, that a nullification by those sovereignties of all unauthorized acts done under color of that instrument, is the rightful remedy.' Jefferson had been even stronger in his original draft, saying 'that every state has a natural right in cases not within the compact [*casus non foederis*] to nullify of their own authority, all assumptions of power by others within their limits.' Thus to Jefferson, the 'Jacob of the transaction' as Professor E. S. Corwin calls him, goes the credit, if any, for the first clear and unequivocal statement of the doctrine of nullification.

The political ties binding men together in political society, someone has observed, are in the nature of slip-knots. In periods of social slack, of general harmony of interests, the constitutional knot seems securely tied. But in times of crisis, or sharp conflict of interests, the case is far otherwise. During the half-century preceding the Civil War, the South could and did nullify federal tariffs, force repeal of legislation limiting extension of slavery,—all this without breaking the bonds of union. It was not until 1861 that the slave states cut loose and attempted secession. Enlisting certain Founding Fathers in their support, they held that the Constitution emanated from the sovereign states, that they therefore had the right to interpose their judgment against any acts of the national government deemed by them to be unauthorized, and might thereafter withdraw from the Union. It was on this theory, complicated by tangled economic interests, that the South went on to Harper's Ferry, Shiloh, and Appomattox.

Long before the South was driven to take up arms in the effort to maintain the slave system, Chief Justice John Marshall's bold assertion of national supremacy had sent John Taylor of Caroline (1753–1824) scurrying to his desk and pen. In his *Construction Construed and Constitutions Vindicated*, published in 1820, one year after McCulloch *v.* Maryland, and excerpted in this chapter, Taylor contended 'that the federal constitution, so far from intending to make its political spheres morally unequal in powers, or to invest the *greatest* with any species of sovereignty over the least, intended the very reverse,—the distribution of equal power between the states and the national government.' 'The reason,' Taylor continued, 'why great spheres derive no authority from magnitude to transgress upon small spheres, is, that both are donations from the same source; and that the donor did not intend, that one donation should pilfer another, because it was smaller.' Taylor accepted Marshall's view that the natural government derived its power from the people, but he added that the people limited power by dividing it, both within the central government and between that government and the states.

Rhetoric, however persuasive, would perhaps not affect the course of events, and Taylor concluded on a fatalistic note, though not without prescience: 'The laws of congress claim a general supremacy, but the supreme court claims and exercises a supremacy over them; . . . the supremacy of congress *and* of the court, in alliance . . . has declared war against the sovereignty of the states; but how it will terminate, is hidden in the womb of time.'

Hugh Swinton Legaré (1797?–1843), of South Carolina, also challenged the great Chief Justice's constitutional jurisprudence. The nationalistic implications of McCulloch *v.* Maryland troubled Legaré no less than they did Taylor. Legaré predicted that if Marshall's broad construction of national power were followed, the Supreme Court could never pronounce unconstitutional any act of the federal government. McCulloch *v.* Maryland 'covers the whole ground of political sovereignty, and consecrates usurpation in advance.' Its rationale, Legaré argued, could not be sound; it 'necessarily converts a government of enumerated into one of indefinite powers, and a confederacy of republics into a gigantic and consolidated empire.'

Legaré's request for the Supreme Court to 'act the part of an umpire in questions of constitutional law,' especially those touching federal-state relations, was answered eight years later when Andrew Jackson appointed Roger Brooke Taney as Chief Justice Marshall's successor. In response to Legaré's plea, Taney ruled that 'judicial power was justly regarded as indispensable, not merely to maintain the supremacy of the laws of the United States, but also to guard the States from any encroachment upon their reserved rights by the General Government.'

> . . . So long . . . as this Constitution shall endure, this tribunal must exist with it, deciding in the peaceful forms of judicial proceedings the angry and irritating controversies between sovereignties, which in other countries have been determined by the arbitrament of force. [Abelman *v.* Booth, 21 Howard 506 (1859), 520–21.]

Legaré's defense of states' rights met with strong opposition from Daniel Webster (1782–1852). In the debate on *Foot's Resolution* in 1830, the Massachusetts Senator eloquently implored:

> . . . may I not see him [Hayne] shining on the broken and dishonored fragments of a once glorious Union; on States dissevered, discordant, belligerent; on a land rent with civil feuds, or drenched, it may be, in fraternal blood! Let their last feeble and lingering glance rather behold the gorgeous ensign of the republic, now known and honored throughout the earth . . . *Liberty and Union,* now and for ever, one and inseparable!

The Resolution that let loose Webster's three days of oratory had proposed an inquiry into the sales and surveys of western lands; during the debate, however, Senator Hayne of South Carolina had broached the doctrine of nullification, criticizing New England 'patriotism,' Massachusetts in particular, and Webster personally. Webster was quick to chide Hayne's errors, especially those concerning the nature of the Union. Nullification, he declared, was based on 'total misapprehension'; it was to exclude nullification that the Constitution was founded. The 'very chief end, the main design, for which the whole Constitution was framed and adopted,' he instructed the gentleman from South Carolina, 'was to establish a government that should not be obliged to act through State agency, or depend on State opinion and State discretion.'

Senator Hayne was unequal to Webster's forensics, but the latter soon met his match. Hayne resigned shortly thereafter to become governor of South Carolina, being succeeded by Webster's most formidable opponent, the 'great nullifier' himself, John C. Calhoun. In Calhoun (1782–1851), Webster was confronted by not only a bold states' rights advocate but also by a brilliant thinker capable of discussing these issues on the most elevated theoretical level. It was in the nature of man, Calhoun argued in his *Disquisition on Government*, herein excerpted, to be either ruler or ruled, and the most stable governments were those in which political power was vested with the small propertied minority rather than with the broad mass of the people. Translating this doctrine into constitutional interpretation. Calhoun argued that the Union had been formed by the several states combining but not submerging their separate sovereignties. And therefore the states inevitably remained free agents armed with the right to give or withdraw their assent to acts of the general government, as they saw fit. He favored an alliance of economic interests in both North and South to the end of preventing control of the government by the 'numerical majority' who, thereafter, would effect 'popular tyranny.'

The German-American political philosopher, Francis Lieber (1800–1872), meeting Calhoun on his own ground of theory, probed Webster's nationalism more deeply. Lieber, who emigrated to this country in 1827, taught history and political economy at South Carolina College for over two decades (1835–56), spending the rest of his life at Columbia University as professor of history, political science, and public law. His most influential books were the *Manual of Political Ethics* (1838–39) and *Civil Liberty and Self-Government* (1853).

Lieber sought to shore up the theoretical underpinnings of national supremacy. Political sovereignty, he argued, was naturally inherent in nations. Depending neither on social contract nor on natural law, sovereignty was the peculiar attribute of nations; the pretensions of the states to sovereignty was 'a modern fiction.'

Lincoln (1809–65), like Lieber, had no respect for Calhoun or for his views. A quasi-Jeffersonian and frontier Unionist, he was at the opposite end of the social-political firmament. Spokesman throughout his career for small farmers and entrepreneurs of the Corn Belt, he proclaimed in 1861, on the eve of the Civil War, his devotion to the ordinary ranks of the people in both the North and the South. 'Is there any better or equal hope in the world,' he asked, in his first inaugural address, '. . . [than] that truth and that justice will surely prevail by the judgment of this great tribunal of the American people'?

Although the first shots had been fired at Sumter and secession was a fact, Lincoln still searched for a theory of the Union that would go deeper than the great constitutional debates then rife. He finally hit upon an idea first advanced by John Jay: that the 'Union is perpetual . . . much older than the Constitution. It was formed, in fact'—'by the Articles of Association in 1744 . . . matured and continued by the Declaration of Independence in 1776. It was further matured . . . by the Articles of Confederation in 1778. And finally, in 1787 one of the declared objects for ordaining and establishing the Constitution was "to form a more perfect Union." ' Eight years later, in Texas *v.* White, the Supreme Court adopted Lincoln's reasoning, almost his words, in establishing the still enduring concept of the nature of the Union. Chief Justice Chase (1803–73) stated:

> Union of the States never was a purely artificial and arbitrary relation. It began among the Colonies . . . and received definite form, and character, and sanction from the Articles of Confederation. By these the Union was solemnly declared to 'be perpetual' . . . the Constitution was ordained 'to form a more perfect Union.' It is difficult to convey the idea of indissoluble unity more clearly than by these words. What can be indissoluble if a perpetual Union, made more perfect, is not?

Through Marshall, Webster, Lieber, and Lincoln, this, the organic view, had steadily advanced. Repeatedly tested by pen and, finally, by musket, the Union was fused, in Chase's words, 'out of common origin, mutual sympathies, kindred principles, similar interests, and geographical relations.' Justice Holmes, himself a soldier in Lincoln's army, reinforced this theory in a Supreme Court opinion of 1919:

> When we are dealing with words that are also a constituent act, like the Constitution of the United States, we must realize that they have called into life a being, the development of which could not have been foreseen completely by the most gifted of its begetters. It was enough for them to realize or to hope that they had created an organism; it has taken a century and has cost their successors much sweat and blood to prove that they created a nation.

The Union, like the Constitution itself, had to be 'extorted from the grinding necessity' of a reluctant people.

1. *The donor did not intend that one donation should pilfer another*

JOHN TAYLOR, *Construction Construed and Constitutions Vindicated,* 1820 *

THE UNION

Who made it? 'We, the people of the United States.' But who were they? The associated inhabitants of each state, or the unassociated inhabitants of all the states. This question is an exposition, either of the ignorance or the design of construction. If there is no difficulty in answering it, construction ought to be laughed at for playing the fool; but if it gives the wrong answer, as supposing it to furnish contrary inferences to the right one, it ought to be suspected of playing the knave. At least an attempt to construe away a fact, known to everybody, is a very fine specimen of its character when aiming at an accession of power. It has been imagined, that by considering the union as the act of the people, in their natural, and not in their political associated capacity, some aspect of consolidation might be shed over the country, and that the federal government might thereby acquire more power. But I cannot discern that the construction of the constitution will be affected in the smallest degree, by deducing it from either source, provided a sound authority is allowed to the source selected. Every stipulation, sentence, word and letter; and every donation, reservation, division and restriction, will be exactly the same, whichever is preferred. A man, having two titles, may distinguish himself by which he pleases, in making a contract; and whichever he uses, he remains himself. So the people having two titles or capacities, one arising from an existing association, the other from the natural right of self-government, may enter into a compact under either, but are themselves still; and their acts are equally obligatory, whichever they may select. Politicians may therefore indulge their taste in deducing the constitution of the union from either, but whichever they may fancy, no sound ground will thence result for their differing in the construction of it. . .

It would be an incivility to the reader . . . to prove, that the term 'state' [as used in various state constitutions] is not in any one instance used in reference to all the people of the United States, either as composing a single state, or as being about to compose a single state. Used geographically, it refers to state territory; used politically, it refers to the inhabitants of this territory, united by mutual consent into a civil society. The sovereignty of this association, the allegiance due to it, and its right to internal government, are all positively asserted. The terms 'state and government' far from being synonymous, are used to convey different ideas; and the latter is never recognized as possessing any species of sovereignty.

It next behooves us to consider whether the term 'states' has changed its

* Richmond, Va., Shepherd and Pollard, 1820, pp. 39–46, 107–8, 120–21, 139–42 *passim.*

meaning, by being transplanted from its original nursery, into the constitution of the United States; and is there used to designate all the inhabitants of the United States, as constituting one great state; or whether it is recognized in the same sense in which it had been previously used by most or all of the state constitutions.

The plural 'states' rejects the idea, that the people of all the states considered themselves as one state. The word 'united' is an averment of pre-existing social compacts, called states; and these consisted of the people of each separate state. It admits the existence of political societies able to contract with each other, and who had previously contracted. And the words 'more perfect union' far from implying that the old parties to the old union were superseded by new parties, evidently mean, that these same old parties were about to amend their old union.

But the parties, though recognized as being the same, were not strictly so. The authority of the people of each state is resorted to in the last union, in preference to that of the government of each state, by which the old confederation was formed. This circumstance by no means weakens the force of the last observation, because the recognition of existing political parties able to contract, remains the same. The states, in referring to the old union, only admit themselves to have been bound by their governments, as they possessed the right of making treaties. But as the state governments were the parties to the first confederation, and as such, had a mutual right to destroy that treaty, this danger suggests another reason for the style and principles of the new union. Among its improvements, that by which it is chiefly made 'more perfect,' was the substitution of the authority of 'the people of the United States' for that of the governments of the United States; not with an intention of excluding from the new union the idea of a compact between the states, but of placing that compact upon better ground, than that upon which it previously rested.

The term 'union' has never been applied to describe a government, established by the consent of individuals; nor do any of our state constitutions use it in that sense. They speak indeed of individuals 'uniting' to form a government, not to form a union; and I do not recollect that a single compact between individuals for the establishment of a government, has ever been called a union; though a multitude of cases exist, in which that name has been given to agreements between independent states. If therefore this term comprised the whole evidence, to prove that our union was the act of distinct bodies politic, composed of the people within different geographical boundaries, and not of a number of people, encircled by one line, without any such discrimination, it would be sufficient.

But the constitution itself furnishes the plainest correspondent evidence, in its origin, establishment and terms. The members of the convention which formed it, were chosen by states, and voted by states, without any regard to the number of people in each state. It was adopted by thirteen votes, without respecting the same principles. Now what was represented by these voters; the territory of each state, or the people of each state? The terms 'United States' must refer to one or the other. If to the former, then the territories of each state entered into a compact 'to form a more perfect union, establish justice, insure domestic tranquillity, provide for the common defence, promote the general welfare, and secure the blessings of liberty to *ourselves* and our *posterity.' The posterity of territories.* If to the latter, it was the people of each state, who by compact in their political capacity, by giving one vote each, formed the union. . .

As the great political departments of the federal government, legislative and executive, emanated from the societies called states, so they are made dependent upon them, in the mode prescribed for amending the constitution of the union; because the authors had the right of altering their own work. Had this constitution originated from, or been made by the people inhabiting the territories of the whole union, its amendment would have remained to them, as the amendment of the state constitutions belongs to the people of a state. But as such a body of associated people, did not exist, the amendment of the union is left in the hands of the existing bodies politic, to which, as its authors, it obviously belonged. No majority in congress can either call a convention, or amend the constitution; but the legislatures of two-thirds of the states may compel congress to call one, and those of three-fourths, may amend it. Thus a supremacy of the states, not only over congress, but over the whole constitution, is twice acknowledged; first, by their power over the legislative and executive departments instituted for executing the union; and secondly, by their power over the union itself. . .

THE SOVEREIGNTY OF SPHERES

When the adoption of the federal constitution was under discussion, its enemies expressed an alarm, on account of the magnitude of the powers conferred on the federal government, and its friends an apprehension of its feebleness, compared with the powers reserved to the states; but neither party contended, that an amplification of the greater division of power, and of course a diminution of the lesser, could constitutionally be made by equipping the giant in all the panoply of means, implication and inference, and compelling the dwarf to appear naked in a combat with his antagonist. On the contrary, it was successfully urged by the warmest friends to the constitution, and in particular by the authors of the *Federalist*, that the supposed inequality of power between the state and federal spheres did not exist; and that either division, especially the state, was able to balance and control the other. In this computation, the comparison was made between the federal sphere, and the state sphere, comprising all the state governments; and the equilibrium of power was deduced from the expectation, that if the rights of one state were assailed by the federal government, the rest would not suffer their copartner to be overwhelmed by the weight of power, and their own rights to be destroyed by a victory, in a contest so unequal. To estimate the magnitude of their relative powers, the state governments ought to be considered as constituting one sphere, and the federal government another. Perhaps a cool philosopher may consider the security of private property, the protection of personal rights, the suppression of crimes, the care of good manners and the catalogue of municipal regulations, as embracing a sphere of action, of greater moral extent, than the powers delegated to congress; and if the two spheres are to be geographically compared, the map demonstrates their equality. If these spheres are equal as to magnitude, one magnitude attracts undefined appurtenances as strongly as the other; and if the framers of the constitution designed to balance magnitude by magnitude, they could not also have designed to destroy the balance, by annexing to either an exclusive privilege of attracting undefined powers.

Be this as it may, I contend, that the federal constitution, so far from intending to make its political spheres morally unequal in powers, or to invest the *greatest* with any species of sovereignty over the least, intended the very reverse; and that the court have recognized the latter intention by avowing its right to declare an unconstitutional law, void. As the powers of congress must be confessed to transcend those of the court, much farther than they do those of the states, it follows, that if they cannot be constitutionally used to contract the powers of the court, they cannot be constitutionally used to contract the powers of the states. The reason why great spheres derive no authority from magnitude to transgress upon small spheres, is, that both are donations from the same source; and that the donor did not intend, that one donation should pilfer another, because it was smaller. . . The laws of congress claim a general supremacy, but the supreme court claims and exercises a supremacy over them. . . The supremacy of congress and of the court, in alliance . . . has declared war against the sovereignty of the states; but how it will terminate, is hidden in the womb of time. . .

2. *The great end of the Supreme Court is to act as an umpire between the States and the Confederacy*

HUGH S. LEGARÉ, *Review of Kent's Commentaries on American Law*, 1828 *

. . . If any one wishes to be convinced how little, even the wisest men, are able to foresee the results of their own political contrivances, let him read the constitution, with the contemporaneous exposition of it contained (even) in *The Federalist;* and then turn to this part of Chancellor Kent's work, to the inaugural speech of the present Executive of the United States [Andrew Jackson], and to some of the records of Congress, during the memorable session which is just past.

He will find that the government has been fundamentally altered by the progress of opinion—that instead of being any longer one of enumerated powers and a circumscribed sphere, as it was beyond all doubt intended to be, it knows absolutely no bounds but the will of a majority of Congress—that instead of confining itself in time of peace to the diplomatic and commercial relations of the country, it is seeking out employment for itself by interfering

* *The Southern Review,* August 1828, vol. II, no. 1, pp. 72–113, Reprinted in *Writings of Hugh Swinton Legaré,* vol. II, pp. 94–9, 101–4, 111–12 *passim.*

in the domestic concerns of society, and threatens in the course of a very few years, to control in the most offensive and despotic manner, all the pursuits, the interests, the opinions and the conduct of men. He will find that this extraordinary revolution has been brought about, in a good degree by the Supreme Court of the United States, which has applied to the constitution—very innocently, no doubt, and with commanding ability in argument—and thus given authority and currency to, such canons of interpretation, as necessarily lead to these extravagant results. Above all, he will be perfectly satisfied that that high tribunal affords, by its own showing, no barrier whatever against the usurpations of Congress—and that the rights of the weaker part of this confederacy may, to any extent, be wantonly and tyrannically violated, under colour of law, (the most grievous shape of oppression) by men neither interested in its destiny nor subject to its control, without any means of redress being left it, except such as are inconsistent with all idea of order and government. . .

M'Cullough's case established a doctrine sufficiently latitudinarian. It gave the government an unbounded discretion in the choice of 'means' to effect its constitutional objects. Nor does it confine the exercise of this arbitrary power to cases of absolute necessity. It declares that Congress has the same latitude in matters even of the most doubtful character, by way *of standing policy*—in time of peace, for example, it may do what could only be justified by the pressing exigencies of war, when the urgency of the case creates its own law and supersedes all others. A national bank, is, no doubt, in many points of view, an excellent institution, but did any one ever before hear of such an establishment being founded for the purpose of collecting revenue? But whether as a *means*, 'it is necessary and proper' it seems, is for the Legislature to decide, and the court has no right to look into that question.

In short, there is no end to the consequences that may and will be deduced from the doctrine in M'Cullough's case. The amount of it really is, that the enumeration of powers in the constitution was a vain attempt to confine what is necessarily illimitable—that such an instrument never can ascertain its objects with any sort of precision—that it can, at most, hint a vague purpose and sketch a sweeping outline, which is to be filled up at discretion—in short, that it is not the plan of a government formed and settled, and circumscribed from the first, as it is intended to continue forever, but is a mere nucleus, around which a government is *to be* formed, according to the circumstances of the times, and the opinions of mankind. Such a principle being once established, no man can pretend to anticipate what shape the constitution of the United States (not that written by the convention, but the other which is to be built upon it) is destined to take. . .

We venture to predict that no act of the federal government (supposing it to have common discretion) will ever be pronounced unconstitutional in that court, for the simple reason that the principle of M'Cullough's case covers the whole ground of political sovereignty, and consecrates usurpation in advance. . . That argument . . . cannot be sound which necessarily converts a government of enumerated into one of indefinite powers, and a confederacy of republics into a gigantic and consolidated empire.

Perhaps it may be said that this would be allowing too much discretion to the court—but we do not see that it would exceed the bounds of a sound, legal discretion, such as is absolutely necessary in every part of the administration of justice. Besides, that discretion would have the inestimable advantage of being in *favorem libertatis*, whereas the uncontrolled discretion of Congress is just the contrary. None but the worst consequences can reasonably be anticipated from it. In a country extending over such an immense territory—already comprising a multitude of commonwealths, differing so widely in interests, in character, and in political opinions, and still going on to increase without any assignable limit—it is preposterous to expect that a central government, which shall attempt to meddle with the domestic concerns of society, can be tolerable to its subjects. It will be inevitably *societas mater discordiarum*; or if two sections should unite to give the law, it would be the most impracticable, impenetrable and reckless tyranny that ever existed. At all events, whether we have pointed out the true causes of the evil, and whether there be any remedy for it or not, we are satisfied that no purity of character, no rectitude of intention, no superiority of judgment and capacity in the judges of the Supreme Court (and we can scarcely expect greater than it is already distinguished by) will ever enable that tribunal to answer its great end, as an umpire between the states and the confederacy. The mischief has already been done—the first step is taken, and the whole *system* is radically wrong. . .

. . . A quick sense of injustice, with a determination to resist it in every shape and under every name and pretext, is of the very essence and definition of liberty, political as well as personal. How far, indeed, this resistance is to be carried in any particular instance, is a question of circumstances and discretion. So dreadful are all revolutions in their immediate effects—so uncertain in their ultimate issues, that a wise man would doubt long—that a moderate and virtuous man would bear much—before he could be prevailed upon to give his consent to extreme measures. We would be any thing rather than apostles of discord and dismemberment, sorely as the government to which South-Carolina, and the south in general, have been so loyal and devoted, is beginning to press upon all our dearest interests and sensibilities. But we feel it to be our duty to exhort our fellow-citizens to renewed exertion, and to a jealous and sleepless vigilance upon this subject. The battle must be fought inch by inch—no concession or compromise must be thought of. The courage and constancy of a free people can never fail, when they are exerted in defense of right. . .

3. *It is, sir, the people's Constitution*

DANIEL WEBSTER, Second Speech on Foot's Resolution,
Reply to Hayne, 26 January 1830 *

. . . I understand the honorable gentleman from South Carolina to maintain, that it is a right of the State legislatures to interfere, whenever, in their judg-

* *The Writings and Speeches of Daniel Webster*, Boston, Little, Brown, and Co., 1903, vol. 6, pp. 3–75 *passim*.

ment, this government transcends its constitutional limits, and to arrest the operation of its laws. . .

What he contends for is, that it is constitutional to interrupt the administration of the Constitution itself, in the hands of those who are chosen and sworn to administer it, by the direct interference, in form of law, of the States, in virtue of their sovereign capacity. The inherent right in the people to reform their government I do not deny; and they have another right, and that is, to resist unconstitutional laws, without overturning the government. It is no doctrine of mine that unconstitutional laws bind the people. The great question is, Whose prerogative is it to decide on the constitutionality or unconstitutionality of the laws? On that, the main debate hinges. The proposition, that, in case of a supposed violation of the Constitution by Congress, the States have a constitutional right to interfere and annul the law of Congress, is the proposition of the gentleman. I do not admit it. If the gentleman had intended no more than to assert the right of revolution for justifiable cause, he would have said only what all agree to. But I cannot conceive that there can be a middle course, between submission to the laws, when regularly pronounced constitutional, on the one hand, and open resistance, which is revolution or rebellion, on the other. I say, the right of a State to annul a law of Congress cannot be maintained, but on the ground of the inalienable right of man to resist oppression; that is to say, upon the ground of revolution. I admit that there is an ultimate violent remedy, above the Constitution and in defiance of the Constitution, which may be resorted to when a revolution is to be justified. But I do not admit, that, under the Constitution and in conformity with it, there is any mode in which a State government, as a member of the Union, can interfere and stop the progress of the general government, by force of her own laws, under any circumstances whatever.

This leads us to inquire into the origin of this government and the source of its power. Whose agent is it? Is it the creature of the State legislatures, or the creature of the people? If the government of the United States be the agent of the State governments, then they may control it, provided they can agree in the manner of controlling it; if it be the agent of the people, then the people alone can control it, restrain it, modify, or reform it. It is observable enough, that the doctrine for which the honorable gentleman contends leads him to the necessity of maintaining, not only that this general goverment is the creature of the States, but that it is the creature of each of the States severally, so that each may assert the power for itself of determining whether it acts within the limits of its authority. It is the servant of four-and-twenty masters, of different wills and different purposes, and yet bound to obey all. This absurdity (for it seems no less) arises from a misconception as to the origin of this government and its true character. It is, Sir, the people's Constitution, the people's government, made for the people, made by the people, and answerable to the people. The people of the United States have declared that this Constitution shall be the supreme law. We must either admit the proposition, or dispute their authority. The States are, unquestionably, sovereign, so far as their sovereignty is not affected by this supreme law. But the State legislatures, as political bodies, however sovereign, are yet not sovereign over the people. So far as the people have given power to the general government so far the grant is unquestionably good, and the government holds of the people, and not of the State governments. We are all agents of the same supreme power, the people. The general government and the State governments derive their authority from the same source. Neither can, in relation to the other, be called primary, though one is definite and restricted, and the other general and residuary. The national government possesses those powers which it can be shown the people have conferred on it, and no more. All the rest belongs to the State governments, or to the people themselves. So far as the people have restrained State sovereignty, by the expression of their will, in the Constitution of the United States, so far, it must be admitted, State sovereignty is effectually controlled. I do not contend that it is, or ought to be, controlled farther. The sentiment to which I have referred propounds that State sovereignty is only to be controlled by its own 'feeling of justice'; that is to say, it is not to be controlled at all, for one who is to follow his own feelings is under no legal control. Now, however men may think this ought to be, the fact is, that the people of the United States have chosen to impose control on State sovereignties. There are those, doubtless, who wish they had been left without restraint; but the Constitution has ordered the matter differently. To make war, for instance, is an exercise of sovereignty; but the Constitution declares that no State shall make war. To coin money is another exercise of sovereign power; but no State is at liberty to coin money. Again, the Constitution says that no sovereign State shall be so sovereign as to make a treaty. These prohibitions, it must be confessed are a control on the State sovereignty of South Carolina, as well as of the other States, which does not arise 'from her own feelings of honorable justice.' The opinion referred to, therefore, is in defiance of the plainest provisions of the Constitution. . .

The people, then, Sir, erected this government. They gave it a Constitution, and in that Constitution they have enumerated the powers which they bestow on it. They have made it a limited government. They have defined its authority. They have restrained it to the exercise of such powers as are granted, and all others, they declare, are reserved to the States or the people. But, Sir, they have not stopped here. If they had, they would have accomplished but half their work. No definition can be so clear, as to avoid possibility of doubt; no limitation so precise, as to exclude all uncertainty. Who, then, shall construe this grant of the people? Who shall interpret their will, where it may be supposed they have left it doubtful? With whom do they repose this ultimate right of deciding on the powers of the government? Sir, they have settled all this in the fullest manner. They have left it with the government itself, in its appropriate branches. Sir, the very chief end, the main design, for which the whole Constitution was framed and adopted, was to establish a government that should not be obliged to act through State agency, or depend on State opinion and State discretion. The people had had quite enough of that kind of government under the Confederation. Under that system, the legal action, the application of law to individuals, belonged exclusively to the States. Congress could only recommend; their acts were not of binding force, till the States had adopted and sanctioned them. Are we in that condition still? Are we yet at the mercy of State discretion and State construction? Sir, if we are, then vain will be our attempt to maintain the Constitution under which we sit.

But, Sir, the people have wisely provided, in the Constitution itself, a proper, suitable mode and tribunal for settling questions of constitutional law. There are in the Constitution grants of powers to Congress, and restrictions on these powers. There are, also, prohibitions on the States. Some authority must, therefore, necessarily exist, having the ultimate jurisdiction to fix and ascertain the interpretation of these grants, restrictions, and prohibitions. The Constitutions has itself pointed out, ordained, and established that authority. How has it accomplished this great and essential end? By declaring, Sir, that '*the Constitution, and the laws of the United States made in pursuance thereof, shall be the supreme law of the land, any thing in the constitution* or *laws of any State to the contrary notwithstanding*.'

This, Sir, was the first great step. By this the supremacy of the Constitution and laws of the United States is declared. The people so will it. No State law is to be valid which comes in conflict with the Constitution, or any law of the United States passed in pursuance of it. But who shall decide this question of interference? To whom lies the last appeal? This, Sir, the Constitution itself decides also by declaring, '*that the judicial power shall extend to all* cases *arising under the Constitution and laws of the United States*.' These two provisions cover the whole ground. They are, in truth, the keystone of the arch! With these it is a government; without them it is a confederation. In pursuance of these clear and express provisions, Congress established, at its very first session, in the judicial act, a mode for carrying them into full effect, and for bringing all questions of constitutional power to the final decision of the Supreme Court. It then, Sir, became a government. It then had the means of self-protection; and but for this, it would, in all probability, have been now among things which are past. Having constituted the government, and declared its powers, the people have further said, that, since somebody must decide on the extent of these powers, the government shall itself decide; subject, always, like other popular governments, to its responsibility to the people. And now, Sir, I repeat, how is it that a State legislature acquires any power to interfere? Who, or what, gives them the right to say to the people, 'We, who are your agents and servants for one purpose, will undertake to decide, that your other agents and servants, appointed by you for another purpose, have transcended the authority you gave them!' The reply would be, I think, not impertinent,—'Who made you a judge over another's servants? To their own masters they stand or fall.'

Sir, I deny this power of State legislatures altogether. It cannot stand the test of examination. Gentlemen may say, that, in an extreme case, a State government might protect the people from intolerable oppression. Sir, in such a case, the people might protect themselves, without the aid of the State governments. Such a case warrants revolution. It must make, when it comes, a law for itself. A nullifying act of a State legislature cannot alter the case, nor make resistance any more lawful. In maintaining these sentiments, Sir, I am but asserting the rights of the people. I state what they have declared, and insist on their right to declare it. They have chosen to repose this power in the general government, and I think it my duty to support it, like other constitutional powers. . .

I have not allowed myself, Sir, to look beyond the Union, to see what might lie hidden in the dark recess behind. I have not coolly weighed the chances of preserving liberty when the bonds that unite us together shall be broken asunder. I have not accustomed myself to hang over the precipice of disunion, to see whether, with my short sight, I can fathom the depth of the abyss below; nor could I regard him as a safe counsellor in the affairs of this government, whose thoughts should be mainly bent on considering, not how the Union may be best preserved, but how tolerable might be the condition of the people when it should be broken up and destroyed. While the Union lasts, we have high, exciting, gratifying prospects spread out before us, for us and our children. Beyond that I seek not to penetrate the veil. God grant that in my day, at least, that curtain may not rise! God grant that on my vision never may be opened what lies behind! When my eyes shall be turned to behold for the last time the sun in heaven, may I not see him shining on the broken and dishonored fragments of a once glorious Union; on States dissevered, discordant, belligerent; on a land rent with civil feuds, or drenched, it may be, in fraternal blood! Let their last feeble and lingering glance rather behold the gorgeous ensign of the republic, now known and honored throughout the earth, still full high advanced, its arms and trophies streaming in their original lustre, not a stripe erased or polluted, nor a single star obscured, bearing for its motto, no such miserable interrogatory as 'What is all this worth?' nor those other words of delusion and folly, 'Liberty first and Union afterwards'; but everywhere, spread all over in characters of living light, blazing on all its ample folds, as they float over the sea and over the land, and in every wind under the whole heavens, that other sentiment, dear to every true American heart,—Liberty *and* Union, now and for ever, one and inseparable!

4. *The numerical majority is as truly a single power as the absolute government of one*

JOHN C. CALHOUN, *A Disquisition on Government*, 1850 *

In order to have a clear and just conception of the nature and object of government, it is indispensable to understand correctly what that constitution or law of our nature is, in which government originates; or, to express it more fully and accurately,—that law, without which government would not, and with which, it must necessarily exist. Without this, it is as impossible to lay any solid foundation for the science of government, as it would be to lay one for that of astronomy, without a like understanding of that constitution or law of the material world, according to which the several bodies composing the solar system mutually act on each other, and by which they are kept in their

* *The Works of John C. Calhoun*, Richard K. Crallé, ed., New York, D. Appleton and Co., 1853–55, vol. 1, pp. 1–70 *passim*.

respective spheres. The first question, accordingly, to be considered is,—What is that constitution or law of our nature, without which government would not exist, and with which its existence is necessary?

In considering this, I assume, as an incontestable fact, that man is so constituted as to be a social being. His inclinations and wants, physical and moral, irresistibly impel him to associate with his kind; and he has accordingly, never been found, in any age or country, in any state other than the social. In no other, indeed, could he exist; and in no other,—were it possible for him to exist,—could he attain to a full development of his moral and intellectual faculties, or raise himself, in the scale of being, much above the level of the brute creation.

I next assume, also, as a fact not less incontestable, that, while man is so constituted as to make the social state necessary to his existence and the full development of his faculties, this state itself cannot exist without government. The assumption rests on universal experience. In no age or country has any society or community ever been found, whether enlightened or savage, without government of some description.

Having assumed these, as unquestionable phenomena of our nature, I shall, without further remark, proceed to the investigation of the primary and important question,—What is that constitution of our nature, which, while it impels man to associate with his kind, renders it impossible for society to exist without government?

The answer will be found in the fact, (not less incontestable than either of the others,) that, while man is created for the social state, and is accordingly so formed as to feel what affects others, as well as what affects himself, he is, at the same time, so constituted as to feel more intensely what affects him directly, than what affects him indirectly through others; or, to express it differently, he is so constituted, that his direct or individual affections are stronger than his sympathetic or social feelings. I intentionally avoid the expression, *selfish* feelings, as applicable to the former; because, as commonly used, it implies an unusual excess of the individual over the social feelings, in the person to whom it is applied; and consequently, something depraved and vicious. My object is, to exclude such inference, and to restrict the inquiry exclusively to facts in their bearings on the subject under consideration, viewed as mere phenomena appertaining to our nature,—constituted as it is; and which are as unquestionable as is that of gravitation, or any other phenomenon of the material world.

In asserting that our individual are stronger than our social feelings, it is not intended to deny that there are instances, growing out of peculiar relations, —as that of a mother and her infant,—or resulting from the force of education and habit over peculiar constitutions, in which the latter have over-powered the former; but these instances are few, and always regarded as something extraordinary. The deep impression they make, whenever they occur, is the strongest proof that they are regarded as exceptions to some general and well understood law of our nature; just as some of the minor powers of the material world are apparently to gravitation.

I might go farther, and assert this to be a phenomenon, not of our nature only, but of all animated existence, throughout its entire range, so far as our knowledge extends. It would, indeed, seem to be essentially connected with the great law of self-preservation which pervades all that feels, from man down to the lowest and most insignificant reptile or insect. In none is it stronger than in man. His social feelings may, indeed, in a state of safety and abundance, combined with high intellectual and moral culture, acquire great expansion and force; but not so great as to overpower this all-pervading and essential law of animated existence.

But that constitution of our nature which makes us feel more intensely what affects us directly than what affects us indirectly through others, necessarily leads to conflict between individuals. Each, in consequence, has a greater regard for his own safety or happiness, than for the safety or happiness of others; and, where these come in opposition, is ready to sacrifice the interests of others to his own. And hence, the tendency to a universal state of conflict, between individual and individual; accompanied by the connected passions of suspicion, jealousy, anger and revenge,—followed by insolence, fraud and cruelty; and, if not prevented by some controlling power, ending in a state of universal discord and confusion, destructive of the social state and the ends for which it is ordained. This controlling power, wherever vested, or by whomsoever exercised, is GOVERNMENT.

It follows, then, that man is so constituted, that government is necessary to the existence of society, and society to his existence, and the perfection of his faculties. It follows, also, that government has its origin in this twofold constitution of his nature; the sympathetic or social feelings constituting the remote,—and the individual or direct, the proximate cause.

If man had been differently constituted in either particular;—if, instead of being social in his nature, he had been created without sympathy for his kind, and independent of others for his safety and existence; or if, on the other hand, he had been so created, as to feel more intensely what affected others than what affected himself, (if that were possible,) or, even, had this supposed interest been equal,—it is manifest that, in either case, there would have been no necessity for government, and that none would ever have existed. But, although society and government are thus intimately connected with and dependent on each other,—of the two society is the greater. It is the first in the order of things, and in the dignity of its object; that of society being primary—to preserve and perfect our race; and that of government secondary and subordinate, to preserve and perfect society. Both are, however, necessary to the existence and well-being of our race, and equally of Divine ordination. . .

But government, although intended to protect and preserve society, has itself a strong tendency to disorder and abuse of its powers, as all experience and almost every page of history testify. The cause is to be found in the same constitution of our nature which makes government indispensable. The powers which it is necessary for government to possess, in order to repress violence and preserve order, cannot execute themselves. They must be administered by men in whom, like others, the individual are stronger than the social feelings. And hence, the powers vested in them to prevent injustice and oppression on the part of others, will, if left unguarded, be by them converted into instruments to oppress the rest of the community. That, by which this is prevented, by whatever name called, is what is meant by CONSTITUTION, in its most comprehensive sense, when applied to GOVERNMENT.

Having its origin in the same principle of our nature, *constitution* stands to *government*, as *government* stands to *society*; and, as the end for which society is ordained, would be defeated without government, so that for which government is ordained would, in a great measure, be defeated without constitution. But they differ in this striking particular. There is no difficulty in forming government. It is not even a matter of choice, whether there shall be one or not. Like breathing, it is not permitted to depend on our volition. Necessity will force it on all communities in some one form or another. Very different is the case as to constitution. Instead of a matter of necessity, it is one of the most difficult tasks imposed on man to form a constitution worthy of the name; while, to form a perfect one,—one that would completely counteract the tendency of government to oppression and abuse, and hold it strictly to the great ends for which it is ordained,—has thus far exceeded human wisdom, and possibly ever will. From this, another striking difference results. Constitution is the contrivance of man, while government is of Divine ordination. Man is left to perfect what the wisdom of the Infinite ordained, as necessary to preserve the race.

With these remarks, I proceed to the consideration of the important and difficult question: How is this tendency of government to be counteracted? Or, to express it more fully,—How can those who are invested with the powers of government be prevented from employing them, as the means of aggrandizing themselves, instead of using them to protect and preserve society? It cannot be done by instituting a higher power to control the government, and those who administer it. This would be but to change the seat of authority, and to make this higher power, in reality, the government; with the same tendency, on the part of those who might control its powers, to pervert them into instruments of aggrandizement. Nor can it be done by limiting the powers of government, so as to make it too feeble to be made an instrument of abuse; for, passing by the difficulty of so limiting its powers, without creating a power higher than the government itself to enforce the observance of the limitations, it is a sufficient objection that it would, if practicable, defeat the end for which government is ordained, by making it too feeble to protect and preserve society. The powers necessary for this purpose will ever prove sufficient to aggrandize those who control it, at the expense of the rest of the community.

In estimating what amount of power would be requisite to secure the objects of government, we must take into the reckoning, what would be necessary to defend the community against external, as well as internal dangers. . .

Self-preservation is the supreme law, as well with communities as individuals. And hence the danger of withholding from government the full command of the power and resources of the state; and the great difficulty of limiting its powers consistently with the protection and preservation of the community. And hence the question recurs,—By what means can government, without being divested of the full command of the resources of the community, be prevented from abusing its powers? . .

There is but one way in which this can possibly be done; and that is, by such an organism as will furnish the ruled with the means of resisting successfully this tendency on the part of the rulers to oppression and abuse. Power can only be resisted by power,—and tendency by tendency. Those who exercise power and those subject to its exercise,—the rulers and the ruled,—stand in antagonistic relations to each other. The same constitution of our nature which leads rulers to oppress the ruled,—regardless of the object for which government is ordained,—will, with equal strength, lead the ruled to resist, when possessed of the means of making peaceable and effective resistance. Such an organism, then, as will furnish the means by which resistance may be systematically and peaceably made on the part of the ruled, to oppression and abuse of power on the part of the rulers, is the first and indispensable step towards *forming* a constitutional government. And as this can only be effected by or through the right of suffrage,—(the right on the part of the ruled to choose their rulers at proper intervals, and to hold them thereby responsible for their conduct,)—the responsibility of the rulers to the ruled, through the right of suffrage, is the indispensable and primary principle in the *foundation* of a constitutional government. . .

I call the right of suffrage the indispensable and primary principle; for it would be a great and dangerous mistake to suppose, as many do, that it is, of itself, sufficient to form constitutional governments. . .

The right of suffrage, of itself, can do no more than give complete control to those who elect, over the conduct of those they have elected. In doing this, it accomplishes all it possibly can accomplish. This is its aim,—and when this is attained, its end is fulfilled. It can do no more, however enlightened the people, or however widely extended or well guarded the right may be. The sum total, then, of its effects, when most successful, is, to make those elected, the true and faithful representatives of those who elected them,—instead of irresponsible rulers,—as they would be without it; and thus, by converting it into an agency, and the rulers into agents, to divest government of all claims to sovereignty, and to retain it unimpaired to the community. But it is manifest that the right of suffrage, in making these changes, transfers, in reality, the actual control over the government, from those who make and execute the laws, to the body of the community; and, thereby, places the powers of the government as fully in the mass of the community, as they would be if they, in fact, had assembled, made, and executed the laws themselves, without the intervention of representatives or agents. The more perfectly it does this, the more perfectly it accomplishes its ends; but in doing so, it only changes the seat of authority, without counteracting in the least, the tendency of the government to oppression and abuse of its powers.

If the whole community had the same interests, so that the interests of each and every portion would be so affected by the action of the government, that the laws which oppressed or impoverished one portion, would necessarily oppress and impoverish all others,—or the reverse,—then the right of suffrage, of itself, would be all-sufficient to counteract the tendency of the government to oppression and abuse of its powers; and, of course, would form, of itself, a perfect constitutional government. The interest of all being the same, by supposition, as far as the action of the government was concerned, all would have like interests as to what laws should be made, and how they should be executed. All strife and struggle would cease as to who should be elected to make and execute them. The only question would be, who was most fit; who the wisest and most capable of understanding the common interest of the whole. This decided, the election would pass off quietly, and without party discord; as no one portion could advance its own peculiar interest without regard to the rest, by electing a favorite candidate.

But such is not the case. On the contrary, nothing is more difficult than to equalize the action of the government, in reference to the various and diversified interests of the community; and nothing more easy than to pervert its powers into instruments to aggrandize and enrich one or more interests by oppressing and impoverishing the others; and this too, under the operation of laws, couched in general terms;—and which, on their face, appear fair and equal. Nor is this the case in some particular communities only. It is so in all; the small and the great,—the poor and the rich,—irrespective of pursuits, productions, or degrees of civilization;—with, however, this difference, that the more extensive and populous the country, the more diversified the condition and pursuits of its population, and the richer, more luxurious, and dissimilar the people, the more difficult is it to equalize the action of the government,—and the more easy for one portion of the community to pervert its powers to oppress and plunder the other.

Such being the case, it necessarily results, that the right of suffrage, by placing the control of the government in the community must, from the same constitution of our nature which makes government necessary to preserve society, lead to conflict among its different interests,—each striving to obtain possession of its powers, as the means of protecting itself against the others;—or of advancing its respective interests, regardless of the interests of others. For this purpose, a struggle will take place between the various interests to obtain a majority, in order to control the government. If no one interest be strong enough, of itself, to obtain it, a combination will be formed between those whose interests are most alike;—each conceding something to the others, until a sufficient number is obtained to make a majority. The process may be slow, and much time may be required before a compact, organized majority can be thus formed; but formed it will be in time, even without preconcert or design, by the sure workings of that principle or constitution of our nature in which government itself originates. When once formed, the community will be divided into two great parties,—a major and minor,—between which there will be incessant struggles on the one side to retain, and on the other to obtain the majority,—and, thereby, the control of the government and the advantages it confers. . .

As, then, the right of suffrage, without some other provision, cannot counteract this tendency of government, the next question for consideration is—What is that other provision? . .

From what has been said, it is manifest, that this provision must be of a character calculated to prevent any one interest, or combination of interests, from using the powers of government to aggrandize itself at the expense of the others. Here lies the evil: and just in proportion as it shall prevent, or fail to prevent it, in the same degree it will effect, or fail to effect the end intended to be accomplished. There is but one certain mode in which this result can be secured; and that is, by the adoption of some restriction or limitation, which shall so effectually prevent any one interest, or combination of interests, from obtaining the exclusive control of the government, as to render hopeless all attempts directed to that end. There is, again, but one mode in which this can be effected; and that is, by taking the sense of each interest or portion of the community, which may be unequally and injuriously affected by the action of the government, separately, through its own majority, or in some other way by which its voice may be fairly expressed; and to require the consent of each interest, either to put or to keep the government in action. This, too, can be accomplished only in one way,—and that is, by such an organism of the government,—and, if necessary for the purpose, of the community also, —as will, by dividing and distributing the powers of government, give to each division or interest, through its appropriate organ, either a concurrent voice in making and executing the laws, or a veto on their execution. It is only by such an organism, that the assent of each can be made necessary to put the government in motion; or the power made effectual to arrest its action, when put in motion;—and it is only by the one or the other that the different interests, orders, classes, or portions, into which the community may be divided, can be protected, and all conflict and struggle between them prevented—by rendering it impossible to put or to keep it in action, without the concurrent consent of all.

Such an organism as this, combined with the right of suffrage, constitutes, in fact, the elements of constitutional government. The one, by rendering those who make and execute the laws responsible to those on whom they operate, prevents the rulers from oppressing the ruled; and the other, by making it impossible for any one interest or combination of interests or class, or order, or portion of the community, to obtain exclusive control, prevents any one of them from oppressing the other. It is clear, that oppression and abuse of power must come, if at all, from the one or the other quarter. From no other can they come. It follows, that the two, suffrage and proper organism combined, are sufficient to counteract the tendency of government to oppression and abuse of power; and to restrict it to the fulfilment of the great ends for which it is ordained. . .

It may be readily inferred, from what has been stated, that the effect of organism is neither to supercede nor diminish the importance of the right of suffrage; but to aid and perfect it. The object of the latter is, to collect the sense of the community. The more fully and perfectly it accomplishes this, the more fully and perfectly it fulfils its end. But the most it can do, of itself, is to collect the sense of the greater number; that is, of the stronger interests, or combination of interests; and to assume this to be the sense of the community. It is only when aided by a proper organism, that it can collect the sense of the entire community,—of each and all its interests; of each, through its appropriate organ, and of the whole, through all of them united. This would truly be the sense of the entire community; for whatever diversity each interest might have within itself,—as all would have the same interest in reference to the action of the government, the individuals composing each would be fully and truly represented by its own majority or appropriate organ, regarded in reference to the other interests. In brief, every individual of every interest might trust, with confidence, its majority or appropriate organ, against that of every other interest.

It results, from what has been said, that there are two different modes in which the sense of the community may be taken; one, simply by the right of suffrage, unaided; the other, by the right through a proper organism. Each collects the sense of the majority. But one regards numbers only, and considers the whole community as a unit, having but one common interest throughout; and collects the sense of the greater number of the whole, as that of the community. The other, on the contrary, regards interests as well as numbers;—considering the community as made up of different and conflicting interests, as far as the action of the government is concerned; and takes the sense of each, through its majority or appropriate organ, and the united sense of all, as the sense of the entire community. The former of these I shall call the numerical, or absolute majority; and the latter, the concurrent, or constitutional majority. I call it the constitutional majority, because it is an essential element in every constitutional government,—be its form what it may. So great is the difference, politically speaking, between the two majorities, that they cannot be confounded, without leading to great and fatal errors; and yet the distinction between them has been so entirely overlooked, that when the term *majority* is used in political discussions, it is applied exclusively to designate the numerical, —as if there were no other. Until this distinction is recognized, and better understood, there will continue to be great liability to error in properly constructing constitutional governments, especially of the popular form, and of preserving them when properly constructed. Until then, the latter will have a strong tendency to slide, first, into the government of the numerical majority, and, finally, into absolute government of some other form. To show that such must be the case, and at the same time to mark more strongly the difference between the two, in order to guard against the danger of overlooking it, I propose to consider the subject more at length.

The first and leading error which naturally arises from overlooking the distinction referred to, is, to confound the numerical majority with the people; and this so completely as to regard them as identical. This is a consequence that necessarily results from considering the numerical as the only majority. All admit, that a popular government, or democracy, is the government of the people; for the terms imply this. A perfect government of the kind would be one which would embrace the consent of every citizen or member of the community; but as this is impracticable, in the opinion of those who regard the numerical as the only majority, and who can perceive no other way by which the sense of the people can be taken,—they are compelled to adopt this as the only true basis of popular government, in contradistinction to governments of the aristocratical or monarchical form. Being thus constrained, they are, in the next place, forced to regard the numerical majority, as, in effect, the entire people; that is, the greater part as the whole; and the government of the greater part as the government of the whole. It is thus the two come to be confounded, and a part made identical with the whole. And it is thus, also, that all the rights, powers, and immunites of the whole people come to be attributed to the numerical majority; and, among others, the supreme, sovereign authority of establishing and abolishing governments at pleasure.

This radical error, the consequence of confounding the two, and of regarding the numerical as the only majority, has contributed more than any other cause, to prevent the formation of popular constitutional governments,—and to destroy them even when they have been formed. It leads to the conclusion that, in their formation and establishment nothing more is necessary than the right of suffrage,—and the allotment to each division of the community a representation in the government, in proportion to numbers. If the numerical majority were really the people; and if, to take its sense truly, were to take the sense of the people truly, a government so constituted would be a true and perfect model of a popular constitutional government; and every departure from it would detract from its excellence. But, as such is not the case,—as the numerical majority, instead of being the people, is only a portion of them,—such a government, instead of being a true and perfect model of the people's government, that is, a people self-governed, is but the government of a part, over a part,—the major over the minor portion.

But this misconception of the true elements of constitutional government does not stop here. It leads to others equally false and fatal, in reference to the best means of preserving and perpetuating them, when, from some fortunate combination of circumstances, they are correctly formed. For they who fall into these errors regard the restrictions which organism imposes on the will of the numerical majority as restrictions on the will of the people, and, therefore, as not only useless, but wrongful and mischievous. And hence they endeavor to destroy organism, under the delusive hope of making government more democratic. . .

A written constitution certainly has many and considerable advantages; but it is a great mistake to suppose, that the mere insertion of provisions to restrict and limit the powers of the government, without investing those for whose protection they are inserted with the means of enforcing their observance, will be sufficient to prevent the major and dominant party from abusing its powers. Being the party in possession of the government, they will, from the same constitution of man which makes government necessary to protect society, be in favor of the powers granted by the constitution, and opposed to the restrictions intended to limit them. As the major and dominant party, they will have no need to these restrictions for their protection. The ballot-box, of itself, would be ample protection to them. Needing no other, they would come, in time, to regard these limitations as unnecessary and improper restraints;—and endeavor to elude them, with the view of increasing their power and influence.

The minor, or weaker party, on the contrary, would take the opposite direction;—and regard them as essential to their protection against the dominant party. And, hence, they would endeavor to defend and enlarge the restrictions, and to limit and contract the powers. But where there are no means by which they could compel the major party to observe the restrictions, the only resort left them would be, a strict construction of the constitution,—that is, a constitution which would confine these powers to the narrowest limits which the meaning of the words used in the grant would admit.

To this the major party would oppose a liberal construction,—one which would give to the words of the grant the broadest meaning of which they were susceptible. It would then be construction against construction; the one to contract, and the other enlarge the powers of the government to the utmost. But of what possible avail could the strict construction of the minor party be, against the liberal interpretation of the major, when the one would have all the powers of the government to carry its construction into effect,—and the other be deprived of all means of enforcing its construction? In a contest so unequal, the result would not be doubtful. The party in favor of the restrictions would be overpowered. . .

The necessary consequence of taking the sense of the community by the concurrent majority is, as has been explained, to give to each interest or portion of the community a negative on the others. It is this mutual negative among its various conflicting interests, which invests each with the power of protecting itself;—and places the rights and safety of each, where only they can be securely placed, under its own guardianship. . . It is, indeed, the negative power which makes the constitution,—and the positive which makes the government. The one is the power of acting;—and the other the power of preventing or arresting action. The two, combined, make constitutional governments.

But, as there can be no constitution without the negative power, and no negative power without the concurrent majority;—it follows, necessarily, that where the numerical majority has the sole control of the government, there can be no constitution; as constitution implies limitation or restriction,—and, of course, is inconsistent with the idea of sole or exclusive power. And hence, the numerical, unmixed with the concurrent majority, necessarily forms, in all cases, absolute government.

It is, indeed, the single, or *one power*, which excludes the negative, and constitutes absolute government; and not the *number* in whom the power is vested. The numerical majority is as truly a *single power*, and excludes the negative as completely as the absolute government of one, or of the few. The former is as much the absolute government of the democratic, or popular form, as the latter of the monarchical or aristocratical. It has, accordingly, in common with them, the same tendency to oppression and abuse of power. . .

The concurrent majority, then, is better suited to enlarge and secure the bounds of liberty, because it is better suited to prevent government from passing beyond its proper limits, and to restrict it to its primary end,—the protection of the community. . . The tendency of government to pass beyond its proper limits is what exposes liberty to danger, and renders it insecure; and it is the strong counteraction of governments of the concurrent majority to this tendency which makes them so favorable to liberty. . .

Such are the many and striking advantages of the concurrent over the numerical majority. Against the former but two objections can be made. The one is, that it is difficult of construction . . . and the other, that it would be impracticable to obtain the concurrence of conflicting interests, where they were numerous and diversified; or, if not, that the process for this purpose, would be too tardy to meet, with sufficient promptness, the many and dangerous emergencies, to which all communities are exposed. This objection is plausible; and deserves a fuller notice than it has yet received.

The diversity of opinion is usually so great, on almost all questions of policy, that it is not surprising, on a slight view of the subject, it should be thought impracticable to bring the various conflicting interests of a community to unite on any one line of policy;—or, that a government, founded on such a principle, would be too slow in its movements and too weak in its foundation to succeed in practice. But, plausible as it may seem at the first glance, a more deliberate view will show, that this opinion is erroneous. It is true, that, when there is no urgent necessity, it is difficult to bring those who differ, to agree on any one line of action. Each will naturally insist on taking the course he may think best;—and, from pride of opinion, will be unwilling to yield to others. But the case is different when there is an urgent necessity to unite on some common course of action; as reason and experience both prove. When something *must* be done,—and when it can be done only by the united consent of all,—the necessity of the case will force to a compromise;—be the cause of that necessity what it may. On all questions of acting, necessity where it exists, is the overruling motive; and where, in such cases, compromise among the parties is an indispensable condition to acting, it exerts an overruling influence in predisposing them to acquiesce in some one opinion or course of action. . .

5. *The Constitution is a national fundamental law, establishing a complete national government—an organism of national life*

FRANCIS LIEBER, *Two Lectures on the Constitution of the United States*, 1851 *

. . . What is the Constitution of the United States? Do the States form a league? Or is the Constitution a pact, a contract—a political partnership of contracting parties? Do we live in a confederacy? and if so, in a confederacy of what degree of unitedness? Or is the Constitution a framework of government for a united country—a political organism of a people, with its own vitality and self-sufficing energy? Do we form a union, or an aggregate of partners at pleasure?

These are momentous questions—not only interesting in an historical or scientific point of view, but important as questions of political life and social existence, of public conscience, of right and truth in the highest spheres of human action and of our civilization. At no time has the very character and essence of our Constitution been so much discussed as in ours. Never before have measures of such importance been so made to depend, in appearance, upon the fundamental character of the document called the Constitution of

* New York, 1861. Written in 1851.

the United States, while never before have those in high authority attended less to its genesis, its contents, and its various provisions, in order to justify actions affecting our entire polity. Never before, either in our own, or in the history of our race, have whole communities seemed to make acts of elementary and national consequence depend upon a single term; upon the question whether the Constitution is a mere contract, or whether the word, derived as it is from *constituere*, must be understood in the sense in which Cicero takes it, when he speaks of *constituere rempublicam*—that is, organizing the common weal, putting it in order and connecting all the parts in mutual organic dependence upon one another. . .

Throughout the Debates of the Constituent Convention we find it expressed —I wish I had counted how often—that there is the most urgent necessity of establishing a national *government*. This is the standing phrase of all the members. They did not mean to make a *nation*. Nations are not made by man, but he may politically stamp a nation; just as government cannot make money, but it may coin commodities that are already values.

Almost as frequently we meet in the debates with the expression, that unless we have a national government we cannot avoid anarchy and convulsion. Those who, like Franklin, did not approve of every feature in the Constitution, declared themselves nevertheless ready to accept it, in order to prevent anarchy and convulsion. Why anarchy? When sovereigns fail to conclude a league, war may follow, but it is not anarchy. Anarchy is absence of law and government where they ought to exist—that is, among and over a people. . .

The Constitution is a law, with all the attributes essential to a law, the first of which is that it must be obeyed, and that there must be an authority that can enforce obedience. It is a law, not a mere adhortation, not a pastoral letter, not a 'proclamation in terrorem.'

It is a national law, having proceeded from the fullness of the national necessity, national consciousness and national will, and is expressive of a national destiny.

It is a national fundamental law, establishing a complete national government,—an organism of national life. It is not a mere league of independent states or nations; it allows of no 'Sonderbund.' It is an organism with living functions; not a string of beads in mere juxtaposition on a slender thread, which may snap at any time and allow the beads to roll in all directions.

The more you study history in candor and good faith, and not in order merely to collect points to make out a case, the more you will be convinced that, as indeed I have indicated before, the general government, nationally uniting a number of States, with the framework of local governments, is that very thing which America has contributed as her share to the political history of our race. . .

Our system, being neither a pure unitary government nor a pure confederacy, is not without its difficulties. It has its very great difficulties, as our own times prove, but neither in our case nor in any other whatsoever, be it of practice, theory, or science, is an elementary difficulty overcome by seizing upon one of the contending elements exclusively, and by carrying it out to a fanatical end irrespective of other elements. Seizing upon the single idea of State-sovereignty—a modern fiction, taken in the sense in which the present extremists take it—denying, as was quite recently done in the Senate of the United States, all allegiance to the United States, and imagining that liberty chiefly consists in denying power and authority to the national government, is very much like an attempt of explaining the planetary system by centrifugal power alone. It is a fact, which you will mark as such for future reflection, that almost all, perhaps actually all, the most prominent extremists on the State-right side—that is to say, of those statesmen who were most perseveringly bent on coercing the national government into the narrowest circle of helplessness—have been at the same time strongly inclined toward centralization and consolidation of power within their respective States. Secessionists by profession would cry 'treason,' indeed, were a portion of a State to intimate a desire to peel off one more skin of the bulb. Yet, suppose Rhode Island to secede, why should not Block Island set up as a nation? I say *suppose!* Have we not had close before our eyes a proposition of secession for our city? And what logical process shall stop us from proceeding to the sejunction of the different wards? One thing seems certain—and I conclude my remarks with this observation—that if ever the American people should be forced to make a choice between a unitary government and an unmitigated confederacy, they would be obliged to select the former type.

6. *The Union is much older than the Constitution*

ABRAHAM LINCOLN, First Inaugural Address, 4 March 1861 *

A disruption of the Federal Union, heretofore only menaced, is now formidably attempted.

I hold that, in contemplation of universal law and of the Constitution, the Union of these States is perpetual. Perpetuity is implied, if not expressed, in the fundamental law of all national governments. It is safe to assert that no government proper ever had a provision in its organic law for its own termination. Continue to execute all the express provisions of our national Constitution, and the Union will endure forever—it being impossible to destroy it except by some action not provided for in the instrument itself.

Again, if the United States be not a government proper, but an association of State in the nature of contract merely, can it as a contract be peaceably unmade by less than all the parties who made it? One party to a contract may violate it—break it, so to speak; but does it not require all to lawfully rescind it?

Descending from these general principles, we find the proposition that in legal contemplation the Union is perpetual confirmed by the history of the Union itself. The Union is much older than the Constitution. It was formed, in fact, by the Articles of Association in 1774. It was matured and continued by the Declaration of Independence in 1776. It was further matured, and the

* *Messages and Papers of the Presidents,* James D. Richardson, ed., vol. VI, pp. 5, 7–12 *passim.*

faith of all the then thirteen States expressly plighted and engaged that it should be perpetual, by the Articles of Confederation in 1778. And finally, in 1787 one of the declared objects for ordaining and establishing the Constitution was 'to form a more perfect Union.'

But if the destruction of the Union by one or by a part only of the States be lawfully possible, the Union is less perfect than before the Constitution, having lost the vital element of perpetuity.

It follows from these views that no State upon its own mere motion can lawfully get out of the Union; that resolves and ordinances to that effect are legally void; and that acts of violence, within any State or States, against the authority of the United States, are insurrectionary or revolutionary, according to circumstances.

I therefore consider that, in view of the Constitution and the laws, the Union is unbroken; and to the extent of my ability I shall take care, as the Constitution itself expressly enjoins upon me, that the laws of the Union be faithfully executed in all the States. Doing this I deem to be only a simple duty on my part; and I shall perform it so far as practicable, unless my rightful masters, the American people, shall withhold the requisite means, or in some authoritative manner direct the contrary. I trust this will not be regarded as a menace, but only as the declared purpose of the Union that it will constitutionally defend and maintain itself.

In doing this there needs to be no bloodshed or violence; and there shall be none, unless it be forced upon the national authority. The power confided to me will be used to hold, occupy, and possess the property and places belonging to the Government, and to collect the duties and imposts; but beyond what may be necessary for these objects, there will be no invasion, no using of force against or among the people anywhere. Where hostility to the United States, in any interior locality, shall be so great and universal as to prevent competent resident citizens from holding the Federal offices, there will be no attempt to force obnoxious strangers among the people, for that object. While the strict legal right may exist in the government to enforce the exercise of these offices, the attempt to do so would be so irritating, and so nearly impracticable withal, that I deem it better to forego for the time the uses of such offices. . .

Before entering upon so grave a matter as the destruction of our national fabric, with all its benefits, its memories, and its hopes, would it not be wise to ascertain precisely why we do it? Will you hazard so desperate a step while there is any possibility that any portion of the ills you fly from have no real existence? Will you, while the certain ills you fly to are greater than all the real ones you fly from—will you risk the commission of so fearful a mistake?

All profess to be content in the Union, if all constitutional rights can be maintained. Is it true, then, that any right, plainly written in the Constitution, has been denied? I think not. Happily the human mind is so constituted, that no party can reach to the audacity of doing this. Think, if you can, of a single instance in which a plainly written provision of the Constitution has ever been denied. If, by the mere force of numbers, a majority should deprive a minority of any clearly written constitutional right, it might, in a moral point of view, justify revolution—certainly would, if such right were a vital one. But such is not our case. All the vital rights of minorities, and of individuals, are so plainly assured to them, by affirmations and negations, guaranties and prohibitions, in the Constitution, that controversies never arise concerning them. But no organic law can ever be framed with a provision specifically applicable to every question which may occur in practical administration. No foresight can anticipate, nor any document of reasonable length contain express provisions for all possible questions. Shall fugitives from labor be surrendered by national or by state authority? The Constitution does not expressly say. *May* Congress prohibit slavery in the territories? The Constitution does not expressly say. *Must* Congress protect slavery in the territories? The Constitution does not expressly say.

From questions of this class spring all our constitutional controversies, and we divide upon them into majorities and minorities. If the minority will not acquiesce, the majority must, or the government must cease. There is no other alternative; for continuing the government, is acquiescence on one side or the other. If a minority, in such case, will secede rather than acquiesce, they make a precedent which in turn, will divide and ruin them; for a minority of their own will secede from them, whenever a majority refuses to be controlled by such minority. For instance, why may not any portion of a new confederacy, a year or two hence, arbitrarily secede again, precisely as portions of the present Union now claim to secede from it. All who cherish disunion sentiments, are now being educated to the exact temper of doing this. Is there such perfect identity of interests among the states to compose a new Union, as to produce harmony only, and prevent renewed secession?

Plainly, the central idea of secession, is the essence of anarchy. A majority, held in restraint by constitutional checks, and limitations, and always changing easily, with deliberate changes of popular opinions and sentiments, is the only true sovereign of a free people. Whoever rejects it, does, of necessity, fly to anarchy or to despotism. Unanimity is impossible; the rule of a minority, as a permanent arrangement, is wholly inadmissible, so that, rejecting the majority principle, anarchy, or despotism in some form, is all that is left.

I do not forget the position assumed by some, that constitutional questions are to be decided by the Supreme Court; nor do I deny that such decisions must be binding in any case, upon the parties to a suit, as to the object of that suit, while they are also entitled to very high respect and consideration, in all parallel cases, by all other departments of the government. And while it is obviously possible that such decision may be erroneous in any given case, still the evil effect following it, being limited to that particular case, with the chance that it may be overruled, and never become a precedent for other cases, can better be borne than could the evils of a different practice. At the same time the candid citizen must confess that if the policy of the government, upon vital questions, affecting the whole people, is to be irrevocably fixed by decisions of the Supreme Court, the instant they are made, in ordinary litigation between parties, in personal actions, the people will have ceased, to be their own rulers, having, to that extent, practically resigned their government, into the hands of that eminent tribunal. Nor is there, in this view, any assault upon the court, or the judges. It is a duty, from which they may not shrink, to decide cases properly brought before them; and it is no fault of theirs, if others seek to turn their decisions to political purposes. . .

One section of our country believes slavery is *right*, and ought to be extended, while the other believes it is *wrong*, and ought not to be extended. This is the only substantial dispute. The fugitive slave clause of the Constitution, and the law for the suppression of the foreign slave trade, are each as well enforced, perhaps, as any law can ever be in a community where the moral sense of the people imperfectly supports the law itself. The great body of the people abide by the dry legal obligation in both cases, and a few break over in each. This, I think, cannot be perfectly cured; and it would be worse in both cases *after* the separation of the sections, than before. The foreign slave trade, now imperfectly suppressed, would be ultimately revived without restriction, in one section; while fugitive slaves, now only partially surrendered, would not be surrendered at all, by the other.

Physically speaking, we cannot separate. We cannot remove our respective sections from each other, nor build an impassable wall between them. A husband and wife may be divorced and go out of the presence and beyond the reach of each other; but the different parts of our country cannot do this. They cannot but remain face to face, and intercourse, either amicable or hostile, must continue between them. . .

This country, with its institutions, belongs to the people who inhabit it. Whenever they shall grow weary of the existing government, they can exercise their *constitutional* right of amending it, or their *revolutionary* right to dismember, or overthrow it. I cannot be ignorant of the fact that many worthy, and patriotic citizens are desirous of having the national Constitution amended. While I make no recommendation of amendment, I fully recognize the rightful authority of the people over the whole subject, to be exercised in either of the modes prescribed in the instrument itself; and I should, under existing circumstances, favor, rather than oppose, a fair opportunity being afforded the people to act upon it. . .

In your hands, my dissatisfied fellow-countrymen, and not in mine, is the momentous issue of civil war. The government will not assail you. You can have no conflict without being yourselves the aggressors. You have no oath registered in heaven to destroy the government, while I shall have the most solemn one to 'preserve, protect, and defend' it.

I am loath to close. We are not enemies, but friends. We must not be enemies. Though passion may have strained, it must not break, our bonds of affection. The mystic chords of memory, stretching from every battle-field and patriot grave to every living heart and hearthstone all over this broad land, will yet swell the chorus of the Union when again touched, as surely they will be, by the better angels of our nature.

7. *The Constitution looks to an indestructible Union of indestructible states*

CHIEF JUSTICE SALMON P. CHASE, in Texas v. White, 1869 *

. . . Texas . . . took part, with the other Confederate States, in the war of the rebellion. . . During the whole of that war there was no governor, or judge, or any other State officer in Texas, who recognized the National authority. Nor was any officer of the United States permitted to exercise any authority whatever under the National government within the limits of the State, except under the immediate protection of the National military forces.

Did Texas, in consequence of these acts, cease to be a State? Or, if not, did the State cease to be a member of the Union?

It is needless to discuss, at length, the question whether the right of a State to withdraw from the Union for any cause regarded by herself as sufficient, is consistent with the Constitution of the United States.

The Union of the States never was a purely artificial and arbitrary relation. It began among the Colonies, and grew out of common origin, mutual sympathies, kindred principles, similar interests, and geographical relations. It was confirmed and strengthened by the necessities of war, and received definite form, and character, and sanction from the Articles of Confederation. By these the Union was solemnly declared to 'be perpetual.' And when these Articles were found to be inadequate to the exigencies of the country, the Constitution was ordained 'to form a more perfect Union.' It is difficult to convey the idea of indissoluble unity more clearly than by these words. What can be indissoluble if a perpetual Union, made more perfect, is not?

But the perpetuity and indissolubility of the Union, by no means implies the loss of distinct and individual existence, or of the right of self-government by the States. Under the Articles of Confederation each State retained its sovereignty, freedom, and independence, and every power, jurisdiction, and right not expressly delegated to the United States. Under the Constitution, though the powers of the States were much restricted, still, all powers not delegated to the United States, nor prohibited to the States, are reserved to the States respectively, or to the people. And we have already had occasion to remark at this term, that 'the people of each State compose a State, having its own government, and endowed with all the functions essential to separate and independent existence,' and that 'without the States in union, there could be no such political body as the United States.' Not only, therefore, can there be no loss of separate and independent autonomy to the States, through their union under the Constitution, but it may be not unreasonably said that the preservation of the States, and the maintenance of their governments, are as much within the design and care of the Constitution as the preservation of the Union and the maintenance of the National government. The Constitution, in all its provisions, looks to an indestructible Union, composed of indestructible States.

* 7 Wallace, 700.

When, therefore, Texas became one of the United States, she entered into an indissoluble relation. All the the obligations of perpetual union, and all the guaranties of republican government in the Union, attached at once to the State. The act which consummated her admission into the Union was something more than a compact; it was the incorporation of a new member into the political body. And it was final. The union between Texas and the other States was as complete, as perpetual, and as indissoluble as the union between the original States. There was no place for reconsideration, or revocation, except through revolution, or through consent of the States.

Considered therefore as transactions under the Constitution, the ordinance of secession, adopted by the convention and ratified by a majority of the citizens of Texas, and all the acts of her legislature intended to give effect to that ordinance, were absolutely null. They were utterly without operation in law. The obligations of the State, as a member of the Union, and of every citizen of the State, as a citizen of the United States, remained perfect and unimpaired. It certainly follows that the State did not cease to be a State, nor her citizens to be citizens of the Union. If this were otherwise, the State must have become foreign, and her citizens foreigners. The war must have ceased to be a war for the suppression of rebellion, and must have become a war for conquest and subjugation.

Our conclusion therefore is, that Texas continued to be a State, and a State of the Union, notwithstanding the transactions to which we have referred. And this conclusion, in our judgment, is not in conflict with any act or declaration of any department of the National government, but entirely in accordance with the whole series of such acts and declarations since the first outbreak of the rebellion. . .

SELECTED REFERENCES

Documents Relating to New-England Federalism, 1800–1815, Henry Adams, ed., Boston, Little, Brown, 1877.

John Quincy Adams, *The Jubilee of the Constitution. A Discourse delivered April 30, 1839, the 50th Anniversary of the Inauguration of George Washington as President of the United States*, New York, Samuel Colman, 1839.

Herman V. Ames, *State Documents on Federal Relations; the State and the United States*, Philadelphia, University of Pennsylvania, 1900.

O. A. Brownson, *The American Republic, Its Constitution, Tendencies and Destiny*, New York, P. O'Shea, 1866.

Jesse T. Carpenter, *The South as a Conscious Minority, 1789–1861: A Study in Political Thought*, New York, New York University Press, 1930.

Chisholm *v.* Georgia, 2 Dallas, 419, 1793. Chief Justice Jay's opinion and concurring opinions by Justices Wilson and Cushing.

Edward S. Corwin, *The Doctrine of Judicial Review: Its Legal and Historical Basis and Other Essays*, Princeton University Press, 1914, chap. 2, 'We the People.'

———, 'National Power and State Interposition, 1781–1861,' *Michigan Law Review*, 1912, vol. x, pp. 535–51.

Gunnar Heckscher, 'Calhoun's Idea of "Concurrent Majority" and the Constitutional Theory of Hegel,' *The American Political Science Review*, 1939, vol. xxiii.

John C. Hurd, *The Theory of Our National Existence, As Shown by the Government of the United States Since 1861*, Boston, Little, Brown, 1881.

Andrew C. McLaughlin, *The Courts, the Constitution, and Parties*, University of Chicago Press, 1912, chap. IV, 'Social Compact and Constitutional Construction,' pp. 189–242.

A. T. Mason, *The States Rights Debate: Antifederalism and the Constitution*, Englewood Cliffs, Prentice-Hall, 1964.

C. E. Merriam, *A History of American Political Theories*, New York: Macmillan, 1918, chap. VII, 'Political Theory in Relation to the Nature of the Union,' pp. 252–302.

Elisha Mulford, *The Nation: The Foundations of Civil Order and Political Life in the United States*, New York, Hurt and Houghton, 1870.

Alexander H. Stephens, *A Constitutional View of the Late War Between the States*, Philadelphia, National Publishing Company, 1868.

Joseph Story, *Commentaries on the Constitution of the United States*, Boston, Charles C. Little & James Brown, 1851, 2nd ed., pp. 137–264.

Abel P. Upshur, *The Federal Government: Its True Nature and Character;* Being a Review of Judge Story's Commentaries on the Constitution of the United States, New York, Van Evrie, Horton, 1868, pp. 97–182.

Ware *v.* Hylton, 3 Dallas, 232. (1796)

E. D. Warfield, *The Kentucky Resolution of 1798*, New York, G. P. Putnam, 1887.

XV

PLUTOCRACY OR SOCIAL DEMOCRACY?

Liberal political thought in the United States from 1820 to 1860 had two main drives: first, to win universal manhood suffrage, and thereby cast off the constitutional safeguards for property embodied in the early state constitutions; second, to abolish Negro slavery. These goals had been won, in large measure, by 1870. One might have then anticipated that the last barrier of privilege would soon be erased. But foreshadowings of a new tyranny, a new slavery, had been observed even while these crusades were being waged.

'I am of the opinion that the manufacturing aristocracy which is growing up under our eyes is one of the harshest which ever existed in the world,' Tocqueville warned in the early 1830's. George Fitzhugh was troubled, as we have seen, by the 'white slave trade,' by 'slaves without masters,' and contrasted 'free labor' unfavorably with Negro slavery. 'The men without property, in a free society (and dependent on those who have property),' he said, 'are in a worse condition than slaves.' In 1871 Charles Francis Adams confirmed Tocqueville's forecast, and lent certain support to Fitzhugh's analysis.

Adams had just returned from England, where he had served as our war-time minister. Among the vast changes wrought by the years, he cited as most noticeable, 'a greatly enlarged grasp of enterprise and increased facility of combination.' The five years following the Civil War, Adams wrote in the *North American Review* of April 1871, 'witnessed some of the most remarkable examples of organized lawlessness, under the forms of law, which mankind has yet had opportunity to study. If individuals have, as a rule, quietly pursued their peaceful vocations, the same cannot be said of certain single men at the head of vast combinations of private wealth.' This had been particularly true, Adams went on, as regards those interests controlling the railroads:

> These modern potentates have declared war, negotiated peace, reduced courts, legislatures, and sovereign states to an unqualified obedience to their will, disturbed trade, agitated the currency, imposed taxes, and, boldly setting both law and public opinion at defiance, have freely exercised many other attributes of sovereignty. . . The strength implied in all this they wielded in practical independence of the control both of governments and of indi-

> viduals; much as petty German despots might have governed their little principalities a century or two ago.

Just as kings had a Sir Robert Filmer or a Thomas Hobbes to explain, rationalize, and justify their power, so our new American industrial oligarchy found an apologist in the English philosopher, bio-sociologist, and agnostic, Herbert Spencer (1820–1903). Spencer, who was 'rejected by professional philosophers as superficial and by scientists as ignorant,' supplied American industrialists with their one and only political creed. By and large, they continue to live in the same mental climate as he did. 'H. Spencer you English never quite do justice to', Justice Holmes wrote Lady Pollock in 1895. 'He writes an ugly, uncharming style, his ideals are those of a lower middle class British Philistine. And yet after all abatements I doubt if any writer of English except Darwin has done so much to affect our whole way of thinking about the universe.'

Spencer's creative endeavors span the years 1850–1900, a half-century in which political democracy forged ahead in both England and the United States. The ever-increasing social legislation disturbed him greatly. How did it come to pass, he wanted to know, that the people, getting more and more into power, began to uphold through their own majorities the Tory policy of dictating the action of private citizens, thus narrowing the range in which individuals are free? How could men think of themselves as liberals in adding restrictions on individual liberty rather than in following the historic liberal policy of casting them off? The suggestion that the restraints before 1820 were imposed by a Tory government, whereas those after 1880 were authorized by a government elected by and responsible to the people, Spencer thrust aside as irrelevant and immaterial, a distinction without difference. 'The liberty which a citizen enjoys is measured,' he said, 'not by the nature of the governmental machinery he lives under, whether representative or other, but by the relative paucity of the restraints it imposes on him.'

Spencer's theory rests on precise views about man and his rights, society, and government. Man is born bad: he is 'shapen in iniquity and conceived in sin.' Human frailties will be manifest and decisive regardless of the political system: 'There is no political alchemy by which you can get golden conduct out of leaden instincts.' Such good as there is in man evolves out of grim, even cruel struggle. Just as universal warfare among lower animals ultimately produces types perfectly adapted to environment, so the same beneficent, though severe discipline, the same 'felicity pursuing law' in social relations, brings forth men adapted to their environment and capable of greatest happiness: 'The poverty of the incapable, the distresses that come upon the improvident, the starvation of the idle, and the shouldering aside of the weak by the strong, which leaves so many in shadows and misery are the decrees of a large, far-seeing benevolence. . .'

The natural process that 'must be undergone, the suffering that must be endured,' ultimately develop a society divided sharply into two classes—the rich and powerful, the poor and weak, the good and the good-for nothing. Certain men triumph in the struggle because they are fittest; they are possessed of natural rights and immune from government control or regulation. Government has neither capacity nor authority to intervene in this divinely ordained struggle: 'No power on earth, no cunningly devised laws of statesmanship, no world rectifying schemes of the humane, no communist panaceas, no reforms that men ever did broach or ever will broach, can diminish them one jot. . .' Instead of lessening suffering, they ultimately increase it.

The privileges rightly won, the rights naturally gained, Spencer declared, can be touched or interfered with by government only at the cost of slavery for all. Government does not and cannot fulfill its functions by creating human rights; it exists solely for more effective protection of historically existing rights, more effective enforcement of nature's existing laws. For enduring progress the functions of government must be confined to repelling invasions, suppressing insurrections and enforcing contracts.

In Spencer one observes old concepts in new dress: *natural law*—the law of struggle, the competitive clash of men with men; *aristocracy*—those who win in the battle that leaves so many in 'shadows and misery'; *natural and inalienable rights*—inherent in those who survive and flourish in this divinely guided order. The total effect was, of course, to place insuperable barriers against any government effort to correct industrial abuses or to regulate the new economic oligarchy. On first reading Herbert Spencer, Andrew Carnegie's reaction was as natural as it was spontaneous: 'Light came as in a flood and all was clear. . . "All is well since all grows better," became my motto.'

Herbert Spencer's philosophy, Cochran and Miller write in their book, *The Age of Enterprise* (1942), 'won America as no philosophy ever won a nation before. To an age singularly engrossed in the competitive pursuit of industrial wealth, it gave cosmic sanction to free competition. In an age of science, it "scientifically" justified ceaseless exploitation. . . Their cupidity (that of American business men), it defended as part of the universal struggle for existence; the wealth, it hallowed as the sign of the fittest.' Zealous American spokesmen spread his creed. Besides industrialists, there were clergymen, lawyers, judges, and educators. The latter included Charles W. Eliot and John Fiske at Harvard, Nicholas Murray Butler at Columbia, Francis A. Walker at the Massachusetts Institute of Technology, and towering high above them, William Graham Sumner (1840–1910) of Yale. His student, William Lyon Phelps, tells an incident of the educator's vehemence in propounding his version of the Spencerian dogma:

'Professor,' a student inquired, 'don't you believe in any government aid to industry?'

'No: it's root, hog, or die.'

'Yes, but hasn't the hog got a right to root?'

'There are no rights. The world owes nobody a living.'

'You believe, then, Professor, in only one system, the contract-competitive system?'

'That's the only sound economic system. All others are fallacies.'

'Well, suppose some professor of political economy came along and took your job away. Wouldn't you be sore?'

'Any other professor is welcome to try. If he gets my job, it's my fault.

My business is to teach the subject so well that no one can take the job away from me.'

Sumner was trained as a clergyman, but when he became convinced that the church was destined to play a diminishing role in American life, he turned to education and to Yale, accepting there, in 1872, a professorship of political economy. From this vantage point, Sumner, by his voluminous writings, Americanized the *laisser-faire* dogmas of Herbert Spencer. In the paper here included, Sumner is as forthright in his preference for the economic power and might of concentrated wealth as in his misgivings about democracy. By enlisting the support of sociology, he fortified the prejudices of Spencer with the stately embellishments of authoritative science. 'If we could get rid of some of our notions about liberty and equality,' Sumner snorted, 'we might get some insight into societal organization; what it does for us and what it makes us do.'

The most forthright and incisive challenge of *laisser-faire* came from Professor Simon N. Patten, economist at the University of Pennsylvania, and Professor Richard T. Ely, economist at the Johns Hopkins University, later at the University of Wisconsin. These men, along with a handful of other forward-looking academicians, in September 1883, organized the American Economic Association. 'We regard the state,' ran the Association's statement of principles, 'as an agency whose positive assistance is one of the indispensable conditions of human progress. . . We believe in a progressive development of economic conditions, which must be met by a corresponding development of legislative policy.' In taking this bold stand they foreshadowed by almost half a century the popular uprising implicit in the election of Franklin D. Roosevelt in 1932, and the broad-gauged legislative program that followed.

But while Patten saw science as the key to 'an age of surplus and pleasure when all things are possible if we but keep our eyes turned towards the future and strip our intelligence for their tasks,' defenders of the Gilded Age, whether clerical, industrial, or academic, found firm and even scientific basis for their faith in the evolutionary doctrines of Darwin and Spencer. It was assumed that these inevitably meant political negativism—*laisser-faire*. Recent research queries this easy conclusion and insists that Darwinism in politics suggests rather the desirability and even the necessity of positive government. Among early voices raised in support of this view was that of the paleobotanist and government bureaucrat Lester W. Ward (1841–1913), who, in 1883, had published his impressive two-volume work *Social Dynamics*. Ward made a frontal attack on Herbert Spencer.

> The laissez-faire school had entrenched itself behind the fortifications of science and while declaring with truth that social phenomena are, like physical phenomena, uniform and governed by laws, they have accompanied this by the false declaration and *non sequitur* that neither physical nor social phenomena are capable of human control, the fact being that all the practical benefits of science are the result of man's control of natural forces and phenomena which would otherwise have run to waste or operated as enemies to human progress. The opposing positive school of econ-

> omists simply demands an opportunity to utilize the social forces for human advantage in precisely the same manner as physical forces have been utilized. It is only through the artificial control of natural phenomena that science is made to minister to human needs; and if social laws are really analogous to physical laws, there is no reason why social science may not receive practical applications such as have been given to physical science.

In his article of 1895, here reprinted, Ward points out that private enterprisers and capitalists, besieging legislatures for subsidies and protective tariffs, have put themselves in the strangely inconsistent position of resorting to politics and paternalism. In his *Twenty Years of the Republic* (1906), Harry Thurston Peck heightened the paradox, saying that 'the Republican party had been essentially socialistic from the outset. . . When in control of government, that party had used the Federal power through tariff legislation to foster special interests, and to enrich particular classes of individuals.' Capitalists preached *laisser-faire*, but they did not practice it. James Bryce noted their willingness to extend the reach of government into 'ever-widening fields.'

Some ten years before Charles Francis Adams noted the emergence of 'modern potentates,' freely exercising many 'attributes of sovereignty,' a tall, lanky boy of nineteen mounted the pulpit in the little Methodist Church of Westfield, Massachusetts, to proclaim the gospel of wealth, giving for the first time his famous lecture, 'Acres of Diamonds.' Without knowing it, the youthful Baptist minister, Russell H. Conwell (1843–1925), many years later president of Temple University, was then beginning a lecture marathon seldom, if ever, equaled. During the half-century following, Dr. Conwell delivered the sentiments, herein excerpted, more than six thousand times. 'Little did he foresee,' writes Conwell's official biographer, Agnes Rush Burr, 'how it would affect the lives of thousands upon thousands of people; nor the *influence it would have upon the industries of this country*.' (Editor's italics)

The title of the lecture comes from an Eastern parable about the Persian Ali Hafed, who sold his land to search for riches abroad—the Golconda diamond mines. It turned out that the wealth he sought was in his own back yard. The moral is simply this, 'that the opportunity to get rich, to attain unto great wealth, is here in Princeton now.' (The locus of the diamond mine shifted with every lecture.) Within the compass of a single glittering phrase Conwell, equating wealth with virtue, made the transition from the feudal emphasis on poverty to the modern preference for material prosperity as the path to godliness.

Dr. Conwell gives us a prescient clue to what Mark Twain dubbed the Gilded Age. Perhaps his lecture is more significant as reinforcing the doctrine of *laisser-faire* than as preaching the gospel of wealth. 'It is *prima facie* evidence of littleness to hold public office under our form of government,' he told the young men in his audience. 'If you only get the privilege of casting one vote, you don't get anything that is worth while. . . This country is not run by votes. . . It is governed by the ambitious and the enterprises which control the votes.' Here is the gospel of *laisser-faire* uttered forty years before it reached its American heyday, and along with it the stern insistence that political democracy in the domains of economic oligarchy is a colossal farce. Conwell had endorsed, unwittingly perhaps, Webster's words of 1820: 'A great equality of condition is the true basis, most certainly, of popular government.'

In 1900 Bishop William Lawrence of Massachusetts rounded out the money-morality thesis. 'In the long run,' Lawrence ordained, 'it is only to the man of morality that wealth comes. We believe in the harmony of God's Universe. . . [I]t is only by working along His laws natural and spiritual that we can work with Efficiency. . . Godliness is in league with riches. . . Material prosperity is helping to make the national character sweeter, more joyous, more unselfish, more Christlike.' 'That is my answer,' Lawrence concluded, 'to the question as to the relation of material prosperity to morality.'

A less flamboyant statement of the Conwell-Lawrence thesis came from the steel magnate, Andrew Carnegie (1835–1910), who contributed the essay, here excerpted, to the *North American Review*, June 1889. 'The finest article I have ever published in the *Review*,' the editor commented. Carnegie concedes that in the historic transition from primitive equality to civilized inequality of industrialism, 'human society loses homogeneity'; the social cost, 'the price we pay,' he admits, is great but the process is 'highly beneficial.'

John D. Rockefeller reinforced Carnegie's endorsement of Social Darwinism: 'The growth of a large business is merely a survival of the fittest.' 'The American Beauty rose,' Rockefeller analogized, 'can be produced in the splendor and fragrance which bring cheer to its beholder only by sacrificing the early buds which grow up around it. This is not an evil tendency in business. It is merely the working out of a law of nature and a law of God.' Wealth, however, implied responsibility. 'The good Lord gave me my money,' the devout Baptist told the first graduating class of the university he had founded, 'and how could I withhold it from the University of Chicago?'

The piece by one of our greatest satirists, Finley Peter Dunne (1867–1936), here reprinted, explores the motivations that underlay Carnegie's philanthropies with devastating effect. But, on the whole, Dunne's analysis of industrial oligarchy was restrained. Running through many of Mr. Dooley's conversations with Mr. Hennessy is the Conwell-Carnegie overtone—politics is a dirty business which honest men would do well to shun.

Less restrained was the concerted attack of Walter Rauschenbusch (1861–1918). Countering the religious support Conwell and Lawrence had given the Darwinian tide, the Reverend Mr. Rauschenbusch, long a professor at the Rochester Theological Seminary, sought to tie religion to the growing reform movement. *Christianity and the Social Crisis* (1907) and *Christianizing the Social Order* (1912) contain the core of his philosophy.

'We cannot join economic inequality and political equality,' Rauschenbusch insisted, arguing much in the manner of Henry George and other 'utopians' whose readings the young minister had devoured. Change, he argued, was inevitable; religion ought to be employed in its service. Prevailing Christian doctrine was merely a rationalization of concentrations of irresponsible wealth. Christianity should be regularly reinterpreted to keep pace with changing social conditions. Recognizing that social stability depended in large measure on material welfare, Rauschenbusch warned: 'Unless the ideal social order can supply men with food, warmth, and comfort more efficiently than our present economic order, back we shall go to Capitalism. . . "The God that answereth by low food prices, let him be God." '

By the dawn of the twentieth century the growing concentration and integration of wealth had become the most conspicuous aspect of American life. The enterprising editor of *The Independent* exploited this trend by publishing a series of articles dealing with the subject from various points of view. He gloried in the 'amazing frankness, the psychological self-revelation of the authors.'

Sumner, the first contributor, 'tried to set forth the economic necessity for the concentration of wealth.'

> . . . What law of nature, religion, ethics, or the State is violated by inequalities of fortune? The inequalities prove nothing. Others argue that great fortunes are won by privileges created by law and not by legitimate enterprise and ability. This statement is true, but it is entirely irrelevant. We have to discuss the concentration of wealth within the facts of the institutions, laws, usages and customs which our ancestors have bequeathed to us and which we allow to stand. If it is proposed to change any of these parts of the societal order, that is a proper subject of discussion, but it is aside from the concentration of wealth. . . The modern [industrial] methods offer very great opportunities, and the rewards of those men who can 'size up' a situation, and develop its controlling elements with sagacity and good judgment, are very great. It is well that they are so, because these rewards stimulate to the utmost all the ambitious and able men, and they make it certain that great and useful inventions will not long remain unexploited as they did formerly. Here comes, then, a new reaction on the economic system. New energy is infused into it, with hope and confidence. We could not spare this stimulus and keep up our work of production. I may add that we could not spare it and keep up the air of contentment and enthusiastic cheerfulness which characterizes our society. No man can acquire a million without helping a million men to increase their little fortunes all the day down through all the social grades. In some points of view it is an error that we fix our attention so much upon the very rich and overlook the prosperous mass, but the compensating advantage is that the great successes stimulate emulation the most powerfully.
>
> What matters it then that some millionaires are idle, or silly, or vulgar, that their ideas are sometimes futile, and their plans grotesque, when they turn aside from money-making? How do they differ in this from any other class? The millionaires are a product of natural selection, acting on the whole body of men, to pick out those who can meet the requirement of certain work to be done. In this respect they are just like the great statesmen, or scientific

> men, or military men. It is because they are thus selected that wealth aggregates under their hands—both their own and that intrusted to them. . . They may fairly be regarded as the naturally selected agents of society for certain work. They get high wages and live in luxury, but the bargain is a good one for society. . .

'Our age is befooled by Democracy,' Spencer's apostle concluded.

The second contributor, John Dewitt Warner (1851–1925), a lawyer by profession, a trustee of Cornell University, and a member of Congress from 1891 to 1895, specialized in tariff and currency problems. The editor of *The Independent* said of him in 1902: 'No one has a better knowledge as a practical and theoretical student of the political dangers of the concentration of wealth.' In conversation with a Cornell instructor in 1905 Warner remarked: 'New York is run by men who believe that a dividend paying stock is the noblest work of God.' Warner questioned the materialistic determinism implicit in the thinking of both Carnegie and Sumner, and especially the former's smug dictum that 'it is a waste of time to criticize the inevitable.' Although no radical himself, Warner foresaw the development of socialism as the reaction against trust abuses.

'This is one of the articles that once published, lives,' the editor said in the issue of *The Independent* that carried William J. Ghent's (1866–1942) article. An editor of *The American Fabian* and a successful lawyer, Ghent was long most prominent in various social reform movements. The burden of his argument, here reprinted, later expanded into a book, *Our Benevolent Feudalism* (1902), is that a realistic examination of current political and economic phenomena in the United States revealed a society having the essential elements of a feudal social order. He conceded that while there would be occasional and determined threats to the industrial baron's power, these would be suppressed or appeased wherever necessary, and the losses, if any, recouped elsewhere, thus circumventing any serious invasion of his power. What Ghent identified in 1902 as 'a mighty, resistless transformation of the old economic individualism into a vast industrial feudalism,' Berle and Means documented a generation later in their *Modern Corporation and Private Property*. 'One Power alone,' Ghent said in 1902, might prevent benevolent economic feudalism—'the collective popular will that it shall not be.' Centering on this loophole, John Bates Clark (1847–1938), economist and professor at Columbia University, took exception to Ghent's prognosis.

Rivaling the Social Darwinism of the Gilded Age, sometimes threatening to displace it entirely, were the Reformers, constituting a less articulated movement that expressed itself in a wide variety of popular creeds. These, indeed, were among the more clamorous tributaries following into the broad river of ideas that we call liberalism. Though wide disagreement dissipated effectiveness, they all pointed at and condemned the new and strange forces subjecting liberty to unprecedented peril. In one way or another, all were rooted in popular power, all believed in man's ability, through government or by other means to master his own destiny.

The most specific reform proposals came from Henry George (1839–97), author of a perpetual best-seller, *Progress and Poverty*, and independent candidate for mayor of New York in 1886 and 1897. Born in Philadelphia, and living in California during the great land boom, George one day asked a teamster about land prices. 'I don't know exactly,' came back the reply, 'but there is a man over there who will sell some land for a thousand dollars an acre.' 'Like a flash.' George later recalled, 'it came upon me that *there* was the reason of advancing poverty with advancing wealth.'

Though largely self-educated, George was a man of tremendous emotional and intellectual power. His moral influence spread far beyond the narrow bonds of the cause he represented. There are still organizations in America spreading his gospel, but the Single Tax Movement George initiated has been highly disappointing even to its promoters.

A decade after the appearance of *Progress and Poverty*, a book was published which exceeded George's by far in popular appeal—Edward Bellamy's (1850–98) runaway best-seller, *Looking Backward*. Son of a Baptist minister, trained as a lawyer, Bellamy spent his life as a newspaper man and novelist. The book, here excerpted, was published early in 1888. By December 1889, some 210,000 copies had been sold and it went on selling 10,000 copies a week. A literary fantasy, the book tells the story of a young man, Julian West, who fell asleep in 1887, and awoke in the house of Dr. Leete in the year 2000, to find himself in a country without poverty, misery, or greed. New environmental conditions alone, we learn as the story unfolds, are capable of creating a more tolerable world in which determination of a man's needs turns not on the quantity of material goods he produces but on the 'fact that he is a man.' Meditative silence seized Dr. Leete when questioned in regard to wages. There was no wage equivalent in this imaginary world of 2000 A.D. 'Desert is a moral question,' Dr. Leete explained. 'The amount of effort alone is pertinent to the question, desert.'

Nor was the society Bellamy envisaged entirely a figment of his imagination. Finding 'the elements which are to develop' in the year 2000 'already in ferment,' Bellamy imparted a larger element of realism than one is likely to discern in the paradise of prosperity conjured up by American followers of Herbert Spencer. The latter evolved, moreover, from a fierce competitive struggle in which only the economically elect may survive. Bellamy's utopia, on the other hand, was all-inclusive in the benefits enjoyed; and men were driven not by the prospect of material gain but by the spirit of co-operation, by the honor of social recognition. 'Bellamy's epic dream', Charles A. Beard wrote, 'served as a torch from which were lighted the aspirations of multitudes in the United States.'

'A venture in realism in a world of realities,' is the way someone has described Henry Demarest Lloyd's (1847–1903) *Wealth Against Commonwealth* of 1894. Born into a household dominated by clergymen, Lloyd was trained in the law, disappointing his mother who wished him to go into the ministry. He moved from New York, where he was brought up, to Chicago, joined the editorial staff of the *Chicago Tribune* and began his career as a reforming publicist.

Lloyd fired his first volley in an attack on the Standard Oil monopoly in an article of 1881, published in the *Atlantic Monthly*, causing that number of the sedate Boston periodical to go through seven editions. His book of 1894, from which the material here reprinted is taken, set a model for latter-day muckrakers, being quarried from official records, decisions of courts, reports of state legislatures, and various other official inquiries, with full documentation throughout. Lloyd, unlike so many of those who followed in his footsteps, was not content merely to expose and deplore. He went out on the firing line and fought for specific remedies that finally covered the ideological span from populism to socialism.

1. *A free man in a free democracy has no duty whatever toward other men of the same rank and standing*

WILLIAM GRAHAM SUMNER, *What Social Classes Owe to Each Other*, 1883 *

. . . I now propose to try to find out whether there is any class in society which lies under the duty and burden of fighting the battles of life for any other class, or of solving social problems for the satisfaction of any other class; also, whether there is any class which has the right to formulate demands on 'society'—that is, on other classes; also, whether there is anything but a fallacy and a superstition in the notion that 'the State' owes anything to anybody except peace, order, and the guarantees of rights. . .

Certain ills belong to the hardships of human life. They are natural. They are a part of the struggle with Nature for existence. We cannot blame our fellow-men for our share of these. My neighbor and I are both struggling to free ourselves from these ills. The fact that my neighbor has succeeded in this struggle better than I constitutes no grievance for me. Certain other ills are due to the malice of men, and to the imperfections or errors of civil institutions. These ills are an object of agitation, and a subject of discussion. The former class of ills is to be met only by manly effort and energy; the latter may be corrected by associated effort. The former class of ills is constantly grouped and generalized, and made the object of social schemes. We shall see, as we go on, what that means. The second class of ills may fall on certain social classes, and reform will take the form of interference by other classes in favor of that one. The last fact is, no doubt, the reason why people have been led, not noticing distinctions, to believe that the same method was applicable to the other class of ills. The distinction here made between the ills which belong to the struggle for existence and those which are due to the faults of human institutions is of prime importance.

It will also be important, in order to clear up our ideas about the notions which are in fashion, to note the relation of the economic to the political significance of assumed duties of one class to another. That is to say, we may discuss the question whether one class owes duties to another by reference to the economic effects which will be produced on the classes and society;

*New York, Harper & Brothers, pp. 12–168 *passim*.

or we may discuss the political expediency of formulating and enforcing rights and duties respectively between the parties. In the former case we might assume that the givers of aid were willing to give it, and we might discuss the benefit or mischief of their activity. In the other case we must assume that some at least of those who were forced to give aid did so unwillingly. Here, then, there would be a question of rights. The question whether voluntary charity is mischievous or not is one thing; the question whether legislation which forces one man to aid another is right and wise, as well as economically beneficial, is quite another question. Great confusion and consequent error is produced by allowing these two questions to become entangled in the discussion. Especially we shall need to notice the attempts to apply legislative methods of reform to the ills which belong to the order of Nature.

There is no possible definition of 'a poor man.' A pauper is a person who cannot earn his living; whose producing powers have fallen positively below his necessary consumption; who cannot, therefore, pay his way. A human society needs the active co-operation and productive energy of every person in it. A man who is present as a consumer, yet who does not contribute either by land, labor, or capital to the work of society, is a burden. On no sound political theory ought such a person to share in the political power of the State. He drops out of the ranks of workers and producers. Society must support him. It accepts the burden, but he must be cancelled from the ranks of the rulers likewise. So much for the pauper. About him no more need be said. But he is not the 'poor man.' The 'poor man' is an elastic term, under which any number of social fallacies may be hidden.

Neither is there any possible definition of 'the weak.' Some are weak in one way, and some in another; and those who are weak in one sense are strong in another. In general, however, it may be said that those whom humanitarians and philanthropists call the weak are the ones through whom the productive and conservative forces of society are wasted. They constantly neutralize and destroy the finest efforts of the wise and industrious, and are a dead-weight on the society in all its struggles to realize any better things. Whether the people who mean no harm, but are weak in the essential powers necessary to the performance of one's duties in life, or those who are malicious and vicious, do the more mischief, is a question not easy to answer.

Under the names of the poor and the weak, the negligent, shiftless, inefficient, silly, and imprudent are fastened upon the industrious and prudent as a responsibility and a duty. On the one side, the terms are extended to cover the idle, intemperate, and vicious, who, by the combination, gain credit which they do not deserve, and which they could not get if they stood alone. On the other hand, the terms are extended to include wage-receivers of the humblest rank, who are degraded by the combination. The reader who desires to guard himself against fallacies should always scrutinize the terms 'poor' and 'weak' as used, so as to see which or how many of these classes they are made to cover.

The humanitarians, philanthropists, and reformers, looking at the facts of life as they present themselves, find enough which is sad and unpromising in the condition of many members of society. They see wealth and poverty side by side. They note great inequality of social position and social chances. They eagerly set about the attempt to account for what they see, and to devise schemes for remedying what they do not like. In their eagerness to recommend the less fortunate classes to pity and consideration they forget all about the rights of other classes; they gloss over all the faults of the classes in question, and they exaggerate their misfortunes and their virtues. They invent new theories of property, distorting rights and perpetrating injustice, as any one is sure to do who sets about the re-adjustment of social relations with the interests of one group distinctly before his mind, and the interests of all other groups thrown into the background. When I have read certain of these discussions I have thought that it must be quite disreputable to be respectable, quite dishonest to own property, quite unjust to go one's own way and earn one's own living, and that the only really admirable person was the good-for-nothing. The man who by his own effort raises himself above poverty appears, in these discussions, to be of no account. The man who has done nothing to raise himself above poverty finds that the social doctors flock about him, bringing the capital which they have collected from the other class, and promising him the aid of the State to give him what the other had to work for. In all these schemes and projects the organized intervention of society through the State is either planned or hoped for, and the State is thus made to become the protector and guardian of certain classes. . .

In our modern state, and in the United States more than anywhere else, the social structure is based on contract, and status is of the least importance. Contract, however, is rational—even rationalistic. It is also realistic, cold, and matter-of-fact. A contract relation is based on a sufficient reason, not on custom, or prescription. It is not permanent. It endures only so long as the reason for it endures. In a state based on contract sentiment is out of place in any public or common affairs. It is relegated to the sphere of private and personal relations, where it depends not at all on class types, but on personal acquaintance and personal estimates. The sentimentalists among us always seize upon the survivals of the old order. They want to save them and restore them. Much of the loose thinking also which troubles us in our social discussions arises from the fact that men do not distinguish the elements of status and of contract which may be found in our society. . .

A society based on contract is a society of free and independent men, who form ties without favor or obligation, and cooperate without cringing or intrigues. A society based on contract, therefore, gives the utmost room and chance for individual development, and for all the self-reliance and dignity of a free man. That a society of free men, co-operating under contract, is by far the strongest society which has ever yet existed; that no such society has ever yet developed the full measure of strength of which it is capable; and that the only social improvements which are now conceivable lie in the direction of more complete realization of a society of free men united by contract, are points which cannot be controverted. It follows, however, that one man, in a free state, cannot claim help from, and cannot be charged to give help to, another. To understand the full meaning of this assertion it will be worth while to see what a free democracy is. . .

The notion of a free state is entirely modern. It has been developed with the development of the middle class, and with the growth of a commercial and industrial civilization. Horror at human slavery is not a century old as a common sentiment in a civilized state. The idea of the 'free man,' as we understand it, is the product of a revolt against mediaeval and feudal ideas; and our notion of equality, when it is true and practical, can be explained only by that revolt. It was in England that the modern idea found birth. It has been strengthened by the industrial and commercial development of that country. It has been inherited by all the English-speaking nations, who have made liberty real because they have inherited it, not as a notion, but as a body of institutions. . .

The notion of civil liberty which we have inherited is that of *a status created for the individual by laws and institutions, the effect of which is that each man is guaranteed the use of all his own powers exclusively for his own welfare*. It is not at all a matter of elections, or universal suffrage, or democracy. All institutions are to be tested by the degree to which they guarantee liberty. It is not to be admitted for a moment that liberty is a means to social ends, and that it may be impaired for major considerations. Any one who so argues has lost the bearing and relations of all the facts and factors in a free state. A human being has a life to live, a career to run. He is a centre of powers to work, and of capacities to suffer. What his powers may be—whether they can carry him far or not; what his chances may be, whether wide or restricted; what his fortune may be, whether to suffer much or little—are questions of his personal destiny which he must work out and endure as he can; but for all that concerns the bearing of the society and its institutions upon that man, and upon the sum of happiness to which he can attain during his life on earth, the product of all history and all philosophy up to this time is summed up in the doctrine, that he should be left free to do the most for himself that he can, and should be guaranteed the exclusive enjoyment of all that he does. If the society, that is to say, in plain terms, if his fellow-men, either individually, by groups, or in a mass—impinge upon him otherwise than to surround him with neutral conditions of security, they must do so under the strictest responsibility to justify themselves. Jealousy and prejudice against all such interferences are high political virtues in a free man. It is not at all the function of the State to make men happy. They must make themselves happy in their own way, and at their own risk. The functions of the State lie entirely in the conditions or chances under which the pursuit of happiness is carried on, so far as those conditions or chances can be affected by civil organization. Hence, liberty for labor and security for earnings are the ends for which civil institutions exist, not means which may be employed for ulterior ends. . .

A free man in a free democracy has no duty whatever toward other men of the same rank and standing, except respect, courtesy, and good will. We cannot say that there are no classes, when we are speaking politically, and then say that there are classes, when we are telling A what it is his duty to do for B. In a free state every man is held and expected to take care of himself and his family, to make no trouble for his neighbor, and to contribute his full share to public interests and common necessities. If he fails in this he throws burdens on others. He does not thereby acquire rights against the others. On the contrary, he only accumulates obligations toward them; and if allowed to make his deficiencies a ground of new claims, he passes over into the position of a privileged or petted person—emancipated from duties, endowed with claims. This is the inevitable result of combining democratic political theories with humanitarian social theories. It would be aside from my present purpose to show, but it is worth noticing in passing, that one result of such inconsistency must surely be to undermine democracy, to increase the power of wealth in the democracy, and to hasten the subjection of democracy to plutocracy; for a man who accepts any share which he has not earned in another man's capital cannot be an independent citizen. . .

The aggregation of large fortunes is not at all a thing to be regretted. On the contrary, it is a necessary condition of many forms of social advance. If we should set a limit to the accumulation of wealth, we should say to our most valuable producers, 'We do not want you to do us the services which you best understand how to perform, beyond a certain point.' It would be like killing off our generals in war. A great deal is said, in the cant of a certain school, about 'ethical views of wealth,' and we are told that some day men will be found of such public spirit that, after they have accumulated a few millions, they will be willing to go on and labor simply for the pleasure of paying the taxes of their fellow-citizens. Possibly this is true. It is a prophecy. It is as impossible to deny it as it is silly to affirm it. For if a time ever comes when there are men of this kind, the men of that age will arrange their affairs accordingly. There are no such men now, and those of us who live now cannot arrange our affairs by what men will be a hundred generations hence. . .

In the United States the opponent of plutocracy is democracy. Nowhere else in the world has the power of wealth come to be discussed in its political aspects as it is here. Nowhere else does the question arise as it does here. . . Nowhere in the world is the danger of a plutocracy as formidable as it is here. To it we oppose the power of numbers as it is presented by democracy. Democracy itself, however, is new and experimental. It has not yet existed long enough to find its appropriate forms. It has no prestige from antiquity such as aristocracy possesses. It has, indeed, none of the surroundings which appeal to the imagination. On the other hand, democracy is rooted in the physical, economic, and social circumstances of the United States. This country cannot be other than democratic for an indefinite period in the future. Its political processes will also be republican. The affection of the people for democracy makes them blind and uncritical in regard to it, and they are as fond of the political fallacies to which democracy lends itself as they are of its sound and correct interpretation, or fonder. Can democracy develop itself and at the same time curb plutocracy?

Already the question presents itself as one of life or death to democracy. Legislative and judicial scandals show us that the conflict is already opened, and that it is serious. The lobby is the army of the plutocracy. An elective judiciary is a device so much in the interest of plutocracy, that it must be regarded as a striking proof of the toughness of the judicial institution that it has resisted the corruption so much as it has. The caucus, convention, and committee lend themselves most readily to the purposes of interested speculators and jobbers. It is just such machinery as they might have invented if they had been trying to make political devices to serve their purpose, and their processes call in question nothing less than the possibility of free self-government under the forms of a democratic republic.

For now I come to the particular point which I desire to bring forward against all the denunciations and complainings about the power of chartered corporations and aggregated capital. If charters have been given which confer undue powers, who gave them? Our legislators did. Who elected these legislators? We did. If we are a free, self-governing people, we must understand that it costs vigilance and exertion to be self-governing. It costs far more vigilance and exertion to be so under the democratic form, where we have no aids from tradition or prestige, than under other forms. If we are a free, self-governing people, we can blame nobody but ourselves for our misfortunes. No one will come to help us out of them. It will do no good to heap law upon law, or to try by constitutional provisions simply to abstain from the use of powers which we find we always abuse. How can we get bad legislators to pass a law which shall hinder bad legislators from passing a bad law? That is what we are trying to do by many of our proposed remedies. The task before us, however, is one which calls for fresh reserves of moral force and political virtue from the very foundations of the social body. Surely it is not a new thing to us to learn that men are greedy and covetous, and that they will be selfish and tyrannical if they dare. The plutocrats are simply trying to do what the generals, nobles, and priests have done in the past—get the power of the State into their hands, so as to bend the rights of others to their own advantage; and what we need to do is to recognize the fact that we are face to face with the same old foes—the vices and passions of human nature. . .

The new foes must be met, as the old ones were met—by institutions and guarantees. The problem of civil liberty is constantly renewed. Solved once, it re-appears in a new form. The old constitutional guarantees were all aimed against king and nobles. New ones must be invented to hold the power of wealth to that responsibility without which no power whatever is consistent with liberty. The judiciary has given the most satisfactory evidence that it is competent to the new duty which devolves upon it. The courts have proved, in every case in which they have been called upon, that there are remedies, that they are adequate, and that they can be brought to bear upon the cases. The chief need seems to be more power of voluntary combination and co-operation among those who are aggrieved. Such co-operation is a constant necessity under free self-government; and when, in any community, men lose the power of voluntary co-operation in furtherance or defence of their own interests, they deserve to suffer, with no other remedy than newspaper denunciations and platform declamations. Of course, in such a state of things, political mountebanks come forward and propose fierce measures which can be paraded for political effect. Such measures would be hostile to all our institutions, would destroy capital, overthrow credit, and impair the most essential interests of society. On the side of political machinery there is no ground for hope, but only for fear. On the side of constitutional guarantees and the independent action of self-governing freemen there is every ground for hope. . .

The amateur social doctors are like the amateur physicians—they always begin with the question of remedies, and they go at this without any diagnosis or any knowledge of the anatomy or physiology of society. They never have any doubt of the efficacy of their remedies. They never take account of any ulterior effects which may be apprehended from the remedy itself. It generally troubles them not a whit that their remedy implies a complete reconstruction of society, or even a reconstitution of human nature. Against all such social quackery the obvious injunction to the quacks is, to mind their own business. . .

Society . . . does not need any care or supervision. If we can acquire a science of society, based on observation of phenomena and study of forces, we may hope to gain some ground slowly toward the elimination of old errors and the re-establishment of a sound and natural social order. Whatever we gain that way will be by growth, never in the world by any reconstruction of society on the plan of some enthusiastic social architect. The latter is only repeating the old error over again and postponing all our chances of real improvement. Society needs first of all to be freed from these meddlers—that is, to be let alone. Here we are, then, once more back at the old doctrine—*laissez faire*. Let us translate it into blunt English, and it will read, Mind your own business. It is nothing but the doctrine of liberty. Let every man be happy in his own way. If his sphere of action and interest impinges on that of any other man, there will have to be a compromise and adjustment. Wait for occasion. Do not attempt to generalize those interferences or to plan for them *a priori*. We have a body of laws and institutions which have grown up as occasion has occurred for adjusting rights. Let the same process go on. Practise the utmost reserve possible in your interferences even of this kind, and by no means seize occasion for interfering with natural adjustments. Try first long and patiently whether the natural adjustment will not come about through the play of interests and the voluntary concessions of the parties. . .

It no doubt wounds the vanity of a philosopher who is just ready with a new solution of the universe to be told to mind his own business. So he goes on to tell us that if we think that we shall, by being let alone, attain to perfect happiness on earth, we are mistaken. The half-way men—the professorial socialists—join him. They solemnly shake their heads, and tell us that he is right—that letting us alone will never secure us perfect happiness. Under all this lies the familiar logical fallacy, never expressed, but really the point of the whole, that we *shall* get perfect happiness if we put ourselves in the hands of the world-reformer. We never supposed that *laissez-faire* would give us perfect happiness. We have left perfect happiness entirely out of our account. If the social doctors will mind their own business, we shall have no troubles but what belong to Nature. Those we will endure or combat as we can. What we desire is, that the friends of humanity should cease to add to them. Our disposition toward the ills which our fellow-man inflicts on us through malice or meddling is quite different from our disposition toward the ills which are inherent in the conditions of human life.

To mind one's own business is a purely negative and unproductive injunction, but, taking social matters as they are just now, it is a sociological principle of the first importance. . .

Social improvement is not to be won by direct effort. It is secondary, and results from physical or economic improvements. That is the reason why schemes of direct social amelioration always have an arbitrary, sentimental, and artificial character, while true social advance must be a product and a growth. The efforts which are being put forth for every kind of progress in the arts and sciences are, therefore, contributing to true social progress. Let any one learn what hardship was involved, even for a wealthy person, a century ago, in crossing the Atlantic, and then let him compare that hardship even with a steerage passage at the present time, considering time and money cost. This improvement in transportation by which 'the poor and weak' can be carried from the crowded centres of population to the new land is worth more to them than all the schemes of all the social reformers. An improvement in surgical instruments or in anaesthetics really does more for those who are not well off than all the declamations of the orators and pious wishes of the reformers. Civil service reform would be a greater gain to the laborers than innumerable factory acts and eight-hour laws. Free trade would be a greater blessing to 'the poor man' than all the devices of all the friends of humanity if they could be realized. . .

We each owe it to the other to guarantee rights. Rights do not pertain to *results*, but only to *chances*. They pertain to the *conditions* of the struggle for existence, not to any of the results of it; to the *pursuit* of happiness, not to the possession of happiness. It cannot be said that each one has a right to have some property, because if one man had such a right some other man or men would be under a corresponding obligation to provide him with some property. Each has a right to acquire and possess property if he can. It is plain what fallacies are developed when we overlook this distinction. Those fallacies run through *all* socialistic schemes and theories. If we take rights to pertain to results, and then say that rights must be equal, we come to say that men have a right to be equally happy, and so on in all the details. Rights should be equal, because they pertain to chances, and all ought to have equal chances so far as chances are provided or limited by the action of society. This, however, will not produce equal results, but it is right just because it will produce unequal results—that is, results which shall be proportioned to the merits of individuals. . .

. . . If there be liberty, some will profit by the chances eagerly and some will neglect them altogether. Therefore, the greater the chances the more unequal will be the fortune of these two sets of men. So it ought to be, in all justice and right reason. The yearning after equality is the offspring of envy and covetousness, and there is no possible plan for satisfying that yearning which can do aught else than rob A to give to B; consequently all such plans nourish some of the meanest vices of human nature, waste capital, and overthrow civilization. . .

2. *Nothing is more obvious than the inability of capital or private enterprise to take care of itself unaided by the state*

LESTER F. WARD, *Plutocracy and Paternalism*, November 1895 *

To judge from the tone of the popular press, the country would seem to be between the devil of state interference and the deep sea of gold. The two epithets, 'plutocracy' and 'paternalism,' so freely applied, are intended to characterize the worst tendencies of the times in these two opposite directions, and are calculated to engender the bitterest feelings in the public mind. If such a thing were possible, it would certainly be useful, standing aloof from the contest, to make a cool, unbiased analysis of the true meaning of these terms in their relation to the existing state of affairs. . .

Justly or unjustly, society has made wealth a measure of worth. It is easy on general principles to prove that it is not such a measure. Every one is personally cognizant of numerous cases to the contrary. All will admit that, taken in the abstract, the principle is unsound, and yet all act upon it. Not rationally, not perhaps consciously, but still they do it. It is 'human nature' to respect those who have, and to care little for those who have not. There is a sort of feeling that if one is destitute there must be a reason for it. It is inevitably ascribed to some personal deficit. In a word, absence of means is, in one form or another, made to stand for absence of merit. Its cause is looked for in character. This is most clearly seen in the marked contrast between the indisposition to help the unsuccessful, and the willingness to help the successful. Aside from the prospect of a *quid pro quo*, no one wants to waste time, energy, or money on what is worthless,—and possession is the primary test of worth. . .

Thus it comes about that wealth, in the existing state of society, is a tremendous power. It gives not only ease, plenty, luxury, but, what is infinitely more, the respect of all and the envy of the less favored. It gives, in a word, superiority; and the strongest craving of man's nature is, in one way or another, to be set over his fellows. When all this is considered, the futility of the proposal of certain reformers to eradicate the passion for proprietary acquisition becomes apparent. It may be assumed that this passion will continue for an indefinite period to be the ruling element of the industrial state. That it has done and is still doing incalculable service to society few will deny. That it may continue to be useful to the end of our present industrial era will probably be admitted by all but a small class.

If the accumulation of wealth, even for the benefit of individuals, were all that is involved in the term 'plutocracy,' the indictment would not be serious. If the governing power implied in the last component of the word were nothing more than the normal influence that wealth exerts, no great injury to society could accrue. Even the amassing of colossal fortunes is not an evil in itself, since the very activity which it requires stimulates industry and benefits a large number. There is, it is true, a danger—in the transmission of such fortunes to inactive and non-productive heirs—of creating a non-industrial class in per-

* *The Forum*, November 1895, vol. 20, pp. 300–310 *passim*.

petuity; but this could be remedied, without hardship to any worthy person, by a wise limitation of inheritance.

So much for plutocracy. Let us now turn to the other pole of public opinion and inquire into the meaning of 'paternalism.' Literally, of course, paternalism in government would be restricted to cases in which the governing power is vested in a single person, who may be regarded as well-disposed and seeking to rule his subjects for their own good, as a father governs his children. But a ruling family, or even a large ruling class, may be supposed to govern from similar motives. In either case the governed are not supposed to have any voice in the matter, but are cared for like children by the assumed wisdom of their rulers. How far from true paternalism is anything that exists in this or any other civilized country to-day may therefore be readily seen. No one will claim that there is any danger, in a representative government with universal suffrage, of any such state being brought about. This shows at the outset that the term is not used in its original and correct sense, but is merely borrowed and applied as a stigma to certain tendencies in republican governments which the users of it do not approve. What are these tendencies? In general it may be said that they are tendencies toward the assumption by the state of functions that are now entrusted to private enterprise.

On the one hand it is logically argued that the indefinite extension of such powers would eventuate in the most extreme socialistic system,—the conduct of all business by the state. On the other hand it is shown with equal logic that the entire relinquishment of the functions which the state has already assumed would be the abolition of government itself. The extremists of one party would land us in socialism; those of the other, in anarchy. But on one side it is said by the more moderate that the true function of government is the protection of society; to which it is replied by the other that such extension of governmental powers is in the interest of protection, viz., protection against the undue rapacity of private enterprise. Here, as almost everywhere else in the realm of politics, it is a question of quantity and not of quality. It is not a difference in principle, but in policy. It is the degree to which the fundamental principle of all government is to be carried out.

If we look for precedents and historical examples we find great diversity. If we take the question of government telegraphy we find that the United States is almost the only country in the civilized world that has not adopted it, while the reports from other countries are practically unanimous in its favor. That such a movement should be called paternalism is therefore quite gratuitous, and must spring from either pecuniary interest or unenlightened prejudice. From this on, up to the question of abolishing the private ownership of land, there is a multitude of problems presenting all shades of difference in the degree to which the principle of state action is to be applied in their solution. They need to be fearlessly investigated, coolly considered, and wisely decided in the true interests of the public. It was not the purpose of this article to discuss any of these questions, but simply to mention them in illustration of the popular use of the term 'paternalism.' It is clear that that term is employed solely to excite prejudice against the extension of the functions of the state, just as the term 'plutocracy' is used to arouse antagonism to the wealthy classes. The words have in these senses no natural meaning, and, with intelligent persons, should have no argumentative weight.

Are there, then, no dangerous or deleterious tendencies in modern society? There certainly are such, and they may be said to be in the direction of both plutocracy and paternalism, giving to these terms not a literal, but a real or scientific meaning, as denoting respectively the too great power of wealth, and the too great solicitude for and fostering of certain interests on the part of government.

The first law of economics is that every one may be depended upon at all times to seek his greatest gain. It is both natural and right that the individual should be ever seeking to acquire for himself and his; and this rather irrespective of the rest of the world. It was so in the olden time, when physical strength was almost the only force. It is so to-day, when business shrewdness is practically supreme. Government was instituted to protect the weak from the strong in this universal struggle to possess; or, what is the same thing, to protect society at large. Originally it was occupied solely with abuses caused by brute force. It is still, so far as this primary function of enforcing justice is concerned, practically limited to this class of abuses, relatively trifling as they are. Crime still means this, as it did in the days of King Arthur, and as it does to-day in barbaric countries. Any advantage gained by force is promptly met by the law; but advantage gained by cunning, by superior knowledge,—if it be only of the technicalities of the law,—is not a crime, though its spirit be as bad as that of highway robbery and its consequences a thousand times worse.

From this point of view, then, modern society is suffering from the very opposite of paternalism,—from undergovernment, from the failure of government to keep pace with the change which civilization has wrought in substituting intellectual for physical qualities as the workers of injustice. Government to-day is powerless to perform its primary and original function of protecting society. There was a time when brigandage stalked abroad throughout Europe and no one was safe in life or property. This was due to lack of adequate government. Man's nature has not changed, but brigandage has succumbed to the strong arm of the law. Human rapacity now works in subtler ways. Plutocracy is the modern brigandage and can be dislodged only by the same power,—the power of the state. All the evils of society are the result of the free flow of natural propensities. The purpose of government is, as far as may be, to prevent this from causing injustice. The physical passions of men are natural and healthy, but they cannot be allowed to go unbridled. Government was established, not to lessen or even to alter them. Exactly the same is needed to be done with the higher acquisitive faculty. It need not be condemned; it cannot be suppressed: but it can and should be directed into harmless ways and restricted to useful purposes. Properly viewed, too, this is to secure its maximum exercise and greatest freedom, for unrestrained license soon leads to conflict, chokes its own free operation, and puts an end to its activity. The true function of government is not to fetter but to liberate the forces of society, not to diminish but to increase their effectiveness. Unbridled competition destroys itself. The only competition that endures is that which goes on under judicious regulations.

If, then, the danger of plutocracy is so largely due to insufficient government, where is the tendency to paternalism in the sense of too much government? This opens up the last and most important aspect of the subject. If there were no influences at work in society but those of unaided nature; if we had a pure physiocracy or government of nature, such as prevails among wild animals, and the weak were thereby sacrificed that the strong might survive to beget the strong, and thus elevate the race along the lines of evolution,—however great the hardship, we might resign ourselves to it as part of the great cosmic scheme. But unfortunately this is not the case. Without stopping to show that, from the standpoint of a civilized society, the qualities which best fit men to gain advantage over their fellows are the ones least useful to society at large, it will be sufficient for the present purpose to point out that in the actual state of society it is not even those who, from this biological point of view, are the fittest, that become in fact the recipients of the greatest favors at the hands of society. This is due to the creation, by society itself, of artificial conditions that destroy the balance of forces and completely nullify all the beneficial effects that are secured by the operation of the natural law on the lower plane. Indeed, the effect is reversed, and instead of developing strength, either physical or mental, through activity incident to emulation, it tends to parasitic degeneracy through the pampered idleness of the favored classes.

What, in the last analysis, are these social conditions? They are at bottom integral parts of government. They are embodied in law. Largely they consist of statute law. Where this is wanting they rest on judicial decisions, often immemorial, and belonging to the *lex non scripta*. In a word, they constitute the great system of jurisprudence relating to property and business, gradually built up through the ages to make men secure in their possessions and safe in their business transactions, but which in our day, owing to entirely changed industrial conditions, has become the means of throwing unlimited opportunities in the way of some and of barring out the rest from all opportunities. This system of artificial props, bolsterings, and scaffoldings has grown so perfect as to make exertion needless for the protected class and hopeless for the neglected mass. . .

And thus we have the remarkable fact, so persistently overlooked in all the discussions of current question, that government, which fails to protect the weak, is devoting all its energies to protecting the strong. It legalizes and promotes trusts and combinations; subsidizes corporations, and then absolves them from their obligations; sustains stockwatering schemes and all forms of speculation; grants without compensation the most valuable franchises, often in perpetuity; and in innumerable ways creates, defends, and protects a vast array of purely parasitic enterprises, calculated directly to foster the worst forms of municipal corruption. The proofs of each one of these counts lie about us on every hand. Only those who are blinded by interest or prejudice can fail to see them.

There is no greater danger to civilization than the threatened absorption by a few individuals of all the natural resources of the earth, so that they can literally extort tribute from the rest of mankind. If half a dozen persons could get possession of all the breadstuffs of a country, it would justify a revolution.

Fortunately, from the nature of this product, this is impossible, although long strides in that direction have from time to time been taken. But it is otherwise with some other products which, if less indispensable, are still among the modern necessaries of life. All the petroleum of this country is owned by a single trust. If men could not live without it there is no telling how high the price would be raised. Nothing limits it but the question of how much the public will pay rather than do without. That indispensable product, coal, has well-nigh reached the same stage through the several railroad combinations that now control it. That which costs sixty cents to mine, and as much more to transport, cannot be obtained by the consumer for less than five or six dollars. Does it speak well for the common sense of a great people that they should continue to submit to such things? There seems to be no remedy except in the power of the nation. . .

The very possession of wealth is only made possible by government. The safe conduct of all business depends upon the certain protection of law. The most powerful business combinations take place under legal forms. Even dishonest and swindling schemes, so long as they violate no penal statute, are protected by law. Speculation in the necessaries of life is legitimate business, and is upheld by the officers of the law though it result in famine; and even then bread riots are put down by the armed force of the state. Thus has society become the victim of its own system, against the natural effects of which it is powerless to protect itself. It has devised the best possible scheme for satisfying the rapacity of human nature.

And now, mark: The charge of paternalism is chiefly made by the class that enjoys the largest share of government protection. Those who denounce state interference are the ones who most frequently and successfully invoke it. The cry of *laissez-faire* mainly goes up from the ones who, if really 'let alone,' would instantly lose their wealth-absorbing power. .

Nothing is more obvious to-day than the signal inability of capital and private enterprise to take care of themselves unaided by the state; and while they are incessantly denouncing 'paternalism,'—by which they mean the claim of the defenceless laborer and artisan to a share in this lavish state protection, —they are all the while besieging legislatures for relief from their own incompetency, and 'pleading the baby act' through a trained body of lawyers and lobbyists. The dispensing of national pap to this class should rather be called 'maternalism,' to which a square, open, and dignified paternalism would be infinitely preferable.

Still all these things must be regarded as perfectly natural, that is, inherent in the nature of man, and not as peculiar to any class. Therefore personalities and vituperation are entirely out of place. It is simply a question of whether they are going to be permitted to go on. The fault is altogether with the system. Nor should any one object to state protection of business interests. Even monopoly may be defended against aggressive competition on the ground of economy. The protection of the strong may not be too great, but there should be at the same time protection of the weak against the protected strong. It is not the purpose of this article to point out remedies, but tendencies, and it seems clear that right here are to be located the two greatest dangers to modern society. Here lies the only plutocracy, and here the only paternalism. The two are really one, and are embodied in the joint fact of state-protected monopoly. . .

3. *I say, get rich, get rich!*

RUSSELL H. CONWELL, *Acres of Diamonds*, 1861 *

I often wish I could see the younger people, and would that the Academy had been filled to-night with our high-school scholars, and our grammar-school scholars, that I could have them to talk to. While I would have preferred such an audience as that, because they are most susceptible, as they have not grown up into their prejudices as we have, they have not gotten into any custom that they cannot break, they have not met with any failures as we have; and while I could perhaps do such an audience as that more good than I can do grown-up people, yet I will do the best I can with the material I have. I say to you that you have 'acres of diamonds' in Philadelphia right where you now live. 'Oh,' but you say, 'you cannot know much about your city if you think there are any "acres of diamonds" here.' . .

I say . . . that the opportunity to get rich, to attain unto great wealth, is here in Philadelphia now, within the reach of almost every man and woman who hears me speak tonight, and I mean just what I say. I have not come to this platform even under these circumstances to recite something to you. I have come to tell you what in God's sight I believe to be the truth, and if the years of life have been of any value to me in the attainment of common sense, I know I am right; that the men and women sitting here, who found it difficult perhaps to buy a ticket to this lecture or gathering to-night, have within their reach 'acres of diamonds,' opportunities to get largely wealthy. There never was a place on earth more adapted than the city of Philadelphia to-day, and never in the history of the world did a poor man without capital have such an opportunity to get rich quickly and honestly as he has now in our city. I say it is the truth, and I want you to accept it as such; for if you think I have come to simply recite something, then I would better not be here. I have no time to waste in any such talk, but to say the things I believe, and unless some of you get richer for what I am saying to-night my time is wasted.

I say that you ought to get rich, and it is your duty to get rich. How many of my pious brethren say to me, 'Do you, a Christian minister, spend your time going up and down the country advising young people to get rich, to get money?' 'Yes, of course I do.' They say, 'Isn't that awful! Why don't you preach the gospel instead of preaching about man's making money?' 'Because to make money honestly is to preach the gospel.' That is the reason. The men who get rich may be the most honest men you find in the community.

'Oh,' but says some young man here to-night, 'I have been told all my life

* New York, Harper & Brothers, 1915, pp. 15–25, 49–59 *passim*.

that if a person has money he is very dishonest and dishonorable and mean and contemptible.' My friend, that is the reason why you have none, because you have that idea of people. The foundation of your faith is altogether false. Let me say here clearly, and say it briefly, though subject to discussion which I have not time for here, ninety-eight out of one hundred of the rich men of America are honest. That is why they are rich. That is why they are trusted with money. That is why they carry on great enterprises and find plenty of people to work with them. It is because they are honest men. . .

For a man to have money, even in large sums, is not an inconsistent thing. We preach against covetousness, and you know we do, in the pulpit, and oftentimes preach against it so long and use the terms about 'filthy lucre' so extremely that Christians get the idea that when we stand in the pulpit we believe it is wicked for any man to have money—until the collection-basket goes around, and then we almost swear at the people because they don't give more money. Oh, the inconsistency of such doctrines as that!

Money is power, and you ought to be reasonably ambitious to have it. You ought because you can do more good with it than you could without it. Money printed your Bible, money builds your churches, money sends your missionaries, and money pays your preachers, and you would not have many of them, either, if you did not pay them. I am always willing that my church should raise my salary, because the church that pays the largest salary always raises it the easiest. You never knew an exception to it in your life. The man who gets the largest salary can do the most good with the power that is furnished to him. Of course he can if his spirit be right to use it for what it is given to him.

I say, then, you ought to have money. If you can honestly attain unto riches in Philadelphia, it is your Christian and godly duty to do so. It is an awful mistake of these pious people to think you must be awfully poor in order to be pious.

Some men say, 'Don't you sympathize with the poor people?' Of course I do, or else I would not have been lecturing these years. I won't give in but what I sympathize with the poor, but the number of poor who are to be sympathized with is very small. To sympathize with a man whom God has punished for his sins, thus to help him when God would still continue a just punishment, is to do wrong, no doubt about it, and we do that more than we help those who are deserving. While we should sympathize with God's poor—that is, those who cannot help themselves—let us remember there is not a poor person in the United States who was not made poor by his own shortcomings, or by the shortcomings of some one else. It is all wrong to be poor, anyhow. . .

I think I will leave that behind me now and answer the question of nearly all of you who are asking, 'Is there opportunity to get rich in Philadelphia?' Well, now, how simple a thing it is to see where it is, and the instant you see where it is it is yours. Some old gentleman gets up back there and says, 'Mr. Conwell, have you lived in Philadelphia for thirty-one years and don't know that the time has gone by when you can make anything in this city?' 'No, I don't think it is.' 'Yes, it is; I have tried it.' 'What business are you in?'

'I kept a store here for twenty years, and never made over a thousand dollars in the whole twenty years.'

'Well, then, you can measure the good you have been to this city by what this city has paid you, because a man can judge very well what he is worth by what he receives; that is, in what he is to the world at this time. If you have not made over a thousand dollars in twenty years in Philadelphia, it would have been better for Philadelphia if they had kicked you out of the city nineteen years and nine months ago. A man has no right to keep a store in Philadelphia twenty years and not make at least five hundred thousand dollars, even though it be a corner grocery up-town.' You say, 'You cannot make five thousand dollars in a store now.' Oh, my friends, if you will just take only four blocks around you, and find out what the people want and what you ought to supply and set them down with your pencil, and figure up the profits you would make if you did supply them, you would very soon see it. There is wealth right within the sound of your voice. . .

But let me hasten to one other greater thought. 'Show me the great men and women who live in Philadelphia.' A gentleman over there will get up and say: 'We don't have any great men in Philadelphia. They don't live here. They live away off in Rome or St. Petersburg or London or Manayunk, or anywhere else but here in our town.' I have come now to the apex of my thought. I have come now to the heart of the whole matter and to the center of my struggle: Why isn't Philadelphia a greater city in its greater wealth? Why does New York excel Philadelphia? People say, 'Because of her harbor.' Why do many other cities of the United States get ahead of Philadelphia now? There is only one answer, and that is because our own people talk down their own city. If there ever was a community on earth that has to be forced ahead, it is the city of Philadelphia. If we are to have a boulevard, talk it down; if we are going to have better schools, talk them down; if you wish to have wise legislation, talk it down; talk all the proposed improvements down. That is the only great wrong that I can lay at the feet of the magnificent Philadelphia that has been so universally kind to me. I say it is time we turn around in our city and begin to talk up the things that are in our city, and begin to set them before the world as the people of Chicago, New York, St. Louis, and San Francisco do. Oh, if we only could get that spirit out among our people, that we can do things in Philadelphia and do them well!

Arise, ye millions of Philadelphians, trust in God and man, and believe in the great opportunities that are right here—not over in New York or Boston, but here—for business, for everything that is worth living for on earth. There was never an opportunity greater. Let us talk up our own city. . .

'When are you going to be great?' 'When I am elected to some political office.' Young man, won't you learn a lesson in the primer of politics that it is a *prima facie* evidence of littleness to hold office under our form of government? Great men get into office sometimes, but what this country needs is men that will do what we tell them to do. . .

I know of a great many young women, now that woman's suffrage is coming, who say, 'I am going to be President of the United States some day.' . . I want to say right here what I say to the young men, that if you only get the privilege of casting one vote, you don't get anything that is worth while. Unless you can control more than one vote, you will be unknown, and your influence so dissipated as practically not to be felt. This country is not run by votes. Do you think it is? It is governed by influence. It is governed by the ambitions and the enterprises which control votes. . .

Greatness consists not in the holding of some future office, but really consists in doing great deeds with little means and the accomplishments of vast purposes from the private ranks of life. To be great at all one must be great here, now, in Philadelphia. He who can give to this city better streets and better sidewalks, better schools and more colleges, more happiness and more civilization, more of God, he will be great any where. Let every man or woman here, if you never hear me again, remember this, that if you wish to be great at all, you must begin where you are and what you are, in Philadelphia, now. He that can give to his city any blessing, he who can be a good citizen while he lives here, he that can make better homes, he that can be a blessing whether he works in the shop or sits behind the counter or keeps house, whatever be his life, he who would be great anywhere must first be great in his own Philadelphia. . .

4. *It is a waste of time to criticize the inevitable*

ANDREW CARNEGIE, *Wealth*, 1889 *

The problem of our age is the proper administration of wealth, so that the ties of brotherhood may still bind together the rich and poor in harmonious relationship. The conditions of human life have not only been changed, but revolutionized, within the past few hundred years. . . The contrast between the palace of the millionaire and the cottage of the laborer with us to-day measures the change which has come with civilization.

This change, however, is not to be deplored, but welcomed as highly beneficial. It is well, nay, essential for the progress of the race, that the houses of some should be homes for all that is highest and best in literature and the arts, and for all the refinements of civilization, rather than that none should be so. Much better this great irregularity than universal squalor. . . But whether the change be for good or ill, it is upon us, beyond our power to alter, and therefore to be accepted and made the best of. It is a waste of time to criticize the inevitable.

It is easy to see how the change has come. One illustration will serve for almost every phase of the cause. In the manufacture of products we have the whole story. It applies to all combinations of human industry, as stimulated and enlarged by the inventions of this scientific age. Formerly articles were manufactured at the domestic hearth or in small shops which formed part of the household. The master and his apprentices worked side by side, the latter living with the master, and therefore subject to the same conditions. When

* *North American Review*, vol. CXLVIII, 1889, pp. 654–64 *passim*.

these apprentices rose to be masters, there was little or no change in their mode of life, and they, in turn, educated in the same routine succeeding apprentices. There was, substantially, social equality, and even political equality, for those engaged in industrial pursuits had then little or no political voice in the State. . .

Today [as a result of industrialization] the world obtains commodities of excellent quality at prices which even the generation preceding this would have deemed incredible. In the commercial world similar causes have produced similar results, and the race is benefited thereby. The poor enjoy what the rich could not before afford. What were then luxuries have become the necessaries of life. The laborer has now more comforts than the farmer had a few generations ago. The farmer has more luxuries than the landlord had, and is more richly clad and better housed. The landlord has books and pictures rarer, and appointments more artistic, than the King could then obtain.

The price we pay for this salutary change is, no doubt, great. We assemble thousands of operatives in the factory, in the mine, and in the counting-house, of whom the employer can know little or nothing, and to whom the employer is little better than a myth. All intercourse between them is at an end. Rigid Castes are formed, and, as usual, mutual ignorance breeds mutual distrust. Each Caste is without sympathy for the other, and ready to credit anything disparaging in regard to it. Under the law of competition, the employer of thousands is forced into the strictest economies, among which the rates paid to labor figure prominently, and often there is friction between the employer and the employed, between capital and labor, between rich and poor. Human society loses homogeneity.

The price which society pays for the law of competition, like the price it pays for cheap comforts and luxuries, is also great; but the advantages of this law are also greater still, for it is to this law that we owe our wonderful material development, which brings improved conditions in its train. But, whether the law be benign or not, we must say of it, as we say of the change in the conditions of men to which we have referred: It is here; we cannot evade it; no substitutes for it have been found; and while the law may be sometimes hard for the individual, it is best for the race, because it insures the survival of the fittest in every department. We accept and welcome, therefore, as conditions to which we must accommodate ourselves, great inequality of environment, the concentration of business, industrial and commercial, in the hands of a few, and the law of competition between these, as being not only beneficial, but essential for the future progress of the race. Having accepted these, it follows that there must be great scope for the exercise of special ability in the merchant and in the manufacturer who has to conduct affairs upon a great scale. That this talent for organization and management is rare among men is proved by the fact that it invariably secures for its possessor enormous rewards, no matter where or under what laws or conditions. The experienced in affairs always rate the MAN whose services can be obtained as a partner as not only the first consideration, but such as to render the question of his capital scarcely worth considering, for such men soon create capital; while, without the special talent required, capital soon takes wings. . . It is a law, is certain as any of the others named, that men possessed of this peculiar talent for affairs, under the free play of economic forces, must, of necessity, soon be in receipt of more revenue than can be judiciously expended upon themselves; and this law is as beneficial for the race as the others.

Objections to the foundations upon which society is based are not in order, because the condition of the race is better with these than it has been with any others which have been tried. Of the effect of any new substitutes proposed we cannot be sure. The Socialist or Anarchist who seeks to overturn present conditions is to be regarded as attacking the foundation upon which civilization itself rests, for civilization took its start from the day that the capable, industrious workman said to his incompetent and lazy fellow, 'If thou dost not sow, thou shalt not reap,' and thus ended primitive Communism by separating the drones from the bees. One who studies this subject will soon be brought face to face with the conclusion that upon the sacredness of property civilization itself depends—the right of the laborer to his hundred dollars in the savings bank, and equally the legal right of the millionaire to his millions. To those who propose to substitute Communism for this intense Individualism the answer, therefore is: The race has tried that. All progress from that barbarous day to the present time has resulted from its displacement. Not evil, but good, has come to the race from the accumulation of wealth by those who have the ability and energy that produce it. But even if we admit for a moment that it might be better for the race to discard its present foundation, Individualism,—that it is a nobler ideal that man should labor, not for himself alone, but in and for a brotherhood of his fellows, and share with them all in common, realizing Swedenborg's idea of Heaven, where, as he says, the angels derive their happiness, not from laboring for self, but for each other,—even admit all this, and a sufficient answer is, This is not evolution, but revolution. . . We might as well urge the destruction of the highest existing type of man because he failed to reach our ideal as to favor the destruction of Individualism, Private Property, the Law of Accumulation of Wealth, and the Law of Competition; for these are the highest results of human experience, the soil in which society so far has produced the best fruit. Unequally or unjustly, perhaps, as these laws sometimes operate, and imperfect as they appear to the Idealist, they are, nevertheless, like the highest type of man, the best and most valuable of all that humanity has yet accomplished.

We start, then, with a condition of affairs under which the best interests of the race are promoted, but which inevitably gives wealth to the few. Thus far, accepting conditions as they exist, the situation can be surveyed and pronounced good. The question then arises,—and, if the foregoing be correct, it is the only question with which we have to deal,—What is the proper mode of administering wealth after the laws upon which civilization is founded have thrown it into the hands of the few? And it is of this great question that I believe I offer the true solution. It will be understood that *fortunes* are here spoken of, not moderate sums saved by many years of effort, the returns from which are required for the comfortable maintenance and education of families. This is not *wealth*, but only *competence*, which it should be the aim of all to acquire.

There are but three modes in which surplus wealth can be disposed of. It can be left to the families of the decedents; or it can be bequeathed for public purposes; or, finally, it can be administered during their lives by its possessors. . . Under republican institutions the division of property among the children is much fairer, but the question which forces itself upon thoughtful men in all lands is: Why should men leave fortunes to their children? If this is done from affection, is it not misguided affection? Observation teaches that, generally speaking, it is not well for the children that they should be so burdened. Neither is it well for the state. . .

It is not suggested that men who have failed to educate their sons to earn a livelihood shall cast them adrift in poverty. If any man has seen fit to rear his sons with a view to their living idle lives, or, what is highly commendable, has instilled in them the sentiment that they are in a position to labor for public ends without reference to pecuniary considerations, then, of course, the duty of the parent is to see that such are provided for *in moderation*. There are instances of millionaires' sons unspoiled by wealth, who, being rich, still perform great services in the community. Such are the very salt of the earth, as valuable as, unfortunately, they are rare; still it is not the exception, but the rule, that men must regard, and, looking at the usual result of enormous sums conferred upon legatees, the thoughtful man must shortly say, 'I would as soon leave to my son a curse as the almighty dollar,' and admit to himself that it is not the welfare of the children, but family pride, which inspires these enormous legacies.

As to the second mode, that of leaving wealth at death for public uses, it may be said that this is only a means for the disposal of wealth, provided a man is content to wait until he is dead before it becomes of much good in the world. . .

There remains, then, only one mode of using great fortunes; but in this we have the true antidote for the temporary unequal distribution of wealth, the reconciliation of the rich and the poor—a reign of harmony—another ideal, differing, indeed, from that of the Communist in requiring only the further evolution of existing conditions, not the total overthrow of our civilization. It is founded upon the present most intense individualism, and the race is prepared to put it in practice by degrees whenever it pleases. Under its sway we shall have an ideal state, in which the surplus wealth of the few will become, in the best sense, the property of the many, because administered for the common good, and this wealth, passing through the hands of the few, can be made a much more potent force for the elevation of our race than if it had been distributed in small sums to the people themselves. Even the poorest can be made to see this, and to agree that great sums gathered by some of their fellow citizens and spent for public purposes, from which the masses reap the principal benefit, are more valuable to them than if scattered among them through the course of many years in trifling amounts. . .

Poor and restricted are our opportunities in this life; narrow our horizon; our best work most imperfect; but rich men should be thankful for one inestimable boon. They have it in their power during their lives to busy themselves in organizing benefactions from which the masses of their fellows will derive lasting advantage, and thus dignify their own lives. . .

This, then, is held to be the duty of the man of Wealth: First, to set an example of modest, unostentatious living, shunning display or extravagance; to provide moderately for the legitimate wants of those dependent upon him; and after doing so to consider all surplus revenues which come to him simply as trust funds, which he is called upon to administer, and strictly bound as a matter of duty to administer in the manner which, in his judgment, is best calculated to produce the most beneficial results for the community—the man of wealth thus becoming the mere agent and trustee for his poorer brethren, bringing to their service his superior wisdom, experience, and ability to administer, doing for them better than they would or could do for themselves. . .

The best uses to which surplus wealth can be put have already been indicated. Those who would administer wisely must, indeed, be wise, for one of the serious obstacles to the improvement of our race is indiscriminate charity. It were better for mankind that the millions of the rich were thrown into the sea than so spent as to encourage the slothful, the drunken, the unworthy. . .

In bestowing charity, the main consideration should be to help those who will help themselves; to provide part of the means by which those who desire to improve may do so; to give those who desire to rise the aids by which they may rise; to assist but rarely or never to do all. Neither the individual nor the race is improved by alms-giving. . . He is the only true reformer who is as careful and as anxious not to aid the unworthy as he is to aid the worthy, and, perhaps, even more so, for in alms-giving more injury is probably done by rewarding vice than by relieving virtue. . .

Thus is the problem of Rich and Poor to be solved. The laws of accumulation will be left free; the laws of distribution free. Individualism will continue, but the millionaire will be but a trustee for the poor; intrusted for a season with a great part of the increased wealth of the community, but administering it for the community far better than it could or would have done for itself. . .

5. *The worst thing ye can do f'r anny man is to do him good*

FINLEY PETER DUNNE, *The Carnegie Libraries*, 1906 *

'Has Andhrew Carnaygie given ye a libry yet?' asked Mr. Dooley.

'Not that I know iv,' said Mr. Hennessy.

'He will,' said Mr. Dooley. 'Ye'll not escape him. Befure he dies he hopes to crowd a libry on ivry man, woman, an' child in th' counthry. He's given thim to cities, towns, villages, an' whistlin' stations. They're tearin' down gas-houses an' poor-houses to put up libries. Befure another year, ivry house in Pittsburg that ain't a blast-furnace will be a Carnaygie libry. In some places

* *Dissertations by Mr. Dooley*, New York, Harper & Brothers, 1906, pp. 177–82 *passim.*

all th' buildin's is libries. If ye write him f'r an autygraft he sinds ye a libry. No beggar is iver turned impty-handed fr'm th' dure. Th' pan-handler knocks an' asts f'r a glass iv milk an' a roll. "No, sir," says Andhrew Carnaygie. "I will not pauperize this onworthy man. Nawthin' is worse f'r a beggar-man thin to make a pauper iv him. Yet it shall not be said iv me that I give nawthin' to th' poor. Saunders, give him a libry, an' if he still insists on a roll tell him to roll th' libry. F'r I'm humorous as well as wise," he says.'

'Does he give th' books that go with it?' asked Mr. Hennessy.

'Books?' said Mr. Dooley. 'What ar-re ye talkin' about? D'ye know what a libry is? I suppose ye think it's a place where a man can go, haul down wan iv his fav'rite authors fr'm th' shelf, an' take a nap in it. That's not a Carnaygie libry. A Carnaygie libry is a large, brown-stone, impenethrible buildin' with th' name iv th' maker blown on th' dure. Libry, fr'm th' Greek wurruds, libus, a book an' ary, sildom,—sildom a book. A Carnaygie libry is archytechooor, not lithrachoor. Lithrachoor will be riprisinted. Th' most cillybrated dead authors will be honored be havin' their names painted on th' wall in distinguished comp'ny, as thus: Andhrew Carnaygie, Shakespeare; Andhrew Carnaygie, Byron; Andhrew Carnaygie, Bobby Burns; Andhrew Carnaygie, an' so on. Ivry author is guaranteed a place next to pure readin' matther like a bakin' powdher advertisemint, so that whin a man comes along that niver heerd iv Shakespeare he'll know he was somebody, because there he is on th' wall. That's th' dead authors. Th' live authors will stand outside an' wish they were dead.

'He's havin' gr-reat spoort with it. I r-read his speech th' other day, whin he laid th' corner-stone iv th' libry at Pianola, Ioway. Th' entire popylation iv this lithry cinter gathered to see an' hear him. There was th' postmaster an' his wife, th' blacksmith an' his fam'ly, the station agent, mine host iv th' Farmers' Exchange, an' some sthray live stock. "Ladies an' gintlemen," says he. "Modesty compels me to say nawthin' on this occasion, but I am not to be bulldozed," he says. "I can't tell ye how much pleasure I take in' disthributin' monymints to th' humble name around which has gathered so manny hon'rable associations with mesilf. I have been a very busy little man all me life, but I like hard wurruk, an' givin' away me money is th' hardest wurruk I iver did. It fairly makes me teeth ache to part with it. But there's wan consolation. I cheer mesilf with th' thought that no matther how much money I give it don't do anny particular person anny good. Th' worst thing ye can do f'r anny man is to do him good. I pass by th' organ-grinder on th' corner with a savage glare. I bate th' monkey on th' head whin he comes up smilin' to me window, an' hurl him down on his impecyoonyous owner. None iv me money goes into th' little tin cup. I cud kick a hospital, an' I lave Wall Sthreet to look afther th' widow an' th' orphan. Th' submerged tenth, thim that can't get hold iv a good chunk iv th' goods, I wud cut off fr'm th' rest iv th' wurruld an' prevint fr'm bearin' th' haughty name iv papa or th' still lovelier name iv ma. So far I've got on'y half me wish in this matther.

' "I don't want poverty an' crime to go on. I intind to stop it. But how? It's been holdin' its own f'r cinchries. Some iv th' gr-reatest iv former minds has undertook to prevint it an' has failed. They didn't know how. Modesty wud prevint me agin fr'm sayin' that I know how, but that' nayether here nor there. I do. Th' way to abolish poverty an' bust crime is to put up a brown-stone buildin' in ivry town in th' counthry with me name over it. That's th' way. I suppose th' raison it wasn't thried befure was that no man iver had such a name. 'Tis thrue me efforts is not apprecyated ivrywhere. I offer a city a libry, an' oftentimes it replies an' asks me f'r something to pay off th' school debt. I rayceive degraded pettyshuns fr'm so-called proud methropolises f'r a gas-house in place iv a libry. I pass thim by with scorn. All I ask iv a city in raythurn f'r a fifty-thousan'-dollar libry is that it shall raise wan millyon dollars to maintain th' buildin' an' keep me name shinny, an' if it won't do that much f'r lithrachoor, th' divvle take it, it's onworthy iv th' name iv an American city. What ivry community needs is taxes an' lithrachoor. I give thim both. Three cheers f'r a libry an' a bonded debt! Lithrachoor, taxation, an' Andhrew Carnaygie, wan an' insiprable, now an' foriver! They'se nawthin' so good as a good book. It's betther thin food; it's betther thin money. I have made money an' books, an' I like me books betther thin me money. Others don't, but I do. With these few wurruds I will con-clude. . ."

'All th' same, I like Andhrew Carnaygie. Him an' me ar-re agreed on that point. I like him because he ain't shamed to give publicly. Ye don't find him puttin' on false whiskers an' turnin' up his coat-collar whin he goes out to be benivolent. No sir. Ivry time he dhrops a dollar it makes a noise like a waither fallin' down-stairs with a tray iv dishes. He's givin' th' way we'd all like to give. I niver put annything in th' poor-box, but I wud if Father Kelly wud rig up like wan iv thim slot-machines, so that whin I stuck in a nickel me name wud appear over th' altar in red letthers. But whin I put a dollar in th' plate I get back about two yards an' hurl it so hard that th' good man turns around to see who done it. Do good be stealth, says I, but see that th' burglar alarm is set. Anny benivolent money I hand out I want to talk about me. Him that giveth to th' poor, they say, lindeth to th' Lord; but in these days we look f'r quick returns on our invistments. I like Andhrew Carnaygie, an', as he says, he puts his whole soul into th' wurruk.'

'What's he mane be that?' asked Mr. Hennessy.

'He manes,' said Mr. Dooley, 'that he's gin-rous. Ivry time he gives a libry he gives himsilf away in a speech.'

6. *The force of the religious spirit should be bent toward asserting the supremacy of life over property*

WALTER RAUSCHENBUSCH, *Christianity and Social Crisis*, 1907 *

As long as the working class simply attempts to better its condition somewhat and to secure a recognized standing for its class organization, it stands on the basis of the present capitalistic organization of industry. Capitalism necessarily divides industrial society into two classes,—those who own the instruments

* New York, The Macmillan Company, pp. 406–10, 413–14 *passim*.

and materials of production, and those who furnish the labor for it. This sharp division is the peculiar characteristic of modern capitalism which distinguishes it from other forms of social organization in the past. These two classes have to coöperate in modern production. The labor movement seeks to win better terms for the working class in striking its bargains. Yet whatever terms organized labor succeeds in winning are always temporary and insecure, like the hold which a wrestler gets on the body of his antagonist. The persistent tendency with capital necessarily is to get labor as cheaply as possible and to force as much work from it as possible. Moreover, labor is always in an inferior position in the struggle. It is handicapped by its own hunger and lack of resources. It has to wrestle on its knees with a foeman who is on his feet. Is this unequal struggle between two conflicting interests to go on forever? Is this insecurity the best that the working class can ever hope to attain?

Here enters socialism. It proposes to abolish the division of industrial society into two classes and to close the fatal chasm which has separated the employing class from the working class since the introduction of power machinery. It proposes to restore the independence of the workingman by making him once more the owner of his tools and to give him the full proceeds of his production instead of a wage determined by his poverty. It has no idea of reverting to the simple methods of the old handicrafts, but heartily accepts the power machinery, the great factory, the division of labor, the organization of the men in great regiments of workers, as established facts in modern life, and as the most efficient method of producing wealth. But it proposes to give to the whole body of workers the ownership of these vast instruments of production and to distribute among them all the entire proceeds of their common labor. There would then be no capitalistic class opposed to the working class; there would be a single class which would unite the qualities of both. Every workman would be both owner and worker, just as a farmer is who tills his own farm, or a housewife who works in her own kitchen. This would be a permanent solution of the labor question. It would end the present insecurity, the constant antagonism, the social inferiority, the physical exploitation, the intellectual poverty to which the working class is now exposed even when its condition is most favorable.

If such a solution is even approximately feasible, it should be hailed with joy by every patriot and Christian, for it would put a stop to our industrial war, drain off the miasmatic swamp of undeserved poverty, save our political democracy, and lift the great working class to an altogether different footing of comfort, intelligence, security and moral strength. And it would embody the principle of solidarity and fraternity in the fundamental institutions of our industrial life. All the elements of coöperation and interaction which are now at work in our great establishments would be conserved, and in addition the hearty interest of all workers in their common factory or store would be immensely intensified by the diffused sense of ownership. Such a social order would develop the altruistic and social instincts just as the competitive order brings out the selfish instincts.

Socialism is the ultimate and logical outcome of the labor movement. When the entire working class throughout the industrial nations is viewed in a large way, the progress of socialism gives an impression of resistless and elemental power. It is inconceivable from the point of view of that class that it should stop short of complete independence and equality as long as it has the power to move on, and independence and equality for the working class must mean the collective ownership of the means of production and the abolition of the present two-class arrangement of industrial society. If the labor movement in our country is only slightly tinged with socialism as yet, it is merely because it is still in its embryonic stages. Nothing will bring the working class to a thorough comprehension of the actual status of their class and its ultimate aim more quickly than continued failure to secure their smaller demands and reactionary efforts to suppress their unions. . .

The coöperation of professional men outside the working class would contribute scientific information and trained intelligence. They would mediate between the two classes, interpreting each to the other, and thereby lessening the strain of hostility. Their presence and sympathy would cheer the working people and diminish the sense of class isolation. By their contact with the possessing classes they could help to persuade them of the inherent justice of the labor movement and so create a leaning toward concessions. No other influence could do so much to prevent a revolutionary explosion of pent-up forces. It is to the interest of all sides that the readjustment of the social classes should come as a steady evolutionary process rather than as a social catastrophe. If the laboring class should attempt to seize political power suddenly, the attempt might be beaten back with terrible loss in efficiency to the movement. If the attempt should be successful, a raw governing class would be compelled to handle a situation so vast and complicated that no past revolution presents a parallel. There would be widespread disorder and acute distress, and a reactionary relapse to old conditions would, by all historical precedents, be almost certain to occur. It is devoutly to be desired that the shifting of power should come through a continuous series of practicable demands on one side and concessions on the other. Such an historical process will be immensely facilitated if there are a large number of men in the professional and business class with whom religious and ethical motives overcome their selfish interests so that they will throw their influence on the side of the class which is now claiming its full rights in the family circle of humanity. . .

The force of the religious spirit should be bent toward asserting the supremacy of life over property. Property exists to maintain and develop life. It is unchristian to regard human life as a mere instrument for the production of wealth.

The religious sentiment can protect good customs and institutions against the inroads of ruthless greed, and extend their scope. It can create humane customs which the law is impotent to create. It can create the convictions and customs which are later embodied in good legislation.

Our complex society rests largely on the stewardship of delegated powers. The opportunities to profit by the betrayal of trust increase with the wealth and complexity of civilization. The most fundamental evils in past history and present conditions were due to converting stewardship into ownership. The keener moral insight created by Christianity should lend its help in scrutinizing all claims to property and power in order to detect latent public rights and to recall the recreant stewards to their duty. . .

The splendid ideal of a fraternal organization of society cannot be realized by idealists only. It must be supported by the self-interest of a powerful class. The working class, which is now engaged in its upward movement, is struggling to secure better conditions of life, an assured status for its class organizations, and ultimately the ownership of the means of production. Its success in the last great aim would mean the closing of the gap which now divides industrial society and the establishment of industry on the principle of solidarity and the method of coöperation. Christianity should enter into a working alliance with this rising class, and by its mediation secure the victory of these principles by a gradual equalization of social opportunity and power.

7. *We must make land common property*

HENRY GEORGE, *Progress and Poverty,* 1879 *

THE PROBLEM

The present century has been marked by a prodigious increase in wealth-producing power. The utilization of steam and electricity, the introduction of improved processes and labor-saving machinery, the greater subdivision and grander scale of production, the wonderful facilitation of exchanges, have multiplied enormously the effectiveness of labor.

At the beginning of this marvelous era it was natural to expect, and it was expected, that labor-saving inventions would lighten the toil and improve the condition of the laborer; that the enormous increase in the power of producing wealth would make real poverty a thing of the past. . .

Now, however, we are coming into collision with facts which there can be no mistaking. From all parts of the civilized world come complaints of industrial depression; of labor condemned to involuntary idleness; of capital massed and wasting; of pecuniary distress among businessmen; of want and suffering and anxiety among the working classes. All the dull, deadening pain, all the keen, maddening anguish, that to great masses of men are involved in the words 'hard times,' afflict the world today. . .

And, unpleasant as it may be to admit it, it is at last becoming evident that the enormous increase in productive power which has marked the present century is still going on with accelerating ratio, has no tendency to extirpate poverty or to lighten the burdens of those compelled to toil. . . The march of invention has clothed mankind with powers of which a century ago the boldest

* New York, D. Appleton & Co., 1882, pp. 3, 11, 148–9, 295–304, 362–6, 490, 495–6 *passim*.

imagination could not have dreamed. But in factories where labor-saving machinery has reached its most wonderful development, little children are at work; wherever the new forces are anything like fully utilized, large classes are maintained by charity or live on the verge of recourse to it; amid the greatest accumulations of wealth, men die of starvation, and puny infants suckle dry breasts; while everywhere the greed of gain, the worship of wealth, shows the force of the fear of want. The promised land flies before us like the mirage. . .

This association of poverty with progress is the great enigma of our times. It is the central fact from which spring industrial, social, and political difficulties that perplex the world, and with which statesmanship and philanthropy and education grapple in vain. . .

I propose in the following pages to attempt to solve by the methods of political economy the great problem I have outlined. I propose to seek the law which associates poverty with progress, and increases want with advancing wealth; and I believe that in the explanation of this paradox we shall find the explanation of those recurring seasons of industrial and commercial paralysis which, viewed independent of their relations to more general phenomena, seem so inexplicable. . .

RENT AND THE LAW OF RENT

The term rent, in its economic sense—that is, when used, as I am using it, to distinguish that part of the produce which accrues to the owners of land or other natural capabilities by virtue of their ownership—differs in meaning from the word rent as commonly used. In some respects this economic meaning is narrower than the common meaning; in other respects it is wider.

It is narrower in this: In common speech, we apply the word rent to payments for the use of buildings, machinery, fixtures, etc., as well as to payments for the use of land or other natural capabilities; and in speaking of the rent of a house or the rent of a farm, we do not separate the price for the use of the improvements from the price for the use of the bare land. But in the economic meaning of rent, payments for the use of any of the products of human exertion are excluded, and of the lumped payments for the use of houses, farms, etc., only that part is rent which constitutes the consideration for the use of the land—that part paid for the use of buildings or other improvements being properly interest, as it is a consideration for the use of capital.

It is wider in this: In common speech we only speak of rent when owner and user are distinct persons. But in the economic sense there is also rent where the same person is both owner and user. Where owner and user are thus the same person, whatever part of his income he might obtain by letting the land to another is rent, while the return for his labor and capital are that part of his income which they would yield him did he hire instead of owning the land. Rent is also expressed in a selling price. When land is purchased, the payment which is made for the ownership, or right to perpetual use, is rent commuted or capitalized. If I buy land for a small price and hold it until I can sell it for a large price, I have become rich, not by wages for my labor or by interest upon my capital, but by the increase of rent. Rent, in short, is the share in the wealth produced which the exclusive right to the use of natural capabilities gives to the owner. Wherever land has an exchange value there is rent in the economic meaning of the term. Wherever land having a value is used, either by owner or hirer, there is rent actual; wherever it is not used, but still has a value, there is rent potential. It is this capacity of yielding rent which gives value to land. Until its ownership will confer some advantage, land has no value.*

Thus rent or land value does not arise from the productiveness or utility of land. It in no wise represents any help or advantage given to production, but simply the power of securing a part of the results of production. No matter what are its capabilities, land can yield no rent and have no value until some one is willing to give labor or the results of labor for the privilege of using it; and what any one will thus give, depends not upon the capacity of the land, but upon its capacity as compared with that of land that can be had for nothing. I may have very rich land, but it will yield no rent and have no value so long as there is other land as good to be had without cost. But when this other land is appropriated, and the best land to be had for nothing is inferior, either in fertility, situation, or other quality, my land will begin to have a value and yield rent. And though the productiveness of my land may decrease, yet if the productiveness of the land to be had without charge decreases in greater proportion, the rent I can get, and consequently the value of my land, will steadily increase. Rent, in short, is the price of monopoly, arising from the reduction to individual ownership of natural elements which human exertion can neither produce nor increase. . .

THE TRUE REMEDY

There is but one way to remove an evil—and that is, to remove its cause. Poverty deepens as wealth increases, and wages are forced down while productive power grows, because land, which is the source of all wealth and the field of all labor, is monopolized. To extirpate poverty, to make wages what justice commands they should be, the full earnings of the laborer, we must therefore substitute for the individual ownership of land a common ownership. Nothing else will go to the cause of the evil—in nothing else is there the slightest hope.

This, then, is the remedy for the unjust and unequal distribution of wealth apparent in modern civilization, and for all the evils which flow from it:

We must make land common property. . .

If the remedy to which we have been led is the true one, it must be consistent with justice; it must be practicable of application; it must accord with the tendencies of social development, and must harmonize with other reforms. . .

I thus propose to show that the laws of the universe do not deny the natural

* In speaking of the value of land I use and shall use the words as referring to the value of the bare land. When I wish to speak of the value of land and improvements I shall use those words.

aspirations of the human heart; that the progress of society might be, and, if it is to continue, must be, toward equality, not toward inequality; and that the economic harmonies prove the truth perceived by the Stoic Emperor—

'We are made for co-operation—like feet, like hands, like eyelids, like the rows of the upper and lower teeth.'

THE INJUSTICE OF PRIVATE PROPERTY IN LAND

When it is proposed to abolish private property in land the first question that will arise is that of justice. Though often warped by habit, superstition, and selfishness into the most distorted forms, the sentiment of justice is yet fundamental to the human mind, and whatever dispute arouses the passions of men, the conflict is sure to rage, not so much as to the question 'Is it wise?' as to the question 'Is it right?'. . .

What constitutes the rightful basis of property? What is it that enables a man to justly say of a thing, 'It is mine!' From what springs the sentiment which acknowledges his exclusive right as against all the world? Is it not, primarily, the right of a man to himself, to the use of his own powers, to the enjoyment of the fruits of his own exertions? Is it not this individual right, which springs from and is testified to by the natural facts of individual organization—the fact that each particular pair of hands obey a particular brain and are related to a particular stomach; the fact that each man is a definite, coherent, independent whole—which alone justifies individual ownership? As a man belongs to himself, so his labor when put in concrete form belongs to him.

And for this reason, that which a man makes or produces is his own, as against all the world—to enjoy or to destroy, to use, to exchange, or to give. No one else can rightfully claim it, and his exclusive right to it involves no wrong to any one else. Thus there is to everything produced by human exertion a clear and indisputable title to exclusive possession and enjoyment, which is perfectly consistent with justice, as it descends from the original producer, in whom it is vested by natural law. The pen with which I am writing is justly mine. No other human being can rightfully lay claim to it, for in me is the title of the producers who made it. It has become mine, because transferred to me by the stationer, to whom it was transferred by the importer, who obtained the exclusive right to it by transfer from the manufacturer, in whom, by the same process of purchase, vested the rights of those who dug the material from the ground and shaped it into a pen. Thus, my exclusive right of ownership in the pen springs from the natural right of the individual to the use of his own faculties. . .

This right of ownership that springs from labor excludes the possibility of any other right of ownership. If a man be rightfully entitled to the produce of his labor, then no one can be rightfully entitled to the ownership of anything which is not the produce of his labor, or the labor of some one else from whom the right has passed to him. If production give to the producer the right to exclusive possession and enjoyment, there can rightfully be no exclusive possession and enjoyment of anything not the production of labor, and the recognition of private property in land is a wrong. For the right to produce of labor cannot be enjoyed without the right to the free use of the opportunities offered by nature, and to admit the right of property in these is to deny the right of property in the produce of labor. When non-producers can claim as rent a portion of the wealth created by producers, the right of the producers to the fruits of their labor is to that extent denied. . .

The moment this distinction is realized, that moment is it seen that the sanction which natural justice gives to one species of property is denied to the other; that the rightfulness which attaches to individual property in the produce of labor implies the wrongfulness of individual property in land; that, whereas the recognition of the one places all men upon equal terms, securing to each the due reward of his labor, the recognition of the other is the denial of the equal rights of men, permitting those who do not labor to take the natural reward of those who do.

Whatever may be said for the institution of private property in land, it is therefore plain that it cannot be defended on the score of justice.

The equal right of all men to the use of land is as clear as their equal right to breathe the air—it is a right proclaimed by the fact of their existence. For we cannot suppose that some men have a right to be in this world and others no right. . .

HOW EQUAL RIGHTS TO THE LAND MAY BE ASSERTED AND SECURED

But a question of method remains. How shall we do it?

We should satisfy the law of justice, we should meet all economic requirements, by at one stroke abolishing all private titles, declaring all land public property, and letting it out to the highest bidders in lots to suit, under such conditions as would sacredly guard the private right to improvements.

Thus we should secure, in a more complex state of society, the same equality of rights that in a ruder state were secured by equal partitions of the soil, and by giving the use of the land to whoever could procure the most from it, we should secure the greatest production. . .

But such a plan, though perfectly feasible, does not seem to me the best. Or rather I propose to accomplish the same thing in a simpler, easier, and quieter way, than that of formally confiscating all the land and formally letting it out to the highest bidders.

To do that would involve a needless shock to present customs and habits of thought—which is to be avoided.

To do that would involve a needless extension of governmental machinery—which is to be avoided.

I do not propose either to purchase or to confiscate private property in land. The first would be unjust; the second, needless. Let the individuals who now hold it still retain, if they want to, possession of what they are pleased to call *their* land. Let them continue to call it *their* land. Let them buy and sell, and bequeath and devise it. We may safely leave them the shell, if we take the kernel. *It is not necessary to confiscate land; it is only necessary to confiscate rent.* . .

What I, therefore, propose, as the simple yet sovereign remedy, which will raise wages, increase the earnings of capital, extirpate pauperism, abolish poverty, give remunerative employment to whoever wishes it, afford free scope to human powers, lessen crime, elevate morals, and taste, and intelligence, purify government and carry civilization to yet nobler heights, is—*to appropriate rent by taxation.*

In this way, the State may become the universal landlord without calling herself so, and without assuming a single new function. In form, the ownership of land would remain just as now. No owner of land need be dispossessed, and no restriction need be placed upon the amount of land any one could hold. For, rent being taken by the State in taxes, land, no matter in whose name it stood, or in what parcels it was held, would be really common property, and every member of the community would participate in the advantages of its ownership.

Now, insomuch as the taxation of rent, or land values, must necessarily be increased just as we abolish other taxes, we may put the proposition into practical form by proposing—

To abolish all taxation save that upon land values. . .

Experience has taught me (for I have been for some years endeavoring to popularize this proposition) that wherever the idea of concentrating all taxation upon land values finds lodgment sufficient to induce consideration, it invariably makes way, but that there are few of the classes most to be benefited by it, who at first, or even for a long time afterwards, see its full significance and power. It is difficult for workingmen to get over the idea that there is a real antagonism between capital and labor. It is difficult for small farmers and homestead owners to get over the idea that to put all taxes on the value of land would be to unduly tax them. It is difficult for both classes to get over the idea that to exempt capital from taxation would be to make the rich richer, and the poor poorer. These ideas spring from confused thought. But behind ignorance and prejudice there is a powerful interest, which has hitherto dominated literature, education, and opinion.

The reform I propose accords with all that is politically, socially, or morally desirable. It has the qualities of a true reform, for it will make all other reforms easier. What is it but the carrying out in letter and spirit of the truth enunciated in the Declaration of Independence—the 'self-evident' truth that is the heart and soul of the Declaration—'*That all men are created equal; that they are endowed by their Creator with certain inalienable rights; that among them are life, liberty, and the pursuit of happiness!*'

These rights are denied when the equal right to land—on which and by which men alone can live—is denied. Equality of political rights will not compensate for the denial of the equal right to the bounty of nature. Political liberty, when the equal right to land is denied, becomes, as population increases and invention goes on, merely the liberty to compete for employment at starvation wages. This is the truth that we have ignored. . .

8. *All men who do their best do the same*

EDWARD BELLAMY, *Looking Backward, 2000–1887*, 1889 *

[DR. LEETE:] 'It was in 1887 that you fell into this sleep, I think you said.'
[MR. WEST:] 'Yes, May 30th, 1887.'

My companion regarded me musingly for some moments. Then he observed, 'And you tell me that even then there was no general recognition of the nature of the crisis which society was nearing? Of course, I fully credit your statement. The singular blindness of your contemporaries to the signs of the times is a phenomenon commented on by many of our historians, but few facts of history are more difficult for us to realize. . . I should be interested, Mr. West, if you would give me a little more definite idea of the view which you and men of your grade of intellect took of the state and prospects of society in 1887. You must, at least, have realized that the widespread industrial and social troubles, and the underlying dissatisfaction of all classes with the inequalities of society, and the general misery of mankind, were portents of great changes of some sort.'

'We did, indeed, fully realize that,' I replied. 'We felt that society was dragging anchor and in danger of going adrift. Whither it would drift nobody could say, but all feared the rocks.'

'Nevertheless,' said Dr. Leete, 'the set of the current was perfectly perceptible if you had but taken pains to observe it, and it was not toward the rocks, but toward a deeper channel.'

. . . 'Since you are in the humor to talk rather than to sleep, as I certainly am, perhaps I cannot do better than to try to give you enough idea of our modern industrial system to dissipate at least the impression that there is any mystery about the process of its evolution. The Bostonians of your day had the reputation of being great askers of questions, and I am going to show my descent by asking you one to begin with. What should you name as the most prominent feature of the labor troubles of your day?'

'Why, the strikes, of course,' I replied.

'Exactly; but what made the strikes so formidable?'

'The great labor organizations.'

'And what was the motive of these great organizations?'

'The workmen claimed they had to organize to get their rights from the big corporations,' I replied.

'That is just it,' said Dr. Leete; 'the organization of labor and the strikes were an effect, merely, of the concentration of capital in greater masses than had ever been known before. Before this concentration began, while as yet commerce and industry were conducted by innumerable petty concerns with small capital, instead of a small number of great concerns with vast capital, the individual workman was relatively important and independent in his relations to the employer. Moreover, when a little capital or a new idea was enough to start a man in business for himself, workingmen were constantly becoming employers

* New York, Houghton Mifflin Company, 1889, pp. 49–244 *passim*.

and there was no hard and fast line between the two classes. Labor unions were needless then, and general strikes out of the question. But when the era of small concerns with small capital was succeeded by that of the great aggregations of capital, all this was changed. The individual laborer, who had been relatively important to the small employer, was reduced to insignificance and powerlessness over against the great corporation, while at the same time the way upward to the grade of employer was closed to him. Self-defense drove him to union with his fellows.

'The records of the period show that the outcry against the concentration of capital was furious. Men believed that it threatened society with a form of tyranny more abhorrent than it had ever endured. They believed that the great corporations were preparing for them the yoke of a baser servitude than had ever been imposed on the race, servitude not to men but to soulless machines incapable of any motive but insatiable greed. . .

'In the United States there was not, after the beginning of the last quarter of the century, any opportunity whatever for individual enterprise in any important field of industry, unless backed by a great capital. During the last decade of the century, such small businesses as still remained were fast-failing survivals of a past epoch, or mere parasites on the great corporations, or else existed in fields too small to attract the great capitalists. Small businesses, as far as they still remained, were reduced to the condition of rats and mice, living in holes and corners, and counting on evading notice for the enjoyment of existence. The railroads had gone on combining till a few great syndicates controlled every rail in the land. In manufactories, every important staple was controlled by a syndicate. These syndicates, pools, trusts, or whatever their name, fixed prices and crushed all competition except when combinations as vast as themselves arose. Then a struggle, resulting in a still greater consolidation, ensued. . .

'The fact that the desperate popular opposition to the consolidation of business in a few powerful hands had no effect to check it proves that there must have been a strong economical reason for it. The small capitalists, with their innumerable petty concerns, had in fact yielded the field to the great aggregations of capital, because they belonged to a day of small things and were totally incompetent to the demands of an age of steam and telegraphs and the gigantic scale of its enterprises. To restore the former order of things, even if possible, would have involved returning to the day of stage-coaches. Oppressive and intolerable as was the regime of the great consolidations of capital, even its victims, while they cursed it, were forced to admit the prodigious increase of efficiency which had been imparted to the national industries, the vast economies effected by concentration of management and unity of organization, and to confess that since the new system had taken the place of the old the wealth of the world had increased at a rate before undreamed of. . .

'Was there, then, no way of commanding the services of the mighty wealth-producing principle of consolidated capital without bowing down to a plutocracy like that of Carthage? As soon as men began to ask themselves these questions, they found the answer ready for them. The movement toward the conduct of business by larger and larger aggregations of capital, the tendency toward monopolies, which had been so desperately and vainly resisted, was recognized at last, in its true significance as a process which only needed to complete its logical evolution to open a golden future to humanity. . .

'In a word, the people of the United States concluded to assume the conduct of their own business, just as one hundred odd years before they had assumed the conduct of their own government, organizing now for industrial purposes on precisely the same grounds that they had then organized for political purposes. At last, strangely late in the world's history, the obvious fact was perceived that no business is so essentially the public business as the industry and commerce on which the people's livelihood depends, and that to entrust it to private persons to be managed for private profit is a folly similar in kind, though vastly greater in magnitude, to that of surrendering the functions of political government to kings and nobles to be conducted for their personal glorification.'

'Such a stupendous change as you describe,' said I, 'did not, of course, take place without great bloodshed and terrible convulsions.'

'On the contrary,' replied Dr. Leete, 'there was absolutely no violence. . . Fifty years before, the consolidation of the industries of the country under national control would have seemed a very daring experiment to the most sanguine. But by a series of object lessons, seen and studied by all men, the great corporations had taught the people an entirely new set of ideas on this subject. They had seen for many years syndicates handling revenues greater than those of states, and directing the labors of hundreds of thousands of men with an efficiency and economy unattainable in smaller operations. It had come to be recognized as an axiom that the larger the business the simpler the principles that can be applied to it; that, as the machine is truer than the hand, so the system, which in a great concern does the work of the master's eye in a small business, turns out more accurate results. Thus it came about that, thanks to the corporations themselves, when it was proposed that the nation should assume their functions, the suggestion implied nothing which seemed impracticable even to the timid. . .'

'Leaving comparison aside,' I said, 'the demagoguery and corruption of our public men would have been considered, in my day, insuperable objections to any assumption by government of the charge of the national industries. We should have thought that no arrangement could be worse than to entrust the politicians with control of the wealth-producing machinery of the country. . .'

'No doubt you were right,' rejoined Dr. Leete, 'but all that is changed now. We have no parties or politicians, and as for demagoguery and corruption, they are words having only an historical significance.'

'Human nature itself must have changed very much,' I said.

'Not at all," was Dr. Leete's reply, 'but the conditions of human life have changed, and with them the motives of human action. The organization of society with you was such that officials were under a constant temptation to misuse their power for the private profit of themselves or others. Under such circumstances it seems almost strange that you dared entrust them with any of your affairs. Nowadays, on the contrary, society is so constituted that there is absolutely no way in which an official, however ill-disposed, could possibly make any profit for himself or any one else by a misuse of his power. Let him be as bad an official as you please, he cannot be a corrupt one. There is no motive to be. The social system no longer offers a premium on dishonesty. . .'

'But you have not yet told me how you have settled the labor problem. It is the problem of capital which we have been discussing,' I said. 'After the nation had assumed conduct of the mills, machinery, railroads, farms, mines, and capital in general of the country, the labor question still remained. In assuming the responsibilities of capital the nation had assumed the difficulties of the capitalist's position.'

'The moment the nation assumed the responsibilities of capital those difficulties vanished,' replied Dr. Leete. 'The national organization of labor under one direction was the complete solution of what was, in your day and under your system, justly regarded as the insoluble labor problem. When the nation became the sole employer, all the citizens, by virtue of their citizenship, became employees, to be distributed according to the needs of industry.' . .

'How, then, do you regulate wages?' I once more asked.

Dr. Leete did not reply till after several moments of meditative silence. . . 'I am a little at loss how to answer you best. You ask me how we regulate wages; I can only reply that there is no idea in the modern social economy which at all corresponds with what was meant by wages in your day.'

'I suppose you mean that you have no money to pay wages in,' said I. 'But the credit given the worker at the government storehouse answers to his wages with us. How is the amount of the credit given respectively to the workers in different lines determined? By what title does the individual claim his particular share? What is the basis of allotment?'

'His title,' replied Dr. Leete, 'is his humanity. The basis of his claim is the fact that he is a man.'

'The fact that he is a man!' I repeated, incredulously. 'Do you possibly mean that all have the same share?'

'Most assuredly.' . .

'How can you do that, I should like to know, when no two men's powers are the same?'

'Nothing could be simpler,' was Dr. Leete's reply. 'We require of each that he shall make the same effort; that is, we demand of him the best service it is in his power to give.'

'And supposing all do the best they can,' I answer, 'the amount of the product resulting is twice greater from one man than from another.'

'Very true,' replied Dr. Leete; 'but the amount of the resulting product has nothing whatever to do with the question, which is one of desert. Desert is a moral question, and the amount of the product a material quantity. It would be an extraordinary sort of logic which should try to determine a moral question by a material standard. The amount of the effort alone is pertinent to the question of desert. All men who do their best, do the same. . . The Creator sets men's tasks for them by the faculties he gives them; we simply exact their fulfillment.' . .

'But what inducement,' I asked, 'can a man have to put forth his best endeavors when, however much or little he accomplishes, his income remains the same? High characters may be moved by devotion to the common welfare under such a system, but does not the average man tend to rest back on his oar, reasoning that it is of no use to make a special effort, since the effort will not increase his income, nor its withholding diminish it?'

'Does it then really seem to you,' answered my companion, 'that human nature is insensible to any motives save fear of want and love of luxury, that you should expect security and equality of livelihood to leave them without possible incentives to effort? . . Not higher wages, but honor and the hope of men's gratitude, patriotism and the inspiration of duty, were the motives which they set before their soldiers when it was a question of dying for the nation, and never was there an age of the world when those motives did not call out what is best and noblest in men. And not only this, but when you come to analyze the love of money which was the general impulse to effort in your day, you find that the dread of want and desire of luxury was but one of several motives which the pursuit of money represented; the others, and with many the more influential, being desire of power, of social position, and reputation for ability and success. So you see that though we have abolished poverty and the fear of it, and inordinate luxury with the hope of it, we have not touched the greater part of the motives which underlay the love of money in former times, or any of those which prompted the supremer sorts of effort. The coarser motives, which no longer move us, have been replaced by higher motives wholly unknown to the mere wage earners of your age. . .' With us, diligence in the national service is the sole and certain way to public repute, social distinction and official power. . .

'What may this badge be?' I asked.

'Every industry has its emblematic device,' replied Dr. Leete, 'and this, in the shape of a metallic badge so small that you might not see it unless you knew where to look, is all the insignia which the men of the army wear, except where public convenience demands a distinctive uniform. This badge is the same in form for all grades of industry, but while the badge of the third grade is iron, that of the second grade is silver, and that of the first is gilt. . .

'It is obviously important that not only the good but also the indifferent and poor workmen should be able to cherish the ambition of rising. Indeed, the number of the latter being so much greater, it is even more essential that the ranking system should not operate to discourage them than that it should stimulate the others. It is to this end that the grades are divided into classes. . .

'It is not even necessary that a worker should win promotion to a higher grade to have at least a taste of glory. While promotion requires a general excellence of record as a worker, honorable mention and various sorts of prizes are awarded for excellence less than sufficient for promotion and also for special feats and single performances in the various industries. There are many minor distinctions of standing, not only within the grades but within the classes, each of which acts as a spur to the efforts of a group. It is intended that no form of merit shall wholly fail of recognition.

'As for actual neglect of work, positively bad work, or other overt remissness on the part of men incapable of generous motives, the discipline of the industrial army is far too strict to allow anything whatever of the sort. A man able to do duty, and persistently refusing, is sentenced to solitary imprisonment on bread and water till he consents. . .

'I should not fail to mention,' resumed the doctor, 'that for those too deficient in mental or bodily strength to be fairly graded with the main body of workers, we have a separate grade, unconnected with the others,—a sort of invalid corps, the members of which are provided with a light class of tasks fitted to their strength. All our sick in mind and body, all our deaf and dumb, and lame and blind and crippled, and even our insane, belong to this invalid corps, and bear its insignia. The strongest often do nearly a man's work, the feeblest, of course, nothing; but none who can do anything are willing quite to give up. In their lucid intervals, even our insane are eager to do what they can.'

"That is a pretty idea of the invalid corps,' I said. 'Even a barbarian from the nineteenth century can appreciate that. It is a very graceful way of disguising charity, and must be grateful to the feelings of its recipients.'

'Charity!' repeated Dr. Leete. 'Did you suppose that we consider the incapable class we are talking of objects of charity?'

'Why, naturally,' I said, 'inasmuch as they are incapable of self-support.'

But here the doctor took me up quickly.

'Who is capable of self-support?' he demanded. 'There is no such thing in a civilized society as self-support. In a state of society so barbarous as not even to know family cooperation, each individual may possibly support himself, though even then for a part of his life only; but from the moment that men begin to live together, and constitute even the rudest sort of society, self-support becomes impossible. As men grow more civilized, and the subdivision of occupations and services is carried out, a complex mutual dependence becomes the universal rule. Every man, however solitary may seem his occupation, is a member of a vast industrial partnership, as large as the nation, as large as humanity. The necessity of mutual dependence should imply the duty and guarantee of mutual support; and that it did not in your day constituted the essential cruelty and unreason of your system.'

'That may all be so,' I replied, 'but it does not touch the case of those who are unable to contribute anything to the product of industry.'

'Surely I told you this morning, at least I thought I did,' replied Dr. Leete, 'that the right of a man to maintenance at the nation's table depends on the fact that he is a man, and not on the amount of health and strength he may have, so long as he does his best.'

'You said so,' I answered, 'but I supposed the rule applied only to the workers of different ability. Does it also hold of those who can do nothing at all?'

'Are they not also men?'

'I am to understand, then, that the lame, the blind, the sick, and the impotent, are as well off as the most efficient, and have the same income?'

'Certainly,' was the reply.

'The idea of charity on such a scale,' I answered, 'would have made our most enthusiastic philanthropists gasp.'

'If you had a sick brother at home,' replied Dr. Leete, 'unable to work, would you feed him on less dainty food, and lodge and clothe him more poorly, than yourself? More likely far, you would give him the preference; nor would you think of calling it charity. Would not the word, in that connection, fill you with indignation?'

'Of course,' I replied; 'but the cases are not parallel. There is a sense, no doubt, in which all men are brothers; but this general sort of brotherhood is not to be compared, except for rhetorical purposes, to the brotherhood of blood, either as to its sentiment or its obligations.'

'There speaks the nineteenth century!' exclaimed Dr. Leete. 'Ah, Mr. West, there is no doubt as to the length of time that you slept. If I were to give you, in one sentence, a key to what may seem the mysteries of our civilization as compared with that of your age, I should say that it is the fact that the solidarity of the race and the brotherhood of man, which to you were but fine phrases, are, to our thinking and feeling, ties as real and as vital as physical fraternity. . .

'A solution which leaves an unaccounted-for residuum is no solution at all; and our solution of the problem of human society would have been none at all had it left the lame, the sick, and the blind outside with beasts, to fare as they might. Better far have left the strong and well unprovided for than these burdened ones, toward whom every heart must yearn, and for whom ease of mind and body should be provided, if for no others. Therefore it is, as I told you this morning, that the title of every man, woman, and child to the means of existence rests on no basis less plain, broad, and simple than the fact that they are fellows of one race—members of one human family. . .

'I think there is no feature of the civilization of your epoch so repugnant to modern ideas as the neglect with which you treated your dependent classes. Even if you had no pity, no feeling of brotherhood, how was it that you did not see that you were robbing the incapable class of their plain right in leaving them unprovided for?'

'I don't quite follow you there,' I said. 'I admit the claim of this class to our pity, but how could they who produced nothing claim a share of the product as a right?'

'How happened it,' was Dr. Leete's reply, 'that your workers were able to produce more than so many savages would have done? Was it not wholly on account of the heritage of the past knowledge and achievements of the race, the machinery of society, thousands of years in contriving, found by you ready-made to your hand? . . You inherited it, did you not. And were not these others, these unfortunate and crippled brothers whom you cast out, joint inheritors, co-heirs with you? What did you do with their share? Did you not rob them when you put them off with crusts, who were entitled to sit with the heirs, and did you not add insult to robbery when you called the crusts charity?' . .

'Your courts must have an easy time of it,' I observed. 'With no private property to speak of, no disputes between citizens over business relations, no real estate to divide or debts to collect, there must be absolutely no civil business at all for them; and with no offenses against property, and mighty few of any sort to provide criminal cases, I should think you might almost do without judges and lawyers altogether.'

'We do without the lawyers, certainly,' was Dr. Leete's reply. 'It would not seem reasonable to us, in a case where the only interest of the nation is to find out the truth, that persons should take part in the proceedings who had an acknowledged motive to color it.'

'But who defends the accused?'

'If he is a criminal he needs no defense, for he pleads guilty in most instances,' replied Dr. Leete. 'The plea of the accused is not a mere formality with us, as with you. It is usually the end of the case.' . .

'That is the most astounding thing you have yet told me,' I exclaimed. 'If lying has gone out of fashion, this is indeed the "new heavens and the new earth wherein dwelleth righteousness," which the prophet foretold.'

'Such is, in fact, the belief of some persons nowadays,' was the doctor's answer. . . 'Because we are now all social equals, and no man either has anything to fear from another or can gain anything by deceiving him, the contempt of falsehood is so universal that it is rarely, as I told you, that even a criminal in other respects will be found willing to lie. . .'

'There being no legal profession to serve as a school for judges,' I said, 'they must, of course, come directly from the law school to the bench.'

'We have no such things as law schools,' replied the doctor smiling. 'The law as a special science is obsolete. It was a system of casuistry which the elaborate artificiality of the old order of society absolutely required to interpret it, but only a few of the plainest and simplest legal maxims have any application to the existing state of the world. Everything touching the relations of men to one another is now simpler, beyond any comparison, than in your day. We should have no sort of use for the hair-splitting experts who presided and argued in your courts. You must not imagine, however, that we have any disrespect for those ancient worthies because we have no use for them. On the contrary, we entertain an unfeigned respect, amounting almost to awe, for the men who alone understood and were able to expound the interminable complexity of the rights of property, and the relations of commercial and personal dependence involved in your system. . .'

'I will readily admit,' I said, 'that our industrial system was ethically very bad, but as a mere wealth-making machine, apart from moral aspects, it seemed to us admirable.'

'As I said,' responded the doctor, 'the subject is too large to discuss at length now, but if you are really interested to know the main criticisms which we moderns make on your industrial system as compared with our own, I can touch briefly on some of them.

'The wastes which resulted from leaving the conduct of industry to irresponsible individuals, wholly without mutual understanding or concert, were mainly four: first, the waste by mistaken undertakings; second, the waste from the competition and mutual hostility of those engaged in industry; third, the waste by periodical gluts and crises, with the consequent interruption of industry; fourth, the waste from idle capital and labor, at all times. Any one of these four great leaks, were all the others stopped, would suffice to make the difference between wealth and poverty on the part of a nation.

'Take the waste by mistaken undertakings, to begin with. In your day the production and distribution of commodities being without concert or organization, there was no means of knowing just what demand there was for any class of products, or what was the rate of supply. Therefore, any enterprise by a private capitalist was always a doubtful experiment. . .

'The next of the great wastes was that from competition. The field of industry was a battle-field as wide as the world, in which the workers wasted, in assailing one another, energies which, if expended in concerted effort, as to-day, would have enriched all. As for mercy or quarter in this warfare, there was absolutely no suggestion of it. To deliberately enter a field of business and destroy the enterprises of those who had occupied it previously, in order to plant one's own enterprise on their ruins, was an achievement which never failed to command popular admiration. . . Your contemporaries, with their mutual throat-cutting, knew very well what they were at. The producers of the nineteenth century were not, like ours, working together for the maintenance of the community, but each solely for his own maintenance at the expense of the community. If, in working to this end, he at the same time increased the aggregate wealth, that was merely incidental. It was just as feasible and as common to increase one's private hoard by practices injurious to the general welfare. One's worst enemies were necessarily those of his own trade, for, under your plan of making private profit the motive of production, a scarcity of the article he produced was what each particular producer desired. It was for his interest that no more of it should be produced than he himself could produce. To secure this consummation as far as circumstances permitted, by killing off and discouraging those engaged in his line of industry, was his constant effort. When he had killed off all he could, his policy was to combine with those he could not kill, and convert their mutual warfare into a warfare upon the public at large by cornering the market, as I believe you used to call it, and putting up prices to the highest point people would stand before going without the goods. The day dream of the nineteenth century producer was to gain absolute control of the supply of some necessity of life, so that he might keep the public at the verge of starvation, and always command famine prices for what he supplied. This, Mr. West, is what was called in the nineteenth century a system of production. . .

'Apart from the waste of labor and capital by misdirected industry, and that from the constant bloodletting of your industrial warfare, your system was liable to periodical convulsions, overwhelming alike the wise and unwise, the successful cut-throat as well as his victim. I refer to the business crises at intervals of five to ten years, which wrecked the industries of the nation, prostrating all weak enterprises and crippling the strongest, and were followed by long periods, often of many years, of so-called dull times, during which the capitalists slowly regathered their dissipated strength while the laboring classes starved and rioted. Then would ensue another brief season of prosperity, followed in turn by another crisis and the ensuing years of exhaustion. . .

'If you would see how needless were these convulsions of business which I have been speaking of, and how entirely they resulted from leaving industry to private and unorganized management, just consider the working of our system. Over-production in special lines, which was the great hobgoblin of your day, is impossible now, for by the connection between distribution and production supply is geared to demand like an engine to the governor which regulates its speed. . .

'After what you have told me,' I said, 'I do not so much wonder that the nation is richer now than then, but that you are not all Croesuses.'

'Well,' replied Dr. Leete, 'we are pretty well off. The rate at which we live is as luxurious as we could wish. The rivalry of ostentation, which in your day led to extravagance in no way conducive to comfort, finds no place, of course, in a society of people absolutely equal in resources, and our ambition stops at the surroundings which minister to the enjoyment of life. . . You have not begun to see how we live yet, Mr. West. At home we have comfort, but the splendor of our life is, on its social side, that which we share with our fellows. . .'

'I suppose,' observed Dr. Leete, as we strolled homeward from the dining hall, 'that no reflection would have cut the men of your wealth-worshipping century more keenly than the suggestion that they did not know how to make money. Nevertheless, that is just the verdict history has passed on them. Their system of unorganized and antagonistic industries was as absurd economically as it was morally abominable. Selfishness was their only science, and in industrial production selfishness is suicide. Competition, which is the instinct of selfishness, is another word for dissipation of energy, while combination is the secret of efficient production; and not till the idea of increasing the individual hoard gives place to the idea of increasing the common stock can industrial combination be realized, and the acquisition of wealth really begin. . .'

9. *Liberty and monopoly cannot live together*

HENRY DEMAREST LLOYD, *Wealth Against Commonwealth*, 1894 *

Nature is rich; but everywhere man, the heir of nature, is poor. Never in this happy country or elsewhere—except in the Land of Miracle, where 'they did all eat and were filled'—has there been enough of anything for the people. Never since time began have all the sons and daughters of men been all warm, and all filled, and all shod and roofed. . .

The world, enriched by thousands of generations of toilers and thinkers, has reached a fertility which can give every human being a plenty undreamed of even in the Utopias. But between this plenty ripening on the boughs of our civilization and the people hungering for it step the 'cornerers,' the syndicates, trusts, combinations, with the cry of 'over-production'—too much of everything. Holding back the riches of earth, sea, and sky from their fellows who famish and freeze in the dark, they declare to them that there is too much

* New York, Harper & Brothers, 1894, pp. 1–6, 494–536 *passim*.

light and warmth and food. They assert the right, for their private profit, to regulate the consumption by the people of the necessaries of life, and to control production, not by the needs of humanity, but by the desires of a few for dividends. The coal syndicate thinks there is too much coal. There is too much iron, too much lumber, too much flour—for this or that syndicate.

The majority have never been able to buy enough of anything; but this minority have too much of everything to sell.

Liberty produces wealth, and wealth destroys liberty. . . Our bignesses, cities, factories, monopolies, fortunes, which are our empires, are the obesities of an age gluttonous beyond its powers of digestion. Mankind are crowding upon each other in the centres, and struggling to keep each other out of the feast set by the new sciences and the new fellowships. Our size has got beyond both our science and our conscience. . . If mankind had gone on pursuing the ideals of the fighter, the time would necessarily have come when there would have been only a few, then only one, and then none left. This is what we are witnessing in the world of livelihoods. . . We are rapidly reaching the stage where in each province only a few are left; that is the key to our times. Beyond the deep is another deep. This era is but a passing phase in the evolution of industrial Caesars, and these Caesars will be of a new type—corporate Caesars. . .

Laws against these combinations have been passed by Congress and by many of the States. There have been prosecutions under them by the State and Federal governments. The laws and the lawsuits have alike been futile. . .

The Attorney-General of the national government gives a large part of his annual report of 1893 to showing 'what small basis there is for the popular impression' 'that the aim and effect of this statute [the Anti-Trust Law] are to prohibit and prevent those aggregations of capital which are so common at the present day, and which sometimes are on so large a scale as to practically control all the branches of an extensive industry.' This executive says of the action of the 'co-ordinate' Legislature: 'It would not be useful, even if it were possible, to ascertain the precise purposes of the framers of the statute.' He is the officer charged with the duty of directing the prosecutions to enforce the law; but he declares that since, among other reasons, 'all ownership of property is a monopoly . . . any literal application of the provisions of the statute is out of the question.' Nothing has been accomplished by all these appeals to the legislatures and the courts, except to prove that the evil lies deeper than any public sentiment or public intelligence yet existent, and is stronger than any public power yet at call. . .

The corn of the coming harvest is growing so fast that, like the farmer standing at night in his fields, we can hear it snap and crackle. We have been fighting fire on the well-worn lines of old-fashion politics and political economy, regulating corporations, and leaving competition to regulate itself. But the flames of a new economic evolution run around us, and we turn to find that competition has killed competition, that corporations are grown greater than the State and have bred individuals greater than themselves, and that the naked issue of our time is with property becoming master instead of servant, property in many necessaries of life becoming monopoly of the necessaries of life. . .

In all this we see at work a 'principle' which will go into the records as one of the historic mistakes of humanity. Institutions stand or fall by their philosophy, and the main doctrine of industry since Adam Smith has been the fallacy that the self-interest of the individual was a sufficient guide to the welfare of the individual and society. Heralded as the final truth of 'science' this proves to have been nothing higher than a temporary formula for a passing problem. It was a reflection in words of the policy of the day. . .

'It is a law of business for each proprietor to pursue his own interest,' said the committee of Congress which in 1893 investigated the coal combinations. 'There is no hope for any of us, but the weakest must go first,' is the golden rule of business. There is no other field of human associations in which any such rule of action is allowed. The man who should apply in his family or his citizenship this 'survival of the fittest' theory as it is practically professed and operated in business would be a monster, and would be speedily made extinct, as we do with monsters. To divide the supply of food between himself and his children, according to their relative powers of calculation, to follow his conception of his own self-interest in any matter which the self-interest of all has taken charge of, to deal as he thinks best for himself with foreigners with whom his country is at war, would be a short road to the penitentiary or the gallows. In trade men have not yet risen to the level of the family life of the animals. The true law of business is that all must pursue the interest of all. In the law, the highest product of civilization, this has long been a commonplace. The safety of the people is the supreme law. We are in travail to bring industry up to this. Our century of the caprice of the individual as the law-giver of the common toil, to employ or disemploy, to start or stop, to open or close, to compete or combine, has been the disorder of the school while the master slept. The happiness, self-interest, or individuality of the whole is not more sacred than that of each, but it is greater. They are equal in quality, but in quantity they are greater. In the ultimate which the mathematician, the poet, the reformer projects the two will coincide.

. . . The perfect self-interest of the perfect individual is an admirable conception, but it is still individual, and the world is social. The music of the spheres is not to be played on one string. Nature does nothing individually. All forces are paired like the sexes, and every particle of matter in the universe has to obey every other particle. When the individual has progressed to a perfect self-interest, there will be over against it, acting and reacting with it, a correspondingly perfect self-interest of the community. Meanwhile, we who are the creators of society have got the times out of joint, because, less experienced than the Creator of the balanced matter of earth, we have given the precedence to the powers on one side. As gods we are but half-grown. For a hundred years or so our economic theory has been one of industrial government by the self-interest of the individual. Political government by the self-interest of the individual we call anarchy. It is one of the paradoxes of public opinion that the people of America, least tolerant of this theory of anarchy in political government, lead in practising it in industry. Politically, we are civilized; industrially, not yet. Our century, given to this *laissez-faire*—'leave the individual alone; he will do what is best for himself, and what is best for him is best for all'—has done one good; it has put society at the mercy of its own ideals, and has produced an actual anarchy in industry which is horrifying us into a change of doctrines. . .

Every community, said Pascal, is a man, and every man, said Plato, is a community. There is a new self-interest—that of the 'man called million,' as Mazzini named him—and with this social motive the other, which has so long had its own way, has now to reckon. Mankind has gone astray following a truth seen only partially, but coronated as a whole truth. Many civilizations must worship good men as gods and follow the divinity of one and another before civilization sees that these are only single stars in a firmament of humanity. Our civilization has followed the self-interest of the individual to learn that it was but one of the complex forces of self-interest.

The true *laissez-faire* is, let the individual do what the individual can do best, and let the community do what the community can do best. The *laissez-faire* of social self-interest, if true, cannot conflict with the individual self-interest, if true, but it must outrank it always. What we have called 'free competition' has not been free, only freer than what went before. The free is still to come. The pressure we feel is notice to prepare for it. Civilization—the process of making men citizens in their relations to each other, by exacting of each that he give to all that which he receives from all—has reached only those forms of common effort which, because most general and most vital, first demanded its harmonizing touch. Men joining in the labors of the family, the mutual sacrifices of the club or the church in the union of forces for self-defence and for the gains of co-operation on the largest scale in labors of universal concern, like letter-carrying, have come to be so far civilized. . .

Where the self-interest of the individual is allowed to be the rule both of social and personal action, the level of all is forced down to that of the lowest. Business excuses itself for the things it does—cuts in wages, exactions in hours, tricks of competition—on the plea that the merciful are compelled to follow the cruel. . . When the self-interest of society is made the standard the lowest must rise to the average. The one pulls down, the other up. That men's hearts are bad and that bad men will do bad things has a truth in it. But whatever the general average of morals, the anarchy which gives such individuals their head and leaves them to set the pace for all will produce infinitely worse results than a policy which applies mutual checks and inspirations. Bad kings make bad reigns, but monarchy is bad because it is arbitrary power, and that, whether it be political or industrial makes even good men bad.

A partial truth universally applied as this of self-interest has been is a universal error. Everything goes to defeat. Highways are used to prevent travel and traffic. Ownership of the means of production is sought in order to 'shut down' production, and the means of plenty make famine. All follow self-interest to find that though they have created marvellous wealth it is not theirs. We pledge 'our lives, our fortunes, and our sacred honor' to establish the rule of the majority and end by finding that the minority—a minority in morals, money, and men—are our masters whichever way we turn. . .

We now have Captains of Industry, with a few aids, rearranging from office chairs this or that industry, by mere contrivances of wit compelling the fruits of the labor of tens of thousands of their fellows, who never saw them, never heard of them, to be every day deposited unwilling and unwitting to their own credit at the bank; setting, as by necromancy, hundreds of properties, large and small, in a score of communities, to flying through invisible ways into their hands; sitting calm through all the hubbub raised in courts, legislatures, and public places, and by dictating letters and whispering words remaining the master magicians of the scene; defying, though private citizens, all the forces and authorities of a whole people; by the mere mastery of compelling brain, without putting hand to anything, opening or closing the earth's treasures of oil or coal or gas or copper or what not; pulling down or putting up great buildings, factories, towns themselves; moving men and their money this way and that; inserting their will as part of the law of life of the people. . .

Syndicates, by one stroke, get the power of selling dear on one side, and producing cheap on the other. Thus they keep themselves happy, prices high, and the people hungry. What model merchant could ask more? The dream of the king who wished that all his people had but one neck that he might decapitate them at one blow is realized to-day in this industrial garrote. The syndicate has but to turn its screw, and every neck begins to break. Prices paid to such intercepters are not an exchange of service; they are ransom paid by the people for their lives. . . Those who have this power to draw the money from the people—from every railroad station, every street-car, every fireplace, every salt-cellar, every bread-pan, wash-board, and coalscuttle—to their own safes have the further incentive to make this money worth the most possible. . . Given, as a ruling motive, the principles of business—to get the most and give the least; given the legal and economic, physical and mechanical control, possible under our present social arrangements, to the few over the many, and the certain end of all this, if unarrested, unreversed, can be nothing less than a return to chattel slavery. . .

Mankind belongs to itself, not to kings or monopolists, and will supersede the one as surely as the other with the institutions of democracy. . . If power could continue paternal and benign, mankind would not be rising through one emancipation after another into a progressive communion of equalities. The individual and society will always be wrestling with each other in a composition of forces. But to just the extent to which civilization prevails, society will be held as inviolable as the individual; not subordinate—indeed inaudible —as now in the counting-room and corporation-office. We have overworked the self-interest of the individual. The line of conflict between individual and social is a progressive one of the discovery of point after point in which the two are identical. Society thus passes from conflict to harmony, and on to another conflict. Civilization is the unceasing accretion of these social solutions. We fight out to an equilibrium, as in the abolition of human slavery; then upon this new level thus built up we enter upon the struggle for a new equilibrium, as now in the labor movement. The man for himself destroys himself and all men; only society can foster him and them. . .

If our civilization is destroyed, as Macaulay predicted, it will not be by his barbarians from below. Our barbarians come from above. Our great money-makers have sprung in one generation into seats of power kings do not know.

The forces and the wealth are new, and have been the opportunity of new men. Without restraints of culture, experience, the pride, or even the inherited caution of class or rank, these men, intoxicated, think they are the wave instead of the float, and that they have created the business which has created them. To them science is but a never-ending répertoire of investments stored up by nature for the syndicate government but a fountain of franchises, the nations but customers in squads, and a million the unit of a new arithmetic of wealth written for them. . .They are gluttons of luxury and power, rough, unsocialized, believing that mankind must be kept terrorized. . .

Competition has ended in combination, and our new wealth takes as it chooses the form of corporation or trust, or corporation again, and with every change grows greater and worse. Under these kaleidoscopic masks we begin at last to see progressing to its terminus a steady consolidation, the end of which is one-man power. The conspiracy ends in one, and one cannot conspire with himself. When this solidification of many into one has been reached, we shall be at last face to face with the naked truth that it is not only the form but the fact of arbitrary power, of control without consent, of rule without representation that concerns us. . .

Monopoly is business at the end of its journey. It has got there. The irrepressible conflict is now as distinctly with business as the issue so lately met was with slavery. Slavery went first only because it was the cruder form of business.

Against the principles, the men embodying them and pushing them to extremes—by which the powers of government, given by all for all, are used as franchises for personal aggrandizement; by which, in the same line, the common toil of all and the common gifts of nature, lands, forces, mines, sites, are turned from service to selfishness, and are made by one and the same stroke to give gluts to a few and impoverishment to the many—we must plan our campaign. . .

Two social energies have been in conflict, and the energy of reform has so far proved the weaker. We have chartered the self-interest of the individual as the rightful sovereign of conduct; we have taught that the scramble for profit is the best method of administering the riches of earth and the exchange of services. Only those can attack this system who attack its central principle, that strength gives the strong in the market the right to destroy his neighbor. Only as we have denied that right to the strong elsewhere have we made ourselves as civilized as we are. And we cannot make a change as long as our songs, customs, catchwords, and public opinions tell all to do the same thing if they can. Society, in each person of its multitudes, must recognize that the same principles of the interest of all being the rule of all, of the strong serving the weak, of the first being the last—'I am among you as one that serves'—which have given us the home where the weakest is the one surest of his rights and of the fullest service of the strongest, and have given us the republic in which all join their labor that the poorest may be fed, the weakest defended, and all educated and prospered, must be applied where men associate in common toil as wherever they associate. Not until then can the forces be reversed which generate those obnoxious persons—our fittest. . .

We have a people like which none has ever existed before. We have millions capable of conscious co-operation. The time must come in social evolution when the people can organize the free-will to choose salvation which the individual has been cultivating for 1900 years, and can adopt a policy more dignified and more effective than leaving themselves to be kicked along the path of reform by the recoil of their own vices. We must bring the size of our morality up to the size of our cities, corporations, and combinations, or these will be brought down to fit our half-grown virtue.

Industry and monopoly cannot live together. Our modern perfection of exchange and division of labor cannot last without equal perfection of morals and sympathy. Every one is living at the mercy of every one else in a way entirely peculiar to our times. Nothing is any longer made by a man; parts of things are made by parts of men, and become wholes by the luck of a good-humor which so far keeps men from flying asunder. It takes a whole company to make a match. A hundred men will easily produce a hundred million matches, but not one of them could make one match. No farm gets its plough from the cross-roads blacksmith, and no one in the chilled-steel factory knows the whole of the plough. . .

Liberty and monopoly cannot live together. What chance have we against the persistent coming and the easy coalescence of the confederated cliques, which aspire to say of all business, 'This belongs to us,' and whose members, though moving among us as brothers, are using against us, through the corporate forms we have given them powers of invisibility, of entail and accumulation, unprecedented because impersonal and immortal, and, most peculiar of all, power to act as persons, as in the commission of crimes, with exemption from punishment as persons? Two classes study and practice politics and government: place hunters and privilege hunters. In a world of relativities like ours size of area has a great deal to do with the truth of principles. America has grown so big—and the tickets to be voted, and the powers of government, and the duties of citizens, and the profits of personal use of public functions have all grown so big—that the average citizen has broken down. No man can half understand or half operate the fulness of this big citizenship, except by giving his whole time to it. This the place hunter can do, and the privilege hunter. Government, therefore—municipal, State, national—is passing into the hands of these two classes, specialized for the functions of power by their appetite for the fruits of power. The power of citizenship is relinquished by those who do not and cannot know how to exercise it to those who can and do—to those who have a livelihood to make to those who make politics their livelihood. . .

Aristotle's lost books of the Republics told the story of two hundred and fifty attempts at free government, and these were but some of the many that had to be melted down in the crucible of fate to teach Hamilton and Jefferson what they knew. Perhaps we must be melted by the same fierce flames to be a light to the feet of those who come after us. For as true as that a house divided against itself cannot stand, and that a nation half slave and half free cannot permanently endure, is it true that a people who are slaves to market-tyrants will surely come to be their slaves in all else, that all liberty begins to be lost when one liberty is lost, that a people half democratic and half plutocratic cannot permanently endure. . .

The wonder of to-day is the modern multiplication of products by the union of forces; the marvel of tomorrow will be the greater product which will follow when that which is co-operatively produced is co-operatively enjoyed. . .

This social debate has gone far beyond the question whether change there must be. What shall the change be? is the subject all the world is discussing. Exposure of abuses no longer excites more than a languid interest. . .

In nothing has liberty justified itself more thoroughly than in the resolute determination spreading among the American people to add industrial to political independence. . . Nowhere else has the new claim to tax without representation been so quickly detected, so intelligently scrutinized, and so bravely fought. . . At the very beginning of this new democratic life among the nations it was understood that to be safe liberty must be complete on its industrial as well as on its political and religious sides. This is the American principle. 'Give a man power over my subsistence,' said Alexander Hamilton, 'and he has power over the whole of my moral being'. . .

In making themselves free of arbitrary and corrupt power in government the Americans prepared themselves to be free in all else, and because foremost in political liberty they have the promise of being the first to realize industrial liberty—the trunk of a tree of which political liberty is the seed, and without which political liberty shrinks back into nothingness. . .

We must either regulate, or own, or destroy, perishing by the sword we take. The possibility of regulation is a dream. As long as this control of the necessaries of life and this wealth remain private with individuals, it is they who will regulate, not we. The policy of regulation, disguise it as we may, is but moving to a compromise and equilibrium within the evil all complain of. It is to accept the principle of the sovereignty of the self-interest of the individual and apply constitutional checks to it. The unprogressive nations palter in this method with monarchy. But the wits of America are equal to seeing that as with kingship and slavery so with poverty—the weeding must be done at the roots. Sir Henry Sumner Maine says mankind moves from status to contract; from society ruled by inherited customs to one ruled by agreement, varied according to circumstances. Present experience suggests the addition that the movement, like all in nature, is pendulous, and that mankind moves progressively from status to contract, and from this stage of contract to another status. We march and rest and march again. . .

Democracy is not a lie. There live in the body of the commonalty the unexhausted virtue and the ever-refreshed strength which can rise equal to any problems of progress. In the hope of tapping some reserve of their powers of self-help this story is told to the people.

10. *Socialism will be government's answer to monopoly*

JOHN DEWITT WARNER, *Consolidation of Wealth: Political Aspects*, 1902 *

Is concentration of wealth a permanent phase of our growth? On this, as on some other points, I note Mr. Carnegie's opinion. . .

> The fashion of Trusts has but a short season longer to run, and then some other equally vain device may be expected to appear when the next period of depression arrives; but there is not the slightest danger that serious injury can result to the sound principles of business from any or all of these movements. The only people who have reason to fear Trusts are those foolish enough to enter into them. The consumer and the transporter, not the manufacturer and the railway owner, are to reap the harvest.

Time has refuted this conclusion. . .

We have seen the Trusts extend their realm until they now control the leading necessaries of life and commerce; until to-day our Federal Government and many States are desperately seeking means to meet the appeal of a people deprived of meat, except at extortion rates. Concentration of wealth has so progressed that, through billion dollar trusts, we see developing the American billionaire—differing from wealthy classes elsewhere in that while, by social or other conditions, they are as much possessed by their wealth as possessors of it, he is wielding it as a power in business and in politics—that is, in government.

In a later article, 'Wealth'—the most famous one Mr. Carnegie ever wrote—he discussed this result, which he already recognized as characteristic of our time. . .

It may well be questioned whether the average citizen is actually profited—that is, made more useful or more happy—by the 'luxuries' referred to, or whether, indeed, his brain was not better stimulated, his social nature better developed, and his relish of life sharper, under the old system than the new; in short, whether in the United States two generations ago the average farmer and craftsman was not a greater factor in the social, political and spiritual life of his community, and raised more children fit for free citizens than does his successor of to-day. . .

But what are the political results? Mr. Carnegie refers to the older times when those engaged in industrial pursuits—master or man—had little or no political voice in the State. Those were the days of oligarchy—of class rule by nobles, priests or soldiers. Was it stable? Or rather, in the case of every civilized nation, has not reform of class rule been forced by the masses, and always to the weal of the State? Has Plutocracy more hold upon the regard, the affection or the prejudices of men than Church, Nobility, or Military Glory? Are our citizens less able or apt to assert themselves than those of other lands and other times? Is our government better framed for class rule and

* *The Independent*, 1 May 1902, vol. 54, pp 1045–9 *passim*.

better fitted to resist popular demands than were the kingdoms and empires before it?

To ask these questions is to answer them. The Church, the Nobility, the Army—each rose from and was rooted in the history and the sentiment of the peoples over which it towered. But Plutocracy has ever been despised by all, hated most of all by those most subservient to it, and ever found most destitute of support, except such as it buys at rapidly rising price. There is no more offensive claim than that of the few who have most dollars to rule the many in right of their dollars. As compared with others, our people are the most able and most ready to resent such a rule. As compared with other governments, ours leaves class rule most at the mercy of popular wrath when roused. All experience has shown that, whatever may have been the merits of individual capitalists, plutocratic rule tends to vulgarity, stupidity and oppression; and that from the dawn of history no nation to which it has been subjected has survived except by casting it out. Politically, therefore, there is nothing more certain than its repudiation by our country. . .

Nor do I forget Mr. Carnegie's picture of the man whom wealth has made unselfish, far-seeing, philanthropic and fitted to dictate their weal to his fellowmen. But I need not suggest how little impressive is the charity that returns to the public a part of what it has taken; how comparatively rare is even such practice; or how much more common are those of plots against the public, debauchery of legislatures and excess of vulgarity and luxury. And all history has shown how prone is Plutocracy to degenerate—made up, as it must be, of mortal men—stirred, as it always has been, by the pride of the wealth that buys and the lust of the power that rests on purchase. . .

Great, however, as is the political danger of this, I believe another to be more certain and closer at hand—the rapid development of State socialism, the excesses of which will be a part of the reaction against Trusts, and the necessity for it a most serious indictment of Trust policy.

The situation is this: As fast as any necessary of life or commerce becomes a private monopoly, Government must regulate or supplant it. And effectively to regulate is practically to supplant. No self-respecting people will permit the supply of its food or the control of its transport facilities to be controlled by private citizens for their own profit. It is futile to discuss legal, even constitutional, barriers. The prerogative involved is as important as any for which governments are organized, and is essentially one of government—none the less so because hitherto supposed checked by free competition, hence left unregulated by law. Once conceded that competition is powerless or forestalled, and our people will vindicate the principle that human law was made for man, and not man for it; and that when it does not fit him, it (not he) must be broken and remade. If our Trusts in steel and many another facility for commerce; in sugar, salt, meat—and many another necessary of food; or in transportation cannot be otherwise checked,—and such in increasing number of directions seems to be the case—then Government must and will supplant them by state monopoly.

I know how serious a problem it would be for a national commission either to fix the rates which the owners of railroads should be permitted to charge, or to compel equal services at equal rates to all citizens; and that national ownership of interstate, and State ownership of all interstate railroads would involve others as grave. But, from the popular standpoint, the choice would be prompt between Government administration for the public benefit by responsible officials, and private extortion for private profit by irresponsible Trust magnates. . .

The political dangers of concentrated wealth as a characteristic of present conditions in this country are, therefore, in the main, those of the state socialism that will naturally develop as government's answer to private monopoly. Those of us who thus believe deprecate the death of business competition. We oppose Trusts because, foreseeing the extension of government functions as the remedy, we dread the consequence of its too rapid application even though it may be a welcome alternative to the evil to be checked. But we find no room for the pessimism that can imagine either acceptance by our people of the dependent position planned for them by Mr. Carnegie, or such delay in effective government intervention as shall necessitate revolution, or but that in the long run we shall relegate wealth to its proper place—as the servant of our people, not their ruler. Indeed the event may show our present fear of the excesses of state socialism to have been groundless; and that the concentrations of wealth that compel resort to it are therefore but blessings in disguise. For the world is fast learning to distinguish between the old socialism that restricted the individual and the new socialism that serves him.

11. *Only the collective popular will can decree it shall not be*

W. J. Ghent, *Benevolent Feudalism*, 1902 *

The next distinct stage in the socio-economic evolution of America may be something entirely different from any of the forms usually predicted. Anarchist prophecies are, of course, futile; and the Tolstoyan Utopia of a return to primitive production, with its prodigal waste of effort and consequent impoverishment of the race, allures but few minds. The Kropotkinian dream of a communistic union of shop industry and agriculture is of a like type; and well-nigh as barren as the Neo-Jeffersonian visions of a general revival of small-farm and small-shop production and the dominance of a middle-class democracy. The orthodox economists, with their notions of a slightly modified Individualism, wherein each unit secures the just reward of his capacity and service, are but worshiping an image which they have created out of their books and which has no real counterpart in life; and finally, the Marxists, who predict the establishment of a co-operative commonwealth, are, to say the least, too sanguine in foreshortening the time of its triumph. Whatever the more distant future may bring to pass, there is but little evidence to prove that collectivism will be the next status of society. Rather, that coming status, of which the contributing forces are now energetically at work and of which

* *The Independent*, 3 April 1902, vol. 54, pt. 2, pp. 781–8 *passim*.

the first phases are already plainly observable, will be something in the nature of a Benevolent Feudalism.

That the concentration of capital and the increase of individual holdings of wealth will continue is almost unanimously conceded. . .

The more the great combinations increase their power, the greater is the subordination of the small concerns. They may, for one reason or another, find it possible, and even fairly profitable, to continue; but they will be more and more confined to particular activities, to particular territories, and in time to particular methods, all dictated and enforced by the pressure of the larger concerns. The petty tradesmen and producers are thus an economically dependent class; and their dependence increases with the years. In a like position, also, are the owners of small and moderate holdings in the trusts. The larger holdings—often the single largest holding—determines the rules of the game; the smaller ones are either acquiescent, or if recalcitrant, are powerless to enforce their will. Especially is this true in America, where the head of a corporation is often an absolute ruler, who determines not only the policy of the enterprise, but the *personnel* of the board of directors.

The tendencies thus make, on the one hand, toward the centralization of vast power in the hands of a few men—the morganization of industry, as it were—and on the other, toward a vast increase in the number of those who compose the economically dependent classes. The latter number is already stupendous. The laborers and mechanics were long ago brought under the yoke through their divorcement from the land and the application of steam to factory operation. They are economically unfree except in so far as their organizations make possible a collective bargaining for wages and hours. The growth of commerce raised up an enormous class of clerks and helpers, perhaps the most dependent class in the community. The growth and partial diffusion of wealth in America has in fifty years largely altered the character of domestic service and increased the number of servants many fold. Railroad pools and farm-implement trusts have drawn a tightening cordon about the farmers. The professions, too, have felt the change. Behind many of our important newspapers are private commercial interests which dictate their general policy, if not, as is frequently the case, their particular attitude upon every public question; while the race for endowments made by the greater number of the churches and by all colleges except a few State-supported ones compels a cautious regard on the part of synod and faculty for the wishes, the views and prejudices of men of great wealth. To this growing deference of preacher, teacher and editor is added that of two yet more important classes—the makers and the interpreters of law. The record of legislation and judicial interpretation regarding slavery previous to the Civil War has been paralleled in recent years by the record of legislatures and courts in matters relating to the lives and health of manual workers, especially in such cases as employer's liability and factory inspection. Thus, with a great addition to the number of subordinate classes, with a tremendous increase of their individual components, and with a corresponding growth of power in the hands of a few score magnates, there is needed little further to make up a socio-economic status that contains all the essentials of a renascent feudalism.

It is, at least in its beginning, less a personal than a class feudalism. History may repeat itself, as the adage runs; but not by identical forms and events. . . The old feudalism exacted faithful service, industrial and martial, from the underling; protection and justice from the overlord. It is not likely that personal fidelity, as once known, can ever be restored: the long period of dislodgment from the land, the diffusion of learning, the exercise of the franchise, and the training in individual effort have left a seemingly unbridgeable chasm between the past and the present forms. But though personal fidelity, in the old sense, is improbable, group fidelity, founded upon the conscious dependence of a class, is already observable, and it grows apace. Out of the sense of class dependence arises the extreme deference which we yield, the rapt homage which we pay—not as individuals, but as units of a class—to the men of wealth. We do not know them personally, and we have no sense of personal attachment. But in most things we grant them priority. We send them or their legates to the Senate to make our laws; we permit them to name our administrators and our judiciary, we listen with eager attention to their utterances and we abide by their judgment. Not always, indeed; for some of us grumble at times and ask angrily where it will all end. We talk threateningly of instituting referendums to curb excessive power; of levying income taxes, or of compelling the Government to acquire the railroads and the telegraphs. We subscribe to newspapers and other publications which criticise the acts of the great corporations, and we hail as a new Gracchus the ardent reformer who occasionally comes forth for a season to do battle for the popular cause. But this revolt is, for the most part, sentimental; it is a mental attitude but rarely transmutable into terms of action. It is, moreover, sporadic and flickering; it dies out after a time, and we revert to our usual moods, concerning ourselves with our particular interests and letting the rest of the world wag as it will.

The new feudalism is thus characterized by a class dependence rather than by a personal dependence. But it differs in still other respects from the old. It is qualified and restricted. . . Democracy tends to restrain it, and ethics to moralize it. Though it has its birth and nurture out of the 'rough and unsocialized barbarians of wealth,' in Mr. Henry D. Lloyd's phrase, its youth and maturity promise a modification of character. More and more it tends to become a *benevolent* feudalism. . .

The limitation which democracy puts upon the new feudalism is . . . important. For democracy will endure, in spite of the new order. 'Like death,' said Disraeli, 'it gives back nothing.' Something of its substance it gives back, it must be confessed; for it permits the most serious encroachments upon its rights; but of its outer forms it yields nothing, and thus it retains the potentiality of exerting its will in whatever direction it may see fit. And this fact, though now but feebly recognized by the feudal barons, will be better understood by them as time runs on, and they will bear in mind the limit of popular patience. It is an elastic limit of a truth; for the mass of mankind, as both Hamlet and Thomas Jefferson observed, are more ready to endure known ills than to fly to others that they know not. It is a limit which, to be heeded, needs only to be carefully studied. Macaulay's famous dictum, that the privileged classes, when their rule is threatened, always bring about their own ruin by making further exactions, is likely, in this case, to prove untrue. . . Our nobility will thus temper their exactions to an endurable limit; and they will distribute benefits to a degree that makes a tolerant, if not a satisfied people. They may even make a working principle of Bentham's maxim, and after, of course, appropriating the first and choicest fruits of industry to themselves, may seek to promote the 'greatest happiness of the greatest number.' For therein will lie their greater security. . .

Popular discontent will naturally follow, and it will be fomented, to some extent, by agitation; but the agitation will be guarded in expression and action, and it will be relatively barren of result. The possible danger therefrom will have been provided against, and a host of economists, preachers and editors will be ready to show indisputably that the evolution taking place is for the best interests of all; that it follows a 'natural and inevitable law;' that those who have been thrown out of work have only their own incompetency to blame; that all who really want work can get it, and that any interference with the prevailing *régime* will be sure to bring on a panic, which will only make matters worse. Hearing this, the multitude will hesitatingly acquiesce and thereupon subside; and though occasionally a radical journal or a radical agitator will counsel revolt, the mass will remain quiescent. . .

In its general aspects shop industry will be carried on much as now. Only the shops will be very much larger, the individual and total output will be greater, the unit cost of production will be lessened. Wages and hours will for a time continue on something like the present level; but, despite the persistence of the unions, no considerable gains in behalf of labor are to be expected. The owners of all industry worth owning, the barons will laugh at threats of striking and boycotting. . . What the barons will most dread will be the collective assertion of the villeins at the polls: but this, from experience, they will know to be a thing of no immediate danger. By the putting forward of a hundred irrevelant issues they can hopelessly divide the voters at each election; or, that failing, there is always to be trusted as a last resort the cry of impending panic. . .

The outlines of the present State loom but feebly through the intricate network of the new system. The nobles will have attained to complete power, and the motive and operation of Government will have become simply the registering and administering of their collective will. . . The present State machinery is admirably adapted for the subtle and extra-legal exertion of power by an autocracy; and while improvements to that end might unquestionably be made, the barons will hesitate to take action which will needlessly arouse popular suspicions. From petty constable to Supreme Court Justice the officials will understand, or be made to understand, the golden mean of their duties; and except for an occasional rascally Jacobin, whom it may for a time be difficult to suppress, they will be faithful and obey. . .

Armed force will, of course, be employed to overawe the discontented and to quiet unnecessary turbulence. Unlike the armed forces of the old feudalism, the nominal control will be that of the State; the soldiery will be regular and not irregular. Not again will the barons risk the general indignation arising from the employment of Pinkertons and other private armies. The worker has unmistakably shown his preference, when he is to be subdued, for the militia and the Federal army. Broadly speaking, it is not an unreasonable attitude; and it goes without saying that it will be respected. The militia of our Benevolent Feudalism will be recruited, as now, mostly from the clerkly class; and it will be officered largely by the sons and nephews of the barons. But its actions will be tempered by a saner policy. Governed by those who have most to fear from popular exasperation, it will show a finer restraint. . .

This, then, in the rough, is our Benevolent Feudalism to be. It is not precisely a Utopia, not an 'island valley of Avilion'; and yet it has its commendable, even its fascinating features. 'The empire is peace,' shouted the partisans of Louis Napoleon; and a like cry, with an equal ardency of enthusiasm, will be uttered by the supporters of the new *régime*. Peace and stability will be its defensive arguments, and peace and stability it will probably bring. But tranquil or unquiet, whatever it may be, its triumph is assured; and existent forces are carrying us toward it with an ever accelerating speed. One power alone might prevent it—the collective popular will that it shall not be. But of this there is no fear on the part of the barons, and but little expectation on the part of the underlings.

12. *The people need not let monopoly develop at all*

JOHN B. CLARK, *Feudalism or Commonwealth*, 1902 *

The able article by Mr. W. J. Ghent in *The Independent* for April the third has presented one of the possible and not unreasonable views concerning the industrial state of the immediate future. . . With a few touches of his pencil Mr. Ghent has given definiteness of outline to a picture which has presented itself, in a nebulous shape, to many minds. Nearly all of us have had a growing sense of subordination, if not of quasi-dependence, as we have watched the growth of private fortunes and that of trusts of the 'billion dollars' type. Standing once in the lobby of a hotel I heard a friend say, 'That is the man who owns us'; and a glance showed me a kindly gentleman, supposed to be worth a vast sum and to control a vaster one, who might have served as the model of one of the benevolent 'barons' of the new system, and yet we knew that, in reality, he had no baronial power over us. We were his customers who, in common with a million others, paid him his price for a service rendered. . .

One often discovers radical differences between things which are so similar that at first they seem to be identical. Mr. Ghent's picture is not a caricature, but a serious portrait, of which one may say that, in certain conspicuous traits, it is 'horribly like the original.' The points of unlikeness, though less conspicuous, are sufficient to impress the beholder with the fact that there is essential inaccuracy in the portrayal. That the so-called capitalistic system has continued until now and that its further continuance is regarded with toleration is enough to prove that it has not the essential quality which the word feudal describes.

* *The Independent*, 29 May 1902, vol. 54, pp. 1275–9 *passim*.

What is that trait? It is an arbitrary rule which destroys freedom and puts the fortunes of the dependent classes at the disposal of the overlord. He can take what he will and let his underlings have the rest. Wages are a residuum in an intolerable sense, for they are gauged, '*ad misericordiam*,' as an old term expressed it, according to the dictates of a pity which moderates the lord's exactions as the condition of his villains approaches the level of starvation. No benevolence could temper such a power so as to make it tolerable; and as for fortifying it by teachings emanating from church or school, using such things to oppose the popular feeling would be like hurling handfuls of chaff at an approaching battle ship. With anything of this kind impending, however, we shall save our freedom before it is lost, instead of waiting to recover it.

It is not worth while here to analyze the class distinctions which were maintained during the feudal period. The single question that is paramount is whether, in the new industrial state, the employe is helpless, and the mere recipient of whatever the employer chooses to leave for him. Is there no economic law which protects him? Is there, in the actual adjustment of wages, say, between a trade union and an average corporation, any gauging of pay '*ad misericordiam*?' Does not the employer give what he must and not what he will? The thing that would enable him more completely to have his way is monopoly, and in order to give him such a power this would have to be far more absolute than any monopoly has become. The whole influence of competition would have to vanish, and the principle on which, to and including the present time, the pay of every kind of labor is determined would have to become inoperative. Such an annihilation of the power of competition is not coming without observation; it will be seen in the distance and its approach will never be permitted. . .

. . . What has been said . . . as to the impossibility of making a democracy submit to a feudal tryranny applies to the *régime* of monopoly; for the people will never endure it. The important fact is that the people do not need to let it develop at all. The laborers are far from being alone in opposition to monopoly, for with them are farmers and independent investors; and, moreover, great natural forces are working on their side. Competition is forever asserting itself, and if hereafter it were to do no more than it is now doing, even this would be enough to hold the power of great corporations within relatively narrow limits. But there is every reason for hoping that competition may do more than this. Laborers, farmers and honest investors ought to be able to have their way in law making; and there are laws that will help to keep the competitive process alive. The monopolist may buy the political boss, and so dictate nominations to office, and make it hard either to enact the laws that we need or to enforce them when they are enacted; but is any one willing to say that, with a union of the forces that demand this, it cannot be done? . . .

The following assertions may be safely made:

(1) A genuine feudalism would never be tolerated by the people, however benevolent it might be.

(2) The tyrannical power which threatens us is that of monopoly, and the working of it is unlike that of a feudal tyranny.

(3) Powerful natural forces are holding this power in control, and, through their government, the people will be able to curb it more completely. . .

What is before us, then, is not a feudalism tempered by benevolence and prudence, but rather a commonwealth menaced by monopoly, but able to meet this danger, and to move on to a state of prosperity and a contentment that is based on justice. . . Laws and even constitutions will undergo changes, and in making the changes the democracy will find its wisdom taxed far more than its ultimate strength. It will be engaged in a struggle against corporate powers, political machines and bosses, and will have to use its forces strategically as well as vigorously. The reclaiming of an industrial state is the end in view, and he has a poor opinion of humanity who does not think it will ever be accomplished. To accept feudalism would be to submit to what is intolerable, while to reclaim the commonwealth will only be doing what is difficult; and there is no uncertainty as to which of these alternatives the people will choose. The society of the future will have great capital and great labor unions, and the two, as they deal with each other in a spirit of independence and under conditions which give just results, will in the end make the industrial commonwealth what it should be. If we were to make a picture that should symbolize the coming state, it would not be that of a portly figure representing capital holding labor under its feet and glancing apprehensively at fierce shapes lurking in the shadows and representing communism and anarchism. Rather would it be a picture of two strong men standing side by side and representing the honest capital and the honest laborer in their natural alliance, looking with displeasure but with no fear at the ugly shape of monopoly which menaces them both. In the contest with that power, at least, they are allies. . .

SELECTED REFERENCES

T. W. Arnold, *The Folklore of Capitalism*, New Haven, Yale University Press, 1937.

Thomas C. Cochran and William Miller, *The Age of Enterprise*, New York, Macmillan, 1942.

Herbert Croly, *Progressive Democracy*, New York, Macmillan, 1914.

Sidney Fine, *Laissez-Faire and the General Welfare State: A Study of Conflict in American Thought, 1865–1901*, Ann Arbor, University of Michigan Press, 1956.

Ralph Henry Gabriel, *The Course of American Democratic Thought*, New York, Ronald Press, 1940, chap. 18.

William J. Ghent, *Mass and Class: A Survey of Social Divisions*, New York, Macmillan, 1903.

Richard Hofstadter, *Social Darwinism in American Thought, 1860–1915*, Philadelphia, University of Pennsylvania Press, 1945.

Matthew Josephson, *The Robber Barons*, New York, Harcourt, Brace, 1934.

Robert G. McCloskey, *American Conservatism in the Age of Enterprise*, Cambridge, Harvard University Press, 1931.

Allan Nevins, *The Emergence of Modern America, 1865–1878*, New York, Macmillan, 1928.

V. L. Parrington, *Main Currents in American Thought*, New York, Harcourt, Brace, 1930, vol. III, chaps. 2 and 3.

Simon N. Patten, *The Theory of Prosperity*, New York, Macmillan, 1902.

———, *The New Basis of Civilization*, New York, Macmillan, 1907.

F. J. Turner, *The Frontier in American History*, New York, Henry Holt, 1920. Chapter 1 embodies the now famous essay on the significance of the frontier in our culture.

XVI

THE PROGRESSIVE IMPULSE

Before 1850 democracy had been, so to speak, on the make; industrialism was in its early phases. But in *The Forum* magazine, November 1889, T. G. Shearman, a New York corporation lawyer, noted that 'the United States of America are practically owned by less than 250,000 persons.' By 1919, he said that it would be owned by less than 50,000 persons. Shearman knew that business had already begun to crystallize into corporate and super-corporate monopoly—and this despite, or because of, the enormous immigrations of the century prior to 1919.

Shearman failed to take into account certain counter-trends. Liberal reaction had already set in. On all sides, new forces were emerging. As Tocqueville had predicted in the 1830's, the masses refused 'to remain miserable and sovereign.' The very action and counteraction Webster had foreseen in 1820 were stimulated. With mounting insistency, trade unionists, greenbackers, grangers, and populists had organized. The truth embodied in Edmund Burke's comment, 'Liberty, when men act in bodies, is power,' was soon realized. Extensive political and philosophical realignments followed, and even the most conservative thinkers began to make pronouncements in the fair and comprehensive name of liberalism. With good reason, these years have gone down in history as the Progressive Era, the Age of Reform.

In the vanguard of Progressivism at the turn of the century was Herbert Croly (1869–1930). Few books have had such impact as *The Promise of American Life*, published in 1909 when Croly was nearly forty. Croly had led a relatively obscure life. From 1900 to 1906 he had worked as editor of the *Architectural Record*, a journal his father had helped found. He had studied at Harvard on and off during a period of eleven years, finally winning a degree in 1910 on the strength of the belated kudos his book brought him.

Influenced at Harvard by the pragmatism of Henry James and the moral philosophy of George Santayana, Croly set out to redirect the course of modern American reform—to channel it from an essentially negative criticism of tycoons and trusts to a positive program. One among the few who rejected the destructive individualism of early Progressivism, Croly saw his fellow reformers as unwitting reactionaries. Tenaciously clinging to Jefferson's notion of 'equal rights for all and special privileges for none,' reformers rarely saw the inevitable conflict between liberty and equality. Absolute liberty in the economic sphere—pure competition—always led to marked inequality; efforts to promote equality risked tyranny of the majority. Progressives, moreover, were nonplussed when arch conservatives hurled back the individualistic slogans they professed.

Croly's chief contribution to American political thought is 'New Nationalism,' a formula combining the use of Hamiltonian means for the pursuit of Jeffersonian ends. His ideas soon found embodiment in the speeches of Theodore Roosevelt. At Osawatomie, Kansas, in August 1910, the former President implored the American people to put into practice nearly every idea Croly had propounded. The 'Rough Rider' called for a stronger, more energetic national government, and advocated military preparedness in the service of world peace.

T.R.'s 'New Nationalism' spurned the extreme demands of more militant reformers. 'Utopians' like Henry Demarest Lloyd had earlier discovered 'the real world' and 'democratic socialism' as the solution for its ills through close study of books, official documents, and keen observation. With little aid from books, Eugene V. Debs (1855–1926), president of the American Railway Union, reached the same goal through practical experience as a labor organizer in Terre Haute, Indiana. A jail sentence imposed on him for violating the blanket injunction issued in the great Pullman strike of 1894 deepened his conviction of the futility of A.F.of L. craft unionism as well as Samuel Gompers's traditional political policy of 'rewarding friends and punishing enemies' within the two major parties. Steering his course between the syndicalist terrorism of the I.W.W. and the A.F.of L.'s compromising labor and political policies, Debs put his trust in democratic socialism, running as the Socialist candidate for President in 1900, 1904, 1908, and 1912. 'There is nothing in our government the ballot cannot remove or amend,' he wrote while serving a six months' jail sentence. 'It can make and unmake presidents and congresses and courts. . . It can sweep over trusts, syndicates, corporations, monopolies. . . The ballot can do all this and more. It can give our civilization its crowning glory—the cooperative commonwealth.'

No such rosy prospect loomed before the eyes of Samuel Gompers (1850–1924), the immigrant cigar maker and American Federation of Labor president. It was enough for labor to work, as he said, 'along the line of least resistance,' and to make each day 'a better day than the one which has gone before.' To achieve this was largely the responsibility of the organized workers themselves rather than of government. Gompers was vehement in his denunciation of 'quack nostrums' and almost as firm as Andrew Carnegie or William Graham Sumner in his conviction that 'permanent changes and progress must come from within man.' 'You can't "save" people—they must save themselves,' Gompers said in words that might have been lifted from the pages of *Man Versus the State*. But Gompers was consistent as many disciples of Spencer were not. He approved the trust 'as the logical and inevitable development of our modern industrial and commercial system,' but insisted that 'constructive and associated effort [among the workers] must check and correct the abuses that have grown so rapidly in this era of concentrated methods of production and distribution.' It remained for labor, largely through voluntary self-help, to get its own fair share of these larger benefits—'more, more, more,' a larger slice of the national economic pie. Gompers headed the A.F.of L. from 1886 to 1924 except for one year, 1895, when a socialist uprising, capitalizing on widespread economic depression, defeated him. As time wore on, the list of things Gompers's A.F.of L. called on government to do lengthened to a point which justifies listing him as a reformer rather than as a defender of the *status quo*.

Intellectuals, seeking the source of the problem in the anthropological and psychological roots of our culture, probed more deeply. Among the most perceptive was the satirical iconoclast, Thorstein Veblen (1857–1929). His *Theory of the Leisure Class* appeared in 1899, followed in 1904 by *The Theory of Business Enterprise*. Of Norwegian ancestry, he was born on the Wisconsin frontier, and was educated at Carleton College, Minnesota. He did graduate work at Johns Hopkins, Cornell, and Yale. After receiving the Ph.D. degree from Yale, where he took William Graham Sumner's courses, Veblen began a hectic teaching career that carried him from Chicago to Stanford, and to the University of Missouri, winding up at the postwar New School for Social Research. Veblen's contribution lay in a torrential flow of books that went to the very heart of industrialism and its dominant rationale. What Spencer and his American disciples saw as the inevitable working of natural forces, Veblen explained in the coldest terms of economics, more particularly as the pecuniary drive for profit. 'Profit is a business proposition, livelihood is not,' he said. 'Industrial man is chained in an economic prison where law and politics bear the pecuniary imprint, to the exclusion of all else.'

In 1921, Veblen developed the social and political implications of industrial oligarchy in his book, *The Engineers and the Price System*, noting that, under eighteenth-century liberal principles, income is 'a sure sign of productive work done.' Businessmen were thus accorded full credit for having created this productive capacity, ignoring contributing factors such as 'continued advance in technology,' 'continued increase of the available natural resources,' and 'continued increase of population.' Observers of the progress of capitalism also overlooked what the 'same captains of industry have been doing in the ordinary course of business to hold productive industry in check.' 'It is today quite an open question,' Veblen observed, 'whether the businesslike management of the captains is not more occupied with checking industry than with increasing its productive capacity'—that is, more interested in making money than in making goods and supplying services.

What Veblen lost sight of, or at least did not take fully into account, was the counter-force—popular power and the dynamic strength latent in freedom under leadership. He did not recognize, as did V. L. Parrington, that 'broadly two great movements were going forward side by side in the unconscious drift of political tendency—the democratic and the plutocratic.' Indeed Veblen's thought was hardly less narrowly deterministic than Spencer's, but whereas the latter saw man driven by the natural urge to survive, the former saw him in the grip of an implacable pecuniary imperative.

While Veblen probed the psychological foundations of industrialism, Brooks Adams (1848–1927) of the famous Adams family (a great-grandson of John Adams, grandson of John Quincy Adams, and youngest son of Charles Francis Adams) showed how the Veblen thesis was grounded in history. 'The modern capitalist not only thinks in terms of history,' Adams wrote, 'but he thinks in terms of money more exclusively than the French aristocrat or lawyer ever thought in terms of caste . . . He may sell his services to whom he pleases and at what price may suit him, and if by so doing he ruins men and cities, it is nothing to him.'

Brooks Adams, like his distinguished ancestors and his brother Henry, was graduated from Harvard. Trained as a lawyer, he waited eight years in vain for clients, and in 1881 embarked on his career as a social and economic historian. Firm grounding enabled him to see, as Veblen never did, that the dominant capitalist hierarchy was precipitating the very conflict it desired most to allay—the rise of popular power, even of revolution. 'I contend,' he wrote in his *Theory of Social Revolution*, 'that no court can, because of the nature of its being, effectively check a popular majority, acting through a coordinate legislative assembly. . . In assuming attributes beyond the limitation of their being, they . . . not only fail in their object, but shake the foundations of authority and immolate themselves.'

Revolution could not be avoided, Adams contended, because the capitalists and their lawyer adjuncts 'think with specialized minds.' It was not likely, it seemed to him in 1913, that they would be able to bring to their support 'a mind which can grasp a multitude of complex relations, and thus preclude drastic social change.' But at the time he was writing a Harvard man and Boston lawyer, Louis D. Brandeis (1856–1941) had been proving, for a full decade, his extraordinary grasp of complex social-economic relations. Brandeis addressed himself to the inconsistency between 'our political liberty and our our industrial absolutism.' In his testimony before the U.S. Commission on Industrial Relations, January 1915, he proposed the solution William Graham Sumner had thrust aside as the one by which his age had been 'befooled'—industrial democracy. Brandeis argued that although it was important for management to share with labor the profits of industry, labor must also be given a share in the management of business; it must share industrial power as well as industrial responsibilities.

Walter E. Weyl (1873–1919), American economist and writer, an associate editor of the *New Republic* from its beginning, published in 1912 a penetrating survey of political and economic tendencies, *The New Democracy* which, like Croly's book, exerted a powerful influence. Many of Croly's and Weyl's specific suggestions were incorporated in T.R.'s Progressive party campaign of 1912, and later found expression in Woodrow Wilson's 'New Freedom.'

Throughout our history popular power, by and large, has been suspect, feared, denounced. Various constitutional devices have been fashioned to purify, frustrate, or defeat it. Leadership rooted in such power and determined to use it in the service of mankind has usually been considered as necessarily demagogic. 'When we extol our Constitution.' Woodrow Wilson (1856–1924) noted in 1893, 'we think of it in static terms, as an admirable reservoir in which the mighty waters of democracy are held at rest, kept back from free destructive force.' 'But after all,' Wilson went on, 'progress is motion, government is action. The waters of democracy are useless in their reservoirs unless they may be made to drive the wheels of policy and administration.' 'We have not made enough of leadership,' Wilson said. The power that lies in the masses must be released, guided and directed, and to do this is, he declared, the function of leadership.

Professor Wilson of 1893 was already within hailing distance of President Wilson of 1913. 'I am not afraid of the American people getting up and doing something,' he said in a campaign speech. 'I am afraid that they will not.' Wilson recognized what the Randolphs, Kents, and Upshurs did not dare face—the inevitable shift of power in America from the few to the many. He did more than that: he developed and advanced a theory of public power and of leadership to support a national program of regulatory legislation that might have changed the course of our history had not World War I intervened and wrought even greater changes.

No survey of Progressive thought can ignore Walter Lippmann, recently hailed as 'perhaps the most important American political thinker of the twentieth century.' So expansive has been his influence, spreading from the second decade of this century to the present moment, that three selections from his thought—each extract separated by two decades—are included in this book. In *Drift and Mastery*, first published in 1914, Lippmann dealt with the relatively new tensions of industrial democracy and attempted to come to grips with the problems they posed for free government. A year earlier, in *A Preface to Politics*, he had expressed opinions on two of the dominant political thinkers of the Progressive period. 'What reality could there be in comments upon American politics,' he queried, 'which ignored the colossal phenomenon of Roosevelt?' T.R. succeeded where President Taft had failed. A 'statesman' and not an 'agitator,' T.R.'s task was 'to meet demands when they had grown to national proportions.' Roosevelt stood 'as the working model for a possible American statesman at the beginning of the twentieth century.'

In Woodrow Wilson, then recently elected President, Lippmann saw 'an elegant and highly refined intellect. . . An urbane civilization produced it, leisure has given it spaciousness, ease has made it generous.' Aloof from the cause he championed, Wilson possessed a 'mind without tension, its roots . . . not in the somewhat barbarous undercurrents of the nation.' 'Woodrow Wilson understands easily,' Lippmann observed, 'but he does not incarnate; he has never been a part of the protest he speaks. . . Like all essentially contemplative men, the world has to be reflected in the medium of his intellect before he can grapple with it.'

Wilson, like T.R., belonged among the statesmen. Roosevelt seemed to the Lippmann of 1913 more 'effective,' more nearly 'complete.' 'Wilson, less complete than Roosevelt, is worthy of our deepest interest because his judgment is subtle where Roosevelt's is crude. He is a foretaste of a more advanced statesmanship.'

1. *The problem belongs to the American national democracy, and its solution must be attempted chiefly by means of official national action*

HERBERT CROLY, *The Promise of American Life*, 1909 *

The only fruitful promise of which the life of any individual or any nation can be possessed, is a promise determined by an ideal. Such a promise is to be fulfilled, not by sanguine anticipations, not by a conservative imitation of past achievements, but by laborious, single-minded, clear-sighted, and fearless work. If the promising career of any individual is not determined by a specific and worthy purpose, it rapidly drifts into a mere pursuit of success; and even if such a pursuit is successful, whatever promise it may have had, is buried in the grave of its triumph. So it is with a nation. . .

No doubt Americans have in some measure always conceived their national future as an ideal to be fulfilled. Their anticipations have been uplifting as well as confident and vainglorious. They have been prophesying not merely a safe and triumphant, but also a better, future. The ideal demand for some sort of individual and social amelioration has always accompanied even their vainest flights of patriotic prophecy. They may never have sufficiently realized that this better future, just in so far as it is better, will have to be planned and constructed rather than fulfilled of its own momentum; but at any rate, in seeking to disentangle and emphasize the ideal implications of the American national Promise, I am not wholly false to the accepted American tradition. Even if Americans have neglected these ideal implications, even if they have conceived the better future as containing chiefly a larger portion of familiar benefits, the ideal demand, nevertheless, has always been palpably present; and if it can be established as the dominant aspect of the American tradition, that tradition may be transformed, but it will not be violated.

Furthermore, much as we may dislike the American disposition to take the fulfillment of our national Promise for granted, the fact that such a disposition exists in its present volume and vigor demands respectful consideration. It has its roots in the salient conditions of American life, and in the actual experience of the American people. The national Promise, as it is popularly understood, has in a way been fulfilling itself. If the underlying conditions were to remain much as they have been, the prevalent mixture of optimism, fatalism, and conservatism might retain a formidable measure of justification; and the changes which are taking place in the underlying conditions and in the scope of American national experience afford the most reasonable expectation that this state of mind will undergo a radical alteration. It is new conditions which are forcing Americans to choose between the conception of their national Promise as a process and an ideal. Before, however, the nature of these novel conditions and their significance can be considered, we must

* Reprinted with permission of the publisher from *The Promise of American Life*, by Herbert Croly, New York, Anchor Books, 1963, pp. 5–7, 17–18, 20–21, 23–44 passim.

examine with more care the relation between the earlier American economic and social conditions and the ideas and institutions associated with them. Only by a better understanding of the popular tradition, only by an analysis of its merits and its difficulties, can we reach a more consistent and edifying conception of the Promise of American life. . .

The fault in the vision of our national future possessed by the ordinary American does not consist in the expectation of some continuity of achievement. It consists rather in the expectation that the familiar benefits will continue to accumulate automatically. In his mind the ideal Promise is identified with the processes and conditions which hitherto have very much simplified its fulfillment, and he fails sufficiently to realize that the conditions and processes are one thing and the ideal Promise quite another. Moreover, these underlying social and economic conditions are themselves changing, in such wise that hereafter the ideal Promise, instead of being automatically fulfilled, may well be automatically stifled. For two generations and more the American people were, from the economic point of view, most happily situated. They were able, in a sense, to slide down hill into the valley of fulfillment. Economic conditions were such that, given a fair start, they could scarcely avoid reaching a desirable goal. But such is no longer the case. Economic conditions have been profoundly modified, and American political and social problems have been modified with them. The Promise of American life must depend less than it did upon the virgin wilderness and the Atlantic Ocean, for the virgin wilderness has disappeared, and the Atlantic Ocean has become merely a big channel. The same results can no longer be achieved by the same easy methods. Ugly obstacles have jumped into view, and ugly obstacles are peculiarly dangerous to a person who is sliding down hill. The man who is clambering up hill is in a much better position to evade or overcome them. Americans will possess a safer as well as a worthier vision of their national Promise as soon as they give it a house on a hill-top rather than in a valley. . .

A numerous and powerful group of reformers has been collecting whose whole political policy and action is based on the conviction that the 'common people' have not been getting the Square Deal to which they are entitled under the American system; and these reformers are carrying with them a constantly increasing body of public opinion. A considerable proportion of the American people is beginning to exhibit economic and political, as well as personal, discontent. A generation ago the implication was that if a man remained poor and needy, his poverty was his own fault, because the American system was giving all its citizens a fair chance. Now, however, the discontented poor are beginning to charge their poverty to an unjust political and economic organization, and reforming agitators do not hesitate to support them in this contention. Manifestly a threatened obstacle has been raised against the anticipated realization of our national Promise. Unless the great majority of Americans not only have, but believe they have, a fair chance, the better American future will be dangerously compromised.

The conscious recognition of grave national abuses casts a deep shadow across the traditional American patriotic vision. The sincere and candid reformer can no longer consider the national Promise as destined to automatic fulfillment. The reformers themselves are, no doubt, far from believing that whatever peril there is cannot be successfully averted. They make a point of being as patriotically prophetic as the most 'old-fashioned Democrat.' They proclaim even more loudly their conviction of an indubitable and a beneficent national future. But they do not and cannot believe that this future will take care of itself. As reformers they are bound to assert that the national body requires for the time being a good deal of medical attendance, and many of them anticipate that even after the doctors have discontinued their daily visits the patient will still need the supervision of a sanitary specialist. He must be persuaded to behave so that he will not easily fall ill again, and so that his health will be permanently improved. Consequently, just in so far as reformers are reformers they are obliged to abandon the traditional American patriotic fatalism. The national Promise has been transformed into a closer equivalent of a national purpose, the fulfillment of which is a matter of conscious work.

The transformation of the old sense of a glorious national destiny into the sense of a serious national purpose will inevitably tend to make the popular realization of the Promise of American life both more explicit and more serious. As long as Americans believed they were able to fulfill a noble national Promise merely by virtue of maintaining intact a set of political institutions and by the vigorous individual pursuit of private ends, their allegiance to their national fulfillment remained more a matter of words than of deeds; but now that they are being aroused from their patriotic slumber, the effect is inevitably to disentangle the national idea and to give it more dignity. The redemption of the national Promise has become a cause for which the good American must fight, and the cause for which a man fights is a cause which he more than ever values. The American idea is no longer to be propagated merely by multiplying the children of the West and by granting ignorant aliens permission to vote. Like all sacred causes, it must be propagated by the Word and by that right arm of the Word, which is the Sword.

The substance of our national Promise has consisted, as we have seen, of an improving popular economic condition, guaranteed by democratic political institutions, and resulting in moral and social amelioration. These manifold benefits were to be obtained merely by liberating the enlightened self-interest of the American people. The beneficent result followed inevitably from the action of wholly selfish motives—provided, of course, the democratic political system of equal rights was maintained in its integrity. The fulfillment of the American Promise was considered inevitable because it was based upon a combination of self-interest and the natural goodness of human nature. On the other hand, if the fulfillment of our national Promise can no longer be considered inevitable, if it must be considered as equivalent to a conscious national purpose instead of an inexorable national destiny, the implication necessarily is that the trust reposed in individual self-interest has been in some measure betrayed. No preëstablished harmony can then exist between the free and abundant satisfaction of private needs and the accomplishment of a morally and socially desirable result. The Promise of American life is to be fulfilled —not merely by a maximum amount of economic freedom, but by a certain measure of discipline; not merely by the abundant satisfaction of individual desires, but by a large measure of individual subordination and self-denial. And this necessity of subordinating the satisfaction of individual desires to the fulfillment of a national purpose is attached particularly to the absorbing occupation of the American people,—the occupation, viz.: of accumulating wealth. The automatic fulfillment of the American national Promise is to be abandoned, if at all, precisely because the traditional American confidence in individual freedom has resulted in a morally and socially undesirable distribution of wealth. . .

I must be content for the present with the bare assertion that the prevailing abuses and sins, which have made reform necessary, are all of them associated with the prodigious concentration of wealth, and of the power exercised by wealth, in the hands of a few men. I am far from believing that this concentration of economic power is wholly an undesirable thing, and I am also far from believing that the men in whose hands this power is concentrated deserve, on the whole, any exceptional moral reprobation for the manner in which it has been used. In certain respects they have served their country well, and in almost every respect their moral or immoral standards are those of the great majority of their fellow-countrymen. But it is none the less true that the political corruption, the unwise economic organization, and the legal support afforded to certain economic privileges are all under existing conditions due to the malevolent social influence of individual and incorporated American wealth; and it is equally true that these abuses, and the excessive 'money power' with which they are associated, have originated in the peculiar freedom which the American tradition and organization have granted to the individual. Up to a certain point that freedom has been and still is beneficial. Beyond that point it is not merely harmful; it is by way of being fatal. Efficient regulation there must be; and it must be regulation which will strike, not at the symptoms of the evil, but at its roots. The existing concentration of wealth and financial power in the hands of a few irresponsible men is the inevitable outcome of the chaotic individualism of our political and economic organization, while at the same time it is inimical to democracy, because it tends to erect political abuses and social inequalities into a system. The inference which follows may be disagreeable, but it is not to be escaped. In becoming responsible for the subordination of the individual to the demand of a dominant and constructive national purpose, the American state will in effect be making itself responsible for a morally and socially desirable distribution of wealth.

The consequences, then, of converting our American national destiny into a national purpose are beginning to be revolutionary. When the Promise of American life is conceived as a national ideal, whose fulfillment is a matter of artful and laborious work, the effect thereof is substantially to identify the national purpose with the social problem. What the American people of the present and the future have really been promised by our patriotic prophecies is an attempt to solve that problem. They have been promised on American soil comfort, prosperity, and the opportunity for self-improvement; and the lesson of the existing crisis is that such a Promise can never be redeemed by an indiscriminate individual scramble for wealth. The individual competition, even when it starts under fair conditions and rules, results, not only, as it should, in the triumph of the strongest, but in the attempt to perpetuate the victory; and it is this attempt which must be recognized and forestalled in the interest of the American national purpose. The way to realize a purpose is, not to leave it to chance, but to keep it loyally in mind, and adopt means proper to the importance and the difficulty of the task. No voluntary association of individuals, resourceful and disinterested though they be, is competent to assume the responsibility. The problem belongs to the American national democracy, and its solution must be attempted chiefly by means of official national action. . .

2. *Whenever the alternative must be faced, I am for men and not for property*

THEODORE ROOSEVELT, Speech at Osawatomie, Kansas, 31 August 1910 *

. . . At many stages in the advance of humanity, this conflict between the men who possess more than they have earned and the men who have earned more than they possess is the central condition of progress. In our day it appears as the struggle of free men to gain and hold the right of self-government as against the special interests, who twist the methods of free government into machinery for defeating the popular will. At every stage, and under all circumstances, the essence of the struggle is to equalize opportunity, destroy privilege, and give to the life and citizenship of every individual the highest possible value both to himself and to the commonwealth. . .

Practical equality of opportunity for all citizens, when we achieve it, will have two great results. First, every man will have a fair chance to make of himself all that in him lies; to reach the highest point to which his capacities, unassisted by special privilege of his own and unhampered by the special privilege of others, can carry him, and to get for himself and his family substantially what he has earned. Second, equality of opportunity means that the commonwealth will get from every citizen the highest services of which he is capable. No man who carries the burden of the special privileges of another can give to the commonwealth that service to which it is fairly entitled.

I stand for the square deal. But when I say that I am for the square deal, I mean not merely that I stand for fair play under the present rules of the game, but that I stand for having those rules changed so as to work for a more substantial equality of opportunity and of reward for equally good service. . .

Now, this means that our government, national and state, must be freed from the sinister influence or control of special interests. Exactly as the special interests of cotton and slavery threatened our political integrity before

* *The New Nationalism*, William E. Leuchtenburg, ed., Englewood Cliffs, N. J., Prentice-Hall, 1961, pp. 25–9, 34–7 *passim*.

the Civil War, so now the great special business interests too often control and corrupt the men and methods of government for their own profit. We must drive the special interests out of politics. That is one of our tasks to-day. Every special interest is entitled to justice—full, fair, and complete,—and, now, mind you, if there were any attempt by mob violence to plunder and work harm to the special interest, whatever it may be, that I most dislike, and the wealthy man, whomsoever he may be, for whom I have the greatest contempt, I would fight for him, and you would if you were worth your salt. He should have justice. For every special interest is entitled to justice, but not one is entitled to a vote in Congress, to a voice on the bench, or to representation in any public office. The Constitution guarantees protection to property, and we must make that promise good. But it does not give the right of suffrage to any corporation.

The true friend of property, the true conservative, is he who insists that property shall be the servant and not the master of the commonwealth; who insists that the creature of man's making shall be the servant and not the master of the man who made it. The citizens of the United States must effectively control the mighty commercial forces which they have themselves called into being. . .

It has become entirely clear that we must have government supervision of the capitalization, not only of public service corporations, including, particularly, railways, but of all corporations doing an interstate business. I do not wish to see the nation forced into the ownership of the railways if it can possibly be avoided, and the only alternative is thoroughgoing and effective regulation, which shall be based on a full knowledge of all the facts, including a physical valuation of property. This physical valuation is not needed, or, at least, is very rarely needed, for fixing rates; but it is needed as the basis of honest capitalization.

We have come to recognize that franchises should never be granted except for a limited time, and never without proper provision for compensation to the public. It is my personal belief that the same kind and degree of control and supervision which should be exercised over public service corporations should be extended also to combinations which control necessaries of life, such as meat, oil, and coal, or which deal in them on an important scale. I have no doubt that the ordinary man who has control of them is much like ourselves. I have no doubt he would like to do well, but I want to have enough supervision to help him realize that desire to do well.

I believe that the officers, and, especially, the directors, of corporations should be held personally responsible when any corporation breaks the law.

Combinations in industry are the result of an imperative economic law which cannot be repealed by political legislation. The effort at prohibiting all combination has substantially failed. The way out lies, not in attempting to prevent such combinations, but in completely controlling them in the interest of the public welfare. For that purpose the Federal Bureau of Corporations is an agency of first importance. Its powers, and, therefore, its efficiency, as well as that of the Interstate Commerce Commission, should be largely increased. . .

But I think we may go still further. The right to regulate the use of wealth in the public interest is universally admitted. Let us admit also the right to regulate the terms and conditions of labor, which is the chief element of wealth, directly in the interest of the common good. The fundamental thing to do for every man is to give him a chance to reach a place in which he will make the greatest possible contribution to the public welfare. Understand what I say there. Give him a chance, not push him up if he will not be pushed. Help any man who stumbles; if he lies down, it is a poor job to try to carry him; but if he is a worthy man, try your best to see that he gets a chance to show the worth that is in him. No man can be a good citizen unless he has a wage more than sufficient to cover the bare cost of living, and hours of labor short enough so that after his day's work is done he will have time and energy to bear his share in the management of the community, to help in carrying the general load. We keep countless men from being good citizens by the conditions of life with which we surround them. We need comprehensive workmen's compensation acts, both state and national laws to regulate child labor and work for women, and, especially, we need in our common schools not merely education in book learning, but also practical training for daily life and work. We need to enforce better sanitary conditions for our workers and to extend the use of safety appliances for our workers in industry and commerce, both within and between the states. Also, friends, in the interest of the workingman himself we need to set our faces like flint against mob violence just as against corporate greed; against violence and injustice and lawlessness by wage workers just as much as against lawless cunning and greed and selfish arrogance of employers. If I could ask but one thing of my fellow countrymen, my request would be that, whenever they go in for reform, they remember the two sides, and that they always exact justice from one side as much as from the other. I have small use for the public servant who can always see and denounce the corruption of the capitalist, but who cannot persuade himself, especially before election, to say a word about lawless mob violence. And I have equally small use for a man, be he a judge on the bench, or editor of a great paper, or wealthy and influential private citizen, who can see clearly enough and denounce the lawlessness of mob violence, but whose eyes are closed so that he is blind when the question is one of corruption in business on a gigantic scale. Also remember what I said about excess in reformer and reactionary alike. If the reactionary man, who thinks of nothing but the rights of property, could have his way, he would bring about a revolution; and one of my chief fears in connection with progress comes because I do not want to see our people, for lack of proper leadership, compelled to follow men whose intentions are excellent, but whose eyes are a little too wild to make it really safe to trust them. . .

I do not ask for overcentralization; but I do ask that we work in a spirit of broad and far-reaching nationalism when we work for what concerns our people as a whole. We are all Americans. Our common interests are as broad as the continent. I speak to you here in Kansas exactly as I would speak in New York or Georgia, for the most vital problems are those which affect us all alike. The national government belongs to the whole American people, and where the whole American people are interested, that interest can be guarded effectively only by the national government. The betterment which we seek must be accomplished, I believe, mainly through the national government.

The American people are right in demanding that New Nationalism, without which we cannot hope to deal with new problems. The New Nationalism puts the national need before sectional or personal advantage. It is impatient of the utter confusion that results from local legislatures attempting to treat national issues as local issues. It is still more impatient of the impotence which springs from overdivision of governmental powers, the impotence which makes it possible for local selfishness or for legal cunning, hired by wealthy special interests, to bring national activities to a deadlock. This New Nationalism regards the executive power as the steward of the public welfare. It demands of the judiciary that it shall be interested primarily in human welfare rather than in property, just as it demands that the representative body shall represent all the people rather than any one class or section of the people.

I believe in shaping the ends of government to protect property as well as human welfare. Normally, and in the long run, the ends are the same; but whenever the alternative must be faced, I am for men and not for property. . . I am far from underestimating the importance of dividends; but I rank dividends below human character. Again, I do not have any sympathy with the reformer who says he does not care for dividends. Of course, economic welfare is necessary, for a man must pull his own weight and be able to support his family. I know well that the reformers must not bring upon the people economic ruin, or the reforms themselves will go down in the ruin. But we must be ready to face temporary disaster, whether or not brought on by those who will war against us to the knife. Those who oppose all reform will do well to remember that ruin in its worst form is inevitable if our national life brings us nothing better than swollen fortunes for the few and the triumph in both politics and business of a sordid and selfish materialism. . .

3. *The goal—to establish the working class republic*

EUGENE DEBS, *Unionism and Socialism*, 1908 *

The labor question, as it is called, has come to be recognized as the foremost of our time. In some form it thrusts itself into every human relation, and directly or indirectly has a part in every controversy. . .

There has always been a labor question since man first exploited man in the struggle for existence, but not until its true meaning was revealed in the development of modern industry did it command serious thought or intelligent

* *Eugene Debs: His Writings and Speeches*, Chicago, Kerr, 1908, pp. 119–41 *passim.*

consideration, and only then came any adequate conception of its importance to the race. . .

A century ago a boy served his apprenticeship and became the master of his trade. The few simple tools with which work was then done were generally owned by the man who used them; he could provide himself with the small quantity of raw material he required, and freely follow his chosen pursuit and enjoy the fruit of his labor. But as everything had to be produced by the work of his hands, production was a slow process, meagre of results, and the worker found it necessary to devote from twelve to fifteen hours to his daily task to earn a sufficient amount to support himself and family.

It required most of the time and energy of the average worker to produce enough to satisfy the physical wants of himself and those dependent upon his labor.

There was little leisure for mental improvement, for recreation or social intercourse. The best that can be said for the workingman of this period is that he enjoyed political freedom, controlled in large measure his own employment, by virtue of his owning the tools of his trade, appropriated to his own use the product of his labor and lived his quiet, uneventful round to the end of his days.

This was a new country, with boundless stretches of virgin soil. There was ample room and opportunity, air and sunlight, for all.

There was no millionaire in the United States; nor was there a tramp. These types are the products of the same system. The former is produced at the expense of the latter, and both at the expense of the working class. They appeared at the same time in the industrial development and they will disappear together with the abolition of the system that brought them into existence.

The application of machinery to productive industry was followed by tremendous and far-reaching changes in the whole structure of society. First among these was the change in the status of the worker, who, from an independent mechanic or small producer, was reduced to the level of a dependent wage worker. The machine had leaped, as it were, into the arena of industrial activity, and had left little or no room for the application of the worker's skill or the use of his individual tools.

The economic dependence of the working class became more and more rigidly fixed—and at the same time a new era dawned for the human race.

The more or less isolated individual artisans were converted into groups of associated workers and marshalled for the impending social revolution. . .

The swift and vast concentration of capital and the unprecedented industrial activity which marked the close of the nineteenth century were followed by the most extraordinary growth in the number and variety of trades-unions in the history of the movement; yet this expansion, remarkable as it was, has not only been equalled, but excelled, in the first years of the new century, the tide of unionism sweeping over the whole country, and rising steadily higher, notwithstanding the efforts put forth from a hundred sources controlled by the ruling class to restrain its march, impair its utility or stamp it out of existence. . .

The enemies of unionism, while differing in method, are united solidly upon one point, and that is in the effort to misrepresent and discredit the men who, scorning and defying the capitalist exploiters and their minions, point steadily the straight and uncompromising course the movement must take if it is to accomplish its allotted task and safely reach its destined port. . .

The more or less open enemies have inaugurated some interesting innovations during the past few years. The private armies the corporations used some years ago, such as Pinkerton mercenaries, coal and iron police, deputy marshals, etc., have been relegated to second place as out of date, or they are wholly out of commission. It has been found after repeated experiments that the courts are far more deadly to trades-unions, and that they operate noiselessly and with unerring precision.

The rapid fire injunction is a great improvement on the gatling gun. Nothing can get beyond its range and it never misses fire.

The capitalists are in entire control of the injunction artillery, and all the judicial gunner has to do is to touch it off at their command.

Step by step the writ of injunction has invaded the domain of trades-unionism, limiting its jurisdiction, curtailing its powers, sapping its strength and undermining its foundations, and this has been done by the courts in the name of the institutions they were designed to safeguard, but have shamelessly betrayed at the behest of the barons of capitalism.

Injunctions have been issued restraining the trades-unions and their members from striking, from boycotting, from voting funds to strikes, from levying assessments to support their members, from walking on the public highway, from asking non-union men not to take their places, from meeting to oppose wage reductions, from expelling a spy from membership, from holding conversation with those who had taken or were about to take their jobs, from congregating in public places, from holding meetings, from doing anything and everything, directly, indirectly or any other way, to interfere with the employing class in their unalienable right to operate their plants as their own interests may dictate, and to run things generally to suit themselves.

The courts have found it in line with judicial procedure to strike every weapon from labor's economic hand and leave it defenseless at the mercy of its exploiter; and now that the courts have gone to the last extremity in this nefarious plot of subjugation, labor, at last, is waking up to the fact that it has not been using its political arm in the struggle at all; that the ballot which it can wield is strong enough not only to disarm the enemy, but to drive that enemy entirely from the field.

The courts, so notoriously in control of capital, and so shamelessly perverted to its base and sordid purpose are, therefore, exercising a wholesome effect upon trades-unionism by compelling the members to note the class character of our capitalist government and driving them to the inevitable conclusion that the labor question is also a political question and that the working class must organize their political power that they may wrest the government from capitalist control and put an end to class rule forever.

Trades-unionists for the most part learn slowly, but they learn surely, and fresh object lessons are prepared for them every day. . .

They have seen the supreme court of the nation turn labor out without a hearing, while the corporation lawyers, who compose this august body, and who hold their commissions in virtue of the 'well done' of their capitalist retainers, solemnly descant upon the immaculate purity of our judicial institutions.

They have seen state legislatures, both Republican and Democratic, with never an exception, controlled bodily by the capitalist class and turn the committees of labor unions empty-handed from their doors.

They have seen state supreme courts declare as unconstitutional the last vestige of law upon the statute books that could by any possibility be construed as affording any shelter or relief to the labor union or its members.

They have seen these and many other things and will doubtless see many more before their eyes are opened as a class; but we are thankful for them all, painful though they be to us in having to bear witness to the suffering of our benighted brethren. . .

The members of a trades-union should be taught the true import, the whole object of the labor movement and understand its entire program.

They should know that the labor movement means more, infinitely more, than a paltry increase in wages and the strike necessary to secure it; that while it engages to do all that possibly can be done to better the working conditions of its members, its higher object is to overthrow the capitalist system of private ownership of the tools of labor, abolish wage-slavery and achieve the freedom of the whole working class and, in fact, of all mankind. . .

The trades-union is an economic organization with distinct economic functions and as such is a part, a necessary part, but a part only of the Labor Movement; it has its own sphere of activity, its own program and is its own master within its economic limitations.

But the labor movement has also its political side and the trades-unionist must be educated to realize its importance and to understand that the political side of the movement must be *unionized* as well as the economic side, and that he is not in fact a union man at all who, although a member of the union on the economic side, is a non-unionist on the political side; and the while striking for, votes against the working class.

The trades-union expresses the economic power and the Socialist party expresses the political power of the Labor movement.

The fully developed labor-unionist uses both his economic and political power in the interest of his class. He understands that the struggle between labor and capital is a *class* struggle; that the working class are in a great majority, but divided, some in trade-unions and some out of them, some in one political party and some in another; that because they are divided they are helpless and must submit to being robbed of what their labor produces, and treated with contempt; that they must unite their class in the trades-union on the one hand and in the Socialist party on the other hand; that industrially and politically they must act together as a class against the capitalist class and that this struggle is a class struggle, and that any workingman who deserts his union in a strike and goes to the other side is a scab, and any workingman who deserts his party on election day and goes over to the enemy is a betrayer of his class and an enemy of his fellowman.

Both sides are organized in this class struggle, the capitalists, however, far more thoroughly than the workers. In the first place the capitalists are, comparatively, few in number, while the workers number many millions. Next, the capitalists are men of financial means and resources, and can buy the best brains and command the highest order of ability the market affords. Then again, they own the earth, and the mills and mines and locomotives and ships and stores and the jobs that are attached to them, and this not only gives them tremendous advantage in the struggle, but makes them for the time the absolute masters of the situation.

The workers, on the other hand, are poor as a rule, and ignorant as a class, *but they are in an overwhelming majority*. In a word, they have the power, but are not conscious of it. This then is the supreme demand; to make them conscious of the power of their class, or class-conscious workingmen. . .

The Socialist party is to the workingman politically what the trades-union is to him industrially; the former is the party of his class, while the latter is the union of his trade.

The difference between them is that while the trades-union is confined to the trade, the Socialist party embraces the entire working class, and while the union is limited to bettering conditions under the wage system, the party is organized to conquer the political power of the nation, wipe out the wage system and make the workers themselves the masters of the earth. . .

4. *The goal—to secure for labor a larger share of the national income*

SAMUEL GOMPERS, *The American Labor Movement, Its Makeup, Achievements and Aspirations*, 1914 *

The workers of the United States do not receive the full product of their labor. It is impossible for any one to say definitely what proportion the workers receive in payment for their labor, but due to the organized labor movement they have received and are receiving a larger share of the product of their labor than ever before in the history of modern industry. One of the functions of organized labor is to increase the share of the workers in the product of their labor. Organized labor makes constantly increasing demands upon society for rewards for the services which the workers give to society and without which civilized life would be impossible. The process of increasing the share is not always gradual, but it is continual. The organized labor movement has generally succeeded in forcing an increase in the proportion the workers receive of the general product.

The working people—and I prefer to say working people and to speak of

* An abstract of the statements made before the United States Commission on Industrial Relations at its hearings in New York City, 21–23 May 1914. Published as a pamphlet.

them as really human beings—are prompted by the same desires, the same hopes of a better life as are all other people. They are not willing to wait for a better life until after they have shuffled off this mortal coil but they want improvements here and now. They want to make conditions better for their children so that they may be prepared to meet other and new problems of their time. The working people are pressing forward, making their demands and presenting their claims with whatever power they can exercise in a natural, normal manner to secure a larger and constantly increasing share of what they produce. They are working toward the highest and the best ideals of social justice.

The intelligent, common-sense workingmen prefer to deal with the problems of to-day, with which they must contend if they want to make advancements, rather than to deal with a picture and a dream which have never had, and, I am sure, will never have, any reality in the affairs of humanity, and which threaten, if they could be introduced, the most pernicious system for circumscribing effort and activity that has ever been invented.

The workers will never stop in any effort, nor will they stop at any point in an effort to secure greater improvements in conditions or for a better life in all its phases. Where these efforts may lead, what that better life may be, I do not care to predict. I decline to permit my mind or my activities to be labeled or limited by any particular ism because of adherence to a theory or a dream. The A.F. of L. is neither governed in its activities by a so-called 'Social Philosophy,' nor does it work 'blindly from day to day.' Its work is well planned to be continually of the greatest benefit to the working people to protect and promote their rights and interest in every field of human activity. . .

In improving conditions from day to day the organized labor movement has no 'fixed program' for human progress. If you start out with a program everything must conform to it. With theorists, if facts do not conform to their theories, then so much the worse for the facts. Their declarations of theories and actions refuse to be hampered by facts. We do not set any particular standard, but work for the best possible conditions immediately obtainable for the workers. When they are obtained then we strive for better.

It does not require any elaborate social philosophy or great discernment to know that a wage of $3 a day and a workday of eight hours in sanitary workshops are better than $2.50 a day and a workday of twelve hours under perilous conditions. The working people will not stop when any particular point is reached; they will never stop in their efforts to obtain a better life for themselves, for their wives, for their children, and for all humanity. The object is to attain complete social justice.

The Socialist party has for its purpose the abolition of the present system of wages. Many employers agree with that purpose—the abolition of wages. But the A.F. of L. goes beyond the system which those dreamers have conceived.

The movement of the working people, whether under the A.F. of L. or not, will simply follow the human impulse for improvement in conditions wherever that may lead, and wherever that may lead they will go without aiming at any theoretical goal. Human impulse for self-betterment will lead constantly to the material, physical, social, and moral betterment of the people. We decline to commit our labor movement to any species of speculative philosophy. . .

The efforts of the American labor movement to secure a larger share of the income are directed against all who illegitimately stand between the workers and the attainment of a better life. This class includes all who have not made honest investment in honest enterprise. Employers, capitalists, stockholders, bondholders—the capitalist class generally—oppose the efforts of the workers in the A.F. of L. and in other organizations to obtain a larger share of the product. Very much of the opposition to the efforts of the working people to secure improved conditions has come from those who obtain what may be called an unearned share in the distribution. The beneficiaries of the present system of distribution desire to retain as much as possible of their present share or to increase that proportion. But an additional reason that leads to opposition is that there are employers who live in the twentieth century, yet who have the mental outlook of the sixteenth century in their attitude toward the working people, and who still imagine that they are 'masters of all they survey.' These employers think that any attempt upon the part of the working people to secure improvements in their condition is a spirit of rebellion that must be frowned down. But we organized workers have found that after we have had some contests with employers, whether we have won the battle or lost it, if we but maintain our organization there is less difficulty thereafter in reaching a joint agreement or a collective bargain involving improved conditions of the workers.

The stronger the organization of the workers the greater the likelihood of their securing concessions. These concessions are not altogether because of the strength shown by the employees, but result in part from the changed attitude of the employer.

An employer changes his policy when he is convinced that the workingmen have demonstrated that they have a right to a voice in determining questions affecting the relations between themselves and their employers. For instance, this was demonstrated in the case of the late Mr. Baer,* who, as may be recalled, once declared that he would not speak with nor confer with the

* George Frederick Baer (1842–1914), President of the Philadelphia and Reading Railway Co. Gompers refers to Baer's letter of 17 July 1902 addressed to W. F. Clark of Wilkes-Barre, who had appealed to him to end the anthracite coal strike of that year.

'I do not know who you are,' Baer wrote Clark. 'I see that you are a religious man; but you are evidently biased in favor of the working man to control business in which he has no other interest than to secure fair wages for the work he does.

'I beg you not to be discouraged. The rights and interests of the laboring man will be protected and cared for—not by labor agitators, but by the Christian men to whom God in His infinite wisdom has given the control of the property interests of the country, and upon whom the successful Management of which so much depends.

'Do not be discouraged. Pray earnestly that right may triumph, always remembering that the Lord God omnipotent still reigns, and that His reign is one of Law and Order, and not of violence and crime.'

For a photograph copy of this letter, see Caro Lloyd, *Henry Demarest Lloyd, 1847–1903*, 1912, vol. II, opposite p. 190. [A.T.M.]

representative of the miners or any one who stood for them; that he and his associates were the 'trustees of God' in the administration of their property and in taking care of the rights and interests of the working people. He, as well as many other employers, lived to revise his judgment and to see the necessity of making agreements with workers.

Because employers as a class are interested in maintaining or increasing their share of the general product and because workers are determined to demand a greater and ever greater share of this same general product the economic interests between these two are not harmonious. Upon this point I have been repeatedly misrepresented by socialist writers and orators whose frequent repetitions of that misrepresentation have finally convinced them of the truth of their assertion. No amount of emphatic repudiation of that statement, no matter how often that repudiation and denial have been expressed, has secured a change in the assertion that my position was contrary to the one I have just stated. . .

In the initial stages of the altered relations between workers and employers improvements are forced upon employers by collective bargains, strikes and boycotts. Later there is a realization upon the part of the employers that it is more costly to enter into long strikes and lockouts than to concede conditions without interrupting the industry. As the vision and the understanding of the employer change, his attitude toward his workmen and the relation between employer and workers also change, so that the sentiments and views of employers are often in entire accord with those of the organizations of working people.

However the gains made by the organized labor movement in this country have generally been wrung from the employing classes. What workingmen of America have obtained in improved conditions, higher wages, shorter hours of labor, was not handed to them on a silver platter. They have had to organize, they have had to show their teeth, they have had to strike, they have had to go hungry, and to make sacrifices in order to impress upon the employers their determination to be larger sharers in the products of labor. . .

It is not the practice of large employers of labor to carry the gospel of their interests wherever they can, particularly into the camp of organized labor. While the National Association of Manufacturers is absolutely hostile to the labor unions and everything they represent, yet it is not an association in which a labor leader is either accepted or tolerated. He therefore cannot take the doctrine and message of Labor there. The avowed purpose of the National Association of Manufacturers is an active organization for warfare against organized labor. It has a severer purpose, which is to prevent organizations of working people from protecting themselves or their interests. As a matter of fact, the president of that organization only a few days ago declared that he was going to form a 'new union' over our heads. It is on a par with pretended friends of labor, but with them it is simply treason to the interests of labor.

Employers in their relation to employes and to the labor movement are generally guided by their own economic interests, and the greater number of employers are not members of the N.A.M. and are not in accord with that association. In addition, I know that there are a number of employers who belong to the N.A.M. because of trade advantages which are secured through other activities of that association. Those of the employing class who have organized for the promotion of their own economic interests which are opposed to those of the working classes are against the organized labor movement. . .

The A.F. of L. has an independent policy, an independent political policy —a policy so independent politically that it is independent of the Socialist party too. It is concerned more about achievements than it is about the instrumentality for achievement. We have achieved through the American labor movement more real betterment for the working people than has been accomplished by any other labor movement in the world.

The entire trade union movement of America is absolutely without any parties and without political affiliation. The large national organizations not affiliated to the A.F. of L. are also absolutely independent politically. . .

There has been for many years an insistent effort to establish for these men some tribunal that would fix by legislation the wages, conditions of service, and hours of labor. Insistence for the enactment of legislation placing in a governmental board such power is always traceable to the larger interests that employ men. There is an underground process constantly at work to devise ways and means ostensibly and superficially wellsounding, but which contain a process and a method by which the status of the workmen can be fixed. The purpose is to tie them to their tasks, that the right of freedom of action shall be first impaired and then denied. Our friends, the members and leaders of the Socialist party, would gladly establish that in the wholesale. They do not understand the real struggle for freedom. . .

The labor movement in this country has already become political as well as economic. I am not prepared to say what the next or the future generations may develop; but to the A.F. of L., and I suppose to the American working people, it is of less consequence what instrumentality is employed in the accomplishment of the purpose than the accomplishment of the purpose itself. We have in the United States secured legislation of the most substantial character without the use or the necessity of a so-called independent labor party. . .

There is no necessity, in the United States at least, for dealing with these problems. Our problems are primarily industrial. I have my day dreams, and build my castles in the air, and sometimes allow my mind to run riot; but when I want to be of some service to my fellow workers now and hereafter I am going to get down to terra firma and help them in their present struggle. . .

5. *In America, as nowhere else, has the sacredness of pecuniary obligation so permeated the common sense of the community*

THORSTEIN VEBLEN, *The Theory of Business Enterprise*, 1904 *

Popular welfare is bound up with the conduct of business; because industry is managed for business ends, and also because there prevails throughout modern

*New York, Charles Scribner's Sons, 1904, pp. 268–92 *passim*.

communities a settled habit of rating the means of livelihood and the amenities of life in pecuniary terms. But apart from their effect in controlling the terms of livelihood from day to day, these principles are also in great measure decisive in the larger affairs of life, both for the individual in his civil relations and for the community at large in its political concerns. Modern (civilized) institutions rest, in great part, on business principles. This is the meaning, as applied to the modern situation, of the current phrases about the Economic Interpretation of History, or the Materialistic Theory of History.

Because of this settled habit of seeing all the conjunctures of life from the business point of view, in terms of profit and loss, the management of the affairs of the community at large falls by common consent into the hands of business men and is guided by business considerations. Hence modern politics is business politics, even apart from the sinister application of the phrase to what is invidiously called corrupt politics. This is true both of foreign and domestic policy. Legislation, police surveillance, the administration of justice, the military and diplomatic service, all are chiefly concerned with business relations, pecuniary interests, and they have little more than an incidental bearing on other human interests. All this apparatus is also charged with the protection of life and personal liberty, but its work in this bearing has much of a pecuniary color.

Legislation and legal decisions are based on the dogma of Natural Liberty. This is peculiarly true as regards the English-speaking peoples, the foundation of whose jurisprudence is the common law, and it holds true in an especial degree of America. In other European communities the sway of natural-rights preconceptions is not so unmitigated, but even with them there is a visibly growing predilection for the natural-rights standpoint in all matters touching business relations. The dogma of natural liberty is peculiarly conducive to an expeditious business traffic and peculiarly consonant with the habits of thought which necessarily prevail in any business community.

The current body of natural-rights preconceptions antedates the modern business situation. The scheme of natural rights grew up and found secure lodgement in the common sense of the community, as well as with its lawgivers and courts, under the discipline of the small industry and petty trade ('domestic industry') whose development culminated in the eighteenth century. In industrial matters the efficient and autonomous factor in the days of the small industry was the individual workman, his personal force, dexterity, and diligence; similarly in the petty trade of the precapitalistic English situation the decisive factor was the discretion and sagacity of the small merchant and the petty employer, who stood in direct personal relations with their customers and their employees. In so far as trade and industry was not restrained by conventional regulations, statutory or customary, both trade and industry was in effect an open field of free competition, in which man met man on a somewhat equable footing. While the competitors were not on a footing of material equality, the industrial system was sufficiently loose-jointed, of a sufficiently diffuse growth, to make competition effective in the absence of mandatory restrictions. The like will hold of the business organization associated with the small industry. Both trade and industry were matters of personal efficiency rather than comprehensively organized process of an impersonal character.

Natural rights, as they found their way into the conceptions of law and equity, were in effect the assumed equal rights of men so situated on a plane of at least constructive equality that the individuals concerned would be left in a position of effectively free choice if conventional restrictions were done away. The organization was not, mechanically, a close-knit one, in the sense that the concatenation of industrial processes or of business transactions was not rigorous either in point of time relations or of the quantity and character of the output or the work. Neither were the place, pace, circumstances, means, or hours of work closely determined for the workman or his employer by mechanical circumstances of the industrial process or of the market. The standardization of life under the old regime was of a conventional character, not of a mechanical kind such as is visible in the more recent development. And this conventional standardization was gradually losing force.

The movement of opinion on natural-rights ground converged to an insistence on the system of natural liberty, so called. But this insistence on natural liberty did not contemplate the abrogation of all conventional prescription. 'The simple and obvious system of natural liberty' meant freedom from restraint on any other prescriptive ground than that afforded by the rights of ownership. In its economic bearing the system of natural liberty meant a system of free pecuniary contract. 'Liberty does not mean license,' which in economic terms would be transcribed, 'The natural freedom of the individual must not traverse the prescriptive rights of property.' Property rights being included among natural rights, they had the indefeasibility which attaches to natural rights. Natural liberty prescribes freedom to buy and sell, limited only by the equal freedom of others to buy and sell; with the obvious corollary that there must be no interference with others' buying and selling, except by means of buying and selling.

This principle of natural (pecuniary) liberty has found its most unmitigated acceptance in America, and has here taken the firmest hold on the legal mind. Nowhere else has the sacredness of pecuniary obligations so permeated the common sense of the community, and nowhere does pecuniary obligation come so near being the only form of obligation that has the unqualified sanction of current common sense. Here, as nowhere else, do obligations and claims of the most diverse kinds, domestic, social, and civil, tend to take the pecuniary form and admit of being fully discharged on a monetary valuation. To a greater extent than elsewhere public esteem is awarded to artists, actors, preachers, writers, scientists, officials, in some rough proportion to the sums paid for their work.

American civil rights have taken an extreme form, with relatively great stress on the inviolability of pecuniary relations, due to the peculiar circumstances under which the American community has grown up. The pioneers, especially in that North-Atlantic seaboard community that has been chiefly effective in shaping American traditions, brought with them a somewhat high-wrought variant of the English preconception in favor of individual discretion, and this tradition they put in practice under circumstances peculiarly favorable to a bold development. They brought little of the remnants of that prescriptive code that once bound the handicraft system, and the conditions of life in the colonies did not foster a new growth of conventional regulations circumscribing private initiative. America is the native habitat of the self-made man, and the self-made man is a pecuniary organism.

Presently, when occasion arose, the metaphysics of natural liberty, pecuniary and other, was embodied in set form in constitutional enactments. It is therefore involved in a more authentic form and with more incisive force in the legal structure of this community than in that of any other. Freedom of contract is the fundamental tenet of the legal creed, so to speak, inviolable and inalienable; and within the province of law and equity no one has competence to penetrate behind this first premise or to question the merits of the natural-rights metaphysics on which it rests. The only principle (attested habit of thought) which may contest its primacy in civil matters is a vague 'general welfare' clause; and even this can effectively contest its claims only under exceptional circumstances. Under the application of any general welfare clause the presumption is and always must be that the principle of free contract be left intact so far as the circumstances of the case permit. The citizen may not be deprived of life, liberty, or property without due process of law, and the due process proceeds on the premise that property rights are inviolable. In its bearing upon the economic relations between individuals this comes to mean, in effect, not only that one individual or group of individuals may not legally bring any other than pecuniary pressure to bear upon another individual or group, but also that pecuniary pressure cannot be barred.

Now, through gradual change of the economic situation, this conventional principle of unmitigated and inalienable freedom of contract began to grow obsolete from about the time when it was fairly installed; obsolescent, of course, not in point of law, but in point of fact. Since about the time when this new conventional standardization of the scheme of economic life in terms of free contract reached its mature development, in the eighteenth century, a new standardizing force, that of the machine process, has invaded the field. The standardization and the constraint of the system of machine industry differs from what went before it in that it has had no conventional recognition, no metaphysical authentication. It has not become a legal fact. Therefore it neither need nor can be taken account of by the legal mind. It is a new fact which fits into the framework neither of the ancient system of prescriptive usage nor of the later system of free personal initiative. It does not exist *de jure*, but only *de facto*. Belonging neither to the defunct system nor to the current legal system, since it neither constitutes nor traverses a 'natural right,' it is, as within the cognizance of the law, non-existent. It is, perhaps, actual, with a gross, material actuality; but it is not real, with a legal, metaphysically competent reality. Such coercion as it may exert, or as may be exercised through its means, therefore, is, in point of legal reality, no coercion.

Where physical impossibility to fulfil the terms of a contract arises out of the concatenation of industrial processes, this physical impossibility may be pleaded as invalidating the terms of the contract. But the pecuniary pressure of price or subsistence which the sequence and interdependence of industrial processes may bring to bear has no standing as such in law or equity; it can reach the cognizance of the law only indirectly, through gross defection of one of the contracting parties, in those cases where the pressure is severe enough to result in insolvency, sickness, or death. The material necessities of a group of workmen or consumers, enforced by the specialization and concatenation of industrial processes, is, therefore, not competent to set aside, or indeed to qualify, the natural freedom of the owners of these processes to let work go on or not, as the outlook for profits may decide. Profits is a business proposition, livelihood is not.

Under the current *de facto* standardization of economic life enforced by the machine industry, it may frequently happen that an individual or a group, e.g., of workmen, has not a *de facto* power of free contract. A given workman's livelihood can perhaps, practically, be found only on acceptance of one specific contract offered, perhaps not at all. But the coercion which in this way bears upon his choice through the standardization of industrial procedure is neither assault and battery nor breach of contract, and it is, therefore, not repugnant to the principles of natural liberty. Through controlling the processes of industry in which alone, practically, given workmen can find their livelihood, the owners of these processes may bring pecuniary pressure to bear upon the choice of the workmen; but since the rights of property which enforce such pressure are not repugnant to the principles of natural liberty, neither is such pecuniary pressure repugnant to the law,—the case is therefore outside the scope of the law. The converse case, where the workmen take similar advantage of their employers to bring them to terms, is similarly outside the scope of the common law,—supposing, of course, that there has in neither case been a surrender of individual liberty, a breach of contract, theft, a resort to violence, or threats of violence. So long as there is no overt attempt on life, liberty of the person, or the liberty to buy and sell, the law cannot intervene, unless it be in a precautionary way to prevent prospective violation of personal or property rights.

The 'natural,' conventional freedom of contract is sacred and inalienable. *De facto* freedom of choice is a matter about which the law and the courts are not competent to inquire. By force of the concatenation of industrial processes and the dependence of men's comfort or subsistence upon the orderly working of these processes, the exercise of the rights of ownership in the interests of business may traverse the *de facto* necessities of a group or class; it may even traverse the needs of the community at large, as, e.g., in the conceivable case of an advisedly instituted coal famine; but since these necessities, of comfort or of livelihood, cannot be formulated in terms of the natural freedom of contract, they can, in the nature of the case, give rise to no cognizable grievance and find no legal remedy.

The discrepancy between law and fact in the matter of industrial freedom has had repeated illustration in the court decisions on disputes between bodies of workmen and their employers or owners. These decisions commonly fall out in favor of the employers or owners; that is to say, they go to uphold property rights and the rights of free contract. The courts have been somewhat broadly taken to task by a certain class of observers for alleged partiality to the owners' side in this class of litigation. It has also been pointed out by faultfinders that the higher courts decide, on the whole, more uniformly in favor of the employer-owner than the lower ones, and especially more so than the juries in those cases where juries have found occasion to pass on the law of the case. The like is true as regards suits for damages arising out of injuries sustained by workmen, and so involving the question of the employer's liability. Even a casual scrutiny of the decisions, however, will show that in most cases the decision of the court, whether on the merits of the case or on the constitutionality of the legal provisions involved, is well grounded on the metaphysical basis of natural liberty. That is to say in other words, the decisions will be found on the side of the maintenance of fundamental law and order, 'law and order' having, of course, reference to the inalienable rights of ownership and contract. As should fairly be expected, the higher courts, who are presumably in more intimate touch with the principles of jurisprudence, being more arduously trained and more thoroughly grounded in the law at the same time that they have also presumably a larger endowment of legal acumen,—these higher courts speak more unequivocally for the metaphysical principles and apply them with a surer and firmer touch. In the view of these higher adepts of the law, free contract is so inalienable a natural right of man that not even a statutory enactment will enable a workman to forego its exercise and its responsibility. By metaphysical necessity its exercise attaches to the individual so indefeasibly that it cannot constitutionally be delegated to collective action, whether legislative or corporate. This extreme consequence of the principle of natural liberty has at times aroused indignation in the vulgar; but their grasp of legal principles is at fault. The more closely the logical sequence is followed up, the more convincingly does the legitimacy of such a decision stand out. . .

The ground of sentiment on which rests the popular approval of a government for business ends may be summed up under two heads: patriotism and property. Both of these terms stand for institutional facts that have come down out of a past which differed substantially from the present situation. The substance of both is of the nature of unreasoning sentiment, in the sense that both are insisted on as a matter of course, as self-legitimating grounds of action which, it is felt, not only give expedient rules of conduct, but admit of no question as to their ulterior consequences or their value for the life-purposes of the community. The former of these fundamental institutional habits of thought (perhaps better, habits of mind) runs back to the discipline of early barbarism, through the feudal days of fealty to the earlier days of clan life and clannish animosity. It has therefore the deep-rooted strength given by an extremely protracted discipline of predation and servitude. Under modern conditions it is to be rated as essentially an institutional survival, so ingrained in the populace as to make any appeal to it secure of a response irrespective of the material merits of the contention in whose behalf the appeal is made.

By force of this happy knack of clannish fancy the common man is enabled to feel that he has some sort of metaphysical share in the gains which accrue to the business men who are citizens of the same 'commonwealth'; so that whatever policy furthers the commercial gains of those business men whose domicile is within the national boundaries is felt to be beneficial to all the rest of the population.

The second institutional support of business politics, viz. property, is similarly an outgrowth of the discipline of the past, and similarly, though perhaps in a less degree, out of touch with the discipline of the more recent cultural situation. In the form in which it prevails in the current popular animus, the principle of ownership comes down from the days of handicraft industry and petty trade, as pointed out above. As it is of less ancient and less unbroken descent, so it seems also to be a less secure cultural heritage than the sense of patriotic solidarity. It says that the ownership of property is the material foundation of human well-being, and that this natural right of ownership is sacred, after the manner in which individual life, and more especially national life, is sacred. The habits of life and thought inculcated by joint work under the manorial system and by joint rules under the handicraft system have apparently contributed much to the notion of a solidarity of economic interests, having given the notion such a degree of consistency as has enabled it to persist in the face of a visible discrepancy of interests in later, capitalistic times. Under this current, business regime, business gains are the basis of individual wealth, and the (pseudo) notion of joint acquisition has taken the place of the manorial notion of joint work. The institutional animus of ownership, as it took shape under the discipline of early modern handicraft, awards the ownership of property to the workman who has produced it. By a dialectical conversion of the terms, this metaphysical dictum is made to fit the circumstances of later competitive business by construing acquisition of property to mean production of wealth; so that a business man is looked upon as the putative producer of whatever wealth he acquires. By force of this sophistication the acquisition of property by any person is held to be, not only expedient for the owner, but meritorious as an action serving the common good. Failure to bargain shrewdly or to accumulate more goods than one has produced by the work of one's own hands is looked upon with a feeling of annoyance, as a neglect, not only of opportunity, but of duty. The pecuniary conscience commonly does not, of course, go to quixotic lengths in a public-spirited insistence on everybody's acquiring more than an aliquot part of the aggregate wealth on hand, but it is felt that he best serves the common good who, other things equal, diverts the larger share of the aggregate wealth to his own possession. His acquiring a defensible title to it makes him the putative producer of it.

The natural-rights basis of ownership is by this paralogism preserved intact, and the common man is enabled to feel that the business men in the community add to the aggregate wealth at least as much as they acquire a title to; and the successful business men are at least as well persuaded that such is their relation to the aggregate wealth and to the material well-being of the community at large. So that both the business men whose gains are sought to be enhanced by business politics and the populace by whose means the business gains are secured work together in good faith towards a well-advised business end,—the accumulation of wealth in the hands of those men who are skilled in pecuniary matters. . .

especially national restraint, believing that his one weapon—money—would b more effective in obtaining what he wanted in state legislatures than in Con gress. Thus, of necessity, he precipitates a conflict, instead of establishing a adjustment. He is, therefore, in essence, a revolutionist without being awar of it. . .

And this leads, advancing in an orderly manner step by step, to what is perhaps, to me, the most curious and interesting of all modern intellectua phenomena connected with the specialized mind,—the attitude of the capi talist toward the law. Naturally the capitalist, of all men, might be suppose to be he who would respect and uphold the law most, considering that he i at once the wealthiest and most vulnerable of human beings, when called upo to defend himself by physical force. How defenceless and how incompeten he is in such exigencies, he proved to the world some years ago when h plunged himself and the country into the great Pennsylvania coal strike, wit absolutely no preparation. Nevertheless, in spite of his vulnerability, he is of al citizens the most lawless.* He appears to assume that the law will always b enforced, when he has need of it, by some special personnel whose duty lie that way, while he may evade the law, when convenient, or bring it int contempt, with impunity. The capitalist seems incapable of feeling his responsibility, as a member of the governing class, in this respect, and that he is bound to uphold the law, no matter what the law may be, in order that others may do the like. If the capitalist has bought some sovereign function, and wishes to abuse it for his own behoof, he regards the law which restrains him as a despotic invasion of his constitutional rights, because, with his specialized mind, he cannot grasp the relation of a sovereign function to the nation as a whole. He, therefore, looks upon the evasion of a law devised for public protection, but inimical to him, as innocent or even meritorious.

If an election be lost, and the legislature, which has been chosen by the majority, cannot be pacified by money, but passes some act which promises to be annoying, the first instinct of the capitalist is to retain counsel, not to advise him touching his duty under the law, but to devise a method by which he may elude it, or, if he cannot elude it, by which he may have it annulled as unconstitutional by the courts. The lawyer who suceeds in this branch of practice is certain to win the highest prizes at the bar. And as capital has had now, for more than one or even two generations, all the prizes of the law within its gift, this attitude of capital has had a profound effect upon shaping the American legal mind. The capitalist, as I infer, regards the constitutional form of government which exists in the United States, as a convenient method of obtaining his own way against a majority, but the lawyer has learned to worship it as a fetish. Nor is this astonishing, for, were written constitutions suppressed, he would lose most of his importance and much of his income. Quite honestly, therefore, the American lawyer has come to believe that a sheet of paper soiled with printers' ink and interpreted by half-a-dozen elderly gentlemen snugly dozing in armchairs, has some inherent and marvellous virtue

* In these observations on the intellectual tendencies of capital I speak generally. Not only individual capitalists, but great corporations, exist, who are noble examples of law-abiding and intelligent citizenship. Their rarity, however, and their conspicuousness, seem to prove the general rule.

6. *The capitalist is essentially a revolutionist*

Brooks Adams, *The Theory of Social Revolutions,* 1913 *

As the universe, which at once creates and destroys life, is a complex of infinitely varying forces, history can never repeat itself. It is vain, therefore, to look in the future for some paraphrase of the past. Yet if society be, as I assume it to be, an organism operating on mechanical principles, we may learn enough of those principles to enable us to view, more intelligently than we otherwise should, the social phenomena about us. What we call civilization is, I suspect, only, in proportion to its perfection, a more or less thorough social centralization, while centralization, very clearly, is an effect of applied science. Civilization is accordingly nearly synonymous with centralization, and is caused by mechanical discoveries, which are applications of scientific knowledge. . . And we perceive on a little consideration that from the first great and fundamental discovery of how to kindle fire, every advance in applied science has accelerated social movement, until the discovery of steam and electricity in the eighteenth and nineteenth centuries quickened movement as movement had never been quickened before. And this quickening has caused the rise of those vast cities, which are at once our pride and our terror.

Social consolidation is, however, not a simple problem, for social consolidation implies an equivalent capacity for administration. I take it to be an axiom, that perfection in administration must be commensurate to the bulk and momentum of the mass to be administered, otherwise the centrifugal will overcome the centripetal force, and the mass will disintegrate. In other words, civilization will dissolve. It is in dealing with administration, as I apprehend, that civilizations have usually, though not always, broken down, for it has been on administrative difficulties that revolutions have for the most part supervened. Advances in administration seem to pre-suppose the evolution of new governing classes, since, apparently, no established type of mind can adapt itself to changes in environment, even in slow-moving civilizations, as fast as environments change. Thus a moment arrives when the minds of any given dominant type fail to meet the demands made upon them, and are superseded by a younger type, which in turn is set aside by another still younger, until the limit of the administrative genius of that particular race has been reached. Then disintegration sets in, the social momentum is gradually relaxed, and society sinks back to a level at which it can cohere. To us, however, the most distressing aspect of the situation is, that the social acceleration is progressive in proportion to the activity of the scientific mind which makes mechanical discoveries, and it is, therefore, a triumphant science which produces those ever more rapidly recurring changes in environment to which men must adapt themselves at their peril. As, under the stimulant of modern science, the old types fail to sustain themselves, new types have to be equally rapidly evolved, and the rise of a new governing class is always synonymous with a social

revolution and a redistribution of property. The Industrial Revolutic
almost precisely a century and a half ago, since when the scientific r
continually gained in power, and, during that period, on an average of
two generations, the environment has so far shifted that a social re
has occurred, accompanied by the advent of a new favored class, a
adjustment of wealth. I think that a glance at American history will sl
estimate to be within the truth. At the same time such rapidity of int
mutation is without precedent, and I should suppose that the mental
tion incident thereto must be very considerable. . .

Administration is the capacity of co-ordinating many, and often co
social energies in a single organism, so adroitly that they shall oper
unity. This presupposes the power of recognizing a series of relations
numerous special social interests, with all of which no single man
intimately acquainted. Probably no very highly specialized class can b
in this intellectual quality because of the intellectual isolation inci
specialization; and yet administration or generalization is not only the
upon which social stability rests, but is, possibly, the highest faculty
human mind. It is precisely in this preeminent requisite for success
ernment that I suspect the modern capitalistic class to be weak. The s
the human intellect is necessarily limited, and modern capitalists appear
been evolved under the stress of an environment which demanded e
specialization in the direction of a genius adapted to money-making
highly complex industrial conditions. To this money-making attribute
has been sacrificed, and the modern capitalist not only thinks in te
money, but he thinks in terms of money more exclusively than the
aristocrat or lawyer ever thought in terms of caste. The modern capitali
upon life as a financial combat of a very specialized kind, regulated by
which he understands and has indeed himself concocted, but which is
nized by no one else in the world. He conceives sovereign powers to
sale. He may, he thinks, buy them; and if he buys them; he may us
as he pleases. He believes, for instance, that it is the lawful, nay m
America, that it is the constitutional right of the citizen to buy the n
highways, and, having bought them, to use them as a common carrier
use a horse and a cart upon a public road. He may sell his service to wh
pleases at what price may suit him, and if by doing so he ruins m
cities, it is nothing to him. He is not responsible, for he is not a trustee
public. If he be restrained by legislation, that legislation is in his eye an
sion and an outrage, to be annulled or eluded by any means which w
lead to the penitentiary. He knows nothing and cares less, for the r
which highways always have held, and always must hold, to every ci
population, and if he be asked to inform himself on such subjects he
the suggestion as an insult. He is too specialized to comprehend a socia
tion, even a fundamental one like this, beyond the narrow circle of his
interests. He might, had he so chosen, have evolved a system of governi
railway regulation, and have administered the system personally, or by hi
agents, but he could never be brought to see the advantage to hims
rational concession to obtain a resultant of forces. He resisted all res

by which it can arrest the march of omnipotent Nature. And capital gladly accepts this view of American civilization, since hitherto capitalists have usually been able to select the magistrates who decide their causes, perhaps directly through the intervention of some president or governor whom they have had nominated by a convention controlled by their money, or else, if the judiciary has been elective, they have caused sympathetic judges to be chosen by means of a mechanism like Tammany, which they have frankly bought.

I wish to make myself clearly understood. Neither capitalists nor lawyers are necessarily, or even probably, other than conscientious men. What they do is to think with specialized minds. All dominant types have been more or less specialized, if none so much as this, and this specialization has caused, as I understand it, that obtuseness of perception which has been their ruin when the environment which favored them has changed. All that is remarkable about the modern capitalist is the excess of his excentricity, or his deviation from that resultant of forces to which he must conform. To us, however, at present, neither the morality nor the present mental excentricity of the capitalist is so material as the possibility of his acquiring flexibility under pressure, for it would seem to be almost mathematically demonstrable that he will, in the near future, be subjected to a pressure under which he must develop flexibility or be eliminated. . .

I find it difficult to believe that capital, with its specialized views of what constitutes its advantages, its duties, and its responsibilities, and stimulated by a bar moulded to meet its prejudices and requirements, will ever voluntarily assent to the consolidation of the United States to the point at which the interference of the courts with legislation might be eliminated; because, as I have pointed out, capital finds the judicial veto useful as a means of at least temporarily evading the law, while the bar, taken as a whole, quite honestly believes that the universe will obey the judicial decree. No delusion could be profounder and none, perhaps, more dangerous. . .

7. *In the long run industrial absolutism and democracy cannot exist in the same community*

Louis D. Brandeis, Testimony before the U.S. Commission on Industrial Relations, 23 January 1915 *

. . . Chairman Walsh: Do . . . financial directors, in your opinion, Mr. Brandeis, have sufficient knowledge of industrial conditions and social conditions to qualify them to direct labor policies involving hundreds of thousands of men?

Mr. Brandeis: I should think most of them did not; but what is perhaps more important or fully as important is the fact that neither these same men nor anybody else can properly deal with these problems without a far more intimate knowledge of the facts than it is possible for men to get who undertake

* *Senate Document*, 64th Congress, 1st session, vol. 26, pp. 7659–68 *passim*.

to have a voice in so many different businesses. They are prevented from obtaining an understanding not so much because of their point of view or motive, but because of human limitations. These men have endeavored to cover far more ground than it is possible for men to cover properly, and without an intimate knowledge of the facts they cannot possibly deal with the problems involved.

Chairman Walsh: Does the fact that many large corporations with thousands of stockholders, among whom are large numbers of employees, in any way whatever affect the policy of large corporations?

Mr. Brandeis: I do not believe that the holding of stock by employees—what is practically almost an insignificant participation, considering their percentage to the whole body of stockholders in large corporations—improves the condition of labor in those corporations. I think its effect is rather the opposite. . .

My observation leads me to believe that while there are many contributing causes to unrest, that there is one cause which is fundamental. That is the necessary conflict—the contrast between our political liberty and our industrial absolutism. We are as free politically, perhaps, as free as it is possible for us to be. Every male has his voice and vote; and the law has endeavored to enable, and has succeeded practically, in enabling him to exercise his political franchise without fear. He therefore has his part; and certainly can secure an adequate part in the government of the country in all of its political relations; that is, in all relations which are determined directly by legislation or governmental administration.

On the other hand, in dealing with industrial problems the position of the ordinary worker is exactly the reverse. The individual employee has no effective voice or vote. And the main objection, as I see it, to the very large corporation is, that it makes possible—and in many cases makes inevitable—the exercise of industrial absolutism. It is not merely the case of the individual worker against the employer which, even if he is a reasonably sized employer, presents a serious situation calling for the interposition of a union to protect the individual. But we have the situation of an employer so potent, so well organized, with such concentrated forces and with such extraordinary powers of reserve and the ability to endure against strikes and other efforts of a union, that the relatively loosely organized masses of even strong unions are unable to cope with the situation. We are dealing here with a question, not of motive, but of condition. Now, the large corporation and the managers of the powerful corporation are probably in large part actuated by motives just the same as an employer of a tenth of their size. Neither of them, as a rule, wishes to have his liberty abridged; but the smaller concern usually comes to the conclusion that it is necessary that it should be, where an important union must be dealt with. But when a great financial power has developed—when there exists these powerful organizations, which can successfully summon forces from all parts of the country, which can afford to use tremendous amounts of money in any conflict to carry out what they deem to be their business principle, and can also afford to suffer large losses—you have necessarily a condition of inequality between the two contending forces. Such contests, though undertaken with the best motives and with strong conviction on the part of the corporate managers that they are seeking what is for the best interests not only of the company but of the community, lead to absolutism. The result, in the cases of these large corporations, may be to develop a benevolent absolutism, but it is an absolutism all the same; and it is that which makes the great corporation so dangerous. There develops within the State a state so powerful that the ordinary social and industrial forces existing are insufficient to cope with it.

I noted, Mr. Chairman, that the question you put to me concerning the employees of these large corporations related to their physical condition. Their mental condition is certainly equally important. Unrest, to my mind, never can be removed—and fortunately never can be removed—by mere improvement of the physical and material condition of the workingmen. If it were possible we should run great risk of improving their material condition and reducing their manhood. We must bear in mind all the time, that however much we may desire material improvement and must desire it for the comfort of the individual, that the United States is a democracy, and that we must have, above all things, men. It is the development of manhood to which any industrial and social system should be directed. We Americans are committed not only to social justice in the sense of avoiding things which bring suffering and harm, like unjust distribution of wealth; but we are committed primarily to democracy. The social justice for which we are striving is an incident of our democracy, not the main end. It is rather the result of democracy—perhaps its finest expression—but it rests upon democracy, which implies the rule by the people. And therefore the end for which we must strive is the attainment of rule by the people, and that involves industrial democracy as well as political democracy. That means that the problem of a trade should be no longer the problems of the employer alone. The problems of his business, and it is not the employer's business alone, are the problems of all in it. The union cannot shift upon the employer the responsibility for conditions, nor can the employer insist upon determining, according to his will, the conditions which shall exist. The problems which exist are the problems of the trade; they are the problems of employer and employee. Profit sharing, however liberal, cannot meet the situation. That would mean merely dividing the profits of business. Such a division may do harm or it might do good, dependent on how it is applied.

There must be a division not only of profits, but a division also of responsibilities. The employees must have the opportunity of participating in the decisions as to what shall be their condition and how the business shall be run. They must learn also in sharing that responsibility that they, too, must bear the suffering arising from grave mistakes, just as the employer must. But the right to assist in making the decisions, the right of making their own mistakes, if mistakes there must be, is a privilege which should not be denied to labor. We must insist upon labor sharing the responsibilities for the result of the business. . .

The grave objection to the large business is that, almost inevitably, the form of organization, the absentee stockholdings, and its remote directorship prevent participation, ordinarily, of the employees in such management. The executive officials become stewards in charge of the details of the operation of the business, they alone coming into direct relation with labor. Thus we lose that necessary co-operation which naturally flows from contact between employers and employees—and which the American aspirations for democracy demand. It is in the resultant absolutism that you will find the fundamental cause of prevailing unrest; no matter what is done with the superstructure, no matter how it may be improved in one way or the other, unless we eradicate that fundamental difficulty, unrest will not only continue, but, in my opinion, will grow worse.

Chairman Walsh: From your observation, Mr. Brandeis, what would you say is the responsibility of these so-called absentee owners of industries for conditions, wages, and other conditions existing in the corporations in which they are financially interested?

Mr. Brandeis: . . . The obligation of a director must be held to be absolute. Of course, I said a little while ago that one of the grave objections to this situation with large corporations was the directors did not know what was going on, and they could not therefore pass an intelligent judgment on these questions of the relations between employer and employee, because they did not have the facts.

Nobody can form a judgment that is worth having without a fairly detailed and intimate knowledge of the facts, and the circumstances of these gentlemen, largely bankers of importance, with a multitude of different associations and occupations—the fact that those men cannot know the facts is conclusive to my mind against a system by which the same men are directors in many different companies. I doubt whether anybody who is himself engaged in any important business has time to be a director in more than one large corporation. If he seeks to know about the affairs of that one corporation as much as he should know, not only in the interest of the stockholders, but in the interest of the community, he will have a field for study that will certainly occupy all the time that he has. . .

Chairman Walsh: For the purpose of illustration, take a corporation such as the Steel Corporation and explain what you mean by the democratization of industry. . .

Mr. Brandeis: I think the difficulty of applying it to that corporation, I mean a corporation as large as that and as powerful as that, is this: The unit is so large that it is almost inconceivable that the men in control can be made to realize the necessity of yielding a part of their power to the employee.

Now, when they resist a particular labor policy—for instance, the unionization of shops—and they do resist it violently, most of the officials do so in absolute good faith, convinced that they are doing what they ought to do. They have in mind the excesses of labor unions and their obligations to stockholders to protect the property; and having those things in mind and exaggerating, no doubt, the dangers of the situation, they conclude that they cannot properly submit to so-called union demands. They are apt to believe that it is 'un-American' to do so—and declare it to be contrary to our conceptions of liberty, and the rest. And they believe they are generally sincere in their statements.

The possession of almost absolute power makes them believe this. It is exactly the same condition that presents itself often in the political world.

No doubt the Emperor of Russia means just as well toward each of his subjects as most rulers of a constitutional government or the executives of a republic. But he is subject to a state of mind that he cannot overcome. The fact that he possesses the power and that he is the final judge of what is right or wrong prevents his seeing clearly and doing that which is necessary to give real liberty and freedom.

It is almost inconceivable to my mind that a corporation with powers so concentrated as the Steel Corporation could get to a point where it would be willing to treat with the employees on equal terms. And unless they treat on equal terms then there is no such thing as democratization. The treatment on equal terms with them involves not merely the making of a contract; it must develop into a continuing relation. The making of a contract with a union is a long step. It is collective bargaining—a great advance. But it is only the first step. In order that collective bargaining should result in industrial democracy it must go further and create practically an industrial government—a relation between employer and employee where the problems as they arise from day to day, or from month to month, or from year to year, may come up for consideration and solution as they come up in our political government.

In that way conditions are created best adapted to securing proper consideration of any question arising. The representative of each party is heard—and strives to advance the interest he represents. It is the conflict of these opposing forces which produces the contract ultimately. But adequately to solve the trade problems there must be some machinery which will deal with these problems as they arise from day to day. You must create something akin to a government of the trade before you reach a real approach to democratization. . .

Chairman Walsh: Past experience indicates that large corporations can be trusted to bring about these reforms themselves?

Mr. Brandeis: I think all of our human experience shows that no one with absolute power can be trusted to give it up even in part. That has been the experience with political absolutism; it must prove the same with industrial absolutism. Industrial democracy will not come by gift. It has got to be won by those who desire it. And if the situation is such that a voluntary organization like a labor union is powerless to bring about the democratization of a business, I think we have in this fact some proof that the employing organization is larger than is consistent with the public interest. I mean by larger, is more powerful, has a financial influence too great to be useful to the State; and the State must in some way come to the aid of the workingmen if democratization is to be secured.

Chairman Walsh: Are workmen employed by large corporations in a position to work out their own salvation by trade-union organization today?

Mr. Brandeis: I think our experience, taking the steel trade as an example, has certainly shown that they are not. And this is true also of many other lines of business. Even in the case of corporations very much smaller than the Steel Corporation, where the unions have found it impossible to maintain their position against the highly centralized, well-managed, highly financed company. Such corporations as a means of overcoming union influence and democratization frequently grant their employees more in wages and comforts than the union standards demands. But 'men cannot live by bread alone.' Men must have industrial liberty as well as good wages.

Chairman Walsh: Do you believe that the existing State and Federal legislation is adequately and properly drawn to provide against abuses in industry, so far as the employees are concerned?

Mr. Brandeis: I have grave doubt as to how much can be accomplished by legislation, unless it be to set a limit upon the size of corporate units. I believe in dealing with this labor problem as in dealing with the problem of credit. We must meet this question.

Chairman Walsh: Of what? Excuse me.

Mr. Brandeis: Size. And in dealing with the problem of industrial democracy there underlies all of the difficulties the question of the concentration of power. This factor so important in connection with the subject of credit and in connection with the subject of trusts and monopolies is no less important in treating the labor problem. As long as there is such concentration of power no effort of the working men to secure democratization will be effective. The statement that size is not a crime is entirely correct when you speak of it from the point of motive. But size may become such a danger in its results to the community that the community may have to set limits. A large part of our protective legislation consists of prohibiting things which we find are dangerous, according to common experience. Concentration of power has been shown to be dangerous in a democracy, even though that power may be used beneficently. For instance, on our public highways we put a limit on the size of an autotruck, no matter how well it is run. It may have the most skillful and considerate driver, but its mere size may make it something which the community cannot tolerate, in view of the other uses of the highway and the danger inherent in its occupation to so large an extent by a single vehicle.

Chairman Walsh: Commissioner Lennon has a few questions he would like to ask. . .

Commissioner Lennon: Now, to apply it to the work that the unions have done for physical betterment, increase of wages and limitation of the hours, and the elimination of children like in the coal industry.

Mr. Brandeis: Oh, I think those are all positive gains, unqualified gains.

Commissioner Lennon: Gains for manhood?

Mr. Brandeis: They are all gains for manhood; and we recognize that manhood is what we are striving for in America. We are striving for democracy; we are striving for the development of men. It is absolutely essential in order that men may develop that they be properly fed and properly housed, and that they have proper opportunities of education and recreation. We cannot reach our goal without those things. But we may have all those things and have a nation of slaves. . .

I think the main mistake that the employers have made has been a failure to acquire understanding of the conditions and facts concerning labor. There has been ignorance in this respect on the part of employers—ignorance due in large part to lack of imagination. Employers have not been able to think themselves into the labor position. They do not understand labor and many successful business men have never recognized that labor presents the most important problem in the business. . .

The other cause of employers' difficulties is a failure to think clearly. The employers' refusal to deal with a union is ordinarily due to erroneous reasoning or false sentiment. The man who refuses to deal with the union acts ordinarily from a good motive. He is impressed with 'union dictation.' He is apt to think 'this is my business and the American has the right of liberty of contract.' He honestly believes that he is standing up for a high principle and is willing often to run the risk of having his business ruined rather than abandon that principle. They have not thought out clearly enough that liberty means exercising one's rights consistently with a like exercise of rights by other people; that liberty is distinguished from license in that it is subject to certain restrictions, and that no one can expect to secure liberty in the sense in which we recognize it in America without having his rights curtailed in those respects in which it is necessary to limit them in the general public interest. The failure of many employers to recognize these simple truths is a potent reason why employers have not been willing to deal with unions. . .

I had my first practical experience in dealing with labor problems while acting for manufacturers in the effort to settle or prevent strikes. I found if I wanted to bring about a settlement it was absolutely necessary that the head of the business be brought into the conference. If the employer was a large corporation, nothing less than the president would do, and on the other hand we required the president of the international union to deal with the man in real authority. My effort was to bring these two men together and make each understand the problems of the other. And when I could bring that about, when I could make the union understand the employers' problem, and the employer the union's problem, a settlement was almost certain. The next step was to make the individual employee feel that whatever the system of dealing, either through superintendents or otherwise, that there was no individual in that employ who was so insignificant but that if he believed a wrong was done him, he could, in the last analysis, appeal to the highest official of the corporation. When once that principle was established, the danger of a rupture between employer and employee was usually passed. . .

8. *Democracy's goal is the socialization of industry*

WALTER WEYL, *The New Democracy*, 1912 *

The new spirit is social. Its base is broad. It involves common action and a common lot. It emphasizes social rather than private ethics, social rather than individual responsibility.

This new spirit, which is marked by a social unrest, a new altruism, a changed patriotism, an uncomfortable sense of social guilt, was not born of

* New York, Macmillan, 1912, pp. 279–80, 348–9 *passim*.

any sudden enthusiasm or quickening revelation. It grew slowly in the dark places of men's minds out of the new conditions. The old individualism—carried to its logical sequence—would have meant impotence and social bankruptcy. Individualism struck its frontier when the pioneer struck his, and society, falling back upon itself, found itself. New problems arose, requiring for their solution slight amendments of our former canons of judgment and modes of action. In many spheres of economic life the individual began to find more profit in his undivided share of the common lot than in his chance of individual gain. On this foundation of an individual interest in the common lot, the new social spirit was laid. This egoistic interest, however, was shared by so many interdependent millions, that men passed insensibly from an ideal of reckless individual gaining to a new ideal, which urged the conservation and thrifty utilization of the patrimony of all in the interest of all.

In obedience to this new spirit we are slowly changing our perception and evaluation of the goods of life. We are freeing ourselves from the unique standard of pecuniary preeminence and are substituting new standards of excellence. We are ceasing solely to adore successful greed, and are evolving a tentative theory of the trusteeship of wealth. We are emphasizing the overlordship of the public over property and rights formerly held to be private. A new insistence is laid upon human life, upon human happiness. What is attainable by the majority—life, health, leisure, a share in our natural resources, a dignified existence in society—is contended for by the majority against the opposition of men who hold exorbitant claims upon the continent. The inner soul of our new democracy is not the unalienable rights, negatively and individualistically interpreted, but those same rights, 'life, liberty, and the pursuit of happiness,' extended and given a social interpretation.

It is this social interpretation of rights which characterizes the democracy coming into being, and makes it different in kind from the so-called individualistic democracy of Jefferson and Jackson. It is this social concept which is the common feature of many widely divergent democratic policies. The close of the merely expansive period of America showed that an individualistic democracy must end in its own negation, the subjection of the individual to an economically privileged class of rich men. The political weapons of our forefathers might avail against political despotism, but were farcically useless against economic aggression. The right of habeas corpus, the right to bear arms, the rights of free speech and free press could not secure a job to the gray-haired citizen, could not protect him against low wages or high prices, could not save him from a jail sentence for the crime of having no visible means of support. The force of our individualistic democracy might suffice to supplant one economic despot by another, but it could not prevent economic despotism.

To-day no democracy is possible in America except a socialized democracy, which conceives of society as a whole and not as a more or less adventitious assemblage of myriads of individuals. . .

To-day the chief restrictions upon liberty are economic, not legal, and the chief prerogatives desired are economic, not political. It is a curious, but not inexplicable, development, moreover, that our constitutional provisions, safeguarding our political liberties, are often used to deprive us of economic liberties. The constitutional provision that 'no one shall be deprived of life, liberty, or property without due process of law' has seldom prevented an Alabama Negro from illegally being sent to the chain gang, but it has often prevented the people of a State from securing relief from great interstate corporations. The restraints upon the liberty of the poor are to-day economic. A law forbidding a woman to work in the textile mills at night is a law increasing rather than restricting *her* liberty, simply because it takes from the employer *his* former right to compel her through sheer economic pressure to work at night when she would prefer to work by day. So a law against adulteration of food products increases the economic liberty of food purchasers, as a tenement house law increases the liberty of tenement dwellers.

In two respects, the democracy towards which we are striving differs from that of to-day. Firstly, the democracy of to-morrow, being a real and not a merely formal democracy, does not content itself with the mere right to vote, with political immunities, and generalizations about the rights of men. Secondly, it is a plenary, socialized democracy, emphasizing social rather than merely individual aims, and carrying over its ideals from the political into the industrial and social fields.

Because of this wideness of its aims, the new spirit, in a curiously cautious, conservative way, is profoundly revolutionary. The mind of the people slowly awakens to the realization of the people's needs; the new social spirit gradually undermines the crust of inherited and promulgated ideas; the rising popular will overflows old barriers and converts former institutions to new uses. It is a deep-lying, potent, swelling movement. It is not noiseless, for rotten iron cracks with a great sound, and clamor accompanies the decay of profit-yielding privileges. It is not uncontested, for men, threatened with the loss of a tithe of their pretensions, sometimes fight harder than the wholly disinherited. It does not proceed everywhere at equal pace; the movement is not uniform nor uninterrupted. And yet, measured by decades, or even by years, the revolution grows. . .

What the democracy desires, however, is not government ownership for itself, but merely as much government ownership, regulation, or control as may be necessary to a true socialization of industry. The democracy's goal —the socialization of industry—is a viewing of our manifold business life from the standpoint of society and not solely from that of the present beneficiaries or directors of industry. It is such a coördination of business as will permanently give the greatest happiness and the highest development to the largest number of individuals, and to society as a whole.

Socialization is thus a point of view. It is less a definite industrial program than the animating ideal of a whole industrial policy. It is a standard by which industrial conditions and industrial developments must be adjudged.

In certain industries socialization may involve a government monopoly. In others, it may mean government operation in competition with private businesses; or a government ownership with private management; or a division of the profits of private industries. Or it may involve a thoroughgoing regulation of an industry, prescribing rates, prices, services, wages, hours, labor conditions, dividends, and the internal economy in general. Or, socialization may mean a lesser regulation; or mere publicity; or encouragement; or subsidies; or legal recognition; or simply the prescribing of a minimum capital or of a preliminary training. Again, socialization may mean a deflection of the stream of wealth which flows from an industry, a deflection accomplished by tax laws, or by laws altering the conditions of conveying property. Finally, socialization may be accomplished without direct governmental regulation. How far the government shall interfere depends on the business. . .

We are now beginning to realize that our present acute social unrest is not due to an attempt to return to the conditions and principles of the eighteenth century, but is merely a symptom of a painfully evolving democracy, at once industrial, political, and social. We are beginning to realize that our stumbling progress towards this democracy of to-morrow results from the efforts, not of a single class, but of the general community; that the movement is not primarily a class war, but, because it has behind it forces potentially so overwhelming, has rather the character of a national adjustment; that the movement does not proceed from an impoverished people, nor from the most impoverished among the people, nor from a people growing, or doomed to grow, continually poorer, but proceeds, on the contrary, from a population growing in wealth, intelligence, political power, and solidarity. We are awakening to the fact that this movement, because of the heterogeneous character of those who further it, is tentative, conciliatory, compromising, evolutionary, and legal, proceeding with a minimum of friction through a series of partial victories; that the movement is influenced and colored by American conditions and traditions, proceeding, with but few violent breaks, out of our previous industrial, political, and intellectual development and out of our material and moral accumulations, and utilizing, even while reforming and reconstituting, our economic and legal machinery. It is a movement dependent upon a large social surplus; a movement which grows in vigor, loses in bitterness, and otherwise takes its character from the growing fund of our national wealth, which gives it its motive and impetus. Finally, it is a movement which in the very course of its fulfillment develops broad and ever broadening industrial, political, and social programs, which aim at the ultimate maintenance of its results.

9. *Men will do almost anything but govern themselves*

WALTER LIPPMANN, *Drift and Mastery*, 1914 *

When the trusts appeared, when the free land was gone, and America had been congested into a nation, the only philosophy with any weight of tradition behind it was a belief in the virtues of the spontaneous, enterprising, untrained and unsocialized man. Trust promoters cried: Let us alone. The

* Copyright 1914 by Henry Holt Co. Reprinted by permission of Holt, Rinehart and Winston, Inc. Pages 178–89, 268–72, 333–4 *passim.*

little business men cried: We're the natural men, so let us alone. And the public cried: We're the most natural of all, so please do stop interfering with us. Muckraking gave an utterance to the small business men and to the larger public, who dominated reform politics. What did they do? They tried by all the machinery and power they could muster to restore a business world in which each man could again be left to his own will—a world that needed no coöperative intelligence. In the Sherman Act is symbolized this deliberate attempt to recreate an undeliberate society. No group of people, except the socialists, wished to take up the enormous task of disciplining business to popular need. For the real American was dreaming of the Golden Age in which he could drift with impunity.

But there has arisen in our time a large group of people who look to the future. They talk a great deal about their ultimate goal. Many of them do not differ in any essential way from those who dream of a glorious past. They put Paradise before them instead of behind them. They are going to be so rich, so great, and so happy some day, that any concern about to-morrow seems a bit sordid. They didn't fall from Heaven, as the reactionaries say, but they are going to Heaven with the radical. Now this habit of reposing in the sun of a brilliant future is very enervating. It opens a chasm between fact and fancy, and the whole fine dream is detached from the living zone of the present. At the only point where effort and intelligence are needed, that point where to-day is turning into to-morrow, there these people are not found. At the point where human direction counts most they do not direct. . .

Then too there are the darlings of evolution. They are quite certain that evolution, as they put it, is ever onward and upward. . .

In a constructive social movement the harm done is immeasurable. The most vivid illustration is that of the old-fashioned, fatalistic Marxian socialists. They have an implicit faith that human destiny is merely the unfolding of an original plan, some of the sketches of which are in their possession, thanks to the labors of Karl Marx. Strictly speaking, these men are not revolutionists as they believe themselves to be; they are the interested pedants of destiny. They are God's audience, and they know the plot so well that occasionally they prompt Him. In their system all that education, unions, leadership and thought can do is to push along what by the theory needs no pushing. These socialists are like the clown Marceline at the Hippodrome, who is always very busy assisting in labor that would be done whether he were there or not. They face the ancient dilemma of fatalism: whatever they do is right, and nothing they do matters. Go to almost any socialist meeting and you'll hear it said that socialism would come if the Socialist Party had never been heard from. Perhaps so. But why organize a Socialist Party?

Of course, socialists don't act upon their theory. They are too deeply impressed with the evil that exists, too eager for the future that they see, to trust entirely in the logic of events. They do try to shape that future. But their old fatalism hampers them enormously the moment any kind of action is proposed. . .

Men will do almost anything but govern themselves. They don't want the responsibility. In the main, they are looking for some benevolent guardian, be it a 'good man in office' or a perfect constitution, or the evolution of nature. They want to be taken in charge. If they have to think for themselves they turn either to the past or to a distant future: but they manage to escape the real effort of the imagination which is to weave a dream into the turning present. They trust to destiny, a quick one or a slow one, and the whole task of judging events is avoided. They turn to automatic devices: human initiative can be ignored. They forbid evil, and then they feel better. They settle on a particular analogy, or a particular virtue, or a particular policy, and trust to luck that everything else will take care of itself.

But no one of these substitutes for self-government is really satisfactory, and the result is that a state of chronic rebellion appears. That is our present situation. The most hopeful thing about it is that through the confusion we can come to some closer understanding of why the modern man lacks stability, why his soul is scattered. We may, perhaps, be able to see a little better just what self-government implies. . .

There is indeed a dreaming quality in life: moved as it is from within by unconscious desires and habits, and from without by the brute forces of climate and soil and wind and tide. There are stretches in every day when we have no sense of ourselves at all, and men often wake up with a start: 'Have I lived as long as I'm supposed to have lived? . . . Here I am, this kind of person who has passed through these experiences—well, I didn't quite know it.'

That, I think, is the beginning of what we call reflection: a desire to realize the drama in which we are acting, to be awake during our own lifetime. When we cultivate reflection by watching ourselves and the world outside, the thing we call science begins. We draw the hidden into the light of consciousness, record it, compare phases of it, note its history, experiment, reflect on error, and we find that our conscious life is no longer a trivial iridescence, but a progressively powerful way of domesticating the brute.

This is what mastery means: the substitution of conscious intention for unconscious striving. Civilization, it seems to me, is just this constant effort to introduce plan where there has been clash, and purpose into the jungles of disordered growth. But to shape the world nearer to the heart's desire requires a knowledge of the heart's desire and of the world. You cannot throw yourself blindly against unknown facts and trust to luck that the result will be satisfactory. . .

There have been fine things produced in the world without intention. Most of our happiness has come to us, I imagine, by the fortunate meeting of events. But happiness has always been a precarious incident, elusive and shifting in an unaccountable world. In love, especially, men rejoice and suffer through what are to them mysterious ways. Yet when it is suggested that the intelligence must invade our unconscious life, men shrink from it as from dangerous and clumsy meddling. It is dangerous and clumsy now, but it is the path we shall have to follow. We have to penetrate the dreaming brute in ourselves, and make him answerable to our waking life.

It is a long and difficult process, one for which we are just beginning to find a method. But there is no other way that offers any hope. To shove our impulses underground by the taboo is to force them to virulent and uncontrolled expression. To follow impulse wherever it leads means the satisfaction of one impulse at the expense of all the others. The glutton and the rake can satisfy only their gluttonous and rakish impulses, and that isn't enough for happiness. What civilized men aim at is neither whim nor taboo, but a frank recognition of desire, disciplined by a knowledge of what is possible, and ordered by the conscious purpose of their lives. . .

There are people who think that rebellion is an inevitable accompaniment of progress. I don't see why it should be. If it is possible to destroy, as I think we are doing, the very basis of authority, then change becomes a matter of invention and deliberate experiment. No doubt there is a long road to travel before we attain such a civilization. But it seems to me that we have every right to look forward to it—to a time when childhood will cease to be assaulted by bogeys, when eagerness for life will cease to be a sin. There is no more reason why everyone should go through the rebellions of our time than that everyone should have to start a suffrage movement to secure his vote.

To idealize rebellion is simply to make a virtue out of necessity. It shows more clearly than anything else that the sheer struggle for freedom is an exhausting thing, so exhausting that the people who lead it are often unable to appreciate its uses. But just as the men who founded democracy were more concerned with the evils of the kingly system than they were with the possibilities of self-government, so it is with working men and women, and with all those who are in revolt against the subtle tyrannies of the school and the home and the creed. Only with difficulty does the affirmative vision emerge.

10. *Human freedom consists in perfect adjustments of human interests, human activities and human energies*

WOODROW WILSON, *The New Freedom*, 1913 *

. . . The life of America is not the life that it was twenty years ago; it is not the life that it was ten years ago. We have changed our economic conditions, absolutely, from top to bottom; and, with our economic society, the organization of our life. The old political formulas do not fit the present problems; they read now like documents taken out of a forgotten age. . . We are facing the necessity of fitting a new social organization, as we did once fit the old organization, to the happiness and prosperity of the great body of citizens; for we are conscious that the new order of society has not been made to fit and provide the convenience or prosperity of the average man. The life of the nation has grown infinitely varied. It does not centre now upon questions of governmental structure or of the distribution of governmental powers. It centres upon questions of the very structure and operation of society itself, of which government is only the instrument. Our development has run so fast and so far along the lines sketched in the earlier day of constitutional definition, has so crossed and interlaced those lines, has piled upon them such novel structures of trust and combination, has elaborated within them a life so manifold, so full of forces which transcend the boundaries of the country itself and fill the eyes of the world, that a new nation seems to have been created which the old formulas do not fit or afford a vital interpretation of.

We have come upon a very different age from any that preceded us. We have come upon an age when we do not do business in the way in which we used to do business,—when we do not carry on any of the operations of manufacture, sale, transportation, or communication as men used to carry them on. There is a sense in which in our day the individual has been submerged. In most parts of our country men work, not for themselves, not as partners in the old way in which they used to work, but generally as employees,—in a higher or lower grade,—of great corporations. There was a time when corporations played a very minor part in our business affairs, but now they play the chief part, and most men are the servants of corporations. . .

Yesterday, and ever since history began, men were related to one another as individuals. . . To-day, the everyday relationships of men are largely with great impersonal concerns, with organizations, not with other individual men. . .

In this new age we find, for instance, that our laws with regard to the relations of employer and employee are in many respects wholly antiquated and impossible. They were framed for another age, which nobody now living remembers, which is, indeed, so remote from our life that it would be difficult for many of us to understand it if it were described to us. The employer is now generally a corporation or a huge company of some kind; the employee is one of hundreds or of thousands brought together, not by individual masters whom they know and with whom they have personal relations, but by agents of one sort or another. Workingmen are marshaled in great numbers for the performance of a multitude of particular tasks under a common discipline. They generally use dangerous and powerful machinery, over whose repair and renewal they have no control. New rules must be devised with regard to their obligations and their rights, their obligations to their employers and their responsibilities to one another. Rules must be devised for their protection, for their compensation when injured, for their support when disabled.

There is something very new and very big and very complex about these new relations of capital and labor. A new economic society has sprung up, and we must effect a new set of adjustments. We must not pit power against weakness. The employer is generally, in our day, as I have said, not an individual, but a powerful group; and yet the workingman when dealing with his employer is still, under our existing law, an individual. . .

Our modern corporations employ thousands, and in some instances hundreds of thousands, of men. The only persons whom you see or deal with are local superintendents or local representatives of a vast organization, which is not like anything that the workingmen of the time in which our laws were framed knew anything about. A little group of workingmen, seeing their employer every day, dealing with him in a personal way, is one thing, and the modern body of labor engaged as employees of the huge enterprises that spread all over the country, dealing with men of whom they can form no personal conception, is another thing. A very different thing. You never saw a corporation, any more than you ever saw a government. Many a workingman to-day never saw the body of men who are conducting the industry in which he is employed. And they never saw him. What they know about him is written in ledgers and books and letters, in the correspondence of the office, in the reports of the superintendents. He is a long way off from them.

So what we have to discuss is, not wrongs which individuals intentionally do,—I do not believe there are a great many of those,—but the wrongs of a system. . . The truth is, we are all caught in a great economic system which is heartless. The modern corporation is not engaged in business as an individual. When we deal with it, we deal with an impersonal element, an immaterial piece of society. A modern corporation is a means of co-operation in the conduct of an enterprise which is so big that no one man can conduct it, and which the resources of no one man are sufficient to finance. . . Men begin to pool their earnings, little piles, big piles. A certain number of men are elected by the stockholders to be directors, and these directors elect a president. This president is the head of the undertaking, and the directors are its managers. . .

And do our laws take note of this curious state of things? Do they even attempt to distinguish between a man's act as a corporation director and as an individual? They do not. Our laws still deal with us on the basis of the old system. The law is still living in the dead past which we have left behind. . .

American industry is not free, as once it was free; American enterprise is not free; the man with only a little capital is finding it harder to get into the field, more and more impossible to compete with the big fellow. Why? Because the laws of this country do not prevent the strong from crushing the weak. That is the reason, and because the strong have crushed the weak the strong dominate the industry and economic life of this country. No man can deny that the lines of endeavor have more and more narrowed and stiffened; no man who knows anything about the development of industry in this country can have failed to observe that the larger kinds of credit are more and more difficult to obtain, unless you obtain them upon the terms of uniting your efforts with those who already control the industries of the country; and nobody can fail to observe that any man who tries to set himself up in competition with any process of manufacture which has been taken under the control of large combinations of capital will presently find himself either squeezed out or obliged to sell and allow himself to be absorbed.

There is a great deal that needs reconstruction in the United States. I should like to take a census of the business men,—I mean the rank and file of the business men,—as to whether they think that business conditions in this country, or rather whether the organization of business in this country, is satisfactory or not. I know what they would say if they dared. If they could vote secretly they would vote overwhelmingly that the present organization of business was meant for the big fellows and was not meant for the little fellows; that it was meant for those who are at the top and was meant to exclude those who are at the bottom; that it was meant to shut out beginners, to prevent new entries in the race, to prevent the building up of competitive enterprises that would interfere with the monopolies which the great trusts have built up. . . .

The originative part of America, the part of America that makes new enterprises, the part into which the ambitious and gifted workingman makes his way up, the class that saves, that plans, that organizes, that presently spreads its enterprises until they have a national scope and character,—that middle class is being more and more squeezed out by the processes which we have been taught to call processes of prosperity. Its members are sharing prosperity, no doubt; but what alarms me is that they are not *originating* prosperity. No country can afford to have its prosperity originated by a small controlling class. The treasury of America does not lie in the brains of the small body of men now in control of the great enterprises that have been concentrated under the direction of a very small number of persons. The treasury of America lies in those ambitions, those energies, that cannot be restricted to a special favored class. It depends upon the inventions of unknown men, upon the originations of unknown men, upon the ambitions of unknown men. Every country is renewed out of the ranks of the unknown, not out of the ranks of those already famous and powerful and in control.

There has come over the land that un-American set of conditions which enables a small number of men who control the government to get favors from the government; by those favors to exclude their fellows from equal business opportunity; by those favors to extend a network of control that will presently dominate every industry in the country, and so make men forget the ancient time when America lay in every hamlet. . .

We used to think in the old-fashioned days when life was very simple that all that government had to do was to put on a policeman's uniform, and say, 'Now don't anybody hurt anybody else.' We used to say that the ideal of government was for every man to be left alone and not interfered with, except when he interfered with somebody else; and that the best government was the government that did as little governing as possible. That was the idea that obtained in Jefferson's time. But we are coming now to realize that life is so complicated that we are not dealing with the old conditions, and that the law has to step in and create new conditions under which we may live, the conditions which will make it tolerable for us to live. . . Whenever bodies of men employ bodies of men, it ceases to be a private relationship. . .

. . . Our government has been for the past few years under the control of heads of great allied corporations with special interests. It has not controlled these interests and assigned them a proper place in the whole system of business; it has submitted itself to their control. As a result, there have grown up vicious systems and schemes of governmental favoritism (the most obvious being the extravagant tariff), far-reaching in effect upon the whole fabric of life, touching to his injury every inhabitant of the land, laying unfair and impossible handicaps upon competitors, imposing taxes in every direction, stifling everywhere the free spirit of American enterprise. . .

The old order changeth—changeth under our very eyes, not quietly and equably, but swiftly and with the noise and heat and tumult of reconstruction. . .

We are upon the eve of a great reconstruction. It calls for creative statesmanship as no age has done since that great age in which we set up the government under which we live, that government which was the admiration of the world until it suffered wrongs to grow up under it which have made many of our own compatriots question the freedom of our institutions and preach revolution against them. I do not fear revolution. I have unshaken faith in the power of America to keep its self-possession. Revolution will come in peaceful guise, as it came when we put aside the crude government of the Confederation and created the great Federal Union which governs individuals, not States, and which has been these hundred and thirty years our vehicle of progress. Some radical changes we must make in our law and practice. Some reconstructions we must push forward, which a new age and new circumstances impose upon us. But we can do it all in calm and sober fashion, like statesmen and patriots. . .

There are two theories of government that have been contending with each other ever since government began. One of them is the theory which in America is associated with the name of a very great man, Alexander Hamilton. A great man, but, in my judgment, not a great American. He did not think in terms of American life. Hamilton believed that the only people who could understand government, and therefore the only people who were qualified to conduct it, were the men who had the biggest financial stake in the commercial and industrial enterprises of the country.

That theory, though few have now the hardihood to profess it openly, has been the working theory upon which our government has lately been conducted. It is astonishing how persistent it is. It is amazing how quickly the political party which had Lincoln for its first leader,—Lincoln, who not only denied, but in his own person so completely disproved the aristocratic theory, —it is amazing how quickly that party, founded on faith in the people, forgot the precepts of Lincoln and fell under the delusion that the 'masses' needed the guardianship of 'men of affairs.'

For indeed, if you stop to think about it, nothing could be a greater departure from original Americanism, from faith in the ability of a confident, resourceful, and independent people, than the discouraging doctrine that somebody has got to provide prosperity for the rest of us. And yet that is exactly the doctrine on which the government of the United States has been conducted lately. . . The gentlemen whose ideas have been sought are the big manufacturers, the bankers, and the heads of the great railroad combinations. The masters of the government of the United States are the combined capitalists and manufacturers of the United States. It is written over every intimate page of the records of Congress, it is written all through the history of conferences at the White House, that the suggestions of economic policy in this country have come from one source, not from many sources. The benevolent guardians, the kind-hearted trustees who have taken the troubles of government off our hands, have become so conspicuous that almost anybody can write out a list of them. They have become so conspicuous that their names are mentioned upon almost every political platform. The men who have undertaken the interesting job of taking care of us do not force us to requite them with anonymously directed gratitude. We know them by name. . .

The government of our country cannot be lodged in any special class. The policy of a great nation cannot be tied up with any particular set of interests. I want to say, again and again, that my arguments do not touch the character of the men to whom I am opposed. I believe that the very wealthy men who have got their money by certain kinds of corporate enterprise have closed in their horizon, and that they do not see and do not understand the rank and file of the people. It is for that reason that I want to break up the little coterie that has determined what the government of the nation should do. . .

No group of men less than the majority has a right to tell me how I have got to live in America. I will submit to the majority, because I have been trained to do it,—though I may sometimes have my private opinion even of the majority. I do not care how wise, how patriotic, the trustees may be, I have never heard of any group of men in whose hands I am willing to lodge the liberties of America in trust. . .

THE LIBERATION OF A PEOPLE'S VITAL ENERGIES

What is liberty? You say of the locomotive that it runs free. What do you mean? You mean that its parts are so assembled and adjusted that friction is reduced to a minimum, and that it has perfect adjustment. . . Human freedom consists in perfect adjustments of human interests and human activities and human energies.

Now, the adjustments necessary between individuals, between individuals and the complex institutions amidst which they live, and between those institutions and the government, are infinitely more intricate to-day than ever before. . . Life has become complex; there are many more elements, more parts, to it than ever before. And, therefore, it is harder to keep everything adjusted,—and harder to find out where the trouble lies when the machine gets out of order.

You know that one of the interesting things that Mr. Jefferson said in those early days of simplicity which marked the beginnings of our government was that the best government consisted in as little governing as possible. And there is still a sense in which that is true. It is still intolerable for the government to interfere with our individual activities except where it necessary to interfere with them in order to free them. But I feel confident that if Jefferson were living in our day he would see what we see: that the individual is caught in a great confused nexus of all sorts of complicated circumstances, and that to let him alone is to leave him helpless as against the obstacles with which he has to contend, and that, therefore, law in our day must come to the assistance of the individual. It must come to his assistance to see that he gets fair play; that is all, but that is much. Without the watchful interference, the resolute interference, of the government, there can be no fair play between individuals and such powerful institutions as the trusts. Freedom to-day is something more than being let alone. The program of a government of freedom must in these days be positive, not negative merely. . .

I believe in human liberty as I believe in the wine of life. There is no salvation for men in the pitiful condescensions of industrial masters. Guardians have no place in a land of freemen. Prosperity guaranteed by trustees has no prospect of endurance. Monopoly means the atrophy of enterprise. If monopoly persists, monopoly will always sit at the helm of the government. I do not expect to see monopoly restrain itself. If there are men in this country big enough to own the government of the United States, they are going to own it; what we have to determine now is whether we are big enough, whether we are men enough, whether we are free enough, to take possession again of the government which is our own. . .

I do not believe that America is securely great because she has great men in her now. America is great in proportion as she can make sure of having great men in the next generation. She is rich in her unborn children; rich, that is to say, if those unborn children see the sun in a day of opportunity, see the sun when they are free to exercise their energies as they will. If they open their eyes in a land where there is no special privilege, then we shall come into a new era of American greatness and American liberty; but if they open their eyes in a country where they must be employees or nothing, if they open their eyes in a land of merely regulated monopoly, where all the conditions of industry are determined by small groups of men, then they will see an America such as the founders of this Republic would have wept to think of. . .

Since their day the meaning of liberty has deepened. But it has not ceased to be a fundamental demand of the human spirit, a fundamental necessity for the life of the soul. And the day is at hand when it shall be realized on this consecrated soil,—a New Freedom,—a Liberty widened and deepened to match the broadened life of man in modern America. . .

SELECTED REFERENCES

John Chamberlain, *Farewell to Reform: Being a History of the Rise, Life and Decay of the Progressive Mind in America*, New York, Liveright, 1932.

Thomas C. Cochran and William Miller, *The Age of Enterprise*, New York, Macmillan, 1942.

A Crossroads of Freedom: The 1912 Campaign Speeches of Woodrow Wilson, John Wells Davidson, ed., New Haven, Yale University Press, 1956.

Chester McArthur Destler, *American Radicalism, 1865–1901*, New London, Connecticut College, 1946.

George Raymond Geiger, *The Philosophy of Henry George*, New York, Macmillan, 1933.

Eric Goldman, *Rendezvous with Destiny: A History of Modern American Reform*, New York, Knopf, 1952.

Richard Hofstadter, *Social Darwinism in American Thought*, Philadelphia, University of Pennsylvania Press, 1945.

———, *The Age of Reform*, New York, Knopf, 1955.

E. R. Lewis, *A History of American Political Thought from the Civil War to the World War*, New York, Macmillan, 1937.

Max Lerner, *The Mind and Faith of Justice Holmes*, Boston, Little, Brown, 1945.

A. T. Mason, 'Liberalism: Dilemma,' *Journal of Social Philosophy*, April 1938.

A. T. Mason (and others), *The Democratic Process: Lectures on the American Liberal Tradition*, New London, Connecticut College, 1948.

Louis S. Reed, *The Labor Philosophy of Samuel Gompers*, New York, Columbia University Press, 1930.

Thomas G. Shearman, 'Henry George's Mistakes,' *The Forum*, September 1889.

Woodrow Wilson, 'The Character of Democracy in the United States.' Published in the volume of essays, *An Old Master and Other Essays*, New York, Scribner's, 1893.

XVII

JUDICIAL RESPONSE

By the turn of the century the Supreme Court had become the crucial factor in the march of social democracy. Rarely had the country been more conscious of that venerable institution. Winning favor were the interventionist views of Associate Justice David J. Brewer (1837–1910). In a speech before the New York State Bar Association, 17 January 1893, he dropped his judicial robes to proclaim Herbert Spencer's eternal verities. 'The many,' Brewer complained, 'attempted to transfer to themselves through political power the wealth they lacked the ability or patience to earn in the ordinary pursuit of their business.' This 'movement of coercion' ran counter to the primary end of free government: private property. The Justice cited 'the black flag of anarchism, flaunting destruction of property,' and 'the red flag of socialism, inviting a redistribution of property.' Whether in the hands of a monarch or a majority, he noted soberly, 'power always chafes at but needs restraint.'

Brewer admitted that, 'within limits,' the movement of coercion in legislative halls and in trade unions was beneficial. Needed were safeguards against excess. What more logical agency 'to lift the restraining hand than the courts of the land?' Brewer was convinced that 'the salvation of the nation, the permanence of government . . . rests upon the independence and vigor of the judiciary.'

Later that year James Bradley Thayer (1854–1902), professor of constitutional law at Harvard and an active member of the American Bar Association, made the now classic retort to judicial aggrandizement. Justice Frankfurter has identified this selection as 'the most important single essay' on American constitutional law.

Ignoring the inflammatory crusades so frightening to Brewer, Thayer calmly addressed himself to the nature and limits of judicial power. The burden of his closely reasoned analysis was a solemn warning that judicial *review* did not imply judicial *supremacy*. So restricted was the scope of judicial review that 'much which is harmful *and* unconstitutional may take effect without any capacity in the courts to prevent it.' (Italics added.) In the face of Brewer's unblushing ukase—'strengthen the judiciary,' Thayer pleaded that the judicial function was 'merely that of fixing the outside border of reasonable legislative action.' Power of such modest dimension would leave the courts 'a great and stately jurisdiction.' 'It will only imperil the whole of it,' Thayer warned, 'if it is sought to give them more.'

In 1894 William Howard Taft, later both President and Chief Justice, entered the fray on the side of property. In a particularly urgent address to the graduating class of the Michigan Law School, entitled 'The Right of Private Property,' the young circuit court judge called for judicial intervention against social legislation. The security of private property against the force of numbers must depend upon the courts, informed and strengthened by the bar. He urged members of the graduating class, at the threshold of their professional careers, to return to their various communities and become molders of public opinion. Whether working as public figures, politicians, or private citizens, they must not cease to be lawyers; they must not forget that the Constitution they are sworn to support and defend 'secured as sacred the right of private property.'

Taft's views were clearly at odds with those of his sometime benefactor, mentor, and adviser—Theodore Roosevelt (1858–1919). 'I do not at all like the social conditions at present,' President Roosevelt observed. T.R. berated the 'dull, purblind folly of the very rich men,' 'their greed and arrogance, and the way in which they have unduly prospered by the help of the ablest lawyers, and too often through the weakness or shortsightedness of judges. . .' For the 'Rough Rider,' moreover, the presidency—not the Court—was the proper locus of power for resolving the conflict between 'political democracy and industrial absolutism.'

As if in response to Taft's plea, the Supreme Court itself rushed to the rescue, the fateful year being 1895. In a single term the Justices hampered enforcement of the Sherman Anti-Trust Act, barred a direct federal income tax, and exalted the injunction-contempt power of the federal courts over organized labor. Ten years later a divided Court struck down a state law regulating the working hours of bakers, provoking Justice Holmes's scathing dissent:

> The Fourteenth Amendment does not enact Mr. Herbert Spencer's *Social Statics* . . . A Constitution is not intended to embody a particular economic theory, whether of paternalism and organic relation of the citizen to the state or of laissez-faire. It was made for people of fundamentally differing views, and the accident of our finding certain opinions natural and familiar or novel and even shocking ought not to conclude our judgment upon the question whether statutes embodying them conflict with the Constitution of the United States. [Dissenting opinion in Lochner *v.* New York, 198 U.S. 45 (1905)]

Oliver Wendell Holmes, Jr., (1841–1935), Boston Brahmin, famous son of a famous father, spent most of his life as a judge, first on the Supreme Judicial Court of Massachusetts, and from 1902 to 1933 as an Associate Justice of the United States Supreme Court. Holmes discerned the stubborn negativism in *status quo* liberals, like Justice Brewer, who forgot that 'to rest upon formula is a slumber that, prolonged, means death.' Holmes also distrusted 'the come-outers,' 'the greatest bores in the world,' 'cocksure of a thousand nostrums.' His liberalism was a by-product of ingrained skepticism that led to rejection of any and all absolutes whether in economics, ethics, or politics. Lacking any sensitivity to the danger of inaction, Holmes was disinclined to shape social forces constructively. His famed liberalism, therefore, must be measured primarily in terms of his rare open-mindedness in an age when most lawyers and judges were singularly obstinate and obtuse.

With the development of substantive due process as a shield against state regulation, solidified by the *Lochner* decision of 1905, the constitutional revolution was complete. The Supreme Court had established itself as final arbiter of social and economic policy. Government at both state and national levels was stymied in its attempts to control the abuses of property. The cautionary warnings of James Bradley Thayer and the forward-looking statesmanship of Theodore Roosevelt had been ignored.

Further warnings against judicial supremacy were expressed in 1908. In a landmark article, 'Common Law and Legislation,' Roscoe Pound took up the cudgels in behalf of judicial restraint:

> Formerly it was argued that common law was superior to legislation because it was customary and rested upon the consent of the governed. Today we recognize that the so-called custom is a custom of judicial decision, not a custom of popular action. We recognize that legislation is the more truly democratic form of law-making. We see in legislation the more direct and accurate expression of the general will. We are told that law-making of the future will consist in putting the sanction of society on what has been worked out in the sociological laboratory. That courts cannot conduct such laboratories is self-evident. Courts are fond of saying that they apply old principles to new situations. But at times they must apply new principles to situations both old and new. The new principles are in legislation. The old principles are in common law. The former are as much to be respected and made effective as the latter—probably more so as our legislation improves. The public cannot be relied upon permanently to tolerate judicial obstruction or nullification of the social policies to which more and more it is compelled to be committed.

The same year Louis D. Brandeis, the militant Boston lawyer, accepted Justice Peckham's challenge in Lochner *v.* New York (1905) that a relation between health and the working hours of bakers could not 'in fact' be established in the legislative laboratory. The famous 'Brandeis Brief' in Muller *v.* Oregon (1908) helped persuade a hostile Court that Oregon lawmakers could have reasonably believed—on the basis of sociological evidence—that working hours of women were *in fact* related to health.

Despite Brandeis's successful invocation of 'living law,' the judicial retreat in *Muller* was more apparent than real. Defenders of the *status quo* were reassured by Arthur Twining Hadley (1856–1930), professor of political economy, Railroad Commissioner of Connecticut, and then—in 1908—president of Yale. To the query—does the Constitution enthrone economic-judicial power?—Hadley answered: 'The fundamental division of powers in the Constitution of the United States is between the voters on the one hand and property owners on the other. . . This theory of American politics has not often been stated, but it has been universally acted upon.'

Among those urging that Hadley's 'theory of American politics' be acted upon was the eminent critic and philosopher, Paul Elmer More (1864–1937). Longtime professor and lecturer at Harvard, Bryn Mawr, and Princeton, he had been editor of *The Nation* (1909–14). In the selection here excerpted, More argued that private property was an absolute right, even '*more important than the right to life*.' The cause and basis of civilization, private property was entitled to all the security law could offer—and then some.

The views of Hadley and More were, of course, anathema to Brandeis, whose role in *Muller* preceded by two years Woodrow Wilson's call in 'The Lawyer and the Community' for 'creative statesmanship' on the bench and at the bar. Brandeis, himself a highly successful corporation lawyer, recognized the explosive nature of popular power and sensed the danger that lay in it for men of wealth like himself. As early as 1905 he anticipated that 'immense wealth would in time develop a hostility from which much trouble will come to us unless the excesses of capital are curbed.' He was acutely conscious of the socialist peril. But whereas conventional corporation lawyers traced this danger to agitators, muckrakers, corrupt politicians, and labor leaders, Brandeis pointed straight at the 'great captains of industry' as 'the chief makers of socialism.'

Brandeis, along with Wilson, Pound, Thayer, Theodore Roosevelt, and Brooks Adams, saw that power was moving irretrievably from the few to the many. Lawyers and judges, if wise, would not try to freeze privilege and indiscriminately thwart change. Here indeed was the signal opportunity for lawyers—'the richest field for those who wish to serve the people.' It lay within their power to set the course of political and social action—'to determine whether it is to be expressed in lines of evolution or in lines of revolution.'

Brandeis never concurred in President Hadley's caveat that democracy, constitutionally, was 'bound to stop short of social democracy.' To satisfy our twentieth-century ideal of 'democracy and social justice' it was not necessary, he said, 'to amend our constitution. It has not lost its capacity for expansion to meet new conditions unless interpreted by rigid minds which have no such capacity. Instead of amending the Constitution, I would amend men's economic and social ideas.'

Defenders of the *status quo* had won staunch support in the courts. The judiciary had yet to heed Learned Hand's counsel. In 'The Speech of Justice' in 1916, he reflected:

> [Courts] stand in a dilemma, because, while no ritualistic piety can save them from the necessity of an active partisanship amid the contests of their time, *their partiality must endure the final test of a genuine social ideal which shall be free from class prejudice*. Like every public functionary, in the end they are charged

> with the responsibility of choosing but of choosing well. Courage and insight alone can win confidence and power. Democracy must learn to value and to trust such qualities or democracy cannot disentangle its true purposes and realize its vaguely formed ideals; but *democracy is quick to understand those who respond to its fundamental feelings, and is ruthless in casting aside those who seek cover behind the protection of the written word,* for which it may, and even in the same breath, itself profess reverence. [Italics added.]

Both aspects of Webster's forecast of 1820 were now fulfilled: 'popular power' in the form of legislation enacted by duly elected representatives had broken in on 'the rights of property,' and the 'influence of property' had found new ways to 'limit and control the exercise of popular power.'

1. *The salvation of the nation—a strengthened judiciary*

JUSTICE DAVID J. BREWER, *The Movement of Coercion,* An Address before the New York State Bar Association, 17 January 1893 *

Three things differentiate the civilized man from the savage—that which he knows, that which he is, and that which he has. That which he knows: The knowledge of the savage is limited to the day, and bounded by the visible horizon. The civilized man looks backward through all history, and beholds the present limits of the universe. The accumulations of the centuries are his. The logic of Aristotle and Bacon determines the processes of his mind. The philosophy of Plato and Herbert Spencer is his wisdom. . .

That which he is: All passions riot in the savage. He grovels through things of earth to satisfy the lusts of the body; and the height of his morality is an eye for an eye and a tooth for a tooth. Civilization lifts the soul above the body, and makes character the supreme possession. It reads into human history the glory and value of self-denial. It catches from the Divine One of Nazareth the nobility of helpfulness, and teaches that the externals are not the man; that accumulations and accomplishments only suggest that which makes both valuable; and that the poet's divination,—'a man's a man for a' that,' is the ultimate fact. . .

That which he has: A hut for a home—a blanket and a breechclout for his apparel—a bow and arrow for his means of support—a canoe and a horse for his travel—and sea-shells for his jewels; these are the possessions of the savage. But for the child of civilization all continents bring food to his table, and decorations to his home. . . The World brings tribute. And the potency of civilization is that it accumulates all the earth produces, and pours it round and into the homes of its children. . .

But that which he has lies within the reach of others. Given power and willingness on the part of those about him, and a man may be stripped of all

* *Proceedings of the New York State Bar Association*, vol. 16, pp. 37–47.

his material possessions. Hence the Eighth and Tenth Commandments:—'Thou shalt not steal,' 'Thou shalt not covet.' Only under their sanction is society possible.

I am not here this evening to defend the Eighth Commandment, or to denounce its grosser violators. . . I wish rather to notice that movement which may be denominated the movement of 'coercion,' and which by the mere force of numbers seeks to diminish protection to private property. . . It is the unvarying law, that the wealth of a community will be in the hands of a few; and the greater the general wealth, the greater the individual accumulations. The large majority of men are unwilling to endure that long self-denial and saving which makes accumulation possible; they have not the business tact and sagacity which bring about large combinations and great financial results; and hence it always has been, and until human nature is remodeled always will be true, that the wealth of a nation is in the hands of a few, while the many subsist upon the proceeds of their daily toil. But security is the chief end of government; and other things being equal, that government is best which protects to the fullest extent each individual, rich or poor, high or low, in the possession of his property and the pursuit of his business. It was the boast of our ancestors in the old country, that they were able to wrest from the power of the king so much security for life, liberty and property. . .

Here there is no monarch threatening trespass upon the individual. The danger is from the multitudes—the majority, with whom is the power. . .

This movement expresses itself in two ways: First, in the improper use of labor organizations to destroy the freedom of the laborer, and control the uses of capital. . . That which I particularly notice is the assumption of control over the employer's property, and blocking the access of laborers to it. The common rule as to strikes is this: Not merely do the employees quit the employment, and thus handicap the employer in the use of his property, and perhaps in the discharge of duties which he owes to the public; but they also forcibly prevent others from taking their places. It is useless to say that they only advise—no man is misled. When a thousand laborers gather around a railroad track, and say to those who seek employment that they had better not, and when that advice is supplemented every little while by a terrible assault on one who disregards it, every one knows that something more than advice is intended. It is coercion, force; it is the effort of the many, by the mere weight of numbers, to compel the one to do their bidding. It is a proceeding outside of the law, in defiance of the law, and in spirit and effect—an attempt to strip from one that has that which of right belongs to him—the full and undisturbed use and enjoyment of his own. It is not to be wondered at, that deeds of violence and cruelty attend such demonstrations as these; nor will it do to pretend that the wrongdoers are not the striking laborers, but lawless strangers who gather to look on. . . It is the attempt to give to the many a control over the few—a step toward despotism. Let the movement succeed; let it once be known that the individual is not free to contract for his personal services . . . and the next step will be a direct effort on the part of the many to seize the property of the few.

The other form of this movement assumes the guise of a regulation of the charges for the use of property subjected, or supposed to be, to a public use. This acts in two directions: One by extending the list of those things, charges for whose use the government may prescribe; until now we hear it affirmed that whenever property is devoted to a use in which the public has an interest, charges for that use may be fixed by law. And if there be any property in the use of which the public or some portion of it has no interest, I hardly know what it is or where to find it. And second, in so reducing charges for the use of property, which in fact is subjected to a public use, that no compensation or income is received by those who have so invested their property. By the one it subjects all property and its uses to the will of the majority; by the other it robs property of its value. Statutes and decisions both disclose that this movement, with just these results, has a present and alarming existence. . .

. . . It may be said that that majority will not be so foolish, selfish and cruel as to strip that property of its earning capacity. I say that so long as constitutional guaranties lift on American soil their buttresses and bulwarks against wrong, and so long as the American judiciary breathes the free air of courage, it cannot.

It must be supposed that the forms in which this movement expresses itself are in themselves bad. . . Labor organizations are the needed and proper complement of capital organizations. They often work wholesome restraints on the greed, the unscrupulous rapacity which dominates much of capital; and the fact that they bring together a multitude of tiny forces, each helpless in a solitary struggle with capital, enables labor to secure its just rights. So also, in regulating the charges of property which is appropriated to a public use, the public is but exercising a legitimate function, and one which is often necessary to prevent extortion in respect to public uses. Within limits of law and justice, labor organizations and state regulation of charges for the use of property which is in fact devoted to public uses are commendable. But with respect to the proposition that the public may rightfully regulate the charges for the use of any property in whose use it has an interest, I am like the lawyer who, when declared guilty of contempt, responded promptly that he had shown no contempt, but on the contrary had carefully concealed his feelings.

Now, conceding that there is this basis of wisdom and justice, and that within limits the movement in both directions will work good to society, the question is how can its excesses, those excesses which mean peril to the nation, be stayed? Will the many who find in its progress temporary and apparent advantages, so clearly discern the ultimate ruin which flows from injustice as voluntarily to desist? or must there be some force, some tribunal, outside so far as possible, to lift the restraining hand? The answer is obvious. Power always chafes at but needs restraint. This is true whether that power be in a single monarch or in a majority. All history attests the former. We are making that which proves the latter. The triple subdivision of governmental powers into legislative, executive and judicial recognizes the truth, and has provided in this last co-ordinate department of government the restraining force. And the question which now arises is whether, in view of this exigency, the functions of the judiciary should be strengthened and enlarged, or weakened and restricted. As might be expected, they who wish to push this movement to the extreme, who would brook no restraint on aught that seems to make for their gain, are unanimous in crying out against judicial interference, and are constantly seeking to minimize the power of the courts. . . The argument is that judges are not adapted by their education and training to settle such matters as these; that they lack acquaintance with affairs and are tied to precedents; that the procedure in the courts is too slow and that no action could be had therein until long after the need of action has passed. It would be folly to assert that this argument is barren of force. . . But the great body of judges are as well versed in the affairs of life as any, and they who unravel all the mysteries of accounting between partners, settle the business of the largest corporations and extract all the truth from the mass of scholastic verbiage that falls from the lips of expert witnesses in patent cases, will have no difficulty in determining what is right and wrong between employer and employees, and whether proposed rates of freight and fare are reasonable as between the public and the owners; while as for speed, is there anything quicker than a writ of injunction?

But the real objection lies deeper. Somehow or other men always link the idea of justice with that of judge. It matters not that an arbitrator or commission may perform the same function, there is not the same respect for the office, nor the same feeling that justice only can be invoked to control the decision. The arbitrator and commission will be approached with freedom by many, with suggestions that the public, or the party, or certain interests demand or will be profited by a decision in one way; but who thus comes near to the court or offers those suggestions to the judge? There is the tacit but universal feeling that justice, as he sees it, alone controls the decision. It is a good thing that this is so; that in the common thought the idea of justice goes hand in hand with that of judge; and that when anything is to be wrought out which it is feared may not harmonize with eternal principles of right and wrong, the cry is for arbitration or commission, or something else whose name is not symbolical or suggestive. . .

So it is that the mischief-makers in this movement ever strive to get away from courts and judges, and to place the power of decision in the hands of those who will the more readily and freely yield to the pressure of numbers, that so-called demand of the majority. . .

And so it is, that because of the growth of this movement, of its development in many directions, and the activity of those who are in it, and especially because of the further fact that, carrying votes in its hand, it ever appeals to the trimming politician and time-serving demagogue, and thus enters into so much of legislation, arises the urgent need of giving to the judiciary the utmost vigor and efficiency. Now, if ever in the history of this country, must there be somewhere and somehow a controlling force which speaks for justice, and for justice only. . .

What, then, ought to be done? My reply is, strengthen the judiciary. How? Permanent tenure of office accomplishes this. . . Judges are but human. If one must soon go before the people for re-election, how loath to rule squarely against public sentiment! There is no need of imputing conscious dishonesty, but the inevitable shrinking from antagonizing popular feeling, or the wishes or interests of some prominent leader or leaders tend to delay or mollify the due decision, while the judge who knows nothing can disturb his position, does not hesitate promptly and clearly to 'lay judgment to the line and righteous-to the plummet.' . .

It is said that the will of the people would often be delayed or thwarted, and that this is against the essential idea of government of and by the people. But for what are written constitutions? They exist, not simply to prescribe modes of action, but because of the restraints and prohibitions they contain. Popular government may imply, generally speaking, that the present will of the majority should be carried in effect, but this is true in no absolute or arbitrary sense, and the limitations and checks which are found in all our written constitutions are placed there to secure the rights of the minority. Constitutions are generally, and ought always to be, formed in times free from excitement. They represent the deliberate judgment of the people as to the provisions and restraints which, firmly and fully enforced, will secure to each citizen the greatest liberty and utmost protection. They are rules prescribed by Philip Sober to control Philip Drunk. When difficulties arise, when the measures and laws framed by a majority are challenged as a violation of these rules and a trespass upon the rights of the minority, common justice demands that the tribunal to determine the question shall be as little under the influence of either as is possible. . . And surely, if the judges hold office by a life tenure and with a salary which cannot be disturbed, it would seem as though we had a tribunal as far removed from disturbing influences as possible. . .

It may be said that this is practically substituting government by the judges for government by the people, and thus turning back the currents of history. The world has seen government by chiefs, by kings and emperors, by priests and by nobles. All have failed, and now government by the people is on trial. Shall we abandon that and try government by judges? But this involves a total misunderstanding of the relations of judges to government. There is nothing in this power of the judiciary detracting in the least from the idea of government of and by the people. The courts hold neither purse nor sword; they cannot corrupt nor arbitrarily control. They make no laws, they establish no policy, they never enter into the domain of popular action. They do not govern. Their functions in relation to the State are limited to seeing that popular action does not trespass upon right and justice as it exists in written constitutions and natural law. So it is that the utmost power of the courts and judges works no interference with true liberty, no trespass on the fullest and highest development of government of and by the people; it only means security to personal rights—the inalienable rights, life, liberty and the pursuit of happiness; it simply nails the Declaration of Independence, like Luther's theses against indulgences upon the doors of the Wittenburg church of human rights, and dares the anarchist, the socialist and every other assassin of liberty to blot out a single word. . .

Who does not see the wide unrest that fills the land? Who does not feel that vast social changes are impending, and realize that those charges must be guided in justice to safety and peace, or they will culminate in revolution? Who does not perceive that the mere fact of numbers is beginning to assert

itself? Who does not hear the old demagogic cry—*vox populi vox dei* (paraphrased to-day, the majority are always right)—constantly invoked to justify disregard of those guaranties which have hitherto been deemed sufficient to give protection to private property? . .
. . . I am firmly persuaded that the salvation of the Nation, the permanence of government of and by the people, rests upon the independence and vigor of the judiciary. To stay the waves of popular feeling, to restrain the greedy hand of the many from filching from the few that which they have honestly acquired, and to protect in every man's possession and enjoyment, be he rich or poor, that which he hath, demands a tribunal as strong as is consistent with the freedom of human action, and as free from all influences and suggestions other than is compassed in the thought of justice, as can be created out of the infirmities of human nature. To that end the courts exist, and for that let all the judges be put beyond the reach of political office, and all fear of losing position or compensation during good behavior. It may be that this is not popular doctrine to-day. . . The black flag of anarchism, flaunting destruction to property, and therefore relapse of society to barbarism; the red flag of socialism, inviting a redistribution of property, which, in order to secure the vaunted equality, must be repeated again and again at constantly decreasing intervals, and that colorless piece of baby-cloth, which suggests that the State take all property and direct all the work and life of individuals, as if they were little children, may seem to fill the air with their flutter. But as against these schemes, or any other plot or vagary of fiend, fool or fanatic, the eager and earnest protest and cry of the Anglo-Saxon is for individual freedom and absolute protection of all his rights of person and property. . . And to help and strengthen that good time, we shall yet see in every State an independent judiciary, made as independent of all outside influences as is possible . . . supreme in fact as in name, holding all, individuals and masses, corporations and States—even the great Nation itself—unswervingly true to the mandates of justice, that justice which is the silver sheen and the golden band in the jeweled diadem of Him to whom all Nations bow and all worlds owe allegiance.

2. *Fixing the outside border of reasonable legislative action leaves the Court a great and stately jurisdiction*

JAMES BRADLEY THAYER, *The Origin and Scope of the American Doctrine of Constitutional Law*, An Address before the Congress on Jurisprudence and Law Reform, 9 August 1893 *

How did our American doctrine, which allows to the judiciary the power to declare legislative Acts unconstitutional, and to treat them as null, come about, and what is the true scope of it?

It is a singular fact that the State constitutions did not give this power to the judges in express terms; it was inferential. In the earliest of these in-

* *Harvard Law Review*, vol. VII, 25 October 1893, pp. 129–56 *passim*.

struments no language was used from which it was clearly to be made out. . .

It is plain that where a power so momentous as this primary authority to interpret is given, the actual determinations of the body to whom it is intrusted are entitled to a corresponding respect; and this not on mere grounds of courtesy or conventional respect, but on very solid and significant grounds of policy and law. The judiciary may well reflect that if they had been regarded by the people as the chief protection against legislative violation of the constitution, they would not have been allowed merely this incidental and postponed control. They would have been let in, as it was sometimes endeavored in the conventions to let them in, to a revision of the laws before they began to operate. As the opportunity of the judges to check and correct unconstitutional Acts is so limited, it may help us to understand why the extent of their control, when they do have the opportunity, should also be narrow.

It was, then, all along true, and it was foreseen, that much which is harmful and unconstitutional may take effect without any capacity in the courts to prevent it, since their whole power is a judicial one. Their interference was but one of many safeguards, and its scope was narrow.

The rigor of this limitation upon judicial action is sometimes freely recognized, yet in a perverted way which really operates to extend the judicial function beyond its just bounds. The court's duty, we are told, is the mere and simple office of construing two writings and comparing one with another, as two contracts or two statutes are construed and compared when they are said to conflict; of declaring the true meaning of each, and, if they are opposed to each other, of carrying into effect the constitution as being of superior obligation,—an ordinary and humble judicial duty, as the courts sometimes describe it. This way of putting it easily results in the wrong kind of disregard of legislative considerations; not merely in refusing to let them directly operate as grounds of judgment, but in refusing to consider them at all. Instead of taking them into account and allowing for them as furnishing possible grounds of legislative action, there takes place a pedantic and academic treatment of the texts of the constitution and the laws. And so we miss that combination of a lawyer's rigor with a statesman's breadth of view which should be found in dealing with this class of questions in constitutional law. . .

The courts have perceived with more or less distinctness that this exercise of the judicial function does in truth go far beyond the simple business which judges sometimes describe. If their duty were in truth merely and nakedly to ascertain the meaning of the text of the constitution and of the impeached Act of the legislature, and to determine, as an academic question, whether in the court's judgment the two were in conflict, it would, to be sure, be an elevated and important office, one dealing with great matters, involving large public considerations, but yet a function far simpler than it really is. Having ascertained all this, yet there remains a question—the really momentous question—whether, after all, the court can disregard the Act. It cannot do this as a mere matter of course,—merely because it is concluded that upon a just and true construction the law is unconstitutional. That is precisely the significance of the rule of administration that the courts lay down. It can only disregard the Act when those who have the right to make laws have not merely made a mistake, but have made a very clear one,—so clear that it is not open to rational question. That is the standard of duty to which the courts bring legislative Acts; that is the test which they apply,—not merely their own judgment as to constitutionality, but their conclusion as to what judgment is permissible to another department which the constitution has charged with the duty of making it. This rule recognizes that, having regard to the great, complex, ever-unfolding exigencies of government, much which will seem unconstitutional to one man, or body of men, may reasonably not seem so to another; that the constitution often admits of different interpretations; that there is often a range of choice and judgment; that in such cases the constitution does not impose upon the legislature any one specific opinion, but leaves open this range of choice; and that whatever choice is rational is constitutional. This is the principle which the rule that I have been illustrating affirms and supports. The meaning and effect of it are shortly and very strikingly intimated by a remark of Judge Cooley, to the effect that one who is a member of a legislature may vote against a measure as being, in his judgment, unconstitutional; and, being subsequently placed on the bench, when this measure, having been passed by the legislature in spite of his opposition, comes before him judicially, may there find it his duty, although he has in no degree changed his opinion, to declare it constitutional. . .

The legislature in determining what shall be done, what it is reasonable to do, does not divide its duty with the judges, nor must it conform to their conception of what is prudent or reasonable legislation. The judicial function is merely that of fixing the outside border of reasonable legislative action, the boundary beyond which the taxing power, the power of eminent domain, police power, and legislative power in general, cannot go without violating the prohibitions of the constitution or crossing the line of its grants. . .

. . . *the ultimate question is not what is the true meaning of the constitution, but whether legislation is sustainable or not.* . .

. . . What really took place in adopting our theory of constitutional law was this: we introduced for the first time into the conduct of government through its great departments a judicial sanction, as among these departments,—not full and complete, but partial. The judges were allowed, indirectly and in a degree, the power to revise the action of other departments and to pronounce it null. In simple truth, while this is a mere judicial function, it involves, owing to the subject-matter with which it deals, taking a part, a secondary part, in the political conduct of government. If that be so, then the judges must apply methods and principles that befit their task. In such a work there can be no permanent or fitting *modus vivendi* between the different departments unless each is sure of the full co-operation of the others, so long as its own action conforms to any reasonable and fairly permissible view of its constitutional power. The ultimate arbiter of what is rational and permissible is indeed always the courts, so far as litigated cases bring the question before them. This leaves to our courts a great and stately jurisdiction. It will only imperil the whole of it if it is sought to give them more. They must not step into the shoes of the law-maker, or be unmindful of the hint that is found in the sagacious remark of an English bishop nearly two centuries ago, quoted lately from Mr. Justice Holmes:—

> 'Whoever hath an absolute authority to interpret any written or spoken laws, it is he who is truly the lawgiver, to all intents and purposes, and not the person who first wrote or spoke them.'

The view which has thus been presented seems to me highly important. I am not stating a new doctrine, but attempting to restate more exactly and truly an admitted one. If what I have said be sound, it is greatly to be desired that it should be more emphasized by our courts, in its full significance. It has been often remarked that private rights are more respected by the legislatures of some countries which have no written constitution, than by ours. No doubt our doctrine of constitutional law has had a tendency to drive out questions of justice and right, and to fill the mind of legislators with thoughts of mere legality, of what the constitution allows. And moreover, even in the matter of legality, they have felt little responsibility; if we are wrong, they say, the courts will correct it. If what I have been saying is true, the safe and permanent road towards reform is that of impressing upon our people a far stronger sense than they have of the great range of possible harm and evil that our system leaves open, and must leave open, to the legislatures, and of the clear limits of judicial power; so that responsibility may be brought sharply home where it belongs. The checking and cutting down of legislative power, by numerous detailed prohibitions in the constitution, cannot be accomplished without making the government petty and incompetent. This process has already been carried much too far in some of our States. Under no system can the power of courts go far to save a people from ruin; our chief protection lies elsewhere. . .

3. *Fear of socialism has influenced judicial decisions*

O. W. Holmes, *The Path of the Law*, 8 January 1897 *

I think that the judges themselves have failed adequately to recognize their duty of weighing considerations of social advantage. The duty is inevitable, and the result of the often proclaimed judicial aversion to deal with such considerations is simply to leave the very ground and foundation of judgments inarticulate, and often unconscious, as I have said. When socialism first began to be talked about, the comfortable classes of the community were a good deal frightened. I suspect that this fear has influenced judicial action both here and in England. . . I think that something similar has led people who no longer hope to control the legislatures to look to the courts as expounders of the Constitutions, and that in some courts new principles have been discovered outside the bodies of those instruments, which may be generalized into acceptance of

* From *Collected Legal Papers* by Oliver Wendell Holmes, copyright 1920 by Harcourt, Brace & World, Inc.; copyright, 1948, by Edward J. Holmes. Reprinted by permission of the publishers. Page 185.

the economic doctrines which prevailed about fifty years ago, and a wholesale prohibition of what a tribunal of lawyers does not think about right. I cannot but believe that if the training of lawyers led them habitually to consider more definitely and explicitly the social advantage on which the rule they lay down must be justified, they sometimes would hesitate where now they are confident, and see that really they were taking sides upon debatable and often burning questions.

4. *We need to learn to transcend our own convictions*

O. W. HOLMES, *Law and the Court*, 15 February 1913 *

Let me turn to . . . palpable realities—to that other visible Court to which for ten now accomplished years it has been my opportunity to belong. We are very quiet there, but it is the quiet of a storm centre, as we all know. Science has taught the world scepticism and has made it legitimate to put everything to the test of proof. Many beautiful and noble reverences are impaired, but in these days no one can complain if any institution, system, or belief is called on to justify its continuance in life. Of course we are not excepted and have not escaped. Doubts are expressed that go to our very being. Not only are we told that when Marshall pronounced an Act of Congress unconstitutional he usurped a power that the Constitution did not give, but we are told that we are the representatives of a class—a tool of the money power. I get letters, not always anonymous, intimating that we are corrupt. Well, gentlemen, I admit that it makes my heart ache. It is very painful, when one spends all the energies of one's soul in trying to do good work, with no thought but that of solving a problem according to the rules by which one is bound, to know that many see sinister motives and would be glad of evidence that one was consciously bad. But we must take such things philosophically and try to see what we can learn from hatred and distrust and whether behind them there may not be some germ of inarticulate truth.

The attacks upon the Court are merely an expression of the unrest that seems to wonder vaguely whether law and order pay. When the ignorant are taught to doubt they do not know what they safely may believe. And it seems to me that at this time we need education in the obvious more than investigation of the obscure. . . Most men think dramatically, not quantitatively, a fact that the rich would be wise to remember more than they do. We are apt to contrast the palace with the hovel, the dinner at Sherry's with the working man's pail, and never ask how much or realize how little is withdrawn to make the prizes of success (subordinate prizes—since the only prize much cared for by the powerful is power. The prize of the general is not a bigger tent, but command). We are apt to think of ownership as a terminus, not as a gateway, and not to realize that except the tax levied for personal consumption large

* *Speeches*, published by Little, Brown and Company, 1913. Reprinted by permission of the Law School of Harvard University.

ownership means investment, and investment means the direction of labor towards the production of the greatest returns—returns that so far as they are great show by that very fact that they are consumed by the many, not alone by the few. If I may ride a hobby for an instant, I should say we need to think things instead of words—to drop ownership, money, etc., and to think of the stream of products; of wheat and cloth and railway travel. When we do, it is obvious that the many consume them; that they now as truly have substantially all there is, as if the title were in the United States; that the great body of property is socially administered now, and that the function of private ownership is to divine in advance the equilibrium of social desires—which socialism equally would have to divine, but which, under the illusion of self-seeking, is more poignantly and shrewdly foreseen.

I should like to see it brought home to the public that the question of fair prices is due to the fact that none of us can have as much as we want of all the things we want; that as less will be produced than the public wants, the question is how much of each product it will have and how much go without; that thus the final competition is between the objects of desire, and therefore between the producers of those objects; that when we oppose labor and capital, labor means the group that is selling its product and capital all the other groups that are buying it. The hated capitalist is simply the mediator, the prophet, the adjuster according to his divination of the future desire. If you could get that believed, the body of the people would have no doubt as to the worth of law.

That is my outside thought on the present discontents. As to the truth embodied in them, in part it cannot be helped. It cannot be helped, it is as it should be, that the law is behind the times. I told a labor leader once that what they asked was favor, and if a decision was against them they called it wicked. The same might be said of their opponents. It means that the law is growing. As law embodies beliefs that have triumphed in the battle of ideas and then have translated themselves into action, while there still is doubt, while opposite convictions still keep a battle front against each other, the time for law has not come; the notion destined to prevail is not yet entitled to the field. It is a misfortune if a judge reads his conscious or unconscious sympathy with one side or the other prematurely into the law, and forgets that what seem to him to be first principles are believed by half his fellow men to be wrong. I think that we have suffered from this misfortune, in State courts at least, and that this is another and very important truth to be extracted from the popular discontent. When twenty years ago a vague terror went over the earth and the word socialism began to be heard, I thought and still think that fear was translated into doctrines that had no proper place in the Constitution or the common law. Judges are apt to be naif, simple-minded men, and they need something of Mephistopheles. We too need education in the obvious—to learn to transcend our own convictions and to leave room for much that we hold dear to be done away with short of revolution by the orderly change of law.

I have no belief in panaceas and almost none in sudden ruin. I believe with Montesquieu that if the chance of a battle—I may add, the passage of a law—has ruined a state, there was a general cause at work that made the state ready to perish by a single battle or a law. Hence I am not much interested one way or the other in the nostrums now so strenuously urged. I do not think the United States would come to an end if we lost our power to declare an Act of Congress void. I do think the Union would be imperiled if we could not make that declaration as to the laws of the several States. For one in my place sees how often a local policy prevails with those who are not trained to national views and how often action is taken that embodies what the Commerce Clause was meant to end. But I am not aware that there is any serious desire to limit the Court's power in this regard. For most of the things that properly can be called evils in the present state of the law I think the main remedy, as for the evils of public opinion, is for us to grow more civilized.

If I am right it will be a slow business for our people to reach rational views, assuming that we are allowed to work peaceably to that end. But as I grow older I grow calm. If I feel what are perhaps an old man's apprehensions, that competition from new races will cut deeper than working men's disputes and will test whether we can hang together and can fight; if I fear that we are running through the world's resources at a pace that we cannot keep, I do not lose my hopes. I do not pin my dreams for the future to my country or even to my race. I think it probable that civilization somehow will last as long as I care to look ahead—perhaps with smaller numbers, but perhaps also bred to greatness and splendor by science. I think it not improbable that man, like the grub that prepares a chamber for the winged thing it never has seen but is to be—that man may have cosmic destinies that he does not understand. And so beyond the vision of battling races and an impoverished earth I catch a dreaming glimpse of peace.

5. *I leave absolute truth for those who are better equipped*

O. W. HOLMES, *Ideals and Doubts*, 1915 *

When I say that a thing is true, I mean that I cannot help believing it. I am stating an experience as to which there is no choice. But as there are many things that I cannot help doing that the universe can, I do not venture to assume that my inabilities in the way of thought are inabilities of the universe. I therefore define the truth as the system of my limitations, and leave absolute truth for those who are better equipped. With absolute truth I leave absolute ideals of conduct equally on one side.

But although one believes in what commonly, with some equivocation, is called necessity; that phenomena always are found to stand in quantitatively fixed relations to earlier phenomena; it does not follow that without such absolute ideals we have nothing to do but to sit still and let time run over us. As I wrote many years ago, the mode in which the inevitable comes to pass is through effort. Consciously or unconsciously we all strive to make the kind of a world that we like. And although with Spinoza we may regard criticism

* *Collected Legal Papers*, op. cit. pp. 303-7.

of the past as futile, there is every reason for doing all that we can to make a future such as we desire.

There is every reason also for trying to make our desires intelligent. The trouble is that our ideals for the most part are inarticulate, and that even if we have made them definite we have very little experimental knowledge of the way to bring them about. The social reformers of today seem to me so far to forget that we no more can get something for nothing by legislation than we can by mechanics as to be satisfied if the bill to be paid for their improvements is not presented in a lump sum. Interstitial detriments that may far outweigh the benefit promised are not bothered about. Probably I am too skeptical as to our ability to do more than shift disagreeable burdens from the shoulders of the stronger to those of the weaker. But I hold to a few articles of a creed that I do not expect to see popular in my day. I believe that the wholesale social regeneration which so many now seem to expect, if it can be helped by conscious, coordinated human effort, cannot be affected appreciably by tinkering with the institution of property, but only by taking in hand life and trying to build a race. That would be my starting point for an ideal for the law. The notion that with socialized property we should have women free and a piano for everybody seems to me an empty humbug.

To get a little nearer to the practical, our current ethics and our current satisfaction with conventional legal rules, it seems to me, can be purged to a certain extent without reference to what our final ideal may be. To rest upon a formula is a slumber that, prolonged, means death. Our system of morality is a body of imperfect social generalizations expressed in terms of emotion. To get at its truth, it is useful to omit the emotion and ask ourselves what those generalizations are and how far they are confirmed by fact accurately ascertained. So in regard to the formulas of the law, I have found it very instructive to consider what may be the postulates implied. They are generically two: that such and such a condition or result is desirable and that such and such means are appropriate to bring it about. In all debatable matters there are conflicting desires to be accomplished by inconsistent means, and the further question arises, which is entitled to prevail in the specific case? Upon such issues logic does not carry us far, and the practical solution sometimes may assume a somewhat cynical shape. But I have found it a help to clear thinking to try to get behind my conventional assumptions as a judge whose first business is to see that the game is played according to the rules whether I like them or not. To have doubted one's own first principles is the mark of a civilized man. To know what you want and why you think that such a measure will help it is the first but by no means the last step towards intelligent legal reform. The other and more difficult one is to realize what you must give up to get it, and to consider whether you are ready to pay the price.

It is fashionable nowadays to emphasize the criterion of social welfare as against the individualistic eighteenth century bills of rights. I may venture to refer to a book * of mine published thirty-four years ago to show that it is no novelty. The trouble with some of those who hold to that modest platitude is that they are apt to take the general premise as a sufficient justification for

* *The Common Law*, pp. 43–8.

specific measures. One may accept the premise in good faith and yet disbelieve all the popular conceptions of socialism, or even doubt whether there is a panacea in giving women votes. Personally I like to know what the bill is going to be before I order a luxury. But it is a pleasure to see more faith and enthusiasm in the young men; and I thought that one of them made a good answer to some of my skeptical talk when he said, 'You would base legislation upon regrets rather than upon hopes.'

6. *Certitude is not the test of certainty*

O. W. Holmes, *Natural Law*, 1915 *

. . . There is in all men a demand for the superlative, so much so that the poor devil who has no other way of reaching it attains it by getting drunk. It seems to me that this demand is at the bottom of the philosopher's effort to prove that truth is absolute and of the jurist's search for criteria of universal validity which he collects under the head of natural law.

I used to say, when I was young, that truth was the majority vote of that nation that could lick all others. . . I think that the statement was correct in so far as it implied that our test of truth is a reference to either a present or an imagined future majority in favor of our view. If, as I have suggested elsewhere, the truth may be defined as the system of my (intellectual) limitations, what gives it objectivity is the fact that I find my fellow man to a greater or less extent (never wholly) subject to the same *Can't Helps*. If I think that I am sitting at a table I find that the other persons present agree with me; so if I say that the sum of the angles of a triangle is equal to two right angles. If I am in a minority of one they send for a doctor or lock me up; and I am so far able to transcend the to me convincing testimony of my senses or my reason as to recognize that if I am alone probably something is wrong with my works.

Certitude is not the test of certainty. We have been cock-sure of many things that were not so. If I may quote myself again, property, friendship, and truth have a common root in time. One can not be wrenched from the rocky crevices into which one has grown for many years without feeling that one is attacked in one's life. What we most love and revere generally is determined by early associations. I love granite rocks and barberry bushes, no doubt because with them were my earliest joys that reach back through the past eternity of my life. But while one's experience thus makes certain preferences dogmatic for one self, recognition of how they came to be so leaves one able to see that others, poor souls, may be equally dogmatic about something else. And this again means scepticism. Not that one's belief or love does not remain. Not that we would not fight and die for it if important—we all, whether we know it or not, are fighting to make the kind of a world that we should like—but that we have learned to recognize that others will fight and die to make a different world, with equal sincerity or belief. Deep-seated preferences can not

* *Collected Legal Papers*, op. cit. pp. 310–16 *passim*.

be argued about—you can not argue a man into liking a glass of beer—and therefore, when differences are sufficiently far reaching, we try to kill the other man rather than let him have his way. But that is perfectly consistent with admitting that, so far as appears, his grounds are just as good as ours.

The jurists who believe in natural law seem to me to be in that naive state of mind that accepts what has been familiar and accepted by them and their neighbors as something that must be accepted by all men everywhere. . .

It is true that beliefs and wishes have a transcendental basis in the sense that their foundation is arbitrary. You can not help entertaining and feeling them, and there is an end of it. As an arbitrary fact people wish to live, and we say with various degrees of certainty that they can do so only on certain conditions. To do it they must eat and drink. That necessity is absolute. It is a necessity of less degree but practically general that they should live in society. If they live in society, so far as we can see, there are further conditions. Reason working on experience does tell us, no doubt, that if our wish to live continues, we can do it only on those terms. But that seems to me the whole of the matter. I see no *a priori* duty to live with others and in that way, but simply a statement of what I must do if I wish to remain alive. If I do live with others they tell me that I must do and abstain from doing various things or they will put the screws on to me. I believe that they will, and being of the same mind as to their conduct I not only accept the rules but come in time to accept them with sympathy and emotional affirmation and begin to talk about duties and rights. . .

. . .The real conclusion is that the part can not swallow the whole—that our categories are not, or may not be, adequate to formulate what we cannot know. If we believe that we come out of the universe, not it out of us, we must admit that we do not know what we are talking about when we speak of brute matter. We do know that a certain complex of energies can wag its tail and another can make syllogisms. These are among the powers of the unknown, and if, as may be, it has still greater powers that we can not understand . . . why should we not be content? Why should we employ the energy that is furnished to us by the cosmos to defy it and shake our fist at the sky? It seems to me silly.

That the universe has in it more than we understand, that the private soldiers have not been told the plan of the campaign, or even that there is one, rather than some vaster unthinkable to which every predicate is an impertinence, has no bearing upon our conduct. We still shall fight—all of us because we want to live, some, at least, because we want to realize our spontaneity and prove our powers, for the joy of it, and we may leave to the unknown the supposed final valuation of that which in any event has value to us. It is enough for us that the universe has produced us and has within it, as less than it, all that we believe and love. If we think of our existence not as that of a little god outside, but as that of a ganglion within, we have the infinite behind us. It gives us our only but our adequate significance. A grain of sand has the same, but what competent person supposes that he understands a grain of sand? That is as much beyond our grasp as man. If our imagination is strong enough to accept the vision of ourselves as parts inseverable from the rest, and to extend our final interest beyond the boundary of our skins, it justifies the sacrifice even of our lives for ends outside of ourselves. The motive, to be sure, is the common wants and ideals that we find in man. Philosophy does not furnish motives, but it shows men that they are not fools for doing what they already want to do. It opens to the forlorn hopes on which we throw ourselves away, the vista of the farthest stretch of human thought, the chords of a harmony that breathes from the unknown.

7. *Democracy is bound to stop short of social democracy*

ARTHUR TWINING HADLEY, *The Constitutional Position of Property in America*, 9 April 1908 *

. . . Our legislatures are often ready to pass drastic measures of regulation; they are rarely willing to pursue a consistent and carefully developed policy for the attainment of an industrial end. The people often declaim against the extent of the powers of private capital; they are seldom willing to put that capital under the direct management of the government itself. The man who talks loudest of the abuses of private railroad management shrinks from the alternative of putting railroads into the direct control and ownership of the State.

The fact is, that private property in the United States, in spite of all the dangers of unintelligent legislation, is constitutionally in a stronger position, as against the Government and the Government authority, than is the case in any country of Europe. However much public feeling may at times move in the direction of socialistic measures, there is no nation which by its constitution is so far removed from socialism or from a socialistic order. This is partly because the governmental means provided for the control or limitation of private property are weaker in America than elsewhere, but chiefly because the rights of private property are more formally established in the Constitution itself. . .

At the time . . . when the United States separated from England, respect for industrial property right was a fundamental principle in the law and public opinion of the land. It was natural enough that this should be so at a period when every man either held property or hoped to do so. The strange thing is that this principle should have survived with so little change down to the present day. But there were certain circumstances connected with the adoption of the Constitution of the United States which provided for the perpetuation of this state of things—which made it difficult for public opinion in another and later age, when property holding was less widely distributed, to alter the legal conditions of the earlier period. . .

The delegates to the convention of 1787 were concerned with questions of constitutional law in the narrower sense. They were not thinking of the legal position of private property. But it so happened that in making mutual limitations upon the powers of the Federal and the State government they unwit-

* *The Independent*, vol. LXIV, January-June 1908, pp. 834–8 *passim*.

tingly incorporated into the Constitution itself certain very extraordinary immunities to the property holders as a body.*

It was in the first place provided that there should be no taking of private property without due process of law. The States Rights men feared that the Federal Government might, under the stress of military necessity, pursue an arbitrary policy of confiscation. The Federalists, or national party, feared that under the influence of sectional jealousy one or more of the States might pursue the same policy. This constitutional provision prevented the legislature or executive, either of the nation or of the individual States from taking property without judicial inquiry as to the necessity, and without making full compensation even in case the result of such inquiry was favorable to the government. No man foresaw the subsequent effect of this provision in preventing a majority of voters, acting in the legislature or thru the executive, from disturbing existing arrangements with regard to railroad building or factory operation until the railroad stockholders or factory owners had had the opportunity to have their case tried in the courts.†

There was another equally important clause in the Constitution providing that no State should pass a law impairing the obligation of contracts. In this case also a provision which was at first intended to prevent sectional strife and to protect the people of one locality against arbitrary legislation in another became a means of strengthening vested rights as a whole against the possibility of legislative or executive interference. Nor was the direct effect of these two clauses in preventing specific acts on the part of the legislature the most important result of their existence. They were a powerful means of establishing the American courts in that position of supremacy which they enjoy under the Constitution. For whenever an act of the legislature or the executive violated, or even seemed to violate, one of these clauses, it came before the courts for review. If the Federal courts said that the act of a legislature violated one of these provisions it was blocked—rendered powerless by a dictum of the judges. I do not mean that these two clauses in the Constitution were the chief source of judicial power. That power has been due primarily to the traditional respect for the judicial office existing in the United States, which has rendered it almost impossible for any but men of learning and character to aspire to it; and, secondarily, to the very great ability that certain of the early American judges—notably Marshall, Story and Kent—showed in expounding the law in such manner as to command universal approval. But if these provisions did not lie at the foundation of the positive authority of the judges, they were unquestionably a most powerful instrument in practically limiting the authority of legislatures, and to that extent in strengthening the rights of the property holders. . .

Under these circumstances, it is evident that large powers and privileges have been constitutionally delegated to private property in general and to cor-

* The student may wish to consult, in this connection, C. A. Beard, *An Economic Interpretation of the Constitution of the United States*, New York, 1913. [A.T.M.]

† President Hadley implies what is not true—that the 'due process' clause was in the original Constitution. It was embodied by the first Congress in the Fifth Amendment as a check on the national government, and nearly seventy-five years later in the Fourteenth Amendment as a limitation on state power. [A.T.M.]

porate property in particular. . .The general status of the property owner under the law cannot be changed by the action of the legislature or the executive, or the people of a State voting at the polls, or all three put together. It cannot be changed without either a consensus of opinion among the judges, which should lead them to retrace their old views, or an amendment of the Constitution of the United States by the slow and cumbersome machinery provided for that purpose, or, last—and I hope most improbable—a revolution.

When it is said, as it commonly is, that the fundamental division of powers in the modern State is into legislative, executive and judicial, the student of American institutions may fairly note an exception. The fundamental division of powers in the Constitution of the United States is between voters on the one hand and property owners on the other. The forces of democracy on one side, divided between the executive and the legislature, are set over against the forces of property on the other side, with the judiciary as arbiter between them; the Constitution itself not only forbidding the legislature and executive to trench upon the rights of property, but compelling the judiciary to define and uphold those rights in a manner provided by the Constitution itself.

This theory of American politics has not often been stated. But it has been universally acted upon. One reason why it has not been more frequently stated is that it has been acted upon so universally that no American of earlier generations ever thought it necessary to state it. It has had the most fundamental and far-reaching effects upon the policy of the country. To mention but one thing among many, it has allowed the experiment of universal suffrage to be tried under conditions essentially different from those which led to its ruin in Athens or in Rome. The voter was omnipotent—within a limited area. He could make what laws he pleased, as long as those laws did not trench upon property right. He could elect what officers he pleased, as long as those officers did not try to do certain duties confided by the Constitution to the property holders. Democracy was complete as far as it went, but constitutionally it was bound to stop short of *social* democracy. I will not go so far as to say that this set of limitations on the political power of the majority in favor of the political power of the property owner has been a necessary element in the success of universal suffrage in the United States, but I will say unhesitatingly that it has been a decisive factor in determining the political character of the nation and the actual development of its industries and institutions.

8. *To the civilized man the rights of property are more important than the right to life*

PAUL ELMER MORE, *Property is the Basis of Civilization,* 1915 *

There has been, as every one knows, a long strike in the mines of Colorado, with violence on both sides and bitter recriminations. . .

Now in regard to the truth of the charges of violence and other misconduct

* *Shelburne Essays,* ninth series, *Aristocracy and Justice,* Boston, Houghton Mifflin, 1915, pp. 127–48 *passim.* Reprinted by permission of Mrs. Harry Fine and Mrs. E. Gilbert Dymond.

urged alternately by the strikers and the owners and by their sympathizers, one may be unable to decide on the evidence; nor is that the question here considered. The remarkable point is that not a single word was uttered on either side for property itself, as at least a substantial element of civilization. Such a silence was no doubt natural on the part of the strikers; but what of the owners? . . . The few whose natural strength has been enhanced by property, seeing that they should still be at the mercy of the united mass of the poor and weak, delude the mass into binding themselves by passing laws in defence of property. Law is thus the support at once of civilization and of injustice.

The syllogism is rigid, and the inevitable conclusion would be: abolish law, and let mankind return to the happier condition of barbarism. But such a conclusion forces us to reconsider our premises, and we immediately see that the argument rests on two assumptions, one true and the other false. It is a *fact* that property has been the basis of civilization, and that with property there has come a change from natural inequality to what is assumed to be unnatural injustice. But it is *not a fact* that barbarism is in general a state of innocence and happiness.

In simple truth, property may rightly be called the *cause* of civilization, but, strictly speaking, it is only the *occasion* of injustice: injustice is inherent in the imperfection of man, and the development of the means of living merely brings into greater prominence what is an unavoidable feature of existence, not for man only but for the whole range of creation, in this puzzling world of ours. Rousseau, by inflaming the passions of men against the wrongs of society, which by his own hypothesis are inevitable, was, and still is, the father of frightful confusions and catastrophes; but he performed a real service to philosophy by stating so sharply the bare truth that *property is the basis of civilization*.

The socialistic theories of communal ownership give the argument, I admit, a new turn. Socialism rests on two assumptions. First, that community of ownership will, for practical purposes, eliminate the greed and injustice of civilized life. This I deny, believing it to be demonstrably false in view of the present nature of most men, and, I might add, in view of the notorious quarrelsomeness of the socialists among themselves. Secondly, that under community of control the material productivity of society will not be seriously diminished. This question I leave to the economists, though here too it would appear to follow demonstrably from the nature of man that the capacity to manage and the readiness to be managed are necessary to efficient production. Certainly, there has been a convincing uniformity in the way in which wealth and civilization have always gone together, and in the fact that wealth has accumulated only when private property was secure. So far as experience or any intelligent outlook goes, there is no sufficient motive for the creation of property but personal ownership, at least in a share of joint property. The burden of proof is entirely on those who assert the sufficiency of communal property; their theory has never been proved, but in innumerable experiments has always failed. And, in fact, the real strength of socialism, the force that some think is driving us along the edge of revolution, is in no sense a reasoned conviction that public ownership is better than private ownership, but rather a profound emotional protest against the *inequalities* of ownership. The serious question is not in regard to the importance of property, but in regard to the justice of its present distribution. Despite all the chatter about the economic interpretation of history, we are to-day driven along by a sentiment, and by no consideration of economics. . .

Unless we are willing to pronounce civilization a grand mistake, as, indeed, religious enthusiasts have ever been prone to do (and humanitarianism is more a perverted religion than a false economics), unless our material progress is all a grand mistake, we must admit, sadly or cheerfully, that any attempt by government or institution to ignore that inequality may stop the wheels of progress or throw the world back into temporary barbarism, but will surely not be the cause of wider and greater happiness.

It is not heartlessness, therefore, to reject the sentiment of the humanitarian, and to avow that the security of property is the first and all-essential duty of a civilized community. And we may assert this truth more bluntly, or, if you please, more paradoxically. Although, probably, the rude government of barbarous chiefs, when life was precarious and property unimportant, may have dealt principally with wrongs to person, yet the main care of advancing civilization has been for property. After all, life is a very primitive thing. Nearly all that makes it more significant to us than to the beast is associated with our possessions—with property, all the way from the food we share with the beasts, to the most refined products of the human imagination. To the civilized man *the rights of property are more important than the right to life.*

It is safer, in the utterance of law, to err on the side of natural inequality than on the side of ideal justice. We can go a little way, very slowly, in the endeavor to equalize conditions by the regulation of property, but the elements of danger are always near at hand and insidious; and undoubtedly any legislation which deliberately releases labor from the obligations of contract, and permits it to make war on property with impunity, must be regarded as running counter to the first demands of society. It is an ugly fact, as the world has always seen, that, under cover of the natural inequality of property, evil and greedy men will act in a way that can only be characterized as legal robbery. It is strictly within the province of the State to prevent such action so far as it safely can. Yet even here, in view of the magnitude of the interests involved, *it is better that legal robbery should exist along with the maintenance of law, than that legal robbery should be suppressed at the expense of law.*

No doubt there is a certain cruelty in such a principle, as there is a factor of cruelty in life itself. But it does not, in any proper sense of the word, involve the so-called economic interpretation of history. On the contrary, this principle recognizes, far more completely than does any humanitarian creed, that there is a large portion of human activity lying quite outside of the domain of physical constraint and legislation, and it is supremely jealous that the arms of government should not extend beyond their true province. All our religious feelings, our aspiring hopes, our personal morality, our conscience, our intellectual pursuits, all these things, and all they mean, lie beyond the law—all our individual life, as distinguished from the material relations of man with man, reaches far beyond the law's proper comprehension.

Our most precious heritage of liberty depends on the safeguarding of that realm of the individual against the encroachments of a legal equalitarianism. For there is nothing surer than that *liberty of the spirit*, if I may use that dubious word, is bound up with the *inequality of men* in their natural relations; and every movement in history to deny the inequalities of nature has been attended, and by a fatal necessity always will be attended, with an effort to crush the liberty of distinction in the ideal sphere.

As the rights of property do not involve the economic interpretation of history, so neither do they result in materialism. The very contrary. For in this matter, as in all other questions of human conduct and natural forces, you may to a certain degree control a fact, but if you deny a fact it will control you. This is the plain paradox of life, and its application is everywhere. Just so sure as you see a feministic movement undertaking to deny the peculiar characteristics and limitations of the female sex, you will see this sex element overriding all bounds—you will, to take an obvious illustration, see women dressing in a manner to exaggerate their relative physical disability and their appeal to the other sex. . .

And the same paradox holds true of property. You may to a certain extent control it and make it subservient to the ideal nature of man; but the moment you deny its rights, or undertake to legislate in defiance of them, you may for a time unsettle the very foundations of society, you will certainly in the end render property your despot instead of your servant, and so produce a materialized and debased civilization. . .

It is in accordance with the law of human nature that the sure way to foster the spirit of materialism is to unsettle the material basis of social life. Manifestly, the mind will be free to enlarge itself in immaterial interests only when that material basis is secure, and without a certain degree of such security a man must be anxious over material things and preponderantly concerned with them. And, manifestly, if this security is dependent on the rights of property, and these rights are denied or belittled in the name of some impossible ideal, it follows that the demands of intellectual leisure will be regarded as abnormal and anti-social, and that he who turns to the still and quiet life will be despised as a drone, if not hated as an enemy of the serious part of the community. There is something at once comical and vicious in the spectacle of those men of property who take advantage of their leisure to dream out vast benevolent schemes which would render their own self-satisfied career impossible.

No doubt the ideal society would be that in which every man should be filled with noble aspirations, and should have the opportunity to pursue them. But I am not here concerned with such Utopian visions, nor, as I have said, am I arguing with those who are honestly persuaded that a socialistic régime is, in our day, or any day, economically or psychologically feasible. My desire is rather to confirm in the dictates of their own reason those who believe that the private ownership of property, including its production and distribution, is, with very limited reservations, essential to the material stability and progress of society. . .

One shudders to think of the bleak pall of anxiety and the rage of internecine materialism that would fall upon society were the laws so altered as to transfer the predominant rights from property acquired to the labor by which it is produced. For *if property is secure, it may be the means to an end, whereas if it is insecure it will be the end itself.*

9. *Society has lost its onetime feeling that law is the basis of its peace, its progress, its prosperity*

Woodrow Wilson, *The Lawyer and the Community,*
An Address before the American Bar Association, 1910 *

You cannot but have marked the recent changes in the relation of lawyers to affairs in this country; and, if you feel as I do about the great profession to which we belong, you cannot but have been made uneasy by the change. Lawyers constructed the fabric of our state governments and of the government of the United States, and throughout the earlier periods of our national development presided over all the larger processes of politics. Our political conscience as a nation was embedded in our written fundamental law. Every question of public policy seemed sooner or later to become a question of law, upon which trained lawyers must be consulted. In all our legislative halls debate thundered in the phrases of the written enactments under which our legislators and our governors exercised authority. Public life was a lawyer's forum. Laymen lent their invaluable counsel, but lawyers guided, and lawyers framed the law.

I am not speaking of the dependence of our political movement upon the judgments of courts. That has not been altered, and cannot be. So long as we have written constitutions courts must interpret them for us, and must be the final tribunals of interpretation. I am speaking of the prominence and ascendency of lawyers in the practical political processes which precede the judgments of the courts. Until the civil war came and the more debatable portions of our fundamental law were cut away by the sword, the very platform of parties centred upon questions of legal interpretation and lawyers were our guiding statesmen. I suppose a more intensely legal polity never existed. . .

In the first place, the debates and constitutional struggles of the first seventy years of our political history settled most of the fundamental questions of our constitutional law. Solid lines of decided cases carry the definite outlines of the structure and make clear the methods of its action. We seemed after the civil war to be released from the demands of formal definition. The life of the nation running upon normal lines, has grown infinitely varied. It does not centre now upon questions of governmental structure or of the distribution of governmental powers. It centres upon economic questions, questions of the very structure and operation of society itself, of which government is only the instrument. . .

Constitutional lawyers have fallen into the background. We have relegated them to the Supreme Court, without asking ourselves where we are to find

* Woodrow Wilson, *Public Papers: College and State, Educational, Literary and Political Papers (1875–1913),* Roy Stannard Baker and William E. Dodd, eds., New York, Harper & Brothers, 1925, pp. 248–67 *passim.*

them when vacancies occur in that great tribunal. A new type of lawyers has been created; and that new type has come to be the prevailing type. Lawyers have been sucked into the maelstrom of the new business system of the country. That system is highly technical and highly specialized. It is divided into distinct sections and provinces, each with particular legal problems of its own. Lawyers, therefore, everywhere that business has thickened and had a large development, have become experts in some special technical field. They do not practise law. They do not handle the general, miscellaneous interests of society. They are not general counsellors of right and obligation. They do not bear the relation to the business of their neighbourhoods that the family doctor bears to the health of the community in which he lives. They do not concern themselves with the universal aspects of society. . . Lawyers are specialists, like all other men around them. The general, broad, universal field of law grows dim and yet more dim to their apprehension as they spend year after year in minute examination and analysis of a particular part of it . . . and yet a province apart, whose conquest necessarily absorbs them and necessarily separates them from the dwindling body of general practitioners who used to be our statesmen.

And so society has lost something, or is losing it,—something which it is very serious to lose in an age of law, when society depends more than ever before upon the lawgiver and the courts for its structural steel, the harmony and coördination of its parts, its convenience, its permanency, and its facility. In gaining new functions, in being drawn into modern business instead of standing outside of it, in becoming identified with particular interests instead of holding aloof and impartially advising all interests, the lawyer has lost his old function, is looked askance at in politics, must disavow special engagements if he would have his counsel heeded in matters of common concern. Society has suffered a corresponding loss,—at least American society has. It has lost its one-time feeling for law as the basis of its peace, its progress, its prosperity. Lawyers are not now regarded as the mediators of progress. Society was always ready to be prejudiced against them; now it finds its prejudice confirmed. . .

The specialization of business and the extraordinary development of corporate organization and administration have led to consequences well worth the lawyer's consideration. Everyone else is considering them, and considering them with deep concern. We have witnessed in modern business the submergence of the individual within the organization, and yet the increase to an extraordinary degree of the power of the individual, of the individual who happens to control the organization. Most men are individuals no longer so far as their business, its activities or its moralities, is concerned. They are not units, but fractions; with their individuality and independence of choice in matters of business they have lost also their individual choice within the field of morals. They must do what they are told to do or lose their connection with modern affairs. They are not at liberty to ask whether what they are told to do is right or wrong. They cannot get at the men who ordered it,—have no access to them. They have no voice of counsel or of protest. They are mere cogs in a machine which has men for its parts. And yet there are men here and there with whom the whole choice lies. There are revenues and command resources which no ancient state possessed, and which some modern bodies politic show no approach to in their budgets. The economic power of society itself is concentrated in them for the conduct of this, that, or the other sort of business. The functions of business are differentiated and divided amongst them, but the power for each function is massed. . .

Society cannot afford to have individuals wield the power of thousands without personal responsibility. It cannot afford to let its strongest men be the only men who are inaccessible to the law. Modern democratic society, in particular, cannot afford to constitute its economic undertakings upon the monarchical or aristocratic principle and adopt the fiction that the kings and great men thus set up can do no wrong which will make them personally amenable to the law which restrains smaller men: that their kingdoms, not themselves, must suffer for their blindness, their follies, and their transgressions of right.

It does not redeem the situation that these kings and chiefs of industry are not chosen upon the hereditary principle (sometimes, alas! they are) but are men who have risen by their own capacity, sometimes from utter obscurity, with the freedom of self-assertion which should characterize a free society. Their power is none the less arbitrary and irresponsible when obtained. That a peasant may become king does not render the kingdom democratic.

I would not have you think that I am speaking with a feeling of hostility towards the men who have in our day given the nation its extraordinary material power and prosperity by an exercise of genius such as in days gone by was used, in each great age, to build empires and alter the boundaries of states. . . I am simply trying to analyze the existing constitution of business in blunt words of truth, without animus or passion of any kind, and with a single, clear purpose.

That purpose is to recall you to the service of the nation as a whole, from which you have been drifting away; to remind you that, no matter what the exactions of modern legal business, no matter what or how great the necessity for specialization in your practice of the law, you are not the servants of special interests, the mere expert counsellors of this, that, or the other group of business men; but guardians of the general peace, the guides of those who seek to realize by some best accommodation the rights of men. With that purpose in view, I am asking you to look again at the corporation.

It is an indispensable convenience; but is it a necessary burden? Modern business is no doubt best conducted upon a great scale, for which the resources of the single individual are manifestly insufficient. Money and men must be massed in order to do the things that must be done for the support and facilitation of modern life. Whether energy or economy be your standard, it is plain enough that we cannot go back to the old competitive system under which individuals were the competitors. Wide organization and coöperation have made the modern world possible and must maintain it. They have developed genius as well as wealth. The nations are richer in capacity and in gifts comparable to the higher gifts of statesmanship because of them and the opportunities they have afforded exceptional men. But we have done things in pursuit of them, and have nursed notions regarding them, which are no necessary part of what we seek. We can have corporations, can retain them in unimpaired efficiency, without depriving law of its ancient searching efficiency, its inexorable mandate that men, not societies, must suffer for wrongs done. The major promise of all law is moral responsibility, the moral responsibility of individuals for their acts and conspiracies; and no other foundation can any man lay upon which a stable fabric of equitable justice can be reared. . .

In respect of the responsibility which the law imposes in order to protect society itself, in order to protect men and communities against wrongs which are not breaches of contract but offences against the public interest, the common welfare, it is imperative that we should regard corporations as merely groups of individuals, from which it may, perhaps, be harder to pick out particular persons for punishment than it is to pick them out of the general body of unassociated men, but from which it is, nevertheless, possible to pick them out,—possible not only, but absolutely necessary if business is ever again to be moralized. Corporations must continue to be used as a convenience in the transaction of business, but they must cease to be used as a covert for wrong-doers. . .

I have used the corporation merely as an illustration. It stands in the foreground of all modern economic questions, so far as the United States are concerned. It is society's present means of effective life in the field of industry. Society must get complete control of its instrument or fail. But I have used it only as an illustration of a great theme, a theme greater than any single illustration could compass,—namely, the responsibility of the lawyer to the community he professes to serve.

You are not a mere body of expert business advisers in the fields of civil law or a mere body of expert advocates for those who get entangled in the meshes of the criminal law. You are servants of the public, of the state itself. You are under bonds to serve the general interest, the integrity and enlightenment of law itself, in the advice you give individuals. It is your duty also to advise those who make the laws,—to advise them in the general interest, with a view to the amelioration of every undesirable condition that the law can reach, the removal of every obstacle to progress and fair dealing that the law can remove, the lightening of every burden the law can lift and the righting of every wrong the law can rectify. The services of the lawyer are indispensable not only in the application of the accepted processes of the law, the interpretation of existing rules in the daily operations of life and business. His services are indispensable also in keeping, and in making, the law clear with regard to responsibility, to organization, to liability, and, above all, to the relation of private rights to the public interest. . .

Just because they have so buried themselves in modern business, just because they have been so intimate a part of it, they know better than any one else knows what legal adjustments have and have not been made,—know the practices that circumvent the law, even the existing law, and the provisions of statute and court procedure that might put a stop to them or square them with what the interests of the whole community demand, theirs is the special responsibility to advise remedies. Theirs has been the part of intimate counsel in all that has been going on. The country holds them largely responsible for it. It distrusts every 'corporation lawyer.' It supposes him in league with persons whom it has learned to dread, to whom it ascribes a degree of selfishness which in effect makes them public enemies, whatever their motives or their private character may be. And the lawyer,—what does he do? He stands stoutly on the defensive. He advises his client how he may make shift, no matter how the law runs. He declares that business would go very well and every man get his due if only legislators would keep their hands off! He keeps his expert advice for private persons and criticises those who struggle without his countenance or assistance along the difficult road of reform. It is not a promising situation.

10. *Our country is not a country of dollars but of ballots*

Louis D. Brandeis, *The Opportunity in the Law*, 1905 *

. . . The leading lawyers of the United States have been engaged mainly in supporting the claims of the corporations; often in endeavoring to evade or nullify the extremely crude laws by which legislators sought to regulate the power or curb the excesses of corporations.

Such questions as the regulation of trusts, the fixing of railway rates, the municipalization of public utilities, the relation between capital and labor, call for the exercise of legal ability of the highest order. Up to the present time the legal ability of a high order which has been expended on those questions has been almost wholly in opposition to the contentions of the people. The leaders of the Bar, without any preconceived intent on their part, and rather as an incident to their professional standing, have, with rare exceptions, been ranged on the side of the corporations, and the people have been represented, in the main, by men of very meagre legal ability.

If these problems are to be settled right, this condition cannot continue. Our country is, after all, not a country of dollars, but of ballots. The immense corporate wealth will necessarily develop a hostility from which much trouble will come to us unless the excesses of capital are curbed, through the respect for law, as the excesses of democracy were curbed seventy-five years ago. There will come a revolt of the people against the capitalists, unless the aspirations of the people are given some adequate legal expression; and to this end cooperation of the abler lawyers is essential.

For nearly a generation the leaders of the Bar have, with few exceptions, not only failed to take part in constructive legislation designed to solve in the public interest our great social, economic and industrial problems; but they have failed likewise to oppose legislation prompted by selfish interests. They have often gone further in disregard of common weal. They have often advocated, as lawyers, legislative measures which as citizens they could not approve, and have endeavored to justify themselves by a false analogy. They have erroneously assumed that the rule of ethics to be applied to a lawyer's advocacy is the same where he acts for private interests against the public, as it is in litigation between private individuals. . .

* An address delivered before the Harvard Ethical Society, 4 May 1905. Published in *Business—A Profession*, 1914, pp. 333–47 *passim*. Reprinted by permission of Charles T. Branford Company.

The lawyer recognizes that in trying a case his prime duty is to present his side to the tribunal fairly and as well as he can, relying upon his adversary to present the other side fairly and as well as he can. Since the lawyers on the two sides are usually reasonably well matched, the judge or jury may ordinarily be trusted to make such a decision as justice demands.

But when lawyers act upon the same principle in supporting the attempts of their private clients to secure or to oppose legislation, a very different condition is presented. In the first place, the counsel selected to represent important private interests possesses usually ability of a high order, while the public is often inadequately represented or wholly unrepresented. Great unfairness to the public is apt to result from this fact. . .

Here, consequently, is the great opportunity in the law. The next generation must witness a continuing and ever-increasing contest between those who have and those who have not. The industrial world is in a state of ferment. The ferment is in the main peaceful, and, to a considerable extent, silent; but there is felt to-day very widely the inconsistency in this condition of political democracy and industrial absolutism. The people are beginning to doubt whether in the long run democracy and absolutism can co-exist in the same community; beginning to doubt whether there is a justification for the great inequalities in the distribution of wealth, for the rapid creation of fortunes, more mysterious than the deeds of Aladdin's lamp. The people have begun to think; and they show evidences on all sides of a tendency to act. Those of you who have not had an opportunity of talking much with laboring men can hardly form a conception of the amount of thinking that they are doing. With many these problems are all-absorbing. Many workingmen, otherwise uneducated, talk about the relation of employer and employee far more intelligently than most of the best educated men in the community. The labor question involves for them the whole of life, and they must in the course of a comparatively short time realize the power which lies in them. Often their leaders are men of signal ability, men who can hold their own in discussion or in action with the ablest and best-educated men in the community. The labor movement must necessarily progress. The people's thought will take shape in action; and it lies with us, with you to whom in part the future belongs, to say on what lines the action is to be expressed; whether it is to be expressed wisely and temperately, or wildly and intemperately; whether it is to be expressed on lines of evolution or on lines of revolution.

11. *The law must keep pace with our longing for social justice*

Louis D. Brandeis, *The Living Law*, 1916 *

The history of the United States, since the adoption of the constitution, covers less than 128 years. Yet in that short period the American ideal of govern-

* An address delivered before the Chicago Bar Association, 3 January 1915. *Illinois Law Review*, vol. 10, 1916, pp. 461–70 *passim*. Reprinted by permission of Charles T. Branford Company.

ment has been greatly modified. At first our ideal was expressed as 'A government of laws and not of men.' Then it became 'A government of the people, by the people, for the people.' Now it is 'Democracy and social justice.'

In the last half century our democracy has deepened. Coincidentally there has been a shifting of our longing from legal justice to social justice, and—it must be admitted—also a waning respect for law. Is there any casual connection between the shifting of our longing from legal justice to social justice and waning respect for law? If so, was that result unavoidable? . . .

Has not the recent dissatisfaction with our law as administered been due, in large measure, to the fact that it had not kept pace with the rapid development of our political, economic and social ideals? In other words, is not the challenge of legal justice due to its failure to conform to contemporary conceptions of social justice?

Since the adoption of the federal constitution, and notably within the last fifty years, we have passed through an economic and social revolution which affected the life of the people more fundamentally than any political revolution known to history. Widespread substitution of machinery for hand labor (thus multiplying a hundredfold man's productivity), and the annihilation of space through steam and electricity, have wrought changes in the conditions of life which are in many respects greater than those which had occurred in civilized countries during thousands of years preceding. The end was put to legalized human slavery—an institution which had existed since the dawn of history. But of vastly greater influence upon the lives of the great majority of all civilized peoples was the possibility which invention and discovery created of emancipating women and of liberating men called free from the excessive toil theretofore required to secure food, clothing and shelter. Yet, while invention and discovery created the possibility of releasing men and women from the thraldom of drudgery, there actually came, with the introduction of the factory system and the development of the business corporation, new dangers to liberty. Large publicly owned corporations replaced small privately owned concerns. Ownership of the instruments of production passed from the workman to the employer. Individual personal relations between the proprietor and his help ceased. The individual contract of service lost its character, because of the inequality in position between employer and employee. The group relation of employee to employer with collective bargaining became common, for it was essential to the workers' protection.

Political as well as economic and social science noted these revolutionary changes. But legal science—the unwritten or judge-made laws as distinguished from legislation—was largely deaf and blind to them. Courts continued to ignore newly arisen social needs. They applied complacently 18th century conceptions of the liberty of the individual and of the sacredness of private property. Early 19th century scientific half-truths, like 'The survival of the fittest,' which translated into practice meant 'The devil take the hindmost,' were erected by judicial sanction into a moral law. Where statutes giving expression to the new social spirit were clearly constitutional, judges, imbued with the relentless spirit of individualism, often construed them away. Where any doubt as to the constitutionality of such statutes could find lodgment, courts all too frequently declared the acts void. Also in other countries the strain upon the law has been great during the last generation, because there also the period has been one of rapid transformation; and the law has everywhere a tendency to lag behind the facts of life. But in America the strain became dangerous, because constitutional limitations were invoked to stop the natural vent of legislation. In the course of relatively few years hundreds of statutes which embodied attempts (often very crude) to adjust legal rights to the demands of social justice were nullified by the courts, on the grounds that the statutes violated the constitutional guaranties of liberty or property. Small wonder that there arose a clamor for the recall of judges and of judicial decisions and that demand was made for amendment of the constitutions and even for their complete abolition. . .

The challenge of existing law does not . . . come only from the working classes. Criticism of the law is widespread among business men. The tone of their criticism is more courteous than that of the working classes, and the specific objections raised by business men are different. Business men do not demand recall of judges or of judicial decisions. Business men do not ordinarily seek constitutional amendments. They are more apt to desire repeal of statutes than enactment. But both business men and working men insist that courts lack understanding of contemporary industrial conditions. Both insist that the law is not 'up to date.' Both insist that the lack of familiarity with the facts of business life results in erroneous decisions. . . Both business men and working men have given further evidence of their distrust of the courts and of lawyers by their efforts to establish non-legal tribunals or commissions to exercise functions which are judicial (even where not legal) in their nature, and by their insistence that the commissions shall be manned with business and working men instead of lawyers. And business men have been active in devising other means of escape from the domain of the courts, as is evidenced by the widespread tendency to arbitrate controversies through committees of business organizations. . .

The remedy so sought is not adequate, and may prove a mischievous one. What we need is not to displace the courts, but to make them efficient instruments of justice; not to displace the lawyer, but to fit him for his official or judicial task. And indeed the task of fitting the lawyer and the judge to perform adequately the functions of harmonizing law with life is a task far easier of accomplishment than that of endowing men, who lack legal training, with the necessary qualifications. . .

The pursuit of the legal profession involves a happy combination of the intellectual with the practical life. The intellectual tends to breadth of view; the practical to that realization of limitations which are essential to the wise conduct of life. Formerly the lawyer secured breadth of view largely through wide professional experience. Being a general practitioner, he was brought into contact with all phases of contemporary life. His education was not legal only, because his diversified clientage brought him, by the mere practice of his profession, an economic and social education. . . The same lawyer was apt to serve at one time or another both rich and poor, both employer and employee. Furthermore—nearly every lawyer of ability took some part in political life. Our greatest judges, Marshall, Kent, Story, Shaw, had secured this training. . .

The last fifty years have wrought a great change in professional life. Industrial development and the consequent growth of cities have led to a high degree of specialization—specialization not only in the nature and class of questions dealt with, but also specialization in the character of clientage. The term 'corporation lawyer' is significant in this connection. The growing intensity of professional life tended also to discourage participation in public affairs, and thus the broadening of view which comes from political life was lost. The deepening of knowledge in certain subjects was purchased at the cost of vast areas of ignorance and grave danger of resultant distortion of judgment. . .

The judge came to the bench unequipped with the necessary knowledge of economic and social science, and his judgment suffered likewise through lack of equipment in the lawyers who presented the cases to him. For a judge rarely performs his functions adequately unless the case before him is adequately presented. Thus were the blind led by the blind. It is not surprising that under such conditions the laws as administered failed to meet contemporary economic and social demands.

We are powerless to restore the general practitioner and general participation in public life. Intense specialization must continue. But we can correct its distorting effects by broader education—by study undertaken preparatory to practice—and continued by lawyer and judge throughout life: study of economics and sociology and politics which embody the facts and present the problems of today.

'Every beneficent change in legislation,' Professor Henderson said, 'comes from a fresh study of social conditions, and social ends, and from such rejection of obsolete laws to make room for a rule which fits the new facts. One can hardly escape from the conclusion that a lawyer who has not studied economics and sociology is very apt to become a public enemy.'

SELECTED REFERENCES

Louis B. Boudin, *Government by Judiciary*, 2 vols., New York, Godwin, 1932.

John A. Garraty, *Constitutional Quarrels That Have Changed History*, New York, Harper and Row, 1964.

A. T. Mason, *Brandeis: A Free Man's Life*, New York, Viking, 1946, VI and XVI.

———, 'The Conservative World of Mr. Justice Sutherland,' *The American Political Science Review*, June 1938.

Arnold M. Paul, *Conservative Crisis and the Rule of Law: Attitudes of Bar and Bench, 1887–1895*, Ithaca, Cornell University Press, 1960.

J. Allen Smith, *The Spirit of American Government*, New York, Macmillan, 1912, chaps. III, V, XI–XIV incl.

Benjamin R. Twiss, *Lawyers and the Constitution: How Laissez-faire Came to the Supreme Court*, Princeton, Princeton University Press, 1942.

XVIII

CYNICISM, NORMALCY, OPTIMISM, REALISM

The program of New Freedom that had begun so auspiciously for liberals in Woodrow Wilson's first administration was suddenly blighted by the chaos of World War I. Its destructive impact, coupled with America's preparation for the conflict and subsequent entrance into it, created profound disillusionment. After 1920, the passion for 'normalcy' became universal. John W. Davis, 1924 presidential candidate on the Democratic ticket, noted that 'the people usually know what they want at a particular time. In 1924 . . . what they wanted was repose.' For our more sensitive liberals, as for British Foreign Minister Earl Grey, 'The lights' seemed to be 'going out all over the world.' Randolph Bourne (1886–1918)—whose *Unfinished Fragment on the State* opens this chapter—a precocious youth and brilliant student at Columbia University, where his literary and intellectual gifts began to flower, has been rated as one of the few men of moral and intellectual stature in our time. 'I know of no other twentieth century American who has compressed so much of suggestive political thinking in such brief compass,' Max Lerner observes. The same writer considers Bourne's *Unfinished Fragment* as 'one of the most notable American attempts at a theory of the state.'

War, described as 'the health of the state,' runs as a monotonous chant through Bourne's pages. He hated war because it aggrandized the power and glory of the state, making it patriotic to silence minorities, force conformity, and destroy those differences and disagreements that in peace time threaten the elite. The 'significant classes' welcomed world conflict, as it enabled them to enjoy the 'peacefulness of being at war.' War also destroys, in the rank and file, those cultural values and variants that make life worth while—individual diversity, creativeness, beauty, reason. 'You feel powerful by conforming, and you feel forlorn and helpless if you are out of the crowd.' In the vanguard promoting the holocaust were the intellectuals, former teachers and friends, 'identifying themselves with the least democratic forces in American life,' giving their 'reactionary opponents a rationalization for the war.'

A hunchback whose life was cut short at thirty-two by influenza, Bourne is in the dissident tradition of William Lloyd Garrison, Henry David Thoreau, Walt Whitman, and Eugene Victor Debs, who during other crucial periods of our history gave moral substance and tenacity to American political thought.

Postwar America, favored by the unhappy exhaustion of her principal business competitors and organized by and for the leadership of high finance, was able to sell a flood of mass-produced goods in the most favorable markets, to draw the gold of the world into her coffers, and pay it out as stock bonus, profit, and wages, thus expanding demand, production, and investment. The incredible boom, and the glow of optimism that ensued, created a golden age for agile industrialists and financiers. Aiding them for twelve years was a serviceably acquiescent Republican administration headed first by Warren G. Harding, then by silent do-nothing Calvin Coolidge, and finally by that high priest of rugged individualism, Herbert Hoover.

A provocative portrayal of the 'rugged individualism' enveloping much of America during the 'twenties is given by Sinclair Lewis (1885–1951), first American to win the Nobel Prize for literature. A small-town Midwesterner, educated at Yale, Lewis has been described as 'a native blend of boldness and enthusiasm, of skepticism and affirmation.' The novelist's fictional town Zenith is largely a reflection of Lewis's conception of Minneapolis. The starkly drawn portrait suggests a caricature, filling out the devastating picture painted by the British essayist, G. Lowes Dickinson. Discerning the endemic anarchism in American individualism, Dickinson wrote in 1914:

> Describe the average Western man and you describe the American; from east to west, from north to south, everywhere and always the same—masterful, aggressive, unscrupulous, egotistic, at once good-natured and brutal, kind if you do not cross him, ruthless if you do, greedy, ambitious, self-reliant, active for the sake of activity, intelligent and unintellectual, quick-witted and crass, contemptuous of ideas but amorous of devices, valuing nothing but success, recognising nothing but the actual, Man in the concrete, undisturbed by spiritual life, the master of methods and slave of things, and therefore the conqueror of the world, the unquestioning, the undoubting, the child with the muscles of a man, the European stripped bare, and shown for what he is, a predatory, unreflecting naïf, precociously accomplished brute.

There is just enough truth in this unvarnished portrait to make the thickest American skin wince. But, like Lewis's Babbitt, it may be slightly exaggerated. In the end Babbitt fails even to convince himself. When his son abandons the creed, paternal blessings are quickly forthcoming.

> I've always wanted you to have a college degree . . . But I've never—Now, for heaven's sake, don't repeat this to your mother, or she'd remove what little hair I've got left, but practically, I've never done a single thing I've wanted to in my whole life! I don't know I've accomplished anything except just get along. I figure out I've made about a quarter of an inch out of a possible hundred rods. Well, maybe you'll carry things further. I don't know. But I do get a kind of sneaking pleasure out of the fact that you knew what you wanted to do and did it. Well, these folks in there will

> try to bully you, and tame you down. Tell 'em to go to the devil! I'll back you. Take your factory job, if you want to. Don't be scared of the family. No, nor of all of Zenith. Nor of yourself, the way I've been. Go ahead, old man! The world is yours!

Far more cynical than Sinclair Lewis is the editor, columnist, and erudite etymologist, H. L. Mencken (1880–1935). Selections from his *Notes on Democracy* are included here, not as a serious discussion of public issues, but as a burlesque of the inglorious Harding-Coolidge-Hoover epoch.

Looking about him in the 1920's, the acidulous *American Mercury* editor and author of *The American Language* found a great deal of wickedness and far too much foolishness abroad in our land. Why should this be so? It is all due, he said in effect, to natural causes—to stupid, boobish, wicked man, and that worst of all human contrivances—'amusing,' 'idiotic' democracy. What Mencken wrote about popular government is a racy rehash of what aristocrats and authoritarians, at home and abroad, had been gossiping for centuries. Sharing Mencken's gloomy outlook were certain level-headed observers. To Ralph Barton Perry 'the moral and intellectual bankruptcy of liberalism in our time needs no demonstration.' 'Liberalism is dead,' Joseph Wood Krutch announced. 'So many people who seem to agree upon nothing else have agreed to accept these three sweeping words.' Will Durant, echoing Mencken, noted that 'self-government has been held up to ridicule, and many observers count it already dead.' 'He suited the age of Coolidge,' Harold Laski wrote of Mencken, 'in which, in the aftermath of the disillusion created by the first World War, a restless and dissatisfied generation was prepared to pull down all idols it had previously worshipped.'

Thanks to George Sutherland (1862–1942), Utah Congressman, Senator, and Associate Justice of the Supreme Court (1922–38), Harding's slogan 'Back to Normalcy' received official endorsement in Supreme Court decisions. Seeing Wilson's New Freedom as presaging an era of political experimentation and ruinous bureaucracy, Sutherland revived and enforced the fears and faith of earlier defenders of the *status quo*. Resisting 'king numbers,' the 'tyranny of the majority,' and 'the forward march of democracy,' he proclaimed that their effect would be to rescue us 'from the absolutism of the king only to hand us over to the tyranny of the majority.' Sutherland's creed denounced positive government as heresy, flying in the face of unconquerable social and economic laws. Such sacrilege is both futile and harmful since these laws are 'beyond the power' and 'beyond the right of human control.' Government interference is also unconstitutional because the owner has 'an inherent, constiutional right to the market price, fixed by what is called the "higgling of the market," irrespective of the extent of his profits.' Yet Sutherland confessed a certain dissatisfaction in thus embracing a theory of society, of government, and of the Constitution that so obviously loaded the economic-legal scales to the advantage of the well-to-do. He could do no more, however, than offer his sympathy to the less well-off, knowing no way, as he said, of making any remedial adjustment 'without the consent of those whose property would be depleted.' Sutherland represents a significant aspect of American character and tradition.

Born in England but himself a product of the great West, he believed implicitly that enduring social progress is built on industry, painful self-denial, and thrift. During his sixteen years on the Supreme Bench, no other Justice spoke for the Court in so many important cases. Of his 320 opinions, 295 represented the majority of the Court. For sixteen years Sutherland's creed was practically synonymous with the supreme law of the land. And when, after 1932, President F. D. Roosevelt and his New Dealers began to violate his basic tenets, Sutherland observed:

> The world is passing through an uncomfortable experience, and in many respects will have to retrace its steps with painful effort. The tendency of many governments is the direction of destroying individual initiative, self-reliance, and other cardinal virtues which I was always taught were necessary to develop a real democracy. The notion that the individual is not to have the full reward of what he does well, and is not to bear the responsibility for what he does badly, apparently is becoming part of our present philosophy of government.

Nor can we be sure that Sutherland's influence or the value of his granite adherence to 'principle' has been fully spent. In 1944, Chief Justice Stone Stone expressed the opinion that

> the time will come when it will be recognized, perhaps more clearly than it is at present, how fortunate it has been for the true progress of the law that at a time when the trend was in the opposite direction [but not until after 1932], there sat upon this Bench a man of stalwart independence, and of the purest character who . . . fought stoutly for the constitutional guaranties of the liberty of the individual.
>
> It is too soon and we are perhaps still too close to the smoke of battle to see clearly or to say with omniscient finality precisely how the great constitutional issues of that period should have been decided. Indeed, who would be so rash as to say now, despite shifting emphases and attitudes and the changes which time has brought and will bring, that Justice Sutherland's influence will not continue, perhaps in greater measure than today, to play its part in directing the current of our legal thinking.

The Chief Justice's appraisal recalls Henry Jones Ford's editorial comment in the New York *Evening Post,* 22 March 1909: 'The statesman in other countries depends upon his success in obtaining results; in this country upon the emotional fervor which he is able to arouse by his good intentions.'

Justice Holmes, believing that the Constitution imposes few restrictions on government, dissented from Sutherland's opinion in the minimum wage case, and disagreed again, in 1927, when Sutherland, speaking for the Court, held that the New York state legislature was powerless to safeguard society against scalpers by forbidding the resale of theater tickets at a price in excess of fifty cents beyond that printed on the face of the ticket. This time Justice Holmes took the opportunity to spell out his contrasting views, warning judges (and he may well have had colleagues such as Sutherland in mind) against the tendency to read their own social and economic preferences into judicial decisions. The excerpt included in this chapter represents a literary gem of judicial tolerance.

Herbert Hoover (1874-   ), mine operator and promoter, Belgium Relief Commissioner, United States Food Administrator, Secretary of Commerce in the Harding and Coolidge administrations, and elected President in 1928, proclaimed and promoted, much as Sutherland did, the dogma of rugged individualism. An incurable optimist (at least prior to 1932) who in 1928 saw poverty banished from the earth, Hoover lacked that incisiveness of mind, as well as the literary craftsmanship that made Sutherland so effective. Hoover's speeches, including the one here reprinted, 'read as if he had been brought up on a steady diet of corporation reports as printed in *The Times* of London.' As Secretary of Commerce, he won a reputation as 'the advance agent' of American businessmen in foreign lands, yet he stubbornly insisted that the profit system should remain comparatively unregulated. 'When industry cures its own abuses,' that, Hoover declared, 'is true self-government.'

Even as depression deepened, the rank and file of financial-political leaders confined themselves to a kind of political Couéism—'every day in every way the economic situation is getting better and better.' President Hoover made so many optimistic predictions that what he said finally became a national joke. Though his views on the proper limits of government belong essentially to the early nineteenth century, he finally took a belated flyer in government planning (the most notable instance being the Reconstruction Finance Corporation, approved 22 January 1932) on such a scale as practically to qualify him as a sort of New Dealer, or at least as the transitional figure from the old order to the new.

Yet Hoover's thinking and planning were fatally crippled partly by his inability to detect any major flaw in America's domestic economy, though it was bankrupt, and even more by his traditional assumptions, widely held, that wealth is tangible goods in the hands of owners who actually control and direct its use, that the profit motive keeps industry going, that the property owner's enterprise, daring, and initiative supply the dynamics of American business. Economic-political statesmanship took no account of the silent revolution that had in the last half-century transformed our basic economic institutions, so as to center control in the managers of a scant two hundred large corporations who frequently owned little or no part of the complex economic empires they governed. These basic facts were ascertained and established by Adolf Berle, Jr., (1895-   ) and the economist Gardiner C. Means (1896-   ) in a book, partly reproduced herein, which Charles A. Beard described as 'the most important work bearing on American statescraft between the publication of the immortal "Federalist" and the opening of the year 1933.' This realistic volume was a fitting prelude, perhaps even a prerequisite, to the administration of Franklin D. Roosevelt and his New Deal.

The role of the scholar in politics is perhaps best exemplified by the contribution of Berle himself. The same year *The Modern Corporation and*

Private Property appeared (1932), Walter Lippmann delivered the Phi Beta Kappa oration at the Columbia University Commencement. Published as 'The Scholar in a Troubled World,' the article suggested that the intellectual in politics was circumscribed by inescapable relativism. Elaborating on *A Preface to Morals,* Lippmann contended that 'we must not expect society to be guided by its professors until, or . . . unless, the fluctuating opinions that now govern affairs are replaced by clear, by settled, moral values.' Lippmann was sure that democracy 'without coherence and purpose' could not last long; 'it must, and inevitably it will, give way to some more settled social order.' Meanwhile, scholars could 'forge the instruments' that Shelley dreamed of:

> Those instruments with which High Spirits call
> The future from its cradle, and the past
> Out of its grave, and make the present last
> In thoughts and joys which sleep, but cannot die
> Folded within their own eternity. . .

Despite Lippmann's thoughtful misgivings, the Brain Trust, including Berle among others, so conspicuous in President Franklin Roosevelt's first administration, was already preparing the would-be Democratic candidate for the presidency.

1. *War is the health of the state*

RANDOLPH BOURNE, *Unfinished Fragment on the State,* 1918 *

. . . Government is the idea of the State put into practical operation in the hands of definite, concrete, fallible men. It is the visible sign of the invisible grace. It is the word made flesh. And it has necessarily the limitations inherent in all practicality. Government is the only form in which we can envisage the State, but it is by no means identical with it. That the State is a mystical conception is something that must never be forgotten. Its glamor and its significance linger behind the framework of Government and direct its activities.

Wartime brings the ideal of the State out into very clear relief, and reveals attitudes and tendencies that were hidden. In times of peace the sense of the State flags in a republic that is not militarized. For war is essentially the health of the State. . . The State is the organization of the herd to act offensively or defensively against another herd similarly organized. The more terrifying the occasion for defense, the closer will become the organization and the more coercive the influence upon each member of the herd. War sends the current of purpose and activity flowing down to the lowest level of the herd, and to its most remote branches. All the activities of society are linked together as fast as possible to this central purpose of making a military offensive or a military defense, and the State becomes what in peace times it has vainly

* *Untimely Papers,* pp. 140–230 *passim.*

struggled to become—the inexorable arbiter and determinant of men's businesses and attitudes and opinions. The slack is taken up, the cross-currents fade out, and the nation moves lumberingly and slowly, but with ever accelerated speed and integration, towards the great end, towards that 'peacefulness of being at war,' of which L. P. Jacks has so unforgettably spoken.

The classes which are able to play an active and not merely a passive role in the organization for war get a tremendous liberation of activity and energy. Individuals are jolted out of their old routine, many of them are given new positions of responsibility, new techniques must be learnt. Wearing home ties are broken and women who would have remained attached with infantile bonds are liberated for service overseas. A vast sense of rejuvenescence pervades the significant classes, a sense of new importance in the world. Old national ideals are taken out, re-adapted to the purpose and used as universal touchstones, or molds into which all thought is poured. Every individual citizen who in peacetimes had no function to perform by which he could imagine himself an expression or living fragment of the State becomes an active amateur agent of the Government in reporting spies and disloyalists, in raising Government funds, or in propagating such measures as are considered necessary by officialdom. Minority opinion, which in times of peace, was only irritating and could not be dealt with by law unless it was conjoined with actual crime, becomes, with the outbreak of war, a case for outlawry. Criticism of the State, objections to war, lukewarm opinions concerning the necessity or the beauty of conscription, are made subject to ferocious penalties, far exceeding in severity those affixed to actual pragmatic crimes. Public opinion, as expressed in the newspapers, and the pulpits and the schools, becomes one solid block. 'Loyalty,' or rather war orthodoxy, becomes the sole test for all professions, techniques, occupations. Particularly is this true in the sphere of the intellectual life. There the smallest taint is held to spread over the whole soul, so that a professor of physics is *ipso facto* disqualified to teach physics or to hold honorable place in a university—the republic of learning—if he is at all unsound on the war. Even mere association with persons thus tainted is considered to disqualify a teacher. Anything pertaining to the enemy becomes taboo. His books are suppressed wherever possible, his language is forbidden. His artistic products are considered to convey in the subtlest spiritual way taints of vast poison to the soul that permits itself to enjoy them. So enemy music is suppressed, and energetic measure of opprobrium taken against those whose artistic consciences are not ready to perform such an act of self-sacrifice. The rage for loyal conformity works impartially, and often in diametric opposition to other orthodoxies and traditional conformities, or even ideals. . .

War is the health of the State. It automatically sets in motion throughout society those irresistible forces for uniformity, for passionate cooperation with the Government in coercing into obedience the minority groups and individuals which lack the larger herd sense. The machinery of government sets and enforces the drastic penalties, the minorities are either intimidated into silence, or brought slowly around by a subtle process of persuasion which may seem to them really to be converting them. Of course the ideal of perfect loyalty, perfect uniformity is never really attained. The classes upon whom the amateur work of coercion falls are unwearied in their zeal, but often their agitation instead of converting, merely serves to stiffen their resistance. Minorities are rendered sullen, and some intellectual opinion bitter and satirical. But in general, the nation in war time attains a uniformity of feeling, a hierarchy of values culminating at the undisputed apex of the State ideal, which could not possibly be produced through any other agency than war. Other values such as artistic creation, knowledge, reason, beauty, the enhancement of life, are instantly and almost unanimously sacrificed, and the significant classes who have constituted themselves the amateur agents of the State, are engaged not only in sacrificing these values for themselves but in coercing all other persons into sacrificing them.

War—or at least modern war waged by a democratic republic against a powerful enemy—seems to achieve for a nation almost all that the most inflamed political idealist could desire. Citizens are no longer indifferent to their Government, but each cell of the body politic is brimming with life and activity. We are at last on the way to full realization of that collective community in which each individual somehow contains the virtue of the whole. In a nation at war, every citizen identifies himself with the whole, and feels immensely strengthened in that identification. The purpose and desire of the collective community live in each person who throws himself whole-heartedly into the cause of war. The impeding distinction between society and the individual is almost blotted out. At war, the individual becomes almost identical with his society. He achieves a superb self-assurance, an intuition of the rightness of all his ideas and emotion, so that in the suppression of opponents or heretics he is invincibly strong; he feels behind him all the power of the collective community. The individual as social being in war seems to have achieved almost his apotheosis. . .

There is nothing invidious in the use of the term 'herd' in connection with the State. It is merely an attempt to reduce closer to first principles the nature of this institution in the shadow of which we all live, move and have our being. . .

This gregarious impulse is the tendency to imitate, to conform, to coalesce together, and is most powerful when the herd believes itself threatened with attack. Animals crowd together for protection, and men become most conscious of their collectivity at the threat of war. Consciousness of collectivity brings confidence and a feeling of massed strength, which in turn arouses pugnacity and the battle is on. In civilized man, the gregarious impulse acts not only to produce concerted action for defense, but also to produce identity of opinion. . .

Just as in modern societies the sex instinct is enormously over-supplied for the requirements of human propagation, so the gregarious impulse is enormously over-supplied for the work of protection which it is called upon to perform. It would be quite enough if we were gregarious enough to enjoy the companionship of others, to be able to cooperate with them, and to feel a slight malaise at solitude. Unfortunately, however, this impulse is not content with these reasonable and healthful demands, but insists that like-mindedness shall prevail everywhere, in all departments of life. So that all human progress, all novelty, and non-conformity, must be carried against the resistance of this tyrannical herd instinct which drives the individual into obedience and conformity with the majority. Even in the most modern and enlightened societies this impulse shows little sign of abating. As it is driven by inexorable economic demand out of the sphere of utility, it seems to fasten itself ever more fiercely in the realm of feeling and opinion, so that conformity comes to be a thing aggressively desired and demanded.

. . . You feel powerful by conforming, and you feel forlorn and helpless if you are out of the crowd. While even if you do not get any access of power by thinking and feeling just as everybody else in your group does, you get at least the warm feeling of obedience, the soothing irresponsibility of protection.

Joining as it does to these very vigorous tendencies of the individual—the pleasure in power and the pleasure in obedience—this gregarious impulse becomes irresistible in society. War stimulates it to the highest possible degree, sending the influences of its mysterious herd-current with its inflations of power and obedience to the farthest reaches of the society, to every individual and little group that can possibly be affected. And it is these impulses which the State—the organization of the entire herd, the entire collectivity—is founded on and makes use of.

. . . A people at war have become in the most literal sense obedient, respectful, trustful children again, full of that naive faith in the all-wisdom and all-power of the adult who takes care of them, imposes his mild but necessary rule upon them and in whom they lose their responsibility and anxieties. In this recrudescence of the child, there is great comfort, and a certain influx of power. On most people the strain of being an independent adult weighs heavily, and upon none more than those members of the significant classes who have had bequeathed to them or have assumed the responsibilities of governing. The State provides the convenientest of symbols under which these classes can retain all the actual pragmatic satisfaction of governing, but can rid themselves of the psychic burden of adulthood. They continue to direct industry and government and all the institutions of society pretty much as before, but in their own conscious eyes and in the eyes of the general public, they are turned from their selfish and predatory ways, and have become loyal servants of society, or something greater than they—the State. The man who moves from the direction of a large business in New York to a post in the war management industrial service in Washington does not apparently alter very much his power or his administrative technique. But psychically, what a transfiguration has occurred! His is now not only the power but the glory! . .

The members of the working-classes, that portion at least which does not identify itself with the significant classes and seek to imitate it and rise to it, are notoriously less affected by the symbolism of the State, or, in other words, are less patriotic than the significant classes. For theirs is neither the power nor the glory. The State in wartime does not offer them the opportunity to regress, for, never having acquired social adulthood, they cannot lose it. If they have been drilled and regimented, as by the industrial regime of the last century, they go out docilely enough to do battle for their State, but they are almost entirely without that filial sense and even without that herd-intellect sense which operates so powerfully among their 'betters.' They live habitually in an industrial serfdom, by which though nominally free, they are in practice as a class bound to a system of machine-production the implements of which they do not own, and in the distribution of whose products they have not the slightest voice, except what they can occasionally exert by a veiled intimidation which draws slightly more of the product in their direction. From such serfdom, military conscription is not so great a change. But into the military enterprise they go, not with those hurrahs of the significant classes whose instincts war so powerfully feeds, but with the same apathy with which they enter and continue in the industrial enterprise.

From this point of view, war can be called almost an upper-class sport. . .

To the spread of that herd-feeling which arises from the threat of war, and which would normally involve the entire nation, the only groups which make serious resistance are those, of course, which continue to identify themselves with the other nation from which they or their parents have come. In times of peace they are for all practical purposes citizens of their new country. They keep alive their ethnic traditions more as a luxury than anything. . . If they are consciously opposed by a too invidious policy of Americanism, they tend to be strengthened. . . This herd-feeling, this newly awakened consciousness of the State, demands universality. The leaders of the significant classes, who feel most intensely this State-compulsion, demand a one hundred per cent. Americanism, among one hundred per cent of the population. The State is a jealous God and will brook no rivals. . .

The whole terrific force of the State is brought to bear against the heretics. The nation boils with a slow insistent fever. A white terrorism is carried on by the Government against pacifists, Socialists, enemy aliens, and a milder unofficial persecution against all persons or movements that can be imagined as connected with the enemy. War, which should be the health of the State, unifies all the bourgeois elements and the common people, and outlaws the rest. . .

Oppression of minorities became justified on the plea that the latter were perversely resisting the rationally constructed and solemnly declared will of a majority of the nation. The herd-coalescence of opinion which became inevitable the moment the State had set flowing the war-attitudes became interpreted as a pre-war popular decision, and disinclination to bow to the herd was treated as a monstrously anti-social act. . . The significant classes with their trailing satellites, identify themselves with the State, so that what the State, through the agency of the Government, has willed, this majority conceives itself to have willed.

All of which goes to show that the State represents all the autocratic, arbitrary, coercive, belligerent forces within a social group, it is a sort of complexus of everything most distasteful to the modern free creative spirit, the feeling for life, liberty and the pursuit of happiness. War is the health of the State. Only when the State is at war does the modern society function with that unity of sentiment, simple uncritical patriotic devotion, cooperation of services, which have always been the ideal of the State lover. . .

The moment war is declared . . . the mass of the people, through some spiritual alchemy, become convinced that they have willed and executed the deed themselves. They then with the exception of a few malcontents, proceed to allow themselves to be regimented, coerced, deranged in all the environments of their lives, and turned into a solid manufactory of destruction toward whatever other people may have, in the appointed scheme of things, come within the range of the Government's disapprobation. The citizen throws off his contempt and indifference to Government, identifies himself with its purposes, revives all his military memories and symbols, and the State once more walks, an august presence, through the imaginations of men. Patriotism becomes the dominant feeling, and produces immediately that intense and hopeless confusion between the relations which the individual bears and should bear towards the society of which he is a part. . .

2. *Irresponsible teachers and professors constitute the worst menace to sound government*

SINCLAIR LEWIS, *Babbitt*, 1922 *

' "Gentlemen, it strikes me that each year at this annual occasion when friend and foe get together and lay down the battle-ax and let the waves of good-fellowship waft them up the flowery slopes of amity, it behooves us, standing together eye to eye and shoulder to shoulder as fellow-citizens of the best city in the world, to consider where we are both as regards ourselves and the common weal.

' "It is true that even with our 361,000, or practically 362,000, population, there are, by the last census, almost a score of larger cities in the United States. But, gentlemen, if by the next census we do not stand at least tenth, then I'll be the first to request any knocker to remove my shirt and to eat the same, with the compliments of G. F. Babbitt, Esquire! . .

' "I don't mean to say we're perfect. We've got a lot to do in the way of extending the paving of motor boulevards, for, believe me, it's the fellow with four to ten thousand a year, say, and an automobile and a nice little family in a bungalow on the edge of town, that makes the wheels of progress go round!

' "That's the type of fellow that's ruling America to-day; in fact, it's the ideal type to which the entire world must tend, if there's to be a decent, well-balanced, Christian, go-ahead future for this little old planet! Once in a while I just naturally sit back and size up this Solid American Citizen, with a whale of a lot of satisfaction.

' "Our Ideal Citizen—I picture him first and foremost as being busier than a bird-dog, not wasting a lot of good time in day-dreaming or going to sassiety teas or kicking about things that are none of his business, but putting the zip into some store or profession or art. At night he lights up a good cigar, and climbs into the little old 'bus, and maybe cusses the carburetor, and shoots out home. He mows the lawn, or sneaks in some practice putting, and then he's ready for dinner. After dinner he tells the kiddies a story, or takes the family to the movies, or plays a few fists of bridge, or reads the evening paper, and a chapter or two of some good lively Western novel if he has a taste for literature, and maybe the folks next-door drop in and they sit and visit about their friends and the topics of the day. Then he goes happily to bed, his conscience clear, having contributed his mite to the prosperity of the city and to his own bank-account.

'"In politics and religion this Sane Citizen is the canniest man on earth; and in the arts he invariably has a natural taste which makes him pick out the best, every time. In no country in the world will you find so many reproductions of the Old Masters and of well-known paintings on parlor walls as in these United States. No country has anything like our number of phonographs, with not only dance records and comic but also the best operas, such as Verdi, rendered by the world's highest-paid singers.

'"In other countries, art and literature are left to a lot of shabby bums living in attics and feeding on booze and spaghetti, but in America the successful writer or picture-painter is indistinguishable from any other decent business man; and I, for one, am only too glad that the man who has the rare skill to season his message with interesting reading matter and who shows both purpose and pep in handling his literary wares has a chance to drag down his fifty thousand bucks a year, to mingle with the biggest executives on terms of perfect equality, and to show as big a house and as swell a car as any Captain of Industry! But, mind you, it's the appreciation of the Regular Guy who I have been depicting which has made this possible, and you got to hand as much credit to him as to the authors themselves.

'"Finally, but most important, our Standardized Citizen, even if he is a bachelor, is a lover of the Little Ones, a supporter of the hearthstone which is the basic foundation of our civilization, first, last, and all the time, and the thing that most distinguishes us from the decayed nations of Europe.

'"I have never yet toured Europe—and as a matter of fact, I don't know that I care to such an awful lot, as long as there's our own mighty cities and mountains to be seen—but, the way I figure it out, there must be a good many of our own sort of folks abroad. Indeed, one of the most enthusiastic Rotarians I ever met boosted the tenets of one-hundred-per-cent pep in a burr that smacked o' bonny Scutlond and all ye bonny braes o' Bobby Burns. But same time, one thing that distinguishes us from our good brothers, the hustlers over there, is that they're willing to take a lot off the snobs and journalists and politicians, while the modern American business man knows how to talk right up for himself, knows how to make it good and plenty clear that he intends to run the works. He doesn't have to call in some highbrow hired-man when it's necessary for him to answer the crooked critics of the sane and efficient life. He's not dumb, like the old-fashioned merchant. He's got a vocabulary and a punch.

'"With all modesty, I want to stand up here as a representative business man and gently whisper, 'Here's our kind of folks! Here's the specifications of the Standardized American Citizen! Here's the new generation of Americans:

fellows with hair on their chests and smiles in their eyes and adding-machines in their offices. We're not doing any boasting, but we like ourselves first-rate, and if you don't like us, look out—better get under cover before the cyclone hits town!'

' "So! In my clumsy way I have tried to sketch the Real He-man, the fellow with Zip and Bang. And it's because Zenith has so large a proportion of such men that it's the most stable, the greatest of our cities.

' "Some time I hope folks will quit handing all the credit to a lot of moth-eaten, mildewed, out-of-date, old European dumps, and give proper credit to the famous Zenith spirit, that clean fighting determination to win Success that has made the little old Zip City celebrated in every land and clime, wherever condensed milk and pasteboard cartons are known! Believe me, the world has fallen too long for these worn-out countries that aren't producing anything but bootblacks and scenery and booze, that haven't got one bathroom per hundred people, and that don't know a loose-leaf ledger from a slip-cover; and it's just about time for some Zenithite to get his back up and holler for a show-down!

' "I tell you, Zenith and her sister-cities are producing a new type of civilization. There are many resemblances between Zenith and these other burgs, and I'm darn glad of it! The extraordinary, growing, and sane standardization of stores, offices, streets, hotels, clothes, and newspapers throughout the United States shows how strong and enduring a type is ours.

' "I always like to remember a piece that Chum Frink wrote for the newspapers about his lecture-tours. . .

> When I am out upon the road, a poet with a pedler's load, I mostly sing a hearty song, and take a chew and hike along, a-handing out my samples fine of Cheero Brand of sweet sunshine, and peddling optimistic pokes and stable lines of japes and jokes to Lyceums and other folks, to Rotarys, Kiwanis' Clubs, and feel I ain't like other dubs. And then old Major Silas Satan, a brainy cuss who's always waitin', he gives his tail a lively quirk, and gets in quick his dirty work. He fills me up with mullygrubs; my hair the backward way he rubs; he makes me lonelier than a hound, on Sunday when the folks ain't round. And then b' gosh, I would prefer to never be a lecturer, a-ridin' round in classy cars and smoking fifty-cent cigars, and never more I want to roam; I simply want to be back home, a-eatin' flap-jacks, hash, and ham, with folks who savvy whom I am!
>
> But when I get that lonely spell, I simply seek the best hotel, no matter in what town I be—St. Paul, Toledo, or K.C., in Washington, Schenectady, in Louisville or Albany. And at that inn it hits my dome that I again am right at home. If I should stand a lengthy spell in front of that first-class hotel, that to the drummers loves to cater, across from some big film theayter; if I should look around and buzz, and wonder in what town I was, I swear that I could never tell! For all the crowd would be so swell, in just the

same fine sort of jeans they wear at home, and all the queens with spiffy bonnets on their beans, and all the fellows standing round a-talkin' always, I'll be bound, the same good jolly kind of guff, 'bout autos, politics and stuff and baseball players of renown that Nice Guys talk in my home town!

Then when I entered that hotel, I'd look around and say, 'Well, well!' For there would be the same news-stand, same magazines and candies grand, same smokes of famous standard brand, I'd find at home, I'll tell! And when I saw the jolly bunch come waltzing in for eats at lunch, and squaring up in natty duds to platters large of French Fried spuds, why then I'd stand right up and bawl, 'I've never left my home at all!' And all replete I'd sit me down beside some guy in derby brown upon a lobby chair of plush, and murmur to him in a rush, 'Hello, Bill, tell me, good old scout, how is your stock a-holdin' out?' Then we'd be off, two solid pals, a-chatterin' like giddy gals of flivvers, weather, home, and wives, lodge-brothers then for all our lives! So when Sam Satan makes you blue, good friend, that's what I'd up and do, for in these States where'er you roam, you never leave your home sweet home. . .

' "I believe, however, in keeping the best to the last. When I remind you that we have one motor car for every five and seven-eighths persons in the city, then I give a rock-ribbed practical indication of the kind of progress and braininess which is synonymous with the name Zenith!

' "But the way of the righteous is not all roses. Before I close I must call your attention to a problem we have to face, this coming year. The worst menace to sound government is not the avowed socialists but a lot of cowards who work under cover—the long-haired gentry who call themselves "liberals" and "radicals" and "non-partisan" and "intelligentsia" and God only knows how many other trick names! Irresponsible teachers and professors constitute the worst of this whole gang, and I am ashamed to say that several of them are on the faculty of our great State University! The U. is my own Alma Mater, and I am proud to be known as an alumni, but there are certain instructors there who seem to think we ought to turn the conduct of the nation over to hoboes and roustabouts.

' "Those profs are the snakes to be scotched—they and all their milk-and-water ilk!

' ". . . let me tell you that during this golden coming year it's just as much our duty to bring influence to have those cusses fired as it is to sell all the real estate and gather in all the good shekels we can.

' "Not till that is done will our sons and daughters see that the ideal of American manhood and culture isn't a lot of cranks sitting around chewing the rag about their Rights and their Wrongs, but a God-fearing, hustling, successful, two-fisted Regular Guy, who belongs to some church with pep and piety to it, who belongs to the Boosters or the Rotarians or the Kiwanis, to the Elks or Moose or Red Men or Knights of Columbus or any one of a score of organizations of good, jolly, kidding, laughing, sweating, upstanding, lend-a-handing Royal Good Fellows, who plays hard and works hard, and whose answer to his critics is a square-toed boot that'll teach the grouches and smart alecks to respect the He-man and get out and root for Uncle Samuel, U.S.A." '

3. *Democracy is idiotic—it destroys itself*

H. L. MENCKEN, *Notes on Democracy*, 1926 *

Whether or not democracy is destined to survive in the world until the corruptible puts on incorruption and the immemorial Christian dead leap out of their graves, their faces shining and their yells resounding—this is something, I confess, that I don't know, nor is it necessary, for the purposes of the present inquiry, that I venture upon the hazard of a guess. My business is not prognosis, but diagnosis. I am not engaged in therapeutics, but in pathology. That simple statement of fact, I daresay, will be accepted as a confession, condemning me out of hand as unfit for my task, and even throwing a certain doubt upon my *bona fides*. For it is one of the peculiar intellectual accompaniments of democracy that the concept of the insoluble becomes unfashionable—nay, almost infamous. To lack a remedy is to lack the very license to discuss disease. The causes of this are to be sought, without question, in the nature of democracy itself. It came into the world as a cure-all, and it remains primarily a cure-all to this day. Any boil upon the body politic, however vast and raging, may be relieved by taking a vote; any flux of blood may be stopped by passing a law. The aim of government is to repeal the laws of nature, and re-enact them with moral amendments. War becomes simply a device to end war. The state, a mystical emanation from the mob, takes on a transcendental potency, and acquires the power to make over the father which begat it. Nothing remains inscrutable and beyond remedy, not even the way of a man with a maid. . .

Democracy becomes a substitute for the old religion, and the antithesis of it. . . It has the power to enchant and disarm; it is not vulnerable to logical attack. I point for proof to the appalling gyrations and contortions of its chief exponents. Read, for example, the late James Bryce's *Modern Democracies*. Observe how he amasses incontrovertible evidence that democracy doesn't work —and then concludes with a stout declaration that it does. Or, if his two fat volumes are too much for you, turn to some school reader and give a judicious perusal to Lincoln's Gettysburg Address, with its argument that the North fought the Civil War to save self-government to the world!—a thesis echoed in falsetto, and by feebler men, fifty years later. It is impossible, by an device known to philosophers, to meet doctrines of that sort; they obviously lie outside the range of logical ideas. There is, in the human mind, a natural taste for such hocus-pocus. It greatly simplifies the process of ratiocination, which is unbearably painful to the great majority of men. What dulls and baffles the teeth may be got down conveniently by an heroic gulp. . . Democracy is shot through with this delight in the incredible, this banal mysticism. One cannot discuss it without colliding with preposterous postulates, all of them cherished like authentic hairs from the whiskers of Moses himself. I have alluded to its touching acceptance of the faith that progress is illimitable and ordained of God—that every human problem, in the very nature of things, may be solved. There are corollaries that are even more naive. One, for example, is to the general effect that optimism is a virtue in itself—that there is a mysterious merit in being hopeful and of glad heart, even in the presence of adverse and immovable facts. This curious notion turns the glittering wheels of Rotary, and is the motive power of the political New Thoughters called Liberals. Certainly the attitude of the average American Liberal toward the so-called League of Nations offered superb clinical material to the student of democratic psychopathology. He began by arguing that the League would save the world. Confronted by proofs of its fraudulence, he switched to the doctrine that believing in it would save the world. So, later on, with the Washington Disarmament Conference. The man who hopes absurdly, it appears, is in some fantastic and gaseous manner a better citizen than the man who detects and exposes the truth. Bear this sweet democratic axiom clearly in mind. It is, fundamentally, what is the matter with the United States.

As I say, my present mandate does not oblige me to conjure up a system that will surpass and shame democracy as a democracy surpasses and shames the polity of the Andaman Islanders or the Great Khan—a system full-blown and perfect, like Prohibition, and ready to be put into effect by the simple adoption of an amendment to the Constitution. Such a system, for all I know, may lie outside the farthest soarings of the human mind, though that mind can weigh the stars and know God. Until the end of the chapter the ants and bees may flutter their sardonic antennae at us in that department, as they do in others: the last joke upon man may be that he never learned how to govern himself in a rational and competent manner. . . I am not even undertaking to prove here that democracy is too full of evils to be further borne. On the contrary, I am convinced that it has some valuable merits, not often described, and I shall refer to a few of them presently. All I argue is that its manifest defects, if they are ever to be got rid of at all, must be got rid of by examining them realistically—that they will never cease to afflict all the more puissant and exemplary nations so long as discussing them is impeded by concepts borrowed from theology. As for me, I have never encountered any actual evidence, convincing to an ordinary jury, that *vox populi* is actually *vox Dei*. The proofs, indeed, run the other way. The life of the inferior man is one long protest against the obstacles that God interposes to the attainment of his dreams, and democracy, if it is anything at all, is simply one way of getting round those obstacles. Thus it represents, not a jingling echo of what seems to be the divine will, but a raucous defiance of it. . .

For all I know, democracy may be a self-limiting disease, as civilization itself seems to be. There are obvious paradoxes in its philosophy, and some of them have a suicidal smack. It offers John Doe a means to rise above his place beside

Richard Roe, and then, by making Roe his equal, it takes away the chief usufructs of the rising. I here attempt no pretty logical gymnastics: the history of democratic states is a history of disingenuous efforts to get rid of the second half of that dilemma. There is not only the natural yearning of Doe to use and enjoy the superiority that he has won; there is also the natural tendency of Roe, as an inferior man, to acknowledge it. Democracy, in fact, is always inventing class distinctions, despite its theoretical abhorrence of them. The baron has departed, but in his place stand the grand goblin, the supreme worthy archon, the sovereign grand commander. Democratic man, as I have remarked, is quite unable to think of himself as a free individual; he must belong to a group, or shake with fear and loneliness—and the group, of course, must have its leaders. It would be hard to find a country in which such brummagem serene highnesses are revered with more passionate devotion than they get in the United States. The distinction that goes with mere office runs far ahead of the distinction that goes with actual achievement. A Harding is regarded as genuinely superior to a Halsted, no doubt because his doings are better understood. But there is a form of human striving that is understood by democratic man even better than Harding's, and that is the striving for money. Thus the plutocracy, in a democratic state, tends to take the place of the missing aristocracy, and even to be mistaken for it. It is, of course, something quite different. It lacks all the essential characters of a true aristocracy: a clean tradition, culture, public spirit, honesty, honour, courage—above all, courage. It stands under no bond of obligation to the state; it has no public duty; it is transient and lacks a goal. Its most puissant dignitaries of to-day came out of the mob only yesterday—and from the mob they bring all its peculiar ignobilities. As practically encountered, the plutocracy stands quite as far from the *honnete homme* as it stands from the Holy Saints. Its main character is its incurable timorousness; it is forever grasping at the straws held out by demagogues. Half a dozen gabby Jewish youths, meeting in a back room to plan a revolution—in other words, half a dozen kittens preparing to upset the Matterhorn—are enough to scare it half to death. Its dreams are of banshees, hobgoblins, bugaboos. The honest, untroubled snores of a Percy or a Hohenstaufen are quite beyond it.

The plutocracy, as I say, is comprehensible to the mob because its aspirations are essentially those of inferior men; it is not by accident that Christianity, a mob religion, paves heaven with gold and precious stones, i.e., with money. There are, of course, reactions against this ignoble ideal among men of more civilized tastes, even in democratic states, and sometimes they arouse the mob to a transient distrust of certain of the plutocratic pretensions. But that distrust seldom arises above mere envy, and the polemic which engenders it is seldom sound in logic or impeccable in motive. What it lacks is aristocratic disinterestedness, born of aristocratic security. There is no body of opinion behind it that is, in the strictest sense, a free opinion. Its chief exponents, by some divine irony, are pedagogues of one sort or another—which is to say, men chiefly marked by their haunting fear of losing their jobs. Living under such terrors, with the plutocracy policing them harshly on one side and the mob congenitally suspicious of them on the other, it is no wonder that their revolt usually peters out in metaphysics, and that they tend to abandon it as their families grow up, and the costs of heresy become prohibitive. The pedagogue, in the long run, shows the virtues of the Congressman, the newspaper editorial writer or the butler, not those of the aristocrat. . . Thus politics, under democracy, resolves itself into impossible alternatives. Whatever the label on the parties, or the war cries issuing from the demagogues who lead them, the practical choice is between the plutocracy on the one side and a rabble of preposterous impossibilists on the other. One must either follow the *New York Times*, or one must be prepared to swallow Bryan and the Bolsheviki. It is a pity that this is so. For what democracy needs most of all is a party that will separate the good that is in it theoretically from the evils that beset it practically, and then try to erect that good into a workable system. What it needs beyond everything is a party of liberty. It produces, true enough, occasional libertarians, just as despotism produces occasional regicides, but it treats them in the same drumhead way. It will never have a party of them until it invents and installs a genuine aristocracy, to breed them and secure them. . .

I have alluded somewhat vaguely to the merits of democracy. One of them is quite obvious: it is, perhaps, the most charming form of government ever devised by man. The reason is not far to seek. It is based upon propositions that are palpably not true—and what is not true, as everyone knows, is always immensely more fascinating and satisfying to the vast majority of men than what is true. Truth has harshness that alarms them, and an air of finality that collides with their incurable romanticism. They turn, in all the great emergencies of life, to the ancient promises, transparently false but immensely comforting, and of all those ancient promises there is none more comforting than the one to the effect that the lowly shall inherit the earth. It is at the bottom of the dominant religious system of the modern world, and it is at the bottom of the dominant political system. The latter, which is democracy, gives it an even higher credit and authority than the former, which is Christianity. More, democracy gives it a certain appearance of objective and demonstrable truth. The mob man, functioning as citizen, gets a feeling that he is really important to the world—that he is genuinely running things. Out of his maudlin herding after rogues and mountebanks there comes to him a sense of vast and mysterious power—which is what makes archbishops, police sergeants, the grand goblins of the Ku Klux and other such magnificoes happy. And out of it there comes, too, a conviction that he is somehow wise, that his views are taken seriously by his betters—which is what makes United States Senators, fortune-tellers and Young Intellectuals happy. Finally, there comes out of it a glowing consciousness of a high duty triumphantly done—which is what makes hangmen and husbands happy.

All these forms of happiness, of course, are illusory. They don't last. The democrat, leaping into the air to flap his wings and praise God, is for ever coming down with a thump. The seeds of his disaster, as I have shown, lie in his own stupidity: he can never get rid of the naive delusion—so beautifully Christian!—that happiness is something to be got by taking it away from the other fellow. But there are seeds, too, in the very nature of things: a promise, after all, is only a promise, even when it is supported by divine revelation, and the chances against its fulfilment may be put into a depressing mathematical formula. Here the irony that lies under all human aspiration shows itself: the quest for happiness, as always, brings only unhappiness in the end. But saying that is merely saying that the true charm of democracy is not for the democrat but for the spectator. That spectator, it seems to me, is favoured with a show of the first cut and calibre. Try to image anything more heroically absurd! What grotesque false pretences! What a parade of obvious imbecilities! What a welter of fraud! But is fraud unamusing? Then I retire forthwith as a psychologist. The fraud of democracy, I contend, is more amusing than any other—more amusing even, and by miles, than the fraud of religion. Go into your praying-chamber and give sober thought to any of the more characteristic democratic inventions: say, Law Enforcement. Or to any of the typical democratic prophets: say, the late Archangel Bryan. If you don't come out paled and palsied by mirth then you will not laugh on the Last Day itself, when Presbyterians step out of the grave like chicks from the egg, and wings blossom from their scapulae, and they leap into interstellar space with roars of joy.

I have spoken hitherto of the possibility that democracy may be a self-limiting disease, like measles. It is, perhaps, something more: it is self-devouring. One cannot observe it objectively without being impressed by its curious distrust of itself—its apparently ineradicable tendency to abandon its whole philosophy at the first sign of strain. I need not point to what happens invariably in democratic states when the national safety is menaced. All the great tribunes of democracy, on such occasions, convert themselves, by a process as simple as taking a deep breath, into despots of an almost fabulous ferocity. Lincoln, Roosevelt and Wilson come instantly to mind: Jackson and Cleveland are in the background, waiting to be recalled. Nor is this process confined to times of alarm and terror: it is going on day in and day out. Democracy always seems bent upon killing the thing it theoretically loves. I have rehearsed some of its operations against liberty, the very cornerstone of its political metaphysic. It not only wars upon the thing itself; it even wars upon mere academic advocacy of it. I offer the spectacle of Americans jailed for reading the Bills of Rights as perhaps the most gaudily humorous ever witnessed in the modern world. Try to imagine monarchy jailing subjects for maintaining the divine right of Kings! Or Christianity damning a believer for arguing that Jesus Christ was the Son of God! This last, perhaps, has been done: anything is possible in that direction. But under democracy the remotest and most fantastic possibility is a commonplace of every day. All the axioms resolve themselves into thundering paradoxes, many amounting to downright contradictions in terms. The mob is competent to rule the rest of us—but it must be rigorously policed itself. There is a government, not of men, but of laws—but men are set upon benches to decide finally what the law is and may be. The highest function of the citizen is to serve the state—but the first assumption that meets him, when he assays to discharge it, is an assumption of his disingenuousness and dishonour. Is that assumption commonly sound? Then the farce only grows the more glorious.

I confess, for my part, that it greatly delights me. I enjoy democracy immensely. It is incomparably idiotic, and hence incomparably amusing. Does it exalt dunderheads, cowards, trimmers, frauds, cads? Then the pain of seeing them go up is balanced and obliterated by the joy of seeing them come down. Is it inordinately wasteful, extravagant, dishonest? Then so is every other form of government: all alike are enemies to laborious and virtuous men. Is rascality at the very heart of it? Well, we have borne that rascality since 1776, and continue to survive. In the long run, it may turn out that rascality is necessary to human government, and even to civilization itself—that civilization, at bottom, is nothing but a colossal swindle. I do not know: I report only that when the suckers are running well the spectacle is infinitely exhilarating. But I am, it may be, a somewhat malicious man: my sympathies, when it comes to suckers, tend to be coy. What I can't make out is how any man can believe in democracy who feels for and with them, and is pained when they are debauched and made a show of. How can any man be a democrat who is sincerely a democrat?

4. *Certain social and economic laws are beyond human direction and control*

GEORGE SUTHERLAND, *Principle or Expedient?* 1921 *

There is nothing more unfortunate in governmental administration than a policy of playing fast and loose with great economic and political principles which have withstood the strain of changing circumstances and the stress of time and have become part of our fundamental wisdom. . . Too little government and too much government lie at the opposite extremities of social management, and both are bad; for if too little government tends toward anarchy, too much government carries us in the direction of tyranny and oppression. . . Obviously, therefore, that government is best which governs neither least nor most, but just enough. But, even that indubitable statement of the matter, while theoretically unobjectionable, does not, for practical purposes, bring us anywhere, since it furnishes no intelligible standard for determining what is just enough government, and no two individuals would be likely to ever agree upon its application in specific instances.

A principle to be of any value, therefore, must be not only sound and just, but capable of practical application to the affairs of life. In other words, it must be definite as well as righteous. Conditions which such a principle governs may change—indeed, in this forward moving world of ours, they must change—but the principle itself is immutable; once righteous it is always righteous. When it ceases to be operative it is not because the principle has become wrong where it was once right, but because under altered conditions it no longer applies. . .

The difficulty with so many of our political reformers is that they lack a proper sense of discrimination. Finding that something has gone wrong with the social organism they are prone to conclude that some fundamental rule

* Annual address, 21 January 1921, before the New York State Bar Association, *Proceedings of the New York State Bar Association*, vol. 44, pp. 263-82 *passim*.

which has theretofore governed its operations is at fault, when, in fact, the trouble lies outside the scope of the rule altogether, or, not infrequently, is due to its violation and not to its enforcement. In consequence, wise and wholesome principles are discarded and unjustly fall under the condemnation of the public with the result that matters grow worse instead of getting better. After a lingering period of inconvenience and suffering, the truth is finally rediscovered and the old principle re-established and society slowly recovers from the effects of its painful and altogether useless experience.

We have a very recent case in point. We have been passing through an unpleasant period of advancing prices which began by being vexatious and ended by becoming intolerable. Laws to punish the profiteer in time of war, crudely framed and hastily enacted, were brought to bear on the situation; government agencies were invoked to search out the offender and expose him to public scorn; irritating regulations were devised; indictments were sought and returned; prosecutions were carried forward and the criminal convicted, or the innocent acquitted under precisely similar facts according to the taste of an impartial jury and the accidental bent of the judicial mind. Now the old principle, proven by centuries of experience under all conceivable circumstances, applicable to such matters in time of peace is that government should confine its activities, as a general rule, to preserving a free market and preventing fraud, but otherwise leave prices to the automatic control of the economic law of supply and demand. But our officials, having first worked themselves into a state of mind on the subject, threw the principle, with all the confirming lessons of the past, into the scrap-heap and turned the matter of price control over to the constabulary. The legal officers of the government in a condition of more or less excitement, made extravagant promises to an equally excited public to the effect that an end would be made of high prices by putting those who exacted them in jail, where they would obviously be unable to charge high prices, being unable to charge any at all.

The profiteer was threatened and prosecuted; penalties, both legal and extralegal were inflicted upon him—all without the least avail so far as the promised relief was concerned. Prices did not fall. On the contrary, they rose, mounting in perverse and insulting disregard of the hopeful speculations of the Department of Justice, and despite all statutes and regulations and prosecutions to the contrary intent. And then all at once this world old economic law brought about the result which statutes and official regulation, and legal fuss and fustian, had been utterly unable to accomplish, and prices began to fall. They have proceeded so far already in their descent that we have become as much alarmed over falling prices as we were theretofore enraged over rising prices, and Congress has been engaged in devising plans to intercept the reverse movement of this great, imperturbable economic force in response to a demand quite as frantic as that which a short time ago had induced the effort on the part of the government to check the advance, and with probable consequences no less disappointing. The whole process has been absurdly futile, but it has also been expensive and in some respects tragic, so that one knows not whether tears or laughter be the more appropriate emotion.

All of which brings me to the point which I want principally to emphasize, namely, that there are certain fundamental social and economic laws which are beyond the power, and certain underlying governmental principles, which are beyond the right of official control, and any attempt to interfere with their operations inevitably ends in confusion, if not disaster. These laws and principles may be compared with the forces of nature whose movements are entirely outside the scope of human power. We may temporarily divert the small tributaries of the Mississippi from their natural channels in the uplands, but who is so vain as to attempt to control the forces of gravity which will finally bring their waters down to the accustomed level or change the course of the great river itself in its majestic journey to the sea? . . .

One trouble, and perhaps the most serious trouble, is that people expect too much of the government. They seem to forget that it is a creature wholly of their own making, and come to look upon it as a species of Providence which can work miracles of beneficence if it only will. But government is neither all wise nor all powerful. I do not agree with some that it is an unnecessary evil that should be abolished, nor with others that it is a necessary evil that must be borne, although I am bound to say that it escapes the latter characterization sometimes by a very narrow margin. It is simply a fallible, human contrivance, under more or less wise and more or less foolish and more or less skillful and more or less stupid management, and consequently a mixture of success and failure. As a result of long and varied experience a fund of useful information has been slowly acquired, and it is the part of prudence that those who are called upon to direct the operations of government should utilize this great store of accumulated wisdom for their guidance, not in slavish adherence to mere use and wont, but with the discriminating intelligence of men who seek the best rather than the newest. In saying this, I hope not to be accused of being old-fashioned, for I sincerely believe myself to be fairly progressive. I know I am not reactionary, unless a perverse tendency to put a good deal of faith in experience and very little in mere experiment, can be so characterized. There are, nevertheless, I may say in passing, some very old fashioned things that are still generally accepted as authoritative: the multiplication-table, the Sermon on the Mount, the American Constitution, for example. One occasionally meets with a person calling himself a progressive who seems to proceed upon the theory that an idea ought to be approved merely because our fathers rejected it, or rejected simply because our fathers believed in it. But that is not progress. It is stupidity; and quite as objectionable as it is to cling to a doctrine simply because our fathers clung to it. . .

In a progressive society, to be sure, government will from time to time require readjustment, but in society, as in nature, there are few cataclysms. Changes come, sometimes slowly, sometimes swiftly, but usually step by step. The face and form of society, like the face and form of nature, as a general rule, change by imperceptible degrees. . . The careful husbandman sprays the infected leaves and lops off the diseased branches in preference to uprooting the tree. The political crusader of our day, on the contrary, goes up and down the land, hoping for the worst, inculcating the gospel of pessimism that 'whatever is is wrong' and seeking to uproot great and noble principles in order to overcome a small evil that needs only to be sprayed, or, perhaps, left alone to work its own cure. . .

A government of laws! These four words, perhaps the most significant in our political language, describe the fundamental quality of the American system of government upon which, for their chief security, all our civil and political liberties depend. They express a principle without which a just relation between the rights of the individual and the requirements of the social organism to which he belongs could not be maintained. The spirit of them has been woven into and through the fabric of our state and national polity, and so long as it abides there we shall never become subject to the arbitrary will of an autocrat, because it precludes the effective operation of the arbitrary will of anybody. That spirit is the inspiration of the Bill of Rights in every American constitution, the fundamental reason for the separation of the three several departments of government, the very soul of the free institutions under which we live. Older than the Union or the Constitution, the principle animates the great charters of English liberty from Magna Charta to the Bill of Rights. The strength of its influence may be measured throughout the history of civilization by the rise and fall of autocratic power, because to the precise extent that official will has from time to time taken the place of standing law as the rule of human conduct, a government of laws has been supplanted by a government of men. . .

Our chief danger lies . . . in the growing extension of vaguely conferred powers in the hands of administrative bodies. In state and nation there is an alarming increase of official agencies whose powers thus tend, more and more, to become arbitrary, and lead us further and further from the rule of law. If anything goes wrong, or a large number of people conclude that something has gone wrong, the remedy almost invariably suggested is an allopathic dose of legislation. The general sentiment is that if we only have a law on the subject, and particularly a rigorous law, everything will immediately be made all right. We do not give ourselves time to study the conditions or consult the precedents so as to determine whether the symptoms point to a serious disorder, or mark a mere irregularity in an otherwise normal and healthful development, or, indeed, whether they simply indicate a perfectly proper but unfamiliar condition, due to the great changes which are continually taking place in our modern life. But the demand at once and imperiously goes forth for the enactment of a statute to be administered and amplified by a bureau or commission. The result is that our political establishment is steadily losing its character as a government of laws, and individuals and corporate bodies are becoming less and less able to determine, by reference to fixed rules, what are their rights and duties and responsibilities, and more and more reduced to the necessity of guessing what they may do with the reasonable hope of satisfying not the law but the views of some more or less intelligent administrative body.

Not only is the growth of personal and bureaucratic government undermining the fundamental qualities of our institutions, and becoming intolerably vexatious by reason of the arbitrary interference in affairs hitherto considered essentially private, but it is becoming exceedingly burdensome by reason of the constantly increasing cost of its maintenance.

The one law which all bureaus and commissions seem to definitely agree upon is the law of expansion. Having been created and set in motion, they defy all efforts of their legislative creators to confine them to their original limits, but reach out and absorb a constantly increasing degree of power and continually add to the number of their agents and employes and the expense of their operations. What succeeding generations will be obliged to face I do not know, but this generation has seen the growth of a comparatively modest official establishment to a vast army, far exceeding, in my judgment, any reasonable public need. It is safe to say that if our various governments were managed in the same spirit of economy and intimate responsibility which actuates the management of our great business concerns, at least one-third of this army could be relegated to private life. . .

We have been compelled, from time to time, to listen to a great deal of nonsense on the subject of property. We have been warned by the demagogue not to exalt property above the man. Of course, the enforcement of the Due Process Clause can have no such effect, for it is not the right of property which is protected, but the right *to* property. Property, *per se*, has no rights; but the individual—the man—has three great rights, equally sacred from arbitrary interference: the right to his life, the right to his liberty, the right to his property. . . To give a man his life but deny him his liberty, is to take from him all that makes his life worth living. To give him his liberty but take from him the property which is the fruit and badge of his liberty, is to still leave him a slave. . .

We cannot maintain a government of laws if the rights of some men are submitted to the test of liberty, and the rights of others to the test of power. We cannot have liberty itself in any real sense if we act upon the theory that liberty is a right to do as we please, and prevent others from doing as *they* please. Hence any law which arbitrarily separates men into classes to be punished or rewarded, not according to what they do but according to the class to which they are assigned, is odious and despotic, no matter how large a majority may have approved it. I have personally the greatest possible sympathy for the farmers of the country who have been first to feel the hardship of falling prices, but legislation which proposes to extend special and exclusive aid to them is almost sure to be, in one way or another, at the expense of other classes of our citizenship. Apart from all other consideration, the danger of all such legislation is that it may constitute the first link in a chain of precedents which, beginning in necessity, passes from one gradation to another until, at length, it rests in mere favor. . .

I have a very firm conviction that the tendency to control our activities by statutory rule is being overemphasized. Too many laws are being passed in haste. Too many that simply reflect a temporary prejudice, a passing fad, a fleeting whim, a superficial view or an exaggerated estimate of the extent, or a mistaken impression of the quality of an evil. Many of the evils sought to be governed by legislation would rectify themselves under the powerful force of public sentiment. Many of them would be automatically corrected as a result of the unpleasant consequences which follow their indulgence. The truth is, that, as we grow in intelligence the consequences which follow good or bad conduct more and more control our behavior. In our dealings with one another we are not controlled by statute law which visits an infraction of its terms by *punishment* more or less uncertain, more or less delayed, and more or less severe, half so often as we are by the unwritten moral law the violation of which automatically imposes certain definite, unpleasant *consequences* upon the violator, which, like the consequences following the violation of a physical law—as, for example, an attack of indigestion after an indiscreet dinner—promote repentance and reformation more surely than a statutory penalty.

In determining whether legislation affecting individual conduct is justified there are always two things to be balanced against one another, namely, the evil of the objectionable conduct and the evil of curtailing individual freedom of action; and the great factor of determination in each case is whether the harm resulting from the objectionable conduct is of so grave a nature as to justify its suppression by a resort to the opposing evil of interference with the freedom of the individual. It is a melancholy fact, but a fact, nevertheless, that a good deal of well intended legislation which has been passed in disregard of this principle, has brought evils greater than they have suppressed. . .

5. *I don't believe in apologies for power*

MR. JUSTICE HOLMES, Tyson *v.* Banton, 1927 *

We fear to grant power and are unwilling to recognize it when it exists . . . and when legislatures are held to be authorized to do anything considerably affecting public welfare it is covered by apologetic phrases like the police power, or the statement that the business concerned has been dedicated to a public use. The former expression is convenient, to be sure, to conciliate the mind to something that needs explanation: the fact that the constitutional requirement of compensation when property is taken cannot be pressed to its grammatical extreme; that property rights may be taken for public purposes without pay if you do not take too much; that some play must be allowed to the joints if the machine is to work. But police power often is used in a wide sense to cover and, as I said, to apologize for the general power of the legislature to make a part of the community uncomfortable by a change.

I do not believe in such apologies. I think the proper course is to recognize that a state legislature can do whatever it sees fit to do unless it is restrained by some express prohibition in the Constitution of the United States or of the State, and that Courts should be careful not to extend such prohibitions beyond their obvious meaning by reading into them conceptions of public policy that the particular Court may happen to entertain. . . The truth seems to me to be that, subject to compensation when compensation is due, the legis-

* Dissenting opinion, 273 U.S. 418, 1927, pp. 446–7.

lature may forbid or restrict any business when it has a sufficient force of public opinion behind it. Lotteries were thought useful adjuncts of the State a century or so ago; now they are believed to be immoral and they have been stopped. Wine has been thought good for man from time of the Apostles until recent years. But when public opinion changed it did not need the Eighteenth Amendment, notwithstanding the Fourteenth, to enable a State to say that the business should end. . . What has happened to lotteries and wine might happen to theatres in some moral storm of the future, not because theatres were devoted to a public use, but because people had come to think that way.

But if we are to yield to fashionable conventions, it seems to me that theatres are as much devoted to public use as anything well can be. We have not that respect for art that is one of the glories of France. But to many people the superfluous is the necessary, and it seems to me that Government does not go beyond its sphere in attempting to make life livable for them. I am far from saying that I think this particular law a wise and rational provision. That is not my affair. But if the people of the State of New York speaking by their authorized voice say that they want it, I see nothing in the Constitution of the United States to prevent their having their will. . .

6. *Poverty will be banished from this nation*

HERBERT HOOVER, Accepting the Republican Nomination for the Presidency, 1928 *

. . . No party ever accepted a more difficult task of reconstruction than did the Republican Party in 1921. The record of these seven and one-half years constitutes a period of rare courage in leadership and constructive action. Never has a political party been able to look back upon a similar period with more satisfaction. Never could it look forward with more confidence that its record would be approved by the electorate.

Peace has been made. The healing processes of good-will have extinguished the fires of hate. Year by year in our relations with other nations we have advanced the ideals of law and of peace, in substitution for force. By rigorous economy Federal expenses have been reduced by two billions per annum. The national debt has been reduced by six and a half billions. The foreign debts have been settled in large part and on terms which have regard for our debtors and for our taxpayers. Taxes have been reduced four successive times. These reductions have been made in the particular interest of the smaller taxpayers. For this purpose taxes upon articles of consumption and popular service have been removed. The income tax rolls today show a reduction of 80 per cent in the total revenue collected on income under $10,000 per year, while they show a reduction of only 25 per cent in revenues from incomes above that amount. Each successive reduction in taxes has brought a reduction in the cost of living to all our people.

Commerce and industry have revived. . . Constructive leadership and co-operation by the Government have released and stimulated the energies of our people. Faith in the future has been restored. Confidence in our form of government has never been greater.

But it is not through the recitation of wise policies in government alone that we demonstrate our progress under Republican guidance. . . In this short time we have equipped nearly 9,000,000 more homes with electricity, and through it drudgery has been lifted from the lives of women. The barriers of time and distance have been swept away and life made freer and larger by the installation of 6,000,000 more telephones, 7,000,000 radio sets, and the service of an additional 14,000,000 automobiles. Our cities are growing magnificent with beautiful buildings, parks and playgrounds. Our countryside has been knit together with splendid roads. . .

One of the oldest and perhaps the noblest of human aspirations has been the abolition of poverty. By poverty I mean the grinding by undernourishment, cold, and ignorance and fear of old age of those who have the will to work. We in America today are nearer to the final triumph over poverty than ever before in the history of any land. The poorhouse is vanishing among us. We have not yet reached the goal, but, given a chance to go forward with the policies of the last eight years, and we shall soon, with the help of God, be in sight of the day when poverty will be banished from this nation. . .

The Republican Party has ever been the exponent of protection to all our people from competition with lower standards of living abroad. We have always fought for tariffs designed to establish this protection from imported goods. We also have enacted restrictions upon immigration for the protection of labor from the inflow of workers faster than we can absorb them without breaking down our wage levels.

The Republican principle of an effective control of imported goods and of immigration has contributed greatly to the prosperity of our country. There is no selfishness in this defense of our standards of living. Other countries gain nothing if the high standards of America are sunk and if we are prevented from building a civilization which sets the level of hope for the entire world. A general reduction in the tariff would admit a flood of goods from abroad. It would injure every home. It would fill our streets with idle workers. It would destroy the returns to our dairymen, our fruit, flax, and livestock growers, and our other farmers. . .

During these past years we have grown greatly in the mutual understanding between employer and employe. We have seen a growing realization by the employer that the highest practicable wage is the road to increased consumption and prosperity and we have seen a growing realization by labor that the maximum use of machines, of effort and of skill is the road to lower production costs and in the end to higher real wages. Under these impulses and the Republican protective system our industrial output has increased as never before and our wages have grown steadily in buying power. . .

With impressive proof on all sides of magnificent progress no one can rightly deny the fundamental correctness of our economic system. Nothing, however, is perfect but it works for progress. Our pre-eminent advance over nations in the last eight years has been due to distinctively American accomplishments. We do not owe these accomplishments to our vast natural resources. These we have always had. They have not increased. What has changed is our ability to utilize these resources more effectively. It is our human resources that have changed. Man for man and woman for woman we are today more capable whether in the work of farm, factory, or business than ever before. It lies in our magnificent educational system, in the hardworking character of our people, in the capacity for far-sighted leadership in industry, the ingenuity, the daring of the pioneers of new inventions, in the abolition of the saloon, and the wisdom of our national policies. . .

Business is practical, but it is founded upon faith—faith among our people in the integrity of business men, and faith that it will receive fair play from the Government. It is the duty of Government to maintain that faith. Our whole business system would break down in a day if there was not a high sense of moral responsibility in our business world. The whole practice and ethics of business has made great strides of improvement in the last quarter of a century, largely due to the effort of business and the professions themselves. One of the most helpful signs of recent years is the stronger growth of associations of workers, farmers, business men and professional men with a desire to cure their own abuses and a purpose to serve public interest. Many problems can be solved through co-operation between Government and these self-governing associations to improve methods and practices. When business cures its own abuses it is true self-government which comprises more than political institutions. . .

There is one of the ideals of America upon which I wish at this time to lay especial emphasis. For we would constantly test our economic, social and governmental system by certain ideals which must control them. The founders of our Republic propounded the revolutionary doctrine that all men are created equal and all should have equality before the law. This was the emancipation of the individual. And since these beginnings, slowly, surely and almost imperceptibly, this nation has added a third ideal almost unique to America—the ideal of equal opportunity. This is the safeguard of the individual. The simple life of early days in our Republic found but few limitations upon equal opportunity. By the crowding of our people and the intensity and complexity of their activities it takes today a new importance.

Equality of opportunity is the right of every American—rich or poor, foreign or native-born, irrespective of faith or color. It is the right of every individual to attain that position in life to which his ability and character entitle him. By its maintenance we will alone hold open the door of opportunity to every new generation, to every boy and girl. It tolerates no privileged classes or castes or groups who would hold opportunity as their prerogative. Only from confidence that this right will be upheld can flow that unbounded courage and hope which stimulate each individual man and woman to endeavor and to achievement. The sum of their achievement is the gigantic harvest of national progress.

This ideal of individualism based upon equal opportunity to every citizen is the negation of socialism. It is the negation of anarchy. It is the negation of despotism. It is as if we set a race. We, through free and universal education, provide the training of the runners; we give to them an equal start; we provide in the Government the umpire of fairness in the race. The winner is he who shows the most conscientious training, the greatest ability and the greatest character. Socialism bids all to end the race equally. It holds back the speedy to the pace of the slowest. Anarchy would provide neither training nor umpire. Despotism picks those who should run and those who should win. . .

Equality of opportunity is a fundamental principle of our nation. With it we must test all our policies. The success or failure of this principle is the test of our Government. . .

7. *The modern industrial corporation is the dominant institution of the modern world*

ADOLF A. BERLE, JR., AND GARDINER C. MEANS, *The Modern Corporation and Private Property*, 1932 *

PROPERTY IN TRANSITION

Corporations have ceased to be merely legal devices through which the private business transactions of individuals may be carried on. Though still much used for this purpose, the corporate form has acquired a larger significance. The corporation has, in fact, become both a method of property tenure and a means of organizing economic life. Grown to tremendous proportions, there may be said to have evolved a 'corporate system'—as there was once a feudal system—which has attracted to itself a combination of attributes and powers, and has attained a degree of prominence entitling it to be dealt with as a major social institution.

We are examining this institution probably before it has attained its zenith. Spectacular as its rise has been, every indication seems to be that the system will move forward to proportions which would stagger imagination today; just as the corporate system of today was beyond the imagination of most statesmen and business men at the opening of the present century. Only by remembering that men still living can recall a time when the present situation was hardly dreamed of, can we enforce the conclusion that the new order may easily become completely dominant during the lifetime of our children. For that reason, if for no other, it is desirable to examine this system, bearing in mind

 Pages 1–9, 345–57 *passim.*

that its impact on the life of the country and of every individual is certain to be great; it may even determine a large part of the behaviour of most men living under it.

Organization of property has played a constant part in the balance of powers which go to make up the life of any era. We need not resolve the controversy as to whether property interests are invariably controlling. The cynical view of many historians insists that property interests have at all times, visible or invisible, been dominant. Following this grim analysis, one commentator on the rise of corporations observed that they had become the 'master instruments of civilization.' * Another expressed his depression at the fact that the system had at length reached a point definitely committing civilization to the rule of a plutocracy.† Still others have seen in the system a transition phase towards ultimate socialism or communism. Acceptance of any of these beliefs may be delayed; but the underlying thought expressed in them all is that the corporate system has become the principal factor in economic organization through its mobilization of property interests.

In its new aspect the corporation is a means whereby the wealth of innumerable individuals has been concentrated into huge aggregates and whereby control over this wealth has been surrendered to a unified direction. The power attendant upon such concentration has brought forth princes of industry, whose position in the community is yet to be defined. The surrender of control over their wealth by investors has effectively broken the old property relationships and has raised the problem of defining these relationships anew. The direction of industry by persons other than those who have ventured their wealth has raised the question of the motive force back of such direction and the effective distribution of the returns from business enterprise.

These corporations have arisen in field after field as the myriad independent and competing units of private business have given way to the few large groupings of the modern quasi-public corporation. The typical business unit of the nineteenth century was owned by individuals or small groups; was managed by them or their appointees; and was, in the main, limited in size by the personal wealth of the individuals in control. These units have been supplanted in ever greater measure by great aggregations in which tens and even hundreds of thousands of workers and property worth hundreds of millions of dollars, belonging to tens or even hundreds of thousands of individuals, are combined through the corporate mechanism into a single producing organization under unified control and management. Such a unit is the American Telephone and Telegraph Company, perhaps the most advanced development of the corporate system. With assets of almost five billions of dollars, with 454,000 employees, and stockholders to the number of 567,694, this company may indeed be called an economic empire—an empire bounded by no geographical limits, but held together by centralized control. One hundred companies of this size would control the whole of American wealth; would employ all of the gainfully employed; and if there were no duplication of stockholders, would be owned by practically every family in the country.

* T. Veblen, *Absentee Ownership and Business Enterprise*, New York, 1923.
† Walter Rathenau, *Die neue Wirtschaft*, Berlin, 1918.

Such an organization of economic activity rests upon two developments, each of which has made possible an extension of the area under unified control. The factory system, the basis of the industrial revolution, brought an increasingly large number of workers directly under a single management. Then, the modern corporation, equally revolutionary in its effect, placed the wealth of innumerable individuals under the same central control. By each of these changes the power of those in control was immensely enlarged and the status of those involved, worker or property owner, was radically changed. The independent worker who entered the factory became a wage laborer surrendering the direction of his labor to his industrial master. The property owner who invests in a modern corporation so far surrenders his wealth to those in control of the corporation that he has exchanged the position of independent owner for one in which he may become merely recipient of the wages of capital.

In and of itself, the corporate device does not necessarily bring about this change. It has long been possible for an individual to incorporate his business even though it still represents his own investment, his own activities, and his own business transactions; he has in fact merely created a legal *alter ego* by setting up a corporation as the nominal vehicle. If the corporate form had done nothing more than this, we should have only an interesting custom according to which business would be carried on by individuals adopting for that purpose certain legal clothing. It would involve no radical shift in property tenure or in the organization of economic activity; it would inaugurate no 'system' comparable to the institutions of feudalism.

The corporate system appears only when this type of private or 'close' corporation has given way to an essentially different form, the quasi-public corporation: a corporation in which a large measure of separation of ownership and control has taken place through the multiplication of owners.

. . . Separation of ownership and control becomes almost complete when not even a substantial minority interest exists, as in the American Telephone and Telegraph Company whose largest holder is reported to own less than one per cent of the company's stock. Under such conditions control may be held by the directors or titular managers who can employ the proxy machinery to become a self-perpetuating body, even though as a group they own but a small fraction of the stock outstanding. In each of these types, majority control, minority control, and management control, the separation of ownership from control has become effective—a large body of security holders has been created who exercise virtually no control over the wealth which they or their predecessors in interest have contributed to the enterprise. In the case of management control, the ownership interest held by the controlling group amounts to but a very small fraction of the total ownership. Corporations where this separation has become an important factor may be classed as quasi-public in character in contradistinction to the private, or closely held corporation in which no important separation of ownership and control has taken place. . .

Though the American law makes no distinction between the private corporation and the quasi-public, the economics of the two are essentially different. The separation of ownership from control produces a condition where the interests of owner and of ultimate manager may, and often do, diverge, and where many of the checks which formerly operated to limit the use of power disappear. Size alone tends to give these giant corporations a social significance not attached to the smaller units of private enterprise. By the use of the open market for securities, each of these corporations assumes obligations towards the investing public which transform it from a legal method clothing the rule of a few individuals into an institution at least nominally serving investors who have embarked their funds in its enterprise. New responsibilities towards the owners, the workers, the consumers, and the State thus rest upon the shoulders of those in control. In creating these new relationships, the quasi-public corporation may fairly be said to work a revolution. It has destroyed the unity that we commonly call property—has divided ownership into nominal ownership and the power formerly joined to it. Thereby the corporation has changed the nature of profit-seeking enterprise. . .

This dissolution of the atom of property destroys the very foundation on which the economic order of the past three centuries has rested. Private enterprise, which has molded economic life since the close of the middle ages, has been rooted in the institution of private property. Under the feudal system, its predecessor, economic organization grew out of mutual obligations and privileges derived by various individuals from their relation to property which no one of them owned. Private enterprise, on the other hand, has assumed an owner of the instruments of production with complete property rights over those instruments. Whereas the organization of feudal economic life rested upon an elaborate system of binding customs, the organization under the system of private enterprise has rested upon the self-interest of the property owner—a self-interest held in check only by competition and the conditions of supply and demand. Such self-interest has long been regarded as the best guarantee of economic efficiency. It has been assumed that, if the individual is protected in the right both to use his own property as he sees fit and to receive the full fruits of its use, his desire for personal gain, for profits, can be relied upon as an effective incentive to his efficient use of any industrial property he may possess.

In the quasi-public corporation, such an assumption no longer holds. As we have seen, it is no longer the individual himself who uses his wealth. Those in control of that wealth, and therefore in a position to secure industrial efficiency and produce profits, are no longer, as owners, entitled to the bulk of such profits. Those who control the destinies of the typical modern corporation own so insignificant a fraction of the company's stock that the returns from running the corporation profitably accrue to them in only a very minor degree. The stockholders, on the other hand, to whom the profits of the corporation go, cannot be motivated by those profits to a more efficient use of the property, since they have surrendered all disposition of it to those in control of the enterprise. The explosion of the atom of property destroys the basis of the old assumption that the quest for profits will spur the owner of industrial property to its effective use. It consequently challenges the fundamental economic principle of individual initiative in industrial enterprise. It raises for re-examination the question of the motive force back of industry, and the ends for which the modern corporation can be or will be run. . .

THE INADEQUACY OF TRADITIONAL THEORY

Underlying the thinking of economists, lawyers and business men during the last century and a half has been the picture of economic life so skillfully painted by Adam Smith. Within his treatise on the *Wealth of Nations* are contained the fundamental concepts which run through most modern thought. Though adjustments in his picture have been made by later writers to account for new conditions, the whole has been painted in the colors which he supplied. Private property, private enterprise, individual initiative, the profit motive, wealth, competition,—these are the concepts which he employed in describing the economy of his time and by means of which he sought to show that the pecuniary self-interest of each individual, if given free play, would lead to the optimum satisfaction of human wants. Most writers of the nineteenth century built on these logical foundations, and current economic literature is, in large measure, cast in such terms.

Yet these terms have ceased to be accurate, and therefore tend to mislead in describing modern enterprise as carried on by the great corporations. Though both the terms and the concepts remain, they are inapplicable to a dominant area in American economic organization. New terms, connoting changed relationships, become necessary.

When Adam Smith talked of 'enterprise' he had in mind as the typical unit the small individual business in which the owner, perhaps with the aid of a few apprentices or workers, labored to produce goods for market or to carry on commerce. Very emphatically he repudiated the stock corporation as a business mechanism, holding that dispersed ownership made efficient operation impossible. 'The directors of such companies . . .' he pointed out, 'being the managers rather of other people's money than of their own, it cannot well be expected that they should watch over it with the same anxious vigilance with which the partners in a private copartnery frequently watch over their own. Like the stewards of a rich man, they are apt to consider attention to small matters as not for their master's honour, and very easily give themselves a dispensation from having it. Negligence and profusion, therefore, must always prevail, more or less, in the management of the affairs of such a company. It is upon this account that joint stock companies for foreign trade [at the time he was writing the only important manifestation of the corporation outside of banks, insurance companies, and water or canal companies] have seldom been able to maintain the competition against private adventurers. They have, accordingly, very seldom succeeded without an exclusive privilege, and frequently have not succeeded with one. Without an exclusive privilege they have commonly mismanaged the trade. With an exclusive privilege they have both mismanaged and confined it.'

Yet when we speak of business enterprise today, we must have in mind primarily these very units which seemed to Adam Smith not to fit into the principles which he was laying down for the conduct of economic activity. . .

PRIVATE ENTERPRISE

To Adam Smith, private enterprise meant an individual or few partners actively engaged and relying in large part on their own labor or their immediate direction. Today we have tens and hundreds of thousands of owners, of workers and of consumers combined in single enterprises. These great associations are so different from the small, privately owned enterprises of the past as to make the concept of private enterprise an ineffective instrument of analysis. It must be replaced with the concept of corporate enterprise, enterprise which is the organized activity of vast bodies of individuals, workers, consumers and suppliers of capital, under the leadership of the dictators of industry, 'control.'

INDIVIDUAL INITIATIVE

As private enterprise disappears with increasing size, so also does individual initiative. The idea that an army operates on the basis of 'rugged individualism' would be ludicrous. Equally so is the same idea with respect to the modern corporation. Group activity, the coordinating of the different steps in production, the extreme division of labor in large scale enterprise necessarily imply not individualism but cooperation and the acceptance of authority almost to the point of autocracy. Only to the extent that any worker seeks advancement within an organization is there room for individual initiative,—an initiative which can be exercised only within the narrow range of function he is called on to perform. At the very pinnacle of the hierarchy of organization in a great corporation, there alone, can individual initiative have a measure of free play. Yet even there a limit is set by the willingness and ability of subordinates to carry out the will of their superiors. In modern industry, individual liberty is necessarily curbed. . .

THE NEW CONCEPT OF THE CORPORATION

Most fundamental to the new picture of economic life must be a new concept of business enterprise as concentrated in the corporate organization. . .

Such a great concentration of power and such a diversity of interest raise the long-fought issue of power and its regulation—of interest and its protection. A constant warfare has existed between the individuals wielding power, in whatever form, and the subjects of that power. Just as there is a continuous desire for power, so also there is a continuous desire to make that power the servant of the bulk of the individuals it affects. The long struggles for the reform of the Catholic Church and for the development of constitutional law in the states are phases of this phenomenon. Absolute power is useful in building the organization. More slowly, but equally sure is the development of social pressure demanding that the power shall be used for the benefit of all concerned. This pressure, constant in ecclesiastical and political history, is already making its appearance in many guises in the economic field. . .

The rise of the modern corporation has brought a concentration of economic power which can compete on equal terms with the modern state—economic power versus political power, each strong in its own field. The state seeks in some aspects to regulate the corporation, while the corporation, steadily becoming more powerful, makes every effort to avoid such regulation. Where its own interests are concerned, it even attempts to dominate the state. The future may see the economic organism, now typified by the corporation, not only on an equal plane with the state, but possibly even superseding it as the dominant form of social organization. . .*

* [A.T.M.] In a national advertising circular of late 1947, Walter S. Gifford, President, American Telephone and Telegraph Company, turned the argument of Berle and Means around so as to justify divorce of ownership and control in terms of the interests of labor, investor and consumer. Mr. Gifford's argument follows:

'It used to be that the owners of practically every business were themselves the managers of the business. Today, as far as large businesses are concerned, a profound change has taken place. In the Bell System, for instance, employee management, up from the ranks, and not owner management, is responsible for running the business.

This management has been trained for its job in the American ideal of respect for the individual and equal opportunity for each to develop his talents to the fullest. A little thought will bring out the important significance of these facts.

Management is, of course, vitally interested in the success of the enterprise it manages, for if it doesn't succeed, it will lose its job.

So far as the Bell System is concerned, the success of the enterprise depends upon the ability of management to carry on an essential nation-wide telephone service in the public interest.

This responsibility requires that management act as a trustee for the interest of all concerned: the millions of telephone users, the hundreds of thousands of employees, and the hundreds of thousands of stockholders. Management necessarily must do the best it can to reconcile the interests of these groups.

Of course, management is not infallible; but with its intimate knowledge of all the factors, management is in a better position than anybody else to consider intelligently and act equitably for each of these groups—and in the Bell System there is every incentive for it to wish to do so.

Certainly in the Bell System there is no reason either to underpay labor or overcharge customers in order to increase the "private profits of private employers," for its profits are limited by regulation. In fact, there is no reason whatever for management to exploit or to favor any one of the three great groups as against the others and to do so would be plain stupid on the part of management.

The business cannot succeed in the long run without well-paid employees with good working conditions, without adequate returns to investors who have put their savings in the interprise, and without reasonable prices to the customers who buy its services. On the whole, these conditions have been well-met over the years in the Bell System.

Admittedly, this has not been and is not an easy problem to solve fairly for all concerned. However, collective bargaining with labor means that labor's point of view is forcibly presented. What the investor must have is determined quite definitely by what is required to attract the needed additional capital, which can only be obtained in competition with other industries.

And in our regulated business, management has the responsibility, together with regulatory authorities, to see to it that the rates to the public are such as to assure the money, credit and plant that will give the best possible telephone service at all times.

More and better telephone service at a cost as low as fair treatment of employees and a reasonable return to stockholders will permit is the aim and responsibility of management in the Bell System.

Walter S. Gifford, President
American Telephone and Telegraph Company'

8. *I doubt whether a student can do a greater work for his nation than to detach himself from its preoccupations*

WALTER LIPPMANN, *The Scholar in a Troubled World*, 1932 *

. . . We assume that a profound study of politics ought to produce a statesman, a profound study of economics ought to produce a man of affairs, a profound study of the law ought to produce a legislator, a judge, or an advocate. Yet we know that it rarely happens. Nevertheless, we continue to assume and expect, and then are disappointed when the scholar is ineffective in affairs, or half-hearted and distracted in his search for truth. Yet the notion that the contemplative life is a preparation for immediate participation in the solution of current problems is by no means to be taken for granted. In fact, the traditions of human wisdom are against it. . .

For, at the point where knowledge is to be applied in action, there is a highly variable and incalculable factor. That factor is the will of the people. Therefore, when the student of politics is asked to recommend a particular course of action, he must say, if he is candid, that his system of ideas rests upon a foundation of assumptions about human conduct; that these assumptions are necessarily generalized and abstract; and that, therefore, they discount the willfulness and uncertainty of the immediate situation. But practical decisions depend in large part upon appraising swiftly just this element of willfulness and uncertainty in public opinion and individual response. A knowledge of the past and reflection upon the behavior of men in analogous circumstance may illuminate and steady the appraisal, but there is as yet no science which controls it.

The art of practical decision, the art of determining which of several ends to pursue, which of many means to employ, when to strike and when to recoil, comes from intuitions that are more unconscious than the analytical judgment. In great emergencies the man of affairs feels his conclusions first, and understands them later. He proceeds by a kind of empathy, relying upon a curious capacity for self-identification with the moods of others and upon a sense of the realities which he can rarely expound. Those who have this gift must be immersed in affairs; they must absorb much more than they analyze; they must be subtly sensitive to the atmosphere about them; they must, like a cat, be able to see in the dark. They pay a price for their capacities. Only the very greatest men of affairs see beyond the moment. But at the instant of decision they can often act with an assurance and sometimes with a rightness which it is impossible to deduce from the principles of any theoretical system.

The political sciences, since they deal with conduct, must rest upon some positive conception of human motives. It is not, I think, possible to formulate principles of government or of economics on the assumption that human motives are incalculable. There are no principles that could be worked out which would

* An address delivered as the Phi Beta Kappa oration, Columbia University, 31 May 1932. *The Atlantic Monthly*, vol. CL (1932), p. 148. Reprinted by permission of Walter Lippmann.

be equally true for a nation of heroes and saints, a community of ascetics and of swindlers or thieves. The political thinker must make some assumptions about the character and the working motives of people. These assumptions must necessarily be simpler and more stable than those which are actually in play at any particular moment of decision. Shall he, for example, assume that each man intelligently pursues his own interest? If he adopts this abstraction, he can produce an imposing and coherent doctrine. The classical economists did that, and, granting the premise, a perfectly intelligible social policy can be deduced from it. But observation soon shows that even if it were true that men desire their own interest exclusively, they are usually too little informed and too gullible to know what it is.

But once the economist admits this, he must go further and admit that practical judgment as to the best course at any moment is dependent upon what to him is mere guesswork, upon a surmise as to what choices are open as a result of the particular mixtures of understanding and ignorance, partisanship and propaganda, national, sectional, sectarian, and class prejudice, then prevailing among the people, as well as upon the personal idiosyncrasies, and special bias, of the men temporarily in power. As an economist he has no particular aptitude for making these surmises. Thus if, for example, he attempts to estimate a nation's capacity to pay a war debt in the course of three generations, no process of economic reasoning will give him the answer. For the capacity to pay is in some important degree a function of the will to pay, and to judge that he must make a guess about the whole political future of a people. He must guess at the evolution of its prejudices.

It appears, then, that our ability to derive practical guidance from theoretical studies is fundamentally limited by the part which transient prejudice plays in human conduct. I venture to think that this is the core of the difficulty which confronts the man of affairs when he turns to the scholar for advice, and the scholar when he seeks to give advice. No theoretical system of political economy has ever been constructed by the mind of man which rests upon incalculable human conduct. Yet in our modern democracies, most particularly in the modern American democracy which is so unsettled in its life and in its convictions, the working motives of men are so highly volatile that they defy theoretical formulation and systematic analysis.

We are compelled, I think, to recognize that in no other critical period of the modern world has transient opinion played so great a role in affairs. If, with this in mind, we examine the deliberations which accompanied the establishment of the Republic, we must be impressed, it seems to me, with the greater capacity of the eighteenth-century thinkers to reach definite practical conclusions from their general principles. I, for one, never read in the *Federalist* without a feeling of envy that no one living today believes in general principles as did the authors of those essays, or is able to use his principles so confidently and effectively. These men possessed an intellectual clarity that we have wholly lost. They were the masters of their subject in a way that we are not.

I do not believe that this is wholly a matter of superior genius. I imagine it must be due, in some measure, to the fact that in their time, and well down into the nineteenth century, the mass of men were, as Gladstone put it, passive.

They had prejudices, but they were stable prejudices. The patterns of popular conduct varied very little, so that political thinkers and men of affairs could reason with some confidence about their behavior.

But by the second half of the nineteenth century the passive democracy had become an active democracy. Under the impact of the Industrial Revolution and of popular education, the popular mode of life became radically unsettled, and with it the fixed prejudices, the normal expectations, the established conventions, the enduring convictions of the older world. They were replaced by new ambitious and transient opinions. An immense uncertainty entered public life, and consequently into the premises of all the sciences that deal with public affairs. The modern world became revolutionary in its essence, for no abiding tradition of any kind remained.

If this analysis is correct, then it follows that we must not expect society to be guided by its professors until, or perhaps I should say unless, the fluctuating opinions that now govern affairs are replaced by clear, by settled, moral values. Either men must have the stable prejudices of the ancestral order or they must have stable conventions they have rationally accepted; on either foundation a political science which actually controlled events might be built up. But upon a foundation of merely transient opinions derived from the impressions of the moment, undirected by any abiding conception of personal and social values, no influential political science can be constructed, and, it may be, no enduring political state.

A recognition of this underlying difficulty—that systematic principles cannot be derived from or applied to a democracy ruled by willful and uncertain opinions—would go a long way toward resolving the conflict which now unsettles the scholar's spirit. It would give him the courage to preserve that detachment which his instinct demands. It would give him the resolution to shut out the distracting demands for interviews and statements and conferences and all the other paraphernalia of active intervention in affairs. If, nevertheless, he is moved to intervene, he can do so at least knowing that in that role he is not a scholar, but merely one more amateur as to things in general, however much he may be the specialist of something in particular. He will no longer be astonished that he is puzzled by the complexity of the actual, or undervalue his own theoretical life and in the presence of the immediate let himself be over-awed by the superior assurance of the man of affairs.

The more fully he understands the real reason why today theory is so divorced from practice, the more he will realize how supremely important it is that those who have the gift for theory should imperturbably cultivate it. For what is most wrong with the world is that the democracy, which at last is actually in power, is a creature of the immediate moment. With no authority above it, without religious, political, or moral convictions which control its opinions, it is without coherence and purpose. Democracy of this kind cannot last long; it must, and inevitably it will, give way to some more settled social order. But in the meanwhile the scholar will defend himself against it. He will build a wall against chaos, and behind that wall, as in other bleak ages of the history of man, he will give his true allegiance, not to the immediate world, but to the invisible empire of reason.

In that realm of being, the scholar makes his genuine contact with the affairs of men. The life of man has other dimensions besides the troubled surface and the present moment. To the controversies arising out of the play of transient prejudice upon circumstances he can perhaps contribute technical knowledge. He can contribute no particular wisdom that is peculiarly his own. His concern is with the formulation and establishment of modes of thought that underlie and might reorganize the prejudiced will, and cure it of that transiency which is the fundamental source of all our troubles. He does not manage the passing moment. He prepares the convictions and the conventions, the hypotheses and the dispositions which might control the purposes of those who will manage future events. Thus in this crisis his chief duty is to understand, so that the next one may be more intelligible. This crisis is what it is. The men who will decide the issues may change their opinions a little; it is too late for them to change their habits, and within the grooves of those habits the immediate decisions will be made.

The true scholar is always radical. He is preoccupied with presumptions, with antecedents and probabilities; he moves at a level of reality under that of the immediate moment, in a world where the choices are more numerous and the possibilities more varied than they are at the level of practical decisions. At the level of affairs the choices are narrow, because prejudice has become set. At the level of thought, in the empire of reason, the choices are wide, because there is no compulsion of events or of self-interest. The immediate has never been the realm of the scholar. His provinces are the past, from which he distills understanding, and the future, for which he prepares insight. The immediate is for his purpose a mere fragment of the past, to be observed and remembered rather than to be dealt with and managed.

This view of the scholar's life will seem to many a mere elegy to a fugitive and cloistered virtue. Yet I doubt whether the student can do a greater work for his nation in this grave moment of its history than to detach himself from its preoccupations, refusing to let himself be absorbed by distractions about which, as a scholar, he can do almost nothing. For this is not the last crisis in human affairs. The world will go on somehow, and more crises will follow. It will go on best, however, if among us there are men who have stood apart, who refused to be anxious or too much concerned, who were cool and inquiring, and had their eyes on a longer past and a longer future. By their example they can remind us that the passing moment is only a moment; by their loyalty they will have cherished those things which only the disinterested mind can use. . .

SELECTED REFERENCES

Frederick Lewis Allen, *Only Yesterday: An Informal History of the Nineteen Twenties*, New York, Harper, 1931.

John Dos Passos, *U.S.A., The Big Money*, New York, Random House, 1930.

Charles N. Fay, *Business in Politics*, Cambridge, Mass., Cosmos Press, 1926.

Richard Hofstadter, *The American Political Tradition and the Men Who Made It*, New York, Knopf, 1948, chap. 11.

Herbert Hoover, *American Individualism*, Garden City, Doubleday, Page, 1922.
Max Lerner, *Ideas for the Ice Age*, New York, Viking, 1941.
Broadus Mitchell, *Depression Decade: From New Era Through New Deal, 1929–1941*, New York, Rinehart & Co., 1947.
Joel Francis Paschal, *Mr. Justice Sutherland: A Man Against the State*, Princeton, Princeton University Press, 1951.
James W. Prothro, *The Dollar Decade: Business Ideas in the 1920s*, Baton Rouge, Louisiana State University Press, 1954.
Karl Shriftgiesser, *This Was Normalcy: An Account of Party Politics During Twelve Republican Years, 1920–1932*, Boston: Atlantic-Little, Brown.
Arthur Schlesinger, Jr., *The Crisis of the Old Order*, Boston, Houghton Mifflin, 1957.
George Soule, *Prosperty Decade: A Chapter from American Economic History, 1917–1929*, London, Pilot Press, 1947.

XIX

THE NEW DEAL

The Great Depression of 1929 cracked the foundations of the Old Deal and the old faith. For the first time men began seriously to doubt the survival of American capitalism. Economic emergency 'more serious than war,' not the musings of a philosopher, produced whatever theory F. D. Roosevelt's New Deal may embody.

Some commentators believe the New Deal lacked the sure sense of direction ideology might be expected to supply. Others contend that Mr. Roosevelt had developed his political philosophy long before the depression struck. However that may be, anyone who considers the administration's feverish activity during the early months of 1933, or takes the trouble to read Hugh Johnson's amazing book, *The Blue Eagle, From Egg to Earth* (1935), may conclude that New Dealers were like the Americans the English author G. Lowes Dickinson described: 'quick-witted and crass,' 'active for the sake of activity, amorous of devices, contemptuous of ideas.'

Frances Perkins tells of the 'superficial young reporter' who confronted Roosevelt with some specific queries:

'Mr. President, are you a Communist?'

'No.'

'Are you a capitalist?'

'No.'

'Are you a socialist?'

'No.'

'Well, what is your philosophy, then?'

'Philosophy?' asked the President, blandly puzzled. 'Philosophy? I am a Christian and a Democrat—that's all.'

The name 'New Deal' is somewhat opaque, resembling T.R.'s Square Deal, Woodrow Wilson's New Freedom. Like these forerunners, it was a shining slogan to advance and solidify the administration politically rather than to usher in any brand new order. At the outset, the New Deal had neither a well-rounded ideology, nor a well integrated, self-consistent program. It was largely a doctrine of action, a policy of bold experimentation. With banks closed or closing, with farm and home owners faced with mortgage foreclosures, and the vast numbers of unemployed mounting daily, the new government could ill-afford the luxury usual among earlier saviors of society—that of mulling over doctrines and tilting with utopias. In any event, much of what was denounced as innovation was built on tradition, and expressed ideas or interests that can be traced far back in American and European history.

The sense of being a new world politically and socially has always permeated the American outlook. Our first comprehensive New Deal was the American Revolution, representing, as Lincoln put it at Gettysburg, a determined effort to settle on this continent a new social-economic order, as well as free government of, by, and for the people. Latter-day immigrants came to our shores by millions in much the same frame of mind, and those already here, forever on the move, have kept alive the pioneering spirit. Tocqueville in the 1830's found Americans breaking fresh ground, launching new experiments with the zest and persistence of a people always 'on the wing.'

Harold Laski observes in his major work, *The American Democracy* (1948): *

> What is remarkable in the New Deal is the degree in which it is, in fact, simply the completion of a continuous development of discontent with traditional individualism which goes back, in a sense, to Shays' Rebellion, and, in another, at least to Populism of the period after the Civil War. In these aspects the struggle waged by Jefferson and Jackson against the financial interests embodied first in the Federalist movement, and then in the bank of the United States, must be regarded in direct line of ancestry. So, too, if from a somewhat different approach, was the tradition of the Republican Progressive movement which Theodore Roosevelt offered to take to Armageddon.

Even if one considers the New Deal revolutionary in doctrine and action, one must contrast it with earlier abrupt turning points in our history. During the months preceding Roosevelt's inauguration in 1933, there was little or none of the theoretical discussion, the arguing and straining in terms of first principles, comparable to that preceding the American Revolution, the Constitutional Revolution of 1787, or the dislocations produced by the Civil War. And yet Governor Franklin D. Roosevelt did far more planning and hard thinking in the months before his campaign for the presidency than is generally supposed. During the spring of 1932, Raymond Moley organized the original 'Brain Trust,' recruited largely from Columbia University's Public Law faculty. Without salary or even traveling expenses, this group spent many hours in Albany working with Roosevelt, hammering a national program into shape in accordance with the New York Governor's political philosophy. And Moley insists that Roosevelt had a political philosophy: 'He believed that government not only could, but should, achieve the subordination of private interests to collective interests, substitute co-operation for the mad-scramble of selfish individualism. He had a profound feeling for the underdog, a real sense of the critical unbalance of economic life, a very keen awareness that political democracy could not exist side by side with economic plutocracy.'

It was not, however, until the now famous Commonwealth Club speech,

23 September 1932, heading this chapter, that Roosevelt undertook a systematic statement of his creed. The Democratic presidential candidate had originally planned to deliver a brief, inconsequential greeting to the distinguished San Francisco Club. But Moley, realizing that this was a rare opportunity for non-partisan discussion of the great public issues before 'extraordinarily intelligent men,' urged Roosevelt to make a major speech, 'to sum up his political philosophy.' A first draft, and a fine one, was prepared by Adolf Berle in forty-eight hours, leaving little time for revision.

In this scholarly analysis of our tradition, Roosevelt gave a hint and more of what was ahead of us. In 1928 Herbert Hoover spoke of 'equality of opportunity' as if it had been realized; that was for him the very essence of our creed. For Roosevelt in 1932, 'a glance at our situation . . . indicates that equality of opportunity as we have known it no longer exists.' Such wide disagreement in assumptions was bound to reflect itself in a more positive program.

Among the most persuasive apostles of New Deal gospel during the early years of the Roosevelt administration, rivaling even the president himself, was Henry Agard Wallace (1889–), erstwhile T.R. Progressive, F.D.R.'s Secretary of Agriculture, and later acknowledged spokesman of 'the Common Man.' Wallace's effectiveness lay partly in his grounding in economics but even more, perhaps, in his ability to give the New Deal program a highly moral, even a religious cast. Elaborating Candidate Roosevelt's theme of 1932, Wallace said in the selections here reproduced that the physical frontiers were gone, and with their passing our economic problems had grown in both number and complexity. To deal with the new issues, we must, he said, equal our forefathers in courage and persistence and conquer the new frontiers of mind and heart. The New Deal's primary objective was to achieve through co-operation and policies, admittedly experimental, a more equitable distribution of the national income, better balance among 'all our major producing groups.' In 1934 Wallace believed it was possible to 'cut a path between the devil of individualism and the deep sea of collectivism.' Others in the New Deal family concurred. 'In a world in which revolutions just now are coming easily,' Adolf Berle remarked, 'the New Deal chose the more difficult course of moderation and rebuilding.' 'It conformed,' as Harold Ickes said, 'to no theory, but it did fit into the American system—a system of taking action step by step.'

For months after the Roosevelt policies were launched, the opposition lay quiescent. The President never got from businessmen the co-operation he sought; rather they implored help, muttered doubts, and awaited anxiously the final collapse they felt was surely coming. By August 1934 the spearhead of the opposition was bitter, outspoken, and organized in the American Liberty League. An outgrowth of the Association against the Prohibition Amendment, this top level industrial-financial body drew its eminent membership from both major parties. After repeal of the Eighteenth Amendment, certain members of the triumphant Association proposed launching a campaign for repeal of the Sixteenth Amendment (Income Tax), but F.D.R. and his New Dealers now constituted such a serious threat as to suggest the need for an educational campaign 'to teach respect for rights of persons and property,' 'to defend and uphold the Constitution of the United States,' etc. The tenor of the Liberty League's attack, and the theory motivating it, comes out in the selection from Raoul E. Desvernine (1891–), New York lawyer and Vice President of the American Liberty League.

In vehemence and persistence none of these New Deal critics can match ex-President Hoover. In books and speeches he has kept up a rapid-fire attack. But, like Desvernine and others, he has been inclined to throw the New Deal and all its works into the general totalitarian cesspool, along with Fascism, Nazism, Sovietism, etc.

The Roosevelt program provoked equally bitter, and not wholly dissimilar criticism, from Communist Earl Browder. 'The New Deal,' he wrote in 1934, 'merely gave a new form to the fundamental Old Deal policies.' Mingled with his onslaughts were barbs of equal sharpness directed against the Hoovers and Desvernines.

Meanwhile, a significant turning point had occurred in the temper and focus of the New Deal. After the Supreme Court overturned the National Industrial Recovery Act and certain other key measures, the fairly even balance heretofore maintained between recovery and reform was tipped in favor of the latter. The President's answer to the Court's decision setting aside N.I.R.A., under which industry received what it had long sought—'the right to act in unison'—was a smashing attack on economic privilege and on the 'nine old men,' stigmatized as its chief defenders. The President struck this bolder note in his New Instruments of Public Power speech, foreshadowing the knock-down, drag-out fight over F.D.R.'s proposal of 1937 to reorganize the Federal Courts.

Even before the lines of attack and counter-attack had been so tightly drawn as to suggest a fundamental inconsistency between capitalism and democracy, Professor John Dewey (1859–1952), America's distinguished philosopher and outstanding liberal, detecting a blinding mote in the eye of both radical and reactionary, had written reasurringly of mankind's possession of a 'new method, that of cooperative and experimental science.' The show-down was still to come. The atomic age had not yet dawned.

1. *New conditions impose new requirements on government*

FRANKLIN D. ROOSEVELT, Campaign Address, Commonwealth Club, San Francisco, 23 September 1932 *

The issue of Government has always been whether individual men and women will have to serve some system of Government or economics, or whether a system of Government and economics exists to serve individual men and women. This question has persistently dominated the discussion of Government for many generations. On questions relating to these things men have

* *The Public Papers and Addresses of Franklin D. Roosevelt*, New York, Random House, Inc., 1938, vol. I, pp. 742–56 *passim*.

differed, and for time immemorial it is probable that honest men will continue to differ.

The final word belongs to no man; yet we can still believe in change and in progress. Democracy, as a dear old friend of mine in Indiana, Meredith Nicholson, has called it, is a quest, a never-ending seeking for better things, and in the seeking for these things and the striving for them, there are many roads to follow. But if we map the course of these roads, we find that there are only two general directions.

When we look about us, we are likely to forget how hard people have worked to win the privilege of Government. . . In many instances the victory of the central Government, the creation of a strong central Government, was a haven of refuge to the individual. The people preferred the master far away to the exploitation and cruelty of the smaller master near at hand.

But the creators of national Government were perforce ruthless men. They were often cruel in their methods, but they did strive steadily toward something that society needed and very much wanted, a strong central State able to keep the peace, to stamp out civil war, to put the unruly nobleman in his place, and to permit the bulk of individuals to live safely. The man of ruthless force had his place in developing a pioneer country, just as he did in fixing the power of the central Government in the development of Nations. Society paid him well for his services and its development. . .

There came a growing feeling that Government was conducted for the benefit of a few who thrived unduly at the expense of all. The people sought a balancing—a limiting force. There came gradually, through town councils, trade guilds, national parliaments, by constitution and by popular participation and control, limitations on arbitrary power.

Another factor that tended to limit the power of those who ruled, was the rise of the ethical conception that a ruler bore a responsibility for the welfare of his subjects.

The American colonies were born in this struggle. The American Revolution was a turning point in it. After the Revolution the struggle continued and shaped itself in the public life of the country. There were those who because they had seen the confusion which attended the years of war for American independence surrendered to the belief that popular Government was essentially dangerous and essentially unworkable. They were honest people, my friends, and we cannot deny that their experience had warranted some measure of fear. The most brilliant, honest and able exponent of this point of view was Hamilton. He was too impatient of slow-moving methods. Fundamentally he believed that the safety of the republic lay in the autocratic strength of its Government, that the destiny of individuals was to serve that Government, and that fundamentally a great and strong group of central institutions, guided by a small group of able and public spirited citizens, could best direct all Government.

But Mr. Jefferson, in the summer of 1776, after drafting the Declaration of Independence turned his mind to the same problem and took a different view. He did not deceive himself with outward forms. Government to him was a means to an end, not an end in itself; it might be either a refuge and a help or a threat and a danger, depending on the circumstances. We find him carefully analyzing the society for which he was to organize a Government. 'We have no paupers. The great mass of our population is of laborers, our rich who cannot live without labor, either manual or professional, being few and of moderate wealth. Most of the laboring class possess property, cultivate their own lands, have families and from the demand for their labor, are enabled to exact from the rich and the competent such prices as enable them to feed abundantly, clothe above mere decency, to labor moderately and raise their families.'

These people, he considered, had two sets of rights, those of 'personal competency' and those involved in acquiring and possessing property. By 'personal competency' he meant the right of free thinking, freedom of forming and expressing opinions, and freedom of personal living, each man according to his own lights. To insure the first set of rights, a Government must so order its functions as not to interfere with the individual. But even Jefferson realized that the exercise of the property rights might so interfere with the rights of the individual that the Government, without whose assistance the property rights could not exist, must intervene, not to destroy individualism, but to protect it.

You are familiar with the great political duel which followed; and how Hamilton, and his friends, building toward a dominant centralized power were at length defeated in the great election of 1800, by Mr. Jefferson's party. Out of that duel came the two parties, Republican and Democratic, as we know them today.

So began, in American political life, the new day, the day of the individual against the system, the day in which individualism was made the great watchword of American life. The happiest of economic conditions made that day long and splendid. On the Western frontier, land was substantially free. No one, who did not shirk the task of earning a living, was entirely without opportunity to do so. Depressions could, and did, come and go; but they could not alter the fundamental fact that most of the people lived partly by selling their labor and partly by extracting their livelihood from the soil, so that starvation and dislocation were practically impossible. At the very worst there was always the possibility of climbing into a covered wagon and moving west where the untilled prairies afforded a haven for men to whom the East did not provide a place. So great were our natural resources that we could offer this relief not only to our own people, but to the distressed of all the world; we could invite immigration from Europe, and welcome it with open arms. Traditionally, when a depression came a new section of land was opened in the West; and even our temporary misfortune served our manifest destiny.

It was in the middle of the nineteenth century that a new force was released and a new dream created. The force was what is called the industrial revolution, the advance of steam and machinery and the rise of the forerunners of the modern industrial plant. The dream was the dream of an economic machine, able to raise the standard of living for everyone; to bring luxury within the reach of the humblest; and to annihilate distance by steam power and later by electricity, and to release everyone from the drudgery of the heaviest manual toil. It was to be expected that this would necessarily affect Government.

Heretofore, Government had merely been called upon to produce conditions within which people could live happily, labor peacefully, and rest secure. Now it was called upon to aid in the consummation of this new dream. There was, however, a shadow over the dream. To be made real, it required use of the talents of men of tremendous will and tremendous ambition, since by no other force could the problems of financing and engineering and new developments be brought to a consummation.

So manifest were the advantages of the machine age, however, that the United States fearlessly, cheerfully and, I think, rightly, accepted the bitter with the sweet. It was thought that no price was too high to pay for the advantages which we could draw from a finished industrial system. The history of the last half century is accordingly in large measure a history of a group of financial Titans, whose methods were not scrutinized with too much care, and who were honored in proportion as they produced the results, irrespective of the means they used. The financiers who pushed the railroads to the Pacific were always ruthless, often wasteful, and frequently corrupt; but they did build railroads, and we have them today. It has been estimated that the American investor paid for the American railway system more than three times over in the process; but despite this fact the net advantage was to the United States. As long as we had free land; as long as population was growing by leaps and bounds; as long as our industrial plants were insufficient to supply our own needs, society chose to give the ambitious man free play and unlimited reward provided only that he produced the economic plant so much desired.

During this period of expansion, there was equal opportunity for all and the business of Government was not to interfere but to assist in the development of industry. This was done at the request of business men themselves. The tariff was originally imposed for the purpose of 'fostering our infant industry,' a phrase I think the older among you will remember as a political issue not so long ago. The railroads were subsidized, sometimes by grants of money, oftener by grants of land; some of the most valuable oil lands in the United States were granted to assist the financing of the railroad which pushed through the Southwest. A nascent merchant marine was assisted by grants of money, or by mail subsidies, so that our steam shipping might ply the seven seas. Some of my friends tell me that they do not want the Government in business. With this I agree; but I wonder whether they realize the implications of the past. For while it has been American doctrine that the Government must not go into business in competition with private enterprises, still it has been traditional, particularly in Republican administrations, for business urgently to ask the Government to put at private disposal all kinds of Government assistance. The same man who tells you that he does not want to see the Government interfere in business—and he means it, and has plenty of good reasons for saying so—is the first to go to Washington and ask the Government for a prohibitory tariff on his product. When things get just bad enough, as they did two years ago, he will go with equal speed to the United States Government and ask for a loan; and the Reconstruction Finance Corporation is the outcome of it. Each group has sought protection from the Government for its own special interests, without realizing that the function of Government must be to favor no small group at the expense of its duty to protect the rights of personal freedom and of private property of all its citizens.

In retrospect we can now see that the turn of the tide came with the turn of the century. We were reaching our last frontier; there was no more free land and our industrial combinations had become great uncontrolled and irresponsible units of power within the State. Clear-sighted men saw with fear the danger that opportunity would no longer be equal; that the growing corporation, like the feudal baron of old, might threaten the economic freedom of individuals to earn a living. In that hour, our anti-trust laws were born. The cry was raised against the great corporations. Theodore Roosevelt, the first great Republican Progressive, fought a Presidential campaign on the issue of 'trust busting' and talked freely about malefactors of great wealth. If the Government had a policy it was rather to turn the clock back, to destroy the large combinations and to return to the time when every man owned his individual small business.

This was impossible; Theodore Roosevelt, abandoning the idea of 'trust busting,' was forced to work out a difference between 'good' trusts and 'bad' trusts. The Supreme Court set forth the famous 'rule of reason' by which it seems to have meant that a concentration of industrial power was permissible if the method by which it got its power, and the use it made of that power, were reasonable.

Woodrow Wilson, elected in 1912, saw the situation more clearly. Where Jefferson had feared the encroachment of political power on the lives of individuals, Wilson knew that the new power was financial. He saw, in the highly centralized economic system, the despot of the twentieth century, on whom great masses of individuals relied for their safety and their livelihood, and whose irresponsibility and greed (if they were not controlled) would reduce them to starvation and penury. The concentration of financial power had not proceeded so far in 1912 as it has today; but it had grown far enough for Mr. Wilson to realize fully its implications. It is interesting, now, to read his speeches. What is called 'radical' today (and I have reason to know whereof I speak) is mild compared to the campaign of Mr. Wilson. 'No man can deny,' he said, 'that the lines of endeavor have more and more narrowed and stiffened; no man who knows anything about the development of industry in this country can have failed to observe that the larger kinds of credit are more and more difficult to obtain unless you obtain them upon terms of uniting your efforts with those who already control the industry of the country, and nobody can fail to observe that every man who tries to set himself up in competition with any process of manufacture which has taken place under the control of large combinations of capital will presently find himself either squeezed out or obliged to sell and allow himself to be absorbed.' Had there been no World War—had Mr. Wilson been able to devote eight years to domestic instead of to international affairs—we might have had a wholly different situation at the present time. However, the then distant roar of European cannon, growing ever louder, forced him to abandon the study of this issue. The problem he saw so clearly is left with us as a legacy; and no one of us on either side of the political controversy can deny that it is a matter of grave concern to the Government.

A glance at the situation today only too clearly indicates that equality of opportunity as we have known it no longer exists. Our industrial plant is built; the problem just now is whether under existing conditions it is not overbuilt. Our last frontier has long since been reached, and there is practically no more free land. More than half of our people do not live on the farms or on lands and cannot derive a living by cultivating their own property. There is no safety valve in the form of a Western prairie to which those thrown out of work by the Eastern economic machines can go for a new start. We are not able to invite the immigration from Europe to share our endless plenty. We are now providing a drab living for our own people.

Our system of constantly rising tariffs has at last reacted against us to the point of closing our Canadian frontier on the north, our European markets on the east, many of our Latin-American markets to the south, and a goodly proportion of our Pacific markets on the west, through the retaliatory tariffs of those countries. It has forced many of our great industrial institutions which exported their surplus production to such countries, to establish plants in such countries, within the tariff walls. This has resulted in the reduction of the operation of their American plants, and opportunity for employment.

Just as freedom to farm has ceased, so also the opportunity in business has narrowed. It still is true that men can start small enterprises, trusting to native shrewdness and ability to keep abreast of competitors; but area after area has been preempted altogether by the great corporations, and even in the fields which still have no great concerns, the small man starts under a handicap. The unfeeling statistics of the past three decades show that the independent business man is running a losing race. Perhaps he is forced to the wall; perhaps he cannot command credit; perhaps he is 'squeezed out,' in Mr. Wilson's words, by highly organized corporate competitors, as your corner grocery man can tell you. Recently a careful study was made of the concentration of business in the United States. It showed that our economic life was dominated by some six hundred odd corporations who controlled two-thirds of American industry. Ten million small business men divided the other third. More striking still, it appeared that if the process of concentration goes on at the same rate, at the end of another century we shall have all American industry controlled by a dozen corporations, and run by perhaps a hundred men. Put plainly, we are steering a steady course toward economic oligarchy, if we are not there already.

Clearly, all this calls for a re-appraisal of values. A mere builder of more industrial plants, a creator of more railroad systems, an organizer of more corporations, is as likely to be a danger as a help. The day of the great promoter or the financial Titan, to whom we granted anything if only he would build, or develop, is over. Our task now is not discovery or exploitation of natural resources, or necessarily producing more goods. It is the soberer, less dramatic business of administering resources and plants already in hand, of seeking to reestablish foreign markets for our surplus production, of meeting the problem of under consumption, of adjusting production to consumption, of distributing wealth and products more equitably, of adapting existing economic organizations to the service of the people. The day of enlightened administration has come.

Just as in older times the central Government was first a haven of refuge, and then a threat, so now in a closer economic system the central and ambitious financial unit is no longer a servant of national desire, but a danger. I would draw the parallel one step farther. We did not think because national Government had become a threat in the 18th century that therefore we should abandon the principle of national Government. Nor today should we abandon the principle of strong economic units called corporations, merely because their power is susceptible of easy abuse. In other times we dealt with the problem of an unduly ambitious central Government by modifying it gradually into a constitutional democratic Government. So today we are modifying and controlling our economic units.

As I see it, the task of Government in its relation to business is to assist the development of an economic declaration of rights, an economic constitutional order. This is the common task of statesman and business man. It is the minimum requirement of a more permanently safe order of things.

Happily, the times indicate that to create such an order not only is the proper policy of Government, but it is the only line of safety for our economic structures as well. We know, now, that these economic units cannot exist unless prosperity is uniform, that is, unless purchasing power is well distributed throughout every group in the Nation. That is why even the most selfish of corporations for its own interest would be glad to see wages restored and unemployment ended and to bring the Western farmer back to his accustomed level of prosperity and to assure a permanent safety to both groups. That is why some enlightened industries themselves endeavor to limit the freedom of action of each man and business group within the industry in the common interest of all; why business men everywhere are asking a form of organization which will bring the scheme of things into balance, even though it may in some measure qualify the freedom of action of individual units within the business. . .

The Declaration of Independence discusses the problem of Government in terms of a contract. Government is a relation of give and take, a contract, perforce, if we would follow the thinking out of which it grew. Under such a contract rulers were accorded power, and the people consented to that power on consideration that they be accorded certain rights. The task of statesmanship has always been the re-definition of these rights in terms of a changing and growing social order. New conditions impose new requirements upon Government and those who conduct Government. . .

I feel that we are coming to a view through the drift of our legislation and our public thinking in the past quarter century that private economic power is, to enlarge an old phrase, a public trust as well. I hold that continued enjoyment of that power by any individual or group must depend upon the fulfillment of that trust. The men who have reached the summit of American business life know this best; happily, many of these urge the binding quality of this greater social contract.

The terms of that contract are as old as the Republic, and as new as the new economic order.

Every man has a right to life; and this means that he has also a right to make a comfortable living. He may by sloth or crime decline to exercise that right; but it may not be denied him. We have no actual famine or death; our industrial and agricultural mechanism can produce enough and to spare. Our Government formal and informal, political and economic, owes to everyone an avenue to possess himself of a portion of that plenty sufficient for his needs, through his own work.

Every man has a right to his own property; which means a right to be assured, to the fullest extent attainable, in the safety of his savings. By no other means can men carry the burdens of those parts of life which, in the nature of things, afford no chance of labor; childhood, sickness, old age. In all thought of property, this right is paramount; all other property rights must yield to it. If, in accord with this principle, we must restrict the operations of the speculator, the manipulator, even the financier, I believe we must accept the restriction as needful, not to hamper individualism but to protect it.

These two requirements must be satisfied, in the main, by the individuals who claim and hold control of the great industrial and financial combinations which dominate so large a part of our industrial life. They have undertaken to be, not business men, but princes of property. I am not prepared to say that the system which produces them is wrong. I am very clear that they must fearlessly and competently assume the responsibility which goes with the power. So many enlightened business men know this that the statement would be little more than a platitude, were it not for an added implication.

This implication is briefly, that the responsible heads of finance and industry instead of acting each for himself, must work together to achieve the common end. They must, where necessary, sacrifice this or that private advantage; and in reciprocal self-denial must seek a general advantage. It is here that formal Government—political Government, if you choose—comes in. Whenever in the pursuit of this objective the lone wolf, the unethical competitor, the reckless promoter, the Ishmael or Insull whose hand is against every man's, declines to join in achieving an end recognized as being for the public welfare, and threatens to drag the industry back to a state of anarchy, the Government may properly be asked to apply restraint. Likewise, should the group ever use its collective power contrary to the public welfare, the Government must be swift to enter and protect the public interest.

The Government should assume the function of economic regulation only as a last resort, to be tried only when private initiative, inspired by high responsibility, with such assistance and balance as Government can give, has finally failed. As yet there has been no final failure, because there has been no attempt; and I decline to assume that this Nation is unable to meet the situation.

The final term of the high contract was for liberty and the pursuit of happiness. We have learned a great deal of both in the past century. We know that individual liberty and individual happiness mean nothing unless both are ordered in the sense that one man's meat is not another man's poison. We know that the old 'rights of personal competency,' the right to read, to think, to speak, to choose and live a mode of life, must be respected at all hazards. We know that liberty to do anything which deprived others of those elemental rights is outside the protection of any compact; and that Government in this regard is the maintenance of a balance, within which every individual may have a place if he will take it; in which every individual may find safety if he wishes it; in which every individual may attain such power as his ability permits, consistent with his assuming the accompanying responsibility.

All this is a long, slow talk. Nothing is more striking than the simple innocence of the men who insist, whenever an objective is present, on the prompt production of a patent scheme guaranteed to produce a result. Human endeavor is not so simple as that. Government includes the art of formulating a policy, and using the political technique to attain so much of that policy as will receive general support; persuading, leading, sacrificing, teaching always, because the greatest duty of a statesman is to educate. But in the matters of which I have spoken, we are learning rapidly, in a severe school. The lessons so learned must not be forgotten, even in the mental lethargy of a speculative upturn. We must build toward the time when a major depression cannot occur again; and if this means sacrificing the easy profits of inflationist booms, then let them go; and good riddance.

Faith in America, faith in our tradition of personal responsibility, faith in our institutions, faith in ourselves demand that we recognize the new terms of the old social contract. We shall fulfill them, as we fulfilled the obligation of the apparent Utopia which Jefferson imagined for us in 1776, and which Jefferson, Roosevelt and Wilson sought to bring to realization. We must do so, lest a rising tide of misery, engendered by our common failure, engulf us all. But failure is not an American habit; and in the strength of great hope we must all shoulder our common load.

2. *An enduring democracy can be secured only by promoting balance among all producing groups*

Henry Wallace, *New Frontiers*, 1934 *

In the old days before the World War our fathers and grandfathers had their troubles and disagreements, but they agreed for the most part that this was a land of unlimited opportunity; that we would have continually more machinery and more inventions; that our cities would be getting bigger, our land values higher, and our opportunities for personal profit greater all the time. . .

In four generations our ancestors did most of the work of cutting the trees, draining the fields, and all the varied building of houses, barns, highways, railroads, skyscrapers and factories. Feverishly they worked, carrying out the injunction of the old hymn, 'Work for the night is coming when man works no more.' . .

Present-day youth is in debt to these pioneers, just as they, in their turn went in debt to a still older generation in the older settled regions of the earth. Pioneers generally pay high interest rates and borrow too much money. One of the reasons they are able to do so much work is that they bring in from outside tremendous quantities of money and labor. They keep the men and pay back the money by sending out the extra stuff they are able to produce. In a thinly settled community, man-labor produces more than pioneers can consume, so they ship out the surplus to pay their debts.

The tragic joke on the United States is that we went to bed as a pioneer debtor nation in 1914 and woke up after a nightmare of world madness as a presumably mature creditor nation in 1920. We were full grown in the same sense that a boy of eighteen is full grown. But ever since 1920 that boy of eighteen has been playing in the sand pile.

We educated our children—among them, millions of unemployed young—in the belief that the United States was still a pioneer country where the rugged, individualistic virtues of hard work and saving would inevitably bring success. We did not tell our sons and daughters that they were caught between two worlds, and that in the new world it will take more than hard work and savings to insure salvation. . .

It is our privilege and disadvantage to look at the Bourbons, the wealthy troglodytes of the preceding generation, repeating in their ignorance outworn phrases, seeking to patch their outworn economic structure and defend it from the poverty-stricken radicals, many of whom are just as ignorant as the troglodytes.

My generation wishes the new generation would spend more time trying to build seaworthy vessels in which to reach a new world and less time bothering with the troglodytes, who are rapidly dying off, anyway. . .

Our young people may wait until we are ready for them to begin, or they may not; but they will not wait forever. During the past four jobless years they have become terribly disillusioned. They are poor in experience, influence, learning, and money. Doubtless they need to know much more than they do about the facts of today. Most of all, they need to have their imaginations aroused to the possibilities of the future. . .

Able men, unequalled resources, inventive genius—here are the materials which the older generation, partly as a result of inept leadership, partly as a result of war, have so terribly foozled. Here is the challenge to all younger adaptable spirits possessing sufficient courage and insight to enter upon a plan of national coordination, realistic, yet idealistic. . .

Our land of tomorrow must be surveyed, and trails hacked out. To go in and take possession means mental and spiritual toil, comparable with the physical toil of those who built the New England stone fences, cleared the Ohio woods, drained northern Iowa and built the great highways of the past and present. Speech makers and enthusiasts prepared the way for all such definite jobs but the actual doing was in the hands of men with a rare capacity for planning. They had no romantic illusions; they knew the cost and decided to pay it. Hearts, minds and wills were set to the accomplishment of definite physical tasks, and the jobs were done with a rather remarkable continuous joy in the accomplishment, even though women folks and the children were often offered up as tragic sacrifices.

What we approach is not a new continent but a new state of heart and mind resulting in new standards of accomplishment. We must invent, build and put to work new social machinery. This machinery will carry out the Sermon on the Mount as well as the present social machinery carries out and intensifies the law of the jungle. . .

Two aspects of the problem stand out clearly. One has to do with planning in the physical sense of the term. The other has to do with changing the rules of the game—with laws governing tariffs, money, the regulation of corporations, taxation, and railroad and public utility rates.

We must control that part of our individualism which produces anarchy and widespread misery. If the majority of us are to have automobiles, we must obey the traffic lights and observe certain rules of common decency in order to get speedily and safely from one place to another. In the process our individuality has been curbed, but once certain habits of mutual consideration are established, we discover that the advantages outweigh the handicaps. The range of individual expression has really been widened. . .

Obviously, certain limits must be placed on competition and individualism. These limits should be placed by a state in the justice of whose acts there is absolute confidence. The limits should not deal with irritating particulars but with broad outlines. On these broad outlines, there should be substantial unanimity of opinion among thinking people in both the Republican and Democratic parties, and among leaders of labor, industry and agriculture. If such agreement can be reached there will be infinite opportunities for the 125 million individuals of the United States to develop their ruggedness to mutual advantage instead of to their competitive disadvantage.

It is important for all, and for younger people especially, to realize that the New Deal spirit ebbs and flows. Ordinarily, the progressive liberals get a real opportunity to change the rules only about once in a generation. Human nature is such that complacency prevails and conservatives stay in the saddle until things get pretty bad. From a logical point of view the leadership of the United States from 1920 to 1930 was bad. But the conservatives stayed in power. Most people resolutely refuse to think politically if they have jobs, a place to sleep and something to eat and wear. The economic well-being of the moment was pumped up by a false statesmanship. It took ten years and an economic smash before the people would heed the warnings of those who said, 'This thing is built on sand.'

Most of the so-called young liberals of today received their first political inspiration between 1906 and 1915 from Woodrow Wilson and Theodore Roosevelt. They saw liberalism go out of date in the '20's and wondered if the American people had permanently accepted a Belly-God. The young men who today are between eighteen and thirty years of age and who are anxious to see America built over fundamentally and completely in line with their dreams, will perhaps also have an opportunity to watch the conservatives get back into power. This may not come for eight, twelve or sixteen years, but it will come almost as surely as prosperity returns. People like to be comfortable and 'let alone.' The conservative is bound to triumph fully half the time.

But it must also be remembered that there is something inherently inadequate and often rotting about comfort. The conservative type of mind is constitutionally incapable of understanding the inevitability of certain changes. . .

I am not suggesting that all our younger people be liberals. There are many who should be conservatives. I am deeply concerned, however, that the leadership of the future, whether liberal or conservative, should grapple more definitely and clearly with the facts and forces involved. . . There are tremendously important problems to be put before the people. It may not be good politics to conduct this education, but it is absolutely vital if our democracy is to survive.

I am hoping we can advance by means of an aroused, educated Democracy. Socialism, Communism, and Fascism, it is true, have the advantage of certain precise rules not available to Democracy. They make the path to the land of tomorrow seem straight and short. The only rules a Democracy can rely upon make the path seem by comparison long and tortuous. But the point is that most Americans think less rigid rules and the clash of free opinion allowed by Democracy will in the long run take us farther than will the precise, decisive dogma of Communism or Fascism. So do I.

There is nothing novel or sensational about the rules of the game I have in mind. Until recently, however, the full significance of such rules has been obscured, and the rules have been manipulated more or less secretly for the benefit of the few at the expense of the many. Now the time seems ripe for a change in behalf of the many.

The first step is to understand these rules in all their significance. They have to do with such devices as the tariff, the balance of international payments, monetary policy, subsidies, taxation, price and production policies, and railroad rate regulations. Their significance lies in the fact that by their manipulation it is possible to direct, stimulate, restrain, and balance those forces which have to do with proportioning the national income. All governments that have advanced beyond the pioneer stage find it necessary to use such controls, in lieu of free competition. In using them, a democracy worthy of the name must be guided by concern for social justice and social charity—in other words, the greatest good for the greatest number.

Reliance upon such devices to redistribute income and opportunity, is not the way of Socialism, of Communism or of Fascism. Neither is it the way of the free-booter capitalists of the neo-Manchester school of economics. With their devotion to unlimited competition, these people seem to think the traffic lights should be removed so motorists and pedestrians might illustrate the doctrine of the survival of the fittest at every street corner. It is necessary in a democracy to furnish the red and green lights to guide the traffic, but not to supply drivers for every car on the road.

Long before the World War, competition was limited by rules, both public and private. Since then, it has been limited increasingly. The vital question is: In whose behalf is competition limited? Is the limitation making the rich richer and the poor poorer? If so, there is danger that a day may come when the extreme left will join hands with the extreme right to bring about that most dangerous of all forms of government, a corrupt oligarchy, maintaining itself in power by pandering to the vices and prejudices of a bitter, materialistic, perennially unemployed multitude.

An enduring democracy can be had only by promoting a balance among all our major producing groups, and in such a way as does not build up a small, inordinately wealthy class. The danger in democracies, as we have known them in the past, is this: All too easily, under pressure of changing conditions, they play into the hands of either the extreme left or the extreme right. The same legislators will allow themselves to be stampeded by scared capitalists toward the extreme right, and by the unemployed toward the extreme left. The complexities and the confusion of modern civilization are such that legislators quickly forget objectives of social and economic balance, and give way to the special pressures of the moment. . .

The old frontier was real. There were Indians and fear of foreign conquest. People in the older Colonies or States had to stand together against actual perils on the edge of a new civilization. . .

For a hundred and fifty years we felt it was manifest destiny to push onward, until the Pacific Coast was reached, until all the fertile lands between had been plowed and bound together by railroads and paved highways.

The obvious physical task to which we set ourselves has been accomplished; and in so doing, we have destroyed in large measure the thing which gave us hope and unity as a people.

We now demand a new unity, a new hope. There are many spiritual and mental frontiers yet to be conquered, but they lead in many different directions and our hearts have not yet fully warmed to any one of them. They do not point in an obvious single direction as did that downright physical challenge which, for so many generations, existed on the Western edge of our life. Now we have come to the time when we must search our souls and the relationship of our souls and bodies to those of other human beings. . .

The keynote of the new frontier is cooperation just as that of the old frontier was individualistic competition. The mechanism of progress of the new frontier is social invention, whereas that of the old frontier was mechanical invention and the competitive seizure of opportunities for wealth. Power and wealth were worshiped in the old days. Beauty and justice and joy of spirit must be worshiped in the new. . .

3. *We have built up new instruments of public power*

FRANKLIN D. ROOSEVELT, Annual Message to Congress, 3 January 1936 *

On the fourth day of March, 1933, on the occasion of taking the oath of office as President of the United States, I addressed the people of our country. . . The crisis of that moment was almost exclusively a national one. In

* *The Public Papers and Addresses of Franklin D. Roosevelt*, vol. v, pp. 8–17 *passim*.

recognition of that fact, so obvious to the millions in the streets and in the homes of America, I devoted by far the greater part of that address to what I called, and the nation called, critical days within our own borders. . .

Were I today to deliver an inaugural address to the people of the United States . . . I should be compelled to devote the greater part to world affairs. . .

The evidence before us clearly proves that autocracy in world affairs endangers peace and that such threats do not spring from those nations devoted to the democratic ideal. If this be true in world affairs, it should have the greatest weight in the determination of domestic policies.

Within democratic nations the chief concern of the people is to prevent the continuation or the rise of autocratic institutions that beget slavery at home and aggression abroad. Within our borders, as in the world at large, popular opinion is at war with a power-seeking minority.

This is no new thing. It was fought out in the Constitutional Convention of 1787. From time to time since then the battle has been continued, under Thomas Jefferson, Andrew Jackson, Theodore Roosevelt and Woodrow Wilson.

In these latter years we have witnessed the domination of government by financial and industrial groups, numerically small but politically dominant in the twelve years that succeeded the World War. The present group of which I speak is indeed numerically small and, while it exercises a large influence and has much to say in the world of business, it does not, I am confident, speak the true sentiments of the less articulate, but more important elements that constitute real American business.

In March, 1933, I appealed to the Congress and to the people . . . in a new effort to restore power to those to whom it rightfully belonged. The response to that appeal resulted in the writing of a new chapter in the history of popular government. You, the members of the legislative branch, and I, the Executive, contended for an established new relationship between government and people.

What were the terms of that new relationship? They were an appeal from the clamor of many private and selfish interests, yes, an appeal from the clamor of partisan interest, to the ideal of public interest. Government became the representative and the trustee of the public interest. Our aim was to build upon essentially democratic institutions, seeking all the while the adjustment of burdens, the help of the needy, the protection of the weak, the liberation of the exploited and the genuine protection of the people's property.

It goes without saying that to create such an economic constitutional order more than a single legislative enactment was called for. We had to build, you in the Congress and I, as the Executive, upon a broad base. Now, after thirty-four months of work, we contemplate a fairly rounded whole. We have returned the control of the Federal Government to the city of Washington.

To be sure, in so doing, we have invited battle. We have earned the hatred of entrenched greed. The very nature of the problem that we faced made it necessary to drive some people from power and strictly to regulate others. I made that plain when I took the oath of office in March, 1933. I spoke of the practices of the unscrupulous money-changers who stood indicted in the court of public opinion. I spoke of the rulers of the exchanges of mankind's goods, who failed through their own stubbornness and their own incompetence. I said that they had admitted their failure and had abdicated.

Abdicated? Yes, in 1933, but now with the passing of danger they forget their damaging admissions and withdraw their abdication.

They seek the restoration of their selfish power. They offer to lead us back round the same old corner into the same old dreary street.

Yes, there are still determined groups that are intent upon that very thing. Rigorously held up to popular examination, their true character reveals itself. They steal the livery of great national constitutional ideals to serve discredited special interests. As guardians and trustees for great groups of individual stockholders, they wrongfully seek to carry the property and the interest entrusted to them into the arena of partisan politics. They seek—this minority in business and industry—to control and often do control and use for their own purposes legitimate and highly honored business associations; they engage in vast propaganda to spread fear and discord among the people—they would 'gang up' against the people's liberties.

The principle that they would instill into government if they succeed in seizing power is well shown by the principles which many of them have instilled into their own affairs: Autocracy toward labor, toward stockholders, toward consumers, toward public sentiment. Autocrats in smaller things, they seek autocracy in bigger things. 'By their fruits ye shall know them.'

If these gentlemen believe, as they say they believe, that the measures adopted by this Congress and its predecessor, and carried out by this administration, have hindered rather than promoted recovery, let them be consistent. Let them propose to this Congress the complete repeal of these measures. The way is open to such a proposal.

Let action be positive and not negative. The way is open in the Congress of the United States for an expression of opinion by yeas and nays. Shall we say that values are restored and that the Congress will, therefore, repeal the laws under which we have been bringing them back? Shall we say that because national income has grown with rising prosperity, we shall repeal existing taxes and thereby put off the day of approaching a balanced budget and of starting to reduce the national debt? Shall we abandon the reasonable support and regulation of banking? Shall we restore the dollar to its former gold content?

Shall we say to the farmer—'The prices for your products are in part restored, now go and hoe your own row'?

Shall we say to the home owners—'We have reduced your rates of interest. We have no further concern with how you keep your home or what you pay for your money. That is your affair'?

Shall we say to the several millions of unemployed citizens who face the very problem of existence—yes, of getting enough to eat—'We will withdraw from giving you work, we will turn you back to the charity of your communities and to those men of selfish power who tell you that perhaps they will employ you if the government leaves them strictly alone'?

Shall we say to the needy unemployed—'Your problem is a local one except that perhaps the Federal Government, as an act of mere generosity, will be willing to pay to your city or to your county a few grudging dollars to help maintain your soup kitchens'? . .

We have been specific in our affirmative action. Let them be specific in their negative attack.

But the challenge faced by this Congress is more menacing than merely a return to the past—bad as that would be. Our resplendent economic autocracy does not want to return to that individualism of which they prate, even though the advantages under that system went to the ruthless and the strong. They realize that in thirty-four months we have built up new instruments of public power. In the hands of a people's government this power is wholesome and proper. But in the hands of political puppets of an economic autocracy such power would provide shackles for the liberties of the people. Give them their way and they will take the course of every autocracy of the past—power for themselves, enslavement for the public.

Their weapon is the weapon of fear. I have said—'The only thing we have to fear is fear itself,' and that is as true today as it was in 1933. But such fear as they instill today is not natural fear, a normal fear; it is a synthetic, manufactured, poisonous fear that is being spread subtly, expensively and cleverly by the same people who cried in those other days—'Save us, save us, else we perish.' . .

In the light of our substantial material progress, in the light of the increasing effectiveness of the restoration of popular rule, I recommend to the Congress that we advance and that we do not retreat. . .

4. *The New Deal—foreign slave trail of arbitrary government*

Raoul E. Desvernine, *Democratic Despotism*, 1936 *

Before his nomination for the presidency, Governor Roosevelt gave no indication of having any decided views of a politically or socially subversive nature, or of any desire on his part fundamentally to readjust our constitutional processes, to bring about any new order, or, in fact, in any way substantially to depart from the existing order. He seemed to look rather only to the perfecting of the existing order. His speeches while Governor of New York were all spoken in the mood of an orthodox constitutionalist seeking the correction of abuses, the reparation of wrongs, and social welfare for the people, through strictly constitutional means. He many times displayed a passionate devotion to States' rights as against Federal encroachments, and was always keen for the defense of individual liberty against governmental oppression. He boasted of being a true Jeffersonian democrat.

He was nominated and conducted his campaign on, and solemnly pledged himself to, the carrying out of all the provisions of the conservative and tradi-

* Copyright 1936 by Raoul E. Desvernine. Reprinted by permission of A. Watkins and of Dodd, Mead and Company, Inc. Pages 139–243 *passim*.

tional platform adopted at the Democratic National Convention in 1932. This platform was declared to be 'a covenant with the people,' to state 'the terms of the contract to which they (the people) are asked to subscribe.' There is not a word in this platform which could, by even the most extravagant exaggeration, be said to foreshadow the 'rounded whole' of his subsequent policies and actions. His campaign speeches did not seriously depart from this platform. Only once (and then merely casually, and, as some of his close advisers explained, unintentionally,) did he show an untraditional attitude toward, or disrespect for, the Supreme Court. As a matter of fact, even in his Inaugural Address, he said: 'Our Constitution is so simple, so practical that it is possible always to meet extraordinary needs by changes in emphasis and arrangement without loss of essential form. That is why our constitutional system has proved itself the most superbly enduring political mechanism the world has ever seen.'

It is clear, therefore, that when he took office in 1933, there was not, even in his own mind in any sense, a constitutional crisis before the country. As a matter of fact no one in a responsible position, or anybody officially identified with the incoming Administration, openly suggested any need or occasion for constitutional reform. The nation heard absolutely nothing which even remotely resembled the recent 'professed objectives' of the members of his official family.

It is difficult for us to put our finger on the exact time, or to fix in our own minds the precise occasion, of the President's departure from the traditional way in our political thinking and of his entrance into the new road of thought and his taking the startlingly different direction thereon, which he is now so perversely pursuing. These changes seem to have developed surreptitiously, 'unconsciously,' as Wallace might say; or, perhaps, by 'attrition,' as Frankfurter, and Berle, would doubtlessly scientifically characterize the method of their development. . .

When and how, therefore, President Roosevelt did develop 'the distrust' for 'the future of essential democracy,' which he so eloquently disclaimed in his Inaugural Address, it is our disagreeable task . . . to try to determine.

It cannot be successfully disputed that he assumed the presidency under most trying, almost desperate, conditions. The people gave him their practically unanimous acclaim. The responsibility he then took upon himself was extraordinary and stupendous, and was unprecedented. His courage gave the nation a renewed confidence. He knew and publicly stated that great sacrifices and drastic remedies were necessary, but he unhesitatingly proclaimed that our Constitution was able to meet 'every stress.'

The only hint of the possibility of any departure by him from our conventional theories and constitutional practices was that contained in the following paragraph of his Inaugural Address: 'It is to be hoped that the normal balance of executive and legislative authority may be wholly adequate to meet the unprecedented task before us. But it may be that an unprecedented demand and need for undelayed action may call for temporary departure from the normal balance of public procedure.' But he immediately made clear that he would seek only measures 'within my constitutional authority.'

It is significant to note that up to this time the Minor Prophets * had not attained the prominence and power which they later did, at least not publicly, and that they had not as yet begun to preach their doctrines, or even their strange political, social, and economic views. Now looking back in retrospect, however, it is safe to assume that their unseen hands were even then at work, because we observe a striking similarity between their teachings and the legislative and executive program that was quickly developed and has since been assiduously pursued. This is surely more than a mere coincidence.

Soon we note that the President himself is conscious of the fact that the Administration policies are undertaking a new order of things and are affecting a permanent change in the existing order. He said 'We have undertaken a new order of things . . . a permanent readjustment of many of our ways of thinking and therefore many of our social and economic arrangements.' The implications of this are best explained by [Henry A.] Wallace, who says: 'The experimental method of democracy may be slow, but it has the advantage of being sure. When you change people's minds you change the course of a nation.' . .

The President said: 'You, the members of the legislative branch, and I, the Executive, contended for and established a new relationship between government and people.'

What is this 'new relationship' of which he so proudly boasts? The relationship between the United States Government and American citizens was established and defined by the written Constitution. This Constitution was the sovereign act of the sovereign people. It prescribes the only method by which it can be amended or changed. Therefore, the relationship which it established between government and people can not be rightfully supplanted by any 'new' relationship, except in the prescribed manner. This is a basic doctrine of Constitutional Democracy. But the President here says that a 'new' relationship has been contended for and established by the concerted action of the legislative and executive branches. This seems a revolutionary method of amending the Constitution. . .

The President further says 'that in thirty-four months we have built up new instruments of public power' 'on a broad base.' Until 'thirty-four months' ago we were content with the constitutional instruments of public power—they were the only instruments of public power the people ever built up—constructed on the fundamental and sole base of our Constitution. . .

Now, how can we reconcile this 'new chapter in the history of popular government' with the preceding chapters written by the Founding Fathers, in the Declaration of Independence and in the Constitution of the United States? . . Where do we find in this 'new chapter' reverence for the sacred rights of man which are his by divine endowment and are beyond interference by the State? Where do we find respect for the distribution of powers into different and independent political units? What has happened to local self-government in the States? What has become of the organic structure of our constitutional machinery, which, as we have seen, was carefully set up to prevent the concentrating of power? Where do we observe any thought that the

* Rexford Tugwell, Henry A. Wallace, Donald Richberg, Adolf Berle, Jr., among others. [A.T.M.]

Constitution is a solemn compact between the people and the Government, which the Government must obey if the people's 'consent' is to be respected? Where are the basic institutions upon which our Government and our traditions have been erected? . . .

We recall the admonition of our ancestors that the concentration of power in any one political unit, no matter how democratic it may be, is despotism. Moreover, the people have never expressed any desire for a dictator even though he be wise and good. Our President, however, seems to revert to the spirit of our ancestors when he wisely observes: 'Give them their way and they will take the course of every autocracy of the past—power for themselves, enslavement for the public.' He might also have added the autocracies of the present to his denunciation of those of the past. Europe demonstrates that this political principle is as true today as it has been throughout the whole course of history.

Another statement in this speech of President Roosevelt further confirms a line of thinking foreign to our political concepts. 'We have returned the control of the Federal Government to the city of Washington.' Heretofore, the control of the Federal Government resided in the forty-eight sovereign States and the people. Part of the machinery and some of its operations have always been conveniently located in Washington. Many of the elected officials, and some of the appointed agents, of the Federal Government also carry on their assigned functions there. But *control* is a different thing. We have tried to make it clear that one of the fundamental concepts of our constitutional philosophy is to prohibit the concentration of power—the deposit of control—in any one political unit, as President Washington said in his Farewell Address, 'by dividing and distributing it into different depositories.' We should again be reminded that the Supreme Court has sounded the warning that the deposit of control in any political unit, no matter how democratic, is despotism. . .

The people having been thus made impressionable and receptive to these new ideas by the distortion of democratic ideas, the next step is to manipulate democratic processes in such a manner as to convert these new ideas into accomplished fact. 'We must go forward with the Constitution'; that is, as long as the Constitution can be molded to their purpose. . .

Thus far they have met with an unsurmountable obstacle in the process of this technique—the Judiciary. Fearing that this is a barrier they cannot jump, they now propose either to remove it as a barrier, or so to impair it, that it will not block their progress. They make a variety of proposals to deprive the Supreme Court of its power to declare legislation and executive acts unconstitutional. Chief among these are: to require a unanimous decision, or a majority opinion of seven, to void such acts; to increase the number of the Justices composing the Supreme Court and to pack it with 'liberals'; and to restrict the judicial power of injunction in all cases against the Government. All of these proposals have the same objectives—to remove restraint on their power to interpret and apply the Constitution in furtherance of their desires. They are resentful, at times bitter, against a supreme law to which their wills must bend and which they must obey. They want a goverment of men—themselves—not of laws. . .

And so, we conclude, we are at the crossroads in the journey toward our national destiny: one road is the old American 'horse and buggy' road of democracy with the Constitution as its foundation; the other, the foreign slave trail of arbitrary government built upon the arbitrary will of a man or a group of men. Which of these two roads we should take depends entirely upon where we want to go. At any rate, the signposts on the road we have been recently traveling should give us a positive understanding of our present direction.

We answer the challenge in the words of Hamilton and Madison, in the Federalist Papers: 'An elective despotism was not the government we fought for': * and emulating the illustrious example set for us, we 'adapt' an historic utterance by inquiring

Delano, Quo vadis?

5. *The New Deal—European planned existence*

HERBERT HOOVER, *The Road to Freedom*, 10 June 1936 †

In this room rests the greatest responsibility that has come to a body of Americans in three generations. In the lesser sense this is a convention of a great political party. But in the larger sense it is a convention of Americans to determine the fate of those ideals for which this nation was founded. That far transcends all partisanship. . .

I have given about four years to research into the New Deal, trying to determine what its ultimate objectives were, what sort of a system it is imposing on this country.

To some people it appears to be a strange interlude in American history in that it has no philosophy, that it is sheer opportunism, that it is a muddle of a spoils system, of emotional economics, of reckless adventure, of unctuous claims to a monopoly of human sympathy, of greed for power, of a desire for popular acclaim and an aspiration to make the front pages of the newspapers. This is the most charitable view.

To other people it appears to be a cold-blooded attempt by starry-eyed boys to infect the American people by a mixture of European ideas, flavored with our native predilection to get something for nothing.

You can choose either one you like best. But the first is the road of chaos which leads to the second. Both of these roads lead over the same grim precipice that is the crippling and possibly the destruction of the freedom of men. . .

In Central Europe the march of Socialist or Fascist dictatorships and their destruction of liberty did not set out with guns and armies. Dictators began their ascent to the seats of power through the elections provided by liberal institutions. Their weapons were promise and hate. They offered the mirage

* Mr. Desvernine should have credited these words to Jefferson's *Notes on Virginia*, 1781-82. [A.T.M.]

† From *Addresses Upon the American Road*, New York, Charles Scribner's Sons. Copyright © 1938 by Edgar Rickard. Reprinted by permission of Charles Scribner's Sons.

of Utopia to those in distress. They flung the poison of class hatred. They may not have maimed the bodies of men, but they maimed their souls.

The 1932 campaign was a pretty good imitation of this first stage of European tactics. You may recall the promises of the abundant life, the propaganda of hate.

Once seated in office, the first demand of these European despotisms was for power and 'action.' Legislatures were told they 'must' delegate their authorities. Their free debate was suppressed. The powers demanded are always the same pattern. They all adopted planned economy. They regimented industry and agriculture. They put the government into business. They engaged in gigantic government expenditures. They created vast organizations of spoils henchmen and subsidized dependents. They corrupted currency and credit. They drugged the thinking of the people with propaganda at the people's expense.

If there are any items in this stage in the march of European collectivism that the New Deal has not imitated it must have been an oversight.

But at this point this parallel with Europe halts—at least for the present. The American people should thank Almighty God for the Constitution and the Supreme Court. They should be grateful to a courageous press. . .

So much for the evidence that the New Deal is a definite attempt to replace the American system of freedom with some sort of European planned existence. But let us assume that the explanation is simply hit-and-run opportunism, spoils system and muddle.

We can well take a moment to explore the prospects of American ideals of liberty and self-government under that philosophy. We may take only seven short examples:

The Supreme Court has reversed some ten or twelve of the New Deal major enactments. Many of these acts were a violation of the rights of men and of self-government. Despite the sworn duty of the Executive and Congress to defend these rights they have sought to take them into their own hands. That is an attack on the foundations of freedom.

More than this, the independence of the Congress, the Supreme Court and the Executive are pillars at the door of liberty. For three years the word 'must' has invaded the independence of Congress. And the Congress has abandoned its responsibility to check even the expenditures of money. They have turned open appropriations into personal power. These are destructions of the very safeguards of free people. . .

Billions have been spent to prime the economic pump. It did employ a horde of paid officials upon the pump handle. We have seen the frantic attempts to find new taxes on the rich. Yet three-quarters of the bill will be sent to the average man and the poor. He and his wife and his grandchildren will be giving a quarter of all their working days to pay taxes. Freedom to work for himself is changed into a slavery of work for the follies of government. . .

We have seen the most elemental violation of economic law and experience. The New Deal forgets it is solely by production of more goods and more varieties of goods and services that we advance the standard of living and security of men. If we constantly decrease costs and prices and keep up earnings, the production of plenty will be more and more widely distributed. These laws may be restitched in new phrases but they are the very shoes of human progress.

We had so triumphed in this long climb of mankind toward plenty that we had reached Mount Pisgah, where we looked over the promised land of abolished poverty. Then men began to quarrel over the division of the goods. The depression produced by war destruction temporarily checked our march toward the promised land.

Then came the little prophets of the New Deal. They announce the striking solution that the way out is to produce less and to increase prices so the people can buy less. . .

Can democracy stand the strain of Mother Hubbard economics for long? Will there be anything left in the economic cupboard but a bone? . . .

The President has constantly reiterated that he will not retreat. For months, to be sure, there has been a strange quiet. . .

But the American people have the right to know now, while they still have power to act. What is going to be done after election with these measures which the Constitution forbids and the people by their votes have never authorized? What do the New Dealers propose to do with these unstable currencies, unbalanced budgets, debts and taxes? . .

There are principles which neither tricks of organization, nor the rigors of depression, nor the march of time, nor New Dealers, nor Socialists, nor Fascists can change. There are some principles which came into the universe along with the shooting stars of which worlds are made, and they have always been and ever will be true. Such are the laws of mathematics, the law of gravitation, the existence of God and the ceaseless struggle of humankind to be free.

Throughout the centuries of history, man's vigil and his quest have been to be free. For this, the best and bravest of earth have fought and died. To embody human liberty in workable government, America was born. Shall we keep that faith? Must we condemn the unborn generations to fight again and to die for the right to be free?

There are some principles that cannot be compromised. Either we shall have a society based upon ordered liberty and the initiative of the individual, or we shall have a planned society that means dictation, no matter what you call it or who does it. There is no half-way ground. They cannot be mixed. Government must either release the powers of the individual for honest achievement or the very forces it creates will drive it inexorably to lay its paralyzing hand more and more heavily upon individual effort. . .

6. *I do not believe that Americans will give up without a wholehearted effort to make democracy a living reality*

JOHN DEWEY, *Liberalism and Social Action,* 1935 *

It is frequently asserted that the method of experimental intelligence can be applied to physical facts because physical nature does not present conflicts of class interests, while it is inapplicable to society because the latter is so deeply marked by incompatible interests. It is then assumed that the 'experimentalist' is one who has chosen to ignore the uncomfortable fact of conflicting interests. Of course, there *are* conflicting interests; otherwise there would be no social problems. The problem under discussion is precisely *how* conflicting claims are to be settled in the interest of the widest possible contribution to the interests of all—or at least of the great majority. The method of democracy—inasfar as it is that of organized intelligence—is to bring these conflicts out into the open where their special claims can be seen and appraised, where they can be discussed and judged in the light of more inclusive interests than are represented by either of them separately. . .

In spite of the existence of class conflicts, amounting at times to veiled civil war, any one habituated to the use of the method of science will view with considerable suspicion the erection of actual human beings into fixed entities called classes, having no overlapping interests and so internally unified and externally separated that they are made the protagonists of history—itself hypothetical. Such an idea of classes is a survival of a rigid logic that once prevailed in the sciences of nature, but that no longer has any place there. This conversion of abstractions into entities smells more of a dialectic of concepts than of a realistic examination of facts, even though it makes more of an emotional appeal to many than do the results of the latter. To say that all past historic social progress has been the result of cooperation and not of conflict would be also an exaggeration. But exaggeration against exaggeration, it is the more reasonable of the two. And it is no exaggeration to say that the measure of civilization is the degree in which the method of cooperative intelligence replaces the method of brute conflict. . .

The argument, drawn from history, that great social changes have been effected only by violent means, needs considerable qualification, in view of the vast scope of changes that are taking place without the use of violence. But even if it be admitted to hold of the past, the conclusion that violence is the method now to be depended upon does not follow—unless one is committed to a dogmatic philosophy of history. The radical who insists that the future method of change must be like that of the past has much in common with the hide-bound reactionary who holds to the past as an ultimate fact. Both overlook the *fact that history in being a process of change generates change not only in details but also in the method of directing social change.* . . Mankind now has in its possession a new method, that of cooperative and

 Pages 79–93 *passim*.

experimental science which expresses the method of intelligence. I should be meeting dogmatism with dogmatism if I asserted that the existence of this historically new factor completely invalidates all arguments drawn from the effect of force in the past. But it is within the bounds of reason to assert that the presence of this social factor demands that the present situation be analyzed on its own terms, and not be rigidly subsumed under fixed conceptions drawn from the past.

Any analysis made in terms of the present situation will not fail to note one fact that militates powerfully against arguments drawn from past use of violence. Modern warfare is destructive beyond anything known in older times. This increased destructiveness is due primarily, of course, to the fact that science has raised to a new pitch of destructive power all the agencies of armed hostility. But it is also due to the much greater interdependence of all the elements of society. The bonds that hold modern communities and states together are as delicate as they are numerous. The self-sufficiency and independence of a local community, characteristic of more primitive societies, have disappeared in every highly industrialized country. The gulf that once separated the civilian population from the military has virtually gone. War involves paralysis of all normal social activities, and not merely the meeting of armed forces in the field. The Communist Manifesto presented two alternatives: *either* the revolutionary change and transfer of power to the proletariat, or the common ruin of the contending parties. Today, the civil war that would be adequate to effect transfer of power and a reconstruction of society at large, as understood by official Communists, would seem to present but one possible consequence: the ruin of all parties and the destruction of civilized life. This fact alone is enough to lead us to consider the potentialities of the method of intelligence. . .

Those who uphold the necessity of dependence upon violence usually much oversimplify the case by setting up a disjunction they regard as self-evident. They say that the sole alternative is putting our trust in parliamentary procedures as they now exist. This isolation of law-making from other social forces and agencies that are constantly operative is wholly unrealistic. Legislatures and congresses do not exist in a vacuum—not even the judges on the bench live in completely secluded sound-proof chambers. The assumption that it is possible for the constitution and activities of law-making bodies to persist unchanged while society itself is undergoing great change is an exercise in verbal formal logic.

It is true that in this country, because of the interpretations made by courts of a written constitution, our political institutions are unusually inflexible. It is also true, as well as even more important (because it is a factor in causing this rigidity) that our institutions, democratic in form, tend to favor in substance a privileged plutocracy. Nevertheless, it is sheer defeatism to assume in advance of actual trial that democratic political institutions are incapable either of further development or of constructive social application. Even as they now exist, the forms of representative government are potentially capable of expressing the public will when that assumes anything like unification. And there is nothing inherent in them that forbids their supplementation by political agencies that represent definitely economic social interests, like those of producers and consumers. . .

I know of no greater fallacy than the claim of those who hold to the dogma of the necessity of brute force that this use will be the method of calling genuine democracy into existence—of which they profess themselves the simon-pure adherents. It requires an unusually credulous faith in the Hegelian dialectic of opposites to think that all of a sudden the use of force by a class will be transmuted into a democratic classless society. Force breeds counterforce; the Newtonian law of action and reaction still holds in physics, and violence is physical. To profess democracy as an ultimate ideal and the suppression of democracy as a means to the ideal may be possible in a country that has never known even rudimentary democracy, but when professed in a country that has anything of a genuine democratic spirit in its traditions, it signifies desire for possession and retention of power by a class, whether that class be called Fascist or Proletarian. In the light of what happens in non-democratic countries, it is pertinent to ask whether the rule of a class signifies the dictatorship of the majority, or dictatorship over the chosen class by a minority party; whether dissenters are allowed even within the class the party claims to represent; and whether the development of literature and the other arts proceeds according to a formula prescribed by a party in conformity with a doctrinaire dogma of history and of infallible leadership, or whether artists are free from regimentation? Until these questions are satisfactorily answered, it is permissible to look with considerable suspicion upon those who assert that suppression of democracy is the road to the adequate establishment of genuine democracy. The one exception—and that apparent rather than real—to dependence upon organized intelligence as the method for directing social change is found when society through an authorized majority has entered upon the path of social experimentation leading to great social change, and a minority refuses by force to permit the method of intelligent action to go into effect. Then force may be intelligently employed to subdue and disarm the recalcitrant minority.

There may be some who think I am unduly dignifying a position held by a comparatively small group by taking their arguments as seriously as I have done. But their position serves to bring into strong relief the alternatives before us. It makes clear the meaning of renascent liberalism. The alternatives are continuation of drift with attendant improvisations to meet special emergencies; dependence upon violence; dependence upon socially organized intelligence. The first two alternatives, however, are not mutually exclusive, for if things are allowed to drift the result may be some sort of social change effected by the use of force, whether so planned or not. Upon the whole, the recent policy of liberalism has been to further 'social legislation'; that is, measures which add performance of social services to the older functions of government. The value of this addition is not to be despised. It marks a decided move away from *laissez faire* liberalism, and has considerable importance in educating the public mind to a realization of the possibilities of organized social control. It has helped to develop some of the techniques that in any case will be needed in a socialized economy. But the cause of liberalism will be lost for a considerable period if it is not prepared to go further and socialize the forces of production, now at hand, so that the liberty of individuals will be supported by the very structure of economic organization. . .

Since liberation of the capacities of individuals for free, self-initiated expression is an essential part of the creed of liberalism, liberalism that is sincere must will the means that condition the achieving of its ends. Regimentation of material and mechanical forces is the only way by which the mass of individuals can be released from regimentation and consequent suppression of their cultural possibilities. The eclipse of liberalism is due to the fact that it has not faced the alternatives and adopted the means upon which realization of its professed aims depends. Liberalism can be true to its ideals only as it takes the course that leads to their attainment. The notion that organized social control of economic forces lies outside the historic path of liberalism shows that liberalism is still impeded by remnants of its earlier *laissez faire* phase, with its opposition of society and the individual. The thing which now dampens liberal ardor and paralyzes its efforts is the conception that liberty and development of individuality as ends exclude the use of organized social effort as means. Earlier liberalism regarded the separate and competing economic action of individuals as the means to social well-being as the end. We must reverse the perspective and see that socialized economy is the means of free individual development as the end. . .

It is no part of my task to outline in detail a program for renascent liberalism. But the question of 'what is to be done' cannot be ignored. Ideas must be organized, and this organization implies an organization of individuals who hold these ideas and whose faith is ready to translate itself into action. Translation into action signifies that the general creed of liberalism be formulated as a concrete program of action. It is in organization for action that liberals are weak, and without this organization there is danger that democratic ideals may go by default. Democracy has been a fighting faith. When its ideals are reenforced by those of scientific method and experimental intelligence, it cannot be that it is incapable of evoking discipline, ardor and organization. To narrow the issue for the future to a struggle between Fascism and Communism is to invite a catastrophe that may carry civilization down in the struggle. Vital and courageous democratic liberalism is the one force that can surely avoid such a disastrous narrowing of the issue. I for one do not believe that Americans living in the tradition of Jefferson and Lincoln will weaken and give up without a whole-hearted effort to make democracy a living reality. . .

SELECTED REFERENCES

T. W. Arnold, *The Folklore of Capitalism*, New Haven, Yale University Press, 1937.

Mario Einaudi, *The Roosevelt Revolution*, New York, Harcourt, Brace, 1959.

Daniel R. Fusfeld, *The Economic Thought of Franklin D. Roosevelt, and the Origins of the New Deal*, New York, Columbia University Press, 1956.

Thomas H. Greer, *What Roosevelt Thought: The Social and Political Ideas of Franklin D. Roosevelt*, East Lansing, Michigan State University Press, 1958.

Herbert Hoover, *The Challenge to Liberty*, New York, Scribner's, 1934.

Thomas Paul Jenkin, *Reactions of Major Groups to Positive Government in the*

United States, 1930–1940; A Study in Contemporary Political Thought, Berkeley, University of California, 1945.

Edgar Kemler, *The Deflation of American Ideals: An Ethical Guide for New Dealers*, Washington, D.C., American Council of Public Affairs, 1941.

Ernest K. Lindley, *The Roosevelt Revolution*, New York, Viking, 1933.

Walter Lippmann, *The New Imperative*, New York, Macmillan, 1935.

David Mitrany, 'The New Deal: An Interpretation of Its Origin and Nature,' *American Interpretations*, London, Contact Publications, 1946.

Ogden L. Mills, *Liberalism Fights On*, New York, Macmillan, 1936.

———, *What of Tomorrow?*, New York, Macmillan, 1935.

Raymond Moley, *After Seven Years*, New York, Harper, 1939.

F. D. Roosevelt, *Looking Forward*, New York, John Day, 1933.

Arthur Schlesinger, Jr., *The Politics of Upheaval*, Boston, Houghton Mifflin, 1960.

Robert Sherwood, *Roosevelt and Hopkins*, New York, Harper, 1948.

Rexford Guy Tugwell, *The Democratic Roosevelt*, Garden City, Doubleday, 1957.

H. A. Wallace, *New Frontiers*, New York, Reynal & Hitchcock, 1935.

Dixon Wecter, *Age of Great Depression*, New York, Macmillan, 1948.

XX

INEVITABLE CONFLICT

Backed by a huge popular mandate in the 1936 presidential election, and faced with a recalcitrant Judiciary determined to stall his entire legislative program, President Roosevelt made a bold proposal for reorganization of the Federal Courts. His plan was to give Supreme Court Justices past seventy, six months to retire. If they failed to do so, they could continue on the bench, but the President would appoint new Justices, presumably younger and better able to carry the heavy load, and thus clear an allegedly crowded court docket. In presenting his plan, 5 February 1937, the President gave no hint of wanting to change 'reactionary' Court decisions, or subordinate the Judiciary to the Executive and Congress. But in his message of 9 March, here reprinted, he stated his position more forthrightly.

The President's unvarnished attack on our most sacrosanct institution aroused the nation to a fury of public discussion and debate. Leading the campaign against 'Court packing,' as F.D.R.'s critics dubbed his proposal, was Senator Burton K. Wheeler, who remarked that 'a liberal cause was never won by stacking a deck of cards, by stuffing a ballot box, or packing a Court.' The upshot was a prolonged discussion that sheds meaningful light on our complex political tradition.

President Roosevelt's attack on the judicial fortress, into which the enemies of positive government had dug in for a last-stand battle, was nothing new. Jefferson, Jackson, Lincoln, and Theodore Roosevelt, confronted with similar situations, had reacted in much the same way; the 1937 conflict was inevitable. Proclaiming his faith in popular majorities, F.D.R. used language that recalled Jefferson's bitter assaults on John Marshall. But the President combined with all this an espousal of positive government in defiance of Jefferson's policy of *laisser-faire*.

A majority of the Judiciary Committee rejected the court proposal. The Committee's reasoning, like F.D.R.'s in favor of the plan, is rooted in tradition. Of course, the Court might be steadily unresponsive to the public will, as expressed at the ballot box and in legislative majorities. All the more reason for leaving such a truly independent body alone—ran the Committee's seemingly impeccable, allegedly 'democratic' logic. 'If the Court of last resort,' the Committee's majority report said, 'is to be made to respond to a prevalent sentiment of a current hour, politically imposed, that Court must ultimately become subservient to the pressures of public opinion of the hour, which might at the moment embrace mob passion abhorrent to a more calm, lasting consideration.'

Uttered in the heyday of the New Deal, these words mark the triumph in 1937 of the aristocratic doctrines of Hamilton, Kent, and Brewer. But it was not an unmixed victory for either interests or numbers. Though the Court reorganization plan was defeated, the President, for all practical purposes, had his way. Even before the fight was concluded, and without any change in the Court's personnel, five to four decisions in crucial cases were going in favor of rather than against Roosevelt's legislative program.

Thurman W. Arnold (1891–) bluntly denied that America had faced up to the issues. In his witty and iconoclastic analysis, Arnold charged that most Americans, instead of coming to grips with the problems confronting the nation, engaged in shadowboxing. Real issues were cloaked by the clichés of myth and folklore. Conservatives, defending the Court, contended that 'Court packing' threatened to destroy the Constitution. But defenders of the faith failed to ask, '*Whose* Constitution?' Nor did they bother to note that the dominant jurisprudence of the Court between 1890 and 1936 had already seriously damaged John Marshall's Constitution. Participants on both sides, Arnold observed, 'denounced government by men, and sought relief by reciting principles.' Published in 1937, Arnold's *Folklore of Capitalism* brought him to President Roosevelt's attention, leading perhaps to his appointment as Assistant Attorney General in charge of the Antitrust Division.

By 1939 the basic problems of recovery were still unsolved, but with war clouding the political horizon the New Deal seemed firmly entrenched. The most vigorous New Deal critic, the American Liberty League, was in precipitous decline. To what new arsenal might the opposition now turn? In 1914, when conservative interests were threatened by Woodrow Wilson's New Freedom, Truxton Beale prepared a new edition of Herbert Spencer's *Man Versus the State* with not only a general introduction by the editor, but a sympathetic foreword to each of Spencer's chapters by eminent Americans, including William Howard Taft, Elihu Root, Nicholas Murray Butler, David Jayne Hill, Henry Cabot Lodge, and Harlan Fiske Stone. So, in 1939, Albert Jay Nock, author and critic, editor of *The Freeman* and biographer of Jefferson, once more turned hopefully to the nineteenth-century tutelary genius of *laisser-faire* —Herbert Spencer. In justification of a new edition the publisher's blurb commented: 'With the powers of government becoming broader with each year, with officialdom growing at a ruinous rate, and with freedom fighting a losing battle, there is still one last intellectual rampart to which the protagonists of freedom have learned to turn'—that is, to Herbert Spencer. He will present, the blurb continues, 'the present lover of freedom with a dialectic basis that will serve him as fundamentally as Marx's *Das Kapital* serves the Communist.' The goblins of Statism will get you, Editor Nock chimed in, if you don't read *Man Versus the State*.

Undaunted, President Roosevelt continued to push his reforms and round out his philosophy. In the Four Freedoms speech of 1944, he gave his creed cosmic application. The words as well as the ideas of this now famous utterance must be credited, Robert Sherwood tells us, to the President himself.

Reaction to Roosevelt's four categories of freedom was prompt and specific. Dr. Nicholas Murray Butler, president of Columbia University (who had found so much to praise in his introductory essay in Beale's 1916 edition of Herbert Spencer), declared that 'Freedom of Enterprise' is the 'keystone of the arch' on which President Roosevelt's Four Freedoms stand or fall. 'I therefore suggest it as a Fifth Freedom,' Dr. Butler said. Ex-President Hoover made the same suggestion and elaborated his reasons in the address here reproduced.

The magnificent account which so-called Free Enterprise gave of itself in World War II revived faith in our economic system and in those who operate and control it. No longer timid, half-apologetic, or defeatist, as businessmen were inclined to be in the years immediately following the 1929 depression, spokesmen for the Free Enterprise system after 1942 were self-confident and increasingly vocal. American industry throughout the war years being rigidly hampered by a variety of controls, advertising space and radio time, normally devoted to selling goods and services, became a medium for selling the gospel of 'Free Enterprise!' In 1943, Merle Thorpe, editor of *Nation's Business*, squarely facing the issue, asked whether America 'at the end of the war will throw off political controls of our lives and livelihoods, or whether the people will accept them as a permanent part of our social and economic structure.'

Meanwhile, President Roosevelt had also turned his attention to the Free Enterprise system, sponsoring in 1938 the Temporary National Economic Committee, whose conclusions are embodied in a mountain of TNEC Monographs, published in 1940–41. But whereas spokesmen for business, such as Merle Thorpe, saw Free Enterprise imperiled by government, President Roosevelt and TNEC Chairman, Senator Joseph C. O'Mahoney (1884–) whose statement is here reprinted, denounced interlocking financial controls, among other things, for robbing American business of 'much of its traditional virility, independence and daring.' This is the thesis that runs through the TNEC Monographs and report. One finds in them no 'subversive' want of faith in capitalism. What TNEC found was 'not that the system of free enterprise for profit had failed in this generation but that it had not been tried.' And in his instructions to the TNEC, Roosevelt said categorically: 'The power of a few to manage the economic life of the nation must be diffused among the many or be transferred to the public and its democratically responsible government.'

By 1944, liberal thought in America seems to have passed through two distinct phases: *laisser-faire* or *status quo*, the theory that man is free only if industry is practically immune from government control, the theory that insists on 'the right of those who own property to control it'; or public control, the theory that freedom is possible under modern conditions of economic dependence and interdependence only if government, rather than industrial management or ownership, is the dominant though not absolute power. The difference consists largely in the values deemed fundamental and the relation of government thereto. The first, failing to recognize that liberty can be, and is, encroached upon by forces other than government, takes liberty as its watchword, and, like Herbert Spencer, measures liberty in terms of the paucity of restraint government places on the individual. The second, sensitive to blighting inequalities of opportunity that exist in the social and economic struggle among private individuals and groups, advocates government intervention to establish greater equality of opportunity. On 11 January 1944, President Roosevelt, harking back to the ideals stated in the Declaration of Independence and in the Preamble to the Constitution of 1787, formulated an Economic Bill of Rights. In it the President reinterpreted Jefferson's verities—liberty, equality, and the idea that free governments derive their just powers from the consent of the governed—for a new age:

Liberty: During a good part of our history, liberty had been, as we have seen, largely a negative concept, comprising little more than the protection of private rights, especially those of property and contract, against invasion by government. In actual practice there had been, prior to 1870, only one notable exception to this narrow view of government's role in relation to liberty—the emancipation of the slaves—but this served to illustrate the tremendous potentialities latent in political democracy, and to demonstrate the possibilities of utilizing government power as an instrument for enlarging individual freedom and opportunity, both against dwarfing conditions, and against submerging forces other than government.

Equality: This, too, is a basic New Deal tenet, no less than in the Declaration of Independence. Never asserted as a statement of biological fact, usually defined as equality of opportunity, it has been largely adhered to as an ideal to be striven for, perhaps never to be fully achieved. During the Jacksonian period it had considerable substance even in the absence of political equality, i.e., full and equal suffrage. After the rise of industrialism it was widely recognized that political equality was not enough in a society marked by vast economic inequalities. We had passed to a subtler civilization with barriers for privilege and against progress unknown in the days of agrarianism. Now, it was argued, government must act positively to repel these inroads on both economic and political equality. The New Deal, building on such knowledge, enacted this theory.

Governments Derive Their Just Powers from the Consent of the Governed: This conviction likewise continues as an article of our political faith. During much of our history, however, this did not mean or require mass consent or even the consent of political majorities. It meant, as we have seen, only popular consent to a government checked, divided, and balanced, and only such legislation as could pass muster with our Supreme Court. Under positive government 'consent of the governed' means much more than that. With the erosion of traditional Constitutional barriers—dual federalism, checks and balances, and even of judicial review—it connotes greater responsiveness to the popular will as expressed at the ballot box, in Congress, and by the President—greater reliance than in the past on the political, as against legal and judicial interference, with government policy and action.

As a consequence of all these major developments, both singly and in combination, the triumph of positive government meant the strengthening of our democracy in the sense of majority rule and in the fundamental sense of equality of opportunity. But, perhaps, the most significant aspect of the New

Deal is the advanced theory of public power it represents, coupled with its recognition of government as a positive instrument in the service of the general welfare. President Roosevelt's confidence in average people helped develop his gift for leadership, enabling him to think, as our Founding Fathers could not, of popular power not as something to be feared and checked but as a natural force needing to be released, guided, and directed.

'Government is action,' Woodrow Wilson wrote in 1893, 'and democratic government more than any other needs organization to escape disintegration.' What is more, democratic government demands leadership. President Roosevelt came close to fulfilling Wilson's specifications of free government.

1. *We want a Supreme Court under the Constitution*

FRANKLIN D. ROOSEVELT, Reorganizing the Federal Judiciary, 9 March 1937 *

Tonight, sitting at my desk in the White House, I make my first radio report to the people in my second term of office.

I am reminded of that evening in March four years ago, when I made my first radio report to you. We were then in the midst of the great banking crisis. . .

In 1933 you and I knew that we must never let our economic system get completely out of joint again—that we could not afford to take the risk of another great depression.

We also became convinced that the only way to avoid a repetition of those dark days was to have a government with power to prevent and to cure the abuses and the inequalities which had thrown that system out of joint.

We then began a program of remedying those abuses and inequalities—to give balance and stability to our economic system—to make it bombproof against the causes of 1929.

Today we are only part way through that program—and recovery is speeding up to a point where the dangers of 1929 are again becoming possible, not this week or month perhaps, but within a year or two.

National laws are needed to complete that program. Individual or local or State effort alone cannot protect us in 1937 any better than 10 years ago. . .

Four years ago action did not come until the eleventh hour. It was almost too late.

If we learned anything from the depression we will not allow ourselves to run around in new circles of futile discussion and debate, always postponing the day of decision.

The American people have learned from the depression. For in the last three national elections an overwhelming majority of them voted a mandate that the Congress and the President begin the task of providing that protection —not after long years of debate, but now.

* *Senate Reports*, 75th Congress, 1st session, 5 January–21 August 1937, vol. 1, pp. 41–4 *passim.*

The courts, however, have cast doubts on the ability of the elected Congress to protect us against catastrophe by meeting squarely our modern social and economic conditions.

We are at a crisis in our ability to proceed with that protection. It is a quiet crisis. There are no lines of depositors outside closed banks. But to the farsighted it is far-reaching in its possibilities of injury to America.

I want to talk with you very simply about the need for present action in this crisis—the need to meet the unanswered challenge of one-third of a nation ill-nourished, ill-clad, ill-housed.

Last Thursday I described the American form of government as a three-horse team provided by the Constitution to the American people so that their field might be plowed. The three horses are, of course, the three branches of government—the Congress, the executive, and the courts. Two of the horses are pulling in unison today; the third is not. Those who have intimated that the President of the United States is trying to drive that team overlook the simple fact that the President, as Chief Executive, is himself one of the three horses.

It is the American people themselves who are in the driver's seat.

It is the American people themselves who want the furrow plowed.

It is the American people themselves who expect the third horse to pull in unison with the other two.

I hope that you have reread the Constitution of the United States. Like the Bible, it ought to be read again and again.

It is an easy document to understand when you remember that it was called into being because the Articles of Confederation under which the Original Thirteen States tried to operate after the Revolution showed the need of a National Government with power enough to handle national problems. In its preamble the Constitution states that it was intended to form a more perfect Union and promote the general welfare; and the powers given to the Congress to carry out those purposes can be best described by saying that they were all the powers needed to meet each and every problem which then had a national character and which could not be met by merely local action.

But the framers went further. Having in mind that in succeeding generations many other problems then undreamed of would become national problems, they gave to the Congress the ample broad powers 'to levy taxes . . . and provide for the common defense and general welfare of the United States.'

That, my friends, is what I honestly believe to have been the clear and underlying purpose of the patriots who wrote a Federal Constitution to create a National Government with national power, intended as they said, 'to form a more perfect union . . . for ourselves and our posterity.'

For nearly twenty years there was no conflict between the Congress and the Court. Then, in 1803, Congress passed a statute which the Court said violated an express provision of the Constitution. The Court claimed the power to declare it unconstitutional and did so declare it. But a little later the Court itself admitted that it was an extraordinary power to exercise and through Mr. Justice Washington laid down this limitation upon it: 'It is but a decent respect due to the wisdom, the integrity, and the patriotism of the legislative body, by which any law is passed, to presume in favor of its validity until its violation of the Constitution is proved beyond all reasonable doubt.' *

But since the rise of the modern movement for social and economic progress through legislation, the Court has more and more often and more and more boldly asserted a power to veto laws passed by the Congress and State legislatures in complete disregard of this original limitation.

In the last four years the sound rule of giving statutes the benefit of all reasonable doubt has been cast aside. The Court has been acting not as a judicial body, but as a policy-making body.

When the Congress has sought to stabilize national agriculture, to improve the conditions of labor, to safeguard business against unfair competition, to protect our national resources, and in many other ways to serve our clearly national needs, the majority of the Court has been assuming the power to pass on the wisdom of these acts of the Congress—and to approve or disapprove the public policy written into these laws.

That is not only my accusation. It is the accusation of most distinguished Justices of the present Supreme Court. I have not the time to quote to you all the language used by dissenting Justices in many of these cases. But in the case holding the Railroad Retirement Act unconstitutional, for instance, Chief Justice Hughes said in a dissenting opinion that the majority opinion was 'a departure from sound principles,' and placed 'an unwarranted limitation upon the commerce clause.' ** And three other Justices agreed with him.

In the case holding the A.A.A. unconstitutional,† Justice Stone said of the majority opinion that it was a 'tortured construction of the Constitution.' And two other Justices agreed with him.

In the case holding the New York Minimum Wage Law unconstitutional,‡ Justice Stone said that the majority were actually reading into the Constitution their own 'personal economic predilections,' and that if the legislative power is not left free to choose the methods of solving the problems of poverty, subsistence, and health of large numbers in the community, then 'government is to be rendered impotent.' And two other Justices agreed with him.

In the case of these dissenting opinions, there is no basis for the claim made by some members of the Court that something in the Constitution has compelled them regretfully to thwart the will of the people.

In the face of such dissenting opinions, it is perfectly clear that as Chief Justice Hughes has said, 'We are under a Constitution, but the Constitution is what the judges say it is.' §

* Ogden *v.* Saunders, 12 Wheaton 213, 1824.

** Railroad Retirement Bd. *et al. v.* Alton R.R. Co., 295 U.S. 330, 1935.

† U. S. *v.* Butler, 297 U.S. 1, 1936.

‡ Morehead *v.* N. Y. *ex rel.* Tipaldo, 298 U.S. 587, 1936.

§ Speech of Governor Hughes before the Elmira, New York, Chamber of Commerce, 3 May 1907. Published in *Addresses*, 1908, p. 139.

In reply to an inquiry (13 January 1948) whether the meaning President Roosevelt gave to Hughes's famous words was the one the then Governor of New York intended, the Chief Justice's secretary commented 2 February 1948: 'The clause is taken entirely out of its context. . . The way this phrase has been quoted and used does a considerable injustice to Mr. Hughes's intent in reference to the court.'

The Court in addition to the proper use of its judicial functions has improperly set itself up as a third House of the Congress—a superlegislature, as one of the Justices has called it—reading into the Constitution words and implications which are not there, and which were never intended to be there.

We have, therefore, reached the point as a Nation where we must take action to save the Constitution from the Court and the Court from itself. We must find a way to take an appeal from the Supreme Court to the Constitution itself. We want a Supreme Court which will do justice under the Constitution—not over it. In our courts we want a government of laws and not of men.

I want—as all Americans want—an independent judiciary as proposed by the framers of the Constitution. That means a Supreme Court that will enforce the Constitution as written—that will refuse to amend the Constitution by the arbitrary exercise of judicial power—amendment by judicial say-so. It does not mean a judiciary so independent that it can deny the existence of facts universally recognized. . .

What is my proposal? It is simply this: Whenever a judge or justice of any Federal Court has reached the age of seventy and does not avail himself of the opportunity to retire on a pension, a new member shall be appointed by the President then in office, with the approval, as required by the Constitution, of the Senate of the United States.

That plan has two chief purposes: By bringing into the judicial system a steady and continuing stream of new and younger blood, I hope, first, to make the administration of all Federal justice speedier and therefore less costly; secondly, to bring to the decision of social and economic problems younger men who have had personal experience and contact with modern facts and circumstances under which average men have to live and work. This plan will save our National Constitution from hardening of the judicial arteries. . .

Those opposing this plan have sought to arouse prejudice and fear by crying that I am seeking to 'pack' the Supreme Court and that a baneful precedent will be established.

What do they mean by the words 'packing the Court'?

Let me answer this question with a bluntness that will end all honest misunderstanding of my purposes.

If by that phrase 'packing the Court' it is charged that I wish to place on the bench spineless puppets who would disregard the law and would decide specific cases as I wished them to be decided, I make this answer: That no President fit for his office would appoint, and no Senate of honorable men fit for their office would confirm, that kind of appointees to the Supreme Court.

But if by that phrase the charge is made that I would appoint and the Senate would confirm Justices worthy to sit beside present members of the Court who understand those modern conditions; that I will appoint Justices who will not undertake to override the judgment of the Congress on legislative policy; that I will appoint Justices who will act as Justices and not as legislators—if the appointment of such Justices can be called 'packing the Courts'—then I say that I, and with me the vast majority of the American people, favor doing just that thing—now. . .

Like all lawyers, like all Americans, I regret the necessity of this controversy. But the welfare of the United States, and indeed of the Constitution itself, is what we all must think about first. Our difficulty with the Court today rises not from the Court as an institution but from human beings within it. But we cannot yield our constitutional destiny to the personal judgment of a few men who, being fearful of the future, would deny us the necessary means of dealing with the present.

This plan of mine is no attack on the Court; it seeks to restore the Court to its rightful and historic place in our system of constitutional government and to have it resume its high task of building anew on the Constitution 'a system of living law.' . .

2. *Let there be no change by usurpation*

Adverse Report of the Senate Judiciary Committee, 1937 *

. . . By this bill, judges who have reached 70 years of age may remain on the bench and have their judgment augmented if they agree with the new appointee, or vetoed if they disagree. This is far from the independence intended for the courts by the framers of the Constitution. This is an unwarranted influence accorded the appointing agency, contrary to the spirit of the Constitution. . . Neither speed nor 'new blood' in the judiciary is the object of this legislation, but a change in the decisions of the Court—a subordination of the views of the judges to the views of the executive and legislative, a change to be brought about by forcing certain judges off the bench or increasing their number. . .

There is a remedy for usurpation or other judicial wrongdoing. If this bill be supported by the toilers of this country upon the ground that they want a Court which will sustain legislation limiting hours and providing minimum wages, they must remember that the procedure employed in the bill could be used in another administration to lengthen hours and to decrease wages. If farmers want agricultural relief and favor this bill upon the ground that it gives them a Court which will sustain legislation in their favor, they must remember that the procedure employed might some day be used to deprive them of every vestige of a farm relief.

When members of the Court usurp legislative powers or attempt to exercise political power, they lay themselves open to the charge of having lapsed from that 'good behavior' which determines the period of their official life. But, if you say, the process of impeachment is difficult and uncertain, the answer is, the people made it so when they framed the Constitution. It is not for us, the servants of the people, the instruments of the Constitution, to find a more easy way to do that which our masters made difficult.

* *Senate Reports*, 75th Congress, 1st session, 5 January–21 August 1937, vol. 1, Report no. 711, 'Reorganization of the Federal Judiciary,' pp. 1, 9–23 *passim*.

But, if the fault of the judges is not so grievous as to warrant impeachment, if their offense is merely that they have grown old, and we feel, therefore, that there should be a 'constant infusion of new blood,' then obviously the way to achieve that result is by constitutional amendment fixing definite terms for the members of the judiciary or making mandatory their retirement at a given age. Such a provision would indeed provide for the constant infusion of new blood, not only now but at all times in the future. The plan before us is but a temporary expedient which operates once and then never again, leaving the Court as permanently expended to become once more a court of old men, gradually year by year falling behind the times. . .

We are told that a reactionary oligarchy defies the will of the majority, that this is a bill to 'unpack' the Court and give effect to the desires of the majority that is to say, a bill to increase the number of Justices for the express purpose of neutralizing the views of some of the present members. In justification we are told, but without authority, by those who would rationalize this program, that Congress was given the power to determine the size of the Court so that the legislative branch would be able to impose its will upon the judiciary. This amounts to nothing more than the declaration that when the Court stands in the way of a legislative enactment, the Congress may reverse the ruling by enlarging the Court. When such a principle is adopted, our constitutional system is overthrown! . .

Even if every charge brought against the so-called 'reactionary' members of this Court be true, it is far better that we await orderly but inevitable change of personnel than that we impatiently overwhelm them with new members. Exhibiting this restraint, thus demonstrating our faith in the American system, we shall set an example that will protect the independent American judiciary from attack as long as this Government stands. . .

We declare for the continuance and perpetuation of government and rule by law, as distinguished from government and rule by men, and in this we are but reasserting the principles basic to the Constitution of the United States. The converse of this would lead to and in fact accomplish the destruction of our form of government, where the written Constitution with its history, its spirit, and its long line of judicial interpretation and construction, is looked to and relied upon by millions of our people. Reduction of the degree of the supremacy of law means an increasing enlargement of the degree of personal government. . .

Courts and the judges thereof should be free from a subservient attitude of mind, and this must be true whether a question of constitutional construction or one of popular activity is involved. If the court of last resort is to be made to respond to a prevalent sentiment of a current hour, politically imposed, that Court must ultimately become subservient to the pressure of public opinion of the hour, which might at the moment embrace mob passion abhorrent to a more calm, lasting consideration.

True it is, that courts like Congresses, should take account of the advancing strides of civilization. True it is that law, being a progressive science must be pronounced progressively and liberally; but the milestones of liberal progress are made to be noted and counted with caution rather than merely to be encountered and passed. Progress is not a mad mob march; rather, it is a steady, invincible stride. . .

If, under the 'hydraulic pressure' of our present need for economic justice, we destroy the system under which our people have progressed to a higher degree of justice and prosperity than that ever enjoyed by any other people in all the history of the human race, then we shall destroy not only all opportunity for further advance but everything we have thus far achieved. . .

Inconvenience and even delay in the enactment of legislation is not a heavy price to pay for our system. Constitutional democracy moves forward with certainty rather than with speed. The safety and the permanence of the progressive march of our civilization are far more important to us and to those who are to come after us than the enactment now of any particular law. The Constitution of the United States provides ample opportunity for the expression of popular will to bring about such reforms and changes as the people may deem essential to their present and future welfare. It is the people's charter of the powers granted those who govern them. . .

Familiar with English history and the long struggle for human liberty, they [the Founding Fathers] held it to be an axiom of free government that there could be no security for the people against the encroachment of political power save a written Constitution and an uncontrolled judiciary.

This has now been demonstrated by 150 years of progressive American history. As a people, Americans love liberty. It may be with truth and pride also said that we have a sensitive regard for human rights. Notwithstanding these facts, during 150 years the citizen over and over again has been compelled to contend for the plain rights guaranteed in the Constitution. Free speech, a free press, the right of assemblage, the right of a trial by jury, freedom from arbitrary arrest, religious freedom—these are among the great underlying principles upon which our democracy rests. But for all these, there have been occasions when the citizen has had to appeal to the courts for protection as against those who would take them away. And the only place the citizen has been able to go in any of these instances, for protection against the abridgment of his rights, has been to an independent and uncontrolled and incorruptible judiciary. Our law reports are filled with decisions scattered throughout these long years, reassuring the citizen of his constitutional rights, restraining States, restraining the Congress, restraining the Executive, restraining majorities, and preserving the noblest in rights of individuals.

Minority political groups, no less than religious and racial groups, have never failed, when forced to appeal to the Supreme Court of the United States, to find in its opinions the reassurance and protection of their constitutional rights. No finer or more durable philosophy of free government is to be found in all the writings and practices of great statesmen than may be found in the decisions of the Supreme Court when dealing with great problems of free government touching human rights. This would not have been possible without an independent judiciary. . .

If ever there was a time when the people of America should heed the words of the Father of Their Country this is the hour. Listen to his solemn warning from the Farewell Address:

> It is important, likewise, that the habits of thinking, in a free country, should inspire caution in those intrusted with its administration, to confine themselves within their respective constitutional spheres, avoiding, in the exercises of the powers of one department, to encroach upon another. The spirit of encroachment tends to consolidate the powers of all the departments in one, and thus to create, whatever the form of government, a real despotism. A first estimate of that love of power, and proneness to abuse it, which predominates in the human heart, is sufficient to satisfy us of the truth of this position. The necessity of reciprocal checks in the exercise of political power, by dividing and distributing it into different depositories, and constituting each the guardian of the public weal, against invasions by the others, has been evinced by experiment, ancient and modern; some of them in our own country, and under our own eyes. To preserve them must be as necessary as to institute them. If, in the opinion of the people, the distribution or modification of the constitutional powers be, in any particular, wrong, let it be corrected by an amendment in the way which the Constitution designates. But let there be no change by usurpation; for though this, in one instance, may be the instrument of good, it is the customary weapon by which free governments are destroyed. The precedent must always greatly overbalance, in permanent evil, any partial or transient benefit which the use can, at any time, yield. . .

We recommend the rejection of this bill as a needless, futile, and utterly dangerous abandonment of constitutional principle. . .

It is a proposal without precedent and without justification.

It would subjugate the courts to the will of Congress and the President and thereby destroy the independence of the judiciary, the only certain shield of individual rights. . .

It points the way to the evasion of the Constitution and establishes the method whereby the people may be deprived of their right to pass upon all amendments of the fundamental law.

It stands now before the country, acknowledged by its proponents as a plan to force judicial interpretation of the Constitution, a proposal that violates every sacred tradition of American democracy. . .

3. *The folklore during the Great Depression was that principles could be more trusted than organizations*

THURMAN W. ARNOLD, *The Folklore of Capitalism*, 1937 *

The effect of the peculiar folklore of 1937 was to encourage the type of organization known as industry or business and discourage the type known as government. Under the protection of this folklore the achievements of American business were remarkable. There was no questioning of myths which supported independent empires by those engaged in those enterprises. So-called private institutions like General Motors never lost their direction through philosophical debate. The pioneer efforts at industrial organization in this country had been wasteful beyond belief, but bold and confident.

With respect to political government, however, our superstitions had the opposite effect. They were not a cohesive force, but a destructive and disintegrating one. The pioneer efforts of the Government were timid, indecisive, and ineffective. When it became necessary for the Government to fill gaps in the national structure in which private business enterprise was an obvious failure, the myths and folklore of the time hampered practical organization at every turn. Men became more interested in planning the culture of the future—in saving posterity from the evils of dictatorship or bureaucracy, in preventing the American people from adopting Russian culture on the one hand, or German culture on the other—than in the day-to-day distribution of food, housing, and clothing to those who needed them. Mystical attacks on practical measures achieved an astonishing degree of success. Debaters and orators rose to the top in such an atmosphere and technicians twiddled their thumbs, unable to use their skills. . .

In the spring of 1936 the writer heard a group of bankers, businessmen, lawyers, and professors, typical of the learned and conservative thinkers of the time, discussing a crisis in the affairs of the bankrupt New York, New Haven, and Hartford Railroad—once the backbone of New England, the support of its institutions and its worthy widows and orphans. They were expressing indignation that a bureaucratic Interstate Commerce Commission, operating from Washington, had decreed that passenger rates be cut almost in half. Every man there would directly benefit from the lower rate. None were stockholders. Yet all were convinced that the reduction in rate should be opposed by all conservative citizens and they were very unhappy about this new outrage committed by a government bent on destroying private business by interfering with the free judgment of its managers.

This sincere indignation and gloom had its roots not in selfishness nor the pursuit of the profit of the moment, but in pure idealism. These men, though they owned no stock, were willing to forego the advantage of lower fares to save the railroad from the consequences of economic sin. They took a long-

* New Haven, Yale University Press, 1937, pp. 46–51, 57–8, 61–71 *passim*. Reprinted by permission of Yale University Press.

range view and decided that in the nature of things the benefits of the lower rates would be only temporary, because they had been lowered in violation of the great principle that government should not interfere with business. Some sort of catastrophe was bound to result from such an action. . .

Trains would keep on running, but with a sinister change in the character of the service. Under government influence, it would become as unpleasant as the income taxes were unpleasant. And in the background was an even more nebulous fear. The Government would, under such conditions, have to take over the railroad, thus ushering in bureaucracy and regimentation. Trains would run, but there would be no pleasure in riding on them any more.

There was also the thought that investors would suffer. This was difficult to put into concrete terms because investors already had suffered. The railroad was bankrupt. Most of the gentlemen present had once owned stock, but had sold it before it had reached its present low. Of course, they wanted the stock to go up again, along with everything else, provided, of course, that the Government did not put it up by "artificial" means, which would be inflation.

The point was raised as to whether the Interstate Commerce Commission was right in believing that the road would actually be more prosperous under the lower rates. This possibility was dismissed as absurd. Government commissions were always theoretical. This was a tenet of pure faith about which one did not even argue. . .

And so the discussion ended on a note of vague worry. No one was happy over the fact that he could travel cheaper. No one was pleased that employment would increase, or that the heavy industries would be stimulated by the reduction of rates. Out of pure mystical idealism, these men were opposing every selfish interest both of themselves and the community, because the scheme went counter to the folklore to which they were accustomed. And since it went counter to that folklore, the same fears resulted from every other current scheme which violated traditional attitudes, whether it was relief, housing, railroad rates, or the Securities Exchange Act. Anything which could be called governmental interference in business necessarily created bureaucracy, regimentation, inflation and put burdens on posterity. . .

The way of thinking illustrated by the above incident is a stereotype. Its pattern is the same to whatever problems it is applied. It starts by reducing a situation, infinitely complicated by human and political factors, to a simple parable which illustrates fundamental and immutable principles. It ends by proving that the sacrifice of present advantage is necessary in order to protect everything we hold most dear. All such discussions end with arguments based on freedom, the home, tyranny, bureaucracy, and so on. All lead into a verbal crusade to protect our system of government. In this way certainty of opinion is possible for people who know nothing whatever about the actual situation. They feel they do not have to know the details. They know the principles. . .

This way of thinking is as old as the desire of men to escape from the hard necessity of making practical judgments in the comfort and certainty of an appeal to priests. It controlled the thinking about the human body in the Middle Ages. It controls our thinking about the body politic today. Out of it have been spun our great legal and economic principles which have made our learning about government a search for universal truth rather than a set of observations about the techniques of human organization.

The great ideological battle in 1937 was whether Capitalism was worth preserving. Most people thought it should be preserved. There were many intelligent humanitarian people, however, who thought that it should be abandoned and a new system inaugurated, usually called Socialism. This new system on paper seemed preferable to Capitalism. Yet it was constantly pointed out by its opponents that if one tried to obtain Socialism, one got either Fascism or Communism, with their attendant evils of regimentation, bureaucracy, dictatorship, and so on, and that individualism disappeared.

It was a complicated business, this preservation of the capitalistic system in 1937 against the other "isms" and alien ideals. There was first the task of defining what Capitalism really was. This was a constant process. It had to be done every day and each new restatement led only to the necessity of further definition. The preservation of Capitalism also required that practical plans be tested by expert economic theorists who looked at each practical measure through the spectacles of economic abstractions, in order not to be confused by immediate objectives. Thus child labor had to be debated, not on the basis of whether it was desirable for children to work, but in the light of its effect on the American home in ten years, if it were followed to its logical conclusion. Measures for the conservation of oil, or regulation of agriculture, had to be considered without relation to immediate benefits either to oil or agriculture. Tendencies were regarded as far more important than immediate effects, and the danger to posterity actually seemed more real than the danger to existing persons.

The capitalistic system in America had two sets of rules, one economic and the other legal, determining what the limits of governmental control should be. Economic theory had no separate institution to speak ex cathedra, other than the two political parties, each of which hired experts to study it and advise them. Whatever was produced by any political platform had to have its background of scholarly research. It was the duty of each party to consult only sound economists. Legal theory, on the other hand, was manufactured by the Supreme Court of the United States. There were two parties in the Supreme Court of the United States, each with its own legal theory. However, it was generally agreed that what the majority of judges thought was the real essence of the Constitution. It was not left to the people to decide between sound and unsound legal theory, and therefore the opinions of dissenting judges, unlike the opinions of dissenting economists, were not available in political debate, at least prior to Roosevelt's attack on the Court. This was because law concerned the spiritual welfare of the people and preserved their form of government, whereas economics concerned only their material welfare. In spiritual things it is essential that men do right according to some final authority. There was thought to be no such compelling reason to prevent them from ruining themselves economically.

The general [picture] of the Supreme Court's function is [one of] the economic and social legislation of the day [being thrown] out of the august portals of the Supreme Court. . . This [is] . . . what the great mass of conservative people thought the Court was doing for them. They did not trust themselves to decide whether a humanitarian or practical scheme was really government by edict, or would lead to government by edict. They knew that such things seldom appeared on the surface, and that they required great learning to analyze. However, more intelligent people required a more complicated explanation, because they preferred long words to pictures. Hence the years of the depression produced thousands of learned dissertations, which came to every possible sort of conclusion as to the constitutionality of various measures. These articles did not make the law clear. They did, however, make it clear that there was such a thing as law, which experts could discover through reason.

It was this faith in a higher law which made the Supreme Court the greatest unifying symbol in American government. Here was the one body which could still the constant debate, and represent to the country the ideal of a government of fundamental principles. On this Court the whole ideal of a government of laws and not of the competing opinions of men appeared to depend. Here only was there a breathing spell from the continual din of arguments about governmental philosophy which were never settled.

The legislative branches of the Government were under constant suspicion, and their acts were presumed to be malevolent. The incompetency of Congress was an assumed fact everywhere. The great trouble with the legislative branches was that they were influenced by an unlearned, untheoretical, illogical, and often corrupt force called "politics." Politics was continually putting unworthy persons in power, as opposed to business, where, because of economic law, only worthy persons rose to the top. A body influenced by political considerations could not give any disinterested judgment as to the soundness of any economic theory. Hence Congress was constantly picking unsound theories, listening to unsound economists, and letting the practical convenience of the moment overweigh the needs of posterity. Politicians were the kind of people who would not care if a thing called bureaucracy was established as long as it gave them jobs.

The only trustworthy check against unsound economic theory was not the politician, but that great body of thinking men and women who composed the better class of the public. Yet even such people were easily confused in those days when the noise of competing theories was loudest. The only way of straightening them out was by constant preaching, which had the weakness of all preaching throughout the centuries, in that sin and heresy were always rising against it. . .

Men could choose between sound and unsound economic theories, but they must not be permitted to choose between sound and unsound constitutional theories. To prevent them from erring on this point, a scholargarchy was set up, with complete autocratic power. To a superficial observer, this might seem a denial of the beauty of group free will, but closer examination showed that it was not. For the function of the Supreme Court was not to prevent people from choosing what kind of constitution they desired, but to prevent them from changing their form of government *without knowing it.* Congress in its ignorance was constantly passing laws with purely practical objectives, which really changed the constitution without giving the people a chance to exercise their free will on that important subject. Therefore, some autocratic power had to be set up to apply the complicated scholarly techniques to such measures, not to prevent the people from exercising their free will on the Constitution, but to prevent them from doing it inadvertently. . .

To find peace, men denounced government by men, and sought relief by reciting principles. The fundamental assumption of the folklore about government during the great depression was that principles could be more trusted than organizations. Organizations were dangerous because of their tendency to err and stray. Principles, provided that they were sound, endured forever, and could alone make up for the constant tendency of social groups to backslide.

All this folklore persisted in a time when the theory of free will, sin, and repentance was disappearing from the thinking about individuals' troubles. Psychiatrists and psychologists no longer explained individual conduct on the basis of a free-will choice between good and evil. Such a way of thinking had led in the past to curing the insane by preaching away the devil which had entered the patient. By 1937 people had lost interest in theoretical ethical principles for maladjusted individuals. The term "sinner" had gone from all sophisticated psychology. The concept of the devil had disappeared from the anatomy of the individual mind. Indeed, the idea that any man was a single integrated individual had disappeared, and it was recognized that each individual was a whole cast of characters, each appearing on the stage under the influence of different stimuli. In diagnosing an individual's maladies, the psychiatrist found out what his fantasies were and, without bothering whether they were true or false, attempted to cure him by recognizing these fantasies as part of the problem.

In 1937 there was little of this point of view in legal or economic thinking. The point of view of the psychiatrist had long been part of the stock in trade of that low class called politicians. However, the attitude seldom was in evidence when respectable people talked or thought about government. There were exceptions here and there in colleges, but that influence had failed to reach the minds of respectable editorial writers, forward-looking reformers, or molders of public opinion. The conception of social institutions as having free will, and winning their salvation by a free-will selection of the right principles; the idea that politics, pressure groups, lobbying, powerful political machines existed because people had sinful yearnings in that direction; the economic idea that depressions were the result of tinkering with economic laws and preventing the automatic working of an abstract law which would have functioned properly had it not been for bad men who threw this law out of gear—these were held as articles of faith by conservatives and radicals alike.

This faith, held so implicitly, was sorely tried during the years of the great depression. As in every time of great travail, from the great plagues on to today, prayers went up in all directions. These prayers, from businessmen, labor leaders, and socialists, had one element in common. They all showed distrust of any form of organized control. No one would admit that man should govern man. No one would observe the obvious fact that lay everywhere under their noses, that human organizations rise to power, not by following announced creeds, but by the development of loyalties and institutional habits. All these devoted people thought that the world could only attain that state of static perfection which alone was worth aiming at, by studying and developing the proper theories, and then following them, not by force, but by their own free will.

Every age has its social philosophy; otherwise it would not develop organizations. The social philosophy of the United States today is that of a great battle in which both sides are fighting each other to attain the same end. The sum total of law and economics which is the literature of our social philosophy today *must* represent the two sets of principles held by opposing camps, in order to justify the struggle. . .

In times when the emotional conflict is not so keenly felt, social philosophy appears more consistent and less confused. Its inconsistencies are concealed by ceremony or literature, instead of emphasized and brought into the open by battle. This is what is meant by a 'rule of law.' Yet the term 'rule of law' would have no meaning except for organizations which had previously developed a mythology and a hierarchy of divinities through a combat.

The social philosophy of today, as in all periods of combat between new institutions and old, is the philosophy of a war to end war. The sum total of its slogans offers an arsenal of weapons with which each side can attack the other. . .

That distinguished and revered priesthood (and we mean no criticism of the Supreme Court by this observation) had up to the time of the last election been devoting itself almost exclusively to protecting the American people from their unholy desires. The Constitution had become a hair shirt, through the wearing of which salvation could be attained. A bare majority of the Court appeared to regard any extension of government power as something fraught with grave danger. Three dissenting justices consistently opposed this policy of obstruction. They felt that the Constitution, if it were to survive, would have to become a sermon of hope rather than a ritual of gloom. They tried to express a faith in national government through their dissents. However, in the bitterness of the controversy, the very fact that these justices could survey the activities of new governmental organizations without either indignation or panic created alarm in the rest of the Court. Things went so far that the learned Justices actually began calling each other names in public in scholarly language from the bench. The Court lost its atmosphere of judicial calm. After the election of Roosevelt it ceased, in its majority opinions, to represent that reconciliation of conflicting ideals which had heretofore made it the greatest symbol of our national unity. Large groups of people in the United

States began to regard the Court as their enemy rather than their impartial judge.

Of course, there were a lot of logical distinctions and nice reasonings back of the two opposing attitudes in the Court. However, the learned details were actually unimportant. Intelligible and plausible briefs could be written on both sides of the political questions which the Court was deciding, even in spite of the fact that the majority in writing each decision tried to settle the questions once for all. The Supreme Court of the United States, which was once the repository of a generally accepted social philosophy, reacted in a time of conflict as such bodies always react. When governmental philosophies became a source of controversy, they provided a set of opposing slogans for each warring group. This always happens in all theologies. Perhaps it was chance that the majority of the Court was fighting for the old world that had disappeared and only the minority recognized the new one. Yet if one observes the history of similar institutions, one finds that this is the rule, not the exception. The conflict in the outside world produced the conflict in the Court. And always in such conflicts respectable institutions hang back, frightened by the exuberance, the lack of respect for old landmarks, and the surge forward of heretofore unrecognized groups which accompany change. . .

In this situation it was inevitable that the purely negative philosophy of the majority finally became untenable. There were only two possible outcomes to the proposal of the President. Either the Court would change or there would be a new Court. Observers generally credit Mr. Chief Justice Hughes with the political skill which accomplished the change. It is represented in two opinions, one sustaining the minimum-wage law for women and the other permitting the Wagner Labor Relations Act to be applied to the Jones and Laughlin Steel Company.

These opinions represent a transition from a negative to a positive philosophy of federal power. They are technical and uninspired. However, they did clear away the underbrush. They showed that the Court was capable of change. . .

In this country the trial of political issues by the Supreme Court of the United States, while it was actually political propaganda, was supposed to be something else. The failure of the unfortunate conservative bloc of the Supreme Court of the United States to realize that they were actually deciding political issues came near to wrecking the Court. The Court was finally compelled to make a public reversal of its former attitude which would have been unnecessary had the majority known, as Mr. Justice Stone knew, the limitation on the judicial function. A most useful social philosophy for the future is one which recognizes the functions which dramatic contests of all sorts perform in giving unity and stability in government. The most primitive type of such contests is war. The most civilized types are games and judicial trial. The frank recognition of this fact is the beginning of knowledge of social institutions. . .

4. *Herbert Spencer's work of 1851 is the answer to Mr. Roosevelt and his entourage*

ALBERT J. NOCK, Introduction to Spencer's *Man Versus the State*, 1940 *

In 1851 Herbert Spencer published a treatise called *Social Statics* or, *The Conditions Essential to Human Happiness Specified.* Among other specifications, this work established and made clear the fundamental principle that society should be organized on the basis of voluntary cooperation, not on the basis of compulsory cooperation, or under the threat of it. In a word, it established a principle of individualism as against Statism—against the principle underlying all the collectivist doctrines which are everywhere dominant at the present time. It contemplated the reduction of State power over the individual to an absolute minimum, and the raising of social power to its maximum; as against the principle of Statism, which contemplates the precise opposite. Spencer maintained that the State's interventions upon the individual should be confined to punishing those crimes against person or property which are recognized as such by what the Scots philosophers called 'the common sense of mankind'; enforcing the obligations of contract; and making justice costless and easily accessible. Beyond this the State should not go; it should put no further coercive restraint upon the individual. All that the State can do for the best interests of society—all it can do to promote a permanent and stable well-being of society—is by way of these purely negative interventions. Let it go beyond them and attempt the promotion of society's well-being by positive coercive interventions upon the citizen, and whatever apparent and temporary social good may be effected will be greatly at the cost of real and permanent social good.

Spencer's work of 1851 is long out of print and out of currency; a copy of it is extremely hard to find. It should be republished, for it is to the philosophy of individualism what the work of the German idealist philosophers is to the doctrine of Statism, what Das Kapital is to Statist economic theory, or what the Pauline Epistles are to the theology of Protestantism. It had no effect, or very little, on checking the riotous progress of Statism in England; still less in staying the calamitous consequences of that progress. From 1851 down to his death at the end of the century, Spencer wrote occasional essays, partly as running comment on the acceleration of Statism's progress; partly as exposition, by force of illustration and example; and partly as remarkably accurate prophecy of what has since come to pass in consequence of the wholesale substitution of the principle of compulsory cooperation—the Statist principle—for the individualist principle of voluntary cooperation. He reissued four of these essays in 1884 under the title, *The Man versus the State*; and these four essays, together with two others, called *Over-legislation* and *From Freedom to Bondage*, are now reprinted here under the same general title.

The first essay, *The New Toryism*, is of primary importance just now, because it shows the contrast between the aims and methods of early Liberalism and those of modern Liberalism. In these days we hear a great deal about Liberalism, Liberal principles and policies, in the conduct of our public life. All sorts and conditions of men put themselves forward on the public stage as Liberals; they call those who oppose them Tories, and get credit with the public thereby. In the public mind, Liberalism is a term of honour, while Toryism—especially 'economic Toryism'—is a term of reproach. Needless to say, these terms are never examined; the self-styled Liberal is taken popularly at the face value of his pretentions, and policies which are put forth as Liberal are accepted in the same unreflecting way. This being so, it is useful to see what the historic sense of the term is, and to see how far the aims and methods of latter-day Liberalism can be brought into correspondence with it; and how far, therefore, the latter-day Liberal is entitled to bear that name.

Spencer shows that the early Liberal was consistenly for cutting down the State's coercive power over the citizen, wherever this was possible. He was for reducing to a minimum the number of points at which the State might make coercive interventions upon the individual. He was steadily enlarging the margin of existence within which the citizen might pursue and regulate his own activities as he saw fit, free of State control or State supervision. Liberal policies and measures, as originally conceived, were such as reflected these aims. The Tory, on the other hand, was opposed to these aims, and his policies reflected this opposition. In general terms, the Liberal was consistently inclined towards the individualist philosophy of society, while the Tory was consistently inclined towards the Statist philosophy.

Spencer shows moreover that as a matter of practical policy, the early Liberal proceeded towards the realization of his aims by the method of repeal. He was not for making new laws, but for repealing old ones. It is most important to remember this. Wherever the Liberal saw a law which enhanced the State's coercive power over the citizen, he was for repealing it and leaving its place blank. There were many such laws on the British statute-books, and when Liberalism came into power it repealed an immense grist of them.

Spencer must be left to describe in his own words, as he does in the course of this essay, how in the latter half of the last century British Liberalism went over bodily to the philosophy of Statism, and abjuring the political method of repealing existent coercive measures, proceeded to outdo the Tories in constructing new coercive measures of ever-increasing particularity. This piece of British political history has great value for American readers, because it enables them to see how closely American Liberalism has followed the same course. It enables them to interpret correctly the significance of Liberalism's influence upon the direction of our public life in the last half-century, and to perceive just what it is to which that influence has led, just what the consequences are which that influence has tended to bring about, and just what are the further consequences which may be expected to ensue.

For example, Statism postulates the doctrine that the citizen has no rights which the State is bound to respect; the only rights he has are those which the State grants him, and which the State may attenuate or revoke at its own pleasure. This doctrine is fundamental; without its support, all the various nominal modes or forms of Statism which we see at large in Europe and America—such as are called Socialism, Communism, Naziism, Fascism, etc.,—would collapse at once. The individualism which was professed by the early Liberals, maintained the contrary; it maintained that the citizen has rights which are inviolable by the State or by any other agency. This was fundamental doctrine; without its support, obviously, every formulation of individualism becomes so much waste paper. Moreover, early Liberalism accepted it as not only fundamental, but also as axiomatic, self-evident. We may remember, for example, that our great charter, the Declaration of Independence takes as its foundation the self-evident truth of this doctrine, asserting that man, in virtue of his birth, is endowed with certain rights which are 'unalienable'; and asserting further that it is 'to secure these rights' that governments are instituted among men. Political literature will nowhere furnish a more explicit disavowal of the Statist philosophy than is to be found in the primary postulate of the Declaration.

But now, in which direction has latter-day American Liberalism tended? Has it tended towards an expanding *régime* of voluntary cooperation, or one of enforced cooperation? Have its efforts been directed consistently towards repealing existent measures of State coercion, or towards the devising and promotion of new ones? Has it tended steadily to enlarge or to reduce the margin of existence within which the individual may act as he pleases? Has it contemplated State intervention upon the citizen at an ever-increasing number of points, or at an ever-decreasing number? In short, has it consistently exhibited the philosophy of individualism or the philosophy of Statism?

There can be but one answer, and the facts supporting it are so notorious that multiplying examples would be a waste of space. To take but a single one from among the most conspicuous, Liberals worked hard—and successfully—to inject the principle of absolutism into the Constitution by means of the Income-tax Amendment. Under that Amendment it is competent for Congress not only to confiscate the citizen's last penny, but also to levy punitive taxation, discriminatory taxation, taxation for 'the equalization of wealth' or for any other purpose it sees fit to promote. Hardly could a single measure be devised which would do more to clear the way for a purely Statist *régime*, than this which puts so formidable a mechanism in the hands of the State, and gives the State *carte blanche* for its employment against the citizen. Again, the present Administration is made up of self-styled Liberals, and its course has been a continuous triumphal advance of Statism. In a preface to these essays, written in 1884, Spencer has a paragraph which sums up with remarkable completeness the political history of the United States during the last six years:

> Dictatorial measures, rapidly multiplied, have tended continually to narrow the liberties of individuals; and have done this in a double way. Regulations have been made in yearly-growing numbers, restraining the citizen in directions where his actions were previously unchecked, and compelling actions which previously he might perform or not as he liked; and at the same time heavier public bur-

> dens, chiefly local, have further restricted his freedom, by lessening that portion of his earnings which he can spend as he pleases, and augmenting the portion taken from him to be spent as public agents please.

Thus closely has the course of American Statism, from 1932 to 1939, followed the course of British Statism from 1860 to 1884. Considering their professions of Liberalism, it would be quite appropriate and by no means inurbane, to ask Mr. Roosevelt and his entourage whether they believe that the citizen has any rights which the State is bound to respect. Would they be willing—*ex animo,* that is, and not for electioneering purposes—to subscribe to the fundamental doctrine of the Declaration? One would be unfeignedly surprised if they were. Yet such an affirmation might go some way to clarify the distinction, if there actually be any, between the 'totalitarian' Statism of certain European countries and the 'democratic' Statism of Great Britain, France and the United States. It is commonly taken for granted that there is such a distinction, but those who assume this do not trouble themselves to show wherein the distinction consists; and to the disinterested observer the fact of its existence is, to say the least, not obvious.

Spencer ends *The New Toryism* with a prediction which American readers today will find most interesting, if they bear in mind that it was written fifty-five years ago in England and primarily for English readers. He says:

> The laws made by Liberals are so greatly increasing the compulsions and restraints exercised over citizens, that among Conservatives who suffer from this aggressiveness there is growing up a tendency to resist it. Proof is furnished by the fact that the 'Liberty and Property Defense League' largely consisting of Conservatives, has taken for its motto, 'Individualism *versus* Socialism.' So that if the present drift of things continues, it may by-and-by really happen that the Tories will be defenders of liberties which the Liberals, in pursuit of what they think popular welfare, trample under foot.

This prophecy has already been fulfilled in the United States.

5. *We look forward to a world founded on four essential freedoms*

FRANKLIN D. ROOSEVELT, *The Four Freedoms Address,* 6 January 1941 *

I address you, the Members of the Seventy-seventh Congress, at a moment unprecedented in the history of the Union. I use the word 'unprecedented,' because at no previous time has American security been as seriously threatened from without as it is today.

Since the permanent formation of our Government under the Constitution, in 1789, most of the periods of crisis in our history have related to our domestic

* *The Public Papers and Addresses of Franklin D. Roosevelt,* New York, The Macmillan Company, 1941, pp. 663–72 *passim.*

affairs. Fortunately, only one of these—the four-year War Between the States—ever threatened our national unity. Today, thank God, one hundred and thirty million Americans in forty-eight States, have forgotten points of the compass in our national unity. . .

Every realist knows that the democratic way of life is at this moment being directly assailed in every part of the world—assailed either by arms, or by secret spreading of poisonous propaganda by those who seek to destroy unity and promote discord in nations that are still at peace.

During sixteen long months this assault has blotted out the whole pattern of democratic life in an appalling number of independent nations, great and small. The assailants are still on the march, threatening other nations, great and small. . .

No realistic American can expect from a dictator's peace international generosity, or return of true independence, or world disarmament, or freedom of expression, or freedom of religion—or even good business. . .

Just as our national policy in internal affairs has been based upon a decent respect for the rights and the dignity of all our fellow men within our gates, so our national policy in foreign affairs has been based on a decent respect for the rights and dignity of all nations, large and small. And the justice of morality must and will win in the end.

Our national policy is this:

First, by an impressive expression of the public will and without regard to partisanship, we are committed to all-inclusive national defense.

Second, by an impressive expression of the public will and without regard to partisanship, we are committed to full support of all those resolute peoples, everywhere, who are resisting aggression and are thereby keeping war away from our Hemisphere. By this support, we express our determination that the democratic cause shall prevail; and we strengthen the defense and the security of our own nation.

Third, by an impressive expression of the public will and without regard to partisanship, we are committed to the proposition that principles of morality and considerations for our own security will never permit us to acquiesce in a peace dictated by aggressors and sponsored by appeasers. We know that enduring peace cannot be bought at the cost of other people's freedom. . .

The happiness of future generations of Americans may well depend upon how effective and how immediate we can make our aid felt. No one can tell the exact character of the emergency situations that we may be called upon to meet. The Nation's hands must not be tied when the Nation's life is in danger.

We must all prepare to make the sacrifices that the emergency—almost as serious as war itself—demands. Whatever stands in the way of speed and efficiency in defense preparations must give way to the national need. . .

As men do not live by bread alone, they do not fight by armaments alone. Those who man our defenses, and those behind them who build our defenses, must have the stamina and the courage which come from unshakable belief in the manner of life which they are defending. The mighty action that we are calling for cannot be based on a disregard of all things worth fighting for.

The Nation takes great satisfaction and much strength from the things which have been done to make its people conscious of their individual stake in the preservation of democratic life in America. Those things have toughened the fibre of our people, have renewed their faith and strengthened their devotion to the institutions we make ready to protect.

Certainly this is no time for any of us to stop thinking about the social and economic problems which are the root cause of the social revolution which is today a supreme factor in the world.

For there is nothing mysterious about the foundations of a healthy and strong democracy. The basic things expected by our people of their political and economic systems are simple. They are:

Equality of opportunity for youth and for others.

Jobs for those who can work.

Security for those who need it.

The ending of special privilege for the few.

The preservation of civil liberties for all.

The enjoyment of the fruits of scientific progress in a wider and constantly rising standard of living. . .

Many subjects connected with our social economy call for immediate improvement.

As examples:

We should bring more citizens under the coverage of old-age pensions and unemployment insurance.

We should widen the opportunities for adequate medical care.

We should plan a better system by which persons deserving or needing gainful employment may obtain it. . .

In the future days, which we seek to make secure, we look forward to a world founded upon four essential human freedoms.

The first is freedom of speech and expression—everywhere in the world.

The second is freedom of every person to worship God in his own way—everywhere in the world.

The third is freedom from want—which, translated into world terms, means economic understandings which will secure to every nation a healthy peacetime life for its inhabitants—everywhere in the world.

The fourth is freedom from fear—which, translated into world terms, means a world-wide reduction of armaments to such a point and in such a thorough fashion that no nation will be in a position to commit an act of physical aggression against any neighbor—anywhere in the world.

That is no vision of a distant millennium. It is a definite basis for a kind of world attainable in our own time and generation. That kind of world is the very antithesis of the so-called new order of tyranny which the dictators seek to create with the crash of a bomb. . .

Since the beginning of our American history, we have been engaged in change—in a perpetual peaceful revolution—a revolution which goes on steadily, quietly adjusting itself to changing conditions—without the concentration camp or the quick-lime in the ditch. . .

6. *There is a fifth freedom*

HERBERT HOOVER, *Address: The Fifth Freedom*, 1941 *

The President of the United States on January 6, 1941, stated that we seek 'everywhere in the world' the four old freedoms: freedom of speech and expression, freedom of religion, freedom from fear, freedom from want.

Soon thereafter I called attention to the fact that there is a Fifth Freedom —economic freedom—without which none of the other four freedoms will be realized.

I have stated many times over the years that to be free, men must choose their jobs and callings, bargain for their own wages and salaries, save and provide by private property for their families and old age. And they must be free to engage in enterprise so long as each does not injure his fellowmen. And that requires laws to prevent abuse. And when I use the term 'Fifth Freedom,' I use it in this sense only, not in the sense of laissez-faire or economic exploitation. Exploitation is the negation of freedom. The Fifth Freedom does not mean going back to abuses.

Laws to prevent men doing economic injury to their fellows were universal in civilized countries long before the First World War. In the United States, for example, the State and Federal Governments had established regulation of banks, railroads, utilities, coinage; prevention of combinations to restrain trade; government support to credit in times of stress; public works; tariffs; limitations on hours of labor and in other directions.

The key of such government action to economic freedom is that government must not destroy but promote freedom. When governments exert regulation of economic life, they must do so by definite statutory rules of conduct imposed by legislative bodies that all men may read as they run and in which they may have at all times the protection of the courts. No final judicial or legislative authority must be delegated to bureaucrats, or at once tyranny begins.

When Government violates these principles, it sooner or later weakens constitutional safeguards of personal liberty and representative government.

When Government goes into business in competition with citizens, bureaucracy always relies upon tyranny to win. And bureaucracy never develops that competence in management which comes from the mills of competition. Its conduct of business inevitably lowers the living standards of the people. Nor does bureaucracy ever discover or invent. A Millikan, Ford, or Edison never came from a bureaucracy.

And inherent in bureaucracy is the grasping spirit of more and more power. It always resents criticism and sooner or later begins directly or indirectly to limit free speech and free press. Intellectual and spiritual freedom will not long survive the passing of economic freedom. One of the illusions of our time is that we can have totalitarian economics and the personal freedoms. . .

We must sacrifice much economic freedom to win the war. That is eco-

* *The Rotarian*, April 1943. Included in Herbert Hoover's *Addresses Upon the American Road: World War II, 1941–1945*, published by D. Van Nostrand Co., 1946, pp. 222–5 *passim*. Reprinted by permission of Herbert Hoover.

nomic Fascism, for Fascist economics were born of just these measures in the last war. But there are two vast differences in the application of this sort of economic system at the hands of democracies or at the hands of dictators. First, in democracies we strive to keep free speech, free press, free worship, trial by jury, and other personal liberties alive. And, second, we want so to design our actions that these Fascist economic measures are not frozen into life, but shall thaw out after the war.

Even the temporary suspension of economic liberty creates grave dangers because liberty rapidly atrophies from disuse. Vested interests and vested habits grow around its restrictions. It would be a vain thing to fight the war and lose our own liberties. If we would have them return, we must hold furiously to the ideals of economic liberty. We must challenge every departure from them. There are just two tests: 'Is this departure necessary to win the war?' 'How are we going to restore these freedoms after the war?' . .

Under the stress of reconstruction after the war, our liberties will be slow in coming back, but the essential thing in this sort of question is the direction in which we travel. We must establish the direction now.

7. *War controls have no place in peacetime economy*

MERLE THORPE, *Freedom is not Free*, Editorial, 1943 *

Students of government have predicted that democracy, in the words of William Flinders Petrie, will ultimately 'eat itself up,' that the majority always chooses the easy road, taking the cash today without thought of what the morrow may bring.

A corollary is that the State never relinquishes its powers voluntarily. 'The mind of man is fond of power, increase his prospects and you increase his desires,' said Gouverneur Morris, urging Executive curbs at the Constitutional Convention in 1787.

History will soon write another page, chronicling a decision American democracy must make. It must decide whether political controls of our lives and livelihoods, accepted by our people as a war measure, shall become a permanent part of our social and economic structure.

Consider recent events in Great Britain. . .

Home Secretary [Herbert] Morrison [makes] dire prediction of 'social and economic catastrophe' if Britain abandons in peace the government controls imposed for the purpose of organizing the Empire for war. If these controls have merit in war, they have no less merit in peace, says Mr. Morrison.

This distrust of democracy is echoed among our own timid souls. Our frontiers are gone. We have reached a rocking-chair maturity. The resourcefulness, courage and moral responsibility of the individual are horse-and-buggy virtues. Private enterprise carries within itself the seed of its own destruction. In its place must come government authority to regiment every citizen with licenses, permits, directives and allocations.

* *Nation's Business*, November 1943. Reprinted by permission of *Nation's Business*.

So runs the argument of the home front Jeremiahs, who call themselves liberals and progressives. In truth, they are reactionaries who would take us back to the conditions in Europe which drove real liberals to cross the ocean and build here a society where the individual was master and the State the servant. . .

Today's men of faith foresee a resurgence of private enterprise, if the people through their representatives permit a program of full production by freeing the individual of handicaps and restrictions.

To those who fear that after this war we may live 'on an island of democracy in a totalitarian world,' they reply: Our ancestors created here an island of democracy in a totalitarian world. We can preserve what they built.

The decision of young America—and its parents—will answer another and more disturbing question: Is the stock of pioneer America deteriorating? Faith in ourselves, grievously beset at times, leads to the belief that America will choose the hard way because it is the free way.

8. *How can we safeguard free enterprise?*

SENATOR JOSEPH C. O'MAHONEY, *The Preservation of Economic Freedom*, 11 March 1941 *

. . . President Roosevelt, in his message of April 29, 1938, recommending that this study be undertaken, asserted in plain words that he was offering 'a program to preserve private enterprise for profit by keeping it free enough to be able to utilize all our resources of capital and labor at a profit.' This purpose has been reasserted in one way or another by every person who has submitted a recommendation to this committee. . .

I believe therefore that our final report should begin with a definite and unequivocal declaration of our faith in free enterprise, a declaration that we do not seek a formula for the establishment of an all powerful government but one by which to preserve opportunity for all the people. We seek the formula by which we may enable the people to increase production and to distribute goods and services more equitably and effectively than ever before. We seek to foster and encourage private business. We are opposed to all arbitrary control of the economic activity of free men, just as we are opposed to all arbitrary control of their thought or speech, and we oppose such control whether it is exercised by private or public authority.

The unalienable rights of life, liberty, and the pursuit of happiness, the preservation of which was described in the Declaration of Independence as the primary reason why governments are instituted among men, belong to people and may not be taken away from people by any institution which man creates. This principle we must recognize as the cornerstone of our economic as well as of our political structure, for without it all freedom is endangered.

We must make it clear . . . that we have no purpose of trying to cure the

* Final Statement of the Temporary National Economic Committee, 77th Congress, 1st session, Senate Doc. no. 39, U.S. Government Printing Office, Washington, D.C., 1941.

evils which have resulted from private restriction of individual opportunity by setting up any system of public restriction to take its place. The recommendations which we shall make will be designed not only to keep government free and responsive to the people, but to keep business free also. . .

There is altogether too much disposition upon the part of men who are engaged in business to look with fear and suspicion upon the spokesmen of government and too much disposition upon the part of some spokesmen in government to denounce and criticize the acts and omissions of business executives. The truth is that the American standards of business ethics and of political ethics are much higher today than at any time in history and we shall not find the way out of our predicament by criticism of one another or by searching out and condemning one another's economic and political sins. The way out lies along the road of tolerance and cooperation. . .

Before [our] task can be accomplished . . . we must first discover the underlying causes of the economic maladjustment with which we have been struggling and to mitigate which, because there was no other alternative, the Government at Washington has been compelled to engage upon a program of deficit-spending which arouses the fears even of those who authorize it. . .

In the beginning our commercial and industrial system, like our political system, was essentially local in almost all its aspects. The means of livelihood, the instruments of production and distribution were all readily commended by each community. So far as commerce was concerned, the functions of the National Government were directed chiefly to that which was carried on with foreign nations. With the passing years, however, local and State boundaries began to mean less and less so far as business was concerned and as this change took place the powers of the National Government began to grow. . .

Certainly this did not come about because the people of America wanted to surrender local powers to Washington. It came about solely because people in every community found themselves dealing with new economic agencies to cope with which their traditional local governments were inadequate. Year by year business became increasingly national in scope and the new organizations by which this national business was carried on became steadily more important. . .

The modern industrial system produced geographical concentration of productive enterprise before it produced the concentration of economic power and wealth. . . As all observers know, when manufacturing was moved from the home to the factory a new era began. It was a natural and in most aspects a wholly desirable development. It was the very development which has provided the present generation with all the marvelous tools which make available the amazing convenience and luxuries in which we take so much pride, but it almost completely robbed commerce of its local aspect and made it a national phenomenon with wholly national effects and national significance. Geographical boundaries have lost most of their importance so far as commerce is concerned.

The inevitable result has been the expansion of national law. Throughout the long period during which this change has been taking place, Congress was reluctant to impose national regulations in the place of local regulations and it made changes but slowly. This generation needs no instruction to understand that commerce among the states is the most important element of our modern economic activity, but the Congress which confronted this problem for the first time more than fifty years ago thought of interstate commerce in terms of railroad transportation only and when it set up the Interstate Commerce Commission it had no thought of 'interfering with private enterprise,' as the phrase goes, except with respect to the railroads. . . From that day to this there has been a steady growth of the government establishment at Washington, but let no one make the mistake of assuming that this growth has taken place because 'politicians' have wanted to take business over. It has grown solely because commerce must be regulated by government in the public interest and because in this country there is no agency except the federal government which is capable of such regulation. . .

But private enterprise is threatened indeed, it has been undermined to an appalling degree not by Government and not so much by business itself, for all the monopolistic practices which have so frequently been condemned, but by a general failure to comprehend the change that has taken place and a failure properly to co-ordinate Government and business in their relation to people. This failure, it has seemed to me, is principally due to the fact that we seem not to realize that modern business is no longer the activity of individuals, but is the activity of organizations of individuals and we have permitted these organizations to grow so large that people are actually helpless before them. We have persisted in treating these organizations as though they were clothed with natural human rights instead of having only the rights which the people, acting through their Government, see fit to bestow upon them. It will be impossible even to begin the task of adjusting Government to business until we realize that the modern business organization has grown to such proportions that neither the people, as individuals, nor through their local governments are able to cope with it. . .

. . . There are only ten sovereign states which have within their respective borders property valued at more than the assets of either the Metropolitan Life Insurance Company or the American Telephone and Telegraph Company. Stated in another way, each of these two corporations is richer than any one of thirty-eight sovereign states. . .

Among the great corporations . . . are banks, insurance companies and industrials. In popular discussion they are regarded as 'private enterprise.' But how private is such enterprise after all? The American Telephone and Telegraph Company, like Commonwealth and Southern, is a public utility and although in recent years there has been a tendency in certain circles to drop the word 'public' when referring to such utilities, it is nevertheless quite clear that each of them is just as public as the thousands of municipal corporations which are likewise chartered by the several states. They are different however, from municipal corporations in that the latter operate within the borders of the states which create them while the modern interstate corporation operates throughout the length and breadth of the land and in the field of commerce 'with foreign nations and among the states,' the power to regulate which was exclusively committed by the Federal Constitution to the Congress of the United States. . .

It might have been imagined that with the change from the individual to the corporate economy there would probably be a large distribution of corporate ownership among individuals. The fact, however, seems to be that this amazing concentration of the corporate ownership of wealth has been accompanied by a similar concentration of dividend distribution. The great and powerful business organizations which dominate the economic scene are owned by a numerically insignificant proportion of the total population. . .

Thus it appears that the great bulk of the wealth and income of this country is owned by corporations, that the overwhelming percentage of this is owned by comparatively few corporations, that the stock ownership of these corporations is not substantially distributed among the people of the country and, finally, that the dividends paid by these corporations go to a very small proportion of the population. . .

For two generations, the concentration of economic power and wealth has proceeded at such a pace that the welfare of the masses in agriculture and industry has been seriously jeopardized. Small business has been swallowed up by big business and big business is now confronted with the danger of being swallowed up by government. The way to reverse this trend is not to be found in further expanding the powers of government, nor in releasing big business from so-called 'government interference.' The only remedy to save a democratic economy is to be found in making the economy democratic. If we are to avoid an all-powerful central government, we have no recourse but to re-establish and encourage free private enterprise, that is to say, private enterprise which will be free from the arbitrary control of private organizations as well as of public organizations. . .

Therefore, I recommend:

1. National charters for national corporations, in order that these agencies may have a definite and a free place in our economy and local business may be differentiated and protected from national business;
2. The effective and thorough enforcement of the antitrust laws to maintain competition and to prevent all combinations and agreements that destroy business;
3. The encouragement of new business and small enterprise by revision of the tax laws for the purpose of encouraging new employment and new industry;
4. A national conference called by Congress of the various organizations representative of business, labor, agriculture, and consumers which have for years been working on diverse phases of this central problem might concentrate public thought and action on the objectives on which there is general agreement instead of, as now, on the objectives concerning which there is only misunderstanding, suspicion, and disagreement.

In an hour of political uncertainty 153 years ago, the Continental Congress called a national convention to draft a national political constitution. That conference of American leaders was successful beyond the dreams of any of those who authorized it. Our need today is a national economic constitution which shall abolish the economic uncertainties which seem to threaten even our political system. I have an abiding faith that the patriotism and ability of the people of America is equal to the task.

9. *We have come to a clear realization that individual freedom cannot exist without economic security and independence*

FRANKLIN D. ROOSEVELT, Address on the State of the Union, 11 January 1944 *

This Nation in the past two years has become an active partner in the world's greatest war against human slavery.

We have joined with like-minded people in order to defend ourselves in a world that has been gravely threatened with gangster rule. . .

We are united in determination that this war shall not be followed by another interim which leads to new disaster—that we shall not repeat the tragic errors of ostrich isolationism—that we shall not repeat the excesses of the wild twenties when this Nation went for a joyride on a roller coaster which ended in a tragic crash. . .

The one supreme objective for the future . . . for each nation individually, and for all the United Nations, can be summed up in one word: Security.

And that means not only physical security which provides safety from attacks by aggressors. It means also economic security, social security, moral security—in a family of nations. . .

It is our duty now to begin to lay the plans and determine the strategy for the winning of a lasting peace and the establishment of an American standard of living higher than ever before known. We cannot be content, no matter how high that general standard of living may be, if some fraction of our people—whether it be one-third or one-fifth or one-tenth—is ill-fed, ill-clothed, ill-housed, and insecure.

This Republic had its beginning, and grew to its present strength, under the protection of certain inalienable political rights—among them the right of free speech, free press, free worship, trial by jury, freedom from unreasonable searches and seizures. They were our rights to life and liberty.

As our Nation has grown in size and stature, however—as our industrial economy expanded—these political rights proved inadequate to assure us equality in the pursuit of happiness.

We have come to a clear realization of the fact that true individual freedom cannot exist without economic security and independence. 'Necessitous men are not free men.' People who are hungry and out of a job are the stuff of which dictatorships are made.

In our day these economic truths have become accepted as self-evident. We have accepted, so to speak, a second Bill of Rights under which a new basis of security and posterity can be established for all—regardless of station, race, or creed.

* *Congressional Record*, 78th Congress, 2nd session, vol. 90, pt. 1, pp. 55–7 *passim.*

Among these are:

The right to a useful and remunerative job in the industries, or shops or farms or mines of the Nation;

The right to earn enough to provide adequate food and clothing and recreation;

The right of every farmer to raise and sell his products at a return which will give him and his family a decent living;

The right of every businessman, large and small, to trade in an atmosphere of freedom from unfair competition and domination by monopolies at home or abroad;

The right of every family to a decent home;

The right to adequate medical care and the opportunity to achieve and enjoy good health;

The right to adequate protection from the economic fears of old age, sickness, accident, and unemployment;

The right to a good education.

All of these rights spell security. And after this war is won, we must be prepared to move forward, in the implementation of these rights, to new goals of human happiness and well-being.

America's own rightful place in the world depends in large part upon how fully these and similar rights have been carried into practice for our citizens. For unless there is security here at home there cannot be lasting peace in the world.

SELECTED REFERENCES

T. W. Arnold, *The Symbols of Government*, New Haven, Yale University Press, 1935.

Joseph Alsop and Turner Catledge, *168 Days*, Garden City, Doubleday, 1938.

Chester Bowles, 'Do Controls Endanger Democracy?' *The New York Times Magazine*, 21 December 1947.

H. S. Commager, *Majority Rule and Minority Rights*, New York, Oxford University Press, 1943.

E. S. Corwin, *Constitutional Revolution, Ltd.*, California, Claremont College, 1941.

Harvey Fergusson, *People and Power: A Study of Political Behavior in America*, New York, William Morrow, 1947.

Walter Hamilton, 'The Smouldering Constitutional Crisis,' *The New Republic*, 18 January 1943.

F. A. Hayek, *The Road to Serfdom*, Chicago, University of Chicago Press, 1942.

Robert H. Jackson, *The Struggle for Judicial Supremacy: A Study of a Crisis in American Power Politics*, New York, Knopf, 1941.

A. T. Mason, *The Supreme Court: Vehicle of Revealed Truth or Power Group*, Boston, Boston University Press, 1953.

Edwin Mims, *The Majority of the People*, New York, Modern Age Book, 1941.

Isabel Paterson, *The God of the Machine*, New York, G. P. Putnam, 1943.

Frances Perkins, *The Roosevelt I Knew*, New York, Viking, 1946.

The Public Papers and Addresses of Franklin D. Roosevelt, New York, The Macmillan Company. The introduction to vol. 7 contains F. D. R.'s analysis of his liberalism.

Edgar M. Queeny, *The Spirit of Enterprise*, New York, Charles Scribner's Sons, 1943.

Samuel I. Rosenman, 'He Gave Strength to Freedom,' *The New Republic*, 15 April 1946.

Arthur M. Schlesinger, Jr., *The Politics of Upheaval*, Boston, Houghton Mifflin, 1960.

XXI

CONTINUING PREDICAMENT

'To make a government requires no great prudence,' Edmund Burke observed. 'Settle the seat of power; teach obedience; and the work is done. To give freedom is still more easy. It is not necessary to guide; it only requires to let go the rein.' 'But,' Burke continued, 'to form a *free government*; that is, *to temper together these opposite elements of liberty and restraint* in one consistent work, requires much thought; deep reflection; a sagacious, powerful, and combining mind.' (Italics added.)

Posed is the continuing predicament of free government—a dilemma that nearly two centuries of American experience has failed to resolve. The principles adumbrated in our Declaration of Independence were almost a reckless affirmation. Resting the foundation of government on reason and consent rather than on coercion and force was a commitment of awesome dimensions, a wager that flew in the face of tremendous odds. It represented faith in man apparently falsified by recorded experience. Not until our own time could the boldness of America's commitment, reaffirmed and refined by the Constitution of 1789, be seen in all its starkness. Still to be determined is whether a government so conceived and so founded can endure. 'The play is still on,' Carl Becker writes, 'and we are still betting on freedom of the mind, but the outcome seems now somewhat more dubious than it did in Jefferson's time.'

Rarely has free government been more severely challenged than in recent years; rarely has the discrepancy between image and reality been more apparent; rarely has the gap between pretensions and performance seemed so cosmic. 'As a living thing,' Louis Hartz writes, political democracy 'turns out to be a mad anomaly, a set of ideals half realized through institutions which contradict them.' Hartz quickly concludes—perhaps too quickly—that, while there may be 'problems,' there is no 'crisis,' no question of 'survival.'

Survival—at what price, and for what? The cost is implicit in any thoughtful consideration of contemporary realities. Commentators are dismayed because democracy in a technological age cannot fulfill the promises of the pristine image. Exposed are thorny challenges—the irresponsible power wielded by giant corporations, by organized labor, by the military—and by an uneasy, sometimes unwitting, confluence of all these groups; the rigid posture of the 'radical right'; the perennial states' rights issue; the dangerous implications of coerced conformity in an era of continuing cold war; the explosive race issue, probably the nation's most pressing domestic problem; the overshadowing blot of violence in our culture. Sobering experience in all these areas (and there are others) queries the vitality, even the viability, of American political thought itself.

Most alarming, perhaps, is the ever-widening spectacle of power without responsibility and responsibility without power. The former condition yields the antithesis of free government; the latter maximizes the difficulty of positive action in an age requiring more and more government. Brandeis worried about interlocking corporate directorates. Today intertwined interests, including the economic, military, and political, are more varied as well as more subtle. Men as widely separated in outlook as former President Eisenhower and the late C. Wright Mills have pointed ominously to the coincidence of this complex. 'If they [the power elite] do not reign,' Mills observed, 'they do govern at many of the vital points of everyday life in America, and no powers effectively and consistently countervail against them, nor have they as corporate-made men developed any effectively restraining conscience.' 'If it is not oligarchy,' Charles Frankel concludes more tentatively, 'it is not what has been envisaged by modern liberal democracy either.' In a sobering search for the perils endangering our liberties, President Eisenhower devoted his farewell address, reprinted in this chapter, to the military-industrial complex.

Theodore K. Quinn (1893-), until the mid 1930's a vice president of General Electric, is highly pessimistic. The story elaborated in this chapter tells why Mr. Quinn resigned:

> I quit monster business because it is undemocratic, because it is inhuman and not socially responsible, because most of it is big only for the sake of bigness or for purposes of concentrated power and control, because it is inefficient and corruptive, because it is causing a dependent society where only masses count, genuine individual freedom languishes and opportunity and expression are restricted, because it glorifies leaders whose interest is too much in themselves, and because through its essentially collectivistic forms and methods and mockery of 'free enterprise,' it is leading our country just as surely as the sunsets to a brand of totalitarianism which is a perversion as far from individualism, civil liberties and the democratic process as Russian Communism.

In the boom year 1929 there were only twenty private corporations with more than a billion dollars in gross assets. By 1939, aften ten years of depression, there were twenty-eight billionaire private corporations, and ten years later forty-eight of them. 'We now have,' Mr. Quinn observes, 'a billionaire private "economic state" for every political state in the union,' and 'many of our states in the union have less total wealth than a number of the economic monsters.'

Adolf A. Berle (1895-) is more relaxed, reminding us that corporate power 'has laws of its own.' 'Almost against its will,' the corporation, he writes, 'has been compelled to assume in appreciable part the role of conscience-carrier of twentieth-century American society.' Berle tempers his optimism, noting 'deadening forces' which 'give every motive to an individual not to let his thought range, not to disagree, not to open unpleasant questions, not to shock or displease the group in which he moves.' To expect corporate interests to coincide with community interest seems both unrealistic and undesirable—unrealistic because inconsistent with the profit motive, undesirable because a politically irresponsible body cannot be safely entrusted with interests involving the community at large. One recalls Brandeis's caveat of 1915: 'Concentration of power has been shown to be dangerous in a democracy, even though that power may be used beneficently.'

Irresponsible power, of whatever orientation, is suspect. 'Government must not tolerate,' Henry C. Simons (1899–1946) warned, 'erection of great private corporate empires or cartel organizations which suppress competition and rival in power great governmental units themselves.' Organized labor no less than organized business is adept at fashioning theories of the public good, which turn out on close scrutiny to be but thin disguises for particular interests. 'It is my basic view,' the late Justice Robert H. Jackson declared, 'that whenever any organization or combination of individuals, whether in a corporation, a labor union or other body, obtains such economic or legal advantage that it can control or, in effect, govern the lives of other people, it is subject to the control of the Government . . . for the Government can suffer no rivals in the field of coercion.' The confrontation of Roger Blough of U.S. Steel with President Kennedy in 1962, and the cancellation of the proposed price increase of steel, is a recent illustration.

Government alone can create and maintain the broad firmament of order under which individuals and groups, including so-called free enterprise, can function for the good of all. 'He that is to govern a whole nation must,' Hobbes said, 'read in himself not this or that particular man, but mankind.'

The 'Welfare State' is now fixed in the American pattern. No longer limited to government care of the sick, the aged, and the needy, 'welfare' now means government responsibility for security, prosperity, and abundance. Its methods are insurance, subsidies, and taxes. Its beneficiaries are everyone—for industrial workers, job security; for farmers, guaranteed prices; for government workers, higher pay; for pensioners, bigger checks; for veterans, windfalls and benefits without number; for foreign governments, billions in cash contributions; for the businessman, government contracts beyond any peacetime record.

As a private citizen Dwight D. Eisenhower had been critical of the bureaucratic trend. 'If all that Americans want is security,' he challenged, 'they can go to prison.' As President, however, he did not turn his back on either the achievements or the theory of the New Deal. On the contrary, he recognized that 'Government must use its vast power to maintain employment and purchasing power as well as to maintain reasonably stable prices'; 'must be alert and sensitive to economic developments, including its own myriad activities'; 'must be prepared to take preventive as well as remedial action'; 'must be ready to cope with new situations that may arise.' 'This is not,' Eisenhower said, 'a start-and-stop responsibility, but a continuous one.' In words that smack of Franklin Roosevelt himself, President Eisenhower boldly proclaimed: 'The arsenal of weapons at the disposal of Government for maintaining economic stability is formidable. . . We shall not hesitate to use any or all of these weapons as the situation may require.'

Politics must be dominant over economics. Official, politically responsible government must insist on monopolizing coercive power, as against any and all private aspirants for such power. It must do this, not because there is special virtue in established authority, or because government is or can be omniscient, but because this is the only way of avoiding chaos, the only way, as Locke's men discovered in his state of nature, to prevent individuals and groups from taking law into their own hands.

The John Birch Society rejects this philosophy *in toto*. Advocating a nineteenth-century approach, the new conservatives 'believe that increasing the size of government, increasing the centralization of government, and increasing the functions of government all act as brakes on material progress and as destroyers of personal freedom.'

The ideology of liberal democracy helped assure the growth of private power centers. Autonomous forces, left substantially unregulated, engendered new and irresponsible accumulations of power, sometimes more dangerous to the freedom of the individual than the power of government itself. Will free government now be able to impose restrictions on private power without achieving a Pyrrhic victory? How can government be made strong enough to protect the freedom of the many without becoming so strong as to destroy the freedom of all? 'It is a melancholy reflection,' Madison wrote, 'that liberty shall be equally exposed to danger whether the Government have too much or too little power, and that the line which divides these extremes should be so inaccurately defined by experience.' 'To be more safe,' Hamilton cautioned in an uncanny adumbration of cold war psychology, 'nations at length become willing to run the risk of being less free.'

Public policy and action since World War II betray the counsel of Madison and Hamilton. Growing evidence indicates that the area in which discussion and debate can be carried on is perilously narrowed. The information prerequisite to a meaningful dialogue is not always available. Complaints are heard on all sides. In vetoing the Internal Security Act of 1950, President Truman lamented the 'cowering and foolish fear' driving us to 'throw away the ideals which are the fundamental basis of our free society.' Speaking at the Dartmouth College commencement exercises in June 1953, President Eisenhower, touching the seamy side of American life, pleaded for calm restraint, lest we ape totalitarian methods. Justice Douglas seizes every opportunity to warn against the pervading sense of insecurity manifesting itself in colleges, in pulpits, in business and politics. George F. Kennan (1904–   ), former Ambassador to the U.S.S.R. and to Yugoslavia, sends us back to the fountainheads of our tradition, cautioning against 'this fear of the untypical.' He deplores the alien forces at large in our society today, suggesting that 'these people would eventually narrow the area of political and cultural respectability to a point where it included only themselves.'

Of course free speech, like other basic rights, is not an absolute. Internal disorder and/or foreign aggression may, under certain circumstances, tip the scales in favor of purposes other than political freedom and unrestricted exchange of ideas. Nevertheless, repression must be recognized as the exception rather than the rule. There is danger lest we become enamoured of the totalitarian notion that security can be found in coercion, that order means the absence of change. 'As a free society,' Adlai Stevenson reminds us, 'we must rely primarily on persuasion. We can use coercion only rarely, and usually only as a defensive measure.' Judge Learned Hand (1872–1961), underscoring our continuing predicament, concluded that 'it is only by trial and error, by insistent scrutiny and by readiness to re-examine presently accredited conclusions that we have risen from our brutish ancestors. . . In our loyalty to these habits lies our only chance, not merely of progress, but even of survival.' In the classic pronouncement reprinted in this chapter, Brandeis presents this as the essence of the American creed.

The Oppenheimer affair of 1954, a dramatic illustration of our quandary, has been called 'the trial of a security system.' 'A great and responsible nation, the greatest and therefore the most responsible,' the late Charles P. Curtis wrote, 'is telling itself to fear itself, advising itself to stand on suspicions, to mistake caution for courage and to take prudence to be better than wisdom.' 'Do you remember what Joan's ghost said to Charles the Seventh?' Curtis asked, perceptively anticipating recent efforts to 'rehabilitate' Dr. Oppenheimer.

> In Shaw's epilogue, Charles was telling Joan that her case was being tried over again, as in the chronicles of time Oppenheimer's case will be. Charles was telling Joan that her judges were to be charged with malice and other things besides. Joan would have none of that. Joan said—and her reply was charitable and precise—'Not they. They were as honest a lot of poor fools as ever burned their betters.'

Experience having demonstrated that men do not always use freedom of speech and of press in rational and disinterested ways, certain commentators argue that drastically changed times and circumstances require reappraisal of the ages-old liberty versus authority antithesis. Holmes's conviction that the best test of truth is the power of thought to get itself accepted in the competition of the market rested on the assumption that the competition would be really free and honestly conducted. What the liberal now fears 'is systematic corruption of the free market of ideas by activities which make intelligent choice impossible. In short, what he fears is not heresy but conspiracy.' For Professor Sidney Hook, as for certain Supreme Court Justices and others, the distinction is of vital importance. Professor Hook puts it this way:

'Communist ideas are heresies, and liberals need have no fear of them where they are freely and openly expressed. They should be studied and evaluated in the light of the relevant evidence. No one should be punished because he holds them. The communist movement, however, is something quite different from a mere heresy, for wherever it exists, it operates along the lines laid down by Lenin as guides to communists of all countries, and perfected in great detail since then.'

Twentieth-century liberalism being confronted by an unfamiliar—indeed unprecedented—situation, must toughen its fiber. 'It must defend the free market in ideas against the racist, the professional patrioteers, and those spokesmen of the *status quo* who would freeze existing inequalities of opportunity and economic power by choking off criticism. It must also be defended against those agents and apologists of communist totalitarianism who instead of honestly defending heresies, resort to conspiratorial methods of anonymity and other techniques of fifth columnists.'

'Extremism in the defense of liberty is no vice,' Senator Barry Goldwater told the Republican National Nominating Convention in his acceptance speech, July 1964. 'Moderation in the pursuit of justice is no virtue.'

Assuming free government can cope with the competing values of liberty and security, assuming power outside formal political institutions can be tamed, how can free society flourish in the face of still another baffling dilemma —the stern imperatives of technology?

> Individuals are stripped of their individuality, not by external compulsion, but by the very rationality under which they live. . . Today the apparatus to which the individual is to adjust and adapt himself is sc rational that individual protest and liberation appear not only as hopeless but as utterly irrational. The system of life created by modern industry is one of the highest expediency, convenience and necessity. Rational behavior becomes identical with a matter-of-factness which teaches reasonable submissiveness, and thus guarantees getting along in the prevailing order. [Herbert Marcuse, 'Some Implications of Modern Technology,' in *Studies in Philosophy and Social Science*, IX (1941), 421.]

Decisions as to when, where, and how to introduce technological change are political decisions. Yet, as Charles Frankel reminds us, they are too often made 'in something close to a social vacuum.'

> A current example is the impact of television. It has affected education and home life, changed the patterns of congressional behavior and political discussion, and fundamentally altered, for better or worse, the operating conditions and purposes of traditional political institutions like legislative investigations and political conventions. But the decisions on how to use television, and how not to use it, have been made almost entirely by men whose area of responsibility is very narrow, and who have to think about only a very few, selected values. . .

'Hardly any question arises in the United States,' Tocqueville noted more than a century ago, 'that is not resolved sooner or later into a judicial question.' Since its withdrawal in 1937 from the status of 'super-legislature' in economic affairs, the Supreme Court (with occasional deviations) has subjected government action threatening civil rights to close scrutiny. Evidence mounts that the 'self-restraint' banner then raised has not blinded Chief Justice Warren to certain positive responsibilities. His Court began to discharge these on 17 May 1954, that historic day the Justices handed down their unanimous decision in the school segregation cases. The anxiously awaited opinion was short and incisive. 'In approaching this problem,' the Chief Justice remarked, 'we must consider public education in the light of its full development and its present place in American life throughout the Nation.' Segregation, he said, may affect hearts and minds in a way unlikely ever to be undone. Redressing the damage done civil rights legislation a century earlier, the Warren Court filled the gap that other branches of government were unable or unwilling to close.

Nor is racial segregation the only field in which the Warren Court has responded to a positive responsibility. At a single sitting, 17 June 1957, the Justices shouldered other tasks in the civil rights orbit. Upheld was the right of anyone to advocate overthrow of the government, so long as the preaching does not openly urge specific action; qualified was the power of Congressional committees to make investigations and require witnesses to testify; limited was the State's power to force witnesses to co-operate in investigations authorized by State law. In 1961, the Justices, reversing a position of only a decade earlier, ruled that unlawfully seized evidence must be excluded, as a matter of due process, in the prosecution of accused persons tried in State courts. In 1963, the Justices vetoed State laws requiring recital of the Lord's Prayer and Bible-reading in public schools. In all these cases the Court took the position that government action restricting or taking away fundamental rights should be examined with special diligence, that 'the Judiciary has the duty of implementing the constitutional safeguards that protect individual rights.'

More recently the Justices asserted their responsibility for maintaining the democratic character of the political process. Reaffirmed in the famous Georgia reapportionment case of 17 February 1964 (Wesberry v. Sanders) was America's bold commitment of 1776. 'As nearly as practicable,' Justice Black wrote for the majority, 'one man's vote in a Congressional election is to be worth as much as another'—in short, 'one man, one vote.' The effect was to provoke one of the sharpest cleavages in our judicial history.

Reacting sharply to the Court's increasing preoccupation with civil rights in an age when pressures multiply to diminish them, Justice Harlan pointedly cautioned against the 'subtle capacity for serious mischief' contained in the view that 'all deficiencies in our society which have failed of correction by other means should find a cure in the courts.' 'The Constitution does not confer on the Court,' Harlan challenged on 17 February, 'blanket authority to step into every situation where the political branch may be thought to have fallen short.' The Justice's concern is well taken. Surely no society can depend exclusively on the judiciary to safeguard it from harm. But, if the political process itself is impeded or corrupted, it would seem unrealistic to look to agencies which assume no responsibility for the breakdown as the sole organs of government empowered to furnish a corrective. Unless the judiciary intervenes, no remedy will be forthcoming.

Certain Supreme Court Justices charge that the judiciary has undertaken to resolve essentially legislative issues. Inside and outside the Court one hears the familiar charge, 'judicial usurpation.' The most dramatic reaction is reflected in the far-reaching amendments proposed in December 1962 by the Council of State Governments. One would undo the 1962 Supreme Court decision striking at the rotten borough scandal. Another would permit state legislatures to amend the Constitution without consideration or discussion in any national forum. The third would set up a super-Supreme Court—consisting of the Chief Justices of the fifty states, empowered to review and override certain Supreme Court decisions. Impressed by the ominous implications of these proposals, and dismayed by the widespread public apathy, Chief Justice Warren called for a 'great national debate.' 'If proposals of such magnitude had been made in the early days of the Republic,' the Chief Justice declared, 'a great debate would be resounding in every legislative hall and in every place where lawyers, scholars, and statesmen gather.' Yet Lloyd W. Lowry's *Statement of Principles*, in presenting the amendments, suggests that they are offered as the logical corrective for a recognized evil. Lowry's words portray states' rights as a hotly contested issue.

Not far beneath the surface of the battle among the Justices and in the country on the Court's role in a free society are profound theoretical issues. Questions debated at Putney over three centuries ago remain unanswered. Does natural law alone furnish the legitimate measure of men's rights in political society? Or must individual rights and civil institutions be shaped by constitutional compact? Must not a written constitution rest ultimately on a generally accepted core of values? Walter Lippmann, contending that no society can long endure without consensus on fundamentals, strongly urges a return to natural law principles—to 'the public philosophy of a free society.' Lippmann recognizes that 'the public philosophy . . . cannot be popular,' since it 'aims to resist and to regulate those very desires and opinions which are most popular.' 'Neither can it,' Lippmann believes, 'be restored by fiat and force.' Underscored is Charles P. Curtis's arresting query: ought we to leave 'our natural law to take its chances without a national prophet'? Should a court decide such questions as segregation? Curtis's answer is somewhat elusive:

> When the legislature asked the judge to decide, the legislature asked *him* to decide, him and no one else. Congress can shirk its duty. A court cannot. And yet such cases as these are not properly judiciable. The Common Law, with more consideration for judges, perhaps naturally so, allowed them to turn such questions over to a jury, where, it seems to me, they belong. But no, we put these questions of natural law, this natural law that we are talking about, to the judge and expect him to have a ready answer. . .

Curtis agreed that it would be preferable for Congress to decide issues having a natural law content, but realized that if the Court had refused to come to grips with the 'separate but equal' doctrine, then awaiting Congressional action, there would have been 'something of an Alphonse-Gaston game, with no one going through the door.'

The role of the Court in a free society, always a live issue, was never more fervently debated both inside and outside the judicial conference room. 'Whether by force of circumstance or deliberate design,' Woodrow Wilson observed, Americans have—for better or for worse—'married legislation with adjudication, and look for statesmanship in Courts.' But is statesmanship enough?

Many observers saw in the *Brown* decision of 1954 judicial statesmanship of the highest order. Yet, by the end of 1962, less than one-half of one per cent of all Negro students in the eleven Southern states were attending integrated public schools. Justifiably impatient with the judicial process—slow, cumbersome, expensive, subject to numerous devices for delaying or avoiding law enforcement—Negroes in 1963 demanded 'equality *now*.' Minimizing token integration in public schools, they sought first-class citizenship in *all* areas.

The so-called Negro Revolution of 1963 and 1964, dramatized by the march on Washington, and manifest in race riots, demonstrations, sit-ins, 'freedom-rides,' etc., suggested that when the political process itself breaks down even the statesmanlike union of judicial review and the Bill of Rights cannot avert resort to violence. The basic social contract, dating from 1776, had been abrogated; the prospect of changing the law through peaceable, orderly means, or the likelihood of enforcing 'the supreme law of the land,' could no longer compel civil obedience. 'Civil disobedience,' often violence, ensued.

Malcolm X, appealing to armed mobs, makes Free Government's predicament seem bizarre: 'We should form rifle clubs that can be used to defend our lives and our properties. . . It is legal and lawful to own a shotgun or a rifle. We believe in obeying the law.' Segregation is indefensible, but integration is no solution. With pride in his race, Malcolm urges Negroes to rise up and separate themselves once and for all from the white man's culture and civilization.

The race issue remains unresolved, perhaps unresolvable. Division prevails within both Negro and white communities, not only on means but also on ultimate ends. In his 'interview with myself' Robert Penn Warren (1905–) a native Southerner, represents the enlightened Southern position. William D. Workman, Jr., assays an intellectual justification of racial segregation. Negro leaders themselves are not united. Booker T. Washington's (1859?–1915) moderate stance of 1895, despite the opprobrium 'Uncle Tomism,' is not wholly lacking in support. Note the striking dissimilarity between the positions of Martin Luther King, Jr. (1929–), and James Baldwin (1924–); both are under attack by Malcolm X.

In 1963, as racial violence became commonplace, the centennial anniversary of Lincoln's Emancipation Proclamation ironically witnessed the assassination of President John F. Kennedy, a tragedy paralleling that of a century earlier. Thoughtful observers were driven to probe underlying causes. Was the assassination merely a tragic accident, the act of a profoundly tormented brain, or the grotesque manifestation of a deeper failing in our culture? Was America —on the crest of the highest wave in the history of civilization—marked with the very flaws so fatal to the tragic heroes of old? Did the ancient Greek concept of *hubris* apply equally to nations? 'How explain our illness?' Henry Steele Commager queried. His explanation is hardly encouraging:

> 'Out of all this,' he concludes, 'the tradition of frontier violence, the special saturation of race relations in the South, the double standard of morality, the assumption that the ordinary rules did not apply to us, that we were exempt from the laws and the processes of history—out of all this has come that bigotry and arrogance and vanity and violence which so deeply shocks us today.'

Man's capacity for inflicting violence on man reached cosmic dimensions with the development of the atom bomb. In 1945, when a reporter broke the news of Hiroshima, Albert Einstein, who initiated creation of this diabolical weapon, commented soberly: 'Ach! The world is not ready for it.' 'Our defense is not in armaments, nor in science, nor in going underground,' this great man of science asserted. 'Our defense is in law and order.' Senator J. William Fulbright (1905–) is optimistic. Citing the 'strain of violence in our culture,' he points hopefully to the 'basic decency and humanity of America' as a corrective for the disabling 'wounds of divisiveness and hate.'

'The poor always ye have with you.' No other social affliction is more widespread or more persistent. It is no respector of nations. The most 'prosperous' societies are plagued by it. Affluence serves to accent rather than alleviate it. It snarls the race issue. If the Negro were to win every item in the Civil Rights Act of 1964, one effect would be to underscore troubles stemming from the stark fact of inescapable poverty. No other single condition is more conducive to the spread of communism. David M. Potter (1910–) shows how poverty hampers America's self-imposed mission to democratize the world. President Johnson has placed it at the very top of the national agenda. It ranks high among Free Government's predicaments. In the piece here reproduced, W. H. Ferry, vice president of the Fund for the Republic, explores various aspects of the problem.

Free Government is threatened by conflicts among men, among groups, among nations, and by an even more baffling war going on within man's own nature. From Reinhold Niebuhr (1892–) comes the sobering reminder that democracy is 'a method of finding proximate solutions for insoluble problems.' The predicament of Free Government, the late President Kennedy (1917–63) prophesied, will not be resolved 'perhaps in our life-time on this planet.' Man will always be engaged in a struggle against the perversities of his own nature. The Founding Fathers' assumptions reflect this complexity.* Political institutions are so organized and arranged that human drives and tensions are mutually self-correcting and self-limiting. The institutionalized tension thus achieved, coupled with the proposition that consent of the people

* Said Madison: 'As there is a degree of depravity in mankind which requires a degree of circumspection and distrust: so there are other qualities in human nature which justify a certain portion of esteem and confidence. Republican government presupposes the existence of these qualities in a higher degree than any other form.' (*Federalist* 55.)

Said Hamilton: 'The supposition of universal venality in human nature is little less an error in political reasoning than the supposition of universal rectitude. The institution of delegated power implies that there is a portion of virtue and honor among mankind, which may be a reasonable foundation of confidence; and experience justifies the theory.' (*Federalist* 76.)

is the only legitimate source of power, constitute the essentials of a free society. 'Vibrations of power,' Hamilton commented in 1802, 'are the genius of our government.'

Continuing predicaments are inherent in the system under which we live. The very liberty a free society recognizes and guarantees induces a condition of unrest, encourages criticism of things as they are, fosters disorder. A free society is naturally torn, as Madison said, by unending war among factions, sects, and creeds. He cited 'zeal for different opinions concerning religion, concerning government, and many other points, as well of speculation as of practice. . . So strong is this propensity of mankind, to fall into mutual animosities, that where no substantial occasion presents itself, the most frivolous and fanciful distinctions have been sufficient to kindle their unfriendly passions, and excite their most violent conflicts.' This, moreover, is a free society's natural condition. The effort to combine individual liberty with social justice, the attempt to reconcile freedom and security, to fuse the initiative necessary for progress with the social cohesion needed for survival—all this creates Free Government's inescapable predicament. No adjustment will ever be perfectly and finally achieved. The only alternative is totalitarianism or the peace of the graveyard. The tediousness of its method and proximate nature of the results place Free Government at seeming disadvantage. 'The wastes of democracy,' Justice Brandeis declared, 'are among the most obvious wastes.' Minds, more disposed to vex each other than to co-operate for the common good, have to be consulted, informed, and brought into agreement. These time-consuming procedures are Free Government's most distinguishing feature, the only assurance that whatever course it may have to take, freedom may endure.

IRRESPONSIBLE POWER

1. *Monster business is undemocratic, inhuman and not socially responsible*

THEODORE K. QUINN, *I Quit Monster Business*, 1948 *

My approach is meant to be factual, moderate and objective. . .I do not intend any attack upon economic commercial or mass production single units which because of the nature of the business must be comparatively big to be efficient and to operate profitably. My quarrel is entirely with the growing system of monster, combination corporations made up of many large units, often entirely unrelated, which are big only for the sake of bigness or for reasons of financial control that are dwarfing and victimizing our people including eventually, as I here undertake to show, those involved in them.

Small, independent, decentralized business of the kind that built this country is disappearing or being made dependent upon the monsters. The monsters continue to swell alarmingly in power and number, and their existence

* New York, Public Relations Inc., 522 Fifth Avenue.

and methods are as constant a threat to everything we hold dear as would be ever present herds of uncaged tigers or elephants running rampant. Any notion that small business can continue indefinitely to compete against the financial, purchasing and advertising power of the monster corporations is a pure myth. It is not a question of efficiency. Buying raw materials or parts at lowest costs is often a matter of sheer power. Suppliers become obliged to accept what the huge companies choose to pay. Volume of advertising is large in amount and impact but low in proportion to enormous sales. And great wealth and credit are frequently matters of favor or accident.

Created by man himself like Frankenstein's brute, economic monsters are essentially undemocratic and destructive by the very nature of their organizations and size, and are leading us unwittingly toward an inevitable collectivistic type rulership. . .

By 'Monster,' I mean a private corporation for gain which has greater assets or more stockholders and employees than a number of states in the Union have wealth or population. It may also be a 'Monster' if it has an effective control in any major or important field of business whether or not it is in the billionaire class. Any giant corporation is included if it engages in various types of business, has hundreds of millions of dollars in assets, and subsidiary companies or divisions, factories or offices located in many States. These corporations are monsters in the sense of enormous, sprawling size with the human qualities necessarily submerged. The brutal elements tend to become controlling through impersonality, and the monsters themselves are heartless gigantic machines driving on relentlessly and regardless to narrow, materialistic objectives. They also breed trade unions and government of corresponding or greater size which become socially desirable because we must have them to oppose and counterbalance the tremendous, selfish industrial and commercial organizations. A one million dollar business is a good sized business and a ten million dollar one is a big business. When we come to one that is from a hundred to a thousand times bigger than either of these we have a 'monster,' and I know of no more descriptive or fitting name for it.

The huge combination, private corporations are monsters too, in that no individual or officer, however tireless, or competent he may believe himself to be, can ever fully understand them, know what they are doing, control them or assume intelligent responsibility for the many thousands of human beings employed. Thus the officers and managers attracted by large salaries or intrigued by mere size are as much the victims of the monsters as are its other employees and the public. They are not entirely to blame for pursuing what to them is only a logical course. Little in our law requires them to regard the effect of their activities upon society and few of them give it a serious thought.

There is no such thing as a 'good' monster or what has been called a big 'good' wolf. Let us not be fooled by the handiwork of the skilled public relations experts hired expressly to make black appear to be white. All monsters are bad because they are monsters. Enormous size is power that can injure by the fact of its existence. The concentration of power which it represents can be and is being used against the public interest. Monster organizations are stupid beasts and are creating an increasingly dependent society where only masses count, genuine individual freedom languishes and individual opportunity and expression are strangled. For big business there is often some good reason and explanation; for monsters there is none. The instability of our economic system has increased along with the increase in the number and power of monsters and monopolies.

We are hell bent toward some kind of collectivist state not primarily because of the highly publicized outside influences or because of the pitiful communists in our midst, but more because our own private and public institutions are swelling to uncontrollable, gigantic proportions and have already assumed huge, collectivistic forms. The threat of communism is real enough, but with strong, free and independent, smaller democratic units and no impoverished people, we would be impregnable against it. Alexander Hamilton prophesied truly that it is not by arms that the liberty of this country is to be destroyed but by a pretense of adhering to all the forms of law and yet by breaking down all the substance of our liberties.

The United States is indeed, as has been effectively if crudely said, 'lousy with greatness.' It is greatness which must be measured more by what we can do than by what we have done. Let no one suppose that in the conditions existing today of restricted individual opportunities and millions of cramped, dependent and underprivileged people, we have approached the great American ideal. Freedom, self government and equality mean infinitely more than we have accomplished, and what we have done would not have been possible under today's limitations. Founded upon the principles of equal opportunity for all, the Bill of Rights and government only by consent of the governed, our future should be unlimited. As it is our whole country is in jeopardy. Prices are rising to prohibitive heights. The wartime savings of most of the people are being rapidly depleted but the wealth and power of the top one percent continues to increase, forcasting greater unbalance and eventual collapse.

Concentrated monster and monopoly capitalism with too few owning and enjoying the good things in life is a perversion, as far from our ideals as Russian Communism. Both are totalitarian, the antithesis of what is inherent in individualism, civil liberties and the democratic process. . .

At this point, lest any agent or follower of any other political or economic system receives the slightest comfort from anything in this book, I hasten to say that even with all its faults, ours is demonstrably the best system on earth. But our responsibility is to keep it so and unhappily we are slipping and slipping too fast into the forms and methods of collectivism. . .

Collectivism in industry begets collectivism in government. It is a collectivism which is only a few steps removed from collectivism as it is now practiced in Russia. What it points toward is the end of free enterprise—the right to risk and profit, and eventually the loss of those civil liberties that are based upon the limitations of governmental power. It is utterly foolish to cry out against big government or big unions while we have monster private business organizations unless we want to place the latter in absolute control.

Those of us who wish to see our traditional American freedoms continued and honest free enterprise maintained for the many, as well as for the few, must act promptly to avoid the oncoming socialization of the entire country. . .

Are we to wait passively and stupidly like the Bourbons of France for the deluge? It may be that a democratic socialistic system would prove to be better than ours but we are not now giving individualistic competitive capitalism a fair chance.

The choice of private enterprise is between becoming bigger in its economic units and subject to more regulation, or remaining smaller and to a much greater extent free. Individuals in monster companies, who insist upon expansion merely to increase their theoretical personal power or prestige, or to gain monopolistic profits, are scuttling the ship of private enterprise. It is a discouraging thing to find these confused and shortsighted men appointed on national committees, sometimes by the President himself where the ostensible purpose is the preservation of freedom or the maintenance of genuine free enterprise.

One of the fallacies standing in the way of action to prevent further concentration of power and wealth is that bigness in business is self-corrective, and that when it reaches a point where the curve of efficiency turns down because of size, it will stop expanding, decentralize or go broke. This is very seldom if ever true. No matter how inefficient General Motors, du Pont, Standard Oil of New Jersey, Metropolitan Life, or any other of their size or importance might become, they could not be permitted to fail. They are too integral a part of our whole economy—quasi public institutions. We keep alive the fiction that the monsters are essentially private in nature, allow them too much power, permit them further to eliminate small business and force us down the road to collectivism.

Big monopolistic business drives government closer to the totalitarian state. And size is more than an invitation to monopoly—it is a practical requirement. The ways and means may be changed, but where there are huge companies operating, we cannot expect any degree of healthy competition. . .

The individual is not happy nor most constructive, as I have tried to show, under conditions of domination in monster private corporations. He may be somewhat more content under a collective authority in which he is a partner, economic or political. But the urgent problem is one of checking the penetrating collectivism now being forced upon us in various forms, with a new determination to preserve the essence of the fundamental rights of the individual as guaranteed in our Constitution. The basic conditions have changed from an agricultural, then a mercantile to an industrial society. We cannot expect the best from the individual in any monopolistic organization, private or public. We need a new declaration of Thomas Paine's Rights of Man, suited to the conditions of our times which will recognize the essential co-operation of the industrial age and reconcile it harmoniously with a reasonable liberty for the individual, leaving him free to grow, move, create and have his being. For it must always be true that progress for all of us depends upon the progress of each, and an organization, public or private, where men are not free is intolerable. . .

2. *We may find an alternative to socialist collectivism in the modern business corporation*

ADOLF A. BERLE, JR., *The Emerging Common Law of Free Enterprise: Antidote to the Omnipotent State*, 1951 *

Examination of the relevant economic data makes clear that private enterprise is likely to include for a good while to come a large proportion of 'big' corporations. I here adopt this assumption. Engineers may, of course, take us out. Some atomic scientist may one day make it possible for anyone to make steel in a backyard blacksmith shop; some inventor may create a strange device permitting anyone to turn out automobiles in a plant the size of a small town garage. But nothing of this is in sight now. Bigness is with us and the technicians tell us it is necessary.

Apparently, then, we are going to have to live with two phenomena: a large sector of industry concentrated in big enterprise; and a number of essential industries in which supply and distribution is dominantly concentrated in a few large concerns.

Now great economic concentration, and great concentration within any essential industry even though privately owned, progressively ceases to be either private, or even free, enterprise. I present the thesis that corporations, under these circumstances, progressively approximate a form of non-statist socialism.

Yet I suggest that the difference between great private concentrations, especially great concentrations within essential industries, and state or publicly-owned industry is less than one would suppose. The two systems are similar in that both strive toward a central planning function. They differ chiefly in the groups that carry on that central planning function, and in the criteria applied to their planning. . .

Economic concentration in industry would be interesting as an event in itself. It happens to have occurred, however, simultaneously with another phenomenon: the phenomenon of government responsibility for the working of the economic system and for conditions of life under it. The twentieth century has thus seen the development of the huge corporation as an economic mechanism, dominant in great sectors of industrial life; but it has also seen the assumption by government of responsibility for the functioning of the economic system. . . In America, at least, the assumption has not been doctrinaire: it has been built up through a series of quite normal and wholly eclectic political movements.

The result may be quite simply stated: unless the American economic system supplies at an acceptable level of prices the current needs for goods, services and employment, the government in power is likely to be voted out of office at the next general election.

Yet the government, endeavoring to maintain a more or less stable and

* Reprinted by permission of The Brandeis Society, 238 South 13th Street, Philadelphia, Pa.

more or less satisfactory economic system, is forced to include the great industrial concentrations in its calculations. Production is needed: this can only be had by small-scale production, by big corporate production, or by socialist operation. Employment must be substantially full: if the government is not itself to be the employer, the private corporation must provide work. If private enterprise balanced by competition does not keep the economy on an even keel, the government must step in with planning and controls.

In much of the world (including most of the continent of Europe), governments have met this situation by socializing in greater or less degree the production of their respective countries. In America we have not—relying on private organization, competitive practice, and private initiative. In tangible fact, at the present state of the industrial revolution, two, and only two, great methods of productive organization have emerged: socialist collectivism, operated by government commissariats, and private collectivisms, operated by great corporations of the American type.

We seem to like it. The system has advantages as well as disadvantages. But it is fair to ask where the system is bound. The problem is whether we shall be able to avoid those developments which led England down a primrose path through concentration to cartels, and thence into state socialism—a socialism perhaps inevitable for the British, but which still seems unnecessary here.

Some commentators have propounded the theory that corporate concentration is a half-way house on the one-way road towards socialism. These believe that if concentration cannot be brought back, if the trend of growth continues, we have only to await the development of the corporate executive into the socialist commissar. The state may take over the corporate concentrates—or the corporate concentrates may take over the state—the result is much the same. This view, it is suggested, leaves out a possible development: the possibility that rules of law and social standards may so govern the internal as well as external functioning of the corporation that a democratic, non-governmental economic system may emerge, capable alike of planning and stabilizing an economy and also of escaping the dangers which come from merging political and economic power. It is my belief that such rules of law and social standards are already appearing, and already are beginning to govern the corporate enterprise. I accordingly suggest—and make this my thesis tonight—that there is coming into being what may be called the 'intra-corporate common law' which does not regulate operations but rather sets up standards by which corporations are judged.

These standards are emerging, partly as common law, and partly as applications of anti-trust and similar statute laws. Enforcement of these standards, apparently, is proving to be the American alternative to the actual conduct of operations by the state. Instead of nationalizing an enterprise or industry, we set up standards of conduct for the managers of the enterprise or industry in such fashion that it will ultimately become immaterial whether it is nationalized or not. Such a result would be in the genius, of the common law, as it is in line with the genius of the United States for, fundamentally, in the United States it is the result, and not the dogma, that interests people.

Here we differ from our trans-Atlantic forebears. In Europe, for years the dogma has grown that nationalization per se was somehow good; that private ownership of production was per se an obstacle to progress. This dogma of the nineteenth century has been carried into, and dominates, most of European politics today. But the average American cares little about dogmatic theory. He wants certain results for his physical satisfaction; he wants certain social demands fulfilled. In method he is a pragmatist.

What results does he want?

In the first place, he wants enough of the product. He will raise all kinds of remonstrance, political and otherwise, if he does not get it, whether it consists of cigarettes or automobiles, housing or an adequate supply of steel, or any other thing that he considers necessary.

Second, he wants to pay not more than an 'acceptable' price. I use the word 'acceptable' because I don't want to use the word 'fair.' Some 'acceptable' prices are anything but fair. He wants a price not so far out of range as to impose on him what he considers privation. This is realistic rather than idealistic.

Recently he has begun to make some relatively new demands. There is public insistence that at least a modicum of the Bill of Rights be applied as the standard of corporate action. Particularly he disapproves of race discrimination, and wants to prevent arbitrary discrimination in choosing customers. He does not think of this as insistence of 'equal protection of the laws'—but that is the origin of his demand.

In the public utility field, of course, we have had that demand for years and have satisfied it by imposing definite legal standards. It is now being extended to quite ordinary industry. I surmise that today, if in any area the only grocery stores were the grocery stores of a particular chain store, and if three or four families happened to be disliked by the chain store management, and if the chain store gave notice that these people were not to be allowed to use the local branch shops, the ensuing fracas would be so great that the chain store would have to change its position. . .

Obviously, in our chain store case, if there were fifty competing grocery stores, and one cut off service, the blacklisted customer would be quite able to do his shopping at the other forty-nine. Here is not enough power in the enterprise to generate necessity for legal action. But where the only available service is in the power of a single concentrate to give or withhold, the management of that concern, if blessed with ordinary common sense, knows today that it is extremely dangerous to indulge in discriminatory policy. Good managements are careful not to permit it. The general practice plus public insistence on non-discrimination is already beginning to work its way into settled law. . .

Still a fourth social demand, much in the news just now, is that compensation for employment shall include provision for pensions for the old age of the employees. In economic analysis, I suppose, this is really a demand for redistribution of cost. Obviously, if a man takes a job at nineteen, and works until he is sixty-three, and then is out of work, he is going to be in the town poorhouse; or it may be by his children or relatives, or it may be by private charity; or it may be by his own savings. The present demand is that it shall be by a pension, charged as part of the cost of his labor.

This is a new demand which some forward-looking business men long ago anticipated and provided for. Now it is being generally asserted by the great labor unions as a plain obligation of business. We cannot adequately analyze this demand as yet. By the time the present round of pension demands is met . . . roughly half the industry of the United States will be governed by pension agreements. An inchoate obligation is appearing, crystallizing into binding standards of practice, this time enforced through collective bargaining.

I surmise that, in addition to this, some day there will arise demand for finishing a job Mr. Brandeis worked at a great many years ago.* This is the demand that business be so handled that employment will be regular instead of seasonal, and unemployment be not as casually permitted as it is today. This is a job of industrial engineering of major proportions. Yet I am certain it will be worked out. This is partly because of the desire of business men to meet the demand as a matter of decency, and partly because there is growing labor pressure for a guaranteed annual wage. . .

I submit that the phenomenon of social demands imposing themselves by process of law has gone far enough so that we are not dealing in a pure surmise when we speak of the emergence of 'intra-corporate' common law.

Of equal interest is what happens when any of these social demands is not met.

Factually, pressure for immediate government intervention appears very rapidly. Such pressure is as likely to come from the corporate or business side as from the side of the public, depending on the group most in line of pressure or fire. The instances are illuminating. Men who claim to have the greatest hostility to government intervention are quite as likely to clamor for it as are socialist orators on the street. . .

The conclusion appears to be that private enterprise in corporate form is the standard, accepted American method of production and distribution. The conclusion is equally inescapable that wherever a social demand appears, its fulfillment is insisted on. Where, to assure the result, planning and control are necessary, private enterprise, as well as public demand, insists on appropriate government intervention. . .

When there is substantial social demand for an economic operation, the present theory seems to be that if the demand is justifiable, it must not be denied merely on financial grounds. After all, the first and great requirement of an economic system is that it shall function: that it shall continuously supply the goods, services and employment a community needs. The private collectivisms known as corporations expect to do this without recourse to the government; but, when they need help, no one is less backward than they in asking for and getting governmental assistance. When all is said and done, the performance of their central function is paramount alike to the government and to them and the same motivations compel government and business alike to move towards practical solutions. . .

It appears, then, that the pragmatic American method of dealing with its

* The reference is to Brandeis's advocacy in 1902 of the annual wage. For a discussion of his reasoning, see Mason, *Brandeis: A Free Man's Life* (New York: Viking, 1946), pp. 143–6. In May 1955 the United Auto Workers successfully insisted on an annual wage provision in its contract with the Ford Motor Company. Other similar agreements seem likely to follow.

economic system prefers private ownership and operation—or, indeed, perhaps is not interested greatly in the question who is owner and who is operator, but is vividly interested in results. Put differently, the doctrine imposed by public opinion is that certain results shall be obtained; if obtained, the method of attaining them—private or public—is of only limited interest. Who cares whether the telephone is owned by the state or by the local telephone company, provided the service is good and the price is a dime? If choice has to be made between a privately-owned and a publicly-owned system, the choice is in favor of the private enterprise. Yet the chief reason is that the American Telephone & Telegraph Company has lived up to, and continues to live up to, certain standards—including not only conventional public utility standards but some others as well—for instance, not tapping your wires, or intruding on your conversations.

General Motors during the recent shortage endeavored to maintain its list prices. It went to trouble and expense trying to prevent its dealers from collecting black market prices so far as it could. I think this was honorably done, and was not an attempt to do good for advertising purposes; in any case, the prices collected yielded a respectable profit. I think General Motors had a very solid fear that if it let prices take their uncontrolled course in a period of shortage, the result would have been either government intervention, or a row so great that General Motors would be years getting over it. . .*

Thus we are on the threshold, it seems to me, of a new superstructure of the law of the economic concentrate. It will largely be corporation law. It will side-step, and perhaps quite properly, the problem of who ought to be the owner or who ought to head the organization. Instead, this emerging law will recognize these inchoate social demands and will translate them into accepted philosophy and workable common law. We may be finding an American answer to a problem which elsewhere has turned on sterile issues of dogma and abstract theory. . .

Americans apparently can get better results from our own methods of handling private enterprise than from the doctrinaire methods being tried in Europe. But this appears to imply understanding of what everybody is expected to do. The emergent economic common law appears to be the true antithesis to collective socialism.

* A dramatic example occurred in the spring of 1962 when, shortly after informal agreement between industry and labor had been reached to 'hold the line' on wages and prices, certain steel companies announced price hikes. President Kennedy was profoundly disillusioned concerning industry's sensitiveness to the public interest: 'My father always told me that all business men are son-of-bitches, but I never believed it till now.' (*New York Times*, 23 April 1962, p. 25.) Roger Blough of the U.S. Steel promptly backed down. [A.T.M.]

3. *A community which fails to preserve the discipline of competition exposes itself to the discipline of absolute authority*

HENRY C. SIMONS, *Some Reflections on Syndicalism*, March 1944 *

Questioning the virtues of the organized labor movement is like attacking religion, monogamy, motherhood, or the home. Among the modern intelligentsia any doubts about collective bargaining admit of explanation only in terms of insanity, knavery, or subservience to 'the interests.' Discussion of skeptical views runs almost entirely in terms of how one came by such persuasions, as though they were symptoms of disease. One simply cannot argue that organization is injurious to labor; one is either for labor or against it, and the test is one's attitude toward unionism. But let me indicate from the outset that my central interest, and the criterion in terms of which I wish to argue, is a maximizing of aggregate labor income and a minimizing of inequality. If unionism were good for labor as a whole, that would be the end of the issue for me, since the community whose welfare concerns us is composed overwhelmingly of laborers.

Our problem here, at bottom, is one of broad political philosophy. Advocates of trade-unionism are, I think, obligated morally and intellectually to present a clear picture of the total political-economic system toward which they would have us move. For my part, I simply cannot conceive of any tolerable or enduring order in which there exists widespread organization of workers along occupational, industrial, functional lines. Sentimentalists view such developments merely as a contest between workers who earn too little and enterprises which earn too much; and, unfortunately, there has been enough monopsony in labor markets to make this view superficially plausible, though not enough to make it descriptively important. What we generally fail to see is the identity of interest between the whole community and enterprises seeking to keep down costs. Where enterprise is competitive—and substantial, enduring restraint of competition in product markets is rare—enterprisers represent the community interest effectively; indeed, they are merely intermediaries between consumers of goods and sellers of services. Thus we commonly overlook the conflict of interest between every large organized group of laborers and the community as a whole. What I want to ask is how this conflict can be reconciled, how the power of strongly organized sellers can be limited out of regard for the general welfare. No insuperable problem arises so long as organization is partial and precarious, so long as most unions face substantial non-union competition, or so long as they must exercise monopoly powers sparingly because of organizational insecurity. Weak unions have no large monopoly powers. But how does a democratic community limit the demands and exactions of strong, secure organizations? Looking at the typographers, the railway brother-

* *The Journal of Political Economy*, vol. 52, March 1944, pp. 1–5, 14–15 *passim*. Reprinted by permission of the University of Chicago Press.

hoods, and metropolitan building trades, among others, one answers simply: 'It doesn't!'

In an economy of intricate division of labor, every large organized group is in a position at any time to disrupt or to stop the whole flow of social income; and the system must soon break down if groups persist in exercising that power or if they must continuously be bribed to forgo its disastrous exercise. There is no means, save internal competition, to protect the whole community against organized labor minorities and, indeed, no other means to protect the common interests of organized groups themselves. The dilemma here is not peculiar to our present economic order; it must appear in any kind of system. This minority-monopoly problem would be quite as serious for a democratic socialism as it is for the mixed individualist-collectivist system of the present. It is the rock on which our present system is most likely to crack up; and it is the rock on which democratic socialism would be destroyed if it could ever come into being at all.

All the grosser mistakes in economic policy, if not most manifestations of democratic corruption, arise from focusing upon the interests of people as producers rather than upon their interests as consumers, i.e., from acting on behalf of producer minorities rather than on behalf of the whole community as sellers of services and buyers of products. One gets the right answers usually by regarding simply the interests of consumers, since we are all consumers; and the answers reached by this approach are presumably the correct ones for laborers as a whole. But one doesn't get elected by approaching issues in this way! People seldom vote in terms of their common interests, whether as sellers or as buyers. There is no means for protecting the common interest save in terms of rules of policy; and it is only in terms of general rules or principles that democracy, which is government by free, intelligent discussion, can function tolerably or endure. Its nemesis is racketeering—tariffs, other subsidies, and patronage dispensations generally and, outside of government, monopoly, which in its basic aspect is impairment of the state's monopoly of coercive power.

Trade-unionism may be attacked as a threat to order under any kind of system. The case against it is crystal clear if one thinks in terms of purer types of systems like democratic collectivism. . .

I am arguing, however, not as a socialist, but as an advocate of the elaborate mixed system of traditional economic liberalism. The essence of this practical political philosophy is a distrust of all concentrations of power. No individual may be trusted with much power, no organization, and no institution save the state itself. The state or sovereign must, of course, possess great reserves of power, if only to prevent other organizations from threatening or usurping its monopoly of violence. But the exercise of power inherent in government must be rigidly economized. Decentralization of government is essential. Indeed, the proper purpose of all large-scale organization or federation—as should be obvious to people facing the problem of world order—is that of dispersing power. . .

Governments can be trusted to exercise large power, broad functions, and extensive control only at levels of small units like American states and under the limitations imposed by freedom of external trade. Especially in the higher levels or larger units of government, action must follow broad general rules or principles. Only by adherence to 'constitutional' principles of policy can the common interest be protected against minorities, patronage, and logrolling; and only in terms of issues of broad principle can government by free, intelligent discussion (democracy) prevail. Most important here are the presumptions in favor of free trade and against dispensations to producer minorities. . .

The government must not tolerate erection of great private corporate empires or cartel organizations which suppress competition and rival in power great governmental units themselves. . .

Finally, and most important for the future, it must guard its powers against great trade-unions, both as pressure groups in government and as monopolists outside.

The danger here is now most ominous, in the very nature of such agencies and also because the danger is least well recognized and commonly denied entirely. In other areas we are, if diffident and careless, at least on our guard; nothing is likely to happen that cannot be undone if we will; but labor monopolies and labor 'states' may readily become a problem which democracy simply cannot solve at all. There must be effective limitations upon their powers; but I do not see how they can be disciplined democratically save by internal competition or how that discipline can be effected without breaking down organization itself. Here, possibly, is an awful dilemma: democracy cannot live with tight occupational monopolies; and it cannot destroy them, once they attain great power, without destroying itself in the process. If democratic governments cannot suppress organized extortion and preserve their monopoly of violence, they will be superseded by other kinds of government. Organized economic warfare is like organized banditry and, if allowed to spread, must lead to total revolution, which will, on very hard terms, restore some order and enable us to maintain some real income instead of fighting interminably over its division among minorities.

A community which fails to preserve the discipline of competition exposes itself to the discipline of absolute authority. Preserving the former discipline, we may govern ourselves and look forward to a peaceful world order; without it, we must submit to arbitrary authority and to hopeless disorder internationally. And, let me suggest again, the problem is quite as critical for democratic socialism as for the decentralized system of orthodox liberalism. An obvious danger in collectivism is that the vast powers of government would be abused in favoritism to particular producer groups, organized to demand favors as the price of maintaining peace, and available to support established authorities against political opposition. Adherence to competitive, productivity norms is, now or under socialism, a means for avoiding arbitrariness and, to my mind, the only feasible means. . .

The basic principle here is freedom of entry—freedom of migration, between localities, between industries, between occupational categories. If such freedom is to exist—and it is limited inevitably by costs and by defects of training and experience—wages must fall to accommodate new workers in any area to which many qualified persons wish to move. Freedom of migration implies freedom of qualified workers, not merely to seek jobs but to get them; free entry implies full employment for all qualified persons who wish to enter. Whether the wage permits an adequate family scale of living, according to social service workers, is simply irrelevant—as, indeed, are the net earnings of employers. What really matters is the judgment of workers, who would be excluded by an excessive wage, as to the *relative* merits of the employment in question and of employment in the less attractive alternatives actually open to them. Other things equal, the wage is too high if higher than the wage in actually alternative employment. Ethically, one cannot go beyond the opinion of qualified workers seeking to transfer. If in large numbers they prefer employment here to the alternatives and cannot get it, the wage is excessive. A case may be made for supplementing, by governmental expenditure, the family incomes of workers of low productivity, but not for keeping them idle or for confining them to less productive as against more productive employment.

Now freedom of entry is peculiarly essential in the case of unusually remunerative employments, if one believes in greater equality of opportunity. Only by permitting the freest movement upward through wage categories can we minimize economic inequality and maximize incomes at the bottom of the scale. But it is exactly the high-wage industries which invite and facilitate organization; and it is the favorably situated who have most to gain by exclusion, restriction, and monopolistic practices. At best, no labor organization is likely to be more unselfish or to make less use of its powers than the American Medical Association; and, considering its loose organization and small power, the comparison is surely alarming.

Organization is a device by which privilege may be entrenched and consolidated. It is a device by which the strong may raise themselves higher by pressing down the weak. Unionism, barring entry into the most attractive employments, makes high wages higher and low wages lower. Universally applied, it gets nowhere save to create disorder. Surely we cannot all get rich by restricting production. Monopoly works when everyone does not try it or when few have effective power. Universally applied, it is like universal uniform subsidy paid out of universal, uniform taxation, save that the latter is merely ridiculous while the former is also incompatible with economy of resources and even with order. But the dictator will be installed long before monopoly or functional organization becomes universal. Must we leave it to the man on horseback, or to popes of the future, to restore freedom of opportunity and freedom of occupational movement? . . .

4. *We must guard against the acquisition of unwarranted influence by the military-industrial complex*

DWIGHT D. EISENHOWER, Farewell Radio and Television Address to the American People, 17 January 1961 *

Throughout America's adventure in free government, our basic purposes have been to keep the peace; to foster progress in human achievement, and to enhance liberty, dignity and integrity among people and among nations. To strive for less would be unworthy of a free and religious people. Any failure traceable to arrogance, or our lack of comprehension or readiness to sacrifice would inflict upon us grievous hurt both at home and abroad.

Progress toward these noble goals is persistently threatened by the conflict now engulfing the world. It commands our whole attention, absorbs our very beings. We face a hostile ideology—global in scope, atheistic in character, ruthless in purpose, and insidious in method. Unhappily the danger it poses promises to be of indefinite duration. To meet it successfully, there is called for, not so much the emotional and transitory sacrifices of crisis, but rather those which enable us to carry forward steadily, surely, and without complaint the burdens of a prolonged and complex struggle—with liberty the stake. Only thus shall we remain, despite every provocation, on our charted course toward permanent peace and human betterment.

Crises there will continue to be. In meeting them, whether foreign or domestic, great or small, there is a recurring temptation to feel that some spectacular and costly action could become the miraculous solution to all current difficulties. A huge increase in newer elements of our defense; development of unrealistic programs to cure every ill in agriculture; a dramatic expansion in basic and applied research—these and many other possibilities, each possibly promising in itself, may be suggested as the only way to the road we wish to travel.

But each proposal must be weighed in the light of a broader consideration: the need to maintain balance in and among national programs—balance between the private and the public economy, balance between cost and hoped for advantage—balance between the clearly necessary and the comfortably desirable; balance between our essential requirements as a nation and the duties imposed by the nation upon the individual; balance between actions of the moment and the national welfare of the future. Good judgment seeks balance and progress; lack of it eventually finds imbalance and frustration.

The record of many decades stands as proof that our people and their government have, in the main, understood these truths and have responded to them well, in the face of stress and threat. But threats, new in kind or degree, constantly arise. I mention two only.

A vital element in keeping the peace is our military establishment. Our

* *Public Papers of the Presidents of the United States*, Washington, D.C., Government Printing Office, 1960–61, Vol. 8, pp. 1036–9 *passim*.

arms must be mighty, ready for instant action, so that no potential aggressor may be tempted to risk his own destruction.

Our military organization today bears little relation to that known by any of my predecessors in peacetime, or indeed by the fighting men of World War II or Korea.

Until the latest of our world conflicts, the United States had no armaments industry. American makers of plowshares could, with time and as required, make swords as well. But now we can no longer risk emergency improvisation of national defense; we have been compelled to create a permanent armaments industry of vast proportions. Added to this, three and a half million men and women are directly engaged in the defense establishment. We annually spend on military security more than the net income of all United States corporations.

This conjunction of an immense military establishment and a large arms industry is new in the American experience. The total influence—economic, political, even spiritual—is felt in every city, every State house, every office of the Federal government. We recognize the imperative need for this development. Yet we must not fail to comprehend its grave implications. Our toil, resources and livelihood are all involved; so is the very structure of our society.

In the councils of government, we must guard against the acquisition of unwarranted influence, whether sought or unsought, by the military-industrial complex. The potential for the disastrous rise of misplaced power exists and will persist.

We must never let the weight of this combination endanger our liberties or democratic processes. We should take nothing for granted. Only an alert and knowledgeable citizenry can compel the proper meshing of the huge industrial and military machinery of defense with our peaceful methods and goals, so that security and liberty may prosper together.

Akin to, and largely responsible for the sweeping changes in our industrial-military posture, has been the technological revolution during recent decades.

In this revolution, research has become central; it also becomes more formalized, complex, and costly. A steadily increasing share is conducted for, by, or at the direction of, the Federal government.

Today, the solitary inventor, tinkering in his shop, has been overshadowed by task forces of scientists in laboratories and testing fields. In the same fashion, the free university, historically the fountainhead of free ideas and scientific discovery, has experienced a revolution in the conduct of research. Partly because of the huge costs involved, a government contract becomes virtually a substitute for intellectual curiosity. For every old blackboard there are now hundreds of new electronic computers.

The prospect of domination of the nation's scholars by Federal employment, project allocations, and the power of money is ever present—and is gravely to be regarded.

Yet, in holding scientific research and discovery in respect, as we should, we must also be alert to the equal and opposite danger that public policy could itself become the captive of a scientific-technological elite.

It is the task of statesmanship to mold, to balance, and to integrate these and other forces, new and old, within the principles of our democratic system —ever aiming toward the supreme goals of our free society.

Another factor in maintaining balance involves the element of time. As we peer into society's future, we—you and I, and our government—must avoid the impulse to live only for today, plundering, for our own ease and convenience, the precious resources of tomorrow. We cannot mortgage the material assets of our grandchildren without risking the loss also of their political and spiritual heritage. We want democracy to survive for all generations to come, not to become the insolvent phantom of tomorrow.

Down the long lane of the history yet to be written America knows that this world of ours, ever growing smaller, must avoid becoming a community of dreadful fear and hate, and be, instead, a proud confederation of mutual trust and respect.

Such a confederation must be one of equals. The weakest must come to the conference table with the same confidence as do we, protected as we are by our moral, economic, and military strength. That table, though scarred by many past frustrations, cannot be abandoned for the certain agony of the battlefield.

Disarmament, with mutual honor and confidence, is a continuing imperative. Together we must learn how to compose differences, not with arms, but with intellect and decent purpose. Because this need is so sharp and apparent I confess that I lay down my official responsibilities in this field with a definite sense of disappointment. As one who has witnessed the horror and the lingering sadness of war—as one who knows that another war could utterly destroy this civilization which has been so slowly and painfully built over thousands of years—I wish I could say tonight that a lasting peace is in sight. . .

5. *This is a republic, not a democracy; let's keep it that way*

Beliefs and Principles of the John Birch Society, 1962 *

I

With very few exceptions the members of the John Birch Society are deeply religious people. A member's particular faith is entirely his own affair. Our hope is to make better Catholics, better Protestants, better Jews—or better Moslems—out of those who belong to the society. Our never-ending concern is with morality, integrity, and purpose. Regardless of the differences between us in creed and dogma, we all believe that man is endowed by a Divine Creator with an innate desire and conscious purpose to improve both his world and himself. We believe that the direction which constitutes improvement is clearly visible and identifiable throughout man's known history, and that this God-

* Reprinted in the *Congressional Record*, 87th Congress, 2nd session, 12 June 1962.

given upward reach in the heart of man is a composite conscience to which we all must listen.

II

We believe that the Communists seek to drive their slaves and themselves along exactly the opposite and downward direction, to the Satanic debasement of both man and his universe. We believe that communism is as utterly incompatible with all religion as it is contemptuous of all morality and destructive of all freedom. It is intrinsically evil. It must be opposed, therefore, with equal firmness, on religious grounds, moral grounds, and political grounds. We believe that the continued coexistence of communism and a Christian-style civilization on one planet is impossible. The struggle between them must end with one completely triumphant and the other completely destroyed. We intend to do our part, therefore, to halt, weaken, rout, and eventually to bury, the whole international Communist conspiracy.

III

We believe that means are as important as ends in any civilized society. Of all the falsehoods that have been so widely and deliberately circulated about us, none is so viciously untrue as the charge that we are willing to condone foul means for the sake of achieving praiseworthy ends. We think that communism as a way of life, for instance, is completely wrong; but our ultimate quarrel with the Communists is that they insist on imposing that way of life on the rest of us by murder, treason, and cruelty rather than by persuasion. Even if our own use of force ever becomes necessary and morally acceptable because it is in self-defense, we must never lose sight of the legal, traditional, and humanitarian considerations of a compassionate civilization. The Communists recognize no such compulsions, but this very ingredient of amoral brutishness will help to destroy them in the end.

IV

We believe in patriotism. Most of us will gladly concede that a parliament of nations, designed for the purpose of increasing the freedom and ease with which individuals, ideals, and goods might cross national boundaries, would be desirable. And we hope that in some future decade we may help to bring about such a step of progress in man's pursuit of peace, prosperity, and happiness. But we feel that the present United Nations was designed by its founders for the exactly opposite purpose of increasing the rigidity of Government controls over the lives and affairs of individual men. We believe it has become, as it was intended to become, a major instrumentality for the establishment of a one-world Communist tryanny over the population of the whole earth. One of our most immediate objectives, therefore, is to get the United States out of the United Nations, and the United Nations out of the United States. We seek thus to save our own country from the gradual and piecemeal surrender of its sovereignty to this Communists-controlled supergovernment, and to stop giving our support to the steady enslavement of other people through the machinations of this Communist agency.

V

We believe that a constitutional Republic, such as our Founding Fathers gave us, is probably the best of all forms of government. We believe that a democracy, which they tried hard to obviate, and into which the liberals have been trying for 50 years to convert our Republic, is one of the worst of all forms of government. We call attention to the fact that up to 1928 the U.S. Army Training Manual still gave our men in uniform the following quite accurate definition, which would have been thoroughly approved by the Constitutional Convention that established our Republic. 'Democracy: A Government of the masses. Authority derived through mass meeting or any form of direct expression results in mobocracy. Attitude toward property is communistic—negating property rights. Attitude towards law is that the will of the majority shall regulate, whether it be based upon deliberation or governed by passion, prejudice, and impulse, without restraint or regard to consequences. Results in demagogism, license, agitation, discontent, anarchy.' It is because all history proves this to be true that we repeat so emphatically: 'This is a Republic, not a democracy; let's keep it that way.'

VI

We are opposed to collectivism as a political and economic system, even when it does not have the police-state features of communism. We are opposed to it no matter whether the collectivism be called socialism or the welfare state or the New Deal or the Fair Deal or the New Frontier, or advanced under some other semantic disguise. And we are opposed to it no matter what may be the framework or form of government under which collectivism is imposed. We believe that increasing the size of government, increasing the centralization of government, and increasing the functions of government all act as brakes on material progress and as destroyers of personal freedom.

VII

We believe that even where the size and functions of government are properly limited, as much of the power and duties of government as possible should be retained in the hands of as small governmental units as possible, as close to the people served by such units as possible. For the tendencies of any governing body to waste, expansion, and despotism all increase with the distance of that body from the people governed; the more closely any governing body can be kept under observation by those who pay its bills and provide its delegated authority, the more honestly responsible it will be. And the diffusion of governmental power and functions is one of the greatest safeguards against tyranny man has yet devised. For this reason it is extremely important in our case to keep our township, city, County and State governments from being bribed and coerced into coming under one direct chain of control from Washington.

VIII

We believe that for any people eternal vigilance is the price of liberty far more as against the insidious encroachment of internal tyranny than against the danger of subjugation from the outside or from the prospect of any sharp and decisive revolution. In a republic we must constantly seek to elect and to keep in power a government we can trust, manned by people we can trust, maintaining a currency we can trust, and working for purposes we can trust (none of which we have today). We think it is even more important for the government to obey the laws than for the people to do so. But for 30 years we have had a steady stream of governments which increasingly have regarded our laws and even our Constitution as mere pieces of paper, which should not be allowed to stand in the way of what they, in their omniscient benevolence, considered to be 'for the greatest good of the greatest number.' (Or in their power-seeking plans pretended so to believe.) We want a restoration of a "government of laws, and not of men" in this country; and if a few impeachments are necessary to bring that about, then we are all for the impeachments.

IX

We believe that in a general way history repeats itself. For any combination of causes, similar to an earlier combination of causes, will lead as a rule to a combination of results somewhat similar to the one produced before. And history is simply a series of causes which produced results, and so on around cycles as clearly discernible as any of the dozens that take place elsewhere in the physical and biological sciences. But we believe that the most important history consists not of the repetitions but of the changes in these recurring links in the series. For the changes mark the extent to which man has either been able to improve himself and his environment, or has allowed both to deteriorate, since the last time around. We think that this true history is largely determined by ambitious individuals (both good and evil) and by small minorities who really know what they want. And in the John Birch Society our sense of gratitude and responsibility (to God and to the noble men of the past), for what we have inherited makes us determined to exert our influence, labor, and sacrifice for changes which we think will constitute improvement.

X

In summary, we are striving, by all honorable means at our disposal and to the limits of our energies and abilities, to bring about less government, more responsibility, and a better world. Because the Communists seek, always and everywhere, to bring about more government, less individual responsibility, and a completely amoral world, we would have to oppose them at every turn, even on the philosophical level. Because they are seeking through a gigantically organized conspiracy to destroy all opposition, we must fight them even more aggressively on the plane of action. But our struggle with the Communists, while the most urgent and important task before us today, is basically only incidental to our more important long-range and constructive purposes. For that very reason we are likely to be more effective against the Communists than if we were merely an ad hoc group seeking to expose and destroy so huge and powerful a gang of criminals. In organization, dedication, and purpose we offer a new form of opposition to the Communists which they have not faced in any other country. We have tried to raise a standard to which the wise and the honest can repair. We welcome all honorable allies in this present unceasing war. And we hope that once they and we and millions like us have won a decisive victory at last, many of these same allies will join us in our long look toward the future.

6. *We believe that grave imbalance now exists*

LLOYD W. LOWRY, Amending the Constitution to Strengthen the States in the Federal System. *Statement of Principles,* December 1962 *

The characteristic of our constitutional government, which has contributed most to the development of democratic processes and the preservation of human rights, is the division of the powers of government between the nation and the states on the one hand and between the executive, legislative and judicial departments of both state and federal governments on the other.

Over the years we have escaped the evils of despotism and totalitarianism. It is only when each division of the whole governmental structure insists upon the right to exercise its powers, unrestrained by any other division, that the proper balance can be maintained and constitutional government, as we understand it, preserved.

It is the responsibility of the central government to protect the people from invasion by the states of those rights which are guaranteed to them by the Federal Constitution. It is equally the obligation of the states to initiate and to prosecute to fruition the necessary procedures to protect the states and the people from unwarranted assumption of power by any department of the federal government.

The most sacred duty of all public officials, whether state or federal, and the highest patriotic responsibility of all citizens is to preserve, protect and defend the Constitution, including that portion of the Constitution intended to guarantee a government of dual sovereignty. When it becomes apparent that purposely or inadvertently, any department or agency of government has embarked upon a course calculated to destroy the balance of power essential to our system, it behooves all other departments and agencies acting within their respective spheres of jurisdiction to take all steps within their power necessary to avert the impending evil. We believe that grave imbalance now exists.

* *State Government,* Winter 1963, vol. XXXVI, no. 1, pp. 10–11. Reprinted by permission of the Council of State Governments.

Some federal judicial decisions involving powers of the federal and state governments carry a strong bias on the federal side, and consequently are bringing about a strong shift toward the extension of federal powers and the restraint of state powers. This shift tends to accelerate as each decision forms the basis and starting point for another extension of federal domination.

A greater degree of restraint on the part of the United States Supreme Court can do much, but experience shows that it is not likely to be sufficient. The basic difficulty is that the Supreme Court's decisions concerning the balance between federal and state power are final and can be changed in practice only if the states can muster sufficient interest in Congress, backed by a three-fourths majority of the states themselves to amend the Constitution. While the founding fathers fully expected and wished the words of the Constitution to have this degree of finality, it is impossible to believe that they envisaged such potency for the pronouncements of nine judges appointed by the President and confirmed by the Senate. The Supreme Court is, after all, an organ of the federal government. It is one of the three branches of the national government, and in conflicts over federal and state power, the Court is necessarily an agency of one of the parties in interest. As such, its decisions should not be assigned the same finality as the words of the Constitution itself. There is need for an easier method of setting such decisions straight when they are unsound.

To amend the Federal Constitution to correct specific decisions of the federal courts on specific points is desirable, but it will not necessarily stop the continuing drift toward more complete federal domination. The present situation has taken a long time to develop and may take a long time to remedy. Accordingly, some more fundamental and far-reaching change in the Federal Constitution is necessary to preserve and protect the states.

We appeal most earnestly to all branches of the federal government, and particularly to the highest federal court, to take diligent and impartial reflection upon the dangers to the nation inherent in the trends herein described. We urge them to evaluate the possibilities of an all-powerful central government with unlimited control over the lives of the people, the very opposite of self government under a federal system.

It is the ultimate of political ingenuity to achieve a vigorous federal system in which dynamic states combine with a responsible central government for the good of the people.

COERCED CONFORMITY

7. *Only an emergency can justify repression. Such must be the rule if authority is to be reconciled with freedom.*

JUSTICE BRANDEIS, concurring in Whitney v. California, 1927 *

. . . Those who won our independence believed that the final end of the state was to make men free to develop their faculties, and that in its government

* 274 U.S. 357 (1927), 374–7.

the deliberative forces should prevail over the arbitrary. They valued liberty both as an end and as a means. They believed liberty to be the secret of happiness and courage to be the secret of liberty. They believed that freedom to think as you will and to speak as you think are means indispensable to the discovery and spread of political truth; that without free speech and assembly discussion would be futile; that with them, discussion affords ordinarily adequate protection against the dissemination of noxious doctrine; that the greatest menace to freedom is an inert people; that public discussion is a political duty; and that this should be a fundamental principle of the American government. They recognized the risks to which all human institutions are subject. But they knew that order cannot be secured merely through fear of punishment for its infraction; that it is hazardous to discourage thought, hope and imagination; that fear breeds repression; that repression breeds hate; that hate menaces stable government; that the path of safety lies in the opportunity to discuss freely supposed grievances and proposed remedies; and that the fitting remedy for evil counsels is good ones. Believing in the power of reason as applied through public discussion, they eschewed silence coerced by law—the argument of force in its worst form. Recognizing the occasional tyrannies of governing majorities, they amended the Constitution so that free speech and assembly should be guaranteed.

Fear of serious injury cannot alone justify suppression of free speech and assembly. Men feared witches and burnt women. It is the function of speech to free men from the bondage of irrational fears. To justify suppression of free speech there must be reasonable ground to fear that serious evil will result if free speech is practiced. There must be reasonable ground to believe that the danger apprehended is imminent. There must be reasonable ground to believe that the evil to be prevented is a serious one. . . The wide difference between advocacy and incitement, between preparation and attempt, between assembling and conspiracy, must be borne in mind. In order to support a finding of clear and present danger it must be shown either that immediate serious violence was to be expected or was advocated, or that the past conduct furnished reason to believe that such advocacy was then contemplated.

Those who won our independence by revolution were not cowards. They did not fear political change. They did not exalt order at the cost of liberty. To courageous, self-reliant men, with confidence in the power of free and fearless reasoning applied through the processes of popular government, no danger flowing from speech can be deemed clear and present, unless the incidence of the evil apprehended is so imminent that it may befall before there is opportunity for full discussion. If there be time to expose through discussion the falsehood and fallacies, to avert the evil by the processes of education, the remedy to be applied is more speech, not enforced silence. Only an emergency can justify repression. Such must be the rule if authority is to be reconciled with freedom. Such, in my opinion, is the command of the Constitution. It is therefore always open to Americans to challenge a law abridging free speech and assembly by showing that there was no emergency justifying it.

Moreover, even imminent danger cannot justify resort to prohibition of these functions essential to effective democracy, unless the evil apprehended is relatively serious. Prohibition of free speech and assembly is a measure so stringent that it would be inappropriate as the means for averting a relatively trivial harm to society. A police measure may be unconstitutional merely because the remedy, although effective as means of protection, is unduly harsh or oppressive. . . The fact that speech is likely to result in some violence or in destruction of property is not enough to justify its suppression. There must be the probability of serious injury to the State. Among free men, the deterrents ordinarily to be applied to prevent crime are education and punishment for violations of the law, not abridgment of the rights of free speech and assembly. . .

8. *We must not sacrifice the liberties of our citizens in a misguided attempt to achieve national security*

HARRY S TRUMAN, Veto message withholding approval of the Internal Security Act of 1950 *

TO THE HOUSE OF REPRESENTATIVES:

I return herewith, without my approval, H.R. 9490, the proposed Internal Security Act of 1950.

The ostensible purpose . . . is to prevent persons who would be dangerous to our national security from entering the country or becoming citizens. In fact, present law already achieves that objective.

What these provisions would actually do is to prevent us from admitting to our country, or to citizenship, many people who could make real contributions to our national strength. The bill would deprive our Government and our intelligence agencies of the valuable services of aliens in security operations. It would require us to exclude and to deport the citizens of some friendly non-Communist countries. Furthermore, it would actually make it easier for subversive aliens to become United States citizens. Only the Communist movement would gain from such actions.

In brief, when all the provisions of H.R. 9490 are considered together, it is evident that the great bulk of them are not directed toward the real and present dangers that exist from communism. Instead of striking blows at communism, they would strike blows at our own liberties and at our position in the forefront of those working for freedom in the world. . .

The idea of requiring Communist organizations to divulge information about themselves is a simple and attractive one. But it is about as practical as requiring thieves to register with the sheriff. Obviously, no such organization as the Communist Party is likely to register voluntarily. . .

Unfortunately, these provisions are not merely ineffective and unworkable. They represent a clear and present danger to our institutions.

* House Document No. 708, 81st Congress, 2nd session, 2 September 1950, pp. 1–10 *passim*.

Insofar as the bill would require registration by the Communist Party itself, it does not endanger our traditional liberties. However, the application of the registration requirements to so-called Communist-front organizations can be the greatest danger to freedom of speech, press and assembly, since the alien and sedition laws of 1798. This danger arises out of the criteria or standards to be applied in determining whether an organization is a Communist-front organization.

There would be no serious problem if the bill required proof that an organization was controlled and financed by the Communist Party before it could be classified as a Communist-front organization. However, recognizing the difficulty of proving those matters, the bill would permit such a determination to be based solely upon 'the extent to which the positions taken or advanced by it from time to time on matters of policy do not deviate from those' of the Communist movement.

This provision could easily be used to classify as a Communist-front organization any organization which is advocating a single policy or objective which is also being urged by the Communist Party or by a Communist foreign government. In fact, this may be the intended result since the bill defines 'organization' to include 'a group of persons * * * permanently or temporarily associated together for joint action on any subject or subjects.' Thus, an organization which advocates low-cost housing for sincere humanitarian reasons might be classified as a Communist-front organization because the Communists regularly exploit slum conditions as one of their fifth-column techniques.

It is not enough to say that this probably would not be done. The mere fact that it could be done shows clearly how the bill would open a Pandora's box of opportunities for official condemnation of organizations and individuals for perfectly honest opinions which happen to be stated also by Communists.

The basic error of these sections is that they move in the direction of suppressing opinion and belief. This would be a very dangerous course to take, not because we have any sympathy for Communist opinions, but because any governmental stifling of the free expression of opinion is a long step toward totalitarianism.

There is no more fundamental axiom of American freedom than the familiar statement: In a free country we punish men for the crimes they commit but never for the opinions they have. And the reason this is so fundamental to freedom is not, as many suppose, that it protects the few unorthodox from suppression by the majority. To permit freedom of expression is primarily for the benefit of the majority, because it protects criticism, and criticism leads to progress.

We can and we will prevent espionage, sabotage, or other actions endangering our national security. But we would betray our finest traditions if we attempted, as this bill would attempt, to curb the simple expression of opinion. This we should never do, no matter how distasteful the opinion may be to the vast majority of our people. The course proposed by this bill would delight the Communists, for it would make a mockery of the Bill of Rights and of our claims to stand for freedom in the world.

And what kind of effect would these provisions have on the normal expression of political views? Obviously, if this law were on the statute books, the part of prudence would be to avoid saying anything that might be construed by someone as not deviating sufficiently from the current Communist-propaganda line. And since no one could be sure in advance what views were safe to express, the inevitable tendency would be to express no views on controversial subjects.

The result could only be to reduce the vigor and strength of our political life—an outcome that the Communists would happily welcome, but that freemen should abhor.

We need not fear the expression of ideas—we do need to fear their suppression.

Our position in the vanguard of freedom rests largely on our demonstration that the free expression of opinion, coupled with government by popular consent, leads to national strength and human advancement. Let us not, in cowering and foolish fear, throw away the ideals which are the fundamental basis of our free society. . .

There should be no room in our laws for such hysterical provisions. The next logical step would be to 'burn the books.' . .

But far more significant—and far more dangerous—is their apparent underlying purpose. Instead of trying to encourage the free movement of people, subject only to the real requirements of national security, these provisions attempt to bar movement to anyone who is, or once was, associated with ideas we dislike and, in the process, they would succeed in barring many people whom it would be to our advantage to admit.

Such an action would be a serious blow to our work for world peace. We uphold—or have upheld till now, at any rate—the concept of freedom on an international scale. That is the root concept of our efforts to bring unity among the free nations and peace in the world.

The Communists, on the other hand, attempt to break down in every possible way the free interchange of persons and ideas. It will be to their advantage, and not ours, if we establish for ourselves an 'iron curtain' against those who can help us in the fight for freedom. . .

I do not undertake lightly the responsibility of differing with the majority in both Houses of Congress who have voted for this bill. We are all Americans; we all wish to safeguard and preserve our constitutional liberties against internal and external enemies. But I cannot approve this legislation, which instead of accomplishing its avowed purpose would actually interfere with our liberties and help the Communist against whom the bill was aimed.

This is a time when we must marshal all our resources and all the moral strength of our free system in self-defense against the threat of Communist aggression. We will fail in this, and we will destroy all that we seek to preserve, if we sacrifice the liberties of our citizens in a misguided attempt to achieve national security.

9. *We are drawing about ourselves a cultural curtain similar to the iron curtain of our adversaries*

GEORGE F. KENNAN, *Seek the Finer Flavor*, 1954 *

There are forces at large in our society today that are too diffuse to be described by their association with the name of any one man or any one political concept.

They have no distinct organizational forms. They are as yet largely matters of the mind and the emotion in large masses of individuals. But they all march, in one way or another, under the banner of an alarmed and exercised anti-communism—but an anti-communism of a quite special variety, bearing an air of excited discovery and proprietorship, as though no one had ever known before that there was a communist danger; as though no one had ever thought about it and taken its measure; as though it had begun about the year 1945 and these people were the first to learn of it.

I have no quarrel to pick with the ostensible purpose of the people in which these forces are manifest. . . But I have the deepest misgivings about the direction and effects of their efforts. . .

They distort and exaggerate the dimensions of the problems with which they profess to deal. They confuse internal and external aspects of the communist threat. They insist on portraying as contemporary realities things that had their actuality years ago. They insist on ascribing to the workings of domestic communism evils and frustrations which, in so far as they were not part of the normal and unavoidable burden of complexity in our life, were the product of our behavior generally as a nation, and should today be the subject of humble and contrite soul-searching on the part of all of us, in a spirit of brotherhood and community, rather than of frantic and bitter recrimination.

And having thus incorrectly stated the problem, it is no wonder that these people constantly find the wrong answers. They tell us to remove our eyes from the constructive and positive purposes and to pursue with fanaticism the negative and vindictive ones. They sow timidity where there should be boldness; fear where there should be serenity; suspicion where there should be confidence and generosity. In this way they impel us—in the name of our salvation from the dangers of communism—to many of the habits of thought and action which our Soviet adversaries, I am sure, would most like to see us adopt and which they have tried unsuccessfully over a period of some thirty-five years to graft upon us through the operations of their Communist party.

These forces are narrowly exclusive in their approach to our world position, and carry this exclusiveness vigorously into the field of international cultural exchanges. They tend to stifle the interchange of cultural impulses that is vital to the progress of the intellectual and artistic life of our people. The people in question seem to feel either that cultural values are not important at all or that America has reached the apex of cultural achievement and no longer needs in

* From *Is the Common Man Too Common?* by Joseph Wood Krutch and others, copyright 1954 by University of Oklahoma Press. Reprinted by permission of the University of Oklahoma Press.

any serious way the stimulus of normal contact with other peoples in the field of arts and letters.

They look with suspicion both on the sources of intellectual and artistic activity in this country and on impulses of this nature coming to us from abroad. The remote pasts of foreign artists and scholars are anxiously scanned before they are permitted to enter our land, and this is done in proceedings so inflexible in concept and offensive in execution that their very existence often constitutes a discouragement to cultural interchange. The personal movements and affairs of great scholars and artists are thus passed upon and controlled by people who have no inkling of understanding for the work these same scholars and artists perform.

In this way, we begin to draw about ourselves a cultural curtain similar in some respects to the Iron Curtain of our adversaries. In doing so, we tend to inflict upon ourselves a species of cultural isolation and provincialism wholly out of accord with the traditions of our nation and destined, if unchecked, to bring to our intellectual and artistic life the same sort of sterility from which the cultural world of our Communist adversaries is already suffering.

Within the framework of our society, as in its relations to external environment, the tendency of these forces is exclusive and intolerant—quick to reject, slow to receive, intent on discovering what ought not to be rather than what ought to be. They claim the right to define a certain area of our national life and cultural output as beyond the bounds of righteous approval. This definition is never effected by vague insinuation and suggestion. And the circle, as I say, tends to grow constantly narrower. One has the impression that, if uncountered, these people would eventually narrow the area of political and cultural respectability to a point where it included only themselves, the excited accusers, and excluded everything and everybody not embraced in the profession of denunciation.

I recall reading recently, twice in one day, the words of individuals who proclaimed that if certain other people did not get up and join actively in the denunciation of Communists or communism, they would thereby themselves be suspect. What sort of arrogance is this? Every one of us has his civic obligations. Every one of us has his moral obligations to principles.

I am not condoning anyone for forgetting these obligations. But to go beyond this—to say that it is not enough to be a law-abiding citizen—to say that we all have some obligation to get up and make statements of this tenor or that with respect to other individuals, or else submit to being classified as suspect in the eyes of our fellow citizens—to assert this is to establish a new species of public ritual, to arrogate to one's individual self the powers of the spiritual and temporal law-giver, to make the definition of social conduct a matter of fear in the face of vague and irregular forces, rather than a matter of confidence in the protecting discipline of conscience and the law.

I have lived more than ten years of my life in totalitarian countries. I know where this sort of things leads. I know it to be the most shocking and cynical disservice one can do to the credulity and to the spiritual equilibrium of one's fellow men. And this sort of thing cannot fail to have its effect on the liberal arts, for it is associated with two things that stand in deepest conflict to the development of mind and spirit: with a crass materialism and anti-intellectualism on the one hand, and with a marked tendency toward a standardization and conformity on the other.

In these forces I have spoken about, it seems to me that I detect a conscious rejection and ridicule of intellectual effort and distinction. They come together here with a deep-seated weakness in the American character: a certain shy self-consciousness that tends to deny interests other than those of business, sport, or war.

There is a powerful strain of our American cast of mind that has little use for the artist or the writer, and professes to see in the pursuits of such people a lack of virility—as though virility could not find expression in the creation of beauty, as though Michelangelo had never wielded his brush, as though Dante had never taken up his pen, as though the plays of Shakespeare were lacking in manliness. The bearers of this neomaterialism seem, indeed, to have a strange self-consciousness about the subject of virility—a strange need to emphasize and demonstrate it by exhibitions of taciturnity, callousness, and physical aggressiveness—as though there were some anxiety lest, in the absence of these exhibitions, it might be found wanting.

What weakness is it in us Americans that so often makes us embarrassed or afraid to indulge the gentle impulse to seek the finer and rarer flavor, to admit frankly and without stammering apologies to an appreciation for the wonder of the poet's word and the miracle of the artist's brush, for all the beauty, in short, that has been recorded in the images of word and line created by the hands of men in past ages? What is it that causes us to huddle together, herd-like, in tastes and enthusiasms that represent only the common denominator of popular acquiescence, rather than to show ourselves receptive to the tremendous flights of creative imagination of which the individual mind has shown itself capable? Is it that we are forgetful of the true sources of our moral strength, afraid of ourselves, afraid to look into the chaos of our own breasts, afraid of the bright, penetrating light of the great teachers?

This fear of the untypical, this quest for security within the walls of secular uniformity—these are traits of our national character we would do well to beware of and to examine for their origins. They receive much encouragement these days, much automatic and unintended encouragement, by virtue of the growing standardization of the cultural and, in many respects, the educational influences to which our people are being subjected.

The immense impact of commercial advertising and the mass media on our lives is—let us make no mistake about it—an impact that tends to encourage passivity, to encourage acquiescence and uniformity, to place handicaps on individual contemplativeness and creativeness. It may not seem to many of us too dangerous that we should all live, dress, eat, hear and read substantially alike. But we forget how easily this uniformity of thought and habit can be exploited, when the will to exploit it is there. We forget how easily it can slip over into the domination of our spiritual and political lives by self-appointed custodians who contrive to set themselves at the head of popular emotional currents.

There is a real and urgent danger here for anyone who values the right to differ from others in any manner whatsoever, be it in his interests or his associations or his faith. There is no greater mistake we of this generation can make than to imagine that the tendencies which in other countries have led to the nightmare of totalitarianism will, as they appear in our midst, politely pause—out of some delicate respect for American tradition—at the point where they would begin to affect our independence of mind and belief.

The forces of intolerance and political demagoguery are greedy forces, and unrestrained. There is no limit to their ambitions or their impudence. They contain within themselves no mechanism of self-control. Like the ills in Pandora's box, once released they can be stopped only by forces external to themselves. The only permanent thing behind them all is still the naked vulnerable, human soul, the scene of the age-old battle between good and evil, assailed with weakness and imperfections, always in need of help and support, and yet sometimes capable of such breath-taking impulses of faith and creative imagination.

Finally, it lies with the devotees of the liberal arts to combat the forces of intolerance in our society: to convince people that these forces are incompatible with the flowering of the human spirit, to remember that the ultimate judgments of good and evil are not ours to make: that the wrath of man against his fellow man must always be tempered by the recollection of his weakness and fallibility and by the example of forgiveness and redemption which is the essence of his Christian heritage.

10. *We need the non-conformist*

LEARNED HAND, *A Plea for the Freedom of Dissent*, 1955 *

What do we mean by 'principles of civil liberties and human rights'? We cannot go far in that inquiry until we have achieved some notion of what we mean by Liberty; and that has always proved a hard concept to define. The natural, though naïve, opinion is that it means no more than that each individual shall be allowed to pursue his own desires without let or hindrance; and that, although it is true that this is practically impossible, still it does remain the goal, approach to which measures our success. Why, then, is not a beehive or an anthill a perfect example of a free society? Surely you have been a curious and amused watcher beside one of these. . .

Why is it that we so positively rebel against the hive and the hill as a specimen of a free society? Why is it that such prototypes of totalitarianisms arouse our deepest hostility? Unhappily it is not because they cannot be realized, or at least because they cannot be approached, for a substantial period. Who can be sure that such appalling forecasts as Aldous Huxley's 'Brave New

* *New York Times Magazine*, 6 February 1955. An address at the forty-eighth annual meeting of the American Jewish Committee, Roosevelt Hotel, 26 January 1955.

World' or Orwell's '1984' are not prophetic? Indeed, there have often been near approaches to such an order. . .

Nor need we be surprised that men so often embrace almost any doctrines, if they are proclaimed with a voice of absolute assurance. In a universe that we do not understand, but with which we must in one way or another somehow manage to deal, and aware of the conflicting desires that clamorously beset us, between which we must choose and which we must therefore manage to weigh, we turn in our bewilderment to those who tell us that they have found a path out of the thickets and possess the scales by which to appraise our needs.

Over and over again such prophets succeed in converting us to unquestioning acceptance; there is scarcely a monstrous belief that has not had its day and its passionate adherents, so eager are we for safe footholds in our dubious course. How certain is any one of us that he, too, might not be content to follow any fantastic creed, if he was satisfied that nothing would ever wake him from the dream? And, indeed, if there were nothing to wake him, how should he distinguish its articles from the authentic dictates of verity? . . .

All discussion, all debate, all dissidence tends to question and in consequence to upset existing convictions: that is precisely its purpose and its justification. He is, indeed, a 'subversive' who disputes those precepts that I most treasure and seeks to persuade me to substitute his own. He may have no shadow of desire to resort to anything but persuasion; he may be of those to whom any forcible sanction of conformity is anathema; yet it remains true that he is trying to bring about my apostasy, and I hate him just in proportion as I fear his success.

Contrast this protective resentment with the assumption that lies at the base of our whole system that the best chance for truth to emerge is a fair field for all ideas. Nothing, I submit, more completely betrays our latent disloyalty to this premise to all that we pretend to believe than the increasingly common resort to this and other question-begging words. Their imprecision comforts us by enabling us to suppress arguments that disturb our complacency and yet to continue to congratulate ourselves on keeping the faith as we have received it from the Founding Fathers.

Heretics have been hateful from the beginning of recorded time; they have been ostracized, exiled, tortured, maimed and butchered; but it has generally proved impossible to smother them, and when it has not, the society that has succeeded has always declined. Façades of authority, however imposing, do not survive after it has appeared that they rest upon the sands of human conjecture and compromise.

And so, if I am to say what are 'the principles of civil liberties and human rights,' I answer that they lie in habits, customs—conventions, if you will—that tolerate dissent and can live without irrefragable certainties; that are ready to overhaul existing assumptions; that recognize that we never see save through a glass, darkly, and that at long last we shall succeed only so far as we continue to undertake 'the intolerable labor of thought'—that most distasteful of all our activities.

If such a habit and such a temper pervade a society, it will not need institutions to protect its 'civil liberties and human rights'; so far as they do not, I venture to doubt how far anything else can protect them: whether it be Bills of Rights, or courts that must in the name of interpretation read their meaning into them. . .

It is still in the lap of the gods whether a society can succeed, based on 'civil liberties and human rights,' conceived as I have tried to describe them; but of one thing at least we may be sure; the alternatives that have so far appeared have been immeasurably worse, and so, whatever the outcome, I submit to you that we must press along. Borrowing from Epictetus, let us say to ourselves: 'Since we are men we will play the part of a Man,' and how can I better end than by recalling to you the concluding passage of 'Prometheus Unbound'?

> To suffer woes which Hope thinks infinite;
> To forgive wrongs darker than death or night;
> To defy Power, which seems omnipotent
> To love, and bear; to hope till Hope creates
> From its own wreck the thing it contemplates;
> Neither to change, nor falter, nor repent;
> This, like thy glory, Titan, is to be
> Good, great and joyous, beautiful and free;
> This is alone Life, Joy, Empire and Victory.

THE RACE ISSUE

11. *In all things that are purely social we can be as separate as the fingers, yet one as the hand in all things essential to mutual progress*

BOOKER T. WASHINGTON, *The Atlanta Exposition Address*, 1895 *

One-third of the population of the South is of the Negro race. No enterprise seeking the material, civil, or moral welfare of this section can disregard this element of our population and reach the highest success. I but convey to you, Mr. President and Directors, the sentiment of the masses of my race when I say that in no way have the value and manhood of the American Negro been more fittingly and generously recognized than by the managers of this magnificent Exposition at every stage of its progress. It is a recognition that will do more to cement the friendship of the two races than any occurrence since the dawn of our freedom.

Our greatest danger is that in the great leap from slavery to freedom we may overlook the fact that the masses of us are to live by the productions of our hands, and fail to keep in mind that we shall prosper in proportion as we learn to dignify and glorify common labour and put brains and skill into the common occupations of life; shall prosper in proportion as we learn to draw the line between the superficial and the substantial, the ornamental gewgaws of

* *Up from Slavery*, New York, Doubleday and Company, 1900, pp. 218–25 *passim*.

life and the useful. No race can prosper till it learns that there is as much dignity in tilling a field as in writing a poem. It is at the bottom of life we must begin, and not at the top. Nor should we permit our grievances to overshadow our opportunities.

To those of the white race who look to the incoming of those of foreign birth and strange tongue and habits for the prosperity of the South, were I permitted I would repeat what I say to my own race, 'Cast down your bucket where you are.' Cast it down among the eight millions of Negroes whose habits you know, whose fidelity and love you have tested in days when to have proved treacherous meant the ruin of your firesides. Cast down your bucket among these people who have, without strikes and labour wars, tilled your fields, cleared your forests, builded your railroads and cities, and brought forth treasures from the bowels of the earth, and helped make possible this magnificent representation of the progress of the South. Casting down your bucket among my people, helping and encouraging them as you are doing on these grounds, and to education of head, hand, and heart, you will find that they will buy your surplus land, make blossom the waste places in your fields, and run your factories. While doing this, you can be sure in the future, as in the past, that you and your families will be surrounded by the most patient, faithful, law-abiding, and unresentful people that the world has seen. As we have proved our loyalty to you in the past, in nursing your children, watching by the sick-bed of your mothers and fathers, and often following them with tear-dimmed eyes to their graves, so in the future, in our humble way, we shall stand by you with a devotion that no foreigner can approach, ready to lay down our lives, if need be, in defence of yours, interlacing our industrial, commercial, civil, and religious life with yours in a way that shall make the interests of both races one. In all things that are purely social we can be as separate as the fingers, yet one as the hand in all things essential to mutual progress.

There is no defence or security for any of us except in the highest intelligence and development of all. If anywhere there are efforts tending to curtail the fullest growth of the Negro, let these efforts be turned into stimulating, encouraging, and making him the most useful and intelligent citizen. . .

The wisest among my race understand that the agitation of questions of social equality is the extremest folly, and that progress in the enjoyment of all the privileges that will come to us must be the result of severe and constant struggle rather than of artificial forcing. No race that has anything to contribute to the markets of the world is long in any degree ostracized. It is important and right that all privileges of the law be ours, but it is vastly more important that we be prepared for the exercises of these privileges. The opportunity to earn a dollar in a factory just now is worth infinitely more than the opportunity to spend a dollar in an opera-house.

In conclusion, may I repeat that nothing in thirty years has given us more hope and encouragement, and drawn us so near to you of the white race, as this opportunity offered by the Exposition; and here bending, as it were, over the altar that represents the results of the struggles of your race and mine, both starting practically empty-handed three decades ago, I pledge that in your effort to work out the great and intricate problem which God has laid at the doors of the South, you shall have at all times the patient, sympathetic help of my race; only let this be constantly in mind, that, while from representations in these buildings of the product of field, of forest, of mine, of factory, letters, and art, much good will come, yet far above and beyond material benefits will be that higher good, that, let us pray God, will come, in a blotting out of sectional differences and racial animosities and suspicions, in a determination to administer absolute justice, in a willing obedience among all classes to the mandates of law. This, this, coupled with our material prosperity, will bring into our beloved South a new heaven and a new earth.

12. *I don't think you can live with yourself when you are humiliating the man next to you*

ROBERT PENN WARREN, *Segregation: The Inner Conflict in the South*, 1956 *

There is one more interview I wish to put on record. I shall enter it by question and answer.

Q. You're a Southerner, aren't you?

A. Yes.

Q. Are you afraid of the power state?

A. Yes.

Q. Do you think the Northern press sometimes distorts Southern news?

A. Yes.

Q. Assuming that they do, why do they do it?

A. They like to feel good.

Q. What do you think the South ought to do about that distortion?

A. Nothing.

Q. Nothing? What do you mean, nothing?

A. The distortion—that's the Yankees' problem, not ours.

Q. You mean they ought to let the South work out a way to live with the Negro?

A. I don't think the problem is to learn to live with the Negro.

Q. What is it then?

A. It is to learn to live with ourselves.

Q. What do you mean?

A. I don't think you can live with yourself when you are humiliating the man next to you.

Q. Don't you think the races have made out pretty well, considering?

A. Yes. By some sort of human decency and charity, God knows how. But there was always an image of something else.

Q. An image?

A. Well, I knew an old lady who grew up in a black county, but a county where relations had been, as they say, good. She had a fine farm and a good brick house, and when she got old she sort of retired from the world. The hottest summer weather and she would lock all the doors and windows at night, and lie there in the airless dark. But sometimes she'd telephone to town in the middle of the night. She would telephone that somebody was burning the Negroes out there on her place. She could hear their screams. Something was going on in her old head which in another place and time would not have been going on in her old head. She had never, I should think, seen an act of violence in her life. But something was going on in her head.

Q. Do you think it is chiefly the red-neck who causes violence?

A. No. He is only the cutting edge. He, too, is a victim. Responsibility is a seamless garment. And the northern boundary of that garment is not the Ohio River.

Q. Are you for desegregation?

A. Yes.

Q. When will it come?

A. Not soon.

Q. When?

A. When enough people, in a particular place, a particular county or state, cannot live with themselves any more. Or realize they don't have to.

Q. What do you mean, don't have to?

A. When they realize that desegregation is just one small episode in the long effort for justice. It seems to me that that perspective, suddenly seeing the business as little, is a liberating one. It liberates you from yourself.

Q. Then you think it is a moral problem?

A. Yes, but no moral problem gets solved abstractly. It has to be solved in a context for possible solution.

Q. Can contexts be changed?

A. Sure. We might even try to change them the right way.

Q. Aren't you concerned about possible racial amalgamation?

A. I don't even think about it. We have to deal with the problem our historical moment proposes, the burden of our time. We all live with a thousand unsolved problems of justice all the time. We don't even recognize a lot of them. We have to deal only with those which the moment proposes to us. Anyway, we can't legislate for posterity. All we can do for posterity is to try to plug along in a way to make them think we—the old folks—did the best we could for justice, as we could understand it.

Q. Are you a gradualist on the matter of segregation?

A. If by gradualist you mean a person who would create delay for the sake of delay, then no. If by gradualist you mean a person who thinks it will take time, not time as such, but time for an educational process, preferably a calculated one, then yes. I mean a process of mutual education for whites and blacks. And part of this education should be in the actual beginning of the process of desegregation. It's a silly question, anyway, to ask if somebody is a gradualist. Gradualism is all you'll get. History, like nature, knows no jumps. Except the jump backward, maybe.

Q. Has the South any contribution to make to the national life?

A. It has made its share. It may again.

Q. How?

A. If the South is really able to face up to itself and its situation, it may achieve identity, moral identity. Then in a country where moral identity is hard to come by, the South, because it has had to deal concretely with a moral problem, may offer some leadership. And we need any we can get. If we are to break out of the national rhythm, the rhythm between complacency and panic.

◄

This is, of course, an interview with myself.

13. *Neither satisfaction nor peace can come from any coercive mingling of the white and black races against the will of either*

WILLIAM D. WORKMAN, JR., *The Case for the South*, 1960 *

The South is being scourged by four pestilential forces which impose an almost intolerable burden upon Americans who cherish state sovereignty, constitutional government, and racial integrity. On the one hand are these three: the Supreme Court of the United States, which has wrought havoc in its injudicious effort to play at sociology; the National Association for the Advancement of Colored People, which has recklessly undertaken to achieve race-mixing by pressure; and the Northern politicians and propagandists who pervert small truths into big lies as they purvey vilification and ignorance on a grand scale. On the other hand is the Ku Klux Klan with its unlovely cohorts who substitute muscle and meanness for the intellect which by rights must be the defense of the South.

The man in the middle is the one whose voice needs to be heard, for too long has his quiet but determined resistance to tyranny from either side been unheralded and unexplained. Yet he has a case, a strong case, rooted in American soil and nurtured in Southern tradition. In plain terms his case is simply this: He demands for his state the right to administer its own domestic affairs, and he demands for himself the right to rear his children in the school atmosphere most conducive to their learning—all without hurt or harm to his Negro neighbor or to the Negro's children. . .

The integrationists have succeeded, through their long years of persistent and persuasive propaganda, in dragging the school segregation question into the realm of morality. In doing so, they may have achieved a major purpose and a major advantage, but they have simultaneously laid the basis for opposition which, by invoking morality on *its* side, becomes all the more resistant to change.

So long as social problems grow out of disputed facts, or even out of contrary

* Published by The Devin-Adair Company, 1960, pp. vii–viii, 121–2, 126–30, 185–7, 299–300 *passim*. Reprinted by permission of The Devin-Adair Company.

opinions, there is hope of reconciliation or compromise. The application of good sense and good will, coupled with a studious examination of the facts of the matter, frequently can resolve differences and result in what the Quakers call, with apt phrase, 'the sense of the meeting.'

But once a controversy becomes enmeshed in opposing *moral* values, the likelihood of an amicable solution fades away into nothingness. For one thing, advocates on each side then promptly discard all thoughts of compromise, saying fervently, albeit sometimes fatuously, that 'right is on our side.' Today's integrationists, like yesterday's abolitionists, proceed on the adamant assumption so virulently stated by the anti-slavery, anti-Southern, anti-segregationist Charles Sumner: 'There is no other side.' When such dogmatic morality enters the picture, reason flies out the window.

In this fight over the issue of racial segregation, the cause of 'morality' so piously advanced by the integrationists falls flat because there is no sense of 'immorality' on the part of the segregationists. Despite the refusal of the NAACP and its colleagues to recognize or acknowledge the fact, there is a widespread and honest conviction among hosts of white Southerners that racial separation is a positive good for BOTH races, at least at this stage of the cultural development of the two. There are, of course, countless Southerners who do not foresee any time when racial intermingling will be desirable or inevitable, but even those who do admit that possibility are for the most part sincerely opposed to integration at present.

Being of that mind, they feel no sense of wrong-doing in seeking to preserve a social structure they genuinely feel to be right, proper, and desirable. Consequently, these Southerners are not being influenced by the efforts of their integrationist preceptors to shame them into another way of life. Instead of giving rise to any sense of condition and correction, all this moralizing by the integrationists simply antagonizes Southerners who are satisfied that their course of conduct is the correct one in this time and in this place. . .

Anything that pits the Southern white against the Southern Negro simply because of color does a disservice to both. If there be any peaceable adjustment of the complex problem of race relations, it must be bi-lateral. Somehow, somewhere, and sometime, there must be a meeting of the minds for the formulation of a pattern of peace, progress, and prosperity for both races. Such a pattern can hardly be expected to emerge from an atmosphere laden with racial animosity. Yet such animosity is bound to spread and deepen with every arbitrary act based solely on racial considerations.

If the integration issue is forced to the point of an ultimate setting of white man against black man on a basis of color alone, then the consequences will indeed be fearful. Yet just that sort of an eventuality is embodied in the constant drive of the NAACP and the rest of the 'Do-gooders Alliance' toward integration by force.

Already the intensity of the controversy has driven most of the 'moderates' from the field of public debate. If the fight gets hotter, then inevitably sides will have to be taken on a basis of color alone, and that means black versus white in every sphere of Southern life. It will mean that nothing will exist between the two opposing camps save a no man's land into which individuals venture at considerable risk. . . .

The News and Courier, of Charleston, S. C., gives this unhappy estimate of such a situation (23 July 1957):

'If and when a showdown is forced on the South, the whites will prove themselves richer, stronger, smarter and more numerous than the Negroes. They are also on home ground. It would be difficult to drive them out of their positions even with the bayonets that President Eisenhower assures the public he has no intention of using. To tear up the South for the sake of empty promises of "equality" would be more ruinous to the Negroes than to the whites.'

Integration, to the non-Southerner, is a matter of hypothesis, perhaps caught up with the stuff of 'brotherhood' and 'democracy' as spuriously applied to the issue. Integration will not affect HIS way of life one whit; it will not compel HIS children to enter a strange and strained school world where cross-currents—cultural, moral, and intellectual—will create such discord as to nullify the learning process; it will not evoke in HIM the perpetual concern over the possibility of physical strife flaring up within or without the classroom, or within the community itself. No, to the non-Southerner, all this is academic—an interesting sociological experiment bedecked with the outward trappings of altruism but internally loaded with explosive potentialities.

Yet this non-Southerner is all too willing to acclaim the Supreme Court for its determination to reorder the life of a quarter of the nation; to applaud the President for dispatching combat-hardened troops into the South to enforce integration; and to sustain self-serving politicians who use the issue as a vote-getting device.

All this makes for an unwholesome rejection of the American belief that government derives its just powers from the consent of the governed. The arbitrary action of nine men who comprised the Supreme Court of the United States in May of 1954 not only swept aside the legal precedents of generations, but in effect established a new form of school government in a large area of the nation, without in any wise seeking the consent of the people most affected by that major alteration in the governmental structure.

There is something essentially repellent to the American sense of fair play in this manifestation of federal authority. As reported time and again by observers on those scenes where integration has actually been achieved, the general public even in those areas remains opposed to that pattern of racial admixture and would much prefer separation of the races in the public schools. Yet the will of the people counts for nothing. Significantly, the federal authorities have not even sought an expression of the will of the people on a national level to determine whether they support the action of the federal judiciary.

The time may come when the federal government will have to decide precisely how ruthless it is willing to be in compelling Southerners to accept race-mixing on terms unacceptable to the South. It must decide whether it is willing to impose a major injustice upon the entire South in order to correct whatever minor injustice may conceivably be involved in requiring Negro students to study among their own kind, if self-association in fact be an injustice. If in reaching that decision, the government places the preferences of Negroes above the rights of whites, a crisis in the exercise of governmental authority inevitably will arise. There are hosts of Southerners who will submit to nothing short of pure, unadulterated force if the issue is pressed to the ultimate. The depth of their feeling on the subject of integration is as great as that which motivated the Roman Catholic Bishops of the United States in their November 16, 1957, statement with respect to obscenity in literature and motion pictures, wherein they argued for 'the right of parents to bring up their children in an atmosphere reasonably free from defilement, the right of children to be protected from grave and insidious moral danger, the right of all not to be assailed at every turn by a display of indecency.'

It may be ferociously denied that there is any analogy between integration and obscenity, but in the minds of a myriad Southerners, the one is to be resisted as fiercely as the other. That is a frame of mind which the non-Southerner, and the federal government, may as well accept as existing, even if it may be incomprehensible to those who have never lived among masses of black folk. . .

It is a fair and practical question to ask now whether anything constructive can be salvaged out of all the unpleasantness which has stemmed from the fight over racial integration. The answer might well be 'Yes,' a qualified 'Yes.'

The prospect of improving race relations in the face of intense resistance to integration is admittedly difficult under present pressures and hostilities; yet there are changes which can and should be made, not only for the improved welfare of Negro Southerners, but also for the justification of many arguments used by white Southerners against forced integration.

In any attempt to approach this delicately balanced situation, the advocate of change or relaxation immediately runs head on into a major division of opinion. There are those who contend that any concession whatever will tend to weaken the South's position, to crack the dike of resistance, and to make for an ultimate flooding as the dam breaks. On the other hand, there are those of equal sincerity who argue that SOME abridgments of the adamant segregation pattern MUST be made if the South is to successfully defend its main line of resistance, i.e., the schools. Despite these contrary positions, there IS some hope of improved race relations by virtue of the fact that these two groups BOTH oppose racial integration in the schools. It may be that in joint resistance against a common foe they might find a basis for agreement on certain changes which might ease the situation, improving the lot of the Negro without damaging the lot of the white man.

For one thing, there should be some relaxation of both the legal and the social barriers which obstruct voluntary association of whites and Negroes. Much of the Southern argument against the Supreme Court decision has been based on the interpretation (whether correct or incorrect is beside the point) that enforcement of the decision would deny to the Southern man a freedom of choice as to where his child should attend school. Along with that has gone an extension of the same line of reasoning and its application into other fields

—housing, churches, and so on. The essence of the white man's argument has been this: The individual should be protected in his right of freedom of association, and correspondingly, of freedom to AVOID unwanted association.

But by the same token, if the Southern segregationist wants to be free in his determination of associates, so should the Southern integrationist be free in HIS determination of associates provided, of course, that such associations are mutually acceptable, and provided further that the circumstances and conditions of integrated associations are not such as to endanger the public peace.

Much of the legislation enacted in the Southern states in both the immediate and the distant past has been aimed basically at preserving domestic tranquility as well as racial integrity. This is especially true in the fields of education and recreation, where indiscriminate mingling of the races is bound to bring discord and strife. Whatever the future may bring, and whatever may be the judgment of non-Southerners, the governmental agencies of the South are acting wisely when they seek to prevent mass mingling of the races in schools, pools, and parks. And distressing though it may be, the closing of such institutions in many cases would be the sensible alternative to the emotional, social, and physical upheaval which would follow on the heels of forced race mixing.

But where there is willingness to mix, and where such mixing would not jeopardize the public peace nor infringe upon the rights of others NOT to mix, some concessions are in order. Neither the written law of the political agency nor the unwritten law of the social community should stand in the way of whites and Negroes foregathering to confer, to discuss, or even to dine together with each other's consent and cooperation. The fact that such bi-racial activities might be distasteful to a large percentage of Southern whites should not be allowed to stand in the way of the integrationists' exercise of the right of peaceable assembly.

If an area of bi-racial activity can be carved out of the no-man's-land which now separates the two races by law in most Southern communities, there seems no cause for undue alarm. If the South is to protect the right of some (most) white people to move within segregated circles, then in all fairness it should permit other white people to move within integrated circles if that be their wish. For many years to come, the impetus of such movement will have to be from the whites to the Negroes, but the Southern argument against compulsory integration should apply with equal validity against compulsory segregation of those inclined, however mistakenly, toward racial commingling, so long as the rights of all are protected with respect to preference of association.

Short of utter amalgamation of the races, a thing utterly unacceptable to white Southerners, there is no *solution* to the problem of race relations: there can only be a continual adjustment and readjustment of relationships. The sense of race, no less than those of religion or of nationality, is so deeply embedded in man's nature—both conscious and unconscious—that it cannot be eradicated in the foreseeable future, if indeed it *should* be eradicated. Some persons, whose impulses can be regulated or whose incentives can be manipulated, may rise above, or descend below, race consciousness, but the masses are not likely ever to shed their recognition of race.

Whatever may be the future of race relations in America, this much seems evident: That neither satisfaction nor peace can come from any coercive mingling of the white and black races against the will of either, and that little hope can be entertained for any assimilation of one in the other. There remains, then, only the prospect of accommodating their differences in a pattern of peaceful co-existence based upon a friendly tolerance and helpful understanding. It is the recognition of racial distinctions, not their denial, which will lessen the tensions and enhance their adjustment.

There is serious need now for a thorough reassessment of the entire picture of race relations—North and South—and for what the phrase-makers might call another "agonizing reappraisal" of the costs and the consequences of the nation's forced march toward integration. The time is ripe for both sides—for all sides—of the several controversies to inventory their successes and their failures. Fresh decisions need to be made in the light of matters as they stand now, and as they seem likely to develop in the near future.

14. *If the inexpressible cruelties of slavery could not stop us, the opposition we now face will surely fail*

MARTIN LUTHER KING, Letter from Birmingham City Jail, 16 April 1963 *

Birmingham is probably the most thoroughly segregated city in the United States. Its ugly record of police brutality is known in every section of this country. Its unjust treatment of Negroes in the courts is a notorious reality. There have been more unsolved bombings of Negro homes and churches in Birmingham than any city in this Nation. . .

You may well ask, 'Why direct action? Why sit-ins, marches, etc.? Isn't negotiation a better path?' You are exactly right in your call for negotiation. Indeed, this is the purpose of direct action. Nonviolent direct action seeks to create such a crisis and establish such creative tension that a community that has constantly refused to negotiate is forced to confront the issue. It seeks so to dramatize the issue that it can no longer be ignored. . .

For years now I have heard the word 'Wait!' It rings in the ear of every Negro with a piercing familiarity. This 'wait' has almost always meant 'never.' It has been a tranquilizing thalidomide, relieving the emotional stress for a moment, only to give birth to an ill-formed infant of frustration.

The nations of Asia and Africa are moving with jet-like speed toward the goal of political independence, and we still creep at horse and buggy pace toward the gaining of a cup of coffee at a lunch counter.

* In answer to eight leading white clergymen of Birmingham who urged negotiation. Published by the American Friends Service Committee, May 1963.

I guess it is easy for those who have never felt the stinging darts of segregation to say wait. But when you have seen vicious mobs lynch your mothers and fathers at will and drown your sisters and brothers at whim;

When you have seen hate-filled policemen curse, kick, brutalize, and even kill your black brothers and sisters with impunity;

When you see the vast majority of your 20 million Negro brothers smothering in an air-tight cage of poverty in the midst of an affluent society;

When you suddenly find your tongue twisted and your speech stammering as you seek to explain to your six-year-old daughter why she can't go to the public amusement park that has just been advertised on television, and see tears welling up in her little eyes when she is told that Funtown is closed to colored children, and see the depressing clouds of inferiority begin to form in her little mental sky, and see her begin to distort her little personality by unconsciously developing a bitterness toward white people;

When you have to concoct an answer for a five-year-old son asking in agonizing pathos: 'Daddy, why do white people treat colored people so mean?'

When you take a cross-country drive and find it necessary to sleep night after night in the uncomfortable corners of your automobile because no motel will accept you;

When you are humiliated day in and day out by nagging signs reading 'white' men and 'colored';

When your first name becomes 'nigger' and your middle name becomes 'boy' (however old you are) and your last name becomes 'John,' and when your wife and mother are never given the respected title 'Mrs.';

When you are harried by day and haunted by night by the fact that you are a Negro, living constantly at tip-toe stance never quite knowing what to expect next, and plagued with inner fears and outer resentments;

When you are forever fighting a degenerating sense of 'nobodiness';—then you will understand why we find it difficult to wait.

You express a great deal of anxiety over our willingness to break laws. This is certainly a legitimate concern. Since we so diligently urge people to obey the Supreme Court's decision of 1954 outlawing segregation in the public schools, it is rather strange and paradoxical to find us consciously breaking laws. One may well ask, 'How can you advocate breaking some laws and obeying others?'

The answer is found in the fact that there are two types of laws: There are just laws and there are unjust laws. I would be the first to advocate obeying just laws. One has not only a legal but moral responsibility to obey just laws. Conversely, one has a moral responsibility to disobey unjust laws. I would agree with Saint Augustine that 'An unjust law is no law at all.'

Now what is the difference between the two? How does one determine when a law is just or unjust? A just law is a man-made code that squares with the moral law or the law of God. An unjust law is a code that is out of harmony with the moral law.

To put it in the terms of Saint Thomas Aquinas, an unjust law is a human law that is not rooted in eternal and natural law. Any law that uplifts human personality is just. Any law that degrades human personality is unjust.

All segregation statutes are unjust because segregation distorts the soul and damages the personality. It gives the segregator a false sense of superiority and the segregated a false sense of inferiority.

Let us turn to a more concrete example of just and unjust laws. An unjust law is a code that a majority inflicts on a minority that is not binding on itself. This is difference made legal. On the other hand a just law is a code that a majority compels a minority to follow that it is willing to follow itself. This is sameness made legal. . .

I must confess that over the last few years I have been gravely disappointed with the white moderate. I have almost reached the regrettable conclusion that the Negroes' great stumbling block in the stride toward freedom is not the White Citizens' 'Counciler' or the Ku Klux Klanner, but the white moderate who is more devoted to 'order' than to justice; who prefers a negative peace which is the absence of tension to a positive peace which is the presence of justice; who constantly says, 'I agree with you in the goal you seek, but I can't agree with your methods of direct action'; who paternalistically feels that he can set the time-table for another man's freedom; who lives by the myth of time and who constantly advises the Negro to wait until a 'more convenient season.'

Shallow understanding from people of good will is more frustrating than absolute misunderstanding from people of ill will. Lukewarm acceptance is much more bewildering than outright rejection. . .

We will reach the goal of freedom in Birmingham and all over the nation, because the goal of America is freedom. Abused and scorned though we may be, our destiny is tied up with the destiny of America. Before the Pilgrims landed at Plymouth, we were here. Before the pen of Jefferson etched across the pages of history the majestic words of the Declaration of Independence, we were here.

For more than two centuries our foreparents labored in this country without wages; they made cotton 'king'; and they built the homes of their masters in the midst of brutal injustice and shameful humiliation—and yet out of a bottomless vitality they continued to thrive and develop.

If the inexpressible cruelties of slavery could not stop us, the opposition we now face will surely fail. . .

15. *Do I really want to be integrated into a burning house?*

JAMES BALDWIN, *Letter from a Region in My Mind*, 1963 *

This innocent country set you down in a ghetto in which, in fact, it intended that you should perish. Let me spell out precisely what I mean by that, for the heart of the matter is here, and the root of my dispute with my country.

* *The Fire Next Time*, published by Dial Press, Inc., New York, 1963, pp. 21–4, 36–7, 39–41, 82–4, 98–102, 107–12, 115–18 *passim*. Copyright © 1963, by James Baldwin. Reprinted by permission of the Dial Press, Inc.

You were born where you were born and faced the future that you faced because you were black and *for no other reason*. The limits of your ambition were, thus, expected to be set forever. You were born into a society which spelled out with brutal clarity, and in as many ways as possible, that you were a worthless human being. You were not expected to aspire to excellence: you were expected to make peace with mediocrity. Wherever you have turned, James, in your short time on this earth, you have been told where you could go and what you could do (and *how* you could do it) and where you could live and whom you could marry. I know your countrymen do not agree with me about this, and I hear them saying, 'You exaggerate.' They do not know Harlem, and I do. So do you. . . The details and symbols of your life have been deliberately constructed to make you believe what white people say about you. Please try to remember that what they believe, as well as what they do and cause you to endure, does not testify to your inferiority but to their inhumanity and fear. . . There is no reason for you to try to become like white people and there is no basis whatever for their impertinent assumption that *they* must accept *you*. The really terrible thing, old buddy, is that *you* must accept *them*. And I mean that very seriously. You must accept them and accept them with love. For these innocent people have no other hope. They are, in effect, still trapped in a history which they do not understand; and until they understand it, they cannot be released from it. They have had to believe for many years, and for innumerable reasons, that black men are inferior to white men. Many of them, indeed, know better, but, as you will discover, people find it very difficult to act on what they know. To act is to be committed, and to be committed is to be in danger. In this case, the danger, in the minds of most white Americans, is the loss of their identity. Try to imagine how you would feel if you woke up one morning to find the sun shining and all the stars aflame. You would be frightened because it is out of the order of nature. Any upheaval in the universe is terrifying because it so profoundly attacks one's sense of one's own reality. Well, the black man has functioned in the white man's world as a fixed star, as an immovable pillar: and as he moves out of his place, heaven and earth are shaken to their foundations. You, don't be afraid. I said that it was intended that you should perish in the ghetto, perish by never being allowed to go behind the white man's definitions, by never being allowed to spell your proper name. You have, and many of us have, defeated this intention; and, by a terrible law, a terrible paradox, those innocents who believed that your imprisonment made them safe are losing their grasp of reality. But these men are your brothers—your lost, younger brothers. And if the word *integration* means anything, this is what it means: that we, with love, shall force our brothers to see themselves as they are, to cease fleeing from reality and begin to change it. For this is your home, my friend, do not be driven from it; great men have done great things here, and will again, and we can make America what America must become. It will be hard, James, but you come from sturdy, peasant stock, men who picked cotton and dammed rivers and built railroads, and, in the teeth of the most terrifying odds, achieved an unassailable and monumental dignity. You come from a long line of great poets, some of the greatest poets since Homer. One of them said, *The very time I thought I was lost, My dungeon shook and my chains fell off.*

People more advantageously placed than we in Harlem were, and are, will no doubt find the psychology and the view of human nature sketched above dismal and shocking in the extreme. But the Negro's experience of the white world cannot possibly create in him any respect for the standards by which the white world claims to live. His own condition is overwhelming proof that white people do not live by these standards. Negro servants have been smuggling odds and ends out of white homes for generations, and white people have been delighted to have them do it, because it has assuaged a dim guilt and testified to the intrinsic superiority of white people. Even the most doltish and servile Negro could scarcely fail to be impressed by the disparity between his situation and that of the people for whom he worked. . . Negroes had excellent reasons for doubting that money was made or kept by any very striking adherence to the Christian virtues; it certainly did not work that way for black Christians. In any case, white people, who had robbed black people of their liberty and who profited by this theft every hour that they lived, had no moral ground on which to stand. They had the judges, the juries, the shotguns, the law—in a word, power. But it was a criminal power, to be feared but not respected, and to be outwitted in any way whatever. And those virtues preached but not practiced by the white world were merely another means of holding Negroes in subjection. . .

Negroes in this country—and Negroes do not, strictly or legally speaking, exist in any other—are taught really to despise themselves from the moment their eyes open on the world. This world is white and they are black. White people hold the power, which means that they are superior to blacks (intrinsically, that is: God decreed it so), and the world has innumerable ways of making this difference known and felt and feared. Long before the Negro child perceives this difference, and even longer before he understands it, he has begun to react to it, he has begun to be controlled by it. Every effort made by the child's elders to prepare him for a fate from which they cannot protect him causes him secretly, in terror, to begin to await, without knowing that he is doing so, his mysterious and inexorable punishment. He must be 'good' not only in order to please his parents and not only to avoid being punished by them; behind their authority stands another, nameless and impersonal, infinitely harder to please, and bottomlessly cruel. And this filters into the child's consciousness through his parents' tone of voice as he is being exhorted, punished, or loved; in the sudden, uncontrollable note of fear heard in his mother's or his father's voice when he has strayed beyond some particular boundary. He does not know what the boundary is, and he can get no explanation of it, which is frightening enough, but the fear he hears in the voices of his elders is more frightening still. The fear that I heard in my father's voice, for example, when he realized that I really *believed* I could do anything a white boy could do, and had every intention of proving it, was not at all like the fear I heard when one of us was ill or had fallen down the stairs or strayed too far from the house. It was another fear, a fear that the child, in challenging the white world's assumptions, was putting himself in the path of destruction. . .

Most Negroes cannot risk assuming that the humanity of white people is more real to them than their color. And this leads, imperceptibly but inevitably, to a state of mind in which, having long ago learned to expect the worst, one finds it very easy to believe the worst. The brutality with which Negroes are treated in this country simply cannot be overstated, however unwilling white men may be to hear it. In the beginning—and neither can this be overstated—a Negro just cannot *believe* that white people are treating him as they do; he does not know what he has done to merit it. And when he realizes that the treatment accorded him has nothing to do with anything he has done, that the attempt of white people to destroy him—for that is what it is—is utterly gratuitous, it is not hard for him to think of white people as devils. For the horrors of the American Negro's life there has been almost no language. The privacy of his experience, which is only beginning to be recognized in language, and which is denied or ignored in official and popular speech—hence the Negro idiom—lends credibility to any system that pretends to clarify it. And, in fact, the truth about the black man, as a historical entity and as a human being, *has* been hidden from him, deliberately and cruelly; the power of the white world is threatened whenever a black man refuses to accept the white world's definitions. So every attempt is made to cut that black man down—not only was made yesterday but is made today. Who, then, is to say with authority where the root of so much anguish and evil lies? Why, then, is it not possible that all things began with the black man and that he was perfect—especially since this is precisely the claim that white people have put forward for themselves all these years? Furthermore, it is now absolutely clear that white people are a minority in the world—so severe a minority that they now look rather more like an invention—and that they cannot possibly hope to rule it any longer. If this is so, why is it not also possible that they achieved their original dominance by stealth and cunning and bloodshed and in opposition to the will of Heaven, and not, as they claim, by Heaven's will? And if *this* is so, then the sword they have used so long against others can now, without mercy, be used against them. Heavenly witnesses are a tricky lot, to be used by whoever is closest to Heaven at the time. And legend and theology, which are designed to sanctify our fears, crimes, and aspirations, also reveal them for what they are. . .

The American Negro is a unique creation; he has no counterpart anywhere, and no predecessors. The Muslims react to this fact by referring to the Negro as 'the so-called American Negro' and substituting for the names inherited from slavery the letter 'X.' It is a fact that every American Negro bears a name that originally belonged to the white man whose chattel he was. I am called Baldwin because I was either sold by my African tribe or kidnapped out of it into the hands of a white Christian named Baldwin, who forced me to kneel at the foot of the cross. I am, then, both visibly and legally the descendant of slaves in a white, Protestant country, and this is what it means to be an American Negro, this is who he is—a kidnapped pagan, who was sold like an animal and treated like one, who was once defined by the American Constitution as 'three-fifths' of a man, and who, according to the Dred Scott decision, had no rights that a white man was bound to respect. And today, a hundred years after his technical emancipation, he remains—with the possible exception of the American Indian—the most despised creature in his country. Now, there is simply no possibility of a real change in the Negro's situation without the most radical and far-reaching changes in the American political and social structure. And it is clear that white Americans are not simply unwilling to effect these changes; they are, in the main, so slothful have they become, unable even to envision them. It must be added that the Negro himself no longer believes in the good faith of white Americans—if, indeed, he ever could have. What the Negro *has* discovered, and on an international level, is that power to intimidate which he has always had privately but hitherto could manipulate only privately—for private ends often, for limited ends always. And therefore when the country speaks of a 'new' Negro, which it has been doing every hour on the hour for decades, it is not really referring to a change in the Negro, which, in any case, it is quite incapable of assessing, but only to a new difficulty in keeping him in his place, to the fact that it encounters him (again! again!) barring yet another door to its spiritual and social ease. This is probably, hard and odd as it may sound, the most important thing that one human being can do for another—it is certainly *one* of the most important things; hence the torment and necessity of love—and this is the enormous contribution that the Negro has made to this otherwise shapeless and undiscovered country. Consequently, white Americans are in nothing more deluded than in supposing that Negroes could ever have imagined that white people would 'give' them anything. It is rare indeed that people give. Most people guard and keep; they suppose that it is they themselves and what they identify with themselves that they are guarding and keeping, whereas what they are actually guarding and keeping is their system of reality and what they assume themselves to be. One can give nothing whatever without giving oneself—that is to say, risking oneself. If one cannot risk oneself, then one is simply incapable of giving. And, after all, one can give freedom only by setting someone free. This, in the case of the Negro, the American republic has never become sufficiently mature to do. White Americans have contented themselves with gestures that are now described as 'tokenism.' For hard example, white Americans congratulate themselves on the 1954 Supreme Court decision outlawing segregation in the schools; they suppose, in spite of the mountain of evidence that has since accumulated to the contrary, that this was proof of a change of heart—or, as they like to say, progress. Perhaps. It all depends on how one reads the word 'progress.' Most of the Negroes I know do not believe that this immense concession would ever have been made if it had not been for the competition of the Cold War, and the fact that Africa was clearly liberating herself and therefore had, for political reasons, to be wooed by the descendants of her former masters. Had it been a matter of love or justice, the 1954 decision would surely have occurred sooner; were it not for the realities of power in this difficult era, it might very well not have occurred yet. This seems an extremely harsh way of stating the case—ungrateful, as it were—but the evidence that supports this way of stating it is not easily refuted. I myself do not think that it can be refuted at all. In any event, the sloppy and fatuous nature of American good will can never be relied upon to deal with hard problems. These have been dealt with, when they have been dealt with at all, out of necessity—and in political terms, anyway, necessity means concessions made in order to stay on top. I think this is a fact, which it serves no purpose to deny, *but, whether it is a fact or not, this is what the black population of the world, including black Americans, really believe.* The word 'independence' in Africa and the word 'integration' here are almost equally meaningless; that is, Europe has not yet left Africa, and black men here are not yet free. And both of these last statements are undeniable facts, related facts, containing the gravest implications for us all. The Negroes of this country may never be able to rise to power, but they are very well placed indeed to precipitate chaos and ring down the curtain on the American dream. . .

America, of all the Western nations, has been best placed to prove the uselessness and the obsolescence of the concept of color. But it has not dared to accept this opportunity, or even to conceive of it as an opportunity. White Americans have thought of it as their shame, and have envied those more civilized and elegant European nations that were untroubled by the presence of black men on their shores. This is because white Americans have supposed 'Europe' and 'civilization' to be synonyms—which they are not—and have been distrustful of other standards and other sources of vitality, especially those produced in America itself, and have attempted to behave in all matters as though what was east for Europe was also east for them. What it comes to is that if we, who can scarcely be considered a white nation, persist in thinking of ourselves as one, we condemn ourselves, with the truly white nations, to sterility and decay, whereas if we could accept ourselves as we are, we might bring new life to the Western achievements, and transform them. The price of this transformation is the unconditional freedom of the Negro; it is not too much to say that he, who has been so long rejected, must now be embraced, and at no matter what psychic or social risk. He is *the* key figure in his country, and the American future is precisely as bright or as dark as his. And the Negro recognizes this, in a negative way. Hence the question: Do I really *want* to be integrated into a burning house?

White Americans find it as difficult as white people elsewhere do to divest themselves of the notion that they are in possession of some intrinsic value that black people need, or want. And this assumption—which, for example, makes the solution to the Negro problem depend on the speed with which Negroes accept and adopt white standards—is revealed in all kinds of striking ways, from Bobby Kennedy's assurance that a Negro can become President in forty years to the unfortunate tone of warm congratulation with which so many liberals address their Negro equals. It is the Negro, of course, who is presumed to have become equal—an achievement that not only proves the comforting fact that perseverance has no color but also overwhelmingly corroborates the white man's sense of his own value. Alas, this value can scarcely be corroborated in any other way; there is certainly little enough in the white man's public or private life that one should desire to imitate. White men, at the bottom of their hearts, know this. Therefore, a vast amount of the energy that goes into what we call the Negro problem is produced by the white man's profound desire not to be judged by those who are not white, not to be seen as he is, and at the same time a vast amount of the white anguish is rooted in the white man's equally profound need to be seen as he is, to be released from the tyranny of his mirror. All of us know, whether or not we are able to admit it, that mirrors can only lie, that death by drowning is all that awaits one there. It is for this reason that love is so desperately sought and so cunningly avoided. Love takes off the masks that we fear we cannot live without and know we cannot live within. I use the word 'love' here not merely in the personal sense but as a state of being, or a state of grace—not in the infantile American sense of being made happy but in the tough and universal sense of quest and daring and growth. And I submit, then, that the racial tensions that menace Americans today have little to do with real antipathy—on the contrary, indeed—and are involved only symbolically with color. These tensions are rooted in the very same depths as those from which love springs, or murder. The white man's unadmitted—and apparently, to him, unspeakable—private fears and longings are projected onto the Negro. The only way he can be released from the Negro's tyrannical power over him is to consent, in effect, to become black himself, to become a part of that suffering and dancing country that he now watches wistfully from the heights of his lonely power and, armed with spiritual traveller's checks, visits surreptitiously after dark. How can one respect, let alone adopt, the values of a people who do not, on any level whatever, live the way they say they do, or the way they say they should? I cannot accept the proposition that the four-hundred-year travail of the American Negro should result merely in his attainment of the present level of the American civilization. I am far from convinced that being released from the African witch doctor was worthwhile if I am now—in order to support the moral contradictions and the spiritual aridity of my life—expected to become dependent on the American psychiatrist. It is a bargain I refuse. The only need of new standards, which will release him from his confusion and place him once again in fruitful communion with the depths of his own being. thing white people have that black people need, or should want, is power —and no one holds power forever. White people cannot, in the generality, be taken as models of how to live. Rather, the white man is himself in sore And I repeat: The price of the liberation of the white people is the liberation of the blacks—the total liberation, in the cities, in the towns, before the law, and in the mind. Why, for example—especially knowing the family as I do —I should *want* to marry your sister is a great mystery to me. But your sister and I have every right to marry if we wish to, and no one has the right to stop us. If she cannot raise me to her level, perhaps I can raise her to mine.

In short, we, the black and the white, deeply need each other here if we are really to become a nation—if we are really, that is, to achieve our identity, our maturity, as men and women. To create one nation has proved to be a hideously difficult task; there is certainly no need now to create two, one black and one white. But white men with far more political power than that possessed by the Nation of Islam movement have been advocating exactly this, in effect, for generations. If this sentiment is honored when it falls from the lips of Senator Byrd, then there is no reason it should not be honored when it falls from the lips of Malcolm X. And any Congressional committee wishing to investigate the latter must also be willing to investigate the former. They are expressing exactly the same sentiments and represent exactly the same danger. There is absolutely no reason to suppose that white people are better equipped to frame the laws by which I am to be governed than I am. It is entirely unacceptable that I should have no voice in the political affairs of my own country, for I am not a ward of America; I am one of the first Americans to arrive on these shores. . .

The American Negro has the great advantage of having never believed that collection of myths to which white Americans cling: that their ancestors were all freedom-loving heroes, that they were born in the greatest country the world has ever seen, or that Americans are invincible in battle and wise in peace, that Americans have always dealt honorably with Mexicans and Indians and all other neighbors or inferiors, that American men are the world's most direct and virile, that American women are pure. Negroes know far more about white Americans than that; it can almost be said, in fact, that they know about white Americans what parents—or, anyway, mothers—know about their children, and that they very often regard white Americans that way. And perhaps this attitude, held in spite of what they know and have endured, helps to explain why Negroes, on the whole, and until lately, have allowed themselves to feel so little hatred. The tendency has really been, insofar as this was possible, to dismiss white people as the slightly mad victims of their own brainwashing. One watched the lives they led. One could not be fooled about that; one watched the things they did and the excuses that they gave themselves, and if a white man was really in trouble, deep trouble, it was to the Negro's door that he came. And one felt that if one had had that white man's worldly advantages, one would never have become as bewildered and as joyless and as thoughtlessly cruel as he. The Negro came to the white man for a roof or for five dollars or for a letter to the judge; the white man came to the Negro for love. But he was not often able to give what he came seeking. The price was too high; he had too much to lose. And the Negro knew this, too. When one knows this about a man, it is impossible for one to hate him, but unless he becomes a man—becomes equal—it is also impossible for one to love him. Ultimately, one tends to avoid him, for the universal characteristic of children is to assume that they have a monopoly on trouble, and therefore a monopoly on *you*. (Ask any Negro what he knows about the white people with whom he works. And then ask the white people with whom he works what they know about *him*.)

How can the American Negro past be used? It is entirely possible that this dishonored past will rise up soon to smite all of us. There are some wars, for example (if anyone on the globe is still mad enough to go to war) that the American Negro will not support, however many of his people may be coerced—and there is a limit to the number of people any government can put in prison, and a rigid limit indeed to the practicality of such a course. A bill is coming in that I fear America is not prepared to pay. 'The problem of the twentieth century,' wrote W. E. B. Du Bois around sixty years ago, 'is the problem of the color line.' A fearful and delicate problem, which compromises, when it does not corrupt, all the American efforts to build a better world—here, there, or anywhere. It is for this reason that everything white Americans think they believe in must now be reëxamined. What one would not like to see again is the consolidation of peoples on the basis of their color. But as long as we in the West place on color the value that we do, we make it impossible for the great unwashed to consolidate themselves according to any other principle. Color is not a human or a personal reality; it is a political reality. But this is a distinction so extremely hard to make that the West has not been able to make it yet. And at the center of this dreadful storm, this vast confusion, stand the black people of this nation, who must now share the fate of a nation that has never accepted them, to which they were brought in chains. Well, if this is so, one has no choice but to do all in one's power to change that fate, and at no matter what risk—eviction, imprisonment, torture, death. For the sake of one's children, in order to minimize the bill that *they* must pay, one must be careful not to take refuge in any delusion—and the value placed on the color of the skin is always and everywhere and forever a delusion. I know that what I am asking is impossible. But in our time, as in every time, the impossible is the least that one can demand—and one is, after all, emboldened by the spectacle of human history in general, and American Negro history in particular, for it testifies to nothing less than the perpetual achievement of the impossible.

REAPPRAISALS

16. *Whoever heard of economic theory with poets, painters, and philosophers among the premises?*

W. H. FERRY, *Caught on the Horn of Plenty*, 1962 *

Strangely enough, Americans are having a hard time getting used to the idea of abundance. Abundance is not only a relatively recent state of affairs. There is also an idea current that it may not last very long. The barriers to general comprehension of the possibilities and demands of abundance are numerous. There is, for example, tradition, and a mythology that seeks to confine the growing abundance of this country inside the old political and social enclosures. Happily there is also the beginning of a less dusty literature on the topic.

As consumers, Americans are joyously sopping up affluence, quarter after

* Published by Center for the Study of Democratic Institutions, *Bulletin*, January 1962. Reprinted by permission of the Center for the Study of Democratic Institutions.

quarter sending private debt for consumer goods to record levels, and inventing new categories of services. But the lesson of abundance is even here ambiguous; for while there is enough to go around for all, not all are sharing. There is enough in our ever-swollen granaries so that no American need to go to bed hungry. Yet millions do, while millions of others are vaguely uneasy and feel guilty about so absurd a situation. The American farm is technology's most notorious victory. That the disaster of abundance on our farms has so far resisted solution is a portent of greater dilemmas in other areas.

For the country may soon be in the same fix with regard to consumer goods and services—more than enough for all, but without the political wit to know how to bring about a just distribution. We may, in fact, be in that situation at present. There is evidence that something like 30 per cent of our productive facilities are standing idle most of the time. Much of our machinery is obsolete. Everyone knows that the steel industry spent about a year in the doldrums of 50 per cent of capacity production. Planned obsolescence, which is the design and sales strategy of many manufacturers, is latent abundance, just as the fields left unturned by wheat and barley and rice farmers are latent abundance. It is not only what is produced that counts up to a total of abundance, but what is capable of being produced.

Not the least of our troubles occurs over definitions. Abundance of this self evident variety, for example, is not the opposite of the classical idea of scarcity. And what are resources? How do you tell when a resource is scarce? Or not scarce? Are people resources? Are people without jobs or skills resources? What is prosperity? This is a particularly hard definition. The recession is said to be past. Newcomers by the millions are thronging into the stock market. The national rate of growth has risen above 3 per cent. Some 5,000,000 people are out of jobs. Is this prosperity? What are today's definitions of work, leisure, play, affluence? Our vocabularly is tuned to yesterday's industrial revolution, not to today's scientific revolution. Abundance might, for instance, be defined as the capacity—here meaning resources, skill, capital, and potential and present production—the capacity to supply every citizen with a minimum decent life. We have the capacity, so this makes us an abundant society. Yet some 30,000,000 Americans are living below the poverty line. . .

The immemorial view is that unemployment is a bad state of affairs. Although all the tendencies in recent generations have been toward leisure—shorter work-days and work-weeks, more pay for less labor, education for constructive use of spare time—the country has assumed that the process would always come to a convenient halt close to the Full Employment sign. It seems not to have occurred to any statesman that leisure might as *readily* be a goal of society as employment. Now that such a possibility exists, no welcome mat is put out for it. On the contrary, dismay is the rule. Instead of embracing the hope that technology may be opening the way into a new style of civilization, one in which work and the economic machinery are not the preeminent concerns of society, the effort today is to show that nothing has been significantly altered by the onrush of technology, that we can lean back comfortably on ancient theories, and that old goals are best after all. . .

The question is whether jobs can be manufactured fast enough to approach full employment, using the present definition of jobs and the means of providing them that are presently regarded as acceptable. The essential contention of this paper is that the answer is no. An apparently unavoidable condition of the Age of Abundance is increasing structural unemployment and under-employment.

The novelty of this proposition is that the majority of victims of technological displacement will be *permanently* out of work. They will not just be "resting between engagements." They will not just be waiting for the next upturn, or for expansion of the industry or company in which they were working. They will no longer be the objects of unemployment insurance plans, for these plans are designed to fill the gap between jobs, not to provide a permanent dole. . .

The unemployed and under-employed are no longer almost exclusively the unskilled, the recent immigrants, the colored, the groups at the end of the economic scale, who have customarily borne the heaviest weight of economic slides. White-collar workers are joining this group as automation reaches the office. There is some reason for thinking that white-collar workers will after a few years comprise most of the growing category of technologically displaced. Herbert Simon has observed that by 1985 machines can do away with all of middle management, 'if Americans want it that way.' Since middle management is considered the ultimate destination of much of the middle-class America, Simon's words have an air of clammy prophecy about them. . .

In an abundant society the problem is not an economic one of keeping the machine running regardless of what it puts out, but a political one of achieving the common good. And planning is one of its major means.

But whether or not we can figure out some such way of taking systematic advantage of the bewildering fact of abundance, we shall within a short while have to discard attitudes that grew up in the dog-eat-dog phase of capitalism and adopt others suitable to modern mercantilism. For example, we shall have to stop automatically regarding the unemployed as lazy, unlucky, indolent, and unworthy. We shall have to find means, public or private, of paying people to do no work.

This suggestion goes severely against the American grain, and it will have to be adopted slowly. The first steps have been taken. Unemployment insurance and supplementary unemployment benefit plans reached by company-union negotiations are examples. As these have come to be accepted as civic-industrial policy, so may plans for six-month work years, or retirement at 50 or 55 at full pay until pension schemes take hold. So may continuation of education well into adult years, at public expense. So may payment from the public treasury for non-productive effort, such as writing novels, painting pictures, composing music, doing graduate work, and taking part in the expanding functions of government. Is a physicist more valuable to the community than a playwright? Why? The responsibility of the individual to the general welfare runs far beyond the purely economic. In his book, *The Challenge of Abundance*, Robert Theobald observes:

'. . . In the last century and a half we have tried to solve two problems with a single mechanism. We have allowed the income received from the production of goods to determine the distribution of wealth. However, this system is no longer suitable for an economy moving toward abundance. The economy of abundance will have rules different from those applying in an economy of scarcity. *The fact that a proposed solution would be impossible in an economy of scarcity does not mean that it is not appropriate for an economy of abundance*. . . In the past, society has claimed that its members were entitled to a living only if they carried out a task society defined as valuable and for which it was willing to pay. The creation of a society of abundance will make it possible to relax this requirement. We will be able to allow people to follow an interest they find vital, but that society would not support through the price mechanism.' . .

The essential change in outlook will be to regard the new leisure—including the leisure of the liberated margin—as desirable, as a good, and to direct public policy to accepting it as a good in itself. . .

It will be hard to look on members of the liberated margin as useful participants in society, no matter how enlightened the arrangements may be, because 'useful' has up to now strictly denoted people who work for economically productive enterprises and ends. Let me emphasize that I am not talking about idleness, only about what most people today regard as idleness, or near to it. The revolution in economic theory that is indicated by abundance is dramatically illustrated here. Whoever heard of economic theory with poets, painters, and philosophers among the premises?

Deliberation on the ways and the standards for getting purchasing power into the hands of the liberated margin may be the beginning of methodical social justice in the American political economy. Abundance may compel social justice as conscience never has. The liberated margin will have to get 'what is its due.' This means developing a basis of distribution of income which is not tied to work as a measure. For decisions about 'due-ness' will have to be made without economic criteria; at least without the criterion of what members of the liberated margin are worth in the employment market, for there is no such market for them. The criteria of capitalism, are, in fact, largely irrelevant to conditions of abundance. Efficiency, administration, progress, success, profit, competition, and private gain are words of high standing in the lexicon of capitalism. Presumably among these terms are some of the 'pseudomoral principles,' that Keynes saw on their way to the ashcan as society progressively solved its economic problems. In any event, a community of abundance will find less use for these ideas, and will turn instead to ideas like justice, law, government, general welfare, virtue, cooperation, and public responsibility as the touchstones of policy.

17. *We supposed that our revelation was 'democracy revolutionizing the world,' but in reality it was 'abundance revolutionizing the world'*

DAVID M. POTTER, *People of Plenty: Economic Abundance and American Character*, 1954 *

From the very inception of the American Republic, the United States has constantly supposed that it had a message for the world, even a mission to perform in the world. That message, we were convinced, was democracy; that mission, the exemplification to all the world of the merit of democratic institutions—even the propagation of such institutions. From the outset, our Declaration of Independence concerned itself not simply with the rights of the colonists or the equality of British subjects but with the equality of all men and their universal right to liberty. . .

Also, from the beginning, the American people have experienced a long succession of disappointments in which prospects for the realization of the American mission appeared to present themselves but were never fulfilled. Our government under the Constitution had not been in operation for more than six weeks when the first hopeful signs appeared that our ideals were about to spread. The Estates-General met outside Paris, and Thomas Jefferson, who was on the scene, rejoiced at the prospect of a French application of American libertarian principles. . .

But after that the revolution entered the phase of the guillotine and the Terror, and America was, for the first time, brought reluctantly to the recognition of what she has been forced to recognize so often since, namely, that American ideals were not working out according to American expectations. American liberals were, for the first time, put on a spot where they have repeatedly found themselves in the last hundred and sixty years—that is, they were compelled to overlook much of the bloodshed, the violence, the exercise of despotic authority in the name of the people and were obliged to make the most of the basic similarity between American revolutionary and French revolutionary principles. After the lapse of a few more years, Napoleon emerged as the supreme power in the land of liberty, equality, and fraternity, and by that time even the most ardent American Jacobin could no longer keep up the pretense that France was merely applying American beliefs in her own distinctively Gallic way.

After a hundred and sixty years, this cycle by which revolts against despotism mature into despotisms under new management has become a painfully familiar story, but it required more than this first disillusionment of the Jeffersonian Francophiles to disillusion the American people. Indeed, faith in America's democratic mission was far too robust to yield to a single disconcerting experience, and we continued to hail the gleam of liberty wherever it showed itself. . .

* Published by The University of Chicago Press, 1954, pp. 128–37, 140–41 *passim*. Reprinted by permission of the University of Chicago Press.

In some respects, the only revolutions with which the American people could feel completely satisfied were the ones that did not succeed. After every revolution that failed, we were free to assume that its success would have fulfilled our ideals and were free to extend our hospitality to the revolutionists who were no longer welcome at home. . .

We continued to hope that American liberty could go abroad and still remain liberty as we knew her, and, in fact, we never faltered in seeking to promote this end. The spectacle of Cuba struggling to be free provided popular support for the Spanish-American War, though it ended in a Platt Amendment for Cuba and an occupation for the Philippine Islands because we could not bear to face what these two aspirants to liberty were likely to do with their freedom. . .

Later still, when we engaged in two major world wars, we could not bring ourselves to confront and accept the sacrifices that would be required, without some conviction that our historic mission would now be fostered on a global scale. Technically, the first World War may have had as its *casus belli* for the United States the question of the violation by submarines of neutral rights, but the dynamic of the war for Americans was not to vindicate the rights of visit and search; it was 'to make the world safe for democracy.' . .

When we were, for the second time, confronted with world war in 1939, Franklin Roosevelt avoided the highly idealistic, highly altruistic formulas which Wilson had invoked, and, indeed, he made a special effort to be 'realistic' and to emphasize America's immediate stake in the result. . .

Although democracy in the American style never seemed to gain ascendancy in other parts of the globe, there was a long interval, extending over most of the nineteenth century, during which American ideals seemed a beacon light to poor and humble folk all over the world. Millions of these poor came to America because it was a refuge for the oppressed, and millions of others who remained at home were inspired by the American dream. The moral authority of our ideals of equality, of freedom, and of opportunity was immense, and we were entitled to believe that for every aristocrat who disparaged us or condescended to us there were scores of plain men and women who shared in and were heartened by our aspirations for human welfare. The rapidity and eagerness with which our immigrants embraced Americanism gave tangible proof of this response, and thus our people, who have always been solicitous for the approval of others, could find comfort in the assurance that the heart of humanity responded to the creed of our democracy. This assurance went far to mitigate our disappointment at the failure of American democracy to take root overseas.

But today this consolation has utterly vanished, and we now harbor few illusions as to the affection which we can command from the mass of humanity. Ever since the days of Calvin Coolidge, when Uncle Sam first heard himself being called 'Uncle Shylock,' we have grown increasingly used to finding American motives misrepresented and American ideals greeted with skepticism and indifference. In the last decade many Americans have come sadly to believe that the only influence which we can command is of that precarious kind which is bought and paid for, not once but repeatedly. . .

The thought is not original with me, but what I would suggest is this: that we have been historically correct in supposing that we had a revolutionary message to offer but we have been mistaken in our concept of what that message was. We supposed that our revelation was 'democracy revolutionizing the world,' but in reality it was 'abundance revolutionizing the world'—a message which we did not preach and scarcely understood ourselves, but one which was peculiarly able to preach its own gospel without words.

It is perhaps significant that it took a European to perceive the true impact which the United States had upon the rest of the world. As early as 1932, André Siegfried, in an address to a group of French Protestant businessmen, made these very pregnant observations: 'The West,' he said, 'has thought for a long time, not without a certain naïveté, that it represented spirituality in the world. But is spirituality really the message we have taken along with us everywhere? What has been borrowed from us, as I have so often observed, is our mechanisms. Today, in the most remote, most ancient villages, one finds the automobile, the cinema, the radio, the telephone, the phonograph, not to mention the airplane, and it is not the white men, nor the most civilized, who display the greatest enthusiasm for them.'

This comment applies to the influence of Western civilization as a whole, but, with specific reference to America, Siegfried said, 'The United States is presiding at a general reorganization of the ways of living throughout the entire world.'

As to what we have imparted, 'the one really new gospel we have introduced is the revelation, after centuries of passively endured privations, that a man may at last free himself of poverty, and, most fantastic innovation of all, that he may actually enjoy his existence. . . And so, without our wishing it, or even knowing it, we appear as the terrible instigators of social change and revolution.' . .

We conceived of democracy as an absolute value largely ideological in content and equally valid in any environment, instead of recognizing that our own democratic system is one of the major products of our abundance, working primarily because of the measure of our abundance. . .

On the international front this fallacy has had most far-reaching results, in that it has consistently impelled us to proselyte for converts to the democratic faith in places where the economic prerequisites for democracy have not been established. This, I believe, has a great deal to do with the widespread impression in the world that the Americans are, somehow, hypocrites. In our own country the promise of equality meant the right to advance, without discrimination, to easily attainable ends. Hence the principle of equality could be upheld with genuine sincerity. Freedom meant the removal of barriers to advancement from one position to another, more advantageous one. But in countries where even decency, much less comfort, lay beyond the point of attainability for most people—where the number of advantageous positions was negligible—it seemed a kind of deception to offer the individual as good a chance as anyone to compete for nonexistent prizes or to assure him of his freedom to go where he wishes, when there was, in fact, nowhere to go. . .

As a result, our message to the world has become involved in a dilemma:

to other peoples, our democracy has seemed attainable but not especially desirable; our abundance has seemed infinitely desirable but quite unattainable. But, if the realities of the relationship between democracy and abundance had been understood by people of other countries or, what is more to the point, by those Americans who were seeking to impart our message, our democracy would have seemed more desirable, and our abundance would have seemed more attainable. . .

18. *In the maintenance of a true community the articulate public philosophy is the thread which holds the pieces of the fabric together*

WALTER LIPPMANN, *The Public Philosophy*, 1955 *

The public philosophy is known as *natural law*, a name which, alas, causes great semantic confusion. This philosophy is the premise of the institutions of the Western society, and they are, I believe, unworkable in communities that do not adhere to it. Except on the premises of this philosophy, it is impossible to reach intelligible and workable conceptions of popular election, majority rule, representative assemblies, free speech, loyalty, property, corporations, and voluntary associations. The founders of these institutions, which the recently enfranchised democracies have inherited, were all of them adherents of some one of the various schools of natural law. . .

To speak of a public philosophy is, I am well aware, to raise dangerous questions, rather like opening Pandora's box. . . Yet the men of the seventeenth and eighteenth centuries who established these great salutary rules would certainly have denied that a community could do without a general public philosophy. They were themselves the adherents of a public philosophy—of the doctrine of natural law, which held that there was law 'above the ruler and the sovereign people . . . above the whole community of mortals.'

The traditions of civility spring from this principle, which was first worked out by the Stoics. . .

These traditions were expounded in the treatises of philosophers, were developed in the tracts of the publicists, were absorbed by the lawyers and applied in the courts. At times of great stress some of the endangered traditions were committted to writing, as in the Magna Carta and the Declaration of Independence. For the guidance of judges and lawyers, large portions were described—as in Lord Coke's examination of the common law. The public philosophy was in part expounded in the Bill of Rights of 1689. It was reenacted in the first ten amendments of the Constitution of the United States. The largest part of the public philosophy was never explicitly stated. Being the wisdom of a great society over the generations, it can never be stated in any single document. But the traditions of civility permeated the peoples of

* Published by Little, Brown and Co., Boston, 1955, chaps. 8, 9, and 11 *passim*. Reprinted by permission of Little, Brown and Co.–Atlantic Monthly Press.

the West and provided a standard of public and private action which promoted, facilitated, and protected the institutions of freedom and the growth of democracy.

The founders of our free institutions were themselves adherents of this public philosophy. When they insisted upon excluding the temporal power from the realm of the mind and the spirit, it was not that they had no public philosophy. It was because experience had taught them that as power corrupts, it corrupts the public philosophy. It was, therefore, a practical rule of politics that the government should not be given sovereignty and proprietorship over the public philosophy. . .

We come, then, to a crucial question. If the discussion of public philosophy has been, so to speak, tabled in the liberal democracies, can we assume that, though it is not being discussed, there is a public philosophy? Is there a body of positive principles and precepts which a good citizen cannot deny or ignore? I am writing this book in the conviction that there is. It is a conviction which I have acquired gradually, not so much from a theoretical education, but rather from the practical experience of seeing how hard it is for our generation to make democracy work. I believe there is a public philosophy. Indeed there is such a thing as the public philosophy of civility. It does not have to be discovered or invented. It is known. But it does have to be revived and renewed. . .

In our time the institutions built upon the foundations of the public philosophy still stand. But they are used by a public who are not being taught, and no longer adhere to, the philosophy. Increasingly, the people are alienated from the inner principles of their institutions. The question is whether and how this alienation can be overcome, and the rupture of the traditions of civility repaired. . .

When we have demonstrated the need for the public philosophy, how do we prove that the need can be satisfied? Not, we may be sure, by exhortation, however eloquent, to rise to the enormity of the present danger, still less by lamentations about the glory and the grandeur that are past. Modern men, to whom the argument is addressed, have a low capacity to believe in the invisible, the intangible, and the imponderable.

Exhortation can capture the will to believe. But of the will to believe there is no lack. The modern trouble is in a low capacity to believe in precepts which restrict and restrain private interests and desire. Conviction of the need of these restraints is difficult to restore once it has been radically impaired. Public principles can, of course, be imposed by a despotic government. But the public philosophy of a free society cannot be restored by fiat and by force. To come to grips with the unbelief which underlies the condition of anomy, we must find a way to reestablish confidence in the validity of public standards. We must renew the convictions from which our political morality springs.

In the prevailing popular culture all philosophies are the instruments of some man's purpose, all truths are self-centered and self-regarding, and all principles are the rationalizations of some special interest. There is no public criterion of the true and the false, of the right and the wrong, beyond that which the preponderant mass of voters, consumers, readers, and listeners happen at the moment to be supposed to want.

There is no reason to think that this condition of mind can be changed until it can be proved to the modern skeptic that there are certain principles which, when they have been demonstrated, only the willfully irrational can deny, that there are certain obligations binding on all men who are committed to a free society, and that only the willfully subversive can reject them.

When I say that the condition of anomy cannot be corrected unless these things are proved to the modern skeptic, I mean that the skeptic must find the proof compelling. His skepticism cannot be cured by forcing him to conform. If he has no strong beliefs, he will usually conform if he is made to conform. But the very fact that he has been forced by the government or by the crowd will prove that the official doctrine lacked something in the way of evidence or of reason to carry full conviction. In the blood of the martyrs to intolerance are the seeds of unbelief.

In order to repair the capacity to believe in the public philosophy, it will be necessary to demonstrate the practical relevance and the productivity of the public philosophy. It is almost impossible to deny its high and broad generalities. The difficulty is to see how they are to be applied in the practical affairs of a modern state. . .

The free political institutions of the Western world were conceived and established by men who believed that honest reflection on the common experience of mankind would always cause men to come to the same ultimate conclusions. Within the Golden Rule of the same philosophy for elucidating their ultimate ends, they could engage with confident hope in the progressive discovery of truth. All issues could be settled by scientific investigation and by free debate if— but only if—all the investigators and the debaters adhered to the public philosophy; if, that is to say, they used the same criteria and rules of reason for arriving at the truth and for distinguishing good and evil.

Quite evidently, there is no clear sharp line which can be drawn in any community or among communities between those who adhere and those who do not adhere to the public philosophy. But while there are many shades and degrees in the spectrum, the two ends are well defined. When the adherence of the whole body of people to the public philosophy is firm, a true community exists; where there is division and dissent over the main principles, the result is a condition of latent war.

In the maintenance and formation of a true community the articulate philosophy is, one might say, like the thread which holds the pieces of the fabric together. . .

The fabrics in the metaphor are the traditions of how the good life is lived and the good society is governed. When they come apart, as they have in the Western democracies, the result is tantamount to a kind of collective amnesia. The liberal democracies have been making mistakes in peace and in war which they would never have made were they not suffering from what is a failure of memory. They have forgotten too much of what their predecessors had learned before them. The newly enfranchised democracies are like men who have kept their appetites but have forgotten how to grow food. They have the perennial human needs for law and order, for freedom and justice, for what only good government can give them. But the art of governing well has to be learned. If it is to be learned, it has to be transmitted from the old to the young, and the habits and the ideas must be maintained as a seamless web of memory among the bearers of the tradition, generation after generation.

When the continuity of the traditions of civility is ruptured, the community is threatened; unless the rupture is repaired, the community will break down into factional, class, racial, and regional wars. For when the continuity is interrupted, the cultural heritage is not being transmitted. The new generation is faced with the task of rediscovering and re-inventing and relearning, by trial and error, most of what the guardians of a society need to know.

No one generation can do this. For no one generation of men are capable of creating for themselves the arts and sciences of a high civilization. Men can know more than their ancestors did if they start with a knowledge of what their ancestors had already learned. They can do advanced experiments if they do not have to learn all over again how to do the elementary ones. That is why a society can be progressive only if it conserves its traditions. The generations are, as Bernard of Chartres said, 'like dwarfs seated on the shoulders of giants,' enabled, therefore, to 'see more things than the Ancients and things more distant.'

But traditions are more than the culture of the arts and sciences. They are the public world to which our private worlds are joined. This continuum of public and private memories transcends all persons in their immediate and natural lives and it ties them all together. In it there is performed the mystery by which individuals are adopted and initiated into membership in the community.

The body which carries this mystery is the history of the community, and its central theme is the great deeds and the high purposes of the great predecessors. From them the new men descend and prove themselves by becoming participants in the unfinished story. . . We come now to the problem of communicating the public philosophy to the modern democracies. The problem has been, to be sure, only too obvious from the beginning. For . . . the public philosophy is in a deep contradiction with the Jacobin ideology, which is, in fact, the popular doctrine of the mass democracies. The public philosophy is addressed to the government of our appetites and passions by the reasons of a second, civilized, and, therefore, acquired nature. Therefore, the public philosophy cannot be popular. For it aims to resist and to regulate those very desires and opinions which are most popular. The warrant of the public philosophy is that while the regime it imposes is hard, the results of rational and disciplined government will be good. And so, while the right but hard decisions are not likely to be popular when they are taken, the wrong and soft decisions will, if they are frequent and big enough, bring on a disorder in which freedom and democracy are destroyed.

If we ask whether the public philosophy can be communicated to the democracies, the answer must begin with the acknowledgment that there must be a doctrine to communicate. The philosophy must first be made clear and pertinent to our modern anxieties. Our reconnaissance has been addressed to that first need.

But beyond it lies the problem of the capacity and the willingness of modern men to receive this kind of philosophy. The concepts and the principles of the public philosophy have their being in the realm of immaterial entities. They cannot be experienced by our sense organs or even, strictly speaking, imagined in visual or tangible terms. Yet these essences, these abstractions, which are out of sight and out of touch, are to have and to hold men's highest loyalties.

The problem of communication is posed because in the modern world, as it is today, most men—not all men, to be sure, but most active and influential men—are in practice positivists who hold that the only world which has reality is the physical world. Only seeing is believing. Nothing is real enough to be taken seriously, nothing can be a matter of deep concern, which cannot, or at least might not, somewhere and sometime, be seen, heard, tasted, smelled, or touched. . .

Early in the history of Western society, political thinkers in Rome hit upon the idea that the concepts of the public philosophy—particularly the idea of reciprocal rights and duties under law—could be given concreteness by treating them as contracts. In this way, freedom emanating from a constitutional order has been advocated, explained, made real to the imagination and the conscience of Western men; by establishing the presumption that civilized society is founded on a public social contract.

A contract is an agreement reached voluntarily, *quid pro quo* and likely, therefore, to be observed—in any event, rightfully enforceable. Being voluntary, it has the consent of the parties. The presumption is not only that one party has acceded to what the other party proposed, but also that, in the original meaning of the word, both parties have consented—that they have thought, felt and judged the matter together. Being a contract, the agreement will, presumably, be specific enough to minimize the quarrels of misunderstanding. It will say what the parties may expect of one another. It will say what are their respective rights and duties. In the field of the contract, their relations will be regulated and criteria will exist for adjudicating issues between them.

These are the essential characteristics of a constitutional system. It can be said to prevail when every man in and out of office is bound by lawful contracts. Without this, that is, without constitutional government, there is no freedom. For the antithesis to being free is to be at the mercy of men who can act arbitrarily. It is not to know what may be done to you. It is to have no right to an accounting, and to have no means of objecting. Despotism and anarchy prevail when a constitutional order does not exist. Both are lawless and arbitrary. Indeed, despotism may be defined as the anarchy of lawless rulers, and anarchy as the despotism of lawless crowds.

The first principle of a civilized state is that power is legitimate only when it is under contract. Then it is, as we say, duly constituted. This principle is of such controlling significance that in the Western world the making of the contracts of government and of society has usually been regarded as marking—historically or symbolically—the crossing of the line which divides barbarity from civility. . .

Men have been laboring with the problem of how to make concrete and real what is abstract and immaterial ever since the Greek philosophers began to feel the need to accommodate the popular Homeric religion to the advance of science. The theologians, says Aristotle, are like the philosophers in that they promulgate certain doctrines; but they are unlike them in that they do so in mythical form.

The method of accommodation employed by the philosophers has been to treat the materialization in the myth as allegory: as translation of the same knowledge into another language. To converse with the devil, for example, could then mean what literally it says—to talk face to face with the devil, a concrete materialized personage. . .

But there are limits beyond which we cannot carry the time-honored method of accommodating the diversity of beliefs. As we know from the variety and sharpness of schisms and sects in our time, we have gone beyond the limits of accommodation. We know, too, that as the divisions grow wider and more irreconcilable, there arise issues of loyalty with which the general principle of toleration is unable to cope.

For the toleration of differences is possible only on the assumption that there is no vital threat to the community. Toleration is not, therefore, a sufficient principle for dealing with the diversity of opinions and beliefs. It is itself dependent upon the positive principle of accommodation. The principle calls for the effort to find agreement beneath the differences.

There is an impressive historical example of how by accommadation it is possible to communicate these difficult truths to a large heterogeneous society. In medieval Christendom a great subject of accommodation was the origin and sanction of the public philosophy itself, of the natural laws of the rational order. . .

But though there was agreement on this, there was deep controversy over whether the natural laws were the commands of God or whether they were the dictates of an eternal reason, grounded on the being of God, and unalterable even by God himself. How were men to imagine, to materialize and make concrete the natural law which is above the Pope and the Kaiser and all mortals? As decrees of an omniscient and omnipotent heavenly king? Or as the principles of the nature of things? There were some who could not conceive of binding laws which had to be obeyed unless there was a lawgiver made in the image of the human lawgivers they had seen or heard about. There were others to whose capacity it was not necessary to condescend with quite that much materialization.

The crucial point, however, is not where the naturalists and supernaturalists disagreed. It is that they did agree that there was a valid law which, whether it was the commandment of God or the reason of things, was transcendent. They did agree that it was not something decided upon by certain men and then proclaimed by them. It was not someone's fancy, someone's prejudice, someone's wish or rationalization, a psychological experience and no more.

It is there objectively, not subjectively. It can be discovered. It has to be obeyed. . .

19. *Man's capacity for justice makes democracy possible; but man's inclination to injustice makes democracy necessary*

REINHOLD NIEBUHR, *The Children of Light and the Children of Darkness*, 1944 *

Democracy has a more compelling justification and requires a more realistic vindication than is given it by the liberal culture with which it has been associated in modern history. The excessively optimistic estimates of human nature and of human history with which the democratic credo has been historically associated are a source of peril to democratic society; for contemporary experience is refuting this optimism and there is danger that it will seem to refute the democratic ideal as well.

A free society requires some confidence in the ability of men to reach tentative and tolerable adjustments between their competing interests and to arrive at some common notions of justice which transcend all partial interests. A consistent pessimism in regard to man's rational capacity for justice invariably leads to absolutistic political theories; for they prompt the conviction that only preponderant power can coerce the various vitalities of a community into a working harmony. But a too consistent optimism in regard to man's ability and inclination to grant justice to his fellows obscures the perils of chaos which perennially confront every society, including a free society. In one sense a democratic society is particularly exposed to the dangers of confusion. If these perils are not appreciated they may overtake a free society and invite the alternative evil of tyranny.

But modern democracy requires a more realistic philosophical and religious basis, not only in order to anticipate and understand the perils to which it is exposed; but also to give it a more persuasive justification. Man's capacity for justice makes democracy possible; but man's inclination to injustice makes democracy necessary.† In all non-democratic political theories the state or the

 Pages x–xii, 1–118 *passim*.

† The text of Niebuhr's thought is taken from Paul's Epistle to the Romans, 7:18–25:
18. For I know that in me (that is, in my flesh) dwelleth no good thing: for to will is present with me; but how to perform that which is good I find not.
19. For the good that I would I do not: but the evil which I would not, that I do.
20. Now if I do that I would not, it is no more I that do it, but sin that dwelleth in me.
21. I find then a law, that, when I would do good, evil is present with me.
22. For I delight in the law of God after the inward man:
23. But I see another law in my members, warring against the law of my mind, and bringing me into captivity to the law of sin which is in my members.
24. O wretched man that I am! Who shall deliver me from the body of this death?
25. I thank God through Jesus Christ our Lord. So then, with the mind I myself serve the law of God; but with the flesh the law of sin. [A.T.M.]

ruler is invested with uncontrolled power for the sake of achieving order and unity in the community. But the pessimism which prompts and justifies this policy is not consistent; for it is not applied, as it should be, to the ruler. If men are inclined to deal unjustly with their fellows, the possession of power aggravates this inclination. That is why irresponsible and uncontrolled power is the greatest source of injustice. . .

Democracy, as every other historic ideal and institution, contains both ephemeral and more permanently valid elements. Democracy is on the one hand the characteristic fruit of a bourgeois civilization; on the other hand it is a perennially valuable form of social organization in which freedom and order are made to support, and not to contradict, each other.

Democracy is a 'bourgeois ideology' in so far as it expresses the typical viewpoints of the middle classes who have risen to power in European civilization in the past three or four centuries. Most of the democratic ideals, as we know them, were weapons of the commercial classes who engaged in stubborn, and ultimately victorious, conflict with the ecclesiastical and aristocratic rulers of the feudal-medieval world. The ideal of equality, unknown in the democratic life of the Greek city states and derived partly from Christian and partly from Stoic sources, gave the bourgeois classes a sense of self-respect in overcoming the aristocratic pretension and condescension of the feudal overlords of medieval society. The middle classes defeated the combination of economic and political power of mercantilism by stressing economic liberty; and, through the principles of political liberty, they added the political power of suffrage to their growing economic power. The implicit assumptions, as well as the explicit ideals, of democratic civilization were also largely the fruit of middle-class existence. The social and historical optimism of democratic life, for instance, represents the typical illusion of an advancing class which mistook its own progress for the progress of the world.

Since bourgeois civilization, which came to birth in the sixteenth to eighteenth centuries and reached its zenith in the nineteenth century, is now obviously in grave peril, if not actualy in *rigor mortis* in the twentieth century, it must be obvious that democracy, in so far as it is a middle-class ideology, also faces its doom.

This fate of democracy might be viewed with equanimity, but for the fact that it has a deeper dimension and broader validity than its middle-class character. Ideally democracy is a permanantly valid form of social and political organization which does justice to two dimensions of human existence: to man's spiritual stature and his social character; to the uniqueness and variety of life, as well as to the common necessities of all men. Bourgeois democracy frequently exalted the individual at the expense of the community; but its emphasis upon liberty contained a valid element, which transcended its excessive individualism. The community requires liberty as much as does the individual; and the individual requires community more than bourgeois thought comprehended. Democracy can therefore not be equated with freedom. An ideal democratic order seeks unity within the conditions of freedom; and maintains freedom within the framework of order.

Man requires freedom in his social organization because he is 'essentially' free, which is to say, that he has the capacity for indeterminate transcendence over the processes and limitations of nature. This freedom enables him to make history and to elaborate communal organizations in boundless variety and in endless breadth and extent. But he also requires community because he is by nature social. He cannot fulfill his life within himself but only in responsible and mutual relations with his fellows. . .

The individual cannot be a true self in isolation. Nor can he live within the confines of the community which "nature" establishes in the minimal cohesion of family and herd. His freedom transcends these limits of nature, and therefore makes larger and larger social units both possible and necessary. It is precisely because of the essential freedom of man that he requires a contrived order in his community.

The democratic ideal is thus more valid than the libertarian and individualistic version of it which bourgeois civilization elaborated. Since the bourgeois version has been discredited by the events of contemporary history and since, in any event, bourgeois civilization is in process of disintegration, it becomes important to distinguish and save what is permanently valid from what is ephemeral in the democratic order.

If democracy is to survive it must find a more adequate cultural basis than the philosophy which has informed the building of the bourgeois world. The inadequacy of the presuppositions upon which the democratic experiment rests does not consist merely in the excessive individualism and libertarianism of the bourgeois world view; though it must be noted that this excessive individualism prompted a civil war in the whole western world in which the rising proletarian classes pitted an excessive collectivism against the false individualism of middle-class life. This civil conflict contributed to the weakness of democratic civilization when faced with the threat of barbarism. Neither the individualism nor the collectivism did justice to all the requirements of man's social life, and the conflict between half-truth and half-truth divided the civilized world in such a way that the barbarians were able to claim first one side and then the other in this civil conflict as their provisional allies.

But there is a more fundamental error in the social philosophy of democratic civilization than the individualism of bourgeois democracy and the collectivism of Marxism. It is the confidence of both bourgeois and proletarian idealists in the possibility of achieving an easy resolution of the tension and conflict between self-interest and the general interest. . .

In the field of domestic politics the war of uncontrolled interests may have been the consequence, but it was certainly not the intention, of middle-class individualists. Nor was the conflict between nations in our modern world their intention. They did demand a greater degree of freedom for the nations; but they believed that it was possible to achieve an uncontrolled harmony between them, once the allegedly irrelevant restrictions of the old religio-political order were removed. In this they proved to be mistaken. They did not make the mistake, however, of giving simple moral sanction to self-interest. They depended rather upon controls and restraints which proved to be inadequate.

In illumining this important distinction more fully, we may well designate the moral cynics, who know no law beyond their will and interest, with a scriptural designation of 'children of this world' or 'children of darkness.' Those who believe that self-interest should be brought under the discipline of a higher law could then be termed 'the children of light.' This is no mere arbitrary device; for evil is always the assertion of some self-interest without regard to the whole, whether the whole be conceived as the immediate community, or the total community of mankind, or the total order of the world. The good is, on the other hand, always the harmony of the whole on various levels. Devotion to a subordinate and premature 'whole' such as the nation, may of course become evil, viewed from the perspective of a larger whole, such as the community of mankind. The 'children of light' may thus be defined as those who seek to bring self-interest under the discipline of a more universal law and in harmony with a more universal good.

According to the scripture 'the children of this world are in their generation wiser than the children of light.' This observation fits the modern situation. Our democratic civilization has been built, not by children of darkness but by foolish children of light. It has been under attack by the children of darkness, by the moral cynics, who declare that a strong nation need acknowledge no law beyond its strength. It has come close to complete disaster under this attack, not because it accepted the same creed as the cynics; but because it underestimated the power of self-interest, both individual and collective, in modern society. The children of light have not been as wise as the children of darkness.

The children of darkness are evil because they know no law beyond the self. They are wise, though evil, because they understand the power of self-interest. The children of light are virtuous because they have some conception of a higher law than their own will. They are usually foolish because they do not know the power of self-will. They underestimate the peril of anarchy in both the national and the international community. Modern democratic civilization is, in short, sentimental rather than cynical. It has an easy solution for the problem of anarchy and chaos on both the national and international level of community, because of its fatuous and superficial view of man. It does not know that the same man who is ostensibly devoted to the 'common good' may have desires and ambitions, hopes and fears, which set him at variance with his neighbor.

It must be understood that the children of light are foolish not merely because they underestimate the power of self-interest among the children of darkness. They underestimate this power among themselves. The democratic world came so close to disaster not merely because it never believed that Nazism possessed the demonic fury which it avowed. Civilization refused to recognize the power of class interest in its own communities. It also spoke glibly of an international conscience; but the children of darkness meanwhile skilfully set nation against nation. They were thereby enabled to despoil one nation after another, without every civilized nation coming to the defence of each. Moral cynicism had a provisional advantage over moral sentimentality. Its advantage lay not merely in its own code of scruple but also in its shrewd assessment of the power of self-interest, individual and national, among the children of light, despite their moral protestations. . .

Our modern civilization . . . was ushered in on a wave of boundless social optimism. Modern secularism is divided into many schools. But all the various schools agreed in rejecting the Christian doctrine of original sin. It is not possible to explain the subtleties or to measure the profundity of this doctrine in this connection. But it is necessary to point out that the doctrine makes an important contribution to any adequate social and political theory the lack of which has robbed bourgeois theory of real wisdom; for it emphasizes a fact which every page of human history attests. Through it one may understand that no matter how wide the perspectives which the human mind may reach, how broad the loyalties which the human imagination may conceive, how universal the community which human statecraft may organize, or how pure the aspirations of the saintliest idealist may be, there is no level of human moral or social achievement in which there is not some corruption of inordinate self-love.

This sober and true view of the human situation was neatly rejected by modern culture. That is why it conceived so many fatuous and futile plans for resolving the conflict between the self and the community; and between the national and the world community. Whenever modern idealists are confronted with the divisive and corrosive effects of man's self-love, they look for some immediate cause of this perennial tendency, usually in some specific form of social organization. One school holds that men would be good if only political institutions would not corrupt them; another believes that they would be good if the prior evil of a faulty economic organization could be eliminated. Or another school thinks of this evil as no more than ignorance, and therefore waits for a more perfect educational process to redeem man from his partial and particular loyalties. But no school asks how it is that an essentially good man could have produced corrupting and tyrannical political organizations or exploiting economic organizations, or fanatical and superstitious religious organizations. . . The survival impulse, which man shares with the animals, is regarded as the normative form of his egoistic drive. If this were a true picture of the human situation man might be, or might become, as harmless as seventeenth- and eighteenth-century thought assumed. Unfortunately for the validity of this picture of man, the most significant distinction between the human and the animal world is that the impulses of the former are 'spiritualized' in the human world. Human capacities for evil as well as for good are derived from this spiritualization. There is of course always a natural survival impulse at the core of all human ambition. But this survival impulse cannot be neatly disentangled from two forms of its spiritualization. The one form is the desire to fulfill the potentialities of life and not merely to maintain its existence. Man is the kind of animal who cannot merely live. If he lives at all he is bound to seek the realization of his true nature; and to his true nature belongs his fulfillment in the lives of others. The will to live is thus transmuted into the will to self-realization; and self-realization involves self-giving in relations to others. When this desire for self-realization is fully explored it becomes apparent that it is subject to the paradox that the highest form of self-realization is the consequence of self-giving, but that it cannot be the intended consequence without being prematurely limited. Thus the will to live is finally transmuted into its opposite in the sense that only in self-giving can the self be fulfilled, for: 'He that findeth his life shall lose it: and he that loseth his life for my sake shall find it.'

On the other hand the will-to-live is also spiritually transmuted into the will-to-power or into the desire for 'power and glory.' Man, being more than a natural creature, is not interested merely in physical survival but in prestige and social approval. Having the intelligence to anticipate the perils in which he stands in nature and history, he invariably seeks to gain security against these perils by enhancing his power, individually and collectively. Possessing a darkly unconscious sense of his insignificance in the total scheme of things, he seeks to compensate for his insignificance by pretensions of pride. The conflicts between men are thus never simple conflicts between competing survival impulses. They are conflicts in which each man or group seeks to guard its power and prestige against the peril of competing expressions of power and pride. Since the very possession of power and prestige always involves some encroachment upon the prestige and power of others, this conflict is by its very nature a more stubborn and difficult one than the mere competition between various survival impulses in nature. It remains to be added that this conflict expresses itself even more cruelly in collective than in individual terms. Human behaviour being less individualistic than secular liberalism assumed, the struggle between classes, races and other groups in human society is not as easily resolved by the expedient of dissolving the groups as liberal democratic idealists assumed.

Since the survival impulse in nature is transmuted into two different and contradictory spiritualized forms, which we may briefly designate as the will-to-live-truly and the will-to-power, man is at variance with himself. The power of the second impulse places him more fundamentally in conflict with his fellowman than democratic liberalism realizes. The fact he cannot realize himself, except in organic relation with his fellows, makes the community more important than bourgeois individualism understands. The fact that the two impulses, though standing in contradiction to each other, are also mixed and compounded with each other on every level of human life, makes the simple distinctions between good and evil, between selfishness and altruism, with which liberal idealism has tried to estimate moral and political facts, invalid. The fact that the will-to-power inevitably justifies itself in terms of the morally more acceptable will to realize man's true nature means that the egoistic corruption of universal ideals is a much more persistent fact in human conduct than any moralistic creed is inclined to admit.

If we survey any period of history, and not merely the present tragic era of world catastrophe, it becomes quite apparent that human ambitions, lusts and desires, are more inevitably inordinate, that both human creativity and human evil reach greater heights, and that conflicts in the community between varying conceptions of the good and between competing expressions of vitality are of more tragic proportions than was anticipated in the basic philosophy which underlies democratic civilization. . . It is the error of a too great reliance upon the human capacity for transcendence over self-interest. There is indeed such a capacity. If there were not, any form of social harmony among men would be impossible; and certainly a democratic version of such harmony would be quite unthinkable. But the same man who displays this capacity also reveals varying degrees of the power of self-interest and of the subservience of the mind to these interests. Sometimes this egotism stands in frank contradiction to the professed ideal or sense of obligation to higher and wider values; and sometimes it uses the ideal as its instrument.

It is this fact which a few pessimists in our modern culture have realized, only to draw undemocratic and sometimes completely cynical conclusions from it. The democratic idealists of practically all schools of thought have managed to remain remarkably oblivious to the obvious facts. Democratic theory therefore has not squared with the facts of history. This grave defect in democratic theory was comparatively innocuous in the heyday of the bourgeois period, when the youth and the power of democratic civilization surmounted all errors of judgment and confusions of mind. But in this latter day, when it has become important to save what is valuable in democratic life from the destruction of what is false in bourgeois civilization, it has also become necessary to distinguish what is false in democratic theory from what is true in democratic life.

The preservation of a democratic civilization requires the wisdom of the serpent and the harmlessness of the dove. The children of light must be armed with the wisdom of the children of darkness but remain free from their malice. They must know the power of self-interest in human society without giving it moral justification. They must have this wisdom in order that they may beguile, deflect, harness and restrain self-interest, individual and collective, for the sake of the community. . . The restraints which all human communities place upon human impulses and ambitions are made necessary by the fact that all man's vitalities tend to defy any defined limits. But since the community may as easily become inordinate in its passion for order, as may the various forces in the community in their passion for freedom, it is necessary to preserve a proper balance between both principles, and to be as ready to champion the individual against the community as the community against the individual. Any definition of a proper balance between freedom and order must always be at least slightly colored by the exigencies of the moment which may make the peril of the one seem greater and the security of the other therefore preferable. Thus even the moral and social principle which sets limits upon freedom and order must, in a free society, be subject to constant re-examination. In our own society this re-examination has actually been too long delayed. That is why economic forces which come within an ace of dominating the community are able to prevent communal control of their power by appealing to traditional conceptions of liberty. . .

A full analysis of these complexities must invalidate any simple solution of the problem of property. Since economic power, as every other form of social power, is a defensive force when possessed in moderation and a temptation to injustice when it is great enough to give the agent power over others, it would seem that its widest and most equitable distribution would make for the highest degree of justice. This gives a provisional justification to the liberal theory.

But bourgeois liberalism assumes a natural equilibrium of economic power in the community which historic facts refute. If the economic process is left severely alone either the strong devour the weak, in which case monopoly displaces competition, or competition breeds chaos in the community. . .

There must, in other words, be a continuous debate on the property question in democratic society and a continuous adjustment to new developments. Such a debate is possible, however, only if there is some common denominator between opposing factions.

The contradictory dogmas about property can be most easily dissolved if the utopianism which underlies both of them, is dispelled. In communities, such as America, where the Marxist dogma has never developed the power to challenge the bourgeois one, the primary requirement of justice is that the dominant dogma be discredited. The obvious facts about property which both liberal and Marxist theories have obscured are: that all property is power; that some forms of economic power are intrinsically more ordinate than others and therefore more defensive, but that no sharp line can be drawn between what is ordinate and what is inordinate; that property is not the only form of economic power and that the destruction of private property does not therefore guarantee the equalization of economic power in a community; that inordinate power tempts its holders to abuse it, which means to use it for their own ends; that the economic, as well as the political, process requires the best possible distribution of power for the sake of justice and the best possible management of this equilibrium for the sake of order.

None of these propositions solves any specific issue of property in a given instance. But together they set the property issue within the framework of democratic procedure. For democracy is a method of finding proximate solutions for insoluble problems.

20. *To overcome violence and bigotry we must alter some of the basic assumptions in American life and politics*

J. William Fulbright, *The Strain of Violence*, 1963 *

Our national life, both past and present, has . . . been marked by a baleful and incongruous strand of intolerance and violence.

It is in evidence all around us; in the senseless and widespread crime that makes the streets of our great cities unsafe; in the malice and hatred of extremist political movements; in the cruel bigotry of race that leads to such tragedies as the killing of Negro children in a church in Alabama.

We must ask ourselves many questions about this element of barbarism in a civilized society. We must ask ourselves what its sources are, in history and in human nature. . .

* Rockefeller Public Service Award Address, *Princeton Alumni Weekly*, 17 March 1964.

We must ask ourselves what, if anything, all this has to do with the death of our President. Finally, and most important, we must ask ourselves what we must do, and how and when, to overcome hatred and bigotry and to make America as decent and humane a society as we would like it to be. . .

Moral absolutism—righteous, crusading, and intolerant—has been a major force in the history of Western civilization. Whether religious or political in form, movements of crusading moralism have played a significant, and usually destructive, role in the evolution of Western societies. Such movements, regardless of the content of their doctrines, have all been marked by a single characteristic: the absolute certainty of their own truth and virtue. Each has regarded itself as having an exclusive pipeline to heaven, to God, or to a deified concept of History—or whatever is regarded as the ultimate source of truth. Each has regarded itself as the chosen repository of truth and virtue and each has regarded all nonbelievers as purveyors of falsehood and evil.

Absolutist movements are usually crusading movements. Free as they are from any element of doubt as to their own truth and virtue, they conceive themselves to have a mission of spreading the truth and destroying evil. They consider it to be their duty to regenerate mankind, however little it may wish to be regenerated. The means which are used for this purpose, though often harsh and sometimes barbaric, are deemed to be wholly justified by the nobility of the end. They are justified because the end is absolute and there can be no element of doubt as to its virtue and its truth. . .

Democratic societies have by no means been free of self-righteousness and the crusading spirit. On the contrary, they have at times engaged in great crusades to spread the gospel of their own ideology. Indeed, no democratic nation has been more susceptible to this tendency than the United States, which in the past generation has fought one war to 'make the world safe for democracy,' another to achieve nothing less than the 'unconditional surrender' of its enemies, and even now finds it possible to consider the plausibility of 'total victory' over communism in a thermonuclear war.

It is clear that democratic nations are susceptible to dogmatism and the crusading spirit. The point, however, is that this susceptibility is not an expression but a denial of the democratic spirit. When a free nation embarks upon a crusade for democracy, it is caught up in the impossible contradiction of trying to use force to make men free. The dogmatic and crusading spirit in free societies is an anti-democratic tendency, a lingering vestige of the strand of dogmatism and violence in the Western heritage.

Although no Western nation has completely dispelled the absolutist spirit of the crusades and the religious wars, some have been more successful than others. The most successful of all, I believe—at least among those nations which have had an important impact on the world beyond their own frontiers—has been England. . . By the time of the establishment of the English colonies in the new world, the evolution toward constitutional democracy was well advanced. The process quickly took hold in the North American colonies and their evolution toward democracy outpaced that of the mother country. This was the basic heritage of America—a heritage of tolerance, moderation, and individual liberty that was implanted from the very beginnings of European settlement in the new world. America has quite rightly been called a nation that was 'born free.'

There came also to the new world the Puritans, a minor group in England who became a major force in American life. Their religion was Calvinism, an absolutist faith with a stern moral code promising salvation for the few and damnation for the many. The intolerant, witch-hunting Puritanism of seventeenth century Massachusetts was not a major religious movement in America. It eventually became modified and as a source of ethical standards made a worthy contribution to American life. But the Puritan *way of thinking*, harsh and intolerant, permeated the political and economic life of the country and became a major secular force in America. Coexisting uneasily with our English heritage of tolerance and moderation, the Puritan way of thinking has injected an absolutist strand into American thought—a strand of stern moralism in our public policy and in our standards of personal behavior. . .

The Puritan way of thinking has had a powerful impact on our foreign policy. It is reflected in our traditional vacillation between self-righteous isolation and total involvement and in our attitude toward foreign policy as a series of idealistic crusades rather than as a continuing defense of the national interest. It is reflected in some of the most notable events of our history: in the unnecessary war with Spain, which was spurred by an idealistic fervor to liberate Cuba and ended with our making Cuba an American protectorate; in the war of 1917, which began with a national commitment to 'make the world safe for democracy' and ended with our repudiation of our own blueprint for a world order of peace and law; in the radical pacifism of the interwar years which ended with our total involvement in a conflict in which our proclaimed objective of 'unconditional surrender' was finally achieved by dropping atomic bombs on Hiroshima and Nagasaki.

Throughout the twentieth century American foreign policy has been caught up in the inherent contradiction between our English heritage of tolerance and accommodation and our Puritan heritage of crusading righteousness. This contradiction is strikingly illustrated by the policy of President Wilson in World War I. In 1914 he called upon the American people to be neutral in thought as well as in their actions; in early 1917, when the United States was still neutral, he called upon the belligerents to compromise their differences and accept a 'peace without victory'; but in the spring of 1918, when the United States had been involved in the war for a year, he perceived only one possible response to the challenge of Germany in the war: 'Force, Force to the utmost, Force without *stint* or limit, the righteous and triumphant Force which shall make Right the law of the world, and cast every selfish dominion down in the dust.'

The danger of any crusading movement issues from its presumption of absolute truth. If the premise is valid, then all else follows. If we know, with absolute and unchallengeable certainty, that a political leader is traitorous, or that he is embarked upon a course of certain ruin for the nation, then it is our right, indeed our duty, to carry our opposition beyond constitutional means and to remove him by force or even murder. The premise, however, is *not* valid. We do not know, nor can we know, with absolute certainty that those who disagree with us are wrong. We are human and therefore fallible, and being fallible, we cannot escape the *element of doubt* as to our own opinions and convictions. This, I believe, is the core of the democratic spirit. When we acknowledge our own fallibility, tolerance and compromise become possible and fanaticism becomes absurd.

Before I comment on recent events, it is necessary to mention another major factor in the shaping of the American national character. That factor is the experience of the frontier, the building of a great nation out of a vast wilderness in the course of a single century. The frontier experience taught us the great value of individual initiative and self-reliance in the development of our resources and of our national economy. But the individualism of the frontier, largely untempered by social and legal restraints, has also had an important influence on our political life and on our personal relations. It has generated impatience with the complex and tedious procedures of law and glorified the virtues of direct individual action. It has instilled in us an easy familiarity with violence and vigilante justice. In the romanticized form in which it permeates the television and other mass media, the mythology of the frontier conveys the message that killing a man is not bad as long as you don't shoot him in the back, that violence is only reprehensible when its purpose is bad and that in fact it is commendable and glorious when it is perpetrated by good men for a good purpose.

The murder of the accused assassin of President Kennedy is a shocking example of the spirit of vigilante justice. Compounding one crime with another, this act has denied the accused individual of one of the most basic rights of a civilized society: the right to a fair trial under established procedures of law. No less shocking are the widespread expressions of sympathy and approval for the act of the man who killed the accused assassin. Underlying these expressions of approval is an assumption that it is not killing that is bad but only certain kinds of killing, that it is proper and even praiseworthy for a citizen to take justice into his own hands when he deems his purpose to be a just one or a righteous act of vengeance. This attitude is a prescription for anarchy. Put into general practice, it would do far more to destroy the fabric of a free society than the evils which it purports to redress. . .

The mythology of the frontier, the moral absolutism of our Puritan heritage, . . . have injected a strand of intolerance and violence into American life. This violent tendency lies beneath the surface of an orderly, law-abiding democratic society, but not far beneath the surface. When times are normal, when the country is prosperous at home and secure in its foreign relations, our violent and intolerant tendencies remain quiescent and we are able to conduct our affairs in a rational and orderly manner. But in times of crisis, foreign or domestic, our underlying irrationality breaks through to become a dangerous and disruptive force in our national life.

Since World War II, times have not been 'normal'; they are not 'normal' now, nor are they likely to be for as far into the future as we can see. In this era of nuclear weapons and cold war, we live with constant crises and the continuing and immediate danger of incineration by hydrogen bombs. We are a people who have faced dangers before but we have always been able to overcome them by direct and immediate action. Now we are confronted with dangers vastly greater than we or any other nation have ever before known and we see no end to them and no solutions to them. Nor are there any solutions. There are only possibilities, limited, intermittent, and ambiguous, to alleviate the dangers of our time. For the rest, we have no choice but to try to live with the unsolved problems of a revolutionary world.

. . . If we are to overcome violence and bigotry in our national life, we must alter some of the basic assumptions of American life and politics. We must recognize that the secular Puritanism which we have practiced, with its principles of absolute good, absolute evil, and intolerance of dissent, has been an obstacle to the practice of democracy at home and the conduct of an effective foreign policy. We must recognize that the romanticized cult of the frontier, with its glorification of violence and of unrestrained individualism, is a childish and dangerous anachronism in a nation which carries the responsibility of the leadership of the free world in the nuclear age.

Finally, we must revive and strengthen the central core of our national heritage, which is the legacy of liberty, tolerance, and moderation that came to us from the ancient world through a thousand years of English history and three centuries of democratic evolution in North America. It is this historic legacy which is the best and the strongest of our endowments. . .

21. *The struggle for security and peace will not be finished perhaps in our lifetime on this planet*

JOHN F. KENNEDY, Inaugural Address, 20 January 1961 *

The world is very different now. For man holds in his mortal hands the power to abolish all forms of human poverty and all forms of human life. And yet the same revolutionary beliefs for which our forebears fought are still at issue around the globe—the belief that the rights of man come not from the generosity of the state but from the hand of God.

We dare not forget today that we are the heirs of that first revolution. Let the word go forth from this time and place, to friend and foe alike, that the torch has been passed to a new generation of Americans—born in this century, tempered by war, disciplined by a hard and bitter peace, proud of our ancient heritage—and unwilling to witness or permit the slow undoing of those human rights to which this nation has always been committed, and to which we are committed today at home and around the world. . .

To those old allies whose cultural and spiritual origins we share, we pledge the loyalty of faithful friends. United, there is little we cannot do in a host of cooperative ventures. Divided, there is little we can do—for we dare not meet a powerful challenge at odds and split asunder.

To those new states whom we welcome to the ranks of the free, we pledge

* *Public Papers of the Presidents of the United States,* Washington, D.C., 1962, pp. 1–2.

our word that one form of colonial control shall not have passed away merely to be replaced by a far more iron tyranny. We shall not always expect to find them supporting our view. But we shall always hope to find them strongly supporting their own freedom—and to remember that, in the past, those who foolishly sought power by riding the back of the tiger ended up inside.

To those peoples in the huts and villages of half the globe struggling to break the bonds of mass misery, we pledge our best efforts to help them help themselves, for whatever period is required—not because the communists may be doing it, not because we seek their votes, but because it is right. If a free society cannot help the many who are poor, it cannot save the few who are rich.

To our sister republics south of our border, we offer a special pledge—to convert our good words into good deeds—in a new alliance for progress—to assist free men and free governments in casting off the chains of poverty. But this peaceful revolution of hope cannot become the prey of hostile powers. Let all our neighbors know that we shall join with them to oppose aggression or subversion anywhere in the Americas. And let every other power know that this Hemisphere intends to remain the master of its own house.

To that world assembly of sovereign states, the United Nations, our last best hope in an age where the instruments of war have far outpaced the instruments of peace, we renew our pledge of support—to prevent it from becoming merely a forum for invective—to strengthen its shield of the new and the weak—and to enlarge the area in which its writ may run.

Finally, to those nations who would make themselves our adversary, we offer not a pledge but a request: that both sides begin anew the quest for peace, before the dark powers of destruction unleashed by science engulf all humanity in planned or accidental self-destruction.

We dare not tempt them with weakness. For only when our arms are sufficient beyond doubt can we be certain beyond doubt that they will never be employed.

But neither can two great and powerful groups of nations take comfort from our present course—both sides overburdened by the cost of modern weapons, both rightly alarmed by the steady spread of the deadly atom, yet both racing to alter that uncertain balance of terror that stays the hand of mankind's final war.

So let us begin anew—remembering on both sides that civility is not a sign of weakness, and sincerity is always subject to proof. Let us never negotiate out of fear. But let us never fear to negotiate.

Let both sides explore what problems unite us instead of belaboring those problems which divide us.

Let both sides, for the first time, formulate serious and precise proposals for the inspection and control of arms—and bring the absolute power to destroy other nations under the absolute control of all nations.

Let both sides seek to invoke the wonders of science instead of its terrors. Together let us explore the stars, conquer the deserts, eradicate disease, tap the ocean depths and encourage the arts and commerce. . .

And if a beach-head of cooperation may push back the jungle of suspicion, let both sides join in creating a new endeavor, not a new balance of power, but a new world of law, where the strong are just and the weak secure and the peace preserved.

All this will not be finished in the first one hundred days. Nor will it be finished in the first one thousand days, nor in the life of this Administration, nor even perhaps in our lifetime on this planet. But let us begin. . .

Now the trumpet summons us again—not as a call to bear arms, though arms we need—not as a call to battle, though embattled we are—but a call to bear the burden of a long twilight struggle, year in and year out, 'rejoicing in hope, patient in tribulation'—a struggle against the common enemies of man: tyranny, poverty, disease and war itself. . .

In the long history of the world, only a few generations have been granted the role of defending freedom in its hour of maximum danger. . . The energy, the faith, the devotion which we bring to this endeavor will light our country and all who serve it—and the glow from that fire can truly light the world. . .

And so, my fellow Americans: ask not what your country can do for you—ask what you can do for your country.

My fellow citizens of the world: ask not what America will do for you, but what together we can do for the freedom of man. . .

SELECTED REFERENCES

Alan Barth, *The Loyalty of Free Men*, New York, Viking, 1951.

———, *Government by Investigation*, New York, Viking, 1955.

Daniel Bell, *The New American Right*, New York, Criterion Books, 1955.

Adolf Berle, Jr., *The 20th Century Capitalist Revolution*, New York, Harcourt, Brace, 1954.

———, *The American Economic Republic*, New York, Harcourt, Brace & World, 1963.

Eleanor Bontecou, *The Federal Loyalty Security Program*, Ithaca, Cornell University Press, 1953.

Daniel Boorstin, *The Genius of American Politics*, Chicago, University of Chicago Press, 1953.

Julian P. Boyd, 'Subversive of What?', *The Atlantic Monthly*, August 1948.

Robert A. Brady, *Business as a System of Power*, New York, Columbia University Press, 1947.

Louis D. Brandeis, *The Curse of Bigness*, Miscellaneous Papers, edited by Osmond K. Fraenkel, New York, Viking, 1934.

Harrison Brown, *The Challenge of Man's Future*, New York, Viking, 1954.

Robert K. Carr, *Federal Protection of Civil Rights: Quest for a Sword*, Ithaca, Cornell University Press, 1947.

———, *The House Committee on Un-American Activities*, Ithaca, Cornell University Press, 1952.

Zechariah Chafee, *Free Speech in the United States*, Cambridge, Harvard University Press, 1942.

Carl Cohen, 'Essence and Ethics of Civil Disobedience,' *The Nation*, March 16, 1964.

Henry Steele Commager, *Freedom, Loyalty, Dissent*, New York, Oxford University Press, 1954.

———, 'How Explain Our Illness,' *The Washington Post*, December 1963. Reprinted in *Current*, January 1964.

Charles P. Curtis, *Law as Large as Life: A Natural Law for Today and the Supreme Court as Its Prophet*, New York, Simon & Schuster, 1959.

Sebastion De Grazia, *Of Time, Work and Leisure*, New York, Twentieth Century Fund, 1962.
Thomas I. Emerson and David M. Helfeld, 'Loyalty among Government Employees,' *Yale Law Journal*, December 1948.
Charles Frankel, *The Democratic Prospect*, New York, Harper, 1962.
———, *The Case for Modern Man*, New York, Harper, 1956.
J. K. Galbraith, *American Capitalism: Concept of Countervailing Power*, Boston, Houghton Mifflin, 1952.
———, *The Affluent Society*, Boston, Houghton Mifflin, 1958.
Walter Gellhorn, *Security, Loyalty and Science*, Ithaca, Cornell University Press, 1950.
Andrew Hacker, *The Corporation Take-Over*, New York, Harper & Row, 1964.
Learned Hand, *The Bill of Rights*, Cambridge, Harvard University Press, 1958.
Sidney Hook, *Heresy, Yes—Compromise, No!*, New York, John Day, 1953.
George Kistiakowsky, quoted in *Science* editorial, 'Footnote to History,' vol. 133, February 10, 1961, p. 355.
Michael Harrington, *The Other America: Poverty in the United States*, New York, Macmillan, 1962.
Harold Lasswell, *National Security and Individual Freedom*, New York, McGraw-Hill, 1950.
David Lilienthal, *Big Business: A New Era*, New York, Harper, 1952.
A. T. Mason, *The States' Rights Debate*, Englewood Cliffs, N. J., Prentice-Hall, 1964.
———, *Security Through Freedom*, Ithaca, N. Y., Cornell University Press, 1955, chapters 5 and 6.
Alexander Meiklejohn, *Free Speech and Its Relation to Self-Government*, New York, Harper, 1948.
———, 'What Does the First Amendment Mean?', *University of Chicago Law Review*, 1953, vol. 20, pp. 461–79.
John Stuart Mill, *On Liberty*, New York, E. P. Dutton, Everyman's Library.
Arthur Miller and Ronald Howell, 'The Myth of Neutrality in Constitutional Adjudication,' 27 *University of Chicago Law Review*, 1960, 661.
C. Wright Mills, *The Power Elite*, New York, Oxford University Press, 1956.
Gunnar Myrdal, *An American Dilemma: The Negro Problem and Modern Democracy*, New York, Harper, 1944.
Bernard D. Nossiter, *The Mythmakers: An Essay on Power and Wealth*, Boston, Houghton Mifflin, 1964.
Challenge to Democracy: The Next Ten Years, Edward Reed, ed., New York, Praeger, 1963.
David Riesman, *Abundance for What?*, New York, Doubleday, 1964.
———, *The Lonely Crowd*, New Haven, Yale University Press, 1950.
Paths of American Thought, Arthur Schlesinger, Jr., and Morton White, eds., Boston, Houghton Mifflin, 1963.
David Spitz, *Patterns of Anti-Democratic Thought*, New York, Macmillan, 1949.
Edmund Stillman and William Pfaff, *The Politics of Hysteria*, New York, Harper & Row, 1964.
W. F. Swindler, 'The Current Challenge to Federalism: The Confederating Proposals,' 52 *Georgetown Law Journal*, 1963, 1–41.
Telford Taylor, *Grand Inquest: The Story of Congressional Investigations*, New York, Simon & Schuster, 1955.
Herbert Wechsler, 'Toward Neutral Principles of Constitutional Law,' 73 *Harvard Law Review*, 1959, 1.
Freedom Now! The Civil Rights Struggle in America, Alan F. Westin, ed., New York, Basic Books, 1964.
W. H. Whyte, *The Organization Man*, New York, Simon & Schuster, 1956.
Norbert Wiener, *Cybernetics*, Cambridge, Mass., Technology Press, 1948.

*

CONSTITUTION OF THE UNITED STATES

We the people of the United States, in order to form a more perfect union, establish justice, insure domestic tranquillity, provide for the common defense, promote the general welfare, and secure the blessings of liberty to ourselves and our posterity, do ordain and establish this Constitution for the United States of America.

ARTICLE I

SECTION 1. All legislative powers herein granted shall be vested in a Congress of the United States, which shall consist of a Senate and House of Representatives.

SECTION 2. 1. The House of Representatives shall be composed of members chosen every second year by the people of the several States, and the electors in each State shall have the qualifications requisite for electors of the most numerous branch of the State legislature.

2. No person shall be a representative who shall not have attained to the age of twenty-five years, and been seven years a citizen of the United States, and who shall not, when elected, be an inhabitant of that State in which he shall be chosen.

3. Representatives and direct taxes [1] shall be apportioned among the several States which may be included within this Union, according to their respective numbers, which shall be determined by adding to the whole number of free persons, including those bound to service for a term of years, and excluding Indians not taxed, *three fifths of all other persons.*[2] The actual enumeration shall be made within three years after the first meeting of the Congress of the United States, and within every subsequent term of ten years, in such manner as they shall by law direct. The number of representatives shall not exceed one for every thirty thousand, but each State shall have at least one representative; and until such enumeration shall be made, the State of New Hampshire shall be entitled to choose three, Massachusetts eight, Rhode Island and Providence Plantations one, Connecticut five, New York six, New Jersey four, Pennsylvania eight, Delaware one, Maryland six, Virginia ten, North Carolina five, South Carolina five, and Georgia three.

4. When vacancies happen in the representation from any State, the executive authority thereof shall issue writs of election to fill such vacancies.

5. The House of Representatives shall choose their speaker and other officers; and shall have the sole power of impeachment.

[1] See the 16th Amendment.
[2] See the 14th Amendment.

SECTION 3. 1. The Senate of the United States shall be composed of two senators from each State, *chosen by the legislature thereof,*[3] for six years; and each senator shall have one vote.

2. Immediately after they shall be assembled in consequence of the first election, they shall be divided as equally as may be into three classes. The seats of the senators of the first class shall be vacated at the expiration of the second year, of the second class at the expiration of the fourth year, and of the third class at the expiration of the sixth year, so that one third may be chosen every second year; and if vacancies happen by resignation, or otherwise, during the recess of the legislature of any State, the executive thereof may make temporary appointments until the next meeting of the legislature, which shall then fill such vacancies.[3]

3. No person shall be a senator who shall not have attained to the age of thirty years, and been nine years a citizen of the United States, and who shall not, when elected, be an inhabitant of that State for which he shall be chosen.

4. The Vice President of the United States shall be President of the Senate, but shall have no vote, unless they be equally divided.

5. The Senate shall choose their other officers, and also a president *pro tempore,* in the absence of the Vice President, or when he shall exercise the office of the President of the United States.

6. The Senate shall have the sole power to try all impeachments. When sitting for that purpose, they shall be on oath or affirmation. When the President of the United States is tried, the chief justice shall preside: and no person shall be convicted without the concurrence of two thirds of the members present.

7. Judgment in cases of impeachment shall not extend further than to removal from office, and disqualification to hold and enjoy any office of honor, trust or profit under the United States: but the party convicted shall nevertheless be liable and subject to indictment, trial, judgment and punishment, according to law.

SECTION 4. 1. The times, places and manner of holding elections for senators and representatives, shall be prescribed in each State by the legislature thereof; but the Congress may at any time by law make or alter such regulations, except as to the places of choosing senators.

2. The Congress shall assemble at least once in every year, and such meeting shall be on the first Monday in December, unless they shall by law appoint a different day.[4]

SECTION 5. 1. Each House shall be the judge of the elections, returns and qualifications of its own members, and a majority of each shall constitute a quorum to do business; but a smaller number may adjourn from day to day, and may be authorized to compel the attendance of absent members, in such manner, and under such penalties as each House may provide.

2. Each House may determine the rules of its proceedings, punish its members for disorderly behavior, and, with the concurrence of two thirds, expel a member.

3. Each House shall keep a journal of its proceedings, and from time to time publish the same, excepting such parts as may in their judgment require secrecy; and the yeas and nays of the members of either House on any question shall, at the desire of one fifth of those present, be entered on the journal.

[3] See the 17th Amendment.
[4] See the 20th Amendment.

4. Neither House, during the session of Congress, shall, without the consent of the other, adjourn for more than three days, nor to any other place than that in which the two Houses shall be sitting.

SECTION 6. 1. The senators and representatives shall receive a compensation for their services, to be ascertained by law, and paid out of the Treasury of the United States. They shall in all cases, except treason, felony, and breach of the peace, be privileged from arrest during their attendance at the session of their respective Houses, and in going to and returning from the same; and for any speech or debate in either House, they shall not be questioned in any other place.

2. No senator or representative shall, during the time for which he was elected, be appointed to any civil office under the authority of the United States, which shall have been created, or the emoluments whereof shall have been increased during such time; and no person holding any office under the United States, shall be a member of either House during his continuance in office.

SECTION 7. 1. All bills for raising revenue shall originate in the House of Representatives; but the Senate may propose or concur with amendments as on other bills.

2. Every bill which shall have passed the House of Representatives and the Senate, shall, before it becomes a law, be presented to the President of the United States; if he approve he shall sign it, but if not he shall return it, with his objections to that House in which it shall have originated, who shall enter the objections at large on their journal, and proceed to reconsider it. If after such reconsideration two thirds of that House shall agree to pass the bill, it shall be sent, together with the objections, to the other House, by which it shall likewise be reconsidered, and if approved by two thirds of that House, it shall become a law. But in all such cases the votes of both Houses shall be determined by yeas and nays, and the names of the persons voting for and against the bill shall be entered on the journal of each House respectively. If any bill shall not be returned by the President within ten days (Sundays excepted) after it shall have been presented to him, the same shall be a law, in like manner as if he had signed it, unless the Congress by their adjournment prevent its return, in which case it shall not be a law.

3. Every order, resolution, or vote to which the concurrence of the Senate and the House of Representatives may be necessary (except on a question of adjournment) shall be presented to the President of the United States; and before the same shall take effect, shall be approved by him, or being disapproved by him, shall be repassed by two thirds of the Senate and House of Representatives, according to the rules and limitations prescribed in the case of a bill.

SECTION 8. The Congress shall have the power

1. To lay and collect taxes, duties, imposts, and excises, to pay the debts and provide for the common defense and general welfare of the United States; but all duties, imposts, and excises shall be uniform throughout the United States;

2. To borrow money on the credit of the United States;

3. To regulate commerce with foreign nations, and among the several States, and with the Indian tribes;

4. To establish a uniform rule of naturalization, and uniform laws on the subject of bankruptcies throughout the United States;

5. To coin money, regulate the value thereof, and of foreign coin, and fix the standard of weights and measures;

6. To provide for the punishment of counterfeiting the securities and current coin of the United States;

7. To establish post offices and post roads;

8. To promote the progress of science and useful arts, by securing for limited times to authors and inventors the exclusive right to their respective writings and discoveries;

9. To constitute tribunals inferior to the Supreme Court;

10. To define and punish piracies and felonies committed on the high seas, and offenses against the law of nations;

11. To declare war, grant letters of marque and reprisal, and make rules concerning captures on land and water;

12. To raise and support armies, but no appropriation of money to that use shall be for a longer term than two years;

13. To provide and maintain a navy;

14. To make rules for the government and regulation of the land and naval forces;

15. To provide for calling forth the militia to execute the laws of the Union, suppress insurrections and repel invasions;

16. To provide for organizing, arming, and disciplining the militia, and for governing such part of them as may be employed in the service of the United States, reserving to the States respectively, the appointment of the officers, and the authority of training the militia according to the discipline prescribed by Congress;

17. To exercise exclusive legislation in all cases whatsoever, over such district (not exceeding ten miles square) as may, by cession of particular States, and the acceptance of Congress, become the seat of the government of the United States, and to exercise like authority over all places purchased by the consent of the legislature of the State in which the same shall be, for the erection of forts, magazines, arsenals, dockyards, and other needful buildings; and

18. To make all laws which shall be necessary and proper for carrying into execution the foregoing powers, and all other powers vested by this Constitution in the government of the United States, or in any department or officer thereof.

SECTION 9. 1. The migration or importation of such persons as any of the States now existing shall think proper to admit, shall not be prohibited by the Congress prior to the year one thousand eight hundred and eight, but a tax or duty may be imposed on such importation, not exceeding ten dollars for each person.

2. The privilege of the writ of *habeas corpus* shall not be suspended, unless when in cases of rebellion or invasion the public safety may require it.

3. No bill of attainder or *ex post facto* law shall be passed.

4. No capitation, or other direct, tax shall be laid, unless in proportion to the census or enumeration hereinbefore directed to be taken.[5]

5. No tax or duty shall be laid on articles exported from any State.

6. No preference shall be given by any regulation of commerce or revenue to the ports of one State over those of another: nor shall vessels bound to, or from, one State be obliged to enter, clear or pay duties in another.

[5] See the 16th Amendment.

7. No money shall be drawn from the treasury, but in consequence of appropriations made by law; and a regular statement and account of the receipts and expenditures of all public money shall be published from time to time.

8. No title of nobility shall be granted by the United States: and no person holding any office or profit or trust under them, shall, without the consent of the Congress, accept of any present, emolument, office, or title, of any kind whatever, from any king, prince, or foreign State.

SECTION 10. 1. No State shall enter into any treaty, alliance, or confederation; grant letters of marque and reprisal; coin money; emit bills of credit; make anything but gold and silver coin a tender in payment of debts; pass any bill of attainder, *ex post facto* law, or law impairing the obligation of contracts, or grant any title of nobility.

2. No State shall, without the consent of the Congress, lay any imposts or duties on imports or exports, except what may be absolutely necessary for executing its inspection laws: and the net produce of all duties and imposts laid by any State on imports or exports, shall be for the use of the Treasury of the United States; and all such laws shall be subject to the revision and control of the Congress.

3. No State shall, without the consent of the Congress, lay any duty of tonnage, keep troops, or ships of war in time of peace, enter into any agreement or compact with another State, or with a foreign power, or engage in war, unless actually invaded, or in such imminent danger as will not admit of delay.

ARTICLE II

SECTION 1. 1. The executive power shall be vested in a President of the United States of America. He shall hold his office during the term of four years, and, together with the Vice President, chosen for the same term, be elected as follows:

2. Each State shall appoint, in such manner as the legislature thereof may direct, a number of electors, equal to the whole number of senators and representatives to which the State may be entitled in the Congress: but no senator or representative, or person holding an office of trust or profit under the United States, shall be appointed an elector.

The electors shall meet in their respective States, and vote by ballot for two persons, of whom one at least shall not be an inhabitant of the same State with themselves. And they shall make a list of all the persons voted for, and of the number of votes for each; which list they shall sign and certify, and transmit sealed to the seat of the government of the United States, directed to the president of the Senate. The president of the Senate shall, in the presence of the Senate and House of Representatives, open all the certificates, and the votes shall then be counted. The person having the greatest number of votes shall be the President, if such number be a majority of the whole number of electors appointed; and if there be more than one who have such majority, and have an equal number of votes, then the House of Representatives shall immediately choose by ballot one of them for President; and if no person have a majority, then from the five highest on the list the said House shall in like manner choose the President. But in choosing the President, the votes shall be taken by States, the representation from each State having one vote; a quorum for this purpose shall consist of a member or members from two thirds of the States, and a majority of all the States shall be necessary to a choice. In every case, after the choice of the President, the person having the greatest number of votes of the electors shall be the Vice President. But if there should remain two or more who have equal votes, the Senate shall choose from them by ballot the Vice President.[6]

3. The Congress may determine the time of choosing the electors, and the day on which they shall give their votes; which day shall be the same throughout the United States.

4. No person except a natural born citizen, or a citizen of the United States, at the time of the adoption of this Constitution, shall be eligible to the office of President; neither shall any person be eligible to that office who shall not have attained to the age of thirty-five years, and been fourteen years a resident within the United States.

5. In case of the removal of the President from office, or of his death, resignation, or inability to discharge the powers and duties of the said office, the same shall devolve on the Vice President, and the Congress may by law provide for the case of removal, death, resignation, or inability, both of the President and Vice President, declaring what officer shall then act as President, and such officer shall act accordingly, until the disability be removed, or a President shall be elected.

6. The President shall, at stated times, receive for his services a compensation, which shall neither be increased nor diminished during the period for which he shall have been elected, and he shall not receive within that period any other emolument from the United States, or any of them.

7. Before he enter on the execution of his office, he shall take the following oath or affirmation:—"I do solemnly swear (or affirm) that I will faithfully execute the office of President of the United States, and will to the best of my ability, preserve, protect and defend the Constitution of the United States."

SECTION 2. 1. The President shall be commander in chief of the army and navy of the United States, and of the militia of the several States, when called into the actual service of the United States; he may require the opinion, in writing, of the principal officer in each of the executive departments, upon any subject relating to the duties of their respective offices, and he shall have power to grant reprieves and pardons for offenses against the United States, except in cases of impeachment.

2. He shall have power, by and with the advice and consent of the Senate, to make treaties, provided two thirds of the senators present concur; and he shall nominate, and by and with the advice and consent of the Senate, shall appoint ambassadors, other public ministers and consuls, judges of the Supreme Court, and all other officers of the United States, whose appointments are not herein otherwise provided for, and which shall be established by law: but the Congress may by law vest the appointment of such inferior officers, as they think proper, in the President alone, in the courts of law, or in the heads of departments.

3. The President shall have power to fill up all vacancies that may happen during the recess of the Senate, by granting commissions which shall expire at the end of their next session.

SECTION 3. He shall from time to time give to the Congress information of the state of the Union, and recommend to their consideration such measures as he shall judge necessary and expedient; he may, on extraordinary occasions, convene both Houses, or either of them, and in case of disagreement between them with

[6] Superseded by the 12th Amendment.

respect to the time of adjournment, he may adjourn them to such time as he shall think proper; he shall receive ambassadors and other public ministers; he shall take care that the laws be faithfully executed, and shall commission all the officers of the United States.

SECTION 4. The President, Vice President, and all civil officers of the United States, shall be removed from office on impeachment for, and conviction of, treason, bribery, or other high crimes and misdemeanors.

ARTICLE III

SECTION 1. The judicial power of the United States shall be vested in one Supreme Court, and in such inferior courts as the Congress may from time to time ordain and establish. The judges, both of the Supreme and inferior courts, shall hold their offices during good behavior, and shall, at stated times, receive for their services, a compensation, which shall not be diminished during their continuance in office.

SECTION 2. 1. The judicial power shall extend to all cases, in law and equity, arising under this Constitution, the laws of the United States, and treaties made, or which shall be made, under their authority;—to all cases affecting ambassadors, other public ministers and consuls;—to all cases of admiralty and maritime jurisdiction;—to controversies to which the United States shall be a party;—to controversies between two or more States;—between a State and citizens of another State; [7]—between citizens of different States;—between citizens of the same State claiming lands under grants of different States, and between a State, or the citizens thereof, and foreign States, citizens or subjects.

2. In all cases affecting ambassadors, other public ministers and consuls, and those in which a State shall be party, the Supreme Court shall have original jurisdiction. In all the other cases before mentioned, the Supreme Court shall have appellate jurisdiction, both as to law and to fact, with such exceptions, and under such regulations as the Congress shall make.

3. The trial of all crimes, except in cases of impeachment, shall be by jury; and such trial shall be held in the State where the said crimes shall have been committed; but when not committed within any State, the trial shall be at such place or places as the Congress may by law have directed.

SECTION 3. 1. Treason against the United States shall consist only in levying war against them, or in adhering to their enemies, giving them aid and comfort. No person shall be convicted of treason unless on the testimony of two witnesses to the same overt act, or on confession in open court.

2. The Congress shall have power to declare the punishment of treason, but no attainder of treason shall work corruption of blood, or forfeiture except during the life of the person attainted.

ARTICLE IV

SECTION 1. Full faith and credit shall be given in each State to the public acts, records, and judicial proceedings of every other State. And the Congress may by

[7] See the 11th Amendment.

general laws prescribe the manner in which such acts, records and proceedings shall be proved, and the effect thereof.

SECTION 2. 1. The citizens of each State shall be entitled to all privileges and immunities of citizens in the several States.

2. A person charged in any State with treason, felony, or other crime, who shall flee from justice, and be found in another State, shall on demand of the executive authority of the State from which he fled, be delivered up, to be removed to the State having jurisdiction of the crime.

3. No person held to service or labor in one State under the laws thereof, escaping into another, shall, in consequence of any law or regulation therein, be discharged from such service or labor, but shall be delivered up on claim of the party to whom such service or labor may be due.[8]

SECTION 3. 1. New States may be admitted by the Congress into this Union; but no new State shall be formed or erected within the jurisdiction of any other State; nor any State be formed by the junction of two or more States, or parts of States, without the consent of the legislatures of the States concerned as well as of the Congress.

2. The Congress shall have power to dispose of and make all needful rules and regulations respecting the territory or other property belonging to the United States; and nothing in this Constitution shall be so construed as to prejudice any claims of the United States, or of any particular State.

SECTION 4. The United States shall guarantee to every State in this Union a republican form of government, and shall protect each of them against invasion; and on application of the legislature, or of the executive (when the legislature cannot be convened) against domestic violence.

ARTICLE V

The Congress, whenever two thirds of both Houses shall deem it necessary, shall propose amendments to this Constitution, or, on the application of the legislatures of two thirds of the several States, shall call a convention for proposing amendments, which in either case, shall be valid to all intents and purposes, as part of this Constitution, when ratified by the legislatures of three-fourths of the several States, or by conventions in three fourths thereof, as the one or the other mode of ratification may be proposed by the Congress; Provided that no amendment which may be made prior to the year one thousand eight hundred and eight shall in any manner affect the first and fourth clauses in the ninth section of the first article; and that no State, without its consent, shall be deprived of its equal suffrage in the Senate.

ARTICLE VI

1. All debts contracted and engagements entered into, before the adoption of this Constitution, shall be as valid against the United States under this Constitution, as under the Confederation.[9]

2. This Constitution, and the laws of the United States which shall be made in pursuance thereof; and all treaties made, or which shall be made, under the

[8] See the 13th Amendment.
[9] See the 14th Amendment, Sec. 4.

authority of the United States, shall be the supreme law of the land; and the judges in every State shall be bound thereby, anything in the Constitution or laws of any State to the contrary notwithstanding.

3. The senators and representatives before mentioned, and the members of the several State legislatures, and all executive and judicial officers, both of the United States and of the several States, shall be bound by oath or affirmation to support this Constitution; but no religious test shall ever be required as a qualification to any office or public trust under the United States.

ARTICLE VII

The ratification of the conventions of nine States shall be sufficient for the establishment of this Constitution between the States so ratifying the same.

Done in Convention by the unanimous consent of the States present the seventeenth day of September in the year of our Lord one thousand seven hundred and eighty-seven, and of the independence of the United States of America the twelfth. In witness whereof we have hereunto subscribed our names.

[Names omitted]

Articles in addition to, and amendment of, the Constitution of the United States of America, proposed by Congress, and ratified by the several States pursuant to the fifth article of the original Constitution.

Amendments

FIRST TEN AMENDMENTS PASSED BY CONGRESS SEPT. 25, 1789.
RATIFIED DECEMBER 15, 1791.

ARTICLE I

Congress shall make no law respecting an establishment of religion, or prohibiting the free exercise thereof; or abridging the freedom of speech, or of the press; or the right of the people peaceably to assemble, and to petition the government for a redress of grievances.

ARTICLE II

A well regulated militia, being necessary to the security of a free State, the right of the people to keep and bear arms, shall not be infringed.

ARTICLE III

No soldier shall, in time of peace be quartered in any house, without the consent of the owner, nor in time of war, but in a manner to be prescribed by law.

ARTICLE IV

The right of the people to be secure in their persons, houses, papers, and effects, against unreasonable searches and seizures, shall not be violated, and no warrants shall issue, but upon probable cause, supported by oath or affirmation, and particularly describing the place to be searched, and the persons or things to be seized.

ARTICLE V

No person shall be held to answer for a capital, or otherwise infamous crime, unless on a presentment or indictment of a grand jury, except in cases arising in the land or naval forces, or in the militia, when in actual service in time of war or public danger; nor shall any person be subject for the same offense to be twice put in jeopardy of life or limb; nor shall be compelled in any criminal case to be a witness against himself, nor be deprived of life, liberty, or property, without due process of law; nor shall private property be taken for public use without just compensation.

ARTICLE VI

In all criminal prosecutions, the accused shall enjoy the right to a speedy and public trial, by an impartial jury of the State and district wherein the crime shall have been committed, which district shall have been previously ascertained by law, and to be informed of the nature and cause of the accusation; to be confronted with the witnesses against him; to have compulsory process for obtaining witnesses in his favor, and to have the assistance of counsel for his defense.

ARTICLE VII

In suits at common law, where the value in controversy shall exceed twenty dollars, the right of trial by jury shall be preserved, and no fact tried by a jury shall be otherwise reëxamined in any court of the United States, than according to the rules of the common law.

ARTICLE VIII

Excessive bail shall not be required, nor excessive fines imposed, nor cruel and unusual punishments inflicted.

ARTICLE IX

The enumeration in the Constitution of certain rights shall not be construed to deny or disparage others retained by the people.

ARTICLE X

The powers not delegated to the United States by the Constitution, nor prohibited by it to the States, are reserved to the States respectively, or to the people.

ARTICLE XI

RATIFIED JANUARY 8, 1798.

The judicial power of the United States shall not be construed to extend to any suit in law or equity, commenced or prosecuted against one of the United States by citizens of another State, or by citizens or subjects of any foreign State.

ARTICLE XII

RATIFIED SEPTEMBER 25, 1804.

The electors shall meet in their respective States and vote by ballot for President and Vice President, one of whom, at least, shall not be an inhabitant of the same State with themselves; they shall name in their ballots the person voted for as President, and in distinct ballots, the person voted for as Vice President, and they shall make distinct lists of all persons voted for as President, and of all persons voted for as Vice President, and of the number of votes for each, which lists they shall sign and certify, and transmit sealed to the seat of the government of the United States, directed to the President of the Senate;—The President of the Senate shall, in the presence of the Senate and House of Representatives, open all the certificates and the votes shall then be counted;—The person having the greatest number of votes for President, shall be the President, if such number be a majority of the whole number of electors appointed; and if no person have such majority, then from the persons having the highest numbers not exceeding three on the list of those voted for as President, the House of Representatives shall choose immediately, by ballot, the President. But in choosing the President, the votes shall be taken by States, the representation from each State having one vote; a quorum for this purpose shall consist of a member or members from two thirds of the States, and a majority of all the States shall be necessary to a choice. And if the House of Representatives shall not choose a President whenever the right of choice shall devolve upon them, before the fourth day of March next following, then the Vice President shall act as President, as in the case of the death or other constitutional disability of the President. The person having the greatest number of votes as Vice President shall be the Vice President, if such number be a majority of the whole number of electors appointed, and if no person have a majority, then from the two highest numbers on the list, the Senate shall choose the Vice President; a quorum for the purpose shall consist of two thirds of the whole number of Senators, and a majority of the whole number shall be necessary to a choice. But no person constitutionally ineligible to the office of President shall be eligible to that of Vice President of the United States.

ARTICLE XIII

RATIFIED DECEMBER 18, 1865.

SECTION 1. Neither slavery nor involuntary servitude, except as punishment for crime whereof the party shall have been duly convicted, shall exist within the United States, or any place subject to their jurisdiction.

SECTION 2. Congress shall have power to enforce this article by appropriate legislation.

ARTICLE XIV

RATIFIED JULY 28, 1868.

SECTION 1. All persons born or naturalized in the United States, and subject to the jurisdiction thereof, are citizens of the United States and of the State wherein they reside. No State shall make or enforce any law which shall abridge the privileges or immunities of citizens of the United States; nor shall any State deprive any person of life, liberty, or property, without due process of law; nor deny to any person within its jurisdiction the equal protection of the laws.

SECTION 2. Representatives shall be apportioned among the several States according to their respective numbers, counting the whole number of persons in each State, excluding Indians not taxed. But when the right to vote at any election for the choice of electors for President and Vice President of the United States, representatives in Congress, the executive and judicial officers of a State, or the members of the legislature thereof, is denied to any of the male inhabitants of such State, being twenty-one years of age, and citizens of the United States, or in any way abridged, except for participation in rebellion, or other crime, the basis of representation therein shall be reduced in the proportion which the number of such male citizens shall bear to the whole number of male citizens twenty-one years of age in such State.

SECTION 3. No person shall be a senator or representative in Congress, or elector of President and Vice President, or hold any office, civil or military, under the United States, or under any State, who having previously taken an oath, as a member of Congress, or as an officer of the United States, or as a member of any State legislature, or as an executive or judicial officer of any State, to support the Constitution of the United States, shall have engaged in insurrection or rebellion against the same, or given aid or comfort to the enemies thereof. But Congress may by a vote of two thirds of each House, remove such disability.

SECTION 4. The validity of the public debt of the United States, authorized by law, including debts incurred for payment of pensions and bounties for services in suppressing insurrection or rebellion, shall not be questioned. But neither the United States nor any State shall assume or pay any debt or obligation incurred in aid of insurrection or rebellion against the United States, or any claim for the loss or emancipation of any slave; but all such debts, obligations, and claims shall be held illegal and void.

SECTION 5. The Congress shall have power to enforce, by appropriate legislation, the provisions of this article.

ARTICLE XV

RATIFIED MARCH 30, 1870.

SECTION 1. The right of citizens of the United States to vote shall not be denied or abridged by the United States or by any State on account of race, color, or previous condition of servitude.

SECTION 2. The Congress shall have power to enforce this article by appropriate legislation.

ARTICLE XVI

RATIFIED FEBRUARY 25, 1913.

The Congress shall have power to lay and collect taxes on incomes, from whatever source derived, without apportionment among the several States, and without regard to any census or enumeration.

ARTICLE XVII

RATIFIED MAY 31, 1913.

The Senate of the United States shall be composed of two senators from each state, elected by the people thereof, for six years; and each senator shall have one vote. The electors in each State shall have the qualifications requisite for electors of the most numerous branch of the State legislature.

When vacancies happen in the representation of any State in the Senate, the executive authority of such State shall issue writs of election to fill such vacancies: *Provided,* That the legislature of any State may empower the executive thereof to make temporary appointments until the people fill the vacancies by election as the legislature may direct.

This amendment shall not be so construed as to affect the election or term of any senator chosen before it becomes valid as part of the Constitution.

ARTICLE XVIII

RATIFIED JANUARY 29, 1919.

After one year from the ratification of this article, the manufacture, sale, or transportation of intoxicating liquors within, the importation thereof into, or the exportation thereof from the United States and all territory subject to the jurisdiction thereof for beverage purposes is hereby prohibited.

The Congress and the several States shall have concurrent power to enforce this article by appropriate legislation.

This article shall be inoperative unless it shall have been ratified as an amendment to the Constitution by the legislatures of the several States, as provided in the Constitution, within seven years from the date of the submission hereof to the States by Congress.

ARTICLE XIX

RATIFIED AUGUST 26, 1920.

The right of citizens of the United States to vote shall not be denied or abridged by the United States or by any State on account of sex.

The Congress shall have power by appropriate legislation to enforce the provisions of this article.

ARTICLE XX

RATIFIED JANUARY 23, 1933.

SECTION 1. The terms of the President and Vice President shall end at noon on the 20th day of January, and the terms of Senators and Representatives at noon on the 3d day of January, of the years in which such terms would have ended if this article had not been ratified; and the terms of their successors shall then begin.

SECTION 2. The Congress shall assemble at least once in every year, and such meeting shall begin at noon on the 3d day of January, unless they shall by law appoint a different day.

SECTION 3. If, at the time fixed for the beginning of the term of the President, the President-elect shall have died, the Vice President-elect shall become President. If a President shall not have been chosen before the time fixed for the beginning of his term, or if the President-elect shall have failed to qualify, then the Vice President-elect shall act as President until a President shall have qualified; and the Congress may by law provide for the case wherein neither a President-elect nor a Vice President-elect shall have qualified, declaring who shall then act as President, or the manner in which one who is to act shall be selected, and such person shall act accordingly until a President or Vice President shall have qualified.

SECTION 4. The Congress may by law provide for the case of the death of any of the persons from whom the House of Representatives may choose a President whenever the right of choice shall have devolved upon them, and for the case of the death of any of the persons from whom the Senate may choose a Vice President whenever the right of choice shall have devolved upon them.

SECTION 5. Sections 1 and 2 shall take effect on the 15th day of October following the ratification of this article.

SECTION 6. This article shall be inoperative unless it shall have been ratified as an amendment to the Constitution by the legislatures of three-fourths of the several States within seven years from the date of its submission.

ARTICLE XXI

RATIFIED DECEMBER 15, 1933.

SECTION 1. The Eighteenth Article of amendment to the Constitution of the United States is hereby repealed.

SECTION 2. The transportation or importation into any State, Territory, or possession of the United States for delivery or use therein of intoxicating liquors in violation of the laws thereof, is hereby prohibited.

SECTION 3. This article shall be inoperative unless it shall have been ratified as an amendment to the Constitution by conventions in the several States, as provided in the Constitution, within seven years from the date of the submission thereof to the States by the Congress.

ARTICLE XXII

RATIFIED FEBRUARY 26, 1951.

SECTION 1. No person shall be elected to the office of the President more than twice, and no person who has held the office of President, or acted as President, for more than two years of a term to which some other person was elected President shall be elected to the office of the President more than once. But this Article shall not apply to any person holding the office of President when this Article was proposed by the Congress, and shall not prevent any person who may be holding the office of President, or acting as President, during the term within which this Article becomes operative from holding the office of President, or acting as President during the remainder of such term.

SECTION 2. This Article shall be inoperative unless it shall have been ratified as an amendment to the Constitution by the legislatures of three-fourths of the several States within seven years from the date of its submission to the States by the Congress.

ARTICLE XXIII

RATIFIED APRIL 3, 1961.

SECTION 1. The District constituting the seat of Government of the United States shall appoint in such manner as the Congress may direct:

A number of electors of President and Vice-President equal to the whole number of Senators and Representatives in Congress to which the District would be entitled if it were a State, but in no event more than the least populous State; they shall be in addition to those appointed by the States, but they shall be considered, for the purposes of the election of President and Vice President, to be electors appointed by a State; and they shall meet in the District and perform such duties as provided by the twelfth article of amendment.

SECTION 2. The Congress shall have power to enforce this article by appropriate legislation.

ARTICLE XXIV

RATIFIED JANUARY 23, 1964.

SECTION 1. The right of citizens of the United States to vote in any primary or other election for President or Vice President, for electors for President or Vice President, or for Senator or Representative in Congress, shall not be denied or abridged by the United States or any State by reason of failure to pay any poll tax or other tax.

SECTION 2. The Congress shall have power to enforce this article by appropriate legislation.